Artificial Intelligence and Quantum Computing
for Advanced Wireless Networks

Artificial Intelligence and Quantum Computing for Advanced Wireless Networks

Savo G. Glisic
Worcester Polytechnic Institute, Massachusetts, USA

Beatriz Lorenzo
University of Massachusetts, Amherst, USA

Registered Offices
John Wiley & Sons, Inc., 111 River Street, Hoboken, NJ 07030, USA
John Wiley & Sons Ltd, The Atrium, Southern Gate, Chichester, West Sussex, PO19 8SQ, UK

Editorial Office
The Atrium, Southern Gate, Chichester, West Sussex, PO19 8SQ, UK

For details of our global editorial offices, customer services, and more information about Wiley products visit us at www.wiley.com.

Wiley also publishes its books in a variety of electronic formats and by print-on-demand. Some content that appears in standard print versions of this book may not be available in other formats.

Library of Congress Cataloging-in-Publication Data Applied for:

HB ISBN: 9781119790297

Cover Design: Wiley
Cover Image: © AF-studio/Getty Images; Courtesy of Savo Glisic; © Yuichiro Chino/Moment/Getty Images

Set in 9.5/12.5pt STIXTwoText by Straive, Pondicherry, India
Printed and bound by CPI Group (UK) Ltd, Croydon, CR0 4YY

C9781119790297_030222

Contents

Preface

At this stage, it is anticipated that 6G wireless networks will be based on massive use of machine learning (ML) and artificial intelligence (AI), while 7G will already include hybrids of classical and quantum computing (QC) technologies. In anticipation of this evolution, we have structured the book to continuously move, through a series of chapters, from the presentation of ML algorithms to the final chapter covering the principles of quantum internet. In this process, we also provide chapters covering the complex relationship between the two technologies, on topics such as quantum ML, quantum game theory, and quantum decision theory. The focus of the book is not on the problem how to construct a quantum computer but rather how QC technology enables new paradigms in the modeling, analysis, and design of communication networks, what is nowadays referred to as QC-enabled communications. These new paradigms benefit from the significant computation speedup enabled by the computing parallelism of quantum computers and the new quantum search algorithms developed so far for big data processing. Quantum cryptography and quantum key distribution (QKD) enable new solutions to the problem of security in advanced networks.

This book is also designed to facilitate a new concept in education in this field. Instead of the classical approach of providing a list of problems at the end of a chapter, we introduce a series of design examples throughout the book that require teamwork by a group of students for solving complex design problems, including reproduction of the results presented in the book. This approach turned out to be rather popular with our students at University of Massachusetts at Amherst. We hope that the book provides useful material for not only students but also for researchers, educators, and regulatory professionals in this field.

The Authors
January 2021
Amherst, Massachusetts

Part I

Artificial Intelligence

1

Introduction

1.1 Motivation

Owing to the increase in the density and number of different functionalities in wireless networks, there is an increasing need for the use of artificial intelligence (AI) in planning the network deployment, running their optimization, and dynamically controlling their operation. Machine learning (ML) algorithms are used to predict traffic and network state in order to reserve resources for smooth communication with high reliability and low latency in a timely fashion. Big data mining is used to predict customer behavior and pre-distribute (caching) the information content across the network in a timely fashion so that it can be efficiently delivered as soon as it is requested. Intelligent agents can search the Internet on behalf of the customer in order to find the best options when it comes to buying any product online. This book reviews ML-based algorithms with a number of case studies supported by Python and R programs. It discusses the learning algorithms used in decision making based on game theory and a number of specific applications in wireless networks such as channel, network state, and traffic prediction.

We begin the book with a comprehensive survey of AI learning algorithms. These algorithms are used in the prediction of the network parameters for efficient network slicing, customer behavior for content caching across the network, or for efficient network control and management. Subsequently, we focus on network applications with an emphasis on AI-based learning algorithms used for reaching equilibria in games used among different parties in a variety of new business models in communication networks. This includes competition between network operators, service providers, or even users in dynamic network architectures of user-provided networks.

The book also covers in detail a number of specific applications of AI for dynamic readjusting network behavior based on the observation of its state, traffic variation, and user behavior. This includes channel and power level selection in cellular networks, network self-organization, proactive caching, big data learning, graph neural network (GNN), and multi-armed bandit estimators.

Why quantum computing? The ever-reducing transistor size following Moore's law is approaching the point where quantum effects predominate in transistor operation. This specific trend implies that quantum effects become unavoidable, hence making research on quantum computing (QC) systems an urgent necessity. In fact, a quantum annealing chipset is already commercially available from D-Wave1.

Apart from the quantum annealing architecture, gate-based architecture, which relies on building computational blocks using quantum gates in a similar fashion to classical logic gates,

Artificial Intelligence and Quantum Computing for Advanced Wireless Networks, First Edition.
Savo G. Glisic and Beatriz Lorenzo.
© 2022 John Wiley & Sons Ltd. Published 2022 by John Wiley & Sons Ltd.

is attracting increasing attention due to the recent advances in quantum stabilizer codes, which are capable of mitigating the de-coherence effects encountered by quantum circuits. In terms of implementation, IBM has initially produced 53-qubits quantum computer [1] and plans to have 1-million qubits by 2030 [2]. D-Wave Two 512 qubit processors [3] are built in Google and NASA quantum computer. With this recent developments, Quantum computing has become a commercial reality and it may be used in wireless communications systems in order to speed up specific processes due to its inherent parallelization capabilities.

Whereas a classical bit may adopt the values 0 or 1, a quantum bit, or qubit, may have the values $|0>$, $|1>$, or any superposition of the two, where the notation $|>$ is the column vector of a quantum state. If two qubits are used, then the composite quantum state may have the values $|00>$, $|01>$, $|10>$, and $|11>$ simultaneously. In general, by employing b bits in a classical register, one out of b^2 combinations is represented at any time. By contrast, in a quantum register associated with b qubits, the composite quantum state may be found in a superposition of all b^2 values simultaneously. Therefore, applying a quantum operation to the quantum register would result in altering all b^2 values at the same time. This represents the parallel processing capability of quantum computing.

In addition to superior computing capabilities, multiple quantum algorithms have been proposed, which are capable of outperforming their classical counterparts in the same categories of problems, by either requiring fewer computational steps, or by finding a better solution to the specific problem. In this book, we will focus on the employment of quantum algorithms in classical communication systems, which is nowadays referred to as quantum-assisted communications.

In the following sections, we revisit the ML methods in the context of quantum-assisted algorithms for ML and the quantum machine learning (QML) framework. Quantum principles based on emerging computing technologies will bring in entirely new modes of information processing. An overview of supervised, unsupervised, and reinforcement learning (RL) methods for QML is presented in this segment of the book.

Currently, 5G networks have entered into the commercialization phase, which makes it appropriate to launch a strong effort to conceptualize the future vision of the next generation of wireless networks. The increasing size, complexity, services, and performance demands of communication networks necessitate planning and consultation for envisioning new technologies to enable and harmonize future heterogeneous networks. An overwhelming interest in AI methods is seen in recent years, which has motivated the provision of essential intelligence to 5G networks. However, this provision is limited to the performance of different isolated tasks of optimization, control, and management. The recent success of quantum-assisted and data-driven learning methods in communication networks has led to their candidature as enablers of future heterogeneous networks. This section reviews a novel framework for 6G/7G networks, where quantum-assisted ML and QML are proposed as the core enablers along with some promising communication technology innovations.

The relevance of the research fields integrated throughout this book can be easily recognized within the National Science Foundation (NSF) list of research priorities in science and technology: These 10 areas specified by NSF include (i) AI and ML; (ii) high performance computing, semiconductors, and advanced computer hardware; (iii) quantum computing and information systems; (iv) robotics, automation, and advanced manufacturing; (v) natural or anthropogenic disaster prevention; (vi) advanced communications technology; (vii) biotechnology, genomics, and synthetic biology; (viii) cybersecurity, data storage, and data management technologies; (ix) advanced energy; and (x) materials science, engineering, and exploration relevant to other key technology areas. The 10 areas would be revisited every four years.

1.2   Book Structure

The first part of the book covers selected topics in ML, and the second part presents a number of topics from QC relevant for networking.

Chapter 2 (Machine Learning Algorithms): This chapter presents an introductory discussion of many basic ML algorithms that are often used in practice and not necessary directly related to networking problems. However, they will present a logical basis for developing more sophisticated algorithms that are used nowadays to efficiently solve various problems in this field. These algorithms include linear regression, logistic regression, decision tree (regression trees vs. classification trees), and working with decision trees [4] in R and Python. In this chapter, we answer the questions: What is bagging? What is random forest? What is boosting? Which is more powerful: GBM or XGBoost? We also explain the basics of working in R and Python with GBM, XGBoost, SVM (support vector machine), Naive Bayes, kNN, K-means, random forest, dimensionality reduction algorithms [5, 6], gradient boosting algorithms, GBM, XGBoost, LightGBM, and CatBoost [7, 8].

Chapter 3 (Artificial Neural Networks): We are witnessing the rapid, widespread adoption of AI [9] in our daily life, which is accelerating the shift toward a more algorithmic society. Our focus is on reviewing the unprecedented new opportunities opened up by using AI in deploying and optimization of communication networks. In this chapter, we will discuss the basis of artificial neural networks (ANNs) [10] including multilayer neural networks, training and backpropagation, finite-impulse response (FIR) architecture spatial temporal representations, derivation of temporal backpropagation, applications in time series prediction, auto-regressive linear prediction, nonlinear prediction, adaptation and iterated predictions as well as multiresolution FIR neural-network-based learning algorithm applied to network traffic prediction. Traffic prediction is important for timely reconfiguration of the network topology or traffic rerouting to avoid congestion or network slicing.

Chapter 4 (Explainable NN): Even with the advancements of AI described in the previous chapter, a key impediment to the use of AI-based systems is that they often lack transparency. Indeed, the black-box nature of these systems allows powerful predictions, but they cannot be directly explained. This problem has triggered a new debate on explainable AI (XAI) [11–14].

XAI is a research field that holds substantial promise for improving the trust and transparency of AI-based systems. It is recognized as the main support for AI to continue making steady progress without disruption. This chapter provides an entry point for interested researchers and practitioners to learn key aspects of the young and rapidly growing body of research related to XAI. Here, we review the existing approaches regarding the topic, discuss trends surrounding related areas, and present major research trajectories covering a number of problems related to Explainable NN. This, in particular, includes such topics as using XAI: the need and the application opportunities for XAI; explainability strategies: complexity-related methods, scoop, and model-related methods; XAI measurement: evaluating explanations; XAI perception: human in the loop; XAI antithesis: explain or predict discussion; toward more formalism; human-machine teaming; explainability methods composition; other explainable intelligent systems; and the economic perspective.

Chapter 5 (Graph Neural Networks): Graph theory is a basic tool for modeling communication networks in the form G(N,E), where N is the set of nodes and E the set of links (edges) interconnecting the nodes. Recently, the methodology of analyzing graphs with ML have been attracting increasing attention because of the great expressive power of graphs; that is, graphs can be used to represent a large number of systems across various areas including social science (social networks) [15, 16], natural science (physical systems [17, 18] and protein–protein interaction networks [19]), knowledge graphs [20], and many other research areas [21] including communication networks, which is our focus in this book. As a unique non-Euclidean data structure for ML, graph analysis focuses on node classification, link prediction, and clustering. GNNs are deep-learning-based methods that operate on graph domain. Due to its convincing performance and high interpretability, GNN has recently been a widely applied graph analysis method. In this chapter, we will illustrate the fundamental motivations of GNNs and demonstrate how we can use these tools to analyze network slicing. The chapter includes GNN modeling, computation of the graph state, the learning algorithm, transition and output function implementations, linear and nonlinear (non-positional) GNN, computational complexity, and examples of Web page ranking and network slicing.

Chapter 6 (Learning Equilibria and Games): A comprehensive network optimization also includes the cost of implementing specific solutions. More generally, all negative effects caused by a certain decision in the choice of network parameters such as congestion, power consumption, and spectrum misuse, can be modeled as a cost. On the other hand, most economic theory relies on equilibrium analysis, making use of either Nash equilibrium or one of its refinements [22–31]. One justification of this is to argue that Nash equilibrium might arise as a result of learning and adaptation. In this chapter, we investigate theoretical models of learning in games. A variety of learning models have been proposed, with different motivations. Some models are explicit attempts to define dynamic processes that lead to Nash equilibrium play. Other learning models, such as stimulus response or reinforcement models, were introduced to capture laboratory behavior. These models differ widely in terms of what prompts players to make decisions and how sophisticated players are assumed to behave. In the simplest models, players are just machines who use strategies that have worked in the past. They may not even realize they are in a game. In other models, players explicitly maximize payoffs given beliefs that may involve varying levels of sophistication. Thus, we will look at several approaches including best response dynamics (BRD), fictitious play (FP), RL, joint utility and strategy learning (JUSTE), trial and error learning (TE), regret matching learning, Q-learning, multi-armed bandits, and imitation learning.

Chapter 7 (AI Algorithms in Networks): Finally, at the end of Part I of the book, in this chapter we present an extensive set of examples of solving practical problems in networks by using AI. This includes a survey of specific AI-based algorithms used in networks, such as for controlled caching in small cell networks; channel and power level selection; controlling network self-organization; proactive caching; big data learning for AI-controlled resource allocation; GNN for prediction of resource requirements; and multi-armed bandit estimators for Markov channels.

In particular, we consider AI-based algorithms for traffic classification, traffic routing, congestion control, resource management, fault management, Quality of Service (QoS) and Quality of Experience (QoE) management, network security, ML for caching in small cell networks, Q-learning-based joint channel and power level selection in heterogeneous cellular networks, stochastic non-cooperative game, multi-agent Q-learning, Q-learning for channel and power level selection, ML for self-organizing cellular networks, learning in self-configuration, RL for SON coordination, SON function model, RL, RL-based caching, system model, optimality conditions, big data analytics in wireless networks, evolution of analytics, data-driven networks optimization, GNNs, network virtualization, GNN-based dynamic resource management, deep reinforcement learning (DRL) for multioperator network slicing, game equilibria by DRL, deep Q-learning for latency limited network virtualization, DRL for dynamic VNF migration, multi-armed bandit estimator (MBE), and network representation learning.

Chapter 8 (Fundamentals of Quantum Communications): During the last few years, the research community has turned its attention to quantum computing [32–36] with the objective of combining it with classical communications in order to achieve certain performance targets, such as through-put, round trip delay, and reliability targets at a low computational complexity. As we will discuss in more detail in this chapter, there are numerous optimization problems in wireless communications systems that may be solved at a reduced number of cost function evaluations (CFEs) by employing quantum algorithms. Although we do not attempt to cover the problems of quantum computer design itself, in this chapter we will discuss the basics of QC technology in order to understand better how this technology can enable significant improvements in the design and optimization of communication networks. These fundamentals include discussions on the qubit system, alge-braic representation of quantum states, entanglement, geometrical (2D, 3D) representation of quantum states, quantum logical gates, tensor computing, the Hadamard operator H, and the Pauli and Toffoli gates.

Chapter 9 (Quantum Channel Information Theory): Quantum information processing exploits the quantum nature of information. It offers fundamentally new solutions in the field of computer science and extends the possibilities to a level that cannot be imagined in classical communication systems. For quantum communication channels, many new capacity definitions were developed in analogy with their classical counterparts. A quantum channel can be used to achieve classical infor-mation transmission or to deliver quantum information, such as quantum entanglement. In this chapter, we review the properties of the quantum communication channel, the various capacity measures, and the fundamental differences between the classical and quantum channels [37–43]. Specifically, we will discuss the privacy and performance gains of quantum channels, the quantum channel map, the formal model, quantum channel capacity, classical capacities of a quantum channel, the quantum capacity of a quantum channel, quantum channel maps, and capacities and practical implementations of quantum channels.

Chapter 10 (Quantum Error Correction): The challenge in creating quantum error correction codes lies in finding commuting sets of stabilizers that enable errors to be detected without disturb-ing the encoded information. Finding such sets is nontrivial, and special code constructions are required to find stabilizers with the desired properties. We will start this section by discussing how a code can be constructed by concatenating two smaller codes. Other constructions include methods for repurposing classical codes to obtain commuting stabilizer checks [44–47]. Here, we will outline a construction known as the surface code [48, 49]. The realization of a surface code logical qubit is a key goal for many quantum computing hardware efforts [50–54]. The codes belong to a broader family of so-called topological codes [55]. In this framework, within this chapter we will discuss stabilizer codes, surface codes, the rotated lattice, fault-tolerant gates, fault tolerance, theoretical framework, classical error correction, and the theory of quantum error correction in addition to some auxiliary material on binary fields and discrete vector spaces, and noise physics.

Chapter 11 (Quantum Search Algorithms): The appetite for faster, more reliable, greener, and more secure communications continues to grow. The state-of-the-art methods conceived for achiev-ing the performance targets of the associated processes may be accompanied by an increase in com-putational complexity. Alternatively, degraded performance may have to be accepted due to the lack of jointly optimized system components. In this chapter, we investigate the employment of quantum computing for solving problems in wireless communication systems. By exploiting the inherent parallelism of quantum computing, quantum algorithms may be invoked for approaching the optimal performance of classical wireless processes, despite their reduced number of CFEs cost-function evaluations. In Chapter 8, we have already discussed the basics of quantum computing using linear algebra, before presenting here the operation of the major quantum algorithms that have been proposed in the literature for improving wireless communications systems. Furthermore, in the following chapters, we will investigate a number of optimization problems encountered both in the physical and network layer of wireless communications, while comparing their classical and quantum-assisted solutions. More specifically, in this chapter we will discuss the following: quantum search algorithms (QSAs) for wireless communications such as the Deutsch algorithm, the Deutsch–Jozsa algorithm, Simon's algorithm, Shor's algorithm, the quantum phase estimation algorithm, Grover's QSA, the Boyer–Brassard–Høyer–Tapp QSA, the Dürr–Høyer QSA, quantum counting algorithm, quantum heuristic algorithm, quantum genetic algorithm, Harrow–Hassidim–Lloyd algorithm, quantum mean algorithm, and quantum-weighted sum algorithm.

Chapter 12 (Quantum Machine Learning): In this chapter, we provide a brief description of quantum machine learning (QML) and its correlation with AI. We will see how the quantum counterpart of ML is much faster and more efficient than classical ML. Training the machine to learn from the algorithms implemented to handle data is the core of ML. This field of computer science and statistics employs AI and computational statistics. The classical ML method, through its subsets of deep learning (supervised and unsupervised), helps to classify images, recognize patterns and speech, handle big data, and many more. Thus, classical ML has received a lot of attention and investments from the industry. Nowadays, due to the huge quantities of data with which we deal every day, new approaches are needed to automatically manage, organize, and classify these data. Classical ML, which is a flexible and adaptable procedure, can recognize patterns efficiently, but some of these problems cannot be efficiently solved by these algorithms. Companies engaged in big databases management are aware of these limitations, and are very interested in new approaches to accomplish this. They have found one of these approaches in quantum ML. However, the interest in implementing these techniques through QC is what paves the way for quantum ML. QML [56–59] aims to implement ML algorithms in quantum systems by using quantum properties such as superposition and entanglement to solve these problems efficiently. This gives QML an edge over the classical ML technique in terms of speed of functioning and data handling. In the QML techniques, we develop quantum algorithms to operate classical algorithms using a quantum computer. Thus, data can be classified, sorted, and analyzed using the quantum algorithms of supervised and unsupervised learning methods. These methods are again implemented through models of a quantum neural network or support vector machine. This is the point where we merge the algorithms discussed in Parts I and II of this book. In particular, we will discuss QML algorithms, quantum neural network preliminaries, quantum, classifiers with ML: near-term solutions, the circuit-centric quantum classifier, training, gradients of parameterized quantum gates, classification with quantum neural networks, representation, learning, the quantum decision tree classifier, and the model of the classifier in addition to some auxiliary material on matrix exponential.

Chapter 13 (Quantum Computing Optimization): Convexity naturally arises in many segments of quantum information theory; the sets of possible preparations, processes, and measurements for quantum systems are all convex sets. Many important quantities in quantum information are defined in terms of a convex optimization problem, such as quantifying entanglement [60, 61]. Since the set of separable or unentangled states is convex, a measure of entanglement may be defined for entangled states outside of this set, given a suitable "distance" measure, such as the minimum distance to a state inside. Perhaps the most well known of these quantities is the relative entropy of entanglement. In addition, in the chapter we discuss a number of optimization algorithms including optimization for hybrid quantum-classical algorithms, the quantum approximate optimization algorithm (QAOA), convex optimization in quantum information theory, relative entropy of entanglement, quantum algorithms for combinatorial optimization problems, QC for linear systems of equations, a design example (QC for multiple regression), and a quantum algorithm for systems of nonlinear differential equations.

Chapter 14 (Quantum Decision Theory): The classical decision-making process is mostly based on expected utility theory, and its performance significantly degrades in scenarios involving risk and uncertainty [62]. In most of the classical decision-making processes, the possibility of making correct predictions can be strongly affected by the nature of the surrounding environment such as the unknown stochastic or varying environment. Furthermore, in scenarios having incomplete or partially reliable information or incomplete preference relations, any prediction is likely to be just partial and qualitative. To address this, quantum decision theory (QDT) seems to be a promising approach and has been already investigated in the existing literature [62, 63]. Also, the process of representing all steps of a decision process mathematically in order to allow quantitative prediction is significant not only for the decision theory but also for developing artificial quantum intelligence, which can work only for the operations defined in mathematical terms [64].

With the recent advances in quantum information and QC, there has been a trend of formulating classical game theory using quantum probability amplitudes toward analyzing the impact of quantum superposition, entanglement, and interference on the agents' optimal strategies [65]. Quantum game theory (QGT) in general replaces the classical probabilities of game theory with quantum amplitudes by creating the possibility of new effects arising from entanglement or superposition. The main difference between the classical game and the quantum game is that classical games perform calculations in the probability space, whereas quantum games operate in the Hilbert space. Quantum game theoretic techniques can be utilized for investigating suitable solutions in quantum communication [66] and quantum information processing [67]. In this regard, an article [65] provided an introduction to quantum theory along with some related works and discussed some well-known quantum games including the quantum penny flip, Eisert's quantum prisoners' dilemma, and quantum Parrondo games. Furthermore, a recent article [68] analyzed the existing works on quantum games from three perspectives, namely, co-authorship, co-occurrence, and co-citation, and also reviewed the main quantum game models and applications. Under this umbrella, the chapter discusses QGT, definitions, quantum games, a design example (quantum routing games), quantum game for spectrum sharing, QDT, a model (QDT), predictions in QDT, utility factors, and classification of lotteries by attraction indices.

Chapter 15 (Quantum Computing in Wireless Networks): In this chapter, we discuss several examples of wireless network design based on the tools enabled by quantum computing. Both satellite and terrestrial networks are considered. Traditional security techniques mostly focus on the encryption of communication, where security depends on the mathematical complexity. However, encryption methodologies are becoming less reliable as eavesdroppers and attackers are gaining powerful computing ability. As already discussed in Chapters 8 and 11, quantum cryptography is a new cryptographic technology for generating random secret keys to be used in secure communication. Quantum cryptography can provide communication security based on the laws of quantum physics (e.g., the no-cloning theorem and uncertainty principle). However, the quantum key has to be distributed over the communication network to be used by the senders and receivers.

Reference [69] demonstrated the feasibility of quantum key distribution (QKD) over optical networks. Such a QKD network can be constructed by distributing end-to-end secret (quantum) keys through trusted repeaters (e.g., based on the point-to-point BB84 protocol). References [70, 71] also reported such optical-fiber-based QKD networks, used to secure metropolitan and backbone networks. Recent studies discussed about the integration of QKD and classical networks, such as QKD over wavelength division multiplexing (WDM) networks [72, 73] and QKD-enabled software-defined networks (SDN) [74]. While implementing QKD in terrestrial optical networks, distributing secret keys over a long distance (e.g., across the globe) is challenging. Single-photon signals transmitted over long-distance optical fiber suffer from high losses and depolarization. Hence, carrying the keys using optical fiber over long distances (e.g., 1000 km) is not an effective solution [75].

To address these limitations, an experimented free-space QKD has been studied in recent years. In contrast to optical fibers, the free-space photon will experience negligible loss in vacuum, making it feasible to distribute secret keys over thousands of kilometers. Although the optical beam of a satellite-to-ground link can suffer from atmospheric loss, most of the space is empty, which makes the channel loss less than that for a long fiber [75, 76]. The quantum satellite *Micius*, launched in 2016 for quantum communication experiments, has successfully demonstrated satellite-to-ground QKD using single-photon source [77]. In 2017, a ground free-space QKD experiment was conducted using telecom wavelength in daylight and demonstrated the feasibility of inter-satellite QKD in daylight [78, 79]. Therefore, satellite-based QKD is a promising method for distributing quantum keys between two ultra-long-distance parties on the ground.

Since the coverage and flyover time of one satellite is limited, a group of quantum satellites can be used as trusted repeaters to serve ground stations. Recently, researchers have proposed a "network of quantum satellites" to realize global-scale quantum communications [80, 81]. The authors of [78] proposed a QKD satellite networks architecture based on quantum repeaters. The researchers also proposed the trusted-repeater-based satellite QKD scheme [79–83]. Their scheme is based on BB84 protocol since quantum repeaters are still far from being implemented. Reference [84] investigates the possible schemes of free-space QKD using inter-satellite links and analyzed the properties of satellite-ground links. These studies motivated the concept presented here [85], which is a contribution toward the advancement of the state of the-art in satellite-based QKD networks.

Prior studies envision that a quantum-capable satellite constellation can be formed to construct global QKD (similar to traditional satellite constellations such as IRIDIUM [86]). In recent proposals, quantum satellites will use a low earth orbit (LEO) to benefit from its low channel loss. But a LEO satellite can access a particular ground station for a limited time of the day [87]. This limited coverage may lead to a shortage of secret keys between satellite and ground. By contrast, geostationary earth orbit (GEO) satellites can access ground stations continuously, all day. However, their signal can suffer from high channel loss and a limited key generation rate.

In 2017, German researchers successfully measured quantum signals that were sent from a GEO to a ground station [88]. Italian researchers have also demonstrated the feasibility of quantum communications between high-orbiting global navigation satellites and a ground station [89]. The Chinese Academy of Sciences has future projects to launch higher-altitude satellites [77–79]. According to the researchers, the future quantum satellite constellation will comprise satellites in high and low orbits [90]. Thus, combining both GEO and LEO satellites to build QKD networks is a research direction worth exploring. Within this scope, in this chapter we will address the following problems: quantum satellite networks, satellite-based QKD system, quantum satellite network architecture, a routing and resource allocation algorithm, QC routing for social overlay networks, social overlay networks, a multiple-objective optimization model, QKD Networks, QoS in QKD overlay networks, adaptive QoS-QKD networks, and a routing protocol for QKD networks.

Chapter 16 (Quantum Network on Graph)

To fully benefit from the advantages of quantum technology, it is necessary to design and implement quantum networks [91, 92] that are able to connect distant quantum processors through remote quantum entanglement distribution. However, despite the tremendous progress of quantum technologies, efficient long-distance entanglement distribution remains a key problem, due to the exponential decay of the communication rate as a function of distance [93, 94]. A solution to counteract the exponential decay loss is the adoption of quantum repeaters [95, 96]. Instead of distributing entanglement over a long link, entanglement will be generated through shorter links. A combination of entanglement swapping [97] and entanglement purification [98] performed at each quantum repeater enables the entanglement to be extended over the entire channel. Now a simple question arises: "when does a repeater ensure higher entanglement distribution over the direct long link?"

Different from classical information, quantum information (e.g., qubits) cannot be copied due to the no-cloning theorem [99, 100]. Hence, quantum networks rely on the quantum teleportation process (Chapter 8), [101] as a unique feasible solution, transmitting a qubit without the need to physically move the physical particle storing the qubit. The quantum teleportation of a single qubit between two different nodes requires (i) a classical communication channel capable of sending two classical bits and (ii) the generation of a pair of maximally entangled qubits, referred to as Einstein–Podolsky–Rosen (EPR) pair, with each qubit stored at each remote node. In the following, the generation of an EPR pair at two different nodes is referred to as remote entanglement generation. Under this umbrella, in this chapter we discuss the following specific problems: optimal routing in quantum networks, network model, entanglement, optimal quantum routing, quantum network on symmetric graph, quantum walks, discrete quantum walks on a line (DQWL), Performance study of DQWL, multidimensional quantum walks, the quantum random walk, *Channel Entropy*, quantum random walks on general graphs, continuous time quantum random walks, and searching large-scale graphs.

Chapter 17 (Quantum Internet): Finally, in this chapter we discuss current progress in building up a quantum Internet [91, 102–104] intended to enable the transmission of quantum bits (qubits) between distant quantum devices to achieve the tasks that are impossible using classical communication. For example, with such a network we can implement cryptographic protocols like long-distance QKD [105, 106], which enables secure communication. Apart from QKD, many other applications in the domain of distributed computing and multi-party cryptography [107] have already been identified at different stages of quantum network development [108].

Like the classical Internet, a quantum Internet consists of network components such as physical communication links, and eventually routers [2, 109–111]. However, due to fundamental differences between classical and quantum bits, these components in a quantum network behave rather differently from their classical counterparts. For example, qubits cannot be copied, which rules out retransmission as a means of overcoming qubit losses [112]. To nevertheless send qubits reliably, a standard method is to first produce quantum entanglement between a qubit held by the sender and a qubit held by the receiver. Once this entanglement has been produced, the qubit can then be sent using quantum teleportation [112, 113]. This requires, in addition, the transmission of two classical bits per qubit from the sender to the receiver. Importantly, teleportation consumes the entanglement, meaning that it has to be re-established before the next qubit can be sent. When it comes to routing qubits in a network, one hence needs to consider routing entanglement [102, 114–117]. In this chapter, we discuss the Internet system model, routing algorithms, the quantum network on general virtual graph, the quantum network on ring and grid graph, quantum network on recursively generated graph (RGG), recursively generated virtual graphs, the quantum network protocol stack, preliminaries, the quantum network protocol stack, Layer 3 – reliable state linking, and Layer 4 – region routing.

References

1 https://www.technologyreview.com/2019/09/18/132956/ibms-new-53-qubit-quantum-computer-is-the-most-powerful-machine-you-can-use/.

2 https://fortune.com/2020/09/15/ibm-quantum-computer-1-million-qubits-by-2030/.

3 https://www.nature.com/articles/nature.2013.12999.

4 Safavin, S.R. and Landgrebe, D. (1991). A survey of decision tree classifier methodology. *IEEE Trans. Syst. Man Cybern.* **21** (3): 660–674.

5 Fodor, I.K. A survey of dimension reduction techniques Lawrence Livermore Natl. Laboratory, 2002

6 C.O.S. Sorzano, Vargas, J., Pascual-Montano, A., et al., A survey of dimensionality reduction techniques, https://arxiv.org/ftp/arxiv/papers/1403/1403.2877.pdf

7 Lin, Y.Y., Liu, T.L., and Fuh, C.S. (2011). Multiple kernel learning for dimensionality reduction. *IEEE Trans. Pattern Anal. Machine Intell.* **33**: 1147–1160.

8 Jolliffe, I.T. (2002). *Principal Component Analysis*. Wiley.

9 Stanford https://cs231n.github.io/neural-networks-1

10 Haykin, S. (1999). *Neural Networks: A Comprehensive Foundation*, 2e. Upper Saddle River, NJ: Prentice-Hall.

11 D. Gunning. Explainable artificial intelligence (XAI), Defense Advanced Research Projects Agency (DARPA). Accessed: Jun. 6, 2018. [Online]. Available: http://www.darpa.mil/program/explainable-artificialintelligence

12 A. Henelius, K. Puolamäki, and A. Ukkonen. (2017). "Interpreting classifiers through attribute interactions in datasets." [Online]. Available: https://arxiv.org/abs/1707.07576

13 Letham, B., Rudin, C., McCormick, T.H., and Madigan, D. (2015). Interpretable classifiers using rules and Bayesian analysis: building a better stroke prediction model. *Ann. Appl. Statist.* **9** (3): 1350–1371.

14 Krening, S., Harrison, B., Feigh, K.M. et al. (2016). Learning from explanations using sentiment and advice in RL. *IEEE Trans. Cogn. Develop. Syst.* **9** (1): 44–55.

15 W. L. Hamilton, Z. Ying, and J. Leskovec, "Inductive representation learning on large graphs," NIPS 2017, pp. 1024–1034, 2017.

16 T. N. Kipf and M. Welling, "Semi-supervised classification with graph convolutional networks," ICLR 2017, 2017.

17 A. Sanchez-Gonzalez, N. Heess, J. T. Springenberg, J. Merel, M. Riedmiller, R. Hadsell, and P. Battaglia, "Graph networks as learnable physics engines for inference and control," arXiv preprint arXiv:1806.01242, 2018.

18 P. Battaglia, R. Pascanu, M. Lai, D. J. Rezende et al., "Interaction networks for learning about objects, relations and physics," in NIPS 2016, 2016, pp. 4502–4510.

19 A. Fout, J. Byrd, B. Shariat, and A. Ben-Hur, "Protein interface prediction using graph convolutional networks," in NIPS 2017, 2017, pp. 6530–6539.

20 T. Hamaguchi, H. Oiwa, M. Shimbo, and Y. Matsumoto, "Knowledge transfer for out-of-knowledge-base entities: A graph neural network approach," in IJCAI 2017, 2017, pp. 1802–1808.

21 H. Dai, E. B. Khalil, Y. Zhang, B. Dilkina, and L. Song, "Learning combinatorial optimization algorithms over graphs," arXiv preprint arXiv:1704.01665, 2017.

22 Borgers, T. and Sarin, R. (1997). Learning through reinforcement and replicator dynamics. *J. Econ. Theory* **77**: 1–14.

23 Brown, G. (1951). Iterative solutions of games by fictitious play. In: *Activity Analysis of Production and Allocation* (ed. T.C. Koopmans), 374–376. New York: Wiley.

24 Erev, I. and Roth, A. (1998). Predicting how play games: reinforcement learning in experimental games with unique mixed-strategy equilibria. *Am. Econ. Rev.* **88**: 848–881.

25 Fudenberg, D. and Kreps, D. (1993). Learning mixed equilibria. *Behav. Ther.* **5**: 320–367.

26 Fudenberg, D. and Kreps, D. (1995). Learning in extensive form games I: self-confirming equilibria. *Games Econ. Behav.* **8**: 20–55.

27 Fudenberg, D. and Levine, D. (1993). Self-confirming equilibrium. *Econometrica* **61**: 523–546.

28 Fudenberg, D. and Levine, D. (1999). *The Theory of Learning in Games*. Cambridge: MIT Press.

29 Kalai, E. and Lehrer, E. (1993). Rational learning leads to Nash equilibria. *Econometrica* **61** (5): 1019–1045.

30 Kalai, E. and Lehrer, E. (1993). Subjective equilibrium in repeated games. *Econometrica* **61** (5): 1231–1240.

31 Robinson, J. (1951). An iterative method of solving a game. *Ann. Math. Stat.* **54**: 296–301.

32 Hanzo, L. et al. (2012). Wireless myths, realities, and futures: from 3G/4G to optical and quantum wireless. *Proc. IEEE* **100**: 1853–1888.

33 Nielsen, M.A. and Chuang, I.L. (2011). *Quantum Computation and Quantum Information*, 10e. New York, NY, USA: Cambridge University Press.

34 Imre, S. and Balázs, F. (2005). *Quantum Computing and Communications: An Engineering Approach*. Chichester, UK: Wiley.

35 Imre, S. and Gyongyosi, L. (2013). *Advanced Quantum Communications: An Engineering Approach*. Hoboken, NJ, USA: Wiley.

36 Lipton, R.J. and Regan, K.W. (2014). *Quantum Algorithms via Linear Algebra: A Primer*. Cambridge, MA, USA: MIT Press.

37 Hsieh, M.-H. and Wilde, M.M. (2010). Entanglement-assisted communication of classical and quantum information. *IEEE Trans. Inf. Theory* **56** (9): 4682–4704.

38 Hsiehand, M.-H. and Wilde, M.M. (2010). Trading classical communication, quantum communication, and entanglement in quantum Shannon theory. *IEEE Trans. Inf. Theory* **56** (9): 4705–4730.

39 Wilde, M.M., Hsieh, M.-H., and Babar, Z. (2014). Entanglement-assisted quantum turbo codes. *IEEE Trans. Inf. Theory* **60** (2): 1203–1222.

40 Takeoka, M., Guha, S., and Wilde, M.M. (2014). The squashed entanglement of a quantum channel. *IEEE Trans. Inf. Theory* **60** (8): 4987–4998.

41 Inoue, K. (2006). Quantum key distribution technologies. *IEEE J. Sel. Topics Quantum Electron.* **12** (4): 888–896.

42 V. Sharma and S. Banerjee, "Analysis of quantum key distribution based satellite communication," in Proc. Int. Conf. Comput., Commun. Netw. Technol., Jul. 2018, pp. 1–5.

43 Piparo, N.L. and Razavi, M. (May 2015). Long-distance trust-free quantum key distribution. *IEEE J. Sel. Topics Quantum Electron.* **21** (3): 123–130.

44 Calderbank, A.R. and Shor, P.W. (1996). Good quantum error-correcting codes exist. *Phys. Rev. A* **54**: 1098–1106.

45 Steane, A. (1996). Error correcting codes in quantum theory. *Phys. Rev. Lett.* **77**: 793–797.

46 Kovalev, A.A. and Pryadko, L.P. (2013). Quantum kronecker sum-product low-density paritycheck codes with finite rate. *Phys. Rev. A* **88** (1) https://doi.org/10.1103/physreva.88.012311.

47 Tillich, J.P. and Zemor, G. (2014). Quantum LDPC codes with positive rate and minimum distance proportional to the square root of the blocklength. *IEEE Trans. Inf. Theory* **60** (2): 1193.

48 Bravyi SB, Kitaev AY. Quantum codes on a lattice with boundary. arXiv:quant-ph/9811052. 1998;.

49 Freedman MH, Meyer DA. Projective plane and planar quantum codes; 1998.

50 Nickerson, N.H., Fitzsimons, J.F., and Benjamin, S.C. (2014). Freely scalable quantum technologies using cells of 5-to-50 qubits with very lossy and noisy photonic links. *Phys. Rev. X* **4** (4): 041041.

51 Kelly, J., Barends, R., Fowler, A.G. et al. (2016). Scalablein situqubit calibration during repetitive error detection. *Phys. Rev. A* **94** (3).

52 Sete EA, Zeng WJ, Rigetti CT. A functional architecture for scalable quantum computing. In: 2016 IEEE International Conference on Rebooting Computing (ICRC). IEEE; 2016.

53 O'Gorman, J., Nickerson, N.H., Ross, P. et al. (2016). A silicon-based surface code quantum computer. *NPJ Quantum Inf.* **2** (1) https://doi.org/10.1038/npjqi.2015.19.

54 Takita, M., Cross, A.W., C'orcoles, A. et al. (2017). Experimental demonstration of fault-tolerant state preparation with superconducting qubits. *Phys. Rev. Lett.* **119** (18): 180501. https://doi.org/10.1103/PhysRevLett.119.180501. Epub 2017 Oct 31. PMID: 29219563. Also arXiv:1705.09259v1 [quant-ph] 25 May 2017.

55 Kitaev, A. (2003). Fault-tolerant quantum computation by anyons. *Ann. Phys. Rehabil. Med.* **303** (1): 2–30. https://doi.org/10.1016/s0003-4916(02)00018-0.

56 S. Lloyd, M. Mohseni, and P. Rebentrost. (2013). "Quantum algorithms for supervised and unsupervised machine learning." [Online]. Available: https://arxiv.org/abs/1307.0411

57 Dunjko, V., Taylor, J.M., and Briegel, H.J. (2016). Quantum-enhancedmachine learning. *Phys. Rev. Lett.* **117** (13): 130501–130506.

58 Wittek, P. (2014). *Quantum Machine Learning: What Quantum Computing Means to Data Mining*. New York, NY, USA: Academic.

59 Oneto, L., Ridella, S., and Anguita, D. (2017). Quantum computing and supervised machine learning: training, model selection, and error estimation. In: *Quantum Inspired Computational Intelligence* (eds. S. Bhattacharyya, U. Maulik and P. Dutta), 33–83. Amsterdam, The Netherlands: Elsevier.

60 Plenio, M.B. and Virmani, S. (2005). An introduction to entanglement measures. *Quantum Inf. Comput.* **7**: 1. arXiv:quant-ph/0504163.

61 Horodecki, R., Horodecki, M., and Horodecki, K. (2009). Quantum entanglement. *Rev. Mod. Phys.* **81**: 865. arXiv:arXiv:quantph/0702225v2.

62 Yukalov, V.I. and Sornette, D. Quantitative predictions in quantum decision theory. *IEEE Trans. Syst.*: 366–381. also arXiv:1802.06348v1 [physics.soc-ph] 18 Feb 2018.

63 Ashtiani, M. and Azgomi, M.A. (2015). A survey of quantum-like approaches to decision making and cognition. *Math. Social Sci.* **75**: 49–80.

64 Yukalov, V.I. and Sornette, D. (2009). Scheme of thinking quantum systems. *Laser Phys. Lett.* **6** (11): 833–839.

65 W. Liu, J. Liu, M. Cui, and M. He, "An introductory review on quantum game theory," in Proc. Int. Conf. Genetic Evol. Comput., Dec. 2010, pp. 386–389.

66 Brandt, H.E. (1999). Qubit devices and the issue of quantum decoherence. *Prog. Quantum Electron.* **22** (5–6): 257–370.

67 Lee, C.F. and Johnson, N.F. (2002). Exploiting randomness in quantum information processing. *Phys. Lett. A* **301** (5–6): 343–349.

68 D. Huang and S. Li, "A survey of the current status of research on quantum games," in Proc. 4th Int. Conf. Inf. Manage., May 2018, pp. 46–52.

69 Qi, B., Zhu, W., Qian, L., and Lo, H.-K. (2010). Feasibility of quantum key distribution through a dense wavelength division multiplexing network. *New J. Phys.* **12** (10): 103042.

70 Patel, K.A., Dynes, J.F., Lucamarini, M. et al. (2014). Quantum key distribution for 10 Gb/s dense wavelength division multiplexing networks. *Appl. Phys. Lett.* **104** (5): 051123.

71 S. Bahrani, M. Razavi, and J. A. Salehi, "Optimal wavelength allocation," in Proc. 24th Eur. Signal Process. Conf., Budapest, Hungary, Aug./Sep. 2016, pp. 483–487.

72 Cao, Y., Zhao, Y., Yu, X., and Wu, Y. (2017). Resource assignment strategy in optical networks integrated with quantum key distribution. *IEEE/OSA J. Opt. Commun. Netw.* **9** (11): 995–1004.

73 Zhao, Y., Cao, Y., Wang, W. et al. (2018). Resource allocation in optical networks secured by quantum key distribution. *IEEE Commun. Mag.* **56** (8): 130–137.

74 Cao, Y., Zhao, Y., Colman-Meixner, C. et al. (2017). Key on demand (KoD) for software-defined optical networks secured by quantum key distribution (QKD). *Opt. Express* **25** (22): 26453–26467.

75 Nauerth, S., Moll, F., Rau, M. et al. (2013). Air-to-ground quantum communication. *Nat. Photon.* **7** (5): 382–386.

76 Vallone, G., Bacco, D., and Dequal, D. (2015, Art. no.). Experimental satellite quantum communications. *Phys. Rev. Lett.* **115** (4): 040502.

77 Liao, S.K., Cai, W.Q., and Liu, W.Y. (2017). Satellite-to-ground quantum key distribution. *Nature* **549** (7670): 43–47.

78 Liao, S.-K. et al. (2017). Long-distance free-space quantum key distribution in daylight towards inter-satellite communication. *Nat. Photon.* **11** (8): 509–513.

79 Liao, S.-K., Cai, W.-Q., and Handsteiner, J. (2018). Satellite-relayed intercontinental quantum network. *Phys. Rev. Lett.* **120** (3): 030501.

80 Bacsardi, L. (2013). On the way to quantum-based satellite communication. *IEEE Commun. Mag.* **51** (8): 50–55.

81 Simon, C. (2017). Towards a global quantum network. *Nat. Photon* **11** (11): 678–680.

82 P. Wang, X. Zhang, and G. Chen, "Quantum key distribution for security guarantees over quantum-repeater-based QoS-driven 3d satellite networks," in Proc. IEEE Global Commun. Conf., Dec. 2014, pp. 728–733.

83 Bedington, R., Arrazola, J.M., and Ling, A. (2017). Progress in satellite quantum key distribution. *NPJ Quantum Inf.* **3** (1): 30.

84 M. Pfennigbauer, W. Leeb, and M. Aspelmeyer, "Free-space optical quantum key distribution using intersatellite links," in Proc. CNESIntersatellite Link Workshop, 2003.

85 Huang, D. et al. (2020). Quantum key distribution over double-layer quantum satellite networks. *IEEE Access* **8**: 16087–16098. IEEE.

86 Pratt, S.R., Raines, R.A., Fossa, C.E., and Temple, M.A. (1999). An operational and performance overview of the IRIDIUM low earth orbit satellite system. *IEEE Commun. Surv. Tuts.* **2** (2): 2–10, 2nd Quart.

87 Bourgoin, J.-P., Meyer-Scott, E., Higgins, B.L. et al. (2013). A comprehensive design and performance analysis of low earth orbit satellite quantum communication. *New J. Phys.* **15** (2): 023006.

88 Günthner, K., Khan, I., Elser, D. et al. (2017). Quantum-limited measurements of optical signals from a geostationary satellite. *Optica* **4** (6): 611–616.

89 Calderaro, L., Agnesi, C., Dequal, D. et al. (2018). Towards quantum communication from global navigation satellite system. *Quantum Sci. Technol.* **4** (1): 015012.

90 F. Yu. ScienceNet.cn, China. Accessed: Aug. 10, 2017. [Online]. Available: http://news.sciencenet.cn/htmlnews/2017/8/384831.shtm?id=384831. http://news.sciencenet.cn/htmlnews/2017/8/384831. 中国科学家 划建"量子星座"—新闻—科学网 (sciencenet.cn)

91 Kimble, H.J. (2008). The quantum internet. *Nature* **453** (7198): 1023–1030.

92 Nguyen, H.V. et al. (2017). Towards the quantum internet: generalized quantum network coding for large-scale quantum communication networks. *IEEE Access* **5**: 17288–17308.

93 Sun, Q.-C. et al. (2016). Quantum teleportation with independent sources and prior entanglement distribution over a network. *Nat. Photon.* **10** (10): 671–675.

94 Yin, J. et al. (2017). Satellite-based entanglement distribution over 1200 kilometers. *Science* **356** (6343): 1140–1144.

95 Briegel, H.-J., Dür, W., Cirac, J.I., and Zoller, P. (1998). Quantum repeaters: the role of imperfect local operations in quantum communication. *Phys. Rev. Lett.* **81**: 5932–5935.

96 Dür, W., Briegel, H.-J., Cirac, J.I., and Zoller, P. (1999). Quantum repeaters based on entanglement purification. *Phys. Rev. A Gen. Phys.* **59**: 169–181.

97 Żukowski, M., Zeilinger, A., Horne, M.A., and Ekert, A.K. (Dec. 1993). "Event-readydetectors" bell experiment via entanglement swapping. *Phys. Rev. Lett.* **71**: 4287–4290.

98 Deutsch, D. et al. (1996). Quantum privacy amplification and the security of quantum cryptography over noisy channels. *Phys. Rev. Lett.* **77**: 2818–2821.

99 Wootters, W.K. and Zurek, W.H. (1982). A single quantum cannot be cloned. *Nature* **299** (5886): 802–803.

100 Dieks, D. (1982). Communication by EPR devices. *Phys. Rev. A Gen. Phys.* **92** (6): 271–272.

101 Bennett, C.H., Brassard, G., Crépeau, C. et al. (Mar. 1993). Teleporting an unknown quantum state via dual classical and Einstein-Podolsky-Rosen channels. *Phys. Rev. Lett.* **70**: 1895–1899.

102 Van Meter, R. (2014). *Quantum Networking*. Wiley.

103 Lloyd, S., Shapiro, J.H., Wong, F.N. et al. (2004). Infrastructure for the quantum internet. *ACM SIGCOMM Computer Commun. Rev.* **34** (5): 9–20.

104 Castelvecchi, D. (2018). The quantum internet has arrived (and it hasn't). *Nature* **554** (7692): 289.

105 Bennett, C.H. and Brassard, G. (2014). Quantum cryptography: public key distribution and coin tossing. *Theor. Comput. Sci.* **560** (P1): 7–11.

106 Ekert, A.K. (1991). Quantum cryptography based on bell theorem. *Phys. Rev. Lett.* **67** (6): 661.

107 Broadbent, A. and Schaffner, C. (2016). Quantum cryptography beyond quantum key distribution. *Des. Codes Cryptogr.* **78** (1): 351–382.

108 Wehner, S., Elkouss, D., and Hanson, R. (2018). Quantum internet: a vision for the road ahead. *Science* **362** (6412): eaam9288.

109 Van Meter, R., Ladd, T.D., Munro, W., and Nemoto, K. (2009). System design for a long-line quantum repeater. *IEEE/ACM Trans. Netw. (TON)* **17** (3): 1002–1013.

110 Simon, C., De Riedmatten, H., Afzelius, M. et al. (2007). Quantum repeaters with photon pair sources and multimode memories. *Phys. Rev. Lett.* **98** (19): 190503.

111 Sangouard, N., Dubessy, R., and Simon, C. (2009). Quantum repeaters based on single trapped ions. *Phys. Rev. A* **79** (4): 042340.

112 M. A. Nielsen and I. Chuang, "Quantum computation and quantum information," 2002.

113 Bennett, C.H., Brassard, G., Crepeau, C. et al. (1993). Teleporting an unknown quantum state via dual classical and Einstein-Podolsky-Rosen channels. *Phys. Rev. Lett.* **70** (13): 1895.

114 Caleffi, M. (2017). Optimal routing for quantum networks. *IEEE Access* **5**: 22 299–22 312.

115 Gyongyosi, L. and Imre, S. (2018). Decentralized base-graph routing for the quantum internet. *Phys. Rev. A* **98** (2): 022310.

116 Van Meter, R., Satoh, T., Ladd, T.D. et al. (2013). Path selection for quantum repeater networks. *Netw. Sci.* **3** (1–4): 82–95.

117 Perseguers, S., Lapeyre, G. Jr., Cavalcanti, D. et al. (2013). Distribution of entanglement in large-scale quantum networks. *Rep. Prog. Phys.* **76** (9): 096001.

2

Machine Learning Algorithms

In the first subsection of this chapter, we briefly present a number of machine learning (ML) algorithms in a rather descriptive way. Only in the second subsection will we go into the details of a limited subset of these algorithms. Due to the massive interest in neural networks, this topic is presented in detail separately in Chapters 3–5.

2.1 Fundamentals

2.1.1 Linear Regression

Regression analysis deals with the problem of fitting straight lines to patterns of data. In a linear regression model, the variable of interest (the so-called "dependent" variable) is predicted from k other variables (the so-called "independent" variables) using a linear equation. If Y denotes the dependent variable and X_1, ..., X_k, are the independent variables, then the assumption is that the value of Y at time t is determined by the linear equation

$$Y_t = \beta_0 + \beta_1 X_{1t} + \beta_2 X_{2t} + ... + \beta_k X_{kt} + \varepsilon_t \tag{2.1}$$

The corresponding equation for predicting Y_t from the corresponding values of the X's is therefore

$$\hat{Y}_t = b_0 + b_1 X_{1t} + b_2 X_{2t} + ... + b_k X_{kt} \tag{2.2}$$

where the b's are estimates of the betas obtained by least squares, that is, minimizing the squared prediction error within the sample. This is about the simplest possible model for predicting one variable from a group of others, and it rests on the assumption that the expected value of Y is a linear function of the X variables. More precisely, the following is assumed:

1) The expected value of Y is a linear function of the X variables. This means: (i) If X_i changes by an amount ΔX_i, holding other variables fixed, then the expected value of Y changes by a proportional amount $\beta_i \Delta X_i$, for some constant β_i (which in general could be a positive or negative number). (ii) The value of β_i is always the same, regardless of values of the other X's. (iii) The total effect of the X's on the expected value of Y is the sum of their separate effects.
2) The unexplained variations of Y are independent random variables (in particular, not "autocorrelated" if the variables are time series).

Artificial Intelligence and Quantum Computing for Advanced Wireless Networks, First Edition.
Savo G. Glisic and Beatriz Lorenzo.
© 2022 John Wiley & Sons Ltd. Published 2022 by John Wiley & Sons Ltd.

3) They all have the same variance ("homoscedasticity").
4) They are normally distributed.

These assumptions will never be exactly satisfied by real data, but you hope that they are not badly wrong. For proper regression modeling, we need to collect data that are relevant and informative with respect to our decision problem, and then define the variables and construct the model in such a way that the assumptions listed above are plausible, at least as a first-order approximation to reality.

If we normalize the values of Y and X as

$$X_t^* = (X_t - E(X))/\sigma_x$$
$$Y_t^* = (Y_t - E(Y))/\sigma_y$$

with the correlation function defined as

$$r_{XY} = \left(X_1^* Y_1^* + X_2^* Y_2^* + \; + X_n^* Y_n^*\right)/n$$

the phenomenon that Galton noted was that the regression line for predicting Y* from X* passes through the origin and has a slope equal to the correlation between Y and X; that is, the regression equation in normalized units is

$$\hat{Y}^* = r_{XY} X^*$$

Figures 2.1 and 2.2 illustrate this equation [1]. When the units of X and Y are standardized and both are also normally distributed, their values are distributed in an elliptical pattern that is symmetric around the 45° line, which has a slope equal to 1.

However, the regression line for predicting Y* from X* is *not* the 45° line. Rather, it is a line passing through the origin whose slope is r_{XY}, the dashed red line in the picture below, which is tilted toward the horizontal because the correlation is less than 1 in magnitude. In other words, it is a line that "regresses" (i.e. moves backward) toward the X-axis.

2.1.2 Logistic Regression

Logistic regression analysis studies the association between a categorical dependent variable and a set of independent (explanatory) variables. The term *logistic regression* is used when the dependent variable has only two values, such as 0 and 1, or Yes and No. Suppose the numerical values of 0 and 1 are assigned to the two outcomes of a binary variable. Often, 0 represents a negative response, and 1 represents a positive response. The mean of this variable will be the proportion of positive responses. If p is the proportion of observations with an outcome of 1, then $1 - p$ is the probability of a outcome of 0. The ratio $p/(1 - p)$ is called the *odds* and the *logit* is the logarithm of the odds, or just *log odds*. Formally, the *logit* transformation is written *as* $l = \text{logit}(p) = \ln(p/(1 - p))$. Note that while p ranges between 0 and 1, the logit ranges between minus and plus infinity. Also, note that the zero logit occurs when p is 0.50. The *logistic* transformation is the inverse of the logit transformation. It is written as $p = \text{logistic}(l) = e^l/(1 + e^l)$

The difference between two log odds can be used to compare two proportions, such as that of boys versus girls. Formally, this difference is written as

$$
\begin{aligned}
l_1 - l_2 &= \text{logit}(p_1) - \text{logit}(p_2) \\
&= \ln(p_1/(1 - p_1)) - \ln(p_2/(1 - p_{12})) \\
&= \ln\left(\left(\frac{p_1}{1 - p_1}\right)\Big/\left(\frac{p_2}{1 - p_2}\right)\right) = \ln\left(\frac{p_1(1 - p_2)}{p_2(1 - p_1)}\right) = \ln(OR_{1,2})
\end{aligned}
\tag{2.3}
$$

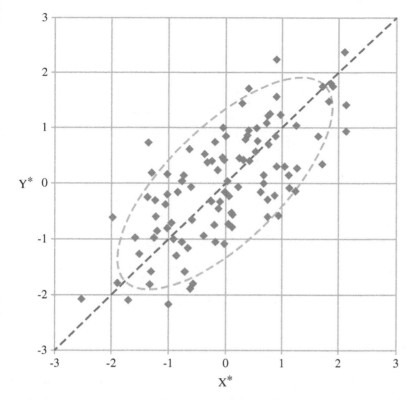

Figure 2.1   If X and Y are two jointly normally distributed random variables, then in standardized units (X^*, Y^*) their values are scattered in an elliptical pattern that is symmetric around the 45° line. *Source:* Modified from Introduction to linear regression analysis [50]. Available at https://people.duke.edu/~rnau/regintro.htm.

This difference is often referred to as the *log odds ratio*. The odds ratio is often used to compare proportions across groups. Note that the logistic transformation is closely related to the odds ratio. The converse relationship is

$$OR_{1,2} = e^{l_1 - l_2} \tag{2.4}$$

In logistic regression, a categorical dependent variable Y having G (usually $G = 2$) unique values is regressed on a set of p independent variables $X_1, X_2, ..., X_p$.

Let $X = (X_1, X_2, ..., X_p)$ and $B_g = (\beta_{g1}, ..., \beta_{gp})^T$; then the logistic regression model is given by the G equations $ln(p_g/p_1) = ln(P_g/P_1) + \beta_{g1}X_1 + \beta_{g2}X_2 + ... + \beta_{gp}X_p = ln(P_g/P_1) + XB_g$. Here, p_g is the probability that an individual with values $X_1, X_2, ..., X_p$ is in outcome g. That is, $p_g = Pr$ $(Y = g \mid X)$. Usually, $X_1 \equiv 1$ (that is, an intercept is included), but this is not necessary. The quantities $P_1, P_2, ..., P_G$ represent the prior probabilities of outcome membership. If these prior probabilities are assumed equal, then the term $ln(P_g/P_1)$ becomes zero and drops out. If the priors are not assumed equal, they change the values of the intercepts in the logistic regression equation.

The first outcome is called the *reference value*. The regression coefficients $\beta_1, \beta_2, ..., \beta_p$ for the reference value are set to zero. The choice of the reference value is arbitrary. Usually, it is the most frequent value or a control outcome to which the other outcomes are to be compared. This leaves $G - 1$ logistic regression equations in the logistic model.

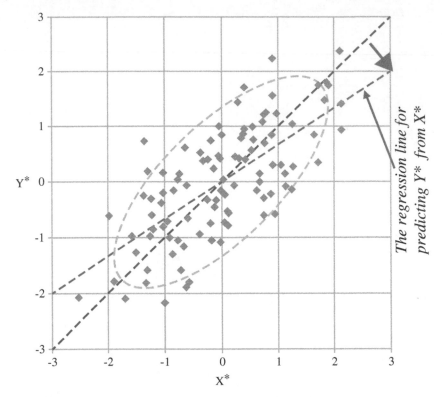

Figure 2.2 The regression line for predicting Y* from X* is *not* the 45° line. It has slope rXY, which is less than 1. Hence it "regresses" toward the X-axis. For this data sample, rXY = 0.69.

The β's are population regression coefficients that are to be estimated from the data. Their estimates are represented by b's. The β's represent unknown parameters to be estimated, whereas the b's are their estimates. These equations are linear in the logits of p. However, in terms of the probabilities, they are nonlinear. The corresponding nonlinear equations are

$$p_g = Prob(Y = g | X) = \frac{e^{XB_g}}{1 + e^{XB_2} + e^{XB_3} + \cdots + e^{XB_G}} \tag{2.5}$$

since $e^{XB_1} = 1$ because all of its regression coefficients are zero. Using the fact that $e^{a+b} = (e^a)(e^b)$, e^{XB} may be reexpressed as follows: $e^{XB} = exp(\beta_1 X_1 + \beta_2 X_2 + \cdots + \beta_p X_p) = e^{\beta_1 X_1} e^{\beta_2 X_2} ... e^{\beta_p X_p}$. This shows that the final value is the product of its individual terms.

2.1.3 Decision Tree: Regression Trees Versus Classification Trees

The decision tree (Figure 2.3) is a type of supervised learning algorithm (having a predefined target variable) that is mostly used in classification problems. It works for both categorical and continuous input and output variables. In this technique, we split the population or sample into two or more homogeneous sets (or sub-populations) based on the most significant splitter/differentiator in the input variables.

Types of decision tree are based on the type of target variable used. If a categorical target variable (zero/one or yes/no) as described in the previous section is used, then we have a *categorical variable*

Figure 2.3 Decision tree.

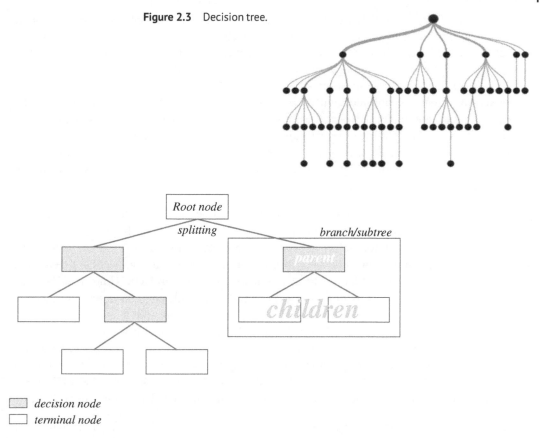

decision node
terminal node

Figure 2.4 Tree terminology.

decision tree. If a continuous target variable is used, then we have a *continuous variable decision tree*. The basic tree terminology is presented in Figure 2.4.

Regression trees versus classification trees: From Figure 2.4 we can see that the terminal nodes (or leaves) lie at the bottom of the decision tree. This means that decision trees are typically drawn upside down such that leaves are the bottom and the roots are the top.

Both the trees work almost similar to each other. Let us look at the primary differences and similarities between classification and regression trees:

- Regression trees are used when the dependent variable is continuous. Classification trees are used when dependent variable is categorical.
- In the case of regression trees, the value obtained by terminal nodes in the training data is the mean response of observations falling in that region. Thus, if an unseen data observation falls in that region, we will make its prediction with the mean value.
- In the case of classification trees, the value (class) obtained by terminal nodes in the training data is the mode of observations falling in that region. Thus, if an unseen data observation falls in that region, we will make its prediction with the mode value.
- Both the trees divide the predictor space (independent variables) into distinct and non-overlapping regions. For the sake of simplicity, we can think of these regions as high-dimensional boxes.

- Both the trees follow a top-down greedy approach known as recursive binary splitting. We call it "top-down" because it begins from the top of the tree when all the observations are available in a single region and successively splits the predictor space into two new branches down the tree. It is known as "greedy" because the algorithm cares about (looks for the best variable available) only the current split, and not about future splits which will lead to a better tree.
- This splitting process is continued until a user-defined stopping criterion is reached. For example, we can tell the algorithm to stop once the number of observations per node becomes less than 50.
- In both the cases, the splitting process results in fully grown trees until the stopping criterion is reached. However, the fully grown tree is likely to overfit data, leading to poor accuracy on unseen data. This is handled by "pruning," which is one of the techniques used to tackle overfitting.

Tree pruning: One of the questions that arises in a decision tree algorithm is the optimal size of the final tree. A tree that is too large risks overfitting the training data and poorly generalizing to new samples. A small tree might not capture important structural information about the sample space. However, it is hard to tell when a tree algorithm should stop because it is impossible to tell if the addition of a single extra node will dramatically decrease error. This problem is known as the horizon effect. A common strategy is to grow the tree until each node contains a small number of instances, and then use pruning to remove nodes that do not provide additional information.

Pruning should reduce the size of a learning tree without reducing predictive accuracy as measured by a cross-validation set. There are many techniques for tree pruning that differ in the measurement that is used to optimize performance. Pruning can occur in a top-down or bottom-up fashion. A top-down pruning will traverse nodes and trim subtrees starting at the root, while a bottom-up pruning will start at the leaf nodes. We now describe two popular pruning algorithms.

Reduced error pruning: One of the simplest forms of pruning is reduced error pruning. Starting at the leaves, each node is replaced with its most popular class. If the prediction accuracy is not affected, then the change is retained. Although somewhat naive, reduced error pruning has the advantage of simplicity and speed.

Cost-complexity pruning: Cost-complexity pruning generates a series of trees $T_0, T_1, ..., T_m$, where T_0 is the initial tree and T_m is the root alone. At step i, the tree is created by removing a subtree from tree $i - 1$ and replacing it with a leaf node having a value chosen as in the tree building algorithm. The subtree that is removed is chosen as follows: (a) Define the error rate of tree T over dataset S as $e(T,S)$. (b) The subtree chosen for removal minimizes

$$\frac{e(prune(T,t),S) - e(T,S)}{|leaves(T)| - |leaves(prune(T,t))|}$$

The function *prune(T,t)* defines the tree obtained by pruning the subtrees *t* from the tree *T*. Once the series of trees has been created, the best tree is chosen by generalized accuracy as measured by a training set or cross-validation.

The decision of making strategic splits heavily affects a tree's accuracy. The decision criterion is different for classification and regression trees. The most popular algorithms used in practice are Gini, Chi-Square, and Reduction in Variance. For details, see Section 2.2.2.

Overfitting in decision trees is one of the key challenges faced while using tree-based algorithms. If no limit is set on the size of a decision tree, it will give you 100% accuracy on the training set because in the worst case it will end up making one leaf for each observation. Thus, preventing overfitting is pivotal while modeling a decision tree, and it can be done in two ways: setting constraints on tree size and tree pruning.

Setting constraints on tree-based algorithms can be done by using various parameters that are used to define a tree, such as the following:

Minimum samples for a node split defines the minimum number of samples (or observations) that are required in a node to be considered for splitting. It is used to control overfitting. Higher values prevent a model from learning relations that might be highly specific to the particular sample selected for a tree. Excessively high values can lead to underfitting.

Minimum samples for a terminal node (leaf) defines the minimum samples (or observations) required in a terminal node or leaf. It is used to control overfitting in a way that is similar to min_samples_split [51]. In general, lower values should be chosen for imbalanced class problems because the regions in which the minority class will be in a majority will be very small.

Maximum depth of tree (vertical depth) is used to control overfitting as a higher depth will allow the model to learn relations that are very specific to a particular sample.

Maximum number of terminal nodes can be defined in place of max_depth [52]. Since binary trees are created, a depth of "n" would produce a maximum of 2^n leaves.

Maximum features to consider for split is the number of features to consider while searching for the best split. These will be randomly selected. As a rule of thumb, the square root of the total number of features works well, but up to 30–40% of the total number of features should be checked. Higher values can lead to overfitting, but this is case specific.

2.1.4 Trees in R and Python

There are multiple packages available in R to implement decision trees, such as ctree, rpart, and tree. Here is an example:

```
> library(rpart)
> x <- cbind(x_train,y_train)
# grow tree
> fit <- rpart(y_train ~ ., data = x,method="class")
> summary(fit)
#Predict Output
> predicted= predict(fit,x_test)
```

In the code above, y_train and x_train represent dependent and independent variables, respectively, and x represents training data. Similarly, in Python we have the following:

```
#Import Library
#Import other necessary libraries like pandas, numpy...
from sklearn import tree
#Assumed you have, X (predictor) and Y (target) for training dataset
and x_test(predictor) of test_dataset
# Create tree object
```

```
model = tree.DecisionTreeClassifier(criterion='gini') # for
classification, here you can change the algorithm as gini or entropy
(information gain) by default it is gini
# model = tree.DecisionTreeRegressor() for regression
# Train the model using the training sets and check score
model.fit(X, y)
model.score(X, y)
#Predict Output
predicted= model.predict(x_test)
```

2.1.5 Bagging and Random Forest

Bagging is a technique used to reduce the variance of our predictions by combining the result of multiple classifiers modeled on different subsamples of the same dataset. The steps followed in bagging are as follows:

Form multiple datasets: Sampling is done *with replacement* on the original data, and new datasets are formed. These new datasets can have a fraction of the columns as well as rows, which are generally hyperparameters in a bagging model. Taking row and column fractions less than one helps in making robust models that are less prone to overfitting.

Develop multiple classifiers: Classifiers are built on each dataset. In general, the same classifier is modeled on each dataset, and predictions are made.

Integrate classifiers: The predictions of all the classifiers are combined using a mean, median, or mode value depending on the problem at hand. The combined values are generally more robust than those from a single model. It can be theoretically shown that the variance of the combined predictions is reduced to *1/n* (*n*: number of classifiers) of the original variance, under some assumptions.

There are various implementations of bagging models. Random forest is one of them, and we will discuss it next.

In random forest, we grow multiple trees as opposed to a single tree. To classify a new object based on attributes, each tree gives a classification, and we say the tree "votes" for that class. The forest chooses the classification having the most votes (over all the trees in the forest), and in case of regression, it takes the average of outputs from different trees.

In R packages, random forests have simple implementations. Here is an example;

```
> library(randomForest)
> x <- cbind(x_train,y_train)
# Fitting model
> fit <- randomForest(Species ~ ., x,ntree=500)
> summary(fit)
#Predict Output
> predicted= predict(fit,x_test)
```

2.1.6   Boosting GBM and XGBoost

By definition, "boosting" refers to a family of algorithms that convert weak learner to strong learners. To convert a weak learner to a strong learner, we will combine the prediction of each weak learner using methods such as average/weighted average or considering a prediction that has a higher vote. So, boosting combines weak learners (base learners) to form a strong rule. An immediate question that arises is how boosting identifies weak rules.

To find a weak rule, we apply base learning (ML) algorithms with a different distribution. Each time a base learning algorithm is applied, it generates a new weak prediction rule. This is an iterative process. After many iterations, the boosting algorithm combines these weak rules into a single strong prediction rule.

For choosing the right distribution, here are the steps: (i) The base learner takes all the distributions and assigns equal weights or attention to each observation. (ii) If any prediction error is caused by the first base learning algorithm, we pay greater attention to observations having prediction error. Then, we apply the next base learning algorithm. (iii) Iterate Step 2 until the limit of the base learning algorithm is reached or higher accuracy is achieved.

Finally, boosting combines the outputs from weak learners and creates a strong learner, which eventually improves the prediction power of the model. Boosting pays greater attention to examples that are misclassified or have higher errors generated by preceding weak learners.

There are many boosting algorithms that enhance a model's accuracy. Next, we will present more details about the two most commonly used algorithms: Gradient Boosting (GBM) and XGBoost. *GBM versus XGBoost:*

- Standard GBM implementation has no regularization as in XGBoost, and therefore it also helps to reduce overfitting.
- XGBoost is also known as a "regularized boosting" technique.
- XGBoost implements parallel processing and is much faster than GBM.
- XGBoost also supports implementation on Hadoop.
- XGBoost allow users to define custom optimization objectives and evaluation criteria. This adds a whole new dimension to the model, and there is no limit to what we can do.
- XGBoost has an in-built routine to handle missing values.

The user is required to supply a value that is different from other observations and pass that as a parameter. XGBoost tries different things as it encounters a missing value on each node and learns which path to take for missing values in the future:

- A GBM would stop splitting a node when it encounters a negative loss in the split. Thus, it is more of a greedy algorithm.
- XGBoost, on the other hand, make splits up to the maximum depth specified and then starts pruning the tree backward, removing splits beyond which there is no positive gain. Another advantage is that sometimes a split of negative loss, say -2, may be followed by a split of positive loss, $+10$. GBM would stop as soon as it encounters -2. However, XGBoost will go deeper, and it will see a combined effect of $+8$ of the split and keep both.
- XGBoost allows user to run a cross-validation at each iteration of the boosting process, and thus it is easy to obtain the exact optimum number of boosting iterations in a single run. This is unlike GBM, where we have to run a grid search, and only limited values can be tested.
- User can start training an XGBoost model from its last iteration of the previous run. This can be a significant advantage in certain specific applications. GBM implementation of sklearn also has this feature, so they are evenly matched in this respect.

GBM in R and Python: Let us first start with the overall pseudocode of the GBM algorithm for two classes:

1) Initialize the outcome.
2) Iterate from 1 to total number of trees.
    2.1 Update the weights for targets based on previous run (higher for the ones misclassified).
    2.2 Fit the model on selected subsample of data.
    2.3 Make predictions on the full set of observations.
    2.4 Update the output with current results taking into account the learning rate.
3) Return the final output.

GBM in R:

```
> library(caret)
> fitControl <- trainControl(method = "cv",
              number = 10, #5folds)
> tune_Grid <-  expand.grid(interaction.depth = 2,
              n.trees = 500,
              shrinkage = 0.1,
              n.minobsinnode = 10)
> set.seed(825)
> fit <- train(y_train ~ ., data = train,
         method = "gbm",
         trControl = fitControl,
         verbose = FALSE,
         tuneGrid = gbmGrid)
> predicted= predict(fit,test,type= "prob") [,2]
```

For GBM and XGBoost in Python, see [2].

2.1.7 Support Vector Machine

Support vector machine (SVM) is a supervised ML algorithm that can be used for both classification and regression challenges [48, 49]. However, it is mostly used in classification problems. In the SVM algorithm, we plot each data item as a point in n-dimensional space (where n is the number of features) with the value of each feature being the value of a particular coordinate. Then, we perform classification by finding the hyperplane that differentiates the two classes very well, as illustrated in Figure 2.5.

Support vectors are simply the coordinates of individual observations. The SVM classifier is a frontier that best segregates the two classes (hyperplane Figure 2.5 (upper part)/line Figure 2.5 (lower part)). The next question is how we identify the right hyperplane. In general, as a rule of thumb, we select the hyperplane that better segregates the two classes, that is,

- If multiple choices are available, choose the option that maximizes the distances between nearest data point (either class) and the hyperplane. This distance is called the **margin**.

Figure 2.5 Data classification.

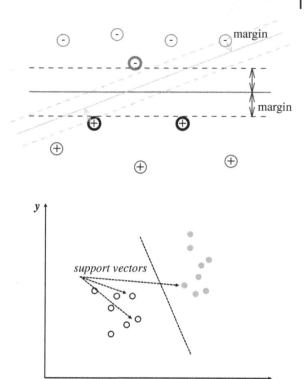

Figure 2.6 Classification with outliers.

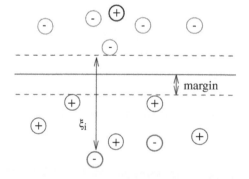

- If the two classes cannot be segregated using a straight line as one of the elements lies in the territory of other class as an outlier (see Figure 2.6), the SVM algorithm has a feature to ignore outliers and find the hyperplane that has the maximum margin. Hence, we can state that SVM classification is robust to outliers.
- In some scenarios, we cannot have a linear hyperplane between the two classes. Linear classifiers are not complex enough sometimes. In such cases, SVM maps data into a richer feature space

$$f(x) = w \cdot \Phi(x) + b$$

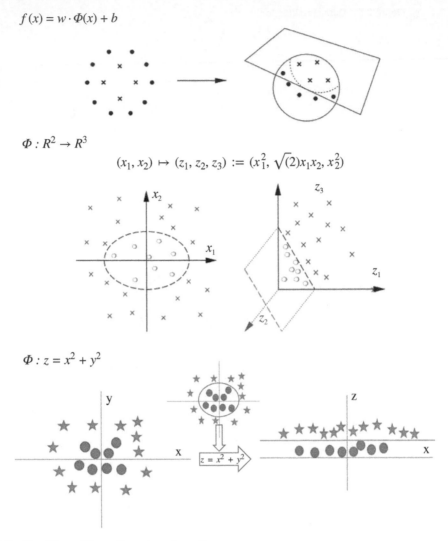

$$\Phi : R^2 \to R^3$$

$$(x_1, x_2) \mapsto (z_1, z_2, z_3) := (x_1^2, \sqrt{(2)}x_1x_2, x_2^2)$$

$$\Phi : z = x^2 + y^2$$

Figure 2.7 Classifiers with nonlinear transformations.

including nonlinear features, and then constructs a hyperplane in that space so that all other equations are identical (Figure 2.7). Formally, it preprocesses data with: $x \to \Phi(x)$ and then learns the map from $\Phi(x)$ to y as follows:

The e1071 package in R is used to create SVMs.
It has helper functions as well as code for the naive Bayes classifier. The creation of an SVM in R and Python follows similar approaches:

```
#Import Library
require(e1071) #Contains the SVM
Train <- read.csv(file.choose())
Test <- read.csv(file.choose())
# there are various options associated with SVM training; like
changing kernel, gamma and C value.
# create model
model <- svm(Target~Predictor1+Predictor2+Predictor3,data=Train,
kernel='linear',gamma=0.2,cost=100)
#Predict Output
preds <- predict(model,Test)
table(preds)
```

2.1.8 Naive Bayes, kNN, k-Means

Naive Bayes algorithm: This is a classification technique based on Bayes' theorem with an assumption of independence among predictors. In simple terms, a naive Bayes classifier assumes that the presence of a particular feature in a class is unrelated to the presence of any other feature.

Example 2.1   An animal may be considered to be a tiger if it has four legs, weighs about 250 pounds, and has yellow fur with black strips. Even if these features depend on each other or upon the existence of the other features, all of these properties independently contribute to the probability that this animal is a tiger, and that is why it is known as "Naive."

Along with simplicity, Naive Bayes is known to outperform even highly sophisticated classification methods. Bayes' theorem provides a way of calculating posterior probability $P(c|x)$ from $P(c)$, $P(x)$ and $P(x|c)$. Here we start with

$$P(c|x) = P(x|c)\,P(c)/P(x) \tag{2.6}$$

where

$P(c|x)$ is the posterior probability of class *(c, target)* given predictor *(x, attributes)*.
$P(c)$ is the prior probability of the class.
$P(x|c)$ is the likelihood, which is the probability of a predictor given the class.
$P(x)$ is the prior probability of the predictor.

Design Example 2.1

Suppose we observe a *street guitar player* who plays different types of music, say, *jazz, rock,* or *country*. Passersby leave a tip in a box in front of him depending on whether or not they like what he is playing. The player chooses to play different songs independent of the tips he receives. Below we have a training dataset of *song* and the corresponding target variable "tip" (which suggests possibilities of getting a tip for a given song). Now, we need to classify whether player will get a tip or not based on the song he is playing. Let us follow the steps involved in this task.

(Continued)

Design Example 2.1 (Continued)

1) Convert the dataset into a frequency table

Data Table

song	jazz	rock	country	jazz	jazz	rock	country	country	jazz
tip	no	yes	yes	yes	yes	yes	no	no	yes

country	jazz	rock	rock	country
yes	no	yes	yes	no

Frequency Table

song	no	yes
rock		4
country	3	2
jazz	2	3
sum	5	9

2) Create a Likelihood table by finding the probabilities, for example, rock probability = 0.29 and probability of getting a tip is 0.64.

Likelihood Table

song	no	yes		
rock		4	=4/14	0.29
country	3	2	=5/14	0.36
jazz	2	3	=5/14	0.36
sum	5	9		
	=5/14	=9/14		
	0.36	0.64		

3) Now, use the Naive Bayesian equation to calculate the posterior probability for each class. The class with the highest posterior probability is the outcome of prediction.

In our case, the player will get a tip if he plays jazz. Is this statement correct? We can solve it using the above method of posterior probability.

$$P(yes \mid jazz) = P(jazz \mid yes)P(yes)/P(jazz)$$
$$P(jazz \mid yes) = 3/9 = 0.33, P(jazz) = 5/14 = 0.36, P(yes) = 9/14 = 0.64$$
$$P(yes \mid jazz) = 0.33^*0.64/0.36 = 0.60,$$

which has a relatively high probability. On the other hand, if he plays rock we have

$$P(yes \mid rock) = P(rock \mid yes)P(yes)/P(rock)$$
$$P(rock \mid yes) = 4/9 = 0.44, P(rock) = 4/14 = 0.29, P(yes) = 9/14 = 0.64$$
$$P(yes \mid rock) = 0.44^*0.64/0.29 = 0.97.$$

R Code for Naive Bayes

```
require(e1071) #Holds the Naive Bayes Classifier
Train <- read.csv(file.choose())
Test <- read.csv(file.choose())
#Make sure the target variable is of a two-class classification
problem only
levels(Train$Item_Fat_Content)
model <- naiveBayes(Item_Fat_Content~., data = Train)
class(model)
pred <- predict(model,Test)
table(pred)
```

Nearest neighbor algorithms: These are among the "simplest" supervised ML algorithms and have been well studied in the field of pattern recognition over the last century. They might not be as popular as they once were, but they are still widely used in practice, and we recommend that the reader at least consider the k-nearest neighbor algorithm in classification projects as a predictive performance benchmark when trying to develop more sophisticated models. In this section, we will primarily talk about two different algorithms, the nearest neighbor (NN) algorithm and the k-nearest neighbor (kNN) algorithm. NN is just a special case of kNN, where $k = 1$. To avoid making this text unnecessarily convoluted, we will only use the abbreviation NN if we talk about concepts that do not apply to kNN in general. Otherwise, we will use kNN to refer to NN algorithms in general, regardless of the value of k.

kNN is an algorithm for supervised learning that simply stores the labeled training examples, $\langle x^{[i]}, y^{[i]} \rangle \in \mathcal{D} (|\mathcal{D}| = n)$, during the training phase and postpones the processing of the training examples until the phase of making predictions. Again, the training consists literally of just storing the training data.

Then, to make a prediction (class label or continuous target), the kNN algorithms find the k nearest neighbors of a query point and compute the class label (classification) or continuous target (regression) based on the k nearest (most "similar") points. The overall idea is that instead of approximating the target function $f(x) = y$ globally, during each prediction, kNN approximates the target function locally. In practice, it is easier to learn to approximate a function locally than globally.

Example 2.2 Figure 2.8 illustrates the NN classification algorithm in two dimensions (features x_1 and x_2). In the left subpanel, the training examples are shown as blue dots, and a query point that we want to classify is shown as a question mark. In the right subpanel, the class labels are also indicated, and the dashed line indicates the nearest neighbor of the query point, assuming a Euclidean distance metric. The predicted class label is the class label of the closest data point in the training set (here: class 0).

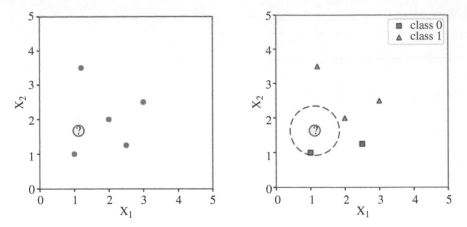

Figure 2.8 Illustration of the nearest neighbor (NN) classification algorithm in two dimensions (features x_1 and x_2).

More formally, we can define the 1-NN algorithm as follows:

```
Training algorithm:
for i = 1, n in the n-dimensional training data set 𝒟(|𝒟| = n):
•store training example ⟨x[i], f(x[i])⟩
Prediction algorithm:
closest point:= None
closest distance:=∞
•for i = 1, n:
    -current distance:=d(x[i], x[q])
    -if current distance < closest distance:
        *closest distance:= current distance
            *closest point:=x[i]
prediction h(x[q]) is the target value of closest point
```

Unless noted otherwise, the default distance metric (in the context of this section) of NN algorithms is the Euclidean distance (also called L^2 distance), which computes the distance between two points, $x^{[a]}$ and $x^{[b]}$:

$$d\left(x^{[a]}, x^{[b]}\right) = \sqrt{\sum_{j=1}^{m}\left(x_j^{[a]} - x_j^{[b]}\right)^2}.$$

Decision boundary: Assuming a Euclidean distance metric, the decision boundary between any two training examples a and b is a straight line. If a query point is located on the decision boundary, this implies its equidistance from both training example a and b. Although the decision boundary between a pair of points is a straight line, the decision boundary of the NN model on a global level, considering the whole training set, is a set of connected, convex polyhedra. All points within a polyhedron are closest to the training example inside, and all points outside the polyhedron are closer to a different training example. Figure 2.9 illustrates the plane partitioning of a two-dimensional

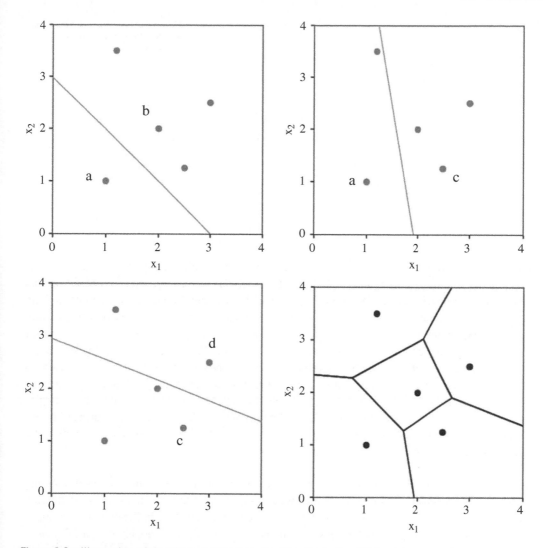

Figure 2.9 Illustration of the plane partitioning of a two-dimensional dataset.

dataset (features x_1 and x_2) via linear segments between two training examples (a & b, a & c, and c & d) and the resulting Voronoi diagram (lower-right corner).

This partitioning of regions on a plane in 2D is also called a Voronoi diagram or Voronoi tessellation. Given a discrete set of points, a Voronoi diagram can also be obtained by a process known as Delaunay triangulation by connecting the centers of the circumcircles.

Whereas each linear segment is equidistant from two different training examples, a vertex (or node) in the Voronoi diagram is equidistant from three training examples. Then, to draw the decision boundary of a two-dimensional NN classifier, we take the union of the pair-wise decision boundaries of instances of the same class. An illustration of the NN decision boundary as the union of the polyhedra of training examples belonging to the same class is shown in Figure 2.10.

k-Means clustering: In this section, we will cover k-means clustering and its components. We will look at clustering, why it matters, and its applications, and then dive into k-means clustering (including how to perform it in Python on a real-world dataset).

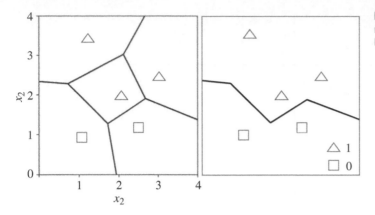

Figure 2.10 Illustration of the nearest neighbor (NN) decision boundary.

Example 2.3 A university wants to offer to its customers (companies in industry) new continuous education type of courses. Currently, they look at the details of each customer and based on this information, decide which offer should be given to which customer. The university can potentially have a large number of customers. Does it make sense to look at the details of each customer separately and then make a decision? Certainly not! It is a manual process and will take a huge amount of time. So what can the university do? One option is to segment its customers into different groups. For instance, each department of the university can group the customers for their field based on their technological level (tl; general education background of the employees), say, three groups high (htl), average (atl), and low (ltl). The department can now draw up three different strategies (courses of different level of details) or offers, one for each group. Here, instead of creating different strategies for individual customers, they only have to formulate three strategies. This will reduce the effort as well as the time.

The groups indicated in the example above are known as clusters, and the process of creating these groups is known as clustering. Formally, we can say that clustering is the process of dividing the entire data into groups (also known as clusters) based on the patterns in the data. Clustering is an unsupervised learning problem! In these problems, we have only the independent variables and no target/dependent variable. In clustering, we do not have a target to predict. We look at the data and then try to club similar observations and form different groups. Hence, it is an unsupervised learning problem.

In order to discuss the properties of the cluster, let us further extend the previous example to include one more characteristic of the customer:

Example 2.4 We will take the same department as before that wants to segment its customers. For simplicity, let us say the department wants to use only the technological level (*tl*) and background mismatch (*bm*) to make the segmentation. Background mismatch is defined as the difference between the content of the potential course and the technical expertise of the customer. They collected the customer data and used a scatter plot to visualize it (see Figure 2.11):

Now, the department can offer a rather focused, high-level course to cluster C_4 since the customer employees have high-level general technical knowledge with expertise that is close to the content of the course. On the other hand, for cluster C_1, the department should offer a course on the broader subject with fewer details.

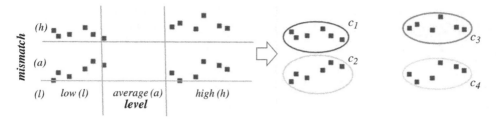

Figure 2.11 Example of clustering.

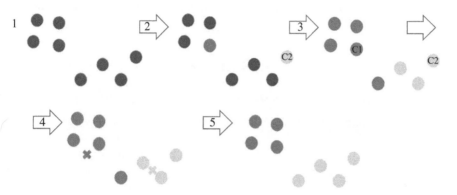

Figure 2.12 k-Means algorithm.

In *k-means*, each cluster is associated with a centroid. The main objective of the k-means algorithm is to minimize the sum of distances between the points and their respective cluster centroid.

As an example, in Figure 2.12 we have eight points, and we want to apply k-means to create clusters for these points. Here is how we can do it:

1) Choose the number of clusters k.
2) Select k random points from the data as centroids.
3) Assign all the points to the closest cluster centroid.
4) Recompute the centroids of newly formed clusters.
5) Repeat steps 3 and 4.

There are essentially three stopping criteria that can be adopted to stop the k-means algorithm:

1) Centroids of newly formed clusters do not change.
2) Points remain in the same cluster.
3) The maximum number of iterations is reached.

Meaning three means (k = 3) clustering on 2D dataset using [3] is shown in Figure 2.13.

2.1.9 Dimensionality Reduction

During the last decade, technology has advanced in tremendous ways, and analytics and statistics have played major roles. These techniques fetch an enormous number of datasets that is usually composed of many variables. For instance, the real-world datasets for image processing, Internet

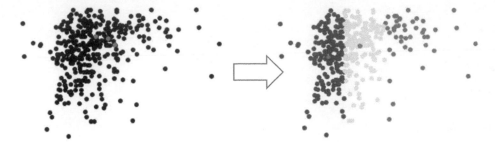

Figure 2.13 k = 3 means clustering on 2D dataset. *Source:* Based on PulkitS01 [3], K-Means implementation, GitHub, Inc. Available at [53] https://gist.github.com/PulkitS01/97c9920b1c913ba5e7e101d0e9030b0e. (for more details see color figure in bins).

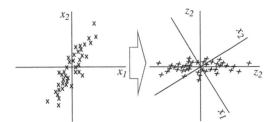

Figure 2.14 Concept of data projection.

search engines, text analysis, and so on, usually have a higher dimensionality, and to handle such dimensionality, it needs to be reduced but with the requirement that specific information should remain unchanged.

Dimensionality reduction [32–34] is a method of converting high-dimensional variables into lower-dimensional variables without changing the specific information of the variables. This is often used as a preprocessing step in classification methods or other tasks.

Linear dimensionality reduction linearly projects n-dimensional data onto a k-dimensional space, $k < n$, often $k << n$ (Figure 2.14).

Design Example 2.2

Principal component analysis (PCA)

The algorithm successively generates principal components (PC): The first PC is the projection direction that maximizes the variance of the projected data. The second PC is the projection direction that is orthogonal to the first PC and maximizes the variance of the projected data. Repeat until k-orthogonal lines are obtained (Figure 2.15).

The projected position of a point on these lines gives the coordinates in k-dimensional reduced space.

Steps in PCA: (i) Compute covariance matrix Σ of the dataset S, (ii) calculate the eigenvalues and eigenvectors of Σ. The eigenvector with the largest eigenvalue λ_1 is the first PC. The eigenvector with the kth largest eigenvalue λ_k is the kth PC. $\lambda_k/\Sigma_i \lambda_i$ = proportion of variance captured by the kth PC.

Design Example 2.2 (Continued)

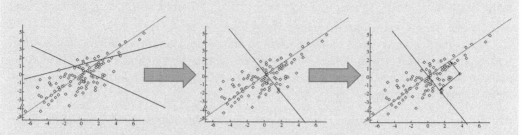

Figure 2.15 Successive data projections.

The full set of PCs comprises a new orthogonal basis for the feature space, whose axes are aligned with the maximum variances of the original data. The projection of original data onto the first k PCs gives a reduced dimensionality representation of the data. Transforming reduced dimensionality projection back into the original space gives a reduced dimensionality reconstruction of the original data. Reconstruction will have some error, but it can be small and often is acceptable given the other benefits of dimensionality reduction. Choosing the dimension k is based on $\Sigma_{i=1,k}\,\lambda_i/\Sigma_{i=1,S}\,\lambda_i > \beta[\%]$, where β is a predetermined value.

2.2 ML Algorithm Analysis

2.2.1 Logistic Regression

In this section, we provide more details on the performance analysis [4] of the logistic regression introduced initially in Section 2.1.2. There, in Eq. (2.5), we provide an expression for the probability that an individual with dataset values $X_1, X_2, ..., X_p$ is in outcome g. That is, $p_g = \Pr(Y = g \mid X)$. For this expression, we need to estimate the parameters β's used in B's. The likelihood for a sample of N observations is given by

$$l = \prod_{j=1}^{N} \prod_{g=1}^{G} \pi_{gj}{}^{y_{gj}} \tag{2.7}$$

where $\pi_{gj} = \mathrm{Prob}\big(Y = g \mid X_j\big) = e^{X_j B_g}/(e^{X_j B_1} + e^{X_j B_2} + \cdots + e^{X_j B_G}) = e^{X_j B_g}/\big(\sum_{s=1}^{G} e^{X_j B_s}\big)$ and y_{gj} is one if the jth observation is in outcome g and zero otherwise. Using the fact that $\sum_{g=1}^{G} y_{gj} = 1$, the log likelihood, L, becomes

$$L = \ln(l) = \sum_{j=1}^{N} \sum_{g=1}^{G} y_{gj}\,\ln\big(\pi_{gj}\big) = \sum_{j=1}^{N} \sum_{g=1}^{G} y_{gj}\,\ln\left(e^{X_j B_g}/\left(\sum_{s=1}^{G} e^{X_j B_s}\right)\right)$$
$$= \sum_{j=1}^{N}\left[\sum_{g=1}^{G} y_{gj} X_j B_g - \ln\left(\sum_{g=1}^{G} e^{X_j B_g}\right)\right] \tag{2.8}$$

Maximum likelihood estimates of the β's are those values that maximize this log likelihood equation. This is accomplished by calculating the partial derivatives and setting them to zero. These equations are $\partial L/\partial \beta_{ik} = \sum_{j=1}^{N} x_{kj}\left(y_{ig} - A_{ig}\right)$ for $g = 1, 2, ..., G$ and $k = 1, 2, ..., p$. Since all coefficients are zero for $g = 1$, the effective range of g is from 2 to G.

Because of the nonlinear nature of the parameters, there is no closed-form solution to these equations, and they must be solved iteratively. The Newton–Raphson [4–7] method is used to solve these equations. This method makes use of the information matrix, $I(\beta)$, which is formed from the matrix of second partial derivatives.

The elements of the information matrix are given by $\partial^2 L/\partial \beta_{ik}\partial \beta_{ik'} = -\sum_{j=1}^{N} x_{kj}x_{k'j}\pi_{ig}\left(1 - \pi_{ig}\right)$

and $\partial^2 L/\partial \beta_{ik}\partial \beta_{i'k'} = \sum_{j=1}^{N} x_{kj}x_{k'j}\pi_{ig}\pi_{i'g}$.

The information matrix is used because the asymptotic covariance matrix of the maximum likelihood estimates is equal to the inverse of the information matrix. That is, $V(\hat{\beta}) = I(\beta)^{-1}$. This covariance matrix is used in the calculation of confidence intervals for the regression coefficients, odds ratios, and predicted probabilities.

The interpretation of the estimated regression coefficients is not straightforward. In logistic regression, not only is the relationship between X and Y nonlinear, but also, if the dependent variable has more than two unique values, there are several regression equations. Consider the usual case of a binary dependent variable, Y, and a single independent variable, X. Assume that Y is coded so it takes on the values 0 and 1. In this case, the logistic regression equation is $ln(p/(1-p)) = \beta_0 + \beta_1 X$. Now consider impact of a unit increase in X. The logistic regression equation becomes $ln(p'/(1-p')) = \beta_0 + \beta_1(X+1) = \beta_0 + \beta_1 X + \beta_1$. We can isolate the slope by taking the difference between these two equations. We have

$$\beta_0 + \beta_1(X+1) - (\beta_0 + \beta_1 X)\, \beta_1 = ln\,(p'/(1-p')) - ln\,(p/(1-p)) =$$
$$ln\left(\frac{p'/(1-p')}{p/(1-p)}\right) = ln\left(\frac{odds'}{odds}\right) \tag{2.9}$$

That is, β_1 is the log of the ratio of the odds at $X+1$ and X. Removing the logarithm by exponentiating both sides gives $e^{\beta_1} = odds'/odds$. The regression coefficient β_1 is interpreted as the log of the odds ratio comparing the odds after a one unit increase in X to the original odds. Note that the interpretation of $\beta 1$ depends on the particular value of X since the probability values, the p' s, will vary for different X.

Inferences about individual regression coefficients, groups of regression coefficients, goodness of fit, mean responses, and predictions of group membership of new observations are all of interest. These inference procedures can be treated by considering hypothesis tests and/or confidence intervals. The inference procedures in logistic regression rely on large sample sizes for accuracy. Two procedures are available for testing the significance of one or more independent variables in a logistic regression: *likelihood ratio tests* and *Wald tests*. Simulation studies usually show that the likelihood ratio test performs better than the Wald test. However, the Wald test is still used to test the significance of individual regression coefficients because of its ease of calculation.

The *likelihood ratio* test statistic is -2 times the difference between the log likelihoods of two models, one of which is a subset of the other. The likelihood ratio is defined as $LR = -2[L_{subset} - L_{full}] = -2[\ln(l_{subset}/l_{full})]$. When the full model in the likelihood ratio test statistic is the saturated model, LR is referred to as the *deviance*. A saturated model is one that includes all possible terms (including interactions) so that the predicted values from the model equal the original data.

The formula for the deviance is $D = -2[L_{\text{Reduced}} - L_{\text{Saturated}}]$. The deviance may be calculated directly using the formula for the deviance residuals:

$$D = 2 \sum_{j=1}^{J} \sum_{g=1}^{G} w_{gj} \ln\left(\frac{w_{gj}}{n_j p_{gj}}\right) \tag{2.10}$$

This expression may be used to calculate the log likelihood of the saturated model without actually fitting a saturated model. The formula is $L_{\text{Saturated}} = L_{\text{Reduced}} + D/2$.

The deviance in logistic regression is analogous to the residual sum of squares in multiple regression. In fact, when the deviance is calculated in multiple regression, it is equal to the sum of the squared residuals. Deviance residuals, to be discussed later, may be squared and summed as an alternative way to calculate the deviance D.

The change in deviance, ΔD, due to excluding (or including) one or more variables is used in logistic regression just as the partial F test is used in multiple regression. Many texts use the letter G to represent ΔD, but we have already used G to represent the number of groups in Y. Instead of using the F distribution, the distribution of the change in deviance is approximated by the chi-square distribution. Note that since the log likelihood for the saturated model is common to both deviance values, ΔD is calculated without actually estimating the saturated model. This fact becomes very important during subset selection. The formula for ΔD that is used for testing the significance of the regression coefficient(s) associated with the independent variable $X1$ is $\Delta D_{X1} = D_{\text{without } X1} - D_{\text{with } X1} = -2 \ [L_{\text{without } X1} - L_{\text{Saturated}}] + 2[L_{\text{with } X1} - L_{\text{Saturated}}] = -2 \ [L_{\text{without} X1} - L_{\text{with} X1}]$.

Note that this formula looks identical to the likelihood ratio statistic. Because of the similarity between the change in deviance test and the likelihood ratio test, their names are often used interchangeably.

The formula for the Wald statistic is $z_j = b_j / s_{b_j}$, where s_{b_j} is an estimate of the standard error of b_j provided by the square root of the corresponding diagonal element of the covariance matrix, $V(\hat{\beta})$. With large sample sizes, the distribution of z_j is closely approximated by the normal distribution. With small and moderate sample sizes, the normal approximation is described as "adequate."

2.2.2 Decision Tree Classifiers

As indicated in Section 2.1, decision trees are considered to be one of the most popular approaches for representing classifiers. Here, we present a number of methods for constructing decision tree classifiers in a top-down manner. This section suggests a unified algorithmic framework for presenting these algorithms and describes the various splitting criteria and pruning methodologies. The material is discussed along the lines presented in [8–11].

Supervised methods are methods that attempt to discover relationship between the input attributes and the target attribute. The relationship discovered is represented in a structure referred to as a model. Usually, models can be used for predicting the value of the target attribute knowing the values of the input attributes. It is useful to distinguish between two main supervised models: *classification* models (classifiers) and *regression* models. Regression models map the input space into a real-valued domain, whereas classifiers map the input space into predefined classes. For instance, classifiers can be used to classify students into two groups: those passing exams on time and those passing exams with a delay. Many approaches are used to represent classifiers. The decision tree is probably the most widely used approach for this purpose.

Terminology: In a typical supervised learning, a training set of labeled examples is given, and the goal is to form a description that can be used to predict previously unseen examples. Most frequently, the training sets are described as a *bag instance* of a certain *bag schema*. The bag schema provides the description of the attributes and their domains. Formally, bag schema is denoted as $R(A \cup y)$, where A denotes the set of n attributes $A = \{a_1, \dots a_i, \dots a_n\}$, and y represents the class variable or the target attribute.

Attributes can be nominal or numeric. When the attribute a_i is nominal, it is useful to denote by $\text{dom}(a_i) = \{v_{i,1}, v_{i,2}, \dots, v_{i,|\text{dom}(a_i)|}\}$ its domain values, where $|\text{dom}(a_i)|$ stands for its finite cardinality. In a similar way, $\text{dom}(y) = \{c_1, \dots, c_{|\text{dom}(y)|}\}$ represents the domain of the target attribute. Numeric attributes have infinite cardinalities. The set of all possible examples is called the instance space, which is defined as the Cartesian product of all the input attributes domains: $X = \text{dom}(a_1) \times \text{dom}(a_2) \times \dots \times \text{dom}(a_n)$. The universal instance space (or the labeled instance space) U is defined as the Cartesian product of all input attribute domains and the target attribute domain, that is, $U = X \times \text{dom}(y)$. The training set is a bag instance consisting of a set of m tuples (also known as *records*). Each tuple is described by a vector of attribute values in accordance with the definition of the bag schema. Formally, the training set is denoted as

$$S(R) = (\langle x_1, y_1 \rangle, \dots, \langle x_m, y_m \rangle) \text{ where } x_q \in X \text{ and } y_q \in \text{dom}(y).$$

Usually, it is assumed that the training set tuples are generated randomly and independently according to some fixed and unknown joint probability distribution D over U. Note that this is a generalization of the deterministic case when a supervisor classifies a tuple using a function $y = f(x)$. Here, we use the common notation of bag algebra to present the projection (π) and selection (σ) of tuples.

The ML community, which is target audience of this book, has introduced the problem of *concept learning*. To learn a concept is to infer its general definition from a set of examples. This definition may be either explicitly formulated or left implicit, but either way it assigns each possible example to the concept or not. Thus, a concept can be formally regarded as a function from the set of all possible examples to the Boolean set {true, false}.

On the other hand, the data mining community prefers to deal with a straightforward extension of the *concept learning*, known as *the classification problem*. In this case, we search for a function that maps the set of all possible examples into a predefined set of class labels and is not limited to the Boolean set.

An *inducer* is an entity that obtains a training set and forms a classifier that represents the generalized relationship between the input attributes and the target attribute.

The notation I represents an inducer and $I(S)$ represents a classifier that was induced by performing I on a training set S. Most frequently, the goal of the classifier's inducers is formally defined as follows: *Given a training set S with input attributes set $A = \{a_1, a_2, \dots a_n\}$ and a target attribute y from a unknown fixed distribution D over the labeled instance space, the goal is to induce an optimal classifier with minimum generalization error.*

Generalization error is defined as the misclassification rate over the distribution D. In case of the nominal attributes, it can be expressed as

$$\sum_{\langle x,y \rangle \in U} D(x,y) \cdot L(y, I(S)(x)) \tag{2.11}$$

where $L(y, I(S)(x)$ is the loss function defined as $L(y, I(S)(x)) = 0$, if $y = I(S)(x)$ *and* 1, if $y \neq I(S)(x)$. In the case of numeric attributes, the sum operator is replaced with the appropriate integral operator.

Tree representation: The initial examples of tree representation including the pertaining terminology are given in Figures 2.3 and 2.4.

Design Example 2.3

The example in Figure 2.16 describes a decision tree that reasons whether or not a potential customer will respond to a direct mailing.

Decision tree induction is closely related to rule induction. Each path from the root of a decision tree to one of its leaves can be transformed into a rule simply by conjoining the tests along the path to form the antecedent part, and taking the leaf's class prediction as the class value. For example, one of the paths in Figure 2.16 can be transformed into the rule: "If customer age <30, and the gender of the customer is "male," then the customer will respond to the mail."

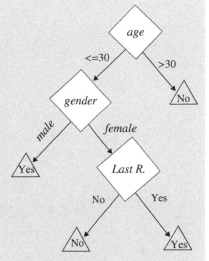

Figure 2.16 Decision tree presenting response to direct mailing.

The goal was to predict whether an email message is spam (junk email) or good.

- *Input features*: Relative frequencies in a message of 57 of the most commonly occurring words and punctuation marks in all the training email messages.
- For this problem, not all errors are equal; we want to avoid filtering out good email, while letting spam get through is not desirable but less serious in its consequences.
- The spam is coded as 1 and email as 0.
- A system like this would be trained for each user separately (e.g. their word lists would be different).
- Forty-eight quantitative predictors – *the percentage of words* in the email that match a given word. Examples include *business, address, Internet, free,* and *George.* The idea was that these could be customized for individual users.
- Six quantitative predictors – *the percentage of characters* in the email that match a given character. The characters are *ch;, ch(, ch[, ch!, ch$, and ch#.*
- The *average* length of uninterrupted sequences of capital letters: CAPAVE.
- The length of the longest uninterrupted sequence of capital letters: CAPMAX.
- The sum of the length of uninterrupted sequences of capital letters: CAPTOT.
- A test set of size 1536 was randomly chosen, leaving 3065 observations in the training set.
- A full tree was grown on the training set, with splitting continuing until a minimum bucket size of 5 was reached.

Algorithmic framework: Decision tree inducers are algorithms that automatically construct a decision tree from a given dataset. Typically, the goal is to find the optimal decision tree by minimizing the generalization error. However, other target functions can be also defined, for instance,

Design Example 2.4

A slightly more sophisticated tree for predicting email spam is shown in Figure 2.17. The results for data from 4601 email messages have been presented in [12].

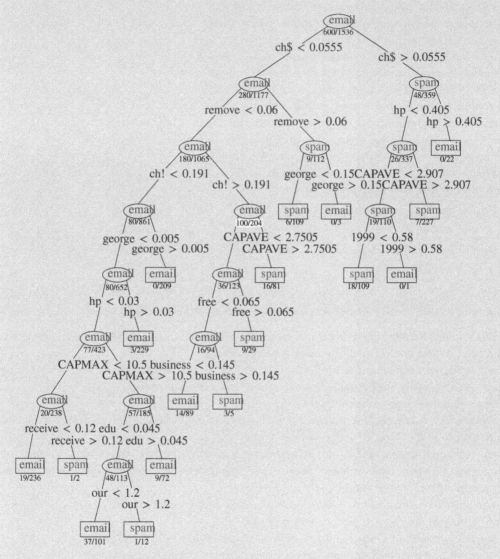

Figure 2.17 Predicting email spam. *Source:* Trevor Hastie [12].

minimizing the number of nodes or minimizing the average depth. Induction of an optimal decision tree from a given dataset is a hard task resulting in an NP hard problem [13–16], which is feasible only in small problems. Consequently, heuristic methods are required for solving the problem. Roughly speaking, these methods can be divided into two groups: top-down and bottom-up, with a clear preference in the literature to the first group. Figure 2.18 presents a typical algorithmic framework for top-down decision tree induction [8].

Splitting criteria: In most of the cases, the discrete splitting functions are univariate. Univariate means that an internal node is split according to the value of a single attribute. Consequently, the inducer searches for the best attribute upon which to split. There are various univariate criteria.

procedure $DTInducer(S, A, y)$
1: $T = TreeGrowing(S, A, y)$
2: Return TreePruning(S,T)

procedure $TreeGrowing(S, A, y)$
1: Create a tree T
2: **if** One of the Stopping Criteria is fulfilled **then**
3:     Mark the root node in T as a leaf with the most common value of y in S as the class.
4: **else**
5:     Find a discrete function $f(A)$ of the input attributes values such that splitting S according to $f(A)$'s outcomes $(v_1,...,v_n)$ gains the best splitting metric.
6:     **if** best splitting metric $\geq$ threshold **then**
7:         Label the root node in T as $f(A)$
8:         **for** each outcome v_i of f(A) **do**
9:             $Subtree_i = TreeGrowing(\sigma_{f(A)=v_i} S, A, y)$.
10:             Connect the root node of T to $Subtree_i$ with an edge that is labelled as v_i
11:         **end for**
12:     **else**
13:         Mark the root node in T as a leaf with the most common value of y in S as the class.
14:     **end if**
15: **end if**
16: Return T

procedure $TreePruning(S, T, y)$
1: **repeat**
2:     Select a node t in T such that pruning it maximally improve some evaluation criteria
3:     **if** $t \neq \emptyset$ **then**
4:         $T = pruned(T, t)$
5:     **end if**
6: **until** t=∅
7: Return T

Figure 2.18 Top-down algorithmic framework for decision tree induction. The inputs are S (training set), A (input feature set), and y (target feature) [8].

These criteria can be characterized in different ways, such as according to the origin of the measure (information theory, dependence, and distance) and according to the measure structure (impurity-based criteria, normalized impurity-based criteria, and binary criteria). Next, we describe the most common criteria in the literature.

Impurity-based criteria: Given a random variable $\dot{x}$ with k discrete values, distributed according to $P = (p_1, p_2, ..., p_k)$, an impurity measure is a function $\phi: [0, 1]^k \rightarrow R$ that satisfies the following conditions: $\phi(P) \geq 0$; $\phi(P)$ is minimum if $\exists i$ such that component $P_i = 1$; $\phi(P)$ is maximum if $\forall i, 1 \leq i \leq k$, $P_i = 1/k$; $\phi(P)$ is symmetric with respect to components of P; $\phi(P)$ is differentiable everywhere in its range. If the probability vector has a component of 1 (the variable x gets only one value), then the variable is defined as pure. On the other hand, if all components are equal the level of impurity reaches a maximum. Given a training set S, the probability vector of the target attribute y is defined as

$$P_y(S) = \left(\frac{|\sigma_{y=c_1}S|}{|S|}, ..., \frac{|\sigma_{y=c_{|dom(y)|}}S|}{|S|} \right) \tag{2.12}$$

The goodness of split due to the discrete attribute a_i is defined as a reduction in impurity of the target attribute after partitioning S according to the values $v_{i,j} \in dom(a_i)$:

$$\Delta\Phi(a_i, S) = \phi(P_y(S)) - \sum_{j=1}^{|dom(a_i)|} \frac{|\sigma_{a_i=v_{i,j}}S|}{|S|} \cdot \phi(P_y(\sigma_{a_i=v_{i,j}}S)). \tag{2.13}$$

Information gain (ig) is an impurity-based criterion that uses the entropy (e) measure (origin from information theory) as the impurity measure:

$$ig(a_i, S) = e(y, S) - \sum_{v_{i,j} \in dom(a_i)} \frac{|\sigma_{a_i=v_{i,j}}S|}{|S|} \cdot e(y, \sigma_{a_i=v_{i,j}}S)$$

where

$$e(y, S) = \sum_{c_j \in dom(y)} -\frac{|\sigma_{y=c_j}S|}{|S|} \log_2 \frac{|\sigma_{y=c_j}S|}{|S|}. \tag{2.14}$$

Gini index: This is an impurity-based criterion that measures the divergence between the probability distributions of the target attribute's values. The Gini (G) index is defined as

$$G(y, S) = 1 - \sum_{c_j \in dom(y)} \left(\frac{|\sigma_{y=c_j}S|}{|S|} \right)^2 \tag{2.15}$$

Consequently, the evaluation criterion for selecting the attribute a_i is defined as the Gini gain (GG):

$$GG(a_i, S) = G(y, S) - \sum_{v_{i,j} \in dom(a_k)} \frac{|\sigma_{a_i=v_{i,j}}S|}{|S|} \cdot G(y, \sigma_{a_i=v_{i,j}}S). \tag{2.16}$$

Likelihood ratio chi-squared statistics: The likelihood ratio (lr) is defined as

$$lr(a_i, S) = 2 \cdot \ln(2) \cdot |S| \cdot ig(a_i, S). \tag{2.17}$$

This ratio is useful for measuring the statistical significance of the information gain criteria. The zero hypothesis (H_0) is that the input attribute and the target attribute are conditionally independent. If H_0 holds, the test statistic is distributed as χ^2 with degrees of freedom equal to $(dom(a_i) - 1) \cdot (dom(y) - 1)$.

Normalized impurity-based criterion: The impurity-based criterion described above is biased toward attributes with larger domain values. That is, it prefers input attributes with many values over attributes with less values. For instance, an input attribute that represents the national security number will probably get the highest information gain. However, adding this attribute to a decision tree will result in a poor generalized accuracy. For that reason, it is useful to "normalize" the impurity-based measures, as described in the subsequent paragraphs.

Gain ratio (gr): This ratio "normalizes" the information gain (ig) as follows: $gr(a_i, S) = ig(a_i, S)/e$ (a_i, S). Note that this ratio is not defined when the denominator is zero. Also, the ratio may tend to favor attributes for which the denominator is very small. Consequently, it is suggested in two stages. First, the information gain is calculated for all attributes. Then, taking into consideration only attributes that have performed at least as well as the average information gain, the attribute that has obtained the best ratio gain is selected. It has been shown that the gain ratio tends to outperform simple information gain criteria both from the accuracy aspect as well as from classifier complexity aspect.

Distance measure: Similar to the gain ratio, this measure also normalizes the impurity measure. However, the method used is different:

$$DM(a_i, S) = \frac{\Delta \Phi(a_i, S)}{-\sum_{v_{i,j} \in \mathrm{dom}(a_i)} \sum_{c_k \in \mathrm{dom}(y)} b \cdot \log_2 b}$$

where

$$b = \frac{|\sigma_{a_i = v_{i,j} \mathrm{and} y = c_k} S|}{|S|} \tag{2.18}$$

Binary criteria: These are used for creating binary decision trees. These measures are based on the division of the input attribute domain into two subdomains.

Let $\beta(a_i, d_1, d_2, S)$ denote the binary criterion value for attribute a_i over sample S when $d1$ and $d2$ are its corresponding subdomains. The value obtained for the optimal division of the attribute domain into two mutually exclusive and exhaustive subdomains, is used for comparing attributes, namely

$$\beta^*(a_i, S) = \max \beta(a_i, d_1, d_2, S)$$
$$\mathrm{s.t.} d_1 \cup d_2 = \mathrm{dom}(a_i) \tag{2.19}$$
$$d_1 \cap d_2 = \emptyset.$$

Twoing criterion: The *Gini* index may encounter problems when the domain of the target attribute is relatively wide. In this case, they suggest using the binary criterion called the twoing (tw) criterion. This criterion is defined as

$$tw(a_i, d_1, d_2, S) = 0.25 \frac{|\sigma_{a_{i \in d_1}} S|}{|S|} \cdot \frac{|\sigma_{a_{i \in d_2}} S|}{|S|} \left(\sum_{c_i \in dom(y)} \left| \frac{|\sigma_{a_{i \in d_1} \cap y = c_i} S|}{|\sigma_{a_{i \in d_1}} S|} - \frac{|\sigma_{a_{i \in d_2} \cap y = c_i} S|}{|\sigma_{a_{i \in d_2}} S|} \right| \right)^2 \tag{2.20}$$

When the target attribute is binary, the Gini and twoing criteria are equivalent. For multiclass problems, the twoing criterion prefers attributes with evenly divided splits.

Orthogonality (ort) criterion: This binary criterion is defined as

$$ort(a_i, d_1, d_2 S) = 1 - \cos \theta(P_{y,1}, P_{y,2})$$

where $\theta(P_{y,1}, P_{y,2})$ is the angle between two distribution vectors $P_{y,1}$ and $P_{y,2}$ of the target attribute y on the bags $\sigma_{a_i \in d_1} S$ and $\sigma_{a_k \in d_2} S$, respectively. It was shown that this criterion performs better than the information gain and the Gini index for specific problem constellations.

Kolmogorov–Smirnov (K–S) criterion: Assuming a binary target attribute, namely, dom(y) = $\{c_1, c_2\}$, the criterion is defined as

$$ks(a_i, d_1, d_2, S) = \left| \frac{\left| \sigma_{a_i \in d_1 \cap y = c_1} S \right|}{\left| \sigma_{y = c_1} S \right|} - \frac{\left| \sigma_{a_i \in d_1 \cap y = c_2} S \right|}{\left| \sigma_{y = c_2} S \right|} \right| \tag{2.21}$$

It was suggest extending this measure to handle target attributes with multiple classes and missing data values. The results indicate that the suggested method outperforms the gain ratio criteria.

Stopping criteria: The tree splitting (growing phase) continues until a stopping criterion is triggered. The following conditions are common stopping rules: (i) all instances in the training set belong to a single value of y, (ii) the maximum tree depth has been reached, (iii) the number of cases in the terminal node is less than the minimum number of cases for the parent nodes, and (iv) if the node were split, the number of cases in one or more child nodes would be less than the minimum number of cases for child nodes. The best splitting criteria is not greater than a certain threshold.

Pruning methods: Employing tightly stopping criteria tends to create small and underfitted decision trees. On the other hand, using loosely stopping criteria tends to generate large decision trees that are overfitted to the training set. Pruning methods were developed to solve this dilemma. There are various techniques for pruning decision trees. Most of them perform top-down or bottom-up traversal of the nodes. A node is pruned if this operation improves a certain criterion. Next, we describe the most popular techniques.

Cost-complexity pruning (pr): This proceeds in two stages. In the first stage, a sequence of trees T_0, $T_1, \ldots T_k$ is built on the training data, where T_0 is the original tree before pruning and T_k is the root tree. In the second stage, one of these trees is chosen as the pruned tree, based on its generalization error estimation. The tree T_{i+1} is obtained by replacing one or more of the subtrees in the predecessor tree T_i with suitable leaves. The subtrees that are pruned are those that obtain the lowest increase in apparent error rate per pruned leaf (l):

$$\alpha = \frac{\varepsilon(pr(T, t), S) - \varepsilon(T, S)}{|\, l(T) \,| - |\, l(pr(T, t)) \,|} \tag{2.22}$$

where $\varepsilon(T, S)$ indicates the error rate of the tree T over the sample S, and $|l(T)|$ denotes the number of leaves in T. The parameter $pr(T, t)$ denote the tree obtained by replacing the node t in T with a suitable leaf. In the second phase, the generalization error of each pruned tree $T_0, T_1, \ldots T_k$ is estimated. The best pruned tree is then selected. If the given dataset is large enough, it is suggested to break it into a training set and a pruning set. The trees are constructed using the training set and evaluated on the pruning set. On the other hand, if the given dataset is not large enough, the *cross-validation* methodology is suggested, despite the computational complexity implications.

Reduced error pruning: While traversing the internal nodes from the bottom to the top, the procedure checks, for each internal node, whether replacing it with the most frequent class reduces the tree's accuracy. If not, the node is pruned. The procedure continues until any further pruning would decrease the accuracy. It can be shown that this procedure ends with the smallest accurate subtree with respect to a given pruning set.

Minimum-error pruning (MEP): It performs bottom-up traversal of the internal nodes. In each node, it compares the l-probability-error rate estimation with and without pruning. The l-probability-error rate estimation is a correction to the simple probability estimation using frequencies. If S_t denote the instances that have reached node t, then the error rate obtained if this node was pruned is

$$\varepsilon'(t) = 1 - \max_{c_i \in \text{dom}(y)} \frac{|\sigma_{y=c_i} S_t| + l \cdot p_{\text{apr}}(y = c_i)}{|S_t| + l} \tag{2.23}$$

where $p_{\text{apr}}(y = c_i)$ is the a priori probability of y getting the value c_i, and denotes the weight given to the a priori probability. A node is pruned if it does not increase the m probability-error rate.

Pessimistic pruning: The basic idea is that the error ratio estimated using the training set is not reliable enough. Instead, a more realistic measure known as continuity correction for binomial distribution should be used: $\varepsilon'(T, S) = \varepsilon(T, S) + |l(T)| / 2 \cdot |S|$. However, this correction still produces an optimistic error rate. Consequently, it was suggested to prune an internal node t if its error rate is within one standard error from a reference tree, namely

$$\varepsilon'(pr(T,t), S) \le \varepsilon'(T,S) + \sqrt{\frac{\varepsilon'(T,S)(1 - \varepsilon'(T,S))}{|S|}}. \tag{2.24}$$

The last condition is based on the statistical confidence interval for proportions. Usually, the last condition is used such that T refers to a subtree whose root is the internal node t, and S denotes the portion of the training set that refers to the node. The pessimistic pruning procedure performs top-down traversing over the internal nodes. If an internal node is pruned, then all its descendants are removed from the pruning process, resulting in a relatively fast pruning.

Error-based pruning (ebp): This is an evolution of pessimistic pruning. As in pessimistic pruning, the error rate is estimated using the upper bound of the statistical confidence interval for proportions:

$$\varepsilon_{UB}(T,S) = \varepsilon(T,S) + Z_\alpha \cdot \sqrt{\frac{\varepsilon(T,S) \cdot (1 - \varepsilon(T,S))}{|S|}} \tag{2.25}$$

where $\varepsilon(T, S)$ denotes the misclassification rate of the tree T on the training set S. Z is the inverse of the standard normal cumulative distribution, and α is the desired significance level. Let subtree (T, t) denote the subtree rooted by the node t. Let $maxchild$ (T, t) denote the most frequent child node of t (namely, most of the instances in S reach this particular child), and let S_t denote all instances in S that reach the node. The procedure performs bottom-up traversal over all nodes and compares the following values:

ε_{UB} (subtree $(T, t), S_t$)

ε_{UB} (pruned (subtree $(T, t), t), S_t$))

ε_{UB} (subtree $(T, maxchild\ (T, t)), S_{maxchild(T,t)}$).

According to the lowest value, the procedure either leaves the tree as is, prunes the node, or replaces the node t with the subtree rooted by $maxchild$ (T, t).

Optimal pruning (opt): Bohanec and Bratko [17] introduced an algorithm guaranteeing optimality called optimal pruning (*opt*). This algorithm finds the optimal pruning based on dynamic programming, with a complexity of $\theta(|l(T)|^2)$, where T is the initial decision tree. Almuallim [18] introduced an improvement of *opt* called opt-2, which also performs optimal pruning using dynamic programming. However, the time and space complexities of *opt-2* are both $\Theta(|l(T^*)||\text{internal}(T)|)$, where T^* is the target (pruned) decision tree, and T is the initial decision tree.

Since the pruned tree is usually much smaller than the initial tree and the number of internal nodes is smaller than the number of leaves, *opt-2* is usually more efficient than *opt* in terms of computational complexity.

Minimum description length (MDL) pruning: Rissanen [19], Quinlan and Rivest [20], and Mehta et al. [21] used the MDL to evaluate the generalized accuracy of a node. This method measures the size of a decision tree by means of the number of bits required to encode the tree. The MDL method prefers decision trees that can be encoded with fewer bits. Mehta et al. [21] indicate that the cost of a split at a leaf t can be estimated as

$$
\text{Cost}(T) = \sum_{c_i \in \text{dom}(y)} |\sigma_{y = c_i} S_t| \cdot \ln \frac{|S_t|}{|\sigma_{y = c_i} S_t|} + \frac{|\text{dom}(y)| - 1}{2} \ln \frac{|S_t|}{2} + \ln \frac{\pi^{\frac{|\text{dom}(y)|}{2}}}{\Gamma\left(\frac{|\text{dom}(y)|}{2}\right)}
$$

(2.26)

where $|S_t|$ denote the number of instances that have reached the node.

The splitting cost of an internal node is calculated based on the cost aggregation of its children.

2.2.3 Dimensionality Reduction Techniques

In this section, we provide an overview of the mathematical properties and foundations of the various dimensionality reduction techniques [22–24]

There are several dimensionality reduction techniques specifically designed for time series. These methods specifically exploit the frequential content of the signal and its usual sparseness in the frequency space. The most popular methods are those based on wavelets [25, 26], and a distant second is *empirical mode decomposition* [27, 28] (the reader is referred to the references above for further details). We do not cover these techniques here since they are not usually applied for the general-purpose dimensionality reduction of data. From a general point of view, we may say that wavelets project the input time series onto a fixed dictionary (see Section 2.3). This dictionary has the property of making the projection sparse (only a few coefficients are sufficiently large), and the dimensionality reduction is obtained by setting most coefficients (the small ones) to zero. Empirical mode decomposition instead constructs a dictionary specially adapted to each input signal.

To maintain the consistency of this review, we do not cover those dimensionality reduction techniques that take into account the class of observations; that is, there are observations from a class A of objects, observations from a class B, ... and the dimensionality reduction technique should maintain, to the extent possible, the separability of the original classes. Fisher's Linear Discriminant Analysis (LDA) was one of the first techniques to address this issue [29, 30]. Many other works have followed since then; for the most recent works and for a bibliographical review, see [31, 35]. Next, we will focus on vector quantization and mixture models and PCA, which was already introduced to some extent in the previous section.

In the following, we will refer to the observations as input vectors x, whose dimension is M. We will assume that we have N observations, and we will refer to the nth observation as x_n. The whole dataset of observations will be **X**, whereas X will be a $M \times N$ matrix with all the observations as columns. Note that non-bold small letters represent vectors (x), whereas capital, non-bold letters (X) represent matrices.

The goal of the dimensionality reduction is to find another representation χ of a smaller dimension m such that as much information as possible is retained from the original set of observations. This involves some transformation operators from the original vectors onto the new vectors, $\chi = T(x)$. These projected vectors are sometimes called *feature vectors*, and the projection of x_n will be denoted as χ_n. There might not be an inverse for this projection, but there must be a way of recovering an approximate value of the original vector, $\hat{x} = R(\chi)$, such that $\hat{x} \approx x$.

An interesting property of any dimensionality reduction technique is to consider its stability. In this context, a technique is said to be ε-stable if for any two input data points, x_1 and x_2, the following inequality holds [36]: $(1 - \mathcal{E})\|x_1 - x_2\|_2^2 \le \|\chi_1 - \chi_2\|_2^2 \le (1 + \mathcal{E})\|x_1 - x_2\|_2^2$. Intuitively, this equation implies that Euclidean distances in the original input space are relatively conserved in the output feature space.

Methods based on statistics and information theory: This family of methods reduces the input data according to some statistical or information theory criterion. Somehow, the methods based on information theory can be seen as a generalization of the ones based on statistics in the sense that they can capture nonlinear relationships between variables, can handle interval and categorical variables at the same time, and many of them are invariant to monotonic transformations of the input variables.

Vector quantization and mixture models: Probably the simplest way of reducing dimensionality is by assigning a class {among a total of K classes) to each one of the observations x_n. This can be seen as an extreme case of dimensionality reduction in which we go from M dimensions to 1 (the discrete class label χ). Each class, χ, has a representative $\bar{x}_\chi$ which is the average of all the observations assigned to that class. If a vector x_n has been assigned to the χ_n-th class, then its approximation after the dimensionality reduction is simply $\hat{x}_n = \bar{x}_{\chi_n}$, (see Figure 2.19).

The goal is thus to find the representatives $\bar{x}_\chi$, and class assignment $u_\chi(x)(u_\chi(x)$ is equal to 1 if the observation x is assigned to the χ-th class, and is 0 otherwise) such that $J_{VQ} = E\left\{\sum_{\chi=1}^{K} u_\chi(x)\|x - \bar{x}_\chi\|^2\right\}$ is minimized. This problem is known as vector quantization or *k-means*, already briefly introduced in Section 2.1. The optimization of this goal function is a combinatorial problem, although there are heuristics to cut down its cost [37, 38]. An alternative formulation of the k-means objective function is $J_{VQ} = \|X - WU\|_F^2$ subject to $U^tU = I$ and $u_{ij} \in \{0, 1\}$ {i.e. that each input vector is assigned to one and only one class). In this expression, W is a $M \times m$ matrix with all representatives as column vectors, U is an $m \times N$ matrix whose ij-th entry is 1 if the j-th input vector is assigned to the i-th class, and $\|\cdot\|_F^2$ denotes the Frobenius norm of a matrix. This intuitive goal function can be put in a probabilistic framework. Let us assume we have a generative model of how the data is produced. Let us assume that the observed data are noisy versions of K vectors x_χ which are equally likely a priori. Let us assume that the observation noise is normally

Figure 2.19 Black circles represent the input data, x_n; red squares represent class representatives, $\bar{x}_\chi$.

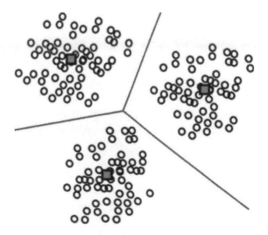

distributed with a spherical covariance matrix $= \sigma^2 I$. The likelihood of observing x_n having produced x_χ is

$$l(x_n | x_\chi, \sigma^2) = \frac{1}{(2\pi)^{\frac{M}{2}} \sigma} \exp\left(-\frac{1}{2} \frac{\|x_n - x_\chi\|^2}{\sigma^2} \right).$$

With our previous definition of $u_\chi(x)$, we can express it as

$$l(x_n | x_\chi, \sigma^2) = \frac{1}{(2\pi)^{\frac{M}{2}} \sigma} \exp\left(-\frac{1}{2} \frac{\sum_{\chi=1}^{K} u_\chi(x_n) \|x_n - x_\chi\|^2}{\sigma^2} \right)$$

The log likelihood of observing the whole dataset $x_n \{n = 1, 2, ..., N\}$ after removing all constants is $L(X | x_\chi) = \sum_{n=1}^{N} \sum_{\chi=1}^{K} u_\chi(x_n) \|x_n - x_\chi\|^2$ We thus see that the goal function of vector quantization J_{VQ} produces the maximum likelihood estimates of the underlying x_l vectors.

Under this generative model, the probability density function of the observations is the convolution of a Gaussian function and a set of delta functions located at the x_χ vectors, that is, a set of Gaussians located at the x_χ vectors. The vector quantization then is an attempt to find the centers of the Gaussians forming the probability density function of the input data. This idea has been further pursued by *Mixture Models*, which are a generalization of vector quantization in which, instead of looking only for the means of the Gaussians associated with each class, we also allow each class to have a different covariance matrix Σ_χ and different a priori probability π_χ. The algorithm looks for estimates of all these parameters by *Expectation–Maximization*, and at the end produces for each input observation x_n, the label χ of the Gaussian that has the maximum likelihood of having generated that observation.

This concept can be extend and, instead of making a hard class assignment, a fuzzy class assignment can be used by allowing $0 \le u_\chi(x) \le 1$ and requiring $\sum_{\chi=1}^{I} u_\chi(x) = 1$ for all x. This is another vector quantization algorithm called *fuzzy k-means*. The k-means algorithm is based on a quadratic objective function, which is known to be strongly affected by outliers. This drawback can be alleviated by taking the l_1 norm of the approximation errors and modifying the problem to $J_{K-medians} = \|X - WU\|_1^2$ subject to $U^t U = I$ and $u_{ij} \in \{0, 1\}$. A different approach can be used to find data representatives less affected by outliers, which we may call robust vector quantization, $J_{RVQ} = E\left\{ \sum_{\chi=1}^{K} u_\chi(x) \Phi\left(\|x - \bar{x}_\chi\|^2 \right) \right\}$, where $\Phi(x)$ is a function less sensitive to outliers than $\Phi(x) = x$, for instance, $\Phi(x) = x^\alpha$ with α about 0.5.

Principal component analysis (PCA): Introduced in Section 2.1, is by far one of the most popular algorithms for dimensionality reduction [39–42]. Given a set of observations x, with dimension M (they lie in $\mathbb{R}^M$), PCA is the standard technique for finding the single best (in the sense of least-square error) subspace of a given dimension, m. Without loss of generality, we may assume the data is zero-mean and the subspace to fit is a linear subspace (passing through the origin).

This algorithm is based on the search for orthogonal directions explaining as much variance of the data as possible. In terms of dimensionality reduction, it can be formulated [43] as the problem of finding the m orthonormal directions w_i minimizing the representation error $J_{PCA} = E\left\{ \|x - \sum_{i=1}^{m} \langle w_i, x \rangle w_i\|^2 \right\}$. In this objective function, the reduced vectors are the projections $\chi = (\langle w_1, x \rangle, ..., \langle w_m, x \rangle)^t$ This can be much more compactly written as $\chi = W^t x$, where W is a $M \times m$ matrix whose columns are the orthonormal directions w_i {or equivalently $W^t W = I$). The approximation to the original vectors is given by $\hat{x} = \sum_{i=1}^{m} \langle w_i, x \rangle w_i$, or equivalently, $\hat{x} = W\chi$.

In Figure 2.15, we have shown a graphical representation of a PCA transformation in only two dimensions ($x \in \mathbb{R}^2$) with a slightly different notation (χ represented by z). As can be seen from Figure 2.15, the variance of the data in the original data space is best captured in the rotated space given by vectors $=W^t x$. χ_1 is the first principal component, and it goes in the direction of most variance; χ_2 is the second principal component, and is orthogonal to the first direction and goes in the second direction with the most variance (in $\mathbb{R}^2$ there is not much choice, but in the general case, $\mathbb{R}^M$, there is). Observe that without loss of generality the data is centered about the origin of the output space. We can rewrite the objective function as

$$J_{PCA} = \left\{ \|x - W\chi\|^2 \right\} = E\left\{ \|x - WW^t x\|^2 \right\} \propto \|X - WW^t X\|_F^2.$$

Note that the class membership matrix (U in vector quantization) has been substituted in this case by $W^t X$, which in general can take any positive or negative value. It, thus, has lost its membership meaning and simply constitutes the weights of the linear combination of the column vectors of W that better approximate each input x. Finally, the PCA objective function can also be written as

$J_{PCA} = \text{Tr}\{W^t \Sigma_X W\}$ [44], where $\Sigma_X = \frac{1}{N} \sum_i (x_i - \bar{x})(x_i - \bar{x})^t$ is the covariance matrix of the observed data. The PCA formulation has also been extended to complex-valued input vectors [45]; the method is called *non-circular PCA*.

The matrix projection of the input vectors onto a lower-dimensional space ($\chi = W^t x$) is a widespread technique in dimensionality reduction. As an illustration, let us look at the following example [46]:

Design Example 2.5

Assume that we are analyzing scientific articles related to a specific domain. Each article will be represented by a vector x of word frequencies; that is, we choose a set of M words representative of our scientific area, and we annotate how many times each word appears in each article. Each vector x is then orthogonally projected onto the new subspace defined by the vectors w_i. Each vector w_i has dimension M, and it can be understood as a "topic" (i.e. a topic is characterized by the relative frequencies of the M different words; two different topics will differ in the relative frequencies of the M words). The projection of x onto each w_i gives an idea of how important topic w_i is for representing the article. Important topics have large projection values and, therefore, large values in the corresponding component of χ.

It can be shown [43, 47], as already indicated in Section 2.1, that when the input vectors, x, are zero-mean (if they are not, we can transform the input data simply by subtracting the sample average vector), then the solution of the minimization of J_{PCA} is given by the m eigenvectors associated to the largest m eigenvalues of the covariance matrix of x $\{C_x = \frac{1}{N} XX^t$, note that the covariance matrix of x is a $M \times M$ matrix with M eigenvalues). If the eigenvalue decomposition of the input covariance matrix is $C_x = W_M \Lambda_M W_M^t$ (since C_x is a real-symmetric matrix), then the feature vectors are constructed as $\chi = \Lambda_m^{-\frac{1}{2}} W_m^t x$, where Λ_m is a diagonal matrix with the m largest eigenvalues of the matrix Λ_M and W_m are the corresponding m columns from the eigenvectors matrix W_M. We could have constructed all the feature vectors at the same time by projecting the whole matrix

$X, U = \Lambda_m^{-\frac{1}{2}} W_m^t X$. Note that the i-th feature is the projection of the input vector x onto the i-th eigenvector, $\chi_i = \lambda_i^{\frac{1}{2}} w_i^t x$. The computed feature vectors have an identity covariance matrix, $C_\chi = I$, meaning that the different features are decorrelated.

Univariate variance is a second-order statistical measure of the departure of the input observations with respect to the sample mean. A generalization of the univariate variance to multivariate variables is the trace of the input covariance matrix. By choosing the m largest eigenvalues of the covariance matrix C_x, we guarantee that we are making a representation in the feature space explaining as much variance of the input space as possible with only m variables. As already indicated in Section 2.1, in fact, w_1 is the direction in which the data exhibit the largest variability, w_2 is the direction with largest variability once the variability along w_1 has been removed, w_3 is the direction with largest variability once the variability along w_1 and w_2 has been removed, and so on. Thanks to the orthogonality of the w_i vectors, and the subsequent decorrelation of the feature vectors, the total variance explained by PCA decomposition can be conveniently measured as the sum of the variances of each feature,

$$\sigma_{PCA}^2 = \sum_{i=1}^{m} \lambda_i = \sum_{i=1}^{m} \text{Var}\{\chi_i\}.$$

References

1 Robert Nau, Statistical forecasting: notes on regression and time series analysis, https://people.duke.edu/~rnau/regintro.htm (accessed 12 May 2021).

2 https://www.analyticsvidhya.com/blog/2016/01/xgboost-algorithm-easy-steps

3 PulkitS01. K-Means implementation. GitHub, Inc. https://gist.github.com/PulkitS01/97c9920b1c913ba5e7e101d0e9030b0e

4 https://pdfslide.net/documents/chapter-321-logistic-regression-ncss-321-logistic-regression-introduction-.html

5 https://iq.opengenus.org/newton-raphson-method

6 https://www.math.ubc.ca/~anstee/math104/newtonmethod.pdf

7 http://mathforcollege.com/nm/mws/gen/03nle/mws_gen_nle_txt_newton.pdf

8 Rokach, L. and Maimon, O. (2005). Top-down induction of decision trees classifiers – a survey. *IEEE Trans. Syst., Man, Cybernet. – Part C: Appl. Rev.* **35** (4): 476–487.

9 Safavin, S.R. and Landgrebe, D. (1991). A survey of decision tree classifier methodology. *IEEE Trans. Syst. Man Cybern.* **21** (3): 660–674.

10 Murthy, S.K. (1998). Automatic construction of decision trees from data: a multidisciplinary survey. *Data Min. Knowl. Discovery* **2** (4): 345–389.

11 Kohavi, R. and Quinlan, J.R. (2002, ch. 16.1.3). Decision-tree discovery. In: *Handbook of Data Mining and Knowledge Discovery* (eds. W. Klosgen and J.M. Zytkow), 267–276. London, U.K.: Oxford University Press.

12 Hastie, T. *Trees, Bagging, Random Forests and Boosting*. Stanford University lecture notes.

13 Hancock, T.R., Jiang, T., Li, M., and Tromp, J. (1996). Lower bounds on learning decision lists and trees. *Inf. Comput.* **126** (2): 114–122.

14 Hyafil, L. and Rivest, R.L. (1976). Constructing optimal binary decision trees is NP-complete. *Inf. Process. Lett.* **5** (1): 15–17.

15 Zantema, H. and Bodlaender, H.L. (2000). Finding small equivalent decision trees is hard. *Int. J. Found. Comput. Sci.* **11** (2): 343–354.

16 Naumov, G.E. (1991). NP-completeness of problems of construction of optimal decision trees. *Sov. Phys. Dokl.* **36** (4): 270–271.

17 Bratko, I. and Bohanec, M. (1994). Trading accuracy for simplicity in decision trees. *Mach. Learn.* **15**: 223–250.

18 Almuallim, H. (1996). An efficient algorithm for optimal pruning of decision trees. *Artif. Intell.* **83** (2): 347–362.

19 Rissanen, J. (1989). *Stochastic Complexity and Statistical Inquiry*. Singapore: World Scientific.

20 Quinlan, J.R. and Rivest, R.L. (1989). Inferring decision trees using the minimum description length principle. *Inf. Comput.* **80**: 227–248.

21 Mehta, R.L., Rissanen, J., and Agrawal, R. (1995). *Proceedings of the 1st International Conference on Knowledge Discovery and Data Mining*, pp. 216–221.

22 Dash, M. and Liu, H. (1997). Feature selection for classification. *Intell. Data Anal.* **1**: 131–156.

23 Guyon, I. and Eliseeff, A. (2003). An introduction to variable and feature selection. *J. Mach. Learn. Res.* **3**: 1157–1182.

24 Saeys, Y., Inza, I., and Larrañaga, P. (2007). A review of feature selection techniques in bioinformatics. *Bioinformatics* **23**: 2507–2517.

25 Rioul, O. and Vetterli, M. (1991). Wavelets and signal processing. *IEEE Signal Process. Mag.* **8**: 14–38.

26 Graps, A. (1995). An introduction to wavelets. *IEEE Comput. Sci. Eng.* **2**: 50–61.

27 Huang, H.E., Shen, Z., Long, S.R. et al. (1998). The empirical mode decomposition and the Hilbert spectrum for nonlinear and non-stationary time series analysis. *Proc. R. Soc. Lond. A* **454**: 903–995.

28 Rilling, G.; Flandrin, P. & Goncalves, P. On empirical mode decomposition and its algorithms Proc. IEEE-EURASIP Workshop on Nonlinear Signal and Image Processing, 2003

29 Fisher, R.A. (1936). The use of multiple measurements in taxonomic problems. *Ann. Eugen.* **7**: 179–188.

30 Fodor, I.K. (2002). *A Survey of Dimension Reduction Techniques*. Lawrence Livermore National Laboratory.

31 Bian, W. and Tao, D. (2011). Max-min distance analysis by using sequential SDP relaxation for dimension reduction. *IEEE Trans. Pattern Anal. Mach. Intell.* **33**: 1037–1050.

32 Cai, H., Mikolajczyk, K., and Matas, J. (2011). Learning linear discriminant projections for dimensionality reduction of image descriptors. *IEEE Trans. Pattern Anal. Mach. Intell.* **33**: 338–352.

33 Kim, M. and Pavlovic, V. (2011). Central subspace dimensionality reduction using covariance operators. *IEEE Trans. Pattern Anal. Mach. Intell.* **33**: 657–670.

34 Lin, Y.Y., Liu, T.L., and Fuh, C.S. (2011). Multiple kernel learning for dimensionality reduction. *IEEE Trans. Pattern Anal. Mach. Intell.* **33**: 1147–1160.

35 Batmanghelich, N.K., Taskar, B., and Davatzikos, C. (2012). Generative-discriminative basis learning for medical imaging. *IEEE Trans. Med. Imaging* **31**: 51–69.

36 Baraniuk, R.G., Cevher, V., and Wakin, M.B. (2012). Low-dimensional models for dimensionality reduction and signal recovery: a geometric perspective. *Proc. IEEE* **98**: 959–971.

37 Gray, R.M. (1984). Vector quantization IEEE acoustics. *Speech Signal Process. Mag.* **1**: 4–29.

38 Gersho, A. and Gray, R.M. (1992). *Vector quantization and signal compression*. Kluwer Academic Publishers.

39 Pearson, K. (1901). On lines and planes of closest fit to systems of points in space. *Philos. Mag.* **2**: 559–572.

40 Wold, S., Esbensen, K., and Geladi, P. (1987). Principal component analysis. *Chemom. Intel. Lab. Syst.* **2**: 37–35.

41 Dunteman, G.H. (1989). *Principal Component Analysis*. Sage Publications.

42 Jollife, I. T. *Principal Component Analysis Wiley*, 2002

43 Hÿvarinen, A., Karhunen, J., and Oja, E. (2001). *Independent Component Analysis*. Wiley.

44 He, R., Hu, B.-G., Zheng, W.-S., and Kong, X.-W. (2011). Robust principal component analysis based on maximum correntropy criterion. *IEEE Trans. Image Process.* **20**: 1485–1494.

45 Li, X.L., Adali, T., and Anderson, M. (2011). Noncircular principal component analysis and its application to model selection. *IEEE Trans. Signal Process.* **59**: 4516–4528.

46 Sorzano, C.O.S., Vargas, J., and Pascual-Montano, A. A survey of dimensionality reduction techniques. https://arxiv.org/ftp/arxiv/papers/1403/1403.2877.pdf

47 Jenssen, R. (2010). Kernel entropy component analysis. *IEEE Trans. Pattern Anal. Mach. Intell.* **32**: 847–860.

48 https://medium.com/machine-learning-101/chapter-2-svm-support-vector-machine-theory-f0812effc72

49 https://cgl.ethz.ch/teaching/former/vc_master_06/Downloads/viscomp-svm-clustering_6.pdf

50 https://people.duke.edu/~rnau/regintro.htm

51 https://discuss.analyticsvidhya.com/t/what-does-min-samples-split-means-in-decision-tree/6233

52 https://medium.com/@mohtedibf/indepth-parameter-tuning-for-decision-tree-6753118a03c3

53 https://gist.github.com/PulkitS01/97c9920b1c913ba5e7e101d0e9030b0e

3

Artificial Neural Networks

3.1 Multi-layer Feedforward Neural Networks

3.1.1 Single Neurons

A biological [1] and mathematical model of a neuron can be represented as shown in Figure 3.1 with the output of the neuron modeled as

$$s = \sum_{i=1}^{N} w_i x_i + w_b, \tag{3.1}$$

$$y = f(s), \tag{3.2}$$

where x_i are the inputs to the neuron, w_i are the synaptic weights, and w_b models a *bias*. In general, f represents the nonlinear *activation function*. Early models used a *sign* function for the activation. In this case, the output y would be $+1$ or -1 depending on whether the total input at the *node s* exceeds 0 or not. Nowadays, a *sigmoid* function is used rather than a hard threshold. One should immediately notice the similarity of Eqs. (3.1) and (3.2) with Eqs. (2.1) and (2.2) defining the operation of a linear predictor. This should suggest that in this chapter we will take the problem of parameter estimation to the next level. The sigmoid, shown in Figure 3.1, is a differentiable squashing function usually evaluated as $y = tanh\,(s)$. This engineering model is an oversimplified approximation to the biological model. It neglects *temporal* relations. This is because the goals of the engineer differ from that of the neurobiologist. The former must use the models feasible for practical implementation. The computational abilities of an isolated neuron are extremely limited.

For electrical engineers, the most popular applications of single neurons are in adaptive finite impulse response (FIR) filters. Here, $s(k) = \Sigma_i^N w_i x(k-i)$, where k represents a discrete time index. Usually, a *linear* activation function is used. In electrical engineering, adaptive filters are used in signal processing with practical applications like adaptive equalization, and active noise cancelation.

Multi-layer neural networks: A neural network is built up by incorporating the basic neuron model into different configurations. One example is the Hopfield network, where the output of each neuron can have a connection to the input of all neurons in the network, including a self-feedback connection. Another option is the *multi-layer feedforward network* illustrated in Figure 3.2. Here, we have layers of neurons where the output of a neuron in a given layer is input to all the neurons in the next layer. We may also have sparse connections or direct connections that may bypass layers. In these networks, no feedback loops exist within the structure. These network are sometimes referred to as *backpropagation networks*.

Artificial Intelligence and Quantum Computing for Advanced Wireless Networks, First Edition.
Savo G. Glisic and Beatriz Lorenzo.
© 2022 John Wiley & Sons Ltd. Published 2022 by John Wiley & Sons Ltd.

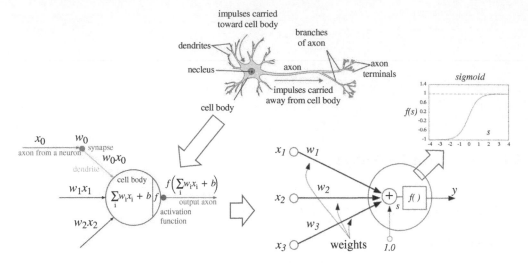

Figure 3.1 From biological to mathematical simplified model of a neuron. *Source:* CS231n Convolutional Neural Networks for Visual Recognition [1].

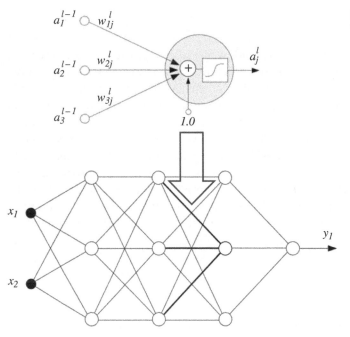

Figure 3.2 Block diagram of feedforward network.

Notation: A single neuron extracted from the l-th layer of an L-layer network is also depicted in Figure 3.2. Parameters w_{ij}^l denote the weights on the links between neuron i in the previous layer and neuron j in layer l. The output of the j-th neuron in layer l is represented by the variable a_j^l. The outputs a_i^L in the last L-th layer represent the overall outputs of the network. Here, we use notation y_i for the outputs as $y_i = a_i^L$. Parameters x_i, defined as inputs to the network, may be viewed as a 0-th layer with notation $x_i = a_i^0$. These definitions are summarized in Table 3.1.

Table 3.1   Multi-layer network notation.

w_{ij}^l	Weight connecting neuron i in layer $l-1$ to neuron j in layer l
w_{bj}^l	Bias weight for neuron j in layer l
$s_j^l = \Sigma_i w_{ij}^l a_i^{l-1} + w_{bj}^l$	Summing junction for neuron j in layer l
$a_j^l = tanh\left(s_j^l\right)$	Activation (output) value for neuron j in layer l
$x_i = a_i^0$	i-th external input to network
$y_i = a_i^L$	i-th output to network

Define an input vector $x = [x_0, x_1, x_2, ... x_N]$ and output vector $y = [y_0, y_1, y_2, ... y_M]$. The network maps, $y = N(w, x)$, the input x to the outputs y using the weights w. Since fixed weights are used, this mapping is *static*; there are no internal dynamics. Still, this network is a powerful tool for computation.

It has been shown that with two or more layers and a sufficient number of internal neurons, any *uniformly* continuous function can be represented with acceptable accuracy. The performance rests on the ways in which this "universal function approximator" is utilized.

3.1.2   Weights Optimization

The specific mapping with a network is obtained by an appropriate choice of weight values. Optimizing a set of weights is referred to as network training. An example of supervised learning scheme is shown in Figure 3.3. A training set of input vectors associated with the desired output vector, $\{(x_1, d_1), ... (x_P, d_P)\}$, is provided. The difference between the desired output and the actual output of the network, for a given input sequence x, is defined as the error

$$e = d - y. \tag{3.3}$$

The overall objective function to be minimized over the training set is the given squared error

$$J = \sum_{p=1}^{P} e_p^T e_p. \tag{3.4}$$

The training should find the set of weights w that minimizes the cost J subject to the constraint of the network topology. We see that training a neural network represent a standard optimization problem.

A stochastic gradient descent (SGD) algorithm is an option as an optimization method. For each sample from the training set, the weights are adapted as

$$\Delta w = -\mu \hat{\nabla}, \tag{3.5}$$

where $\hat{\nabla} = \partial e^T e / \partial w$ is the error gradient for the current input pattern, and μ is the learning rate.

Backpropagation: This is a standard way to find $\partial e^T e / \partial w_{ij}^l$ in Eq. (3.5). Here we provide a formal derivation.

Single neuron case – Consider first a *single* linear neuron, which we may describe compactly as

$$y = \sum_{i=0}^{N} w_i x_i = w^T x, \tag{3.6}$$

where $w = [w_0, w_1, ... w_N]$ and $x = [1, x_1, ... x_N]$. In this simple setup

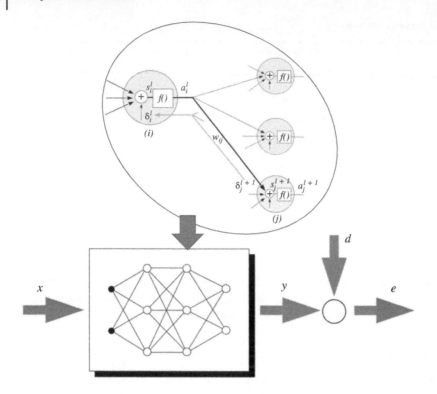

Figure 3.3 Schematic representation of supervised learning.

$$\hat{\nabla} = \frac{\partial e^2}{\partial w} = 2e\frac{\partial(d-y)}{\partial w} = -2ex, \tag{3.7}$$

so that $\Delta w = 2\mu ex$. From this, we have $\Delta w_i = 2\mu ex_i$, which is the least mean square (LMS) algorithm. In a *multi-layer network*, we just formally extend this procedure. For this we use the chain rule

$$\frac{\partial(e^T e)}{\partial w_{ij}^l} = \frac{\partial(e^T e)}{\partial s_j^l}\frac{\partial s_j^l}{\partial w_{ij}^l} = \delta_j^i a_i^{l-1}, \tag{3.8}$$

with $\delta_j^i = \partial(e^T e)/\partial s_j^l$ leading to the weight update $\Delta w_{ij}^l = -\mu\delta_j^l a_i^{l-1}$.

Parameters δ are derived recursively starting from the output layer:

$$\delta_j^L = \nabla\frac{\partial(e^T e)}{\partial s_j^L} = \frac{\partial(e^T e)}{\partial a_j^L}\frac{\partial a_j^L}{\partial s_j^L} = \frac{\partial(e^T e)}{\partial y_j}f'(s_i^L), \tag{3.9}$$

where $f'(s_i^L)$ is the derivative of the sigmoid function of s. We have also used for the output layer $y_j = a_j^L$. With this, at the output layer, each neuron has an explicit desired response, so we can write

$$\frac{\partial(e^T e)}{\partial y_j} = \frac{\partial e_j^2}{\partial y_j} = 2e_j\frac{\partial\left(d_j - y_j\right)}{\partial y_j} = -2e_j. \tag{3.10}$$

Substituting into Eq. (3.9) yields $\delta_j^L = -2e_j f'\left(s_j^L\right)$.

To calculate the $\delta's$, we note that $e^T e$ is influenced through s_i^l indirectly through all node values s_j^{l+1} in the next layer. Referring to the upper part of Figure 3.3, we again employ the chain rule

$$\delta_i^l = \frac{\partial(e^T e)}{\partial s_i^l} = \sum_j \left(\frac{\partial(e^T e)}{\partial s_j^{l+1}} \right) \left(\frac{\partial s_j^{l+1}}{\partial s_i^l} \right) \tag{3.11}$$

with

$$\frac{\partial s_j^{l+1}}{\partial s_i^l} = \left(\frac{\partial s_j^{l+1}}{\partial a_i^l} \right) \left(\frac{\partial a_i^l}{\partial s_i^l} \right) = w_{ij}^{l1} f'(s_i^l). \tag{3.12}$$

Recalling that $\partial(e^T e)/\partial s_j^{l+1} = \delta_j^{l+1}$, we get $\delta_j^i = f'(s_i^l) \sum_j \delta_j^{i+1} w_{ij}^{l+1}$. In summary, we have

$$\nabla w_{ij}^l = -\mu \delta_j^l a_x^{l-1} \tag{3.13}$$

$$\delta_i^l = \begin{cases} -2e_i f'(s_i^L) & l = L \\ f'(s_i^l) \cdot \sum_j \delta_j^{i+1} . w_{ij}^{l+1} & 1 \le l \le L-1, \end{cases} \tag{3.14}$$

For the bias weight w_b^l we note that $a_x^{l-1} = 1$ in Eq. (3.13). The above processing is illustrated in Figure 3.4, indicating the symmetry between the forward propagation of neuron activation values and the backward propagation of δ terms.

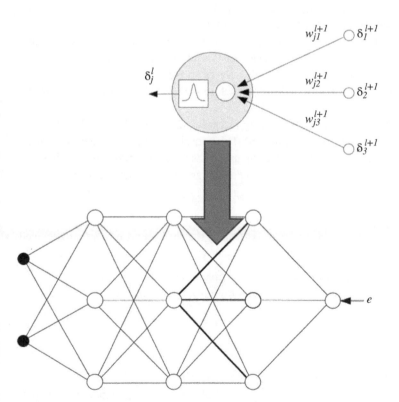

Figure 3.4 Illustration of backpropagation.

3.2 FIR Architecture

3.2.1 Spatial Temporal Representations

Most often in engineering, prior to becoming a member of the observation set, the input signals to the neural network have gone through some form of filtering. This also coincides with the form of *potential* maintained at the axon hillock region of the neural cell. With this in mind, we may modify Eq. (3.1) as

$$s(t) = \sum_i \int_0^t w_i(\tau)x_i(t-\tau)d\tau + w_b = \sum_i w_i(t) * x_i(t) + w_b, \tag{3.15}$$

By adding filtering operations, we have included the equally important *temporal* dimension in the static model. For our purposes, we will now be interested in adapting the filters. To this end, we assume a discrete FIR representation for each filter. This yields

$$s(k) = \sum_i \sum_{n=0}^M w_i(n)x_i(k-n) + w_b = \sum_i w_i x_i(k) + w_b, \tag{3.16}$$

with k being the discrete time index for some sampling rate Δt, and $w_i(n)$ being the coefficients for the FIR filters. In the following, we will represent the vector $w_i = [w_i(0), w_i(1), \dots, w_i(M)]$ and the delayed states as $x_i(k) = [x_i(k), x_i(k-1), \dots, x_i(k-M)]$. Now, a filter operation is written as the vector dot product $w_i x_i(k)$, with time implicitly included in the notation.

The top part of Figure 3.5 shows a standard representation of an FIR filter as a tap delay line. Although this filter represents several biological processes, as well as many engineering solutions, for ease of reference to a real neuron network we will refer to an FIR filter as a *synaptic* filter or simply a *synapse*. The output of the neuron will be as before $y(k) = f(s(k))$ with $f(x) = tanh(x)$, and we have added only a time index k.

We use the same approach to network modeling as in the previous section. Each link in the network is now created using an FIR filter (see Figure 3.5). The neural network no longer performs a simple static mapping from input to output; internal memory has now been added to simple static mapping from input to output. At the same time, since there are no feedback loops, the overall network is still FIR [2–5]. The notation now becomes $w_{ij}^l = \left[w_{ij}^l(0), w_{ij}^l(1), \dots w_{ij}^l(M^l) \right]$.

For all filters in a given layer, we will assume that the order M^l is the same. The activation value $a_j^l(k)$, representing the output of a neuron in a layer, is given by the corresponding vector of delayed activations written as $a_i^l(k) = \left[a_i^l(k), a_i^l(k-1)_1 \dots a_i^l(k-M^{l+1}) \right]$. Again, at the edges we have $x_i(k) = a_i^0(k)$ and $y_i(k) = a_i^L(k)$. Instead of Table 3.1, a complete set of definitions is summarized in Table 3.2. The form of the two tables demonstrates a high level of similarity.

3.2.2 Neural Network Unfolding

An interesting, more insightful, representation of the FIR network is derived by using a concept known as *unfolding in time*. The general strategy is to remove all time delays by expanding the network into a larger equivalent static structure.

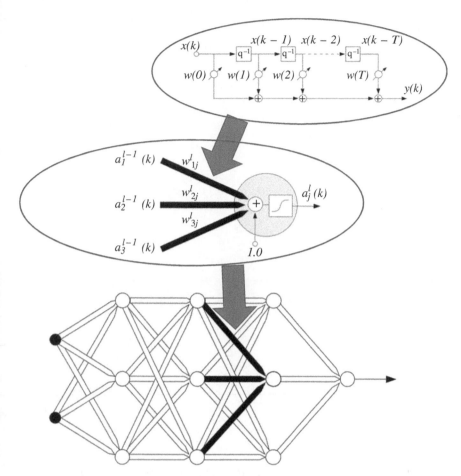

Figure 3.5 Finite impulse response (FIR) neuron and neural network.

Table 3.2 Finite impulse response (FIR) multi-layer network notation.

$\mathbf{w}_{i,j}^{l} = \left[w_{i,j}^{l}(0), w_{i,j}^{l}(1), .. w_{i,j}^{l}(M^{l}) \right]$	Weight connecting neuron i in layer $l-1$ to neuron j in layer l
w_{bj}^{l}	Bias weight for neuron j in layer l
$s_{j}^{l}(k) = \Sigma_{i} \mathbf{w}_{ij}^{l} \cdot \mathbf{a}_{i}^{l-1}(k) + w_{bj}^{l}$	Summing junction or neuron j in layer l
$a_{j}^{l}(k) = tanh\left(s_{j}^{l} \right)$	Activation value for neuron j in layer l
$\mathbf{a}_{i}^{l}(k) = \left[a_{i}^{l}(k), a_{i}^{l}(k-1), .. a_{i}^{l}(k-M^{l+1}) \right]$	Vector of delayed activation values
$x_{i}(k) = a_{i}^{0}(k)$	i-th external input to network
$y_{i}(k) = a_{i}^{L}(k)$	i-th output of network

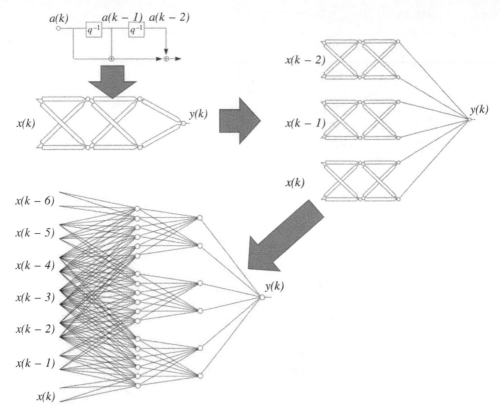

Figure 3.6 Finite impulse response (FIR) network unfolding.

Example For the network shown in Figure 3.6, all connections are made by second-order (three tap) FIRs. Although at first sight it looks as though we have only 10 connections in the network, in reality there are a total of 30 variable filter coefficients (not counting five bias weights). Starting at the output, each tap delay can be interpreted as a "virtual neuron," whose input is delayed by the given number of time steps. A tap delay can be "removed" by replicating the previous layers of the network and delaying the input to the network as shown in Figure 3.6. The procedure is then carried on backward throughout each layer until all delays have been removed. The final unfolded structure is depicted in the bottom of Figure 3.6.

3.2.3 Adaptation

For supervised learning with input sequence x(k), the difference between the desired output at time k and the actual output of the network is the error

$$e(k) = d(k) - y(k). \tag{3.17}$$

The total squared error over the sequence is given by

$$J = \sum_{k=1}^{K} e(k)^T e(k). \tag{3.18}$$

The objective of training is to determine the set of FIR filter coefficients (weights) that minimizes the cost J subject to the constraint of the network topology. A gradient descent approach will be utilized again in which the weights are iteratively updated.

For *instantaneous gradient descent*, FIR filters may be updated at each time slot as

$$w_{ij}^l(k+1) = w_{ij}^l(k) - \mu \frac{\partial e^T(k)e(k)}{\partial w_{ij}^l(k)}, \tag{3.19}$$

where $\partial e^T(k)e(k)/\partial w_{ij}^l(k)$ is the *instantaneous* gradient estimate, and μ is the learning rate. However, deriving an expression for this parameter results in an overlapping of number of chain rules. A simple *backpropagation-like* formulation does not exist anymore.

Temporal backpropagation is an alternative approach that can be used to avoid the above problem. To discuss it, let us consider two alternative forms of the true gradient of the cost function:

$$\frac{\partial J}{\partial w_{ij}^l} = \sum_{k=1}^{K} \frac{\partial e^T(k)e(k)}{\partial w_{ij}^l} = \sum_{k=1}^{K} \frac{\partial J}{\partial s_j^l(k)} \frac{\partial s_j^l(k)}{\partial w_{ij}^l}. \tag{3.20}$$

Note that

$$\frac{\partial J}{\partial s_j^l(k)} \frac{\partial s_j^l(k)}{\partial w_{ij}^l} \neq \frac{\partial e^T(k)e(k)}{\partial w_{ij}^l},$$

only their sum over all k is equal. Based on this new expansion, each term in the sum is used to form the following stochastic algorithm:

$$w_{ij}^l(k+1) = w_{ij}^l(k) - \mu \frac{\partial J}{\partial s_j^l(k)} \frac{\partial s_j^l(k)}{\partial w_{ij}^l}. \tag{3.21}$$

For small learning rates, the total accumulated weight change is approximately equal to the true gradient. This training algorithm is termed *temporal backpropagation*.

To complete the algorithm, recall the summing junction is defined as

$$s_j^l(k) = \sum_i w_{ij}^l a_i^{l-1}(k) + w_b^l = \sum_i s_{ij}^l(k) + w_b^l, \tag{3.22}$$

where intermediate variable s_{ij}^l are defined for convenience. The partial derivative $\partial s_j^l(k)/\partial w_{ij}^l$ in Eq. (3.21) is easily evaluated as

$$\frac{\partial s_j^l(k)}{\partial w_{ij}^l} = \frac{\partial \left(w_{ij}^l \cdot a_i^{l-1}(k) \right)}{\partial w_{ij}^l} = a_i^{l-1}(k). \tag{3.23}$$

This holds for all layers in the network. Defining $\partial J/\partial s_j^l(k) = \delta_j^l(k)$ allows us to rewrite Eq. (3.21) as

$$w_{ij}^l(k+1) = w_{ij}^l(k) - \mu \delta_j^l(k) \cdot a_i^{l-1}(k). \tag{3.24}$$

We now show that a simple recursive formula exists for finding $\delta_j^l(k)$. Starting with the output layer, we observe that $s_j^L(k)$ influences only the instantaneous output node error $e_j(k)$. Thus, we have

$$\delta_j^L(k) = \frac{\partial J}{\partial s_j^L(k)} = \frac{\partial[\Sigma_k e^T(k)e(k)]}{\partial s_j^L(k)} = \frac{\partial e_j^2(k)}{\partial s_j^L(k)}$$

$$= \frac{\partial e_j^2(k)}{\partial a_j^L(k)} \frac{\partial a_j^L(k)}{\partial s_j^L(k)} = \frac{\partial e_j^2(k)}{\partial y_j(k)} f'\left(s_j^L(k)\right) = -2e_j(k)f'\left(s_j^L(k)\right) \qquad (3.25)$$

For a hidden layer, $s_j^l(k)$ has an impact on the error indirectly through all node values $s_m^{l+1}(k)$ in the subsequent layer. Due to the tap delay lines, $s_j^l(k)$ also has an impact on the error across time. Therefore, the chain rule now becomes

$$\delta_j^l(k) = \frac{\partial J}{\partial s_j^l(k)} = \sum_m \sum_t \frac{\partial J}{\partial s_m^{l+1}(t)} \frac{\partial s_m^{l+1}(t)}{\partial s_j^l(k)} \qquad (3.26)$$

where by definition $\partial J/\partial s_m^{l+1}(t) = \delta_m^{l+1}(t)$. Continuing with the remaining term

$$\frac{\partial s_m^{l+1}(t)}{\partial s_j^l(k)} = \frac{\partial s_m^{l+1}(t)}{\partial a_j^l(k)} \frac{\partial a_j^l(k)}{\partial s_j^l(k)} = \frac{\partial s_m^{l+1}(t)}{\partial a_j^l(k)} f'\left(s_j^l(k)\right). \qquad (3.27)$$

Now

$$\frac{\partial s_m^{l+1}(t)}{\partial a_j^l(k)} = \frac{\partial s_{jm}^{l+1}(t)}{\partial a_j^l(k)} \qquad (3.27a)$$

since the only influence $a_j^l(k)$ has on $s_m^{l+1}(t)$ is via the synapse connecting unit j in layer l to unit m in layer $l+1$. The definition of the synapse is explicitly given as

$$s_{jm}^{l+1}(t) = \sum_{p=0}^{M^{l+1}} w_{jm}^{l+1}(p)a_j^l(t-p). \qquad (3.28)$$

Thus

$$\frac{\partial s_{jm}^{l+1}(t)}{\partial a_j^l(k)} = w_{jm}^{l+1}(p) \text{ for } t-p = k \qquad (3.29)$$

$$= \begin{cases} w_{jm}^{l+1}(t-k) & \text{for } 0 \leq t-k \leq M^{l+1} \\ 0 & \text{otherwise.} \end{cases} \qquad (3.30)$$

Making all substitutions into Eq. (3.26), we get

$$\delta_j^l(k) = f'\left(s_j^l(k)\right) \sum_m \sum_{t=k}^{A} \delta_m^{l+1}(t)w_{jm}^{l+1}(t-k); \quad A = M^{l+1} + k$$

$$= f'\left(s_j^l(k)\right) \sum_m \sum_{n=0}^{B} \delta_m^{l+1}(k+n)w_{jm}^{l+1}(n); \quad B = M^{l+1} \qquad (3.31)$$

$$= f'\left(s_j^l(k)\right) \sum_m \delta_m^{l+1}(k) \, w_{jm}^{l+1},$$

where we have defined the vector

$$\delta_m^l(k) = \left[\delta_m^l(k), \delta_m^l(k+1), ..., \delta_m^l(k+M^l)\right]. \qquad (3.32)$$

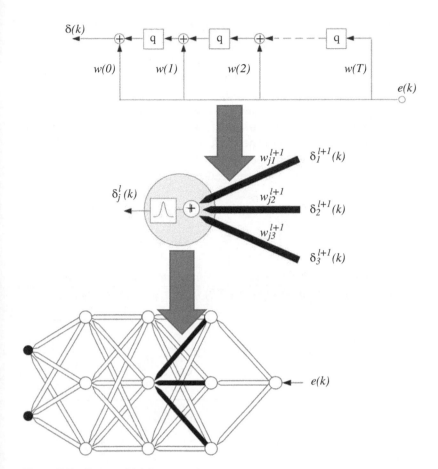

Figure 3.7 Temporal backpropagation.

Each term $\delta_m^{l+1}(k)w_{jm}^{l+1}$ within the sum corresponds to a *reverse* FIR filter. This is illustrated in Figure 3.7. The filter is drawn in such a way to emphasize the reversal of signal propagation through the FIR. Representing the forward propagation of states and the backward propagation of error terms requires simply reversing the direction of signal flow. In this process, unit delay operators q^{-1} should be replaced with unit advances q^{+1}. The complete adaptation algorithm can be summarized as follows:

$$\Delta w_{ij}^l(k) = -\mu \delta_j^{l+1}(k)a_i^l(k) \tag{3.33}$$

$$\delta_j^i(k) = \begin{cases} -2e_j(k)f'\left(s_j^L(k)\right) & l = L \\ f'\left(s_j^l(k)\right) \cdot \sum_m \delta_m^{l+1}(k) \cdot w_{jm}^{l+1} & 1 \le l \le L-1. \end{cases} \tag{3.34}$$

The bias weight w_b^l may again be adapted by letting $a_i^l(k) = 1$ in Eq. (3.33). Observe the similarities between these equations and those for standard backpropagation. In fact, by replacing the vectors a, w, and δ by scalars, the previous equations reduce to precisely the backpropagation algorithm for static networks. Differences in the temporal version are due to implicit time relations. To find $\delta_j^l(k)$, we filter the δ's from the next layer backward through the FIR (see Figure 3.7). In other words, δ's are created not only by taking weighted sums, but also by backward filtering. For each x(k) and desired vector d(k), the forward filters are incremented one time step, producing the current output y(k) and corresponding error e(k). Next, the backward filters are incremented one time step, advancing the δ(k) terms and allowing the filter coefficients to be updated. The process is then repeated for a new input at time k + 1.

The symmetry between the forward propagation of states and the backward propagation of error terms is preserved in temporal backpropagation. The number of operations per iteration now grows linearly with the number of layers and synapses in the network. This savings is due to the efficient recursive formulation. Each coefficient enters into the calculation only once, in contrast to the redundant use of terms when applying standard backpropagation to the unfolded network.

Design Example 3.1

As an illustration of the computations involved, we consider a simple network consisting of only two segments (cascaded linear FIR filters shown in Figure 3.8). The first segment is defined as

$$u(k) = \sum_{i=0}^{M} a_i x(k-i) = ax(k). \tag{3.35}$$

For simplicity, the second segment is limited to only three taps:

$$y(k) = b_0 u(k) + b_1 u(k-1) + b_2 u(k-2) = bu(k). \tag{3.36}$$

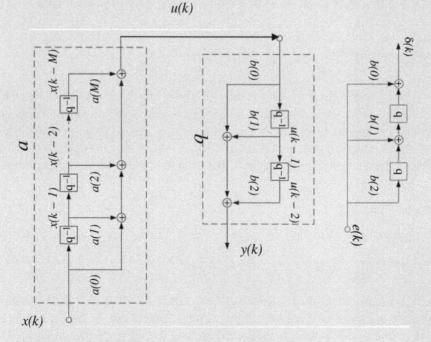

Figure 3.8 Oversimplified finite impulse response (FIR) network.

Design Example 3.1 (Continued)

Here (a is the vector of filter coefficient and should not be confused with the variable for the activation value used earlier). To adapt the filter coefficients, we evaluate the gradients $\partial e^2(k)/\partial a$ and $\partial e^2(k)/\partial b$. For filter b, the desired response is available directly at the output of the filter of interest and the gradient is $\partial e^2(k)/\partial b = -2e(k)u(k)$, which yields the standard LMS update $\Delta b(k) = 2\mu e(k)u(k)$. For filter a, we have

$$
\begin{aligned}
\partial e^2(k)/\partial a &= -2e(k)\partial y(k)/\partial a \\
&= -2e(k)\partial(b_0 u(k) + b_1 u(k-1) + b_2 u(k-2))/\partial a \\
&= -2e(k)[b_0 \partial u(k)/\partial a + b_1 \partial u(k-1)/\partial a + b_2 \partial u(k-2)/\partial a] \\
&= -2e(k)[b_0 x(k) + b_1 x(k-1) + b_2 x(k-2)].
\end{aligned}
\tag{3.37}
$$

which yields

$$
\Delta a(k) = 2\mu e(k)[b_0 x(k) + b_1 x(k-1) + b_2 x(k-2)].
\tag{3.38}
$$

Here, approximately $3M$ multiplications are required at each iteration of this update, which is the product of the orders of the two filters. This computational inefficiency corresponds to the original approach of unfolding a network in time to derive the gradient. However, we observe that at each iteration this weight update is repeated. Explicitly writing out the product terms for several iterations, we get

Iteration			Calculation					
k	$e(k)$	[	$\boxed{b_0 \mathbf{x}(k)}$	+	$b_1 x(k-1)$	+	$b_2 x(k-2)$	]
$k+1$	$e(k+1)$	[	$b_0 \mathbf{x}(k+1)$	+	$\boxed{b_1 \mathbf{x}(k)}$	+	$b_2 x(k-1)$	]
$k+2$	$e(k+2)$	[	$b_0 \mathbf{x}(k+2)$	+	$b_1 x(k-1)$	+	$\boxed{b_2 \mathbf{x}(k)}$	]
$k+3$	$e(k+3)$	[	$b_0 \mathbf{x}(k+3)$	+	$b_1 x(k-2)$	+	$b_2 \mathbf{x}(k+1)$	]

Therefore, rather than grouping along the horizontal in the above equations, we may group along the diagonal (boxed terms). Gathering these terms, we get

$$
[b_0 e(k) + b_1 e(k+1) + b_2 e(k+2)]x(k) = \delta(k)x(k)
\tag{3.39}
$$

where $\delta(k)$ is simply the error filtered backward through the second cascaded filter as illustrated in Figure 3.8. The alternative weight update is thus given by

$$
\Delta a(k) = 2\mu\delta(k)x(k).
\tag{3.40}
$$

Equation (3.40) represents temporal backpropagation. Each update now requires only $M+3$ multiplications, the sum of the two filter orders. So, we can see that a simple reordering of terms results into a more efficient algorithm. This is the major advantage of the temporal backpropagation algorithm.

3.3 Time Series Prediction

In general, here we deal with the problem of predicting future samples of a time series using a number of samples from the past [6, 7]. Given M samples of the series, autoregression (AR) is fit to the data as

$$y(k) = \sum_{n=1}^{M} a(n)y(k-n) + e(k). \tag{3.41}$$

The model assumes that $y(k)$ is obtained by summing up the past values of the sequence plus a modeling error $e(k)$. This error represents the difference between the actual series $y(k)$ and the single-step prediction

$$\hat{y}(k) = \sum_{n=1}^{M} a(n)y(k-n). \tag{3.42}$$

In nonlinear prediction, the model is based on the following nonlinear AR:

$$y(k) = g(y(k-1), y(k-2), \dots y(k-M)) + e(k), \tag{3.43}$$

where g is a nonlinear function. The model can be used for both scalar and vector sequences. The one time step prediction can be represented as

$$\hat{y}(k) = g(y(k-1), y(k-2), \dots y(k-M)) = y(k) - e(k). \tag{3.44}$$

Given the focus of this chapter, we discuss how the network models studied so far can be used when the inputs to the network correspond to the time window $y(k-1)$ through $(k-M)$. Using neural networks for predictions in this case has become increasingly popular. For our purposes, g will be realized with an FIR network. Thus, the prediction $\hat{y}(k)$ corresponding to the output of an FIR network with input $y(k-1)$ can be represented as

$$\hat{y}(k) = N_M(y(k-1)), \tag{3.45}$$

where N_M is an FIR network with total memory length M.

3.3.1 Adaptation and Iterated Predictions

The basic predictor training configuration for the FIR network is shown in Figure 3.9 with a known value of $y(k-1)$ as the input, and the output $\hat{y}(k) = N_M(y(k-1))$ as the single-step estimate of the

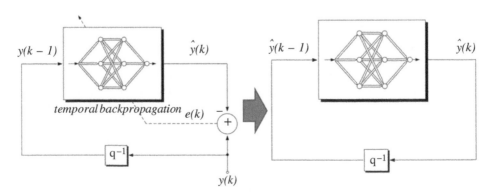

Figure 3.9 Network prediction configuration.

true series value $y(k)$. During training, the squared error $e(k)^2 = (y(k) - \hat{y}(k))^2$ is minimized by using the temporal backpropagation algorithm to adapt the network ($y(k)$ acts as the desired response). Training consists of finding a least-squares solution. In a stochastic framework, the optimal neural network mapping is simply the conditional running mean

$$N^* = E[y(k) \mid y(k-1), y(k-2), \dots y(k-M)], \tag{3.46}$$

where $y(k)$ is viewed as a stationary ergodic process, and the expectation is taken over the joint distribution of $y(k)$ through $y(k-M)$. N^* represents a closed-form optimal solution that can only be approximated due to finite training data and constraints in the network topology.

Iterated predictions: Once the network is trained, *iterated* prediction is achieved by taking the estimate $\hat{y}(k)$ and feeding it back as input to the network:

$$\hat{y}(k) = N_M[\hat{y}(k-1)]. \tag{3.47}$$

as illustrated in Figure 3.9. Equation (3.47) can be now iterated forward in time to achieve predictions as far into the future as desired. Suppose, for example, that we were given only N points for some time series of interest. We would train the network on those N points. The single-step estimate $\hat{y}(N+1)$, based on known values of the series, would then be fed back to produce the estimate $\hat{y}(N+2)$, and continued iterations would yield future predictions.

3.4 Recurrent Neural Networks

3.4.1 Filters as Predictors

Linear filters: As already indicated so far in this chapter, linear filters have been exploited for the structures of predictors. In general, there are two families of filters: those without feedback, whose output depends only upon current and past input values; and those with feedback, whose output depends upon both input values and past outputs. Such filters are best described by a constant coefficient difference equation, as

$$y(k) = \sum_{i=1}^{p} a_i y(k-i) + \sum_{j=0}^{q} b_j e(k-j), \tag{3.48}$$

where $y(k)$ is the output, $e(k)$ is the input, $a_i, i = 1, 2, \dots, p$, are the AR feedback coefficients and b_j, $j = 0, 1, \dots, q$, are the moving average (MA) feedforward coefficients. Such a filter is termed an *autoregressive moving average* (ARMA (p, q)) filter, where p is the order of the autoregressive, or feedback, part of the structure, and q is the order of the MA, or feedforward, element of the structure. Due to the feedback present within this filter, the impulse response – that is, the values of $(k), k \geq 0$, when $e(k)$ is a discrete time impulse – is infinite in duration, and therefore such a filter is referred to as an infinite impulse response (IIR) filter.

The general form of Eq. (3.48) is simplified by removing the feedback terms as

$$y(k) = \sum_{j=0}^{q} b_j e(k-j). \tag{3.49}$$

Such a filter is called MA (q) and has an FIR that is identical to the parameters $b_j, j = 0, 1, \dots, q$. In digital signal processing, therefore, such a filter is called an FIR filter. Similarly, Eq. (3.48) is simplified to yield an autoregressive (AR(p)) filter

$$y(k) = \sum_{i=1}^{p} a_i y(k-i) + e(k), \tag{3.50}$$

which is also an IIR filter. The filter described by Eq. (3.50) is the basis for modeling the speech generating process. The presence of feedback within the AR(p) and ARMA (p, q) filters implies that selection of the a_i, $i = 1, 2, \ldots, p$, coefficients must be such that the filters are *bounded input bounded output (BIBO)* stable. The most straightforward way to test stability is to exploit the $\mathcal{Z}$-domain representation of the transfer function of the filter represented by (3.48):

$$H(z) = \frac{Y(z)}{E(z)} = \frac{b_0 + b_1 z^{-1} + \cdots + b_q z^{-q}}{1 - a_1 z^{-1} - \cdots - a_p z^{-p}} = \frac{N(z)}{D(z)}. \tag{3.51}$$

To guarantee stability, the p roots of the denominator polynomial of (z), that is, the values of z for which $D(z) = 0$, the poles of the transfer function, must lie within the unit circle in the z-plane, $|z| < 1$.

Nonlinear predictors: If a measurement is assumed to be generated by an ARMA (p, q) model, the optimal conditional mean predictor of the discrete time random signal $\{y(k)\}$

$$\hat{y}(k) = E[y(k) \mid y(k-1), y(k-2), \ldots, y(0)] \tag{3.52}$$

is given by

$$\hat{y}(k) = \sum_{i=1}^{p} a_i y(k-i) + \sum_{j=1}^{q} b_j \hat{e}(k-j), \tag{3.53}$$

where the residuals $\hat{e}(k-j) = y(k-j) - \hat{y}(k-j)$, $j = 1, 2, \ldots, q$. The feedback present within Eq. (3.53), which is due to the residuals $\hat{e}(k-j)$, results from the presence of the MA (q) part of the model for $y(k)$ in Eq. (3.48). No information is available about $e(k)$, and therefore it cannot form part of the prediction. On this basis, the simplest form of *nonlinear autoregressive moving average (NARMA (p, q))* model takes the form

$$y(k) = \Theta\left(\sum_{i=1}^{p} a_i y(k-i) + \sum_{j=1}^{q} b_j e(k-j)\right) + e(k), \tag{3.54}$$

where $\Theta(\cdot)$ is an unknown differentiable zero-memory nonlinear function. Notice $e(k)$ is not included within $\Theta(\cdot)$ as it is unobservable. The term NARMA (p, q) is adopted to define Eq. (3.54), since except for the (k), the output of an ARMA (p, q) model is simply passed through the zero-memory nonlinearity $\Theta(\cdot)$.

The corresponding NARMA (p, q) predictor is given by

$$\hat{y}(k) = \Theta\left(\sum_{i=1}^{p} a_i y(k-i) + \sum_{j=1}^{q} b_j \hat{e}(k-j)\right), \tag{3.55}$$

where the residuals $\hat{e}(k-j) = y(k-j) - \hat{y}(k-j)$, $j = 1, 2, \ldots, q$. Equivalently, the simplest form of nonlinear autoregressive (NAR(p)) model is described by

$$y(k) = \Theta\left(\sum_{i=1}^{p} a_i y(k-i)\right) + e(k) \tag{3.56}$$

and its associated predictor is

$$\hat{y}(k) = \Theta\left(\sum_{i=1}^{p} a_i y(k-i)\right). \tag{3.57}$$

The two predictors are shown together in Figure 3.10, where it is clearly indicated which parts are included in a particular scheme. In other words, feedback is included within the NARMA (p, q) predictor, whereas the NAR(p) predictor is an entirely feedforward structure. In control applications, most generally, NARMA (p, q) models also include also external (exogeneous) inputs, $(k-s)$, $s = 1, 2, \ldots, r$, giving

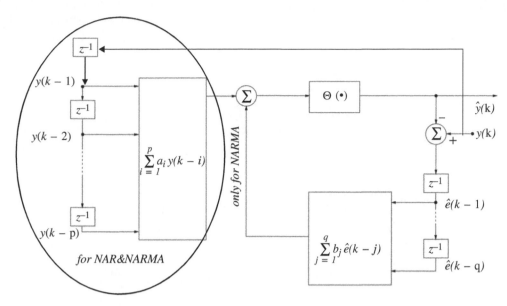

Figure 3.10 Nonlinear AR/ARMA predictors.

$$y(k) = \Theta\left(\sum_{i=1}^{p} a_i y(k-i) + \sum_{j=1}^{q} b_j e(k-j) + \sum_{s=1}^{r} c_s u(k-s)\right) + e(k) \qquad (3.58)$$

and referred to as a NARMA with exogenous inputs model, *NARMAX* (*p, q, r*), with associated predictor

$$\hat{y}(k) = \Theta\left(\sum_{i=1}^{p} a_i y(k-i) + \sum_{j=1}^{q} b_j \hat{e}(k-j) + \sum_{s=1}^{r} c_s u(k-s)\right), \qquad (3.59)$$

which again exploits feedback.

3.4.2 Feedback Options in Recurrent Neural Networks

Feedbacks in recurrent neural networks: In Figure 3.11, the inputs to the network are drawn from the discrete time signal (*k*). Conceptually, it is straightforward to consider connecting the delayed versions of the output, $\hat{y}(k)$, of the network to its input. Such connections, however, introduce feedback into the network, and therefore *the stability of such networks must be considered.* The provision of feedback, with delay, introduces memory to the network and so is appropriate for prediction. The feedback within recurrent neural networks can be achieved in either a local or global manner. An example of a recurrent neural network is shown in Figure 3.11 with connections for both local and global feedback. The local feedback is achieved by the introduction of feedback within the hidden layer, whereas the global feedback is produced by the connection of the network output to the network input. Interneuron connections can also exist in the hidden layer, but they are not shown in Figure 3.11. Although explicit delays are not shown in the feedback connections, they are assumed to be present within the neurons for the network to be realizable. The operation of a recurrent neural network predictor that employs global feedback can now be represented by

$$\hat{y}(k) = \Phi(y(k-1), y(k-2), \dots, (k-p), \hat{e}(k-1), \dots, \hat{e}(k-q)), \qquad (3.60)$$

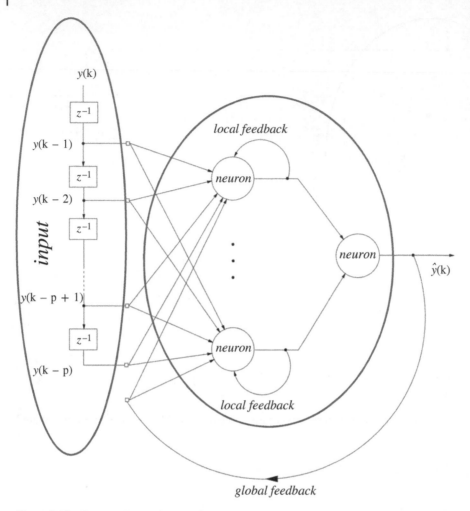

Figure 3.11 Recurrent neural network.

where again $\Phi(\cdot)$ represents the nonlinear mapping of the neural network and $\hat{e}\,(k-j) = y(k-j) - \hat{y}(k-j), j = 1, \ldots, q$.

State-space representation and canonical form: Any feedback network can be cast into a canonical form that consists of a feedforward (static) network (FFSN) (i) whose outputs are the outputs of the neurons that have the desired values, and the values of the state variables, and (ii) whose inputs are the inputs of the network and the values of the state variables, the latter being delayed by one time unit.

The general canonical form of a recurrent neural network is represented in Figure 3.12. If the state is assumed to contain N variables, then a state vector is defined as $s(k) = [s_1(k), s_2(k), \ldots, s_N(k)]^T$, and a vector of p external inputs is given by $y(k-1) = [y(k-1), y(k-2), \ldots, y(k-p)]^T$. The state evolution and output equations of the recurrent network for prediction are given, respectively, by

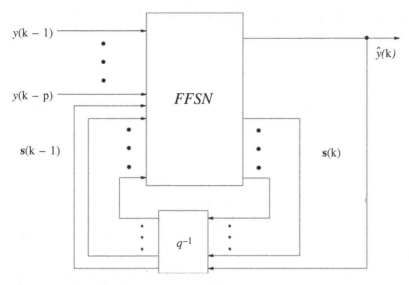

Figure 3.12 Canonical form of a recurrent neural network for prediction.

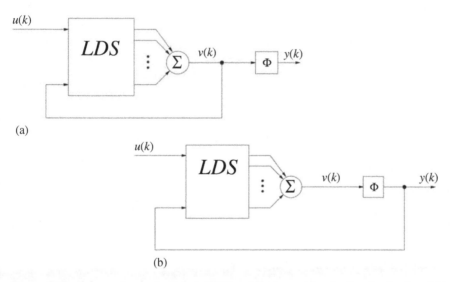

Figure 3.13 Recurrent neural network (RNN) architectures: (a) activation feedback and (b) output feedback.

$$s(k) = \varphi(s(k-1), y(k-1), \hat{y}(k-1)), \tag{3.61}$$

$$\hat{y}(k) = \psi(s(k-1), y(k-1), \hat{y}(k-1)), \tag{3.62}$$

where φ and Ψ represent general classes of nonlinearities.

Recurrent neural network (RNN) architectures: Activation feedback and *output feedback* are two ways to include recurrent connections in neural networks, as shown in Figure 3.13a and b, respectively.

The output of a neuron shown in Figure 3.13a can be expressed as

$$v(k) = \sum_{i=0}^{M} \omega_{u,i}(k)u(k-i) + \sum_{i=0}^{M} \omega_{v,j}(k)v(k-j)$$

$$y(k) = \Phi(v(k))$$

(3.63)

where $\omega_{u,i}$ and $\omega_{v,i}$ are the weights associated with u and v, respectively. In the case of Figure 3.13b, we have

$$v(k) = \sum_{i=0}^{M} \omega_{u,i}(k)u(k-i) + \sum_{i=0}^{M} \omega_{y,j}(k)y(k-j)$$

$$y(k) = \Phi(v(k))$$

(3.64)

where $\omega_{y,j}$ are the weights associated with the delayed outputs. The previous networks exhibit a locally recurrent structure, but when connected into a larger network, they have a feedforward architecture and are referred to as *locally recurrent–globally feedforward (LRGF)* architectures. A general LRGF architecture is shown in Figure 3.14. It allows dynamic synapses to be included within both the input (represented by $H_1, \ldots, H_M$) and the output feedback (represented by H_{FB}), some of the aforementioned schemes. Some typical examples of these networks are shown in Figures 3.15–3.18.

The following equations fully describe the RNN from Figure 3.17

$$y_n(k) = \Phi(v_n(k)), \quad n = 1, 2, \ldots, N$$

$$v_n(k) = \sum_{l=0}^{p+N+1} \omega_{n,l}(k)u_l(k)$$

$$u_n^T(k) = [s(k-1), \ldots, s(k-1), 1, y_1(k-1), y_2(k-1), \ldots, y_N(k-1)]$$

(3.65)

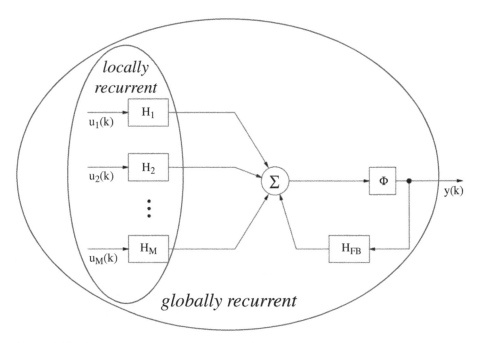

Figure 3.14 General locally recurrent–globally feedforward (LRGF) architecture.

Figure 3.15 An example of Elman recurrent neural network (RNN).

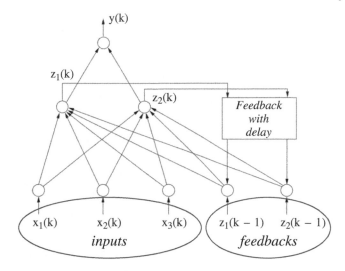

Figure 3.16 An example of Jordan recurrent neural network (RNN).

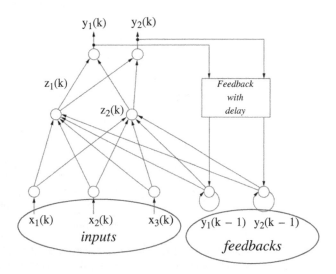

where the $(p + N + 1) \times 1$ dimensional vector u comprises both the external and feedback inputs to a neuron, as well as the unity valued constant bias input.

Training: Here, we discuss training the single fully connected RNN shown in Figure 3.17. The nonlinear time series prediction uses only one output neuron of the RNN. Training of the RNN is based on minimizing the instantaneous squared error at the output of the first neuron of the RNN which can be expressed as

$$\min \left(e^2(k)/2\right) = \min \left([s(k) - y_1(k)]^2/2\right) \tag{3.66}$$

where $e(k)$ denotes the error at the output y1 of the RNN, and $s(k)$ is the training signal. Hence, the correction for the l-th weight of neuron k at the time instant k is

$$\Delta \omega_{n,l}(k) = -\frac{\eta}{2} \frac{\partial}{\partial \omega_{n,l}(k)} e^2(k) = -\eta e(k) \frac{\partial e(k)}{\partial \omega_{n,l}(k)} \tag{3.67}$$

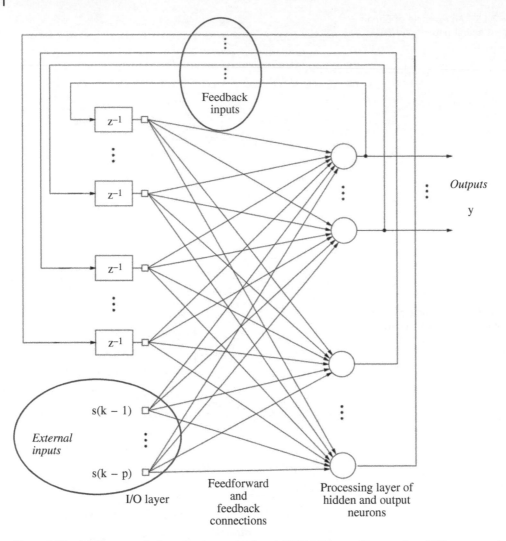

Figure 3.17 A fully connected recurrent neural network (RNN; Williams–Zipser network) The neurons (nodes) are depicted by circles and incorporate the operation Φ (sum of inputs).

Since the external signal vector s does not depend on the elements of W, the error gradient becomes $\partial e(k)/\partial \omega_{n,l}(k) = -\partial y_1(k)/\partial \omega_{n,l}(k)$. Using the chain rule gives

$$\partial y_1(k)/\partial \omega_{n,l}(k) = \Phi'(v_1(k))\partial v_1(k)/\partial \omega_{n,l}(k)$$

$$= \Phi'(v_1(k))\left(\sum_{\alpha=1}^{N} \frac{\partial y_\alpha(k)}{\partial \omega_{n,l}(k)} \omega_{1,\alpha+p+1}(k) + \delta_{nl}u_l(k) \right) \tag{3.68}$$

where $\delta_{nl} = 1$ if $n = 1$ and 0 otherwise. When the learning rate η is sufficiently small, we have $\partial y_\alpha(k-1)/\partial \omega_{n,l}(k) \approx \partial y_\alpha(k-1)/\partial \omega_{n,l}(k-1)$. By introducing the notation $\theta_{n,l}^j = \partial y_j(k)/\partial \omega_{n,l}(k)$; $1 \leq j, n \leq N, 1 \leq l \leq p+1+N$, we have recursively for every time step k and all appropriate j, n and l

$$\theta_{n,l}^j(k+1) = \Phi'(v_j(k))\left(\sum_{m=1}^{N} \omega_{j,m+p+1}(k)\theta_{n,l}^m(k) + \delta_{nj}u_l(k) \right) \tag{3.69}$$

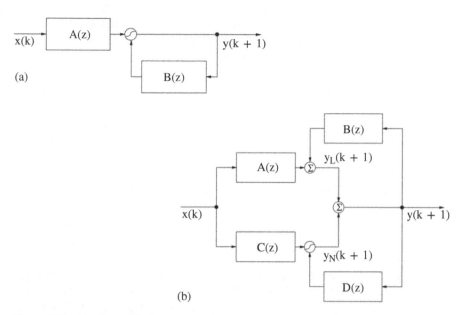

Figure 3.18 Nonlinear IIR filter structures. (a) A recurrent nonlinear neural filter, (b) a recurrent linear/nonlinear neural filter structure.

with the initial conditions $\theta_{n,l}^{j}(0) = 0$. We introduce three new matrices, the $N \times (N + p + 1)$ matrix $\Theta_j(k)$, the $N \times (N + p + 1)$ matrix $U_j(k)$, and the $N \times N$ diagonal matrix $F(k)$, as

$$\Theta_j(k) = \frac{\partial y(k)}{\partial \omega_j(k)}, \ y(k) = [y_1(k), ..., y_N(k)], j = 1, 2, ..., N$$

$$U_j(k) = \begin{bmatrix} 0 \\ \vdots \\ u(k) \\ \vdots \\ 0 \end{bmatrix} \leftarrow jth \ row, j = 1, 2, .., N \tag{3.70}$$

$$F(k) = diag\left[\Phi'\left(u(k)^T \omega_1(k)\right), ..., \Phi'\left(u(k)^T \omega_N(k)\right)\right]$$

With this notation, the gradient updating equation regarding the recurrent neuron can be symbolically expressed as

$$\Theta_j(k + 1) = F(k)\left[U_j(k) + W_\alpha(k)\Theta_\alpha(k)\right], j = 1, 2, .., N \tag{3.71}$$

where W_α denotes the set of those entries in W that correspond to the feedback connections.

3.4.3 Advanced RNN Architectures

The most popular RNN architectures for sequence learning evolved from *long short-term memory (LSTM)* [8] and *bidirectional recurrent neural networks (BRNNs)* [9] schemes. The former introduces the memory cell, a unit of computation that replaces traditional nodes in the hidden layer of a network. With these memory cells, networks are able to overcome difficulties with training encountered by earlier recurrent networks. The latter introduces an architecture in which information from both the future and the past are used to determine the output at any point in the sequence. This is in contrast to previous networks, in which only past input can affect the output, and has been used successfully for sequence labeling tasks in natural language processing, among others. The two schemes are not mutually exclusive, and have been successfully combined for phoneme classification [10] and handwriting recognition [11]. In this section, we explain the LSTM and BRNN, and we describe the *neural Turing machine* (NTM), which extends RNNs with an addressable external memory [12].

LSTM scheme: This was introduced primarily in order to overcome the problem of vanishing gradients. This model resembles a standard RNN with a hidden layer, but each ordinary node in the hidden layer is replaced by a *memory cell* (Figure 3.19). Each memory cell contains a node with a self-connected recurrent edge of fixed weight one, ensuring that the gradient can pass across many time steps without vanishing or exploding. To distinguish references to a memory cell and not an ordinary node, we use the subscript c.

Simple RNNs have long-term memory in the form of weights. The weights change slowly during training, encoding general knowledge about the data. They also have short-term memory in the form of ephemeral activations, which pass from each node to successive nodes. The LSTM model introduces an intermediate type of storage via the memory cell. A memory cell is a composite unit, built from simpler nodes in a specific connectivity pattern, with the novel inclusion of

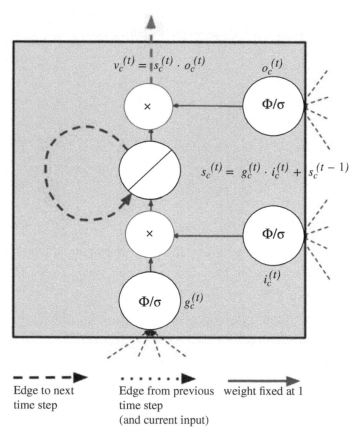

Figure 3.19 A long short-term memory (LSTM) memory cell.

$$v_c^{(t)} = s_c^{(t)} \cdot o_c^{(t)}$$

$$o_c^{(t)}$$

$$s_c^{(t)} = g_c^{(t)} \cdot i_c^{(t)} + s_c^{(t-1)}$$

$$i_c^{(t)}$$

$$g_c^{(t)}$$

Edge to next time step

Edge from previous time step (and current input)

weight fixed at 1

multiplicative nodes, represented in diagrams by the letter X. All elements of the LSTM cell are enumerated and described below.

Note that when we use vector notation, we are referring to the values of the nodes in an entire layer of cells. For example, s is a vector containing the value of s_c at each memory cell c in a layer. When the subscript c is used, it is to index an individual memory cell.

Input node: This unit, labeled g_c, is a node that takes activation in the standard way from the input layer $x^{(t)}$ at the current time step and (along recurrent edges) from the hidden layer at the previous time step $h^{(t-1)}$. Typically, the summed weighted input is run through a tanh activation function, although in the original LSTM paper, the activation function is a sigmoid.

Input gate: Gates are a distinctive feature of the LSTM approach. A gate is a sigmoidal unit that, like the input node, takes activation from the current data point $x^{(t)}$ as well as from the hidden layer at the previous time step. A gate is so called because its value is used to multiply the value of another node. It is a *gate* in the sense that if its value is 0, then flow from the other node is cut off. If the value of the gate is 1, all flow is passed through. The value of the *input gate* i_c multiplies the value of the *input node*.

Internal state: At the heart of each memory cell is a node s_c with linear activation, which is referred to in the original work as the "internal state" of the cell. The internal state s_c has a self-connected recurrent edge with fixed unit weight. Because this edge spans adjacent time steps with constant weight, error can flow across time steps without vanishing or exploding. This edge is often called the *constant error carousel*. In vector notation, the update for the internal state is $s^{(t)} = g^{(t)} \odot i^{(t)} + s^{(t-1)}$ where $\odot$ is pointwise multiplication.

Forget gate: These gates f_c were introduced to provide a method by which the network can learn to flush the contents of the internal state. This is especially useful in continuously running networks. With forget gates, the equation to calculate the internal state on the forward pass is $s^{(t)} = g^{(t)} \odot i^{(t)} + f^{(t)} \odot s^{(t-1)}$.

Output gate: The value v_c ultimately produced by a memory cell is the value of the internal state s_c multiplied by the value of the *output gate* o_c. It is customary that the internal state first be run through a *tanh* activation function, as this gives the output of each cell the same dynamic range as an ordinary *tanh* hidden unit. However, in other works, rectified linear units, which have a greater dynamic range, are easier to train. So it seems plausible that the nonlinear function on the internal state might be omitted.

In the original paper and in most subsequent work, the input node is labeled g. We adhere to this convention but note that it may be confusing as g does not stand for *gate*. In the original paper, the gates are called y_{in} and y_{out}, but this is confusing because y generally stands for output in the machine learning literature. In the interests of clarity, we break with this convention and use *i, f, and o to refer to input, forget, and output* gates, respectively.

Computation in the LSTM model is presented by the following equations, performed at each time step. These equations give the full algorithm for a modern LSTM with forget gates:

$$g^{(t)} = \Phi\left(W^{gx}x^{(t)} + W^{gh}h^{(t-1)} + b_g\right)$$

$$i^{(t)} = \sigma\left(W^{ix}x^{(t)} + W^{ih}h^{(t-1)} + b_i\right)$$

$$f^{(t)} = \sigma\left(Wx + Wh + b_f\right)$$

$$o^{(t)} = \sigma\left(W^{ox}x^{(t)} + W^{oh}h^{(t-1)} + b_o\right)$$

$$s^{(t)} = g^{(t)} \odot i^{(i)} + s^{(t-1)} \odot f^{(t)}$$

$$h^{(t)} = \phi(s(t)) \odot o^{(t)} \tag{3.72}$$

The value of the hidden layer of the LSTM at time t is the vector $h^{(t)}$, while $h^{(t-1)}$ is the values output by each memory cell in the hidden layer at the previous time. Note that these equations include the forget gate. The calculations for the simpler LSTM without forget gates are obtained by setting $f^{(t)} = 1$ for all t. We use the *tanh* function ϕ for the input node g. However, in the original LSTM paper, the activation function for g is the sigmoid σ.

BRNNs: Besides the LSTM, one of the most used RNN architectures is the BRNN (Figure 3.20).

In this architecture, there are two layers of hidden nodes. Both hidden layers are connected to input and output. Only the first layer has recurrent connections from the past time steps, while in the second layer, the direction of recurrent connections is flipped, passing activation backward along the sequence. Given an input sequence and a target sequence, the BRNN can be trained by ordinary backpropagation after unfolding across time. The following three equations describe a BRNN:

$$
\begin{aligned}
h^{(t)} &= \sigma\left(W^{\mathrm{hx}}x^{(t)} + W^{\mathrm{hh}}h^{(t-1)} + b_h\right) \\
z^{(t)} &= \sigma\left(W^{\mathrm{zx}}x^{(t)} + W^{\mathrm{zz}}z^{(t+1)} + b_z\right) \\
\hat{y}^{(t)} &= soft\,max\, W^{\mathrm{yh}}h^{(t)} + W^{\mathrm{yz}}z^{(t)} + b_y
\end{aligned}
\tag{3.73}
$$

where $h^{(t)}$ and $z^{(t)}$ are the values of the hidden layers in the forward and backward directions, respectively.

NTMs: The NTM extends RNNs with an addressable external memory [12]. This enables RNNs to perform complex algorithmic tasks such as sorting. This is inspired by the theories in cognitive science that suggest humans possess a "central executive" that interacts with a memory buffer [13]. By analogy with a Turing machine, in which a program directs *read heads* and *write heads* to interact with external memory in the form of a tape, the model is called an NTM.

The two primary components of an NTM are a *controller* and a *memory matrix*. The controller, which may be a recurrent or feedforward neural network, takes input and returns output to the outside world, as well as passing instructions to and reading from the memory. The memory is represented by a large matrix of N memory locations, each of which is a vector of dimension M. Additionally, a number of read and write heads facilitate the interaction between the controller

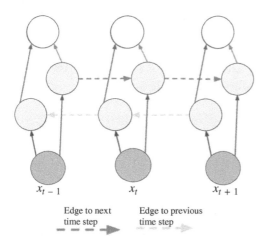

Figure 3.20 A bidirectional recurrent neural network (BRNN). (for more details see the color figure in the bins).

x_{t-1} x_t x_{t+1}

Edge to next time step

Edge to previous time step

and the memory matrix. Despite these additional capabilities, the NTM is differentiable end-to-end and can be trained by variants of SGD using Backpropagation through Time (BPTT).

In [12], five algorithmic tasks are used to test the performance of the NTM model. By *algorithmic* we mean that for each task, the target output for a given input can be calculated by following a simple program, as might be easily implemented in any universal programming language. One example is the *copy* task, where the input is a sequence of fixed length binary vectors followed by a delimiter symbol. The target output is a copy of the input sequence. In another task, *priority sort*, an input consists of a sequence of binary vectors together with a distinct scalar priority value for each vector. The target output is the sequence of vectors sorted by priority. The experiments test whether an NTM can be trained via supervised learning to implement these common algorithms correctly and efficiently. Interestingly, solutions found in this way generalize reasonably well to inputs longer than those presented in the training set. By contrast, the LSTM without external memory does not generalize well to longer inputs. The authors compare three different architectures, namely an LSTM RNN, and NTM, with a feedforward controller, and an NTM with an LSTM controller. On each task, both NTM architectures significantly outperform the LSTM RNN both in training set performance and in generalization to test data.

3.5 Cellular Neural Networks (CeNN)

A spatially invariant CeNN architecture [14, 15] is an $M \times N$ array of identical cells (Figure 3.21 [top]). Each cell, C_{ij}, $(i, j) \in \{1, M\} \times \{1, N\}$, has identical connections with adjacent cells in a predefined neighborhood, $N_r(i, j)$, of radius r. The size of the neighborhood is $m = (2r + 1)^2$, where r is a positive integer.

A conventional analog CeNN cell consists of one resistor, one capacitor, $2m$ linear voltage-controlled current sources (VCCSs), one fixed current source, and one specific type of nonlinear voltage-controlled voltage source (Figure 3.21 [bottom]). The input, state, and output of a given cell

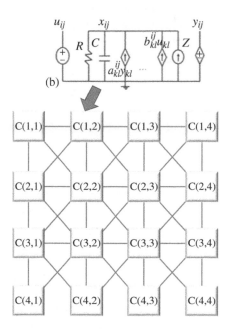

Figure 3.21 (Top) Cellular neural networks (CeNN) architecture, (bottom) circuitry in CeNN cell.

C_{ij} correspond to the nodal voltages u_{ij}, x_{ij}, and y_{ij} respectively. VCCSs controlled by the input and output voltages of each neighbor deliver feedback and feedforward currents to a given cell. The dynamics of a CeNN are captured by a system of $M \times N$ ordinary differential equations, each of which is simply the Kirchhoff's current law (KCL) at the state nodes of the corresponding cells per Eq. (3.74).

$$C\frac{dx_{ij}(t)}{dt} = -\frac{x_{ij}(t)}{R} + \sum_{C_{kl} \in N_r(i,j)} a_{ij,kl} y_{kl}(t)$$
$$+ \sum_{C_{kl} \in N_r(i,j)} b_{ij,kl} u_{kl} + Z \tag{3.74}$$

CeNN cells typically employ a nonlinear sigmoid-like transfer function at the output to ensure fixed binary output levels. The parameters $a_{ij,kl}$ and $b_{ij,kl}$ serve as weights for the feedback and feedforward currents from cell C_{kl} to cell C_{ij}. Parameters $a_{ij,kl}$ and $b_{ij,kl}$ are space invariant and are denoted by two $(2r+1) \times (2r+1)$ matrices. (If $r = 1$, they are captured by 3×3 matrices.) The matrices of a and b parameters are typically referred to as the feedback template (A) and the feedforward template (B), respectively. Design flexibility is further enhanced by the fixed bias current Z that provides a means to adjust the total current flowing into a cell. A CeNN can solve a wide range of image processing problems by carefully selecting the values of the A and B templates (as well as Z). Various circuits, including inverters, Gilbert multipliers, operational transconductance amplifiers (OTAs), etc. [15, 16], can be used to realize VCCSs. OTAs provide a large linear range for voltage-to-current conversion, and can implement a wide range of transconductances allowing for different CeNN templates. *Nonlinear* templates/OTAs can lead to CeNNs with richer functionality. For more information, see [14, 17–19].

Memristor-based cellular nonlinear/neural network (MCeNN): The memristor was theoretically defined in the late 1970s, but it garnered renewed research interest due to the recent much-acclaimed discovery of nanocrossbar memories by engineers at the Hewlett-Packard Labs. The memristor is a nonlinear passive device with variable resistance states. It is mathematically defined by its constitutive relationship of the charge q and the flux ϕ, that is, $d\phi/dt = (d\phi(q)/dq)\cdot dq/dt$. Based on the basic circuit law, this leads to $v(t) = (d\phi(q)/dq)\cdot i(t) = M(q)i(t)$, where $M(q)$ is defined as the resistance of a memristor, called the *memristance*, which is a function of the internal current i and the state variable x. The Simmons tunnel barrier model is the most accurate physical model of TiO_2/TiO_{2-x} memristor, reported by Hewlett-Packard Labs [20].

The memristor is expected to be co-integrated with nanoscale CMOS technology to revolutionize conventional von Neumann as well as neuromorphic computing. In Figure 3.22, a compact convolutional neural network (CNN) model based on memristors is presented along with its performance analysis and applications. In the new CNN design, the memristor bridge circuit acts as the synaptic circuit element and substitutes the complex multiplication circuit used in traditional CNN architectures. In addition, the negative differential resistance and nonlinear current–voltage characteristics of the memristor have been leveraged to replace the linear resistor in conventional CNNs. The proposed CNN design [21–26] has several merits, for example, high density, nonvolatility, and programmability of synaptic weights. The proposed memristor-based CNN design operations for implementing several image processing functions are illustrated through simulation and contrasted with conventional CNNs.

Training MCeNN: In the classical representation, the conductance of a memristor G depends directly on the integral over time of the voltage across the device, sometimes referred to as the flux. Formally, a memristor obeys $i(t) = G(s(t))v(t)$ and $\dot{s}(t) = v(t)$. A generalization of the memristor model, called a *memristive system*, was proposed in [27]. In memristive devices, s is a general state

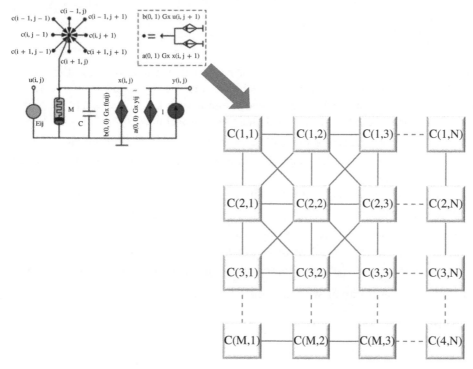

Figure 3.22 Memristor-based cellular nonlinear/neural network (MCeNN).

variable, rather than an integral of the voltage. Such memristive models, which are more commonly used to model actual physical devices, are discussed in [20, 28, 29]. For simplicity, we assume that the variations in the value of $s(t)$ are restricted to be small so that $G(s(t))$ can be linearized around some point s^*, and the conductivity of the memristor is given, to first order, by $G(s(t)) = \bar{g} + \hat{g}s(t)$, where $\hat{g} = [dG(s)/ds]_{s=s}*$ and $\bar{g} = G(s^*) - \hat{g}s^*$. Such a linearization is formally justified if sufficiently small inputs are used, so that s does not stray far from the fixed point (i.e. $2\hat{g}/[d^2G(s)/ds^2]_{s=s}* \gg |s(t) - s^*|$, making second-order contributions negligible). The only (rather mild) assumption is that $G(s)$ is differentiable near s^*. Despite this linearization, the memristor is still a nonlinear component, since from the previous relations we have $i(t) = \bar{g}v(t) + \hat{g}s(t)v(t)$. Importantly, this nonlinear product $s(t)v(t)$ underscores the key role of the memristor in the proposed design, where an input signal $v(t)$ is being multiplied by an *adjustable* internal value $s(t)$. Thus, the memristor enables an efficient implementation of trainable multilayered neural networks (MNNs) in hardware, as explained below.

Online gradient descent learning, which was described earlier, can be used here as well. With the notation used here, we assume a learning system that operates on K discrete presentations of inputs (trials), indexed by $k = 1, 2, \ldots, K$. For brevity, the iteration number is sometimes not indexed when it is clear from the context. On each trial k, the system receives empirical data, a pair of two real column vectors of sizes M and N: a *pattern* $\mathbf{x}^{(k)} \in \mathbb{R}^M$; and a *desired* label $\mathbf{d}^{(k)} \in \mathbb{R}^N$, with all pairs sharing the same desired relation $\mathbf{d}^{(k)} = \mathbf{f}(\mathbf{x}^{(k)})$. Note that two distinct patterns can have the same label. The objective of the system is to estimate (learn) the function $\mathbf{f}(\cdot)$ using the empirical data. As a simple example, suppose W is a tunable $N \times M$ matrix of parameters, and consider the estimator

$$r^{(k)} = W^{(k)} x^{(k)}$$
$$\text{or } r_n^{(k)} = \sum_m W_{nm}^{(k)} x_m^{(k)} \tag{3.75}$$

which is a single-layer NN. The *result* of the estimator $r = Wx$ should aim to predict the correct *desired* labels $d = f(x)$ for new unseen *patterns* x. As before, to solve this problem, W is tuned to minimize some measure of error between the estimated and desired labels, over a K_0-long subset of the training set (for which $k = 1, \ldots, K_0$). If we define the *error* vector as $y^{(k)\Delta} = d^{(k)} - r^{(k)}$, then a common measure is the mean square error: MSE $= \sum_{k=1}^{K_0} \left\| y^{(k)} \right\|^2$. Other error measures can be also be used. The performance of the resulting estimator is then tested over a different subset called the test set ($k = K_0 + 1, \ldots, K$).

As before, a reasonable iterative algorithm for minimizing this objective is the online gradient descent (*SGD*) iteration $W^{(k+1)} = W^{(k)} - \eta \nabla_{W^{(k)}} \left\| y^{(k)} \right\|^2 / 2$, where the $1/2$ coefficient is written for mathematical convenience, η is the *learning rate*, a (usually small) positive constant; and at each iteration k, a single empirical sample $x^{(k)}$ is chosen randomly and presented at the input of the system. Using $\nabla_{W^{(k)}} \left\| y^{(k)} \right\|^2 = -2 \left(d^{(k)} - W^{(k)} x^{(k)} \right) \left(x^{(k)} \right)^{\mathrm{T}}$ and defining $\Delta W^{(k)} = W^{(k+1)} - W^{(k)}$ and $(\cdot)^{\mathrm{T}}$ to be the transpose operation, we obtain the *outer product*

$$\Delta W^{(k)} = \eta y^{(k)} \left(x^{(k)} \right)^{\mathrm{T}}$$
$$W_{nm}^{(k+1)} = W_{nm}^{(k)} + \eta x_m^{(k)} y_n^{(k)}. \tag{3.76}$$

The parameters of more complicated estimators can also be similarly tuned (trained), using backpropagation, as discussed earlier in this chapter.

3.6 Convolutional Neural Network (CoNN)

Notations: In the following, we will use $x \in \mathbb{R}^D$ to represent a column vector with D elements and a capital letter to denote a matrix $X \in \mathbb{R}^{H \times W}$ with H rows and W columns. The vector x can also be viewed as a matrix with 1 column and D rows. These concepts can be generalized to higher-order matrices, that is, tensors. For example, $x \in \mathbb{R}^{H \times W \times D}$ is an order-3 (or third-order) tensor. It contains HWD elements, each of which can be indexed by an index triplet (i, j, d), with $0 \leq i < H$, $0 \leq j < W$, and $0 \leq d < D$. Another way to view an order-3 tensor is to treat it as containing D channels of matrices.

For example, a color image is an order-3 tensor. An image with H rows and W columns is a tensor of size $H \times W \times 3$; if a color image is stored in the RGB format, it has three channels (for R, G and B, respectively), and each channel is an $H \times W$ matrix (second-order tensor) that contains the R (or G, or B) values of all pixels.

It is beneficial to represent images (or other types of raw data) as a tensor. In early computer vision and pattern recognition, a color image (which is an order-3 tensor) is often converted to the grayscale version (which is a matrix) because we know how to handle matrices much better than tensors. The color information is lost during this conversion. But color is very important in various image- or video-based learning and recognition problems, and we do want to process color information in a principled way, for example, as in CoNNs.

Tensors are essential in CoNN. The input, intermediate representation, and parameters in a CoNN are all tensors. Tensors with order higher than 3 are also widely used in a CoNN. For example, we will soon see that the convolution kernels in a convolution layer of a CoNN form an order-4 tensor.

Given a tensor, we can arrange all the numbers inside it into a long vector, following a prespecified order. For example, in MATLAB, the (:) operator converts a matrix into a column vector in the column-first order as

$$A = \begin{bmatrix} 1 & 2 \\ 3 & 4 \end{bmatrix}, \ A(:) = (1, 3, 2, 4)^T \tag{3.77}$$

We use the notation "*vec*" to represent this vectorization operator. That is, $vec(A) = (1, 3, 2, 4)^T$ in the example. In order to vectorize an order-3 tensor, we could vectorize its first channel (which is a matrix, and we already know how to vectorize it), then the second channel, ... , and so on, until all channels are vectorized. The vectorization of the order-3 tensor is then the concatenation of the vectorizations of all the channels in this order. The vectorization of an order-3 tensor is a recursive process that utilizes the vectorization of order-2 tensors. This recursive process can be applied to vectorize an order-4 (or even higher-order) tensor in the same manner.

Vector calculus and the chain rule: The CoNN learning process depends on vector calculus and the chain rule. Suppose z is a scalar (i.e., $z \in \mathbb{R}$) and $y \in \mathbb{R}^H$ is a vector. If z is a function of y, then the partial derivative of z with respect to y is defined as $[\partial z/\partial y]_i = \partial z/\partial y_i$. In other words, $\partial z/\partial y$ is a vector having *the same size* as y, and its i-th element is $\partial z/\partial y_i$. Also, note that $\partial z/\partial y^T = (\partial z/\partial y)^T$.

Suppose now that $x \in \mathbb{R}^W$ is another vector, and y is a function of x. Then, the partial derivative of y with respect to x is defined as $[\partial y/\partial x^T]_{ij} = \partial y_i/\partial x_j$. This partial derivative is a $H \times W$ matrix whose entry at the intersection of the i-th row and j-th column is $y_i/\partial x_j$.

It is easy to see that z is a function of x in a chain-like argument: a function maps x to y, and another function maps y to z. The chain rule can be used to compute $\partial z/\partial x^T$ as

$$\frac{\partial z}{\partial x^T} = \frac{\partial z}{\partial y^T} \frac{\partial y}{\partial x^T}. \tag{3.78}$$

3.6.1 CoNN Architecture

A CoNN usually takes an order-3 tensor as its input, for example, an image with H rows, W columns, and three channels (R, G, B color channels). Higher-order tensor inputs, however, can be handled by CoNN in a similar fashion. The input then goes through a series of processing steps. A processing step is usually called a layer, which could be a *convolution layer, a pooling layer, a normalization layer, a fully connected layer, a loss layer,* etc. We will introduce the details of these layers later.

For now, let us give an abstract description of the CNN structure first. Layer-by-layer operation in a forward pass of a CoNN can be formally represented as $x^1 \rightarrow w^1 \rightarrow x^2 \rightarrow \cdots \rightarrow x^{L-1} \rightarrow w^{L-1} \rightarrow x^L \rightarrow w^L \rightarrow z$. This will be referred to as the *operation chain*. The input is x^1, usually an image (an order-3 tensor). It undergoes the processing in the first layer, which is the first box. We denote the parameters involved in the first layer's processing collectively as a tensor w^1. The output of the first layer is x^2, which also acts as the input to the second-layer processing. This processing continues until all layers in the CoNN have been processed, upon which x^L is outputted.

An additional layer, however, is added for backward error propagation, a method that learns good parameter values in the CoNN. Let us suppose the problem at hand is an image classification problem with C classes. A commonly used strategy is to output x^L as a C-dimensional vector, whose i-th entry encodes the prediction (the posterior probability of x^1 comes from the i-th class). To make x^L a probability mass function, we can set the processing in the $(L-1)$-th layer as a *softmax* transformation of x^{L-1}. In the other applications, the output x^L may have other forms and interpretations.

The last layer is a loss layer. Let us suppose t is the corresponding target (ground truth) value for the input x^1; then a cost or loss function can be used to measure the discrepancy between the CoNN prediction x^L and the target t. For example, a simple loss function could be $z = \|t - x^L\|^2/2$, although more complex loss functions are usually used. This squared ℓ_2 loss can be used in a regression problem. In a classification problem, the cross-entropy loss is often used. The ground truth in a classification problem is a categorical variable t. We first convert the categorical variable t to a C-dimensional vector . Now both t and x^L are probability mass functions, and the cross-entropy loss measures the distance between them. Hence, we can minimize the cross-entropy. The operation chain explicitly models the loss function as a loss layer whose processing is modeled as a box with parameters w^L. Note that some layers may not have any parameters; that is, w^i may be empty for some i. The softmax layer is one such example.

The forward run: If all the parameters of a CoNN model $w^1, \dots, w^{L-1}$ have been learned, then we are ready to use this model for prediction, which only involves running the CNN model forward, that is, in the direction of the arrows in the operational chain. Starting from the input x^1, we make it pass the processing of the first layer (the box with parameters w^1), and get x^2. In turn, x^2 is passed into the second layer, and so on. Finally, we achieve $x^L \in \mathbb{R}^C$, which estimates the posterior probabilities of x^1 belonging to the C categories. We can output the CNN prediction as *arg max$_i$* x_i^L.

SGD: As before in this chapter, the parameters of a CoNN model are optimized to minimize the loss z; that is, we want the prediction of a CoNN model to match the ground-truth labels. Let us suppose one training example x^1 is given for training such parameters. The training process involves running the CoNN network in both directions. We first run the network in the forward pass to get x^L to achieve a prediction using the current CoNN parameters. Instead of outputting a prediction, we need to compare the prediction with the target t corresponding to x^1, that is, continue running the forward pass until the last loss layer. Finally, we achieve a loss z. The loss z is then a supervision signal, guiding how the parameters of the model should be modified (updated). And the SGD method of modifying the parameters is $w^i \leftarrow w^i - \eta \partial z/\partial w^i$. Here, the $\leftarrow$ sign implicitly indicates that the parameters w^i (of the i-layer) are updated from time t to $t+1$. If a time index t is explicitly used, this equation will look like $(w^i)^{t+1} = (w^i)^t - \eta \partial z/\partial (w^i)^t$.

Error backpropagation: As before, the last layer's partial derivatives are easy to compute. Because x^L is connected to z directly under the control of parameters w^L, it is easy to compute $\partial z/\partial w^L$. This step is only needed when w^L is not empty. Similarly, it is also easy to compute $\partial z/\partial x^L$. If the squared ℓ_2 loss is used, we have an empty $\partial z/\partial w^L$ and $\partial z/\partial w^L = x^L - t$. For every layer i, we compute two sets of gradients: the partial derivatives of z with respect to the parameters w^i and that layer's input x^i. The term $\partial z/\partial w^i$ can be used to update the current (i-th) layer's parameters, while $\partial z/\partial x^i$ can be used to update parameters backward, for example, to the $(i-1)$-th layer. An intuitive explanation is that x^i is the output of the $(i-1)$-th layer and $\partial z/\partial x^i$ is how x^i should be changed to reduce the loss function. Hence, we could view $\partial z/\partial x^i$ as the part of the "error" supervision information propagated from z backward until the current layer, in a layer-by-layer fashion. Thus, we can continue the backpropagation process and use $\partial z/\partial x^i$ to propagate the errors backward to the $(i-1)$-th layer. This layer-by-layer backward updating procedure makes learning a CoNN much easier. When we are updating the i-th layer, the backpropagation process for the $(i+1)$-th layer must have been completed. That is, we must already have computed the terms $\partial z/\partial w^{i+1}$ and $\partial z/\partial x^{i+1}$. Both are stored in memory and ready for use. Now our task is to compute $\partial z/\partial w^i$ and $\partial z/\partial x^i$. Using the chain rule, we have

$$
\frac{\partial z}{\partial \left(\text{vec}(w^i)^T \right)} = \frac{\partial z}{\partial \left(\text{vec}(x^{i+1})^T \right)} \frac{\partial \text{vec}(x^{i+1})}{\partial \left(\text{vec}(w^i)^T \right)},
$$

$$
\frac{\partial z}{\partial \left(\text{vec}(x^i)^T \right)} = \frac{\partial z}{\partial \left(\text{vec}(x^{i+1})^T \right)} \frac{\partial \text{vec}(x^{i+1})}{\partial \left(\text{vec}(x^i)^T \right)}.
$$

(3.79)

Since $\partial z/\partial x^{i+1}$ is already computed and stored in memory, it requires just a matrix reshaping operation (vec) and an additional transpose operation to get $\partial z/\partial(\text{vec}(x^{i+1})^T)$. As long as we can compute $\partial \text{vec}(x^{i+1})/\partial(\text{vec}(w^i)^T)$ and $\text{vec}(x^{i+1})/\partial(\text{vec}(x^i)^T)$, we can easily get Eq. (3.79). The terms $\partial \text{vec}(x^{i+1})/\partial(\text{vec}(w^i)^T)$ and $\partial \text{vec}(x^{i+1})/\partial(\text{vec}(x^i)^T)$ are much easier to compute than directly computing $\partial z/\partial(\text{vec}(w^i)^T)$ and $\partial \text{vec}(x^{i+1})/\partial(\text{vec}(x^i)^T)$ because x^i is directly related to x^{i+1} through a function with parameters w^i. The details of these partial derivatives will be discussed in the following sections.

3.6.2 Layers in CoNN

Suppose we are considering the l-th layer, whose inputs form an order-3 tensor x^l with $x^l \in \mathbb{R}^{H^l \times W^l \times D^l}$. A triplet index set (i^l, j^l, d^l) is used to locate any specific element in x^l. The triplet (i^l, j^l, d^l) refers to one element in x^l, which is in the d^l-th channel, and at spatial location (i^l, j^l) (at the i^lth row, and j^l-th column). In actual CoNN learning, the mini-batch strategy is usually used. In that case, x^l becomes an order-4 tensor in $\mathbb{R}^{H^l \times W^l \times D^l \times N}$, where N is the mini-batch size. For simplicity we assume for the moment that $N = 1$. The results in this section, however, are easy to adapt to mini-batch versions. In order to simplify the notations that will appear later, we follow the zero-based indexing convention, which specifies that $0 \le i^l < H^l, 0 \le j^l < W^l$, and $0 \le d^l < D^l$. In the l-th layer, a function will transform the input x^l to an output $= x^{l+1}$. We assume the output has size $H^{l+1} \times W^{l+1} \times D^{l+1}$, and an element in the output is indexed by a triplet $(i^{l+1}, j^{l+1}, d^{l+1}), 0 \le i^{l+1} < H^{l+1}, 0 \le j^{l+1} < W^{l+1}, 0 \le d^{l+1} < D^{l+1}$.

The Rectified Linear Unit (ReLU) layer: An ReLU layer does not change the size of the input; that is, x^l and y share the same size. The ReLU can be regarded as a truncation performed individually for every element in the input: $y_{i,j,d} = \max \left\{ 0, x^l_{i,j,d} \right\}$ with $0 \le i < H^l = H^{l+1}, 0 \le j < W^l = W^{l+1}$, and $0 \le d < D^l = D^{l+1}$. There is no parameter inside a ReLU layer, and hence there is no need for parameter learning in this layer.

The convolution layer: Figure 3.23 illustrates a convolution of the input image (3×4 matrix) and the convolution kernel of size 2×2. For order-3 tensors, the convolution operation is defined similarly. Figure 3.24 illustrates an RGB (red/green/blue) image with three channels and three kernels. Suppose the input in the l-th layer is an order-3 tensor of size $H^l \times W^l \times D^l$. A convolution kernel is also an order-3 tensor of size $H \times W \times D^l$. When we overlap the kernel on top of the input tensor at the spatial location $(0, 0, 0)$, we compute the products of the corresponding elements in all the D^l channels and sum the HWD^l products to get the convolution result at this spatial location. Then, we move the kernel from top to bottom and from left to right to complete the convolution. In a convolution layer, multiple convolution kernels are usually used. Assuming D kernels are used and each kernel is of spatial span $H \times W$, we denote all the kernels as f. f is an order-4 tensor in $\mathbb{R}^{H \times W \times D^l \times D}$. Similarly, we use index variables $0 \le i < H, 0 \le j < W, 0 \le d^l < D^l$ and $0 \le d < D$ to pinpoint a specific element in the kernels.

Stride is another important concept in convolution. At the bottom of Figure 3.23, we convolve the kernel with the input at every possible spatial location, which corresponds to the stride $s = 1$.

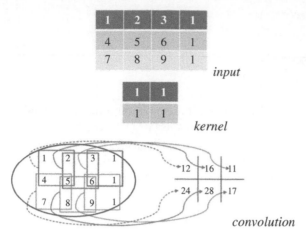

input

kernel

convolution

Figure 3.23 Illustration of the convolution operation. If we overlap the convolution kernel on top of the input image, we can compute the product between the numbers at the same location in the kernel and the input, and we get a single number by summing these products together. For example, if we overlap the kernel with the top-left region in the input, the convolution result at that spatial location is $1 \times 1 + 1 \times 4 + 1 \times 2 + 1 \times 5 = 12$. (for more details see the color figure in the bins).

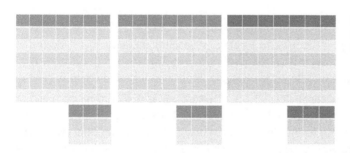

Figure 3.24 RGB image/three channels and three kernels. (for more details see the color figure in the bins).

However, if $s > 1$, every movement of the kernel skips $s - 1$ pixel locations (i.e., the convolution is performed once every s pixels both horizontally and vertically). In this section, we consider the simple case when the stride is 1 and no padding is used. Hence, we have y (or x^{l+1}) in $\mathbb{R}^{H^{l+1} \times W^{l+1} \times D^{l+1}}$, with $H^{l+1} = H^l - H + 1$, $W^{l+1} = W^l - W + 1$, and $D^{l+1} = D$. For mathematical rigor, the convolution procedure can be expressed as an equation:

$$y_{i^{l+1}, j^{l+1}, d} = \sum_{i=0}^{H} \sum_{j=0}^{W} \sum_{d^l=0}^{D^l} f_{i,j,d^l,d} \times x^l_{i^{l+1}+i, j^{l+1}+j, d^l}. \tag{3.80}$$

Convolution as matrix product: There is a way to expand x^l and simplify the convolution as a matrix product. Let us consider a special case with $D^l = D = 1$, $H = W = 2$, and $H^l = 3$, $W^l = 4$. That is, we consider convolving a small single-channel 3×4 matrix (or image) with one 2×2 filter. Using the example in Figure 3.23, we have

$$\begin{bmatrix} 1 & 2 & 3 & 1 \\ 4 & 5 & 6 & 1 \\ 7 & 8 & 9 & 1 \end{bmatrix} * \begin{bmatrix} 1 & 1 \\ 1 & 1 \end{bmatrix} = \begin{bmatrix} 12 & 16 & 11 \\ 24 & 28 & 17 \end{bmatrix} \tag{3.81}$$

where the first matrix is denoted as A, and $*$ is the convolution operator.

The MATLAB command $B = \text{im2col}(A, [2 \ 2])$ gives the B matrix, which is an expanded version of A:

$$
B = \begin{bmatrix} 1 & 4 & 2 & 5 & 3 & 6 \\ 4 & 7 & 5 & 8 & 6 & 9 \\ 2 & 5 & 3 & 6 & 1 & 1 \\ 5 & 8 & 6 & 9 & 1 & 1 \end{bmatrix} \tag{3.82}
$$

Note that the first column of B corresponds to the first 2×2 region in A, in a column-first order, corresponding to $(i^{l+1}, j^{l+1}) = (0, 0)$. Similarly, the second to last column in B correspond to regions in A with (i^{l+1}, j^{l+1}) being $(1, 0)$, $(0, 1)$, $(1, 1)$, $(0, 2)$ and $(1, 2)$, respectively. That is, the MATLAB im2col function explicitly expands the required elements for performing each individual convolution to create a column in the matrix B. The transpose, B^T, is called the im2row expansion of A. If we vectorize the convolution kernel itself into a vector (in the same column-first order) $(1, 1, 1, 1)^T$, we find that

$$
B^T \begin{bmatrix} 1 \\ 1 \\ 1 \\ 1 \end{bmatrix} = \begin{bmatrix} 12 \\ 24 \\ 16 \\ 28 \\ 11 \\ 17 \end{bmatrix} \tag{3.83}
$$

If we reshape this resulting vector properly, we get the exact convolution result matrix in Eq. (3.81).

If $D^l > 1$ (x^l has more than one channel, e.g., in Figure 3.24 of RGB image/three channels), the expansion operator could first expand the first channel of x^l, then the second, ... , until all D^l channels are expanded. The expanded channels will be stacked together; that is, one row in the im2row expansion will have $H \times W \times D^l$ elements, rather than $H \times W$.

Suppose x^l is a third-order tensor in $\mathbb{R}^{H^l \times W^l \times D^l}$, with one element in x^l represented by (i^l, j^l, d^l), and f is a set of convolution kernels whose spatial extent are all $H \times W$. Then, the expansion operator (im2row) converts x^l into a matrix $\varphi(x^l)$ with elements indexed as (p, q). The expansion operator copies the element at (i^l, j^l, d^l) in x^l to the (p, q)-th entry in $\varphi(x^l)$. From the description of the expansion process, given a fixed (p, q), we can calculate its corresponding (i^l, j^l, d^l) triplet from the relation

$$
\begin{aligned}
p &= i^{l+1} + \left(H^l - H + 1\right) \times j^{l+1} \\
q &= i + H \times j + H \times W \times d^l \\
i^l &= i^{l+1} + i \\
j^l &= j^{l+1} + j
\end{aligned} \tag{3.84}
$$

As an example, dividing q by HW and take the integer part of the quotient, we can determine which channel (d^l) belongs to.

We can use the standard *vec* operator to convert the set of convolution kernels f (an order-4 tensor) into a matrix. Starting from one kernel, which can be vectorized into a vector in $\mathbb{R}^{HWD^l}$, all convolution kernels can be reshaped into a matrix with HWD^l rows and D columns with $D^{l+1} = D$ referred to as matrix F. With these notations, we have an expression to calculate convolution results (in Eq. (3.83), $\varphi(x^l)$ is B^T):

$$
\text{vec}(y) = \text{vec}(x^{l+1}) = \text{vec}\left(\varphi(x^l)F\right). \tag{3.85}
$$

with $\text{vec}(y) \in \mathbb{R}^{H^{l+1}W^{l+1}D}$, $\varphi(x^l) \in \mathbb{R}^{(H^{l+1}W^{l+1}) \times (HWD^l)}$, and $F \in \mathbb{R}^{(HWD^l) \times D}$. The matrix multiplication $\varphi(x^l)F$ results in a matrix of size $(H^{l+1}W^{l+1}) \times D$. The vectorization of this resultant matrix generates a vector in $\mathbb{R}^{H^{l+1}W^{l+1}D}$, which matches the dimensionality of $\text{vec}(y)$.

The Kronecker product: Given two matrices $A \in \mathbb{R}^{m \times n}$ and $B \in \mathbb{R}^{p \times q}$, the Kronecker product $A \otimes B$ is a $mp \times nq$ matrix, defined as a block matrix

$$A \otimes B = \begin{Bmatrix} a_{11}B & ...... & a_{1n}B \\ \vdots & \ddots & \vdots \\ a_{m1}B & .... & a_{mn}B \end{Bmatrix} \tag{3.86}$$

The Kronecker product has the following properties that will be useful for us:

$$(A \otimes B)^T = A^T \otimes B^T, \tag{3.87}$$

$$\text{vec}(AXB) = (B^T \otimes A)\text{vec}(X), \tag{3.88}$$

The last equation can be utilized from both directions. Now we can write down

$$\text{vec}(y) = \text{vec}(\varphi(x^l)FI) = (I \otimes \varphi(x^l)) \text{vec}(F), \tag{3.89}$$

$$\text{vec}(y) = \text{vec}(I\varphi(x^l)F) = (F^T \otimes I) \text{vec}(\varphi(x^l)), \tag{3.90}$$

where I is an identity matrix of appropriate size. In Eq. (3.89), the size of I is determined by the number of columns in F, and hence $I \in \mathbb{R}^{D \times D}$. In Eq. (3.90), $I \in \mathbb{R}^{(H^{l+1}W^{l+1}) \times (H^{l+1}W^{l+1})}$. For the derivation of the gradient computation rules in a convolution layer, the notation summarized in Table 3.3 will be used.

Update the parameters – backward propagation: First, we need to compute $\partial z/\partial \text{vec}(x^l)$ and $z/\partial \text{vec}(F)$, where the first term will be used for backward propagation to the previous $(l-1)$th layer, and the second term will determine how the parameters of the current $(l$–th) layer will be updated. Keep in mind that f, F, and w^i refer to the same thing (modulo reshaping of the vector or matrix or tensor). Similarly, we can reshape y into a matrix $Y \in \mathbb{R}^{(H^{l+1}W^{l+1}) \times D}$; then y, Y, and x^{l+1} refer to the same object (again, modulo reshaping).

Table 3.3 Variables, for the derivation of gradient with $\phi \leftrightarrow \varphi$.

	Alias	Size and Meaning
X	x^l	$H^lW^l \times D^l$, the input tensor
F	f, w^l	$HW D^l \times D$, D kernels, each $H \times W$ and D^l channels
Y	y, x^{l+1}	$H^{l+1}W^{l+1} \times D^{l+1}$, the output, $D^{l+1} = D$
$\phi(x^l)$		$H^{l+1}W^{l+1} \times HW D^l$, the im2row expansion of x^l
M		$H^{l+1}W^{l+1}HW D^l \times H^lW^l D^l$, the indictor matrix for $\phi(x^l)$
$\dfrac{\partial z}{\partial Y}$	$\dfrac{\partial z}{\partial \text{vec}(y)}$	$H^{l+1}W^{l+1} \times D^{l+1}$, gradient for y
$\dfrac{\partial z}{\partial F}$	$\dfrac{\partial z}{\partial \text{vec}(f)}$	$HW D^l \times D$, gradient to update the convolution kernels
$\dfrac{\partial z}{\partial X}$	$\dfrac{\partial z}{\partial \text{vec}(x^l)}$	$H^lW^l \times D^l$, gradient for x^l, useful for back propagation

From the chain rule, it is easy to compute $\partial z/\partial \mathrm{vec}(F)$ as

$$\frac{\partial z}{\partial(\mathrm{vec}(F))^T} = \frac{\partial z}{\partial\left(\mathrm{vec}(Y)^T\right)} \frac{\partial \mathrm{vec}(y)}{\partial\left(\mathrm{vec}(F)^T\right)} \tag{3.91}$$

The first term on the right in Eq. (3.91) is already computed in the $(l+1)$-th layer as $\partial z/\partial(\mathrm{vec}(x^{l+1}))^T$. Based on Eq. (3.89), we have

$$\frac{\partial \mathrm{vec}(y)}{\partial\left(\mathrm{vec}(F)^T\right)} = \frac{\partial\left((I\otimes\varphi(x^l))\mathrm{vec}(F)\right)}{\partial\left(\mathrm{vec}(F)^T\right)} = I\otimes\varphi(x^l). \tag{3.92}$$

We have used the fact that $\partial Xa^T/\partial a = X$ or $\partial Xa/\partial a^T = X$ so long as the matrix multiplications are well defined. This equation leads to

$$\frac{\partial z}{\partial(\mathrm{vec}(F))^T} = \frac{\partial z}{\partial\left(\mathrm{vec}(y)^T\right)}\left(I\otimes\varphi(x^l)\right). \tag{3.93}$$

Taking the transpose, we get

$$\begin{aligned}\frac{\partial z}{\partial \mathrm{vec}(F)} &= \left(I\otimes\varphi(x^l)\right)^T \frac{\partial z}{\partial \mathrm{vec}(y)} = \left(I\otimes\varphi(x^l)^T\right)\mathrm{vec}\left(\frac{\partial z}{\partial Y}\right)\\ &= \mathrm{vec}\left(\varphi(x^l)^T\frac{\partial z}{\partial Y}I\right) = \mathrm{vec}\left(\varphi(x^l)^T\frac{\partial z}{\partial Y}\right).\end{aligned} \tag{3.94}$$

Both Eqs. (3.87) and (3.88) are used in the above derivation giving $\partial z/\partial F = \varphi(x^l)^T \partial z/\partial Y$, which is a simple rule to update the parameters in the l–th layer: the gradient with respect to the convolution parameters is the product between $\varphi(x^l)^T$ (the im2col expansion) and $\partial z/\partial Y$ (the supervision signal transferred from the $(l+1)$-th layer).

Function $\varphi(x^l)$ has dimension $H^{l+1}W^{l+1}HWD^l$. From the above, we know that its elements are indexed by a pair p,q. So far, from Eq. (3.84) we know: (i) from q we can determine d^l, the channel of the convolution kernel that is used; and we can also determine i and j, the spatial offsets inside the kernel; (ii) from p we can determine i^{l+1} and j^{l+1}, the spatial offsets inside the convolved result x^{l+1}; and (iii) the spatial offsets in the input x^l can be determined as $i^l = i^{l+1} + i$ and $j^l = j^{l+1} + j$. In other words, the mapping $m: (p, q) \rightarrow (i^l, j^l, d^l)$ is one to one, and thus is a valid function. The inverse mapping, however, is one to many (and thus not a valid function). If we use m^{-1} to represent the inverse mapping, we know that $m^{-1}(i^l, j^l, d^l)$ is a set S, where each $(p, q) \in S$ satisfies $m(p, q) = (i^l, j^l, d^l)$. Now we take a look at $\varphi(x^l)$ from a different perspective.

The question: What information is required in order to fully specify this function? It is obvious that the following three types of information are needed (and only those). *The answer:* For *every* element of $\varphi(x^l)$, we need to know

(A) Which region does it belong to, or what is the value of $(0 \leq p < H^{l+1}W^{l+1})$?

(B) Which element is it inside the region (or equivalently inside the convolution kernel); that is, what is the value of $q(0 \leq q < HWDl)$? The above two types of information determine a location (p, q) inside $\varphi(x^l)$. The only missing information is (C) What is the value in that position, that is, $[\varphi(x^l)]pq$?

Since every element in $\varphi(x^l)$ is a verbatim copy of one element from x^l, we can reformulate question (C) into a different but equivalent one:

(C.1) Where is the value of a given $[\varphi(x^l)]pq$ copied from? Or, what is its original location inside x^l, that is, an index u that satisfies $0 \leq u < H^lW^lD^l$? (C.2) The entire x^l.

It is easy to see that the collective information in [A, B, C.1] (for the entire range of p, q, and u, and (C.2) (x^l) contains exactly the same amount of information as $\varphi(x^l)$. Since $0 \leq p < H^{l+1}W^{l+1}$, $0 \leq q < HWD^l$, and $0 \leq u < H^lW^lD^l$, we can use a a matrix $M \in \mathbb{R}^{\left(H^{l+1}W^{l+1}HWD^l\right) \times \left(H^lW^lD^l\right)}$ to encode the information in [A, B, C.1]. One row index of this matrix corresponds to one location inside $\varphi(x^l)$ (a(p, q) pair). One row of M has $H^lW^lD^l$ elements, and each element can be indexed by (i^l, j^l, d^l). Thus, each element in this matrix is indexed by a 5-tuple: (p, q, i^l, j^l, d^l).

Then, we can use the "indicator" method to encode the function $m(p, q) = (i^l, j^l, d^l)$ into M. That is, for any possible element in M, its row index x determines a(p, q) pair, and its column index y determines a(i^l, j^l, d^l) triplet, and M is defined as

$$M(x, y) = \begin{cases} 1 \text{ if } m(p, q) = \left(i^l, j^l, d^l\right) \\ 0 \text{ otherwise} \end{cases} \tag{3.95}$$

The M matrix is very high dimensional. At the same time, it is also very sparse: there is only one nonzero entry in the $H^lW^lD^l$ elements in one row, because m is a function. M, which uses information [A, B, C.1], encodes only the one-to-one correspondence between any element in $\varphi(x^l)$ and any element in x^l; it does not encode any specific value in x^l. Putting together the one-to-one correspondence information in M and the value information in x^l, we have

$$\text{vec}\left(\varphi\left(x^l\right)\right) = M\text{vec}\left(x^l\right). \tag{3.96}$$

Supervision signal for the previous layer: In the l-th layer, we need to compute $\partial z/\partial \text{vec}(x^l)$. For that, we want to reshape x^l into a matrix $\in \mathbb{R}^{\left(H^lW^l\right) \times D^l}$, and use these two equivalent forms (modulo reshaping) interchangeably. By the chain rule, $\partial z/\partial(\text{vec}(x^l)^T) = [\partial z/\partial(\text{vec}(y)^T)][\partial \text{vec}(y)/\partial(\text{vec}(x^l)^T)]$.

By utilizing Eqs. (3.90) and (3.96), we have

$$\frac{\partial \text{vec}(y)}{\partial\left(\text{vec}(x^l)^T\right)} = \frac{\partial\left(F^T \otimes I\right)\text{vec}\left(\varphi\left(x^l\right)\right)}{\partial\left(\text{vec}(x^l)^T\right)} = \left(F^T \otimes I\right)M. \tag{3.97}$$

$$\frac{\partial z}{\partial\left(\text{vec}(x^l)^T\right)} = \frac{\partial z}{\partial\left(\text{vec}(y)^T\right)}\left(F^T \otimes I\right)M. \tag{3.98}$$

Since by using Eq. (3.88)

$$\frac{\partial z}{\partial\left(\text{vec}(y)^T\right)}\left(F^T \otimes I\right) = \left((F \otimes I)\frac{\partial z}{\partial \text{vec}(y)}\right)^T = \left((F \otimes I)\,\text{vec}\left(\frac{\partial z}{\partial Y}\right)\right)^T$$

$$= \text{vec}\left(I\frac{\partial z}{\partial Y}F^T\right)^T = \text{vec}\left(\frac{\partial z}{\partial Y}F^T\right)^T, \tag{3.99}$$

we have

$$\frac{\partial z}{\partial\left(\text{vec}(x^l)^T\right)} = \text{vec}\left(\frac{\partial z}{\partial Y}F^T\right)^T M, \tag{3.100}$$

or equivalently

$$\frac{\partial z}{\partial(\text{vec}(x^l))} = M^T \text{vec}\left(\frac{\partial z}{\partial Y}F^T\right). \tag{3.101}$$

In Eq. (3.101), $(\partial z/\partial Y)F^T \in \mathbb{R}^{(H^{l+1}W^{l+1})\times(HWD^l)}$, and $\text{vec}((\partial z/\partial Y)F^T)$ is a vector in $\mathbb{R}^{H^{l+1}W^{l+1}HWD^l}$. At the same time, M^T is an indicator matrix in $\mathbb{R}^{(H^lW^lD^l)\times(H^{l+1}W^{l+1}HWD^l)}$. In order to locate one element in $\text{vec}(x^l)$ or one row in M^T, we need an index triplet (i^l, j^l, d^l), with $0 \le i^l < H^l$, $0 \le j^l < W^l$, and $0 \le d^l < D^l$. Similarly, to locate a column in M^T or an element in $\partial z/\partial Y)F^T$, we need an index pair p, q, with $0 \le p < H^{l+1}W^{l+1}$ and $\le q < HWD^l$. Thus, the (i^l, j^l, d^l)-th entry of $\partial z/\partial(\text{vec}(x^l))$ is the product of two vectors: the row in M^T (or the column in M) that is indexed by (i^l, j^l, d^l), and $\text{vec}((\partial z/\partial Y)F^T)$. Since M^T is an indicator matrix, in the row vector indexed by (i^l, j^l, d^l), only those entries whose index (p, q) satisfies $m(p, q) = (i^l, j^l, d^l)$ have a value 1, and all other entries are 0. Thus, the (i^l, j^l, d^l)-th entry of $\partial z/\partial(\text{vec}(x^l))$ equals the sum of these corresponding entries in $\text{vec}((\partial z/\partial Y)F^T)$. Therefore, we get the following succinct equation:

$$[\partial z/\partial X]_{(i^l, j^l, d^l)} = \sum_{(p,q)\in m^{-1}(i^l, j^l, d^l)} [(\partial z/\partial Y)F^T]_{(p,q)}. \tag{3.102}$$

In other words, to compute $\partial z/\partial X$, we do not need to explicitly use the extremely high-dimensional matrix M. Instead, Eqs. (3.102) and (3.84) can be used to efficiently find it. The convolution example from Figure 3.23 is used to illustrate the inverse mapping m^{-1} in Figure 3.25.

In the right half of Figure 3.25, the 6×4 matrix is $\partial z/\partial Y)F^T$. In order to compute the partial derivative of z with respect to one element in the input X, we need to find which elements in $\partial z/\partial Y)F^T$ are involved and add them. In the left half of Figure 3.25, we see that the input element 5 (shown in larger font) is involved in four convolution operations, shown by the red, green, blue and black boxes, respectively. These four convolution operations correspond to $p = 1, 2, 3, 4$. For example, when $p = 2$ (the green box), 5 is the third element in the convolution, and hence $q = 3$ when $p = 2$, and we put a green circle in the (2, 3)-th element of the $(\partial z/\partial Y)F^T$ matrix. After all four circles are put in the matrix $(\partial z/\partial Y)F^T$, the partial derivative is the sum of elements in these four locations of $(\partial z/\partial Y)F^T$. The set $m^{-1}(i^l, j^l, d^l)$ contains at most HWD^l elements. Hence, Eq. (3.102) requires at most HWD^l summations to compute one element of $\partial z/\partial X$.

The pooling layer: Let $x^l \in \mathbb{R}^{H^l \times W^l \times D^l}$ be the input to the l-th layer, which is now a pooling layer. The pooling operation requires no parameter (i.e., w^i is null, and hence parameter learning is not needed for this layer). The spatial extent of the pooling $(H \times W)$ is specified in the design of the CoNN structure. Assume that H divides H^l and W divides W^l and the stride equals the pooling spatial extent, the output of pooling (y or equivalently x^{l+1}) will be an order-3 tensor of size $H^{l+1} \times W^l{}^{+1} \times D^{l+1}$, with $H^{l+1} = H^l/H$, $W^{l+1} = W^l/W$, $D^{l+1} = D^l$. A pooling layer operates upon x^l channel by channel independently. Within each channel, the matrix with $H^l \times W^l$ elements is divided into $H^{l+1} \times W^{l+1}$ nonoverlapping subregions, each subregion being $H \times W$ in size. The pooling operator then maps a subregion into a single number. Two types of pooling operators are widely used:

Figure 3.25 Computing $\partial z/\partial X$. (for more details see the color figure in the bins).

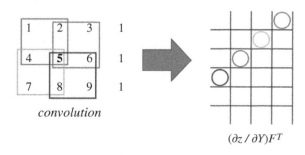

convolution

$(\partial z / \partial Y)F^T$

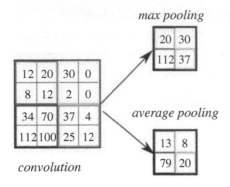

max pooling

Figure 3.26 Illustration of pooling layer operation. (for more details see the color figure in the bins).

max pooling and average pooling. In max pooling, the pooling operator maps a subregion to its maximum value, while the average pooling maps a subregion to its average value as illustrated in Figure 3.26.

Formally this can be represented as

$$\text{max} : y_{i^{l+1}, j^{l+1}, d} = MAX_{0 \le i < H, 0 \le j < W} \left(x_{i^{l+1} \times H + i, j^{l+1} \times W + j, d}^{l} \right)$$

$$\text{average} : y_{i^{l+1}, j^{l+1}, d} = \frac{1}{HW} \sum_{0 \le i < H, 0 \le j < W} \left(x_{i^{l+1} \times H + i, j^{l+1} \times W + j, d}^{l} \right),$$

(3.103)

where $0 \le i^{l+1} < H^{l+1}$, $0 \le j^{l+1} < W^{l+1}$, and $0 \le d < D^{l+1} = D^{l}$.

Pooling is a local operator, and its forward computation is straightforward. When focusing on the backpropagation, only max pooling will be discussed and we can resort to the indicator matrix again. All we need to encode in this indicator matrix is: for every element in y, where does it come from in x^l?

We need a triplet (i^l, j^l, d^l) to locate one element in the input x^l, and another triplet $(i^{l+1}, j^{l+1}, d^{l+1})$ to locate one element in y. The pooling output $y_{i^{l+1}, j^{l+1}, d^{l+1}}$ comes from x_{i^l, j^l, d^l}^l, if and only if the following conditions are met: (i) they are in the same channel; (ii) the (i^l, j^l)-th spatial entry belongs to the (i^{l+1}, j^{l+1})-th subregion; and (iii) the (i^l, j^l)-th spatial entry is the largest one in that subregion. This can be represented as

$$d^{l+1} = d^l, \left\lfloor i^l / H \right\rfloor = i^{l+1}, \left\lfloor j^l / W \right\rfloor = j^{l+1}, x_{i^l, j^l, d^l}^l \ge y_{i + i^{l+1} \times H, \ j + j^{l+1} \times W, d^l},$$

$$\forall 0 \le i < H, 0 \le j < W,$$

where $\lfloor \cdot \rfloor$ is the floor function. If the stride is not $H(W)$ in the vertical (horizontal) direction, the equation must be changed accordingly. Given a $(i^{l+1}, j^{l+1}, d^{l+1})$ triplet, there is only one (i^l, j^l, d^l) triplet that satisfies all these conditions. So, we define an indicator matrix $(x^l) \in \mathbb{R}^{\left(H^{l+1} W^{l+1} D^{l+1} \right) \times \left(H^l W^l D^l \right)}$.

One triplet of indexes $(i^{l+1}, j^{l+1}, d^{l+1})$ specifies a row in S, while (i^l, j^l, d^l) specifies a column. These two triplets together pinpoint one element in (x^l). We set that element to 1 if $d^{l+1} = d^l$ and $x_{i^l, j^l, d^l}^l \ge y_{i + i^{l+1} \times H, \ j + j^{l+1} \times W, d^l}, \forall 0 \le i < H, 0 \le j < W$, are simultaneously satisfied, and 0 otherwise. One row of $S(x^l)$ corresponds to one element in y, and one column corresponds to one element in x^l. By using this indicator matrix, we have $\text{vec}(y) = S(x^l)\text{vec}(x^l)$ and

$$\frac{\partial \text{vec}(y)}{\partial \left(\text{vec}(x^l)^T \right)} = S(x^l), \quad \frac{\partial z}{\partial \left(\text{vec}(x^l)^T \right)} = \frac{\partial z}{\partial \left(\text{vec}(y)^T \right)} S(x^l)$$

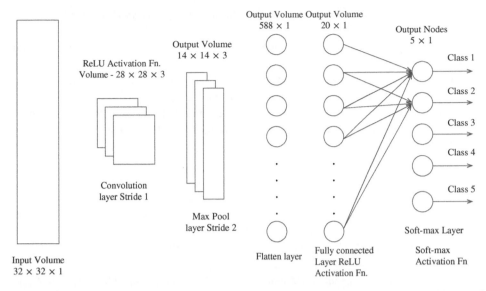

Figure 3.27 Illustration of preprocessing in a cooperative neural network (CoNN)-based image classifier.

resulting in

$$\frac{\partial z}{\partial \text{vec}(x^l)} = S(x^l)^T \frac{\partial z}{\partial \text{vec}(y)}. \tag{3.104}$$

$S(x^l)$ is very sparse since it has only one nonzero entry in every row. Thus, we do not need to use the entire matrix in the computation. Instead, we just need to record the locations of those nonzero entries – there are only $H^{l+1}W^{l+1}D^{l+1}$ such entries in $S(x^l)$. Figure 3.27 illustrates preprocessing in a CoNN-based image classifier.

For further readings on CoNNs, the reader is referred to [30].

References

1 CS231n Convolutional Neural Networks for Visual Recognition. Stanford University. https://cs231n.github.io/neural-networks-1

2 Haykin, S. (1996). *Adaptive Filter Theory*, 3e. Upper Saddle River, NJ: Prentice-Hall.

3 Haykin, S. (1996). Neural networks expand SP's horizons. *IEEE Signal Process. Mag.* **13** (2): 24–49.

4 Haykin, S. (1999). *Neural Networks: A Comprehensive Foundation*, 2e. Upper Saddle River, NJ: Prentice-Hall.

5 Wan, E.A. (1993). Finite impulse response neural networks with applications in time series prediction, Ph.D. dissertation. Department of Electrical Engineering, Stanford University, Stanford, CA.

6 Box, G. and Jenkins, G.M. (1976). *Time Series Analysis: Forecasting and Control*. San Francisco, CA: Holden-Day.

7 Weigend, A.S. and Gershenfeld, N.A. (1994). *Time Series Prediction: Fore- Casting the Future and Understanding the Past*. Reading, MA: Addison-Wesley.

8 Hochreiter, S. and Schmidhuber, J. (1997). Long short-term memory. *Neural Comput.* **9** (8): 1735–1780.

9 Schuster, M. and Paliwal, K.K. (1997). Bidirectional recurrent neural networks. *IEEE Trans. Signal Process.* **45** (11): 2673–2681.

10 Graves, A. and Schmidhuber, J. (2005). Framewise phoneme classification with bidirectional LSTM and other neural network architectures. *Neural Netw.* **18** (5): 602–610.

11 Graves, A., Liwicki, M., Fernandez, S. et al. (2009). A novel connectionist system for unconstrained handwriting recognition. *IEEE Trans. Pattern Anal. Mach. Intell.* **31** (5): 855–868.

12 Graves, A., Wayne, G., and Danihelka, I. (2014). Neural Turing machines. arXiv preprint arXiv:1410.5401.

13 Baddeley, A., Sala, S.D., and Robbins, T.W. (1996). Working memory and executive control [and discussion]. *Philos. Trans. R. Soc. B: Biol. Sci.* **351** (1346): 1397–1404.

14 Chua, L.O. and Roska, T. (2002). *Cellular Neural Networks and Visual Computing: Foundations and Applications*. New York, NY: Cambridge University Press.

15 Chua, L.O. and Yang, L. (1988). Cellular neural network: theory. *IEEE Trans. Circuits Syst.* **35**: 1257–1272.

16 Molinar-Solis, J.E., Gomez-Castaneda, F., Moreno, J. et al. (2007). Programmable CMOS CNN cell based on floating-gate inverter unit. *J. VLSI Signal Process. Syst. Signal, Image, Video Technol.* **49**: 207–216.

17 Pan, C. and Naeemi, A. (2016). A proposal for energy-efficient cellular neural network based on spintronic devices. *IEEE Trans. Nanotechnol.* **15** (5): 820–827.

18 Wang, L. et al. (1998). Time multiplexed color image processing based on a CNN with cell-state outputs. *IEEE Trans. VLSI Syst.* **6** (2): 314–322.

19 Roska, T. and Chua, L.O. (1993). The CNN universal machine: an analogic array computer. *IEEE Trans. Circuits Systems II: Analog Digital Signal Process.* **40** (3): 163–173.

20 Pickett, M.D. et al. (2009). Switching dynamics in titanium dioxide memristive devices. *J. Appl. Phys.* **106** (7): 074508.

21 Hu, X., Duan, S., and Wang, L. (2012). A novel chaotic neural network using memristive synapse with applications in associative memory. *Abstract Appl. Anal.* **2012**: 1–19. https://doi.org/10.1155/2012/405739.

22 Kim, H. et al. (2012). Memristor bridge synapses. *Proc. IEEE* **100** (6): 2061–2070.

23 Adhikari, S.P., Yang, C., Kim, H., and Chua, L.O. (2012). Memristor bridge synapse-based neural network and its learning. *IEEE Trans. Neural Netw. Learn. Syst.* **23** (9): 1426–1435.

24 Corinto, F., Ascoli, A., Kim, Y.-S., and Min, K.-S. (2014). Cellular nonlinear networks with memristor synapses. In: *Memristor Networks*, ed. Andrew Adamatzky, Leon Chua 267–291. New York, NY: Springer-Verlag.

25 Wang, L., Drakakis, E., Duan, S., and He, P. (2012). Memristor model and its application for chaos generation. *Int. J. Bifurcation Chaos* **22** (8): 1250205.

26 Liu, S., Wang, L., Duan, S. et al. (2012). Memristive device based filter and integration circuits with applications. *Adv. Sci. Lett.* **8** (1): 194–199.

27 Chua, L.O. and Kang, S.M. (1976). Memristive devices and systems. *Proc. IEEE* **64** (2): 209–223.

28 Kvatinsky, S., Friedman, E.G., Kolodny, A., and Weiser, U.C. (2013). TEAM: threshold adaptive memristor model. *IEEE Trans. Circuits Syst. I, Reg. Papers* **60** (1): 211–221.

29 Strachan, J. et al. (2013). State dynamics and modeling of tantalum oxide memristors. *IEEE Trans. Electron Devices* **60** (7): 2194–2202.

30 Saha, S. A Comprehensive Guide to Convolutional Neural Networks. https://towardsdatascience.com/a-comprehensive-guide-to-convolutional-neural-networks-the-eli5-way-3bd2b1164a53

4

Explainable Neural Networks

In many applications, the value of the results obtained by machine learning (ML), that is, artificial intelligence (AI), especially implemented by deep neural networks (DNN), would be significantly higher if users could understand, appropriately trust, and effectively manage AI results. This need has generated an interest in explainable AI (XAI), and in our case we would be especially interested in explainable neural networks (*xNN*).

In the past, there have been multiple controversies over AI/ML enabled systems yielding biased or discriminatory results [1, 2]. That implies an increasing need for explanations to ensure that AI-based decisions were not made erroneously. When we talk about an explanation for a decision, we generally mean the need for reasons or justifications for that particular outcome, rather than a description of the inner workings or the logic of the reasoning underlying the decision-making process in general. XAI systems are expected to provide the required information to justify results, particularly when unexpected decisions are made. It also ensures that there is an auditable and provable way of defending algorithmic decisions as being fair and ethical, which helps build trust.

AI needs to provide justifications in order to be in compliance with legislation, for instance, the "right to explanation," which is a regulation included in the General Data Protection Regulation (GDPR) [3].

Explainability can also help to prevent things from going wrong. A better understanding of system behavior provides greater visibility of unknown vulnerabilities and flaws, and helps to rapidly identify and correct errors in critical situations, which enables better control.

Another reason for building explainable models is the need to continuously improve them. A model that can be explained and understood is one that can be more easily improved. Because users know why the system produced specific outputs, they will also know how to make it smarter. Thus, XAI could be the foundation for ongoing iterative improvements in the interaction between human and machine.

Asking for explanations is a helpful tool to learn new facts, to gather information, and thus to gain knowledge. Only explainable systems can be useful for that. For example, if AlphaGo Zero [4] can perform much better than human players at the game of Go, it would be useful if the machine could explain its learned strategy (knowledge) to us. Following this line of thought, we may expect in the future, XAI models will teach us about new and hidden laws in biology, chemistry, and physics. In general, XAI can bring significant benefit to a large range of domains relying on AI systems.

Transportation: Automated vehicles should decrease traffic deaths and providing enhanced mobility, but also pose challenges in addressing the explainability of AI decisions. Autonomous vehicles have to make very fast decisions based on how they classify the objects in the scene in front

Artificial Intelligence and Quantum Computing for Advanced Wireless Networks, First Edition.
Savo G. Glisic and Beatriz Lorenzo.

of them. If a self-driving car suddenly behaves abnormally because of some misclassification problem, the consequences can be serious. This is not just a possibility; it is already happening. Only an explainable system can clarify the ambiguous circumstances of such situations and eventually prevent them from happening. Transportation is a potential application domain of XAI. Work on explaining self-driving vehicle behavior has already begun [5, 6], but there is a long way to go.

Health care: The medical diagnosis model is responsible for human life. How can we be confident enough to treat a patient as instructed by an artificial neural network (ANN) model? In the past, such a model was trained to predict which pneumonia patients should be admitted to hospitals and which patients should be treated as outpatients. Initial findings indicated that neural nets were far more accurate than classical statistical methods. However, after an extensive test, it turned out that the neural net had inferred that pneumonia patients with asthma have a lower risk of dying, and should not be admitted. Medically, this is counterintuitive; however, it reflected a real pattern in the training data – asthma patients with pneumonia usually were admitted not only to the hospital but directly to the intensive care unit (ICU), treated aggressively, and survived [1]. It was then decided to abandon the AI system because it was too dangerous to use it clinically. Only by interpreting the model can we discover such a crucial problem and avoid it. Recently, researchers have conducted preliminary work aiming to make clinical AI-based systems explainable [1, 7–9]. The increasing number of these works confirms the challenge of – and the interest in – applying XAI approaches in the healthcare domain.

Legal: In criminal justice, AI has the potential to improve assessment of risks for recidivism and reduce costs associated with both crime and incarceration. However, when using a criminal decision model to predict the risk of recidivism at the court, we have to make sure the model behaves in an equitable, honest, and nondiscriminatory manner. Transparency of how a decision is made is a necessity in this critical domain, yet very few works have investigated making automated decision making in legal systems explainable [10–12].

Finance: In financial services, the benefits of using AI tools include improvements related to wealth-management activities, access to investment advice, and customer service. However, these tools also pose questions around data security and fair lending. The financial industry is highly regulated, and loan issuers are required by law to make fair decisions. Thus, one significant challenge of using AI-based systems in credit scores and models is that it is harder to provide the needed "reason code" to borrowers – the explanation of why they were denied credit – especially when the basis for denial is the output from an ML algorithm. Some credit bureau agencies are working on promising research projects to generate automated reason codes and make AI credit-based score decisions more explainable and auditor friendly [13].

Military: Originally, the current famous XAI's initiative was begun by military researchers [14], and the growing visibility of XAI today is due largely to the call for research by Defense Advanced Research Projects Agency (DARPA) and the solicitation of DARPA projects. AI in the military arena also suffers from the AI explainability problem. Some of the challenges of relying on autonomous systems for military operations are discussed in [15]. As in the healthcare domain, this often involves life and death decisions, which again leads to similar types of ethical and legal dilemmas. The academic AI research community is well represented in this application domain with the DARPA Ambitious XAI program, along with some research initiatives that study explainability in this domain [16].

XAI can also find interesting applications in other domains like cybersecurity, education, entertainment, government, and image recognition. An interesting chart of potential harms from automated decision making was presented by Future of Privacy Forum [17]: it depicts the various spheres of life where automated decision making can cause injury and where providing automated explanations can turn them into trustworthy processes; these areas include employment, insurance and social benefits, housing, and differential pricing of goods and services.

4.1 Explainability Methods

The majority of works classify the methods according to three criteria: (i) the complexity of interpretability, (ii) the scope of interpretability, and (iii) the level of dependency on the used ML model. Next, we will describe the main features of each class and give examples from current research.

4.1.1 The Complexity and Interoperability

The complexity of an ML model is directly related to its interpretability. In general, the more complex the model, the more difficult it is to interpret and explain. Thus, the most straightforward way to get to interpretable AI/ML would be to design an algorithm that is inherently and intrinsically interpretable. Many works have been reported in that direction. Letham et al. [18] presented a model called Bayesian Rule Lists (BRL) based on decision tree; the authors claimed that preliminary interpretable models provide concise and convincing capabilities to gain domain experts' trust. Caruana et al. [1] described an application of a learning method based on generalized additive models to the pneumonia problem. They proved the intelligibility of their model through case studies on real medical data.

Xu et al. [19] introduced an attention-based model that automatically learns to describe the content of images. They showed through visualization how the model is able to interpret the results. Ustun and Rudin [20] presented a sparse linear model for creating a data-driven scoring system called SLIM. The results of this work highlight the interpretability capability of the proposed system in providing users with qualitative understanding due to their high level of sparsity and small integer coefficients. A common challenge, which hinders the usability of this class of methods, is the trade-off between interpretability and accuracy [21]. As noted by Breiman [22], "accuracy generally requires more complex prediction methods … [and] simple and interpretable functions do not make the most accurate predictors." In a sense, intrinsic interpretable models come at the cost of accuracy.

An alternative approach to interpretability in ML is to construct a highly complex uninterpretable black-box model with high accuracy and subsequently use a separate set of techniques to perform what we could define as a reverse engineering process to provide the needed explanations without altering or even knowing the inner works of the original model. This class of methods offers, then, a post-hoc explanation [23]. Though it could be significantly complex and costly, most recent work done in the XAI field belongs to the post-hoc class and includes natural language explanations [24], visualizations of learned models [25], and explanations by example [26].

So, we can see that interpretability depends on the nature of the prediction task. As long as the model is accurate for the task, and uses a reasonably restricted number of internal components, intrinsic interpretable models are sufficient. If, however, the prediction target involves complex and highly accurate models, then considering post-hoc interpretation models is necessary. It should also be noted that in the literature there is a group of intrinsic methods for complex uninterpretable models. These methods aim to modify the internal structure of a complex black-box model that are not primarily interpretable (which typically applies to a DNN that we are interested in) to mitigate their opacity and thus improve their interpretability [27]. The used methods may either be components that add additional capabilities, components that belong to the model architecture [28, 29], for example, as part of the loss function [30], or as part of the architecture structure, in terms of operations between layers [31, 32].

4.1.2 Global Versus Local Interpretability

Global interpretability facilitates the understanding of the whole logic of a model and follows the entire reasoning leading to all the different possible outcomes. This class of methods is helpful when ML models are crucial to inform population-level decisions, such as drugs consumption trends or climate change [33]. In such cases, a global effect estimate would be more helpful than many explanations for all the possible idiosyncrasies. Works that propose globally interpretable models include the aforementioned additive models for predicting pneumonia risk [1] and rule sets generated from sparse Bayesian generative models [18]. However, these models are usually specifically structured and thus limited in predictability to preserve uninterpretability. Yang et al. [33] proposed a Global model Interpretation via Recursive Partitioning called GIRP to build a global interpretation tree for a wide range of ML models based on their local explanations. In their experiments, the authors highlighted that their method can discover whether a particular ML model is behaving in a reasonable way or is overfit to some unreasonable pattern. Valenzuela-Escárcega et al. [34] proposed a supervised approach for information extraction that provides a global, deterministic interpretation. This work supports the idea that representation learning can be successfully combined with traditional, pattern-based bootstrapping yielding models that are interpretable. Nguyen et al. [35] proposed an approach based on activation maximization – synthesizing the preferred inputs for neurons in neural networks – via a learned prior in the form of a deep generator network to produce a global interpretable model for image recognition. The activation maximization technique was previously used by Erhan et al. [36]. Although a multitude of techniques is used in the literature to enable global interpretability, global model interpretability is difficult to achieve in practice, especially for models that exceed a handful of parameters. In analogy with humans, who focus their effort on only part of the model in order to comprehend the whole of it, local interpretability can be more readily applied.

Explaining the reasons for a specific decision or single prediction means that interpretability is occurring locally. Ribeiro et al. [37] proposed LIME for Local Interpretable Model-Agnostic Explanation. This model can approximate a black-box model locally in the neighborhood of any prediction of interest. Work in [38], extends LIME using decision rules. Leave-one covariate-out (LOCO) [39] is another popular technique for generating local explanation models that offer local variable importance measures. In [40], the authors present a method capable of explaining the local decision taken by arbitrary nonlinear classification algorithms, using the local gradients that characterize how a data point has to be moved to change its predicted label. A set of works using similar methods for image classification models was presented in [41–44]. It is a common approach to understanding the decisions of image classification systems by finding regions of an image that are particularly influential for the final classification. Also called sensitivity maps, saliency maps, or pixel attribution maps [45], these approaches use occlusion techniques or calculations with gradients to assign an "importance" value to individual pixels that are meant to reflect their influence on the final classification. On the basis of the decomposition of a model's predictions on the individual contributions of each feature, Robnik- Šikonja and Kononenko [46] proposed explaining the model prediction for one instance by measuring the difference between the original prediction and the one made with omitting a set of features. A number of recent algorithms can be also found in [47–58].

4.1.3 Model Extraction

Model-specific interpretability methods are limited to specific model classes. Here, when we require a particular type of interpretation, we are limited in terms of choice to models that provide it, potentially at the expense of using a more predictive and representative model. For that reason, there has been a recent surge of interest in model-agnostic interpretability methods as they are model-free and not tied to a particular type of ML model. This class of methods separates prediction from explanation. Model-agnostic interpretations are usually post-hoc; they are generally used to interpret ANN and could be local or global interpretable models. In the interest of improving interpretability AI models, a large number of model-agnostic methods have been developed recently using a range of techniques from statistics, ML, and data science. Here, we group them into four technique types: visualization, knowledge extraction, influence methods, and example-based explanation (EBE).

1) *Visualization:* A natural way to understand an ML model, especially DNN, is to visualize its representations to explore the pattern hidden inside a neural unit. The largest body of research employs this approach with the help of different visualization techniques in order to see inside these black boxes. Visualization techniques are essentially applied to supervised learning models. The popular visualization techniques are surrogate models, partial dependence plot (PDP), and individual conditional expectation (ICE).

   A *surrogate model* is an interpretable model (like a linear model or decision tree) that is trained on the predictions of the original black-box model in order to interpret the latter. However, there are almost no theoretical guarantees that the simple surrogate model is highly representative of the more complex model. The aforementioned [37] approach is a prescribed method for building local surrogate models around single observations. In [59], a surrogate model approach was used to extract a decision tree that represents model behavior. In [60], an approach to building Tree-View visualizations using a surrogate model was proposed.

   PDP is a graphical representation that helps in visualizing the average partial relationship between one or more input variables and the predictions of a black-box model. In [61], PDP is used to understand the relationship between predictors and the conditional average treatment effect for a voter mobilization experiment, with the predictions being made by Bayesian Additive Regression Trees [62]. The approach in [63], which relies on stochastic gradient boosting, used PDPs to understand how different environmental factors influence the distribution of a particular freshwater. Work in [12] demonstrates the advantage of using random forests and the associated PDPs to accurately model predictor-response relationships under asymmetric classification costs that often arise in criminal justice settings. Work in [64] proposed a methodology called Forest Floor to visualize and interpret random forest models, the proposed techniques rely on the feature contributions method rather than on PDP. It was argued by the authors that the advantages of Forest Floor over PDP is that interactions are not masked by averaging, making it is possible to locate interactions that are not visualized in a given projection.

   ICE plots extended PDP. Whereas PDPs provide a coarse view of a model's workings, ICE plots reveal interactions and individual differences by disaggregating the PDP output. Recent works use ICE rather than the classical PDP. For instance, [65] introduced ICE techniques and proved its advantage over PDP. Later, [66] proposed a local feature importance-based approach that uses both partial importance (PI) and individual conditional importance (ICI) plots as visual tools.

2) *Knowledge extraction:* It is difficult to explain how ML models work, especially when the models are based on ANN. The task of extracting explanations from the network is therefore to extract

the knowledge acquired by an ANN during training and encoded as an internal representation. Several works propose methods to extract the knowledge embedded in the ANN that mainly rely on two techniques: rule extraction and model distillation.

Rule extraction is an effort to gain insight into highly complex models [67–69] by extracting rules that approximate the decision-making process in ANN by utilizing the input and output of the ANN. The survey in [27] based on [70, 71] proposed three modes to extract rules: pedagogical, decompositional, and eclectic rule extraction. Decompositional approaches focus on extracting rules at the level of individual units within the trained ANN; that is, the view of the underlying ANN is one of transparency [46–48]. On the other hand, pedagogical approaches treat the trained ANN as a black-box; that is, the view of the underlying ANN is opaque. The Orthogonal Search-based Rule Extraction algorithm (OSRE) from [72] is a successful pedagogical methodology often applied in biomedicine. The third type (eclectic) is a hybrid approach for rule extraction that incorporates elements of the previous rule-extraction techniques [73].

Model distillation is another technique that falls in the knowledge extraction category. Distillation is a model compression to transfer information (dark knowledge) from deep networks (the "teacher") to shallow networks (the "student") [74, 75]. Model compression was originally proposed to reduce the computational cost of a model runtime, but has later been applied for interpretability.

Tan et al. [10] investigated how model distillation can be used to distill complex models into transparent models. Che et al. [76] introduced a knowledge-distillation approach called Interpretable Mimic Learning to learn interpretable phenotype features for making robust prediction while mimicking the performance of deep learning models. A recent work by Xu et al. [77] presented DarkSight, a visualization method for interpreting the predictions of a black-box classifier on a dataset in a way that is inspired by the notion of dark knowledge. The proposed method combines ideas from knowledge distillation, dimension reduction, and visualization of DNN [78–80].

3) *Influence techniques* estimate the importance or the relevance of a feature by changing the input or internal components and recording how much the changes affect model performance. Influence techniques are often visualized. There are three alternative methods to obtain an input variable's relevance: sensitivity analysis (SA), layer-wise relevance propagation (LRP), and feature importance.

SA searches for the answer to the question of how an ANN output is influenced by its input and/or weight perturbations [81]. It is used to verify whether model behavior and outputs remain stable when data are intentionally perturbed or other changes are simulated in data. Visualizing the results of SA is considered an agnostic explanation technique, since displaying a model's stability as data change over time enhances trust in ML results. SA has been increasingly used in explaining ANN in general and DNN classification of images in particular [82, 83]. However, it is important to note that SA does not produce an explanation of the function value itself, but rather a variation of it. The purpose of performing an SA is thus usually not to actually explain the relationship but to test models for stability and trustworthiness, either as a tool to find and remove unimportant input attributes or as a starting point for some more powerful explanation technique (e.g., decomposition).

LRP was proposed in [84] as the LRP algorithm. It redistributes the prediction function backward, starting from the output layer of the network and backpropagating up to the input layer. The key property of this redistribution process is referred to as relevance conservation. In contrast to SA, this method explains predictions relative to the state of maximum uncertainty; that is, it identifies properties that are pivotal for the prediction.

Feature importance quantifies the contribution of each input variable (feature) to the predictions of a complex ML model. The increase in the model's prediction error is calculated after permuting the feature in order to measure its importance. Permuting the values of important features increases the model error, whereas permuting the values of unimportant features does not affect the model and thus keeps the model error unchanged. Using this technique, Fisher et al. [85] proposed a model-agnostic version of the algorithm called Model Class Reliance (MCR), while [66] proposed a local version of the algorithm called SFIMP for permutation-based Shapley feature importance. LOCO [39] uses local feature importance as well.

4) *EBE* techniques select particular instances of the dataset to explain the behavior of ML models. The approach is mostly model agnostic since they make any ML model more interpretable. The slight difference from model-agnostic methods is that the *EBE* methods interpret a model by selecting instances of the dataset and not by acting on features or transforming the model.

Two versions of this technique are (i) Prototypes and Criticisms and (ii) Counterfactual Explanations (CE).

Prototypes and criticisms: Prototypes are a selection of representative instances from the data [86–88]; thus, item membership is determined by its similarity to the prototypes, which leads to overgeneralization. To avoid this, exceptions have to be identified also, called criticisms: instances that are not well represented by those prototypes. Kim [89] developed an unsupervised algorithm for automatically finding prototypes and criticisms for a dataset, called Maximum Mean Discrepancy-critic (MMD-critic). When applied to unlabeled data, it finds prototypes and critics that characterize the dataset as a whole.

Counterfactual explanations (CE): Wachter et al. [90] presented the concept of "unconditional counterfactual explanations" as a novel type of explanation of automated decisions. CE describe the minimum conditions that would have led to an alternative decision (e.g., a bank loan being or not being approved), without the need to describe the full logic of the algorithm. The focus here is on explaining a single prediction in contrast to adversarial examples, where the emphasis is on reversing the prediction and not explaining it [91]. As the research contributions in this class of methods are actively growing, new model-agnostic techniques are regularly proposed. In the next section, we will present in more detail some of the techniques listed in this section.

4.2 Relevance Propagation in ANN

Classification of images has become a key ingredient in many computer vision applications, for example, image search, robotics, medical imaging, object detection in radar images, or face detection. A particularly popular approach to the problem is based on the use of neural networks.

This lack of interpretability in these solutions is due to the nonlinearity of the various mappings that process the raw image pixels to its feature representation and from that to the final classifier function. This is a considerable drawback in classification applications, as it prevents human experts from carefully verifying the classification decision. A simple yes or no answer is sometimes of limited value in applications where questions like where something occurs or how it is structured are more relevant than a binary or real-valued one-dimensional assessment of mere presence or absence of a certain structure. In this section, we aim to explain in more detail the relation between classification and interpretability for multilayered neural networks discussed in the previous chapter.

4.2.1 Pixel-wise Decomposition

We start with the concept of pixel-wise image decomposition, which is designed to understand the contribution of a single pixel of an image x to the prediction $f(x)$ made by a classifier f in an image classification task. We would like to find out, separately for each image x, which pixels contribute to what extent to a positive or negative classification result. In addition, we want to express this extent quantitatively by a measure. We assume that the classifier has real-valued outputs with mapping $f: \mathbb{R}^V \to \mathbb{R}^1$ such that $f(x) > 0$ denotes the presence of the learned structure. We are interested in finding out the contribution of each input pixel $x_{(d)}$ of an input image x to a particular prediction $f(x)$. The important constraint specific to classification consists in finding the differential contribution relative to the state of maximal uncertainty with respect to classification, which is then represented by the set of root points $f(x_0) = 0$. One possible way is to decompose the prediction $f(x)$ as a sum of terms of the separate input dimensions x_d:

$$f(x) \approx \sum_{d=1}^{V} R_d \tag{4.1}$$

Here, the qualitative interpretation is that $R_d < 0$ contributes evidence against the presence of a structure that is to be classified, whereas $R_d > 0$ contributes evidence for its presence. More generally, positive values should denote positive contributions and negative values, negative contributions.

LRP: Returning to multilayer ANNs, we will introduce LRP as a concept defined by a set of constraints. In its general form, the concept assumes that the classifier can be decomposed into several layers of computation, which is a structure used in Deep NN. The first layer are the inputs, the pixels of the image; and the last layer is the real-valued prediction output of the classifier f. The l-th layer is modeled as a vector $z = \left(z_d^{(l)}\right)_{d=1}^{V(l)}$ with dimensionality $V(l)$. LRP assumes that we have a relevance score $R_d^{(l+1)}$ for each dimension $z_d^{(l+1)}$ of the vector z at layer $l+1$. The idea is to find a relevance score $R_d^{(l)}$ for each dimension $z_d^{(l)}$ of the vector z at the next layer l which is closer to the input layer such that the following equation holds:

$$f(x) = \dots = \sum_{d \in l+1} R_d^{(l+1)} = \sum_{d \in l} R_d^{(l)} = \dots = \sum_{d} R_d^{(1)} \tag{4.2}$$

Iterating Eq. (4.2) from the last layer, which is the classifier output $f(x)$, back to the input layer x consisting of image pixels then yields the desired Eq. (4.1). The relevance for the input layer will serve as the desired sum decomposition in Eq. (4.1). In the following, we will derive further constraints beyond Eqs. (4.1) and (4.2) and motivate them by examples. A decomposition satisfying Eq. (4.2) per se is neither unique, nor it is guaranteed that it yields a meaningful interpretation of the classifier prediction.

As an example, suppose we have one layer. The inputs are $x \in \mathbb{R}^V$. We use a linear classifier with some arbitrary and dimension-specific feature space mapping φ_d and a bias b:

$$f(x) = b + \sum_{d} \alpha_d \varphi_d(x_d) \tag{4.3}$$

Let us define the relevance for the second layer trivially as $R_1^{(2)} = f(x)$. Then, one possible LRP formula would be to define the relevance $R^{(1)}$ for the inputs x as

$$R_d^{(1)} = \begin{cases} f(x)^{\frac{|\alpha_d \varphi_d(x_d)|}{\sum_d |\alpha_d \varphi_d(x_d)|}} & \text{if } \sum_d |\alpha_d \varphi_d(x_d)| \neq 0 \\[2mm] \dfrac{b}{V} & \text{if } \sum_d |\alpha_d \varphi_d(x_d)| = 0 \end{cases} \tag{4.4}$$

This clearly satisfies Eqs. (4.1) and (4.2); however, the relevances $R^{(1)}(x_d)$ of all input dimensions have the same sign as the prediction $f(x)$. In terms of pixel-wise decomposition interpretation, all inputs point toward the presence of a structure if $f(x) > 0$ and toward the absence of a structure if $f(x) < 0$. This is for many classification problems not a realistic interpretation. As a solution, for this example we define an alternative

$$R_d^{(1)} = \frac{b}{V} + \alpha_d \varphi_d(x_d) \tag{4.5}$$

Then, the relevance of a feature dimension x_d depends on the sign of the term in Eq. (4.5). This is for many classification problems a more plausible interpretation. This second example shows that LRP is able to deal with nonlinearities such as the feature space mapping φ_d to some extent and how an example of LRP satisfying Eq. (4.2) may look like in practice.

The above example gives an intuition about what relevance R is, namely, the local contribution to the prediction function $f(x)$. In that sense, the relevance of the output layer is the prediction itself: $f(x)$. This first example shows what one could expect as a decomposition for the linear case. The linear case is not a novelty; however, it provides a first intuition. A more graphic and nonlinear example is given in Figure 4.1. The upper part of the figure shows a neural-network-shaped classifier with neurons and weights w_{ij} on connections between neurons. Each neuron i has an output a_i from an activation function. The top layer consists of one output neuron, indexed by 7. For each neuron i we would like to compute a relevance R_i. We initialize the top layer relevance $R_7^{(3)}$ as the function value; thus, $R_7^{(3)} = f(x)$. LRP in Eq. (4.2) requires now to hold

$$R_7^{(3)} = R_4^{(2)} + R_5^{(2)} + R_6^{(2)} \tag{4.6}$$

$$R_4^{(2)} + R_5^{(2)} + R_6^{(2)} = R_1^{(1)} + R_2^{(1)} + R_3^{(1)} \tag{4.7}$$

We will make two assumptions for this example. First, we express the layer-wise relevance in terms of messages $R_{i \leftarrow j}^{(l, l+1)}$ between neurons i and j which can be sent along each connection. The messages are, however, directed from a neuron toward its input neurons, in contrast to what happens at prediction time, as shown in the lower part of Figure 4.1. Second, we define the relevance of any neuron except neuron 7 as the sum of incoming messages ($k : i$ is input for neuron k):

$$R_i^{(l)} = \sum_{i \leftarrow k} R_{i \leftarrow k}^{(l, l+1)} \tag{4.8}$$

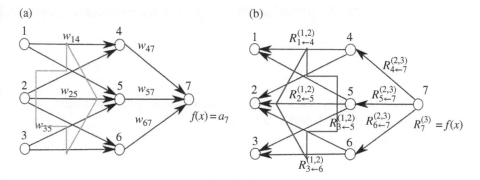

Figure 4.1 (a) Neural network (NN) as a classifier, (b) NN during the relevance computation.

For example, $R_3^{(1)} = R_{3\leftarrow5}^{(1;2)} + R_{3\leftarrow6}^{(1;2)}$. Note that neuron 7 has no incoming messages anyway. Instead, its relevance is defined as $R_7^{(3)} = f(x)$. In Eq. (4.8) and the following text, the terms *input* and *source* have the meaning of being an input to another neuron in the direction defined during the time of classification, not during the time of computation of LRP. For example in Figure 4.1, neurons 1 and 2 are the inputs and source for neuron 4, while neuron 6 is the *sink* for neurons 2 and 3. Given the two assumptions encoded in Eq. (4.8), the LRP by Eq. (4.2) can be satisfied by the following sufficient condition:

$R_7^{(3)} = R_{4\leftarrow7}^{(2;3)} + R_{5\leftarrow7}^{(2;3)} + R_{6\leftarrow7}^{(2;3)};$ $R_4^{(2)} = R_{1\leftarrow4}^{(1;2)} + R_{2\leftarrow4}^{(1;2)};$ $R_5^{(2)} = R_{1\leftarrow5}^{(1;2)} + R_{2\leftarrow5}^{(1;2)} + R_{3\leftarrow5}^{(1;2)}$ and $R_6^{(2)} = R_{2\leftarrow6}^{(1;2)} + R_{3\leftarrow6}^{(1;2)}$. In general, this condition can be expressed as

$$R_k^{(l+1)} = \sum_{i:i \text{ is input for neuron } k} R_{i\leftarrow k}^{(l;l+1)} \tag{4.9}$$

The difference between condition (4.9) and definition (4.8) is that in condition (4.9) the sum runs over the sources at layer l for a fixed neuron k at layer $l + 1$, whereas in definition (4.8) the sum runs over the sinks at layer $l + 1$ for a fixed neuron i at a layer l. When using Eq. (4.8) to define the relevance of a neuron from its messages, then condition (4.9) is a sufficient condition I order to ensure that Eq. (4.2) holds. Summing over the left hand side in Eq. (4.9) yields

$$\sum_k R_k^{(l+1)} = \sum_k \sum_{i:i \text{ is input for neuron } k} R_{i\leftarrow k}^{(l;l+1)}$$
$$= \sum_i \sum_{k:i \text{ is input for neuron } k} R_{i\leftarrow k}^{(l;l+1)} = \sum_i R_i^{(l)}$$

One can interpret condition (4.9) by saying that the messages $R_{i\leftarrow k}^{(l;l+1)}$ are used to distribute the relevance $R_k^{(l+1)}$ of a neuron k onto its input neurons at layer l. In the following sections, we will use this notion and the more strict form of relevance conservation as given by definition (4.8) and condition (4.9). We set Eqs. (4.8) and (4.9) as the main constraints defining LRP. A solution following this concept is required to define the messages $R_{i\leftarrow k}^{(l;l+1)}$ according to these equations.

Now we can derive an explicit formula for LRP for our example by defining the messages $R_{i\leftarrow k}^{(l;l+1)}$. The LRP should reflect the messages passed during classification time. We know that during classification time, a neuron i inputs $a_i w_{ik}$ to neuron k, provided that i has a forward connection to k. Thus, we can rewrite expressions for $R_7^{(3)}$ and $R_4^{(2)}$ so that they match the structure of the right-hand sides of the same equations by the following:

$$R_7^{(3)} = R_7^{(3)} \frac{a_4 w_{47}}{\sum_{i=4,5,6} a_i w_{i7}} + R_7^{(3)} \frac{a_5 w_{57}}{\sum_{i=4,5,6} a_i w_{i7}} + R_7^{(3)} \frac{a_6 w_{67}}{\sum_{i=4,5,6} a_i w_{i7}} \tag{4.10}$$

$$R_4^{(2)} = R_4^{(2)} \frac{a_1 w_{14}}{\sum_{i=1,2} a_i w_{i4}} + R_4^{(2)} \frac{a_2 w_{24}}{\sum_{i=1,2} a_i w_{i4}} \tag{4.11}$$

The match of the right-hand sides of the initial expressions for $R_7^{(3)}$ and $R_4^{(2)}$ against the right-hand sides of Eqs. (4.10) and (4.11) can be expressed in general as

$$R_{i\leftarrow k}^{(l;l+1)} = R_k^{(l+1)} \frac{a_i w_{ik}}{\sum_h a_h w_{hk}} \tag{4.12}$$

Although this solution, Eq. (4.12), for message terms $R_{i\leftarrow k}^{(l;l+1)}$ still needs to be adapted such that it is usable when the denominator becomes zero, the example given in Eq. (4.12) gives an idea of what a message $R_{i\leftarrow k}^{(l;l+1)}$ could be, namely, the relevance of a sink neuron $R_k^{(l+1)}$ that has been already computed, weighted proportionally by the input of neuron i from the preceding layer l.

Taylor-type decomposition: An alternative approach for achieving a decomposition as in Eq. (4.1) for a general differentiable predictor f is a first-order Taylor approximation:

$$f(x) \approx f(x_0) + Df(x_0)[x - x_0]$$
$$= f(x_0) + \sum_{d=1}^{V} \frac{\partial f}{\partial x_{(d)}}(x_0)\left(x_{(d)} - x_{0(d)}\right) \tag{4.13}$$

The choice of a Taylor base point x_0 is a free parameter in this setup. As stated above, in the case of classification, we are interested in finding out the contribution of each pixel relative to the state of maximal uncertainty of the prediction given by the set of points $f(x_0) = 0$, since $f(x) > 0$ denotes the presence and $f(x) < 0$ denotes the absence of the learned structure. Thus, x_0 should be chosen to be a root of the predictor f. Thus, the above equation simplifies to

$$f(x) \approx \sum_{d=1}^{V} \frac{\partial f}{\partial x_{(d)}}(x_0)\left(x_{(d)} - x_{0(d)}\right) \text{ such that } f(x_0) = 0 \tag{4.14}$$

The pixel-wise decomposition contains a nonlinear dependence on the prediction point x beyond the Taylor series, as a close root point x_0 needs to be found. Thus, the whole pixel-wise decomposition is not a linear, but a locally linear algorithm, as the root point x_0 depends on the prediction point x.

4.2.2 Pixel-wise Decomposition for Multilayer NN

Pixel-wise decomposition for multilayer networks: In the previous chapter, we discussed NN networks built as a set of interconnected neurons organized in a layered structure. They define a mathematical function when combined with each other that maps the first-layer neurons (input) to the last-layer neurons (output). In this section, we denote each neuron by x_i, where i is an index for the neuron. By convention, we associate different indices for each layer of the network. We denote by Σ_i the summation over all neurons of a given layer, and by Σ_j the summation over all neurons of another layer. We denote by $x_{(d)}$ the neurons corresponding to the pixel activations (i.e., with which we would like to obtain a decomposition of the classification decision). A common mapping from one layer to the next one consists of a linear projection followed by a nonlinear function: $z_{ij} = x_i w_{ij}$, $z_j = \sum_i z_{ij} + b_j$, $x_j = g(z_j)$, where w_{ij} is a weight connecting neuron x_i to neuron x_j, b_j is a bias term, and g is a nonlinear activation function. Multilayer networks stack several of these layers, each of them being composed of a large number of neurons. Common nonlinear functions are the hyperbolic tangent $g(t) = \tanh(t)$ or the rectification function $g(t) = \max(0, t)$

Taylor-type decomposition: Denoting by $f : \mathbb{R}^M \mapsto \mathbb{R}^N$ the vector-valued multivariate function implementing the mapping between input and output of the network, a first possible explanation of the classification decision $x \mapsto f(x)$ can be obtained by Taylor expansion at a near root point x_0 of the decision function f:

$$R_d^{(1)} = (x - x_0)_{(d)} \cdot \frac{\partial f}{\partial x_{(d)}}(x_0) \tag{4.15}$$

The derivative $\partial f(x)/\partial x_{(d)}$ required for pixel-wise decomposition can be computed efficiently by reusing the network topology using the backpropagation algorithm discussed in the previous chapter. Having backpropagated the derivatives up to a certain layer j, we can compute the derivative of the previous layer i using the chain rule:

$$\frac{\partial f}{\partial x_i} = \sum_j \frac{\partial f}{\partial x_j} \cdot \frac{\partial x_j}{\partial x_i} = \sum_j \frac{\partial f}{\partial x_j} \cdot w_{ij} \cdot g'(z_j). \tag{4.16}$$

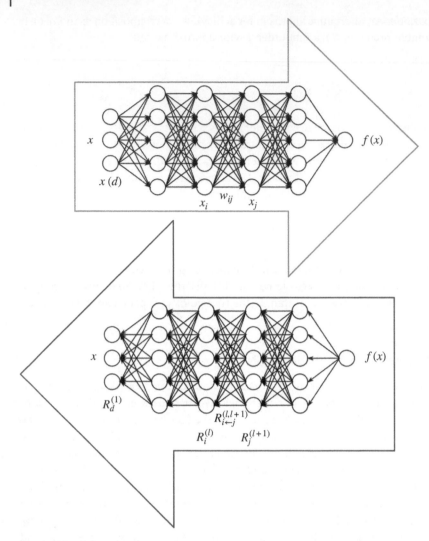

Figure 4.2 Relevance propagation.

Layer-wise relevance backpropagation: As an alternative to Taylor-type decomposition, it is possible to compute relevances at each layer in a backward pass, that is, express relevances $R_i^{(l)}$ as a function of upper-layer relevances $R_j^{(l+1)}$, and backpropagating relevances until we reach the input (pixels). Figure 4.2 depicts a graphic example. The method works as follows: Knowing the relevance of a certain neuron $R_j^{(l+1)}$ for the classification decision $f(x)$, one would like to obtain a decomposition of this relevance in terms of the messages sent to the neurons of the previous layers. We call these messages $R_{i \leftarrow j}$. As before, the conservation property

$$\sum_i R_{i \leftarrow j}^{(l,l+1)} = R_j^{(l+1)} \tag{4.17}$$

must hold. In the case of a linear network $f(x) = \Sigma_i z_{ij}$ where the relevance $R_j = f(x)$, such a decomposition is immediately given by $R_{i \leftarrow j} = z_{ij}$. However, in the general case, the neuron activation x_j is a nonlinear function of z_j. Nevertheless, for the hyperbolic tangent and the rectifying function – two simple monotonically increasing functions satisfying $g(0) = 0$-the pre-activations z_{ij} still provide a sensible way to measure the relative contribution of each neuron x_i to R_j. A first possible choice of relevance decomposition is based on the ratio of local and global pre-activations and is given by

$$R_{i\leftarrow j}^{(l,l+1)} = \frac{z_{ij}}{z_j} \cdot R_j^{(l+1)} \tag{4.18}$$

These relevances $R_{i\leftarrow j}$ are easily shown to approximate the conservation properties, in particular:

$$\sum_i R_{i\leftarrow j}^{(l,l+1)} = R_j^{(l+1)} \cdot \left(1 - \frac{b_j}{z_j}\right) \tag{4.19}$$

where the multiplier accounts for the relevance that is absorbed (or injected) by the bias term. If necessary, the residual bias relevance can be redistributed onto each neuron x_i. A drawback of the propagation rule of Eq. (4.18) is that for small values z_j, relevances $R_{j\leftarrow j}$ can take unbounded values. Unboundedness can be overcome by introducing a predefined stabilizer $\varepsilon \geq 0$:

$$R_{i\leftarrow j}^{(l,l+1)} = \begin{cases} \dfrac{z_{ij}}{z_j + \varepsilon} \cdot R_j^{(l+1)} & z_j \geq 0 \\[2ex] \dfrac{z_{ij}}{z_j - \varepsilon} \cdot R_j^{(l+1)} & z_j < 0 \end{cases} \tag{4.20}$$

The conservation law then becomes

$$\sum_i R_{i\leftarrow j}^{(l,l+1)} = \begin{cases} R_j^{(l+1)} \cdot \left(1 - \dfrac{b_j + \varepsilon}{z_j + \varepsilon}\right) & z_j \geq 0 \\[2ex] R_j^{(l+1)} \cdot \left(1 - \dfrac{b_j - \varepsilon}{z_j - \varepsilon}\right) & z_j < 0 \end{cases} \tag{4.21}$$

where we can observe that some further relevance is absorbed by the stabilizer. In particular, relevance is fully absorbed if the stabilizer ε becomes very large.

An alternative stabilizing method that does not leak relevance consists of treating negative and positive pre-activations separately. Let $z_j^+ = \sum_i z_{ij}^+ + b_j^+$ and $z_j^- = \sum_i z_{ij}^- + b_j^-$, where – and + denote the negative and positive parts of z_{ij} and b_j. Relevance propagation is now defined as

$$R_{i\leftarrow j}^{(l,l+1)} = R_j^{(l+1)} \cdot \left(\alpha \cdot \frac{z_{ij}^+}{z_j^+} + \beta \cdot \frac{z_{ij}^-}{z_j^-}\right) \tag{4.22}$$

where $\alpha + \beta = 1$. For example, for $\alpha\beta = 1/2$, the conservation law becomes

$$\sum_i R_{i\leftarrow j}^{(l,l+1)} = R_j^{(l+1)} \cdot \left(1 - \frac{b_j^+}{2z_j^+} - \frac{b_j^-}{2z_j^-}\right) \tag{4.23}$$

which has a similar form as Eq. (4.19). This alternative propagation method also allows one to manually control the importance of positive and negative evidence, by choosing different factors α and β.

Once a rule for relevance propagation has been selected, the overall relevance of each neuron in the lower layer is determined by summing up the relevances coming from all upper-layer neurons in agreement with Eqs. (4.8) and (4.9):

$$R_i^{(l)} = \sum_j R_{i\leftarrow j}^{(l,l+1)} \tag{4.24}$$

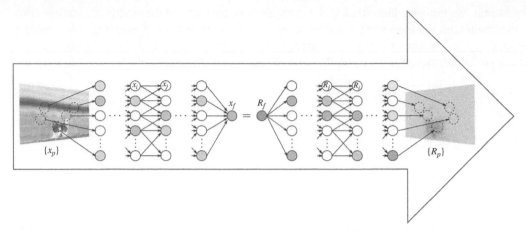

Figure 4.3 Relevance propagation (heat map; relevance is presented by the intensity of the red color). *Source:* Montavon et al. [92]. (For more details see color figure in bins).

The relevance is backpropagated from one layer to another until it reaches the input pixels $x_{(d)}$, and where the relevances $R_d^{(1)}$ provide the desired pixel-wise decomposition of the decision $f(x)$. A practical example of relevance propagation obtained by Deep Taylor decomposition is shown in Figure 4.3 [92].

4.3 Rule Extraction from LSTM Networks

In this section, we consider long short term memory networks (LSTMs), which were discussed in Chapter 3, and described an approach for tracking the importance of a given input to the LSTM for a given output. By identifying consistently important patterns of words, we are able to distill state-of-the-art LSTMs on sentiment analysis and question answering into a set of representative phrases. This representation is then quantitatively validated by using the extracted phrases to construct a simple rule-based classifier that approximates the output of the LSTM.

Word importance scores in LSTMS: Here, we present a decomposition of the output of an LSTM into a product of factors, where each term in the product can be interpreted as the contribution of a particular word. Thus, we can assign importance scores to words according to their contribution to the LSTM's prediction. We have introduced the basics of LSTM networks in the Chapter 3. Given a sequence of word embeddings $x_1, x_T \in \mathbb{R}^d$, an LSTM processes one word at a time, keeping track of cell and state vectors $(c_1, h_1), (c_T, h_T)$, which contain information in the sentence up to word i. h_t and c_t are computed as a function of x_t, c_{t-1} using the updates given by Eq. (3.72) of Chapter 3, which we repeat here with slightly different notation:

$$
\begin{aligned}
f_t &= \sigma\left(W_f x_t + V_f h_{t-1} + b_f\right) \\
i_t &= \sigma\left(W_i x_t + V_i h_{t-1} + b_i\right) \\
o_t &= \sigma\left(W_o x_t + V_o h_{t-1} + b_o\right) \\
\tilde{c}_t &= \tanh\left(W_c x_t + V_c h_{t-1} + b_c\right) \\
c_t &= f_t c_{t-1} + i_t \tilde{c}_t \\
h_t &= o_t \odot \tanh\left(c_t\right)
\end{aligned}
\tag{4.25}
$$

As initial values, we define $c_0 = h_0 = 0$. After processing the full sequence, a probability distribution over C classes is specified by p, with

$$p_i = SoftMax(Wh_T) = \frac{e^{W_i h_T}}{\sum_{j=1}^{C} e^{W_j h_t}} \tag{4.26}$$

where W_i is the i-th row of the matrix W.

Decomposing the output of an LSTM: We now decompose the numerator of p_i in Eq. (4.26) into a product of factors and show that we can interpret those factors as the contribution of individual words to the predicted probability of class i. Define

$$\beta_{i,j} = \exp\big(W_i \big(o_T \odot \big(\tanh(c_j) - \tanh(c_{j-1})\big)\big)\big), \tag{4.27}$$

so that

$$\exp(W_i h_T) = \exp\left(\sum_{j=1}^{T} W_i\left(o_T \odot \big(\tanh(c_j) - \tanh(c_{j-1})\big)\right)\right) = \prod_{j=1}^{T} \beta_{i,j}.$$

As $\tanh(c_j) - \tanh(c_{j-1})$ can be viewed as the update resulting from word j, so $\beta_{i,j}$ can be interpreted as the multiplicative contribution to p_i by word j.

An additive decomposition of the LSTM Cell: We will show below that $\beta_{i,j}$ captures some notion of the importance of a word to the LSTM's output. However, these terms fail to account for how the information contributed by word j is affected by the LSTM's forget gates between words j and T. Consequently, it was empirically found [93] that the importance scores from this approach often yield a considerable amount of false positives. A more nuanced approach is obtained by considering the additive decomposition of c_T in Eq. (4.28), where each term e_j can be interpreted as the contribution to the cell state c_T by word j. By iterating the equation $c_t = f_t c_{t-1} + i_t \tilde{c}_t$, we obtain that

$$c_T = \sum_{i=1}^{T} \left(\prod_{j=i+1}^{T} f_j\right) i_i \tilde{c}_i = \sum_{i=1}^{T} e_{i,T} \tag{4.28}$$

This suggests a natural definition of an alternative score to $\beta_{i,j}$, corresponding to augmenting the c_j terms with the products of the forget gates to reflect the upstream changes made to c_j after initially processing word j:

$$\exp(W_i h_T) = \prod_{j=1}^{T} \exp\left(W_i\left(o_T \odot \left(\tanh\left(\sum_{k=1}^{j} e_{k,T}\right) - \tanh\left(\sum_{k=1}^{j-1} e_{k,T}\right)\right)\right)\right)$$

$$= \prod_{j=1}^{T} \exp\left(W_i\left(o_T \odot \left(\tanh\left(\left(\prod_{k=j+1}^{t} f_k\right) c_j\right) - \tanh\left(\left(\prod_{k=j}^{t} f_k\right) c_{j-1}\right)\right)\right)\right)$$

$$= \prod_{j=1}^{T} \gamma_{i,j} \tag{4.29}$$

We now introduce a technique for using our variable importance scores to extract phrases from a trained LSTM. To do so, we search for phrases that consistently provide a large contribution to the prediction of a particular class relative to other classes. The utility of these patterns is validated by using them as input for a rules-based classifier. For simplicity, we focus on the binary classification case.

Phrase extraction: A phrase can be reasonably described as predictive if, whenever it occurs, it causes a document to both be labeled as a particular class and not be labeled as any other. As our importance scores introduced above correspond to the contribution of particular words to class predictions, they can be used to score potential patterns by looking at a pattern's average contribution to the prediction of a given class relative to other classes. In other words, given a collection of D documents $\left\{ \{x_{i,j}\}_{i=1}^{N_d} \right\}_{j=1}^{D}$, for a given phrase $w_1, ..., w_k$ we can compute scores S_1, S_2 for classes 1 and 2, as well as a combined score S and class C as

$$
\begin{aligned}
S_1(w_1, ..., w_k) &= \frac{\mathcal{E}_{j,b}\left\{ \prod_{l=1}^{k} \beta_{1,b+l,j} \mid x_{b+i,j} = w_i, i = 1, ..., k \right\}}{\mathcal{E}_{j,b}\left\{ \prod_{l=1}^{k} \beta_{2,b+l,j} \mid x_{b+i,j} = w_i, i = 1, ..., k \right\}}; \\
S_2(w_1, w_k) &= \frac{1}{S_1(w_1, ..., w_k)} \\
S(w_1, w_k) &= \max_i(S_i(w_1, w_k)); C(w_1, w_k) = \arg \max_i(S_i(w_1, w_k))
\end{aligned}
\tag{4.30}
$$

where $\beta_{i,j,k}$ denotes $\beta_{i,j}$ applied to document k and $\mathcal{E}$ stands for average.

The numerator of S_1 denotes the average contribution of the phrase to the prediction of class 1 across all occurrences of the phrase. The denominator denotes the same statistic, but for class 2. Thus, if S_1 is high, then $w_1, ..., w_k$ is a strong signal for class 1, and likewise for S_2. It was proposed [93] to use S as a score function in order to search for high-scoring representative phrases that provide insight into the trained LSTM, and C to denote the class corresponding to a phrase.

In practice, the number of phrases is too large to feasibly compute the score for all of them. Thus, we approximate a brute force search through a two-step procedure. First, we construct a list of candidate phrases by searching for strings of consecutive words j with importance scores $\beta_{i,j} > c$ for any i and some threshold c. Then, we score and rank the set of candidate phrases, which is much smaller than the set of all phrases.

Rules-based classifier: The extracted patterns from Section 4.1 can be used to construct a simple rules-based classifier that approximates the output of the original LSTM. Given a document and a list of patterns sorted by descending score given by S, the classifier sequentially searches for each pattern within the document using simple string matching. Once it finds a pattern, the classifier returns the associated class given by C, ignoring the lower-ranked patterns. The resulting classifier is interpretable, and despite its simplicity, retains much of the accuracy of the LSTM used to build it.

4.4 Accuracy and Interpretability

This section focuses on the accuracy and interpretability trade-off in fuzzy model-based solutions. A fuzzy model based on an experience-oriented learning algorithm is presented that is designed to balance the trade-off between both of the above aspects. It combines support vector regression (SVR) to generate the initial fuzzy model and the available experience on the training data and standard fuzzy model solution.

Fuzzy systems have been used for modeling or control in a number of applications. They are able to incorporate human knowledge, so that the information mostly provided for many real-world systems could be discovered or described by fuzzy statements. Fuzzy modeling (FM) considers model structures in the form of fuzzy rule-based systems and constructs them by means of different parametric system identification techniques. In recent years, the interest in data-driven approaches to FM has increased. On the basis of a limited training data set, fuzzy systems can be effectively modeled by means of some learning mechanisms, and the fuzzy model after learning tries to infer the true information. In order to assess the quality of the obtained fuzzy models, there are two contradictory requirements: (i) *interpretability*, the capability to express the behavior of the real system in a way that humans can understand, and (ii) *accuracy*, the capability to faithfully represent the real system. In general, the search for the desired trade-off is usually performed from two different perspectives, mainly using certain mechanisms to improve the interpretability of initially accurate fuzzy models, or to improve the accuracy of good interpretable fuzzy models. In general, improving interpretability means reducing the accuracy of initially accurate fuzzy models.

It is well known that support vector machine (SVM) has been shown to have the ability of generalizing well to unseen data, and giving a good balance between approximation and generalization. Thus, some researchers have been inspired to combine SVM with FM in order to take advantage of both of approaches: human interpretability and good performance. Therefore, support vector learning for FM has evolved into an active area of research. Before we discuss this hybrid algorithm, we discuss separately the basics of the FM and SVR approach.

4.4.1 Fuzzy Models

A descriptive (linguistic) fuzzy model captures qualitative knowledge in the form of *if-then rules* [106]:

$$\mathcal{R}_i : \text{If } \tilde{x} \text{ is } A_i \text{ then } \tilde{y} \text{ is } B_i, i = 1, 2, ..., K \tag{4.31}$$

Here, $\tilde{x}$ is the input (antecedent) linguistic variable, and A_i are the antecedent descriptive (linguistic) terms (constants). Similarly, $\tilde{y}$ is the output (consequent) linguistic variable, and B_i are the consequent linguistic terms. The values of $\tilde{x}(\tilde{y})$ and the linguistic terms $A_i(B_i)$ are fuzzy sets defined in the domains of their respective base variables: $x \in X \subset R^p$ and $y \in Y \subset R^q$. The membership functions of the antecedent (consequent) fuzzy sets are then the mappings: $\mu(x) : X \rightarrow [0, 1]$, $\mu(y) : Y \rightarrow [0, 1]$. Fuzzy sets A_i define fuzzy regions in the antecedent space, for which the respective consequent propositions hold. The linguistic terms A_i and B_i are usually selected from sets of predefined terms, such as Small, Medium, and so on. By denoting these sets by $\mathcal{A}$ and $\mathcal{B}$, respectively, we have $A_i \in \mathcal{A}$ and $B_i \in \mathcal{B}$. The rule base $\mathcal{R} = \{\mathcal{R}_i \mid i = 1, 2, ..., K\}$ and the sets $\mathcal{A}$ and $\mathcal{B}$ constitute the knowledgebase of the linguistic model.

Design Example 4.1

Consider a simple fuzzy model that qualitatively describes how the throughput in data network using the Aloha protocol depends on the traffic volume. We have a scalar input – the traffic volume (*x*) – and a scalar output – the network throughput (*y*). Define the set of antecedent linguistic terms: $\mathcal{A}$ = {Low, Moderate, High}= {L, M, H}, and the set of consequent linguistic terms: $\mathcal{B}$ = {Low, High} = {L, H}. The qualitative relationship between the model input and output can be expressed by the following rules:

$\mathcal{R}_1$: If the traffic volume is Low, then the network throughput is Low.
$\mathcal{R}_2$: If the traffic volume is Moderate, then the network throughput is High.
$\mathcal{R}_3$: If the traffic volume is High, then the network throughput is Low (due to the excessive collisions).

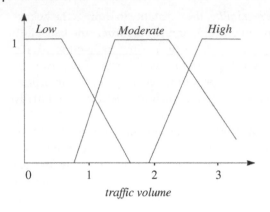

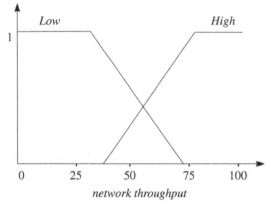

Figure 4.4 Example of membership functions versus the traffic volume and network throughput.

The meaning of the linguistic terms is defined by their membership functions, depicted in Figure 4.4. The numerical values along the base variables are selected somewhat arbitrarily. Note that no universal meaning of the linguistic terms can be defined. For this example, it will depend on the type of the traffic, network size and the topology, MAC protocol, and so on. Nevertheless, the qualitative relationship expressed by the rules remains valid.

Relational representation of a linguistic model: Each rule in Eq. (4.31) can be regarded as a fuzzy relation (fuzzy restriction on the simultaneous occurrences of values x and y): $R_i : (X \times Y) \rightarrow [0, 1]$. This relation can be computed in two basic ways: by using fuzzy conjunctions and by using fuzzy implications (fuzzy logic method). Fuzzy implications are used when the if-then rule, Eq. (4.31), is strictly regarded as an implication $A_i \rightarrow B_i$, that is, "*A* implies *B*." In classical logic, this means that if *A* holds, *B* must hold as well for the implication to be true. Nothing can, however, be said about *B* when *A* does not hold, and the relationship also cannot be inverted.

When using a conjunction, $A \wedge B$, the interpretation of the if-then rules is "it is true that *A* and *B* simultaneously hold." This relationship is symmetric and can be inverted. For simplicity, in this text we restrict ourselves to the conjunction method. The relation *R* is computed by the *minimum* ($\wedge$) operator:

$$R_i = A_i \times B_i, \text{ that is, } \mu_{R_i}(x, y) = \mu_{A_i}(x) \wedge \mu_{B_i}(y). \tag{4.32}$$

Note that the minimum is computed on the Cartesian product space of *X* and *Y*, that is, for all possible pairs of x and y. The fuzzy relation *R* representing the entire model, Eq. (4.31), is given by the disjunction (union) of the *K* individual rule's relations R_i:

$$R = \cup_{i=1}^{K} R_i, \text{that is,} \mu_R(x, y) = \max\left[\mu_{A_i}(x) \wedge \mu_{B_i}(y)\right] \tag{4.33}$$

Now the entire rule base is encoded in the fuzzy relation R, and the output of the linguistic model can be computed by the relational *max-min* composition ($\circ$):

$$\widetilde{y} = \widetilde{x} \circ R. \tag{4.34}$$

Design Example 4.2

Let us compute the fuzzy relation for the linguistic model of Figure 4.4. First, we discretize the input and output domains, for instance: $X = \{0, 1, 2, 3\}$ and $Y = \{0, 25, 50, 75, 100\}$. The (discrete) membership functions are given in Table 4.1 for both antecedent linguistic terms, and for the consequent terms.

Table 4.1 An example of the (discrete) membership functions for both antecedent linguistic terms, and for the consequent terms.

Antecedent				
Domain element				
Linguistic term	0	1	2	3
Low	1.0	0.6	0.0	0.0
Moderate	0.0	0.4	1.0	0.4
High	0.0	0.0	0.1	1.0
Consequent				
Domain element				
Linguistic term	0	25	50	75	100
Low	1.0	1.0	0.6	0.0	0.0
Moderate High	0.0	0.0	0.3	0.9	1.0

The fuzzy relations R_i corresponding to the individual rule can now be computed by using Eq. (4.32). For rule $\mathcal{R}_1$, we have $R_1 = Low \times Low$; for rule $\mathcal{R}_2$, we obtain $R_2 = Moderate \times High$; and finally for rule $\mathcal{R}_3$, $R_3 = High \times Low$. The fuzzy relation R, which represents the entire rule base, is the union (element-wise maximum) of the relations R_i:

(Continued)

Design Example 4.2 (Continued)

$R_i = A_i \times B_i$, that is, $\mu_{R_i}(x, y) = \mu_{A_i}(x) \wedge \mu_{B_i}(y)$

As an example $R_1 = A_1 \times B_1 = Low \times Low$

$\mu_{A_1}(x) \wedge \mu_{B_1}(y) = (1.0\ 0.6\ 0.0\ 0.0) \wedge (1.0\ 1.0\ 0.6\ 0.0\ 0.0)$

$$= (1.0) \wedge (1.0\ 1.0\ 0.6\ 0.0\ 0.0)$$
$$(0.6) \wedge (1.0\ 1.0\ 0.6\ 0.0\ 0.0)$$
$$(0.0) \wedge (1.0\ 1.0\ 0.6\ 0.0\ 0.0)$$
$$(0.0) \wedge (1.0\ 1.0\ 0.6\ 0.0\ 0.0)$$

$$= (1.0\ 1.0\ 0.6\ 0.0\ 0.0)$$
$$(0.6\ 0.6\ 0.6\ 0.0\ 0.0)$$
$$(0.0\ 0.0\ 0.0\ 0.0\ 0.0)$$
$$(0.0\ 0.0\ 0.0\ 0.0\ 0.0)$$

Similarly

$$R_1 = \begin{bmatrix} 1.0 & 1.0 & 0.6 & 0 & 0 \\ 0.6 & 0.6 & 0.6 & 0 & 0 \\ 0 & 0 & 0 & 0 & 0 \\ 0 & 0 & 0 & 0 & 0 \end{bmatrix}$$

$$R_2 = \begin{bmatrix} 0 & 0 & 0 & 0 & 0 \\ 0 & 0 & 0.3 & 0.4 & 0.4 \\ 0 & 0 & 0.3 & 0.9 & 1.0 \\ 0 & 0 & 0.3 & 0.4 & 0.4 \end{bmatrix} \Bigg\} R = \begin{bmatrix} 1.0 & 1.0 & 0.6 & 0 & 0 \\ 0.6 & 0.6 & 0.6 & 0.4 & 0.4 \\ 0.1 & 0.1 & 0.3 & 0.9 & 1.0 \\ 1.0 & 1.0 & 0.6 & 0.4 & 0.4 \end{bmatrix} \quad (4.35)$$

$$R_3 = \begin{bmatrix} 0 & 0 & 0 & 0 & 0 \\ 0 & 0 & 0 & 0 & 0 \\ 0.1 & 0.1 & 0.1 & 0 & 0 \\ 1.0 & 0 & 0.6 & 0 & 0 \end{bmatrix}$$

where from Eq. (4.33) $R = \bigcup_{i=1}^{K} R_i$, that is, $\mu_R(x, y) = \max\left[\mu_{A_i}(x) \wedge \mu_{B_i}(y)\right]$.

Design Example 4.3

Now consider an input fuzzy set to the model, $A' = [1, 0.6, 0.3, 0]$, which can be denoted as SomewhatLow traffic volume, as it is close to Low but does not equal Low. The result of *max-min* composition defined by Eq. (4.34) gives

$$\tilde{y} = \tilde{x} \circ R.$$

$$B' = \max(A' \wedge R)$$

$$A' \wedge R = [1, 0.6, 0.3, 0] \wedge \begin{bmatrix} 1.0 & 1.0 & 0.6 & 0 & 0 \\ 0.6 & 0.6 & 0.6 & 0.4 & 0.4 \\ 0.1 & 0.1 & 0.3 & 0.9 & 1.0 \\ 1.0 & 1.0 & 0.6 & 0.4 & 0.4 \end{bmatrix}$$

$$= \begin{bmatrix} 1.0 & 1.0 & 0.6 & 0.0 & 0.0 \\ 0.6 & 0.6 & 0.6 & 0.4 & 0.4 \\ 0.1 & 0.1 & 0.3 & 0.3 & 0.3 \\ 0.0 & 0.0 & 0.0 & 0.0 & 0.0 \end{bmatrix}$$

$$B' = \max(A' \wedge R) = [1.0, \quad 1.0, \quad 0.6, \quad 0.4, \quad 0.4]$$

Similarly, by using the same procedure for the input set $A' = [0, 0.2, 1, 0.2]$ we obtain $B' = \max(A' \wedge R) = [0.2, 0.2, 0.3, 0.9, 1]$.

Max-min (Mamdani) inference: In the previous section, we have seen that a rule base can be represented as a fuzzy relation. The output of a rule-based fuzzy model is then computed by the max-min relational composition. In this section, it will be shown that the relational calculus can be bypassed. This is advantageous, as the discretization of domains and storing of the relation R can be avoided. To show this, suppose an input fuzzy value $\tilde{x} = A'$, for which the output value B' is given by the relational composition:

$$\mu_{B'}(y) = \max[\mu_{A'}(x) \wedge \mu_R(x, y)]. \tag{4.36}$$

After substituting for $\mu_R(x, y)$ from Eq. (4.33), the following expression is obtained:

$$\mu_{B'}(y) = \max\{\mu_{A'}(x) \wedge \max[\mu_{A_i}(x) \wedge \mu_{B_i}(y)]\}. \tag{4.37}$$

Since the max and min operations are taken over different domains, their order can be changed as follows:

$$\mu_{B'}(y) = \max\{\max[\mu_{A'}(x) \wedge \mu_{A_i}(x)] \wedge \mu_{B_i}(y)\}. \tag{4.38}$$

Denote $\beta_i = \max_X[\mu_{A'}(x) \wedge \mu_{A_i}(x)]$ as the *degree of fulfillment* of the i-th rule's antecedent. The output fuzzy set of the linguistic model is thus

$$\mu_{B'}(y) = \max[\beta_i \wedge \mu_{B_i}(y)], y \in Y. \tag{4.39}$$

The entire algorithm, called the *max-min* or *Mamdani inference*, is summarized in Algorithm 4.1 and visualized in Figure 4.5.

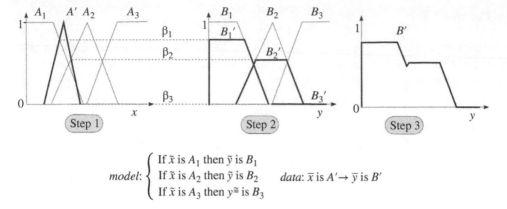

$$model: \begin{cases} \text{If } \tilde{x} \text{ is } A_1 \text{ then } \tilde{y} \text{ is } B_1 \\ \text{If } \tilde{x} \text{ is } A_2 \text{ then } \tilde{y} \text{ is } B_2 \\ \text{If } \tilde{x} \text{ is } A_3 \text{ then } y^{\cong} \text{ is } B_3 \end{cases} \quad data: \bar{x} \text{ is } A' \rightarrow \bar{y} \text{ is } B'$$

Figure 4.5 A schematic representation of the Mamdani inference algorithm.

Algorithm 4.1 Mamdani (max-min) inference

1. Compute the degree of fulfillment by $\beta_i = max_X[\mu_{A'}(x) \wedge \mu_{A_i}(x)]$, $1 \le i \le K$. Note that for a singleton fuzzy set ($\mu_{A'}(x) = 1$ for $x = x_0$ and $\mu_{A'}(x) = 0$ otherwise) the equation for β_i simplifies to $\beta_i = \mu_{A_i}(x_0)$.
2. Derive the output fuzzy sets $B'_i : \mu_{B'_i}(y) = \beta_i \wedge \mu_{B_i}(y)$, $y \in Y$, $1 \le i \le K$.
3. Aggregate the output fuzzy sets $B'_i : \mu_{B'}(y) = max_{1 \le i \le K} \mu_{B'_i}(y)$, $y \in Y$.

Design Example 4.4

Let us take the input fuzzy set $A' = [1, 0.6, 0.3, 0]$ from the previous example and compute the corresponding output fuzzy set by the Mamdani inference method. Step 1 yields the following degrees of fulfillment:

$$\beta_1 = max[\mu_{A'}(x) \wedge \mu_{A_1}(x)] = max([1, 0.6, 0.3, 0] \wedge [1, 0.6, 0, 0]) = 1,$$
$$\beta_2 = max[\mu_{A'}(x) \wedge \mu_{A_2}(x)] = max([1, 0.6, 0.3, 0] \wedge [0, 0.4, 1, 0.4]) = 0.4,$$
$$\beta_3 = max[\mu_{A'}(x) \wedge \mu_{A_3}(x)] = max([1, 0.6, 0.3, 0] \wedge [0, 0, 0.1, 1]) = 0.1.$$

In step 2, the individual consequent fuzzy sets are computed:

$$B'_1 = \beta_1 \wedge B_1 = 1 \wedge [1, 1, 0.6, 0, 0] = [1, 1, 0.6, 0, 0]$$
$$B'_2 = \beta_2 \wedge B_2 = 0.4 \wedge [0, 0, 0.3, 0.9, 1] = [0, 0, 0.3, 0.4, 0.4],$$
$$B'_3 = \beta_3 \wedge B_3 = 0.1 \wedge [1, 1, 0.6, 0, 0] = [0.1, 0.1, 0.1, 0, 0].$$

Finally, step 3 gives the overall output fuzzy set:

$$B = max \, \mu_{B_i} = [1, 1, 0.6, 0.4, 0.4],$$

which is identical to the result from the previous example.

Multivariable systems: So far, the linguistic model was presented in a general manner covering both the single-input and single-output (SISO) and multiple-input and multiple-output (MIMO) cases. In the MIMO case, all fuzzy sets in the model are defined on vector domains by multivariate membership functions. It is, however, usually more convenient to write the antecedent and consequent propositions as logical combinations of fuzzy propositions with univariate membership functions. Fuzzy logic operators, such as the conjunction, disjunction, and negation (complement), can be used to combine the propositions. Furthermore, a MIMO model can be written as a set of multiple-input and single-output (MISO) models, which is also convenient for the ease of notation. Most common is the *conjunctive form* of the antecedent, which is given by

$$\mathcal{R}_i: \text{If } x_1 \text{ is } A_{i1} \text{ and } x_2 \text{ is } A_{i2} \text{ and } \dots \text{ and } x_p \text{ is } A_{ip} \text{ then } y \text{ is } B_i, i = 1, 2, \dots, K. \tag{4.40}$$

Note that the above model is a special case of Eq. (4.31), as the fuzzy set A_i in Eq. (4.31) is obtained as the Cartesian product of fuzzy sets $A_{ij} : A_i = A_{i1} \times A_{i2} \times \cdots \times A_{ip}$. Hence, the degree of fulfillment (step 1 of Algorithm 4.1) is given by

$$\beta_i = \mu_{A_{i1}}(x_1) \wedge \mu_{A_{i2}}(x_2) \wedge \cdots \wedge \mu_{A_{ip}}(x_p), 1 \leq i \leq K. \tag{4.41}$$

Other conjunction operators, such as the product, can be used. A set of rules in the conjunctive antecedent form divides the input domain into a lattice of fuzzy hyper-boxes, parallel with the axes. Each of the hyper-boxes is a Cartesian product-space intersection of the corresponding univariate fuzzy sets. The number of rules in the conjunctive form needed to cover the entire domain is given by $K = \Pi_{i=1}^{p} N_i$, where p is the dimension of the input space, and N_i is the number of linguistic terms of the i-th antecedent variable.

By combining conjunctions, disjunctions, and negations, various partitions of the antecedent space can be obtained; the boundaries are, however, restricted to the rectangular grid defined by the fuzzy sets of the individual variables. As an example, consider the rule "If x_1 is not A_{13} and x_2 is A_{21} then ..."

The degree of fulfillment of this rule is computed using the complement and intersection operators:

$$\beta = \left[1 - \mu_{A_{13}}(x_1)\right] \wedge \mu_{A_{21}}(x_2). \tag{4.42}$$

The antecedent form with multivariate membership functions, Eq. (4.31), is the most general one, as there is no restriction on the shape of the fuzzy regions. The boundaries between these regions can be arbitrarily curved and opaque to the axes. Also, the number of fuzzy sets needed to cover the antecedent space may be much smaller than in the previous cases. Hence, for complex multivariable systems, this partition may provide the most effective representation.

Defuzzification: In many applications, a crisp output y is desired. To obtain a crisp value, the output fuzzy set must be defuzzified. With the Mamdani inference scheme, the *center of gravity* (COG) defuzzification method is used. This method computes the y coordinate of the COG of the area under the fuzzy set B':

$$y' = \text{cog}(B') = \frac{\sum\limits_{j=1}^{F} \mu_{B'}\left(y_j\right)y_j}{\sum\limits_{j=1}^{F} \mu_{B'}\left(y_j\right)}, \tag{4.43}$$

where F is the number of elements y_j in Y. The continuous domain Y thus must be discretized to be able to compute the COG.

Design Example 4.5

Consider the output fuzzy set $B' = [0.2, 0.2, 0.3, 0.9, 1]$ from the previous example, where the output domain is $Y = [0, 25, 50, 75, 100]$. The defuzzified output obtained by applying Eq. (4.43) is

$$y' = \frac{0.2 \cdot 0 + 0.2 \cdot 25 + 0.3 \cdot 50 + 0.9 \cdot 75 + 1 \cdot 100}{0.2 + 0.2 + 0.3 + 0.9 + 1} = 72.12.$$

The network throughput (in arbitrary units), computed by the fuzzy model, is thus 72.12.

4.4.2 SVR

The basic idea: Let $\{(x_1, y_1), \ldots, (x_l, y_l)\} \subset X \times \mathbb{R}$, be a given training data, where X denotes the space of the input patterns (e.g., $X = \mathbb{R}^d$). In ε-SV regression, the objective is to find a function $f(x)$ that has at most a deviation of ε from the actually obtained targets y_i for all the training data, and at the same time is as flat as possible. In other words, we do not care about errors as long as they are less than ε, but will not accept any deviation larger than this. We begin by describing the case of linear functions, f, taking the form

$$f(x) = \langle w, x \rangle + b \text{ with } w \in x, b \in \mathbb{R} \tag{4.44}$$

where $\langle , \rangle$ denotes the dot product in X. *Flatness* in the case of Eq. (4.44) means that one seeks a small w. One way to ensure this is to minimize the norm, that is, $\|w\|^2 = \langle w, w \rangle$. We can write this problem as a convex optimization problem:

$$
\begin{aligned}
&minimize \frac{1}{2}\|w\|^2 \\
&subject\ to \begin{cases} y_i - \langle w, x_i \rangle - b \leq \varepsilon \\ \langle w, x_i \rangle + b - y_i \leq \varepsilon \end{cases}
\end{aligned}
\tag{4.45}
$$

The tacit assumption in Eq. (4.45) was that such a function f actually exists that approximates all pairs (x_i, y_i) with ε precision, or in other words, that the convex optimization problem is feasible. Sometimes, the problem might not have a solution for the given ε, or we also may want to allow for some errors. In analogy with the "soft margin" (see Figure 2.7 of Chapter 2), one can introduce slack variables ξ_i, ξ_i^* to cope with possibly infeasible constraints of the optimization problem: Eq. (4.45). So we have

$$
\begin{aligned}
&minimize \frac{1}{2}\|w\|^2 + C\Sigma_{(i=1)}^p \left(\xi_i + \xi_i^*\right) \\
&subject\ to \begin{cases} y_i - \langle w, x_i \rangle - b & \leq \varepsilon + \xi_i \\ \langle w, x_i \rangle + b - y_i & \leq \varepsilon + \xi_i^* \\ \xi_i, \xi_i^* & \geq 0 \end{cases}
\end{aligned}
\tag{4.46}
$$

The constant $C > 0$ determines the trade-off between the flatness of f and the amount up to which deviations larger than ε are tolerated. This corresponds to dealing with a so-called ε-insensitive loss function $|\xi|_\varepsilon$ described by

Figure 4.6 Illustration of the soft margin for a linear support vector machine (SVM).

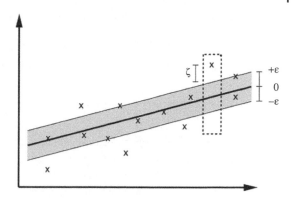

$$|\xi|_\varepsilon := \begin{cases} 0 & \text{if } |\xi| \le \varepsilon \\ |\xi| - \varepsilon & \text{otherwise.} \end{cases} \tag{4.47}$$

Figure 2.7 of Chapter 2 is modified to reflect better the definitions introduced in this section and presented as Figure 4.6. Often, the optimization problem, Eq. (4.46), can be solved more easily in its dual formulation. The dual formulation provides also the key for extending SV machine to nonlinear functions.

Lagrange function: The key idea here is to construct a Lagrange function from the objective function (*primal* objective function) and the corresponding constraints, by introducing a dual set of variables [95]. It can be shown that this function has a saddle point with respect to the primal and dual variables at the solution. So we have

$$L := \frac{1}{2}\|w\|^2 + C\sum_{i=1}^{p}(\xi_i + \xi_i^*) - \sum_{i=1}^{p}(\eta_i\xi_i + \eta_i^*\xi_i^*)$$
$$- \sum_{i=1}^{p}\alpha_i(\varepsilon + \xi_i - y_i + \langle w, x_i\rangle + b) \tag{4.48}$$
$$- \sum_{i=1}^{p}\alpha_i^*(\varepsilon + \xi_i^* + y_i - \langle w, x_i\rangle - b)$$

Here, L is the Lagrangian, and η_i, η_i^*, α_i, α_i^* are Lagrange multipliers. Hence, the dual variables in Eq. (4.48) have to satisfy positivity constraints, that is, $\alpha_i^{(*)}, \eta_i^{(*)} \ge 0$, where by $\alpha_i^{(*)}$, we jointly refer to α_i and α_i^*. In the saddle point, the partial derivatives of L with respect to the primal variables (w, b, ξ_i, ξ_i^*) have to vanish; that is, $\partial_b L = \sum_{i=1}^{l}(\alpha_i^* - \alpha_i) = 0$, $\partial_w L = w - \sum_{i=1}^{l}(\alpha_i - \alpha_i^*)x_i = 0$ and $\partial_{\xi_i^{(*)}} L = C - \alpha_i^{(*)} - \eta_i^{(*)} = 0$. Substituting these conditions into Eq. (4.48) yields the dual optimization problem:

$$\textit{Maximize} \left[-\frac{1}{2}\sum_{i,j=1}^{l}(\alpha_i - \alpha_i^*)(\alpha_j - \alpha_j^*)\langle x_i, x_j\rangle \right.$$
$$\left. -\varepsilon\sum_{i=1}^{l}(\alpha_i + \alpha_i^*) + \sum_{i=1}^{l}y_i(\alpha_i - \alpha_i^*) \right] \tag{4.49}$$

$$\textit{subject to } \sum_{i=1}^{l}(\alpha_i - \alpha_i^*) = 0 \text{ and } \alpha_i, \alpha_i^* \in [0, C]$$

In deriving Eq. (4.49), we already eliminated the dual variables η_i, η_i^* through condition $\partial_{\xi_i^{(*)}} L = C - \alpha_i^{(*)} - \eta_i^{(*)} = 0$, which can be reformulated as $\eta_i^{(*)} = C - \alpha_i^{(*)}$. Equation $\partial_w L = w - \sum_{i=1}^{l} (\alpha_i - \alpha_i^*) x_i = 0$ can be rewritten as $w = \sum_{i=1}^{p} (\alpha_i - \alpha_i^*) x_i$, giving

$$f(x) = \sum_{i=1}^{l} (\alpha_i - \alpha_i^*) \langle x_i, x \rangle + b. \tag{4.50}$$

This is the so-called *support vector expansion*; that is, w can be completely described as a linear combination of the training patterns x_i. In a sense, the complexity of a function's representation by SVs is independent of the dimensionality of the input space X, and depends only on the number of SVs. Moreover, note that the complete algorithm can be described in terms of dot products between the data. Even when evaluating $f(x)$, we need not compute w explicitly. These observations will come in handy for the formulation of a nonlinear extension.

Computing b: Parameter b can be computed by exploiting the so-called Karush–Kuhn–Tucker (KKT) conditions stating that at the point of the solution the product between dual variables and constraints has to vanish, giving $\alpha_i(\varepsilon + \xi_i - y_i + \langle w, x_i \rangle + b) = 0$, $\alpha_i^* (\varepsilon + \xi_i^* + y_i - \langle w, x_i \rangle - b) = 0$, $(C - \alpha_i)\xi_i = 0$ and $(C - \alpha_i^*)\xi_i^* = 0$. This allows us to draw several useful conclusions:

i) Only samples (x_i, y_i) with corresponding $\alpha_i^{(*)} = C$ lie outside the ε-insensitive tube.
ii) $\alpha_i \alpha_i^* = 0$; that is, there can never be a set of dual variables α_i, α_i^* that are both simultaneously nonzero. This allows us to conclude that

$$\varepsilon - y_i + \langle w, x_i \rangle + b \geq 0 \text{ and } \xi_i = 0 \text{ if } \alpha_i < C \tag{4.51}$$

$$\varepsilon - y_i + \langle w, x_i \rangle + b \leq 0 \text{ if } \alpha_i > 0 \tag{4.52}$$

In conjunction with an analogous analysis on α_i^*, we have for b

$$\begin{aligned} \max \{ -\varepsilon + y_i - \langle w, x_i \rangle \mid \alpha_i < C \text{ or } \alpha_i^* > 0 \} \leq b \\ \leq \min \{ -\varepsilon + y_i - \langle w, x_i \rangle \mid \alpha_i > 0 \text{ or } \alpha_i^* < C \} \end{aligned} \tag{4.53}$$

Kernels: We are interested in making the SV algorithm nonlinear. This, for instance, could be achieved by simply preprocessing the training patterns x_i by a map $\Phi: X \to F$ into some feature space F, as already described in Chapter 2, and then applying the standard SV regression algorithm. Let us have a brief look at the example given in Figure 2.8 of Chapter 2. We had (quadratic features in $\mathbb{R}^2$) with the map $\Phi: \mathbb{R}^2 \to \mathbb{R}^3$ with $\Phi(x_1, x_2) = (x_1^2, \sqrt{2} x_1 x_2, x_2^2)$. It is understood that the subscripts in this case refer to the components of $x \in \mathbb{R}^2$. Training a linear *SV* machine on the preprocessed features would yield a quadratic function as indicated in Figure 2.8. Although this approach seems reasonable in the particular example above, it can easily become computationally infeasible for both polynomial features of higher order and higher dimensionality.

Implicit mapping via kernels: Clearly this approach is not feasible, and we have to find a computationally cheaper way. The key observation [96] is that for the feature map of the above example we have

$$\left\langle \left(x_1^2, \sqrt{2} x_1 x_2, x_2^2 \right), \left(x_1'^2, \sqrt{2} x_1' x_2', x_2'^2 \right) \right\rangle = \langle x, x' \rangle^2 \tag{4.54}$$

As noted in the previous section, the SV algorithm only depends on the dot products between patterns x_i. Hence, it suffices to know $k(x, x') := \langle \Phi(x), \Phi(x') \rangle$ rather than Φ explicitly, which allows us to restate the SV optimization problem:

$$Maximize\left[-\frac{1}{2}\sum_{i,j=1}^{p}\left(\alpha_i-\alpha_i^*\right)\left(\alpha_j-\alpha_j^*\right)k(x_i,x_j)\right.$$

$$\left.-\varepsilon\sum_{i=1}^{p}(\alpha_i+\alpha_i^*)+\sum_{i=1}^{p}y_i\left(\alpha_i-\alpha_i^*\right)\right] \tag{4.55}$$

$$subject\ to\ \sum_{i=1}^{l}(\alpha_i-\alpha_i^*)=0\ and\ \alpha_i,\alpha_i^*\in[0,C]$$

Now the expansion for f in Eq. (4.50) may be written as $w=\sum_{i=1}^{p}\left(\alpha_i-\alpha_i^*\right)\Phi(x_i)$ and

$$f(x)=\sum_{i=1}^{p}(\alpha_i-\alpha_i^*)k(x_i,x)+b. \tag{4.56}$$

The difference to the linear case is that w is no longer given explicitly. Also, note that in the non-linear setting, the optimization problem corresponds to finding the *flattest* function in the *feature* space, not in the input space.

4.4.3 Combination of Fuzzy Models and SVR

Given observation data from an unknown system, data-driven methods aim to construct a decision function $f(x)$ that can serve as an approximation of the system. As seen from the previous sections, both fuzzy models and SVR are employed to describe the decision function. Fuzzy models characterize the system by a collection of interpretable if-then rules, and a general fuzzy model that consists of a set of rules with the following structure will be used here:

$$R_i:\ If\ x_1\ is\ A_{i1}\ and\ x_2\ is\ A_{i2}\ and...x_d\ is\ A_{id},$$
$$then\ y_i=g_i(x,\beta_i)\ for\ i=1,2...,c. \tag{4.57}$$

Here, parameter d is the dimension of the antecedent variables $x=[x_1,x_2,\dots,x_d]^T$, R_i is the i-th rule in the rule base, and $A_{i1},\dots,A_{ipx}$ are fuzzy sets defined for the respective antecedent variable. The rule consequent $g_i(x,\beta_i)$ is a function of the inputs with parameters β_i. Parameter c is the number of fuzzy rules. By modification of Eq. (4.41) to product form and Eq. (4.43), the decision function in terms of the fuzzy model by fuzzy mean defuzzification becomes

$$f_{FM}(x)=\frac{\sum_{i=1}^{c}\left(\prod_{j=1}^{d}\mu_i(x_j)\right)g_i(x,\beta_i)}{\sum_{i=1}^{c}\left(\prod_{j=1}^{d}\mu_i(x_j)\right)} \tag{4.58}$$

where $\prod_{j=1}^{d}\mu_i(x_j)$ is the antecedent firing strength, and $\mu_i(x_j)$ is the membership of x_j in the fuzzy set A_{i1}. By the generalization of Eqs. (4.46) and (4.56), SVR is formulated as minimization of the following functional:

$$\frac{1}{2}\|\omega\|^2+C\sum_{i=1}^{n}(\xi_i+\xi_i^*)$$
$$s.t.\ -y_i+f(x_i,\omega)+b\le\varepsilon+\xi_i$$
$$-y_i+f(x_i,\omega)+b\le\varepsilon+\xi_i \tag{4.59}$$
$$\xi_i,\xi_i^*\ge0,i=1,2...n$$

where C is the regularization parameter. The solution of (4.59) is used to determine the decision function $f(x)$, and is given by (see Eq. (4.56)):

$$f_{SVR}(x) = \sum_{i=1}^{c} \theta_i' k(x, x_i) + b \tag{4.60}$$

where $\theta_i' = \alpha_i - \alpha_i^*$ are subjected to constraints $0 \le \alpha_i,\ \alpha_i^* \le C$, c is the number of support vectors, and the kernel $k(x, x_i) = \langle \Phi(x), \Phi(x_i) \rangle$ is an inner product of the images in the feature space. The model given by Eq. (4.60) is referred to as the SVR model.

Motivated by the underlying concept of granularity, both the kernel in Eq. (4.60) and the fuzzy membership function in Eq. (4.59) are information granules. The kernel is a similarity measure between the support vector and the non-support vector in SVR, and fuzzy membership functions associated with fuzzy sets are essentially linguistic granules, which can be viewed as linked collections of fuzzy variables drawn together by the criterion of similarity. Hence, [97–99] regarded kernels as the Gaussian membership function of the t-norm-based algebra product

$$k(x, x_i) = \prod_{j=1}^{d} \exp\left(-\left(\frac{x_i - x_{ij}}{\sigma_j} \right)^2 \right) \tag{4.61}$$

and incorporated SVR in FM. In Eq. (4.61), $x_i = [x_{i1}, x_{i2}, \ldots x_{id}]^T$ denotes the support vector in the framework of SVR, but x_{ij} is referred as to the center of the Gaussian membership function. Parameter σ_j is a hyperparameter of the kernel, whereas it represents the dispersion of the Gaussian membership function in fuzzy set theory.

Fuzzy model based on SVR: Combining the fuzzy model with SVR, we can build a fuzzy system that can use the advantages that each technique offers, so the trade-off could be well balanced under this combination. Such a model is developed to extract support vectors for generating fuzzy rules, so c is equal in both Eqs. (4.58) and (4.60). Sometimes there are too many support vectors, which will lead to a redundant and complicated rule base even though the model performance is good. Alternatively, we could reduce the number of support vectors and utilize them to generate a transparent fuzzy model. Simultaneously, we make the fuzzy model retain the original performance of the SVR model, and learn the experience already acquired from SVR. In such a way, an experience-oriented learning algorithm is created. So, a simplification algorithm is employed to obtain reduced-set vectors instead of support vectors for constructing the fuzzy model, and the parameters are adjusted by a hybrid learning mechanism considering the experience of the SVR model on the same training data set. The obtained fuzzy model retains the acceptable performances of the original SVR solutions, and at the same time possesses high transparency. This enables a good compromise between the interpretability and accuracy of the fuzzy model.

Constructing interpretable kernels: Besides Gaussian kernel functions such as Eq. (4.61), there are some other common forms of membership functions:

The triangle membership function:

$$\mu_t(x, b, \gamma) = \max\left\{ 1 - \frac{|x - b|}{\gamma}, 0 \right\}, y > 0.$$

The generalized bell-shaped membership function:

$$\mu_b(x, b, a) = \frac{1}{1 + \left(\dfrac{x - b}{a} \right)^2}, a > 0$$

The trapezoidal-shaped membership function:

$$\mu_{tr}(x, b, a, c) = \begin{cases} 1 & b - a \leq x \leq b + a \\ \max\left\{ 1 - \dfrac{|x - b| - a}{c}, 0 \right\} & \text{otherwise}, a > 0, c > 0. \end{cases}$$

where b is the center of the membership functions, and parameters γ, a, and c are mean values of the dispersion for the three examples of membership functions.. Could the above functions also be used for constructing an admissible Mercer kernel? Note that they are translation invariant functions, so the multidimensional function created by these kinds of functions based on product t-norm operator is also translation invariant. Furthermore, if we regard the multidimensional functions as translation invariant kernels, then the following theorem can be used to check whether these kernels are admissible Mercer kernels:

A translation-invariant kernel $k(x, x_i) = k(x - x_i)$ is an admissible Mercer kernel if and only if the Fourier transform

$$F[k](w) = (2\pi)^{-px/2} \int_{R^{px}} \exp\left(-j(w \cdot x)\right) k(x) dx$$

is non-negative [100]. For the case of the triangle and generalized bell-shaped membership functions, the Fourier transform is respectively as follows:

$$F[k](w) = (2\pi)^{-d/2} \prod_{j=1}^{d} \frac{2\left(1 - \cos w_j \gamma_j\right)}{w_j^2 \gamma_j}$$

and

$$F[k](w) = \left(\frac{\pi}{2}\right)^{d/2} \prod_{j=1}^{d} \exp\left(-a_j |w_j|\right) a_j.$$

Since both of them are non-negative, we can construct Mercer kernels with triangle and generalized bell-shaped membership functions. But the Fourier transform in the case of the trapezoidal-shaped membership function is

$$F[k](w) = (2\pi)^{-d/2} \prod_{j=1}^{d} \frac{2\left(\cos w_j a_j - \cos w_j (a_j + c_j)\right)}{w_j^2 c_j}$$

which is not always non-negative. In conclusion, the kernel can also be regarded as a product-type multidimensional triangle or a generalized bell-shaped membership function, but not the trapezoidal-shaped one. The notation $\prod_{a}^{b} x$ is also considered as a fuzzy logical operator, namely, the *t-norm-based algebra product* [101, 102]. The obtained Mercer kernels could be understood by means of the conjunction (and) used in the previous sections. Thus, one can assign some meanings to the constructed Mercer kernels to obtain linguistic interpretability.

Experience-oriented FM via reduced-set vectors: Given n training data $\{(x_1, y_1), \ldots, (x_n, y_n)\} \subset \Re^d \times \Re$, the goal of experience-oriented FM is to construct a fuzzy model such as Eq. (4.58) that has a good trade-off between interpretability and accuracy. We examine the trade-off using the proposed algorithm with two objectives: to minimize the number of fuzzy rules and maximize the accuracy, that is, the approximation and generalization performance.

Given the good performance of SVR, it is reasonable to share the successful experience of SVR in FM. So, SVR with Mercer kernels is employed to generate the initial fuzzy model and the available experience on the training data. It is also expected that a reduction in the number of rules could make the resulting rule base more interpretable and transparent. Thus, a simplification algorithm is introduced to generate reduced-set vectors for simplifying the structure of the initial fuzzy model, and at the same time the parameters of the derived simplified model are adjusted by a hybrid learning algorithm including the linear ridge regression algorithm and the gradient descent method based on a new performance measure. As a start, let us reformulate Eq. (4.60) through a simple equivalent algebra transform to obtain

$$f_{SVR}(x) = \left[\sum_{i=1}^{c} k(x, x_i) g_i'(x, \beta_i') c \right] \Big/ \left\{ \sum_{i=1}^{c} k(x, x_i) \right\} \tag{4.62}$$

where c is the number of support vectors, $\beta_i^f = (\theta_i', b, x_j, \Theta')$ are the parameters of the function $g_i'(x, \beta_i') = \sum_{j=1}^{c} k(x, x_j)\theta_i' + b$, and $\Theta' = (\Theta_1', \dots, \Theta_d')$ denote the kernel parameters. Obviously, if $k(x, x_i)$ is created by a Gaussian, triangle, or generalized bell-shaped membership function, then Eq. (4.62) is consistent with the TS fuzzy inference structure, and exhibits good performance under the optimal model selection procedures. However, c, that is, the number of support vectors, usually becomes quite large so that the fuzzy model suffers from being uninterpretable. To compensate for this drawback, c should be replaced by a smaller c^f. Thus, a simplified fuzzy model is used:

$$f_{FM}(x) = \left[\sum_{i=1}^{c'} \prod_{j=1}^{d} \mu_i(x_j, z_{ij}, \Theta_i) g_i(x, \beta_i) \right] \Big/ \left[\sum_{i=1}^{c'} \prod_{j=1}^{d} \mu_i(x_j, z_{ij}, \Theta_j) \right] \tag{4.63}$$

where c' is the number of rules, $\beta_i = (\theta_i, \theta_{0i}, z_j, \Theta)$ are the consequent parameters of the rule $g_i(x, \beta_i) = \sum_{i=1}^{c'} \prod_{j=1}^{d} \mu_i(x_j, z_{ij}, \Theta_j)\theta_i + \theta_{0i}$, and $\Theta = (\Theta_1, \dots, \Theta_d)$ denote the dispersion parameters of the membership functions. The consequent parameter b does not remain unchanged anymore, and it is replaced by θ_{0i} in order to increase the adjustment ability of each consequent.

Rather than directly extracting support vectors to generate fuzzy rules, the FM problem is solved by learning the parameters in Eq. (4.63) while considering the experience of Eq. (4.62). It is expected that Eq. (4.63) would be able to describe the input–output behavior in the same way as Eq. (4.62). However, the experience acquired heavily depends on the selection of the hyperparameters [103, 104]. Improper selection of these hyperparameters may result in bad performance and bring on useless experience and information. Here, some selection methods are suggested:

1) The regularization parameter C can be given by following prescription according to the range of output values of the training data [103]: $C = max\{|\bar{y} - 3\sigma_y|, |\bar{y} + 3\sigma_y|\} \cdot n$, where $\bar{y}$ and σ_y are the mean and the standard deviation of the training data y, and n is the number of training data.

2) v-*SVR* is employed instead of ε-*SVR*, since it is easy to determine of the number of support vectors by the adjustment of v. The adjustment of parameter v can be determined by an asymptotically optimal procedure, and the theoretically optimal value for Gaussian noise is 0.54 [104]. For the kernel parameter Θ', the k-fold cross-validation method is utilized [104].

Reduced-set vectors: In order to share the experience, we are interested in constructing Eq. (4.63) such that the original Eq. (4.62) is approximated. In the following, $k(x, x_i)$ is written as $k'(x, x_i)$, considering its kernel parameters Θ' in Eq. (4.62). Similarly, in Eq. (4.63), $\prod_{j=1}^{d} \mu_i(x_j, z_{ij}, \Theta_j)$ is replaced by $k(x, z_i)$ according to the kernels constructed in the previous paragraph. Then, let $G(x) = \sum_{i=1}^{c} \theta_i' k'(x, x_i) - \sum_{i=1}^{c'} \theta_i \cdot k(x, z_j) + b$. With this we have

$$| f_{SRV}(x) - f_{FM}(x) | = | \sum_{i=1}^{c} \theta'_i k'(x, x_i) + b - \sum_{i=1}^{c'} \theta_i k(x, z_i) - \frac{\sum_{i=1}^{c'} \theta_{0i} k(x, z_i)}{\sum_{i=1}^{c} k(x, z_i)} | \tag{4.64}$$

$$= \sum_{i=1}^{c'} \frac{k(x, z_i)}{\sum_{i=1}^{c'} k(x, z_i)} | G(x) - \theta_{0i} | .$$

If we let the consequent parameter θ_{0i} be $G(x_{0i})$, we have

$$| f_{SRV}(x) - f_{FM}(x)| \leq \max_{i=1,\dots,c'} | G(x) - G(x_{0i}) |$$

$$\leq \max_{i=1,\dots,c'} \left(\begin{array}{c} |(\nabla_{\Phi(x)} G(x) \cdot (\Phi(x) - \Phi(x_{0i})))| \\ + \left| \sum_{j=1}^{c'} \theta_j (k'(x, z_j) - k'(x_{0i}, z_j) - k(x, z_j) + k(x_{0i}, z_j)) \right| \end{array} \right) .$$

For a smaller upper bound, we assume that $\Theta' = \Theta$. Then, according to the Cauchy–Schwartz inequality, the right side of the above inequality is simplified to

$$\max_{i=1,\dots,c'} \|\nabla_{\Phi(x)} G(x)\| \|\Phi(x) - \Phi(x_{0i})\| = \rho \max_{i=1,\dots,c'} \sqrt{k(x,x) + k(x_{0i}, x_{0i}) - 2k(x, x_{0i})}$$

where $\rho > 0, \rho^2 = \left\| \sum_{i=1}^{c} \theta'_i \Phi(x_i) - \sum_{i=1}^{c'} \theta_i \Phi(z_i) \right\|^2$, giving

$$| f_{SRV}(x) - f_{FM}(x) | \leq \rho \max_{i=1,\dots,c'} \sqrt{2 - 2k(x, x_{0i})}.$$

If we use the notation $\|\cdot\|_\infty$ as $\left\| d(x) \right\| = \sup_{x \in R^d} | d(x) |$, we can write

$$\| f_{SVR} - f_{FM} \|_\infty < \sqrt{2}\rho. \tag{4.65}$$

It is expected to obtain a small ρ in order to make a good approximation.

Hybrid learning algorithm: Parameter ρ in Eq. (4.65) is not small enough in many situations. In order to obtain a better approximation, a hybrid learning algorithm including a linear ridge regression algorithm and the gradient descent method can be used to adjust Θ and θ_{0i} according to the experience of Eq. (4.62) [105]. The performance measure is defined as

$$E = \frac{1}{2} \sum_{k=1}^{n} (e_1(x_k))^2 + \frac{\alpha}{2} \sum_{k=1}^{n} (e_2(x_k))^2 \tag{4.66}$$

where α is a weighted parameter that defines the relative trade-off between the squared error loss and the experienced loss, and $e_1(x_k) = y_k - f_{FM}(x_k)$, $e_2(x_k) = f_{SVR}(x_k) - f_{FM}(x_k)$. Thus, the error between the desired output and actual output is characterized by the first term, and the second term measures the difference between the actual output and the experienced output of SVR. Therefore, each epoch of the hybrid learning algorithm is composed of a forward pass and a backward pass which implement the linear ridge regression algorithm and the gradient descent method in E over parameters Θ and θ_{0i}. Here, θ_{0i} are identified by the linear ridge regression in the forward pass. In addition, it is assumed that the Gaussian membership function is employed, and thus Θ_j is referred as to σ_j. Using Eqs. (4.62) and (4.63), and defining

$$\varphi_i(x_k) = \frac{\prod_{j=1}^{d} \exp\left(-\left(\frac{x_j - z_{ij}}{\sigma_j}\right)^2\right)}{\sum_{i=1}^{c} \prod_{j=1}^{d} \exp\left(-\left(\frac{x_j - z_{ij}}{\sigma_j}\right)^2\right)}, \tag{4.67}$$

then, at the minimum point of Eq. (4.66) all derivatives with respect to θ_{0i} should vanish:

$$\frac{\partial E}{\partial \theta_{0i}} = \sum_{k=1}^{n} \varphi_i(x_k)(f_{FM}(x_k) - y_k) + \sum_{k=1}^{n} \alpha \varphi_i(x_k)(f_{FM}(x_k) - f_{SVR}(x_k)) = 0. \tag{4.68}$$

These conditions can be rewritten in the form of normal equations:

$$\theta_{01} \sum_{k=1}^{n} \varphi_m(x_k)\varphi_i(x_k) + \dots + \theta_{0c'} \sum_{k=1}^{n} \varphi_m(x_k)\varphi_c'(x_k)$$

$$= \sum_{k=1}^{n} \varphi_m(x_k) \left(\frac{y_k}{1+\alpha} + \frac{\alpha}{1+\alpha} \left(\sum_{i=1}^{c} k(x_k, x_i)\theta_i' + b \right) \right. \tag{4.69}$$

$$\left. - \sum_{i=1}^{c'} \theta_i \prod_{j=1}^{d} \exp\left(-\left(\frac{x_j - z_{ij}}{\sigma_j}\right)^2 \right) \right)$$

where $m = 1, \dots, c'$. This is a standard problem that forms the grounds for linear regression, and the most well-known formula for estimating $\theta = [\theta_{01}\theta_{02} \cdots \theta_{0c'}]^T$ uses the ridge regression algorithm:

$$\theta = [X^T X + \delta I_n]^{-1} X^T Y \tag{4.70}$$

where δ is a positive scalar, and

$$X = \begin{bmatrix} \psi(x_1)^T \\ \psi(x_2)^T \\ \vdots \\ \psi(x_n)^T \end{bmatrix} \quad Y = \begin{bmatrix} y_1' \\ y_2' \\ \vdots \\ y_n' \end{bmatrix} \tag{4.71}$$

where $y_k' = \frac{y_k}{1+\alpha} + \frac{\alpha}{1+\alpha} \left(\sum_{i=1}^{c} k(x_k, x_i)\theta_i' + b \right) - \sum_{i=1}^{c'} \theta_i \prod_{j=1}^{d} \exp\left(-\left(\frac{x_j - z_{ij}}{\sigma j}\right)^2 \right)$,

$\psi(x_k) = [\varphi_1(x_k), \varphi_2(x_k), \cdots, \varphi_{c'}(x_k)]^T, k = 1, \dots n$. In the backward pass, the error rates propagate backward and σ_j are updated by the gradient descent method. The derivatives with respect to σ_j^{-2} are calculated from

$$\frac{\partial E}{\partial \sigma_j^{-2}} = - \sum_{k=1}^{n} e_1(x_k) \frac{\partial f_{FM}(x_k)}{\partial \sigma_j^{-2}} - \alpha \sum_{k=1}^{n} e_2(x_k) \frac{\partial f_{FM}(x_k)}{\partial \sigma_j^{-2}} \tag{4.72}$$

where

$$\frac{\partial f_{FM}(x_k)}{\partial \sigma_j^{-2}} = - \sum_{i=1}^{c'} (x_{kj} - z_{ij})^2 \lambda_i(x_k)\theta_i + \left(\sum_{i=1}^{c'} (x_{kj} - z_{ij})^2 \varphi_i(x_k) \right) \left(\sum_{i=1}^{c'} \varphi_i(x_k)\theta_{0i} \right)$$

$$- \left(\sum_{i=1}^{c'} (x_{kj} - z_{ij})^2 \varphi_i(x_k)\theta_{0i} \right) \left(\sum_{i=1}^{c'} \varphi_i(x_k) \right) \tag{4.73}$$

$$\lambda_i(x_k) = \prod_{j=1}^{d} \exp\left(-\left(\frac{x_{kj} - z_{ij}}{\sigma j}\right)^2 \right).$$

and σ_j are updated as

$$\sigma_j^{-2} = \sigma_j^{-2} - \eta \frac{\partial E}{\partial \sigma_j^{-2}} \tag{4.74}$$

where η is the constant step size.

References

1 R. Caruana, Y. Lou, J. Gehrke, P. Koch, M. Sturm, and N. Elhadad, "Intelligible models for healthcare: Predicting pneumonia risk and hospital 30-day readmission," in Proc. 21th ACM SIGKDD Int. Conf. Knowl. Discovery Data Mining, 2015, pp. 1721–1730.

2 A. Howard, C. Zhang, and E. Horvitz, "Addressing bias in machine learning algorithms: A pilot study on emotion recognition for intelligent systems," in Proc. Adv. Robot. Social Impacts (ARSO), Mar. 2017, pp. 1–7.

3 (2016). European Union General Data Protection Regulation (GDPR). Accessed: Jun. 6, 2018. [Online]. Available: http://www.eugdpr.org

4 D. Silver, J. Schrittwieser, K. Simonyan, et al., "Mastering the game of go without human knowledge," *Nature*, vol. **550**, no. 7676, pp. 354–359, 2017.

5 M. Bojarski, D. Del Testa, D. Dworakowski, et al. (2016). "End to end learning for self-driving cars." [Online]. Available: https://arxiv.org/abs/1604.07316

6 J. Haspiel, J. Meyerson, L.P. Robert Jr, et al. (2018). Explanations and Expectations: Trust Building in Automated Vehicles, http://deepblue.lib.umich.edu. [Online]. Available: https://doi.org/10.1145/3173386.3177057

7 A. Holzinger, C. Biemann, C. S. Pattichis, and D. B. Kell. (2017). "What do we need to build explainable AI systems for the medical domain?" [Online]. Available: https://arxiv.org/abs/1712.09923

8 G. J. Katuwal and R. Chen. (2016). Machine Learning Model Interpretability for Precision Medicine. [Online]. Available: https://arxiv. org/abs/1610.09045

9 Z. Che , S. Purushotham, R. Khemani, and Y. Liu, "Interpretable deep models for ICU outcome prediction," in Proc. AMIA Annu. Symp., 2017, pp. 371–380

10 S. Tan, R. Caruana, G. Hooker, and Y. Lou. (2018). "Detecting bias in black-box models using transparent model distillation." [Online]. Available: https://arxiv.org/abs/1710.06169

11 C. Howell, "A framework for addressing fairness in consequential machine learning," in Proc. FAT Conf., Tuts., 2018, pp. 1–2.

12 Berk, R. and Bleich, J. (2013). Statistical procedures for forecasting criminal behavior: a comparative assessment. *Criminol. Public Policy* **12** (3): 513–544.

13 Equifax. (2018). Equifax Launches NeuroDecision Technology. Accessed: Jun. 6, 2018. [Online]. Available: https://investor.equifax.com news-and-events/news/2018/03-26-2018-143044126

14 D. Gunning. Explainable artificial intelligence (XAI), Defense Advanced Research Projects Agency (DARPA). Accessed: Jun. 6, 2018. [Online]. Available: http://www.darpa.mil/program/explainable-artificialintelligence

15 W. Knight. (2017). The U.S. military wants its autonomous machines to explain themselves, MIT Technology Review. Accessed: Jun. 6, 2018. [Online]. Available: https://www.technologyreview.com/s/603795/theus-military-wants-its-autonomous-machines-to-explain-themselves

16 A. Henelius, K. Puolamäki, and A. Ukkonen. (2017). "Interpreting classifiers through attribute interactions in datasets." [Online]. Available: https://arxiv.org/abs/1707.07576

17 Future of Privacy Forum. (2017). Unfairness by Algorithm: Distilling the Harms of Automated Decision-Making. Accessed: Jun. 6, 2018. [Online]. Available: https://fpf.org/wp-content/uploads/2017/12/FPF-AutomatedDecision-Making-Harms-and-Mitigation-Charts.pdf

18 Letham, B., Rudin, C., McCormick, T.H., and Madigan, D. (2015). Interpretable classifiers using rules and Bayesian analysis: building a better stroke prediction model. *Ann. Appl. Stat.* **9** (3): 1350–1371.

19 K. Xu, J. Lei Ba, R. Kiros, et al., "Show, attend and tell: Neural image caption generation with visual attention," in Proc. Int. Conf. Mach. Learn. (ICML), 2015, pp. 1–10

20 Ustun, B. and Rudin, C. (2015). Supersparse linear integer models for optimized medical scoring systems. *Mach. Learn.* **102** (3): 349–391.

21 S. Sarkar, "Accuracy and interpretability trade-offs in machine learning applied to safer gambling," in Proc. CEUR Workshop, 2016, pp. 79–87.

22 Breiman, L. (2001). Statistical modeling: the two cultures (with comments and a rejoinder by the author). *Stat. Sci.* **16** (3): 199–231.

23 Z. C. Lipton, "The mythos of model interpretability," in Proc. ICML Workshop Hum. Interpretability Mach. Learn., 2016, pp. 96–100.

24 Krening, S., Harrison, B., Feigh, K.M. et al. (2016). Learning from explanations using sentiment and advice in RL. *IEEE Trans. Cogn. Develop. Syst.* **9** (1): 44–55.

25 A. Mahendran and A. Vedaldi, "Understanding deep image representations by inverting them," in Proc. IEEE Conf. Comput. Vis. Pattern Recognit. (CVPR), Jun. 2015, pp. 5188–5196.

26 T. Mikolov, I. Sutskever, K. Chen, G. S. Corrado, and J. Dean, "Distributed representations of words and phrases and their compositionality," in Proc. Adv. Neural Inf. Process. Syst. (NIPS), 2013, pp. 3111–3119.

27 G. Ras, M. van Gerven, and P. Haselager. (2018). "Explanation methods in deep learning: Users, values, concerns and challenges." [Online]. Available: https://arxiv.org/abs/1803.07517

28 A. Santoro, D. Raposo, D.G.T. Barret, et al. (2017). "A simple neural network module for relational reasoning." [Online]. Available: https://arxiv.org/abs/1706.01427

29 R. B. Palm, U. Paquet, and O. Winther. (2017). "Recurrent relational networks for complex relational reasoning." [Online]. Available: https://arxiv.org/abs/1711.08028

30 Y. Dong, H. Su, J. Zhu, and B. Zhang, "Improving interpretability of deep neural networks with semantic information," in Proc. IEEE Conf. Comput. Vis. Pattern Recognit. (CVPR), Mar. 2017, pp. 4306–4314.

31 C. Louizos, U. Shalit, J. M. Mooij, D. Sontag, R. Zemel, and M. Welling, "Causal effect inference with deep latent-variable models," in Proc. Adv. Neural Inf. Process. Syst. (NIPS), 2017, pp. 6446–6456.

32 O. Goudet, D. Kalainathan, P. Caillou, et al. (2017). "Learning functional causal models with generative neural networks." [Online]. Available: https://arxiv.org/abs/1709.05321

33 C. Yang, A. Rangarajan, and S. Ranka. (2018). "Global model interpretation via recursive partitioning." [Online]. Available: https://arxiv.org/abs/1802.04253

34 M. A. Valenzuela-Escárcega, A. Nagesh, and M. Surdeanu. (2018). "Lightly-supervised representation learning with global interpretability." [Online]. Available: https://arxiv.org/abs/1805.11545

35 A. Nguyen, A. Dosovitskiy, J. Yosinski, T. Brox, and J. Clune, "Synthesizing the preferred inputs for neurons in neural networks via deep generator networks," in Proc. Adv. Neural Inf. Process. Syst. (NIPS), 2016, pp. 3387–3395.

36 D. Erhan, A. Courville, and Y. Bengio, "Understanding representations learned in deep architectures," Dept. d'Informatique Recherche Operationnelle, Univ. Montreal, Montreal, QC, Canada, Tech. Rep. 1355, 2010

37 M. T. Ribeiro, S. Singh, and C. Guestrin, "'Why should I trust you?' Explaining the predictions of any classifier," 22nd ACM SIGKDD Int. Conf. Knowl. Discovery Data Mining, 2016, pp. 1135–1144

38 M. T. Ribeiro, S. Singh, and C. Guestrin, "Anchors: High-precision model-agnostic explanations," in Proc. AAAI Conf. Artif. Intell., 2018, pp. 1–9.

39 J. Lei, M. G'Sell, A. Rinaldo, R. J. Tibshirani, and L. Wasserman, "Distribution-free predictive inference for regression," J. Amer. Stat. Assoc., to be published. [Online]. Available: http://www.stat.cmu.edu/~ryantibs/papers/conformal.pdf

40 Baehrens, D., Schroeter, T., Harmeling, S. et al. (2010). How to explain individual classification decisions. *J. Mach. Learn. Res.* **11** (6): 1803–1831.

41 K. Simonyan, A. Vedaldi, and A. Zisserman. (2013). "Deep inside convolutional networks: Visualising image classification models and saliency maps." [Online]. Available: https://arxiv.org/abs/1312.6034

42 M. D. Zeiler and R. Fergus, "Visualizing and understanding convolutional networks," in Proc. Eur. Conf. Comput. Vis. Zurich, Switzerland: Springer, 2014, pp. 818–833.

43 B. Zhou, A. Khosla, A. Lapedriza, A. Oliva, and O. Torralba, "Learning deep features for discriminative localization," IEEE Conf. Comput. Vis. Pattern Recognit., Jun. 2016, pp. 2921–2929.

44 M. Sundararajan, A. Taly, and Q. Yan. (2017). "Axiomatic attribution for deep networks." [Online]. Available: https://arxiv.org/abs/1703.01365

45 D. Smilkov, N. Thorat, B. Kim, F. Viégas, and M. Wattenberg. (2017). "SmoothGrad: Removing noise by adding noise." [Online]. Available: https://arxiv.org/abs/1706.03825

46 Robnik-Šikonja, M. and Kononenko, I. (2008). Explaining classifications for individual instances. *IEEE Trans. Knowl. Data Eng.* **20** (5): 589–600.

47 Montavon, G., Lapuschkin, S., Binder, A. et al. (2017). Explaining nonlinear classification decisions with deep Taylor decomposition. *Pattern Recog.* **65**: 211–222.

48 S. Bach, A. Binder, K.-R. Müller, and W. Samek, "Controlling explanatory heatmap resolution and semantics via decomposition depth," IEEE Int. Conf. Image Process. (ICIP), Sep. 2016, pp. 2271–2275.

49 R. Fong and A. Vedaldi. (2017). "Interpretable explanations of black boxes by meaningful perturbation." [Online]. Available: https://arxiv.org/abs/1704.03296

50 P. Dabkowski and Y. Gal, "Real time image saliency for black box classifiers," in Proc. Adv. Neural Inf. Process. Syst., 2017, pp. 6970–6979.

51 P.-J. Kindermans, K.T. Schütt, M. Alber, et al., "Learning how to explain neural networks: PatternNet and patternAttribution," in Proc. Int. Conf. Learn. Represent., 2018, pp. 1–16. Accessed: Jun. 6, 2018. [Online]. Available: https://openreview.net/forum?id=Hkn7CBaTW

52 A. Shrikumar, P. Greenside, A. Shcherbina, and A. Kundaje. (2016). "Not just a black box: Interpretable deep learning by propagating activation differences." [Online]. Available: http://arxiv.org/abs/1605.01713

53 A. Ross, M. C. Hughes, and F. Doshi-Velez, "Right for the right reasons: Training differentiable models by constraining their explanations," in Proc. Int. Joint Conf. Artif. Intell., 2017, pp. 2662–2670.

54 S. M. Lundberg and S. I. Lee, "A unified approach to interpreting model predictions," in Proc. Adv. Neural Inf. Process. Syst., 2017, pp. 4768–4777.

55 R. Guidotti, A. Monreale, S. Ruggieri, D. Pedreschi, F. Turini, and F. Giannotti. (2018). "Local rule-based explanations of black box decision systems." [Online]. Available: https://arxiv.org/abs/1805.10820

56 D. Linsley, D. Scheibler, S. Eberhardt, and T. Serre. (2018). "Globaland-local attention networks for visual recognition." [Online]. Available: https://arxiv.org/abs/1805.08819

57 S. Seo, J. Huang, H. Yang, and Y. Liu, "Interpretable convolutional neural networks with dual local and global attention for review rating prediction," in Proc. 11th ACM Conf. Recommender Syst. (RecSys), 2017, pp. 297–305.

58 C. Molnar. (2018). Interpretable Machine Learning: A Guide for Making Black Box Models Explainable. Accessed: Jun. 6, 2018. [Online]. Available: https://christophm.github.io/interpretable-ml-book

59 O. Bastani, C. Kim, and H. Bastani. (2017). "Interpretability via model extraction." [Online]. Available: https://arxiv.org/abs/1706.09773

60 J. J. Thiagarajan, B. Kailkhura, P. Sattigeri, and K. N. Ramamurthy. (2016). "TreeView: Peeking into deep neural networks via feature-space partitioning." [Online]. Available: https://arxiv.org/abs/1611.07429

61 D. P. Green and H. L. Kern, "Modeling heterogeneous treatment effects in large-scale experiments using Bayesian additive regression trees," in Proc. Annu. Summer Meeting Soc. Political Methodol., 2010, pp. 1–40.

62 Chipman, H.A., George, E.I., and McCulloch, R.E. (2010). BART: Bayesian additive regression trees. *Appl. Statist.* **4** (1): 266–298.

63 Elith, J., Leathwick, J., and Hastie, T. (2008). A working guide to boosted regression trees. *J. Anim. Ecol.* **77** (4): 802–813.

64 S. H. Welling, H. H. F. Refsgaard, P. B. Brockhoff, and L. H. Clemmensen. (2016). "Forest floor visualizations of random forests." [Online]. Available: https://arxiv.org/abs/1605.09196

65 Goldstein, A., Kapelner, A., Bleich, J., and Pitkin, E. (2015). Peeking inside the black box: visualizing statistical learning with plots of individual conditional expectation. *J. Comput. Graph. Stat.* **24** (1): 44–65. https://doi.org/10.1080/10618600.2014.907095.

66 G. Casalicchio, C. Molnar, and B. Bischl. (2018). "Visualizing the feature importance for black box models." [Online]. Available: https://arxiv.org/abs/1804.06620

67 U. Johansson, R. König, and I. Niklasson, "The truth is in there—Rule extraction from opaque models using genetic programming," in Proc. FLAIRS Conf., 2004, pp. 658–663.

68 M. H. Aung, P. Lisboa, T. Etchells, et al., "Comparing analytical decision support models through Boolean rule extraction: A case study of ovarian tumour malignancy," in Proc. Int. Symp. Neural Netw. Berlin, Germany: Springer, 2007, pp. 1177–1186.

69 T. Hailesilassie. (2017). "Rule extraction algorithm for deep neural networks: A review." [Online]. Available: https://arxiv.org/abs/1610.05267

70 Andrews, R., Diederich, J., and Tickle, A.B. (1995). Survey and critique of techniques for extracting rules from trained artificial neural networks. *Knowl.-Based Syst.* **8** (6): 373–389.

71 GopiKrishna, T. (2014). Evaluation of rule extraction algorithms. *Int. J. Data Mining Knowl. Manage. Process* **4** (3): 9–19.

72 Etchells, T.A. and Lisboa, P.J.G. (Mar. 2006). Orthogonal search-based rule extraction (OSRE) for trained neural networks: a practical and efficient approach. *IEEE Trans. Neural Netw.* **17** (2): 374–384.

73 Barakat, N. and Diederich, J. (2005). Eclectic rule-extraction from support vector machines. *Int. J. Comput. Intell.* **2** (1): 59–62.

74 P. Sadowski, J. Collado, D. Whiteson, and P. Baldi, "Deep learning, dark knowledge, and dark matter," in Proc. NIPS Workshop High-Energy Phys. Mach. Learn. (PMLR), vol. 42, 2015, pp. 81–87.

75 G. Hinton, O. Vinyals, and J. Dean. (2015). "Distilling the knowledge in a neural network." [Online]. Available: arXiv:1503.02531v1 [stat.ML]

76 Z. Che, S. Purushotham, R. Khemani, and Y. Liu. (2015). "Distilling knowledge from deep networks with applications to healthcare domain." [Online]. Available: arXiv:1512.03542v1 [stat.ML]

77 K. Xu, D. H. Park, D. H. Yi, and C. Sutton. (2018). "Interpreting deep classifier by visual distillation of dark knowledge." [Online]. Available: https://arxiv.org/abs/1803.04042

78 S. Tan, "Interpretable approaches to detect bias in black-box models," in Proc. AAAI/ACM Conf. AI Ethics Soc., 2017, pp. 1–2.

79 S. Tan, R. Caruana, G. Hooker, and Y. Lou. (2018). "Auditing blackbox models using transparent model distillation with side information." [Online]. Available: arXiv:1710.06169v4 [stat.ML]

80 S. Tan, R. Caruana, G. Hooker, and A. Gordo. (2018). "Transparent model distillation." [Online]. Available: https://arxiv.org/abs/1801.08640

81 Y. Zhang and B. Wallace. (2016). "A sensitivity analysis of (and practitioners' Guide to) convolutional neural networks for sentence classification." [Online]. Available: https://arxiv.org/abs/1510.03820

82 Cortez, P. and Embrechts, M.J. (2013). Using sensitivity analysis and visualization techniques to open black box data mining models. *Inform. Sci.* **225**: 1–17.

83 P. Cortez and M. J. Embrechts, "Opening black box data mining models using sensitivity analysis," in Proc. IEEE Symp. Comput. Intell. Data Mining (CIDM), Apr. 2011, pp. 341–348.

84 Bach, S., Binder, A., Montavon, G. et al. (2015). On pixel-wise explanations for non-linear classifier decisions by layer-wise relevance propagation. *PLoS One* **10** (7): e0130140.

85 A. Fisher, C. Rudin, and F. Dominici. (2018). "Model class reliance: Variable importance measures for any machine learning model class, from the 'rashomon' perspective." [Online]. Available: https://arxiv.org/abs/1801.01489

86 Bien, J. and Tibshirani, R. (2011). Prototype selection for interpretable classification. *Ann. Appl. Statist.* **5** (4): 2403–2424.

87 B. Kim, C. Rudin, and J. A. Shah, "The Bayesian case model: A generative approach for case-based reasoning and prototype classification," in Proc. Adv. Neural Inf. Process. Syst., 2014, pp. 1952–1960.

88 K. S. Gurumoorthy, A. Dhurandhar, and G. Cecchi. (2017). "ProtoDash: Fast interpretable prototype selection." [Online]. Available: https://arxiv.org/abs/1707.01212

89 B. Kim, R. Khanna, and O. O. Koyejo, "Examples are not enough, learn to criticize! criticism for interpretability," in Proc. 29th Conf. Neural Inf. Process. Syst. (NIPS), 2016, pp. 2280–2288.

90 S. Wachter, B. Mittelstadt, and C. Russell. (2017). "Counterfactual explanations without opening the black box: Automated decisions and the GDPR." [Online]. Available: https://arxiv.org/abs/1711.00399

91 X. Yuan, P. He, Q. Zhu, and X. Li. (2017). "Adversarial examples: Attacks and defenses for deep learning." [Online]. Available: https://arxiv.org/abs/1712.07107

92 G. Montavon, S. Bach, A. Binder, W. Samek, and K.-R. Muller Explaining NonLinear Classification Decisions with Deep Taylor Decomposition, arXiv:1512.02479v1 [cs.LG] 8 Dec 2015, also in Pattern Recognition, vol. 65 May 2017, Pages pp. 211–222.

93 W. J. Murdoch, A. Szlam, Automatic Rule Extraction from Long Short Term Memory Networks, ICLR 2017 Conference

94 R. Babuska, Fuzzy Systems, Modeling and Identification https://www.researchgate.net/profile/Robert_Babuska/publication/228769192_Fuzzy_Systems_Modeling_and_Identification/links/02e7e5223310e79d19000000/Fuzzy-Systems-Modeling-and-Identification.pdf

95 Glisic, S. (2016). *Advanced Wireless Networks: Technology and Business Models*. Wiley.

96 B. E. Boser, I. Guyon, V. N. Vapnik A training algorithm for optimal margin classifiers. In D. Haussler, editor, *Proceedings of the Annual Conference on Computational Learning Theory*, pages 144–152, Pittsburgh, PA, 1992. ACM Press.

97 Chan, W.C. et al. (2001). On the modeling of nonlinear dynamic systems using support vector neural networks. *Eng. Appl. Artif. Intel.* **14** (2): 105–113.

98 Chiang, J.H. and Hao, P.Y. (2004). Support vector learning mechanism for fuzzy rule-based modeling: a new approach. *IEEE Trans. Fuzzy Syst.* **12** (1): 1–12.

99 Shen, J., Syau, Y., and Lee, E.S. (2007). Support vector fuzzy adaptive network in regression analysis. *Comput. Math. Appl.* **54** (11–12): 1353–1366.

100 Smola, A.J. and Schölkopf, B. (1998). The connection between regularization operators and support vector kernels. *Neural Netw.* **10**: 1445–1454.

101 https://en.wikipedia.org/wiki/T-norm_fuzzy_logics

102 https://en.wikipedia.org/wiki/Construction_of_t-norms

103 Cherkassky, V. and Ma, Y. (2004). Practical selection of SVM parameters and noise estimation for SVM regression. *Neural Netw.* **17** (1): 113–126.

104 Chalimourda, A., Schölkopf, B., and Smola, A.J. (2004). Experimentally optimal v in support vector regression for different noise models and parameters settings. *Neural Netw.* **17** (1): 127–141.

105 Yu, L. and Xiao, J. (2009). Trade-off between accuracy and interpretability: experience-oriented fuzzy modeling via reduced-set vectors. *Comput. Math. Appl.* **57**: 885–895.

5

Graph Neural Networks

5.1   Concept of Graph Neural Network (GNN)

As a start, in this section we present a brief overview of the GNN and then in the subsequent sections discuss some of the most popular variants in more detail.

The basic idea here is to extend existing neural networks for the purpose of processing the data represented in graph domains [1]. In a graph, each node is defined by its own features and the features of the related nodes. The target of GNN is to learn a state embedding $h_v \in \mathbb{R}^s$ that contains information on the neighborhood for each node. The state embedding h_v is an s-dimension vector of node v and can be used to produce an output o_v. Let f be a parametric function, called the *local transition function*, that is shared among all nodes and updates the node state according to the input neighborhood. Let g be the *local output function* that describes how the output is produced. Then, h_v and o_v are defined as

$$h_v = f\left(x_v, x_{co[v]}, h_{ne[v]}, x_{ne[v]}\right); \quad o_v = g(h_v, x_v) \tag{5.1}$$

where x_v, $x_{co[v]}$, $h_{ne[v]}$, and $x_{ne[v]}$ are the features of v, the features of its edges, the states, and the features of the nodes in the neighborhood of v, respectively. If H, O, X, and X_N are the vectors constructed by stacking all the states, all the outputs, all the features, and all the node features, respectively, then we can write

$$H = F(H, X); O = G(H, X_N) \tag{5.2}$$

In Eq. (5.2), F, the *global transition function*, and G, the *global output function*, are stacked versions of f and g for all nodes in a graph, respectively. The value of H is the fixed point of Eq. (5.2) and is uniquely defined with the assumption that F is a contraction map. GNN uses the following iterative scheme for computing the state (Banach's fixed-point theorem [2])

$$H^{t+1} = F(H^t, X) \tag{5.3}$$

where H^t denotes the t-th iteration of H. The dynamical system (Eq. (5.3)) converges exponentially fast to the solution of Eq. (5.2) for any initial value H(0) . Note that the computations described in f and g can be interpreted as feedforward neural networks (FNNs). Given the framework of GNN, how do we learn the parameters of f and g? With the target information (t_v for a specific node) for the supervision, the loss can be written as follows:

$$loss = \sum_{i=1}^{p}(t_i - o_i) \tag{5.4}$$

Artificial Intelligence and Quantum Computing for Advanced Wireless Networks, First Edition.
Savo G. Glisic and Beatriz Lorenzo.

where p is the number of supervised nodes. The learning algorithm is based on a gradient-descent strategy and is composed of the following steps:

---

1) The states h_v^t are iteratively updated by Eq. (5.1) until a time T.
   They approach the fixed-point solution of Eq. (5.2) $H(T) \approx H$.
2) The gradient of weights W is computed from the loss.
3) The weights W are updated according to the gradient computed in the last step.

5.1.1 Classification of Graphs

Directed graphs: Directed edges can yield more information than undirected edges. For example, in a knowledge graph where the edge starts from the head entity and ends at the tail entity, the head entity is the parent class of the tail entity, which suggests we should treat the information propagation process from parent classes and child classes differently. Here, we use two kinds of weight matrix, W_p and W_c, to incorporate more precise structural information. The propagation rule is [3]

$$H^t = \sigma\left(D_p^{-1}A_p\sigma\left(D_c^{-1}A_cH^{t-1}W_c\right)W_p\right) \tag{5.5}$$

where $D_p^{-1}A_p$, and $D_c^{-1}A_c$ are the normalized adjacency matrix for parents and children, respectively, and σ denotes a nonlinear activation function.

Heterogeneous graphs: These have several kinds of nodes. The simplest way to process heterogeneous graphs is to convert the type of each node to a one-hot feature vector that is concatenated with the original feature. *GraphInception* [4] introduces the concept of metapath into propagation on the heterogeneous graph. With metapath, we can group neighbors according to their node types and distances. For each neighbor group, GraphInception treats it as a subgraph in a homogeneous graph to perform propagation and concatenates the propagation results from different homogeneous graphs to arrive at a collective node representation. In [5], the heterogeneous graph attention network (HAN) was proposed, which utilizes node-level and semantic-level attention. The model has the ability to consider node importance and meta-paths simultaneously.

Graphs with edge information: Here, each edge has additional information like the weight or the type of the edge. There are two ways to handle this kind of graph:

1) We can convert the graph to a bipartite graph where the original edges also become nodes and one original edge is split into two new edges, which means there are two new edges between the edge node and begin/end nodes. The encoder of GS2 (Graph to Sequence) [6] uses the following aggregation function for neighbors:

$$h_v^t = \rho\left(\frac{1}{|\mathcal{N}_v|}\sum_{u\in\mathcal{N}_v}W_r\left(r_v^t \odot h_u^{t-1}\right) + b_r\right) \tag{5.6}$$

where W_r and b_r are the propagation parameters for different types of edges (relations r), ρ is a nonlinearity, $\odot$ stands for the Hadamard product and $\mathcal{N}_v$ is the set of neighboring nodes.

2) We can adapt different weight matrices for propagation on different kinds of edges. When the number of relations is very large, r-GCN (Relational Data with Graph Convolutional Networks) [7] introduces two kinds of regularization to reduce the number of parameters for modeling

relations: *basis-* and *block-diagonal*-decomposition. With the basis decomposition, each W_r is defined as follows:

$$W_r = \sum_{b=1}^{B} a_{rb} V_b \tag{5.7}$$

Here each W_r is a linear combination of basis transformations $V_b \in \mathbb{R}^{d_{in} \times d_{out}}$ with coefficients a_{rb}. In the blockdiagonal decomposition, r-GCN defines each W_r through the direct sum over a set of low-dimensional matrices, which needs more parameters than the first one.

Dynamic graphs: These have a static graph structure and dynamic input signals. To capture both kinds of information, diffusion convolutional recurrent NN (DCRNN) [8] and spatial-temporal graph convolutional networks (STGCN) [9] first collect spatial information by GNNs, then feed the outputs into a sequence model like sequence-to-sequence model or convolutional neural networks (CNNs). On the other hand, structural-recurrent NN [10] and STGCN [11] collect spatial and temporal messages at the same time. They extend the static graph structure with temporal connections so that they can apply traditional GNNs to the extended graphs.

5.1.2 Propagation Types

The propagation step and output step in the model define the hidden states of nodes (or edges). Several major modifications have been made to the propagation step from the original GNN model, whereas in the output step a simple feedforward neural network setting is the most popular. The variants utilize different aggregators to gather information from each node's neighbors and specific updaters to update nodes' hidden states.

Convolution has been generalized to the graph domain as well. Advances in this direction are often categorized as spectral approaches and non-spectral (spatial) approaches. Spectral approaches work with a spectral representation of the graphs.

Spectral network: The spectral network was proposed in Bruna et al. [12]. The convolution operation is defined in the Fourier domain by computing the eigen decomposition of the graph Laplacian. For the basics of these techniques, see Appendix 5.A. The operation can be defined as the multiplication of a signal $x \in \mathbb{R}^N$ (a scalar for each node) with a filter $g_\theta = \text{diag}(\theta)$ parameterized by $\theta \in \mathbb{R}^N$:

$$g_\theta \star x = U g_\theta(\Lambda) U^T x \tag{5.8}$$

where U is the matrix of the eigenvectors of the normalized graph Laplacian $L = I_N - D^{-\frac{1}{2}} A D^{-\frac{1}{2}} = U \Lambda U^T$ (D is the degree matrix, and A is the adjacency matrix of the graph), with a diagonal matrix of its eigenvalues Λ.

ChebyshevNet [13] truncates $g_\theta(\Lambda)$ in terms of Chebyshev polynomials $T_k(x)$ up to K^{th} order as

$$g_\theta \star x \approx \sum_{k=0}^{K} \theta_k T_k(\tilde{L}) x \tag{5.9}$$

with $\tilde{L} = 2(L - I_N)/\lambda_{max}$. Parameter λ_{max} denotes the largest eigenvalue of L. $\theta \in \mathbb{R}^K$ is now a vector of Chebyshev coefficients. The Chebyshev polynomials are defined as $T_k(x) = 2x T_{k-1}(x) - T_{k-2}(x)$, with $T_0(x) = 1$ and $T_1(x) = x$. It can be observed that the operation is K-localized since it is a Kth-order polynomial in the Laplacian.

Graph convolutional network (GCN) [14] : This limits the layer-wise convolution operation to $K = 1$ to alleviate the problem of overfitting on local neighborhood structures for graphs with very wide node degree distributions. By approximating $\lambda_{max} \approx 2$, the equation simplifies to

$$g_{\theta'} \star x \approx \theta'_0 x + \theta'_1 (L - I_N) x = \theta'_0 x - \theta'_1 D^{-\frac{1}{2}} A D^{-\frac{1}{2}} x \tag{5.10}$$

with two free parameters θ_0' and θ_1'. After constraining the number of parameters with $\theta = \theta_0' = -\theta_1'$, we get

$$g_\theta \star x \approx \theta\left(I_N + D^{-\frac{1}{2}}AD^{-\frac{1}{2}}\right)x \tag{5.11}$$

Non-spectral approaches define convolutions directly on the graph, operating on spatially close neighbors. The major challenge with non-spectral approaches is defining the convolution operation with differently sized neighborhoods and maintaining the local invariance of CNNs.

Neural fingerprints (FP) [15] use different weight matrices for nodes with different degrees,

$$x = h_v^{t-1} + \sum_{i=1}^{|\mathcal{N}_v|} h_i^{t-1}$$
$$h_v^t = \sigma\left(xW_t^{|\mathcal{N}_v|}\right) \tag{5.12}$$

where $W_t^{|\mathcal{N}_v|}$ is the weight matrix for nodes with degree $|\mathcal{N}_v|$ at layer t. The main drawback of the method is that it cannot be applied to large-scale graphs with more node degrees.

Diffusion-convolutional neural networks (DCNNs) were proposed in [16].Transition matrices are used to define the neighborhood for nodes in DCNN. For node classification, it has the form

$$H = f(W^c \odot P^*X) \tag{5.13}$$

where X is an $N \times F$ tensor of input features (N is the number of nodes, and F is the number of features). P^* is an $N \times K \times N$ tensor that contains the power series $\{P, P^2, ..., P^K\}$ of matrix P, and P is the degree-normalized transition matrix from the graph adjacency matrix A. Each entity is transformed to a diffusion convolutional representation that is a $K \times F$ matrix defined by K hops of graph diffusion over F features. It will then be defined by a $K \times F$ weight matrix and a nonlinear activation function f. Finally, H (which is $N \times K \times F$) denotes the diffusion representations of each node in the graph. As for graph classification, DCNN simply takes the average of nodes' representation,

$$H = f\left(W^c \odot 1_N^T P^*X/N\right) \tag{5.14}$$

and 1_N here is an $N \times 1$ vector of ones. DCNN can also be applied to edge classification tasks, which requires converting edges to nodes and augmenting the adjacency matrix.

Dual graph convolutional network (DGCN) [17]: This jointly considers the local consistency and global consistency on graphs. It uses two convolutional networks to capture the local/global consistency and adopts an unsupervised loss function to ensemble them. As the first step, let us note that stacking the operator in Eq. (5.11) could lead to numerical instabilities and exploding/vanishing gradients, so [14] introduces the *renormalization trick*: $I_N + D^{-\frac{1}{2}}AD^{-\frac{1}{2}} \to \widetilde{D}^{-\frac{1}{2}}\widetilde{A}\widetilde{D}^{-\frac{1}{2}}$, with $\widetilde{A} = A + I_N$ and $\widetilde{D}_{ij} = \sum_j \widetilde{A}_{ij}$. Finally, [14] generalizes the definition to a signal $X \in \mathbb{R}^{N \times C}$ with C input channels and F filters for feature maps as follows:

$$Z = \widetilde{D}^{-\frac{1}{2}}\widetilde{A}\widetilde{D}^{-\frac{1}{2}}X\Theta \tag{5.15}$$

where $\Theta \in \mathbb{R}^{C \times F}$ is a matrix of filter parameters, and $Z \in \mathbb{R}^{N \times F}$ is the convolved signal matrix. The first convolutional network for *DGCN* is the same as Eq. (5.15). The second network replaces the adjacency matrix with a positive pointwise mutual information (PPMI) matrix:

$$H' = \rho\left(D_P^{-\frac{1}{2}}X_P D_P^{-\frac{1}{2}}H\Theta\right) \tag{5.16}$$

where X_P is the PPMI matrix, and D_P is the diagonal degree matrix of X_P.

When dealing with large-scale networks, low-dimensional vector embeddings of nodes in large graphs have proved extremely useful as feature inputs for a wide variety of prediction and graph analysis tasks [18–22]. The basic idea behind node-embedding approaches is to use dimensionality reduction techniques to distill the high-dimensional information about a node's graph neighborhood into a dense vector embedding. These node embeddings can then be fed to downstream machine learning systems and aid in tasks such as node classification, clustering, and link prediction [19–21].

GraphSAGE (SAmple and aggreGatE) [23] is a general inductive framework. The framework generates embeddings by sampling and aggregating features from a node's local neighborhood.

$$
\begin{aligned}
h^t_{N_v} &= AG_t\left(\left\{h^{t-1}_u, \forall u \in \mathcal{N}_v\right\}\right) \\
h^t_v &= \sigma\left(W^t \cdot \left[h^{t-1}_v \big\| h^t_{N_v}\right]\right)
\end{aligned}
\tag{5.17}
$$

However, the original work utilizes in Eq. (5.17) only a fixed-size set of neighbors by uniformly sampling. Three aggregator functions are used.

The mean aggregator could be viewed as an approximation of the convolutional operation from the transductive GCN framework [14], so that the inductive version of the GCN variant could be derived by

$$
h^t_v = \sigma\left(W \cdot mean\left(\left\{h^{t-1}_v\right\} \cup \left\{h^{t-1}_u, \forall u \in \mathcal{N}_v\right\}\right)\right)
\tag{5.18}
$$

The mean aggregator is different from other aggregators because it does not perform the concatenation operation that concatenates h^{t-1}_v and $h^t_{N_v}$ in Eq. (5.17). It could be viewed as a form of "skip connection" [24] and could achieve better performance.

The long short-term memory (LSTM) aggregator, which has a larger expressive capability, is also used. However, LSTMs process inputs in a sequential manner so that they are not permutation invariant. Reference [23] adapts LSTMs to operate on an unordered set by permutating the node's neighbors.

Pooling aggregator: In the pooling aggregator, each neighbor's hidden state is fed through a fully connected layer, after which a max -pooling operation is applied to the set of the node's neighbors:

$$
h^t_{N_v} = \max\left(\left\{\sigma\left(W_{pool} h^{t-1}_u + b\right), \forall u \in \mathcal{N}_v\right\}\right)
\tag{5.19}
$$

Note that any symmetric function could be used in place of the max -pooling operation here. The operation of *GraphSAGE* is illustrated in Figure 5.1 [23].

Gate: Several works have attempted to use a gate mechanism such as gate recurrent units (GRUs) [25] or LSTM [26] in the propagation step to mitigate the restrictions in the former GNN models and improve the long-term propagation of information across the graph structure.

Gated graph neural network (GGNN) [27] uses GRUs in the propagation step, unrolls the recurrence for a fixed number of steps T, and uses backpropagation through time in order to compute gradients. So, the propagation model can be presented as

$$
\begin{aligned}
a^t_v &= A^T_v \left[h^{t-1}_1 ... h^{t-1}_N\right]^T + b \\
z^t_v &= \sigma\left(W^z a^t_v + U^z h^{t-1}_v\right) \\
r^t_v &= \sigma\left(W^r a^t_v + U^r h^{t-1}_v\right) \\
\overline{h^t_v} &= \tanh\left(W a^t_v + U\left(r^t_v \odot h^{t-1}_v\right)\right) \\
h^t_v &= \left(1 - z^t_v\right) \odot h^{t-1}_v + z^t_v \odot \overline{h^t_v}
\end{aligned}
\tag{5.20}
$$

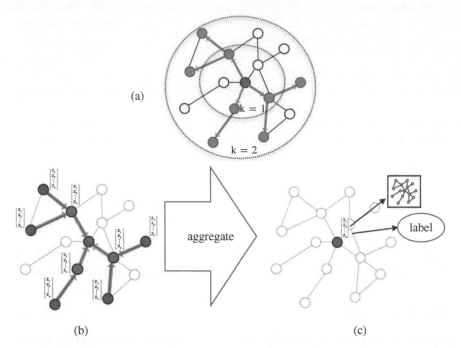

Figure 5.1 Operation of GraphSAGE: (a) sample neighborhood, (b) aggregate feature information from neighbors, (c) predict graph context and label using aggregated information. *Source:* Hamilton et al. [23].

The node v first aggregates message from its neighbors, where A_v is the submatrix of the graph adjacency matrix A and denotes the connection of node v with its neighbors. The GRU-like update functions incorporate information from the other nodes and from the previous time step to update each node's hidden state. Matrix a gathers the neighborhood information of node v, and z and r are the update and reset gates.

LSTM architecture extensions, referred to as the *Child-Sum Tree-LSTM* and the *N-ary Tree-LSTM*, are presented in [28]. As in standard LSTM units, each Tree-LSTM unit (indexed by v) contains input and output gates i_v and o_v, a memory cell c_v, and a hidden state h_v. Instead of a single forget gate, the Tree-LSTM unit contains one forget gate f_{vk} for each child k, allowing the unit to selectively incorporate information from each child. The Child-Sum Tree-LSTM transition equations are given as

$$\overline{h_v^{t-1}} = \sum_{k \in \mathcal{N}_v} h_k^{t-1}; \quad i_v^t = \sigma\left(W^i x_v^t + U^i \overline{h_v^{t-1}} + b^i\right)$$
$$f_{vk}^t = \sigma\left(W^f x_v^t + U^f h_k^{t-1} + b^f\right)$$
$$o_v^t = \sigma\left(W^o x_v^t + U^o \overline{h_v^{t-1}} + b^o\right) \tag{5.21}$$
$$u_v^t = \tanh\left(W^u x_v^t + U^u \overline{h_v^{t-1}} + b^u\right)$$
$$c_v^t = i_v^t \odot u_v^t + \sum_{k \in \mathcal{N}_v} f_{vk}^t \odot c_k^{t-1}; \quad h_v^t = o_v^t \odot \tanh\left(c_v^t\right)$$

x_v^t is the input vector at time t in the standard LSTM setting. If the branching factor of a tree is at most K and all children of a node are ordered, – that is, they can be indexed from 1 to K – then the N-ary Tree-LSTM can be used. For node v, h_{vk}^t and c_{vk}^t denote the hidden state and memory cell of its k-th child at time t, respectively. The transition equations are now

$$i_v^t = \sigma\left(W^i x_v^t + \sum_{l=1}^{K} U_l^i h_{vl}^{t-1} + b^i\right)$$

$$f_{vk}^t = \sigma\left(W^f x_v^t + \sum_{l=1}^{K} U_{kl}^f h_{vl}^{t-1} + b^f\right)$$

$$o_v^t = \sigma\left(W^o x_v^t + \sum_{l=1}^{K} U_l^o h_{vl}^{t-1} + b^o\right) \qquad (5.22)$$

$$u_v^t = \tanh\left(W^u x_v^t + \sum_{l=1}^{K} U_l^u h_{vl}^{t-1} + b^u\right)$$

$$c_v^t = i_v^t \odot u_v^t + \sum_{l=1}^{K} f_{vl}^t \odot c_{vl}^{t-1}; h_v^t = o_v^t \odot \tanh\left(c_v^t\right)$$

The introduction of separate parameter matrices for each child k allows the model to learn more fine-grained representations conditioning on the states of a unit's children than the Child-Sum Tree-LSTM.

The two types of Tree-LSTMs can be easily adapted to the graph. The graph-structured LSTM in [29] is an example of the N-ary Tree-LSTM applied to the graph. However, it is a simplified version since each node in the graph has at most two incoming edges (from its parent and sibling predecessor). Reference [30] proposed another variant of the Graph LSTM based on the relation extraction task. The main difference between graphs and trees is that edges of graphs have labels. Work in [30] utilizes different weight matrices to represent different labels:

$$i_v^t = \sigma\left(W^i x_v^t + \sum_{k\in\mathcal{N}_v} U_{m(v,k)}^i h_k^{t-1} + b^i\right)$$

$$f_{vk}^t = \sigma\left(W^f x_v^t + U_{m(v,k)}^f h_k^{t-1} + b^f\right)$$

$$o_v^t = \sigma\left(W^o x_v^t + \sum_{k\in\mathcal{N}_v} U_{m(v,k)}^o h_k^{t-1} + b^o\right) \qquad (5.23)$$

$$u_v^t = \tanh\left(W^u x_v^t + \sum_{k\in\mathcal{N}_v} U_{m(v,k)}^u h_k^{t-1} + b^u\right)$$

$$c_v^t = i_v^t \odot u_v^t + \sum_{k\in\mathcal{N}_v} f_{vk}^t \odot c_k^{t-1}; h_v^t = o_v^t \odot \tanh\left(c_v^t\right)$$

where $m(v, k)$ denotes the edge label between node v and k.

The attention mechanism has been successfully used in many sequence-based tasks such as machine translation [31–33] and machine reading [34]. Work in [35] proposed a graph attention network (GAT) that incorporates the attention mechanism into the propagation step. It computes the hidden states of each node by attending to its neighbors, following a *self-attention* strategy. The work defines a single *graph attentional layer* and constructs arbitrary GATs by stacking this layer. The layer computes the coefficients in the attention mechanism of the node pair (i, j) by

$$\alpha_{ij} = \exp\left(\text{LeakyReLU}\left(a^T\left[Wh_i \| Wh_j\right]\right)\right) / \left(\sum_{j\in\mathcal{N}_i} \exp\left(\text{LeakyReLU}\left(a^T\left[Wh_i \| Wh_k\right]\right)\right)\right) \qquad (5.24)$$

where α_{ij} is the attention coefficient of node j to i, and $\mathcal{N}_i$ represents the neighborhoods of node i in the graph. The input set of node features to the layer is $h = \{h_1, h_2, ..., h_N\}$, $h_i \in \mathbb{R}^F$, where N is the number of nodes, and F is the number of features of each node; the layer produces a new set of node features (of potentially different cardinality F'), $h' = \{h'_1, h'_2, ..., h'_N\}$, $h'_i \in \mathbb{R}^{F'}$, as its output. $W \in \mathbb{R}^{F' \times F}$ is the *weight matrix* of a shared linear transformation that is applied to every node, and a $\in \mathbb{R}^{2F'}$ is the weight vector of a single-layer FNN. It is normalized by a softmax function, and the LeakyReLU nonlinearity (with negative input slope $\alpha = 0.2$) is applied. After applying a non-linearity, the final output features of each node can be obtained as

$$h'_i = \sigma\left(\sum\nolimits_{j \in \mathcal{N}_i} \alpha_{ij} \mathrm{W} h_j\right) \tag{5.25}$$

The layer utilizes *multi-head attention* similarly to [33] to stabilize the learning process. It applies K independent attention mechanisms to compute the hidden states and then concatenates their features (or computes the average), resulting in the following two output representations:

$$h'_i = \mathop{\|}_{k=1}^{K} \sigma\left(\sum\nolimits_{j \in \mathcal{N}_i} \alpha_{ij}^k \mathrm{W}^k h_j\right) concatenates \tag{5.26}$$

$$h'_i = \sigma\left(\frac{1}{K}\sum\nolimits_{k=1}^{K}\sum\nolimits_{j \in \mathcal{N}_i} \alpha_{ij}^k \mathrm{W}^k h_j\right) or\ averages \tag{5.27}$$

where α_{ij}^k is the normalized attention coefficient computed by the k-th attention mechanism. The attention architecture in [35] has several properties: (i) the computation of the node-neighbor pairs is parallelizable, thus making the operation efficient; (ii) it can be applied to graph nodes with different degrees by specifying arbitrary weights to neighbors; and (iii) it can be easily applied to inductive learning problems.

Apart from different variants of GNNs, several general frameworks have been proposed that aim to integrate different models into a single framework.

Message passing neural networks (MPNNs) [36]: This framework abstracts the commonalities between several of the most popular models for graph-structured data, such as spectral approaches and non-spectral approaches in graph convolution, gated GNNs, interaction networks, molecular graph convolutions, and deep tensor neural networks. The model contains two phases, a *message passing phase* and a *readout phase*. The message passing phase (namely, the propagation step) runs for T time steps and is defined in terms of th message function M_t and the vertex update function U_t. Using messages m_v^t, the updating functions of the hidden states h_v^t are

$$\begin{aligned} m_v^{t+1} &= \sum\nolimits_{w \in \mathcal{N}_v} M_t\left(h_v^t, h_w^t, e_{vw}\right) \\ h_v^{t+1} &= U_t\left(h_v^t, m_v^{t+1}\right) \end{aligned} \tag{5.28}$$

where e_{vw} represents features of the edge from node v to w. The readout phase computes a feature vector for the whole graph using the readout function R according to

$$\hat{y} = R\left(\{h_v^T \mid v \in G\}\right) \tag{5.29}$$

where T denotes the total time steps. The message function M_t, vertex update function U_t, and readout function R could have different settings. Hence, the MPNN framework could generalize several different models via different function settings. Here, we give an example of generalizing GGNN, and other models' function settings could be found in Eq. (5.36). The function settings for GGNNs are

$$\begin{aligned} M_t\left(h_v^t, h_w^t, e_{vw}\right) &= A_{e_{vw}} h_w^t \\ U_t &= GRU\left(h_v^t, m_v^{t+1}\right) \\ R &= \sum_{v \in V} \sigma\left(i\left(h_v^T, h_v^0\right)\right) \odot \left(j\left(h_v^T\right)\right) \end{aligned} \tag{5.30}$$

where $A_{e_{vw}}$ is the adjacency matrix, one for each edge label e. The GRU is the gated recurrent unit introduced in [25]. i and j are neural networks in function R.

Non-local neural networks (NLNN) are proposed for capturing long-range dependencies with deep neural networks by computing the response at a position as a weighted sum of the features at all positions (in space, time, or spacetime). The generic non-local operation is defined as

$$h'_i = \frac{1}{\mathcal{C}(h)} \sum_{\forall j} f(h_i, h_j) g(h_j) \tag{5.31}$$

where i is the index of an output position, and j is the index that enumerates all possible positions. $f(h_i, h_j)$ computes a scalar between i and j representing the relation between them. $g(h_j)$ denotes a transformation of the input h_j, and a factor $1/\mathcal{C}(h)$ is utilized to normalize the results.

There are several instantiations with different f and g settings. For simplicity, the linear transformation can be used as the function g. That means $g(h_j) = W_g h_j$, where W_g is a learned weight matrix. *The Gaussian function* is a natural choice for function f, giving $f(h_i, h_j) = e^{h_i^T h_j}$, where $h_i^T h_j$ is dot-product similarity and $\mathcal{C}(h) = \sum_{\forall j} f(h_i, h_j)$. It is straightforward to extend the Gaussian function by computing similarity in the embedding space giving $f(h_i, h_j) = e^{\theta(h_i)^T \varphi(h_j)}$ with $\theta(h_i) = W_\theta h_i$, $\varphi(h_j) = W \varphi h_j$, and $\mathcal{C}(h) = \sum_{\forall j} f(h_i, h_j)$. The function f can also be implemented as a dot-product similarity $f(h_i, h_j) = \theta(h_i)^T \varphi(h_j)$. Here, the factor $\mathcal{C}(h) = N$, where N is the number of positions in h. Concatenation can also be used, defined as $f(h_i, h_j) = \text{ReLU}\left(w_f^T \left[\theta(h_i) \| \varphi(h_j)\right]\right)$, where w_f is a weight vector projecting the vector to a scalar and $\mathcal{C}(h) = N$.

5.1.3 Graph Networks

The Graph Network (GN) framework [37] generalizes and extends various GNN, MPNN, and NLNN approaches. A graph is defined as a 3-tuple $G = (u, H, E)$ (H is used instead of V for notational consistency). u is a global attribute, $H = \{h_i\}_{i=1:N^v}$ is the set of nodes (of cardinality N^v), where each h_i is a node's attribute. $E = \{(e_k, r_k, s_k)\}_{k=1:N^e}$ is the set of edges (of cardinality N^e), where each e_k is the edge's attribute, r_k is the index of the receiver node, and s_k is the index of the sender node.

GN block contains three "update" functions, φ, and three "aggregation" functions, ρ,

$$\begin{aligned}
e'_k &= \varphi^e(e_k, h_{r_k}, h_{s_k}, u); & \bar{e}'_i &= \rho^{e \to h}(E'_i) \\
h'_i &= \varphi^h(\bar{e}'_i, h_i, u); & \bar{e}' &= \rho^{e \to u}(E') \\
u' &= \varphi^u(\bar{e}', \bar{h}', u); & \bar{h}' &= \rho^{h \to u}(H')
\end{aligned} \tag{5.32}$$

where $E'_i = \{(e'_k, r_k, s_k)\}_{r_k=i,k=1:N^e}$, $H' = \{h'_i\}_{i=1:N^v}$, and $E' = \bigcup_i E'_i = \{(e'_k, r_k, s_k)\}_{k=1:N^e}$. The ρ functions must be invariant to permutations of their inputs and should take variable numbers of arguments.

The computation steps of a GN block:

---

1) φ^e is applied per edge, with arguments $(e_k, h_{r_k}, h_{s_k}, u)$, and returns e'_k. The set of resulting per-edge outputs for each node i is, $E'_i = \{(e'_k, r_k, s_k)\}_{r_k=i,k=1:N^e}$, and $E' = \bigcup_i E'_i = \{(e'_k, r_k, s_k)\}_{k=1:N^e}$ is the set of all per-edge outputs.

2) $\rho^{e \to h}$ is applied to E'_i, and aggregates the edge updates for edges that project to vertex i, into $\bar{e}'_i$, which will be used in the next step's node update.

3) φ^h is applied to each node i, to compute an updated node attribute, h'_i. The set of resulting per-node outputs is $H' = \{h'_i\}_{i=1:N^v}$.

4) $\rho^{e \to u}$ is applied to E', and aggregates all edge updates, into $\bar{e}'$, which will then be used in the next step's global update.
5) $\rho^{h \to u}$ is applied to H', and aggregates all node updates, into $\bar{h}'$, which will then be used in the next step's global update.
6) φ^u is applied once per graph and computes an update for the global attribute, u'.

5.2 Categorization and Modeling of GNN

In the previous section, we have briefly surveyed a number of GNN designs with the very basic description of their principles. Here, we categorize these options into recurrent graph neural networks (*RecGNNs*), convolutional graph neural networks (*ConvGNNs*), graph autoencoders (*GAEs*), and spatial-temporal graph neural networks (*STGNNs*) and provide more details about their operations.

Figures 5.2–5.5, inspired by [38], give examples of various model architectures. In the following, we provide more information for each category, mainly on *computation of the state, the learning algorithm*, and *transition and output function implementations*.

5.2.1 RecGNNs

These networks go back to the beginnings of GNNs. They apply the same set of parameters recurrently over nodes in a graph to extract high-level node representations. Limited by computational power, earlier research mainly focused on directed acyclic graphs, while later works extended these models to handle general types of graphs, for example, acyclic, cyclic, directed, and undirected graphs [1]. Based on an information diffusion mechanism, this particular GNN (in the sequel referred to as GNN*) updates nodes' states by exchanging neighborhood information recurrently until a stable equilibrium is reached. A node's hidden state is recurrently updated by

$$h_v^{(t)} = \sum_{u \in N(v)} f\left(x_v, x_{(v,u)}^e, x_u, h_u^{(t-1)}\right), \tag{5.33}$$

where $f(\cdot)$ is a parametric function, and $h_v^{(0)}$ is initialized randomly. The sum operation enables GNN* to be applicable to all nodes, even if the number of neighbors differs and no neighborhood ordering is known. To ensure convergence, the recurrent function $f(\cdot)$ must be a contraction mapping, which shrinks the distance between two points after projecting them into a latent space. If $f(\cdot)$ is a neural network, a penalty term has to be imposed on the Jacobian matrix of parameters. When a convergence criterion is satisfied, the last step node's hidden states are forwarded to a readout layer. GNN* alternates the stage of node state propagation and the stage of parameter gradient computation to minimize a training objective. This strategy enables GNN to handle cyclic graphs.

Graph Echo State Network (GraphESN), developed in follow-up works [40], extends echo state networks to improve the training efficiency of GNN*. GraphESN consists of an encoder and an output layer. The encoder is randomly initialized and requires no training. It implements a contractive state transition function to recurrently update node states until the global graph state reaches convergence. Afterward, the output layer is trained by taking the fixed node states as inputs.

Figure 5.2 Illustrations of ConvGNN network: (a) A ConvGNN with multiple graph convolutional layers. A graph convolutional layer encapsulates each node's hidden representation by aggregating feature information from its neighbors. After feature aggregation, a nonlinear transformation is applied to the resulted outputs. By stacking multiple layers, the final hidden representation of each node receives messages from a further neighborhood. (b) Recurrent Graph Neural Networks (RecGNNs) use the same graph recurrent layer (Grec) to update node representations. (c) Convolutional Graph Neural Networks (ConvGNNs) use a different graph convolutional layer (Gconv) to update node representations. *Source:* Wu et al. [38]. (For more details see color figure in bins).

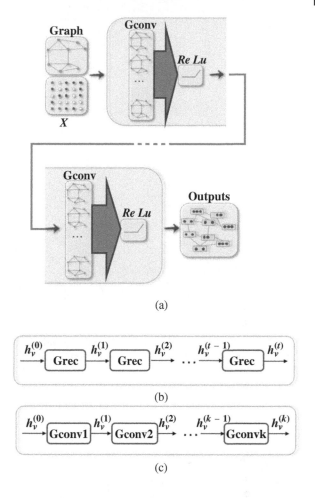

(a)

(b)

(c)

Figure 5.3 2D Convolution versus graph convolution: (a) 2D convolution. Analogous to a graph, each pixel in an image is taken as a node where neighbors are determined by the filter size. The 2D convolution takes the weighted average of pixel values of the red node along with its neighbors. The neighbors of a node are ordered and have a fixed size. (b) Graph convolution. To get a hidden representation of the red node, one simple solution of the graph convolutional operation is to take the average value of the node features of the red node along with its neighbors. Unlike image data, the neighbors of a node are unordered and variable in size. *Source:* Wu et al. [38].

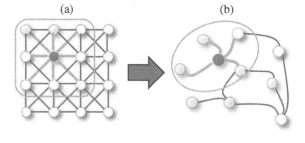

GGNN [41] employs a GRU [42] as a recurrent function, reducing the recurrence to a fixed number of steps. The advantage is that it no longer needs to constrain parameters to ensure convergence. A node's hidden state is updated by its previous hidden states and its neighboring hidden states, defined as

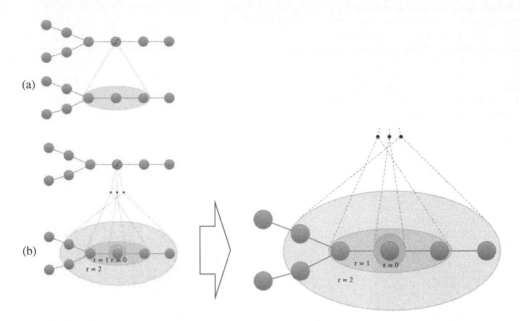

Figure 5.4 Parametric graph convolution: (a) Conventional graph convolutional concept. (b) Parametric graph convolution, where r controls the maximum distance of the considered neighborhood, and the dimensionality of the output [39].

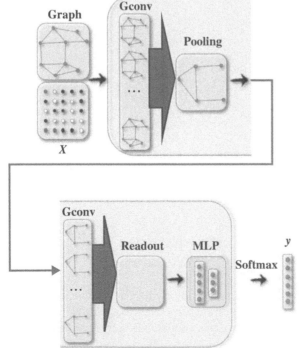

Figure 5.5 A ConvGNN with pooling and readout layers for graph classification. A graph convolutional layer is followed by a pooling layer to coarsen a graph into subgraphs so that node representations on coarsened graphs represent higher graph-level representations. A readout layer summarizes the final graph representation by taking the sum/mean of hidden representations of subgraphs. *Source:* Wu et al. [38]. (For more details see color figure in bins).

$$h_v^{(t)} = GRU\left(h_v^{(t-1)}, \sum_{u \in N(v)} W h_u^{(t-1)}\right),$$ (5.34)

where $h_v^{(0)} = x_v$. Unlike GNN and GraphESN, GGNN uses the backpropagation through time (BPTT) algorithm to learn the model parameters. This can be problematic for large graphs, as GGNN needs to run the recurrent function multiple times over all nodes, requiring the intermediate states of all nodes to be stored in memory.

Stochastic Steady-state Embedding (SSE) uses a learning algorithm that is more scalable to large graphs [43]. It updates a node's hidden states recurrently in a stochastic and asynchronous fashion. It alternatively samples a batch of nodes for state update and a batch of nodes for gradient computation. To maintain stability, the recurrent function of SSE is defined as a weighted average of the historical states and new states, which takes the form

$$h_v^{(t)} = (1-\alpha)h_v^{(t-1)} + \alpha W_1 \sigma\left(W_2\left[x_v, \sum_{u \in N(v)}\left[h_u^{(t-1)}, x_u\right]\right]\right),$$ (5.35)

where α is a hyperparameter, and $h_v^{(0)}$ is initialized randomly. Although conceptually important, SSE does not theoretically prove that the node states will gradually converge to fixed points by applying Eq. (5.35) repeatedly.

5.2.2 ConvGNNs

These networks are closely related to recurrent GNNs. Instead of iterating node states with contractive constraints, they address the cyclic mutual dependencies architecturally using a fixed number of layers with different weights in each layer, as illustrated in Figure 5.2a. This key distinction from recurrent GNNs is illustrated in Figures 5.2b and 5.2c. As graph convolutions are more efficient and convenient to composite with other neural networks, the popularity of ConvGNNs has been rapidly growing in recent years. These networks fall into two categories, spectral-based and spatial-based. Spectral-based approaches define graph convolutions by introducing filters from the perspective of graph signal processing [44] where the graph convolutional operation is interpreted as removing noise from graph signals. Spatial-based approaches inherit ideas from RecGNNs to define graph convolutions by information propagation. Since GCN [14] bridged the gap between spectral-based approaches and spatial-based approaches, spatial-based methods have developed rapidly recently due to their attractive efficiency, flexibility, and generality.

Spectral-based ConvGNNs assume graphs to be undirected. The normalized graph Laplacian matrix is a mathematical representation of an undirected graph, defined as $L = I_n - D^{-\frac{1}{2}}AD^{-\frac{1}{2}}$, where D is a diagonal matrix of node degrees, $D_{ii} = \sum_j(A_{i,j})$. For details, see Appendix 5.A. The normalized graph *Laplacian matrix* possesses the property of being real symmetric positive semidefinite. With this property, the normalized Laplacian matrix can be factored as $L = U\Lambda U^T$, where $U = [u_0, u_1, \cdots, u_{n-1}] \in R^{n \times n}$ is the matrix of eigenvectors ordered by eigenvalues, and Λ is the diagonal matrix of eigenvalues (spectrum), $\Lambda_{ii} = \lambda_i$. The eigenvectors of the normalized Laplacian matrix form an orthonormal space, in mathematical words $U^T U = I$. In graph signal processing, a graph signal $x \in R^n$ is a feature vector of all nodes of a graph where x_i is the value of the i-th node. The *graph Fourier transform* to a signal x is defined as $\mathcal{F}(x) = U^T x$, and the inverse graph Fourier transform is defined as $\mathcal{F}^{-1}(\hat{x}) = U\hat{x}$, where $\hat{x}$ represents the resulting signal from the graph Fourier transform. For more details, see Appendix 5.A. The graph Fourier transform projects the input graph signal to the orthonormal space where the basis is formed by eigenvectors of the normalized graph Laplacian. Elements of the transformed signal $\hat{x}$ are the coordinates of the graph signal in the new space so that the input signal can be represented as $x = \sum_i \hat{x}_i u_i$, which is exactly the inverse graph Fourier transform. Now, the graph convolution $*_G$ of the input signal x with a filter $g \in R^n$ is defined as

$$x *_G g = \mathcal{F}^{-1}(\mathcal{F}(x) \odot \mathcal{F}(g)) = U(U^T x \odot U^T g), \tag{5.36}$$

where $\odot$ denotes the element-wise product. If we denote a filter as $g_\theta = diag(U^T g)$, then the *spectral graph convolution* $*_G$ is simplified as

$$x *_G g_\theta = U g_\theta U^T x. \tag{5.37}$$

Spectral-based ConvGNNs all follow this definition. The key difference lies in the choice of the filter g_θ.

Spectral Convolutional Neural Network (Spectral CNN) [12] assumes the filter $g_\theta = \Theta_{i,j}^{(k)}$ is a set of learnable parameters and considers graph signals with multiple channels. The graph convolutional layer of Spectral CNN is defined as

$$H_{:,j}^{(k)} = \sigma\left(\sum_{i=1}^{f_{k-1}} U\Theta_{i,j}^{(k)} U^T H_{:,i}^{(k-1)}\right) f(\ j = 1, 2, \cdots, f_k), \tag{5.38}$$

where k is the layer index, $H^{(k-1)} \in R^{n \times f_{k-1}}$ is the input graph signal, $H^{(0)} = X$, f_{k-1} is the number of input channels and f_k is the number of output channels, and $\Theta_{i,j}^{(k)}$ is a diagonal matrix filled with learnable parameters. Due to the eigen decomposition of the Laplacian matrix, spectral CNN faces three limitations: (i) any perturbation to a graph results in a change of eigenbasis; (ii) the learned filters are domain dependent, meaning they cannot be applied to a graph with a different structure; and (iii) eigen decomposition requires $O(n^3)$ computational complexity. In follow-up works, ChebNet [45] and GCN [14, 46] reduced the computational complexity to $O(m)$ by making several approximations and simplifications.

Chebyshev Spectral CNN (ChebNet) [45] approximates the filter g_θ by Chebyshev polynomials of the diagonal matrix of eigenvalues, that is, $g_\theta = \sum_{i=0} \theta_i T_i(\tilde{\Lambda})$, where $\tilde{\Lambda} = 2\Lambda/\lambda_{max} - I_n$, and the values of $\tilde{\Lambda}$ lie in $[-1, 1]$. The Chebyshev polynomials are defined recursively by $T_i(x) = 2xT_{i-1}(x) - T_{i-2}(x)$ with $T_0(x) = 1$ and $T_1(x) = x$. As a result, the convolution of a graph signal x with the defined filter g_θ is

$$x *_G g_\theta = U\left(\sum_{i=0}^{K} \theta_i T_i(\tilde{\Lambda})\right) U^T x, \tag{5.39}$$

where $\tilde{L} = 2L/\lambda_{max} - I_n$. As $T_i(\tilde{L}) = UT_i(\tilde{\Lambda})U^T$, which can be proved by induction on i. ChebNet takes the form

$$x *_G g_\theta = \sum_{i=0}^{K} \theta_i T_i(\tilde{L}) x, \tag{5.40}$$

As an improvement over spectral CNN, the filters defined by ChebNet are localized in space, which means filters can extract local features independently of the graph size. The spectrum of ChebNet is mapped to $[-1, 1]$ linearly. CayleyNet [47] further applies Cayley polynomials, which are parametric rational complex functions, to capture narrow frequency bands. The spectral graph convolution of CayleyNet is defined as

$$x *_G g_\theta = c_0 x + 2 Re\left\{\sum_{j=1}^{r} c_j (hL - iI)^j (hL + iI)^{-j} x\right\}, \tag{5.41}$$

where $Re(\cdot)$ returns the real part of a complex number, c_0 is a real coefficent, c_j is a complex coefficent, i is the imaginary number, and h is a parameter that controls the spectrum of a Cayley filter. While preserving spatial locality, CayleyNet shows that ChebNet can be considered as a special case of CayleyNet.

GCN [14] introduces a first-order approximation of ChebNet. Assuming $K = 1$ and $\lambda_{max} = 2$, Eq. (5.40) is simplified as

$$x*_G g_\theta = \theta_0 x - \theta_1 D^{-\frac{1}{2}} A D^{-\frac{1}{2}} x. \tag{5.42}$$

To restrict the number of parameters and avoid overfitting, GCN further assume $\theta = \theta_0 = -\theta_1$, leading to the following definition of a graph convolution:

$$X*_G g_\theta = \theta \left(I_n + D^{-\frac{1}{2}} A D^{-\frac{1}{2}} \right) x. \tag{5.43}$$

To allow multi-channels of inputs and outputs, GCN modifies Eq. (5.43) into a compositional layer, defined as

$$H = X*_G g_\theta = f(\bar{A} X \Theta), \tag{5.44}$$

where $\bar{A} = I_n + D^{-\frac{1}{2}} A D^{-\frac{1}{2}}$ and $f(\cdot)$ is an activation function. Using $I_n + D^{-\frac{1}{2}} A D^{-\frac{1}{2}}$ empirically causes numerical instability to GCN. To address this problem, GCN applies a normalization to replace $\bar{A} = I_n + D^{-\frac{1}{2}} A D^{-\frac{1}{2}}$ by $\bar{A} = \tilde{D}^{-\frac{1}{2}} \tilde{A} \tilde{D}^{-\frac{1}{2}}$ with $\tilde{A} = A + I_n$ and $\tilde{D}_{ii} = \sum_j \tilde{A}_{ij}$. Being a spectral-based method, GCN can be also interpreted as a spatial-based method. From a spatial-based perspective, GCN can be considered as aggregating feature information from a node's neighborhood. Equation (5.44) can be expressed as

$$h_v = f \left(\Theta^T \left(\sum_{u \in \{N(v) \cup v\}} \bar{A}_{v,u} x_u \right) \right) \forall v \in V. \tag{5.45}$$

Several recent works made incremental improvements over GCN [14] by exploring alternative symmetric matrices.

Adaptive Graph Convolutional Network (AGCN) [16] learns hidden structural relations unspecified by the graph adjacency matrix. It constructs a so-called residual graph adjacency matrix through a learnable distance function that takes two nodes' features as inputs.

DGCN [17] introduces a dual graph convolutional architecture with two graph convolutional layers in parallel. While these two layers share parameters, they use the normalized adjacency matrix $\bar{A}$ and the PPMI matrix, which capture nodes' co-occurrence information through random walks sampled from a graph. The PPMI matrix is defined as

$$PPMI_{v_1, v_2} = max \left(log \left(\frac{count(v_1, v_2) \cdot |D|}{count(v_1) count(v_2)} \right), 0 \right), \tag{5.46}$$

where $v_1, v_2 \in V$, $|D| = \sum_{v_1, v_2} count(v_1, v_2)$, and the $count(\cdot)$ function returns the frequency with which node v and/or node u co-occur/occur in sampled random walks. By ensembling outputs from dual graph convolutional layers, DGCN encodes both local and global structural information without the need to stack multiple graph convolutional layers.

Spatial-based ConvGNNs: Analogous to the convolutional operation of a conventional CNN on an image, spatial-based methods define graph convolutions based on a node's spatial relations. Images can be considered as a special form of graph with each pixel representing a node. Each pixel is directly connected to its nearby pixels, as illustrated in Figure 5.3a (adopted from [38]). A filter is applied to a 3×3 patch by taking the weighted average of pixel values of the central node and its neighbors across each channel. Similarly, the spatial-based graph convolutions convolve the central node's representation with its neighbors' representations to derive the updated representation for the central node, as illustrated in Figure 5.3b. From another perspective, spatial-based ConvGNNs share the same idea of information propagation/message passing with RecGNNs. The spatial graph convolutional operation essentially propagates node information along edges.

Neural Network for Graphs (NN4G) [48]: Proposed in parallel with GNN∗, this is the first work toward spatial-based ConvGNNs. Distinctively different from RecGNNs, NN4G learns graph mutual dependency through a compositional neural architecture with independent parameters at each layer. The neighborhood of a node can be extended through incremental construction of the architecture. NN4G performs graph convolutions by summing up a node's neighborhood information directly. It also applies residual connections and skips connections to memorize information over each layer. As a result, NN4G derives its next layer node states by

$$\mathbf{h}_v^{(k)} = f\left(\mathbf{W}^{(k)^T}\mathbf{x}_v + \sum_{i=1}^{k-1}\sum_{u \in N(v)} \Theta^{(k)^T}\mathbf{h}_u^{(k-1)}\right),\tag{5.47}$$

where $f(\cdot)$ is an activation function and $\mathbf{h}_v^{(0)} = 0$. The equation can also be written in a matrix form:

$$\mathbf{H}^{(k)} = f\left(\mathbf{X}\mathbf{W}^{(k)} + \sum_{i=1}^{k-1}\mathbf{A}\mathbf{H}^{(k-1)}\Theta^{(k)}\right),\tag{5.48}$$

which resembles the form of GCN [14]. One difference is that NN4G uses the unnormalized adjacency matrix, which may potentially cause hidden node states to have extremely different scales.

Contextual Graph Markov Model (CGMM) [20] proposes a probabilistic model inspired by NN4G. While maintaining spatial locality, CGMM has the benefit of probabilistic interpretability

DCNN [16] regards graph convolutions as a diffusion process. It assumes that information is transferred from one node to one of its neighboring nodes with a certain transition probability so that information distribution can reach equilibrium after several rounds. DCNN defines the diffusion graph convolution (DGC) as

$$\mathbf{H}^{(k)} = f\left(\mathbf{W}^{(k)} \odot \mathbf{P}^k\mathbf{X}\right),\tag{5.49}$$

where $f(\cdot)$ is an activation function, and the probability transition matrix $\mathbf{P} \in \mathbf{R}^{n \times n}$ is computed by $\mathbf{P} = \mathbf{D}^{-1}\mathbf{A}$. Note that in DCNN, the hidden representation matrix $\mathbf{H}^{(k)}$ remains the same dimension as the input feature matrix $\mathbf{X}$ and is not a function of its previous hidden representation matrix $\mathbf{H}^{(k-1)}$. DCNN concatenates $\mathbf{H}^{(1)}$, $\mathbf{H}^{(2)}$, $\cdots$, $\mathbf{H}^{(K)}$ together as the final model outputs. As the stationary distribution of a diffusion process is the sum of the power series of probability transition matrices, DGC [49] sums up outputs at each diffusion step instead of concatenating them. It defines the DGC by

$$\mathbf{H} = \sum_{k=0}^{K} f\left(\mathbf{P}^k\mathbf{X}\mathbf{W}^{(k)}\right),\tag{5.50}$$

where $\mathbf{W}^{(k)} \in \mathbf{R}^{D \times F}$ and $f(\cdot)$ is an activation function. Using the power of a transition probability matrix implies that distant neighbors contribute very little information to a central node.

Parametric graph convolution (parametric GC-DGCNN) [12, 39] increases the contributions of distant neighbors based on shortest paths. It defines a shortest path adjacency matrix $\mathbf{S}^{(j)}$. If the shortest path from a node v to a node u is of length j, then $\mathbf{S}_{v,u}^{(j)} = 1$ otherwise 0. With a hyperparameter r to control the receptive field size, PGC-DGCNN introduces a graph convolutional operation as follows:

$$H^{(k)} = \|^r_{j=0} f\left(\left(\widetilde{D}^{(j)}\right)^{-1} S^{(j)} H^{(k-1)} W^{(j,k)}\right),$$ (5.51)

where $\widetilde{D}^{(j)} = \sum_i S^{(j)}_{i,l}$, $H^{(0)} = X$, and $\|$ represents the concatenation of vectors. The calculation of the shortest path adjacency matrix can be expensive with $O(n^3)$ at maximum. An illustration of parameter r is given in Figure 5.4 [39]

Partition graph convolution (PGC) [50] partitions a node's neighbors into Q groups based on certain criteria not limited to shortest paths. PGC constructs Q adjacency matrices according to the defined neighborhood by each group. Then, PGC applies GCN [14] with a different parameter matrix to each neighbor group and sums the results:

$$H^{(k)} = \sum^Q_{j=1} \bar{A}^{(j)} H^{(k-1)} W^{(j,k)},$$ (5.52)

where $H^{(0)} = X$, $\bar{A}^{(j)} = \left(\widetilde{D}^{(j)}\right)^{-\frac{1}{2}} \widetilde{A}^{(j)} \left(\widetilde{D}^{(j)}\right)^{-\frac{1}{2}}$ and $\widetilde{A}^{(j)} = A^{(j)} + I$.

MPNN [51] outlines a general framework of spatial-based ConvGNNs. It treats graph convolutions as a message passing process in which information can be passed from one node to another along edges directly. MPNN runs K-step message passing iterations to let information propagate further. The message passing function (namely the spatial graph convolution) is defined as

$$h^{(k)}_v = U_k\left(h^{(k-1)}_v, \sum_{u \in N(v)} M_k\left(h^{(k-1)}_v, h^{(k-1)}_u, x^e_{vu}\right)\right),$$ (5.53)

where $h^{(0)}_v = x_v$, $U_k(\cdot)$ and $M_k(\cdot)$ are functions with learnable parameters. After deriving the hidden representations of each node, $h^{(K)}_v$ can be passed to an output layer to perform node-level prediction tasks or to a readout function to perform graph-level prediction tasks. The readout function generates a representation of the entire graph based on node hidden representations. It is generally defined as

$$h_G = R\left(h^{(K)}_v \mid v \in G\right),$$ (5.54)

where $R(\cdot)$ represents the readout function with learnable parameters. MPNN can cover many existing GNNs by assuming different forms of $U_k(\cdot)$, $M_k(\cdot)$, and $R(\cdot)$.

Graph Isomorphism Network (GIN): Reference [52] finds that previous MPNN-based methods are incapable of distinguishing different graph structures based on the graph embedding they produced. To amend this drawback, GIN adjusts the weight of the central node by a learnable parameter $\varepsilon^{(k)}$. It performs graph convolutions by

$$h^{(k)}_v = MLP\left(\left(1 + \varepsilon^{(k)}\right) h^{(k-1)}_v + \sum_{u \in N(v)} h^{(k-1)}_u\right),$$ (5.55)

where $MLP(\cdot)$ represents a multi-layer perceptron. As the number of neighbors of a node can vary from one to a thousand or even more, it is inefficient to take the full size of a node's neighborhood. GraphSAGE [23] adopts sampling to obtain a fixed number of neighbors for each node. It performs graph convolutions by

$$h_v(k) = \sigma\left(W^{(k)} \cdot f_k\left(h^{(k-1)}_v, \left\{h^{(k-1)}_u, \forall u \in S_{N(v)}\right\}\right)\right),$$ (5.56)

where $h^{(0)}_v = x_v$, $f_k(\cdot)$ is an aggregation function, $S_{N(v)}$ is a random sample of the node v's neighbors. The aggregation function should be invariant to the permutations of node orderings such as a mean, sum, or max function.

GAT [53] assumes that contributions of neighboring nodes to the central node are neither identical like GraphSAGE [23], nor pre-determined like GCN [14]. GAT adopts attention mechanisms to learn the relative weights between two connected nodes. The graph convolutional operation according to GAT is defined as

$$h_v^{(k)} = \sigma\left(\sum_{u \in N(v) \cup v} \alpha_{vu}^{(k)} W^{(k)} h_u^{(k-1)}\right),$$

(5.57)

where $h_v^{(0)} = x_v$. The attention weight $\alpha_{vu}^{(k)}$ measures the connective strength between the node v and its neighbor u:

$$\alpha_{vu}^{(k)} = softmax\left(g\left(a^T\left[W^{(k)}h_v^{(k-1)} \big\| W^{(k)}h_u^{(k-1)}\right]\right)\right),$$

(5.58)

where $g(\cdot)$ is a LeakyReLU activation function and a is a vector of learnable parameters. The softmax function ensures that the attention weights sum up to one over all neighbors of the node v.

Graph pooling modules: After a GNN generates node features, we can use them for the final task. But using all these features directly can be computationally challenging, and thus a downsampling strategy is needed. Depending on the objective and the role it plays in the network, different names are given to this strategy: (i) the pooling operation aims to reduce the size of parameters by downsampling the nodes to generate smaller representations and thus avoid overfitting, permutation invariance, and computational complexity issues and (ii) the readout operation is mainly used to generate graph-level representation based on node representations (see Figure 5.5). Their mechanism is very similar. In this section, we use pooling to refer to all kinds of downsampling strategies applied to GNNs. Nowadays, mean/max/sum pooling, already illustrated in Section 5.1, is the most primitive and effective way to implement downsampling since calculating the mean/ max /sum value in the pooling window is fast:

$$h_G = mean/\max/sum\left(h_1^{(K)}, h_2^{(K)}, .., h_n^{(K)}\right)$$

(5.59)

where K is the index of the last graph convolutional layer.

5.2.3 Graph Autoencoders (GAEs)

These are deep neural architectures that map nodes into a latent feature space and decode graph information from latent representations. GAEs can be used to learn network embeddings or generate new graphs.

Network embedding (encoding) is a low-dimensional vector representation of a node that preserves a node's topological information. GAEs learn network embeddings using an encoder to extract network embeddings and using a decoder to enforce network embeddings to preserve the graph topological information such as the PPMI matrix and the adjacency matrix (see Figure 5.6).

Earlier approaches mainly employ multi-layer perceptrons to build GAEs for network embedding learning. Deep Neural Network for Graph Representations (DNGR) uses a stacked denoising autoencoder to encode and decode the PPMI matrix via multi-layer perceptrons. Concurrently, Structural Deep Network Embedding (SDNE) uses a stacked autoencoder to jointly preserve the node first-order proximity and second-order proximity. SDNE proposes two loss functions on the outputs of the encoder and the outputs of the decoder separately. The first loss function enables the learned network embeddings to preserve the node's first-order proximity by minimizing the distance

Figure 5.6 A graph autoencoder (GAE) for network embedding. The encoder uses graph convolutional layers to get a network embedding for each node. The decoder computes the pairwise distance given network embeddings. After applying a nonlinear activation function, the decoder reconstructs the graph adjacency matrix. The network is trained by minimizing the discrepancy between the real adjacency matrix and the reconstructed adjacency matrix. *Source:* Wu et al. [38].

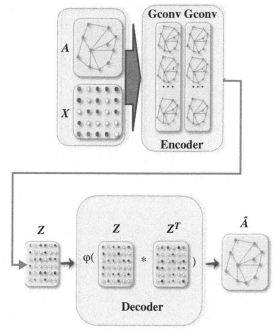

between a node's network embedding and its neighbors' network embeddings. The first loss function L_{1st} is defined as

$$L_{1st} = \sum_{(v,u) \in E} A_{v,u} \| enc(\mathbf{x}_v) - enc(\mathbf{x}_u) \|^2, \tag{5.60}$$

where $\mathbf{x}_v = A_{v,:}$ and $enc(\cdot)$ is an encoder that consists of a multi-layer perceptron. The second loss function enables the learned network embeddings to preserve the node's second-order proximity by minimizing the distance between a node's inputs and its reconstructed inputs and is defined as

$$L_{2nd} = \sum_{v \in V} \| (dec(enc(\mathbf{x}_v)) - \mathbf{x}_v) \odot \mathbf{b}_v \|^2, \tag{5.61}$$

where $b_{v,u} = 1$ if $A_{v,u} = 0$, $b_{v,u} = \beta > 1$ if $A_{v,u} = 1$, and $dec(\cdot)$ is a decoder that consists of a multi-layer perceptron.

DNGR [54] and *SDNE* [55] only consider node structural information about the connectivity between pairs of nodes. They ignore the fact that the nodes may contain feature information that depicts the attributes of nodes themselves. Graph Autoencoder (GAE∗) [56] leverages GCN [14] to encode node structural information and node feature information at the same time. The encoder of GAE∗ consists of two graph convolutional layers, which takes the form

$$Z = enc(\mathbf{X}, \mathbf{A}) = Gconv(\, f(Gconv(\mathbf{A}, \mathbf{X}; \Theta_1)); \Theta_2), \tag{5.62}$$

where Z denotes the network embedding matrix of a graph, $f(\cdot)$ is a ReLU activation function, and the $Gconv\,(\cdot)$ function is a graph convolutional layer defined by Eq. (5.44). The decoder of GAE∗ aims to decode node relational information from their embeddings by reconstructing the graph adjacency matrix, which is defined as

$$\hat{A}_{v,u} = dec(\mathbf{z}_v, \mathbf{z}_u) = \sigma(\mathbf{z}_v^T \mathbf{z}_u), \tag{5.63}$$

where z_v is the embedding of node v. GAE* is trained by minimizing the negative cross-entropy given the real adjacency matrix A and the reconstructed adjacency matrix Â.

Simply reconstructing the graph adjacency matrix may lead to overfitting due to the capacity of the autoencoders. The variational graph autoencoder (VGAE) [56] is a variational version of GAE that was developed to learn the distribution of data. The VGAE optimizes the variational lower bound L:

$$L = E_{q(Z|X,A)}[\ \log p(A \mid Z)] - KL\Big[q(Z \mid X,A)\big\|p(Z)\Big], \tag{5.64}$$

where $KL(\cdot)$ is the Kullback–Leibler divergence function, which measures the distance between two distributions; $p(Z)$ is a Gaussian prior $p(Z) = \prod_{i=1}^{n} p(z_i) = \prod_{i=1}^{n} N(z_i \mid 0, I)$, $p(A_{ij} = 1 \mid z_i, z_j) = dec(z_i, z_j) = \sigma(z_i^T z_j)$, $q(Z \mid X, A) = \prod_{i=1}^{n} q(z_i \mid X, A)$ with $q(z_i \mid X, A) = N(z_i \mid \mu_i, diag\,(\sigma_i^2))$.

The mean vector μ_i is the i-th row of an encoder's outputs defined by Eq. (5.62), and $\log \sigma_i$ is derived similarly as μ_i with another encoder. According to Eq. (5.64), VGAE assumes that the empirical distribution $q(Z \mid X, A)$ should be as close as possible to the prior distribution $p(Z)$. To further enforce this, the empirical distribution $q(Z \mid X, A)$ is chosen to approximate the prior distribution $p(Z)$.

Like GAE*, GraphSAGE [23] encodes node features with two graph convolutional layers. Instead of optimizing the reconstruction error, GraphSAGE shows that the relational information between two nodes can be preserved by negative sampling with the loss:

$$L(z_v) = -\log\big(dec(z_v, z_u)\big) - Q E_{v_n \sim P_n(v)}\ \log\big(-dec(z_v, z_{v_n})\big), \tag{5.65}$$

where node u is a neighbor of node v, node v_n is a distant node to node v and is sampled from a negative sampling distribution $P_n(v)$, and Q is the number of negative samples. This loss function essentially imposes similar representations on close nodes and dissimilar representations on distant nodes.

Deep Recursive Network Embedding (DRNE) [57] assumes that a node's network embedding should approximate the aggregation of its neighborhood network embeddings. It adopts an LSTM network [26] to aggregate a node's neighbors. The reconstruction error of DRNE is defined as

$$L = \sum_{v \in V} \big\|z_v - LSTM(\{z_u \mid u \in N(v)\})\big\|^2, \tag{5.66}$$

where z_v is the network embedding of node v obtained by a dictionary look-up, and the LSTM network takes a random sequence of node v's neighbors ordered by their node degree as inputs. As suggested by Eq. (5.66), DRNE implicitly learns network embeddings via an LSTM network rather than by using the LSTM network to generate network embeddings. It avoids the problem that the LSTM network is not invariant to the permutation of node sequences.*Network representations with adversarially regularized autoencoders (NetRA)* [58] proposes a graph encoder-decoder framework with a general loss function, defined as

$$L = -E_{z \sim P_{data}(z)}\big(dist(z, dec(enc(z)))\big), \tag{5.67}$$

where $dist\,(\cdot)$ is the distance measure between the node embedding z and the reconstructed z. The encoder and decoder of NetRA are LSTM networks *with random walks* rooted on each node $v \in V$ as inputs.

Graph generation (decoding): With multiple graphs, GAEs are able to learn the generative distribution of graphs by encoding graphs into hidden representations and decoding a graph structure given the hidden representations. These methods either propose a new graph in a sequential manner or in a global manner.

Sequential approaches generate a graph by proposing nodes and edges step by step.

Deep Generative Model of Graphs (DeepGMG) [59] assumes that the probability of a graph is the sum over all possible node permutations:

$$p(G) = \sum_{\pi} p(G, \pi), \tag{5.68}$$

where π denotes a node ordering. It captures the complex joint probability of all nodes and edges in the graph. DeepGMG generates graphs by making a sequence of decisions, namely, whether to add a node, which node to add, whether to add an edge, and which node to connect to the new node. The decision process of generating nodes and edges is conditioned on the node states and the graph state of a growing graph updated by an RecGNN.

Global approaches output a graph all at once.

Graph variational autoencoder (GraphVAE) [60] models the existence of nodes and edges as independent random variables. By assuming the posterior distribution $q_\varphi(z|G)$ defined by an encoder and the generative distribution $p_\theta(G \mid z)$ defined by a decoder, GraphVAE optimizes the variational lower bound:

$$L\left(\varphi, \theta; G\right) = E_{q_\varphi}(z \mid G)[-\log p_\theta(G \mid z)] + KL\Big[q_\varphi(z \mid G)p(z)\Big], \tag{5.69}$$

where $p(z)$ follows a Gaussian prior, φ and θ are learnable parameters. With a ConvGNN as the encoder and a simple multi-layer perception as the decoder, GraphVAE outputs a generated graph with its adjacency matrix, node attributes, and edge attributes

5.2.4 STGNNs

These networks are designed to capture the dynamics of graphs. STGNNs follow two directions, recurrent neural network (RNN)-based methods and CNN-based methods. Most RNN-based approaches capture spatial-temporal dependencies by filtering inputs and hidden states passed to a recurrent unit using graph convolutions. To illustrate this (see Figure 5.7), suppose a simple RNN takes the form

$$H^{(t)} = \sigma\Big(WX^{(t)} + UH^{(t-1)} + b\Big), \tag{5.70}$$

where $X^{(t)} \in R^{n \times d}$ is the node feature matrix at time step t. After inserting graph convolution, Eq. (5.70) becomes

$$H^{(t)} = \sigma\Big(Gconv\Big(X^{(t)}, A; W\Big) + Gconv\Big(H^{(t-1)}, A; U\Big) + b\Big), \tag{5.71}$$

where $Gconv(\cdot)$ is a graph convolutional layer. The Graph Convolutional Recurrent Network (GCRN) combines a LSTM network with ChebNet. DCRNN incorporates a proposed DGC layer (Eq. (5.50)) into a GRU network.

Previous methods all use a predefined graph structure. They assume the predefined graph structure reflects the genuine dependency relationships among nodes. However, with many snapshots of

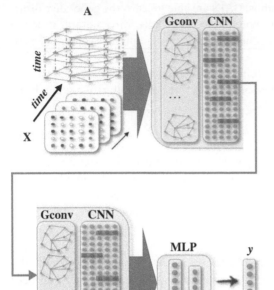

Figure 5.7 A STGNN for spatial-temporal graph forecasting. A graph convolutional layer is followed by a 1D-CNN layer. The graph convolutional layer operates on A and X(t) to capture the spatial dependency, while the 1D-CNN layer slides over X along the time axis to capture the temporal dependency. The output layer is a linear transformation, generating a prediction for each node, such as its future value at the next time step. *Source:* Wu et al. [38]. (For more details see color figure in bins).

graph data in a spatial-temporal setting, it is possible to learn latent static graph structures automatically from data. To realize this,

Graph WaveNet [61] proposes a self-adaptive adjacency matrix to perform graph convolutions. The self-adaptive adjacency matrix is defined as

$$A_{adp} = SoftMax\left(ReLU\left(E_1 E_2^T\right)\right), \tag{5.72}$$

where the softmax function is computed along the row dimension, E1 denotes the source node embedding, and E2 denotes the target node embedding with learnable parameters. By multiplying E1 with E2, one can get the dependency weight between a source node and a target node. With a complex CNN-based spatial-temporal neural network, Graph WaveNet performs well without being given an adjacency matrix.

5.3 Complexity of NN

In order to analyze the network complexity, we need a more detailed definition of both network topologies and network parameters. For this, we will use the original definitions introduced in [1], one of the first papers in this field. For this reason, in this section we will revisit the description of the GNN with more details on the specific model of the network, computation of the states, the learning process, and specific transition and output function implementations, and to facilitate a better understanding of these processes, we will provide a comparison with random walks and recursive neural nets. When discussing computational complexity issues, we will look at the complexity of instructions and the time complexity of the GNN mode. The illustrations will be based on the results presented in [1].

5.3.1 Labeled Graph NN (LGNN)

Here, a graph G is a pair (N, E), where N is the set of nodes and E is the set of edges. The set $ne[n]$ stands for the neighbors of n, that is, the nodes connected to n by an arc, while $co[n]$ denotes the set of arcs having n as a vertex. Nodes and edges may have *labels* represented by real vectors. The labels attached to node n and edge (n_1, n_2) will be represented by $l_n \in R^{l_N}$ and $l_{(n_1, n_2)} \in R^{l_E}$, respectively. Let l denote the vector obtained by stacking together all the labels of the graph.

If y is a vector that contains data from a graph and S is a subset of the nodes (the edges), then y_S denotes the vector obtained by selecting from y the components related to the node (the edges) in S.

For example, $l_{ne[n]}$ stands for the vector containing the labels of all the neighbors of n. Labels usually include features of objects related to nodes and features of the relationships between the objects. No assumption is made regarding the arcs: directed and undirected edges are both permitted. However, when different kinds of edges coexist in the same dataset, it is necessary to distinguish them. This can be easily achieved by attaching a proper label to each edge. In this case, different kinds of arcs turn out to be just arcs with different labels.

The considered graphs may be either positional or nonpositional. Nonpositional graphs are those that have been described thus far; positional graphs differ from them since a unique integer identifier is assigned to each neighbor of a node n to indicate its logical position. Formally, for each node n in a positional graph, there exists an injective function ν_n: $ne[n] \to \{1, ..., |N|\}$, which assigns to each neighbor u of n a position $\nu_n(u)$.

The domain is the set $\mathcal{D}$ of pairs of a graph and a node, that is, $\mathcal{D} = \mathcal{G} \times \mathcal{N}$, where $\mathcal{G}$ is a set of the graphs and $\mathcal{N}$ is a subset of their nodes. We assume a supervised learning framework with the learning set

$$\mathcal{L} = \left\{ (G_i, n_{i,j}, t_{i,j}) \middle|, G_i = (N_i, E_i) \in G; n_{i,j} \in N_i; t_{i,j} \in R^m, 1 \le i \le p, 1 \le j \le q_i \right\} \tag{5.73}$$

where $n_{i,j} \in N_i$ denotes the j-th node in the set $N_i \in \mathcal{N}$ and $t_{i,j}$ is the desired target associated with $n_{i,j}$. Finally, $p \le |\mathcal{G}|$ and $q_i \le |N_i|$. All the graphs of the learning set can be combined into a unique disconnected graph, and therefore one might think of the learning set as the pair $\mathcal{L} = (G, \mathcal{I})$, where $G = (N, E)$ is a graph and $\mathcal{I}$ is a set of pairs $\{(n_i, t_i) \mid n_i \in N, t_i \in R^m, 1 \le i \le q\}$. It is worth mentioning that this compact definition is useful not only for its simplicity, but that it also directly captures the very nature of some problems where the domain consists of only one graph, for instance, a large portion of the Web (see Figure 5.8).

The model: As before, the nodes in a graph represent objects or concepts, and edges represent their relationships. Each concept is naturally defined by its features and the related concepts. Thus, we can attach a *state* $x_n \in R^s$ to each node n that is based on the information contained in the neighborhood of n (see Figure 5.9). The state x_n contains a representation of the concept denoted by n and can be used to produce an *output* o, that is, a decision about the concept. Let f_w be a parametric function, called the *local transition function*, that expresses the dependence of a node n on its neighborhood, and let g_w be the *local output function* that describes how the output is produced. Then, x_n and o_n are defined as follows:

$$x_n = f_w\left(l_n, l_{co[n]}, x_{ne[n]}, l_{ne[n]}\right); \quad o_n = g_w(x_n, l_n) \tag{5.74}$$

where l_n, $l_{co[n]}$, $x_{ne[n]}$, and $l_{ne[n]}$ are the label of n, the labels of its edges, the states, and the labels of the nodes in the neighborhood of n, respectively.

Let x, o, l and l_N be the vectors constructed by stacking all the states, all the outputs, all the labels, and all the node labels, respectively. Then, a compact form of Eq. (5.74) becomes

$$x = F_w(x, l); \quad o = G_w(x, l_N) \tag{5.75}$$

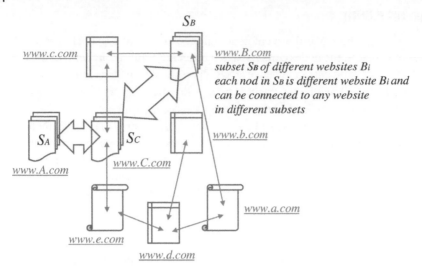

Figure 5.8 A subset of the Web.

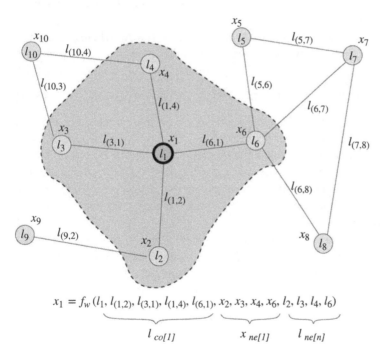

Figure 5.9 Graph and the neighborhood of a node. The state x_1 of node 1 depends on the information contained in its neighborhood. *Source:* Scarselli et al. [1].

$$x_1 = f_w\,(l_1, l_{(1,2)}, l_{(3,1)}, l_{(1,4)}, l_{(6,1)}, x_2, x_3, x_4, x_6, l_2, l_3, l_4, l_6)$$

$$\underbrace{\phantom{l_1, l_{(1,2)}, l_{(3,1)}, l_{(1,4)}, l_{(6,1)}}}_{l_{\,co[1]}} \quad \underbrace{}_{x_{\,ne[1]}} \quad \underbrace{}_{l_{\,ne[n]}}$$

where F_w, the *global transition function*, and G_w, the *global output function*, are stacked versions of $|N|$ instances of f_w and g_w, respectively. For us, the case of interest is when x, o are uniquely defined and Eq. (5.75) defines a map $\phi_w : \mathcal{D} \to R^m$ that takes a graph as input and returns an output o_n for each node. Banach's fixed-point theorem [62] provides a sufficient condition for the existence and uniqueness of the solution of a system of equations. According to Banach's theorem, Eq. (5.75) has a unique solution provided that F_w is a *contraction map* with respect to the state; that is, there exists μ, $0 \leq \mu < 1$ such that $\|F_w(x, l) - F_w(y, l)\| \leq \mu \|x - y\|$ holds for any x, y, where $\| \, . \, \|$ denotes a vectorial norm. Thus, for the moment, let us assume that F_w is a contraction map. Later, we will show that, in GNNs, this property is enforced by an appropriate implementation of the transition function.

For *positional graphs*, f_w must receive the positions of the neighbors as additional inputs. In practice, this can be easily achieved provided that information contained in $x_{ne[n]}$, $l_{co[n]}$, and $l_{ne[n]}$ is sorted according to neighbors' positions and is appropriately padded with special null values in positions corresponding to nonexistent neighbors. For example, $x_{ne[n]} = [y_1, ..., y_M]$, where $M = \max_{n, u} \nu_n(u)$ is the maximum number of neighbors of a node; $y_i = x_u$ holds, if u is the i-th neighbor of $n(\nu_n(u) = i)$; and $y_i = x_0$, for some predefined null state x_0, if there is no i-th neighbor.

For *nonpositional graphs*, it is useful to replace function f_w of Eq. (5.74) with

$$x_n = \sum_{u \in ne[n]} h_w(l_n, l_{(n,u)}, x_u, l_u), n \in N \tag{5.76}$$

where h_w is a parametric function. This transition function, which has been successfully used in recursive NNs, is not affected by the positions and the number of the children. In the following, Eq. (5.76) is referred to as the *nonpositional form*, and Eq. (5.74) is called the *positional form*. To implement the GNN model, we need (i) a method to solve Eq. (5.74)); (ii) a learning algorithm to adapt f_w and g_w using examples from the training dataset; and (iii) an implementation of f_w and g_w. These steps will be considered in the following paragraphs.

Computation of the state: Banach's fixed-point theorem does not only ensure the existence and the uniqueness of the solution of Eq. (5.74), but it also suggests the following classic iterative scheme for computing the state:

$$x(t + 1) = F_w(x(t), l) \tag{5.77}$$

where $x(t)$ denotes the t-th iteration of x. The dynamical system (Eq. (5.77)) converges exponentially fast to the solution of Eq. (5.75) for any initial value (0). We can, therefore, think of $x(t)$ as the state that is updated by the transition function F_w. In fact, Eq. (5.77) implements the Jacobi iterative method for solving nonlinear equations [63]. Thus, the outputs and the states can be computed by iterating

$$x_n(t + 1) = f_w(l_n, l_{co[n]}, x_{ne[n]}(t), l_{ne[n]}); \quad o_n = g_w(x_n(t), l_n), \ n \in N \tag{5.78}$$

Note that the computation described in Eq. (5.78) can be interpreted as the representation of a network consisting of units that compute f_w and g_w. Such a network is called an *encoding network*, following an analogous terminology used for the recursive neural network model [64]. In order to build the encoding network, each node of the graph is replaced by a unit computing the function f_w (see Figure 5.10). Each unit stores the current state $x_n(t)$ of node n, and when activated it calculates the state $x_n(t + 1)$ using the node label and the information stored in the neighborhood. The simultaneous and repeated activation of the units produce the behavior described in Eq. (5.78). The output of node n is produced by another unit, which implements g_w. When f_w and g_w are implemented by FNNs, the encoding network turns out to be a recurrent neural network where the connections between the neurons can be divided into internal and external connections. The internal connectivity is determined by the neural network architecture used to implement the unit. The external connectivity depends on the edges of the processed graph.

The learning algorithm: Learning in GNNs consists of estimating the parameter w such that ϕ_w approximates the data in the learning dataset Eq. (5.73) where q_i is the number of supervised nodes in G_i. For graph-focused tasks, one special node is used for the target ($q_i = 1$ holds), whereas for node-focused tasks, in principle, the supervision can be performed on every node. The learning task can be posed as the minimization of a quadratic cost function

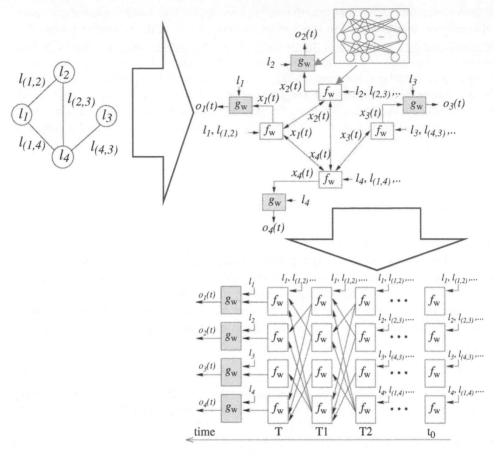

Figure 5.10 Graph (on the top, left), the corresponding encoding network (top right), and the network obtained by unfolding the encoding network (at the bottom). The nodes (the circles) of the graph are replaced, in the encoding network, by units computing f_w and g_w (the squares). When f_w and g_w are implemented by FNNs, the encoding network is a recurrent neural network. In the unfolding network, each layer corresponds to a time instant and contains a copy of all the units of the encoding network. Connections between layers depend on encoding network connectivity.

$$e_w = \sum_{i=1}^{p} \sum_{j=1}^{q_i} \left(t_{i,j} - \phi_w(G_i, n_{i,j}) \right)^2 \tag{5.79}$$

The learning algorithm is based on a gradient-descent strategy and is composed of the following steps:

1) The states $x_n(t)$ are iteratively updated by Eq. (5.78) until at time T they approach the fixed-point solution of Eq. (5.75): $x(T) \approx x$.
2) The gradient $\partial e_w(T)/\partial w$ is computed.
3) The weights w are updated according to the gradient computed in Step 2.

When it comes to Step 1, note that the hypothesis that F_w is a contraction map ensures convergence to the fixed point. Step 3 is carried out within the traditional framework of gradient descent. We will show in the following that Step 3 can be carried out in a very efficient way by exploiting the diffusion process that takes place in GNNs. This diffusion process is very much related to the process that occurs in recurrent neural networks, for which the gradient computation is based on the BPTT algorithm (see Chapter 3). In this case, the encoding network is unfolded from time T back to an initial time t_0. The unfolding produces the layered network shown in Figure 5.10. Each layer corresponds to a time instant and contains a copy of all the units f_w of the encoding network. The units of two consecutive layers are connected following graph connectivity. The last layer corresponding to time T also includes the units g_w and computes the output of the network.

Backpropagation through time consists of carrying out the traditional backpropagation step (see Chapter 3) on the unfolded network to compute the gradient of the cost function at time T with respect to all the instances of f_w and g_w. Then, $\partial e_w(T)/\partial w$ is obtained by summing the gradients of all instances. However, backpropagation through time requires storing the states of every instance of the units. When the graphs and $T - t_0$ are large, the memory required may be considerable. On the other hand, in this case, a more efficient approach is possible, based on the Almeida–Pineda algorithm [65, 66]. Since Eq. (5.78) has reached a stable point x before the gradient computation, we can assume that $x(t) = x$ holds for any $t \geq t_0$. Thus, backpropagation through time can be carried out by storing only x. The following two theorems show that such an intuitive approach has a formal justification. The former theorem proves that function ϕ_w is differentiable.

Theorem 5.1   (Differentiability) [1]: Let F_w and G_w be the global transition and the global output functions of a GNN, respectively. If $F_w(x, l)$ and $G_w(x, l_N)$ are continuously differentiable w.r.t. x and w, then ϕ_w is continuously differentiable w.r.t. w (for the proof, see [1]).

Theorem 5.2   (Backpropagation): Let F_w and G_w be the transition and the output functions of a GNN, respectively, and assume that $F_w(x, l)$ and $G_w(x, l_N)$ are continuously differentiable w.r.t. x and w. Let $z(t)$ be defined by

$$z(t) = z(t + 1)\frac{\partial F_w}{\partial x}(x, l) + \frac{\partial e_w}{\partial o}\frac{\partial G_w}{\partial x}(x, l_N) \tag{5.80}$$

Then, the sequence $z(T), z(T-1)\ldots.$ converges to a vector $z = lim_{t \to -\infty} z(t)$, and the convergence is exponential and independent of the initial state (T). In addition, we have

$$\frac{\partial e_w}{\partial w} = \frac{\partial e_w}{\partial o}\frac{\partial G_w}{\partial w}(x, l_N) + z\frac{\partial F_w}{\partial w}(x, l) \tag{5.81}$$

where x is the stable state of the GNN (for the proof, see [1]).

The relationship between the gradient defined by Eq. (5.81) and the gradient computed by the Almeida–Pineda algorithm can be easily recognized. The first term on the right-hand side of Eq. (5.81) represents the contribution to the gradient due to the output function G_w. Backpropagation calculates the first term while it is propagating the derivatives through the layer of the functions g_w (see Chapter 3, Figure 3.10). The second term represents the contribution due to the transition function F_w. In fact, from Eq. (5.80)

$$z(t) = z(t + 1)\cdot\frac{\partial F_w}{\partial x}(x, l) + \frac{\partial e_w}{\partial o}\frac{\partial G_w}{\partial x}(x, l_N)$$

$$= z(T)\left(\frac{\partial F_w}{\partial x}(x, l)\right)^{T-t} + \sum_{i=0}^{T-t-1}\frac{\partial e_w}{\partial o}\frac{\partial G_w}{\partial x}(x, l_N)\cdot\left(\frac{\partial F_w}{\partial x}(x, l)\right)^{i}$$

If we assume $z(T) = \partial e_w(T)/\partial o(T) \cdot (\partial G_w/\partial x(T))(x(T), l_N)$ and $x(t) = x$, for $t\, 0 \leq t \leq T$, it follows that

$$z(t) = \sum_{i=0}^{T-t} \frac{\partial e_w(T)}{\partial o(T)} \frac{\partial G_w}{\partial x(T)}(x(T), l_N) \cdot \prod_{j=1}^{i} \left(\frac{\partial F_w}{\partial x(T-j)}(x(T-j), l) \right)$$

$$= \sum_{i=0}^{T-t} \frac{\partial e_w(T)}{\partial x(T-i)} = \sum_{i=T}^{t} \frac{\partial e_w(T)}{\partial x(i)}$$

So, Eq. (5.80) accumulates the $\partial e_w(T)/\partial x(i)$ into the variable z. This mechanism corresponds to backpropagating the gradients through the layers containing the f_w units. The learning algorithm is detailed in Table 5.1 [1]. It consists of a main procedure and of two functions: FORWARD and BACKWARD. The function FORWARD takes as input the current set of parameters w and iterates to find the convergent fixed point. The iteration is stopped when $\|x(t) - x(t-1)\|$ is less than a given threshold ε_f according to a given norm $\| \cdot \|$. The function BACKWARD computes the gradient: system Eq. (5.80) is iterated until $\|z(t-1) - z(t)\|$ is smaller than a threshold ε_b; then, the gradient is calculated by Eq. (5.81).

The function FORWARD computes the states, whereas BACKWARD calculates the gradient. The procedure MAIN minimizes the error by calling FORWARD and BACKWARD iteratively. *Transition and output function implementations*: The implementation of the local output function g_w does not need to fulfill any particular constraint. In GNNs, g_w is a multilayered FNN. On the other hand, the local transition function f_w plays a crucial role in the proposed model, since its implementation determines the number and the existence of the solutions of Eq. (5.74). The assumption underlying GNN is that the design of f_w is such that the global transition function F_w is a contraction map with respect to the state x. In the following, we describe two neural network models that fulfill this purpose using different strategies. These models are based on the nonpositional form described by Eq. (5.76). It can be easily observed that there exist two corresponding models based on the positional form as well.

1) *Linear (nonpositional) GNN.* Eq. (5.76) can naturally be implemented by

$$h_w(l_n, l_{(n,u)}, x_u, l_u) = A_{n,u} x_u + b_u \tag{5.82}$$

where the vector $b_n \in R^s$ and the matrix $A_{n,u} \in R^{s \times s}$ are defined by the output of two FNNs, whose parameters correspond to the parameters of the GNN. More precisely, let us call the *transition network* an FNN that has to generate $A_{n,u}$ and the *forcing network* another FNN that has to generate b_n. Let $\varphi_w: R^{2l_N + l_E} \to R^{s^2}$ and $\rho_w: R^{l_N} \to R^s$ be the functions implemented by the transition and the forcing network, respectively. Then, we define

$$A_{n,u} = \frac{\mu}{s \,|\, ne[u] \,|} . \Theta, b_n = \rho_w(l_n) \tag{5.83}$$

where $\mu \in (0, 1)$ and $\Theta = \text{resize}((\varphi_w(l_n, l_{(n, u)}, l_u))$ hold, and resize $(\cdot)$ denotes the operator that allocates the elements of an s^2-dimensional vector into an $s \times s$ matrix. Thus, $A_{n,u}$ is obtained by arranging the outputs of the transition network into the square matrix Θ and by multiplication with the factor $\mu/s \,|\, ne[u]\,|$. On the other hand, b_n is just a vector that contains the outputs of the forcing network. In the following, we denote the 1-norm of a matrix $M = \{m_{i,j}\}$ as $\|M\|_1 = \max_j \sum |m_{i,j}|$ and assume that $\|\varphi_w(l_n, l_{(n, u)}, l_u)\|_1 \leq s$ holds; this can be straightforwardly verified if the output neurons of the transition network use an appropriately bounded activation function, for example, a hyperbolic tangent.

Table 5.1 [1] Learning algorithm.

MAIN
  initialize $\boldsymbol{w}$;
  $\boldsymbol{x}$ = Forward($\boldsymbol{w}$);
  repeat
      $\frac{\partial e_w}{\partial w}$ = BACKWARD $(\boldsymbol{x}, \boldsymbol{w})$;
      $\boldsymbol{w} = \boldsymbol{w} - \lambda \cdot \frac{\partial e_w}{\partial w}$;
      $\boldsymbol{x}$ = FORWARD $(\boldsymbol{w})$;
  until (a stopping criterion);
  return $\boldsymbol{w}$;
end

FORWARD $(\boldsymbol{w})$
  Initialize $\boldsymbol{x}(0)$, t = 0;
  repeat
      $\boldsymbol{x}(t+1)$ = $F_w(\boldsymbol{x}(t), \boldsymbol{1})$;
      t = $t+1$;
  until $\|\boldsymbol{x}(t) - \boldsymbol{x}(t-1)\| \le \varepsilon_f$
  return $\boldsymbol{x}(t)$;
end

BACKWARD $(\boldsymbol{x}, \boldsymbol{w})$
  $\boldsymbol{o}$ = $G_w(\boldsymbol{x}, \boldsymbol{1}_N)$;
  $A = \frac{\partial F_w}{\partial x}(x, 1)$;
  $b = \frac{\partial e_w}{\partial o} \cdot \frac{\partial G_w}{\partial x}(\boldsymbol{x}, \boldsymbol{1}_N)$
  initialize $\boldsymbol{z}(0)$, t = 0;
  repeat
      $z(t)$ = $z(t+1) \cdot \boldsymbol{A} + \boldsymbol{b}$;
      t = $t-1$;
  until $\|z(t-1) - z(t)\| \le \varepsilon_b$;
  $c = \frac{\partial e_w}{\partial o} \cdot \frac{\partial G_w}{\partial w}(x, 1_N)$;
  $d = z(t) \cdot \frac{\partial F_w}{\partial w}(x, 1)$;
  $\frac{\partial e_w}{\partial w}$ = $c + d$;
  return $\frac{\partial e_w}{\partial w}$;
end

The function FORWARD computes the states, whereas BACKWARD calculates the gradient. The procedure MAIN minimizes the error by calling FORWARD and BACKWARD iteratively.

Note that in this case $F_w(x, l) = Ax + b$, where b is the vector constructed by stacking all the b_n, and A is a block matrix $\{\bar{A}_{n,u}\}$, with $\bar{A}_{n,u} = A_{n,u}$ if u is a neighbor of n and $\bar{A}_{n,u} = 0$ otherwise. Vectors b_n and matrices $A_{n,u}$ do not depend on the state x, but only on the node and edge labels. Thus, $\partial F_w / \partial x = A$, and, by simple algebra we have

$$\left\| \frac{\partial F_w}{\partial x} \right\|_1 = \|A\|_1 \leq \max_{u \in N} \left(\sum_{n \in ne[u]} \|A_{n,u}\|_1 \right) \leq \max_{u \in N} \left(\frac{\mu s}{s|ne[u]|} \cdot \sum_{n \in ne[u]} \|\Theta\|_1 \right) \leq \mu$$

which implies that F_w is a contraction map (w.r.t. $\| \ \|_1$) for any set of parameters w.

2) *Nonlinear (nonpositional) GNN.* In this case, h_w is realized by a multilayered feedforward NN. Since three-layered neural networks are universal approximators [67], h_w can approximate any desired function. However, not all the parameters w can be used, because it must be ensured that the corresponding transition function F_w is a contraction map. This can be achieved by adding a penalty term to Eq. (5.79), that is

$$e_w = \sum_{i=1}^{p} \sum_{j=1}^{q_i} \left(t_{i,j} - \phi_w(G_i, n_{i,j}) \right)^2 + \beta L \left(\left\| \frac{\partial F_w}{\partial x} \right\| \right)$$

where the penalty term $L(y)$ is $(y - \mu)^2$ if $y > \mu$ and 0 otherwise, and the parameter $\mu \in (0, 1)$ defines the desired contraction constant of F_w. More generally, the penalty term can be any expression, differentiable with respect to w, that is monotone increasing with respect to the norm of the Jacobian. For example, in our experiments, we use the penalty term $p_w = \sum_{i=1}^{s} L\left(\|A^i\|_1 \right)$, where A^i is the i-th column of $\partial F_w / \partial x$. In fact, such an expression is an approximation of $L(\|\partial F_w / \partial x\|_1) = L(\max_i \|A^i\|_1)$.

5.3.2 Computational Complexity

Here, we derive an analysis of the computational cost in GNN. The analysis will focus on three different GNN models: *positional GNNs*, where the functions f_w and g_w of Eq. (5.74) are implemented by FNNs; *linear (nonpositional) GNNs*; and *nonlinear (nonpositional) GNNs*.

First, we will describe with more details the most complex instructions involved in the learning procedure (see Table 5.2 reproduced from [1]). Then, the complexity of the learning algorithm will be defined. For the sake of simplicity, the cost is derived assuming that the training set contains just one graph G. Such an assumption does not cause any loss of generality, since the graphs of the training set can always be merged into a single graph. The complexity is measured by the order of floating point operations. By the common definition of time complexity, an algorithm requires $O(l(a))$ operations, if there exist $\alpha > 0$, $\bar{a} \geq 0$, such that $c(a) \leq \alpha l(a)$ holds for each $a \geq \bar{a}$, where $c(a)$ is the maximal number of operations executed by the algorithm when the length of the input is a.

We will assume that there exist two procedures FP and BP, which implement the forward phase and the backward phase of the back propagation procedure, respectively. Formally, given a function $l_w: R^a \to R^b$ implemented by an FNN, we have

$$l_w(y) = FP(l_w, y) \ ; \ \left[\delta \frac{\partial l_w}{\partial w}(y), \delta \frac{\partial l_w}{\partial y}(y) \right]$$

Here, $y \in R^a$ is the input vector, and the row vector $\delta \in R^b$ is a signal that suggests how the network output must be adjusted to improve the cost function. In most applications, the cost function is $e_w(y) = (t - y)^2$ and $\delta = (\partial e_w / \partial o)(y) = 2(t - o)$, where $o = l_w(y)$ and t (target) is the vector of the desired output corresponding to input y. On the other hand, $\delta(\partial l_w / \partial y)(y)$ is the gradient of e_w with respect to the network input and is easily computed as a side product of backpropagation. Backpropagation computes for each neuron v the *delta* value $(\partial e_w / \partial a_v)(y) = \delta(\partial l_w / \partial a_v)(y)$, where e_w is the cost

Table 5.2 Time complexity of the most expensive instructions of the learning algorithm. For each instruction and each GNN model, a bound on the order of floating point operations is given. The table also displays the number of times per epoch that each instruction is executed. *Source:* Scarselli et al. [1].

Instruction	Positional	Nonlinear	Linear	Execs.
$z(t+1) = z(t) \cdot A + b$	$s^2\,|E|$	$s^2\,|E|$	$s^2\,|E|$	it_b
$o = G_w(x(t), l_w)$	$|N|\,\vec{C}_g$	$|N|\,\vec{C}_g$	$|N|\,\vec{C}_g$	1
$x(t+1) = F_w(x(t), l)$	$|N|\,\vec{C}_f$	$|E|\,\vec{C}_h$	$s^2\,|E|$	it_f
			$|N|\,\vec{C}_\rho + |E|\,\vec{C}_\phi$	1
$A = \frac{\partial F_w}{\partial x}(x, l)$	$s\,|N|\,\overleftarrow{C}_f$	$s\,|E|\,\overleftarrow{C}_h$	–	1
$\frac{\partial e_w}{\partial o}$	$|N|$	$|N|$	$|N|$	1
$\frac{\partial p_w}{\partial w}$	$t_R \cdot \max\left(s^2 \cdot hi_f, \overleftarrow{C}_f\right)$	$t_R \cdot \max\left(s^2 \cdot hi_h, \overleftarrow{C}_h\right)$	–	1
$b = \frac{\partial e_w}{\partial o}\frac{\partial G_w}{\partial x}(x, l_N)$	$|N|\,\overleftarrow{C}_g$	$|N|\,\overleftarrow{C}_g$	$|N|\,\overleftarrow{C}_g$	1
$c = \frac{\partial e_w}{\partial o}\frac{\partial G_w}{\partial w}(x, l_N)$	$|N|\,\overleftarrow{C}_g$	$|N|\,\overleftarrow{C}_g$	$|N|\,\overleftarrow{C}_g$	1
$d = z(t)\frac{\partial F_w}{\partial w}(x, l)$	$|N|\,\overleftarrow{C}_f$	$|E|\,\overleftarrow{C}_h$	$|N|\,\overleftarrow{C}_\rho + |E|\,\overleftarrow{C}_\phi$	1

function and a_v the activation level of neuron v. Thus, $\delta(\partial l_w/\partial y)(y)$ is just a vector stacking all the delta values of the input neurons. Finally, $\vec{C}_l$ and $\overleftarrow{C}$ denote the computational complexity required by the application of FP and BP on l_w, respectively. For example, if l_w is implemented by a multi-layered FNN with a inputs, b hidden neurons, and c outputs, then $\vec{C}_l = \overleftarrow{C} = O(ab + ac)$ holds.

Complexity of Instructions

1) *Instructions $z(t+1) = z(t) \cdot A + b$, $0 = G_w(x, l_N)$, and $x(t+1) = F_w(x(t), l)$*: Since A is a matrix having at most $s^2\,|E|$ nonnull elements, the multiplication of $z(t)$ by A, and as a consequence, the instruction $z(t+1) = z(t) \cdot A + b$, costs $O(s^2\,|E|)$ floating points operations. The state $x(t+1)$ and the output vector o are calculated by applying the local transition function and the local output function to each node n. Thus, in positional GNNs and in nonlinear GNNs, where f_w, h_w, and g_w are directly implemented by FNNs, $x(t+1)$ and o are computed by running the forward phase of backpropagation once for each node or edge (see Table 5.2). On the other hand, in linear GNNs, $x_n(t)$ is calculated in two steps: the matrices A_n of Eq. (5.82) and the vectors b_n of Eq. (5.83) are evaluated; then, $x(t)$ is computed. The former phase, the cost of which is $\left(|E|\,\vec{C}_\varphi + |N|\,\vec{C}_\rho\right)$, is executed once for each epoch, whereas the latter phase, the cost of which is $O(s^2\,|E|)$, is executed at every step of the cycle in the function FORWARD.

2) *Instruction $=(\partial F_w/\partial x)(x, l)$*: This instruction requires the computation of the Jacobian of F_w. Note that $A = \{A_{n,u}\}$ is a block matrix where the block $A_{n,u}$ measures the effect of node u on node n if there is an arc (n,u) from u to n, and is null otherwise. In the linear model, the matrices $A_{n,u}$ correspond to those displayed in Eq. (5.82) and are used to calculate $x(t)$ in the forward phase. Thus, such an instruction has no cost in the backward phase in linear GNNs.

In nonlinear GNNs, $A_{n,u} = (\partial h_w/\partial x_n)(l_n, l_{(n,u)}, x_u, l_u)$ is computed by appropriately exploiting the backpropagation procedure. In other words, let $q_i \in R^s$ be a vector where all the components are zero except for the i-th one, which equals one, that is, $q_1 = [1, 0, ..., 0]$, $q_2 = [0, 1, 0, ..., 0]$, and so on. Note that BP, when it is applied to l_w with $\delta = b_i$, returns $A^i_{n,u} = q_i(\partial l_w/\partial y)(y)$, that is, the i-th column of the Jacobian $(\partial l_w/\partial y)(y)$. Thus, $A_{n,u}$ can be computed by applying BP on all the q_i, that is,

$$A_{n,u} = \left[A^1_{n,u}, A^2_{n,u}, ..., A^s_{n,u}\right]; \quad A^1_{n,u} = BP_2(h_w, y, q_i) \tag{5.84}$$

where BP_2 indicates that we are considering only the first component of the output of BP. A similar reasoning can also be used with positional GNNs. The complexity of these procedures is easily derived and is displayed in the fourth row of Table 5.2.

3) Computation of $\partial e_w/\partial o$ and $\partial p_w/\partial w$: In linear GNNs, the cost function is $e_w = \sum_{i=1}^q (t_i - \phi_w(G, n_i))^2$, and as a consequence, $\partial e_w/\partial o_k = 2(t_k - o_{n_k})$ if n_k is a node belonging to the training set, and 0 otherwise. Thus, $\partial e_w/\partial o$ is easily calculated by $O(|N|)$ operations.

In positional and nonlinear GNNs, a penalty term p_w is added to the cost function to force the transition function to be a contraction map. In this case, it is necessary to compute $\partial p_w/\partial w$, because such a vector must be added to the gradient. Let $A^{i,j}_{n,u}$ denote the element in position i,j of the block $A_{n,u}$. Recalling the definition of p_w, we have

$$p_w = \sum_{u \in N} \sum_{j=1}^s L\left(\sum_{n,u \in E} \sum_{i=1}^s |A^{i,j}_{n,u}| - \mu\right) = \sum_{u \in N} \sum_{j=1}^s \alpha_{u,j}$$

where $\alpha_{u,j} = \sum_{(n,u) \in E} \sum_{i=1}^s |A^{i,j}_{n,u}| - \mu$ if the sum is larger than 0, and 0 otherwise. It follows that

$$\frac{\partial p_w}{\partial w} = 2\sum_{u \in N} \sum_{j=1}^s \alpha_{u,j} \sum_{(n,u) \in E} \sum_{i=1}^s \mathrm{sgn}\left(A^{i,j}_{n,u}\right) \frac{\partial A^{i,j}_{n,u}}{\partial w} = 2\sum_{u \in N} \sum_{(n,u) \in E} \sum_{j=1}^s \sum_{i=1}^s \alpha_{u,j} \mathrm{sgn}\left(A^{i,j}_{n,u}\right) \frac{\partial A^{i,j}_{n,u}}{\partial w}$$

where sgn is the sign function. Let $R_{n,u}$ be a matrix whose element in position i,j is $\alpha_{u,j} \cdot \mathrm{sgn}\left(A^{i,j}_{n,u}\right)$, and let vec be the operator that takes a matrix and produces a column vector by stacking all its columns one on top of the other. Then

$$\frac{\partial p_w}{\partial w} = 2\sum_{u \in N} \sum_{n,u \in E}^s (vec(R_{n,u}))' \cdot \frac{\partial vec(A_{n,u})}{\partial w} \tag{5.85}$$

holds. The vector $\partial vec(A_{n,u})/\partial w$ depends on selected implementation of h_w or f_w. For the sake of simplicity, let us restrict our attention to nonlinear GNNs and assume that the transition network is a three-layered FNN. σ_j, a_j, V_j, and t_j are the activation function, the vector of the activation levels, the matrix of the weights, and the thresholds of the j-th layer, respectively. σ_j is a vectorial function that takes as input the vector of the activation levels of neurons in a layer and returns the vector of the outputs of the neurons of the same layer. The following reasoning can also be extended to positional GNNs and networks with a different number of layers. The function h_w is formally defined in terms of σ_j, a_j, V_j, and t_j

$$a_1 = \left[l_n, x_u, l_{(n,u)}, l_u\right]$$
$$a_2 = V_1 a_1 + t_1$$
$$a_3 = V_2 \sigma_2(a_2) + t_2$$
$$h_w\left(l_n, l_{(n,u)}, x_u, l_u\right) = \sigma_3(a_3)$$

By the chain differentiation rule, we get

$$vec(A_{n,u}) = vec\left(\frac{\partial h_w}{\partial x_u}\left(l_n, l_{(n,u)}, x_u, l_u\right)\right)$$

$$= vec\left(diag(\sigma'_3(a_3)) \cdot V_2 \cdot diag(\sigma'_2(a_2)) \cdot \bar{V}_1\right)$$

where σ'_j is the derivative of σ_j, *diag* is an operator that transforms a vector into a diagonal matrix having such a vector as diagonal, and $\bar{V}_1$ is the submatrix of V_1 that contains only the weights that connect the inputs corresponding to x_u to the hidden layer. The parameters w affect four components of $vec(A_{n,u})$, that is, a_3, V_2, a_2, and $\bar{V}_1$. By the properties of derivatives for matrix products and the chain rule

$$(vec(R_{u,v}))' \cdot \frac{\partial vec(A_{n,u})}{\partial w} = (vec(R_{u,v}))' \cdot \frac{\partial vec(A_{n,u})}{\partial \sigma'_3(a_3)} \cdot \frac{\partial \sigma'_3(a_3)}{\partial w}$$

$$+ (vec(R_{u,v}))' \cdot \frac{\partial vec(A_{n,u})}{\partial vec(V_2)} \cdot \frac{\partial vec(V_2)}{\partial w}$$

$$+ (vec(R_{u,v}))' \cdot \frac{\partial vec(A_{n,u})}{\partial \sigma'_2(a_2)} \cdot \frac{\partial \sigma'_2(a_2)}{\partial w} \qquad (5.86)$$

$$+ (vec(R_{u,v}))' \cdot \frac{\partial vec(A_{n,u})}{\partial vec(\bar{V}_1)} \cdot \frac{\partial vec(\bar{V}_1)}{\partial w}$$

holds. Thus, $(vec(R_{u,v}))' \cdot \partial vec(A_{n,u})/\partial w$ is the sum of four contributions. In order to derive a method of computing those terms, let I_a denote the $a \times a$ identity matrix. Let $\otimes$ be the Kronecker product, and suppose that P_a is a $a^2 \times a$ matrix such that $vec(diag(v)) = P_a v$ for any vector $v \in R^a$. By the Kronecker product's properties, $vec(AB) = (B' \otimes I_a) \cdot vec(A)$ holds for matrices A, B, and I_a having compatible dimensions [67]. Thus, we have

$$vec(A_{n,u}) = ((V_2 \cdot diag(\sigma'_2(a_2)) \cdot V_1)' \otimes I_s) \cdot P_s \cdot \sigma'_3(a_3)$$

which implies

$$\frac{\partial vec(A_{n,u})}{\partial \sigma'_3(a_3)} = ((V_2 \cdot diag(\sigma'_2(a_2)) \cdot V_1)' \otimes I_s) \cdot P_s$$

Similarly, using the properties $vec(ABC) = (C' \otimes A) \cdot vec(B)$ and $vec(AB) = (I_a \otimes A) \cdot vec(B)$, it follows that

$$\frac{\partial vec(A_{n,u})}{\partial vec(V_2)} = (diag(\sigma'_2(a_2)) \cdot V_1)' \otimes diag(\partial \sigma'_3(a_3))$$

$$\frac{\partial vec(A_{n,u})}{\partial \sigma'_2(a_2)} = (vec(R_{u,v}))' \cdot (V'_1 \otimes (diag(\sigma'_3(a_3)) \cdot V_2)) P_{d_h}$$

$$\frac{\partial vec(A_{n,u})}{\partial vec(\bar{V}_1)} = (I_s \otimes (diag(\sigma'_3(a_3)) \cdot V_2) \cdot diag(\sigma'_2(a_2)))$$

where d_h is the number of hidden neurons. Then, we have

$$(vec(R_{u,v}))' \cdot \frac{\partial vec(A_{n,u})}{\partial \sigma'_3(a_3)} \cdot \frac{\partial \sigma'_3(a_3)}{\partial w} = \left(vec\left(R_{u,v} \cdot \bar{V}_1 \cdot diag(\sigma'_2(a_1)) V'_2\right)\right)' P_s \cdot \frac{\partial \sigma'_3(a_3)}{\partial w} \qquad (5.87)$$

$$(vec(R_{u,v}))' \cdot \frac{\partial vec(A_{n,u})}{\partial vec(V_2)} \cdot \frac{\partial vec(A_{n,u})}{\partial w} = \left(vec\left(diag(\sigma'_3(a_3)) \cdot R_{u,v} \cdot \bar{V}_1 \cdot diag(\sigma'_2(a_2))\right)\right)' \cdot \frac{\partial vec(A_{n,u})}{\partial w}$$

$$(5.88)$$

$$(vec(R_{u,v}))' \cdot \frac{\partial vec(A_{n,u})}{\partial \sigma'_2(a_2)} \cdot \frac{\partial \sigma'_2(a_2)}{\partial w} = (vec(V'_2 \cdot diag(\sigma'_3(a_3))R_{u,v} \cdot V'_1))' \cdot P_{d_h} \cdot \frac{\partial \sigma'_2(a_2)}{\partial w} \quad (5.89)$$

$$(vec(R_{u,v}))' \cdot \frac{\partial vec(A_{n,u})}{\partial vec(\overline{V}_1)} \cdot \frac{\partial vec(\overline{V}_1)}{\partial w} = (vec(diag(\sigma'_2(a_2)) \cdot V'_2 \cdot diag(\sigma'_3(a_3)) \cdot R_{u,v}))' \cdot \frac{\partial vec(\overline{V}_1)}{\partial w}$$

$$(5.90)$$

where the aforementioned Kronecker product properties have been used.

It follows that $(vec\,(R_{u,v}))' \cdot \partial vec(A_{n,u})/\partial w$ can be written as the sum of the four contributions represented by Eqs. (5.87)–(5.90). The second and the fourth terms – Eqs. (5.88) and (5.90) – can be computed directly using the corresponding formulas. The first one can be calculated by observing that $\sigma'_3(a_3)$ looks like the function computed by a three-layered FNN that is the same as h_w except for the activation function of the last layer. In fact, if we denote by $\overline{h}_w$ such a network, then

$$(vec(R_{u,v}))' \cdot \frac{\partial vec(A_{n,u})}{\partial \sigma'_3(a_3)} \cdot \frac{\partial \sigma'_3(a_3)}{\partial w} = BP_1(\overline{h}_w, a_1, \delta) \quad (5.91)$$

holds, where $\delta = (vec(R_{u,v}))' \cdot \partial vec(A_{n,u})/\partial \sigma'_3(a_3)$. A similar reasoning can be applied also to the third contribution.

Required number of operations: The above method includes two tasks: the matrix multiplications of Eqs. (5.87)–(5.90) and the backpropagation as defined by Eq. (5.91). The former task consists of several matrix multiplications. By inspection of Eqs. (5.87)–(5.90), the number of floating point operations is approximately estimated as $2s^2 + 12s\,hi_h + 10s^2 \cdot hi_h$, where hi_h denotes the number of hidden-layer neurons implementing the function h. The second task has approximately the same cost as a backpropagation phase through the original function h_w. Such a value is obtained from the following observations: for an $a \times b$ matrix C and a $b \times c$ matrix D, the multiplication CD requires approximately $2abc$ operations; more precisely, abc multiplications and $ac(b-1)$ sums. If D is a diagonal $b \times b$ matrix, then CD requires $2ab$ operations. Similarly, if C is an $a \times b$ matrix, D is a $b \times a$ matrix, and P_a is the $a^2 \times a$ matrix defined above and used in Eqs. (5.87)–(5.90), then computing $vec(CD)P_c$ costs only $2ab$ operations provided that a sparse representation is used for P_a. Finally, a_1, a_2, a_3 are already available, since they are computed during the forward phase of the learning algorithm. Thus, the complexity of computing $\partial p_w/\partial w$ is $O(|E| \max(s^2 \cdot hi_h, \overleftarrow{C}_h))$. Note, however, that even if the sum in Eq. (5.85) ranges over all the arcs of the graph, only those arcs (n, u) such that $R_{n,u} \neq 0$ have to be considered. In practice, $R_{n,u} \neq 0$ is a rare event, since it happens only when the columns of the Jacobian are larger than μ, and a penalty function was used to limit the occurrence of these cases. As a consequence, a better estimate of the complexity of computing $\partial p_w/\partial w$ is $O(t_R \cdot \max(s^2 \cdot hi_h, \overleftarrow{C}_h))$, where t_R is the average number of nodes u such that $R_{n,u} \neq 0$ holds for some n.

4) *Instructions* $b = (\partial e_w/\partial o)(\partial G_w/\partial x)(x, l_N)$ *and* $=(\partial e_w/\partial o)(\partial G_w/\partial w)(x, l_N)$: The terms b and c can be calculated by the backpropagation of $\partial e_w/\partial o$ through the network that implements g_w. Since such an operation must be repeated for each node, the time complexity of instructions $b = (\partial e_w/\partial o)(\partial G_w/\partial x)(x, l_N)$ and $c = (\partial e_w/\partial o)(\partial G_w/\partial w)(x, l_N)$ is $O(|N| \overleftarrow{C}_g)$ for all the GNN models.

5) *Instruction = $z(t)(\partial F_w/\partial w)(x, l)$:* By definition of $F_w, f_w,$ and BP, we have

$$z(t) \cdot \frac{\partial F_w}{\partial w}(x, l) = \sum_{n \in N} z_n(t) \frac{\partial f_w}{\partial w} \left(l_n, l_{co[n]}, x_u, l_{ne[n]} \right)$$
$$= \sum_{n \in N} BP_1 \left(f_w, y, z_n(t) \right) \tag{5.92}$$

where $y = [l_n, x_u, l_{(n,\,u)}, l_u]$ and BP_1 indicates that we are considering only the first part of the output of BP. Similarly

$$z(t) \cdot \frac{\partial F_w}{\partial w}(x, l) = \sum_{n \in N} \sum_{u \in ne[n]} z_n(t) \frac{\partial h_w}{\partial w} \left(l_n, l_{(n,u)}, x_u, l_u \right)$$
$$= \sum_{n \in N} \sum_{u \in ne[n]} BP_1 \left(h_w, y, z_n(t) \right) \tag{5.93}$$

where $y = [l_n, x_u, l_{(n,\,u)}, l_u]$. These two equations provide a direct method to compute d in positional and nonlinear GNNs, respectively.

For linear GNNs, let h_w^i denote the the output of h_w and note that

$$h_w^i \left(l_n, l_{(n,u)}, x_u, l_u \right) = b_u^i + \sum_{j=1}^{s} A_{n,u}^{i,j} x_u^i$$
$$= \rho_u^i(l_n) + \frac{\mu}{s|ne[u]|} \cdot \sum_{j=1}^{s} x_u^j \varphi_w^{i,j} \left(l_n, l_{(n,u)}, l_u \right)$$

holds where $A_{n,u}^{i,j}$ and $\varphi_w^{i,j}$ are the element in position i, j of matrix $A_{n,\,u}$ and the corresponding output of the transition network, respectively, while b_u^i is the the element of vector b_u, ρ_u^i is the corresponding output of the forcing network (see Eq. (5.83))], and x_u^i is the i-th element of x_u. Then

$$z(t) \cdot \frac{\partial F_w}{\partial w}(x, l) = \sum_{n \in N} \sum_{u \in ne[n]} z_n(t) \frac{\partial h_w}{\partial w} \left(l_n, l_{(n,u)}, x_u, l_u \right)$$
$$= \sum_{n \in N} \sum_{u \in ne[n]} \sum_{i=1}^{s} z_n^i(t) \frac{\partial h_w^i}{\partial w} \left(l_n, l_{(n,u)}, x_u, l_u \right)$$
$$= \sum_{n \in N} BP_1(\rho_w, y, \delta) + \sum_{n \in N} \sum_{u \in ne[n]} BP_2 \left(\varphi_w, \bar{y}, \bar{\delta} \right)$$

where $y = l_n, \bar{y} = \left[l_n, l_{(n,u)}, l_u \right], \delta = |ne[n]| \cdot z'(t),$ and $\bar{\delta}$ is a vector that stores $z_n^i(t) \cdot \mu/s |ne[u]| \cdot x_u^j$ in the position corresponding to i, j, that is, $\bar{\delta} = (\mu/s|ne[u]|) \text{vec} \left(z_n(t) \cdot x_u' \right)$. Thus, in linear GNNs, d is computed by calling the backpropagation procedure on each arc and node.

Time complexity of the GNN model: Formally, the complexity is easily derived from Table 5.2: it is $O\left(|N| \vec{C_g} + \text{it}_f \cdot |N| \vec{C_f} \right)$ for positional GNNs, $O\left(|N| \vec{C_g} + \text{it}_f \cdot |\Phi| \vec{C_h} \right)$ for nonlinear GNNs, and $O\left(|N| \vec{C_g} + \text{it}_f \cdot |E| s^2 + |N| \vec{C_\rho} + |E| \vec{C_\varphi} \right)$ for linear GNNs. In practice, the cost of the test phase is mainly due to the repeated computation of the state $x(t)$. The cost of each iteration is linear with respect to both the dimension of the input graph (the number of edges) and the dimension of the employed FNNs and the state, with the sole exception of linear GNNs, whose single iteration cost is quadratic with respect to the state. The number of iterations required for the convergence of the state depends on the problem at hand, but Banach's theorem ensures that the convergence is exponentially fast, and experiments have shown that 5–15 iterations are generally sufficient to approximate the fixed point [1].

In positional and nonlinear GNNs, the transition function must be activated $it_f \cdot |N|$ and $it_f \cdot |E|$ times, respectively. Even if such a difference may appear significant, in practice, the complexity of the two models is similar, because the network that implements the f_w is larger than the one that implements h_w. In fact, f_w has $M(s + l_E)$ input neurons, where M is the maximum number of neighbors for a node, whereas h_w has only $s + l_E$ input neurons. A significant difference can be noticed only for graphs where the number of neighbors of nodes is highly variable, since the inputs of f_w must be sufficient to accommodate the maximum number of neighbors, and many inputs may remain unused when f_w is applied. On the other hand, it is observed that in the linear model the FNNs are used only once for each iteration, so that the complexity of each iteration is $O(s^2 |E|)$ instead of $\left(|E| |\vec{C_h}| \right)$. Note that $\vec{C_h} = O((s + l_E + 2l_N) \cdot hi_h) = O(s \cdot hi_h)$ holds, when h_w is implemented by a three-layered FNN with hi_h hidden neurons. In practical cases, where hi_h is often larger than s, the linear model is faster than the nonlinear model. As confirmed by the experiments, such an advantage is mitigated by the smaller accuracy that the model usually achieves.

In GNNs, the learning phase requires much more time than the test phase, mainly due to the repetition of the forward and backward phases for several epochs. The experiments have shown that the time spent in the forward and backward phases is not very different. Similarly, to the forward phase, the cost of the function BACKWARD is mainly due to the repetition of the instruction that computes $z(t)$. Theorem 5.2 ensures that $z(t)$ converges exponentially fast, and experiments have confirmed that it_b is usually a small number.

Formally, the cost of each learning epoch is given by the sum of all the instructions times the iterations in Table 5.2. An inspection of the table shows that the cost of all instructions involved in the learning phase are linear with respect to both the dimension of the input graph and of the FNNs. The only exceptions are due to the computation of $z(t + 1) = z(t) \cdot A + b$, $(\partial F_w / \partial x)(x, l)$ and $\partial p_w / w$, which depend quadratically on s.

The most expensive instruction is apparently the computation of $\partial p_w / w$ in nonlinear GNNs, which costs $O\left(t_R \cdot \max \left(s^2 \cdot hi_h, \overleftarrow{C_h} \right) \right)$. On the other hand, the experiments have shown [1] that t_R is usually a small number. In most epochs, t_R is 0, since the Jacobian does not violate the imposed constraint, and in the other cases, t_R is usually in the range 1–5. Thus, for a small state dimension s, the computation of $\partial p_w / w$ requires few applications of backpropagation on h and has a small impact on the global complexity of the learning process. On the other hand, in theory, if s is very large, it might happen that $s^2 \cdot hi_h \gg \overleftarrow{C_h} \approx (s + l_E + 2l_N) \cdot hi_h$ and at the same time $t_R \gg 0$, causing the computation of the gradient to be very slow.

Appendix 5.A   Notes on Graph Laplacian

Let $G = (V, E)$ be an undirected graph with vertex set $V = \{v_1, ..., v_n\}$. In the following, we assume that the graph G is weighted, that is, each edge between two vertices v_i and v_j carries a non-negative weight $w_{ij} \geq 0$. The weighted *adjacency matrix* of the graph is the matrix $W = (w_{ij})_{i, j = 1, ..., n}$. If

$w_{ij} = 0$, this means that the vertices v_i and v_j are not connected by an edge. As G is undirected, we require $w_{ij} = w_{ji}$. The degree of a vertex $v_i \in V$ is defined as

$$d_i = \sum_{j=1}^{n} w_{ij}.$$

Note that, in fact, this sum only runs over all vertices adjacent to v_i, as for all other vertices v_j the weight w_{ij} is 0. The *degree matrix D* is defined as the diagonal matrix with the degrees $d_1, ..., d_n$ on the diagonal. Given a subset of vertices $A \subset V$, we denote its complement $V \backslash A$ by $\bar{A}$. We define the indicator vector $I_A = (f_1, ..., f_n)' \in \mathbb{R}^n$ as the vector with entries $f_i = 1$ if $v_i \in A$ and $f_i = 0$ otherwise. For convenience, we introduce the shorthand notation $i \in A$ for the set of indices $\{i \mid v_i \in A\}$, in particular when dealing with a sum like $\sum_{i \in A} w_{ij}$. For two not necessarily disjoint sets $A, B \subset V$ we define

$$W(A, B) := \sum_{i \in A, j \in B} w_{ij}.$$

We consider two different ways of measuring the "**size**" of a subset $\subset A$:
$|A| :=$ the number of vertices in A; $\mathrm{vol}(A) := \sum_{i \in A} d_i$.

Intuitively, $|A|$ measures the size of A by its number of vertices, whereas $\mathrm{vol}(A)$ measures the size of A by summing over the weights of all edges attached to vertices in A. A subset $A \subset V$ of a graph is connected if any two vertices in A can be joined by a path such that all intermediate points also lie in A. A subset A is called a connected component if it is connected and if there are no connections between vertices in A and $\bar{A}$. The nonempty sets $A_1, ..., A_k$ form a partition of the graph if $A_i \cap A_j = \emptyset$ and $A_1 \cup ... \cup A_k = V$.

Similarity graphs: There are several popular constructions to transform a given set $x_1, ..., x_n$ of data points with pairwise similarities s_{ij} or pairwise distances d_{ij} into a graph. When constructing similarity graphs, the goal is to model the local neighborhood relationships between the data points.

The ε-neighborhood graph: Here, we connect all points whose pairwise distances are smaller than ε. As the distances between all connected points are roughly of the same scale (at most ε), weighting the edges would not incorporate more information about the data to the graph. Hence, the ε-neighborhood graph is usually considered an unweighted graph.

k-nearest neighbor graphs: Here, the goal is to connect vertex v_i with vertex v_j if v_j is among the k-nearest neighbors of v_i. However, this definition leads to a directed graph, as the neighborhood relationship is not symmetric. There are two ways of making this graph undirected. The first way is to simply ignore the directions of the edges, that is, we connect v_i and v_j with an undirected edge if v_i is among the k-nearest neighbors of v_j or if v_j is among the k-nearest neighbors of v_i. The resulting graph is what is usually called the k-nearest neighbor graph. The second choice is to connect vertices v_i and v_j if both of the following are true: (i) v_i is among the k-nearest neighbors of v_j and (ii) v_j is among the k-nearest neighbors of v_i. The resulting graph is called the mutual k-nearest neighbor graph. In both cases, after connecting the appropriate vertices, we weight the edges by the similarity of their endpoints.

The fully connected graph: Here, we simply connect all points with positive similarity with each other, and we weight all edges by s_{ij}. As the graph should represent the local neighborhood relationships, this construction is useful only if the similarity function itself models local neighborhoods. An example of such a similarity function is the Gaussian similarity function $s(x_i, x_j) = \exp(-\|x_i - x_j\|^2/(2\sigma^2))$, where the parameter σ controls the width of the neighborhoods. This parameter plays a similar role as the parameter ε in the case of the ε-neighborhood graph.

Graph Laplacians: The main tools for spectral clustering are graph Laplacian matrices. There exists a whole field dedicated to the study of those matrices, called spectral graph theory. In this section, we want to define different graph Laplacians and point out their most important properties. Note that in the literature there is no unique convention that governs exactly which matrix is called "graph Laplacian." Usually, every author just calls "his" matrix the graph Laplacian. Hence, a lot of care is needed when reading the literature on graph Laplacians.

In the following, we always assume that G is an undirected, weighted graph with weight matrix W, where $w_{ij} = w_{ji} \geq 0$. When using the eigenvectors of a matrix, we will not necessarily assume that they are normalized. For example, the constant vector 1 and a multiple a1 for some $a \neq 0$ will be considered the same eigenvectors. Eigenvalues will always be ordered in ascending order, respecting multiplicities. By "the first k eigenvectors" we refer to the eigenvectors corresponding to the k smallest eigenvalues.

The unnormalized graph Laplacian is defined as $L = D - W$.

The following proposition summarizes the most important facts needed for spectral clustering.

Proposition 5.1 (Properties of L) The matrix L satisfies the following properties:

1) For every vector $f \in \mathbb{R}^n$ we have

$$f'Lf = \frac{1}{2} \sum_{i,j=1}^{n} w_{ij} \left(f_i - f_j \right)^2.$$

2) L is symmetric and positive semidefinite.
3) The smallest eigenvalue of L is 0, and the corresponding eigenvector is the constant one vector *1*.
4) L has *n* non-negative, real-valued eigenvalues $0 = \lambda_1 \leq \lambda_2 \leq \dots \leq \lambda_n$.

Proof:
Part (1): By the definition of d_i,

$$f'\,Lf = f'\,Df - f'\,Wf = \sum_{i=1}^{n} d_i f_i^2 - \sum_{i,j=1}^{n} f_i f_j w_{ij}$$

$$= \frac{1}{2} \left(\sum_{i=1}^{n} d_i f_i^2 - 2 \sum_{i,j=1}^{n} f_i f_j w_{ij} + \sum_{j=1}^{n} d_j f_j^2 \right) = \frac{1}{2} \sum_{i,j=1}^{n} w_{ij} \left(f_i - f_j \right)^2.$$

Part (2): The symmetry of L follows directly from the symmetry of W and D. The positive semi-definiteness is a direct consequence of Part (1), which shows that $f'Lf \geq 0$ for all $f \in \mathbb{R}^n$.

Part (3): Self-evident.

Part (4) is a direct consequence of Parts (1)–(3).

The normalized graph Laplacians: There are two matrices that are called normalized graph Laplacians in the literature. Both matrices are closely related to each other and are defined as

$$L_{\text{sym}} := D^{-1/2} L D^{-1/2} = I - D^{-1/2} W D^{-1/2}$$
$$L_{\text{rw}} := D^{-1} L = I - D^{-1} W.$$

We denote the first matrix by L_{sym} as it is a symmetric matrix, and the second one by L_{rw} as it is closely related to a random walk. In the following, we summarize several properties of L_{sym} and L_{rw}.

Proposition 5.2 (Properties of L_{sym} and L_{rw}) The normalized Laplacians satisfy the following properties:

1) For every $f \in \mathbb{R}^n$ we have

$$f'L_{\text{sym}}f = \frac{1}{2}\sum_{i,j=1}^{n} w_{ij}\left(\frac{f_i}{\sqrt{d_i}} - \frac{f_j}{\sqrt{d_j}}\right)^2.$$

2) λ is an eigenvalue of L_{rw} with eigenvector u *if* and only if λ is an eigenvalue of L_{sym} with eigenvector $w = D^{1/2}u$.

3) λ is an eigenvalue of L_{rw} with eigenvector u if and only if λ and u solve the generalized eigen problem $Lu = \lambda Du$.

4) 0 is an eigenvalue of L_{rw} with the constant one vector I as eigenvector. 0 is an eigenvalue of L_{sym} with eigenvector $D^{1/2}I$.

5) L_{sym} and L_{rw} are positive semidefinite and have n non-negative real-valued eigenvalues $0 = \lambda_1 \leq, ... \leq \lambda_n$.

Proof. Part (1) can be proved similarly to Part (1) of Proposition 5.1.

Part (2) can be seen immediately by multiplying the eigenvalue equation $L_{\text{sym}}w = \lambda w$ with $D^{-1/2}$ from the left and substituting $u = D^{-1/2}w$.

Part (3) follows directly by multiplying the eigenvalue equation $L_{\text{rw}}u = \lambda u$ with D from the left.

Part (4): The first statement is obvious as $L_{\text{rw}}I = 0$, the second statement follows from (2).

Part (5): The statement about L_{sym} follows from (1), and then the statement about L_{rw} follows from (2).

Part (5): The statement about L_{sym} follows from (1), and then the statement about L_{rw} follows from (2).

Appendix 5.B Graph Fourier Transform

Graph signals: A graph signal is a collection of values defined on a complex and irregular structure modeled as a graph. In this appendix, a graph is represented as $= (\mathcal{V}, W)$, where $\mathcal{V} = \{v_0, v_1, ..., v_{N-1}\}$ is the set of vertices (or nodes) and W is the weight matrix of the graph in which an element w_{ij} represents the weight of the directed edge from node j to node i. A graph signal is represented as an

N-dimensional vector $f = [f(1), f(2), ..., f(N)]^T \in \mathbb{C}^N$, where f(i) is the value of the graph signal at node i and $N = |\mathcal{V}|$ is the total number of nodes in the graph.

Directed Laplacian: As discussed in Appendix 5.A, the graph Laplacian for undirected graphs is a symmetric difference operator $L = D - W$, where D is the degree matrix of the graph, and W is the weight matrix of the graph. In the case of directed graphs (or digraphs), the weight matrix W of a graph is not symmetric. In addition, the degree of a vertex can be defined in two ways: in-degree and out-degree. The in-degree of a node i is estimated as $d_i^{\text{in}} = \sum_{j=1}^{N} w_{ij}$, whereas the out-degree of the node i can be calculated as $d_i^{\text{out}} = \sum_{j=1}^{N} w_{ji}$. We consider an in-degree matrix and define the directed Laplacian L of a graph as

$$L = D_{\text{in}} - W, \tag{5.B.1}$$

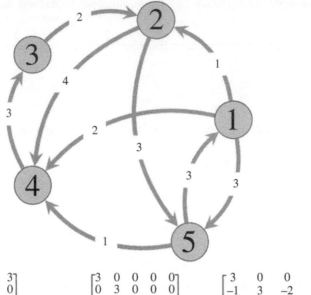

$$W = \begin{bmatrix} 0 & 0 & 0 & 0 & 3 \\ 1 & 0 & 2 & 0 & 0 \\ 0 & 0 & 0 & 3 & 0 \\ 2 & 4 & 0 & 0 & 1 \\ 3 & 3 & 0 & 0 & 0 \end{bmatrix} \qquad D_{in} = \begin{bmatrix} 3 & 0 & 0 & 0 & 0 \\ 0 & 3 & 0 & 0 & 0 \\ 0 & 0 & 3 & 0 & 0 \\ 0 & 0 & 0 & 7 & 0 \\ 0 & 0 & 0 & 0 & 6 \end{bmatrix} \qquad L = \begin{bmatrix} 3 & 0 & 0 & 0 & -3 \\ -1 & 3 & -2 & 0 & 0 \\ 0 & 0 & 3 & -3 & 0 \\ -2 & -4 & 0 & 7 & -1 \\ -3 & -3 & 0 & 0 & 6 \end{bmatrix}$$

Figure 5.B.1 A directed graph and the corresponding matrices.

where D_{in}= diag $\left(\{d_i^{in}\}_{i=1}^N \right)$ is the in-degree matrix. Figure 5.B.1 shows an example of weighted directed graph, with the corresponding matrices [68]. The Laplacian for a directed graph is not symmetric; nevertheless, it follows some important properties: (i) the sum of each row is zero, and hence $\lambda = 0$ is certainly an eigenvalue, and (ii) real parts of the eigenvalues are non-negative for a graph with positive edge weights.

Graph Fourier transform based on directed Laplacian: Using Jordan decomposition, the graph Laplacian is decomposed as

$$L = VJV^{-1}, \tag{5.B.2}$$

where J, known as the Jordan matrix, is a block diagonal matrix similar to L, and the Jordan eigenvectors of L constitute the columns of V. We define the graph Fourier transform (GFT) of a graph signal f as

$$\hat{f} = V^{-1}f. \tag{5.B.3}$$

Here, V is treated as the graph Fourier matrix whose columns constitute the graph Fourier basis. The inverse graph Fourier transform can be calculated as

$$f = V\hat{f}. \tag{5.B.4}$$

In this definition of GFT, the eigenvalues of the graph Laplacian act as the graph frequencies, and the corresponding Jordan eigenvectors act as the graph harmonics. The eigenvalues with a small absolute value correspond to low frequencies and vice versa. Before discussing the ordering of frequencies, we consider a special case when the Laplacian matrix is diagonalizable.

Diagonalizable Laplacian matrix: When the graph Laplacian is diagonalizable, Eq. (5.B.2) is reduced to

$$L = V\Lambda V^{-1}. \tag{5.B.5}$$

Here, $\Lambda \in \mathbb{C}^{N \times N}$ is a diagonal matrix containing the eigenvalues $\lambda_0, \lambda_1, ..., \lambda_{N-1}$ of L, and $V = [v_0, v_1, ..., v_{N-1}] \in \mathbb{C}^{N \times N}$ is the matrix with columns as the corresponding eigenvectors of L. Note that for a graph with real non-negative edge weights, the graph spectrum will lie in the right half of the complex frequency plane (including the imaginary axis).

Undirected graphs: For an undirected graph with real weights, the graph Laplacian matrix L is real and symmetric. As a result, the eigenvalues of L turn out to be real, and L constitutes ortho-normal set of eigenvectors. Hence, the Jordan form of the Laplacian matrix for undirected graphs can be written as

$$L = V\Lambda V^{T}, \tag{5.B.6}$$

where $V^{T} = V^{-1}$, because the eigenvectors of L are orthogonal in th undirected case. Consequently, the GFT of a signal f can be given as $\hat{f} = V^{T}f$, and the inverse can be calculated as $f = V\hat{f}$. One can show that for the example from Figure 5.B.1 for the signal $f = [0.12\ 0.38\ 0.81\ 0.24\ 0.88]$ we have the GFT as

$$\hat{f} = V^{T}f = \begin{bmatrix} 0.447 & 0.447 & 0.447 & 0.447 & 0.447 \\ 0.680 & -0.502 & -0.502 & -0.108 & 0.146 \\ -0.232-0.134i & 0.232+0.312i & -0.502-0.201i & 0.618-0.089i & 0.309 \\ -0.232+0.134i & 0.232-0.312i & -0.502+0.201i & 0.618+0.089i & 0.309 \\ -0.535 & 0.080 & 0.080 & -0.125 & 0.828 \end{bmatrix} \begin{bmatrix} 0.12 \\ 0.38 \\ 0.81 \\ 0.24 \\ 0.88 \end{bmatrix}$$

References

1 Scarselli, F., Gori, M., Tsoi, A.C. et al. (2009). The graph neural network model. *IEEE Trans. Neural Netw.* **20** (1): 61–80.

2 Khamsi, M.A. and Kirk, W.A. (2011). *An Introduction to Metric Spaces and Fixed Point Theory*, vol. **53**. Wiley.

3 M. Kampffmeyer, Y. Chen, X. Liang, H. Wang, Y. Zhang, and E. P. Xing, "Rethinking knowledge graph propagation for zero-shot learning," arXiv preprint arXiv:1805.11724, 2018.

4 Y. Zhang, Y. Xiong, X. Kong, S. Li, J. Mi, and Y. Zhu, "Deep collective classification in heterogeneous information networks," in WWW 2018, 2018, pp. 399–408.

5 X. Wang, H. Ji, C. Shi, B. Wang, Y. Ye, P. Cui, and P. S. Yu, "Heterogeneous graph attention network," WWW 2019, 2019.

6 D. Beck, G. Haffari, and T. Cohn, "Graph-to-sequence learning using gated graph neural networks," in ACL 2018, 2018, pp. 273–283.

7 M. Schlichtkrull, T. N. Kipf, P. Bloem, R. van den Berg, I. Titov, and M. Welling, "Modeling relational data with graph convolutional networks," in ESWC 2018. Springer, 2018, pp. 593–607

8 Y. Li, R. Yu, C. Shahabi, and Y. Liu, "Diffusion convolutional recurrent neural network: Data-driven traffic forecasting," arXiv preprint arXiv:1707.01926, 2017.

9 B. Yu, H. Yin, and Z. Zhu, "Spatio-temporal graph convolutional networks: A deep learning framework for traffic forecasting," arXiv preprint arXiv:1709.04875, 2017. 20

10 A. Jain, A. R. Zamir, S. Savarese, and A. Saxena, "Structural-rnn: Deep learning on spatio-temporal graphs," in CVPR 2016, 2016, pp. 5308–5317.

11 S. Yan, Y. Xiong, and D. Lin, "Spatial temporal graph convolutional networks for skeleton-based action recognition," in Thirty Second AAAI Conference on Artificial Intelligence, 2018.

12 J. Bruna, W. Zaremba, A. Szlam, and Y. Lecun, "Spectral networks and locally connected networks on graphs," ICLR 2014, 2014.

13 Hammond, D.K., Vandergheynst, P., and Gribonval, R. (2011). Wavelets on graphs via spectral graph theory. *Appl. Comput. Harmonic Anal.* **30** (2): 129–150.

14 T. N. Kipf and M. Welling, "Semi-supervised classification with graph convolutional networks," in Proc. of ICLR 2017, 2017.

15 D. K. Duvenaud, D. Maclaurin, J. Aguileraiparraguirre, R. Gomezbombarelli, T. D. Hirzel, A. Aspuruguzik, and R. P. Adams, "Convolutional networks on graphs for learning molecular fingerprints," NIPS 2015, pp. 2224–2232, 2015.

16 J. Atwood and D. Towsley, "Diffusion-convolutional neural networks," in Proc. of NIPS 2016, 2016, pp. 1993–2001.

17 C. Zhuang and Q. Ma, "Dual graph convolutional networks for graph-based semi-supervised classification," in WWW 2018, 2018.

18 S. Cao, W. Lu, and Q. Xu. Grarep: Learning graph representations with global structural information. In KDD, 2015.

19 A. Grover and J. Leskovec. node2vec: Scalable feature learning for networks. In KDD, 2016.

20 B. Perozzi, R. Al-Rfou, and S. Skiena. Deepwalk: Online learning of social representations. In KDD, 2014

21 J. Tang, M. Qu, M. Wang, M. Zhang, J. Yan, and Q. Mei. Line: Large-scale information network embedding. In WWW, 2015.

22 D. Wang, Daixin Wang, Peng Cui, Wenwu Zhu Structural deep network embedding. In KDD, 2016.

23 W. L. Hamilton, Z. Ying, and J. Leskovec, "Inductive representation learning on large graphs," NIPS 2017, pp. 1024–1034, 2017. https://arxiv.org/pdf/1706.02216.pdf

24 K. He, X. Zhang, S. Ren, and J. Sun, "Identity mappings in deep residual networks," in ECCV 2016. Springer, 2016, pp. 630–645.

25 K. Cho, B. Van Merrienboer, C. Gulcehre, D. Bahdanau, F. Bougares, H. Schwenk, and Y. Bengio, "Learning phrase representations using rnn encoder–decoder for statistical machine translation," EMNLP 2014, pp. 1724–1734, 2014.

26 Hochreiter, S. and Schmidhuber, J. (1997). Long short-term memory. *Neural Comput.* **9** (8): 1735–1780.

27 Y. Li, D. Tarlow, M. Brockschmidt, and R. S. Zemel, "Gated graph sequence neural networks," arXiv: Learning, 2016.

28 K. S. Tai, R. Socher, and C. D. Manning, "Improved semantic representations from tree-structured long short-term memory networks," IJCNLP 2015, pp. 1556–1566, 2015.

29 V. Zayats and M. Ostendorf, "Conversation modeling on reddit using a graph-structured lstm," TACL 2018, vol. 6, pp. 121–132, 2018.

30 N. Peng, H. Poon, C. Quirk, K. Toutanova, and W.-t. Yih,"Cross-sentence n-ary relation extraction with graph lstms," arXiv preprint arXiv:1708.03743, 2017.

31 D. Bahdanau, K. Cho, and Y. Bengio, "Neural machine translation by jointly learning to align and translate," ICLR 2015, 2015.

32 J. Gehring, M. Auli, D. Grangier, and Y. N. Dauphin, "A convolutional encoder model for neural machine translation," ACL 2017,vol. 1, pp. 123–135,

33 A. Vaswani, N. Shazeer, N. Parmar, L. Jones, J. Uszkoreit, A. N. Gomez, and L. Kaiser, "Attention is all you need," NIPS 2017, pp.5998–6008, 2017.

34 J. Cheng, L. Dong, and M. Lapata, "Long short-term memory-networks for machine reading," EMNLP 2016, pp. 551–561, 2016.

35 P. Velickovic, G. Cucurull, A. Casanova, A. Romero, P. Lio, and Y. Bengio, "Graph attention networks," ICLR 2018, 2018.

36 J. Gilmer, S. S. Schoenholz, P. F. Riley, O. Vinyals, and G. E. Dahl, "Neural message passing for quantum chemistry," arXiv preprint arXiv:1704.01212, 2017.

37 P. W. Battaglia, J. B. Hamrick, V. Bapst, A. Sanchez-Gonzalez,V. Zambaldi, M. Malinowski, A. Tacchetti, D. Raposo, A. Santoro,R. Faulkner et al., "Relational inductive biases, deep learning, and graph networks," arXiv preprint arXiv:1806.01261, 2018.

38 Z. Wu, Zonghan Wu, Shirui Pan, Fengwen Chen, Guodong Long, Chengqi Zhang, Philip S. Yu, A Comprehensive Survey on Graph Neural Networks, arXiv:1901.00596v4 [cs.LG] 4 Dec 2019, also in in IEEE Transactions on Neural Networks and Learning Systems, doi: 10.1109/TNNLS.2020.2978386

39 D. V. Tran, A. Sperduti Dinh V. Tran, Nicol'o Navarin, Alessandro Sperduti, "On filter size in graph convolutional networks," in SSCI. IEEE, 2018, pp. 1534–1541.

40 C. Gallicchio and A. Micheli, "Graph echo state networks," in IJCNN. IEEE, 2010, pp. 1–8

41 Y. Li, D. Tarlow, M. Brockschmidt, and R. Zemel, "Gated graph sequence neural networks," in Proc. of ICLR, 2015

42 K. Cho, B. Van Merrienboer, C. Gulcehre, D. Bahdanau, F. Bougares, ¨ H. Schwenk, and Y. Bengio,"Learning phrase representations using rnn encoder-decoder for statistical machine translation," in Proc. of EMNLP, 2014, pp. 1724–1734.

43 H. Dai, Z. Kozareva, B. Dai, A. Smola, and L. Song, "Learning steadystates of iterative algorithms over graphs," in Proc. of ICML, 2018, pp. 1114–1122.

44 Shuman, D.I., Narang, S.K., Frossard, P. et al. (2013). The emerging field of signal processing on graphs: extending high-dimensional data analysis to networks and other irregular domains. *IEEE Signal Process. Mag.* **30** (3): 83–98.

45 M. Defferrard, X. Bresson, and P. Vandergheynst, "Convolutional neural networks on graphs with fast localized spectral filtering," in Proc. of NIPS, 2016, pp. 3844–3852.

46 M. Henaff, J. Bruna, and Y. LeCun, "Deep convolutional networks on graph-structured data," arXiv preprint arXiv:1506.05163, 2015.

47 Levie, R., Monti, F., Bresson, X., and Bronstein, M.M. (2017). Cayleynets: graph convolutional neural networks with complex rational spectral filters. *IEEE Trans. Signal Process.* **67** (1): 97–109.

48 Micheli, A. (2009). Neural network for graphs: a contextual constructive approach. *IEEE Trans. Neural Netw.* **20** (3): 498–511.

49 Y. Li, R. Yu, C. Shahabi, and Y. Liu, "Diffusion convolutional recurrent neural network: Data-driven traffic forecasting," in Proc. of ICLR, 2018

50 S. Yan, Y. Xiong, and D. Lin, "Spatial temporal graph convolutional networks for skeleton-based action recognition," in Proc. of AAAI, 2018.

51 J. Gilmer, S. S. Schoenholz, P. F. Riley, O. Vinyals, and G. E. Dahl, "Neural message passing for quantum chemistry," in Proc. of ICML, 2017, pp. 1263–1272.

52 K. Xu, W. Hu, J. Leskovec, and S. Jegelka, "How powerful are graph neural networks," in Proc. of ICLR, 2019

53 P. Velickovic, G. Cucurull, A. Casanova, A. Romero, P. Lio, and Y. Bengio, "Graph attention networks," in Proc. of ICLR, 2017

54 S. Cao, W. Lu, and Q. Xu, "Deep neural networks for learning graph representations," in Proc. of AAAI, 2016, pp. 1145–1152

55 D. Wang, P. Cui, and W. Zhu, "Structural deep network embedding," in Proc. of KDD. ACM, 2016, pp. 1225–1234.

56 T. N. Kipf and M. Welling, "Variational graph auto-encoders," NIPS Workshop on Bayesian Deep Learning, 2016.

57 K. Tu, P. Cui, X. Wang, P. S. Yu, and W. Zhu, "Deep recursive network embedding with regular equivalence," in Proc. of KDD. ACM, 2018, pp. 2357–2366.

58 W. Yu, C. Zheng, W. Cheng, C. C. Aggarwal, D. Song, B. Zong, H. Chen, and W. Wang, "Learning deep network representations with adversarially regularized autoencoders," in Proc. of AAAI. ACM, 2018, pp. 2663–2671.

59 Y. Li, O. Vinyals, C. Dyer, R. Pascanu, and P. Battaglia, "Learning deep generative models of graphs," in Proc. of ICML, 2018.

60 M. Simonovsky and N. Komodakis, "Graphvae: Towards generation of small graphs using variational autoencoders," in ICANN. Springer, 2018, pp. 412–422

61 Z. Wu, S. Pan, G. Long, J. Jiang, and C. Zhang, "Graph wavenet for deep spatial-temporal graph modeling," in Proc. of IJCAI, 2019

62 Khamsi, M.A. (2001). *An Introduction to Metric Spaces and Fixed Point Theory*. New York: Wiley.

63 Powell, M.J.D. (1964). An efficient method for finding the minimum of a function of several variables without calculating derivatives. *Comput. J.* **7**: 155–162.

64 Frasconi, P., Gori, M., and Sperduti, A. (1998). A general framework for adaptive processing of data structures. *IEEE Trans. Neural Netw.* **9** (5): 768–786.

65 L. Almeida, "A learning rule for asynchronous perceptrons with feedback in a combinatorial environment," in Proc. IEEE Int. Conf. Neural Netw., M. Caudill and C. Butler, Eds., San Diego, 1987, vol. 2, pp. 609–618.

66 Pineda, F. (1987). Generalization of back-propagation to recurrent neural networks. *Phys. Rev. Lett.* **59**: 2229–2232.

67 Graham, A. (1982). *Kronecker Products and Matrix Calculus: With Applications*. New York: Wiley.

68 R. Singh, A. Chakraborty and B. S. Manoj, Graph Fourier Transform based on Directed Laplacian, https://arxiv.org/pdf/1601.03204.pdf

6

Learning Equilibria and Games

6.1 Learning in Games

Most optimization processes in advanced networks rely on an equilibrium analysis, making use of either Nash equilibrium or one of its refinements. One defense of this approach is to argue that Nash equilibrium might arise as a result of learning and adaptation. In this chapter, we investigate theoretical models of learning in games. A variety of learning models have been proposed, with different motivations. Some models are explicit attempts to define dynamic processes that lead to Nash equilibrium play. Other learning models, such as stimulus response or reinforcement models, were introduced to capture laboratory behavior. These models differ widely in terms of what prompts players to make decisions and how sophisticated players are assumed to be. In the simplest models we are interested in within the machine learning (ML) concept, players are just machines who use strategies that have worked in the past. They may not even realize they are in a game. In other models, players explicitly maximize payoffs given beliefs; these beliefs may involve varying levels of sophistication. In a systematic way, we will look at several approaches, focusing on the strategies that can be implemented as an ML process for network optimization and control.

Fictitious Play was one of the earliest learning rules to be studied. It is a "belief-based" learning rule, meaning that players form beliefs about opponent play and behave rationally with respect to these beliefs [22].

Fictitious Play Two players, $i = 1, 2$, play the game G at times $t = 0, 1, 2, \ldots$ Player 1 plays U (up) or D (down) while player 2 plays L (left) or R (right) as indicated in the table in Design Example 6.1 Define $\eta_i^t : S_{-i} \to \mathbb{N}$ to be the number of times i has observed s_{-i} in the past, and let $\eta_i^0(s_{-i})$ represent a starting point (or fictitious past). For example, if $\eta_1^0(U) = 3$ and $\eta_1^0(D) = 5$, and player 2 plays U, U, D in the first three periods, then $\eta_1^3(U) = 5$ and $\eta_1^3(D) = 6$.

Each player assumes that his opponent is using a stationary mixed strategy.

So, beliefs in the model are given by a distribution v_i^t on $\Delta(S_j)$.

The standard assumption is that v_i^t has a Dirichlet distribution, so

$$v_i^0(\sigma_{-i}) = k \prod_{s_{-i} \in S_{-i}} \sigma_{-i}(s_{-i})^{\eta_i^0(s_{-i})}$$

Artificial Intelligence and Quantum Computing for Advanced Wireless Networks, First Edition.
Savo G. Glisic and Beatriz Lorenzo.

Expected play can then be defined as

$$\mu_i^t(s_{-i}) = \mathbb{E}_{v_i^t}\sigma_{-i}(s_{-i})$$

The Dirichlet distribution has particularly nice updating properties, so that Bayesian updating implies that

$$\mu_i^t(s_{-i}) = \frac{\eta_i^t(s_{-i})}{\sum_{s_{-i} \in S_{-i}} \eta_i^t(s_{-i})} \tag{6.1}$$

In other words, this states that i forecasts j's strategy at time t to be the empirical frequency distribution of past play. The whole updating story can also be dropped in favor of the direct assumption that players just forecast today's play using the naive forecast rule (Eq. (6.1)). Note that even though updating is done correctly, forecasting is not fully rational. The reason is that i assumes (incorrectly) that j is playing a stationary mixed strategy. One way to think about this is that i's *prior* belief about j's strategy is wrong, even though he updates correctly from this prior.

Given i's forecast rule, he chooses his action at time t to maximize his payoffs, and so

$$s_i^t \in arg\ max_{s_i \in S_{-i}}\ g_i\left(s_i, \mu_i^t\right)$$

This choice is myopic. However, note that myopia is consistent with the assumption that opponents are using stationary mixed strategies. Under this assumption, there is no reason to do anything else.

Design Example 6.1

Consider fictitious play of the following game:

	L	R
U	3,3	0,0
D	4,0	1,1

t: Suppose $\eta_1^0 = (3,0)$ and $\eta_2^0 = (1, 2.5)$.
Then $\mu_1^0 = L$ with probability 1, and $\mu_2^0 = \frac{1}{3.5}U + \frac{2.5}{3.5}D$, so
play follows $s_1^0 = D$ and $s_2^0 = L$.
t + 1: $\eta_1^1 = (4,0)$ and $\eta_2^1 = (1, 3.5)$, so $\mu_1^1 = L$ and $\mu_2^1 = \frac{1}{4.5}U + \frac{3.5}{4.5}D$.
Play follows $s_1^1 = D$ and $s_2^1 = R$.
t + 2: $\eta_1^2 = (4,1)$ and $\eta_2^2 = (1, 4.5)$, so $\mu_1^2 = \frac{4}{5}L + \frac{1}{5}R$ and $\mu_2^2 = \frac{1}{5.5}U + \frac{4.5}{5.5}D$.
Play follows $s_1^1 = D$ and $s_2^1 = R$.

Basically, D is a dominant strategy for player 1, so he *always* plays D, and eventually $\mu_2^t \to D$ with probability 1. At this point, player 2 will end up playing R.

Definition 6.1 The sequence $\{s^t\}$ converges to s if there exists T such that $s^t = s$ for all $t \geq T$.

Definition 6.2 The sequence $\{s^t\}$ converges to σ in the time-average sense if for all i, s_i: $\lim_{T \to \infty} \frac{1}{T+1}$[# times $s_i^t = s_i$ in $\{0, 1, T\}$] $= \sigma_i(s_i)$

Proposition 6.1 Suppose a fictitious play sequence $\{s^t\}$ converges to σ in the time-average sense. Then σ is a Nash equilibrium of G.

Proof [22]. Suppose $s^t \to \sigma$ in the time-average sense and σ is not a Nash equilibrium. Then there is some i, s_i, s_i' such that $\sigma_i(s_i) > 0$ and $g_i(s_i', \sigma_{-i}) > g_i(s_i, \sigma_{-i})$. Pick $\varepsilon > 0$ such that $\varepsilon < \left[g_i(s_i', \sigma_{-i}) - g_i(s_i, \sigma_{-i}) \right] / 2$ and choose T such that whenever $t \geq T$, $| \mu_i^t(s_{-i}) - \sigma_{-i}(s_{-i}) | < \varepsilon/2N$, where N is the number of pure strategies. We can find such a T since $\mu_i^t \to \sigma_{-i}$. But then for any $t \geq T$:

$$g_i(s_i, \mu_i^t) = \sum g_i(s_i, s_{-i}) \mu_i^t(s_{-i}) \leq \sum g_i(s_i, s_{-i}) \sigma_{-i}(s_{-i}) + \varepsilon$$
$$\sum g_i(s_i', s_{-i}) \sigma_{-i}(s_{-i}) - \varepsilon \leq \sum g_i(s_i', s_{-i}) \mu_i^t(s_{-i}) = g_i(s_i', \mu_i^t)$$

So after t, s_i is never played, which implies that as $T \to \infty$, $\mu_j^t(s_i) \to 0$ for all $j \neq i$. But then it cannot be that $\sigma_i(s_i) > 0$, so we have a contradiction.

Reinforcement learning derives from psychology and builds on the idea that people will tend to use strategies that have worked well in the past. These adaptive learning models do not incorporate beliefs about opponent's strategies or require players to have a "model" of the game. Instead, players respond to positive or negative stimuli.

Let $q_{ik}(t)$ denote player i's propensity to play his k-th pure strategy at time t. Initially, player i has the uniform propensities across strategies: $q_{i1}(1) = q_{i2}(1) = \cdots = q_{iK}(1)$. After each period, propensities are updated using a *reinforcement* function. Suppose that at time t, player i employed strategy k_t and obtained a payoff x. Then [22],

$$q_{ik}(t+1) = \begin{cases} q_{ik}(t) + R(x) & \text{if } k = k_t \\ q_{ik}(t) & \text{otherwise} \end{cases} \tag{6.2}$$

for some increasing function $R(\cdot)$. The idea is that if k_t was successful, the player is more likely to use it again. If it was unsuccessful, he will be less likely to use it. Propensities are mapped into choices using a choice rule. For instance, letting $p_{ik}(t)$ denote the probability that i will choose k at time t, a simple rule would be

$$p_{ik}(t) = \frac{q_{ik}(t)}{\sum_j q_{ij}(t)}. \tag{6.3}$$

Although this sort of model is very simple, it can sometimes explain experimental results very well. Not surprisingly, these models tend to fit the data better with more free parameters.

6.1.1 Learning Equilibria of Games

As a generalization of the above introductory discussion, we will now study *empirical game-theoretical analysis*, in which we have partial knowledge of a game, consisting of observations of a subset of the pure-strategy profiles and their associated payoffs to players. The aim is to find an exact or approximate Nash equilibrium of the game, based on these observations. It is usually assumed that the strategy profiles may be chosen in an online manner by the algorithm. We study a corresponding computational learning model, and the query complexity of learning equilibria for various classes of games. We give basic results for exact equilibria of *bimatrix* and *graphical games*. We then study the query complexity of approximate equilibria in bimatrix games. Finally, we study the query complexity of exact equilibria in symmetric network *congestion* games.

Suppose that we have a game G with a known set of players, and known strategy sets for each player. We want to design an algorithm to solve G, where the algorithm can only obtain information about G via *payoff queries*. In a payoff query, the algorithm proposes pure strategies for the players, and is told the resulting payoffs. The general research problem is to identify bounds on the number of payoff queries needed to find an equilibrium, subject to the assumption that G belongs to some given class of games.

Here, along the lines presented in [1], we cover the study of payoff queries for *strategic-form games*, *graphical games* where players are nodes in a given graph and the payoff of a player depends only on the strategies of its neighbors in the graph, and *symmetric network congestion games*, where the strategy space of the players corresponds to the set of paths that connect two nodes in a network. For a strategic-form game, we assume that initially the querying algorithm knows only n, the number of players, and k, the number of pure strategies that each player has.

Definition 6.3 A payoff query to a strategic-form game G selects a pure-strategy profile s for G, and is given as response the payoffs that G's players derive from s.

There are k^n pure-strategy profiles in a game, and one could learn the game exhaustively using this many payoff queries. We are interested in algorithms that require only a small fraction of this trivial upper bound on the number of queries required. Here, we assume that initially the algorithm knows only the number of players n, and the set of pure strategies, given by a graph and the common origin–destination pair. We will consider two different query models, which are described in the following definition.

Definition 6.4 For a symmetric congestion game with m pure strategies and n players, a query is a tuple $q = (q_1, q_2, ..., q_m)$, where for each pure strategy $i = 1, 2, ..., m$, we have that $q_i \in \{0, 1, 2, ..., n\}$ is the number of players assigned to i under the query. In response to the query q, the querier learns the costs of each pure strategy under the assigned loads. Let $Q = \sum_{1 < i < m} q_i$. We consider two different types of queries:

- In a normal-query, we require that $Q = n$;
- In an under-query, we require that $Q < n$.

Normal-queries correspond to the query model that we use for strategic-form games. For a congestion game, m, which is the number of paths from the origin to the destination in a graph, may be exponential. While we defined a query for congestion as a tuple of length m, both normal-queries and under-queries require at most n positions of this tuple to be nonzero, so the query can be specified succinctly. We use under-queries in our query algorithm for games played on directed acyclic graphs. It is understood that under-queries are a reasonable query model for congestion games, because we can ask some players to refrain from playing when we conduct our query.

Definition 6.5 The payoff query complexity of a class of games $\mathcal{G}$, with respect to some solution concept such as exact or approximate Nash equilibrium, is defined as follows. It is the smallest N such that there is some algorithm $\mathcal{A}$ that, given N payoffs queries to any game $G \in \mathcal{G}$ (where initially none of the payoffs of G are known) can find a solution of G.

Note that $\mathcal{A}$ may select the queries in an online manner, so queries can depend on the responses to previous queries.

A *Bimatrix game* is a pair (R, C) of two $k \times k$ matrices: R gives payoffs to the *row player*, and C gives payoffs to the *column player*. We use $[n]$ to denote the set $\{1, 2, ..., n\}$. A *mixed strategy* is a probability distribution over $[k]$. A *mixed strategy profile* is a pair s $= (x, y)$, where x is a mixed strategy for the row player, and y is a mixed strategy for the column player.

Let s $= (x, y)$ be a mixed strategy profile in a $k \times k$ bimatrix game (R, C). We say that a row $i \in [k]$ is a *best response* for the row player if $R_i \cdot y = \max_{j \in [k]} R_j \cdot y$. We say that a column $i \in [k]$ is a best response for the column player if $(x \cdot C)_i = \max_{j \in [k]} (x \cdot C)_j$. We define the row player's *regret* under s $= (x, y)$ as the difference between the payoff of a best response and the payoff that the row player obtains under s. More formally, the regret that the row player suffers under *s* is

$$\max\nolimits_{j \in [k]} \left(R_j \cdot y \right) - x \cdot R \cdot y.$$

Similarly, the column player's regret is defined to be

$$\max\nolimits_{j \in [k]} \left((x \cdot C)_j \right) - x \cdot C \cdot y.$$

We say that s is a *mixed Nash equilibrium* if both players have regret 0 under s. An *ε-Nash equilibrium* is an approximate solution concept: for every $\varepsilon \in [0, 1]$, we say that s is an ε-Nash equilibrium if both players suffer regret at most ε under s.

In the following, we list a number of theorems pertaining to this kind of games; for the proofs, see [1].

Theorem 6.1 The payoff query complexity of finding an exact Nash equilibrium of a zero-sum $k \times k$ bimatrix game is k^2.

Theorem 6.2 Let i be chosen such that $2 \leq i \leq k - 1$. The payoff query complexity of finding a$\left(1 - \frac{1}{i}\right)$-approximate equilibrium of a $k \times k$ bimatrix game is at most $2k - i + 1$.

Lemma 6.1 Suppose that all payoff queries return 0 for both players. Let i be chosen such that $2 \leq i \leq k - 1$, and let s be a$\left(1 - \frac{1}{i}\right)$-Nash equilibrium. Any column that receives no queries must be assigned at least $\frac{1}{i}$ probability by s.

Theorem 6.3 Let i be chosen such that $2 \leq i \leq k - 1$. The payoff query complexity of finding a$\left(1 - \frac{1}{i}\right)$-approximate Nash equilibrium of a $k \times k$ bimatrix game is at least $k - i + 1$.

Definition 6.6 Let $\mathcal{G}_\ell$ be the class of strategic-form games where the column player has ℓ pure strategies and the row player has $\binom{\ell}{\ell/2}$ pure strategies (where we assume ℓ is even).

Let $G_\ell \in \mathcal{G}_\ell$ be the win-lose constant-sum game in which each row of the row player's payoff matrix has $\ell/2$ 1's and $\ell/2$ 0's, all rows being distinct. The column player's payoffs are one minus the row player's payoffs.

Lemma 6.2 Suppose that in game $G_\ell \in \mathcal{G}_\ell$, the column player places probability $\alpha > 1/\ell$ on some column. Then the row player can obtain a payoff strictly greater than $\frac{1}{2} + \frac{\alpha}{2} - \frac{1}{2\ell}$.

Corollary 6.1 Let $\alpha > 1/k$, and let $\varepsilon = \frac{1}{4}\left(\alpha - \frac{1}{k}\right)$. In every ε-Nash equilibrium of $G_\ell \in \mathcal{G}_\ell$, the column player plays each individual column with probability at most α.

Lemma 6.3 For any $\varepsilon < 1/12$, and any even $\ell \geq 8$, the payoff query complexity of finding an ε-Nash equilibrium for the games in $\mathcal{G}_\ell$ is at least $\frac{1}{2} \cdot \binom{\ell}{\ell/2} \cdot \left(\frac{1}{16\varepsilon + 4/\ell}\right)$.

Lemma 6.4 For $k \times k$ bimatrix games, the payoff query complexity of finding an ε-Nash equilibrium for $\varepsilon \leq 1/8$ is at least $\left(\frac{1}{32/\log k + 64\varepsilon}\right)$.

Theorem 6.4 For $k \times k$ bimatrix games, the payoff query complexity of finding an ε-Nash equilibrium for $\varepsilon \in \mathcal{O}\left(\frac{1}{\log k}\right)$ is $\Omega(k \cdot \log k)$.

Corollary 6.2 There is a constant value of $\varepsilon > 0$ for which finding an ε-Nash equilibrium of a $k \times k$ bimatrix game requires strictly more than $2k - 1$ payoff queries.

Graphical games: In an n-player *graphical game*, the players lie at the vertices of a degree-d graph, and a player's payoff is a function of the strategies of just himself and his neighbors. If every player has k pure strategies, then the number of payoff values needed to specify such a game is $n \cdot k^{d+1}$, which, in contrast with strategic-form games, is polynomial (assuming d is a constant).

Theorem 6.5 For constant d, the payoff query complexity of degree d graphical games is polynomial.

Algorithm 1 learns the entire payoff function with polynomially many queries, but there are a couple of important details. Although the payoff query complexity is polynomial, the computational complexity is probably not polynomial, since it is PPAD-complete to actually compute an approximate Nash equilibrium for graphical games. While Algorithm 1 [1] avoids querying all of the exponentially many pure strategy profiles, it works in a brute-force manner that learns the entire payoff function. It is natural to prefer algorithms that find a solution without learning the entire game, such as those that we give later.

6.1.2 Congestion Games

This kind of game is of special interest for network design and analysis. In this chapter, we will revisit the problem in a few iterations, each time providing additional details on the game modeling and analysis. In this section, we start by giving bounds on the payoff query complexity of finding a pure Nash equilibrium in symmetric network congestion games. A congestion game is defined by a

---

Algorithm 1 GRAPHICALGAMES

```
1: Initialize graph G's vertices to be the player set, with no edges
2: Let S be the set of pure profiles in which at least n - (d+1)
players play 1.
3: Query each element of S.
4: for all players p, p' do
5:   if ∃s, s' ∈ S that differ only in p's payoff and p''s strategy then
6:     add directed edge (p, p') to graph
7:   end if
8: end for
9: for all players p do
10:  Let N_p be p's neighborhood in G
11:  Use elements of S to find p's payoffs as a function of
strategies of N_p
12: end for
```

Source: J. Fearnley et al. [1].

---

tuple $\Gamma = (N, E, (S_i)_{i \in N}, (f_e)_{e \in E})$. Here, $N = \{1, 2, ..., n\}$ is a set of n players, and E is a set of resources. Each player chooses as her *strategy* a set $s_i \subseteq E$ from a given *set of available strategies* $s_i \subseteq 2^E$. Associated with each resource $e \in E$ is a nonnegative, nondecreasing function $f_e \colon \mathbb{N} \to \mathbb{R}^+$. These functions describe *costs* (latencies) to be charged to the players for using resource e. An outcome (or strategy profile) is a choice of strategies s$= (s_1, s_2, \ldots, s_n)$ by players with $s_i \in S_i$. For an outcome s define $n_e(s) = |i \in N \colon e \in s_i|$ as the number of players that use resource e. The *cost* for player i is defined by $c_i(s) = \sum_{e \in s_i} f_e(n_e(s))$. A *pure Nash equilibrium* is an outcome s where no player has an incentive to deviate from her current strategy. Formally, s is a pure Nash equilibrium if for each player $i \in N$ and $s_i' \in S_i$, which is an alternative strategy for player i, we have $c_i(s) \leq c_i(s_{-i}, s_i')$. Here (s_{-i}, s_i') denotes the outcome that results when player i changes her strategy in s from s_i to s_i'.

In a *network congestion game*, resources correspond to the edges in a directed multigraph $G = (V, E)$. Each player i is assigned an origin node o_i, and a destination node d_i. A strategy for player i consists of a sequence of edges that form a directed path from o_i to d_i, and the strategy set S_i consists of all such paths. In a *symmetric* network congestion game, all players have the same origin and destination nodes. We write a symmetric network congestion game as $\Gamma = (N, V, E, (f_e)_{e \in E}, o, d)$, where collectively, , o, and d succinctly define the strategy space $(S_i)_{i \in N}$. We consider two types of network: directed acyclic graphs and the special case of parallel links. We assume that initially we only know the number of players n and the strategy space. The latency functions are completely unknown initially. We use several different querying models for congestion games.

Parallel links: Here, we consider congestion games on m parallel links. We are interested in a lower bound and an upper bound on the query complexity of finding an exact pure equilibrium of these games. For simplicity we introduce a stronger type of query referred to as *over-query*. Earlier, for a query $q = (q_1, q_2, ..., q_m)$, we denoted by Q the total number of players used in the query, that is, $Q = \sum_{1 \leq i \leq m} q_i$.

Definition 6.7   An over-query is a query with $n < Q \leq mn$.

First, we present a simple lower bound. Then, we present an algorithm, Algorithm 2, which uses over-queries. Finally, we extend Algorithm 2 to Algorithm 3, which uses only normal-queries.

Lower bound: In the following construction, we show that, if there are two links, the querier can do no better than perform binary search in order to find an equilibrium, which gives a lower bound of $\log (n)$ many queries.

Theorem 6.6:   A querier must make $\log (n)$ queries to determine a pure equilibrium of a symmetric network congestion game played on parallel links.

Corollary 6.3   If over-queries are not allowed, then $\log (n) + m$ queries are required to determine a pure equilibrium of a symmetric network congestion game played on parallel links.

Upper bound: In the rest of the section, we provide an upper bound, by constructing a payoff query algorithm that finds a pure Nash equilibrium using $\mathcal{O}\big(\log (n) \cdot \big(\log^2(m)/\log \ \log (m)\big) + m\big)$ normal-queries. In order to simplify the presentation, we first present an algorithm that makes use of over-queries; later, we show how this can be translated into an algorithm that uses only normal-queries.

The algorithm with over-queries is depicted in Algorithm 2 [1], and it was shown that this algorithm can be implemented with $\mathcal{O}\big(\log (n) \cdot \log^2(m)/\log \ \log (m)\big)$ queries. The integer k is a parameter of the algorithm that determines the block size: in each round, a block of size k^t is considered for some t. To deal with the fact that n may not be an exact power of k, the algorithm will maintain a special link a. This link is defined to be the link upon which all n players are placed at the start of the algorithm. Since every subsequent step of the algorithm only moves players in blocks of size k^t for some t, link a will be the only like where the number of players is not a multiple of the block size.

We start by formalizing the notion of an equilibrium with respect to a certain block size. For a congestion game Γ, an integer δ, and a special link a we define a δ-equilibrium as follows:

Definition 6.8   *(δ-equilibrium):*A strategy profile s is δ-equilibrium if $\delta \mid n_i(s)$ for all $i \in [m]/\{a\}$, and for all links $i, j \in [m]$ with $n_i(s) \geq \delta$ we have $f_i(n_i(s)) \leq f_j(n_j(s) + \delta)$.

Intuitively, we can think of a δ-equilibrium s as a Nash equilibrium in a transformed game where the players (of the original game) are partitioned into blocks of size δ and each block represents a player in the transformed game, and the remaining ($n \bmod \delta$) players are fixed to link a.

We start with an informal description of Algorithm 2. In line 1, we initialize the algorithm by using one over-query to find the cheapest link a, and assigning all n players to link a. Note that a is the special link, as discussed earlier. The algorithm then works in $T + 1$ phases, where Algorithm 1.

$T = \lfloor \log (n)/\log (k)\rfloor$. Each phase is one iteration of the for loop. The for loop is governed by a variable t, which is initially T and decreases by 1 in each iteration. Within any iteration, the algorithm uses the function REFINEPROFILE to transform a k^{t+1}-equilibrium into a k^t-equilibrium.

It was observed that when $k = 2$, each link can receive at most one block when we transform a 2^{t+1}-equilibrium into a 2^t-equilibrium. In the following lemma, we establish a similar property for the case $k \neq 2$: each link can receive at most $2k$ blocks. Intuitively, one might expect each link to receive at most k blocks, but the extra factor of two here arises due to the special link a.

Algorithm 2 PARALLELLINKS

1: $a \leftarrow \arg\min_{i \in [m]} f_i(n)$ ◄ 1 over-query
2: initialize strategy profile s by putting all players on line a
3: $T \leftarrow \left\lfloor \frac{\log(n)}{\log(k)} \right\rfloor$
4: **for** $t = T$, $T-1$, …, 1, 0 **do**
5:    $\delta \rightarrow k^t$
6:    $s \leftarrow$ REFINEPROFILE $(s, \delta, 0, km)$
7: **end for**
8: **return** s
9: **function** REFINEPROFILE $(s, \delta, q_{min}, q_{max})$
10:    $q \leftarrow \left\lfloor \frac{q_{min} + q_{max}}{2} \right\rfloor$
11:    **Parallel** for all links $i \in [m]$
12:      Query for costs $f_i(n_i(s) + r\delta)$ for all integer $1 \leq r \leq 2k$ ► 2k queries
13:    **EndParallel**
14:    $Q \leftarrow$ the ordered multi-set of $2km$ nondecreasing costs from the above queries
15:    $C_{min}(q) \leftarrow (q+1)$-th smallest element of Q
16:    $p_i \leftarrow$ number of times $i \in [m]$ contributes a cost of the q smallest elements of Q
17:    **Parallel** for all links $i \in [m]$
18:      **if** $f_i\left(n_i(s) - \left\lfloor \frac{n_i(s)}{\delta} \right\rfloor \cdot \delta\right) > C_{min}(q)$ **then**   ► 1 query; only relevant for link a
19:        $q_i \leftarrow \left\lfloor \frac{n_i(s)}{\delta} \right\rfloor$
20:      **else** (using binary search on $q_i \in \left[0, \min\left\{km, \left\lfloor \frac{n_i(s)}{\delta} \right\rfloor\right\}\right]$)
21:        $q_i \leftarrow \min\left\{q_i : f_i(n_i(s) - q_i\delta) \leq C_{min}(q)\right\}$ ► $\log(km)$ queries
22:      **end if**
23:    **EndParallel**
24:    **if** $\sum_{i \in [m]} q_i = q$ **then**
25:      modify s by removing q_i and adding p_i blocks of δ players to every link $i \in [m]$
26:      **return** s
27:    **else if** $\sum_{i \in [m]} q_i < q$ **then**
28:      **return** REFINEPROFILE $(s, \delta, q_{min}, q-1)$
29:    **else** $(\sum_{i \in [m]} q_i > q)$
30:      **return** REFINEPROFILE $(s, \delta, q+1, q_{max})$
31:    **end if**
32: **end function**

Source: J. Fearnley et al. [1].

Lemma 6.5 We can convert a k^{t+1}-equilibrium s into a k^t-equilibrium s' by moving at most $2k$ blocks of $\delta = k^t$ players to any individual link and at most km blocks of δ players in total.

REFINEPROFILE determines the number of blocks q that have to be moved by binary search on q in $[0, km]$. Since, by Lemma 6.5, each link receives at most $2k$ blocks of players, we spend $2k$ over-queries to determine the cost function values $f_i(n_i(s) + r \cdot \delta)$ for all integers $r \leq 2k$ and all links $i \in [m]$. We define Q as the multi-set of these cost function values and $C_{\min}(q)$ as the $(q + 1)$-th smallest value in Q. Intuitively, $C_{\min}(q)$ is the cost of the $(q + 1)$-th block of players that we would move. We use $C_{\min}(q)$ to find out how many blocks of players q_i we need to remove from each link $i \in [m]$ so that on each link $i \in [m]$ the cost is at most $C_{\min}(q)$ or we cannot remove any further blocks as there are fewer than δ players assigned to it (which can only happen on link a). By Lemma 6.5, we need to remove at most km blocks of players in all. Therefore, we can determine $q_i \in [0, \min\{km, \lfloor n_i(s)/\delta \rfloor\}]$ by binary search in parallel on all links, with $\mathcal{O}(\log(km))$ under-queries. Now, if $\sum_{i=1}^{m} q_i = q$, we can construct a k^t-equilibrium by removing q_i and adding p_i blocks of δ players to link $i \in [m]$; note that for every $i \in [m]$, either $q_i = 0$ or $p_i = 0$. If $\sum_{i=1}^{m} q_i \neq q$, our guess for q was not correct, and we have to continue the binary search on q. The algorithm maintains the following invariant:

Lemma 6.6   *REFINEPROFILE* (s, δ, 0, km) returns a δ-equilibrium.

Lemma 6.7   *REFINEPROFILE* (s, δ, 0, km) can be implemented to make $2k$ over-queries and $\mathcal{O}(\log^2(km))$ non-over-queries.

Using Lemmas 6.6 and 6.7, we can prove the following.

Theorem 6.7:   *ALGORITHM* PARALLELLINKS returns a pure Nash equilibrium and can be implemented with $\mathcal{O}(\log(n) \cdot \log^2(m)/\log \log(m))$ queries, of which $2k \cdot \log(m)/\log \log(m)$ are over-queries.

Using only normal-queries: We now show how Algorithm 2 can be implemented without the use of over-queries. Before doing so, we remark that in the parallel links setting, we can also avoid using under-queries.

Lemma 6.8   If a parallel links congestion game has at least two links, then every under-query can be translated into two normal-queries.

We now turn our attention to over-queries. The following lemma gives a general method for translating over-queries into non-over-queries.

Lemma 6.9   Suppose we have a parallel links game with m links and n players. Let $q = (i_1, i_2, ..., i_m)$ be an over-query, and define $n' = \sum_{j=1}^{m} i_j$. We can translate q into a sequence of $\mathcal{O}(n'/n)$ non-over-queries.

In order to optimize the number of non-over-queries, we have to adjust Algorithm 2 slightly, because with $k = \Theta(\log(m))$ in early iterations of the for loop, that is, when T is large, the number of players used in the over-queries in line 12 is large and applying Lemma 6.9 would yield a total of $\mathcal{O}(\log(n) \cdot \log^2(m)/\log \log(m) + m \log(m))$ non-over-queries. By contrast, we will now show that our adjusted Algorithm 3 [1] can be implemented to do at most $\mathcal{O}(\log(n) \cdot \log^2(m)/\log \log(m) + m)$ non-over-queries. The main idea is to divide the block size by 2 until the number of players in a block is small enough and then switch to $k = \Theta(\log(m))$.

Algorithm 3 PARALLELLINKS AVOIDING OVER-QUERIES

1: $a \leftarrow \arg \min_{i \in [m]} f_i(n)$ ▶1 over-query
2: initialize strategy profile s by putting all players on link a
3: $T \leftarrow \left\lfloor \frac{\log(n/m)}{\log(k)} \right\rfloor$
4: $T_0 \leftarrow$ largest t such that $k^T 2^t < n$
5: **for** $t = T_0, T_0 - 1, \ldots, 1$ **do**
6: $\delta \leftarrow k^T 2^t$
7: s $\leftarrow$ REFINEPROFILE (s, δ, 0, 2m)
8: **end for**
9: **for** $t = T, T-1, \ldots, 1, 0$ **do**
10: $\delta \leftarrow k^t$
11: s $\leftarrow$ REFINEPROFILE (s, δ, 0, km)
12: **end for**
13: **return** s

Source: J. Fearnley et al. [1].

To initialize the algorithm, we make an over-query that uses $m \cdot n$ players. By Lemma 6.9, we can translate this into $\mathcal{O}(m)$ non-over-queries. In each iteration of the first for loop with value t, by Lemma 6.6, we make $\mathcal{O}(1)$ over-queries. Each of these uses at most $n + m \cdot 4 \cdot k^T 2^t$ players. By Lemma 6.9, these can be simulated by $\mathcal{O}(1 + mk^T 2^t/n)$ non-over-queries. Summing up over all iterations and using the definition of T_0, we can argue that all over-queries of the first for loop can be simulated by

$$\sum_{t=1}^{T_0} \mathcal{O}\left(1 + \frac{mk^T 2^t}{n}\right) = \mathcal{O}(T_0) + \mathcal{O}\left(\frac{mk^T 2^{T_0}}{n}\right) = \mathcal{O}(m)$$

non-over-queries. In each iteration of the second for loop with value t, by Lemma 6.6, we make $2k$ over-queries that each use at most $n + m \cdot 2k \cdot k^t$ players. By Lemma 6.9, these can be simulated by $\mathcal{O}(mk^{t+1}/n)$ non-over-queries. Summing up over all iterations, we can argue that all over-queries of the second for loop can be simulated by

$$\sum_{t=0}^{\lfloor \log(n/m)/\log(k) \rfloor} \mathcal{O}\left(\frac{mk^{t+1}}{n}\right) = \mathcal{O}\left(\frac{m}{n} \cdot k^{\frac{\log(n/m)}{\log(k)} + 1}\right)$$
$$= \mathcal{O}\left(\frac{m}{n} \cdot k^{\frac{\log(n) - \log(m) + \log(k)}{\log(k)}}\right) = \mathcal{O}\left(\frac{m}{n} \cdot k^{\frac{\log(n)}{\log(k)}}\right) = \mathcal{O}(m)$$

non-over-queries. Combining this discussion with Theorem 6.7, we get the following result:

Theorem 6.8 Algorithm 3 returns a pure Nash equilibrium and can be implemented with $\mathcal{O}\left(\log(n) \cdot \log^2(m)/\log \log(m) + m\right)$ queries.

Symmetric network congestion games on directed acyclic graphs: We consider the game $\Gamma = (N, V, E, (f_e)_{e \in E}, o, d)$, where (V, E) is a directed acyclic graph (DAG). We use the $\prec$ relation to denote a topological ordering over the vertices in V. We assume that, for every vertex $v \in V$, there exists a path from o to v, and there exists a path from v to d. If either of these conditions does not hold for some vertex v, then v cannot appear on an o-d path, and so it is safe to delete v.

We present an algorithm that discovers a cost function for each edge.

The algorithm proceeds inductively over the number of players in the game. For the base case, we give an algorithm that finds an equivalent cost function f' such that $f'_e(1)$ is defined for every edge e. This corresponds to learning all the costs in a one-player congestion game played on Γ. Then, for the inductive step, we show how the costs for an i-player game can be used to find the costs in an $i + 1$ player game. That is, we use the known values of $f'_e(j)$ for $j \leq i$ to find the cost of $f'_e(i + 1)$ for every edge e. Therefore, at the end of the algorithm, we have an equivalent cost function f' for an n-player game on Γ, and we can then apply a standard congestion game algorithm in order to solve our game.

Unlike the algorithm on parallel links, in this section we will not use over-queries at all. In each inductive step, when we are considering an i-player congestion game, we will make queries that use exactly i players. Thus, in the first $n - 1$ rounds we will use under-queries, and in the final round we will use normal-queries. For the sake of brevity, in this section we will use the word "query" to refer to both normal-queries and under-queries. As a shorthand for defining queries, we use notation of the form $s \leftarrow (1 \rightarrow p, 3 \rightarrow q)$. This example defines s to be a four-player query that assigns one player to p and three players to q, where p and q are paths from the origin to the destination in a symmetric network congestion game. We use Query(s) to denote the outcome of querying s. It returns a function c_s, which gives the cost of each strategy when s is played.

Preprocessing: The algorithm requires a preprocessing step. We say that edges e and e' are *dependent* if visiting one implies that we must visit the other. More formally, e and e' are dependent if, for every o-d path p, we either have $e, e' \in p$, or we have $e, e' \notin p$. We preprocess the game to ensure that there are no pairs of dependent edges. To do this, we check every pair of edges e and e', and test whether they are dependent. If they are, then we *contract* e', that is, if $e' = (v, u)$, then we delete e', and set $v = u$. The following lemma shows that this preprocessing is valid, and therefore, from now on, we can assume that our congestion game contains no pair of dependent edges.

Lemma 6.10 There is an algorithm that, given a congestion game Γ, where (V, E) is a DAG, produces a game Γ' with no pair of dependent edges, such that every Nash equilibrium of Γ' can be converted to a Nash equilibrium of Γ. The algorithm and conversion of equilibria take polynomial time and make zero payoff queries. Moreover, payoff queries to Γ' can be trivially simulated with payoff queries to Γ.

Equivalent cost functions: As we have mentioned, we cannot hope to find the actual cost function of Γ using payoff queries. To deal with this, we introduce the following notion of equivalence.

Definition 6.9 (Equivalence): Two cost functions f and f' are equivalent if for every strategy profile $s = (s_1, s_2, ..., s_n)$, we have $\sum_{e \in s_i} f_e(n_e(s)) = \sum_{e \in s_i} f'_e(n_i(s))$, for all i.

Clearly, the Nash equilibria of a game cannot change if we replace its cost function f with an equivalent cost function f'. We say that:

- $\left(f'_e \right)_{e \in E}$ is a *partial* cost function if for some $e \in E$ and some $i \leq n$, $f'_e(i)$ is undefined.
- f'' is an *extension* of f' if f'' is a partial cost function, and if $f''_e(i) = f'_e(i)$ for every $e \in E$ and $i \leq n$ for which $f'_e(i)$ is defined.

- f'' is a *total extension* of f' if f'' is an extension of f', and if $f''_e(i)$ is defined for all $e \in E$ and all $i \leq n$.

Definition 6.10 (Partial equivalent cost function): Let f be a cost function. We say that f' is a partial equivalent of f if f' is a partial cost function, and if there exists a total extension f'' of f' such that f'' is equivalent to f.

The goal is to find a total equivalent cost function by learning the costs one edge at a time. Thus, the algorithm will begin with a partial cost function f^0 such that $f^0_e(i)$ is undefined for all $e \in E$ and all $i \leq n$. Since it is undefined everywhere, it is obvious that f^0 is a partial equivalent of f. At every step of the algorithm, we will take a partial equivalent cost function f' of f, and produce an extension f'' of f', such that f'' is still a partial equivalent of f. This guarantees that when the algorithm terminates, the final cost function is equivalent to f.

(1) The one-player case: For the one-player case, the algorithm is relatively straightforward. It proceeds iteratively by processing the vertices according to their topological order, starting from the origin vertex o, and moving toward the destination vertex d. Each time we process a vertex k, we determine the cost of every incoming edge (u, k). There are two different cases: the case where $k \neq d$ and the case where $k = d$. For the latter case, we will observe that once we know the cost of every edge other than the incoming edges to d, we can easily find the cost of the incoming edges to d.

The former case is slightly more complicated. When we consider a vertex $k \neq d$, it turns out that we cannot find the actual costs for the incoming edges at k. Instead, we can use payoff queries to discover the difference in cost between each pair of incoming edges, and therefore we can find the cheapest incoming edge e to k. We proceed by fixing the cost of e to be 0. Once we have done this, we can then set the cost of each other incoming edge e' according to the difference between the cost of e and the cost of e', which we have already discovered. It can be proved that this approach is correct by showing that it yields a partial equivalent cost function.

Algorithm 4: The algorithm begins with the partial cost function f^0 and processes vertices iteratively according to the topological ordering $\prec$. Suppose that we are in iteration $a + 1$ of the algorithm, and that we are processing a vertex $\in V$. We have a partial equivalent cost function f^a such that $f^a_e(1)$ is defined for every edge $e = (v, u)$ with $u \prec k$, for some vertex k. We then produce a partial equivalent cost function f^{a+1} such that $f^{a+1}_e(1)$ is defined for every edge $e = (v, u)$ with $u \preccurlyeq k$. We now consider two cases.

(2) The $k \neq d$ case: We use the procedure shown in Algorithm 4 to process k. Lines 1 through 3 simply copy the old cost function f^a into the new cost function f^{a+1}. This ensures that f^{a+1} is an extension of f^a. The algorithm then picks an arbitrary k-d path p. The loop in lines 5 through 10 compute the function t, which for each incoming edge $e = (v, k)$ gives the cost $t(ep)$ of allocating one player to ep. Note, in particular, that the value of the expression $\sum_{e' \in p} f^a_{e'}(1)$ is known to the algorithm, because every vertex visited by p' has already been processed. The algorithm then selects e' to be the edge that minimizes t, and sets the cost of e' to be 0. Once it has done this, lines 13 through 15 compute the costs of the other edges relative to e'.

When we set the cost of e' to be 0, we are making use of equivalence. Suppose that the actual cost of e' is $c_{e'}$. Setting the cost of e' to be 0 has the following effects:

- Every incoming edge at k has its cost reduced by $c_{e'}$.
- Every outgoing edge at k has its cost increased by $c_{e'}$.

This maintains equivalence with the original cost function, because for every path p that passes through k, the total cost of p remains unchanged. The following lemma formalizes this and proves that f^{a+1} is indeed a partial equivalent cost function.

Algorithm 4 ProcessK

```
Input: A partial equivalent cost function f^a, such that f_e^a (1) is
defined for all edges (v, u) with u < k.
Output: A partial equivalent cost function f^{a+1}, such that f_e^{a+1} (1)
is defined for all edges (v, u) with u ≤ k.
 1: for all e for which f_e^a(1) is defined do
 2:    f_e^{a+1}(1) ← f_e^a(1)
 3: end for
 4: p ← an arbitrary k-d path
 5: for all e = (v, k) ∈ E do
 6:    p' ← an arbitrary o-v path
 7:    s ← (1 ↦ p'ep)
 8:    c_s ← Query(s)
 9:    t(ep) ← c_s(p'ep) - Σ_{e'∈p'} f_{e'}^a(1)
10: end for
11: e' ← edge e = (v, k) that minimizes t(ep)
12: f_{e'}^{a+1}(1) ← 0
13: for all e = (v, k) ∈ E with e ≠ e' do
14:    f_e^{a+1}(1) ← t(ep) - t(e'p)
15: end for
```

Source: J. Fearnley et al. [1].

Lemma 6.11 Let $k \neq d$ be a vertex, and let f^a be a partial equivalent cost function such that $f_e^a(1)$ is defined for all edges $e = (v, u)$ with $u < k$. When given these inputs, Algorithm 4 computes a partial equivalent cost function f^{a+1} such that $f_e^{a+1}(1)$ is defined for all edges $e = (v, u)$ with $u \leq k$.

The k = d case: When the algorithm processes d, it will have a partial cost function f^a such that $f_e^a(1)$ is defined for every edge $e = (v, u)$ with $u \neq d$. The algorithm is required to produce a partial cost function f^{a+1} such that $f_e^{a+1}(1)$ is defined for all $e \in E$. We use Algorithm 5 to do this. Lines 1 through 3 ensure that f^{a+1} is equivalent to f^a. Then, the algorithm loops through each incoming edge $= (v, d)$, and line 8 computes $f_e^{a+1}(1)$. Note, in particular, that $f_{e'}^a(1)$ is defined for every edge $e' \in p$, and thus the computation in line 8 can be performed. Lemma 6.12 shows that Algorithm 5 is correct.

Lemma 6.12 Let $k \neq d$ be a vertex and let f^a be a partial equivalent cost function defined for all edges (v, u) with $u < d$. When given these inputs, Algorithm 5 computes a partial equivalent cost function f^{a+1}.

Query complexity: The algorithm makes exactly $|E|$ payoff queries in order to find the one-player costs. When Algorithm 4 processes a vertex k, it makes exactly one query for each incoming edge (v, k) at k. The same property holds for Algorithm 5. This implies that, in total, the algorithm makes $|E|$ queries.

The many-player case: It assumes that we have a partial equivalent cost function f^a such that $f_e^a(j)$ is defined whenever $j \leq i$. We will describe an algorithm that goes through a sequence of iterations and produces a partial cost function $f^{a'}$, such that $f_e^{a'}(j)$ is defined whenever $j \leq i + 1$.

Algorithm 5 ProcessD

Input: A partial equivalent cost function f^a, such that $f^a_e(1)$ is defined for all edges $e = (v, u)$ with $u < d$.
Output: A partial equivalent cost function f^{a+1}, such that $f^a_e(1)$ is defined for all edges $e \in E$.
1: **for all** e for which $f^a_e(1)$ is defined **do**
2:    $f^{a+1}_e(1) \leftarrow f^a_e(1)$
3: **end for**
4: **for all** $e = (v, d) \in E$ **do**
5:    $p \leftarrow$ an arbitrary $o - v$ path
6:    $s \leftarrow (1 \mapsto pe)$
7:    $c_s \leftarrow Queru(s)$
8:    $f^{a+1}_e(1) \leftarrow c_s(pe) - \sum_{e' \in p} f^a_{e'}(1)$
9: **end for**

Source: J. Fearnley et al. [1].

The algorithm for the many-player case proceeds in a similar fashion to the algorithm for the one-player case. The algorithm is still iterative, and it still processes vertices according to their topological order, starting from the origin o, and moving toward the destination d. In this algorithm, when we process a vertex k, we will discover for each incoming edge e to k, the cost of placing $i + 1$ players on e.

In this case, there is an additional complication. The technique for discovering the cost of placing $i + 1$ players on the incoming edge at k requires two edge disjoint paths from k to d, but there is no reason at all to assume that two such paths exist. We say that an edge e is a bridge between two vertices v and u if every v-u path contains e. Furthermore, if we fix a vertex $k \in V$, then we say that an edge e is a k-bridge if e is a bridge between k and d. The following lemma can be proved using the max-flow min-cut theorem.

Lemma 6.13 Let v and u be two vertices. There are two edge disjoint paths between v and u if, and only if, there is no bridge between v and u.

As a consequence of Lemma 6.13, we can process k only if there are no k-bridges. To resolve this, before attempting to process k, we first use a separate algorithm to determine the cost of placing $i + 1$ players on each k-bridge. After doing this, we can then find two k-d paths that are edge disjoint *except for k bridges*. This, combined with the fact that we know the cost of placing $i + 1$ players on each k-bridge, is sufficient to allow us to process k.

Bridges: Given a vertex k, we show how to determine the cost of the k-bridges. Let $b_1, b_2, ..., b_m$ denote the list of k-bridges sorted according to the topological ordering $\preceq$. That is, if $b_1 = (v_1, u_1)$, and $b_2 = (v_2, u_2)$, then we have $v_1 \prec v_2$, and so on. The algorithm is given a partial cost function f^a, such that $f^a_e(j)$ is defined for all $j \leq i$, and returns a cost function f^{a+1} that is an extension of f^a where, for all ℓ, we have that $f^{a+1}_{b_\ell}(i + 1)$ is defined. The algorithm processes the k-bridges in reverse topological order, starting with the final bridge b_m. Suppose that we are processing the bridge $b_j = (v, u)$. We will make one payoff query to find the cost of b_j, which is described by the following diagram.

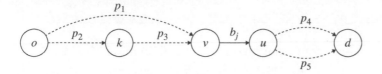

The dashed lines in the diagram represent paths. They must satisfy some special requirements, which we now describe. The paths p_4 and p_5 must be edge disjoint, apart from k-bridges. The following lemma shows that we can always select two such paths.

Lemma 6.14 For each k-bridge $b_j = (v, u)$, there exist two paths p_4 and p_5 from u to d such that $p_4 \cap p_5 = \{b_{j+1}, b_{j+2}, ...b_m\}$.

On the other hand, the paths p_1, p_2, and p_3 must satisfy a different set of constraints, which are formalized by the following lemma.

Lemma 6.15 Let $b_j = (v, u)$ be a k-bridge, and let p_2 be an arbitrarily chosen o-k path. There exist an o-k path p_1 and a k-v path p_3 such that p_1 and p_3 are edge disjoint; and if p_1 visits k, then p_2 and p_1 use different incoming edges for k.

Algorithm 6 shows how the cost of placing $i+1$ players on each of the k-bridges can be discovered. Note that on line 9, since s assigns one player to p_1, we have $n_e(s) = 1$ for every $e \in p_1$. Therefore, $f_e^{a+1}(n_e(s))$ is known for every edge $e \in p_1$. In addition, for every edge $e \in p_4$, we have that $n_e(s) = i+1$ if e is a k-bridge, and we have $n_e(s) = 1$, otherwise. Since the algorithm processes the k-bridges in reverse order, we have that $f_e^{a+1}(n_e(s))$ is defined for every edge $e \in p_4$. The following lemma shows that line 9 correctly computes the cost of b_j.

Algorithm 6 FINDKBRIDGES (k)

Input: A vertex k, and a partial equivalent cost function f^a, such that $f_e^a(j)$ is defined for every $j \leq i$.
Output: A partial equivalent cost function f^{a+1}, such that f^{a+1} is an extension of f^a, and f_e^{a+1} is defined for every e that is a k bridge.
1: **for all** e and j for which $f_e^a(j)$ is defined **do**
2: $\quad f_e^{a+1}(j) \leftarrow f_e^a(j)$
3: **end for**
4: **for** j = m to 1 **do**
5: $\quad p_4, p_5 \leftarrow$ paths chosen according to Lemma 6.14
6: $\quad p_1, p_2, p_3 \leftarrow$ paths chosen according to Lemma 6.15
7: $\quad s \leftarrow (1 \mapsto p_1 b_j p_4, \ i \mapsto p_2 p_3 b_j p_5)$
8: $\quad c_s \leftarrow$ Query(s)
9: $\quad f_{b_j}^{a+1}(i+1) \leftarrow c_S(p_1 b_j p_4) - \sum_{e \in p_1} f_e^{a+1}(n_e(s)) - \sum_{e \in p_4} f_e^{a+1}(n_e(s))$
10: **end for**

Source: J. Fearnley et al. [1].

Lemma 6.16 Let k be a vertex, and let f^a be a partial equivalent cost function, such that $f_e^a(j)$ is defined for every $j \leq i$. Algorithm 6 computes a partial equivalent cost function f^{a+1}, such that f^{a+1} is an extension of f^a, and f_e^{a+1} is defined for every e that is a k-bridge.

Incoming edges of k: We now describe the second part of the many-player case. After finding the cost of each k-bridge, we find the cost of each incoming edge at k. The following diagram describes how we find the cost of $e = (v, k)$, an incoming edge at k.

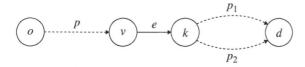

The path p is an arbitrarily chosen path from o to v. The paths p_1 and p_2 are chosen according to the following lemma.

Lemma 6.17 There exist two k-d paths p_1, p_2 such that every edge in $p_1 \cap p_2$ is a k-bridge.

Algorithm 7 shows how we find the cost of putting $i + 1$ players on each edge e that is incoming at k. Apart from the consideration of k-bridges, this algorithm uses the same technique as Algorithm 4. Consider line 9. Note that every vertex in p is processed before k is processed, and therefore $f_e^{a+1}(i+1)$ is known for every $e' \in p$. Moreover, for every edge $e' \in p_1$, we have that $n_{e'}(s) = i + 1$ if e' is a k-bridge, and we have $n_{e'}(s) = 1$ otherwise. In either case, the $f_{e'}^{a+1}(n_{e'}(s))$ is known for every edge $e' \in p_1$. The following lemma show that line 9 correctly computes $f_e^{a+1}(i+1)$.

Algorithm 7 MULTIPROCESSK

Input: A vertex k, and a partial equivalent cost function f^a, such that $f_e^a(j)$ is defined for all $e \in E$ when $j \leq i$, all $e = (v, u)$ with $u < k$ when $j = i+1$, and all k-bridges when $j = i+1$.

Output: A partial equivalent cost function f^a, such that $f_e^a(j)$ is defined for all $e \in E$ when $j \leq i$, and for all $e = (v, u)$ with $u \leqslant k$ when $j = i+1$.

1: **for all** e and j for which $f_e^a(j)$ is defined **do**
2: $f_e^{a+1}(j) \leftarrow f_e^a(j)$
3: **end for**
4: **for all** $e = (v, k) \in E$ **do**
5: $p \leftarrow$ and arbitrary o-v path
6: p_1, p_2 paths chosen according to Lemma 6.17
7: $s \leftarrow (1 \mapsto pep_1, i \mapsto pep_2)$
8: $c_s \leftarrow \text{Query}(s)$
9: $f_e^{a+1}(i+1) \leftarrow c_s(pep_1) - \sum_{e' \in p} f_{e'}^{a+1}(i+1) - \sum_{e' \in p_1} f_{e'}^{a+1}(n_{e'}(s)).$
10: **end for**

Source: J. Fearnley et al. [1].

Lemma 6.18 Let k be a vertex, and let f^a be a partial equivalent cost function such that $f_e^a(j)$ is defined for all $e \in E$ when $j \leq i$, all $e = (v, u)$ with $u \prec k$ when $j = i + 1$, and all k-bridges when $j = i + 1$. Algorithm 7 produces a partial equivalent cost function f^{a+1} such that $f_e^{a+1}(j)$ is defined for all $e \in E$ when $j \leq i$, and for all $e = (v, u)$ with $u \preccurlyeq k$ when $j = i + 1$.

Query complexity: It is argued that the algorithm can be implemented so that the costs for $(i + 1)$ players can be discovered using at most $|E|$ many payoff queries. Every time Algorithm 6 discovers the cost of placing $i + 1$ players on a k-bridge, it makes exactly one payoff query. Every time Algorithm 7 discovers the cost of an incoming edge (v, k), it makes exactly one payoff query. The key observation is that the costs discovered by Algorithm 6 do not need to be rediscovered by Algorithm 7. That is, we can modify Algorithm 7 so that it ignores every incoming edge (v, k) that has already been processed by Algorithm 6. This modification ensures that the algorithm uses precisely $|E|$ payoff queries to discover the edge costs for $i + 1$ players. This gives us the following theorem.

Theorem 6.9 Let Γ be a symmetric network congestion game with n-players played on a *DAG* with $|E|$ edges. The payoff query complexity of finding a Nash equilibrium in Γ is at most $n \cdot |E|$.

6.2 Online Learning of Nash Equilibria in Congestion Games

We will start by establishing a rather general concept of congestion games that model the interaction of players who share resources. We will then use examples to narrow down such a model to the routing games in the networks, which is the focus of the book. In general, the material is organized along the lines presented in [2]. In the congestion game, a finite set $\mathcal{R}$ of resources is shared by a set $\mathcal{X}$ of players. The set of players is endowed with a structure of measure space, $(\mathcal{X}, \mathcal{M}, m)$, where $\mathcal{M}$ is a σ-algebra of measurable subsets [3][1], and m is a finite Lebesgue measure [4][2]. The player set is partitioned into K populations, $\mathcal{X} = \mathcal{X}_1 \cup \cdots \cup \mathcal{X}_K$. For all k, the total mass of population $\mathcal{X}_k$ is assumed to be finite and nonzero. Each player $x \in \mathcal{X}_k$ has a task to perform, characterized by a collection of bundles $\mathcal{P}_k \subset \mathcal{P}$, where $\mathcal{P}$[3] is the power set of $\mathcal{R}$. The task can be accomplished by choosing any bundle of resources $p \in \mathcal{P}_k$. The action set of any player in $\mathcal{X}_k$ is then simply $\mathcal{P}_k$.

The joint actions of all players can be represented by an action profile: $\mathcal{X} \to \mathcal{P}$ such that for all $x \in \mathcal{X}_k$, $a(x) \in \mathcal{P}_k$ is the bundle of resources chosen by player x.

The function $x \to a(x)$ is assumed to be $\mathcal{M}$-measurable ($\mathcal{P}$ is equipped with the counting measure). The action profile a determines the bundle loads and resource loads, defined as follows: for all $k \in \{1, ..., K\}$ and $p \in \mathcal{P}_k$, the *load of bundle* p under population $\mathcal{X}_k$ is the total mass of players in $\mathcal{X}_k$ who chose that bundle

$$f_p^k(a) = \int_{x \in \mathcal{X}_k} 1_{(a(x) = p)} dm(x). \tag{6.4}$$

---

1 In mathematics, the *power set* (or *powerset*) of any set S is the set of all subsets of S, including the empty set and S itself.

2 The *measurable subsets* of a measure space (X, μ) are those *subsets* A of the underlying *set X* for which the measure $\mu(A)$ is defined.

3 The *Lebesgue measure* is the standard way of assigning a measure to subsets of n-dimensional Euclidean space. For $n = 1, 2,$ or 3, it coincides with the standard measure of length, area, or volume.

For any $r \in \mathcal{R}$, the *resource load* is defined to be the total mass of players utilizing r

$$\varphi_r(a) = \sum_{k=1}^{K} \sum_{p \in \mathcal{P}_k : r \in p} f_p^k(a). \tag{6.5}$$

The resource loads determine the losses of all players: the loss associated with a resource r is given by $c_r(\varphi_r(a))$, where the congestion functions c_r are assumed to be nonnegative, nondecreasing Lipschitz-continuous functions.

The total loss of a player x such that $a(x) = p$ is $\sum_{r \in p} c_r(\varphi_r(a))$. The congestion model is given by the tuple $\left(K, (\mathcal{X}_k)_{1 \leq k \leq K}, \mathcal{R}, (\mathcal{P}_k)_{1 \leq k \leq K}, (c_r)_{r \in \mathcal{R}}\right)$. The congestion game is determined by the action set and the loss function for every player: for all $x \in \mathcal{X}_k$, the action set of x is $\mathcal{P}_k$, and the loss function of x, given the action profile a, is $\sum_{r \in a(x)} c_r(\varphi_r(a))$.

A macroscopic view: The action profile a specifies the bundle of each player x. A more concise description of the joint action of players is given by the bundle distribution: the proportion of players choosing bundle p in population $\mathcal{X}_k$ is denoted by $\mu_p^k(a) = f_p^k(a)/m(\mathcal{X}_k)$, which defines a bundle distribution for population $\mathcal{X}_k$, $\mu^k(a) = \left(\mu_p^k(a)\right)_{p \in \mathcal{P}_k} \in \Delta^{\mathcal{P}_k}$, and a bundle distribution across populations, given by the product distribution $\mu(a) = (\mu^1(a), ..., \mu^K(a)) \in \Delta^{\mathcal{P}_1} \times \cdots \times \Delta^{\mathcal{P}_K}$. We say that the action profile a induces the distribution (a). Here, $\Delta^{\mathcal{P}_k}$ denotes the simplex of distributions over $\mathcal{P}_k$, that is, $\Delta^{\mathcal{P}_k} = \left\{\mu \in \mathbb{R}_+^{\mathcal{P}_k} : \sum_{p \in \mathcal{P}_k} \mu_p = 1\right\}$.

The product of simplexes $\Delta^{\mathcal{P}_1} \times \cdots \times \Delta^{\mathcal{P}_K}$ will be denoted by Δ. This macroscopic representation of the joint actions of players is useful in the analysis. We will also view the resource loads as linear functions of the product distribution $\mu(a)$. From Eq. (6.5) and the definition of $\mu_p^k(a)$, we have

$$\varphi_r(a) = \sum_{k=1}^{K} m(\mathcal{X}_k) \sum_{p \in \mathcal{P}_k : r \in p} \mu_p^k(a) = \sum_{k=1}^{K} m(\mathcal{X}_k) \left(M^k \mu^k(a)\right)_r,$$

where for all k, $M^k \in \mathbb{R}^{\mathcal{R} \times \mathcal{P}_k}$ is an incidence matrix defined as follows: for all $r \in \mathcal{R}$ and all $p \in \mathcal{P}_k$,

$$M_{r,p}^k = \begin{cases} 1, & \text{if } r \in p, \\ 0, & \text{otherwise.} \end{cases}$$

We write in vector form $\varphi(a) = \sum_{k=1}^{K} m(\mathcal{X}_k) M^k \mu^k(a)$, and by defining the scaled incidence matrix $\bar{M} = \left(m(\mathcal{X}_1) M^1 \mid ... \mid m(\mathcal{X}_K) M^K\right)$, we have $\varphi(a) = \bar{M} \mu(a)$

For simplicity, the dependence on the action profile a will be omitted, so we will write μ instead of $\mu(a)$ and φ instead of $\varphi(a)$. Also, we define the loss function of a bundle $p \in \mathcal{P}_k$ as

$$\ell_p^k(\mu) = \sum_{r \in p} c_r(\varphi_r) = \sum_{r \in p} c_r\left((\bar{M}\mu)_r\right) = M^T c(\bar{M}\mu), \tag{6.6}$$

where M is the incidence matrix $M = (M^1 \mid .... \mid M^K)$, and $c(\varphi)$ is the vector $(c_r(\varphi_r))_{r \in \mathcal{R}}$. We denote by $\ell^k(\mu)$ the vector of losses $\left(\ell_p^k(\mu)\right)_{p \in \mathcal{P}_k}$ and by $\ell(\mu)$ the K-tuple $\ell(\mu) = (\ell^1(\mu), ..., \ell^K(\mu))$.

Nash equilibria of the congestion game: A product distribution μ is a Nash equilibrium of the congestion game if for all k, and all $p \in \mathcal{P}_k$ such that $\mu_p^k > 0$, $\ell_{p'}^k(\mu) \geq \ell_p^k(\mu)$ for all $p' \in \mathcal{P}_k$ [2]. The set of Nash equilibria will be denoted by $\mathcal{N}$. A distribution μ is a Nash equilibrium if and only if for any joint action a that induces the distribution μ, almost all players have no incentive to unilaterally deviate from a. This also implies that, for a population $\mathcal{X}_k$, all bundles with nonzero mass have equal losses, and bundles with zero mass have greater losses. Therefore, almost all players incur the same loss.

Mixed strategies: The Nash equilibria we have described so far are *pure strategy* equilibria, since each player x deterministically plays a single action $a(x)$. We now extend the model to allow mixed strategies. That is, the action of a player x is a random variable $A(x)$ with distribution $\pi(x)$ and with realization $a(x)$.

We show that when players use mixed strategies, provided they randomize independently, the resulting Nash equilibria are, in fact, the same as those given above. The key observation is that under independent randomization, the resulting bundle distributions μ^k are random variables with zero variance, and thus they are essentially deterministic. To formalize the probabilistic setting, let $(\Omega, \mathcal{F}, \mathbb{P})$ be a probability space. A mixed strategy profile is a function $A: \mathcal{X} \to \Omega \to \mathcal{P}$, such that for all k and all $x \in \mathcal{X}_k$, $A(x)$ is a $\mathcal{P}_k$-valued random variable, such that the mapping $(x, \omega) \to A(x)(\omega)$ is $\mathcal{M} \times \mathcal{F}$-measurable. For all $x \in \mathcal{X}_k$ and $p \in \mathcal{P}_k$, let $\pi_p^k(x) = \mathbb{P}[A(x) = p]$. As in the deterministic case, the mixed strategy profile A determines the bundle distributions μ^k, which are, in this case, random variables, as we recall that $\mu_p^k = \int_{\mathcal{X}_k} 1_{(A(x) = p)} dm(x) / m(\mathcal{X}_k)$. Under independent randomization, $\forall k$, almost surely, $\mu^k = \mathbb{E}[\mu^k] = \int_{\mathcal{X}_k} \pi^k(x) dm(x) / m(\mathcal{X}_k)$ [2].

The Rosenthal potential function: This formulates the set of Nash equilibria as the solution of a convex optimization problem. Consider the function

$$V(\mu) = \sum_{r \in \mathcal{R}} \int_0^{(\bar{M}\mu)_r} c_r(u) du, \tag{6.7}$$

defined on the product of simplexes $\Delta^{\mathcal{P}_1} \times \cdots \times \Delta^{\mathcal{P}_k}$, which will be denoted by Δ. V is called the Rosenthal potential function and was introduced in [5] for the congestion game. It can be viewed as the composition of the function $\bar{V}: \varphi \in \mathbb{R}_+^{\mathcal{R}} \to \sum_{r \in \mathcal{R}} \int_0^{\varphi_r} c_r(u) du$ and the linear function $\mu \to \bar{M}\mu$. Since for all r, c_r is, by assumption, nonnegative, $\bar{V}$ is differentiable and nonnegative and $\nabla \bar{V}(\varphi) = (c_r(\varphi_r))_{r \in \mathcal{R}}$. And since c_r are nondecreasing, $\bar{V}$ is convex. (One way to see this is by Taylor's theorem: for all φ^0, φ, t such that $\varphi^0 \in \mathbb{R}_+^{\mathcal{R}}$ and $\varphi^0 + t\varphi \in \mathbb{R}_+^{\mathcal{R}}$, there exists t' between 0 and t such that

$$\bar{V}(\varphi^0 + t\varphi) = \bar{V}(\varphi^0) + t\langle \nabla \bar{V}(\varphi^0 + t'\varphi), \varphi \rangle \geq \bar{V}(\varphi^0) + t\langle \nabla \bar{V}(\varphi^0), \varphi \rangle;$$

Thus, $\bar{V}$ satisfies the first-order convexity condition. Therefore, V is convex as the composition of a convex and a linear function. A simple application of the chain rule gives $\nabla V(\mu) = \bar{M}^T c(\bar{M}\mu)$. If we denote by $\nabla_{\mu^k} V(\mu)$ the vector of partial derivatives with respect to μ_p^k, $p \in \mathcal{P}_k$, we have $\nabla_{\mu^k} V(\mu) = m(\mathcal{X}_k) M^{k^T} c(\bar{M}\mu) = m(\mathcal{X}_k) \ell^k(\mu)$. Thus,

$$\forall k, \forall p \in \mathcal{P}_k, \quad \frac{\partial V}{\partial \mu_p^k}(\mu) = m(\mathcal{X}_k) \ell_p^k(\mu), \tag{6.8}$$

and V is a potential function for the congestion game. $\mathcal{N}$ is the set of minimizers of V on the product of simplexes Δ. It is a nonempty convex compact set [5]. We will denote by $V_{\mathcal{N}}$ the value of V on $\mathcal{N}$.

The online learning framework. Suppose that the game is played repeatedly for infinitely many iterations, indexed by $\tau \in \mathbb{N}$. During iteration τ, each player chooses a bundle simultaneously. The decision of all players can be represented, as defined above, by an action profile $a^{(\tau)}: \mathcal{X} \to \mathcal{P}$. This induces, at the level of each population $\mathcal{X}_k$, a bundle distribution $\mu^{k(\tau)}$. These, in turn, determine the resource loads and the bundle losses $\ell_p^k(\mu^{(\tau)})$. The losses for bundles $p \in \mathcal{P}_k$ are revealed to all players in population $\mathcal{X}_k$, which marks the end of iteration τ. Players can then use this information to update their strategies before the start of the next iteration.

Each player $x \in \mathcal{X}_k$ is assumed to draw her bundle from a randomized strategy $\pi^{(\tau)}(x) \in \Delta^{\mathcal{P}_k}$. An online learning algorithm (or update rule) for the congestion game, applied by a player $x \in \mathcal{X}_k$, is a

Design Example 6.2

Routing games are congestion games with an underlying graph $\mathcal{G} = (\mathcal{V}, \mathcal{E})$, with vertex set $\mathcal{V}$ and edge set $\mathcal{E} \subset \mathcal{V} \times \mathcal{V}$. In this case, the resource set is equal to the edge set, $\mathcal{R} = \mathcal{E}$. Routing games are used to model congestion on communication networks. Each population $\mathcal{X}_k$ is characterized by a common source vertex $s_k \in \mathcal{V}$ and a common destination vertex $t_k \in \mathcal{V}$. In a communication setting, players send packets from s_k to t_k. The action set $\mathcal{P}_k$ is a set of paths connecting s_k to t_k. In other words, each player chooses a path connecting his or her source and destination vertices. The bundle load f_p^k is then called the flow on path p. The resource load φ_r is called the total edge flow. Finally, the congestion functions $\varphi_r \mapsto c_r(\varphi_r)$ determine the delay (or latency) incurred by each player. In [2], the routing game given in Figure 6.1 is used as an example to illustrate two populations of players sharing the network; the first population sends packets from v_0 to v_1, and the second population from v_2 to v_3. The paths (bundles) available to each population are given by

$$\mathcal{P}_1 = \{(v_0, v_1), (v_0, v_4, v_5, v_1), (v_0, v_5, v_1)\},$$
$$\mathcal{P}_2 = \{(v_2, v_3), (v_2, v_4, v_5, v_3), (v_2, v_4, v_3)\}.$$

Figure 6.1 Routing game with two populations of players. Source: Krichene et al. [2].

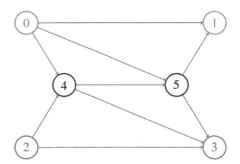

sequence of functions $(\,^xU^{(\tau)})_{\tau \in \mathbb{N}}$, fixed a priori, that is, before the start of the game, such that for each τ,

$$^xU^{(\tau)} : \left(\mathbb{R}^{\mathcal{P}_k}\right)^\tau \times \Delta^{\mathcal{P}_k} \longrightarrow \Delta^{\mathcal{P}_k}$$

$$\left(\left(\ell^k\left(\mu^{(t)}\right)\right)_{t \le \tau}, \pi^{(\tau)}(x)\right) \rightarrow \pi^{(\tau+1)}(x)$$

is a function that maps, given the history of bundle losses $(\ell^k(\mu^{(t)}))_{t \le \tau}$, the strategy on the current day $\pi^{(\tau)}(x)$ to the strategy on the next day $\pi^{(\tau+1)}(x)$. The online learning framework is summarized in Algorithm 8 [2].

Discounted regret: On iteration τ, a player $x \in \mathcal{X}_k$ who draws an action $A^{(\tau)}(x) \sim \pi^{(\tau)}(x)$ incurs a discounted loss given by $\gamma_\tau \ell_{A(\tau)}^k(x)(\mu^{(\tau)})$, where $\mu^{(\tau)}$ is the distribution induced by the profile $A^{(\tau)}$. The cumulative discounted loss for player x up to iteration T is then defined as

$$L^{(T)}(x) = \sum_{\tau=0}^{T} \gamma_\tau \ell_{A^{(\tau)}(x)}^k\left(\mu^{(\tau)}\right). \tag{6.9}$$

Algorithm 8 Online Learning Framework for the Congestion Game

---

1: For every player $x \in \mathcal{P}_k$, and initial mixed strategy $\pi^{(0)}(x) \in \Delta^{\mathcal{P}_k}$ and an online learning algorithm $({}^x U^{(\tau)})_{\tau \in \mathbb{N}}$
2: **for** each iteration $\tau \in \mathbb{N}$ **do**
3:   Every player x independently draws a bundle according to her strategy $\pi^{(\tau)}(x)$, i.e., $A^{(\tau)}(x) \sim \pi^{(\tau)}(x)$.
4:   The vector of bundle losses $\ell^k(\mu^{(\tau)})$ is revealed to all players in $\mathcal{P}_k$. Each player incurs the loss of the bundle she chose.
5:   Players update their mixed strategies:

$$\pi^{(\tau+1)}(x) = {}^x U^{(\tau)}\left(\left(\ell^k_p(\mu^{(t)})\right)_{t \le \tau}, \pi^{(\tau)}(x)\right).$$

6: **end for**

Source: Krichene et al. [2].

We observe that this is a random variable, since the action $A^{(\tau)}(x)$ of player x is random, drawn from a distribution $\pi^{(\tau)}(x)$. The expectation of the cumulative discounted loss is then

$\mathbb{E}\left[L^{(T)}(x)\right] = \sum_{\tau=0}^{T} \gamma_\tau \mathbb{E}\left[\ell^k_{A(\tau)(x)}(\mu^{(\tau)})\right] = \sum_{\tau=0}^{T} \gamma_\tau \langle \pi^{(\tau)}(x), \ell^k(\mu^{(\tau)})\rangle$, where $\langle \cdot, \cdot \rangle$ denotes the Euclidean inner product on $\mathbb{R}^{\mathcal{P}_k}$. Similarly, we define the cumulative discounted loss for a fixed bundle $p \in \mathcal{P}_k$,

$$\mathcal{L}^{k(T)}_p = \sum_{\tau=0}^{T} \gamma_\tau \ell^k_p\left(\mu^{(\tau)}\right) \tag{6.10}$$

Let $x \in \mathcal{X}_k$, and consider an online learning algorithm for the congestion game, given by the sequence of functions $({}^x U^{(\tau)})_{\tau \in \mathbb{N}}$. Let $(\mu^{(\tau)})_{\tau \in \mathbb{N}}$ be the sequence of distributions determined by the mixed strategy profile of all players. Then the discounted regret up to iteration T for player x under algorithm U is the random variable

$$R^{(T)}(x) = L^{(T)}(x) - \min_{p \in \mathcal{P}_k} \mathcal{L}^{k(T)}_p \tag{6.11}$$

The algorithm U is said to have sublinear discounted regret if for any sequence of distributions $(\mu^{(\tau)})_{\tau \in \mathbb{N}}$, and any initial strategy $\pi^{(0)}$,

$$\left[R^{(T)}(x)\right]^+ / \sum_{\tau=0}^{T} \gamma_\tau \to 0 \; almost \; surely \; as \; T \to \infty. \tag{6.12}$$

If there is convergence in the L^1-norm, $\left[\mathbb{E}\left[R^{(T)}(x)\right]\right]^+ / \sum_{\tau=0}^{T} \gamma_\tau \to 0$, it is said that the algorithm has sublinear discounted regret in expectation.

It should be observed that in the definition of the regret, one can replace the minimum over the set $\mathcal{P}_k$ by a minimum over the simplex $\Delta^{\mathcal{P}_k}$, $\min_{p \in \mathcal{P}_k} L^{(T)}_p = \min_{\pi \in \Delta^{\mathcal{P}_k}} \langle \pi, L^{(T)}\rangle$, since the minimizers of a bounded linear function lie on the set of extremal points of the feasible set. So, the discounted regret compares the performance of the online learning algorithm to the *best stationary strategy in hindsight*. Indeed, $\langle \pi, L^{(T)}\rangle$ is the cumulative discounted loss of a stationary strategy π, and minimizing this expression over $\pi \in \Delta^{\mathcal{P}_k}$ yields the best stationary strategy in hindsight: one cannot know a priori which strategy will minimize the expression until all losses up to T are revealed. If the algorithm has sublinear regret, its average performance is, asymptotically, as good as the performance of any stationary strategy, regardless of the sequence of distributions $(\mu^{(\tau)})_{\tau \in \mathbb{N}}$. It should be observed that the cumulative discounted loss and regret are bounded, uniformly in x, since the congestion functions are continuous on a compact set. So, there exists $\rho \geq 0$ such that for all k, all $p \in \mathcal{P}_k$, and all $\mu \in \Delta$, $\mathcal{P}_p^k(\mu) \in [0, \rho]$; and for all $x \in \mathcal{X}_k$, $L^{(T)}(x)/\Sigma_{\tau=0}^T \gamma_\tau \in [0, \rho]$ and $[R^{(T)}(x)]^+/\Sigma_{\tau=0}^T \gamma_\tau \in [0, \rho]$.

Population-wide regret: In the previous section, the discounted regret $R^{(T)}(x)$ was defined for a single player x. Here, we define a population-wide cumulative discounted loss $L^{k(T)}$ and discounted regret $R^{k(T)}$ as

$$L^{k(T)} = \frac{1}{m(\mathcal{X}_k)} \int_{\mathcal{X}_k} L^{(T)}(x) dm(x), \tag{6.13}$$

$$R^{k(T)} = \frac{1}{m(\mathcal{X}_k)} \int_{\mathcal{X}_k} R^{(T)}(x) dm(x) = L^{k(T)} - \min_{p \in \mathcal{P}_k} \mathcal{L}_p^{k(T)} \tag{6.14}$$

Since $L^{(T)}(x)$ is random for all x, $L^{k(T)}$ is also a random variable. However, it is, in fact, almost surely equal to its expectation. By recalling that $\mu_p^{k(\tau)}$ is the proportion of players who chose bundle p at iteration τ (also a random variable), we can write

$$L^{k(T)} = \sum_{\tau=0}^T \gamma_\tau \frac{1}{m(\mathcal{X}_k)} \sum_{p \in \mathcal{P}_k} \int_{\{x \in \mathcal{X}_k : A^{(\tau)}(x) = p\}} \ell_p^k\left(\mu^{(\tau)}\right) dm(x) = \sum_{\tau=0}^T \gamma_\tau \sum_{p \in \mathcal{P}_k} \mu_p^{k(\tau)} \ell_p^k\left(\mu^{(\tau)}\right),$$

thus assuming players randomize independently, $\mu^{(\tau)}$ is almost surely deterministic, and so is $L^{k(T)}$. The same holds for $R^{k(T)}$. If almost every player $x \in \mathcal{X}_k$ applies an online learning algorithm with sublinear regret in expectation, then the population-wide regret is also sublinear [2].

Hedge algorithm: This is *applied by player* $x \in \mathcal{X}_k$, in a congestion game, with an upper bound on the losses ρ, with initial distribution $\pi^{(0)} \in \Delta^{\mathcal{P}_k}$ and learning rates $(\eta_\tau)_{\tau \in \mathbb{N}}$, is an online learning algorithm $(^xU^{(\tau)})_{\tau \in \mathbb{N}}$ such that the $\tau - th$ update function is given by

$$^xU^{(\tau)}\left(\left(\ell^k\left(\mu^{(t)}\right)\right)_{t \leq \tau}, \pi^{(\tau)}(x)\right)$$
$$= \pi^{(\tau+1)}(x) \propto \left(\pi_p^{(\tau)}(x) \exp\left(-\eta_\tau \ell_p^k\left(\frac{\mu^{(\tau)}}{\rho}\right)\right)\right)_{p \in \mathcal{P}_k} \tag{6.15}$$

The Hedge algorithm updates the distribution by computing, at each iteration, a set of bundle weights, then normalizing the vector of weights. The weight of a bundle p is obtained by multiplying the probability at the previous iteration, $\pi_p^{(\tau)}$, by a term that is exponentially decreasing in the bundle loss $\ell_p^k(\mu^{(\tau)})$; thus, the higher the loss of bundle p at iteration τ, the lower the probability of selecting p at the next iteration. The parameter η_τ can be interpreted as a learning rate, as the Hedge update rule (Eq. (6.15)) is the solution to the following optimization problem:

$$\pi^{(\tau+1)} \in \arg \min_{\pi \in \Delta^{\mathcal{P}_k}} \left\langle \pi, \frac{\ell^k\left(\mu^{(\tau)}\right)}{\rho} \right\rangle + \frac{1}{\eta_\tau} D_{KL}\left(\pi \| \pi^{(\tau)}\right), \tag{6.16}$$

where $D_{KL}(\pi \| v) = \sum_{p \in \mathcal{P}_k} \pi_p \log \frac{\pi_p}{v_p}$ is the Kullback–Leibler divergence of distribution π with respect to v [6].

The objective function in Eq. (6.16) is the sum of an instantaneous loss term $\langle \pi, \ell^k(\mu^{(\tau)})/\rho \rangle$ and a regularization term $D_{KL}(\pi\|\pi^{(\tau)})/\eta_\tau$ that penalizes deviations from the previous distribution $\pi^{(\tau)}$, with a regularization coefficient $1/\eta_\tau$. The greedy problem (with no regularization term) would yield a pure strategy that concentrates all the mass on the bundle with minimal loss on the previous iteration. With the regularization term, the player "hedges her bet" by penalizing too much deviation from the previous distribution. The coefficient η_τ determines the relative importance of the two terms in the objective function. In particular, as $\eta_\tau \to 0$, the solution to the problem (Eq. (6.16)) converges to $\pi^{(\tau)}$ since the regularization term dominates the instantaneous loss term. In other words, as η_τ converges to 0, the player stops learning from new observations, which justifies calling η_τ a *learning rate*. From Eq. (6.15), we also have

$$\pi^{(\tau+1)} \propto \left(\pi_p^{(0)} \exp \left(-\sum_{t=0}^{\tau} \eta_t \frac{\ell_p^k(\mu^{(t)})}{\rho} \right) \right)_{p \in \mathcal{P}_k} \tag{6.17}$$

In particular, when $\eta_\tau = \gamma_\tau$, the term $\sum_{t=0}^{\tau} \eta_t \ell_p^k(\mu^{(t)})$ coincides with the cumulative discounted loss $\mathcal{L}_p^{k(\tau)}$ defined in Eq. (6.10). This motivates the use of the discount factors γ_τ as learning rates.

Consider a congestion game with a sequence of discount factors $(\gamma_\tau)_{\tau \in \mathbb{N}}$. The Hedge algorithm with learning rates (γ_τ) satisfies the following regret bound: for any sequence of distributions $(\mu^{(\tau)})_\tau$ and any initial strategy $\pi^{(0)}$,

$$\mathbb{E}\left[R^{(T)}(x) \right] \leq -\rho \log \pi_{\min}^{(0)} + \frac{\rho}{8} \sum_{\tau=0}^{T} \gamma_\tau^2,$$

where $\pi_{\min}^{(0)} = \min_{p \in \mathcal{P}_k} \pi_p^{(0)}$ [2]. For the convergence of these algorithms and the problem of the dynamics, see [2].

6.3 Minority Games

The minority game [7–10] is a simple congestion game in which the players' main goal is to choose among two options the one that is adopted by the smallest number of players. In the network routing problem, we are primary interested in, that means sending the traffic on less congested routes.

Here, we will characterize the set of Nash equilibria and the limiting behavior of several well-known learning processes in the minority game with an arbitrary odd number of players so that the player set is $N = \{1, ..., 2k+1\}$, with $k \in \mathbb{N}$. Each player $i \in N$ has a set of pure strategies $A_i = \{-1, +1\}$: agents have to choose between two options. The set of mixed strategies of player i is denoted by (A_i). We denote a mixed strategy profile by $\alpha \in \times i \in N\Delta(A_i)$, and we use the standard notation $\alpha_{-i} \in \times_{j \in N\backslash\{i\}}\Delta(A)$ to denote a strategy profile of players other than $i \in N$. With each action $a \in \{-1, +1\}$, a function $f_a : \{1, ...2k+1\} \to \mathbb{R}$ can be associated that indicates for each $n \in \{1, ..., 2k+1\}$ the payoff $f_a(n)$ to a player choosing a when the total number of players choosing a equals n. The von Neumann–Morgenstern utility function of a player is then given by

$$u_i(a) = f_{a_i}\left(| \{ j \in N : a_j = a_i \} |\right), \tag{6.18}$$

where $a \times_{j \in N} A_j$. Payoffs are extended to mixed strategies in the usual way. The function $f_a(\cdot)$, $a \in \{-1, +1\}$ can have several forms. We make the common assumptions that congestion is costly: (*i*) f_{-1} and f_{+1} are strictly decreasing functions, and that the congestion effect is the same across alternatives: (*ii*) $f_{-1} = f_{+1}$. A player who uses a mixed strategy that assigns a positive probability to both pure strategies is referred to as a mixer. We call a player that assigns a full probability mass to the alternative -1 as a(-1)-player; similarly, the player that assigns a full probability mass to the alternative $+1$ is called a$(+1)$-player.

Nash equilibria: Throughout this section, let $k \in \mathbb{N}$ and consider a minority game with $2k + 1$ players. Here, a pure strategy profile is a Nash equilibrium if and only if one of the alternatives -1 or $+1$ is chosen by exactly k of the $2k + 1$ players. It can be shown that if $\alpha \in \times_{i \in N}\Delta(A_i)$ is a Nash equilibrium with a nonempty set of mixers, then all mixers use the same strategy: for all i, $j \in N$, if $\alpha_i, \alpha_j \notin \{(1, 0), (0, 1)\}$, then $\alpha_i = \alpha_j$ [11]. Since all mixers use the same strategy and player labels are irrelevant by assumption (ii) $(f_{-1} = f_{+1})$ (if α is a Nash equilibrium, so is every permutation of α), a non-pure Nash equilibrium can be summarized by its type (ℓ, r, λ), where $\ell, r \in \{0, 1, ..., 2k + 1\}$ denote the number of players choosing pure strategy -1 or $+1$, respectively, and $\lambda \in (0, 1)$ the probability that the remaining $m(\ell, r, \lambda) := (2k + 1) - (p + r) > 0$ mixers choose -1. Let also $v_{-1}(\ell, r, \lambda)$ denote the expected payoff to a player choosing -1; $v_{+1}(\ell, r, \lambda)$ is defined similarly. For convenience, write $m := m(\ell, r, \lambda)$. Letting one of the mixers in (ℓ, r, λ) deviate to a pure strategy, this implies in particular that

$$v_{-1}(\ell + 1, r, \lambda) = \sum_{s=0}^{m-1} \binom{m-1}{s} \lambda^s (1 - \lambda)^{m-1-s} f_{-1}(\ell + 1 + s), \tag{6.19}$$

$$v_{+1}(\ell, r + 1, \lambda) = \sum_{s=0}^{m-1} \binom{m-1}{s} \lambda^s (1 - \lambda)^{m-1-s} f_{+1}((r + 1) + (m - 1 - s))$$
$$= \sum_{s=0}^{m-1} \binom{m-1}{s} \lambda^s (1 - \lambda)^{m-1-s} f_{+1}(r + m - s). \tag{6.20}$$

For instance, a profile of type $(\ell + 1, r, \lambda)$ is obtained from type (ℓ, r, λ) if a mixer switches to pure strategy -1. In that case, there are $m - 1$ mixers left. To obtain the expected payoffs, note that the probability that $s \in \{0, ..., m - 1\}$ of these mixers choose -1 is $\binom{m-1}{s} \lambda^s (1 - \lambda)^{m-1-s}$. Using this notation, the Nash equilibria with at least one mixer are characterized as follows.

(i) Let $\ell, r \in \{0, 1, ..., 2k + 1\}$ be such that $\ell + r < 2k + 1$ and $\lambda \in (0, 1)$. A strategy profile of type (ℓ, r, λ) is a Nash equilibrium if and only if $v_{-1}(\ell + 1, r, \lambda) = v_{+1}(\ell, r + 1, \lambda)$.

(ii) There exist equilibria with exactly one mixer. These equilibria are of type (k, k, λ) with arbitrary $\in (0, 1)$; that is, the mixer uses an arbitrary mixed strategy, whereas the remaining $2k$ players are spread evenly over the two pure strategies.

(iii) Let $\ell, r \in \{0, 1, ..., 2k + 1\}$ be such that $\ell + r \leq 2k - 1$. There is a Nash equilibrium of type (ℓ, r, λ) if and only if $\max\{l, r\} < k$. The corresponding probability $\lambda \in (0, 1)$ solving the equation in (i) is unique.

Some consequences of this characterization of the game's non-pure Nash equilibria:

1) There are no Nash equilibria where the number of mixers is two, since in that case, $\max\{\ell, r\} \geq k$.

2) Substitution in the equation in (ii) gives a strategy profile in which the number of (-1)-players is equal to the number of $(+1)$-players and the remaining players mix with probability ½; that is, a

profile of type $(t, t, 1/2)$ with $t \in \{0, ..., k\}$ is a Nash equilibrium. In addition, the set of Nash equilibria with at most one mixer is connected [11–13].

6.4 Nash Q-Learning

The Nash-Q algorithm generalizes single-agent Q-learning [14] to stochastic games by employing an equilibrium operator in place of expected utility maximization [15]. The description presented here adopts notation and terminology from the established frameworks of Q-learning and game theory.

Markov decision process: It is a tuple $\langle S, A, r, p \rangle$, where S is the discrete state space, A is the discrete action space, $r : S \times A \to R$ is the reward function of the agent, and $p : S \times A \to \Delta(S)$ is the transition function, where $\Delta(S)$ is the set of probability distributions over state space S.

In a Markov decision process, an agent's objective is to find a strategy (policy) π so as to maximize the sum of discounted expected rewards,

$$v(s, \pi) = \sum\nolimits_{t=0}^{\infty} \beta^t E(r_t \mid \pi, s_0 = s), \tag{6.21}$$

where s is a particular state, s_0 indicates the initial state, r_t is the reward at time t, and $\beta \in [0, 1)$ is the discount factor. $v(s, \pi)$ represents the *value* for state s under strategy π. A *strategy* is a plan for playing a game. Here $\pi = (\pi_0, ..., \pi_t, ...)$ is defined over the entire course of the game, where π_t is called the *decision rule* at time t. A decision rule is a function $\pi_t: \mathbf{H}_t \to \Delta(A)$, where $\mathbf{H}_t$ is the space of possible histories at time t, with each $H_t \in \mathbf{H}_t$, $H_t = (s_0, a_0, ..., s_{t-1}, a_{t-1}, s_t)$, and $\Delta(A)$ is the space of probability distributions over the agent's actions. π is called a *stationary strategy* if $\pi_t = \bar{\pi}$ for all t. In other words, the decision rule is independent of time. π is called a *behavior strategy* if its decision rule may depend on the history of the game play, $\pi_t = f_t(H_t)$. The standard solution to the problem above is through an iterative search method [16] that searches for a fixed point of the following *Bellman* equation:

$$v(s, \pi^*) = \max_a \left\{ r(s, a) + \beta \sum\nolimits_{s'} p(s' \mid s, a) v(s', \pi^*) \right\}, \tag{6.22}$$

where $r(s, a)$ is the reward for taking action a at state s, s' is the next state, and $p(s' \mid s, a)$ is the probability of transiting to state s' after taking action a in state s. A solution π^* that satisfies Eq. (6.22) is guaranteed to be an optimal policy. A learning problem arises when the agent does not know the reward function or the state transition probabilities. If an agent directly learns about its optimal policy without knowing either the reward function or the state transition function, such an approach is called *model-free reinforcement learning*, of which Q-learning is one example. The basic idea of Q-learning is that we can define a function Q such that

$$Q^*(s, a) = r(s, a) + \beta \sum\nolimits_{s'} p(s' \mid s, a) v(s', \pi^*). \tag{6.23}$$

By this definition, $Q^*(s, a)$ is the total discounted reward of taking action a in state s and then following the optimal policy thereafter. From Eq. (6.22), we have

$$v(s, \pi^*) = \max_a Q^*(s, a).$$

If we know $Q^*(s, a)$, then the optimal policy π^* can be found by simply identifying the action that maximizes $Q^*(s, a)$ under the state s. The problem is then reduced to finding the function $Q^*(s, a)$ instead of searching for the optimal value of $v(s, \pi^*)$. Q-learning provides us with a simple updating procedure in which the agent starts with arbitrary initial values of $Q(s, a)$ for all $s \in S$, $a \in A$, and updates the Q-values as follows:

$$Q_{t+1}(s_t, a_t) = (1 - \alpha_t)Q_t(s_t, a_t) + \alpha_t[r_t + \beta \max_a Q_t(s_{t+1}, a)], \tag{6.24}$$

where $\alpha_t \in [0, 1)$ is the learning rate sequence. It was proved in [14] that sequence Eq. (6.24) converges to $Q^*(s, a)$ under the assumption that all states and actions have been visited infinitely often and the learning rate satisfies certain constraints.

Stochastic games: These games model multi-agent systems with discrete time and a noncooperative nature. We employ the term "noncooperative" in the technical game-theoretic sense, where it means that agents pursue their individual goals and cannot form an enforceable agreement on their joint actions (unless this is modeled explicitly in the game itself). In a stochastic game, agents choose actions simultaneously. The state space and action space are assumed to be discrete. In a standard formal definition we have:

An n-player stochastic game Γ is a tuple $\langle S, A^1, .., A^n, r^1, .., r^n, p \rangle$, where S is the state space, A^i is the action space of player $i (i = 1, ..., n)$, $r^i : S \times A^1 \times \times A^n \rightarrow R$ is the payoff function for player i, $p : S \times A^1 \times, ..., \times A^n \rightarrow \Delta(S)$ is the transition probability map, where $\Delta(S)$ is the set of probability distributions over state space S.

Given state s, agents independently choose actions $a^1, ..., a^n$, and receive rewards $r^i(s, a^1, ..., a^n)$, $i = 1, .., n$. The state then transits to the next state s' based on fixed transition probabilities, satisfying the constraint $\sum_{s' \in S} p(s' \mid s, a1, ..., a^n) = 1$.

In a *discounted stochastic game*, the objective of each player is to maximize the discounted sum of rewards, with discount factor $\beta \in [0, 1)$. Let π^i be the strategy of player i. For a given initial state s, player i tries to maximize $v^i(s, \pi^1, \pi^2, ..., \pi^n) = \sum_{t=0}^{\infty} \beta^t E(r_t^1 \mid \pi^1, \pi^2, ..., \pi^n, s_0 = s)$.

Equilibrium strategies: A Nash equilibrium is a joint strategy where each agent's action is a best response to the others' responses. For a stochastic game, each agent's strategy is defined over the entire time horizon of the game.

In stochastic game Γ, a Nash equilibrium point is a tuple of n strategies $(\pi_*^1, ..., \pi_*^n)$ such that for all $s \in S$ and $i = 1, n, v^i(s, \pi_*^1, ..., \pi_*^n) \geq v^i(s, \pi_*^1, ..., \pi_*^{i-1}, \pi^i, \pi_*^{i+1}, ..., \pi_*^n)$ for all $\pi^i \in \Pi^i$, where Π^i is the set of strategies available to agent i.

The strategies that constitute a Nash equilibrium can in general be behavior strategies or stationary strategies.

Every n-player discounted stochastic game possesses at least one Nash equilibrium point in stationary strategies [16].

6.4.1 Multi-agent Q-Learning

Here we extend Q-learning to multi-agent systems, based on the framework of stochastic games. First, we redefine Q-values for the multi-agent case, and then present the algorithm for learning such Q-values.

Nash Q-values: To adapt Q-learning to the multi-agent context, the first step is recognizing the need to consider joint actions, rather than merely individual actions. For an n-agent system, the Q-function for any individual agent becomes $(s, a^1, ..., a^n)$, rather than the single-agent Q-function, $Q(s, a)$. Given the extended notion of Q-function, and Nash equilibrium as a solution concept, we define a *Nash Q-value* as the expected sum of discounted rewards when all agents follow specified Nash equilibrium strategies from the next period onward. This definition differs from the single-agent case, where the future rewards are based only on the agent's own optimal strategy. We refer to Q_*^i as a *Nash Q-function* for agent i.

Agent i's Nash Q-function is defined over $(s, a^1, ..., a^n)$, as the sum of Agent i's current reward plus its future rewards when all agents follow a joint Nash equilibrium strategy. That is,

$$Q_*^i(s, a^1, ..., a^n) = r^i(s, a^1, ..., a^n) + \beta \sum_{s' \in S} p(s' \mid s, a^1, ..., a^n) v^i(s', \pi_*^1, ..., \pi_*^n), \qquad (6.25)$$

where $(\pi_*^1, ..., \pi_*^n)$ is the joint Nash equilibrium strategy, $r^i(s, a^1, ..., a^n)$ is agent i's one–period reward in state s and under joint action $(a^1, ..., a^n)$, $v^i(s', \pi_*^1, ..., \pi_*^n)$ is agent i's total discounted reward over infinite periods starting from state s' given that agents follow the equilibrium strategies.

The Nash Q-Learning Algorithm: It resembles standard single-agent Q-learning in many ways, but differs in one crucial element: how to use the Q-values of the next state to update those of the current state. The multi-agent Q-learning algorithm updates with future Nash equilibrium payoffs, whereas single-agent Q-learning updates are based on the agent's own maximum payoff. In order to learn these Nash equilibrium payoffs, the agent must observe not only its own reward, but those of others as well. For environments where this is not feasible, some observable proxy for other-agent rewards must be identified, with results dependent on how closely the proxy is related to actual rewards.

Before presenting the algorithm, we need to clarify the distinction between Nash equilibria for a *stage game* (one-period game), and for the stochastic game (many periods).

An n-player stage game is defined as $(M^1, .., M^n)$, where for $k = 1, .., n$, M^k is agent k's payoff function over the space of joint actions, $M^k = \{r^k(a^1, ..., a^n) \mid a^1 \in A^1, .., a^n \in A^n\}$, and r^k is the reward for agent k.

Let σ^{-k} be the product of strategies of all agents other than k, $\sigma^{-k} \equiv \sigma^1 \cdots \sigma^{k-1} \cdot \sigma^{k+1} \cdots \sigma^n$.

A joint strategy $(0^1, ..., 0^n)$ constitutes a Nash equilibrium for the stage game $(M^1, .., M^n)$ if, for $k = 1, n$, $\sigma^k \sigma^{-k} M^k \geq \hat{\sigma}^k \sigma^{-k} M^k$ for all $\sigma^k \in \hat{\sigma}(A^k)$.

Our learning agent, indexed by i, learns about its Q-values by forming an arbitrary guess at time 0. One simple guess would be letting $Q_0^i(s, a^1, ..., a^n) = 0$ for all $s \in S$, $a^1 \in A^1, .., a^n \in A^n$. At each time t, agent i observes the current state, and takes its action. After that, it observes its own reward, actions taken by all other agents, others' rewards, and the new state s'. It then calculates a Nash equilibrium $\pi^1(s') \cdots \pi^n(s')$ for the stage game $(Q_t^1(s'), ..., Q_t^n(s'))$, and updates its Q-values according to

$$Q_{t+1}^i(s, a^1, ..., a^n) = (1 - \alpha_t)Q_t^i(s, a^1, ..., a^n) + \alpha_t[r_t^i + \beta NQ_t^i(s')], \tag{6.26}$$

where

$$NQ_t^i(s') = \pi^1(s') \cdots \pi^n(s') \cdot Q_t^i(s'), \tag{6.27}$$

is referred to as the *Nash Q-function* and denoted as *NQ*. Different methods for selecting among multiple Nash equilibria will in general yield different updates. $NQ_t^i(s')$ is agent i's pay off in state s' for the selected equilibrium. Note that $\pi^1(s'), \cdots \pi^n(s') \cdot Q_t^i(s')$ is a scalar.

In order to calculate the Nash equilibrium $(\pi^1(s'), ..., \pi^n(s'))$, agent i would need to know $Q_t^1(s'),..., Q_t^n(s')$. Information about other agents' Q-values is not given, so agent i must learn about them too. Agent i forms conjectures about those Q-functions at the beginning of play, for example, $Q_0^j(s, a^1, ..., a^n) = 0$ for all j and all s, a^1, a^n. As the game proceeds, agent i observes other agents' immediate rewards and previous actions. That information can then be used to update agent i's conjectures on other agents' Q-functions. Agent i updates its beliefs about agent j's Q-function, according to the same updating rule (Eq. (6.26)) it applies to its own:

$$Q_{t+1}^j(s, a^1, ..., a^n) = (1 - \alpha_t)Q_t^j(s, a^1, ..., a^n) + \alpha_t[r_t^j + \beta NQ_t^j(s')]. \tag{6.28}$$

Note that $\alpha_t = 0$ for $(s, a^1, ..., a^n) \neq (s_t, a_t^1, ..., a_t^n)$. Therefore, Eq. (6.28) does not update all the entries in the Q-functions. It updates only the entry corresponding to the current state and the actions chosen by the agents. Such updating is called *asynchronous updating*.

6.4.2 Convergence

We need to prove the convergence of Q_t^i to an equilibrium Q_*^i for the learning agent i. The value of Q_*^i is determined by the joint strategies of all agents. That means our agent has to learn Q-values of all the agents and derive strategies from them. The learning objective is $(Q_*^1, ..., Q_*^n)$, and we have to show the convergence of $(Q_t^1, ..., Q_t^n)$ to $(Q_*^1, ..., Q_*^n)$.

The convergence proof requires two basic assumptions about infinite sampling and decaying of learning rate. These two assumptions are similar to those in single-agent Q-learning.

---

i) Every state $s \in S$ and action $a^k \in A^k$ for $k=1, . . . , n$, are visited infinitely often.

ii) The learning rate α_t satisfies the following conditions for all $s, t, a^1, ..., a^n$:

  1. $0 \leq \alpha_t(s, a^1, ..., a^n) < 1$, $\Sigma_{t=0}^{\infty} \alpha_t(s, a^1, ..., a^n) = \infty$, $\Sigma_{t=0}^{\infty}[\alpha_t(s, a^1, ..., a^n)]^2 < \infty$, and the latter two hold uniformly and with probability 1.

  2. $\alpha_t(s, a^1, ..., a^n) = 0$ if $(s, a^1, ..., a^n) \neq (s_t, a_t^1, ..., a_t^n)$.

The second item in ii) states that the agent updates only the Q-function element corresponding to the current state s_t and actions a_t^1, a_t^n. The proof relies on the following lemma [17]:

Assume that α_t satisfies ii) and the mapping $P_t : \mathbb{Q} \to \mathbb{Q}$ satisfies the following condition: there exists a number $0 < \gamma < 1$ and a sequence $\lambda_t \geq 0$ converging to zero with probability 1 such that $\|P_t Q - P_t Q_*\| \leq \gamma \|Q - Q_*\| + \lambda_t$ for all $Q \in \mathbb{Q}$ and $Q_* = E[P_t Q_*]$, then the iteration defined by

$$Q_{t+1} = (1 - \alpha_t)Q_t + \alpha_t[P_t Q_t] \tag{6.29}$$

converges to Q_* with probability 1.

Note that P_t in the previous lemma is a pseudo-contraction operator because a "true" contraction operator should map every two points in the space closer to each other, which means $\left\| P_t Q - P_t \hat{Q} \right\| \leq \gamma \left\| Q - \hat{Q} \right\|$ for all Q, $\hat{Q} \in \mathbb{Q}$. Even when $\lambda_t = 0$, P_t is still not a contraction operator because it only maps every $Q \in \mathbb{Q}$ closer to Q_*, not mapping any two points in $\mathbb{Q}$ closer. For an n-player stochastic game, we define the operator P_t as follows:

Let $Q = (Q^1, ..., Q^n)$, where $Q^k \in \mathbb{Q}^k$ for $k = 1, .., n$, and $\mathbb{Q} = \mathbb{Q}^1 \times \times \mathbb{Q}^n$. $P_t : \mathbb{Q} \to \mathbb{Q}$ is a mapping on the complete metric space $\mathbb{Q}$ into $\mathbb{Q}$, $P_t Q = (P_t Q^1, ..., P_t Q^n)$, where

$$P_t Q^k (s, a^1, ..., a^n) = r_t^k (s, a^1, ..., a^n) + \beta \pi^1(s')...\pi^n(s')Q^k(s'),$$

for k = 1, n, where s' is the state at time $t + 1$, and $(\pi^1(s'), ..., \pi^n(s'))$ is a Nash equilibrium solution for the stage game $(Q^1(s'), ..., Q^n(s'))$.

In the sequel, the equation $Q_* = E[P_t Q_*]$ is given as Lemma 6.19, which depends on the following assertions [18].

i) $\left(\pi_*^1, ..., \pi_*^n \right)$ is a Nash equilibrium point in a discounted stochastic game with equilibrium payoff $\left(v^1\left(\pi_*^1, ..., \pi_*^n \right), ..., v^n\left(\pi_*^1, ..., \pi_*^n \right) \right)$, where $v^k\left(\pi_*^1, ..., \pi_*^n \right) = \left(v^k\left(s^1, \pi_*^1, ..., \pi_*^n \right), ..., v^k\left(s^m, \pi_*^1, .., \pi_*^n \right) \right)$, k = 1, ..., n.

ii) For each $s \in S$, the tuple $\left(\pi_*^1(s), ..., \pi_*^n(s) \right)$ constitutes a Nash equilibrium point in the stage game $\left(Q_*^1(s), ..., Q_*^n(s) \right)$ with Nash equilibrium payoffs $\left(v^1\left(s, \pi_*^1, ..., \pi_*^n \right), ..., v^n\left(s, \pi_*^1, ..., \pi_*^n \right) \right)$, where for k = 1, ..., n,

$$Q_*^k (s, a^1, ..., a^n) = r^k (s, a^1, ..., a^n) + \beta \sum_{s' \in S} p(s' \mid s, a^1, ..., a^n) v^k (s', \pi_*^1, ..., \pi_*^n). \tag{6.30}$$

This links agent k's optimal value v^k in the entire stochastic game to its Nash equilibrium payoff in the stage game $\left(Q_*^1(s), ..., Q_*^n(s) \right)$. In other words, $v^k(s) = \pi^1(s) \cdots \pi^n(s) Q_*^k(s)$. This relationship leads to the following lemma:

Lemma 6.19 For an n-player stochastic game, $E[P_t Q_*] = Q_*$, where $Q_* = (Q_*^1, ..., Q_*^n)$ [11].

Now we need to show that the P_t operator is a pseudo-contraction operator. Our P_t satisfies $\left\| P_t Q - P_t \hat{Q} \right\| \leq \beta \left\| Q - \hat{Q} \right\|$ for all $Q, \hat{Q} \in \mathbb{Q}$. In other words, P_t is a *real* contraction operator. For this condition to hold, we have to restrict the domain of the Q-functions during learning. Our restrictions focus on stage games with special types of Nash equilibrium points: *global optima* and *saddles*.

A joint strategy $(\sigma^1, ..., \sigma^n)$ of the stage game $(M^1, .., M^n)$ is a global optimal point if every agent receives its highest payoff at this point. That is, for all $k, \sigma M^k \geq \hat{\sigma} M^k$ for all $\hat{\sigma} \in \sigma(A)$.

A global optimal point is always a Nash equilibrium. It is easy to show that all global optima have equal values.

A joint strategy $(\sigma^1, ..., \sigma^n)$ of the stage game $(M^1, ..., M^n)$ is a saddle point if (i) it is a Nash equilibrium, and (ii) each agent would receive a higher payoff when at least one of the other agents deviates. In other words

$$\sigma^k \sigma^{-k} M^k \geq \hat{\sigma}^k \sigma^{-k} M^k \text{ for all } \hat{\sigma}^k \in \sigma(A^k); \text{ for all } k$$

$$\sigma^k \sigma^{-k} M^k \leq \sigma^k \hat{\sigma}^{-k} M^k \text{ for all } \hat{\sigma}^{-k} \in \sigma(A^{-k}); \text{ for all } k$$

All saddle points of a stage game are equivalent in their values.

Let $\sigma = (\sigma^1, ..., \sigma^n)$ and $\delta = (\delta^1, ..., \delta^n)$ be saddle points of the n-player stage game $(M^1, ..., M^n)$. Then for all $k, \sigma M^k = \delta M^k$ [11].

Examples of stage games that have a global optimal point or a saddle point are shown in Figure 6.2.

In each stage game, player 1 has two action choices: *Up* and *Down*. Player 2's action choices are *Left* and *Right*. Player 1's payoffs are the first numbers in each cell, with the second number denoting player 2's payoff. The first game has only one Nash equilibrium, with values (10, 9), which is a global optimal point. The second game also has a unique Nash equilibrium, in this case a saddle point, valued at (2, 2). The third game has two Nash equilibria: a global optimum, (10, 9), and a saddle, (2, 2).

The convergence proof requires that the stage games encountered during learning have global optima, or alternatively, that they all have saddle points. In addition, it mandates that the learner consistently choose either global optima or saddle points in updating its Q-values.

Assumption[*])- One of the following conditions holds during learning.

i) Every stage game $\left(Q_t^1(s), ..., Q_t^n(s) \right)$, for all t and s, has a global optimal point, and agents 2 payoffs in this equilibrium are used to update their Q-functions.
ii) Every stage game $\left(Q_t^1(s), ..., Q_t^n(s) \right)$, for all t and s, has a saddle point, and agents' payoffs in this equilibrium are used to update their Q-functions.

player 2

Figure 6.2 Examples of different types of stage games.

game 1	Left	Right
Up	10,9	0,3
Down	3,0	−1,2

game 2	Left	Right
Up	5,5	0,6
Down	6,0	2,2

game 3	Left	Right
Up	10,9	0,3
Down	3,0	2,2

player 1

We further define the distance between two Q-functions.

Definition: For $Q, \hat{Q} \in \mathbb{Q}$, define

$$\left\| Q - \hat{Q} \right\| \equiv \max_j \max_s \left\| Q^j(s) - \hat{Q}^j(s) \right\|_{(j,s)}$$

$$\equiv \max_j \max_s \max_{a^1,\dots,a^n} \left| Q^j(s, a^1, \dots, a^n) - \hat{Q}^j(s, a^1, \dots, a^n) \right|.$$

Given Assumption[*], it was established [11] that P_t is a contraction mapping operator.

Lemma 6.20 $\left\| P_t Q - P_t \hat{Q} \right\| \leq \beta \left\| Q - \hat{Q} \right\|$ *for all $Q, \hat{Q} \in \mathbb{Q}$.*

We can now present the main result of this section: that the process induced by NQ updates in Eq. (6.28) converges to NQ-values [11].

Under the assumptions defined in this section, the sequence $Q_t = (Q_t^1, \dots, Q_t^n)$, updated by

$$Q_{t+1}^k(s, a^1, \dots, a^n) = (1 - \alpha_t) Q_t^k(s, a^1, \dots, a^n) + \alpha_t \left(r_t^k + \beta \pi^1(s') \cdots \pi^n(s') Q_t^k(s') \right)$$

for k = 1, ..., n, where $(\pi^1(s'), \dots, \pi^n(s'))$ is the appropriate type of Nash equilibrium solution for the stage game $(Q_t^1(s'), \dots, Q_t^n(s'))$, converges to the NQ-value $Q_* = (Q_*^1, \dots, Q_*^n)$.

6.5 Routing Games

In this section, we study the inefficiency of equilibria in *noncooperative routing games*, in which self-interested players route traffic through a congested network. The section introduces the most important models and examples of routing games, surveys optimal bounds on the price of anarchy (POA) in these models, and presents techniques that are useful for bounding the inefficiency of equilibria in a number of applications. A majority of the current literature on the inefficiency of equilibria concerns routing games. One reason for this popularity is that routing games shed light on an important practical problem: how to route traffic in a large communication network, such as the Internet, which has no central authority. The routing games studied in this section are relevant for networks with "source routing," in which each end user chooses a full route for its traffic, and also for networks in which traffic is routed in a distributed, congestion-sensitive manner.

This section focuses on two different models of routing games. The first model, *nonatomic* selfish routing refers to the assumption that there are a very large number of players, each controlling a negligible fraction of the overall traffic. We also study *atomic* selfish routing, where each player controls a non-negligible amount of traffic. We single out these two models for three reasons:

1) Both models are conceptually simple but quite general.
2) The POA is well understood in both of these models.
3) Third, the two models are superficially similar, but different techniques are required to analyze the inefficiency of equilibria in each of them.

6.5.1 Nonatomic Selfish Routing

In general, we will consider a selfish routing game in a *multi-commodity flow network*, or simply a *network*. A network is given by a directed graph $G=(V, E)$, with vertex set V and directed edge set E, together with a set $(s_1, t_1), \ldots, (s_k, t_k)$ of source–sink vertex pairs. We also call such pairs *commodities*. Each player is identified with one commodity; different players can originate from different source vertices and travel to different sink vertices. We use $\mathcal{P}_i$ to denote the $s_i - t_i$ paths of a network. We consider only networks in which $\mathcal{P}_i \neq \emptyset$ for all i, and define $\mathcal{P} = \bigcup_{i=1}^{k} \mathcal{P}_i$. We allow the graph G to contain parallel edges, and a vertex can participate in multiple source–sink pairs.

We describe the routes chosen by players using a flow, which is simply a nonnegative vector indexed by the set $\mathcal{P}$ of source–sink paths. For a flow f and a path $\in \mathcal{P}_i$, we interpret f_P as the amount of traffic of commodity i that chooses the path P to travel from s_i to t_i. Traffic is "inelastic," in that there is a prescribed amount r_i of traffic identified with each commodity i. A flow f is *feasible* for a vector r if it routes all of the traffic: for each $i \in \{1, 2, ..., k\}$, $\sum_{P \in \mathcal{P}_i} f_P = r_i$. In particular, we do not impose explicit edge capacities.

Finally, each edge e of a network has a *cost function* $c_e: \mathcal{R}^+ \to \mathcal{R}^+$. We always assume that cost functions are nonnegative, continuous, and nondecreasing. All of these assumptions are reasonable in applications where cost represents a quantity that only increases with the network congestion; delay is one natural example. We define a *nonatomic selfish routing game*, or simply a *nonatomic instance*, by a triple of the form (G, r, c).

To formalize the notion of equilibrium in nonatomic selfish routing games, we define the cost of a path P with respect to a flow f as the sum of the costs of the constituent edges: $c_P(f) = \sum_{e \in P} c_e(f_e)$, where $f_e = \sum_{P \in \mathcal{P}_i : e \in P} f_P$ denotes the amount of traffic using paths that contain the edge e. Since we expect selfish traffic to attempt to minimize its cost, we arrive at the following definition:

Let f be a feasible flow for the nonatomic instance (G, r, c). The flow f is an equilibrium flow if, for every commodity $i \in \{1, 2, ..., k\}$ and every pair $P, \tilde{P} \in \mathcal{P}_i$ of $s_i - t_i$ paths with $f_P > 0$, $c_P(f) \leq c_{\tilde{P}}(f)$.

In other words, all paths in use by an equilibrium flow f have the minimum possible cost (given their source, sink, and the congestion caused by f). In other words, all paths of a given commodity used by an equilibrium flow have equal cost.

When we quantify the inefficiency of equilibrium flows, we consider only the utilitarian objective of minimizing the total cost incurred by traffic. Since the cost incurred by a player choosing the path P in the flow f is $c_P(f)$, and f_P denotes the amount of traffic choosing the path P, we define the *cost* of a flow f as

$$C(f) = \sum_{P \in \mathcal{P}} c_P(f) f_P. \tag{6.31}$$

Expanding $c_P(f)$ as $\sum_{e \in P} c_e(f_e)$ and reversing the order of summation in Eq. (6.31) gives a useful alternative definition of the cost of a flow:

$$C(f) = \sum_{e \in E} c_e(f_e) f_e. \tag{6.32}$$

For an instance (G, r, c), we call a feasible flow *optimal* if it minimizes the cost over all feasible flows.

Given an objective function and an equilibrium concept, a game may have different equilibria and objective function values, so we will study to what extent it is different. In this case, the optimization goal is to minimize the cost of a flow. We will consider two important measures of the inefficiency of an equilibria that are used in routing games, and in order to introduce them, we study Pigou's example. In this example, there are many outcomes: If all of the traffic takes the upper edge, then the cost function $c_1(x) = 1 \times 1 + x \times 0 = 1$. If all of the traffic takes the lower edge, then $c_2(x) = 1 \times 0 + x \times 1 = x$. In the case where the traffic is split between the upper and the lower edges,

---

Design Example 6.3

Let us compute the optimal flow in original Pigou's example shown in Figure 6.3a. Here, we have $c_1(x) = 1$, the cost of the upper edge does not depend on the traffic, and $c_2(x) = x$ the cost of the lower edge is directly proportional to the traffic on the path. In the case where they split their traffic between the upper and the lower edge with $f_1 = \alpha$ being the proportion of the flow that take the upper edge, $f_2 = (1 - \alpha)$ is the proportion of flow that take the lower edge: In this case, the cost function is $C(\alpha) = c_1(f_1) \cdot f_1 + c_2(f_2) \cdot f_2 = 1 \cdot \alpha + (1-\alpha)^2 = \alpha^2 - \alpha + 1$. The optimal flow f^* minimizes the cost function $C(f) \cdot C'(\alpha) = 2\alpha - 1$. Now $C'(\alpha) = 0 \Rightarrow 2\alpha = 1 \Rightarrow \alpha = \frac{1}{2} \Rightarrow f^* = (1/2; 1/2)$. Thus, splitting the traffic equally between the two edges is the optimal outcome.

Figure 6.3 In brackets: original version of Pigou's network. no brackets: nonlinear version of Pigou's network. (For more details see color figure in bins).

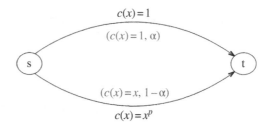

we have already seen that the optimal flow f^* that minimizes the cost function $c(f)$ is $f^* = (1/2; 1/2)$; that is, splitting the traffic equally between the two edges is the optimal outcome. Hence, in this case, half of the traffic has a cost of 1, and the other has a cost of 1/2, the average cost of the traffic in this optimal flow is ¾, and hence $c(f_{WorstEqu})/c(f_{opt}) = 1/(3/4) = 4/3$, where $C(f_{WorstEqu})$ is the cost of the worst Nash equilibrium flow (i.e., with the highest cost) and $C(f_{opt})$ the cost of an optimal flow.

The POA (POA) is defined as $POA = c(f_{WorstEqu})/c(f_{opt})$, where $C(f_{WorstEqu})$ is the cost of the worst Nash equilibrium flow (i.e., with the highest cost) and $C(f_{opt})$ the cost of an optimal flow. In other words, it is the proportion between the worst possible social utility from a Nash equilibrium and the optimal social utility. It is the most popular measure of the inefficiency of equilibria, which adopts a worst-case approach.

To further emphasize the importance of POA problem, let us return to the Pigou's example with the slight modifications indicated in Figure 6.3 in black. The upper edge has a constant cost function $c(x) = 1$, and the lower edge has a highly nonlinear variable cost $c(x) = x^p$ for a large p. If we again split the traffic equally between the two links, then the average cost tends to 1/2 as p *tends to* $+\infty$.

If there was a dictator that could force a small fraction x of the traffic to travel along the lower edge, then the average cost would be $C(x) = 1 \cdot (1\text{-}x) + x^p \cdot x = 1\text{-}x + x^{p+1}$, and hence $C'(x) = -1 + (p+1)x^p = 0 \Rightarrow 1/(p+1) = x^p \Leftrightarrow x = \sqrt[p]{1/(1+p)}$.

For $p = 1$, we have indeed $x = 1/2$, which is the previous result. If p tends to $+\infty$, then $\lim_{p \to +\infty} \sqrt[p]{1/(1+p)} = \lim_{p \to +\infty} (p+1)^{-1/p} = \lim_{p \to +\infty} \exp\left(-(\ln(p+1))/p\right)$. We have that $\lim_{p \to +\infty}(\ln(p+1))/p = 0$, hence $\lim_{p \to +\infty} \sqrt[p]{1/(1+p)} = 1$. This implies that as p tends to $+\infty$, the optimal flow will have an increasing percentage of traffic over the lower edge. Thus, the cost of the network with an optimal flow is $C(\sqrt[p]{1/(1+p)}) = 1 - \sqrt[p]{1/(1+p)} + \left(\sqrt[p]{1/(1+p)}\right)^{p+1}$.

Since the cost of the network with the equilibrium flow is 1, we have that the $POA = 1/(1 - \sqrt[p]{1/(1+p)} + \left(\sqrt[p]{1/(1+p)}\right)^{p+1})$ and $\lim_{p \to +\infty} 1/\left(1 - \sqrt[p]{1/(1+p)} + \left(\sqrt[p]{1/(1+p)}\right)^{p+1}\right)$ $= 1/(1 - 1 + 1/\infty) = 1/0 = +\infty$.

In conclusion, the POA tends to infinity as p tends to $+\infty$, so the equilibrium can be arbitrarily inefficient. We will be looking for games for which the POA is close to 1. Hence, in those games, selfish behavior will not have consequences over the cost function, and so optimality will remain.

The price of stability (POS) is defined as $POS = c(f_{BestEqu})/c(f_{opt})$, where $C(f_{BestEqu})$ is the cost of the best Nash equilibrium flow (i.e., with the lowest cost) and $C(f_{opt})$ the cost of an optimal flow. In other words, it is the proportion between the best possible social utility of a Nash equilibrium and the optimal social utility.

There is the following link between POS and the POA: (i) Consider a game with multiple equilibria that has at least one highly inefficient equilibrium. This game will have a large POA. The POS measures the inefficiency of games but differentiate between games in which all equilibria are inefficient and those in which some equilibrium is inefficient. (ii) In a game with an unique equilibrium, POA = POS, but in a general case for a game with multiple equilibria, $1 \leq POS \leq POA$.

Design Example 6.4 Braess's Paradox

At this point, it would be of interest to look at one more phenomenon in this type of networks. Consider the four-node network shown in Figure 6.4a. There are two disjoint routes from s to t, each with combined cost $1 + x$, where x is the amount of traffic that uses the route. Assume that there is one unit of traffic. In the equilibrium flow, the traffic is split evenly between the two routes, and all of the traffic experiences 3/2 units of cost.

Now suppose that in an effort to decrease the cost encountered by the traffic, we build a zero-cost edge connecting the midpoints of the two existing routes. The new network is shown in Figure 6.4b. What is the new equilibrium flow? The previous equilibrium flow does not persist in the new network: the cost of the new route $s \rightarrow v \rightarrow w \rightarrow t$ is never worse than that along the two original paths, and it is strictly less whenever some traffic fails to use it. As a consequence, the unique equilibrium flow routes all of the traffic on the new route. Because of the ensuing heavy congestion on the edges (s, v) and (w, t), all of the traffic now experiences two units of cost. Braess's Paradox thus shows that the intuitively helpful action of adding a new zero-cost edge can increase the cost experienced by all of the traffic!

The optimal flow in the network from Figure 6.4b is the same as the equilibrium flow in the first network. The POA in the second network is therefore 4/3, the same as that in Pigou's example.

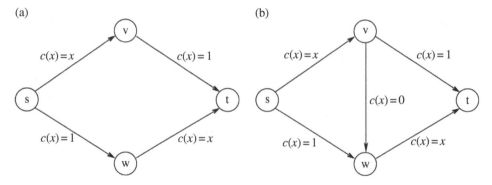

Figure 6.4 Braess's paradox. (a) Initial network, (b) augmented network. The addition of an intuitively helpful edge can have a negative impact on all of the traffic.

6.5.2 Atomic Selfish Routing

An *atomic selfish routing game* or *atomic instance* is defined by the same parameters as a nonatomic one: a directed graph $G = (V, E)$, k source–sink pairs $(s_1, t_1), \ldots, (s_k, t_k)$, a positive amount r_i of traffic for each pair (s_i, t_i), and a nonnegative, continuous, nondecreasing cost function $c_e \colon \mathcal{R}^+ \rightarrow \mathcal{R}^+$ for each edge e.

We also use a triple (G, r, c) to denote an atomic instance. The intuitive difference between the two instances is that in the nonatomic instance, each commodity represents a large population of individuals, each of whom controls a negligible amount of traffic, whereas in the atomic instance, each commodity represents a single player who must route a significant amount of traffic on a single path.

In atomic instances, there are k players, one for each source–sink pair. Different players can have identical source–sink pairs. The strategy set of player i is the set $\mathcal{P}_i$ of $s_i - t_i$ paths, and if player i chooses the path P, then it routes its r_i units of traffic on P. A *flow* is now a nonnegative vector indexed by players and paths, with $f_P^{(i)}$ denoting the amount of traffic that player i routes on the $s_i - t_i$ path P. A flow f is *feasible* for an atomic instance if it corresponds to a strategy profile: for each player i, $f_P^{(i)}$ equals r_i for exactly one $s_i - t_i$ path and equals 0 for all other paths. The cost $c_P(f)$ of a path P with respect to a flow f and the cost $C(f)$ of a flow f are defined as in Section 6.5.1. An equilibrium flow of an atomic selfish routing game is a feasible flow such that no player can strictly decrease its cost by choosing a different path for its traffic.

Atomic equilibrium flow: Let f be a feasible flow for the atomic instance (G, r, c). The flow f is an equilibrium flow if, for every player $i \in \{1, 2, ..., k\}$ and every pair $P, \widetilde{P} \in \mathcal{P}_i$ of $s_i - t_i$ paths with $f_P^{(i)} > 0$, $c_P(f) \leq c_{\widetilde{P}}(\widetilde{f})$, where $\widetilde{f}$ is the flow identical to f except that $\widetilde{f}_P^{(i)} = 0$ and $\widetilde{f}_{\widetilde{P}}^{(i)} = r_i$.

Although the definitions of nonatomic and atomic instances are very similar, the two models are technically quite different. The next example illustrates two of these differences. (i) Different equilibrium flows of an atomic instance can have different costs; all equilibrium flows of a nonatomic instance have equal cost. (ii) The POA in atomic instances can be larger than in their nonatomic counterparts. The following atomic instance has affine cost functions of the form $ax + b$ and its POA is 5/2; in every nonatomic instance with affine cost functions, the POA is at most 4/3.

Design Example 6.5

Consider the bidirected triangle network shown in Figure 6.5a. We assume that there are four players, each of whom needs to route one unit of traffic. The first two have source u and sinks v and w, respectively; the third has source v and sink w; and the fourth has source w and sink v. Each player has two strategies, a one-hop path and a two-hop path. In the optimal flow, all players route on their one-hop paths, and the cost of this flow is 4. This flow is also an equilibrium flow. On the other hand, if all players route on their two-hop paths, then we obtain a second equilibrium flow. Since the first two players each incur three units of cost and the last two players each incur two units of cost, this equilibrium flow has a cost of 10. The price of anarchy of this instance is therefore 10/4 = 2.5.

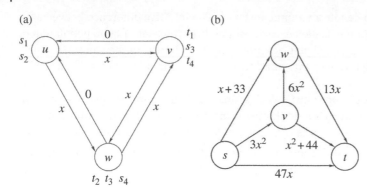

Figure 6.5 (a) In atomic instances with affine cost functions, different equilibrium flows can have different costs, and the price of anarchy can be as large as 5/2. (b) An atomic instance with no equilibrium flow.

Nonexistence of equilibrium in weighted atomic instances: Next, we study the even more basic problem of the existence of equilibrium flows. The equilibrium flows for atomic instances correspond to pure-strategy Nash equilibria, which do not always exist in arbitrary finite games. Do they always exist in atomic selfish routing games? Our second example, in Figure 6.5b, shows that they do not.

Consider the network shown in Figure 6.5b with two players engaged in an atomic selfish routing game, both with source s and sink t, with traffic amounts $r_1 = 1$ and $r_2 = 2$. It can be shown that there is no equilibrium flow in this atomic instance. To prove this, let P_1, P_2, P_3, and P_4 denote the paths $s \rightarrow t$, $s \rightarrow v \rightarrow t$, $s \rightarrow w \rightarrow t$, and $s \rightarrow v \rightarrow w \rightarrow t$, respectively. The following four statements then imply the claim.

(i) If player 2 takes path P_1 or P_2, then the unique response by player 1 that minimizes its cost is the path P_4. (ii) If player 2 takes path P_3 or P_4, then the unique best response by player 1 is the path P_1.(iii) If player 1 takes the path P_4, then the unique best response by player 2 is the path P_3. (iv) If player 1 takes the path P_1, then the unique best response by player 2 is the path P_2.

These statements can be easily verified by inspection. On the other hand, the next section proves that every atomic instance in which all players route the same amount of traffic admits at least one equilibrium flow. We call instances of this type *unweighted*. Figure 6.5a is an example of an unweighted instance, whereas Figure 6.5b is not.

6.5.3 Existence of Equilibrium

In this section, we summarize results on the existence and uniqueness of equilibrium flows in nonatomic and atomic selfish routing games. We also introduce the potential function method, a fundamental proof technique.

Nonatomic selfish routing: Equilibrium flows always exist and are essentially unique (have the same cost). In particular, the POS and the POA coincide in every nonatomic instance. Formally, this can be stated thus: A nonatomic instance (G, r, c) (a) admits at least one equilibrium flow. (b) If f and $\tilde{f}$ are equilibrium flows of (G, r, c), then $c_e(f_e) = c_e(\tilde{f}_e)$ for every edge e.

These statements are proved by the *potential function method*. The idea of this method is to exhibit a real-valued "potential function," defined on the outcomes of a game, such that the equilibria of the game are precisely the outcomes that optimize the potential function.

Potential functions are useful because they enable the application of optimization techniques to the study of equilibria. When a game admits a potential function, there are typically consequences for the existence, uniqueness, and inefficiency of equilibria. To motivate the potential functions corresponding to nonatomic selfish routing games, we present a characterization of optimal flows in such games. We assume that for every edge e of the given nonatomic instance, the function $x \cdot c_e(x)$ is continuously differentiable and convex. Note that $x \cdot c_e(x)$ is the contribution to the social cost function Eq. (6.32) by traffic on the edge e. Let $c_e^*(x) = (x \cdot c_e(x))' = c_e(x) + x \cdot c_e'(x)$ denote the *marginal cost function* for the edge e. For example, if $c(x)$ denotes the cost function $c(x) = ax^p$ for some a, $p \geq 0$, then the corresponding marginal cost function is $c^*(x) = (p+1)ax^p$.

Let $c_P^*(f) = \sum_{e \in P} c_e^*(f)$ denote the sum of the marginal costs of the edges in the path P with respect to the flow f. Let (G, r, c) be a nonatomic instance such that, for every edge e, the function $x \cdot c_e(x)$ is convex and continuously differentiable. Let c_e^* denote the marginal cost function of the edge e. Then f*is an optimal flow for (G, r, c) if and only if, for every commodity $i \in \{1, 2, ..., k\}$ and every pair $P, \tilde{P} \in \mathcal{P}_i$ of $s_i - t_i$ paths with $f_P^* > 0$, $c_P^*(f^*) \leq c_{\tilde{P}}^*(f^*)$.

Under the above assumption, f*is an optimal flow for (G, r, c) if and only if it is an equilibrium flow for (G, r, c^*).

For instance, in Pigou's example (Figure 6.3a), the marginal cost functions of the two edges are $c^*(x) = 1$ and $c^*(x) = 2x$. The equilibrium flow with respect to the marginal cost functions splits the traffic equally between the two links, equalizing their marginal costs at 1; we have shown that this flow is optimal in the original network. In the nonlinear variant of Pigou's example (Figure 6.3b), the marginal cost functions are $c^*(x) = 1$ and $c^*(x) = (p+1)x^p$; the optimal flow therefore routes $(p+1)^{-1/p}$ units of traffic on the second link and the rest on the first. In Braess's Paradox with the zero-cost edge added (Figure 6.4b), routing half of the traffic on each of the paths $s \to v \to t$ and $s \to w \to t$ equalizes the marginal costs of all three paths at 2, and therefore provides an optimal flow for the original instance.

To construct a potential function for equilibrium flows, we seek a function $h_e(x)$ for each edge$-$ playing the previous role of $x \cdot c_e(x)-$ such that $h_e'(x) = c_e(x)$. Setting $h_e(x) = \int_0^x c_e(y)dy$ for each edge e thus yields the desired potential function. Moreover, since c_e is continuous and nondecreasing for every edge e, every function h_e is both continuously differentiable and convex.

Precisely, call

$$\Phi(f) = \sum_{e \in E} \int_0^{f_e} c_e(x)dx \tag{6.33}$$

the *potential function* of a nonatomic instance (G, r, c). Invoking the definition of the optimal flow, with each function $x \cdot c_e(x)$ replaced by $h_e(x) = \int_0^x c(y)dy$, yields the same condition as in definition of the equilibrium flow; we have therefore characterized equilibrium flows as the global minimizers of the potential function Φ. Formally, we have:

Let (G, r, c) be a nonatomic instance. A flow feasible for (G, r, c) is an equilibrium flow if and only if it is a global minimum of the corresponding potential function Φ given in Eq. (6.33).

Atomic selfish routing: We now consider equilibrium flows in atomic instances. The example from Figure 6.5a suggests that no interesting uniqueness results are possible in such instances, so we focus instead on the existence of equilibrium flows. Similarly, the example from Figure 6.5b demonstrates that a general atomic instance need not admit an equilibrium flow. There are two approaches to circumventing this counterexample. The first, taken in this section, is to place additional restrictions on atomic instances so that equilibrium flows are guaranteed to exist. The second approach, discussed in later, is to relax the equilibrium concept so that an equilibrium exists in every atomic instance.

The key results in this section are summarized in the following theorems [19]:

Theorem 6.10 Let (G, r, c) be an atomic instance in which every traffic amount r_i is equal to a common positive value R. Then (G, r, c) admits at least one equilibrium flow.

Theorem 6.11 Let (G, r, c) be an atomic instance with affine cost functions. Then (G, r, c) admits at least one equilibrium flow.

6.5.4 Reducing the POA

As we have seen, the POA can be large in both nonatomic and atomic selfish routing games when cost functions are highly nonlinear. This motivates the question of how can we design or modify a selfish routing network, without explicitly imposing an optimal solution, to minimize the inefficiency of its equilibria? Can modest intervention significantly reduce the POA? We briefly discuss two techniques for mitigating the inefficiency of selfish routing in nonatomic instances: influencing traffic with edge taxes and increasing the capacity of the network.

Marginal cost pricing is an approach to reducing the POA in nonatomic selfish routing games by using *marginal cost taxes* on the edges of the network. The idea of marginal cost pricing is to charge each network user on each edge for the additional cost its presence imposes on the other users of the edge. Formally, we allow each edge e of a nonatomic selfish routing network to possess a nonnegative *tax* τ_e. We denote a nonatomic instance (G, r, c) with edge taxes τ by $(G, r, c + \tau)$. An equilibrium flow for such an instance $(G, r, c + \tau)$ is defined as before, with all traffic traveling on routes that minimize the sum of the edge costs and edge taxes. Equivalently, it is an equilibrium flow for the nonatomic instance (G, r, c^τ), where the cost function c_e^τ is a shifted version of the original cost function $c_e : c_e^\tau(x) = c_e(x) + \tau_e$ for all $x \geq 0$.

The principle of marginal cost pricing asserts that for a flow f feasible for a nonatomic instance (G, r, c), the tax τ_e assigned to the edge e should be $\tau_e = f_e \cdot c'_e(f_e)$, where c'_e denotes the derivative of c_e. (Assume for simplicity that the cost functions are differentiable.) The term $c'_e(f_e)$ corresponds to the marginal increase in cost caused by one user of the edge, and the term f_e is the amount of traffic that suffers from this increase. Formally [19]:

Theorem 6.12 Let (G, r, c) be a nonatomic instance such that, for every edge e, the function $x \cdot c_e(x)$ is convex and continuously differentiable. Let f*be an optimal flow for (G, r, c) and let $\tau_e = f_e^* \cdot c'_e(f_e^*)$ denote the marginal cost tax for edge e with respect to f*. Then f*is an equilibrium flow for $(G, r, c + \tau)$.

Marginal cost taxes thus induce an optimal flow as an equilibrium flow; in this sense, such taxes reduce the POA to 1. Theorem 6.12 also holds with weaker assumptions on the cost functions; in particular, the convexity hypothesis is not needed.

Capacity augmentation provides a bound on the inefficiency of equilibrium flows in nonatomic selfish routing games with arbitrary cost functions. This bound does not involve the POA, which is unbounded in such networks, and instead shows that the cost of an equilibrium flow is at most that of an optimal flow that is forced to route twice as much traffic between each source–sink pair. As we will see, this result implies that in lieu of centralized control, the inefficiency of selfish routing can be offset by a moderate increase in link speed.

Design Example 6.6

Consider the nonlinear variant of Pigou's example (Figure 6.3b). When there is one unit of traffic, the equilibrium flow routes all of the flow on the lower edge, while the optimal flow routes ε units of flow on the upper edge and the rest on the lower edge (where $\varepsilon \to 0$ as $p \to \infty$). When the amount r of traffic to be routed exceeds 1, an optimal flow assigns the additional $r - 1$ units of traffic to the upper link, incurring a cost that tends to $r - 1$ as $p \to \infty$. In particular, for every p an optimal flow feasible for twice the original traffic amount ($r = 2$) has a cost of at least 1, the cost of the equilibrium flow in the original instance. It was shown in [19] that the upper bound stated in above example for the nonlinear variant of Pigou's example holds in every nonatomic instance.

Theorem 6.13 If f is an equilibrium flow for (G, r, c) and f^* is feasible for $(G, 2r, c)$, then $C(f) \leq C(f^*)$.

Proof: Along the lines presented in [19], let f and f^* denote an equilibrium flow for (G, r, c) and a feasible flow for $(G, 2r, c)$, respectively. For each commodity i, let d_i denote the minimum cost of an $s_i - t_i$ path with respect to the flow f. The definition of cost imply that $C(f) = \sum_i r_i d_i$.

Let us define a set of cost functions $\bar{c}$ that satisfies two properties: lower-bounding the cost of f^* relative to that of f is easy with respect to $\bar{c}$; and the new cost functions $\bar{c}$ approximate the original ones c. Specifically, we set $\bar{c}_e(x) = \max\{c_e(f_e), c_e(x)\}$ for each edge e. Let $\bar{C}(\cdot)$ denote the cost of a flow in the instance $(G, r, \bar{c})$. Note that $\bar{C}(f^*) \geq C(f^*)$ while $\bar{C}(f) = C(f)$. We first upper-bound the amount by which the new cost $\bar{C}(f^*)$ of f^* can exceed its original cost $C(f^*)$. For every edge e, $\bar{c}_e(x) - c_e(x)$ is zero for $x \geq f_e$ and bounded above by $c_e(f_e)$ for $x < f_e$, so $x(\bar{c}_e(x) - c_e(x)) \leq c_e(f_e)f_e$ for all $x \geq 0$. Thus

$$\bar{C}(f^*) - C(f^*) = \sum_{e \in E} f_e^* (\bar{c}_e(f_e^*) - c_e(f_e^*)) \leq \sum_{e \in E} c_e(f_e)f_e = C(f). \tag{6.34}$$

In other words, evaluating f^* with cost functions $\bar{c}$, rather than with c, increases its cost by at most an additive $C(f)$ factor.

Now we lower-bound $\bar{C}(f^*)$. By construction, the modified cost $\bar{c}_e(\cdot)$ of an edge e is always at least $c_e(f_e)$, so the modified cost $\bar{c}_P(\cdot)$ of a path $P \in \mathcal{P}_i$ is always at least $c_P(f)$, which in turn is at least d_i. The modified cost $\bar{C}(f^*)$ therefore equals

$$\sum_{P \in \mathcal{P}} \bar{c}_P(f^*)f_P^* \geq \sum_{i=1}^{k} \sum_{P \in \mathcal{P}_i} d_i f_P^* = \sum_{i=1}^{k} 2r_i d_i = 2C(f). \tag{6.35}$$

The theorem now follows immediately from the inequalities Eqs. (6.34) and (6.35). $\square$

Another interpretation of Theorem 6.13 is that the benefit of centralized control is equaled or exceeded by the benefit of a sufficient improvement in link technology.

Corollary 6.4 Let (G, r, c) be an instance and define the modified cost function $\tilde{c}_e$ by $\tilde{c}_e(x) = c_e(x/2)/2$ for each edge e. Let $\tilde{f}$ be an equilibrium flow for $(G, r, \tilde{c})$ with cost $\tilde{C}(\tilde{f})$, and f^* a feasible flow for (G, r, c) with cost $C(f^*)$. Then $\tilde{C}(\tilde{f}) \leq C(f^*)$.

Simple calculations show that Theorem 6.13 and Corollary 6.4 are equivalent [19]. The corollary takes on a particularly nice form in instances in which all cost functions are $M/M/1$ *delay functions*. Such a cost function has the form $c_e(x) = (u_e - x)^{-1}$, where u_e can be interpreted as an edge capacity or a queue service rate; the function is defined to be $+\infty$ when $x \geq u_e$. In this case, the modified function $\tilde{c}_e$ of the corollary is $\tilde{c}_e(x) = 1/2(u_e - x/2) = 1/(2u_e - x)$. The corollary thus suggests the following design principle for selfish routing networks with $M/M/1$ delay functions: *to outperform optimal routing, just double the capacity of every edge.*

6.6 Routing with Edge Priorities

The routing game is played on a directed network $G = (V, E)$, where V is the node set with $n = |V|$ nodes and E is the edge set with $m = |E|$ arcs. In the model, multiple edges, that is, more than one edge starting at the same node and ending at the same node, as well as loops, that is, an edge starting and ending at the same node are allowed. Further, $u: E \rightarrow \mathbb{N}$ are *integral capacities* on the edges. This capacity limits the inflow rate, that is, the amount of flow entering an edge $e \in E$ per time unit. Furthermore, the edges of G are equipped with *integral transit times* $\tau: E \rightarrow \mathbb{N}_0$. The transit time or costs $\tau(e)$ denotes the time a player needs to traverse edge $e \in E$. We use constant transit times here; that is, players use edges independently of other players, and there is no delay due to congestion. We allow edges with transit time zero, since they are useful to model capacities on nodes. The throughput capacity of a node v can be limited by replacing this node by an edge (v', v'') with the desired capacity and zero cost. We restrict ourselves to integral transit times, since each player blocks exactly one capacity unit for one time unit on each edge of its path. In addition, each routing game fixes two distinguished nodes, a source s and a sink t. We assume that the source has no incoming edges, that is, $\deg^-(s) = 0$. Every *player* in the set $N = \{1, \ldots, k\}$ of players chooses a path P_i from the set of s-t-paths $\mathcal{P}_{st}$ and travels over time through the network. To be more specific, a player can leave an edge e at the earliest $\tau(e)$ time units after entering e. Moreover, we consider only discrete time steps, since we have integral transit times. Note that we do not restrict ourselves to simple paths, since it may be advantageous for a player to choose a path containing a cycle as we will see in the upcoming analysis. Since all the players have the same set of strategies, we call it a *symmetric* or *single-commodity* game.

When traveling through the network over time, it might happen that more than $u(e)$ players try to enter an edge $e = (v, w)$ at the same time. To decide which players are allowed to proceed directly and which players need to wait for at least one time unit, we define a *priority order* $\pi(e) = (e_1, e_2, \ldots, e_{\deg^-(v)})$; that is, for every $v \in V$ we assign an ordered list $\pi(e)$ of all incoming edges $e_i = (u_i, v) \in \delta^-(v)$ of v to each outgoing edge $(v, w) \in \delta^+(v)$ of v. If edge e has remaining capacity at time T, a player seeking to enter edge e at time T may do so, if the incoming edge of this player has the lowest possible index in the ordered list $\pi(e)$ among all players who want to enter the link e. This applies iteratively. Thus, after the first player has entered the link, we choose the next player with the lowest possible incoming edge in $\pi(e)$ from the remaining players, if e still has capacity left.

Among the players waiting on an edge e', the *first-in first-out* rule (FIFO) applies. This means that if Player i and Player j both try to enter edge e from the same edge e', the player who arrived on edge e' first will be preferred. If several players have entered e' at the same time, but the desired edge e does not provide enough capacity for all of them, we use the number of the player as a global tie-breaker. That is, in case of a tie, Player i moves before Player j if $i < j$. This rule especially applies at the source; that is, Player 1 is always the first player to leave source s.

If for every node $v \in V$ holds $\pi(e) = \pi(e')$ for all priority lists of outgoing edges, $e' \in \delta^+(v)$, then we call a game *global*; else we call it *local*. In case of a global game, we may simply define a total order on all edges, since such an order canonically defines the priority list of each edge. This total order is, of course, not unique. For the sake of simplicity in a global game, we always relabel the edges of G to $e_1, e_2, \ldots, e_m$ such that e_i has higher priority than e_j whenever $i < j$. In summary, we determine priority in the order *edge list > FIFO > player ID*. A *routing game with edge priorities* is defined as a tuple (G, u, τ, N, π).

In the game, a *strategy* of a Player i is an s-t path P_i. Let P be the *profile* or *state* of the game with the strategies of all the players; that is, P consists of k paths P_1 to P_k. Now, we denote the *arrival time* of

(a)

(b)

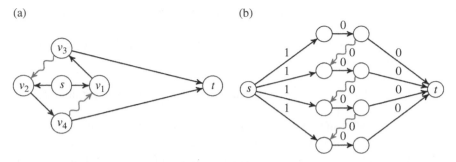

Figure 6.6 (Left) Example of embedding problems with zero-cost cycles. Wavy edges have higher priority. (Right) The 4-Braess graph, where the value of a PNE is not unique. Wavy edges have higher priority.

Player i as $C_i(P)$, which consists of the transit times $\tau(e)$ of all the edges of the chosen path P_i and the *waiting time* on those edges. Obviously, the former is independent of the strategies of the other players due to constant transit times, but the latter significantly depends on P.

A profile P is *socially optimal* if it minimizes the total costs $C(P) = \sum_{i \in N} C_i(P)$. However, we assume players to behave selfishly; that is, each player aims to minimize his own arrival time. We call a state a (pure) Nash equilibrium (PNE) if the chosen strategies separately minimize the players' costs for every player. Let P_{-i} be the state P without the strategy of Player i. Furthermore, with P_i', P_{-i} we denote replacing the strategy of Player i in P by P_i'. More formally, a routing game with state P and strategy P_i for Player i is in a PNE if $C_i(P_i, P_{-i}) \leq C_i(P_i', P_{-i}) \forall P_i' \in \mathcal{P}_{st}$, for all players $i \in N$. In other words, no player can reduce her costs by switching from P_i to another path P_i'.

For a well-defined game, it is important to have a unique mapping of a strategy profile P to costs $C(P)$ of the players. Unfortunately, the current model can still lead to some paradoxical situations in connection with zero-cost cycles. An example with two players is given in Figure 6.6 (top). Assume, Player 1 chooses the path $(s, v_1, v_3, v_2, v_4, t)$ and Player 2 chooses $(s, v_2, v_4, v_1, v_3, t)$. Note that the paths intersect twice. Player i hits node v_i before node v_{3-i} on the respective path.

Now, assume the red wavy edges (v_4, v_1) and (v_3, v_2) in the cycle have priority over the black straight entering edges (s_1, v_1) and (s_2, v_2) to proceed on (v_1, v_3) and (v_2, v_4), respectively. Furthermore, all edges have zero transit time. On the one hand, Player 1 could reach v_2 in zero time and block Player 2 there. If Player 2 is blocked at v_2, he cannot block Player 1 at v_1. Thus, Player 1 reaches t_1 at time 0, and Player 2 reaches t_2 at time 1. On the other hand, the converse argument also holds. Since Player 2 can reach v_1 in zero time, Player 1 is blocked. Hence, Player 2 reaches t_2 at time 0, and Player 1 reaches t_1 at time 1. In other words, there is no unique embedding of the paths, and therefore there is no unique mapping from the strategy P to the arrival times of players $C(P)$.

Note: Since we do not want to forbid zero transit times in general, we exclude all networks with directed zero-cost cycles from our consideration. Moreover, we will compute the ratios of various solutions, for example, the POA. To avoid division by zero, we also exclude all games where source s and sink t have distance zero.

Equilibria: In this section, we highlight some major properties of equilibria in routing games with edge priorities along the lines presented in [20], where it was shown that a PNE always exists in every symmetric game and the bound of its costs with respect to the social optimum was derived.

First, the existence of a pure-strategy Nash equilibrium (PNE) in a symmetric game was proved.

Theorem 6.14 In every symmetric routing game with edge priorities there exists a PNE.

An equilibrium in terms of the profile is not unique. But for a given game, the value $C(P)$ of equilibria is also not unique.

Proposition [*)]. The value of equilibria in a routing game with edge priorities is not unique.

Proof. For the proof, a graph based on Braess's example [21] was used. We refer to the graph with b parallel paths from s to t as a b-*Braess graph*. Each path consists of three edges. Furthermore, edges connect the third node of the i-th path with the second node of the $(i + 1)$-th path for all $1 \leq i < b$.

A 4-Braess graph is depicted in Figure 6.6 (bottom). Consider the b-Braess graph where all s-leaving edges have transit time one and all the other edges have zero cost, while all edges have unit capacity. In this network, the priority follows the scheme depicted in Figure 6.6 (bottom); that is, the wavy edges connecting the parallel paths are always prioritized over the edges in the direct paths. The game with $k = b$ players was studied. Obviously, using the b parallel paths in this network is a PNE. No player can improve her arrival time by switching to another path. This PNE is also socially optimal, yielding total costs $C(P) = k$. However, it is also a PNE for all players to go along the zigzag path; that is, every player uses all the wavy edges, in the order of the player IDs. If Player 1 chooses this path, her arrival time is still 1. Player 2 cannot arrive at time 1 with this choice of Player 1, so Player 2 can decide to follow Player 1, arriving at time 2. The same argument applies to all other players. In this case, Player i has cost i and no improving move. In total $C(P) = k(k + 1)/2$. $\square$

This result also holds if we forbid edges with costs equal to zero. Change the transit times in the b-Braess graph as follows. The outgoing edges of s get costs 1, 3, ..., $2b - 1$ from top to bottom. On the other hand, the incoming edges of t get these costs from the bottom to the top. Each other edge is assigned a transit time of 1. Now, the parallel paths have the same costs, like the zigzag path $c(P) = 2b + 1$. Thus, the same argument as above applies.

Bounding the POS and the POA: In the following, we present a tight bound of the POA for routing games with edge priorities and show that there are instances of these games where every social optimum is not stable, and we present a lower-bound example of the POS. Formal proofs for these results can be found in [20]

Theorem 6.15 The price of anarchy in a symmetric routing game with edge priorities is at most $(k + 1)/2$, where k is the number of players. This upper bound is tight.

Theorem 6.16 The price of stability in a symmetric routing game with edge priorities can be $\geq (k + 1)/4$, where k is the number of players.

6.6.1 Computing Equilibria

In this section, we present an efficient algorithm for computing PNEs in symmetric routing games with edge priorities. We start with a summary of the main ideas, and then we provide an algorithm in form of pseudocode as presented in [20].

> The algorithm itself mainly consists of three steps:
>
> i) Initialize a kind of shortest path network and this step is executed only once.
> ii) A path for the next player is found within this shortest path network.
> iii) The network is updated to renew the earliest arrival property for the upcoming player.

Steps ii and iii are executed once for each player. In detail:

1) A modified Dijkstra search is executed starting in s. Two functions are determined $d: V \rightarrow \mathbb{N}_0$ and $\varepsilon: E \rightarrow \mathbb{N}_0$. Here, $d(v)$ describes at which time step node v can be reached at the earliest; that is, at this initialization step $d(v)$ is the standard label set by Dijkstra's algorithm. The function value $\varepsilon(e)$ defines the earliest point in time at which edge e can be left. Hence, $d(v) \leq \varepsilon(e)$ where $e = (u, v)$. In the initialization, $\varepsilon(e) = d(u) + \tau(e)$ holds for $e = (u, v)$, since there are no waiting times. Moreover, the Dijkstra search is not stopped when the final label of node t is found. Instead, we explore the whole network to prepare the data structure for even longer paths of subsequent players. Please note that the sub-network $G' = (V, E')$, where $E' = \{e \in E: e = (u, v)$ and $\varepsilon(e) = d(v)\}$ contains all shortest paths from s to t. More precisely, every path from s to t in this sub-network is the shortest path in the original network.

2) We now perform a backward search in this sub-network $G' = (V, E')$ to find a path p for every Player i, starting with Player 1. Additionally, we introduce or reset the function $\Delta: V \rightarrow \mathbb{N}_0$. For each node $v \in V$, $\Delta(v)$ is the time step at which we are going to leave node v via an edge $e = (v, w)$. Initially, we set $\Delta(t) = d(t)$ and $\Delta(v) = \text{NaN}$ for $v \neq t$. Any player cannot reach the sink t before $d(t)$. Since we may enter t from every incoming edge immediately, we choose an arbitrary edge $e = (v, t)$ with $\varepsilon(e) = d(t)$ as the last edge of the path p. Consequently, we have to leave v at $d(t) - \tau(e) =: \Delta(v)$. More generally, assume we have chosen an edge $e = (u, v)$ to reach node v at time $\Delta(v)$ at the latest. From all available options we choose the earliest possible time to traverse this edge. This yields the time $\Delta(u)$ at which we want to leave node u. Hence, as predecessor of edge e, we have to consider only edges $e' = (w, u)$ with $\varepsilon(e') \leq \Delta(u)$. Among these edges, we choose the one with the lowest index in $\pi(e)$, that is, the edge e' with the highest priority to enter e. We add $e' = (w, u)$ to the path. Again, we use it at the earliest possible time and update $\Delta(w)$ accordingly. Thanks to the definition of d and ε, we can always find a feasible edge. Thus, we eventually reach the source s by iteratively adding preceding edges.

3) After assigning Player i to the path p constructed in step 2, we have to update the values of d and ε. If player i exhausted the capacity of an edge $e = (u, v)$, we increment $\varepsilon(e)$ by 1. We now perform a modified Dijkstra search to check whether we have to increment other labels $d(v)$ and $\varepsilon(e)$, too. In detail, the new values are $\varepsilon(e) := \max\{\varepsilon(e), d(u) + \tau(e)\}$ and $d(v) := \min\{\varepsilon(e) : e = (u, v)\}$ starting with $d(s) = 0$. Finally, we reset Δ.

Now, we can go back to step 2 to compute the path for the next Player $i + 1$.

These steps are summarized in *Algorithm 9* in the form of a pseudocode [20].

Algorithm 9: PATHFINDER

Input: $G = (V, E)$ with priorities π, $s, t \in V$ and set of players $N = \{1, \ldots, k\}$
Output: A walk for every player $i \in N$

1   calculate $d(v)$ and $\varepsilon(e)$ $\forall v \in V, \forall e \in E$;
2   **for** $i := 1$ **to** k **do**
3      $e :=$ arbitrary edge of $\delta_{\mathrm{in}}(t)$ with $\varepsilon(e) = d(t)$;
4      $v := \mathrm{tail}(e)$;
5      $\Delta(v) := d(t) - \tau(e)$;
6      $p := \{e\}$;
7   **while** $v \neq s$ **do**
8   let $e' \in \delta_{in}(v)$, with $\varepsilon(e') \leq \Delta$ and maximal priority for e;
9          $v := \mathrm{tail}(e')$;
10         $\Delta(v) := \varepsilon(e') - \tau(e')$;
11         $p := p \cup \{e'\}$;
12         $e := e'$;
13   print "Path of player i is p";
14   **foreach** $e \in p$ **do**
15   **if** *capacity of e at entry time $\Delta(\mathrm{tail}(e))$ is exhausted* **then**
16          $\varepsilon(e) := \varepsilon(e) + 1$;
17      $d(s) := 0$;
18      $d(v) := \infty$ $\forall v \in V, v \neq s$;
19      $\Pi := \mathrm{heap}(V, d)$;
20   **while** $\Pi \neq \varnothing$ **do**
21          $v := \mathrm{getMin}(\Pi)$;
22   remove v from Π;
23   **foreach** $e \in \delta_{\mathrm{out}}(v)$ **do**
24              $\varepsilon(e) := \max\{\varepsilon(e), d(v) + \tau(e)\}$;
25              $d(\mathrm{head}(e)) := \min\{d(\mathrm{head}(e)), \varepsilon(e)\}$;

Source: Scheffler et al. [20].

References

1 Fearnley, J., Gairing, M., Goldberg, P. et al. (2015). Learning equilibria of games via payoff queries. *J. Mach. Learn. Res.* **16**: 1305–1344.

2 Krichene, W. et al. (2015). Online learning of Nash equilibria in congestion games. *SIAM J. Control. Optim.* **53** (2): 1056–1081.

3 https://www.math.arizona.edu/~faris/probtheoryweb/measure.pdf

4 http://www.stat.rice.edu/~dobelman/courses/Lebesgue_Measure.Meisters.pdf

5 Rosenthal, R.W. (1973). A class of games possessing pure-strategy Nash equilibria. *Internat. J. Game Theory* **2**: 65–67.

6 Kivinen, J. and Warmuth, M.K. (1997). Exponentiated gradient versus gradient descent for linear predictors. *Inform. Comput.* **132**: 1–63.

7 Bottazzi, G. and Devetag, G. (2007). Competition and coordination in experimental minority games. *J. Evol. Econ.* **17**: 241–275.

8 Challet, D., Marsili, M., and Zhang, Y.-C. (2004). *Minority Games: Interacting Agents in Financial Markets*. Oxford: Oxford University Press.

9 Chmura, T. and Pitz, T. (2006). Successful strategies in repeated minority games. *Physica A* **363**: 477–480.

10 Coolen, A. (2005). *The Mathematical Theory of Minority Games: Statistical Mechanics of Interacting Agents*. Oxford: Oxford University Press.

11 W. Ket, M. Voorneveld, Congestion, equilibrium and learning: The minority game http://tuvalu.santafe.edu/~willemien.kets/GMG.pdf

12 https://web.stanford.edu/~jdlevin/Econ%20202/Uncertainty.pdf

13 https://ocw.mit.edu/courses/economics/14-03-microeconomic-theory-and-public-policy-fall-2016/lecture-notes/MIT14_03F16_lec16.pdf

14 Watkins, C.J.C.H. and Dayan, P. (1992). Q-learning. *Mach. Learn.* **3**: 279–292.

15 Hu, J. and Wellman, M.P. (2003). Nash Q-learning for general-sum stochastic games. *J. Mach. Learn. Res.* **4**: 1039–1069.

16 Fink, A.M. (1964). Equilibrium in a stochastic n-person game. *J. Sci. Hiroshima Univ., Ser. A-I* **28**: 89–93.

17 Szepesvari, C. and Littman, M.L. (1999). A unified analysis of value-function-based reinforcement-learning algorithms. *Neural Comput.* **11** (8): 2017–2059.

18 Filar, J. and Vrieze, K. (1997). *Competitive Markov Decision Processes*. Springer-Verlag.

19 Nisan, N. et al. (2011). *Algorithmic Game Theory*. Cambridge University Press.

20 R. Scheffler, M. Strehler, L. V. Koch, Nash equilibria in routing games with edge priorities, arXiv:1803.00865v3 [cs.GT] 21 Aug 2018

21 Braess, D. (1968). Uber ein Paradoxon aus der Verkehrsplanung. *Unternehmensforschung* **12**: 258–268.

22 Jonathan Levin, Learning in Games https://web.stanford.edu/~jdlevin/Econ%20286/Learning.pdf

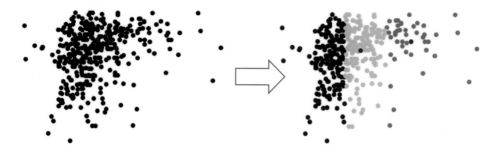

Figure 2.13 k = 3 means clustering on 2D dataset. *Source:* Based on PulkitS01 [3], K-Means implementation, GitHub, Inc. Available at [54] https://gist.github.com/PulkitS01/97c9920b1c913ba5e7e101d0e9030b0e.

Figure 3.20 A bidirectional recurrent neural network (BRNN).

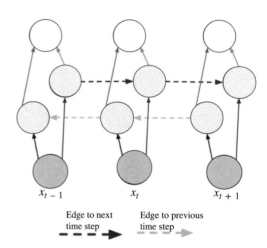

Figure 3.23 Illustration of the convolution operation. If we overlap the convolution kernel on top of the input image, we can compute the product between the numbers at the same location in the kernel and the input, and we get a single number by summing these products together. For example, if we overlap the kernel with the top-left region in the input, the convolution result at that spatial location is $1 \times 1 + 1 \times 4 + 1 \times 2 + 1 \times 5 = 12$.

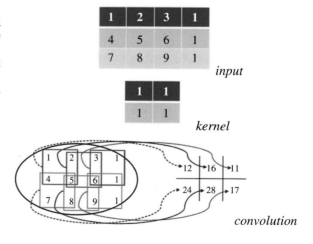

Artificial Intelligence and Quantum Computing for Advanced Wireless Networks, First Edition.
Savo G. Glisic and Beatriz Lorenzo.
© 2022 John Wiley & Sons Ltd. Published 2022 by John Wiley & Sons Ltd.

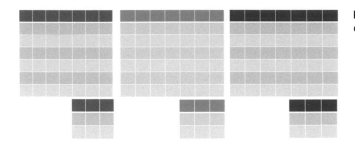

Figure 3.24 RGB image/three channels and three kernels.

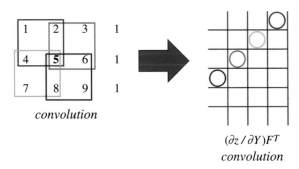

convolution

$(\partial z / \partial Y)F^T$
convolution

Figure. 3.25 Computing $\partial z/\partial X$.

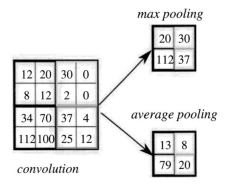

max pooling

average pooling

convolution

Figure 3.26 Illustration of pooling layer operation.

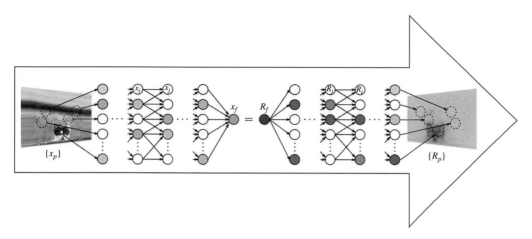

Figure 4.3 Relevance propagation (heat map; relevance is presented by the intensity of the red color). *Source:* Montavon et al. [92].

Figure 5.2 Illustrations of ConvGNN network: (a) A ConvGNN with multiple graph convolutional layers. A graph convolutional layer encapsulates each node's hidden representation by aggregating feature information from its neighbors. After feature aggregation, a nonlinear transformation is applied to the resulted outputs. By stacking multiple layers, the final hidden representation of each node receives messages from a further neighborhood. (b) Recurrent Graph Neural Networks (RecGNNs) use the same graph recurrent layer (Grec) to update node representations. (c) Convolutional Graph Neural Networks (ConvGNNs) use a different graph convolutional layer (Gconv) to update node representations. *Source:* Wu et al. [38].

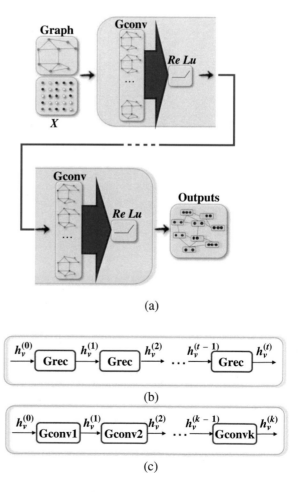

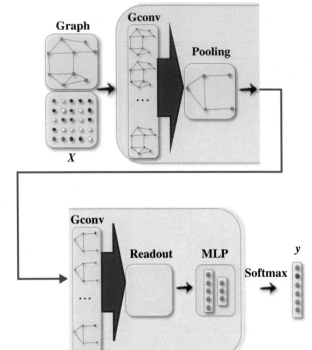

Figure 5.5 A ConvGNN with pooling and readout layers for graph classification. A graph convolutional layer is followed by a pooling layer to coarsen a graph into subgraphs so that node representations on coarsened graphs represent higher graph-level representations. A readout layer summarizes the final graph representation by taking the sum/mean of hidden representations of subgraphs. *Source:* Wu et al. [38].

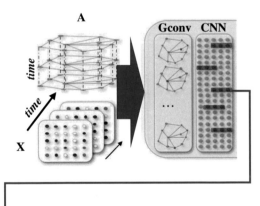

Figure 5.7 A STGNN for spatial-temporal graph forecasting. A graph convolutional layer is followed by a 1D-CNN layer. The graph convolutional layer operates on A and X(t) to capture the spatial dependency, while the 1D-CNN layer slides over X along the time axis to capture the temporal dependency. The output layer is a linear transformation, generating a prediction for each node, such as its future value at the next time step. *Source:* Wu et al. [38].

Figure 6.3 In red: original version of Pigou's network. In black: nonlinear version of Pigou's network.

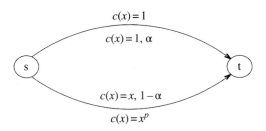

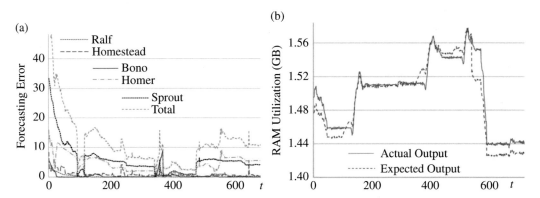

Figure 7.17 (a) Total forecasting error (t-training iteration each involving 103 examples), (b) Ralf RAM utilization (t-test number).

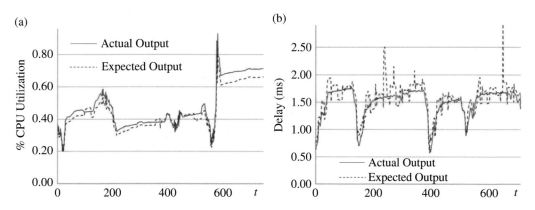

Figure 7.18 (a) Homer CPU utilization, (b) Homestead processing delay (t-test number).

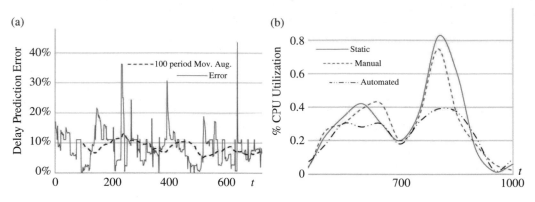

Figure 7.19 (a) Percentage error on delay prediction, (b) percentage CPU for Homer (t-test number).

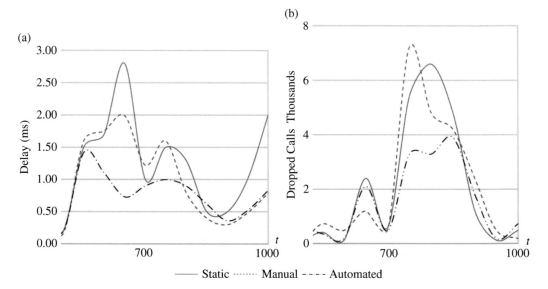

Figure 7.20 (a) Effect on processing latency, (b) effect on calls dropped (t-test number).

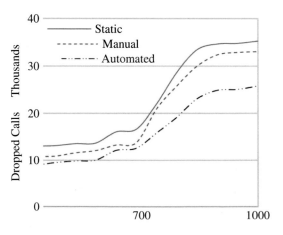

Figure 7.21 Cumulative call drops (t-test number).

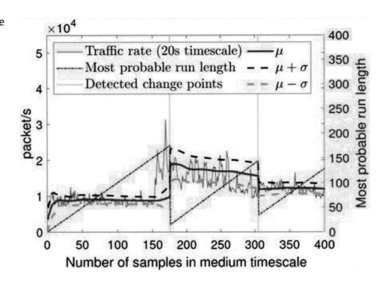

Figure 7.22 Results of change point detection for a nonstationary traffic segment. *Source:* Kaige Qu et al. [231].

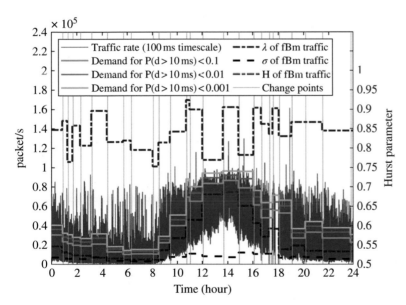

Figure 7.23 Learned traffic parameters and predicted resource demands for daily traffic. *Source:* Kaige Qu et al. [231].

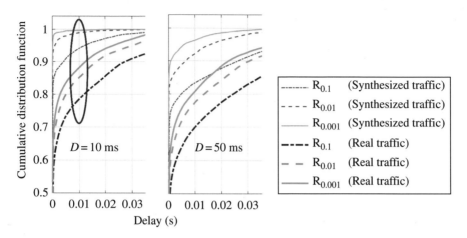

Figure 7.24 Distribution of VNF packet processing delay for both the synthesized traffic and the real traffic. *Source:* Kaige Qu et al. [231].

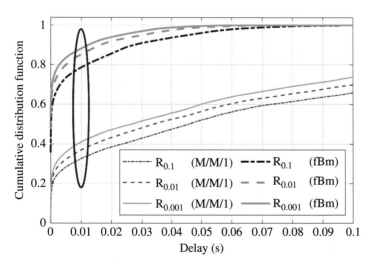

Figure 7.25 QoS performance comparison between resource demand prediction schemes based on the fBm model and M/M/1 model. *Source:* Kaige Qu et al. [231].

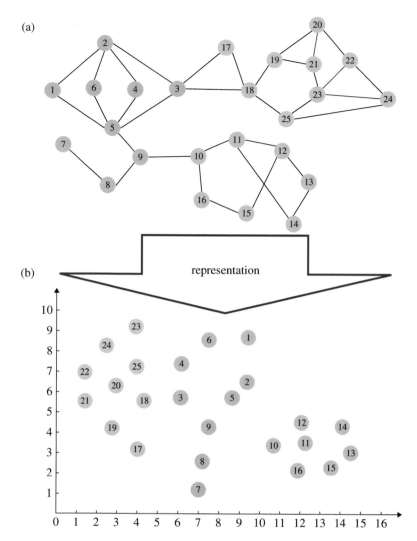

(a)

(b)

Figure 7.30 Conceptual view of network representation learning (NRL).

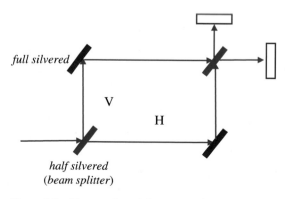

Figure 8.5 Wave and particle nature of light.

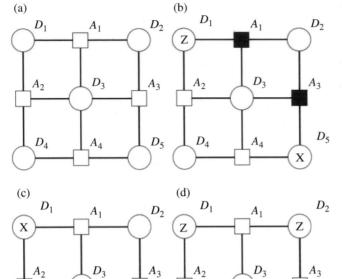

Figure 10.7 (a) The $[[5,1,2]]$ surface code formed by putting together 4 four cycles in a square lattice. (b) Examples of error detection in the $[[5,1,2]]$ surface code. (c) The Pauli-X logical operator $\bar{X} = X_{D_1} X_{D_4}$ acts along the boundary along which Z-type stabilizers are measured. (d) The Pauli-Z logical operator $\bar{Z} = Z_{D_1} Z_{D_2}$ acts along the boundary along which X-type stabilizers are measured. The two logical operators anti-commute with one another.

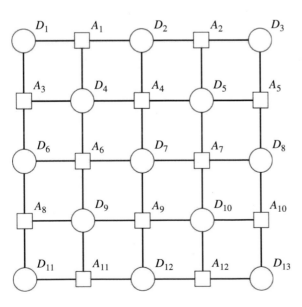

Figure 10.8 A distance-three surface code with parameters $[13, 1, 3]$.

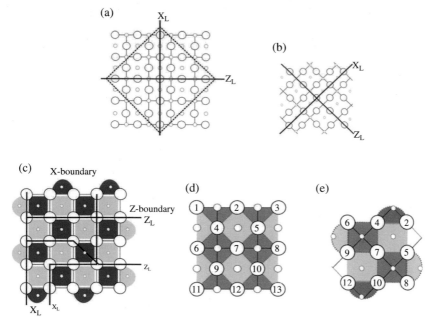

Figure 10.9 (a),(b),(c) Rotating a distance 5 lattice to produce another distance 5 encoded qubit. (a) The original surface. The red square shows the area of the rotated surface. (b) The rotated surface. (c) The rotated plaquettes (vertex plaquettes are marked brown, face plaquettes as yellow), new example logical operators, and boundaries. X(Z) logical operators are shown as red(blue) lines. (d), (e) Two lattices encoding a single qubit with distance 3: d) standard planar lattice; e) the rotated lattice. Light (dark) plaquettes show Z(X) syndrome measurements. *Source:* Horsman et al. [24].

Figure 12.5a Parameter t_1 and its derivative.

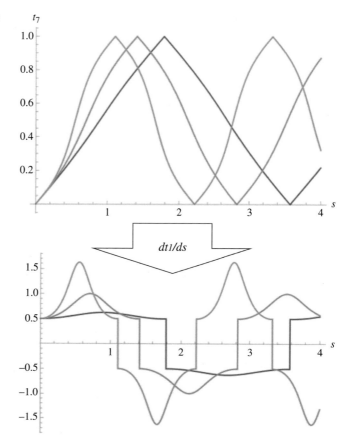

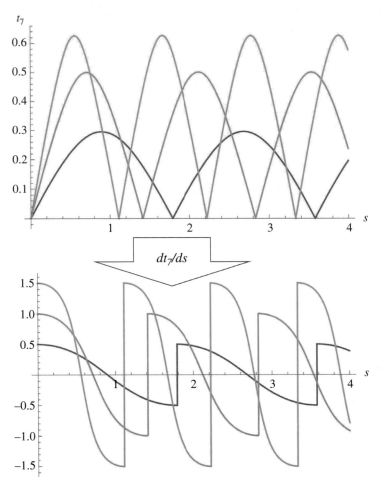

Figure 12.5b Parameter t_7 and its derivative.

dt_7/ds

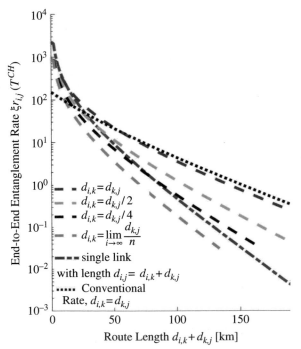

Figure 16.3 Expected end-to-end entanglement rate $\xi_{r_{i,j}}\left(T^{ch}\right)$ between nodes v_i and v_j through route $r_{i,j} = \{e_{i,k}, e_{k,j}\}$ as a function of the total path length $d_{i,k} + d_{k,j}$ for different values of $d_{i,k}$. Atom cooling time τ^d and decoherence time T^{ch} are equal to 100 μs and 1 ms, respectively. *Source:* Caleffi [21].

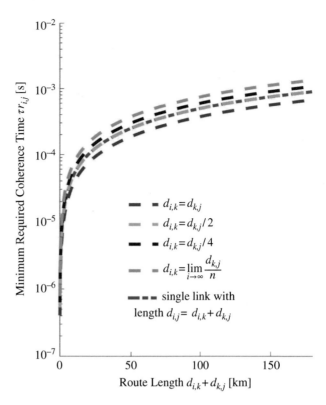

Figure 16.4 Minimum coherence time $\tau_{r_{i,j}}$ required for the successful utilization of an end-to-end entanglement between nodes v_i and v_j through route $r_{i,j} = \{e_{i,k}, e_{k,j}\}$ as a function of the total path length $d_{i,k} + d_{k,j}$ for different values of $d_{i,k}$. Atom cooling time τ^d is equal to 100 µs. Logarithmic scale for y axis. *Source:* Caleffi [21].

Legend:
- $d_{i,k} = d_{k,j}$
- $d_{i,k} = d_{k,j}/2$
- $d_{i,k} = d_{k,j}/4$
- $d_{i,k} = \lim\limits_{i \to \infty} \dfrac{d_{k,j}}{n}$
- single link with length $d_{i,j} = d_{i,k} + d_{k,j}$

Minimum Required Coherence Time $\tau_{r_{i,j}}$ [s]

Route Length $d_{i,k} + d_{k,j}$ [km]

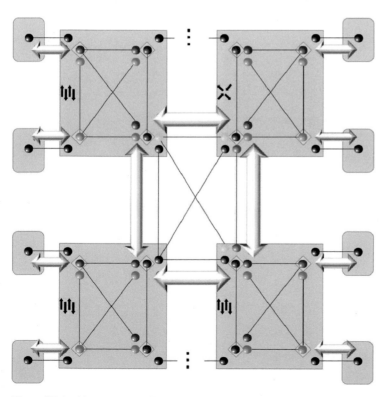

Figure 17.6 Network example with three switches (boxes with multiple vertical arrows) and a router (the box with diagonal arrows) connected in a network via Greenberger–Horne–Zeilinger (GHZ) states of decreasing size (black lines indicate entanglement). *Source:* Pirker and Dür [42].

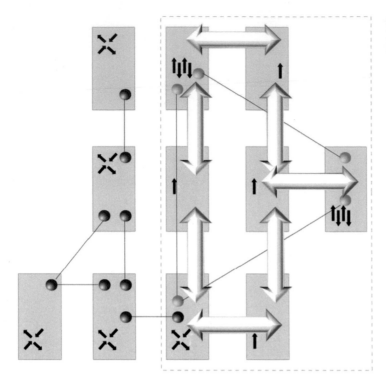

Figure 17.9 Settings of layers 3 and 4. *Source:* Pirker and Dür [42].

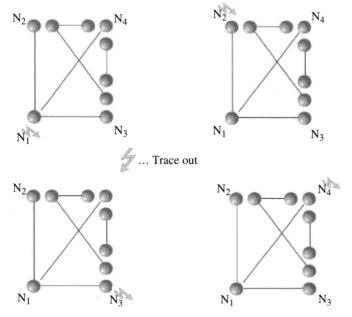

... Trace out

Figure 17.10 Greenberger–Horne–Zeilinger (GHZ) states are very fragile. *Source:* Pirker and Dür [42].

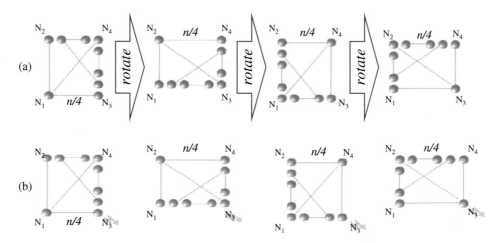

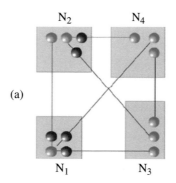

Figure 17.11 (a) Static phase, (b) adaptive phase. *Source:* Pirker and Dür [42].

Figure 17.12 (a) Static phase, (b) adaptive phase. *Source:* Pirker and Dür [42].

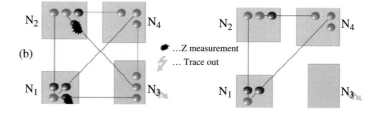

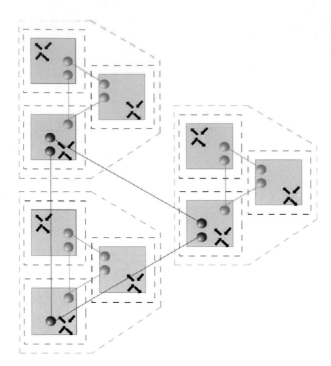

Figure 17.15 The state for connecting nine networks in hierarchical regions for m = 3. *Source:* Pirker and Dür [42].

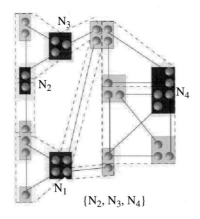

$\{N_2, N_3, N_4\}$

Figure 17.17 Example network for illustration of Protocol 2. *Source:* Pirker and Dür [42].

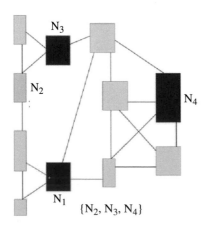

$\{N_2, N_3, N_4\}$

7

AI Algorithms in Networks

7.1 Review of AI-Based Algorithms in Networks

This section presents the application of diverse machine learning (ML) techniques in various key areas of networking across different network technologies. In this way, readers will benefit from a comprehensive discussion on the application of the different learning paradigms and ML techniques covered so far in this book to fundamental problems in networking, including traffic prediction, routing and classification, congestion control, resource and fault management, quality of service (QoS) and quality of experience (QoE) management, and network security.

7.1.1 Traffic Prediction

Network traffic prediction plays a key role in network operations and management for today's increasingly complex and diverse networks. It entails forecasting future traffic and traditionally has been addressed via time series forecasting (TSF). The objective in TSF is to construct a regression model capable of drawing an accurate correlation between future and previously observed traffic volumes. Existing TSF models for traffic prediction can be broadly divided into statistical analysis and supervised ML models. The former are typically built upon the generalized autoregressive integrated moving average (ARIMA) model, whereas most of the latter are implemented via supervised NNs. Generally, the ARIMA model is a popular approach for TSF, where autoregressive (AR) and moving average (MA) models are applied in tandem to perform auto-regression on the differenced and "stationarized" data. However, with the rapid growth of networks and the increasing complexity of network traffic, traditional TSF models are seemingly compromised, giving rise to more advanced ML models. More recently, efforts have been made to reduce overhead and/or improve accuracy in traffic prediction by employing features other than traffic volume from flows.

Traffic prediction as a pure TSF problem: In the last decade, different types of NNs have been employed for TSF of network traffic. Work in [1] proposes an MLP-NN-based bandwidth prediction system for grid environments and compares it to the Network Weather Service (NWS) [2] bandwidth forecasting AR models for traffic monitoring and measurement. The goal of the system is to forecast the available bandwidth on a given path by feeding the NN with the minimum, maximum, and average number of bits per second used on that path in the last epoch (ranging from 10 to 30 s). Experiments on the dotresearch.org network and the 40 gigabit/s NSF TeraGrid network datasets show that the NN outperforms the NWS bandwidth forecasting models with an error rate of up to 8 and 121.9% for MLP-NN and NWS, respectively. Although the proposed NN-based forecasting system shows better learning ability than NWS's, no details are provided for the

Artificial Intelligence and Quantum Computing for Advanced Wireless Networks, First Edition.
Savo G. Glisic and Beatriz Lorenzo.
© 2022 John Wiley & Sons Ltd. Published 2022 by John Wiley & Sons Ltd.

characteristics of the MLP employed in the study, nor the time complexity of the system compared to NWS. For additional works on ML-based traffic prediction via TSF, see [3–6].

Traffic prediction as a non-TSF problem: In contrast to TSF methods, network traffic can be predicted leveraging other methods and features. For instance, work in [7] proposes a frequency-domain-based method for network traffic flows, instead of just traffic volume. The focus is on predicting incoming and outgoing traffic volume on an inter-data center link dominated by extremely large flows (ELFs). Their models incorporate feedforward neural network (FNN), trained with BP using simple gradient descent and the wavelet transform to capture both the time and frequency features of the traffic time series. ELFs are added as separate feature dimensions in the prediction. However, collecting all ELFs at high frequencies is more expensive than byte count for traffic volume. Therefore, ELF flow information is collected at lower frequencies and interpolated to fill in the missing values, overcoming the overhead for ELF collection.

The dataset contains the total incoming and outgoing traffic collected in 30 s intervals using Simple Network Management Protocol (SNMP) counters on the data center (DC) edge routers and the inter-DC links at Baidu over a six-week period. The top five applications account for 80% of the total incoming and outgoing traffic data, which is collected every 5 min and interpolated to estimate missing values at the 30 s scale. The time series is decomposed using a level 10 wavelet transform, leading to 120 features per timestamp. Thus, k-step ahead predictions feed $k \times 120$ features into the NN and show a relative RMSE (RRMSE) ranging from 4 to 10% for the NN–wavelet transformation model as the prediction horizon varies from 30 s to 20 min. Evidently, wavelet transformation reduces the average prediction errors for different prediction horizons by 5.4 and 2.9% for incoming and outgoing traffic, respectively. By contrast, the linear ARIMA model has a prediction error of approximately 8.5 and 6.9% for incoming and outgoing traffic, respectively. The combined NN–wavelet transform model reduces the peak inter-DC link utilization, that is, the ISP's billed utilization, by about 9%. However, the model does not seem to fully consider the features related to the ELF, which may explain the inexplicable good performance of the 0-interpolation, a simple method that fills zeros for all unknown points. Additional works in this segment are presented in [8–12].

7.1.2 Traffic Classification

Traffic classification is important for network operators to perform a wide range of network operation and management activities. These include capacity planning, security and intrusion detection, QoS and service differentiation, performance monitoring, and resource provisioning, and so on. For example, an operator of an enterprise network may want to prioritize traffic for business critical applications, identify unknown traffic for anomaly detection, or perform workload characterization for designing efficient resource management schemes that satisfy diverse application performance and resource requirements.

Traffic classification requires the ability to accurately associate network traffic with predefined classes of interest. These classes of interest can be classes of applications (HTTP, FTP, WWW, DNS, and P2P), applications (e.g., Skype [15], YouTube [16], and Netflix [13]), or class of service [14]. A class of service, for instance one based on QoS, encompasses all applications or classes of applications that have the same QoS requirements. Therefore, it is possible for applications that apparently behave differently to belong to the same class of service [17].

Generally, network traffic classification methodologies can be decomposed into four broad categories that leverage port number, packet payload, host behavior, or flow features [18, 19]. The classical approach to traffic classification simply associates Internet Assigned Numbers Authority (IANA)-registered [20] port numbers with applications. However, this option is no longer used in practice, nor does it lend itself to learning due to trivial lookup. Furthermore, relying solely on port numbers has been shown to be ineffective [21], largely due to the use of dynamic port negotiation, tunneling, and misuse of port numbers assigned to well-known applications for obfuscating traffic and avoiding firewalls [22]. Nevertheless, various classifiers leverage port numbers in conjunction with other techniques [18] to improve the performance of the traffic classifiers.

Payload-based traffic classification is an alternate to port-based traffic classification. However, since it searches through the payload for known application signatures, it incurs higher computation and storage costs. Also, it is cumbersome to manually maintain and adapt the signatures to the ever-growing number of applications and their dynamics [24]. Furthermore, with the rise in security and privacy concerns, the payload is often encrypted and its access is prohibited due to privacy laws. This makes it nontrivial to infer a signature for an application class using a payload [23, 24].

Host-behavior-based traffic classification leverages the inherent behavioral characteristics of hosts on the network to predict the classes of interest. It overcomes the limitations of unregistered or misused port numbers and encrypted packet payload, by moving the observation point to the edge of the network and examining traffic between hosts (e.g., how many hosts are contacted, by which transport protocol, how many different ports are involved). These classifiers rely on the notion that applications generate different communication patterns. For example, a P2P host may contact several different peers using a different port number for each peer, whereas a webserver may be contacted by different clients on the same port. For some solutions in this class, see [25–28].

Flow-feature-based traffic classification: In contrast to payload-based and host-behavior-based traffic classifiers, flow-feature-based classifiers have a different perspective. They step back and consider a communication session that consists of a pair of complete flows. A complete flow is a unidirectional exchange of consecutive packets on the network between a port at an IP address and another port at a different IP address using a particular application protocol [29]. The protocol is defined by four parameters: *srcIP, destIP, srcPort,* and *destPort.*

For example, a complete flow in an online game session would consist of all sequential packets sent from sources to destination (e.g., host to game server). Therefore, a complete flow includes all packets pertaining to session setup, data exchange, and session tear-down. A sub-flow is a subset of a complete flow and can be collected over a time window in an ongoing session. A feature is an attribute representing a unique characteristic of a flow, such as *packet length, packet inter-arrival time, flow duration,* and *the number of packets in a flow.* Flow-feature-based technique uses flow features as discriminators to map flows to classes of interest. In essence, flow-feature-based traffic classification exploits the diversity and distinguishable characteristics of the traffic footprint generated by different applications [30]. It has the potential to overcome numerous limitations of other techniques, such as unregistered port numbers, encrypted packet payload, routing asymmetries, high storage, and computational overhead [31].

Supervised complete flow-feature-based traffic classification is one of the earliest works in network traffic classification using ML [390, 32]. The authors employ k-NN and linear discriminant analysis (LDA) to map network traffic into different classes of interest based on QoS requirements. Their traffic classification framework uses statistics that are insensitive to the application protocol. The authors employ both packet-level and flow-level features. However, they observe that the average packet size and flow duration act as good discriminators, and hence used these in their preliminary evaluation. In their evaluation, k-NN outperforms LDA with the lowest error rate of 5.1 and 9.4% for four- and seven-class classification, respectively. They notice that streaming applications often behave very similarly to bulk data transfer applications. Therefore, either a prioritization rule is necessary to break the tie, or extended/derivative features must be employed to act as good discriminators. In their extended evaluation, the authors employ inter-arrival variability to distinguish between streaming and bulk data transfer applications. Their work was followed up by a number of works like [31–34].

Unsupervised complete flow-feature-based [35] and early and sub-flow-based traffic classification [36, 37] are two additional options used in practice.

Encrypted traffic classification: Various applications employ encryption, obfuscation, and compression techniques that make it difficult to detect the corresponding traffic. Different algorithms for classification of such traffic are presented in [38–40].

NFV and SDN for traffic classification: Recent advances in network paradigms, such as network function virtualization (NFV) and SDN, enable flexible and adaptive techniques for traffic classification. It is well known that the performance of classifiers varies significantly based on the type of flow features used. Furthermore, flows inherently exhibit specific characteristics of network applications and protocols. Therefore, finding the ideal set of features is fundamental to achieving efficiency in traffic classification. Work in [41] proposes an NFV-based traffic-driven learning framework for traffic classification called *vTC*. The framework consists of a controller, and a set of ML classifiers and feature collectors as virtual network functions (VNFs). Their objective is to dynamically select the most effective ML classifiers and the most cost-efficient flow features by leveraging a controller and a group of VNFs for traffic classification. The vTC framework strives to achieve a balance between classification accuracy and speed, and the choice of features has a significant impact on these criteria. Therefore, it is critical to determine the most suitable classifier and dynamically adjust feature collection for a given flow protocol (e.g., TCP, UDP, ICMP). For additional work in this area, see [42, 43].

7.1.3 Traffic Routing

In the previous chapter, we explicitly discussed ML algorithms for finding equilibria in routing and congestion games. Network traffic routing is fundamental in networking, and entails selecting a path for packet transmission. Selection criteria are diverse and primarily depend on the operation policies and objectives, such as cost minimization, maximization of link utilization, and QoS provisioning. Traffic routing requires challenging abilities for the ML models, such as the ability to cope and scale with complex and dynamic network topologies, the ability to learn the correlation between the selected path and the perceived QoS, and the ability to predict the consequences of routing decisions. In the existing literature, one family of ML techniques has dominated research in traffic routing: reinforcement learning (RL).

Recall from the previous chapter that RL employs learning agents to explore, with no supervision, the surrounding environment, usually represented as a Markov decision process (MDP) with finite states, and learns from trial and error the optimal action policy that maximizes a cumulative reward. In the previous chapter, RL models were defined based on a set of states S, a set of actions per state $\mathcal{A}(s_t)$, and the corresponding rewards (or costs/regrets) r_t. When S is associated with the network, a state s_t represents the status at time t of all nodes and links in the network. However, when it is associated with the packet being routed, s_t represents the status of the node holding the packet at time t. In this case, $\mathcal{A}(s_t)$ represents all the possible next-hop neighbor nodes that may be selected to route the packet to a given destination node. With each link or forwarding action within a route, an immediate static or dynamic reward (respectively cost) r_t may be associated according to a single or multiple reward (respectively cost) metric, such as queuing delay, available bandwidth, congestion level, packet loss rate, energy consumption level, link reliability, retransmission count, and so on.

At routing time, the cumulative reward, that is, the total reward accumulated by the time the packet reaches its destination, is typically unknown. In Q-learning, a simple yet powerful model-free technique in RL, an estimate of the *remaining* cumulative reward, also known as the *Q-value*, is associated with each state-action pair. A Q-learning agent learns the best action-selection policy by greedily selecting at each state the action a_t with highest expected Q–value, defined as $\max_{a \in A(s_t)} Q(s_t, a)$. Once the action a_t is executed and the corresponding reward r_t is known, the node updates the Q-value $Q(s_t, a_t)$ accordingly as follows: $Q(s_t, a_t) \leftarrow (1 - \alpha) Q(s_t, a_t) + \alpha (r_t + \gamma \max_{a \in A(s_{t+1})} Q(s_{t+1}, a))$ where $\alpha(0 < \alpha \le 1)$ and $\gamma(0 \le \gamma \le 1)$ denote the learning rate and the discount factor, respectively. The closer α is to 1, the greater is the impact of the most recently learned Q-value. Higher γ values make the learning agent aim for longer-term high rewards. Indeed, the greedy action-selection approach is optimal only if the learning agent knows the current Q-values of all possible actions. The agent can then *exploit* this knowledge to select the most rewarding action. If not, an ε-greedy approach may be used such that with probability ε the agent chooses to *explore* a random action rather than deterministically choosing the action with highest Q-value. Although RL has been gaining a lot of attention these days, its application in network traffic routing dates back to the early 1990s. Boyan and Littman's [44, 45] seminal work introduced Q-routing, a straightforward application of the Q-learning algorithm to packet routing. In Q-routing, a router x learns to map a routing policy, such as routing to destination d via neighbor y, to its Q-value. The Q-value is an estimate of the time it will take for the packet to reach *d* through *y*, including any time the packet would have to spend in node *x*'s queue plus the transmission time over the link *x*, *y*. Upon reception of the packet, y sends back to *x* the new estimated remaining routing delay, and x accordingly adjusts its Q-value based on a learning rate. After convergence of the algorithm, optimal routing policies are learned.

Since then, a number of routing algorithms based on Q-learning have been developed [46–51]. These algorithms can be further subdivided into the following:

1) Routing as a decentralized operation function [52, 53]
2) Routing as a partially decentralized operation function [54, 55]
3) Routing as a centralized control function [56]

7.1.4 Congestion Control

Congestion control is fundamental to network operations and is responsible for controlling the number of packets entering the network. It ensures network stability, fairness in resource utilization, and an acceptable packet loss ratio. Different network architectures deploy their own set of congestion control mechanisms. The most well-known congestion control mechanisms are those implemented in TCP, since TCP along with IP constitute the basis of the current Internet. TCP congestion control mechanisms operate in the end systems of the network to limit the packet sending rate when congestion is detected. Another well-known congestion control mechanism is queue management [57], which operates inside the intermediate nodes of the network (e.g., switches and routers) to complement TCP. There have been several improvements in congestion control mechanisms for the Internet and evolutionary network architectures, such as delay-tolerant networks (DTN) and Named Data Networking (NDN). Despite these efforts, there are various shortcomings in areas such as packet loss classification, queue management, congestion window (CWND) update, and congestion inference.

Several research works demonstrate the potential of applying ML to enhance congestion control in different networks. Most of these techniques have been applied to TCP/IP networks. It is important to note that the first ML-based approaches for congestion control were proposed in the context of Asynchronous Transfer Mode (ATM) networks [58–61].

Packet loss classification: In theory, TCP works well regardless of the underlying transmission medium, such as wired, wireless, and optical. In practice, the standard TCP congestion control mechanism has been optimized for wired networks. However, the major problem in TCP is that it recognizes and handles all packet losses as network congestion, that is, buffer overflow. Hence, unjustified congestion control is performed when a loss is due to other reasons, such as packet reordering [62], fading and shadowing in wireless networks [63], and wavelength contention in optical networks [64]. Consequently, TCP unnecessarily reduces its transmission rate at each detected packet loss, lowering the end-to-end throughput. Various ML-based solutions have been proposed for packet loss classification in end systems for different networks, such as hybrid wired–wireless [65–68] and wired [62] networks. Generally, the classifier is trained offline, leveraging diverse supervised and unsupervised ML algorithms for binary classification. Most of these techniques use the metrics readily available at end systems, and evaluate their classifier on synthetic data on network simulators, such as Network Simulator (Version 2), NS2. The interested reader should check additional work in [69–72].

Queue management is a mechanism in the intermediate nodes of the network that complements TCP congestion control mechanisms. Specifically, queue management is in charge of dropping packets when appropriate, to control the queue length in the intermediate nodes [57]. The conventional technique for queue management is Drop-tail, which adopts the first-in-first-out (FIFO) scheme to handle packets that enter a queue. In Drop-tail, each queue establishes a maximum length for accepting incoming packets. When the queue becomes full, the subsequent incoming packets are dropped until the queue becomes available again. However, the combination of Drop-tail with the TCP congestion avoidance mechanism leads to TCP synchronization, which may cause serious problems [73, 57]: (i) inefficient link utilization and excessive packet loss due to a simultaneous decrease in TCP rate, (ii) unacceptable queuing delay due to a continuous full queue state; and (iii) TCP unfairness due to a few connections that monopolize the queue space (i.e., lock-out phenomenon).

Active Queue Management (AQM) is a proactive approach that mitigates the limitations of Drop-tail by dropping packets (or marking them for drop) before a queue becomes full. This allows end systems to respond to congestion before the queue overflows, and it also allows intermediate nodes to manage packet drops. *Random early detection* (RED) is the earliest and most well-known AQM scheme. RED continually adjusts a dropping (marking) probability according to a predicted congestion level. This congestion level is based on a predefined threshold and a computed average queue length. However, RED suffers from poor responsiveness, fails to stabilize the queue length to a target value, and its performance (link utilization and packet drop) greatly depends on its parameter tuning, which has not been successfully addressed. Many AQM schemes have been proposed to improve these shortcomings. However, they rely on fixed parameters that are insensitive to the time-varying and nonlinear network conditions. For this reason, significant research has been conducted to apply ML for building an effective and reliable AQM scheme that is capable of intelligently managing the queue length and tuning its parameters based on network and traffic conditions [73–81].

CWND update is one of the TCP per-connection state variables that limits the amount of data a sender can transmit before receiving an ACK [82]. The other state variable is the receiver window (RWND), which is a limit advertised by a receiver to a sender for communicating the amount of data it can receive. The TCP congestion control mechanisms use the minimum between these state variables to manage the amount of data injected into the network. However, TCP was designed based on specific network conditions and assumes all losses as congestion. Therefore, TCP in wireless lossy links unnecessarily lowers its rate by reducing CWND at each packet loss, negatively affecting the end-to-end performance. Furthermore, the CWND update mechanism of TCP is not suitable for the diverse characteristics of different network technologies. For example, networks with a high bandwidth delay product (BDP), such as satellite networks, require a more aggressive CWND increase, whereas networks with a low BDP, such as wireless ad hoc networks (WANET), call for a more conservative CWND increase.

A number of approaches based on RL have been proposed to cope with the problems of properly updating CWND (or sending rate) according to the network conditions. Some of these approaches are particularly designed for resource-constrained networks, including WANETs [83–85] and IoT [86], while others address a wider range of network architectures [87–89], such as satellite, cellular, and data center networks.

Congestion inference: Network protocols adapt their operation based on estimated network parameters that allow one to infer the congestion state. For example, some multicast and multipath protocols rely on predictions of TCP throughput to adjust their behavior, and the TCP protocol computes the retransmission timeout based on RTT estimations. However, the conventional mechanisms for estimating these network parameters remain inaccurate, primarily because the relationships between the various parameters are not clearly understood. This is the case of analytic and history-based models for predicting the TCP throughput and the exponential weighted moving average (EWMA) algorithm used by TCP for estimating RTT.

For these reasons, several ML-based approaches have addressed the limitations of inferring the congestion in various network architectures by estimating different network parameters: throughput [90–92], RTT [93, 94], and mobility [95] in TCP-based networks, table entries rate in NDNs [96], and congestion level in DTNs [97].

7.1.5 Resource Management

Resource management in networking entails controlling the vital resources of the network, including the CPU, memory, disk, switches, routers, bandwidth, AP, and radio channels and their frequencies. These are leveraged collectively or independently to offer services. Naïvely, network service providers can provision a fixed amount of resources that satisfies an expected demand for a service. However, it is nontrivial to predict demand, while over- and underestimation can lead to both poor utilization and loss in revenue. Therefore, a fundamental challenge in resource management is predicting demand and dynamically provisioning and re-provisioning resources such that the network is resilient to variations in service demand. Despite the widespread application of ML for load prediction and resource management in cloud data centers [98], various challenges still exist for different networks, including cellular networks, wireless networks, and ad hoc networks. Although there are various challenges in resource management, here, we consider two broad categories: *admission control* and *resource allocation*.

Admission control is an indirect approach to resource management that does not need demand prediction. The objective in admission control is to optimize the utilization of resources by monitoring and managing the resources in the network. For example, new requests for computing and network resources are initiated for a VoIP call or connection setup. In this case, admission control dictates whether the new incoming request should be granted or rejected based on the available network resources, QoS requirements of the new request, and its consequence for the existing services utilizing the resources in the network. Evidently, accepting a new request generates revenue for the network service provider. However, it may degrade the QoS of existing services due to scarcity of resources and consequentially violate service-level agreement (SLA), incurring penalties and loss in revenue. Therefore, there is a clear trade-off between accepting new requests and maintaining or meeting QoS. Admission control addresses this challenge and aims to maximize the number of requests accepted and served by the network without violating SLA.

By contrast, resource allocation is a decision problem that actively manages resources to maximize a long-term objective, such as revenue or resource utilization. The underlying challenge in resource allocation is to adapt resources for long-term benefits in the face of unpredictability. General model-driven approaches to resource allocation have fallen short in keeping up with the velocity and volume of the resource requests in the network. However, resource allocation serves to highlight the advantages of ML, which can learn and manage resource provisioning in various ways.

Admission control has leveraged ML extensively in a variety of networks, including ATM networks [99–102], wireless networks [103–105], cellular networks [106–110], ad hoc networks [111], and next-generation networks [112].

Resource allocation: For an ML-based solution to the resource allocation problem, see [113–115].

7.1.6 Fault Management

Fault management involves detection, isolation, and correction of an abnormal condition of a network. It requires network operators and administrators to have a detailed knowledge of the entire network, its devices, and all the applications running in the network. This is an unrealistic expectation. Furthermore, recent advances in technology, such as virtualization and softwarization, makes today's network monumental in size, complexity, and dynamism. Therefore, fault management is becoming increasingly challenging in today's networks. Naïve fault management is reactive and can be perceived as a cyclic process of detection, localization, and mitigation of faults. First, fault detection jointly correlates different network symptoms to determine whether one or more network failures or faults have occurred. For example, faults can occur due to reduced switch capacity, increased rate of packet generation for a certain application, a disabled switch, and disabled links. The next step in fault management is localization of the root cause of the fault(s), which requires pinpointing the physical location of the faulty network hardware or software element, and determining the reason for the fault. Finally, fault mitigation aims to repair or correct the network behavior.

By contrast, fault prediction is proactive and aims to prevent faults or failures in the future by predicting them and initiating mitigation procedures to minimize performance degradation. ML-based techniques have been proposed to address these challenges and promote cognitive fault management in the areas of fault prediction, detection, localization of root cause, and mitigation of faults.

Fault prediction solutions based on ML are described in [116–119].

Fault detection, unlike fault prediction, is reactive and identifies, or classifies, a failure after it has occurred, using network symptoms, performance degradation, and other parameters. Rao [120] proposes fault detection for cellular networks that can detect faults at different levels: the base station, sector, carrier, and channel. They employ a statistical hypothesis testing framework that combines parametric, semi-parametric, and non-parametric test statistics to model expected behavior. In parametric and semi-parametric statistical tests, a fault is detected when significant deviations from the expected activity are observed. In the case of non-parametric statistical tests, where the expected distribution is not known a priori, the authors use a combination of empirical data and statistical correlations to conduct the hypothesis test. The test is dependent on a threshold value that is initially set through a statistical analysis of traffic patterns. Hence, the threshold should be adapted to changing traffic patterns due to spatial, temporal, and seasonal effects. Solutions based on ML are described in [121–125].

Localizing the root cause of fault: The next step in fault management is to identify the root cause and physically locate the fault to initiate mitigation. This minimizes the mean time to repair in a network that does not deploy a proactive fault prediction mechanism. The authors in [126, 127] use DTs (decision trees) and clustering to diagnose faults in large network systems. The DTs are trained using a new learning algorithm, MinEntropy [126], on datasets of failure-prone network traces. To minimize convergence time and computational overhead, MinEntropy uses an early stopping criterion and follows the most suspicious path in the DT. Chen et al. [126] complement the DT with heuristics, to correlate features with the number of detected failures to aid in feature selection and fault localization. MinEntropy was validated against actual failures observed for several months on eBay [127]. For single fault cases, the algorithm identifies more than 90% of the faults with low FPRs. By contrast, Chen et al. [127] employ clustering to group the successes and failures of requests. A faulty component is detected and located by analyzing the components that are only used in the failed requests. In addition to the single fault cases, the clustering approach can also locate faults occurring due to interactions among multiple components, with a high accuracy and relatively low number of false positives. For other solutions based on ML, see [128–133].

Automated mitigation improves fault management by minimizing, or eliminating, human intervention and reducing downtime. For proactive fault prediction, automated mitigation involves gathering information from the suspected network elements to help find the origin of the predicted fault. For building this information base, a fault manager may either actively poll selected network elements, or rely on passive submission of alarms from them. In both cases, actions should be selected carefully since frequent polling wastes network resources, while too many false alarms diminish the effectiveness of automated mitigation. On the other hand, in the case of reactive fault detection, automated mitigation selects a workflow for troubleshooting the fault. Therefore, the fundamental challenge in automated mitigation is to select the optimal set of actions or workflow in a stochastic environment.

He et al. [134] address this fundamental challenge for proactive fault management using a POMDP, to formulate the trade-off between monitoring, diagnosis, and mitigation. They assume partial observability, to account for the fact that some monitored observations might be missing or delayed in a communication network. They propose an RL algorithm to obtain approximate solutions to the POMDP with a large number of states representing real-life networks. The authors devise a preliminary policy where the states are completely observable. Then, they fine-tune this policy by updating the belief space and transition probabilities in the real world, where the states are incompletely observed. For additional reading, see [135].

7.1.7 QoS and QoE Management

Statistical and ML techniques have been found useful in linking QoE to network- and application-level QoS, and understanding the impact of the latter on the former. Linear and nonlinear regression (e.g., exponential, logarithmic, power regression) was used to quantify the individual and collective impact of network- and application- level QoS parameters (e.g., packet loss ratio, delay, throughput, round-trip time, video bitrate, and frame rate) on the user's QoE. In the literature, simple regression models with a single feature are most dominant [136, 137], although the collective impact of different QoS parameters was also considered [138]. *Simple regression* is used in a number of works for studying correlation between QoS and QoE [139] and multi-parameter regression in

[140]. QoE/QoS correlation with supervised ML is studied in [141, 142]. For QoE prediction under QoS impairments, see [143] and for QoS/QoE prediction for HTTP adaptive streaming, see [144, 145].

7.1.8 Network Security

Security experts are constantly developing new measures to shield the network from known attacks, and most importantly, new attacks. Examples of such security measures include (i) Encryption of network traffic, especially the payload, to protect the integrity and confidentiality of the data in the packets traversing the network. (ii) Authorization using credentials, to restrict access to authorized personnel only. (iii) Access control, for instance, using security policies to grant different access rights and privileges to different users based on their roles and authorities. (iv) Antiviruses, to protect end systems against malwares, for example, Trojan horse and ransomware. (v) Firewalls, hardware- or software-based, to allow or block network traffic based on a predefined set of rules.

However, encryption keys and login credentials can be breached, exposing the network to all kinds of threats. In addition, the prevention capabilities of firewalls and antiviruses are limited by the prescribed set of rules and patches. Hence, it is imperative to include a second line of defense that can detect early symptoms of cyber-threats and react quickly enough before any damage is done. Such systems are commonly referred to as *intrusion detection/prevention systems (IDSs/IPSs)*. IDSs monitor the network for signs of malicious activities and can be broadly classified into two categories: misuse- and anomaly-based systems. While the former rely on signatures of known attacks, the latter are based on the notion that intrusions exhibit a behavior that is quite distinctive from normal network behavior. Hence, the general objective of anomaly-based IDSs is to define the "normal behavior" in order to detect deviations from this norm. When it comes to the application of ML for network security, most works have focused on the application of ML for intrusion detection. Here, intrusion detection refers to detecting any form of attacks that may compromise the network, for example, probing, phishing, DoS, and DDoS. This can be seen as a classification problem.

Here, we focus on network-based intrusion detection and we classify the works into three categories: *misuse, anomaly, and hybrid network IDS*s. We focus on recently published ML-based approaches related to SDN and RL.

Misuse-based IDSs consist of monitoring the network and matching the network activities against the expected behavior of an attack. The key component of such a system is the comprehensiveness of the attack signatures. Typically, the signatures fed to a misuse-IDS rely on expert knowledge [146]. The source of this knowledge can be human experts, or it can be extracted from data. However, the huge volume of generated network traces renders manual inspection practically impossible. Furthermore, attack signatures extracted by sequentially scanning network traces will fail to capture advanced persistent threats or complex attacks with intermittent symptoms. Intruders can easily evade detection if the signatures rely on a stream of suspicious activities by simply inserting noise in the data. In light of the above, ML became the tool of choice for misuse-based IDSs. Its ability to find patterns in big datasets fits the need to learn signatures of attacks from collected network traces. Hence, it comes as no surprise that a fair number of studies in the literature [147–154] rely on ML for misuse detection.

Anomaly-based intrusion detection: Though misuse-based IDSs are very successful at detecting known attacks, they fail to identify new ones. Network cyber-threats are constantly changing and evolving, making it crucial to identify "zero-day" attacks. This is where anomaly-based intrusion detection comes in. Anomaly-based IDS models normal network behavior, and identify anomalies as a deviation from the expected behavior. A big problem with anomaly-based IDSs is false alarms, since it is difficult to obtain a complete representation of normality. ML for anomaly detection has received significant attention, due to the autonomy and robustness it offers in learning and adapting profiles of normality as they change over time. With ML, the system can learn patterns of normal behavior across environments, applications, group of users, and time. In addition, it offers the ability to find complex correlations in the data that cannot be deduced from mere observation. Though anomaly detection can be broadly divided into flow-feature- or payload-based detection, recently, deep learning and RL are being exploited. This is primarily due to their intrinsic ability to extrapolate data from limited knowledge.

Flow-based anomaly detection techniques rely on learning the expected (benign) network activities from flow features. The immediate observation in contrast to misuse detection is the application of unsupervised learning and hybrid supervised/unsupervised learning. Some works employed supervised learning for anomaly detection as well. The main difference is that instead of teaching the model the expected behavior, in unsupervised learning the model is fed an unlabeled training set to find a structure, or a hidden pattern, in the data. In anomaly detection, the notion is that benign network behavior is more common and will naturally group together, whereas anomalous behavior is more sparse and will appear as outliers in the dataset. Hence, the larger and more dense clusters will indicate normal connections, while the smaller more distant data points (or clusters of data points) will indicate malicious behavior. For the most influential work in the application of flow feature-based ML for anomaly detection, see [155–160].

Payload-based anomaly detection systems learn patterns of normality from the packet payload. This provides the ability to detect attacks injected inside the payload that can easily evade flow-feature-based IDSs. In this subsection, we discuss ML techniques that have been employed to detect anomalies using the packet payload alone or in conjunction with flow features.

As an example, PAYL [161] use the 1-g method to model packet payloads. The n-gram is widely used for text analysis. It consists of a sliding window of size n that scans the payload while counting the occurrence/frequency of each n-gram.

In addition to counting the frequency of each byte in the payload, the mean and the standard deviation are computed. As the payload exhibits different characteristics for different services, PAYL generates a payload model for each service, port, direction of payload, and payload length range. Once the models are generated, the Mahalanobis distance is used to measure the deviation between incoming packets and the payload models. The larger the distance, the higher the likelihood that the newly arrived packet is abnormal. Additional works of this type can be found in [161–166].

Deep and reinforcement learning for intrusion detection: Over the past decade, anomaly detection has particularly benefited from self-taught learning (STL) [168], DBN [169], and RNN [170]. Once more, all these works have been evaluated using KDD dataset, and its enhanced version, the NSL-KDD [167] dataset. For RL for intrusion detection, see [171] and for hybrid intrusion detection, see [172].

7.2 ML for Caching in Small Cell Networks

In this section, we consider a heterogeneous network with base stations (BSs), small base stations (SBSs), and users distributed according to independent Poisson point processes. SBS nodes are assumed to possess high storage capacity and to form a distributed caching network. Popular files are stored in local caches of SBSs, so that a user can download the desired files from one of the SBSs in its vicinity. The off-loading loss is captured via a cost function that depends on the random caching strategy considered here [173]. The popularity profile of the cached content is unknown and estimated using instantaneous demands from users within a specified time interval. An estimate of the cost function is obtained from which an optimal random caching strategy is devised.

7.2.1 System Model

In this section, we will use the following notation: Φ_u, Φ_s and Φ_b (λ_u, λ_s and λ_b) – the points (densities) corresponding to the user, SBSs and BS, respectively; k_x – the number of requests in $[0, \tau]$ by the user at x; $X_x^{(l)}$ – the lth request of the user x; λ_r – the average number of requests per unit time. A heterogeneous cellular network is considered where the set $\Phi_u \subseteq \mathbb{R}^2$ of users, the set $\Phi_b \subseteq \mathbb{R}^2$ of BSs, and the set $\Phi_s \subseteq \mathbb{R}^2$ of SBSs are distributed according to independent PPPs with densities λ_u, λ_b, and λ_s, respectively, in two-dimensional space. Each user independently requests a data file of size B bits from the set $F = \{f_1, f_2, \dots, f_N\}$; the popularity of data files is specified by the distribution $P = \{p_1, \dots, p_N\}$, where $\sum_{i=1}^{N} p_i = 1$ and is assumed to be stationary across time. In a typical heterogenous cellular network, the BS fetches a file using its backhaul link to serve a user. During peak data traffic hours, this results in an information bottleneck both at the BS as well as in its backhaul link. As a possible solution of this problem, caching the most popular files (either at the user nodes or at the SBSs) is used. The requested file will be served directly by one of the neighboring SBSs depending on the availability of the file in its local cache. The performance of caching depends on the density of the SBS nodes, cache size, users' request rate, and the caching strategy. It is assumed that the SBS can cache up to M files, each of length B bits. Each SBS in Φ_s caches its content in an independent and identically distributed (i.i.d.) fashion by generating M indices distributed according to $\Pi\{\pi_i : f_i \in F, i = 1, 2, \dots, N\}$, $\sum_{i=1}^{N} \pi_i = 1$. One way of generating this is to roll an N–sided die M times in an i.i.d. fashion, where the outcomes correspond to the index of the file to be cached. Although this approach is suboptimal, it is mathematically tractable, and the corresponding time complexity serves as a lower bound, albeit pessimistic, for optimal strategies. We let each SBS at location $y \in \Phi_s$ communicate with a user at location $x \in \Phi_u$ if $\|y - x\| < \gamma$, ($\gamma > 0$); this condition determines the communication radius. In this protocol, we have ignored the interference constraint. The set of neighbors of the user at location x is denoted

$$N_x = \left\{ y \in \Phi_s : \left\| y - x \right\| < \gamma \right\}. \tag{7.1}$$

The user located at $x \in \Phi_u$ requests a data file from the set F, with the popularity profile chosen from the probability distribution function P. The requested file will be served directly by a neighboring SBS at location $y \in \Phi_s$ depending on the availability of the file in its local cache, and following the protocol described in the previous paragraph. The problem of caching involves minimizing the time overhead incurred due to the unavailability of the requested file. Without loss of generality and for ease of analysis, we focus on the performance of a typical user located at the origin, denoted by $o \in \Phi_u$. The *unavailability* of the requested file from a user located at o is given by

$$T(\Pi, P) = \frac{B}{R_0} \mathbb{E}_{\Phi_u, \Phi_s, P} \sum_{i=1}^{N} [1\{ f_i \notin N_o \}] 1\{ f_i \text{ requested} \}, \tag{7.2}$$

where N_o is as defined in Eq. (7.1), R_0 is the rate supported by the BS for the user, and B/R_0 is the time overhead incurred in transmitting the file from the BS to the user. Further, we use $f_i \notin N_o$ to denote the event that the file f_i is not stored in any of the SBSs in N_o. The expectation is with respect to Φ_u, Φ_s, and P. The indicator function $1\{A\}$ is equal to one if the event A occurs, and zero otherwise. We refer to $T(\Pi, P)$ as the "off-loading loss," which we seek to minimize:

$$\min_{\Pi \geq 0} T(\Pi, P)$$
$$\text{subject to } \sum_{i=1}^{N} \pi_i = 1, \tag{7.3}$$

where $\pi_i \geq 0$, for $i = 1, ..., N$. To solve the optimization problem Eq. (7.3), we need an analytical expression for $T(\Pi, P)$ which is derived in [173] as

$$T(\Pi, P) = \frac{B}{R_0} \left[\sum_{i=1}^{N} \exp\left\{ -\lambda_s \pi \gamma^2 \left[1 - (1 - \pi_i)^M \right] \right\} p_i \right]. \tag{7.4}$$

We will deal with the optimization problem defined by Eq. (7.3) and its further generalizations later in Section 7.5. Here, we focus only on analyzing the training time required to obtain a good estimate of the popularity profile that results in an off-loading loss that is within ε of the optimal off-loading loss.

In practice, the popularity profile P is generally unknown and has to be estimated. Denoting the estimated popularity profile *by* $\hat{P} = \{\hat{p}_1, ..., \hat{p}_N\}$ and the corresponding off-loading loss by $T(\Pi, \hat{P})$, Eq.(7.3) becomes

$$\min_{\Pi \geq 0} T(\Pi, \hat{P})$$
$$\text{subject to } \sum_{i=1}^{N} \pi_i = 1, \tag{7.5}$$

with $\pi_i \geq 0$, for $i = 1, ..., N$. Naturally, the solution to Eq. (7.5) differs from that of the original problem Eq. (7.3). Let Π^* and $\hat{\Pi}^*$ denote the optimal solutions to the problems in Eqs. (7.3) and (7.5), respectively, and let the throughput achieved using $\hat{\Pi}^*$ be denoted $\hat{T}^* = T(\hat{\Pi}^*, \hat{P})$. Here, the focus is on the analysis of the off-loading loss difference, that is, $\hat{T}^* - T^*$, where $T^* = T(\Pi^*, P)$ is the minimum off-loading loss incurred with perfect knowledge of the popularity profile P.

In [173], two methods for estimating the popularity profile were presented, and the corresponding training time was analyzed. Here, we reproduce some of these results and refer the reader to the original work for details. The efficiency of the estimate $\hat{P}$ of the popularity profile depends on the number of available data samples, which in turn is related to the number of requests made by the users.

Request model: Each user requests a file $f \in F$ at a random time $t \in [0, \infty]$ following an independent Poisson arrival process with density $\lambda_r > 0$. The same density is assumed across all the users. The following centralized scheme is used where the BS collects the requests from all the users in its coverage area in a time interval $[0, \tau]$ to estimate the popularity profile of the requested files: Let the number of users in the coverage area of the BS $z \in \Phi_b$ of radius $R > 0$ be n_R, which is distributed according to a PPP with density λ_u. Let the number of requests made by the user at the location $x \in \{\Phi_u \cap \mathbb{B}(0, R)\}$ in the time interval $[0, \tau]$ be k_x, where $\mathbb{B}(0, R)$ is a two-dimensional ball of radius R centered at 0. We assume that requests across the users are known at the BS. The requests from the user x is denoted as $X_x = \{X_x^{(1)}, ..., X_x^{(k_x)}\}$, where $X_x^{(l)} \in \{1, ..., N\}$ denotes the indices of the files in F, $l = 0, ..., k_x$. After receiving X_x, $x \in \{\Phi_u \cap \mathbb{B}(0, R)\}$, in the time interval $[0, \tau]$, the BS computes an estimate of the popularity profile as follows:

$$\hat{p}_i = \frac{1}{\sum_{x \in \{\mathbb{B}(0, R) \cap \Phi_u\}} k_x} \sum_{x \in \{\mathbb{B}(0, R) \cap \Phi_u\}} \sum_{l=0}^{k_x} 1\{X_x^{(l)} = i\}, \tag{7.6}$$

$i = 1, ..., N$. Given the number n_R of users in the coverage area of the BS, the sum $\sum_{x \in \{\mathbb{B}(0,R) \cap \Phi_u\}} k_x$ is a PPP with density $n_R \lambda_r$. Also, $\left\{ \hat{p}_i \middle\| \{\Phi_u \cap \mathbb{B}(0, R)\} \mid = n_R \right\} = p_i$, which leads us to conclude that $\hat{p}_i$ is an unbiased estimator. The estimated popularity profile $\hat{p}_i$ given by Eq. (7.6) is shared with every SBS in the coverage area of the BS, and is then used in Eq. (7.5) to find the optimal caching probability.

The described estimator can be improved by using samples from other related domains, for example, a social network. The term *target domain* is used when samples are obtained only from users in the coverage area of the BS. In the following, we present the minimum training time τ, corresponding to the estimator in Eq. (7.6), required to achieve the desired estimation accuracy $\varepsilon > 0$.

A lower bound on the training time τ: For any $\varepsilon > 0$, with a probability of at least $1 - \delta$, a throughput of $\hat{T}^* \leq T^* + \varepsilon$ can be achieved using the estimate in Eq. (7.6) provided [173].

$$\tau \geq \left\{ \frac{1}{\lambda_r g^*} \, \log \left(\frac{1}{1 - \frac{1}{\lambda_u \pi R^2} \log \frac{2N}{\delta}} \right) \right\}^+ \quad \text{if } \lambda_u > L, \tag{7.7}$$

otherwise, ∞; where $\{x\}^+ = \max\{x, 0\}$, $g^* = \left(1 - \exp\{-2\bar{\varepsilon}^2\} \right)$, $L = \frac{1}{\pi R^2} \, \log \left(\frac{2N}{\delta} \right)$ and

$$\bar{\varepsilon} = \frac{R_0 \varepsilon}{2B \sup_\Pi \sum_{i=1}^N g(\pi_i)}, \tag{7.8}$$

with $g(\pi_i) = \exp\{-\lambda_s \pi \gamma^2 [1 - (1 - \pi_i)^M]\}$.

To achieve a finite training time that results in an estimation accuracy $\varepsilon > 0$, the user density λ_u has to be greater than a threshold. Further insights into Eq. (7.7) are obtained by making the following approximation: $1 - x \leq e^{-x}$ for all $x \geq 0$. This is combined with $\sup_{\Pi:\Pi \succeq 0, 1^T \Pi = 1} \sum_{i=1}^N g(\pi_i) \leq N$, yielding the following lower bound on the training time τ:

$$\tau \geq \frac{2B^2}{\pi R^2 \lambda_u \lambda_r R_0^2 \varepsilon^2} N^2 \, \log \left(\frac{2N}{\delta} \right). \tag{7.9}$$

The lower bound (Eq. (7.9)) enables us to make the following observations:

1) The training time τ to achieve an ε-off-loading loss difference scales as $N^2 \log N$,
2) τ is inversely proportional to (λ_u, λ_r), and
3) as the coverage radius increases, the delay decreases as $1/R^2$, and
4) as the data file size B increases, the training time scales as B^2.

The bound in Eq. (7.9) is a lower bound on the training time per request per user, since the off-loading loss is derived for a given request per user. There are on average λ_r requests per unit time per user. Thus, to obtain the training time per user, the off-loading loss has to be multiplied by λ_r. This amounts to replacing ε by $/\lambda_r$. Therefore, Eq. (7.9) becomes

$$\tau \geq \frac{2B^2 \lambda_r}{\pi R^2 \lambda_u R_0^2 \varepsilon^2} N^2 \, \log \left(\frac{2N}{\delta} \right). \tag{7.10}$$

So, the training time scales linearly with λ_r. Although the training time per user per request tends to zero as $\lambda_r \to \infty$, the training time per user tends to ∞. This is because the number of requests per unit time approaches ∞, and thus a small fraction of errors results in an infinite difference in off-loading loss, leading to an infinite training time. With the increasing demand for providing higher QoS for the end user, the question of whether it is possible to improve (i.e., decrease) the training time τ to achieve the desired estimation accuracy ε deserves attention. In the next subsection, we show that the lower bound on the training time can indeed be improved by employing a *transfer learning* -based approach.

Transfer learning to improve the training time: In practice, the minimum training time required to achieve an estimation accuracy of $\varepsilon > 0$ can be expected to be very large. An approach to overcoming this drawback is to utilize the knowledge obtained from users' interactions with a social community (termed the "source domain"). Specifically, by cleverly combining samples from the source domain and users' request pattern (target domain), one can potentially reduce the training time. In fact, the estimation accuracy is indicative of the dependence between the source and target domains. These techniques are commonly referred to as transfer learning (TL)-based approaches, and have implications for the achievement of a given estimation accuracy by the training time to. The TL-based approach considered here comprises two sources, namely, the source domain and target domain, from which the samples are acquired. An estimate of the popularity profile is obtained in a stepwise manner as follows:

1) Using target domain samples, the following parameter is computed at the BS:

$$\hat{S}_i^{(tar)} = \sum_{x \in B(0,R) \cap \Phi_u} \sum_{l=0}^{k_x} \mathbb{1}\{X_x^{(l)} = i\}, i = 1, ..., N. \tag{7.11}$$

Recall that k_x is the number of requests made by the user at the location x. The corresponding l-th request by the user at the location x in the time interval $[0, \tau]$ is denoted as $X_x^{(l)}$, $l = 1, 2, ..., k_x$.

2) The source domain samples $X^s = \{X_1^s, ..., X_m^s\}$ are drawn i.i.d. from a distribution Q, where $X_i^s = i$ ($i = , ..., N$) denotes that the user corresponding to the l-th sample has requested the file f_i. The nature of the distribution will be made precise in the sequel. Using this, the BS computes

$$\hat{S}_i^s = \sum_{(k=1)}^{m} \mathbb{1}\{X_k^s = i\}, i = 1, 2, ..., N. \tag{7.12}$$

3) The BS uses Eqs. (7.11) and (7.12) to compute an estimate of $\hat{p}_i^{(tl)}$ (the superscript tl indicates transfer learning TL) given by

$$\hat{p}_i^{(tl)} = \frac{\hat{S}_i^{(tar)} + \hat{S}_i^s}{\sum_{x \in B(0,R) \cap \Phi_u} k_x + m}. \tag{7.13}$$

Using the estimate given by Eq. (7.13), a lower bound on the training time is obtained as Let $g(\pi_i) = \exp\{-\lambda_s \pi \gamma^2 [1 - (1 - \pi_i)^M]\}$. Then, for any accuracy

$$\varepsilon > \frac{2B \sup_{\Pi} \left\{ \sum_{i=1}^{N} g(\pi_i) \right\}}{R_0} \|P - Q\|_\infty, \tag{7.14}$$

with a probability of at least $1 - \delta$, a throughput of $\hat{T}^* \leq T^* + \varepsilon$ can be achieved using the estimate in Eq. (7.13) provided the training time τ satisfies the following condition:

$$\tau \geq \begin{cases} \left\{ \left\{ \frac{1}{\lambda_r \left(1 - e^{-2\varepsilon_{pq}^2}\right)} \log\left(\frac{1}{1-\Lambda}\right) \right\}^+ \right. & , \text{if } \lambda_u > \rho, \\ \infty , & \text{otherwise,} \end{cases} \tag{7.15}$$

where $\rho = \frac{1}{\pi R^2}\left(\log\frac{2N}{\delta} - 2\varepsilon_{pq}^2 m\right)$, $\varepsilon_{pq} = \bar{\varepsilon} - \|P - Q\|_\infty$, $\Lambda = \frac{1}{\lambda_u \pi R^2}\left(\log\frac{2N}{\delta} - 2\varepsilon_{pq}^2 m\right)$, and $\bar{\varepsilon} = \dfrac{R_0\varepsilon}{2B\sup_\Pi\left\{\Sigma_{i=1}^N g(\pi_i)\right\}}$.

From Eq. (7.15), we see that under suitable conditions the TL-based approach performs better than the source domain sample-based agnostic approach. The following inferences are drawn:

1) The minimum user density to achieve a finite delay is reduced by a positive offset $2\varepsilon_{pq}^2 m$ In fact,

   for $m > \dfrac{\log\left(\frac{2N}{\delta}\right)}{2\left(\bar{\varepsilon} - \|P - Q\|_\infty\right)^2}$, a finite delay can be achieved for all user densities, which provides a significant advantage.

2) The finite delay achieved is smaller compared to the source domain sample-based agnostic approach for large enough numbers of source samples, and the distributions are "close." More precisely, for any $\varepsilon > 0$ and $\delta \in [0, 1]$, the TL-based approach performs better than the source-sample-based agnostic approach provided the number m of source samples satisfies $m \geq \frac{1}{2\varepsilon_{pq}^2}\left[\log\left(\frac{2N}{\delta}\right) - F\right]^+$, and the distributions satisfy the following condition:

$$\|P - Q\|_\infty < \frac{\varepsilon R_0}{2B\lambda_u \pi \gamma^2 N}, \tag{7.16}$$

where $F = \lambda_u \pi R^2\left(1 - \exp\left\{\dfrac{1 - e^{-2\varepsilon_{pq}^2}}{1 - e^{-2\bar{\varepsilon}^2}}\log(1 - L)\right\}\right)$ and $L = \dfrac{1}{\lambda_u \pi R^2}\log\left(\dfrac{2N}{\delta}\right)$.

In fact, Eq. (7.16) provides the guiding principle to decide if the samples drawn from the distribution Q should be used to estimate the distribution P. In general, the distance between the distributions has to be estimated from the available samples (relative to the distribution on P).

An estimate of the popularity profile can also be obtained by linearly combining its estimates obtained from the source domain and target domain samples. In particular, we have

$$\hat{p}_i = \alpha\hat{p}_i^{(s)} + (1 - \alpha)\hat{p}_i^{(t)}, \tag{7.17}$$

where $\hat{p}_i^{(s)}$ and $\hat{p}_i^{(t)}$ are the estimates of the popularity profile obtained from the source domain samples and the target domain samples, respectively. The estimates are given by

$$\hat{p}_i^{(t)} = \frac{\hat{S}_i^{(tar)}}{\sum\limits_{u \in \left\{\mathbb{B}(0, R) \cap \Phi_u\right\}} k_u}, \tag{7.18}$$

$$\hat{p}_i^{(s)} = \frac{\hat{S}_i^s}{m}. \tag{7.19}$$

Note that in this case the coefficients are independent of the realization of the network. For the estimate proposed in Eq. (7.17), we have the following result:

For any accuracy

$$\varepsilon > \frac{2B\sup_\Pi\left\{\sum\limits_{i=1}^N g(\pi_i)\right\}}{R_0}\|P - Q\|_\infty, \tag{7.20}$$

with a probability of at least $1 - \delta$, a throughput of $\hat{T}^* \leq T^* + \varepsilon$ can be achieved using the estimate in Eq. (7.17) provided the training time τ satisfies the condition specified by [173]

$$\begin{cases} \dfrac{1}{\lambda_r g_t^*} \log \left[\dfrac{1}{1 - \dfrac{1}{\lambda_u \pi R^2} \left(\log\left(\dfrac{2N}{\delta}\right) + \log\left\{ \dfrac{1}{1 - \left(\dfrac{2N}{\delta}\right) \exp\{-2\bar{\omega}^2 m\}} \right\} \right)} \right], & \lambda_u > \rho_{\text{thres}}, \\ \\ \infty, & \text{otherwise,} \end{cases}$$

where

$$\rho_{\text{thresh}} \triangleq \dfrac{1}{\pi R^2} \left(\log\left(\dfrac{2N}{\delta}\right) + \log\left\{ \dfrac{1}{1 - \left(\dfrac{2N}{\delta}\right) \exp\{-2\bar{\omega}^2 m\}} \right\} \right),$$

$$\bar{\varepsilon} = \dfrac{R_0 \varepsilon}{2B \sup_{\Pi} \{\Sigma_{i=1}^N g(\pi_i)\}}, \quad g_t^* \triangleq (1 - \exp\{-2\eta^2\}),$$

$$g(\pi_i) = \exp\left\{ -\lambda_s \pi \gamma^2 \left[1 - (1 - \pi_i)^M\right] \right\}$$

and, $\omega = \dfrac{\bar{\varepsilon} - (1-\alpha)\eta}{\alpha} > 0$. This valid for all $0 < \alpha < \min\left\{\dfrac{\bar{\varepsilon}}{G}, 1\right\}$ and $0 \leq \eta < \dfrac{\bar{\varepsilon} - \alpha G}{1-\alpha}$, where

$$G = \|P - Q\|_\infty + \sqrt{\dfrac{1}{2m} \log\dfrac{2N}{\delta}}.$$

7.3 Q-Learning-Based Joint Channel and Power Level Selection in Heterogeneous Cellular Networks

Network model: In this section, we consider a device-to-device (D2D)-enabled heterogeneous cellular network that consists of N BSs, numbered BS_1, ..., BS_N. We denote by $\mathbf{N} = \{1, ..., N\}$ the set of BS indices. Each BS in the network can be either a high-power BS serving the macrocell or a low-power BS serving the small (micro, pico, or femto) cell. It is assumed that the BSs operate on their own licensed spectrum bands that may overlap with each other. The BSs serve M D2D pairs and L cellular users. For notational consistency, the D2D pairs are numbered, interchangeably, as PU_{M+1}, ..., PU_{N+M} or $(U_{N+1}, U_{N+1'})$, ..., $(U_{N+M}, U_{N+M'})$, with $\mathbf{M} = \{N+1, ..., N+M\}$ being the set of the D2D pairs' indices. The cellular users are denoted as U_{N+M+1}, ..., U_{N+M+L}, with $\mathbf{L} = \{N+M+1, ..., N+M+L\}$ being the set of the cellular users' indices.

The described system runs on a slotted-time basis with the time axis partitioned into the equal non-overlapping time intervals (slots) of the length T_s, with t denoting an integer-valued slot index. We follow the same approach as [174] and assume that the communication of cellular and D2D users is synchronized by the timing signals sent by a cellular network or the global positioning system (GPS). The wireless channels are allocated to cellular users by the associated BSs according to some predetermined scheduling procedure (based on the global CSI, which can be obtained using conventional pilot signals). Unlike cellular users, the D2D users operate fully autonomously (without any cooperation or information exchange among each other and with the BSs). Hence, they have neither precise nor statistical knowledge about the operating environment (such as channel quality or network traffic) and have to select the wireless channels and adjust their transmission power independently based only on their own local observations. It is assumed that each D2D pair decides its channel and power level at the beginning of each time slot. We also assume that each cellular/D2D user stays in the system for an indefinitely long time. That is, although the users eventually leave the network, they are uncertain about the exact duration of their stay.

Here, we present two different scenarios of D2D communication. In the first scenario, the D2D pairs and cellular users operate on different frequency bands (hence creating no interference to each other). In the second scenario, the D2D pairs and cellular users transmit over the same channels. Consequently, we consider the network where K orthogonal channels, numbered $C_1..., C_K$, are available for D2D communication, with $\mathbf{K} = \{1, ..., K\}$ being the set of the corresponding channel indices. Note that in the first scenario, only the D2D users are allowed to transmit over the channels from the set K. The cellular users operate on their dedicated channels belonging to some set K^C, such that $K^C \cap K = \emptyset$, and the total available network bandwidth consists of the channels from the union set $K^C \cup K$. In the second scenario, both the cellular and D2D users can transmit over the channels in the set K (that is, the total spectrum band of the network comprises the channels in the set K).

In the following, for each D2D pair PU_m and cellular user U_m, we define the binary channel allocation vector $c_t^m = \left(c_1^m(t), ..., c_K^m(t)\right)$, $m \in M \cup L$, with the elements $c_k^m(t)$, $k \in K$, equaling 1 if PU_m/U_m transmits over the channel C_k at slot t, and 0 otherwise. For each cellular user U_l, we also define the binary BS association vector $b_t^l = \left(b_1^l(t), ..., b_N^l(t)\right)$, $l \in L$, with the elements $b_n^l(t)$, $n \in N$, equaling 1 if U_l is associated with the BS_n at slot t, and 0 otherwise. In our network model, the number of D2D pairs operating (simultaneously) on the same channels is unlimited. However, at any slot, each D2D user can select at most one channel within the available bandwidth. That is,

$$\sum_{k \in \mathbf{K}} c_k^m(t) \leq 1, \forall m \in \mathbf{M}. \tag{7.21a}$$

In the first scenario, all the channels in the set K are reserved for D2D communication only and we have

$$c_k^l(t) = 0, \forall l \in \mathbf{L}, \forall k \in \mathbf{K}, \tag{7.21b}$$

at any slot t. We also introduce the finite sets of possible channel selection decisions made by each PU_m, defined as

$$C^m = \left\{ c_t^m \sum_{k \in \mathbf{K}} c_k^m(t) \leq 1 \right\}, \forall m \in \mathbf{M}. \tag{7.22}$$

Channel model: Let $G_{m,j}^k(t)$, $j \in MUL$, $m \in M$, $k \in K$ denote the link gain of the channel between U_m and U_j operating on C_k at slot t, and let $G_{n,j}^k(t)$, $n \in N$ be the link gain of the channel between the BS_n and U_j operating on C_k at slot . Note that the instantaneous values of $G_{n,l}^k(t)$ can be measured by all cellular users and the BSs for any $n \in N$, $l \in L$, $k \in K$, using the pilot signals. The D2D users, however, do not possess any prior information on the wireless channel quality. Therefore, the exact values of $G_{m,j}^k(t)$ and $G_{n,j}^k(t)$ are unknown to all D2D pairs (and the BSs).

In the first scenario, the interference to each D2D pair is created by the other D2D users operating on the same channel. Consequently, the SINR for a D2D pair PU_m transmitting over the wireless channel C_k is

$$SINR_k^m(t) = \frac{S_k^m(t)}{I_{m,k}^D(t) + \sigma^2}, \forall m \in \mathbf{M}, \forall k \in \mathbf{K} \tag{7.23a}$$

at any slot t. In Eq. (7.23a), σ^2 is the variance of zero-mean additive white Gaussian noise power; $S_k^m(t)$ is the useful signal power of PU_m over the channel C_k at slot, given by

$$S_k^m(t) = G_{m,m'}^k(t)c_k^m(t)P^m(t), \tag{7.23b}$$

where $P^m(t) \leq P_{\max}$ is the transmission power (that should not exceed some maximal allowed power level $P_{\max}$) selected by PU_m at slot t; $I_{m,k}^D(t)$ is the interference to PU_m from the D2D users operating on the channel C_k, defined, at any slot t, as

$$I_{m,k}^D(t) = \sum_{j \in M \setminus \{m\}} G_{j,m'}^k(t)c_k^j(t)P^j(t). \tag{7.23c}$$

In the second scenario, the interference to the D2D pairs is caused not only by other D2D users but also by cellular users operating on the same channels and associated with different BSs. The SINR for a D2D pair PU_m transmitting over the wireless channel C_k is equal to

$$SINR_k^m(t) = \frac{S_k^m(t)}{I_{(m,k)}^D(t) + I_{(m,k)}^C(t) + \sigma^2} \forall m \in M, \forall k \in K \tag{7.24a}$$

at any slot t, with $I_{m,k}^C(t)$ being the interference to PU_m from the cellular users operating on the channel C_k, given by

$$I_{m,k}^C(t) = \sum_{i \in N} \sum_{j \in L} G_{i,m'}^k(t)b_i^j(t)c_k^j(t)P^j(t), \tag{7.24b}$$

where $P^j(t)$ is the instantaneous transmission power in the DL channel between the cellular user U_j and its associated BS.

To be compatible with the proposed multi-agent Q-learning framework, we discretize the transmission power of the D2D pairs, as follows. For each PU_m, we consider J power levels, numbered P_1, ..., P_J, and define the binary power level selection vector $\mathbf{p}_t^m = (p_1^m(t), ..., p_J^m(t))$, with the elements $p_j^m(t), j \in J = \{1, ..., J\}$, equaling 1 if PU_m chooses to transmit at a power level P_j at slot t, and 0 otherwise. Since only one power level can be selected at any slot, we have

$$\sum_{j \in J} p_j^m(t) \leq 1, \forall m \in M. \tag{7.25a}$$

Given Eq. (7.25a), the instantaneous transmission power of each PU_m can be calculated according to

$$P^m(t) = \frac{P_{\max}}{J} \sum_{j \in J} j \cdot p_j^m(t), \forall m \in M. \tag{7.25b}$$

We also define a finite set of possible power level selection decisions made by PU_m, as

$$P^m = \left\{ \mathbf{p}_t^m \mid \sum_{j \in J} p_j^m(t) \leq 1 \right\}, \forall m \in M. \tag{7.26}$$

Optimization problem: The main goal of the autonomous scheme for joint channel and power level selection is to ensure that there are no D2D pairs with the SINRs falling below some predefined thresholds. That is,

$$SINR^m(t) = \sum_{k \in K} SINR_k^m(t) \geq SINR_{\min}^m, \forall m \in M \tag{7.27}$$

where $SINR_{\min}^m$ is the minimal satisfactory SINR level of PU_m. If, at the current slot t, the constraint in Eq. (7.27) is satisfied for some PU_m then this D2D pair obtains a reward u_t^m, defined as the difference between the throughput and the cost of power consumption achieved by selecting the specific channel and power level. Otherwise (if the constraint in Eq. (7.27) is not satisfied for PU_m), it receives a zero reward. Consequently, we can express the reward u_t^m obtained by PU_m at slot, as

$$u_t^m = \begin{cases} R^m(t) - v^m P^m(t), & \text{if } SINR^m(t) \geq SINR_{\min}^m \\ 0, & \text{otherwise,} \end{cases} \tag{7.28a}$$

for all $m \in$ M. In Eq. (7.28a), $v_m \geq 0$ is the cost per unit (watt) level of power, the throughput $R^m(t)$ is given by

$$R^m(t) = \omega \log(1 + SINR^m(t))$$
$$= \omega \log\Big(1 + \sum_{k \in K} SINR_k^m(t)\Big), \tag{7.28b}$$

where ω is the channel bandwidth, and the transmission power $P^m(t)$ is calculated using Eq. (7.25b). Note that at any slot, the instantaneous reward of PU_m in Eq. (7.28a) depends on

- the individual channel and power level decisions of PU_m, c_t^m, and $\mathbf{p}_t^m$, and the current link gain in its channel $G_{m,m^f}^k(t)$ (which are known or can be measured by PU_m); and
- the channels and power levels selected by the other users and the link gains in their channels (which cannot be observed by PU_m).

In our network, at any slot, each PU_m selects the transmission channel and power level to maximize its long-term reward U_t^m, defined as a sum of the instantaneous rewards that this D2D pair receives over the infinite (indefinitely long) period in the future. To ensure the finiteness of this sum, we introduce the discounting of the future rewards relative to the earlier rewards, which is used to model the situations where the users are uncertain about the duration of their stay in the system. A common assumption is that a user wants to maximize a weighted sum of its future instantaneous rewards where the weights of the later periods are less than the weights of the earlier periods. For simplicity, this assumption often takes a particular form that the sequence of weights forms a geometric progression: for some fixed $\gamma \in [0, 1)$, each weighting factor is γ times the previous weight (γ is called the discount rate). In this case, the long-term reward of the D2D pair PU_m can be expressed as

$$U_t^m = \sum_{\tau = t}^{+\infty} \gamma^{t-\tau} u_\tau^m. \tag{7.29}$$

We now introduce the set of possible channel and power level decisions made by each D2D pair PU_m, defined as $\mathbf{A}^m = \mathbf{C}^m \times \mathbf{P}^m$ (where $\times$ denotes the Cartesian product). Then, the objective of each PU_m is to select, at any slot, the pair $(\bar{\mathbf{c}}_t^m, \bar{\mathbf{p}}_t^m) \in \mathbf{A}^m$ that maximizes its long-term reward in Eq. (7.29). That is,

$$(\bar{\mathbf{c}}_t^m, \bar{\mathbf{p}}_t^m) = arg \ max_{(\bar{\mathbf{c}}_t^m, \bar{\mathbf{p}}_t^m) \in \mathbf{A}^m} U_t^m \tag{7.30}$$

In the following, we will use the subscript t to denote the values of the parameters and functions at a time slot. We will ignore the subscript t when focusing on one slot of the decision process, to simplify the notation.

7.3.1 Stochastic Noncooperative Game

Game formulation: Here, we formulate the considered joint channel and power level selection problem as a dynamic noncooperative game with M players (D2D pairs) having no information about the operating environment (channel quality and network traffic). It is assumed that all players are selfish and rational and, at any slot, execute their actions (determined by the players' decisions regarding their transmission channels and power levels) with the objective of maximizing their long-term rewards in Eq. (7.29). Consequently, the action space of the player PU_m is equivalent to the finite set of its possible channel and power level decisions, $\mathbf{A}^m = \mathbf{C}^m \times \mathbf{P}^m$. The action executed by PU_m at slot $a_t^m = \left(\mathbf{c}_t^m, \mathbf{p}_t^m \right) \in \mathbf{A}^m$ consists of two parts representing, respectively, the channel and power level selected by this player at a given time slot. For each PU_m, we also introduce the vector of actions taken by the other $M-1$ players at slot t, defined as $\mathrm{a}_t^{-m} = \left(a_t^1, ..., a_t^{m-1}, a_t^{m+1}, ..., a_t^M \right) \in \mathbf{A}^{-m}$, where $\mathbf{A}^{-m} = \times_{i \in M \setminus \{m\}} \mathbf{A}^i$.

In the network, at any slot t, the throughput $R^m(t)$ of the player PU_m depends on the current SINR in its channel (see Eq. (7.28b)), which is determined by the players' actions $\left(a_t^m, \mathbf{a}_t^{-m} \right)$ and the instantaneous values of the link gain coefficient matrix $\mathbf{G}_t^m$, given by

$$
\mathbf{G}_t^m = \left\{ \begin{matrix} G_{1,m^f}^1(t) & \cdots & G_{1,m^f}^K(t) \\ \vdots & \vdots & \vdots \\ G_{N+M,m}^1(t) & \cdots & G_{N+M,m}^K(t) \end{matrix} \right\}, \forall m \in M. \tag{7.31}
$$

So, the instantaneous SINR for each D2D pair (i.e., $SINR^m(t)$) in the first and second scenarios can be expressed, for all $m \in M$, as

$$
SINR^m \left(a_t^m, \mathbf{a}_t^{-m}, \mathbf{G}_t^m \right) = \sum_{k \in K} \frac{S_k^m \left(a_t^m, \mathbf{G}_t^m \right)}{I_{m,k}^D \left(\mathbf{a}_t^{-m}, \mathbf{G}_t^m \right) + \sigma^2} \tag{7.32a}
$$

and

$$
SINR^m \left(a_t^m, \mathbf{a}_t^{-m}, \mathbf{G}_t^m \right) = \sum_{k \in K} \frac{S_k^m \left(a_t^m, \mathbf{G}_t^m \right)}{I_{m,k}^D \left(\mathbf{a}_t^{-m}, \mathbf{G}_t^m \right) + I_{m,k}^C + \sigma^2} \tag{7.32b}
$$

respectively, where $S_k^m(t)$ and $I_{m,k}^D(t)$ are presented explicitly as the functions of a_t^m, $\mathbf{a}_t^{-m}$, and G_t^m. Note that at any slot, each player PU_m can measure its current SINR level $SINR^m(t)$.

The instantaneous reward u_t^m obtained by PU_m after taking some action a_t^m equals zero if the current SINR in its channel is less than the predefined threshold $SINR_{min}^m$ (see Eq. (7.28a)). Accordingly, at any slot, for each PU_m we can define the state of the game s_t^m, as

$$
s_t^m = \begin{cases} 1, & \text{if } SINR^m \left(a_t^m, \mathbf{a}_t^{-m}, \mathbf{G}_t^m \right) \geq SINR_{min}^m \\ 0, & \text{otherwise} \end{cases} \forall m \in \mathbf{M} \tag{7.33}
$$

The state s_t^m is fully observable (since it depends on the values of $SINR^m(t)$ that can be measured at any slot t). Using Eq. (7.33), the instantaneous reward u_t^m received by PU_m at slot, can be expressed as

$$
u_t^m = u^m \left(a_t^m, \mathbf{a}_t^{-m}, s_t^m \right) = s_t^m \left[R^m \left(a_t^m, \mathbf{a}_t^{-m}, \mathbf{G}_t^m \right) - v^m P^m \left(a_t^m \right) \right], \tag{7.34a}
$$

for all $m \in \mathbf{M}$, where

$$
R^m \left(a_t^m, \mathbf{a}_t^{-m}, \mathbf{G}_t^m \right) = \omega \log \left(1 + SINR^m \left(a_t^m, \mathbf{a}_t^{-m}, \mathbf{G}_t^m \right) \right), \tag{7.34b}
$$

$SINR^m(a_t^m, \mathbf{a}_t^{-m}, \mathbf{G}_t^m)$ is determined from Eq. (7.32a) or (7.32b) (depending on the considered scenario), and the instantaneous transmission power $P^m(t)$ is expressed explicitly as a function of a_t^m.

It follows from Eq. (7.34a) that, at any slot, the reward u_t^m obtained by PU_m depends on the current (fully observable) state s_t^m and partially observable actions $(a_t^m, \mathbf{a}_t^{-m})$. At the next slot, the game moves to a new random state s_{t+1}^m whose distribution depends on the previous state s_t^m and the selected actions $(a_t^m, \mathbf{a}_t^{-m})$. This procedure repeats for the indefinite number of slots. At any time slot t, the player PU_m can observe its state s_t^m and action a_t^m but does not know the actions of other players, $\mathbf{a}_t^{-m}$, and the precise values of $\mathbf{G}_t^m$. The state transition probabilities (from the current state s_t^m to next state s_{t+1}^m given the executed actions $(a_t^m, \mathbf{a}_t^{-m})$) are also unknown to each player PU_m. Consequently, the considered game is stochastic. Hence, we can characterize this game by the tuple

$\Gamma = (\mathbf{S}, \mathbf{M}, \mathbf{A}, T, \mathbf{U})$ comprising the following respective components:

- the finite set of possible states, $\mathbf{S} = X_{m \in M} \mathbf{S}^m$, with $\mathbf{S}^m = \{0, 1\}$, for all $m \in M$;
- the finite set of players $\mathbf{M}$;
- the finite set of action profiles, $\mathbf{A} = X_{m \in M} \mathbf{A}^m$;
- the state transition probability function $T(s^m, \mathbf{a}, s'^m) = Pr\{s'^m \mid s^m, \mathbf{a}\}$, defined as the probability of transitioning to the next state $s'^m = s_{t+1}^m \in \mathbf{S}^m$ given the joint action $\mathbf{a} = (a_t^1, ..., a_t^M) \in \mathbf{A}$, executed in state $s^m = s_t^m \in \mathbf{S}^m$;
- the vector of player rewards, $\mathbf{U} = (u^1, ..., u^M)$.

A solution to this game is represented by some action vector $(\overline{a}^m, \overline{\mathbf{a}}^{-m}) \in \mathbf{A}$ that corresponds to the Nash equilibrium (NE) where the following inequalities hold for each PU_m in any $s^m \in \mathbf{S}^m$:

$$u^m(\overline{a}^m, \overline{\mathbf{a}}^{-m}, s^m) \geq u^m(a^m, \overline{\mathbf{a}}^{-m}, s^m), \forall a^m \in \mathbf{A}^m. \tag{7.35}$$

That is, in the NE state, the action of each player is the best response to the actions of the other players. Hence, no players can gain by unilateral deviation.

Mixed strategy profile $\pi^m: \mathbf{S}^m \rightarrow \mathbf{A}^m$ (mapping from states to actions) of the player PU_m in state s^m, denoted as $\pi^m(s^m) = \{\pi^m(s^m, a^m)\}_{a^m \in \mathbf{A}^m}$, will be also introduced. Each element $\pi^m(s^m, a^m)$ of $\pi^m(s^m)$ is the probability with which a D2D pair PU_m selects an action $a^m \in \mathbf{A}^m$ in state $s^m \in \mathbf{S}^m$. For each PU_m, we also define the vector of strategies $\pi^{-m}(s) = (\pi^1(s^1), ..., \pi^{m-1}(s^{m-1}), \pi^{m+1}(s^{m+1}), ..., \pi^M(s^M))$ of the other $M - 1$ players. The presence of incomplete information (about the reward structure and state transition probabilities) in a formulated noncooperative game provides opportunities for the players to learn their optimal strategies through repeated interactions with the stochastic environment, and each player PU_m becomes a learning agent whose task is to find an NE strategy $\overline{\pi}^m$ for any state s^m.

In the next subsection, we model the dynamic of our game using a finite-state MDP and derive the multi-agent Q-learning process for joint channel and power level selection by D2D pairs.

7.3.2 Multi-Agent Q-Learning

Q-learning is an RL method for solving the problems modeled after MDPs, where a learning agent operates in an unknown stochastic environment. In multi-agent Q-learning, each m-th agent

1) observes its environment, using some representation of the environment state s^m,
2) selects one of the available actions a^m, and
3) receives, as a consequence of its action a^m, the immediate
4) response from the environment in the form of reward u^m.

When the rewards are based only on the current state and action (without being influenced by the previous states and actions), the task of the m-th agent is said to satisfy the Markov property and can be formally defined as the MDP consisting of

1) a discrete set of environment states S^m,
2) a discrete set of possible actions A^m, and
3) a one-slot dynamics of the environment given by the state transition probabilities

$T_{s^m s'^m} = T(s^m, \boldsymbol{a}, s'^m)$, for all $a^m \in A^m$ and $s^m, s'^m \in \boldsymbol{S}^m$.

The solution to the above MDP is then to select, for each state $s^m \in \boldsymbol{S}^m$, an optimal strategy $\bar{\pi}^m(s^m)$ that maximizes its value-state function V, formally defined as [174]

$$
\begin{aligned}
V(s^m, \pi^m, \boldsymbol{\pi}^{-m}) &= \mathrm{E}\left\{ \sum_{\tau=t}^{+\infty} \gamma^{t-\tau} u_\tau^m \mid s_t^m = s^m \right\} \\
&= \mathrm{E}\{u^m[\pi^m(s^m), \boldsymbol{\pi}^{-m}(s^m), s^m]\} \\
&\quad + \gamma \sum_{s'^m \in \boldsymbol{S}^m} T_{s^m s'^m}[\pi^m(s^m), \boldsymbol{\pi}^{-m}(s^m)] V(s'^m, \pi^m, \boldsymbol{\pi}^{-m}),
\end{aligned}
\tag{7.36a}
$$

for all $m \in \mathbf{M}$, where $\mathrm{E}\{x\}$ is the expectation of x, and

$$
\begin{aligned}
&\mathrm{E}\{u^m(\pi^m(s^m), \boldsymbol{\pi}^{-m}(s^m), s^m)\} \\
&= \sum_{s'^m \in \boldsymbol{S}^m} T_{s^m s'^m}[\pi^m(s^m), \boldsymbol{\pi}^{-m}(s^m)] \\
&\quad \times \sum_{(a^m, \mathbf{a}^{-m}) \in \mathbf{A}} \left\{ u^m(a^m, \mathbf{a}^{-m}, s^m) \prod_{i \in \mathbf{M}} \pi^i(s^i, a^i) \right\}.
\end{aligned}
\tag{7.36b}
$$

Note that the value-state function determines the expected return (the sum of the expected discounted rewards that an agent receives over the infinite time in the future) that can be obtained from each state on every possible policy.

Consequently, a strategy tuple $(\bar{\pi}^m, \bar{\boldsymbol{\pi}}^{-m})$, with $\bar{\boldsymbol{\pi}}^{-m} = (\bar{\pi}^1, .., \bar{\pi}^{m-1}, \bar{\pi}^{m+1}, .., \bar{\pi}^M)$, is an NE if the following inequalities hold for any π^m:

$$
V(s^m, \bar{\pi}^m, \bar{\boldsymbol{\pi}}^{-m}) \geq V(s^m, \pi^m, \bar{\boldsymbol{\pi}}^{-m}), \forall s^m \in \boldsymbol{S}^m.
\tag{7.37}
$$

Since any finite game in a strategic form has the mixed strategy equilibrium [29], there always exists an NE in our game that satisfies the following Bellman's optimality equation:

$$
\bar{V}(s^m, \pi^m, \boldsymbol{\pi}^{-m}) = V(s^m, \bar{\pi}^m, \bar{\boldsymbol{\pi}}^{-m})
$$

$$
= max_{a^m \in \mathbf{A}^m} \left[\mathrm{E}\{u^m[a^m, \bar{\boldsymbol{\pi}}^{-m}(s^m), s^m]\} + \gamma \sum_{s'^m \in \boldsymbol{S}^m} T_{s^m s'^m}[a^m, \bar{\boldsymbol{\pi}}^{-m}(s^m)] V(s'^m, \bar{\pi}^m, \bar{\boldsymbol{\pi}}^{-m})] \right]
$$

$$
\tag{7.38a}
$$

for all $m \in \mathbf{M}$, where

$$
\mathrm{E}\{u^m(a^m, \overline{\pi}^{-m}(s^m), s^m)\} = \sum_{s'^m \in \mathbf{S}^m} T_{s^m s'^m}[a^m, \overline{\pi}^{-m}(s^m)]
$$

$$
\times \sum_{\mathbf{a}^{-m} \in \mathbf{A}^{-m}} \left\{ u^m(a^m, \mathbf{a}^{-m}, s^m) \prod_{i \in \mathrm{M} \setminus \{m\}} \overline{\pi}^i(s^i, a^i) \right\} \tag{7.38b}
$$

Let us further define the function

$$
\begin{aligned}
\overline{Q}(s^m, a^m) &= \mathrm{E}\left\{ \sum_{\tau=t}^{+\infty} \gamma^{t-\tau} u_\tau^m \mid s_t^m = s^m, a_t^m = a^m \right\} \\
&= \mathrm{E}\{u^m[a^m, \overline{\pi}^{-m}(s^m), s^m]\} \\
&\quad + \gamma \sum_{s'^m \in \mathbf{S}^m} T_{s^m s'^m}[a^m, \overline{\pi}^{-m}(s^m)] V(s'^m, \overline{\pi}^m, \overline{\pi}^{-m})
\end{aligned} \tag{7.39}
$$

which is called an optimal action-value function (or simply, an action-value) and measures the maximum expected return for taking an action a^m in state s^m, and thereafter following an optimal strategy (see Chapter 6). Although more than one NE strategy $\overline{\pi}^m(s^m)$ can exist for each learning agent, all of them will have the same action-values $\overline{Q}(s^m, a^m)$ and

$$
V(s^m, \overline{\pi}^m, \overline{\pi}^{-m}) = \max_{a^m \in \mathbf{A}^m} \overline{Q}(s^m, a^m). \tag{7.40}
$$

From Eqs. (7.38a) and (7.40), we get [175]

$$
\begin{aligned}
\overline{Q}(s^m, a^m) &= \mathrm{E}\{u^m[a^m, \overline{\pi}^{-m}(s^m), s^m]\} \\
&\quad + \gamma \sum_{s'^m \in \mathbf{S}^m} T_{s^m s'^m}[a^m, \overline{\pi}^{-m}(s^m)] \max_{a'^m \in \mathbf{A}^m} \overline{Q}(s'^m, a'^m).
\end{aligned} \tag{7.41}
$$

In other words, an optimal action-value function can be obtained recursively from the corresponding action-values. In Q-learning, each agent learns the optimal action-values using the updating rule, described by [174]

$$
\begin{aligned}
& Q_{t+1}(s^m, a^m) \leftarrow Q_t(s^m, a^m) \\
& + \begin{cases} \alpha_t \left[\sum_{\mathbf{a}^{-m} \in \mathbf{A}^{-m}} \left\{ u^m[a^m, \mathbf{a}^{-m}, s^m] \prod_{i \in \mathrm{M} \setminus \{m\}} \pi^i(s^i, a^i) \right\} + \gamma \max_{a'^m \in \mathbf{A}^m} Q_t(s'^m, a'^m) - Q_t(s^m, a^m) \right], \\ \quad \text{if } s_t^m = s^m, a_t^m = a^m \\ 0, \text{otherwise}; \end{cases}
\end{aligned}
$$

$$
\tag{7.42}
$$

for all $s^m \in \mathbf{S}^m$, $a^m \in \mathbf{A}^m$, $m \in \mathbf{M}$, with $\alpha_t \in [0, 1)$ and Q_t being, respectively, the learning rate and action-value at slot t.

7.3.3 Q-Learning for Channel and Power Level Selection

Note that the multi-agent Q-learning algorithm given by Eq. (7.42) implies that each D2D pair has to possess not only the local information about its own strategy and reward but also the information regarding the strategies of the other players. In the following, we present a fully autonomous channel selection algorithm (which will not rely on the availability of the global information about the strategies of the players) based on the multi-agent Q-learning process in Eq. (7.42).

Autonomous Q-learning based on players' beliefs: The Q-learning method formulated in Eq. (7.42) can be applied to our channel selection game to learn the players' rewards. The corresponding recursive learning process for each player PU_m is given by

$$
\hat{u}_{t+1}^m(s^m, a^m) \leftarrow \hat{u}_t^m(s^m, a^m) + I_{s_t^m = s^m, a_t^m = a^m}\alpha_t
$$

$$
\times \left[\begin{array}{l} \sum_{\mathbf{a}^{-m} \in \mathbf{A}^{-m}} \{u^m[a^m, \mathbf{a}^{-m}, s^m]Y(s^m, \mathbf{a}^{-m})\} + \\ \gamma \, max_{a'^m \in \mathbf{A}^m}\hat{u}_t^m(s'^m, a'^m) - \hat{u}_t^m(s^m, a^m) \end{array} \right], \forall m \in \mathbf{M}. \tag{7.43}
$$

for all $s^m \in \mathbf{S}^m$, $a^m \in \mathbf{A}^m$. In Eq. (7.43), $\hat{u}_t^m(s^m, a^m) \leftarrow Q_t(s^m, a^m)$ is the estimated reward of a player PU_m obtained by playing the action a_t^m in state s_t^m, I is the indicator function, and the function $Y(s^m, \mathbf{a}^{-m})$ is given by

$$
Y(s^m, \mathbf{a}^{-m}) = \prod_{i \in \mathbf{M}/\{m\}} \pi^i(s^i, a^i), \forall m \in \mathbf{M}. \tag{7.44}
$$

In a NE state, the strategies of the players remain unaltered. Each player in this state can be viewed as a learning agent behaving optimally with respect to his beliefs about the strategies of all the other players (that is, with respect to $(s^m, \mathbf{a}^{-m})$). The probability that PU_m achieves a reward $u^m(a^m, \mathbf{a}^{-m}, s^m)$ at slot t is equal to the product $\eta^m = \pi^m(s^m, a^m)Y(s^m, \mathbf{a}^{-m})$. In the following, we use the notation t_c to denote the number of slots between any two consecutive events of PU_m achieving the same reward value $u^m(a^m, \mathbf{a}^{-m}, s^m)$. Note that t_c has an independent and identical distribution with η^m and we have

$$
E\{\eta^m\} = \frac{1}{E\{t_c\}}. \tag{7.45a}
$$

Based on Eq. (7.25a), each PU_m can estimate $Y(s^m, \mathbf{a}^{-m})$ as

$$
\hat{Y}(s^m, \mathbf{a}^{-m}) \approx \frac{1}{E\{t_c\}\pi^m(s^m, a^m)}, \forall m \in \mathbf{M}. \tag{7.45b}
$$

Let us further introduce the reference points $\dot{Y}(s^m, a^{-m})$ and $\dot{\pi}^m(s^m, a^m)$, which represent some specific values of the belief $Y(s^m, \mathbf{a}^{-m})$ and strategy $\pi^m(s^m, a^m)$, respectively. Then,

$$
\hat{Y}(s^m, \mathbf{a}^{-m}) - \dot{Y}(s^m, \mathbf{a}^{-m})
$$

$$
\approx \frac{1}{E\{t_c\}}\left\{ \frac{1}{\pi^m(s^m, a^m)} - \frac{1}{\dot{\pi}^m(s^m, a^m)} \right\} \tag{7.46a}
$$

$$
= \beta_t^m[\dot{\pi}^m(s^m, a^m) - \dot{\pi}^m(s^m, a^m)], \forall m \in \mathbf{M}
$$

where

$$
\beta_t^m = \frac{1}{E\{t_c\}\pi^m(s^m, a^m)\dot{\pi}^m(s^m, a^m)}, \forall m \in \mathbf{M} \tag{7.46b}
$$

is some positive scalar. When operating fully autonomously, the players can modify the reference points based on their past local observations. Here, we update the reference points as

$$
\dot{Y}(s^m, \mathbf{a}^{-m}) = Y_{t-1}(s^m, \mathbf{a}^{-m}), \dot{\pi}^m(s^m, a^m) = \pi_{t-1}^m(s^m, a^m) \tag{7.47}
$$

where $Y_{t-1}(s^m, \mathbf{a}^{-m})$ and $\pi_{t-1}^m(s^m, a^m)$ are, respectively, the belief and strategy reference points at past slot $t - 1$. Using Eqs. (7.46a) and (7.47), we get the following updating rule for belief estimation:

$$\hat{Y}(s^m, \mathbf{a}^{-m}) = Y_{t-1}(s^m, \mathbf{a}^{-m})$$
$$- \beta_t^m \left[\pi^m(s^m, a^m) - \pi_{t-1}^m(s^m, a^m) \right] \tag{7.48}$$

for all $m \in \mathbf{M}$. Then, the autonomous multi-agent Q-learning method given by Eq. (7.43) becomes

$$\hat{u}_{t+1}^m(s^m, a^m) \leftarrow \hat{u}_t^m(s^m, a^m) + I_{s_t^m = s^m, a_t^m = a^m} \alpha_t$$
$$\times \left[\begin{array}{c} \sum_{\mathbf{a}^{-m} \in \mathbf{A}^{-m}} \{ u^m[a^m, \mathbf{a}^{-m}, s^m] \hat{Y}(s^m, \mathbf{a}^{-m}) \} \\ + \gamma \ max_{a'^m \in \mathbf{A}^m} \ \hat{u}_t^m(s'^m, a'^m) - \hat{u}_t^m(s^m, a^m) \end{array} \right], \forall m \in \mathbf{M}. \tag{7.49}$$

for all $s^m \in S^m$, $a^m \in A^m$, where the belief estimates are obtained from Eq. (7.48).

Another challenging problem with Q-learning is the trade-off between exploration and exploitation. To obtain a higher reward, a learning agent must exploit the actions that had been effective in the past. But to discover such actions, it has to explore the actions that have not been selected previously. Hence, both exploration and exploitation should be used jointly to complete the learning task.

A rather typical approach of dealing with the problem of exploration/exploitation is ε-greedy selection. With this approach, the best action is selected for a proportion $1 - \varepsilon$ of the trials; any other action is chosen uniformly at random for a proportion ε.

On the other hand, the probability of selecting an action can be expressed as a function of the respective action-value (in our case, the estimated reward $\hat{u}_t^m (s^m, a^m)$). Then, all actions will be weighted according to their action-value, so that the best action will be selected with higher probability. The most common way to implement such action selection is by using the Boltzmann–Gibbs (BG) distribution, given by

$$\pi^m(s^m, a^m) = \frac{e^{\hat{u}_t^m(s^m, a^m)/T_B}}{\sum_{a'^m \in \mathbf{A}^m} e^{\hat{u}_t^m(s^m, a'^m)/T_B}}, \forall m \in \mathbf{M} \tag{7.50}$$

where T_B is the Boltzmann temperature. High temperatures make all actions almost equiprobable, whereas low temperatures result in the large difference of selection probabilities.

The proof of the convergence of the presented autonomous multi-agent Q-learning method given by Eq. (7.49) is provided in [174]. The learning rate α_t and the parameters β_t^m are set in accordance with

$$\alpha_t = \frac{1}{(t + c_\alpha)^{\zeta_\alpha}} \beta_t^m = \frac{1}{(t + c_\beta)^{\zeta_\beta^m}}, \forall m \in \mathbf{M} \tag{7.51}$$

where $c_\alpha > 0$, $c_\beta > 0$, $\zeta_\alpha \in (1/2, 1]$, $\zeta_\beta^m \in (1/2, 1]$. The algorithm for autonomous channel and power level selection by D2D pairs is outlined in Figure 7.1 [174].

7.4 ML for Self-Organizing Cellular Networks

In this section, we discuss different aspects of using ML algorithms for self-organizing cellular networks. For future networks to overcome the current limitations and address the problems of current cellular systems, it is clear that more intelligence needs to be deployed, so that a fully autonomous and flexible network can be enabled. This section focuses on the learning perspective of self-organizing network (SON) solutions and first provides an overview of the most common ML techniques encountered in SONs and then some specific examples in more detail.

Algorithm: Autonomous multi-agent Q-learning Process Based on Players' Beliefs
Initialization:

Set time $t \leftarrow 0$ and the parameters γ, c_α, c_β, ζ_α;

For all $m \in \mathbf{M}$ **do**
{

Set the parameter ζ^m_β;

For all $s^m \in \mathbf{S}^m$, $a^m \in \mathbf{A}^m$ **do**
{

Initialize the action-value $\hat{u}^m_t (s^m, a^m) \leftarrow 0$,

$$\text{strategy } \pi^m (s^m, a^m) \leftarrow \frac{1}{|\mathbf{A}^m|} = \frac{1}{KJ}, \text{ and belief Y } (s^m, a^m) \leftarrow 0;$$

Initialize the state $s^m \leftarrow s^m_t = 0$;

}
Main Loop:

While $(t < T)$ **do**
{

For all PU_m, $m \in \mathbf{M}$ **do**
{

Update the learning rate α_t and the parameter β^m_t according to **(7.51)**

Select an action a^m according to the strategy $\pi^m (s^m)$;

Measure the achieved SINR at the receiver;

If ($SINR^m (t) \geq SIMR^m_{\min}$) **then set** $s^m_t \leftarrow 1$ **else set** $s^m_t \leftarrow 0$;

Update the instantaneous reward umt according to **(7.34a)**

Update the action-value $\hat{u}^m_{t+1} (s^m, a^m)$ according to **(7.49)**

Update the strategy $\pi^m (s^m, a^m)$ according to **(7.50)**

Update the belief $\hat{Y} (s^m, \mathbf{a}^{-m})$ according to **(7.48)**

Upate time $t \leftarrow t + 1$ and the state $s^m \leftarrow s^m_t$;

}

}

Figure 7.1 Algorithm for autonomous channel and power level selection. *Source:* Asheralieva and Miyanaga [174].

A SON can be defined as an adaptive and autonomous network that is also scalable, stable, and agile enough to maintain its desired objectives [176, 177]. Hence, these networks are not only able to independently decide when and how certain actions will be triggered, based on their continuous interaction with the environment, but are also able to learn and improve their performance based on previous actions taken by the system. The concept of SON in mobile networks can also be divided into three main categories – self-configuration, self-optimization, and self-healing – and are commonly denoted jointly as self-x functions.

Self-configuration can be defined as all the configuration procedures necessary to make the network operable. These configuration parameters can come in the form of individual BS configuration parameters, such as IP configuration, neighbor cell list (NCL) configuration, radio and cell parameter configuration, or configurations that will be applied to the whole network, such as policies. Self-configuration is mainly activated whenever a new BS is deployed in the system, but it can also be activated if there is a change in the system (for example, a BS failure or change of service or network policies). After the system has been correctly configured, the self-optimization function is triggered. *Self-optimization phase* can be defined as the functions that continuously optimize the BSs and network parameters in order to guarantee a near-optimal performance. Self-optimization can occur in terms of backhaul optimization, caching, coverage and capacity optimization, antenna parameter optimization, interference management, mobility optimization, handover (HO) parameter optimization, load balancing, resource optimization, Call Admission Control, energy efficiency optimization, and coordination of SON functions. By monitoring the system continuously, and using reported measurements to gather information, self-optimization functions can ensure that the objectives are maintained and that the overall performance of the network is near optimum.

Self-healing function can also be triggered in parallel to self-optimization. Since no system is perfect, faults and failures can occur unexpectedly, and it is no different with cellular systems. Whenever a fault or failure occurs, for whatever reason (e.g., software or hardware malfunction), the self-healing function is activated. Its objective is to continuously monitor the system in order to ensure a fast and seamless recovery. Self-healing functions should be able not only to detect the failure events but also to diagnose the failure (i.e., determine why it happened) and also trigger the appropriate compensation mechanisms, so that the network can return to function properly. Self-healing in cellular systems can occur in terms of network troubleshooting (fault detection), fault classification, and cell outage management [177–180].

Also, each SON function can be divided into subsections, commonly known as use cases. Figure 7.2 shows an outline of the most common use cases of each SON task.

7.4.1   Learning in Self-Configuration

Self-configuration can be defined as the process of automatically configuring all the parameters of network equipment, such as BSs, relay stations, and femtocells. In addition, self-configuration can also be deployed after the network is already operable. This may happen whenever a new BS is

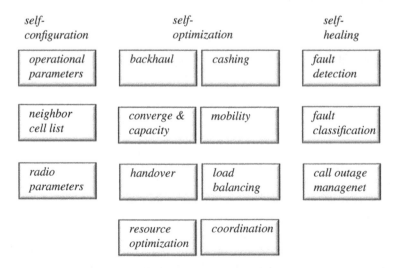

Figure 7.2   Major use cases of each self-organizing network (SON) function. *Source:* Based on Aliu et al. [176].

added to the system or if the network is recovering from a fault and needs to reconfigure its parameters. In [181], for example, the authors propose a generic framework in order to tackle the problem of self-configuration, self-optimization, and self-healing. From the perspective of self-configuration, the authors provide some basic steps that are needed to achieve an autonomous deployment of the network:

---

1) The authors assert that a BS should already have its basic operational parameters configured before being deployed, so that professionals are not required to deploy it.
2) The second stage consists of scanning and determining the BS's neighbors and creating an NCL.
3) The new deployed BS configures its remaining parameters, and the network adjusts the topology to accommodate it.

Other authors, such as in [182], propose a solution based on an assisted approach, in which after the deployment of a new BS, it senses and chooses a neighbor and requests it to download all the necessary operational parameters. After that, the BS configures its remaining parameters automatically. Regardless of the approach taken, it can be seen that both solutions have a few steps in common:

---

1) Configuration of operational parameters.
2) Determination of new BS neighbors and creation of NCL.
3) Configuration of the remaining radio-related parameters and adjustment of network topology.

To perform self-configuration, several learning techniques are being applied not only to configure basic operational parameters but also to discover BSs' neighbors and perform an initial configuration of radio parameters. However, due to the increasingly complexity of BSs, which are expected to have thousands of different parameters that can be configured (many with dependencies between each other) and the possibility of new BSs joining the network or existing ones failing and disappearing from their neighbors' lists, the process of self-configuration still poses quite a challenge for researchers. Based on these steps, three major use cases of self-configuration can be defined and are reviewed below, together with their ML solutions.

Operational parameter configuration is the first stage of self-configuration and consists of the basic configuration of a BS, in which it learns its parameters so that it can become operable. These parameters can be the IP address, access GateWay (aGW), Cell IDentity (CID), and Physical Cell Identity. In addition to these parameters, other authors, such as in [183] and [184], also propose to perform network planning in an autonomous way. In [183], the authors propose a framework to characterize the main key performance indicators (KPIs) in an LTE cellular system. After that, the authors' hybrid approach, which combines holistic planning with a semi-analytic model, is used to formulate a multi-objective optimization problem and determine the best cell planning parameters, such as BS location, number of sectors, antenna height, antenna azimuth, antenna tilt, transmission power, and frequency reuse factor. On the other hand, authors from [184] develop a SOM solution to optimize the network parameters of a Code Division Multiple Access network. The solution optimizes not only planning parameters, such as the number of BSs in a certain area and their location, but also radio parameters, like an antenna's maximum transmit power and its beam pattern. Regarding the configuration of basic parameters, several works have been proposed, such as in [185–187]. In [185], the authors develop a last-hop backhaul-oriented solution covering all aspects of SON: self-configuration, self-optimization, and self-healing. In [186, 187], the authors propose a self-configuring assisted solution for the deployment of a new BS without a dedicated backhaul interface for LTE networks. According to the authors, first, the new BS should get the IP addresses of itself and the Operation, Administration and Maintenance center. This can be done via the Dynamic Host Configuration Protocol (DHCP), BOOTstrap Protocol, or by multicast by using the Internet Group Management Protocol. After that, the new BS searches nearby neighbors and connects with one of them to request and download the remaining operational and radio parameters.

An illustration of using TL for updating state information is shown in Figure 7.3. For additional information on ML techniques used for implementing SON functions from Figure 7.2, see [177].

7.4.2   RL for SON Coordination

To bring down the capital and operational expenditures, an operator can automate the parameter tuning on the small cells through the so-called SON functionalities, such as cell range expansion, mobility robustness optimization, or enhanced Inter-Cell Interference Coordination. Having several of these functionalities in the network will surely create conflicts, as, for example, they may try to change the same parameter in the opposite directions. This raises a need for a SON COordinator (SONCO) whose role is to arbitrate the parameter change requests of the SON functions, ensuring some degree of fairness. In this section, we present SON optimization using this approach mainly along the lines presented in [188].

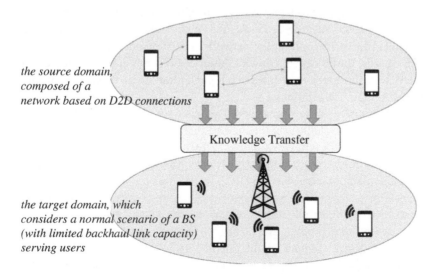

the source domain, composed of a network based on D2D connections

Knowledge Transfer

the target domain, which considers a normal scenario of a BS (with limited backhaul link capacity) serving users

Figure 7.3   Transfer learning (TL)-based network state information updating. *Source:* Based on *P.V. Klaine, et al.* [176].

7.4.3 SON Function Model

Consider a network segment composed of N cells, macro and pico, indexed by $n \in N = \{1, \dots, N'\}$. We define a set of K parameters (e.g., *Cell Individual Offset, Hysteresis, antenna tilt*) that can be tuned on every cell. We index them by $k \in K = \{1, \dots, K\}$. Each parameter k on cell n belongs to a finite set of values $P_n(k)$. Let P_t denote the network parameter configuration at time t. We note $P_t = (P_{t,n})_{n \in N}$, where $P_{t,n} = (P_{t,n}(1), \dots, P_{t,n}(K))$ is the set of parameters corresponding to cell n at time. We denote by $P = \prod_n P_n$ the set of possible values of P_t, where $P_n = \prod_k P_n(k)$.

Consider Z SON functions (e.g., CRE (*Cell Range Expansion*), MRO (*Mobility Robustness Optimization*), eICIC (*enhanced Inter-Cell Interference Coordination*)) indexed by $z \in Z = \{1, \dots, Z'\}$. Each SON function is instantiated on each and every cell. The instance of SON function z on cell n creates an update request $U_{t,n,z}$ to increase/decrease/maintain some of the parameters of cell n. We use the notation $U_{t,n,z} = (U_{t,n,z}(1), \dots, U_{t,n,z}(K))$, where $U_{t,n,z}(k)$ is the request targeting parameter k. In the literature, we typically find update requests encompassing three possible values representing the request to increase, decrease, and maintain the value of the targeted parameter. It also specifies by how much the value should be changed. In [188], update requests also include the information on how critical they are. This sort of information allows one to judiciously tackle a conflict in favor of the most critical request, thus enforcing a certain degree of fairness among the SON functions.

Here, the update is a real value for which we adopt the following convention:

- The case $U_{t,n,z}(k) > 0$ is an increase request. The bigger $|U_{t,n,z}(k)|$ is, the more critical the request is.
- The case $U_{t,n,z}(k) < 0$ is a decrease request. Again, the bigger $|U_{t,n,z}(k)|$ is, the more critical the request is.
- The case $U_{t,n,z}(k) = 0$ is a maintain request.
- The case $U_{t,n,z}(k) =$ void: we say that there is no request, meaning that the SON instance has no incentive to increase, decrease, or maintain the value of parameter k.

Let $U_t = (U_{t,n,z})_{n, z}$ be the vector of all requests at time t. Formally, U_t belongs to a set $U = (\mathbb{R} \cup \{\text{void}\})^{NZK}$.

SON coordination: Instead of directly executing the desired parameter changes in the network, the SON instances send update requests to a SONCO instance, which decides if they are accepted (and immediately enforced) or denied. The SON instances are seen as black boxes by the SONCO, so it does not know the algorithm running inside them. It knows only the current update requests (U_t) and the current network parameter configuration (P_t). The task of the SONCO is to find an equitable conflict resolution to ensure some degree of fairness among the SON instances. To be precise, by being fair we mean that in case we are faced with a conflict situation, we will choose which requests to accept such that at the next time step the maximum criticalness ($\max_{n,k,z} |U_{t,n,z}(k)|$) among all requests is minimized.

The SON instances are considered to be synchronized. They send the update requests simultaneously at the end of a periodic time window. The SONCO is also synchronized with the SON instances. It receives the update requests from all the SON instances and decides which requests are accepted and which are denied. An RL approach is employed as it enables us to incorporate the past experience into the decision process; thus, we make use of the time dimension in this optimization. This information is stored in value functions that reflect how satisfied the SON functions were with a given configuration. RL is founded on the MDP, which we describe in the following.

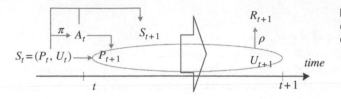

Figure 7.4 Transition kernel: Markov decision process model of the system dynamics.

MDP models the system dynamics as an interplay between the current network parameter configuration P_t, the SON update requests U_t, and the SONCO decisions A_t. To that end, we interpret them as stochastic processes on some probability space, which are governed by the following MDP (see also in Figure 7.4):

1) *State space:* A state s is written as $s = (s_1, \ldots, s_{N'})$, where for any $n \in N$, $s_n = (p_n, u_{n,1}, \ldots, u_{n,z})$ contains the network parameter configuration (p_n) and update requests $(u_{n,z}, \forall z)$ corresponding to cell n. We denote the state space by S. We define $S_t = (P_t, U_t)$ as the state process.

2) *Action space:* $A = A_1 \times \ldots \times A_{N'}$, where $\forall n \in N$, $A_n = \{\pm 1, 0\}^K$. An action $a \in A$ is written as $a = (a_1, \ldots, a_{N'})$, where for each $n \in N$, $a_n = (a_n(1), \ldots, a_n(K))$ is a vector of size K. The action component $a_n(k)$ allows one to increase/decrease the value of a parameter k on cell n only if there exists at least one request to do so, and if the value is not already the maximum/minimum value in the set of possible values $P_n(k)$. To be specific, the next value of parameter k of cell n given the current value $p_n(k)$ is

$$
p'_n(k) = \begin{cases}
\min\,\{x \in P_n(k) : x > p_n(k)\}, \\
\quad \text{if } a_n(k) > 0, p_n(k) \neq \max P_n(k) \\
\quad \text{and } \exists z \in Z \text{ s.t. } u_{n,z}(k) > 0 \\
\max\{x \in P_n(k) : x < p_n(k)\}, \\
\quad \text{if } a_n(k) < 0, p_n(k) \neq \min P_n(k) \\
\quad \text{and } \exists z \in Z \text{ s.t. } u_{n,z}(k) < 0, \\
p_n(k), \text{otherwise.}
\end{cases}
\tag{7.52}
$$

As can be seen from Eq. (7.52), the vector p' representing the next network parameter configuration is a deterministic function of the current parameter configuration p, the update requests u, and the actions a; that is,

$$
p' = g((p, u), a),
\tag{7.53}
$$

where the function $g: P \times U \times A \to P$ is detailed in Eq. (7.52).

3) *Transition kernel:* Let us describe the probability that $s' = (p', u')$ is the next state given that $s = (p, u)$ is the current state and the action is a. Recall the key specificity of our transition kernel mentioned above: p' is entirely determined by $(s, a): p' = g(s, a)$. Random effects are used only to model the values of the next update requests. Recall also that the algorithm inside the SON functions is assumed to be unknown, and so this lack of knowledge is grasped by the transition kernel. Moreover, we make the assumption that the SON functions are memory-less: their output at time $t + 1$ depends only on their inputs at time $t + 1$, which depend only on the network parameter configuration at time $t + 1$. This is typically the case for early SON function designs. Formally stated, we assume for state transition probability

$$\mathbb{P}(U_{t+1} = u' \mid S_t = s, A_t = a, P_{t+1} = p')$$
$$= \mathbb{P}(U_{t+1} = u' \mid P_{t+1} = p'). \tag{7.54}$$

Now, from Eq. (7.53) and the chain rule, our transition kernel model is

$$\mathbb{P}(P_{t+1} = p', U_{t+1} = u' \mid S_t = s, A_t = a)$$
$$= \mathbb{I}_{\{p' = g(s,a)\}}\mathbb{P}(U_{t+1} = u' \mid P_{t+1} = p'), \tag{7.55}$$

where $\mathbb{I}$ is the indicator function $\left(\mathbb{I}_{\{\text{true}\}} = 1, \mathbb{I}_{\{\text{false}\}} = 0\right)$.

4) *Regret:* $r(s, a)$ is the regret associated with the state-action pair (s, a). We introduce $(R_t)_t$ as the process of instantaneous regrets. We consider that $\forall t$

$$\mathbb{E}[R_{t+1} \mid S_t = s, A_t = a] = r(s,a), \text{where } R_t = \rho(U_t), \tag{7.56}$$

for some function $\rho : U \to \mathbb{R}$. Typically, the lower the number of increase/decrease requests (or the lower in absolute value they are), the smaller the regret. As an application of the transition kernel, using Eqs. (7.56) and (7.54), note that

$$r(s,a) = \mathbb{E}[\rho(U_{t+1}) \mid P_{t+1} = g(s,a)]. \tag{7.57}$$

A policy π is a transition kernel π on $S \times 2^A$, such that $\pi(s, \{a\})$ represents the probability of taking action a when the current state is s:

$$\mathbb{P}_\pi(A_t = a \mid S_t = s) = \pi(s,a). \tag{7.58}$$

Value function definitions: For any policy π, to measure its performance, we introduce the state-value function (V^π) and the action-value function (Q^π):

$$V^\pi(s) = \mathbb{E}_\pi\left[\sum_{t=0}^\infty \gamma^t \, R_{t+1} \mid S_0 = s\right], \tag{7.59}$$

$$Q^\pi(s, a) = \mathbb{E}_\pi\left[\sum_{t=0}^\infty \gamma^t \, R_{t+1} \mid S_0 = s, A_0 = a\right], \tag{7.60}$$

where $0 \leq \gamma < 1$ is the regret sum discount factor, and $\mathbb{E}_\pi$ is the expectation given that the followed policy is π. $V^*(s)$ is the *optimal value* of state $s \in S$, if it returns the smallest achievable expected value when the process starts from state s:

$$V^*(s) \leq V^\pi(s), \tag{7.61}$$

for any policy π. Similarly, the *optimal action-value* corresponding to state-action pair (s, a), $Q^*(s, a)$ is defined as the minimum expected regret given that the process starts in state s and the first action is a.

Action-value function simplification: We first define $\hat{r} : P \to \mathbb{R}$, where

$$\hat{r}(p) = \mathbb{E}[\rho(U_1) \mid P_1 = p]. \tag{7.62}$$

It was shown in [188] that for any policy π there exists a function $W^\pi : P \to \mathbb{R}$, such that for any

$$(s, a) \in S \times A,$$
$$Q^\pi(s, a) = W^\pi(g(s,a)). \tag{7.63}$$

Moreover, W^π solves the following fixed-point equation:

$$W^\pi(p) = \hat{r}(p) + \gamma \sum_{u \in U} \mathbb{P}[U_1 = u \mid P_1 = p]$$
$$\times \sum_{a \in A} \pi((p, u), a) \cdot W^\pi(g((p, u), a)). \tag{7.64}$$

This allows us to reduce the action-value function domain size (i.e., the state-action space) to $|P|$ as W^π is defined on P. The optimal policy π^* is known to be a deterministic policy, that is (using a small notation abuse) $\pi^*: S \to A$ and we have: $\pi^*(s) = \arg\min_a Q^*(s, a)$, where Q^* is the *optimal action-value function*. The optimal policy can be derived as

$$W^*(p) = \hat{r}(p) + \gamma \sum_{u \in U} \mathbb{P}[U_1 = u \mid P_1 = p] W^*(p^*),$$
$$p^* = g((p, u), a^*), \tag{7.65}$$
$$a^* = \pi^*(p, u) = \arg\min_{a \in A} W^*(g((p, u), a))$$

Linear function approximation: Although the above discussion allows to simplify Eq. (7.60) to a set of functions with a reduced domain (*state space*) P, the complexity still scales exponentially with the number of cells N'. Therefore, in the following we perform a linear function approximation (LFA), which comes at the cost of possible performance losses.

We approximate $W^*(p)$ by some $\overline{W}^*(p)$ that depends on p through a linear function of some features (p). Let J be the number of features, that is, $P \to \mathbb{R}^J$. The choice of the features is very important, and it is case specific. We provide examples in the sequel. Thus, $\overline{W}^*$ is given by

$$\overline{W}^*(p) = \langle \theta^*, F(p) \rangle, \tag{7.66}$$

where $\langle x, y \rangle$ is the scalar product of x and y, and θ^* should minimize the mean square error:

$$\theta^* = \arg\min_{\theta \in \mathbb{R}^J} \sum_{p \in P'} (W^*(p) - \langle \theta, F(p) \rangle)^2. \tag{7.67}$$

Under these conditions, we have to provide a method of estimating θ^* and approximating the optimal policy. For this, the next section presents a method based on RL.

7.4.4 Reinforcement Learning

Algorithm: We cannot directly calculate $\overline{W}^*$ as we have only partial knowledge of the transition kernel. Instead, according to [189], we can use the flowing recursion:

$$\theta_{t+1} = \theta_t + \alpha[R_t + \gamma \min_{a \in A} \langle \theta_t, F(g((P_t, U_t), a)) \rangle - \langle \theta_t, F(P_t) \rangle] F(P_t). \tag{7.68}$$

Consequently, it would be natural to define the action at time t as

$$\bar{A}_t = \arg\min_{a \in A} \langle \theta_t, F(g((P_t, U_t), a)) \rangle. \tag{7.69}$$

In practice, the construction of the feature function F (as suggested earlier) is insensitive to certain components of the parameter P_t and their associated actions. This means that we may have several potential outputs of the *arg min* in Eq. (7.69). One option is to randomly choose one of them. However, we choose to select the one that leads to the biggest number of parameter changes, or in other words, we select the output that maximizes the number of change requests.

To ensure that the entire state space is explored (see [189]), we choose an ε-greedy policy with respect to $\bar{A}_t$ as follows:

$$\pi_t((P_t, U_t), \{a\}) = \left((1-\varepsilon)\mathbb{I}_{\{a = \bar{A}_t\}} + \frac{\varepsilon}{3^{NK}}\right). \tag{7.70}$$

This means that during $100\varepsilon\%$ of the time we *explore* and during the rest of the time we *exploit*. The SONCO algorithm is summarized in Algorithm 1.

Algorithm 1 SONCO $(\alpha, \gamma, \epsilon)$

Function Init:
Initialize $\theta = \mathbf{0}$
Function SONCO:
Observe current parameter configurations p and update requests u, calculate regret $r = \rho(u)$.
Compute $\bar{a} = \arg\min_{a \in \mathcal{A}} \langle \theta, F(g((p, u), a)) \rangle$.
Update $\theta = \theta + \alpha \left[r + \gamma \langle \theta, F(g((p, u), \bar{a})) \rangle - \langle \theta, F(p) \rangle \right]$
$F(p)$.
Choose current action a using the ϵ-greedy policy:
$\pi((p, u), \{a\}) = (1 - \epsilon)\mathbb{I}_{\{a=\bar{a}\}} + \frac{\epsilon}{3^{NK}}$.
Take action a.

Source: Iacoboaiea et al. [188].

Multidimensional regret: In one of our example scenarios, which will be fully detailed later, we want to make use of linear features (where $F(p)$ is a linear function of the components of the vector p), as it is a widely used method to reduce the state space [189]. However, not every function can be approximated accurately enough by means of linear features. If we look at our regret expression $R_t = \rho(U_t)$, we presume that this would likely be the case, as it is a function of all the update requests. Thus, it was proposed to have a vector of regrets of size $D : R_t = (R_{t, d})_{d \in \mathcal{D}} \in \mathbb{R}^D (\mathcal{D} = \{1, \dots, D\})$. In this case, each component $R_{t,d}$ would be defined as a function ρ_d that takes as argument the value of only one (or a small number of) update request(s). For example, for some $d \in D$ such that ρ_d is a function of only $U_{n, z}(k)$ $(n, z, k$ arbitrarily chosen), we could have

$$\rho_d(U_t) = |U_{n,k}(z)| \mathbb{I}_{\{U_{n,k}(z) > 0\}}. \tag{7.71}$$

More details will be presented later on in section examples. Now that we have clarified the importance of this multidimensional regret, we analyze how this impacts the above framework.

For $D = 1$, obviously we remain within the above framework. For $D > 1$, the framework is still valid up to a certain point. The extension of the definitions of the value functions V in Eq. (7.59) and Q in Eq. (7.60) is straightforward; they simply become vectors of size D. The first bottleneck is the optimal policy as *arg min* no longer has a sense for the multidimensional Q-function. To solve this problem, we first define a methodology to compare vectors.

Consider two vectors of size $D : x, y \in \mathbb{R}^D$. Let $x', y' \in \mathbb{R}^D$ be x and y sorted in descending order, respectively; that is, $x'(1) > x'(2) > \dots$ If $x'(1) > y'(1)$, we say that x is larger than y (we write $x \succ y$). If $x'(1) < y'(1)$, we say that x is smaller than y (we write $x \prec y$). If $x'(1) = y'(1)$, then we compare $x'(2)$ and $y'(2)$ in the same way, and so on. If $x'(d) = y'(d)$ for all $d \in \mathcal{D}$, than we say that the two vectors are *equal* (we write $x \asymp y$). Note that $x \asymp y$ is not the same thing as $x = y$. For $D = 1$, this is consistent with the scalar comparison rules.

By extending the previous framework for any value of D, we say that a policy π^* is optimal if it achieves the optimal value function ($V^*(s)$) in all states ($\forall s \in S$); that is, for any policy π:

$$V^*(s) \leq V^\pi(s). \tag{7.72}$$

To simplify matters for $D > 1$, we consider only the cases with $\gamma = 0$, that is, myopic policies. It is straightforward to see that the value function of any policy (including the optimal) is given by

$$Q^*(s,a) = Q^\pi(s,a) = r(s,a). \tag{7.73}$$

Using the same reasoning as in the unidimensional case, we end up estimating a $W^*(p)$ that is a vector of size D; that is, $W^*(p) = \left(W_d^*(p)\right)_{d \in D}$. In this case, we will approximate each component $W_d^*(p)$ using a set of linear features $F_d(p): P \to \mathbb{R}^J$; that is, $\overline{W}_d^*(p) = \langle \theta_d^*, F_d(p) \rangle$. Thus, $F(p)$ and θ become matrices of size $[D \times J]$. Finally, Algorithm 1 still holds, but we extend the definition of $\langle x, y \rangle$ for x, y matrices of size $[D \times J]$ as

$$\langle x,y \rangle = \left(\left\langle \left(x_{d,j}\right)_j, \left(y_{d,j}\right)_j \right\rangle \right)_{d \in D} = \left(x_{d,1}y_{d,1} + \ldots + x_{d,J}y_{d,J}\right)_{d \in D}. \tag{7.74}$$

Note that this is coherent with the unidimensional case ($D = 1$).

Design Example 7.1

The simulation results for the scenario specified in Figure 7.5 obtained in [188] are shown in Figure 7.6. Before we discuss the results, let us look more closely at the assumptions used in the simulation.

As indicated in Figure 7.5, we have a network segment with macro and pico cells. The pico cells are intended to help the macro cells by providing them with a capacity increase. In this sense, we say that a macro cell may have several *slave* pico cells when the pico cells are under the coverage of the macro cell.

In this scenario, a pico cell is assumed to be the slave of one and only one macro cell. We identify a *cell cluster* to be composed of a macro cell and its slave pico cells. On this note, we consider one independent SONCO instance to govern each cell cluster; that is, we apply the previously described framework per cell cluster. First, we describe in detail the design of such an instance, and afterward we present the scenario that contains several cell clusters (as shown in Figure 7.5) and which implicitly makes use of several independent SONCO instances.

To simplify the SONCO instance description, we limit the view to one cell cluster. As mentioned above, a cell cluster contains one macro cell and several pico cells. We consider that the macro cell has the index $n = 1$; see Figure 7.7. Thus, let $N_M = \{1\}$ and $N_P = \{N - N_M\}$.

Before introducing the SON functions that we use, we introduce some network parameters. There are three parameters ($K = \{1, 2, 3\}$) of interest: the *Cell Individual Offset* (CIO, $k = 1$), the *HandOver* (HO) *Hysteresis* (HYS, $k = 2$), and the number of *Almost Blank Subframes* (ABS, $k = 3$). The CIO and the HYS are used in mobility management as follows: a user equipment (UE) that wants to transmit data will attach to cell $n_0 = \arg\max_{n \in N}(RSRP_n + CIO_n)$, where $RSRP_n$ is the Reference Signal Received Power from cell n, and CIO_n is the CIO of cell n [190]. When attached to a serving cell $n_S(\forall n_S \in N)$, a UE performs an HO to a target cell $n_T \neq n_S$ if $n_T = \arg\max_{n \in N}\left(RSRP_n + CIO_n + HYS_{n_S}\mathbb{I}_{\{n = n_S\}}\right)$, where HYS_{n_S} is the HYS of cell n_S.

Design Example 7.1 (Continued)

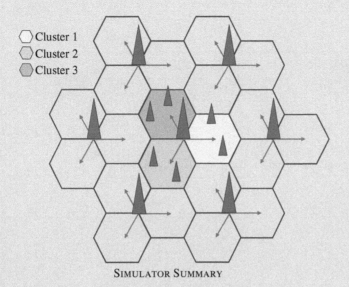

Cluster 1
Cluster 2
Cluster 3

SIMULATOR SUMMARY

Parameter	Value
Number cells	21 macro cells, 6 pico cells
Propagation Model	3GPP Case 3 [34],
HetNet	macro + pico
Carrier	2 GHz
Bandwidth	10 MHz
TxPow	49 dBm/30 dBm
Traffic type	FTP-like, constant file size
File size	16[Mb/UE]
$\Lambda_G \cdot FS$	14[Mb/s/Macro Hexagons Area]
$\Lambda_{HS} \cdot FS$	14[Mb/s/Pico HS Area]

Figure 7.5 Simulation scenario: network and traffic parameters. *Source:* Iacoboaiea et al. [188].

The ABS establishes the number of subframes where the cell will not transmit data to reduce interference to the neighbors [191]. It is used to protect the UEs that are at the cell edge.

Three SON functions ($z = \{1, 2, 3\}$) are defined for a cell cluster: the (MLB via) CRE function ($z = 1$), the MRO function ($z = 2$), and the eICIC function ($z = 3$).

In brief, the CRE is a function that keeps the load of the macro cell lower than a given threshold by tuning the CIOs of the slave pico cells so that part of the load can be off-loaded to them when needed. The MRO aims to reduce the number of ping-pong HOs and of too late HOs [188] originating from the pico cells by tuning the CIO and the HYS on the pico cells. The eICIC aims to protect the users that have been forced to HO from the macro cell to the slave pico cells by tuning the number of ABSs on the macro cell.

(Continued)

Design Example 7.1 (Continued)

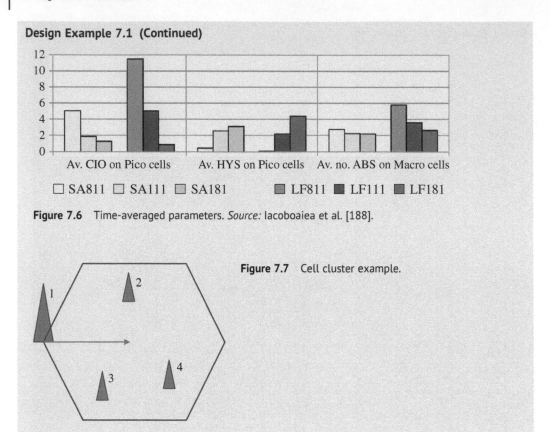

Figure 7.6 Time-averaged parameters. *Source:* Iacoboaiea et al. [188].

Figure 7.7 Cell cluster example.

Design Example 7.2

In this design example, we apply the described framework and elaborate on two SONCO designs [188]:

- *The State Aggregation (SA) design*
- *The Linear Features (LF) design*

1) *SA Design:* In this case, we consider $D = 1$. We compute the (unidimensional) regret as the maximum of the absolute values of the non-void update requests that target the CIO ($k = 1$) or the ABS ($k = 3$). The update requests targeting the HYS ($k = 2$) are not included as we assume that they do not create significant conflict problems; such requests are sent only by the MRO, and they do not significantly affect the inputs of the CRE or of the eICIC. Thus:

$$R_t = \rho(U_t) = \max_{(n,k,z) \in O} w_z \mid U_{t,n,z}[k] \mid , \tag{7.75}$$

where w_z represent the weight per SON function and $O = N_M \times \{3\} \times \{3\} \cup N_P \times \{1\} \times \{1, 2\}$ is composed of the $(n, k, z) \in N \times K \times Z$ pairs of interest. The weights are to be chosen by the network operator according to its priorities. For example, if the HO failures must be avoided at all cost, then the operator should give a bigger weight to the SON functions that optimize this, say MRO. In a realistic setting, it will be necessary to even define such weights on a per-SON-instance basis, to assess the numerous deployment-specific factors such as the environment (rural/urban) and the network lifecycle time (new/mature). Thus, a translation is needed from the high

Design Example 7.2 (Continued)

operator objectives to the low technical objectives. Such details can be found in [192]. Next, we set the number of features J to be the number of possible values corresponding to the set of parameters $\bar{p} = (p_n(k))_{(n,k) \in \bar{O}}$ where $O = (n,k)\{(n,k)\} : \exists z$ s.t. $(n,k,z) \in O\} = N_M \times \{3\} \cup N_P \times \{1\}$ represents the targeted parameters of the update requests in O. Thus, $J = \prod_{(n,k) \in \bar{O}} |P_n(k)|$ and let $\tau : \{1, ..., J\} \rightarrow \prod_{(n,k) \in \bar{O}} P_n(k)$ be a bijection that attributes an index to the mentioned values. Finally, we define the feature vector as $(p) = \left(\mathbb{I}_{\{\bar{p} = \tau(j)\}}\right)_j$. This is equivalent to what is called in the literature an *SA* ([189]). More details can be found in the following table [188].

SONCO Designs: State Aggregation (SA) and Linear Features (LFs)		
SONCO design	SA	LFs
SON functions	CRE ($z = 1$), MRO ($z = 2$), eICIC ($z = 3$), $\mathcal{Z}=\{1,2,3\}$	
Tuned parameters	CIO ($k = 1$), HYS ($k = 2$), ABS($k = 3$), $\mathcal{K} = (1,2,3)$	
CIO set [dB] $\mathcal{P}_n[1]$	$\{0,2, ..., 12\}$ if n > 1	$\{0, 1, ..., 12\}$ if n > 1
	$\{0\}$ if n = 1	$\{0\}$ if n = 1
HYS set [dB] $\mathcal{P}_n[2]$	$\{0,1, ..., 12\}$ if n > 1	
	$\{2\}$ if n = 1	
ABS set [#]	$\{0\}$ if n > 1	(out of 10)
	$\{0, 1, 8\}$ if n = 1,	
Time window T	5 minutes	
SONCO (α, γ, ε)	(0.2, 0.5, 0.1)	(0.5, 0.0, 0.1)
Regret dimension D	1	$2 (1 + 2|\mathcal{N}_p|)$

Note that we choose to use a smaller number of CIO possible values (thus reducing the state space) as the memory requirements for the SA design are very large and the convergence is very slow. Even with this assistance, SA design is still considerably slower than LF design.

2) *LF Design:* In this case, we consider $D = 2 |O| = 2(2N - 1) > 1$, more precisely two regret components for each of the previously mentioned update requests. Thus, the regret becomes $R_t = (R_{t, d})_{d \in D}$. Let η be a bijection: $O \times \{-1, 1\} \rightarrow D$. Thus, for $d \in D$ we consider

$$R_{t,d} = w_z \mid U_{t,n,z}(k) \mid \mathbb{I}_{\{U_{t,n,z}(k) \cdot h \geq 0\}}, \tag{7.76}$$

where $(n, k, z, h) = \eta(d)$. So (for $R_{t,d}$) the corresponding value function component, that is, W_d^* (the d-th sub-component of the vector W^*) is approximated as follows:

- For $z = 1$ (CRE signature), $k = 1$ (target CIO) and $n \in N_P$ (pico cells); and for $z = 3$ (eICIC signature), $k = 3$ (target ABS) and $n = 1$ (macro cell) we approximate W_d^* with a linear function of the CIOs of the cells $n' \in N_P$, the *ABS* cell $n' = 1$, and a constant,
- For $z = 2$ (MRO signature), $k = 1$ (target CIO), and $n \in N_P$ (pico cells) we approximate W_d^* with a linear function of the CIO of cell n and a constant,

Thus, for the feature vector we set $J = N + 1$ and define $F_d(p)$, where $\eta^{-1}(d) = (n, z, k, h)$, as:

$$F_d(p) = \begin{cases} (1 \quad 0.1p_1(3) \quad 0.1p_2(1) \dots 0.1p_N(1)), & \text{if } z \neq 2 \\ (1 \quad 0.1p_n(1) \quad 0 \dots 0), & \text{if } z = 2. \end{cases} \tag{7.77}$$

Note that we use a 0.1 coefficient for some features to reduce the size of the update of the corresponding components of θ. This makes the algorithm more stable in the sense that it does not diverge. The size of $F(p)$ (disregarding the zero padding for $z = 2$) is $(N + 1)$

(Continued)

Design Example 7.2 (Continued)

$(|N_P| + 1) + 2 |N_P| = N'^2 + 3N' - 2$. More details on SONCO parameters for SA and LF can be found in the above table titled "SONCO Designs: State Aggregation (SA) and Linear Features (LFs)." As mentioned earlier, the LF design is myopic; that is, $\beta = 0$. The parameter α was chosen bigger than in the SA design to compensate the 0.1 coefficient from the feature vector (Eq. (7.77)).

3) *SA versus LF Design:*

  a) *Optimization target:* Leaving aside the approximations performed in the two designs, a closer look reveals a small difference in regard to what they optimize. The two targets can be summarized as follows:

- SA: minimization of the expected worst regret:

$$min_{\pi} \mathbb{E}_{\pi} \left[\sum_{t} \gamma^t \ max_{(n,k,z)\in 0} \ \mathrm{w}_z \mid U_{t,z,n}(k) \mid \right]$$

$$= min_{\pi} \mathbb{E}_{\pi} \left[\sum_{t} \gamma^t \ max_{(n,k,z)\in 0 \times \{\pm 1\}} \ \mathrm{w}_z \mid U_{t,z,n}(k) \mid \mathbb{I}_{\{u_{z,n}(k)h > 0\}} \right], \tag{7.78}$$

- LF: minimization of the worst expected regret:

$$min_{\pi} \ max_{(n,k,z)\in 0 \times \{\pm 1\}} \mathbb{E}_{\pi} \left[\sum_{t} \gamma^t w_z \mid U_{t,z,n}(k) \mid \mathbb{I}_{\{U_{t,z,n}(k)h > 0\}} \right], \tag{7.79}$$

with a myopic approach; that is, $\gamma = 0$. One can see that the outcomes of the two approaches are mathematically different but they have the same purpose, which is to provide a sense of fairness among the SON functions, as they minimize the maximum *criticalness* among the requests of the SON functions.

Results: As pointed out at the beginning of this section, the authors in [188] used the network topology from Figure 7.5 to demonstrate the performance of the designs. Tree cell clusters are identified, each of which is composed of one macro cell and two *slave* pico cells. As mentioned earlier, one independent SONCO instance governing each of the cell clusters is considered. An elastic FTP-like traffic is considered with background UE arrival rate $\Lambda_G[\text{UE/s}/m^2]$ together with an additional HotSpot (HS) arrival rate $\Lambda_{HS}[\text{UE/s}/m^2]$ (such that the resulting arrival rate in the HS is $\Lambda_G + \Lambda_{HS}$). Space Poisson point processes are used for the UE arrivals. A UE arriving in the network goes through a Connection-Establishment procedure to attach to a cell, transmits its file (fixed size $FS[Mb/UE]$), and then leaves the network. During the data transmission, the UE may go through Connection Reconfiguration in case it gets attached to a different cell (HO) due to mobility or through Connection Re-Establishment in case it suffers a radio link failure or a handover failure (HOF) due to bad radio channel conditions. The HSs are disk surfaces with a radius of $HSR = 40$ m.

  1. *Fairness biasing:* In this subsection, we show the results aimed at proving the effectiveness of the biasing mechanism, that is, the capability of favoring one SON function or another. For this, we perform simulations with stationary traffic λ (see the table in Figure 7.5) for a period of 20 days. We consider the first 10 days as a sufficiently large time interval for the algorithms to reach a steady state, and we evaluate the network parameters during the last 10 days. Figure 7.6 shows averages over the parameters controlled by the SON functions: the average CIO (over time and all pico cells), the average HYS (over time and all pico cells), and the average number of ABS (over time and all macro cells), respectively, for different weights w.

The three digits after the "SA" or "LF" indication identify the weight of the three SON functions in the following order: CRE, MRO, and eICIC (e.g., "LF181" refers to the LF design with the weights 1, 8, and 1 for CRE, MRO, and eICIC, respectively). For simplicity, we focus only on the conflict between CRE and MRO.

One can see how different weights impact the mentioned parameters. First, we try to give some intuition to help the reader interpret the graphs. The CIO is the main target of CRE. To off-load the macro cell, we increase the CIO of the pico cells. However, if the CIO of the pico cell increases too much, we create the risk of having many too late HOs, which can suffocate the MRO. This is why the MRO also tunes the CIO: to prevent this extreme off-loading. We expect that a higher priority on the CRE should lead to more aggressive off-loading – that is, bigger values of the CIO of pico cells – and on the other hand a bigger priority of the MRO would restrict this off-loading – that is, lower CIO values. The number of ABS will also have the same trend as eICIC reacts to the changes of the CRE: the bigger the CIO, the more UEs there are to protect and thus the bigger the number of ABS subframes.

This trend can be seen in Figure 7.6 for the two scenarios SA and LF. The average HYS is also impacted by the different weights; for example, a small CIO value would reduce the number of too late HOs and would thus allow for bigger HYS values to also reduce the ping-pong HOs. As mentioned earlier, a bigger weight on the CRE leads to higher average CIO values. This forces the MRO to reduce the values of HYS, as can be seen in Figure 7.6, to reduce the number of too late HOs. Naturally, a bigger weight on the MRO will have the opposite effect: that is, the average HYS values will be bigger as the number of too late HOs will not be so critical. MRO will profit from this by increasing the HYS to reduce the number of ping-pong HOs.

7.5 RL-Based Caching

Here, we continue our discussion initiated in Section 7.3 and go into more details of caching optimization in SBSs that have potential to handle the unprecedented demand growth in heterogeneous networks. Through low-rate, backhaul connections with the backbone, SBs can prefetch popular files during off-peak traffic hours, and service them to the edge at peak periods. To intelligently prefetch, each SB must learn what and when to cache, while taking into account SB memory limitations, the massive number of available contents, the unknown popularity profiles, as well as the space–time popularity dynamics of user file requests. Along the lined presented in [193], in this section, local and global Markov processes model user requests, and an RL framework is used for finding the optimal caching policy when the transition probabilities involved are unknown. Joint consideration of global and local popularity demands along with cache-refreshing costs allow for a simple, yet practical asynchronous caching approach. RL-based caching relies on a Q-learning algorithm to implement the optimal policy in an online fashion, thus enabling the cache control unit at the SB to learn, track, and possibly adapt to the underlying dynamics. To impart scalability to the algorithm, an LFA of the Q-learning scheme is introduced, offering faster convergence as well as reduced complexity and memory requirements. A design example is used to further elaborate the approach in various realistic settings.

7.5.1 System Model

Consider a local section of a HetNet with a single SBS connected to the backbone network through a low-bandwidth, high-delay backhaul link. The SBS is equipped with M units to store contents (files) that are assumed for simplicity to have unit size. Caching will be carried out in a slotted fashion over slots $t = 1, 2, \ldots$, where at the end of each slot, the caching control unit CCU-enabled SBS intelligently selects M files from the total of $F \gg M$ available ones at the backbone, and prefetches them for possible use in subsequent slots.

---

1) At the beginning of every time slot, the user file requests are revealed, and the "content delivery" phase takes place.
2) The second phase pertains to "information exchange," where the SBSs transmit their locally observed popularity profiles to the network operator, and in return receive the estimated global popularity profile.
3) Finally, "cache placement" is carried out, and the optimal selection of files is stored for the next time slot.

Generally, a slot starts when the network is at an off-peak period, and its duration coincides with the peak traffic time when the costs of serving users are high. During the content delivery phase of slot t, each user locally requests a subset of files from the set $\mathcal{F} := \{1, 2, ..., F\}$. If a requested file has been stored in the cache, it will be simply served locally, thus incurring (almost) zero cost. Conversely, if the requested file is not available in the cache, the SBS must fetch it from the cloud through its cheap backhaul link, thus incurring a considerable cost due to possible electricity price surges, processing cost, or a sizable delay resulting in low QoE and user dissatisfaction. The CCU wishes to intelligently select the cache contents so that costly services from the cloud can be avoided as often as possible.

Let $a(t) \in \mathcal{A}$ denote the $F \times 1$ binary *caching action vector* at slot t, where $\mathcal{A} := \{a \mid a \in \{0,1\}^F, a^T 1 = M\}$ is the set of all feasible actions; that is, $[a(t)]_f = 1$ indicates that file f is cached for the duration of slot t, and $[a(t)]_f = 0$ otherwise. Depending on the received requests from locally connected users during content delivery phase, the CCU computes the $F \times 1$-vector of *local popularity profile* $p_L(t)$ per slot t, whose f-th entry indicates the expected local demand for file f, defined as

$$[p_L(t)]_f := (\text{number of local requests for } f \text{ at slot } t)/(\text{number of all local requests for } f \text{ at slot } t)$$

Similarly, suppose that the backbone network estimates the $F \times 1$ *global popularity profile* vector $p_G(t)$, and transmits it to all CCUs. Having observed the local and global user requests by the end of the information exchange phase of slot t, our overall system state is $s(t) := \left[p_G^T(t), p_L^T(t), a^T(t)\right]^T$. Being at slot $t-1$, our *objective* is to leverage historical observations of states, $\{s(\tau)\}_{\tau=0}^{t-1}$, and pertinent costs to learn the optimal action for the next slot, namely $a^*(t)$. Explicit expressions for the incurred costs and an analytical formulation of the objective will be elaborated in the following subsections.

Cost functions and caching strategies' efficiency will be measured by how well they utilize the available storage of the local SB to keep the most popular files, versus how often local user requests are met via fetching through the more expensive backhaul link. The overall cost incurred will be modeled as the superposition of three types of costs.

1) *The first type*, $c_{1,t}$, corresponds to the cost of refreshing the cache contents. In its general form, $c_{1,t}(\cdot)$ is a function of the upcoming action, $a(t)$, and the available contents at the cache according to the current caching action $a(t-1)$, where the subscript t captures the possibility of a time-varying cost for refreshing the cache. A reasonable choice of $c_{1,t}(\cdot)$ is

$$c_{1,t}(a(t), a(t-1)) := \lambda_{1,t} a^T(t)[1 - a(t-1)] \tag{7.80a}$$

which, upon recalling that the action vectors $a(t-1)$ and $a(t)$ have binary $\{0, 1\}$ entries, implies that $c_{1,t}$ counts the number of files to be fetched and cached prior to slot t, which were not stored according to action $a(t-1)$.

2) *The second type* of cost is incurred during the operational phase of slot t to satisfy user requests. With $c_{2,t}(s(t))$ denoting this type of cost, a prudent choice must (i) penalize requests for files already cached much less than requests for files not stored; and (ii) be a nondecreasing function of popularities $[p_L]_f$. Here, for simplicity, we assume that the transmission cost of cached files is relatively negligible, and choose

$$c_{2,t}(s(t)) := \lambda_{2,t}[1 - a(t)]^T p_L(t) \tag{7.80b}$$

which penalizes only the non-cached files in descending order of their local popularities.

3) *The third type* of cost captures the "mismatch" between caching action, $a(t)$, and the global popularity profile, $p_G(t)$. Indeed, it is reasonable to consider the global popularity of files as an acceptable representative of what the local profiles will look like in the near future; thus, keeping the caching action close to $p_G(t)$ may reduce future possible costs. Note also that a relatively small number of local requests may only provide a crude estimate of local popularities, while the global popularity profile can serve as side information in tracking the evolution of content popularities over the network. Moreover, in networks with highly mobile users, storing globally popular files, might be a better caching decision than the local ones. This has prompted the advocation of TL approaches, where content popularities in a surrogate domain are utilized for improving estimates of popularity. However, this approach is limited by the degree the surrogate (source) domain, for example, Facebook or Twitter, is a good representative of the target domain requests. When it is not, the techniques will misguide caching decisions while imposing excess processing overhead on the network operator or on the SB. To account for this problem, we introduce the third type of cost as

$$c_{3,t}(s(t)) := \lambda_{3,t}[1 - a(t)]^T p_G(t) \tag{7.80c}$$

which penalizes the files not cached according to the global popularity profile $p_G(\cdot)$ provided by the network operator, thus promoting adoption of caching policies close to global demand trends. So, upon taking action $a(t)$ for slot t, the *aggregate cost conditioned* on the revealed popularity vectors, used in [188], can be expressed as

$$
\begin{aligned}
C_t(s(t-1), a(t) \mid p_G(t), p_L(t)) \\
:= c_{1,t}(a(t), a(t-1)) + c_{2,t}(s(t)) + c_{3,t}(s(t)) \\
= \lambda_{1,t} a^T(t)(1 - a(t-1)) + \lambda_{2,t}(1 - a(t))^T p_L(t) + \lambda_{3,t}(1 - a(t))^T p_G(t).
\end{aligned} \tag{7.81}
$$

Weights $\lambda_{1,t}$, $\lambda_{2,t}$, and $\lambda_{3,t}$ control the relative significance of the corresponding summands, whose tuning influences the optimal caching policy at the CCU. As asserted earlier, the cache-refreshing cost at off-peak periods is considered to be less than the cost of fetching the contents during slots, which justifies the choice $\lambda_{1,t} \ll \lambda_{2,t}$. In addition, setting $\lambda_{3,t} \ll \lambda_{2,t}$ is of interest when the local popularity profiles are of acceptable accuracy, or if tracking local popularities is more important.

Popularity profile dynamics including user requests (and thus popularities) at both global and local scales is modeled using Markov chains. Global popularity profiles will be assumed generated by an underlying Markov process with $|\mathcal{P}_G|$ states collected in the set $\mathcal{P}_G := \left\{ p_G^1, ..., p_G^{|\mathcal{P}_G|} \right\}$; and likewise for the set of all local popularity profiles $\mathcal{P}_L := \left\{ p_L^1, ..., p_L^{|\mathcal{P}_L|} \right\}$. Although $\mathcal{P}_G$ and $\mathcal{P}_L$ are known, the underlying transition probabilities of the two Markov processes are considered unknown.

Given $\mathcal{P}_G$ and $\mathcal{P}_L$ as well as feasible caching decisions in set $\mathcal{A}$, the overall set of states in the network is $\mathcal{S} := \left\{ s \mid s = [p_G^T, p_L^T, a^T]^T, p_G \in \mathcal{P}_G, p_L \in \mathcal{P}_L, a \in \mathcal{A} \right\}$.

In the RL-based caching presented in the following, the underlying transition probabilities for global and local popularity profiles are considered *unknown*, which is a practical assumption. In this approach, the learner seeks the optimal policy by interactively making sequential decisions, and observing the corresponding costs. The caching task is formulated in the following subsection, and an efficient solver is developed to cope with the dimensionality problem typically emerging with RL problems.

The RL formulation assumes that at the end of time slot $t - 1$ the CCU takes caching action $a(t)$ to meet the upcoming requests, and by the end of the content delivery as well as information exchange phases of slot t, the profiles $p_G(t)$ and $p_L(t)$ become available, so that the system state is updated to $s(t)$, and the conditional cost $C_t(s(t-1), a(t) \mid p_G(t), p_L(t))$ is revealed. Given the random nature of user requests locally and globally, C_t in Eq. (7.81) is a random variable with mean E( )

$$
\begin{aligned}
\overline{C}_t(s(t-1), a(t)) &:= E_{p_G(t), p_L(t)}[C_t(s(t-1), a(t) \mid p_G(t), p_L(t))] \\
&= \lambda_1 a^T(t)[1 - a(t-1)] + \lambda_2 E\left[(1 - a(t))^T p_L(t)\right] \\
&\quad + \lambda_3 E\left[(1 - a(t))^T p_G(t)\right]
\end{aligned}
\tag{7.82}
$$

where the expectation is taken with respect to $p_L(t)$ and $p_G(t)$, while the weights are selected as $\lambda_{1,t} = \lambda_1$, $\lambda_{2,t} = \lambda_2$, and $\lambda_{3,t} = \lambda_3$ for simplicity.

Let us now define the policy function $\pi : \mathcal{S} \rightarrow \mathcal{A}$, which maps any state $s \in \mathcal{S}$ to the action set. Under policy $(\cdot)$, for the current state $s(t)$, caching is carried out via action $a(t+1) = \pi(s(t))$ dictating the files state value to be stored for the $(t+1) - $st slot. Caching performance is measured through the so-called function

$$
V_\pi(s(t)) := \lim_{T \to \infty} E\left[\sum_{\tau=t}^{T} \gamma^{\tau - t} \overline{C}(s[\tau], \pi(s[\tau])) \right]
\tag{7.83}
$$

which is the total average cost incurred over an infinite time horizon, with future terms discounted by the factor $\gamma \in [0, 1)$. Since taking action $a(t)$ influences the SB state in future slots, future costs are always affected by past and present actions. The discount factor γ captures this effect, whose tuning trades off current versus future costs. Moreover, γ also accounts for modeling uncertainties, as well as imperfections, or dynamics. For instance, if there is ambiguity about future costs, or if the system changes very fast, setting γ to a small value enables one to prioritize current costs, whereas in a stationary setting one may prefer to demote future costs through a larger γ. Our objective is to find the optimal policy π^* such that the average cost of any state s is minimized

$$
\pi^* = \arg \min_{\pi \in \Pi} V_\pi(s), \forall s \in \mathcal{S}
\tag{7.84}
$$

where Π denotes the set of all feasible policies. The optimization in Eq. (7.84) is a sequential decision-making problem. In the sequel, we present optimality conditions (known as Bellman equations) for our problem, and introduce a Q-learning approach for solving Eq. (7.84).

7.5.2 Optimality Conditions

Bellman equations: Also known as dynamic programming equations, they provide necessary conditions for optimality of a policy in a sequential decision-making problem. For the $(t-1)$st slot, let $[P^a]_{ss'}$ denote the transition probability of going from the current state s to the next state s' under action a; that is, $[P^a]_{ss'} := \Pr\{s(t) = s' \mid s(t-1) = s, \pi(s(t-1)) = a\}$. Bellman equations express the state-value function by Eq. (7.83) in a recursive fashion as

$$V_\pi(s) = \overline{C}(s, \pi(s)) + \gamma \sum_{s' \in S} \left[P^{\pi(s)} \right]_{ss'} \forall s, s' \tag{7.85}$$

which amounts to the superposition of $\overline{C}$ plus a discounted version of future state-value functions under a given policy π. Specifically, after dropping the current slot index $t-1$ and indicating with prime quantities of the next slot t, $\overline{C}$ in Eq. (7.82) can be written as

$$\overline{C}(s, \pi(s)) = \sum_{s' := [p'_G, p'_L, a'] \in S} \left[P^{\pi(s)} \right]_{ss'} C\left(s, \pi(s) \mid p'_G, p'_L \right)$$

where $C\left(s, \pi(s) \mid p'_G, p'_L\right)$ is found as in Eq. (7.81). It turns out that, with $[P^a]_{ss'}$ given $\forall s, s'$, one can readily obtain $\{V_\pi(s), \forall s\}$ by solving Eq. (7.85), and eventually the optimal policy π^* in Eq. (7.87) using the policy iteration algorithm. To outline how this algorithm works in our context, define the state-action value function that we will rely on under policy π as

$$Q_\pi(s, a') := \overline{C}(s, a') + \gamma \sum_{s' \in S} \left[P^{a'} \right]_{ss'} V_\pi(s'). \tag{7.86}$$

As discussed in Chapter 6, the "Q-function," $Q_\pi(s, \alpha)$, basically captures the expected current cost of taking action α when the system is in state s, followed by the discounted value of the future states, provided that the future actions are taken according to policy π. In our setting, the policy iteration algorithm initialized with π_0, proceeds with the following updates at the i-th iteration:

- *Policy evaluation:* Determine $V_{\pi_i}(s)$ for all states $s \in S$ under the current (fixed) policy π_i, by solving the system of linear equations in Eq. (7.85) $\forall s$.
- *Policy update:* Update the policy using

$$\pi_{i+1}(s) := \arg \min_\alpha Q_{\pi_i}(s, \alpha), \forall s \in S.$$

Optimal caching via Q-learning: Q-learning is an online scheme to jointly infer the optimum policy π^* and estimate the optimal state-action value function $Q^*(s, a') := Q_{\pi^*}(s, a') \forall s, a'$. Utilizing Eq. (7.85) for the optimal policy π^*, it can be shown that

$$\pi^*(s) = \arg \min_\alpha Q^*(s, a'), \forall s \in S \tag{7.87}$$

The Q-function and V( ) under π^* are related by

$$V^*(s) := V_{\pi^*}(s) = \min_\alpha Q^*(s, \alpha) \tag{7.88}$$

which gives

$$Q^*(s, a') = \overline{C}(s, a') + \gamma \sum_{s' \in S} [P^a]_{ss'} \min_{\alpha \in A} Q^*(s, \alpha) \tag{7.89}$$

Using Eqs. (7.86)–(7.89), the following algorithm (Algorithm 1) has been developed in [193]. In this algorithm, the agent updates its estimated $\hat{Q}(s(t-1), a(t))$ as

$C(s(t-1), a(t) \mid p_G(t), p_L(t))$ is observed. That is, given $s(t-1)$, Q-learning takes action a(t), and upon observing s(t), it incurs cost $C(s(t-1), a(t) \mid p_G(t), p_L(t))$. Based on the instantaneous error

$$\varepsilon(s(t-1), a(t)) := \left(C(s(t-1), a(t)) + \gamma \min{}_{\alpha} \hat{Q}_t(s(t), \alpha) - \hat{Q}_t(s(t-1), \ a(t)) \right)^2 / 2 \qquad (7.90)$$

the Q-function is updated using stochastic gradient descent as

$$
\begin{aligned}
\hat{Q}_t(s(t-1), a(t)) = {} & (1 - \beta_t)\hat{Q}_{-1}(s(t-1), a(t)) \\
& + \beta_t \left[C(s(t-1), a(t) \mid p_G(t), p_L(t)) + \gamma \ min{}_{\alpha} \ \hat{Q}_{t-1}(s(t), \alpha) \right]
\end{aligned}
\qquad (7.91)
$$

while keeping the rest of the entries in $\hat{Q}_t(\cdot, \cdot)$ unchanged.

Algorithm 2 Caching via Q-learning at CCU

Initialize s(0) randomly and $\hat{Q}_0(\mathbf{s}, \mathbf{a}) = 0 \ \forall \mathbf{s}, \mathbf{a}$

for $t = 1, 2, \dots$ **do**
    Take action $a(t)$ chosen probabilistically by

$$
\mathbf{a}(t) = \begin{cases} \arg\min\limits_{\mathbf{a}} \hat{Q}_{t-1}\left(\mathbf{s}(t-1), \mathbf{a}\right) & \text{w.p.} \quad 1 - \epsilon_t \\ \text{random } \mathbf{a} \in \mathcal{A} & \text{w.p.} \quad \epsilon_t \end{cases}
$$

    $\mathbf{p}_L(t)$ and $\mathbf{p}_G(t)$ are revealed based on user requests

    Set $\quad \mathbf{s}(t) = \left[\mathbf{p}_G^\top(t), \mathbf{p}_L^\top(t), \mathbf{a}(t)^\top \right]^\top$
    Incur cost $C\left(\mathbf{s}(t-1), \mathbf{a}(t) \big| \mathbf{p}_G(t), \mathbf{p}_L(t) \right)$
    Update

$$
\begin{aligned}
\hat{Q}_t\left(\mathbf{s}(t-1), \mathbf{a}(t)\right) = {} & (1 - \beta_t)\hat{Q}_{t-1}\left(\mathbf{s}(t-1), \mathbf{a}(t)\right) \\
& + \beta_t \Big[C\left(\mathbf{s}(t-1), \mathbf{a}(t) \big| \mathbf{p}_G(t), \mathbf{p}_L(t) \right) \\
& \qquad + \gamma \min\limits_{\boldsymbol{\alpha}} \hat{Q}_{t-1}\left(\mathbf{s}(t), \boldsymbol{\alpha}\right) \Big]
\end{aligned}
$$

end for

Source: [188].

Design Example 7.3

In this section, the performance of the Q-learning algorithm is described in different scenarios. To compare the proposed algorithms with the optimal caching policy, which is the best policy under known transition probabilities for global and local popularity Markov chains, a small network with F = 10 information (media) items, and caching capacity M = 2 at the local SB was first simulated in [193]. The global popularity profile is modeled by a two-state Markov chain with states p_G^1 and p_G^2, which are drawn from Zipf distributions having parameters $\eta_1^G = 1$ and $\eta_2^G = 1.5$, respectively [194]; see also Figure 7.8. That is, for state $i \in \{1, 2\}$, the F contents are assigned a random ordering of popularities, and then sorted accordingly in a descending order. Given this ordering and the Zipf distribution parameter η_i^G, the popularity of the *f*-th content is set to

Design Example 7.3 (Continued)

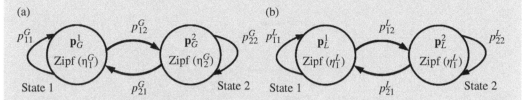

(a)   (b)

Figure 7.8 Popularity profiles modeled as Markov chains. (a) Global popularity Markov chain, (b) local popularity Markov chain. *Source:* Sadeghi et al. [193].

$$[\mathrm{p}_G^i]_f = \frac{1}{f^{\eta_i^G} \sum_{l=1}^{F} 1/l^{\eta_i^G}} \text{ for } i = 1, 2$$

where the summation normalizes the components so that they follow a valid probability mass function, while $\eta_i^G \geq 0$ controls the skewness of popularities. Specifically, $\eta_i^G = 0$ yields a uniform spread of popularity among contents, while a large value of η_i generates more skewed popularities. Furthermore, state transition probabilities of the Markov chain modeling global popularity profiles are

$$P^G := \begin{Bmatrix} p_{11}^G & p_{12}^G \\ p_{21}^G & p_{22}^G \end{Bmatrix} = \begin{Bmatrix} 0.8 & 0.2 \\ 0.75 & 0.25 \end{Bmatrix}.$$

Similarly, local popularities are modeled by a two-state Markov chain, with states p_L^1 and p_L^2, whose entries are drawn from Zipf distributions with parameters $\eta_1^L = 0.7$ and $\eta_2^L = 2.5$, respectively. The transition probabilites of the local popularity Markov chain are

$$P^L := \begin{Bmatrix} p_{11}^L & p_{12}^L \\ p_{21}^L & p_{22}^L \end{Bmatrix} = \begin{Bmatrix} 0.6 & 0.4 \\ 0.2 & 08 \end{Bmatrix}.$$

Caching performance is assessed under three cost-parameter settings:

(s1) $\lambda_1 = 10$, $\lambda_2 = 600$, $\lambda_3 = 1000$,
(s2) $\lambda_1 = 600$, $\lambda_2 = 10$, $\lambda_3 = 1000$, and
(s3) $\lambda_1 = 10$, $\lambda_2 = 10$, $\lambda_3 = 1000$.

In all numerical tests, the optimal caching policy is found by utilizing the policy iteration algorithm with known transition probabilities. In addition, Q-learning in Algorithm 1 is run with $\beta_t = 0.8$, $\alpha_G = \alpha_L = \alpha_R = 0.005$, and $\varepsilon_t = 0.05$. Figure 7.9 depicts the observed cost versus iteration (time) index averaged over 1000 realizations. It is seen that the caching cost via Q-learning, and through its scalable approximation [193], converges to that of the optimal policy. As anticipated, even for the small size of this network, namely $|\mathcal{P}_G| = |\mathcal{P}_L| = 2$ and $|\mathcal{A}| = 45$, the Q-learning algorithm converges slowly to the optimal policy, especially under s1, while its scalable approximation exhibits faster convergence. The reason for the slower convergence under (s1) is that the corresponding cost parameters of local and global popularity mismatch are set high, and

(Continued)

Design Example 7.3 (Continued)

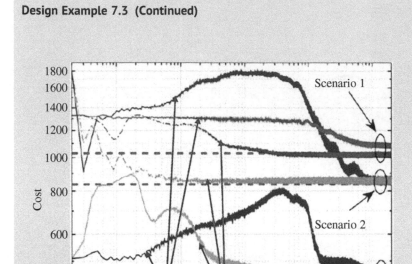

Figure 7.9 Performance of the algorithms. *Source:* Sadeghi et al. [193].

thus the convergence of the Q-learning algorithm as well as the caching policy essentially relies on learning both global and local popularity Markov chains. By contrast, under (s2), λ_2 corresponding to a local popularity mismatch is low, and thus the impact of the local popularity Markov chain on the optimal policy is reduced, giving rise to a simpler policy and thus a faster convergence. To shed more light on this topic, simulations are carried out under a simpler scenario (s3). In this setting, having $\lambda_1 = 10$ further reduces the effect of the cache-refreshing cost, and thus it becomes more important to learn the Markov chain of global popularities. Indeed, the simulations present a slightly faster convergence for (s3) compared to (s2), while both demonstrate much faster convergence than (s1).

7.6 Big Data Analytics in Wireless Networks

Wireless networks are evolving into very complex systems because of the highly diversified service requirements and heterogeneity in applications, devices, and networks. A novel paradigm of proactive, self-aware, self-adaptive, and predictive networking is the need of the hour. The network operators have access to large amounts of data, especially from the network and the subscribers. Systematic exploitation of *the big data* dramatically helps in making the system smart and intelligent, and facilitates efficient as well as cost-effective operation and optimization. It is envisioned that next-generation wireless networks will be data driven, where the network operators employ advanced data analytics, ML, and artificial intelligence. Here, we discuss the data sources and strong drivers for the adoption of the data analytics, and the role of ML and artificial intelligence in making the system intelligent with regard to being self-aware, self-adaptive, proactive, and prescriptive. A set of network design and optimization schemes are presented concerning data analytics.

7.6.1 Evolution of Analytics

Datasets and the sources of data available to the network operators for big data analytics, ML, and artificial intelligence are summarized in Figure 7.10 [195]. There exists a succession of evolutionary advances in big data analytics, starting from descriptive analytics to diagnostic analytics to predictive analytics, and culminating in prescriptive analytics. The network operators currently are in the *descriptive phase* and mainly use visualization tools to get insights into what has happened, the network performance, traffic profile, and so on. The network operators can employ *diagnostic analytics* to figure out the root causes of the network anomalies and discover the faulty KPIs and network functions/elements. To obtain the diagnostic analytics, the analytics tool employs techniques like drill-down, deep learning, data discovery, correlations, and so on.

Predictive analytics is an excellent tool for making predictions. Note that it can never report or be precise about what will happen; however, predictive analytics can only produce forecasting about what might occur, for example, the future locations of subscribers, future traffic patterns, network congestion, and so on. Predictive analytics deliver predictions regarding events based on real-time and archived data by making use of various statistical techniques such as ML, data mining, analytical modeling, and game-theoretic analysis. *Prescriptive analytics* goes steps ahead of just

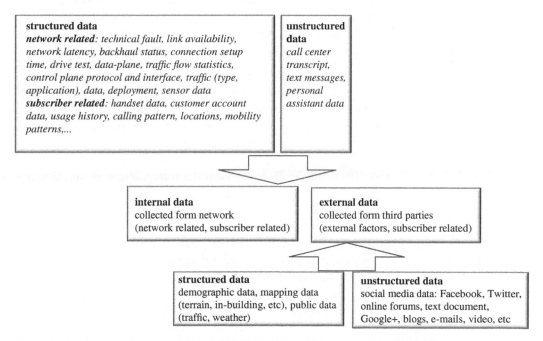

Figure 7.10 Datasets and the sources of data available to the network operators for big data analytics, machine learning, and artificial intelligence. *Source:* Kibria et al. [195].

predicting the future events by suggesting decision options for slicing (i.e., how to slice, how many slices), virtualization, edge computing, and so on, along with the implications of each decision option. Therefore, prescriptive analytics needs a useful predictive model, actionable data, and a feedback system for tracking down the results generated by the action taken. The decision options (e.g., for network expansion, resource usage) are produced considering the network operator's preferences, system constraints (backhaul, fronthaul, spectrum, transmission power), and so on. Prescriptive analytics can also suggest the best course of action for any predefined target, for example, of a particular KPI.

The network operators have access to large amounts of data, which can be categorized into two classes such as internal data and external data, as shown in Figure 7.10. The internal data correspond to data belonging to the network operators and produced in the network, which are network related and subscriber related. The external data are collected from the third parties. Both the internal and external data can be further classified into two categories: structured data and unstructured data. The structured data are stored in a relational database; that is, each field in the database has a name, and the relationships between the areas are well defined. On the other hand, unstructured data (for example, call center transcripts, messages) is not usually saved in a relational database. Comprehensive coverage of the features and sources of mobile big data can be found in [196] and [197].

7.6.2 Data-Driven Network Optimization

The conventional network-centric architecture cannot capture all of the nuances that can affect service quality. Mobile operators need solutions that provide them with analytical capability that captures all the information relating to the network and subscribers into a single enterprise geolocation platform that can help eliminate the assumptions involved in fault isolation and reduce the mean time to repair. Network operators are suitably positioned to exploit big data analytics because of their access to huge amounts of data. The big data analytics engine/agent can produce/predict the following analytics based on its data, primarily from two sources, such as network data and subscriber data, which are then exploited to design and optimize the network.

- *Subscriber Profile:* In this context, the subscriber profile consists of the device profile, SLA, subscriber's affordability (price per unit of data rate), QoS/policy, behavioral profile, and so on. It plays a vital role in the abovementioned controlling and optimization process. The priority of the subscriber in the network is defined in the subscriber profile when resource allocation, congestion control, and traffic off-loading are performed. Behavioral data provide information on how the user behaves when using various applications/services. For example, how frequently and when does the user make video/audio calls and what is the average length of the call duration? Through analytics, we can investigate many of these user attributes.
- *Subscriber Perspective (Sub-P):* This is an attribute/measure that associates the network operator's network activity with the user's SLA, pricing, QoS, QoE, and so on. It delivers a subscriber-centric view of the network for analytics [198]. The subscriber perspective is, in general, defined by the *Cost Over Quality Ratio*, which sometimes gets fine-tuned through a variety of attributes linked to the requested service class and the perceived user-friendliness of the service, that is, QoS violation, delay violation, and so on. It enables the network operator to measure or arrive at a perception about the radio access network (RAN) quality from the subscriber point of view and enables them to provide a high QoE.
- *RAN Perspective (RAN-P):* This is a measure that gives the network operator an indication of the subscriber-centric RAN quality, that is, the RAN performance from the subscriber's point of view

[199]. The UE's view of signaling information (such as signal strength, error codes, available networks, etc.) helps the network operator from the standpoint of analytics. From the user's predicted trajectory, spatial deployment of the BSs, and signaling metrics, the network operator can generate a heat map for coverage and determine the RAN quality. Advanced cell mining that statistically analyzes the performance data enables the network operator to identify radio cell irregularities and other negative syndromes (i.e., SLA violation) via anomaly diagnosis and trend study of the time series data, and control traffic and RAN congestion problems. With the RAN perspective, the full end-to-end subscriber experience can be measured regarding *service availability* and correspondingly mapped to the exact location in the network. The network operator can also use the *Subscriber Satisfaction Coefficient* to define the RAN perspective. Note that the signaling metric cannot be easily retrieved from mobile gateways or by network probes. An efficient retrieval method is discussed in [199] that uses a SIM-based applet stored in users' devices to collect the signal strength and quality metrics. Thus, the subscriber devices act as network probes in measuring the RAN perspective.

- *Subscriber Mobility Pattern (SMP):* To guarantee the QoS requirements and to efficiently maintain resource utilization, traffic off-loading, and routing, advance knowledge of the mobility information of a user is crucial. Human travel pattern analyses reveal that people travel along specific paths with reasonably high predictability [200]. The trajectory of a mobile user can be predicted based on the user's present location, the movement direction, and the aggregate history of SMP. It is possible to predict the spatiotemporal trajectory (trajectory with both spatial and temporal information); that is, not only the mobile user's future location but also the time of arrival and the duration of stay can be predicted. The mobility pattern is based on user positioning, which can be estimated using the signals from the cellular system.

- *Radio Environment Map (REM):* Network operators can better plan, build, control, and optimize their networks conforming to the spatiotemporal radio atmosphere by predicting radio signal attenuation. Many schemes have been developed that give network operators the means to predict the distribution of radio signal attenuation at different operating frequencies and in many different radio environments. The radio map along with the mobile user's predicted trajectory facilitates the prediction of average channel gains. There are several different methods of constructing the radio map, for example, a radio map based on drive test measurements and a radio map based on measurements through a GPS-equipped user terminal.

- *Traffic Profile (TP):* To obtain as well as predict the network's congestion status, temporal-spatial traffic load variation needs to be known; the temporal traffic trace, BS spatial deployment, and BSs' operating characteristics (transmission power, height, etc.) are critical. The authors in [201, 202] report that the network's traffic load dynamics demonstrates periodic characteristics over days and hours, thus implying high predictability of the traffic load. The TP along with the SMP can be used to estimate and predict the traffic arrival rate and congestion status of the network with the required time resolution/granularity.

It is crucial to have a well-balanced load distributed cellular system in a dynamic network and radio environment with mobile users using bursty applications and services. The next-generation network can employ systems analytics, user and service analytics, and radio analytics for control and optimization of the network [203] in the following scenarios.

- *Resource Allocation Strategy:* Advanced resource allocation is crucial for enhancing the spectrum and power utilization efficiency of communication systems. Leveraging big-data-analytics-based prediction ability in optimizing resource allocation has been reported to be very advantageous. With the help of SMP and TP, the network operator can approximate the typical resource usage per cell per user in the network. Because (i) the average channel gains can be predicted from the trajectory of the user and (ii) based on content popularity, a user's behavioral profile, and the currently running application, the preferred content can be predicted even before the individual users put forward their service requests (see the sections on caching). As a result, with the help of big data predictive analytics, operators can predict changes in users' service demands and thus can manage and optimize the resource allocation in real time in integrated backhaul and access mmWave network.

- *Subscriber-Centric Traffic Routing:* Providing the best QoE as end users' subjective perception is one of the most important requirements. Service delay and jitter affect mobile users' QoE severely. Data-driven solutions can deliver traffic to different users depending on their subscription profile, types of applications, and preferences. An AQoE-aware network continuously adopts the changing environment to provide acceptable QoE. The SMP, the network utilization profile, and TP can help the operator devise an efficient routing protocol while considering the backhaul load, the SLA, and the corresponding cost. Depending on users' preferences and interests, and the currently running application, the system can proactively cache the favorite content, and use the backhaul route that is closer to the local caching server.

- *Subscriber-Centric Wireless Off-load:* Due to an exponential surge in mobile data traffic carrier over macrocell layer, network operators are increasingly discovering approaches to optimize the traffic in the network while ensuring seamless connectivity and minimum guaranteed QoS to their subscribers. Traffic off-loading from the macrocell layer to the small cell layer (specifically toward WiFi networks) is a great way to relieve congestion in the macro layer and enhance the overall network throughput. Blindly off-loading mobile users may result in dissatisfaction of the higher-tier subscribers and SLA breaches. Therefore, it is necessary to devise practical solutions that help network operators decide and off-load mobile users to WiFi, based on user profile and network congestion conditions. Data-driven contextual intelligence derived by correlating the customer profile (types of application, spending pattern, SLA) with SMP, TP, and REM can decide which customer should be off-loaded, and even to which small cell/WiFi the customer needs to be unloaded.

- *Optimized Cell Placement:* Small cell placement plays a vital role in defining the capacity of a heterogeneous network. Strategic small cell placement is crucial in areas where subscribers are concentrated and takes care of coverage goals, radio frequency interference problems, and can potentially relieve congestion from the macro layer by off-loading traffic. Rapidly placing the small cells at the very best locations is a complex problem as the number of small cells is much larger than the number of macro cells. A traditional macro cell layer management tool and even the SON tool may not compensate for improper cell placement. However, a data-driven solution can efficiently administer the small cell placement problem by exploiting knowledge of the long-term user density and traffic intensity. In data-driven solutions incorporating the long-term TP, REM can devise an optimized dynamic small cell placement strategy that identifies key locations where small cells need to be deployed and re-arranged to enhance the network capacity, minimize interference, and improve the traffic off-loading capability. A 3D geolocator tool that uses predictive "fingerprinting" algorithms to locate traffic hotspots can simplify the cell placement task.

- *Radio Access Network Congestion Control:* The combination of limited network resources and ever-growing demands result in unavoidable RAN congestion, which degrades users' quality of experience. Expansion of existing RANs provides a solution to this problem, but it is expensive. A flexible, as well as cost-effective, solution is to deploy a proactive policy control mechanism that prevents a deficiency of RAN resources. Smart congestion control solution considering location information, the load level of network elements, and users' SLAs can deliver perceptibility at a particular sub-cell level and confer priority to some set of subscribers based on their tiers. The congestion events are short-lived (typically congestion occurs at busy times of the day), and users' future locations are predictable. With the help of data-driven predictive analytics incorporating the correlation between SMP, radio maps, and the TP, an advanced proactive RAN congestion control mechanism can be deployed where the occurrence of RAN congestion is predicted. RAN congestion control can be achieved in many ways, for example, by reducing the QoS for subscribers belonging to the lowest tier of users, rejecting new session establishment, and terminating specific sessions.

- *Advanced Load Balancing:* Note that the profile of mobile users and the traffic in each cell is distinctive, and the patterns change from time to time. When some users disassociate with one cell and move to the neighboring cell, the network's traffic load distribution, that is, the TP, may change severely, and consequently, some cells in the network may get overloaded, degrading the service. Currently, the load-balancing methods employed by network operators are almost manual, and thus not efficient, and at the same time, they are not accurate enough. Predictive analytics by data mining and correlating the network and subscriber data such TP and SMP can not only help in understanding the cells' current load situation, but also in identifying the heavily loaded parts of the network and predicting the traffic variation in advance. Consequently, network operators can perform advanced load balancing and cell planning by adding capacity, expanding the coverage of unloaded or lightly loaded cells to unburden the neighboring overburdened/overloaded cells. The data-driven advanced load balancing will enable network operators to optimize the utilization of the available network resources.
- *Advanced Beamforming:* This is an integral technology component of next-generation communication systems for enhancing the coverage and data rates. A BS with multiple antennas can generate many beams simultaneously [204]. Under static beamforming (a fixed beam pattern without beam steering), for a mobile user, the quality of the serving beam may deteriorate, and hence a different beam from the same BS (from the same sector or different sector) or from an adjacent BS that serves the user well needs to be selected. ML can help the serving node choose the best beam for the user dynamically. ML also enables dynamic ON/OFF switching of the beams based on TP and SMP for energy and interference minimization. Holographic beamforming1 (with electronic speed beam switching/beam steering) along with data analytics and ML can help in dynamic traffic rerouting, dynamic adjacent cell access, and steering coverage where it is needed to accommodate usage patterns, for example, rush hour traffic, events, and so on.

7.7 Graph Neural Networks

7.7.1 Network Virtualization

NFV is designed to separate network function from traditional middle boxes (physical resources), and in this way provide more agile services. However, one of the main challenges to achieving these objectives is how physical resources can be efficiently, autonomously, and dynamically allocated to VNFs, whose resource requirements change over time. In this section, we discuss a graph-neural-network-based algorithm that exploits VNF forwarding graph topology information to predict future resource requirements for each VNF component (VNFC). The topology information of each VNFC is derived by combining its past resource utilization as well as the modeled effect on the same from VNFCs in its neighborhood. The model will be evaluated again in the form of a design example using the deployment of a virtualized IP multimedia subsystem and real VoIP traffic traces.

Service provision in the telecommunications industry has traditionally been based on the use of specialized network appliances (NAs) for each network function (NF). This tight coupling usually means that even slight changes in the operation of a given NF could necessitate replacement of the NA on which it runs. The main idea of NFV [206, 207] is to take advantage of recent advances in virtualization technologies to decouple NFs (e.g., firewalls, load balancers) from dedicated NAs so as to run them in generic servers that may be located in datacenters or at centralized telecommunications service provider oints of presence. Thanks to NFV, different NFs can evolve independently of each other, and of hardware. Furthermore, by running VNFs in virtualized resources (e.g., virtual machines [VMs]), network resources can be efficiently allocated through dynamic scaling. Finally, NFV promises to lead to more efficient operations through automated and centralized management of networks and services.

In this section, we discuss a topology-aware, dynamic, and autonomous system for managing resources in NFV based on the concept of graph neural networks (GNNs). The method is motivated by the fact that in NFV, services are composed of one or more VNFs arranged in a specific order to create what is known as a service function chain (SFC). Network traffic traverses the VNFs in a given SFC sequentially. This implies that resource requirements of a given VNF may be predicted by observing those of other VNFs in the chain. Therefore, the GNN approach involves modeling each VNFC in an SFC as two parametric functions, each implemented by an FNN. The task of each pair of FNNs representing a given VNFC is to learn (in a supervised way) the trend of resource requirements of the VNFC. This is achieved by combining historical local VNFC resource utilization information with the information collected from its neighbors to forecast future resource requirements of the VNFC. In particular, the first FNN expresses the dependence of the resource requirements of each VNFC on the resource requirements of the VNFCs in its neighborhood. This is input into the second FNN, which forecasts the resource requirements of the VNFC. The resource requirement forecast is in turn used to automatically spin up and configure new VNFCs or turn them off as required.

System Model: The delivery of end-to-end services often requires packets, frames, and/or flows to traverse an ordered or partially ordered set of abstract NFs in what is known as an SFC. In NFV, such NFs are deployed in virtualized resources, and are hence known as VNFs. An example of such a SFC is shown in Figure 7.11, in which the SFC is composed of four VNFs each connected to others by a directed link. Each VNF may be composed of one or more VNFCs, each hosted in a virtualization container (VMs, Linux containers, etc.).

To implement the SFC shown in Figure 7.11, a number of problems should be solved. First, physical infrastructure must be deployed. Then, algorithms must be devised to optimize the placement of virtual containers (or VNFs) onto the available physical servers. Finally, throughout the lifetime of the SFC, it is necessary to determine the actual amount of resources allocated to each virtualization container and/or how many virtualization containers are used for each VNFC. These three problems are referred to as server placement, function placement, and dynamic resource allocation, respectively.

In this section, we focus on dynamic resource allocation. We consider that the VNFs (and hence VNFCs) have already been placed/mapped in the respective virtual resources on which they run. This discussion is motivated by the fact that the resource requirements of each VNF change over time with changes in traffic, which calls for ways to increase and reduce the resources allocated to the VNFCs as needed. Furthermore, since there is a non-negligible delay in spinning up new resources (such as VMs), waiting until the system is overloaded to scale resources up could negatively impact user QoS.

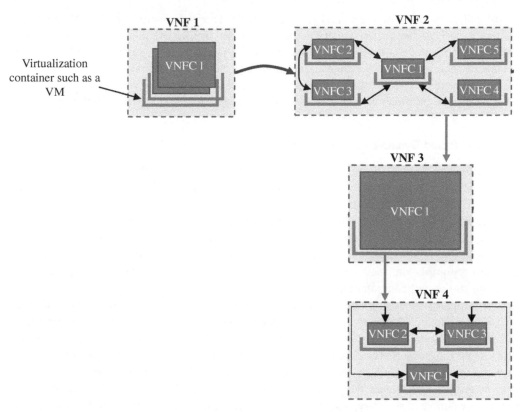

Figure 7.11   Network function virtualization (NFV) service function chain.

So, later, we introduce the concept of GNNs and explain how it has been used to develop a system that forecasts the resource requirements of each VNFC to obtain advance information of the VNFC's upcoming resource needs, allowing an orchestration entity to satisfy such needs just in time. We have discussed GNN in the previous chapters of the book, and here we give only a few more details of the parameters of the GNN when it is used for forecasting the resource requirements of each VNFC. The main idea of GNNs in this context is to define each node n in the graph based on its *features*, f_n, and to complement this by the information (features) observed in the *neighborhood*, n^*, of the node. By neighborhood, here we mean a set of nodes directly connected to node n. Using these two information sources, the GNN model determines a *state* s_n for each node n, which is then used to determine an *output* o_n for the same node. The determination of the state and output for each node is governed by

$$s_n = \sum_{m \in n^*} h_w(f_n, f_m, s_m), \forall n \tag{7.92}$$

$$o_n = g_w(s_n, f_n), \forall n \tag{7.93}$$

where f_m and s_m are the features and state of neighbor $m \in n^*$, respectively. It is possible to also include the features f_{mn} of the direct link between n and m in Eq. (7.92), which only produces a problem with more dimensions. h_w and g_w are parametric functions that express, respectively, the dependence of the state at each node on the state of its neighborhood, and the dependence of the node output on its state, respectively. h_w is known as the *transition function*, while g_w is known as the *output function*. Equations (7.92) and (7.93) represent the activity of a network consisting of units that compute h_w and g_w for each node. This is the main idea of GNNs, an information diffusion mechanism, in which a graph is processed by a set of units (h_w and g_w), each one corresponding to a node of the graph, which are linked according to the graph connectivity. These units update their states and exchange information until they reach a stable equilibrium. It should suffice to say here that by directing the diffusion process, the model is expected to converge exponentially fast, and be stable while determining the node states, and hence the GNN output.

7.7.2 GNN-Based Dynamic Resource Management

Since neighboring VNFCs will usually be part of the same SFC, resource fluctuations at one VNFC are expected to influence resource requirements at its neighbors as traffic flows from one VNFC to the other. This dependency of VNFCs on their neighborhood makes the connectionist approach derived from the GNN model an interesting fit as an approach for managing resources in NFV. Therefore, the GNN-based dynamic resource management system discussed in this section is derived from Eqs. (7.92) and (7.93), and is shown in Figure 7.12 for a single VNFC. As can be seen, the system comprises four main components: (i) SFC features, (ii) VNFC states, (iii) state computation, and (iv) output computation.

SFC features are the observations or monitoring data from the VNFCs, and constitute the input to both h_w and g_w. In an NFV environment, these features represent the network parameters (such as CPU or RAM utilization levels) that can be measured. The SFC in Figure 7.11 may be represented as a VNF-FG. In this section, we consider the resulting VNF-FG at the granularity of VNFCs, that is, the nodes represented in the VNF-FG are VNFCs rather than VNFs. Specifically, we model a SFC as a directed graph (N, L), where N represents the set of VNFCs and L the set of links between these VNFCs. An example of such a representation is given in Figure 7.13, which is based on the SFC in Figure 7.11. As can be seen in the figure, subsets of VNFCs make up a VNF (e.g., $n1$, $n2$, $n3$, $n4$, and $n5$ make up VNF 2 from Figure 7.11). Each VNFC $n \in N$ has a set of features $f_n \in \mathbb{R}^{D_N}$ that represent a measurable resource for the VNFC, such as VNFC memory m_n, CPU c_n, processing delay d_n, and so on. In the same way, each link $l_{nm} \in L$ that connects VNFC n to m is characterized by a set $f_{nm} \in \mathbb{R}^{D_L}$ of features, which could represent link delay d_{nm}, bandwidth b_{nm}, and so on. D_N and D_L refer to the dimensions of the feature sets for VNFCs and links, respectively. Equations (7.94) and (7.95) show example feature sets for VNFC n and link l_{nm}, respectively, for which $D_N = 3$ and $D_L = 2$.

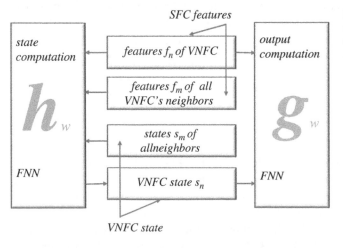

Figure 7.12 Graph neural network (GNN)-based resource forecasting model for a single VNFC. *Source:* Mijumbi et al. [205].

Figure 7.13 Service function chain (SFC) modeling: virtualized network function component (VNFC) directed graph.

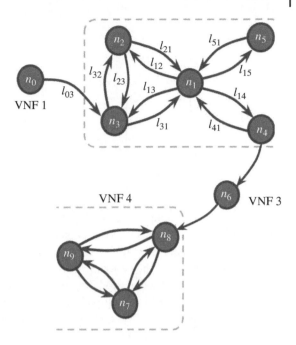

$$f_n = \begin{bmatrix} c_n \\ m_n \\ d_n \end{bmatrix} \qquad (7.94)$$

$$f_{nm} = \begin{bmatrix} b_{nm} \\ d_{nm} \end{bmatrix} \qquad (7.95)$$

The objective is to monitor the features of each VNFC over time, and to use such historical observations, as well as the historical observations from the VNFC's neighbors, to predict its subsequent features, which – in this case – represent future VNFC resource requirements. To define both historic and future resource utilization, we refer to the VNFC and connected link features at (discrete) time step t by $f_n(t)$ and $f_{nm}(t)$, respectively. At any time t, we should be able to predict future resource utilization using a finite horizon of past resource utilization measurements. We denote the number of past measurements included in such a horizon as π. An example of current ($c_n(t)$, $m_n(t)$, and $d_n(t)$) and π previous measurements is shown by the vectors in Eq. (7.96) and (7.97):

$$f_n(t) = \begin{bmatrix} c_n(t) \\ m_n(t) \\ d_n(t) \\ . \\ . \\ . \\ c_n(t-\pi) \\ m_n(t-\pi) \\ d_n(t-\pi) \end{bmatrix} \qquad (7.96)$$

$$f_{nm}(t) = \begin{bmatrix} b_{nm}(t) \\ d_{nm}(t) \\ b_{nm}(t-1) \\ d_{nm}(t-1) \\ \cdot \\ \cdot \\ \cdot \\ b_{nm}(t-\pi) \\ d_{nm}(t-\pi) \end{bmatrix} \qquad (7.97)$$

Using the observations represented by Eq. (7.96) and (7.97), the objective is to predict – say – the CPU requirement $c_n(t+\tau)$ of VNFC n at a time τ time steps after t. In the rest of this section, wherever f_n or f_{nm} is used, it should be interpreted to mean the set containing $f_n(t)$ or $f_{nm}(t)$ plus the full history of features over the period π.

It is important to note that modeling of links and their features is included here only for completeness of the model, as the link features will not be used as neighborhood information for VNFCs. The reason is that we consider that the resource utilization profile of a directed link is directly dependent on that of the VNFC at its source from which the traffic originates, and hence the information obtained from a VNFC would be similar to that obtained from the link.

VNFC States: We consider that VNFCs can be *stateful*, with each VNFC $n \in N$ having a state $s_n \in \mathbb{R}^{S_D}$ of dimension S_D. The state s_n is derived from combining the features of a given VNFC with those from other VNFCs in its neighborhood using the function h_w. This implies that the state of a given VNFC is dependent on the topology or connectivity of the VNF-FG. Such topology awareness is represented in Figure 7.14, which shows the dependencies of VNFCs in VNF 2 on each other.

The figure shows that, for example, the state $S1$ of VNFC $n1$ is dependent on the states s_2, s_3, s_4, and $s5$ of all directly connected VNFCs, as well as the corresponding features f_2, f_3, f_4, and f_5. The state s_n is determined using Eq. (7.92). This means that, considering Figure 7.14, the state $s3$ of VNFC $n3$ is given by Eq. (7.98):

$$s_3 = h_w(f_3, f_2, s_2) + h_w(f_3, f_1, s_1). \qquad (7.98)$$

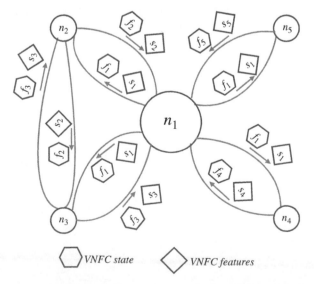

Figure 7.14 States and features from the virtualized network function component (VNFC) neighborhood.

VNFC state   VNFC features

State computation involves using Eq. (7.92) to determine the state for each VNFC. However, as can be observed from the equation, for any given pair of directly connected VNFCs, the state of each of them depends on that of the other. Therefore, the main task of state computation is to find a method to solve Eq. (7.92). The existence and uniqueness of a solution to Eq. (7.92) is guaranteed by Banach's fixed-point theorem [208, 209]. However, this requires that the global function h_w be a contraction map with respect to s; that is, Eq. (7.99) must hold for some constant $0 \leq \rho < 1$ and any two state vectors $s_a, s_b \in \mathbb{R}^{S_D}$, where $\| \cdot \|$ represents a vector norm:

$$\left\| h_w(s_a) - h_w(s_b) \right\| \leq \rho \left\| s_a - s_b \right\| \tag{7.99}$$

When Eq. (7.99) is satisfied, state computation is achieved using the classic iterative scheme given in Eq. (7.100), where $s(i)$ is the i–th iteration of the computation. This way, the function h_w stores the current state (i), and when called, calculates the next state $s(i+1)$. It can be observed that this makes the current state $s_n(i)$ of a VNFC n dependent on the previous state $s_m(i-1)$ of its neighbor m:

$$s_n(i+1) = \sum_{m \in n^*} h_w(f_n, f_m, s_m(i)), \forall n \tag{7.100}$$

Output computation involves taking as input the states calculated by the h_w functions in the iterative process described in the previous subsection, and combining it with the feature set of the VNFC to forecast a future resource requirement. The final output (forecast resource requirement) of a given VNFC is produced by another unit, which implements g_w for all VNFCs using Eq. (7.101):

$$o_n(i) = g_w(s_n(i), f_n), \forall n \tag{7.101}$$

The function g_w can be any general parametric function as long as it can be trained in a supervised manner, and the gradient of its output with respect to its input can be calculated. The straightforward approach is to use an FNN for g_w.

7.7.3 Learning and Adaptation

To achieve forecasts that correctly approximate actual resource requirements, the two functions h_w and g_w must be trained. This involves using data that has both inputs f and target outputs ξ, to adapt the weights w of the FNNs to the task under consideration. In the case of the problem addressed in this section, we need to have sample data that shows for a given resource utilization profile (i.e., historic and current features $f_n(t - \pi), \ldots f_n(t)$), the resource utilization $o_n(t + \tau)$ at a given time in the future. This learning task can be posed as the minimization of a penalized quadratic cost function

$$e_w = \sum_{n \in N} \left((o_n - \xi_n)^2 / 2 + \beta L(o_n) \right) \tag{7.102}$$

The first term in Eq. (7.102) is the standard error term usually used for training FNNs. The second term is a penalty function that is added to the error function to ensure that the function h_w is a contraction map. The relative importance of the second term can be adjusted using the constant β. The second term is meant to limit the values that can be assumed by the weights w to low values. This is achieved by using the function L (defined below) to penalize the FNN whenever its output is above a given threshold μ, known as the contraction constant. In this segment, since all inputs to the system are first scaled to the range $(0, 1)$, the constants μ and β are set to 1:

$$L(y) = \begin{cases} (y - \mu)^2 & \text{if } y > \mu \\ 0 & 0 \end{cases} \tag{7.103}$$

The learning objective is to find the weights w for each h_w and g_w such that the cost function (Eq. (7.102)) is minimized.

Design Example 7.4

Here we chose to present the experimental setup and measurements results from [205] based on Clearwater's cloud IMS [210] (Figure 7.15).

Clearwater's cloud IMS, an open source IMS core developed by Metaswitch Networks, is an example of a practical VNF that is composed from VNFCs.

As shown in Figure 7.15, it is composed of five core nodes named Bono, Sprout, Homestead, Homer, and Ralf. Bono is a Session Initiation Protocol (SIP) edge proxy that provides a Web Real-Time Communications (WebRTC) interface to UEs. It is the anchor point for UEs to the Clearwater system. Sprout is an SIP registrar and authoritative routing proxy that handles UE authentication. It includes a memcached cluster storing client registration data. Homestead provides a Web services interface to Sprout for retrieving authentication credentials and user profile information. It runs as a cluster using Cassandra as the store for mastered/cached data. Homer is a standard XML Document Management Server (XDMS) used to store multimedia telephony (MMTEL) service settings documents for each user of the system using Cassandra as the data store. Ralf provides the Rf Charging Trigger Function (CTF), which is used in IMS to provide offline billing. Bono and Sprout report P-CSCF and I/S-CSCF chargeable events respectively to Ralf, which then reports these over Rf to an external Charging Data Function (CDF). It uses a memcached client to store and manage session state. As shown in the figure, communication is initiated by the UE attaching to Bono. Bono then requests for UE authentication from Sprout, which does this by querying the database in Homestead. During a call, Sprout uses user media settings stored in Homer, and the calls are charged by Ralf. From this flow of communications (for just one VNF), it is clear that if Bono is overloaded by too many UEs trying to attach to the system, then Sprout would likely get more requests as well, and so would Homestead. Moreover, if each of these UE attachments is successful, both Homer and Ralf would also get overloaded. It is these interactions between VNFCs that motivate the approach described in the previous sections. While this illustration considers mainly control plane signaling, a similar effect is expected

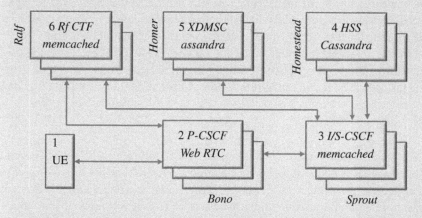

Figure 7.15 Virtualized network function 2 (VNF 2): Clearwater cloud IP multimedia subsystem. *Source:* Mijumbi et al. [205].

Design Example 7.4 (Continued)

by considering the data plane, for example, in an SFC where user packets have to be processed by one VNF before they move to the next.

The experimental setup, based on Clearwater's cloud IMS and used in [205], is shown in Figure 7.16. The deployment comprises six main components: the Clearwater cloud IMS described in Figure 7.15, OpenStack, UE, Monitoring, Domain Name System (DNS), and the algorithms being tested. In the implementation, UE is realized using SIPp [211]. SIPp is an open source test tool/traffic generator for the SIP protocol. Two SIPp instances were created each running in a VM. Each SIPp instance has 50 000 unique registered users. Calls originate from users on one SIP instance to users on the other. To monitor the resource utilization of the VNFCs in the system, Cacti [212], an open source Web-based network monitoring and graphing tool that polls all system nodes using SNMP was used. Finally, BIND [213] an open source implementation of DNS, was used to allow Clearwater nodes to identify each other, and for load distribution when any of the nodes has more than one instance.

In the experiments, each of the Clearwater nodes represents a VNFC, and is hosted in a VM running in OpenStack. Therefore, the basic evaluation system deployment included 10 VMs running in OpenStack (five for Clearwater nodes, two for UEs, one for DNS, one for Cacti monitoring, and one hosting the system under test (the algorithms)). These VMs, and additional ones (for horizontal scaling of Clearwater), were automatically deployed in OpenStack using Heat Orchestration Templates (HOTs) [214].

Setup Parameters: Each VM used in the tests has a 1vCPU, 2 GB RAM, and 8 GB storage, each running Ubuntu 14.04. Calls were generated from one UE to the other following a Poisson distribution with an average arrival rate of 10 calls per second, and each call lasting an average of 180 s following a negative exponential distribution. To model a time-of-day effect on traffic

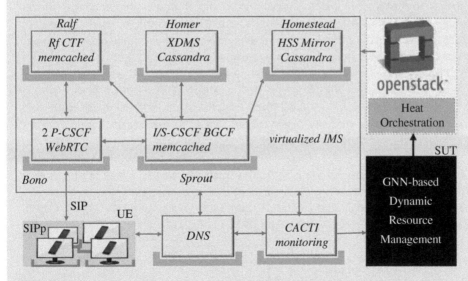

Figure 7.16 Network function virtualization (NFV) implementation used for evaluations. *Source:* Mijumbi et al. [205].

(Continued)

Design Example 7.4 (Continued)

arrivals, the above arrival pattern is repeated after every 50 000 calls, with the arrival rate and call duration parameters being halved and doubled alternately. During the duration of each call, real voice and video media are transmitted between the UEs. The voice/video content is derived from VoIP (Skype) traces [215] that contain network traffic captured on the main link of Politecnico di Torino involving Skype traffic from students, researchers, professors, and administration staff. The original 3.75 GB of end-to-end voice only and voice +video calls traces with about 40 million packets was split into 40 .pcap files, each with about 1 million packets. For each established call, one of these media files (chosen at random) was played to simulate real voice or video media.

Experiments: Three sets of experiments were performed. In each experiment, measurements of resource parameters (CPU, RAM, latency, call drops) for all Clearwater nodes were taken every 15 s.

The first experiment was used to collect 10 000 data points, which were used to train the FNNs. The history and forecasting periods used were $\pi = \tau = 20$, implying that for each VNFC, the last 20 observations were used to predict the resource requirement 20 time units in the future.

In the second experiment, the trained system was tested to determine its prediction accuracy over 1000 measurements, in which case, every 15 s, the system was run to determine an output, and its output compared to the actual resource requirements 20 time units later. This was used as a prediction accuracy test without performing any resource allocations.

Finally, in the third set of experiments, the system predictions were used to actually effect resource allocations in the Clearwater system. In this case, the system was programmed to effect a deployment of a new VNFC whenever it predicted that the % CPU utilization of a given VNFC would exceed 40%, and where possible (if more than one are available), to reduce the number of deployed VNFCs when the predicted utilization is 20%. The motivation behind using 40% and 20% respectively as the thresholds is VNF specific. In the monitoring of the normal operation of the Clearwater VNF, it was observed that the VMs had a relatively low CPU utilization most of the time, but that beyond 40% of CPU utilization, performance (call drops) would degrade, whereas below 20% of CPU utilization, the call drop rate remained almost unchanged. It is worth noting that these thresholds may be different for a different VNF.

Comparisons: The GNN system was compared with two alternatives: a static approach in which the resources were not changed at all, and a manual approach where VNFC deployments were programmed to be performed when the system crossed the (40%) resource utilization threshold. The main difference between the manual programming and the GNN system is that in the manual approach, the process of scaling resources is only started after a given threshold is reached, whereas in the GNN system, the reaching of this threshold is predicted ahead of time, and the scaling process started before the threshold is actually reached. In addition, the prediction accuracy of the GNN system was compared with that resulting from a simple FNN. To compare the differences in prediction accuracies between the FNN and the GNN, the mean absolute percentage error (MAPE) defined as

$$MAPE = \left(\frac{1}{k} \sum_{t=1}^{k} | \frac{\xi_n(t) - o_n(t)}{\xi_n(t)} | \times 100 \right). \tag{7.104}$$

was used.

Design Example 7.4 (Continued)

Neural Network Architectures: The evaluations include three neural network architectures. The first is the basic FNN whose performance is compared against that of the GNN. The other two are also FNNs, but with their architectures designed in line with the requirements of the functions h_w and g_w. The h_w, g_w, and FNN neural networks were implemented in architectures with (i) one hidden layer, and (ii) a number of neurons in the hidden layer equal to the average of the neurons in the input and output layers. Such an architecture has been shown to produce universal approximators [216, 217]. With these guiding rules, the resulting neural network parameters are given in following Table 7.1.

It can be observed that each architecture has three layers. Since we consider three VNFC features (i.e., CPU, memory, and processing delay), the dimension of the state is 3 (one for each feature). This is the reason why the output layer for each of the architectures is 3. The number of neurons in the input layer is determined based on the inputs that should be accepted. For example, for the FNN, since we have three SFC features and since we consider both the current value of each of the parameters plus the 20 previous values, the total number of inputs is $3 \times (20 + 1) = 63$. For h_w, the inputs contain two sets of the features (one from a neighboring VNFC) as well as the state from the neighboring VNFC. This gives $(3 + 3) \times (20 + 1) + 3 = 129$. For g_w, the inputs contain one set of features (from the VNFC under consideration) as well as the state of the VNFC. This gives $(3) \times (20 + 1) + 3 = 66$.

Finally, the number of neurons in the hidden layers for each architecture is determined as the average of the number in the input and output layers. The evaluation results, shown in Figures 7.17–7.21 are self-explanatory.

Table 7.1 Neural network architecture parameters.

Neural network	FNN		GNN
	FNN for each VNFC	h_ω	g_ω
Number of layers	3	3	3
Number of neurons in output layer	3	3	3
Number of neurons in input layer	63	129	66
Number of neurons in hidden layer	33	66	35

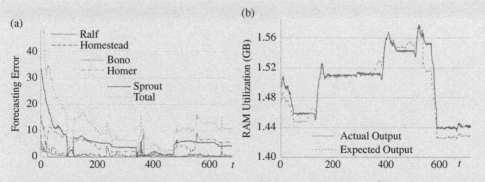

Figure 7.17 (a) Total forecasting error (t-training iteration each involving 10^3 examples), (b) Ralf RAM utilization (t-test number). (For more details see color figure in bins).

(Continued)

Design Example 7.4 (Continued)

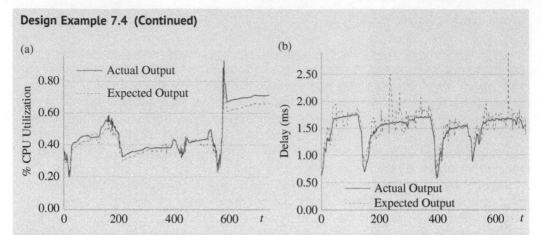

Figure 7.18 (a) Homer CPU utilization, (b) Homestead processing delay (t-test number). (For more details see color figure in bins).

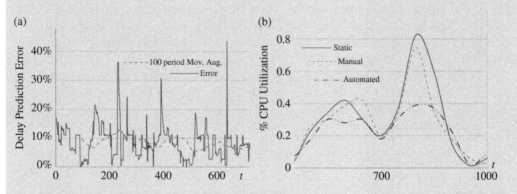

Figure 7.19 (a) Percentage error on delay prediction, (b) percentage CPU for Homer (t-test number). (For more details see color figure in bins).

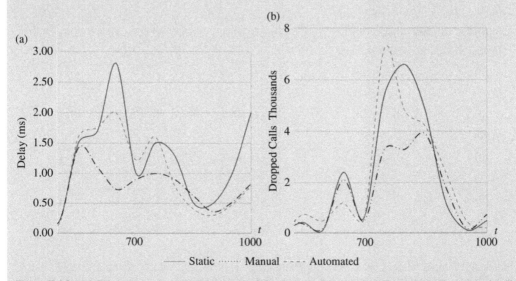

Figure 7.20 (a) Effect on processing latency, (b) effect on calls dropped (t-test number). (For more details see color figure in bins).

Design Example 7.4 (Continued)

Figure 7.21 Cumulative call drops (t-test number). (For more details see color figure in bins).

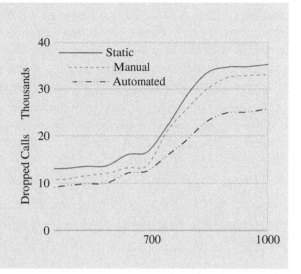

7.8 DRL for Multioperator Network Slicing

In this section, network slicing is considered in a more complex setup. We consider a system where a limited number of channels are auctioned across scheduling slots to mobile users (MUs) of multiple service providers (SPs). Each SP behaves selfishly to maximize the expected long-term payoff from the competition with other SPs for the orchestration of channels, which provides its MUs with the opportunities to access the computation and communication slices. This problem is modeled as a stochastic game, in which the decision making process of an SP depends on the global network dynamics as well as on the joint control policy of all SPs. To approximate the NE solutions, an abstract stochastic game with the local conjectures of channel auction among the SPs is first developed. Then the per-SP MDP is linearly decomposed to simplify the decision making process at an SP, and an online scheme based on deep RL is derived to approach the optimal abstract control policies.

7.8.1 System Model

The physical network infrastructure is split into virtual computation and communication slices tailored to heterogeneous mobile service requests, which can be basically categorized as the emerging Multi-access Edge Computing (MEC) and the traditional mobile services. The shared RAN, which consists of a set B of physical BSs, covers a service region with a set $\mathcal{L}$ of locations (or small areas) with each being characterized by uniform signal propagation conditions. We choose $\mathcal{L}_b$ to designate the set of locations covered by a BS $b \in B$. For any two BSs in the RAN, we assume that $\mathcal{L}_b \cap \mathcal{L}_{b'} = \emptyset$, where $b' \in B$ and $b' \neq b$. We represent the geographical distribution of BSs by a topological graph $\mathcal{TG} = \langle B, \mathcal{E} \rangle$, where $\mathcal{E} = \{e_{b,b'} : b \neq b', b, b' \in B\}$ represents the relative locations between the BSs with

$$e_{b,b'} = \begin{cases} 1, \text{if BSs } b \text{ and } b' \text{ are neighbors;} \\ 0, \text{otherwise.} \end{cases} \tag{7.105}$$

Different SPs provide different mobile services, and each MU can subscribe to only one SP $i \in \mathcal{I}$ = $\{1, ..., I\}$. Let $\mathcal{N}_i$ be the set of MUs of SP i; then $\mathcal{N} = \bigcup_{i \in \mathcal{I}} \mathcal{N}_i$ denotes the set of all MUs across the whole network.

Inter-SP Channel Auction: We consider a system with a set $\mathcal{J} = \{1, ..., J\}$ of non-overlapping orthogonal channels with the same bandwidth η [Hz]. The whole system operates across discrete scheduling slots, each of which is indexed by an integer $k \in \mathrm{IN}+$ and is assumed to be of equal time duration δ (seconds). Over the time horizon, the MUs move in the service region $\mathcal{L}$ following a Markov mobility model. Such a mobility model is widely used in the literature. Let $\mathcal{N}_{b,i}^k$ be the set of MUs appearing in the coverage of a BS $b \in \mathrm{B}$ at a scheduling slot $k \in \mathrm{IN}+$ that are subscribed to SP $i \in \mathcal{I}$; then $\mathcal{N}_i = \bigcup_{b \in \mathrm{B}} \mathcal{N}_{b,i}^k, \forall k \in \mathrm{IN} +$. We assume that during a scheduling slot, an MU at a location can only be associated with the BS that covers the location. The SPs compete for the limited number of channels to provide their MUs access to the virtual computation and communication slices. Specifically, at the beginning of each scheduling slot k, each SP i submits to the SDN orchestrator a bid given by $\hat{\beta}_i^k = \left(\hat{\nu}_i^k, \hat{\mathrm{C}}_i^k \right)$, which is not necessarily equal to $\beta_i^k = \left(\nu_i^k, \mathrm{C}_i^k \right)$. Herein, $\mathrm{C}_i^k = \left(\mathrm{C}_{b,i}^k : b \in \mathcal{B} \right)$, with $\mathrm{C}_{b,i}^k$ being the number of potentially needed channels within the coverage of a BS b and ν_i^k is the true value over C_i^k. Upon receiving the auction bids $\hat{\beta}^k = \left(\hat{\beta}_i^k : i \in \mathcal{I} \right)$ from all SPs, the SDN orchestrator proceeds to allocate the channels to MUs and computes the payment τ_i^k for each SP i. Let $\rho_n^k = \left(\rho_{n,j}^k : j \in \mathcal{J} \right)$ be the channel allocation vector for a MU $n \in \mathcal{N}$, where

$$
\rho_{n,j}^k = \begin{cases} 1, \text{if channel } j \text{ is allocated to} \\ \quad \text{MU } n \in \mathcal{N} \text{ at scheduling slot } k; \\ 0, \text{otherwise}. \end{cases} \tag{7.106}
$$

The following constraints are imposed for the centralized channel allocation at the SDN orchestrator during a single slot:

$$
\left(\sum_{i \in \mathcal{I}} \sum_{n \in \mathcal{N}b, ik} \rho_{n,j}^k \right) \cdot \left(\sum_{i \in \mathcal{I}} \sum_{n \in \mathcal{N}b', ik} \rho_{n,j}^k \right) = 0, \tag{7.107}
$$
$$
\text{if } e_{b,b'} = 1, \forall e_{b,b'} \in \mathcal{E}, \forall j \in \mathcal{J};
$$

$$
\sum_{i \in \mathcal{I}} \sum_{n \in \mathcal{N}b, ik} \rho_{n,j}^k \leq 1, \forall b \in \mathcal{B}, \forall j \in \mathcal{J}; \tag{7.108}
$$

$$
\sum_{j \in \mathcal{I}} \rho_{n,j}^k \leq 1, \forall b \in \mathcal{B}, \forall i \in \mathcal{I}, \forall n \in \mathcal{N}_{b,i}, \tag{7.109}
$$

to ensure that a channel cannot be allocated to the coverage areas of two adjacent BSs to avoid interference in data transmissions, and in the coverage of a BS, an MU can be assigned at most one channel and a channel can be assigned to at most one MU. As we will see later in this section, such assumptions couple the decision making processes from SPs only during the channel auctions.

We denote by $\varphi^k = \left(\varphi_i^k : i \in \mathcal{I} \right)$ the winner determination in the channel auction at a scheduling slot k, where $\varphi_i^k = 1$ if SP i wins the channel auction and $\varphi_i^k = 0$ indicates that no channel is allocated to the MUs of SP i during the slot. The SDN orchestrator calculates φ^k through the Vickrey–Clarke–Groves (VCG) mechanism that maximizes the true value of all SPs:

$$
\varphi^k = \arg_{\varphi} \max \sum_{i \in \mathcal{I}} \varphi_i \cdot \hat{\nu}_i^k
$$

s.t. constraints (7.107), (7.108) and (7.109); $\tag{7.110}$

$$
\sum_{n \in \mathcal{N}bik} \varphi_n^k = \varphi_i \cdot \mathrm{C}_{b,i}^k, \forall b \in \mathcal{B}, \forall i \in \mathcal{I},
$$

where $\varphi = (\varphi_i \in \{0, 1\} : i \in \mathcal{I})$, and $\varphi_n^k = \sum_{j \in \mathcal{I}} \rho_{n,j}^k$ is a channel allocation variable that equals 1 if MU n is assigned a channel and 0, otherwise. Moreover, the payment for each SP i is calculated as

$$\tau_i^k = max_{\varphi_{-i}} \sum_{i' \in \mathcal{I} - \{i\}} \varphi_{i'} \cdot \hat{v}_{i'}^k - max_\varphi \sum_{i' \in \mathcal{I} - \{i\}} \varphi_{i'} \cdot \hat{v}_{i'}^k \tag{7.111}$$

where $-i$ denotes all the other SPs in I without the presence of SP i. The economic properties of the VCG-based channel auction at a scheduling slot k are

- *Efficiency* – When all SPs announce their true bids, the SDN orchestrator allocates the channels to maximize the sum of values, resulting in efficient channel utilization.
- *Individual Rationality* – Each SP i can expect a nonnegative payoff $\hat{v}_i^k - \tau_i^k$ at any scheduling slot k.
- *Truthfulness* – No SP can improve its payoff by bidding differently from its true value, which implies that the optimal bid at any slot k is $\hat{\beta}_i^k = \beta_i^k$, $\forall i \in \mathcal{I}$.

Computation and Communication Models: Let $L_n^k \in \mathcal{L}$ be the location of an MU $n \in \mathcal{N}$ during a scheduling slot k; the average channel gain $H_n^k = h(L_n^k)$ experienced by MU n during the slot is determined by the physical distance between the MU and the associated BS. At the beginning of each scheduling slot k, each MU n independently generates a random number $A_{n,(t)}^k \in \mathcal{A} = \left\{0, 1, ..., A_{(t)}^{(max)}\right\}$ of computation tasks. We represent a computation task by $(\mu_{(t)}, \vartheta)$ with $\mu_{(t)}$ and ϑ being, respectively, the input data size (in bits) and the number of CPU cycles required to process one input bit of the computation task. This work assumes that the task arrival sequence $\left\{A_{n,(t)}^k : k \in \mathrm{IN}_+\right\}$ follows a Markov process. Two options are available for each computation task: (i) local processing at the MU; and (ii) off-loading to the logical MEC gateway in the computation slice. In other words, the arriving computation tasks must be executed during the scheduling slot. The computation off-loading decision for MU n at a slot k specifies the number $R_{n,(t)}^k$ of tasks to be transmitted to the MEC server. So, the final number of tasks to be processed by the mobile device is $A_{n,(t)}^k - \varphi_n^k \cdot R_{n,(t)}^k$. Meanwhile, a data queue is maintained at each MU to buffer the packets coming from the mobile service. The arriving packets are queued until transmission, and we assume that every data packet has a constant size of $\mu_{(p)}$ (bits). Let W_n^k and $A_{n,(p)}^k$ be, respectively, the queue length and the random new packet arrivals for MU n at the beginning of slot k. The packet arrival process is assumed to be independent among the MUs and i.i.d. across the scheduling slots. Let $R_{n,(p)}^k$ be the number of data packets that are to be removed from the queue of MU n at slot k. Then the number of packets that are eventually transmitted via the communication slice is $\varphi_n^k \cdot R_{n,(p)}^k$, and the queue evolution of MU n can be written in the form of

$$W_n^{k+1} = min\left\{W_n^k - \varphi_n^k \cdot R_{n,(p)}^k + A_{n,(p)}^k, W^{(max)}\right\}, \tag{7.112}$$

where $W^{(max)}$ is the maximum buffer size that restricts $W_n^k \in \mathcal{W} = \left\{0, W^{(max)}\right\}$.

The energy (in Joules) consumed by an MU $n \in \mathcal{N}$ for reliably transmitting input data of $\varphi_n^k \cdot R_{n,(t)}^k$ computation tasks and $\varphi_n^k \cdot R_{n,(p)}^k$ packets during a scheduling slot k can be calculated as [219]

$$P_{n,(tr)}^k = \frac{\delta \cdot \eta \cdot \sigma^2}{H_n^k} \cdot \left(2^{\frac{\varphi_n^k\left(\mu_{(t)} \cdot R_{n,(t)}^k + \mu_{(p)} \cdot R_{n,(p)}^k\right)}{\eta\delta}} - 1\right), \tag{7.113}$$

where σ^2 is the noise power spectral density. Let $\Omega^{(max)}$ be the maximum transmit power for all MUs, namely, $P_{n,(tr)}^k \leq \Omega^{(max)} \cdot \delta$, $\forall n$ and $\forall k$. For the remaining number $A_{n,(t)}^k - \varphi_n^k \cdot R_{n,(t)}^k$ of computation tasks that are processed at the mobile device of MU n, the CPU energy consumption is given by

$$P_{n,(CPU)}^k = \varsigma \cdot \mu_{(t)} \cdot \vartheta \cdot \varrho^2 \left(A_{n,(t)}^k - \varphi_n^k \cdot R_{n,(t)}^k \right) \tag{7.114}$$

where ς is the effective switched capacitance that depends on the chip architecture of the mobile device, and ϱ is the CPU cycle frequency at a mobile device.

Control Policy: We denote by $\chi_n^k = \left(L_n^k, A_{n,(t)}^k, W_n^k \right) \in \mathcal{X} = \mathcal{L} \times \mathcal{A} \times \mathcal{W}$ the local network state observed at a MU $n \in \mathcal{N}$. Thus, $\chi^k = \left(\chi_n^k : n \in \mathcal{N} \right) \in \mathcal{X}^{|\mathcal{N}|}$ characterizes the global state of the network, where $|\mathcal{N}|$ stands for the cardinality of the set $\mathcal{N}$. Each SP $i \in \mathcal{I}$ aims to design a control policy $\pi_i = (\pi_{i,(c)}, \pi_{i,(t)}, \pi_{i,(p)})$, where $\pi_{i,(c)}$, $\pi_{i,(t)} = (\pi_{n,(t)} : n \in \mathcal{N}_i)$ and $\pi_{i,(p)} = \left(\pi_{n,(p)} : n \in \mathcal{N}_i \right)$ are the channel auction, the computation off-loading, and the packet scheduling policies, respectively. Note that the computation off-loading policy $\pi_{n,(t)}$ as well as the packet scheduling policy $\pi_{n,(p)}$, are specified by the MU and hence both $\pi_{i,(t)}$ and $\pi_{i,(p)}$ depend only on $\chi_i^k = \left(\chi_n^k : n \in \mathcal{N}_i \right) \in \mathcal{X}_i = \mathcal{X}^{|\mathcal{N}_i|}$. The joint control policy of all SPs is given by $\pi = (\pi_i : i \in \mathcal{I})$. With the observation of χ^k at the beginning of each scheduling slot k, SP i announces the auction bid β_i^k to the SDN orchestrator for channel allocation and decides the numbers of computation tasks $R_{i,(t)}^k$ to be off-loaded and packets $R_{i,(p)}^k$ to be transmitted following π_i, that is, $\pi_i(\chi^k) = \left(\pi_{i,(c)}(\chi^k), \pi_{i,(t)}(\chi_i^k), \pi_{i,(p)}(\chi_i^k) \right) = \left(\beta_i^k, R_{(i,(t))}^k, R_{(i,(p))}^k \right)$, where $R_{i,(t)}^k = \left(R_{n,(t)}^k : n \in \mathcal{N}_i \right)$ and $R_{i,(p)}^k = \left(R_{n,(p)}^k : n \in \mathcal{N}_i \right)$. We define an instantaneous payoff function for SP $i \in \mathcal{I}$ at a slot k as

$$
\begin{aligned}
& F_i \left(\chi^k, \varphi_i^k, R_{i,(t)}^k, R_{i,(p)}^k \right) \\
& = \sum_{n \in \mathcal{N}_i} \alpha_n \cdot U_n \left(\chi_n^k, \varphi_n^k, R_{n,(t)}^k, R_{n,(p)}^k \right) - \tau_i^k,
\end{aligned}
\tag{7.115}
$$

where $\varphi_i^k = \left(\varphi_n^k : n \in \mathcal{N}_i \right)$, and $\alpha_n \in \mathbb{R}_+$ can be treated herein as the unit price to charge an MU n for realizing utility $U_n \left(\chi_n^k, \varphi_n^k, R_{n,(t)}^k, R_{n,(p)}^k \right)$ from consuming power to process the arriving computation tasks and transmit the queued packets to avoid packet overflows, which is chosen to be

$$
\begin{aligned}
& U_n \left(\chi_n^k, \varphi_n^k, R_{n,(t)}^k, R_{n,(p)}^k \right) \\
& = U_n^{(1)} \left(W_n^{k+1} \right) + U_n^{(2)} \left(D_n^k \right) \\
& + l_n \cdot \left(U_n^{(3)} \left(P_{n,(CPU)}^k \right) + U_n^{(4)} \left(P_{n,(tr)}^k \right) \right),
\end{aligned}
\tag{7.116}
$$

where $D_n^k = \max \left\{ W_n^k - \varphi_n^k \cdot R_{n,(p)}^k + A_{n,(p)}^k - W^{(\max)}, 0 \right\}$ defines the number of packet drops that occur when the queue vacancy is less than the number of arriving packets. The positive and monotonically decreasing functions $U_n^{(1)}(\cdot)$, $U_n^{(2)}(\cdot)$, $U_n^{(3)}(\cdot)$, and $U_n^{(4)}(\cdot)$ measure the satisfactions of the packet queuing delay, the packet drops, the CPU energy consumption, and the transmit energy consumption. Finally, $l_n \in \mathbb{R}_+$ is a constant weighting factor that balances the importance of the energy consumption within a scheduling slot.

7.8.2 System Optimization

In this section, we first formulate the competitive channel auction, computation off-loading, and packet scheduling interaction (referred to as *cross-slice resource orchestration*) among the noncooperative SPs across the time horizon as a stochastic game and then discuss the best-response solution from a game-theoretic perspective.

Stochastic Game SG Formulation: Due to the limited radio resources and the stochastic nature of the networking environment, we formulate the problem of cross-slice resource orchestration among multiple noncooperative SPs over the time horizon as a stochastic game, SG, in which I SPs are the competitive players, and there is a set $\mathcal{X}^{|\mathcal{N}|}$ of global network states and a collection of control policies $\{\pi_i : \ \forall i \in \mathcal{I}\}$. The joint control policy π induces a probability distribution over the sequence of global network states $\{\chi^k : \ k \in IN_+\}$ and the sequences of per-slot instantaneous payoffs $\{F_i(\chi^k, \varphi_i^k, R_{i,(t)}^k, R_{i,(p)}^k) : \ k \in IN_+\}$, $\forall i \in \mathcal{I}$. From assumptions regarding the mobility of an MU and the random computation task and data packet arrivals, the randomness present in $\{\chi^k : \ k \in IN_+\}$ is hence Markovian with the following state transition probability:

$$\mathbb{P}\left(\chi^{k+1} \mid \chi^k, \varphi\left(\pi_{(c)}\left(\chi^k\right)\right), \pi_{(t)}\left(\chi^k\right), \pi_{(p)}\left(\chi^k\right)\right)$$
$$= \prod_{n \in \mathcal{N}} \mathbb{P}\left(L_n^{k+1} \mid L_n^k\right) \cdot \mathbb{P}\left(A_{n,(t)}^{k+1} \mid A_{n,(t)}^k\right) \tag{7.117}$$
$$\mathbb{P}\left(W_n^{k+1} \mid W_n^k, \varphi_n\left(\pi_{(c)}\left(\chi^k\right)\right), \pi_{n,(t)}\left(\chi_n^k\right), \pi_{n,(p)}\left(\chi_n^k\right)\right),$$

where $\mathbb{P}(\cdot)$ is the probability of an event, $\varphi = (\varphi_i : i \in \mathcal{I})$ is the global channel allocation by the SDN orchestrator, while $\pi_{(c)} = (\pi_{i,\,(c)} : i \in \mathcal{I})$, $\pi_{(t)} = (\pi_{i,\,(t)} : \ i \in \mathcal{I})$, and $\pi_{(p)} = (\pi_{i,\,(p)} : i \in \mathcal{I})$ are, respectively, the joint channel auction, the joint computation off-loading, and the joint packet scheduling policies. Taking expectation with respect to the sequence of per-slot instantaneous payoffs, the expected long-term payoff of a SP $i \in \mathcal{I}$ for a given initial global network state $\chi^1 = \chi = (\chi_n = (L_n, A_{n,(t)}, W_n) : \ n \in \mathcal{N})$ can be expressed as

$$V_i(\chi, \pi) = (1 - \gamma) \cdot E_\pi \left[\sum_{k=1}^{\infty} (\gamma)^{k-1} \cdot F_i\left(\chi^k, \varphi_i\left(\pi_{(c)}\left(\chi^k\right)\right), \pi_{i,(t)}\left(\chi_i^k\right), \pi_{i,(p)}\left(\chi_i^k\right)\right) \mid \chi^1 = \chi \right]$$

$$\tag{7.118}$$

where $\gamma \in [0, 1)$ is a discount factor. $V_i(\chi, \pi)$ is the state-value function of SP i in a global network state χ under a joint control policy π. The aim of each SP i is to desine a best-response control policy π_i^* that maximizes $V_i(\chi, \pi_i, \pi_{-i})$ for any given initial network state χ, which can be formally formulated as

$$\pi_i^* = argmax_{\pi_i} V_i(\chi, \pi_i, \pi_{-i}), \forall \chi \in \mathcal{X}^{|\mathcal{N}|}. \tag{7.119}$$

An NE describes the rational behaviors of the SPs in a stochastic game. In our formulated stochastic game, SG, an NE is a tuple of control policies $\langle \pi_i^* : i \in \mathcal{I} \rangle$, where each π_i^* of an SP i is the best response to the other SPs' π_{-i}^*. For the I-player stochastic game SG with expected infinite-horizon discounted payoffs, there always exists an NE in stationary control policies [220]. From Eq. (7.118), the optimal state-value function $V_i(\chi) = V_i(\chi, \pi_i^*, \pi_{-i}^*)$, $\forall i \in \mathcal{I}$ and $\forall \chi \in \mathcal{X}^{|\mathcal{N}|}$, the expected long-term payoff of an SP $i \in \mathcal{I}$ depends on information of not only the global network state across the time horizon but also the joint control policy π. In other words, the decision making processes from all SPs is coupled in SG.

Best Response: Suppose that in the *SG*, the global network state information is known and all SPs play the NE control policies π^*; then the best response of a SP $i \in \mathcal{I}$ under $\chi \in \mathcal{X}^{|\mathcal{N}|}$ can be obtained as

$$V_i(\chi) = max_{\pi_i(\chi)} \{(1-\gamma) \cdot F_i\Big(\chi, \varphi_i\Big(\pi_{i,(c)}(\chi), \pi^*_{-i,(c)}(\chi)\Big), \pi_{i,(t)}(\chi_i), \pi_{i,(p)}(\chi_i)\Big) +$$

$$+ \gamma \cdot \sum_{\chi' \in \mathcal{X}^{|\mathcal{N}|}} \mathbb{P}\Big(\chi' \mid \chi, \varphi\Big(\pi_{i,(c)}(\chi), \pi^*_{-i,(c)}(\chi)\Big), \Big(\pi_{i,(t)}(\chi_i), \pi^*_{-i,(t)}(\chi_{-i})\Big), \Big(\pi_{i,(p)}(\chi_i), \pi^*_{-i,(p)}(\chi_{-i})\Big)\Big) \cdot V_i(\chi')$$

(7.120)

where $\chi_i = (\chi_n : n \in \mathcal{N}_i)$ and $\chi' = \Big(\chi'_n = \big(L'_n, A'_{n,(t)}, W'_n\big) : n \in \mathcal{N}\Big)$ is the next global network state. One can see that it is a challenging task to find the NE for the *SG*. To operate the NE, all SPs have to know the global network dynamics, which is prohibited in our noncooperative networking environment.

7.8.3 Game Equilibria by DRL

In this section, we elaborate on how SPs play the above stochastic game with limited information. We reformulate an abstract stochastic game with the conjectures regarding the interactions among the competing SPs. By linearly decomposing the abstract state-value functions of an SP, we derive a DRL-based online learning scheme to approximate the optimal control policies.

Stochastic Game Abstraction via Conjectures: To capture the coupling of decision making processes among the competing SPs, we abstract *SG* as $\mathcal{AG}$ [221–224]. In the abstract stochastic game $\mathcal{AG}$, an SP $i \in \mathcal{I}$ behaves on the basis of on its own local network dynamics and abstractions of states at other competing SPs. Let $\Sigma_i = \{1, S_i\}$ be the abstraction of state space $\mathcal{X}_{-i}$, where $S_i \in IN + \cdot$ We allow each SP i in $\mathcal{AG}$ to construct S_i by classifying the value region $[0, \Gamma_i]$ of payments into S_i intervals, namely, $[0, \Gamma_{i,1}], (\Gamma_{i,1}, \Gamma_{i,2}], (\Gamma_{i,2}, \Gamma_{i,3}],$ and $(\Gamma_{i,S_i-1}, \Gamma_{i,S_i}]$, where $\Gamma_{i,S_i} = \Gamma_i$ is the maximum payment value, and we let $\Gamma_{i,1} = 0$ for a special case in which SP i wins the auction but pays nothing to the SDN orchestrator. With this in mind, a global network state $(\chi_i, \chi_{-i}) \in \mathcal{X}^{|\mathcal{N}|}$ is conjectured as $\widetilde{\chi}_i = (\chi_i, s_i) \in \widetilde{\chi}_i$ if SP i receives a payment τ_i in $(\Gamma_{i,s_i-1}, \Gamma_{i,s_i}]$ from the channel auction in a previous scheduling slot, where $\widetilde{\mathcal{X}}_i = \mathcal{X}_i \times \Sigma_i$ and $s_i \in \Sigma_i$. Hence, Σ_i can be treated as an approximation of $\mathcal{X}_{-i}$ but with size $S_i \ll |\mathcal{X}_{-i}|$. To ease the analysis in the following, we mathematically represent the conjecture by a surjective mapping function $g_i : \mathcal{X}_{-i} \rightarrow S_i$. Classifying the payment values brings the immediate benefit of a much reduced abstract state space for an SP. More importantly, the conjecture makes it possible to predict the expected future payment, which is needed when we specify an auction bid in the next section.

Let $\widetilde{\pi}_i = \big(\widetilde{\pi}_{i,(c)}, \pi_{i,(t)}, \pi_{i,(p)}\big)$ be the abstract control policy in the abstract stochastic game $\mathcal{AG}$ played by an SP $i \in \mathcal{I}$ over the abstract network state space $\widetilde{\mathcal{X}}_i$, where $\widetilde{\pi}_{i,(c)}$ is the abstract channel auction policy. In the abstraction from stochastic game *SG* to $\mathcal{AG}$ for SP i, we have

$$\Gamma_{i,s_i} - \Gamma_{i,s_i-1} \geq \max_{\{\chi : g_i(\chi_{-i}) = s_i\}} | F_i\big(\chi, \varphi_i\big(\pi_{(c)}(\chi)\big), \pi_{i,(t)}(\chi_i), \pi_{i,(p)}(\chi_i)\big)$$
$$- \widetilde{F}_i\big(\widetilde{\chi}_i, \varphi_i\big(\widetilde{\pi}_{(c)}(\widetilde{\chi})\big), \pi_{i,(t)}(\chi_i), \pi_{i,(p)}(\chi_i)\big) |$$

(7.121)

where $\widetilde{F}_i\big(\widetilde{\chi}_i, \varphi_i\big(\widetilde{\pi}_{(c)}(\widetilde{\chi})\big), \pi_{i,(t)}(\chi_i), \pi_{i,(p)}(\chi_i)\big)$ is the payoff of SP i in $\widetilde{\chi}_i \in \widetilde{\mathcal{X}}_i$ under $\widetilde{\pi}_i$, $\widetilde{\chi} = (\widetilde{\chi}_i : i \in \mathcal{I})$, $\widetilde{\pi}_{(c)} = \big(\widetilde{\pi}_{i,(c)} : i \in \mathcal{I}\big)$, and $\pi_{(c)}$ is the original joint channel auction policy in *SG*. Likewise, the abstract state-value function for SP i under $\widetilde{\pi} = (\widetilde{\pi}_i : i \in \mathcal{I})$ can be defined as

$$\widetilde{V}_i(\widetilde{\chi}_i, \widetilde{\pi}) = (1-\gamma) \cdot \mathrm{E}_{\widetilde{\pi}}\left[\sum_{k=1}^{\infty} (\gamma)^{k-1} \cdot \widetilde{F}_i\left(\widetilde{\chi}_i^k, \varphi_i\left(\widetilde{\pi}_{(c)}\left(\widetilde{\chi}^k\right)\right), \pi_{i,(t)}\left(\chi_i^k\right), \pi_{i,(p)}\left(\chi_i^k\right)\right) \mid \widetilde{\chi}_i^1 = \widetilde{\chi}_i\right]$$

(7.122)

$\forall \widetilde{\chi}_i \in \widetilde{\mathcal{X}}_i$, where $\widetilde{\chi}^k = \left(\widetilde{\chi}_i^k = (\chi_i^k, s_i^k) : i \in \mathcal{I}\right)$ with s_i^k being the abstract state at slot k. We will shortly see in Lemma 7.1 that the expected long-term payoff achieved by SP i from the $\widetilde{\pi}_i$ in $\mathcal{AG}$ is not far from the original π_i in $\mathcal{SG}$. Let $\mathrm{T}_i = \max_{s_i \in \mathcal{S}_i}(\Gamma_{i,s_i} - \Gamma_{i,s_i-1})$.

Lemma 7.1 For an original control policy π and the corresponding abstract policy $\widetilde{\pi}$ in games $\mathcal{SG}$ and $\mathcal{AG}$, we have $\forall i \in \mathcal{I}$, $\mid V_i(\chi, \pi) - \widetilde{V}_i(\widetilde{\chi}_i, \widetilde{\pi}) \mid \le \mathrm{T}_i$, $\forall \chi \in \mathcal{X}^{|N|}$, where $\widetilde{\chi}_i = (\chi_i, s_i)$ with $s_i = g_i(\chi_{-i})$ [218].

Instead of playing the original joint control policy π^* in the stochastic game $\mathcal{SG}$, Theorem 7.1 shows that the NE joint abstract control policy given by $\widetilde{\pi}^* = \left(\widetilde{\pi}_i^* : i \in \mathcal{I}\right)$ in the abstract stochastic game $\mathcal{AG}$ leads to a bounded regret, where $\widetilde{\pi}_i^* = \left(\widetilde{\pi}_{i,(c)}^*, \pi_{i,(t)}^*, \pi_{i,(p)}^*\right)$ denotes the best-response abstract control policy of SP $i \in \mathcal{I}$.

Theorem 7.1 For an *SP* $i \in \mathcal{I}$, let π_i be the original control policy corresponding to an abstract control policy $\widetilde{\pi}_i$. The original joint control policy π^* corresponding to a joint abstract control policy $\widetilde{\pi}^*$ satisfies $V_i\left(\chi, (\pi_i, \pi_{-i}^*)\right) \le V_i(\chi) + 2 \cdot \mathrm{T}_i$, $\forall \chi \in \mathcal{X}^{|N|}$, where (π_i, π_{-i}^*) is the joint control policy that results from *SP* i unilaterally deviating from π_i^* to π_i in the original stochastic game $\mathcal{SG}$ [218].

In the sequel, we switch our focus from the stochastic game $\mathcal{SG}$ to the abstract stochastic game $\mathcal{AG}$. Suppose all SPs play the NE joint abstract control policy $\widetilde{\pi}^*$ in the abstract stochastic game $\mathcal{AG}$. Denote $\widetilde{V}_i(\widetilde{\chi}_i) = \widetilde{V}_i(\widetilde{\chi}_i, \widetilde{\pi}^*)$, $\forall \widetilde{\chi}_i \in \widetilde{\mathcal{X}}_i$ and $\forall i \in \mathcal{I}$. The best-response abstract control policy of a SP i can be computed as

$$\widetilde{V}_i(\widetilde{\chi}_i) = \max_{\widetilde{\pi}_i(\widetilde{\chi}_i)}\Big\{(1-\gamma) \cdot \widetilde{F}_i\left(\widetilde{\chi}_i, \varphi_i\left(\widetilde{\pi}_{i,(c)}(\widetilde{\chi}_i), \widetilde{\pi}_{-i,(c)}^*(\widetilde{\chi}_{-i})\right), \pi_{i,(t)}(\chi_i), \pi_{i,(p)}(\chi_i)\right)$$

$$+ \gamma \cdot \sum_{\widetilde{\chi}_i' \in \widetilde{\mathcal{X}}_i} \mathbb{P}\left(\widetilde{\chi}_i' \mid \widetilde{\chi}_i, \varphi_i\left(\widetilde{\pi}_{i,(c)}(\widetilde{\chi}_i), \widetilde{\pi}_{-i,(c)}^*(\widetilde{\chi}_{-i})\right), \pi_{i,(t)}(\chi_i), \pi_{i,(p)}(\chi_i)\right) \cdot \widetilde{V}_i(\widetilde{\chi}_i')$$

(7.123)

$\forall \widetilde{\chi}_i \in \widetilde{\mathcal{X}}_i$, which is based on the local information alone. There remain two challenges involved in solving Eq. (7.123) for each SP $i \in \mathcal{I}$: (i) a priori knowledge of the abstract network state transition probability, which incorporates the statistics of MU mobilities, the computation task, packet arrivals, and the conjectures of other competing SPs' local network information (i.e., the statistics of Σ_i), is not feasible; and (ii) given a specific classification of the payment values, the size of the decision-making space $\{\widetilde{\pi}_i(\widetilde{\chi}_i): \widetilde{\chi}_i \in \widetilde{\mathcal{X}}_i\}$ grows exponentially as $\mid \mathcal{N}_i \mid$ increases.

Abstract State-Value Function: Let us recall that (i) the channel auction decision as well as the computation off-loading and packet scheduling decisions are made sequentially and are independent across an SP and its subscribed MUs; and (ii) the per-slot instantaneous payoff function (Eq. (7.115)) of an SP is of an additive nature, hence we are motivated to decompose the per-SP MDP described by Eq. (7.123) into $\mid \mathcal{N}_i \mid + 1$ independent single-agent MDPs. More specifically, for an SP $i \in \mathcal{I}$, the abstract state-value function $\widetilde{V}_i(\widetilde{\chi}_i)$, $\forall \widetilde{\chi}_i \in \widetilde{\mathcal{X}}_i$, can be expressed as

$$\widetilde{V}_i(\widetilde{\chi}_i) = \sum_{n \in N_i} \alpha_n \cdot \mathrm{U}_n(\chi_n) - \mathrm{U}_i(s_i),$$

(7.124)

where the per-MU expected long-term utility $U_n(\chi_n)$ and the expected long-term payment $U_i(s_i)$ of SP i satisfy, respectively,

$$U_n(\chi_n) = max_{R_{n,(t)}, R_{n,(p)}} \left\{ (1-\gamma) \cdot U_n\left(\chi_n, \varphi_n\left(\tilde{\pi}^*_{(c)}(\tilde{\chi})\right), R_{n,(t)}, R_{n,(p)}\right) \right.$$
$$\left. + \gamma \cdot \sum_{\chi n' \in \mathcal{X}} \mathbb{P}\left(\chi'_n \mid \chi_n, \varphi_n\left(\tilde{\pi}^*_{(c)}(\tilde{\chi})\right), R_{n,(t)}, R_{n,(p)}\right) \cdot U_n\left(\chi'_n\right) \right) \tag{7.125}$$

and

$$U_i(s_i) = (1-\gamma) \cdot \tau_i$$
$$+ \gamma \cdot \sum_{si' \in \mathcal{S}_i} \mathbb{P}\left(s'_i \mid s_i, \varphi_i\left(\tilde{\pi}^*_{(c)}(\tilde{\chi})\right)\right) \cdot U_i(s'_i), \tag{7.126}$$

with $\tilde{\pi}^*_{(c)}(\tilde{\chi}) = \left(\tilde{\pi}^*_{i,(c)}(\tilde{\chi}_i) : i \in \mathcal{I}\right)$, while $R_{n,(t)}$ and $R_{n,(p)}$ are the computation off-loading and packet scheduling decisions under a current local network state χ_n of MU $n \in \mathcal{N}_i$. It is worth noting that the winner determination and the payment calculation from the VCG auction at the SDN orchestrator deduce the derivation of Eq. (7.126). The linear decomposition approach in Eq. (7.124) offers two key advantages:

1) Simplified decision making: The linear decomposition motivates an SP $i \in \mathcal{I}$ to let the MUs locally make the computation off-loading and packet scheduling decisions, which reduces the action space of size $(\mathcal{A} \times \mathcal{W})^{|\mathcal{N}_i|}$ at SP i to $|\mathcal{N}_i|$ local spaces of size $\mathcal{A} \times \mathcal{W}$ at the MUs.
2) Near-optimality: The linear decomposition approach, which can be viewed as a special case of the feature-based decomposition method, provides an accuracy guarantee of the approximation of the abstract state-value function.

With the decomposition of the abstract state-value function as in Eq. (7.124), we can now specify the number of requested channels by an SP $i \in \mathcal{I}$ in the coverage of a BS $b \in B$ as

$$C_{b,i} = \sum_{\{n \in \mathcal{N}_i : L_n \in \mathcal{L}_b\}} z_n, \tag{7.127}$$

and the true value of obtaining $\mathcal{C}_i = (C_{b,i} : b \in \mathcal{B})$ across the service region as

$$\nu_i = \frac{1}{1-\gamma} \cdot \sum_{n \in \mathcal{N}_i} \alpha_n \cdot U_n(\chi_n)$$
$$- \frac{\gamma}{1-\gamma} \cdot \sum_{s_i \in \mathcal{S}_i} \mathbb{P}\left(s'_i \mid s_i, 1_{\{\Sigma_{b \in B} C_{bi} > 0\}}\right) \cdot U_i(s'), \tag{7.128}$$

which together constitute the optimal bid $\tilde{\pi}^*_{i,(c)}(\tilde{\chi}_i) = \beta_i = (\nu_i, \mathcal{C}_i)$ of SP i under a current abstract network state $\tilde{\chi}_i \in \tilde{\mathcal{X}}_i$, where for an MU $n \in \mathcal{N}_i$, z_n given by

$$z_n = argmax_{z \in \{0,1\}} \left\{ (1-\gamma) \cdot U_n\left(\chi_n, z, \pi^*_{n,(t)}(\chi_n), \pi^*_{n,(p)}(\chi_n)\right) \right.$$
$$\left. + \gamma \sum_{\chi n' \in \mathcal{X}} \mathbb{P}\left(\chi'_n \mid \chi_n, z, \pi^*_{n,(t)}(\chi_n), \pi^*_{n,(p)}(\chi_n)\right) \cdot U_n\left(\chi'_n\right) \right\} \tag{7.129}$$

indicates the preference of obtaining one channel, and $1_{\{x\}}$ is an indicator function that equals 1 if the condition x is satisfied and 0 otherwise. We can easily find that the calculation of the optimal bid β_i at SP i needs the private information of $(s_i, \mathbb{P}(s' \mid s, \iota - 1))$ and $(U_n(\chi_n), z_n, L_n)$ from each subscribed MU $\in \mathcal{N}_i$, where $s' \in \Sigma_i$ and $\iota \in \{1, 2\}$.

Learning Optimal Abstract Control Policy: In the calculation of the true value as in Eq. (7.128) for an SP $i \in \mathcal{I}$ at the beginning of each scheduling slot k, the abstract network state transition probability $\mathbb{P}(s' \mid s, \iota - 1)$, which is necessary for the prediction of the value of expected future payments, is unknown. SP i maintains over the scheduling slots a three-dimensional table Y_i^k of size $S_i \cdot S_i \cdot 2$. Each entry $y_{s,s',\iota}^k$ in table Y_i^k represents the number of transitions from $s_i^{k-1} = s$ to $s_i^k = s'$ when $\varphi_i^{k-1} = \iota - 1$ up to scheduling slot k. Y_i^k is updated using the channel auction outcomes from the SDN orchestrator. Then, the abstract network state transition probability at scheduling slot k can be estimated as

$$\mathbb{P}\big(s_i^k = s' \mid s_i^{k-1} = s, \varphi_i^{k-1} = \iota - 1\big) \frac{y_{s,s',\iota}^k}{\sum\limits_{s'' \in \mathcal{S}_i} y_{s'',s',\iota}^k} \tag{7.130}$$

Applying the union bound and the weak law of large numbers [225], we get

$$\lim_{k \to \infty} \mathbb{P}\big(\mid \mathbb{P}\big(s_i^{k+1} = s' \mid s_i^k = s, \varphi_i^k = \iota - 1\big) - \mathbb{P}\big(s_i^k = s' \mid s_i^{k-1} = s, \varphi_i^{k-1} = \iota - 1\big) \mid > \omega\big) = 0 \tag{7.131}$$

for an arbitrarily small constant $\omega \in \mathbb{R}+$, $\forall s, s' \in \Sigma_i$ and $\forall \iota \in \{1, 2\}$. The state-value function $U_i(s_i)$, $\forall s_i \in \Sigma_i$, is learned according to

$$U_i^{k+1}(s_i) =$$

$$\begin{cases} (1 - \zeta^k)\, U_i^k(s_i) + \zeta^k \left((1-\gamma)\tau_i^k + \gamma \sum\limits_{s_i^{k+1} \in \mathcal{E}_i} \mathbb{P}\big(s_i^{k+1} \mid s_i, \varphi_i^k\big) U_i^k\big(s_i^{k+1}\big) \right), & \text{if } s_i = s_i^k \\ U_i^k(s_i), & \text{otherwise} \end{cases} \tag{7.132}$$

based on φ_i^k and τ_i^k from the channel auction, where $\zeta^k \in [0, 1)$ is the learning rate. The convergence of Eq. (7.132) is guaranteed by $\sum_{k=1}^{\infty} \zeta^k = \infty$ and $\sum_{k=1}^{\infty} (\zeta^k)^2 < \infty$ [226]. Given that all SPs deploy the best-response channel auction policies, the well-known value iteration [226] can be used by the MUs to find the optimal per-MU state-value functions (Eq. (7.125)). However, this method requires complete knowledge of the local network state transition probabilities, which is challenging without a priori statistical information of MU mobility, computation task arrivals, and packet arrivals.

1) *Conventional Q-Learning:* One attractive feature of the Q-learning is that it assumes no a priori knowledge of the local network state transition statistics. Combining Eqs. (7.125) and (7.129), we define for each MU $n \in \mathcal{N}$ the optimal state-action value function $Q_n : \mathcal{X} \times \{0, 1\} \times \mathcal{A} \times \mathcal{W} \to \mathbb{R}$,

$$\begin{aligned} &Q_n\big(\chi_n, \varphi_n, R_{n,(t)}, R_{n,(p)}\big) \\ &= (1 - \gamma) \cdot U_n\big(\chi_n, \varphi_n, R_{n,(t)}, R_{n,(p)}\big) \\ &+ \gamma \cdot \sum\limits_{\chi_{n'} \in \mathcal{X}} \mathbb{P}\big(\chi_n' \mid \chi_n, \varphi_n, R_{n,(t)}, R_{n,(p)}\big) \cdot U_n\big(\chi_n'\big), \end{aligned} \tag{7.133}$$

where an action $(\varphi_n, R_{n,(t)}, R_{n,(p)})$ under a current local network state χ_n consists of the channel allocation, computation off-loading, and packet-scheduling decisions. The optimal state-value function $U_n(\chi_n)$ can be hence derived from

$$U_n(\chi_n) = \max\nolimits_{\varphi_n, R_{n,(t)}, R_{n(p)}} Q_n\big(\chi_n, \varphi_n, R_{n,(t)}, R_{n,(p)}\big). \tag{7.134}$$

By substituting Eq. (7.134) into Eq. (7.133), we get

$$Q_n(\chi_n, \varphi_n, R_{n,(t)}, R_{n,(p)}) = (1-\gamma)U_n(\chi_n, \varphi_n, R_{n,(t)}, R_{n,(p)})$$
$$+ \gamma \sum_{\chi_n' \in \mathcal{X}} \mathbb{P}(\chi_n' \mid \chi_n, \varphi_n, R_{n,(t)}, R_{n,(p)}) \tag{7.135}$$
$$\cdot \max_{\varphi_n', R_{n(t)}', R_{n(p)}'} Q_n(\chi_n', \varphi_n', R_{n,(t)}', R_{n,(p)}')$$

where $\left(\varphi_n', R_{n,(t)}', R_{n,(p)}'\right)$ is an action under χ_n'. Using Q-learning, the MU finds $Q_n(\chi_n, \varphi_n, R_{n,(t)}, R_{n,(p)})$ iteratively using observations of the local network state $\chi_n = \chi_n^k$ at a current scheduling slot k, the action $(\varphi_n, R_{n,(t)}, R_{n,(p)}) = \left(\varphi_n^k, R_{n,(t)}^k, R_{n,(p)}^k\right)$, the achieved utility $U_n(\chi_n, \varphi_n, R_{n,(t)}, R_{n,(p)})$, and the resulting local network state $\chi_n' = \chi_n^{k+1}$ at the next slot $k+1$. The learning rule is given as

$$Q_n^{k+1}(\chi_n, \varphi_n, R_{n,(t)}, R_{n,(p)}) = Q_n^k(\chi_n, \varphi_n, R_{n,(t)}, R_{n,(p)})$$
$$+ \zeta^k\left((1-\gamma)U_n(\chi_n, \varphi_n, R_{n,(t)}, R_{n,(p)}) + \gamma \max_{\varphi_n', R_{n(t)}', R_{n(p)}'} Q_n^k(\chi_n', \varphi_n', R_{n,(t)}', R_{n,(p)}')\right.$$
$$\left. - Q_n^k(\chi_n, \varphi_n, R_{n,(t)}, R_{n,(p)})\right) \tag{7.136}$$

which converges to the optimal control policy if (i) the local network state transition probability is stationary; and (ii) all state-action pairs are visited infinitely often [227]. Condition (ii) can be satisfied when the probability of choosing any action in any local network state is nonzero (i.e., *exploration*). Meanwhile, to behave well, an MU has to exploit the most recently learned Q-function (i.e., *exploitation*). A classical way to balance *exploration* and *exploitation* is the ε-greedy strategy [226].

The tabular representation of Q-function values makes the conventional Q-learning not readily applicable to high-dimensional scenarios with a very large state space, where the learning process can be extremely slow. In the system discussed here, the sizes of the local network state space $\mathcal{X}$ and action space $\{0,1\} \times \mathcal{A} \times \mathcal{W}$ are calculated as $|\mathcal{L}| \cdot \left(1 + A_{(t)}^{(\max)}\right) \cdot \left(1 + W^{(\max)}\right)$ and $2 \cdot \left(1 + A_{(t)}^{(\max)}\right) \cdot \left(1 + W^{(\max)}\right)$, respectively. Consider a service region of 1.6×10^3 locations (like the network simulated in [228]), $A_{(t)}^{(\max)} = 5$ and $W^{(\max)} = 10$: the MU has to update a total of 1.39392×10^7 Q-function values, which the conventional Q-learning process cannot converge to within a limited number of scheduling slots.

2) *Deep RL:* The advances in neural networks and the success of deep neural networks in modeling an optimal state-action Q-function inspired us to resort to a double deep Q-network (DQN) to address the massive local network state space $\mathcal{X}$ at each MU $n \in \mathcal{N}_i$ of an SP $i \in \mathcal{I}$ in our considered system [229]. That is, the Q-function in Eq. (7.135) can be approximated by $Q_n(\chi_n, \varphi_n, R_{n,(t)}, R_{n,(p)}) \approx Q_n(\chi_n, \varphi_n, R_{n,(t)}, R_{n,(p)}; \theta_n)$, where θ_n denotes a vector of parameters associated with the DQN of MU n. More specifically, each MU $n \in \mathcal{N}_i$ of an SP $i \in \mathcal{I}$ is equipped with a replay memory of a finite size M to store the experience m_n^k given by

$$\mathrm{m}_n^k = \left(\chi_n^k, \left(\varphi_n^k, R_{n,(t)}^k, R_{n,(p)}^k\right), U_n\left(\chi_n^k, \varphi_n^k, R_{n,(t)}^k, R_{n,(p)}^k\right), \chi_n^{k+1}\right), \tag{7.137}$$

which occurred at the transition between two consecutive scheduling slots k and $k+1$ during the DRL process. The memory of experiences can be encapsulated as $\mathrm{M}_n^k = \{\mathrm{m}_n^{k-M+1}, \mathrm{m}_n^k\}$. Each MU n maintains a DQN as well as a target DQN, namely, $Q_n(\chi_n, \varphi_n, R_{n,(t)}, R_{n,(p)}; \theta_n^k)$ and $Q_n(\chi_n, \varphi_n, R_{n,(t)}, R_{n,(p)}; \theta_{n,-}^k)$, with θ_n^k and $\theta_{n,-}^k$ being the associated parameters at a current scheduling slot k and a certain previous scheduling slot before slot k, respectively. According to the experience replay technique [230], at each scheduling slot k, MU n randomly samples a mini-batch

$\mathcal{O}_n^k \subseteq M_n^k$ of size $O < M$ from the replay memory M_n^k to train the DQN. The training objective is to update the parameters θ_n^k in the direction of minimizing the loss function given by

$$LOSS_n\left(\theta_n^k\right) = E_{\left(\chi_n,\left(\varphi_n, R_{n,(t)}, R_{n,(p)}\right), U_n\left(\chi_n, \varphi_n, R_{n,(t)}, R_{n,(p)}\right), \chi_n'\right) \in \mathcal{O}_n^k}$$

$$\left[\left(\left(1-\gamma\right) \cdot U_n\left(\chi_n, \varphi_n, R_{n,(t)}, R_{n,(p)}\right)\right.\right.$$

$$+ \gamma . Q_n\left(\chi_n', argmax_{\varphi_n', R_{n,(t)}', R_{n,(p)}'} Q_n\left(\chi_n', \varphi_n', R_{n,(t)}', R_{n,(p)}'; \theta_n^k\right); \theta_{n,-}^k\right)$$

$$\left.\left. - Q_n\left(\chi_n, \varphi_n, R_{n,(t)}, R_{n,(p)}; \theta_n^k\right)\right)^2\right] \tag{7.138}$$

Algorithm 3 Online DRL for Approximating Optimal State Action-Value Q-Functions of an MU $n \in \mathcal{N}_i$ of an SP $i \in \mathcal{I}$

1: **initialize** the replay memory $\mathcal{M}_n^k$ of size $M \in \mathbb{N}_+$, the mini-batch $\mathcal{O}_n^k$ of size $O < M$, a DQN and a target DQN with two sets $\boldsymbol{\theta}_n^k$ and $\boldsymbol{\theta}_{n,-}^k$ of parameters, and the local network state $\boldsymbol{\chi}_n^k$, for $k = 1$.

2: **repeat**

3:   At the beginning of scheduling slot k, the MU observes the packet arrivals $A_{n,(p)}^k$, takes χ_n^k as an input to the DQN with parameters $\boldsymbol{\theta}_n^k$, and then selects a random action $(z_n^k, R_{n,(t)}^k, R_{n,(p)}^k)$ with probability ϵ or with probability $1 - \epsilon$, an action $(z_n^k, R_{n,(t)}^k, R_{n,(p)}^k)$ with the maximum value $Q_n(\chi_n^k, z_n^k, R_{n,(t)}^k, R_{n,(p)}^k; \boldsymbol{\theta}_n^k)$.

4:   MU n sends $[Q_n(\chi_n^k, z_n^k, R_{n,(t)}^k, R_{n,(p)}^k; \boldsymbol{\theta}_n^k), z_n^k, L_n^k)$ to the subscribing SP i. SP i submits its bidding vector $\beta_i = (\nu_i, \mathbf{C}_i)$ to the SDN orchestrator, where ν_i is given by (25) and $\mathbf{C}_i = (C_{b,i} : b \in \mathcal{B})$ with each $C_{b,i}$ given by (24).

5:   With the bids from all SPs, the SDN orchestrator determines the auction winners ϕ^k and channel allocation $\rho_i^k = (\rho_n^k : n \in \mathcal{N}_i)$ according to (6), and calculates the payments τ_i^k according to (7) for SP i.

6:   With the channel allocation ρ_i^k, winner determination ϕ_n^k, and payment τ_i^k, SP i updates $\mathbf{Y}_i^k$ and $\mathbf{U}_i^{k+1}(s_i^k)$ according to (29), and MU n performs computation off-loading $\varphi_n^k R_{n,(t)}^k$ and packet scheduling $\varphi_n^k R_{n,(p)}^k$.

7:   MU n achieves utility $U_n(\chi_n^k, \varphi_n^k, R_{n,(t)}^k, R_{n,(p)}^k)$ and observes χ_n^{k+1} at the next slot $k + 1$.

8:   MU n updates $\mathcal{M}_n^k$ with $\mathbf{m}_n^k = (\chi_n^k, (\varphi_n^k, R_{n,(t)}^k, R_{n,(p)}^k), U_n(\chi_n^k, \varphi_n^k, R_{n,(t)}^k, R_{n,(p)}^k), \chi_n^{k+1})$.

9:   With a randomly sampled $\mathcal{O}_n^k$ from $\mathcal{M}_n^k$, MU n updates the DQN parameters $\boldsymbol{\theta}_n^k$ with the gradient in (36).

10:   MU n regularly resets the target DQN parameters with $\boldsymbol{\theta}_{n,-}^{k+1} = \boldsymbol{\theta}_n^k$, and otherwise $\boldsymbol{\theta}_{n,-}^{k+1} = \boldsymbol{\theta}_{n,-}^k$.

11:   The scheduling slot index is updated by $k \leftarrow k + 1$.

12: **until** A predefined stopping condition is satisfied.

---

which is a mean-squared measure of the Bellman equation error at a scheduling slot k. By differentiating $LOSS_n(\theta_n^k)$ with respect to θ_n^k, we obtain the gradient as

$$\nabla_{\theta_n^k} \text{LOSS}_n\left(\theta_n^k\right) = \text{E}_{\left(\chi_{n'}\left(\varphi_n, R_{n,(t)}, R_{n,(p)}\right), U_n\left(\chi_{n'} \varphi_n, R_{n,(t)}, R_{n,(p)}\right) \chi_n'\right) \in \mathcal{O}_n^k}$$

$$\left[\left((1-\gamma).U_n\left(\chi_n, \varphi_n, R_{n,(t)}, R_{n,(p)}\right)\right.\right.$$

$$+ \gamma.Q_n\left(\chi_n', \arg\max \varphi_n', R_{n,(t)}', R_{n,(p)}' Q_n\left(\chi_n', \varphi_n', R_{n,(t)}', R_{n,(p)}'; \theta_n^k\right); \theta_{n,-}^k\right)$$

$$\left.- Q_n\left(\chi_n, \varphi_n, R_{n,(t)}, R_{n,(p)}; \theta_n^k\right).\nabla_{\theta_n^k} Q_n\left(\chi_n, \varphi_n, R_{n,(t)}, R_{n,(p)}; \theta_n^k\right)\right] \tag{7.139}$$

Algorithm 3 details the online training procedure of MU n [218].

7.9 Deep Q-Learning for Latency-Limited Network Virtualization

In this section, the VNF scalability issue is studied to meet the QoS requirement in the presence of nonstationary traffic, through joint VNF migration and resource scaling. A traffic parameter learning method based on change point detection and Gaussian process regression (GPR) is discussed, to learn traffic parameters in a fractional Brownian motion (fBm) traffic model for each stationary traffic segment within a nonstationary traffic trace. Then, the time-varying VNF resource demand is predicted from the learned traffic parameters based on an fBm resource provisioning model. With the detected change points and predicted resource demands, a VNF migration problem is formulated as an MDP with variable-length decision epochs, to maximize the long-term reward integrating load balancing, migration cost, and the resource overloading penalty. A penalty-aware *deep Q-learning algorithm* is described to incorporate awareness of the resource overloading penalty, with improved performance over benchmarks in terms of training loss reduction and cumulative reward maximization. This section is organized along the lines presented in [231].

With time-varying traffic, the processing resource demand of a VNF is dependent on both the statistics of traffic arrivals and the QoS requirement. Here, we consider delay-sensitive VNF chains with a stringent end-to-end (E2E) delay requirement. Suppose that the E2E delay requirement is decomposed into a per-hop delay requirement at each VNF. For example, the probability of packet processing (including queuing) delay at a VNF exceeding a certain delay bound should not be beyond an upper limit. With changes in traffic statistics, the processing resource demand of a VNF varies for a certain QoS requirement. Existing studies usually assume prior knowledge of the time-varying resource demands or predict the future resource demands based on historical resource demand information. The average traffic rate over a certain time duration is usually considered as the resource demand. However, resource allocation/scaling according to the average traffic rate is not sufficient to satisfy a stringent delay requirement. In reality, a resource demand trace with an inherent QoS guarantee is difficult to obtain. Instead, a traffic trace with packet arrival information is usually available. Therefore, a resource demand prediction scheme is required to predict the *time-varying QoS-aware resource demands* following the statistical traffic changes detected in an available packet arrival traffic trace. Then, VNF scaling decisions can be made to scale up/down the amount of resources allocated to the VNFs according to the predicted resource demands and update the placement of VNFs among several candidate NFV nodes. There can be overlapping among the sets of candidate NFV nodes for different VNFs. Here, we consider one VNF in a neighborhood with several candidate NFV nodes, and treat the dynamics of other VNFs as background traffic at the NFV nodes. The dynamics of other VNFs are attributed to dynamics in both their traffic arrivals and scaling decisions.

There are several existing studies on *dynamic* VNF placement and traffic routing, based on decisions made in a proactive or reactive manner at consecutive non-overlapping decision epochs of equal length, for example, 30 min. The selection of epoch length is difficult and is usually based on experience.

If the decision epoch is too long, traffic burstiness in different time granularities within an epoch cannot be captured, resulting in challenges for continuous QoS guarantee; if the decision epoch is too short, decisions are made frequently, possibly resulting in unnecessary expensive VNF migrations for temporal short traffic bursts. A better method is to adopt the *adaptive epoch length* depending on changes in traffic statistics (e.g., mean and variance) and resource demands. Several change point detection algorithms, either retrospective or online, have been developed for detecting structural breaks in a nonstationary time series [232–234]. Online algorithms provide inferences about change points as each data sample arrives, which is more appropriate for detecting statistical traffic changes, based on which VNF scaling decisions can be made reactively without a significant latency [233, 234]. Under the assumption that a nonstationary traffic trace can be partitioned into consecutive stationary traffic segments with unknown change points, decision epochs with variable lengths are to be identified based on change point detection. Each stationary traffic segment corresponds to one decision epoch. Traffic arrivals of a VNF are from a service-level flow that is an aggregation of the traffic flows of different users. In core and backbone networks, the aggregation level is high, which makes Gaussian traffic approximation work well beyond a timescale of around 100 ms [235]. Gaussianity of a certain distribution can be checked by a quantile-quantile plot versus a standard Gaussian distribution [236]. Fractional Brownian motion (fBm) is a Gaussian process with properties such as self-similarity and long-range dependence (LRD) that comply with the properties of real-world network traffic [235, 236].

Hence, we adopt the fBm traffic model, based on which the characteristic traffic parameters of each stationary traffic segment are learned, and the corresponding resource demands are predicted.

At each decision epoch, a VNF scaling decision is made, which possibly requires VNF migrations. We use the VNF scaling decision and the VNF migration decision interchangeably. A VNF migration incurs a migration cost, such as signaling overhead to reroute traffic and resource overhead to transfer VNF states associated with the VNF, which should be minimized [238]. On the other hand, a balanced load distribution among the candidate NFV nodes makes the network more robust to future traffic variations, which is beneficial for long-term efficient resource utilization [238, 239]. There is a trade-off between the two goals. For example, a pure load-balancing solution may result in frequent and expensive VNF migrations. Therefore, we jointly consider the two objectives, by jointly minimizing the migration cost and the maximum resource loading factor among all candidate NFV nodes. Moreover, there is another trade-off between cost minimizations in the short term and in the long run. When a VNF migration is required, the VNF is migrated to the current most lightly loaded NFV node for cost minimization in the current decision epoch. However, a lightly loaded NFV node can become heavily loaded in the future due to increasing background resource usage, resulting in further migrations to avoid performance degradation. By contrast, for cost minimization in the long run, the VNF should be migrated to an NFV node that is expected to not be heavily loaded in the current and successive decision epochs. RL provides an approach for long-run cost minimization, with the ability to capture inherent patterns in network dynamics and to make intelligent decisions accordingly.

So, in this section, a dynamic VNF scaling problem is studied to meet the delay requirement in the presence of nonstationary traffic.

- To provide a QoS guarantee for the VNF with nonstationary traffic input, a change-point-driven traffic parameter learning and resource demand prediction scheme is presented. First, the prior-unknown change points of the nonstationary traffic are detected online, using a Bayesian online change point detection (BOCPD) algorithm with post-processing, which identifies the boundaries between consecutive stationary traffic segments. Then, the fBm traffic parameters are learned for the upcoming stationary traffic segment after each newly detected change point, using GPR with an fBm kernel (covariance) function. Afterward, the resource demand of the upcoming stationary traffic segment is predicted based on an fBm resource provisioning model.
- With the detected change points and predicted resource demands, a VNF migration problem is formulated as an MDP with variable-length decision epochs to minimize the overall cost, integrating imbalanced loading, migration cost, and resource overloading penalty in the long run. A *deep Q-learning* algorithm with penalty-aware prioritized experience replay is used to solve the MDP, with performance gains in terms of both cost and training loss reduction compared with benchmark algorithms.

7.9.1 System Model

Network Scenario: A service request is represented as a VNF chain, originating from a source node and traversing through a number of VNFs in sequence toward a destination node. The source and destination nodes are seen as dummy VNFs. The aggregate traffic stream between two consecutive VNFs is referred to as an inter-VNF sub-flow. We consider one VNF in the VNF chain, with an incoming sub-flow from its upstream VNF, and an outgoing sub-flow toward its downstream VNF. For packet processing at the VNF, it is required that the delay violation probability should not exceed an upper limit, that is, $\Pr(d > D) \leq \varepsilon$, where d is a random variable denoting the experienced VNF packet processing (including queuing) delay, D is the delay bound, and ε is the maximum delay violation probability. For the E2E latency specification and possible variable per node latency, see [240]. The VNF can be placed at an NFV node in a candidate set $\mathcal{N}_C$. The considered VNF is initially placed at the NFV node $n_0 \in \mathcal{N}_C$.

Nonstationary Traffic Model with Multi-Timescale Time Series: Traffic arrivals at the VNF can be represented as a time series, with each traffic sample being the number of packet arrivals in non-overlapping, successive time intervals. We consider traffic arrivals in different timescales, including a medium timescale with interval length (in second) equal T_M (e.g., 20 s), and a small timescale with interval length (in seconds) equal to T_S (e.g., 0.1 s). Let x_M denote the time series in the medium timescale, given by

$$x_M = [x_M(0), x_M(1), \cdots, x_M(m), \cdots] \tag{7.140}$$

where $m(\geq 0)$ is an index for the medium time interval, and $x_M(m)$ is the m-th traffic sample in the medium timescale, representing the number of packet arrivals in the m-th medium time interval. A series of traffic samples between medium time intervals m and m' (inclusive) is given by

$$x_M[m : m'] = [x_M(m), x_M(m+1), \cdots, x_M(m'-1), x_M(m')], m' > m. \tag{7.141}$$

Similarly, a small-timescale time series is represented as

$$x_S = [x_S(0), x_S(1), \cdots, x_S(t), \cdots] \tag{7.142}$$

where $t(\geq 0)$ is an index for the small time interval, and $x_S(t)$ is the t-th traffic sample in small time-scale. Let $x_S[t: t']$ denote a series of traffic samples between small time intervals t and t' (inclusive), given by

$$x_S[t : t'] = [x_S(t), x_S(t + 1), \cdots, x_S(t' - 1), x_S(t')], t' > t. \tag{7.143}$$

Let $A(t)$ denote the cumulative number of packet arrivals before the small time interval t, given by

$$A(t) = \begin{cases} \sum_{t'=1}^{t} x_S(t' - 1), & t \geq 1 \\ 0, & t = 0. \end{cases} \tag{7.144}$$

Letting Λ be the long-term average traffic rate in packet/s, the following relationship holds:

$$\Lambda = \lim_{m' \to \infty} \frac{1}{m'} \sum_{m=0}^{m'} \frac{x_M(m)}{T_M} = \lim_{t' \to \infty} \frac{1}{t'} \sum_{t=0}^{t'} \frac{x_S(t)}{T_S} \tag{7.145}$$

where $x_M(m)/T_M$ and $x_S(t)/T_S$ are average traffic rates (in packet/s) in the m-th medium time interval and the t-th small time interval, respectively. Assume that T_M consists of multiples of T_S. As illustrated in Figure 7.22 [231], a medium-timescale time series can be mapped to a small-timescale time series within the same time duration, represented as

$$x_M[m : m'] \Rightarrow x_S\left[\frac{mT_M}{T_S} : \left(\frac{(m'+1)T_M}{T_S} - 1\right)\right]. \tag{7.146}$$

Stationary Traffic Segments with Unknown Change Points: Real-world network traffic usually exhibits nonstationarity. Here, we consider nonstationary traffic arrivals for the VNF. Assume that the nonstationary traffic time series can be partitioned into non-overlapping stationary traffic segments with unknown change points in time. Between two neighboring change points, traffic statistics such as the mean and variance do not change. Let the integer $k(\geq 0)$ indicate the k-th stationary traffic segment. Consider that the change points can be located by a change point detection algorithm based on traffic statistical changes in the medium-timescale time series. Let $\mathcal{C}_M(k)$ be the index of the k-th change point in the medium timescale; that is, $x_M(\mathcal{C}_M(k))$ is the first traffic

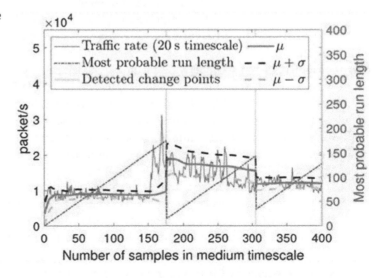

Figure 7.22 Results of change point detection for a nonstationary traffic segment. *Source:* Kaige Qu et al. [231]. (For more details see color figure in bins).

sample (in the medium timescale) of the k-th stationary traffic segment. We have $C_M(0) = 0$ to indicate the beginning of the timeline. Correspondingly, the k-th change point in the small timescale, $C_S(k)$, is given by $C_S(k) = C_M(k)T_M/T_S$.

Factional Brownian Motion for a Stationary Traffic Segment: A standard fBm process $\{Z_s(t), t = 0, 1, \cdots\}$ is a centered Gaussian process with $Z_s(0) = 0$ and covariance function

$$\psi_{Z_s}(t_1, t_2) = \left(t_1^{2H} + t_2^{2H} - |t_1 - t_2|^{2H}\right)/2 \tag{7.147}$$

where $H \in (0, 1)$ is the Hurst parameter [237]. For $H \in [0.5,1)$, the fBm process is both self-similar and LRD. A general fBm process $\{Z(t), t = 0, 1, \cdots\}$, denoting the the cumulative number of packet arrivals before the t-th time unit in a stationary traffic time series, is represented by $Z(t) = \lambda t + \sigma Z_s(t)$, where $\lambda = \mathrm{E}(Z(t)/t)$ is the mean of the packet arrivals in a time unit, and σ is the standard deviation of packet arrivals in a time unit [237]. Here, a time unit corresponds to a small time interval. The covariance function of $Z(t)$ is given by $\psi_Z(t_1, t_2) = \sigma^2\left(t_1^{2H} + t_2^{2H} - |t_1 - t_2|^{2H}\right)/2$.

The fBm traffic model is adopted for a stationary traffic segment. For the k-th stationary traffic segment, we consider a shifted discrete timeline in the small timescale, $\dot{i}$, starting at the beginning of the k-th stationary traffic segment, with $\dot{i} = t - C_S(k)$. Then, we have $\dot{x}_S(\dot{i}) = x_S(t - C_S(k))$, representing the number of packet arrivals in the $\dot{i}$-th shifted small time interval. The cumulative number of packet arrivals in the k-th stationary traffic segment before $\dot{i}$ is modeled as an fBm process with traffic parameters $\{\lambda(k), \sigma(k), H(k)\}$, given by

$$\dot{A}_k(\dot{i}) = \sum_{\dot{i}' = 1}^{\dot{i}} \dot{x}_S(\dot{i}' - 1), \; 1 \le \dot{i} \le C_S(k + 1) - C_S(k) - 1 \text{ and } = 0, \text{ for } \dot{i} = 0 \tag{7.148}$$

7.9.2 Learning and Prediction

Since traffic statistics change across different stationary traffic segments, the amount of processing resources allocated to the VNF for a probabilistic QoS guarantee, that is, $\Pr(d > D) \le \varepsilon$, should be dynamically adjusted. Here, a change-point-driven traffic parameter learning and resource demand prediction scheme is discussed, to predict resource demands from the learned fBm traffic parameters of stationary traffic segments between detected change points. It provides a triggering signal for dynamic VNF migration to be discussed in the sequel.

BOCPD: This algorithm was first introduced in [233]. Central to the BOCPD algorithm is the run length denoted by L. A run is defined as a traffic segment with the same statistics. An online inference about the run length is performed at every time step, given a conditional prior distribution over the run length and an underlying predictive model. Here, we use the BOCPD algorithm to detect statistical changes in the mean and variance of the nonstationary medium-timescale time series x_M, under the assumption that the medium-timescale traffic samples are from an i.i.d Gaussian distribution $\mathcal{N}(\mu, v^2)$, with unknown (and perhaps changing) mean μ and variance v^2.

A time step in the BOCPD algorithm corresponds to a medium time interval. The i.i.d Gaussian assumption is used to detect change points. For traffic parameter learning, we do not rely on such an assumption.

The run length at the m-th time step, denoted by L_m, represents the number of traffic samples before the m-th traffic sample, $x_M(m)$, within the same run. The run length L_m is a random variable taking values from $\{0, 1, \cdots, m\}$. From time step $(m - 1)$ to m, the run length either increases by 1 or resets to 0. For notational simplification, we omit the subscript M denoting the medium timescale, and use x_m to denote $x_M[0 : m]$. We also use $x_m^{(L)}$ to denote $x_M[(m - L_m) : m]$, which is a time series in the same run before the $(m + 1)$-th traffic sample, given the run length L_m at time step m.

The joint probability of the run length and the observed time series at time step m, that is, $\Pr(L_m, x_m)$, is updated recursively from the joint probability at the previous time step, that is, $\Pr(L_{m-1}, x_{m-1})$, for $m \geq 1$, given by

$$\Pr(L_m, x_m) = \sum_{L_{m-1}} \Pr(L_m | L_{m-1}) \Pr\left(x_m \middle| L_{m-1}, x_{m-1}^{(L)}\right) \Pr(L_{m-1}, x_{m-1})$$

$$\Pr(L_m, x_m) \rightarrow m'\text{th iteration}$$
$$\Pr(L_m | L_{m-1}) \rightarrow \text{conditional prior to run length} \tag{7.149}$$
$$\Pr\left(x_m \middle| L_{m-1}, x_{m-1}^{(L)}\right) \rightarrow \text{predictive model}$$
$$\Pr(L_{m-1}, x_{m-1}) \rightarrow (m-1)'\text{th iteration}$$

With initialization $\Pr(L_0 = 0, x_0) = 1$, for any observed value of x_0, the joint probability represents a relative likelihood. The underlying condition for Eq. (7.149) is that the run length L_m is independent of x_m, given L_{m-1}. The conditional prior on run length, that is, $\Pr(L_m | L_{m-1})$, is a probability mass distribution with two outcomes, that is, $L_m = L_{m-1} + 1$ and $L_m = 0$, as given in [231]. The predictive model, that is, $\Pr\left(x_m | L_{m-1}, x_{m-1}^{(L)}\right)$, evaluates the probability that x_m belongs to the same run as $x_{m-1}^{(L)}$ (i.e., $x_M[(m-1-L_{m-1}):(m-1)]$), given L_{m-1}. With a Gaussian-inverse-gamma prior on the unknown mean, μ, and variance, v^2, of the i.i.d Gaussian distribution, the predictive model is described by a student-t distribution with mean $\mu_{m-1}^{(L)}$ and standard deviation $v_{m-1}^{(L)}$. For each possible value of L_{m-1}, both $\mu_{m-1}^{(L)}$ and $v_{m-1}^{(L)}$ take different values. Through normalization, the posterior distribution of the run length, $\Pr(L_m | x_m)$, is given by

$$\Pr(L_m = m' | x_m) = \frac{\Pr(L_m = m', x_m)}{\sum\limits_{L_m = 0}^{m} \Pr(L_m | x_m)}; \forall m^l = 0, 1, \cdots, m. \tag{7.150}$$

For traffic parameter learning and resource demand prediction, deterministic change points are required. Define the most probable run length at time step m as

$$\hat{L}_m = \arg \max_{L_m = \{0, \cdots, m\}} \Pr(L_m | x_m). \tag{7.151}$$

The mean and standard deviation of the student-t predictive model corresponding to the most probable run length at time step m, that is, $\hat{L}_m$, is seen as the estimated mean and standard deviation of the nonstationary medium-timescale time series at time step m, denoted by $\mu_m^{(\hat{L}_m)}$ and $v_m^{(\hat{L}_m)}$, respectively. Time step m is identified as a change point if the following two conditions are satisfied:

1) The gap between the most probable run lengths at time steps $(m-1)$ and m, that is, $\hat{L}_{m-1}$ and $\hat{L}_m$, is larger than a threshold Δ_L, given by $\hat{L}_{m-1} - \hat{L}_m > \Delta_L$.

2) The normalized absolute difference between the estimated mean plus standard deviation at time step m and $(m-1)$ is beyond a predefined threshold Δ_d, given by

$$\frac{\left| \left(\mu_m^{(\hat{L}_m)} + v_m^{(\hat{L}_m)}\right) - \left(\mu_{m-1}^{(\hat{L}_{m-1})} + v_{m-1}^{(\hat{L}_{m-1})}\right) \right|}{\mu_{m-1}^{(\hat{L}_{m-1})} + v_{m-1}^{(\hat{L}_{m-1})}} > \Delta_d. \tag{7.152}$$

The k-th detected change point, denoted by $\hat{\mathcal{C}}_M(k)$, is the estimated value of the real change point $\mathcal{C}_M(k)$, that is, the index of the first medium-timescale traffic sample in the k-th stationary traffic segment. The BOCPD algorithm has a linear space and time complexity per time step in the number of medium-timescale traffic samples after the previously detected change point [233]. The stochastic BOCPD method results in a latency between $\mathcal{C}_M(k)$ and $\hat{\mathcal{C}}_M(k)$. The latency cannot be avoided since it is inherent to the BOCPD algorithm. We exploit the latency for *look-back* traffic parameter learning.

Traffic Parameter Learning: Let m_0 be a small integer such that $(m_0 - 1)$ medium-timescale traffic samples before the $\hat{\mathcal{C}}_M(k)$-th one belong to the k-th stationary traffic segment. The m_0 medium-timescale traffic samples including the $\hat{\mathcal{C}}_M(k)$-th one correspond to $m_0 T_M/T_S$ small-timescale traffic samples within the same time duration, given by

$$
x_M\Big[\Big(\hat{\mathcal{C}}_M(k) - m_0 + 1\Big) : \hat{\mathcal{C}}_M(k)\Big] \Rightarrow
$$
$$
x_S\Big[\Big(\hat{\mathcal{C}}_M(k) - m_0 + 1\Big)T_M/T_S : \Big(\big(\hat{\mathcal{C}}_M(k) + 1\big)T_M/T_S - 1\Big)\Big] \tag{7.153}
$$
$$
= x_S\Big[\hat{\mathcal{C}}_S(k) : \Big(\hat{\mathcal{C}}_S(k) + m_0 T_M/T_S - 1\Big)\Big]
$$

where $\hat{\mathcal{C}}_S(k) = \Big(\hat{\mathcal{C}}_M(k) - m_0 + 1\Big)T_M/T_S$ is the estimated k-th change point in the small timescale. The $m_0 T_M/T_S$ traffic samples are used to learn fBm traffic parameters of the k-th stationary traffic segment. Compared with a *look-ahead* counterpart, the *look-back* mechanism avoids another latency after the detected change point, for collecting sufficient traffic samples.

We consider a modified shifted discrete timeline, $\tilde{t}$, with $\tilde{t} = t - \hat{\mathcal{C}}_S(k)$, for the k-th stationary traffic segment. Correspondingly, we have $\tilde{x}_S(\tilde{t}) = x_S\big(t - \hat{\mathcal{C}}_S(k)\big)$, representing the number of packet arrivals in the $\tilde{t}$-th modified-shifted small time interval. The cumulative number of packet arrivals in the k-th stationary traffic segment before $\tilde{t}$, is given by $\tilde{A}_k(\tilde{t}) = \sum_{\tilde{t}'=1}^{\tilde{t}} \tilde{x}_S(\tilde{t}' - 1)$, $1 \le \tilde{t} \le \hat{\mathcal{C}}_S(k+1) - \hat{\mathcal{C}}_S(k) - 1$ and $\tilde{A}_k(\tilde{t}) = 0$, $for \tilde{t} = 0$. We use $\Big\{\tilde{A}_k(\tilde{t}), 0 \le \tilde{t} \le m_0 T_M/T_S - 1\Big\}$ to learn fBm traffic parameters of the k-th stationary traffic segment. Consider the following GPR model:

$$
\tilde{A}_k(\tilde{t}) \sim \mathcal{GP}\big(\lambda(k)\tilde{t}, \psi_k(\tilde{t}_1, \tilde{t}_2)\big) \tag{7.154}
$$

where $\lambda(k)\tilde{t}$ is the mean function, and $\psi_k(\tilde{t}_1, \tilde{t}_2)$ is the fBm covariance function given by $\psi_k(\tilde{t}_1, \tilde{t}_2) = \dfrac{G^2(k)}{2}\Big(\tilde{t}_1^{2H(k)} + \tilde{t}_2^{2H(k)} - |\tilde{t}_1 - \tilde{t}_2|^{2H(k)}\Big)/2$. The fBm traffic parameters $\{\lambda(k), \sigma(k), H(k)\}$ are referred to as hyper-parameters in the GPR framework [236]. Let $t_k = [0, 1, \cdots, (m_0 T_M/T_S - 1)]$ be training inputs and $A_k = \Big[\tilde{A}_k(0), \tilde{A}_k(1), \cdots, A_k(m_0 T_M/T_S - 1)\Big]$ be training outputs. Then, we have the following joint Gaussian distribution $A_k \sim \mathcal{N}(\lambda(k)t_k, \Psi_k)$, where Ψ_k is a $m_0 T_M/T_S$-by-$m_0 T_M/T_S$ covariance matrix, with $\Psi_k(i, j) = \psi_k(i, j)$. The GPR model is trained; that is, the hyper-parameters are learned, by maximizing the following log-marginal likelihood function with a gradient optimizer

$$
\log\mathrm{Pr}(A_k \mid t_k; \{\lambda(k), \sigma(k), H(k)\}) = -\frac{1}{2}\Big[(A_k - \lambda(k)t_k)^T \Psi_k^{-1}(A_k - \lambda(k)t_k)
$$
$$
+ \log|\Psi_k| + \frac{m_0 T_M}{T_S}\log 2\pi\Big] \tag{7.155}
$$

For traffic parameter learning, it has $\mathcal{O}(m_0 T_M^3/T_S)$ time complexity and $\mathcal{O}(m_0 T_M^2/T_S)$ space complexity due to the inversion of a covariance matrix in Eq. (7.155). Such a complexity is feasible

on a desktop computer for dataset sizes up to a few thousands [241]. There are sparse approximation algorithms to reduce the complexity of GPR [241]. To evaluate the learning accuracy, one-step-
ahead predictions for t_0 subsequent small time intervals are performed using the trained
GPR model. The one–step ahead prediction at time $\widetilde{t}\left(m_0 T_M/T_S - 1 \le \widetilde{t} \le m_0 T_M/T_S + t_0 - 2\right)$
is to predict $\widetilde{A}_k\left(\widetilde{t}^*\right)$ given $\widetilde{t}^* = \widetilde{t} + 1$ and a set of observed data $\mathcal{D} = (t, A)$ with $t = [0, 1, \cdots, \widetilde{t}]$
and $A = \left[\widetilde{A}_k(0), \widetilde{A}_k(1), \cdots, \widetilde{A}_{k,\sim}\left(\widetilde{t}\right)\right]$. The GPR gives a Gaussian posterior distribution of $A_k\left(\widetilde{t}^*\right)$ conditioned on $\widetilde{t}^*$ and $\mathcal{D}$ as

$$\Pr\left(\widetilde{A}_k\left(\widetilde{t}^*\right) \mid \widetilde{t}^*, \mathcal{D}\right) \sim \mathcal{N}\left(\mu_{\mathcal{GP};k}\left(\widetilde{t}^*\right), \sigma^2_{\mathcal{GP};k}\left(\widetilde{t}^*\right)\right) \tag{7.156}$$

with

$$\begin{cases} \mu_{\mathcal{GP};k}\left(\widetilde{t}^*\right) = \psi_k\left(t, \widetilde{t}^*\right)^T (\Phi)^{-1} A \\ \sigma^2_{\mathcal{GP};k}\left(\widetilde{t}^*\right) = \psi_k\left(\widetilde{t}^*, \widetilde{t}^*\right) - \psi_k\left(t, \widetilde{t}^*\right)^T (\Phi)^{-1} \psi_k\left(t, \widetilde{t}^*\right). \end{cases} \tag{7.157}$$

where $\psi_k\left(t, \widetilde{t}^*\right)$ is a $\left(\widetilde{t} + 1\right)$-by-1 vector with the i-th component equal to $\psi_k\left(i, \widetilde{t}^*\right)$, and Φ is
a $\left(\widetilde{t} + 1\right)$–by–$\left(\widetilde{t} + 1\right)$ covariance matrix with $\Phi(i, j) = \psi_k(i, j)$. The mean, $\mu_{\mathcal{GP};k}\left(\widetilde{t}^*\right)$, is taken as a
point estimate for the prediction output, and the variance, $\sigma^2_{\mathcal{GP};k}\left(\widetilde{t}^*\right)$, provides an uncertainty meas-
ure for the point estimate. With the predictive distribution for $\widetilde{A}_k\left(\widetilde{t}^*\right)$, the traffic sample in time
interval $\widetilde{t}^*$, that is, $\widetilde{x}_S\left(\widetilde{t}^*\right)$, is predicted as

$$\hat{\widetilde{x}}_S\left(\widetilde{t}^*\right) = \mu_{\mathcal{GP};k}\left(\widetilde{t}^*\right) - \widetilde{A}_k$$

The prediction error of the t_0 traffic samples in the k-th stationary traffic segment, ϱ_k, is defined as
the normalized root-mean-squared deviation between the t_0 predicted traffic samples and the corresponding ground truth, given by

$$\varrho_k = \frac{\sqrt{\displaystyle\sum_{\widetilde{t} = m_0 T_M/T_S}^{m_0 T_M/T_S + t_0 - 1} \left(\hat{\widetilde{x}}_S\left(\widetilde{t}^*\right) - \widetilde{x}_S\left(\widetilde{t}^*\right)\right)^2}}{\left(x_S^{\max} - x_S^{\min}\right)\sqrt{t_0}}.$$

The normalization constant is the scale of small-timescale traffic samples, that is, $\left(x_S^{\max} - x_S^{\min}\right)$.
A smaller ϱ_k value indicates a higher learning accuracy for traffic parameters.

Resource Demand Prediction: With the learned fBm traffic parameters, the resource demand of
the k-th stationary traffic segment can be predicted. Consider an fBm traffic input with parameters
$\{\lambda, \sigma, H\}$ to an infinite buffer, with a constant service rate of R packets per small time interval. The
buffer overflow probability, that is, the probability that queue length q is beyond a threshold q_B, is
approximately given by [237]

$$\Pr(q > q_B) \simeq \exp\left(-\inf_{t \ge 0} \frac{[q_B + (R - \lambda)t]^2}{2\sigma^2 t^{2H}}\right) \tag{7.158}$$

which has been shown accurate even for a small value of q_B by simulation studies. Correspondingly,
the delay violation probability can be approximated by

$$\Pr(d_S > D_S) \simeq \exp\left(-\inf_{t \ge 0} \frac{[RD_S + (R - \lambda)t]^2}{2\sigma^2 t^{2H}}\right) \tag{7.159}$$

where $d_S = d/T_S$ is the random VNF packet processing delay in the number of small time intervals, and $D_S = D/T_S$ is the corresponding delay bound. To provide a probabilistic QoS guarantee (i.e., Pr $(d_S > D_S) \leq \varepsilon$) to the VNF with minimum resources, we should find $min\{R \mid \forall t \geq 0, [RD_S + (R - \lambda) t]^2 \geq (-2 \log \varepsilon)\sigma^2 t^{2H}\}$ which leads to

$$R_{\min} = \sup_{t \geq 0} \frac{\lambda t + \sqrt{-2 \log \varepsilon}\, \sigma t^H}{t + D_S}. \tag{7.160}$$

The value of t achieving the supremum can be obtained by setting the derivative of $R_{\min}$ with respect to t to zero, that is, $\left(\sqrt{-2 \log \varepsilon}\sigma D_S H t^{H-1} + \sqrt{-2 \log \varepsilon}\sigma(H-1)t^H + \lambda D_S\right)/(t + D_S)^2 = 0$.

With the fBm resource provisioning model given in Eq. (7.160), the predicted resource demand (in packet/s) of the k-th stationary traffic segment, denoted by (k), is calculated from the learned fBm traffic parameters, that is, $\{\lambda(k), \sigma(k), H(k)\}$, the QoS requirement, and the small time interval length, that is, T_S.

7.9.3 DRL for Dynamic VNF Migration

The BOCPD algorithm locates the prior-unknown change points of the nonstationary traffic, which determines the boundaries between consecutive stationary traffic segments. They are also boundaries between consecutive decision epochs (with variable lengths) for VNF scaling and necessary VNF migrations. The length of decision epoch k is equal to $\left(\hat{C}_M(k + 1) - \hat{C}_M(k)\right)T_M$. Once change point $\hat{C}_M(k)$ is detected, the resource demand $R(k)$ of the upcoming k-th stationary traffic segment is predicted, based on which a VNF migration decision is made.

Migration Problem Formulation: For VNF migration, we jointly consider the migration cost and load balancing. Let $\{a_k^n, n \in \mathcal{N}_C\}$ be a binary variable set, with $a_k^n = 1$ if the VNF is placed at NFV node n during the k-th decision epoch, and $a_k^n = 0$ otherwise. Let $a_k(0 \leq a_k \leq |\mathcal{N}_C| - 1)$ be an integer denoting the VNF location during decision epoch k, with $a_k = n$ if the VNF is placed at NFV node n. The relationship between $\{a_k^n\}$ and a_k is given by $a_k^n = 1$ if $a_k = n$, and 0 otherwise.

Define the background resource loading factor of NFV node n during decision epoch k, denoted by $\eta_n^B(k)$, as the average ratio between the amount of processing resources (in packet/s) allocated to background traffic at NFV node n during decision epoch k and the processing resource capacity $R^{(n)}$ (in packet/s) of NFV node n. The resource loading factor of NFV node n during decision epoch k, denoted by $\eta_n(k)$, depends on both $\eta_n^B(k)$ and VNF placement and is given by $\eta_n(k) = \eta_n^B(k) + a_k^n R(k)/R(n)$.

The cost of imbalanced loading during decision epoch k defined as the maximum resource loading factor among all NFV nodes in $\mathcal{N}_C$, given by $c_k^{(1)} = \max$ as index $\eta_n(k)$ since minimizing $c_k^{(1)}$ achieves load balancing among all the candidate NFV nodes. Assume that each VNF migration incurs the same migration cost. Then, we can use the total number of migrations to denote the total migration cost, given by

$$c_k^{(2)} = \begin{cases} \sum_{n \in \mathcal{N}_C} \sum_{n' \in \mathcal{N}_C - n} a_{k-1}^n a_k^{n'}, & \text{if } k > 0 \\ 0, & \text{if } k = 0 \end{cases} \tag{7.161}$$

where a_{k-1}^n is a known value at decision epoch $k(>0)$. In the single VNF scenario, we have $c_k^{(2)} = 1$ for $k > 0$ if the VNF placement changes from decision epoch $(k-1)$ to decision epoch k, and $c_k^{(2)} = 0$ otherwise. The total cost is a weighted combination of the two costs, given by $c_k = \omega c_k^{(1)} + (1 - \omega)c^{(2)}$, where ω is a weighting factor in $(0, 1)$. In stepwise optimization for cost minimization in the short term, the total cost c_k is minimized at each decision epoch k, subject to processing resource capacity constraints at the NFV nodes; that is, the resource loading factors of all NFV nodes should not exceed 1. For cost minimization in the long run, the VNF migration problem can be formulated as an MDP, with the state, action, and reward defined as follows:

- *State* – At decision epoch k, the state is composed of four parts: the k-th change point, the predicted resource demand of the k-th stationary traffic segment, the background resource loading factors of all candidate NFV nodes during decision epoch k, and the previous VNF placement a_{k-1}. Thus, the state for decision epoch k is represented as $s_k = \left[\hat{C}(k), R(k), \{\eta_n^B(k)\}, a_{k-1} \right]$. Here, $\hat{C}(k)$ is a real number representing the k-th estimated change point in hour, given by $\hat{C}(k) = \left(\hat{C}_M(k)T_M/3600 \right) \mod 24$, where the modulo operation limits $\hat{C}(k)$ in $[0, 24)$.

- *Action* – The action at decision epoch k is the new VNF placement, that is, a_k. We use a_k instead of $\{a_k^n\}$ as the action to limit the dimensionality of action space.

- *Reward* – In an unconstrained MDP, the violation of resource capacity constraints is penalized by an extra term in reward. Hence, the reward for decision epoch k is $r_k = -(c_k + c^{(v)}v_k)$, where c_k is the total cost of VNF migration at decision epoch k given as $c_k = \omega c_k^{(1)} + (1 - \omega)c^{(2)}$, v_k is a binary flag indicating whether there is penalty due to resource overloading, and $c^{(v)}$ is a constant representing the level of penalty. Assume that resource overloading is due to improper VNF placement alone; that is, the background traffic does not overload the NFV nodes $(\eta_n^B(k) < 1)$. Then, the penalty flag is defined as $v_k = 1$, if $c_k^{(1)} > \eta_U$ and 0, otherwise, where $\eta_U(0 < \eta_U \leq 1)$ is an upper limit for the maximum resource loading factor without penalty. In practice, we select η_U as a number close to but smaller than 1, for example, $\eta_U = 0.95$, to penalize loading factors close to 1, since the penalty cannot be completely avoided in a learning-based solution due to exploration. Moreover, if the predicted resource demand is very large, it is possible that there is no feasible VNF placement without resource overloading. A potential solution is to throttle the traffic when resource overloading is foreseen to happen. Here, we assume that the VNF placement without resource overloading is always feasible and do not consider traffic throttling.

Penalty-Aware DQL Algorithm: We solve the MDP by an RL approach, when transition probabilities among states are unavailable. Consider an episodic task, in which an RL agent interacts with the VNF migration environment in a sequence of episodes, with a finite number of learning steps in each episode. Here, a learning step corresponds to a decision epoch, and an episode corresponds to a time duration such as one day, one week, or one month. At the beginning of an episode, the VNF placement is initialized at NFV node n_0. Within an episode, an agent observes state s_k and takes action a_k at the beginning of decision epoch k. At the end of decision epoch k, the agent receives reward r_k, and sees the new state s_{k+1}. The goal is to find a policy, (s), mapping a state to an action, to maximize the expected cumulative (episodic) discounted reward $E\left(\sum_{k=0}^K \gamma^k r_k \right)$, where K is the number of variable-length decision epochs in an episode, and $\gamma \in (0, 1]$ is the discount factor. In Q-learning, a state-action value function is defined as

$$Q(s_k, a_k) = \mathrm{E}\left[\sum_{k'=k}^{K-1} \gamma^{k'-k} r_{k'} \mid s_k, a_k\right]$$

The Q-learning is an off-policy algorithm adopting the ε−greedy policy

$$\pi(s_k) = \begin{pmatrix} argmax_a Q(s_k, a), with\ probability\ (1-\varepsilon) \\ random\ action, with\ probability\ \varepsilon \end{pmatrix} \tag{7.162}$$

where ε is the exploration probability. We use a gradually decreasing ε from 1 to a minimum value ε_0, with step size Δ_ε, to transit smoothly from exploration to exploitation. The formulated MDP is characterized by a high-dimensional combinational state space and a low-dimensional discrete action space. To tackle the curse of dimensionality, deep Q-learning employs two deep Q-networks (DQNs) with the same neural network structure as Q function approximators, that is, evaluation $DQN\,(Q)$ with weights θ and target $DQN\,(\hat{Q})$ with slowly updated weights $\hat{\theta}$[242]. Every K_θ learning steps, $\hat{\theta}$ is replaced by θ. The policy in Eq. (7.162) is based on evaluation DQN, which is trained by minimizing a loss function

$$L(\theta) = E\left[(y_k - Q(s_k, a_k; \theta))^2\right]$$

through gradient descent on θ, where y_k is a target value estimated by target DQN, given by $y_k = r_k + \gamma\,\max_a \hat{Q}(s_{k+1}, a; \hat{\theta})$. If an episode terminates at the k-th learning step, y_k is set as r_k. A gradient descent on θ is performed by $\theta \leftarrow \theta - \xi\nabla_\theta L(\theta)/2 = \theta + \xi\delta_k\nabla_\theta Q(s_k, a_k)$, where ξ is the learning rate, and $\delta_k = y_k - Q(s_k, a_k; \theta)$ is the temporal-difference (TD) error.

Experience replay is introduced in deep Q-learning for stable convergence [242]. At each learning step, θ is updated with a mini-batch (size equal J) of experiences (s_j, a_j, r_j, s_{j+1}) uniformly sampled from a replay memory. Experience replay breaks the temporal correlation among experiences, and liberates RL agents from learning with transitions in the same order that they appear. Prioritized experience replay improves learning efficiency by further liberating RL agents from considering transitions in the same frequency that they appear [243, 244]. It assigns a priority, p_j, for transition j sampled from the replay memory, which is the magnitude of the TD error δ_j plus a very small value o. The sampling probability of transition j is $\Pr(j) = p_j^{\varsigma_0}/\sum_{j=1}^{M} p_j^{\varsigma_0}$, where M is the size of the replay memory, and ς_0 determines the level of prioritization.

In the VNF migration problem, it is desired that the deep Q-learning algorithm converge to a solution without incurring a resource overloading penalty in the whole episode. However, such experiences are rare at the early learning stage with a lot of exploration, especially if an episode contains a large number of transitions. To learn more from such rare desired experiences, we extend the prioritized experience replay technique to consider penalty awareness. Among the original prioritized transitions with high absolute TD errors, we prioritize those transitions with zero penalty, given by $p_j = \varphi\,|\,\delta_j\,| + (1 - \varphi)(1 - v_j) + o$, where $\varphi \in [0, 1]$ is a parameter that controls the relative importance of TD error and penalty avoidance. In practice, we select φ close to 1, for example, 0.99, to incorporate penalty awareness without significantly degrading the convergence speed. Correspondingly, a five-tuple transition $(s_j, a_j, r_j, v_j, s_{j+1})$ instead of the original four-tuple transition (s_j, a_j, r_j, s_{j+1}) is stored in the replay memory at every learning step. A deep Q-learning algorithm with penalty-aware prioritized experience replay is presented in Algorithm 1 [231]. The prioritization leads to a loss of diversity, which can be corrected with an importance-sampling weight w_j, given by [244]:

$w_j = (B \cdot \Pr(j))^{-\varsigma_1} / max_j (w_{j'})$, where ς_1 controls the level of compensation. The TD error δ_j is replaced by a weighted TD error $w_j\delta_j$ in a gradient descent step with transition j, as given in line 13 of Algorithm 1 [231].

Design Example 7.5

For the system parameters specified in [231], in this section, we present a few major results obtained by running simulations using the algorithms presented above on DQN. Figure 7.22 shows the results of change point detection for a nonstationary traffic segment in 8000 s, corresponding to 400 medium time intervals. A zigzag trend is observed for the most probable run length. We also observe that the change points are detected after the occurrence of statistical changes, which verifies the effectiveness of the look-back traffic parameter learning.

Figure 7.23 shows the results of the proposed change-point-driven traffic parameter learning and resource demand prediction scheme for a real-world daily traffic trace. The detected change points identify different stationary traffic segments. For each stationary traffic segment, the three learned fBm traffic parameters $\{\lambda(k), \sigma(k), H(k)\}$ are plotted. We observe that the Hurst parameter is within $[0.5, 1)$, indicating the self-similarity and LRD of the traffic. The predicted resource demands for the identified stationary traffic segments are given, for QoS requirements $\Pr(d > 10ms) \leq \varepsilon$ with $\varepsilon = 0.1$, 0.01, and 0.001. As expected, the resource demand increases when ε decreases.

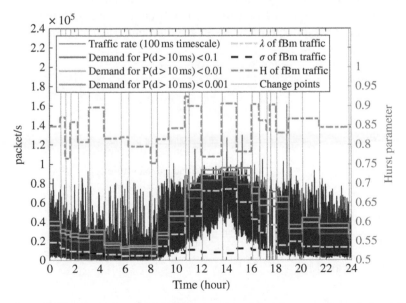

Figure 7.23 Learned traffic parameters and predicted resource demands for daily traffic. *Source:* Kaige Qu et al. [231]. (For more details see color figure in bins).

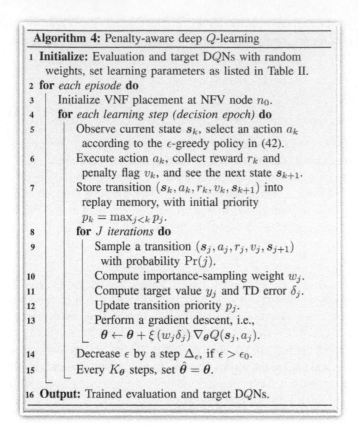

Algorithm 4: Penalty-aware deep Q-learning

1 **Initialize:** Evaluation and target DQNs with random weights, set learning parameters as listed in Table II.
2 **for** *each episode* **do**
3   Initialize VNF placement at NFV node n_0.
4   **for** *each learning step (decision epoch)* **do**
5   Observe current state s_k, select an action a_k according to the ϵ-greedy policy in (42).
6   Execute action a_k, collect reward r_k and penalty flag v_k, and see the next state s_{k+1}.
7   Store transition $(s_k, a_k, r_k, v_k, s_{k+1})$ into replay memory, with initial priority $p_k = \max_{j<k} p_j$.
8   **for** J *iterations* **do**
9   Sample a transition $(s_j, a_j, r_j, v_j, s_{j+1})$ with probability $\Pr(j)$.
10   Compute importance-sampling weight w_j.
11   Compute target value y_j and TD error δ_j.
12   Update transition priority p_j.
13   Perform a gradient descent, i.e., $\theta \leftarrow \theta + \xi (w_j \delta_j) \nabla_\theta Q(s_j, a_j)$.
14   Decrease ϵ by a step Δ_ϵ, if $\epsilon > \epsilon_0$.
15   Every K_θ steps, set $\hat{\theta} = \theta$.
16 **Output:** Trained evaluation and target DQNs.

Figure 7.24 shows the distribution of the VNF packet processing delay for both traffic traces. Two groups of delay requirements with different delay bounds, that is, $D = 10$ ms and $D = 50$ ms, are used for QoS evaluation. In each group, ε is set as 0.1, 0.01, and 0.001. For the same QoS requirement, the amount of resources allocated for both traffic traces are the same. However, the delay

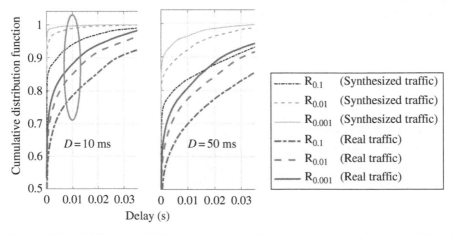

Figure 7.24 Distribution of VNF packet processing delay for both the synthesized traffic and the real traffic. *Source:* Kaige Qu et al. [231]. (For more details see color figure in bins).

performance of the synthesized traffic is better than that of the real traffic, due to less traffic burstiness in time granularities smaller than 0.1 s. For the synthesized traffic, the delay violation probability lies within the corresponding upper limits. For the real traffic, the delay violation probability occasionally exceeds the required upper limit, especially for the stringent QoS requirements such as $\Pr(d > 10ms) \leq 0.001$, due to traffic burstiness in time granularities below 0.1 s.

In addition, we compare the QoS performance of the proposed resource demand prediction scheme based on the fBm model with the performance of a benchmark scheme based on the M/M/1 model [238]. Both methods use the learned traffic parameters for resource demand prediction. In the proposed scheme, the resource demand is predicted from all three learned traffic parameters, that is, $\{\lambda, \sigma, H\}$, based on the fBm resource provisioning model given by Eq. (7.160). In the benchmark scheme, the resource demand is predicted from the first learned traffic parameter, that is, λ, based on an M/M/1 resource provisioning model. For an M/M/1 queue with arrival rate λ (in packet/s) and service rate R (in packet/s), the delay violation probability is $\Pr(d > D) = e^{-(R-\lambda)}$ ^{D}[245]. Hence, the minimum amount of resources (in packet/s) = to guarantee the QoS requirement $\Pr(d > D) \leq \varepsilon$ is $R_{min} = \lambda - \log \varepsilon/D$. Figure 7.25 shows theVNF packet delay distribution with the real packet arrivals and with different amount of resources allocated to the VNF, based on the predicted resource demands given by the two models. A gap is observed between the delay performance of the two models. The *DQN* model, with its ability to capture the bursty nature of traffic, gives a better estimation of resource demands. The performance of the deep Q-learning algorithm with *penalty-aware prioritized* experience replay (PP-*DQN*) is compared with two benchmark algorithms, that is, deep Q-learning with uniformly sampled experience replay (*DQN*) and deep Q-learning with prioritized experience relay (*P-DQN*). All three deep Q-learning algorithms are compared with a common benchmark, that is, stepwise optimization.

Figure 7.26 shows the evolution of the episodic average reward with respect to the number of episodes during the learning process, using the three deep Q-learning algorithms. Both the full reward including penalty and the partial reward without penalty are plotted, with a gap indicating the penalty. It is observed that *DQN* converges to a poor solution that is worse than the stepwise optimization benchmark in terms of the episodic average reward. The penalty is high, which means that *DQN* does not learn a solution that minimizes the resource overloading penalty in the long run. Both the P-*DQN* and PP-*DQN* algorithms take advantage of the prioritized experience replay for convergence to solutions that outperform the stepwise optimization benchmark most of the time

Figure 7.25 QoS performance comparison between resource demand prediction schemes based on the fBm model and M/M/1 model. *Source:* Kaige Qu et al. [231]. (For more details see color figure in bins).

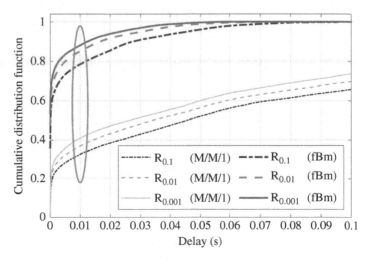

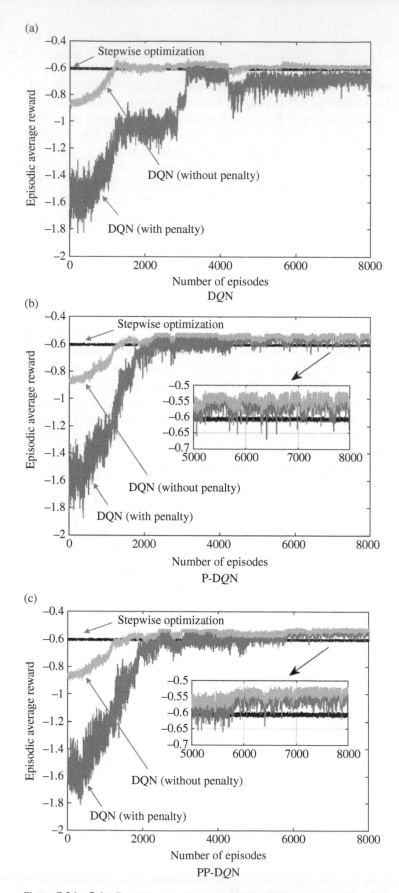

Figure 7.26 Episodic average reward versus the episode number for the three deep Q-learning algorithms: prioritized experience relay (P-DQN) and penalty-aware prioritized experience replay (PP-DQN). *Source:* Kaige Qu et al. [231].

after convergence. It demonstrates that both P-*DQN* and PP-*DQN* after convergence can capture the weekly traffic patterns (both change points and resource demands) and background resource loading patterns at the candidate NFV nodes, and make intelligent VNF migration decisions accordingly. By contrast, when a VNF migration is required, the stepwise optimization benchmark favors VNF migration to a lightly loaded NFV node in the current decision epoch, which can be heavily loaded in the following decision epochs. As illustrated in Figures 7.26b and c, PP-*DQN* achieves a slightly higher gain in terms of penalty suppression compared with P-*DQN*. The episodic average rewards (with penalty) of P-*DQN* and PP-*DQN* after convergence are −0.5502 and −0.5408, respectively.

7.10 Multi-Armed Bandit Estimator (MBE)

In this section, we discuss dynamic channel allocation for remote state estimation of multi-agent systems. For each subsystem, a sensor measures its state and transmits the data via a packet-dropping channel, which is dynamically allocated by the remote estimator. We first formulate the problem as an MDP. Given the difficulty of obtaining an optimal policy for large-scale problems, we develop a suboptimal heuristic policy based on the Whittle index for the restless multi-armed bandit (RMAB) problem. The performance of the Whittle index policy is evaluated from both the theoretical and practical aspects. The strong performance of the Whittle index policy is illustrated by the numerical examples in Design Example 7.6.

7.10.1 System Model

We consider a wireless network consisting of N independent subsystems, as shown in Figure 7.27a. For the i-th subsystem, a sensor measures an independent linear time invariant system

$$x_{k+1}^{(i)} = A^{(i)}x_k^{(i)} + w_k^{(i)} \quad ; y_k^{(i)} = C^{(i)}x_k^{(i)} + v_k^{(i)} \tag{7.163}$$

Figure 7.27 (a) System model, (b) local control loop used to stabilize the unstable subsystem.

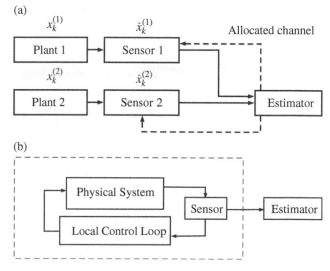

where $x_k^{(i)} \in \mathbb{R}^{n_i}$ is the system state, and $y_k^{(i)} \in \mathbb{R}^{m_i}$ is the measurement. The noises $w_k^{(i)} \in \mathbb{R}^{n_i}$, $v_k^{(i)} \in \mathbb{R}^{m_i}$ are assumed to be i.i. d. zero-mean Gaussian random variables with a finite covariance $\Sigma_w^{(i)} \succeq 0$, $\Sigma_v^{(i)} \succ 0$, respectively. The initial state $x_0^{(i)}$ is a zero-mean Gaussian random vector with covariance Σ_0, uncorrelated with $w_k^{(i)}$, $v_k^{(i)}$. The pair $\left(A^{(i)}, \Sigma_w^{(i)}\right)$ is assumed to be controllable and $(A^{(i)}, C)$ observable.

The system matrix $\{A^{(i)}\}$ is assumed to be stable; that is, $\rho(A^{(i)}) < 1$. (For a matrix X, X^{T}, $\mathrm{Tr}X$, and $\rho(X)$ denote its transpose, trace, and special radius, respectively.) In this section, only stable subsystems are considered. As shown in Figure 7.27b, for each unstable subsystem, a local control loop can be deployed to stabilize the system, which results in a controlled stable subsystem [247].

The sensor is assumed to be "smart," in the sense that it has enough computation capability to compute the MSE estimate of the system state locally via a Kalman filter. The optimal state estimate at the sensor is denoted by $\widetilde{x}_k^{(i)} = \mathbb{E}\left[x_k^{(i)} \mid y_0, \cdot\cdot y_k\right]$.

Under the assumption that $\left(A^{(i)}, \Sigma_w^{(i)}\right)$ is controllable and $(A^{(i)}, C)$ is observable, by Theorem 7.5 in [248], the estimation error covariance associated with each local Kalman filter converges exponentially fast to a steady state. Therefore, we assume that the error covariance of $\widetilde{x}_k^{(i)}$ has reached the steady state at $k = 0$. We denote by $\bar{P}^{(i)}$ the steady state of the error covariance of $\widetilde{x}_k^{(i)}$; that is,

$$\bar{P}^{(i)} = \mathbb{E}\left[\left(x_k^{(i)} - \widetilde{x}_k^{(i)}\right)\left(x_k^{(i)} - \widetilde{x}_k^{(i)}\right)^{\mathrm{T}} \mid y_0, \cdot\cdot y_k)\right] \tag{7.164}$$

which can be obtained by solving a Riccati equation. The sensor sends the local estimate $\widetilde{x}_k^{(i)}$ to the remote estimator via the allocated fading channels. We denote by $\gamma_k^{(i)} \in \{1, 0\}$ whether the data transmission of the i-th subsystem is successful or not. To facilitate the analysis, without loss of generality, we assume that the initial data transmission is successful; that is, $\gamma^{(i)} = 1$. The MSE estimate of the i-th system state at the remote estimator is given by $\hat{x}_k^{(i)} = \mathbb{E}$ $\left(x_k^{(i)} \mid \gamma_0^{(i)} \widetilde{x}_0^{(i)}, \cdot\cdot, \gamma_k^{(i)} \widetilde{x}_k^{(i)}, \gamma_0^{(i)}, \cdot\cdot, \gamma_k^{(i)}\right)$. We denote by $\tau_k^{(i)}$ the number of successive packet drops of the i-th subsystem at time k : $\tau_k^{(i)} = k - \max\left\{j \mid \gamma_j^{(i)} = 1\right\}$. The optimal estimate $\hat{x}_k^{(i)}$ at the remote estimator and the corresponding error covariance $P_k^{(i)}$ can be computed as follows:

$$\hat{x}_k^{(i)} = \begin{cases} \widetilde{x}_k^{(i)}, & \text{if } \gamma_k^{(i)} = 1 \\ A^{(i)}\hat{x}_{k-1}^{(i)}, & \text{otherwise.} \end{cases}$$

$$P_k^{(i)} = h_i^{\tau^{(i)}}\left(\bar{P}^{(i)}\right)$$

where $h_i(X) = A^{(i)}XA^{(i)\mathrm{T}} + \Sigma_w^{(i)}$, and h_i^j is the j-th functional power of h_i.

Dynamic Channel Allocation Mechanism assumes that M identical channels are to be allocated to N sensors by the remote estimator. Due to the capacity limitation, each sensor can be allocated at most one channel at each time step. To avoid trivial problems, we consider only the case where $M < N$. Once the i-th sensor is allocated with the channel, the i-th sensor will transmit the data packets to the remote estimator, which incurs an energy consumption $\mathcal{E}_i > 0$. We denote by $u_k^{(i)} = 1$, $u_k^{(i)} = 0$ whether at time k the i-th subsystem is allocated a channel or not, respectively. We assume that the transmission processes are independent among different subsystems. Furthermore, the following equalities hold:

$$\Pr\left(\gamma_k^{(i)} = 1 \mid u_k^{(i)} = 1\right) = \alpha_i$$

$$\Pr\left(\gamma_k^{(i)} = 1 \mid u_k^{(i)} = 0\right) = 0 \qquad (7.165)$$

where $0 < \alpha_i \leq 1$. We denote by $c^{(i)}$ the one-stage cost of the i-th subsystem

$$c^{(i)}\left(\tau_k^{(i)}\left(, u_k^{(i)}\right)\right) = \mathrm{Tr} h^{\tau_k^{(i)}} \cdot \left(\bar{P}^{(i)}\right) + \lambda_i u_k^{(i)} \mathcal{E}_i \qquad (7.166)$$

where λ_i can be interpreted as a Lagrange multiplier balancing the estimation quality and energy consumption of the i-th subsystem. The transmission decision of the system at time k is denoted by $U_k = \left\{u_k^{(1)}, \ldots, u_k^{(N)} \mid \sum_i^N u_k^{(i)} \leq M\right\}$. We note that the estimation quality of the i-th subsystem is fully characterized by its holding time $\tau_k^{(i)}$, and thus the system determines the transmission decision U_k based on the collection of the holding time of systems, which is defined as $\tau_k = \left\{\tau_k^{(1)}, \ldots, \tau_k^{(N)}\right\}$. It is well known that the stationary policies are complete for infinite-horizon problems for time-homogeneous processes [249]. Without loss of generality, we restrict the scheduling polices to be stationary. An admissible policy π is a mapping from τ_k to the probability measure over the transmission decision U_k; that is,

$$\Pr(U_k = U \mid \tau_k = \tau, \pi) = \pi(U \mid \tau) \qquad (7.167)$$

where for a given τ, $\pi(\cdot \mid \tau)$ is a probability measure over $U = \{u^{(1)}, \ldots, u^{(N)}\}$. For the deterministic policy π, which does not involve any randomization in selecting the transmission decision, we simply write $U_k = \pi(\tau_k)$. We denote by Π the collection of all admissible policies that assign the probability only over the feasible transmission decision $\left\{U \mid \sum_i^N u^{(i)} \leq M\right\}$. In this section, we consider the performance measure as the expected total discounted cost over the infinite horizon. The motivation of studying discounted problems mainly comes from many applications where the costs in the future are less important than the current ones. The expected total discounted cost over the infinite horizon is defined as

$$J_\beta(\pi, \tau_0) = \mathbb{E}_{\tau_0}^\pi \left[\sum_{k=0}^\infty \beta^k \sum_{i=1}^N c^{(i)}\left(\tau_k^{(i)}, u_k^{(i)}\right)\right]$$

where $\beta(0 < \beta < 1)$ is a discount factor, τ_0 is the initial state of the system, and π is the policy. We are interested in finding the optimal policy π^* that achieves the minimal expected total discounted cost by solving the following optimization problems:

$$\inf_{\pi \in \Pi} J_\beta(\pi, \tau_0). \qquad (7.168)$$

In this section, we formulate Eq. (7.168) as an MDP problem, and address the computational complexity in solving the MDP. We continue to relax the MDP problem and obtain a lower bound of the cost of any feasible policy satisfying the constraint $\sum_i^N u_k^{(i)} \leq M$.

We formulate Problem (7.168) as an MDP problem with a countable state space and finite action space. We define a tuple $\{\mathbb{S}, \mathbb{U}, \mathbb{P}(\cdot \mid \cdot, \cdot), c(\cdot, \cdot)\}$ to describe the MDP [246].

1) The state space $\mathbb{S}$ is the collection of the holding time of the system $\tau_k = \left(\tau_k^{(1)}, \ldots, \tau_k^{(N)} \right)$.

2) The action space $\mathbb{U}$: the action is the channel allocation $U_k = \left(u_k^{(1)}, \ldots, u_k^{(N)} \right)$. The constraint is $\sum_{i=1}^{N} u_k^{(i)} \leq M$.

3) The transition kernel $\mathbb{P}(\cdot \mid \cdot, \cdot)$: $\mathbb{P}(\tau_{k+1} \mid \tau_k, U_k)$ is the probability of moving from state τ_{k+1} to τ_k if action U_k is chosen at time step k. Under Eq. (7.165), we have

$$\mathbb{P}(\tau_{k+1} \mid \tau_k, U_k) = \prod_{i=1}^{N} Pr\left(\tau_{k+1}^{(i)} \mid \tau_k^{(i)}, u_k^{(i)} \right) \tag{7.169}$$

where $Pr\left(\tau_{k+1}^{(i)} \mid \tau_k^{(i)}, u_k^{(i)} \right)$

$$= \alpha_i, \text{ if } \tau_{k+1}^{(i)} = 0, u_k^{(i)} = 1$$

$$= 1 - \alpha_i, \text{ if } \tau_{k+1}^{(i)} = \tau_k^{(i)} + 1, u_k^{(i)} = 1$$

$$= 1, \text{ if } \tau_{k+1}^{(i)} = \tau_k^{(i)} + 1, u_k^{(i)} = 0$$

$$= 0, \text{ otherwise.}$$

4) The one-stage reward function $c(\cdot, \cdot)$ is defined as

$$c(\tau_k, U_k) = \sum_{i=1}^{N} c^{(i)} \left(\tau_k^{(i)}, u_k^{(i)} \right)$$

$$= \sum_{i=1}^{N} \left[Trh^{\tau^{(i)}} \left(\bar{P}^{(i)} \right) + \lambda_i u_k^{(i)} \mathcal{E}_i \right] \tag{7.170}$$

where $c^{(i)} \left(\tau_k^{(i)}, u_k^{(i)} \right)$ is defined in Eq. (7.166). For the given initial state τ_0 and policy π, the expected total discounted cost is defined as

$$C_\beta(\pi, \tau_0) = \mathbb{E}_{\tau_0}^{\pi} \left[\sum_{k=0}^{\infty} \beta^k c(\tau_k, U_k) \right].$$

Problem (7.168) is reformulated as an MDP problem as

$$\inf_{\pi \in \Pi} C_\beta(\pi, \tau_0). \tag{7.171}$$

When the scale of the system is small, the optimal policy of an MDP problem can be easily found using the standard value iteration. However, as the number of the subsystems grows linearly, the number of states increases exponentially. The classic value iteration algorithm is no longer amenable for solving the large-scale MDP problems, and obtaining the optimal policy is shown to be PSPACE-hard. In this section, we use the relaxation method in [250] to decompose the original N-dimensional optimization problem into N independent 1D optimization problems, which significantly reduces the computation complexity.

Whittle introduced a relaxation method for restless multi-armed bandits (RMABs) in [250] by replacing the constraint $\sum_{i=1}^{N} u_k^{(i)} \leq M$ with a soft one that requires only that the expected total discounted number of allocated channels should not exceed M.

We denote by $\bar{\Pi}$ the collection of all policies that are able to assign the probability over inadmissible transmission decisions. The collection of feasible policies Π is a subset of $\bar{\Pi}$. We employ this method to derive the following relaxed program of Problem (7.171):

$$min_{\pi \in \bar{\Pi}} C_\beta(\pi, \tau_0)$$

$$\text{s.t. } \mathbb{E}_{\tau_0}^\pi \left[\sum_{k=0}^\infty \beta^k \sum_{i=1}^N \left(1 - u_k^{(i)}\right) \right] \geq \frac{N - M}{1 - \beta}. \tag{7.172}$$

We note that under the relaxed constraint of Eq. (7.172), the number of allocated channels at each time step is allowed to be larger than M, but the expected total discounted number of allocated channels is less than or equal to M. Thus, the optimal policy under this relaxed constraint provides a lower bound to any feasible policies of Eq. (7.171). The main advantage of considering the soft constraint is that the relaxed program can be decomposed into N subproblems by dual decomposition [251].

Whittle [250] proposed a relaxation method of RMABs in which the original constraint is replaced with its discounted version, and a heuristic called the Whittle index policy is developed based on the solution to the relaxed program. The Whittle index policy is based on the solution of the subproblems under a given subsidy φ. If the subsystem does not get the channel, then the subsystem receives a subsidy φ. For convenience of notation, in this section we omit the subscript *(i)* in the notation of the i-th subsystem. We intend to derive the closed-form solution of the subproblems by utilizing the threshold structure of the optimal policy, which is influenced by the value of subsidy φ. The one-stage cost with subsidy φ is defined as

$$c_\varphi(\tau, u) = c(\tau, u) - (1 - u)\,\varphi$$
$$= \mathrm{Trh}^\tau(\bar{P}) + \lambda u \mathcal{E} - (1 - u)\,\varphi \tag{7.173}$$

and recall that $c(\tau, u)$ is the one-stage cost without subsidy φ (7.166). The stochastic property of the subsystem is characterized by the following transition probability:

$$\Pr(\tau_{k+1} \mid \tau_k, u_k)$$
$$= \alpha, \text{ if } \tau_{k+1} = 0, u_k = 1$$
$$= 1 - \alpha, \text{ if } \tau_{k+1} = \tau_k + 1, u_k = 1$$
$$= 1, \text{ if } \tau_{k+1} = \tau_k + 1, u_k = 0$$
$$= 0, \qquad \text{otherwise.}$$

Under the subsidy φ, we denote by $V_{\beta,\varphi}^f(\tau_0)$ the expected discounted cost under policy f with the initial state τ_0:

$$V_{\beta,\varphi}^f(\tau_0) = E_{\tau_0}^f \left[\sum_{k=0}^\infty \beta^k c_\varphi(\tau_k, u_k) \right]$$

Let $f_{\beta,\varphi}^*$ denote the optimal policy of the subsystem, and $V_{\beta,\varphi}^*$ be the associated optimal expected discounted cost. We denote by $Q_{\beta,\varphi}(\tau, u)$ the function describing the quality of a state-action combination:

$$Q_{\beta,\varphi}(\tau, u) = c_\varphi(\tau, u) + \beta \sum_{\tau' \in \mathbb{N}} \Pr(\tau' \mid \tau, u) V_{\beta,\varphi}^*(\tau'). \tag{7.174}$$

From the definition, we have $V_{\beta,\varphi}^*(\tau) = \min_{u \in \{0,1\}} Q_{\beta,\varphi}(\tau, u)$. Let the passivity set $\mathcal{P}(\varphi)$ be the set of states where the optimal action is not allocating the channel, that is,

$$\mathcal{P}(\varphi) = \left\{ j \mid f_{\beta,\varphi}^*(j) = 0 \right\}. \tag{7.175}$$

Before deriving the Whittle index for each subsystem, we shall first verify that the subsystem satisfies the Whittle *indexability* property, whose definition is adopted from [250] as follows.

A subsystem is Whittle indexable if and only if as φ increases from $-\infty$ to ∞, the passivity set $\mathcal{P}(\varphi)$ monotonically expands from $\emptyset$ to $\mathbb{N}$. A system is Whittle indexable if all its subsystems are Whittle indexable.

Under the indexability property of the subsystem, the Whittle index $W_\beta(\tau)$ is the value of the subsidy φ under which both actions lead to the same quality of a state-action combination, that is,

$$W_\beta(\tau) = \inf \left\{ \varphi \mid Q_{\beta,\varphi}(\tau, 0) \leq Q_{\beta,\varphi}(\tau, 1) \right\}. \tag{7.176}$$

The indexability of the system implies that there exists a potential priority order in each subsystem, which is related to the criticality of each subsystem being in its own state (the holding time τ in our case). To measure the criticality, the subsidy φ is introduced to offer an extra reward when the action "no channel allocation" is taken. The Whittle index $W_\beta(\tau)$, which serves as a measure of the criticality of each state of the subsystem, corresponds to the exact value of the subsidy φ leading to no potential benefits of channel allocation. The Whittle index policy is to allocate at most M channels to those subsystems with the currently largest and *nonnegative* Whittle indices at each time step [252]. We note that the Whittle index could be negative, which means that there is no need to allocate the channel, and in this case the total number of actually allocated channels at each time step could be less than M.

Threshold Structure of Optimal Policies: In this section, we show that under a fixed subsidy φ, the optimal policy $f^*_{\beta,\varphi}$ processes a threshold structure, which serves as a preliminary result to prove the indexability of a single bandit arm (subsystem). Before showing the threshold structure of $f^*_{\beta,\varphi}$, we need some preliminary results about the properties of $h(\cdot)$. The following lemmas are introduced in [246].

Lemma 7.2 The function h satisfies $h^\tau(\bar{P}) \preccurlyeq h^{\tau'}(P), \forall \tau \leq \tau'$. The following limit of function composition exists, that is, $\lim_{j \to \infty} h^j(\bar{P}) = Y$, where Y is the solution to the Lyapunov function $YA^T + \Sigma_w = Y$. Furthermore, for any $0 < \beta \leq 1$, $\sum_{j=0}^{\infty} \beta^j \left[Y - h^j(\bar{P}) \right]$ is the unique solution to the Lyapunov function $\beta AXA^T + Y - \bar{P} = X$. The following lemma shows that the optimal policy $f^*_{\beta,\varphi}$ possesses a threshold structure.

Lemma 7.3 The optimal policy $f^*_{\beta,\varphi}$ of a single bandit arm with subsidy φ has a threshold structure, that is, $\exists \tau^*_\varphi \in \mathbb{N}$ such that

$$f^*_{\beta,\varphi}(\tau) = \begin{cases} 0, \text{ if } \tau < \tau^* \\ 1, \text{ if } \tau \geq \tau^*. \end{cases}$$

The threshold τ^*_φ monotonically increases from 0 to ∞ as the subsidy φ increases from $-\infty$ to ∞.

Based on the threshold structure of $f^*_{\beta,\varphi}$, we are ready to derive the closed form of the value function $V^*_{\beta,\varphi}$. Note that the unknown parameter τ^*_φ in the closed-form expression of $V^*_{\beta,\varphi}$ depends on the subsidy φ. In the sequel (Theorem 7.2), we will derive the Whittle index by analyzing the relation between τ^*_φ and φ.

Lemma 7.4 Given that the threshold of the policy $f^*_{\beta,\varphi}$, is $\tau^*_\varphi \in \mathbb{N}$, then $V^*_{\beta,\varphi}$ can be computed as

$$V^*_{\beta,\varphi}(0) = \frac{1}{\Gamma_\beta\left(\tau^*_\varphi\right)} \left[\frac{\beta^{\tau^*_\varphi} - 1}{1 - \beta}\,\varphi + \Delta_\beta\left(\tau^*_\varphi\right)\right] \tag{7.177}$$

where

$$\Gamma_\beta\left(\tau^*_\varphi\right) = 1 - \frac{\alpha\beta^{\tau^*_\varphi + 1}}{1 - \beta(1 - \alpha)} \tag{7.178}$$

$$\Delta_\beta\left(\tau^*_\varphi\right) = \sum_{j=0}^{\tau^*_\varphi - 1} \beta^j \mathrm{Trh}^j(\bar{P})$$

$$+ \sum_{j=\tau^*_\varphi}^{\infty} \beta^j (1-\alpha)^{j-\tau^*_\varphi}\left[\mathrm{Trh}^j(\bar{P}) + \lambda\mathcal{E}\right]. \tag{7.179}$$

and, as the expected total discounted time is passive, it is given by

$$\delta_{\beta,\,\varphi}(0) = \mathbb{E}_\tau^{f^*_{\beta,\varphi}}\left[\sum_{k=0}^{\infty} \beta^k(1 - u_k)\right]$$

$$= \frac{\left(1 - \beta^{\tau^*_\varphi}\right)[1 - \beta(1 - \alpha)]}{(1 - \beta)\left[1 - \beta(1 - \alpha) - \alpha\beta^{\tau^*_\varphi + 1}\right]}. \tag{7.180}$$

Indexability and Whittle Index: With the preliminary results in Lemmas 7.3 and 7.4, we are ready to establish the indexability of the RMAB under the expected total discounted cost criterion and derive the closed-form expression of the Whittle index.

Theorem 7.2: The system is Whittle indexable. Furthermore, the Whittle index for the subsystem at state τ is given by [246]

$$W_\beta(\tau) = \inf\left\{\varphi | v_{\beta,\varphi}(\tau; u = 0) \leq v_{\beta,\varphi}(\tau; u = 1)\right\}$$

$$= (1 - \beta)\frac{\Gamma_\beta(\tau)\Delta_\beta(\tau + 1) - \Gamma_\beta(\tau + 1)\Delta_\beta(\tau)}{(1 - \beta^{\tau + 1})\Gamma_\beta(\tau) - (1 - \beta^\tau)\Gamma_\beta(\tau + 1)} \tag{7.181}$$

At each time step, the (generalized) Whittle index policy is to allocate channels to those subsystems having currently the largest, but *nonnegative*, Whittle indices [252]. We denote by π_w the Whittle index policy for Problem (7.168). We note that in some cases, the number of subsystems to which the channels have been allocated can be less than M. By Theorem 7.2, we have the following properties of the Whittle indices.

Corollary 7.1 C.1 The Whittle index $W_\beta(\tau)$ is monotonically nondecreasing on $\mathbb{N}$. Furthermore, the limit of $W_\beta(\tau)$ exists, that is, $\lim_{\tau \to \infty} W_\beta(\tau) = \alpha\beta TrZ_\beta - \lambda\mathcal{E}$, where Z_β is the unique solution to the Lyapunov function $\beta AXA^T + Y - \bar{P} = X$. Recall that Y is the solution to the Lyapunov function $AXA^T + \Sigma_w = X$.

C.2 If $\mathcal{E} = 0$, then the Whittle index $W_\beta(\tau)$ is nonnegative for any $\tau \in \mathbb{N}$.

C.3 If $\mathcal{E} > \alpha\beta TrZ_\beta$, then the Whittle index $W_\beta(\tau)$ is always negative for any $\tau \in \mathbb{N}$. This subsystem will be made to be passive for all time; that is, $f^*_{\beta,\varphi}(\tau) = 0$, $\forall \tau \in \mathbb{N}$.

7.10.2 System Performance

In this section, along the lines presented in [246], the performance of the Whittle index policy is evaluated from two viewpoints. From the theoretical viewpoint, the asymptotic optimality of the Whittle index policy for indexable systems is stated. From the practical viewpoint, a performance lower bound is derived based on the finite-state approximation, and this bound serves as a numerical benchmark for the Whittle index policy. The performance of the Whittle index policy and the tightness of the performance bound will be shown in Design Example 7.6.

Asymptotic Optimality: For large-scale applications, the performance of the Whittle index policy can be evaluated under the fluid-scaling regime; we scale by $l \in \mathbb{N}$ both the number of subsystems and the number of channels M. After the fluid-scaling procedure, the number of subsystems of class-i is l, and the total number of subsystems is lN. The policy π of the fluid-scaling model is a mapping from the collection of the holding time of all the lN subsystems to the probability measure over the transmission decision of the whole system. In brief, at each time at most lM subsystems get the channels based on the policy π and the collection of holding times of all lN subsystems. The initial state (holding time) τ_0 is not affected by the fluid-scaling procedure, in the sense that all class-i subsystems have the initial state $\tau_0^{(i)}$.

For a given policy π, $S_{i,\tau}^{\pi,u}(k)$ denotes the number of class-i subsystems at time k that have the holding time τ, and transmission decision is u. The expected discounted cost of the fluid-scaling model after normalization is defined as

$$J_\beta(\pi, \tau_0, l) =$$

$$\mathbb{E}_{\tau_0^l}^\pi \left[\sum_{k=0}^\infty \sum_{i=1}^N \sum_{\tau \in \mathbb{N}} \sum_{u \in \{0,1\}} \beta^k c^{(i)}(\tau, u) \frac{S_{i,\tau}^{\pi,u}(k)}{l} \right]$$

The definition of the asymptotic optimality is then adopted from [252].

Definition [2]   The policy π' is asymptotically optimal if for any admissible policy π and any initial state τ_0, $\lim \sup_{l \to \infty} J_\beta(\pi', \tau_0, l) \leq \lim \sup_{l \to \infty} J_\beta(\pi, \tau_0, l)$.

Lower Bound: For a specific application, we are interested in how to numerically evaluate the performance gap between the Whittle index policy and the optimal policy. As the computational complexity of obtaining the optimal policy is formidable, we intend to use the value of the optimal solution to Problem (7.172), which is a lower bound for the value of the optimal solution to Problem (7.171), as the benchmark for the Whittle index policy.

To facilitate the calculation of the solution to Problem (7.172), we introduce a truncated procedure that is characterized by the set of integers $\{t^{(1)}, \dots, t^{(N)} \mid t^i \in \mathbb{N}, \forall i \in [1:N]\}$. For each subsystem, a modified one-state cost $\bar{c}^{(i)}$ (Eq.(7.166)) can be defined as

$$\bar{c}^{(i)}\left(\tau_k^{(i)}, u_k^{(i)} \mid t^{(i)}\right) = \begin{cases} \mathrm{Tr}h_i^{\tau_k^{(i)}}\left(\bar{P}^{(i)}\right) + \lambda_i u_k^{(i)}\mathcal{E}_i, & \text{if } \tau_k^i < t^{(i)} \\ \mathrm{Tr}h_i^{t^{(i)}}\left(\bar{P}^{(i)}\right) + \lambda_i u_k^{(i)}\mathcal{E}_i, & \text{if } \tau_k^i \geq t^{(i)}. \end{cases} \tag{7.182}$$

With this modified one-state cost $\bar{c}^{(i)}$, $i \in [1:N]$, the truncated version can be constructed by embedding the collection of the holding time $\tau^{(i)}$ satisfying $\{\tau^{(i)} \mid \tau^{(i)} \geq t^{(i)}\}$ as a single holding time $t^{(i)}$. For the given initial state τ_0 and policy π, the expected total discounted cost of the truncated program is defined as

$$\bar{C}_\beta(\pi, \tau_0) = \mathbb{E}_{\tau_0}^\pi \left[\sum_{k=0}^\infty \beta^k \bar{c}(\tau_k, U_k) \right] \tag{7.183}$$

where $\bar{c}(\tau_k, U_k)$ is defined as

$$\bar{c}(\tau_k, U_k) = \sum_{i=1}^{N} \bar{c}^{(i)}\left(\tau_k^{(i)}, u_k^{(i)}\right). \tag{7.184}$$

We define the truncated program with the truncation parameters $\{t^{(1)}, \dots, t^{(N)} \mid t^i \in \mathbb{N}, \forall i \in [1: N]\}$ as

$$min_{\pi \in \bar{\Pi}} \bar{\mathcal{C}}_\beta(\pi, \tau_0)$$

$$\text{s.t. } \mathbb{E}_{\tau_0}^{A}\left[\sum_{k=0}^{\infty} \beta^k \sum_{i=1}^{N}\left(1 - u_k^{(i)}\right)\right] \geq \frac{N - M}{1 - \beta}. \tag{7.185}$$

The approximation error between Problems (7.172) and (7.185) is defined as $\sup_{\pi \in \bar{\Pi}}\left[\mathcal{C}_\beta(\pi, \tau_0) - \bar{\mathcal{C}}_\beta(\pi, \tau_0)\right]$. The following lemma characterizes the approximation error induced by the truncation procedure.

Lemma 7.5 The approximation error induced by the truncation procedure satisfies

$$0 < \sup_{\pi \in \bar{\Pi}}\left[\mathcal{C}_\beta(A, \tau_0) - \bar{\mathcal{C}}_\beta(\pi, \tau_0)\right] \leq$$

$$\frac{N}{1 - \beta} \max_i\left\{\mathrm{Tr}Y^{(i)}(i) - \mathrm{Tr}h_i^{(i)}\left(\bar{P}^{(i)}\right)\right\} \tag{7.186}$$

where $Y^{(i)}$ is the solution to the Lyaponov equation $A^{(i)}Y^{(i)}A^{(i)^{\mathrm{T}}} + \Sigma_w^{(i)} = Y^{(i)}$. For any $\varepsilon > 0$, there exist the truncation parameters $\{t^{(1)}, \dots, t^{(N)} \mid t^i \in \mathbb{N}, \forall i \in [1: N]\}$ such that $0 < \sup_{\pi \in \bar{\Pi}}\left[\mathcal{C}_\beta(\pi, \tau_0) - \bar{\mathcal{C}}_\beta(\pi, \tau_0)\right] \leq \varepsilon$.

Problem (7.185) can be decomposed into several subproblems by dual decomposition. Recall that the Whittle indices of the subsystems are directly related to the solutions of the subproblems, and the Whittle index for the truncated problem can be computed in the same way as that in Theorem 7.2 by replacing the one-stage cost function c (Eq. (7.170)) with $\bar{c}$ (Eq.(7.182). The parallel results for the truncated problem can be easily derived. If the threshold of the optimal policy is $\leq t^{(i)}$, the value function $V_{\beta,\varphi}^*{}^{(i)}(0)$ (Eq. (7.177)) for the truncated program can be computed as

$$\bar{V}_{\beta,\varphi}^*(0) = \frac{1}{\bar{\Gamma}_\beta^{(i)}(\tau)}\left[\frac{\beta^\tau - 1}{1 - \beta}\varphi + \bar{\Delta}_\beta^{(i)}(\tau)\right] \tag{7.187}$$

where

$$\bar{\Gamma}_\beta^{(i)}(\tau) = 1 - \frac{\alpha_i \beta^{\tau + 1}}{1 - \beta(1 - \alpha_i)}$$

$$\bar{\Delta}_\beta^{(i)}(\tau) = \sum_{j=0}^{\tau-1} \beta^j \mathrm{Tr}h^j(\bar{P})$$

$$+ \sum_{j=\tau}^{t^{(i)}-1} \beta^j (1 - \alpha_i)^{j-\tau}\left[\mathrm{Tr}h^j(\bar{P}) + \lambda\mathcal{E}\right]$$

$$+ \frac{\beta^{t^{(i)}}(1-\alpha_i)^{t^{(i)}-\tau}}{1 - \beta(1-\alpha_i)}\left[\mathrm{Tr}h^{t^{(i)}}(\bar{P}) + \lambda\mathcal{E}\right].$$

Similarly, the Whittle index for the truncated problem is given by

$$\overline{W}_\beta^{(i)}(\tau) = (1 - \beta)\frac{\bar{\Gamma}_\beta^{(i)}(\tau)\bar{\Delta}_\beta^{(i)}(\tau + 1) - \bar{\Gamma}_\beta^{(i)}(\tau + 1)\bar{\Delta}_\beta^{(i)}(\tau)}{(1 - \beta^{\tau + 1})\bar{\Gamma}_\beta^{(i)}(\tau) - (1 - \beta^\tau)\bar{\Gamma}_\beta^{(i)}(\tau + 1)}. \tag{7.188}$$

The truncation procedure does not change the structure of the state transition, and thus as the expected total discounted time is passive, $\delta_{\beta,\,\varphi}(0)$ (Eq. (7.180)) of the truncated problem is the same with that of untruncated problem. As the Whittle index $\overline{W}_{\beta}^{(i)}(\tau)$ and the expected total discounted time are passive, $\delta_{\beta,\,\varphi}(0)$ can be utilized to efficiently compute the value of the optimal solution to Problem (7.172) within any required approximation error $\varepsilon > 0$. The algorithm in [253] is designed to compute the performance lower bound for the general indexable RMABs with nonnegative Whittle indices, and it can be applied after minor modifications [254] to the problem considered here as well.

Design Example 7.6

To compare the results under a different discounted factor, we normalize the expected value by multiplying it with $(1 - \beta)$, and the normalized expected discounted cost will approach the expected time-average cost as the discounted factor β approaches 1. The required approximation error ε is set to 10^{-4}, and we compute the following values:

1) J_{Greedy}: Expected value of the myopic policy after normalization, and the value is estimated via the simulation.
2) J_{Whittle}: Expected value of the Whittle index policy π_w after normalization.
3) J^*: The algorithm in [255] is utilized to compute the performance lower bound (Problem (7.185)) after normalization.

We consider a large-scale sensor network with 100 first-order systems ($N = 100$). The system parameters $A^{(i)}, C^{(i)}, Q^{(i)}, R^{(i)}$, and α_i are uniformly distributed over $(0,1)$, and $\lambda_i \mathcal{E}_i$ is uniformly distributed over $(0,3)$. Because the scale of this example is large, the classic value iteration fails in this case. We computed $J_{\text{Greedy}}, J_{\text{Whittle}}$, and J^* as defined above. In Figure 7.28, we report the simulation results obtained in [246] with different M ($N = 100$). From the results, we have the following observations:

1) As expected, the degeneration in the performance of the myopic policy becomes more significant when the discounted factor β approaches 1. The Whittle index policy always outperforms the myopic policy.
2) The gap between J^* and J_{Whittle} is small (within 2%) for all M. Recall that the performance of the optimal policy is between J^* and J_{Whittle}, and we conclude that the gap between J_{Whittle} and the performance of the optimal policy is small, and J^* serves as a good benchmark for any feasible policies.
3) The performance of the Whittle index policy is nearly optimal. The simulation results show that the gap between the performance of the Whittle index policy and that of the optimal policy can be neglected.
4) Both J^* and J_{Whittle} decrease monotonically as M increases. We note that the performance of the myopic policy could be worse for larger M. The reason is that the myopic policy neglects the long-term effect, and the energy wasted on the data transmissions is larger for larger M.
5) For the large-scale problems that cannot be solved by the value iteration, the Whittle index policy is nearly optimal. Even for the small-scale problems ($4 \leq N \leq 7$), from the running time we observe that the computation load of computing the Whittle indices is almost the same with the

Figure 7.28 Numerical experiments with different M under N = 100.

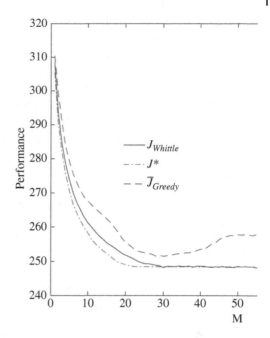

myopic policy, and it is nearly 1% of the value iteration. In the results of the simulation of systems with different sizes ($4 \leq N \leq 7$), we observe the occurrence of the *curse of dimensionality* in the classic value iteration method, as the computation time of value iteration for a system with $N = 7$ is over 500 times longer than that for the system with $N = 4$.

7.11   Network Representation Learning

Recently, network representation learning (NRL) has attracted a lot of research interest. NRL aims to learn latent, low-dimensional representations of network vertices, while preserving network topology structure, vertex content, and other side information. After new vertex representations are learned, network analytic tasks can be easily and efficiently carried out by applying conventional vector-based ML algorithms to the new representation space. This obviates the necessity of deriving complex algorithms that are applied directly to the original network. In this section, due to the limited space and the large number of available algorithms used for NRF, we will present an initial overview of the methodologies by briefly describing the algorithms, introducing only the objective function for the system optimization and providing the main reference for the details. In the subsequent sections, we will discuss only some of these algorithms in more detail. The overall section is organized along the lines presented in [306].

Preliminaries: In this context, an information network is defined as $G = (V, E, X, Y)$, where V denotes a set of vertices, and $|V|$ denotes the number of vertices in network G. $E \subseteq (V \times V)$ denotes a set of edges connecting the vertices. $X \in \mathbb{R}^{|V| \times m}$ is the vertex attribute matrix, where m is the number of attributes, and the element X_{ij} is the value of the i-th vertex on the j-th attribute. $Y \in \mathbb{R}^{|V| \times |\mathcal{Y}|}$ is the vertex label matrix, with $\mathcal{Y}$ being a set of labels. If the i-th vertex has the k-th label, the element $Y_{ik} = 1$; otherwise, $Y_{ik} = -1$. Due to privacy concerns or information access difficulty, the vertex attribute matrix X is often sparse, and the vertex label matrix Y is usually unobserved or partially observed. For each $(v_i, v_j) \in E$, if information network G is undirected, we have $(v_j, v_i) \in E$; if G is directed, (v_j, v_i) unnecessarily belongs to E. Each edge $(v_i, v_j) \in E$ is also associated with a weight w_{ij}, which is equal to 1 if the information network is binary (unweighted).

The generation of information networks is guided or dominated by certain latent mechanisms. Although these latent mechanisms are hardly known, they can be reflected by some network properties that exist widely in information networks. Therefore, the common network properties are essential for the learning of vertex representations that help accurately interpret information networks.

7.11.1 Network Properties

First-order proximity is the local pairwise proximity between two connected vertices. For each vertex pair (v_i, v_j), if $(v_i, v_j) \in E$, the first-order proximity between v_i and v_j is w_{ij}; otherwise, the first-order proximity between v_i and v_j is 0. First-order proximity captures the direct neighbor relationships between vertices.

Second-order proximity captures the two-step relations between each pair of vertices. For each vertex pair (v_i, v_j), second-order proximity is determined by the number of common neighbors shared by the two vertices, which can also be measured by the two-step transition probability from v_i to v_j equivalently. Compared with second-order proximity, high-order proximity captures more global structure, which explores the k-step $(k \geq 3)$ relations between each pair of vertices. For each vertex pair (v_i, v_j), the higher-order proximity is measured by the k-step $(k \geq 3)$ transition probability from vertex v_i to vertex v_j, which can also be reflected by the number of k-step $(k \geq 3)$ paths from v_i to v_j. Second-order and high-order proximities capture the similarity between a pair of indirectly connected vertices with similar structural contexts.

Structural role proximity depicts the similarity between vertices playing similar roles in their neighborhood, such as the edge of a chain, center of a star, and a bridge between two communities. In communication and traffic networks, vertices' structural roles are important to characterize their properties. Unlike first-order, second-order, and high-order proximities, which capture the similarity between vertices close to each other in the network, structural role proximity tries to discover the similarity between distant vertices that share the equivalent structural roles. As shown in Figure 7.29, although vertices 4, 12, and 16 are located far away from each other, they play the same structural role: the center of a star. Thus, they have high structural role proximity.

Intra-community proximity is the pairwise proximity between vertices in the same community. Many networks have a community structure, where vertex–vertex connections within the same community are dense, but connections to vertices outside the community are sparse. A community preserves certain kinds of common properties of vertices within it as cluster structure. For example, in social networks, communities might represent social groups by interest or background; in citation networks, communities might represent related papers on the same topic. The intra-community proximity captures such cluster structure by preserving the common property shared by vertices within the same community.

Vertex attribute: In addition to network structure, vertex attributes can provide direct evidence to measure *content-level similarity* between vertices. Vertex attributes and network structure can help each other filter out noisy information and compensate each other to jointly learn informative vertex representations.

Vertex label: Vertex labels provide direct information about the semantic categorization of each network vertex to certain classes or groups. Vertex labels are strongly influenced by, and inherently correlated to, both network structure and vertex attributes. Though vertex labels are usually

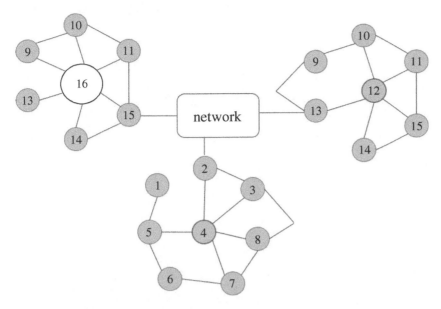

Figure 7.29 Illustrative example of structural role proximity.

partially observed, when coupled with network structure and vertex attributes, they encourage consistent labeling of network structures and vertex attributes, and help learn informative and discriminative vertex representations.

NRL. Given an information network $G= (V, E, X, Y)$, by integrating the network structure in E, vertex attributes in X, and vertex labels in Y (if available), the task of NRL is to learn a mapping function $f\colon v \rightarrow r_v \in \mathbb{R}^d$, where r_v is the learned representation of vertex v, and d is the dimension of the learned representation. The transformation f preserves the original network information such that two vertices similar in the original network should also be represented similarly in the learned vector space.

The learned vertex representations should satisfy the following conditions:

1) Low-dimensional, that is, $d \ll |V|$; in other words, the dimension of the learned vertex representations should be much smaller than the dimension of the original adjacency matrix representation for memory efficiency and the scalability of subsequent network analysis tasks.
2) Informative; that is, the learned vertex representations should preserve the vertex proximity reflected by the network structure and vertex attributes and/or vertex labels (if available).
3) Continuous; that is, the learned vertex representations should have continuous real values to support subsequent network analytic tasks, like vertex classification, vertex clustering, or anomaly detection, and have smooth decision boundaries to ensure the robustness of these tasks.

Figure 7.30 demonstrates a conceptual view of NRL, using a simple network. In this case, only the network structure is considered to learn vertex representations. Given an information network shown in Figure 7.30a, the objective of NRL is to embed all network vertices into a low-dimensional space, as depicted in Figure 7.30b. In the embedding space, vertices with structural proximity are

(a)

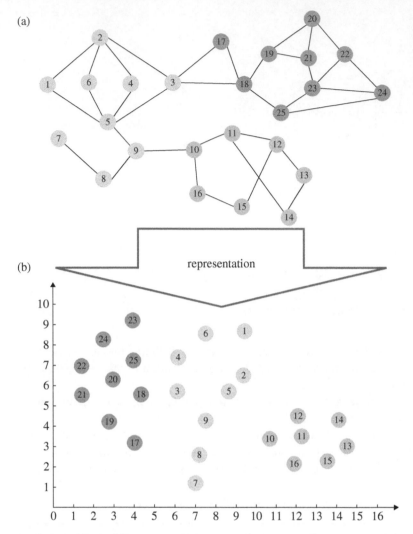

(b)

Figure 7.30 Conceptual view of network representation learning (NRL). (For more details see color figure in bins).

represented close to each other. For example, as vertex 7 and vertex 8 are directly connected, the first-order proximity dictates that they are embedded close to each other in the embedding space. Though vertex 2 and vertex 5 are not directly connected, they are also embedded close to each other because they have high second-order proximity, which is reflected by four common neighbors shared by these two vertices. Vertex 20 and vertex 25 are not directly connected and neither do they share common direct neighbors. However, they are connected by many k-step paths ($k \geq 3$), which proves that they have high-order proximity. Because of this, vertex 20 and vertex 25 also are embedded close to each other. Unlike other vertices, vertices 10–16 clearly belong to the same community in the original network. This intra-community proximity guarantees that the images of these vertices also exhibit a clear cluster structure in the embedding space.

Categorization: Here, we present a taxonomy used to categorize existing NRL techniques. The general overview is shown in Figure 7.31.

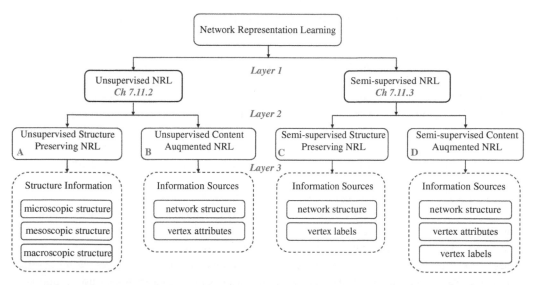

Figure 7.31 Taxonomy to summarize network representation learning (NRL) techniques. Adapted from [306].

Layer 1 of the taxonomy is based on whether vertex labels are provided for learning. According to this, we categorize NRL into two groups: *unsupervised* and *semi-supervised NRL*.

Unsupervised NRL refers to the setting where there no labeled vertices are provided for learning vertex representations. NRL is therefore considered a generic task independent of subsequent learning, and vertex representations are learned in an unsupervised manner. Most of the existing NRL algorithms fall into this category. After vertex representations are learned in a new embedded space, they are taken as features to any vector-based algorithms for various learning tasks such as vertex clustering. Unsupervised NRL algorithms can be further divided into two subgroups based on the type of network information available for learning: (i) unsupervised structure preserving methods that preserve only network structure and (ii) unsupervised content augmented methods that incorporate vertex attributes and network structure to learn joint vertex embeddings.

In *semi-supervised network representation learning (SS NRL)*, some labeled vertices exist for representation learning. Because vertex labels play an essential role in determining the categorization of each vertex with strong correlations to network structure and vertex attributes, *SS NRL* is proposed to take advantage of the vertex labels available in the network to seek more effective joint vector representations. In this setting, *NRL* is coupled with supervised learning tasks such as vertex classification. A unified objective function is often formulated to simultaneously optimize the learning of vertex representations and the classification of network vertices. Therefore, the learned vertex representations can be both informative and discriminative with respect to different categories. *SS* NRL algorithms can also be categorized into two subgroups: *SS* structure preserving methods and *SS* content augmented methods. In general, there are three main types of information sources: network structure, vertex attributes, and vertex labels. Most of the unsupervised NRL algorithms focus on preserving network structure for learning vertex representations, and only a few algorithms attempt to leverage vertex attributes. By contrast, in the *SS* learning setting, half of the algorithms couple vertex attributes with network structure and vertex labels to learn vertex representations. In both settings, most of the algorithms focus on preserving microscopic structure, and very few algorithms attempt to take advantage of the mesoscopic and macroscopic structure.

Approaches to NRL in the above two different settings can be summarized into five categories from algorithmic perspectives:

1) *Matrix factorization-based methods* represent the connections between network vertices in the form of a matrix and use matrix factorization to obtain the embeddings. Different types of matrices are constructed to preserve network structure, such as the k-step transition probability matrix, the modularity matrix, or the vertex-context matrix [256]. By assuming that such high-dimensional vertex representations are only affected by a small number of latent factors, matrix factorization is used to embed the high-dimensional vertex representations into a latent low-dimensional structure preserving space. Factorization strategies vary across different algorithms according to their objectives.

2) *Random-walk-based methods* are exploited for scalable vertex representation learning to capture structural relationships between vertices. By performing truncated random walks, an information network is transformed into a collection of vertex sequences, in which, the occurrence frequency of a vertex-context pair measures the structural distance between them.

3) Edge-modeling-based methods directly learn vertex representations from vertex–vertex connections. For capturing the first-order and second-order proximities, Large-scale Information Network Embedding (LINE) [257, 258] models a joint probability distribution and a conditional probability distribution, respectively, on connected vertices.

4) Deep-learning-based methods are also applied to NRL to extract complex structure features and learn deep, highly nonlinear vertex representations,

5) Hybrid methods: Some other methods employ a mixture of the above methods to learn vertex representations.

7.11.2 Unsupervised NRL

Methods are reviewed by separating them into two subsections, as outlined in Figure 7.31. After that, we summarize key characteristics of the methods and compare their differences across the two categories.

7.11.2.1 Unsupervised Structure Preserving
NRL refers to methods intended to preserve network structure, in the sense that vertices close to each other in the original network space should be represented similarly in the new embedding space. In this category, research efforts have focused on designing various models to capture as much structure information conveyed by the original network as possible.

We summarize network structure considered for learning vertex representations into three types: (i) microscopic structure, which includes local closeness proximity, that is, the first-order, second-order, and high-order proximity; (ii) mesoscopic structure, which captures structural role proximity and the intra-community proximity; and (iii) macroscopic structure, which captures global network properties, such as the scale-free property or small world property. The following subsections are organized according to our categorization of network structure, which is depicted in Figure 7.32.

7.11.2.1.1 Microscopic Structure Preserving NRL
Algorithms aim to preserve local structure information among directly or indirectly connected vertices in their neighborhood, including first-order, second-order, and high-order proximity. The first-order proximity captures the homophily – that is, directly connected vertices tend to be similar to each other – while second-order and high-order proximities capture the similarity between

Figure 7.32 Categorization of network structure. Adapted from [306].

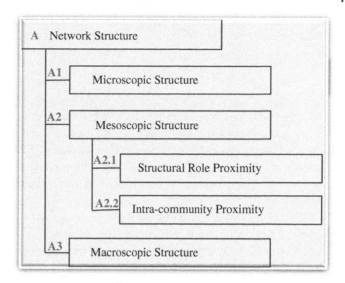

vertices sharing common neighbors. Most of structure preserving NRL algorithms fall into this category.

DeepWalk [259] generalizes the idea of the Skip-gram [268, 269] model, which utilizes word context in sentences to learn latent representations of words, to the learning of latent vertex representations in networks, by making an analogy between a natural language sentence and a short random walk sequence. Given a random walk sequence with length L, $\{v_1, v_2, \cdots, v_L\}$, following Skip-gram, DeepWalk learns the representation of vertex v_i by using it to predict its context vertices, which is achieved by the optimization problem:

$$min_f - \log \mathrm{Pr}(\{v_{i-t}, \cdots, v_{i+t}\} \backslash v_i \mid f(v_i)), \tag{7.189}$$

where $\{v_{i-t}, \cdots, v_{i+t}\} \backslash v_i$ are the context vertices of vertex v_i within t window size. Making the conditional independence assumption, the probability $\mathrm{Pr}(\{v_{i-t}, \cdots, v_{i+t}\} \backslash v_i \mid f(v_i))$ is approximated as

$$\mathrm{Pr}(\{v_{i-t}, \cdots, v_{i+t}\} \backslash v_i \mid f(v_i)) = \prod_{j=i-t, j \neq i}^{i+t} \mathrm{Pr}(v_j \mid f(v_i)). \tag{7.190}$$

Following DeepWalk's learning architecture, vertices that share similar context vertices in a random walk sequences should be represented close to each other in the new embedding space. Considering the fact that context vertices in random walk sequences describe neighborhood structure, DeepWalk actually represents vertices sharing similar neighbors (direct or indirect) that are embedded close to each other, so the second-order and high-order proximities are preserved.

Large-scale Information Network Embedding (LINE): Instead of exploiting random walks to capture network structure, LINE [260] learns vertex representations by explicitly modeling first-order and second-order proximities. To preserve first-order proximity, LINE minimizes the following objective:

$$O_1 = d(\hat{p}_1(\cdot, \cdot), p_1(\cdot, \cdot)). \tag{7.191}$$

For each vertex pair v_i and v_j with $(v_i, v_j) \in E$, $p_1(\cdot, \cdot)$ is the joint distribution modeled by their latent embeddings r_{v_i} and r_{v_j}. $\hat{p}_1(v_i, v_j)$ is the empirical distribution between them. $d(\cdot, \cdot)$ is the distance between two distributions. To preserve second-order proximity, LINE minimizes the following objective:

$$O_2 = \sum_{v_i \in V} \lambda_i d(\hat{p}_2(\cdot \mid v_i), p_2(\cdot \mid v_i)), \tag{7.192}$$

where $p_2(\cdot \mid v_i)$ is the context conditional distribution for each $v_i \in V$ modeled by vertex embeddings, $\hat{p}_2(\cdot \mid v_i)$ is the empirical conditional distribution, and λ_i is the prestige of vertex v_i. Here, the vertex context is determined by its neighbors; that is, for each v_j, v_j is v_i's context if and only if $(v_i, v_j) \in E$. By minimizing these two objectives, LINE learns two kinds of vertex representations that preserve first-order and second-order proximity, and take their concatenation as the final vertex representation.

GraRep. Following the idea of DeepWalk, GraRep [261] extends the Skip-gram model to capture high-order proximity; that is, vertices sharing common k-step neighbors ($k \geq 1$) should have similar latent representations. Specifically, for each vertex, GraRep defines its k-step neighbors ($k \geq 1$) as context vertices, and for each $1 \leq k \leq K$, to learn k-step vertex representations, GraRep employs the matrix factorization version of Skip-gram:

$$[U^k, \Sigma^k, V^k] = SVD(X^k). \tag{7.193}$$

where X^k is the log k-step transition probability matrix. The k-step representation for vertex v_i is constructed as the i-th row of matrix $U_d^k (\Sigma_d^k)^{0.5}$, where U_d^k is the first-d columns of U^k, and Σ_d^k is the diagonal matrix composed of the top d singular values. After k-step vertex representations are learned, GraRep concatenates them together as the final vertex representations.

Deep Neural Networks for Graph Representations (DNGR). To overcome the weakness of truncated random walks in exploiting vertex contextual information, that is, the difficulty in capturing correct contextual information for vertices at the boundary of sequences and the difficulty in determining the walk length and the number of walks, DNGR [262] utilizes the random surfing model to capture contextual relatedness between each pair of vertices and preserves them as $|V|$-dimensional vertex representations X. To extract complex features and model nonlinearities, DNGR applies *stacked denoising autoencoders* (SDAE) to the high-dimensional vertex representations X to learn deep low-dimensional vertex representations.

Structural Deep Network Embedding (SDNE) [263] is a deep-learning-based approach that uses a semi-supervised deep autoencoder model to capture nonlinearity in network structure. In the unsupervised component, SDNE learns the second-order-proximity-preserving vertex representations by reconstructing the $|V|$−dimensional vertex adjacent matrix representations, which tries to minimize

$$\mathcal{L}_{2nd} = \sum_{i=1}^{|V|} \left\| \left(r_{v_i}^{(0)} - \hat{r}_{v_i}^{(0)} \right) \odot b_i \right\| \tag{7.194}$$

where $r^{(0)} = S_{i:}$ is the input representation, and $\hat{r}_{v_i}^{(0)}$ is the reconstructed representation. Vector b_i is a weight vector used to penalize construction error more on the nonzero elements of S. In the supervised component, SDNE imports first-order proximity by penalizing the distance between connected vertices in the embedding space. The loss function for this objective is defined as

$$\mathcal{L}_{1st} = \sum_{i,j=1}^{|V|} S_{ij} \left\| r_{v_i}^{(K)} - r_{v_j}^{(K)} \right\|_2^2, \tag{7.195}$$

where $r_{v_i}^{(K)}$ is the K-th layer representation of vertex v_i, with K being the number of hidden layers. SDNE minimizes the joint objective function

$$\mathcal{L} = \mathcal{L}_{2nd} + \alpha\mathcal{L}_{1st} + \nu\mathcal{L}_{reg}, \tag{7.196}$$

where $\mathcal{L}_{reg}$ is a regularization term to prevent overfitting. After solving the minimization of Eq. (7.196), for vertex v_i, the K-th layer representation $r_{v_i}^{(K)}$ is taken as its representation r_{v_i}.

Node 2vec: In contrast to the rigid strategy of defining neighborhood (context) for each vertex, node 2vec [264] designs a flexible neighborhood sampling strategy, that is, biased random walk, which smoothly interpolates between two extreme sampling strategies: Breadth-first Sampling and Depth-first Sampling. The biased random walk exploited in *node 2vec* can better preserve both the second-order and high-order proximities. Following the Skip-gram architecture, given the set of neighborhood vertices $N(v_i)$ generated by biased random walk, *node2vec* learns the vertex representation $f(v_i)$ by optimizing the occurrence probability of neighbor vertices $N(v_i)$ conditioned on the representation of vertex v_i, $f(v_i)$:

$$\max_f \sum_{v_i \in V} \log\Pr(N(v_i) \mid f(v_i)). \tag{7.197}$$

High-order Proximity Preserved Embedding (HOPE) [265] learns vertex representations that capture the asymmetric high-order proximity in directed networks. In undirected networks, the transitivity is symmetric, but it is asymmetric in directed networks. For example, in a directed network, if there is a directed link from vertex v_i to vertex v_j and from vertex v_j to vertex v_k, it is more likely to have a directed link from v_i to v_k, but not from v_k to v_i. To preserve the asymmetric transitivity, HOPE learns two vertex embedding vectors $U^s, U^t \in \mathbb{R}^{|V| \times d}$, which are called the source and target embedding vectors, respectively. After constructing the high-order proximity matrix S from four proximity measures, HOPE learns vertex embeddings by solving the following matrix factorization problem:

$$\min_{U^s, U^t} \|S - U_s \cdot U_t^{\mathrm{T}}\|_F^2. \tag{7.198}$$

Asymmetric Proximity Preserving graph embedding (APP) [266] is another NRL algorithm designed to capture asymmetric proximity, by using a Monte Carlo approach to approximate the asymmetric Rooted PageRank proximity [267]. Similar to HOPE, APP has two representations for each vertex v_i: a source role $r_{v_i}^s$ and a target role $r_{v_i}^t$. For each sampled path starting from v_i and ending with v_j, the representations are learned by maximizing the target vertex v_j occurrence probability conditioned on the source vertex v_i:

$$\Pr(v_j \mid v_i) = \frac{\exp\left(r_{v_i}^s \cdot r_{v_j}^t\right)}{\sum\limits_{v \in V} \exp\left(r_{v_i}^s \cdot r_v^t\right)}. \tag{7.199}$$

GraphGAN [270] learns vertex representations by modeling the connectivity behavior through an adversarial learning framework. Inspired by GAN (Generative Adversarial Nets) [271], GraphGAN works through two components: (i) Generator $(v \mid v_c)$, which fits the distribution of the vertices connected to v_c across V and generates the likely connected vertices, and (ii) Discriminator $D(v, v_c)$, which outputs a connecting probability for the vertex pair (v, v_c), to differentiate the vertex pairs generated by $G(v \mid v_c)$ from the ground truth. $G(v \mid v_c)$ and $D(v, v_c)$ compete in such a way that $G(v \mid v_c)$ tries to fit the true connecting distribution as much as possible and generates fake connected vertex pairs to fool $D(v, v_c)$, while $D(v, v_c)$ tries to increase its discriminative power to distinguish the vertex pairs generated by $G(v \mid v_c)$ from the ground truth. The competition is achieved by the following *minimax* game:

$$\min_{\theta_G} \ \max_{\theta_D} \sum_{v_c \in V} \left(\mathbb{E}_{v \sim \mathrm{Pr}_{true}(\cdot \mid v_c)} \left[\log D(v, v_c; \theta_D) \right] \right. \tag{7.200}$$

$$\left. + \ \mathbb{E}_{v \sim G(\cdot \mid v_c; \theta_G)} \left[\log(1 - D(v, v_c; \theta_D)) \right] \right).$$

where $G(v \mid v_c; \theta_G)$ and $D(v, v_c; \theta_D)$ are defined as follows:

$$G(v \mid v_c; \theta_G) = \frac{\exp(g_v \cdot g_{v_c})}{\sum\limits_{v \neq v_c} \exp(g_v \cdot g_{v_c})},$$

$$D(v, v_c; \theta_D) = \frac{1}{1 + \exp(d_v \cdot d_{v_c})}, \tag{7.201}$$

where $g_v \in \mathbb{R}^k$ and $d_v \in \mathbb{R}^k$ are the representation vectors for the generator and discriminator, respectively, and $\theta_D = \{d_v\}$, $\theta_G = \{g_v\}$. After the minimax game in Eq. (7.200) is solved, g_v serves as the final vertex representations.

7.11.2.1.2 Mesoscopic Structure

Besides local connectivity patterns, vertices often share similar structural roles at a mesoscopic level, such as centers of stars or members of cliques.

Structural Role Proximity Preserving NRL   Aims to embed vertices that are far away from each other but share similar structural roles close to each other. This not only facilitates the downstream structural role-dependent tasks but also enhances microscopic structure preserving NRL.

Struct 2vec [272]: It first encodes the vertex structural role similarity into a multilayer graph, where the weights of the edges at each layer are determined by the structural role difference at the corresponding scale. DeepWalk is then performed on the multilayer graph to learn vertex representations, such that vertices close to each other in the multilayer graph (with high structural role similarity) are embedded close to each other in the new representation space. For each vertex pair (v_i, v_j), considering their k-hop neighborhood formed by their neighbors within k steps, their structural distance at scale k, $D_k(v_i, v_j)$, is defined as

$$D_k(v_i, v_j) = D_{k-1}(v_i, v_j) + g\big(s(R_k(v_i)), s(R_k(v_j))\big), \tag{7.202}$$

where $R_k(v_i)$ is the set of vertices in its k-hop neighborhood, $s(R_k(v_i))$ is the ordered degree sequence of the vertices in $R_k(v_i)$, and $g(s(R_k(v_i)), s(R_k(v_j)))$ is the distance between the ordered degree sequences $s(R_k(v_i))$ and $s(R_k(v_j))$. When $k = 0$, $D_0(v_i, v_j)$ is the degree difference between vertex v_i and v_j, which captures the structural role dissimilarity between v_i and v_j.

GraphWave: By making use of the spectral graph wavelet diffusion patterns, *GraphWave* [273] embeds vertex neighborhood structure into a low-dimensional space and preserves structural role proximity. The assumption is that if two vertices residing far away in the network share similar structural roles, the graph wavelets starting from them will diffuse similarly across their neighbors.

For vertex v_k, its spectral graph wavelet coefficients Ψ_k is defined as

$$\Psi_k = U Diag\big(g_s(\lambda_1), \cdots, g_s(\lambda_{|V|})\big) U^{\mathrm{T}} \delta_k, \tag{7.203}$$

where U is the eigenvector matrix of the graph Laplacian L and $\lambda_1, \cdots, \lambda_{|V|}$ are the eigenvalues, $g_s(\lambda) = \exp(-\lambda s)$ is the heat kernel, and δ_k is the one-hot vector for k. By taking Ψ_k as a probability distribution, the spectral wavelet distribution pattern in Ψ_k is then encoded into its empirical function:

$$\varphi_k(t) = \frac{1}{|V|} \sum_{m=1}^{|V|} e^{it\Psi_{km}}. \tag{7.204}$$

The v_k's low-dimensional representation is then obtained by sampling the two-dimensional parametric function of $\varphi_k(t)$ at d evenly separated points $t_1, t_2, \cdots, t_d$ as

$$f(v_k) = [\operatorname{Re}(\varphi_k(t_1)), \cdots, \operatorname{Re}(\varphi_k(t_d)), \operatorname{Im}(\varphi_k(t_1)), \cdots, \operatorname{Im}(\varphi_k(t_d))]. \tag{7.205}$$

Structural and neighborhood similarity preserving network embedding (SNS) [274] enhances the random-walk-based method with structural role proximity. To preserve vertex structural roles, SNS represents each vertex as a *Graphlet Degree Vector* with each element being the number of times the given vertex is touched by the corresponding orbit of graphlets. The *Graphlet Degree Vector* is used to measure the vertex structural role similarity. Given a vertex v_i, SNS uses its context vertices $\mathcal{C}(v_i)$ and structurally similar vertices $\mathcal{S}(v_i)$ to predict its existence, which is achieved by maximizing the following probability:

$$\Pr\big(v_i \mid \mathcal{C}(v_i), \mathcal{S}(v_i)\big) = \frac{\exp\big(r'_{v_i} \cdot h_{v_i}\big)}{\sum\limits_{u \in V} \exp\big(r'_u \cdot h_{v_i}\big)}, \tag{7.206}$$

where r'_{v_i} is the output representation of v_i, and h_{v_i} is the hidden layer representation for predicting v_i, which is aggregated from the input representations r_u for each u in $\mathcal{C}(v_i)$ and $\mathcal{S}(v_i)$.

Intra-community Proximity Preserving NRL   Another interesting feature that real-world networks exhibit is the community structure, where vertices are densely connected to each other within the same community, but sparsely connected to vertices from other communities. For example, in social networks, people from the same interest group or affiliation often form a community. In citation networks, papers on similar research topics tend to frequently cite each other. Intra-community preserving NRL aims to leverage the community structure that characterizes key vertex properties to learn informative vertex representations.

Learning Latent Social Dimensions: The social-dimension-based NRL algorithms try to construct social actors' embeddings through their membership or affiliation to a number of social dimensions. To infer these latent social dimensions, the phenomenon of "community" in social networks is considered, stating that social actors sharing similar properties often form groups with denser within-group connections. Thus, the problem boils down to one classical network analytic task – community detection – that aims to discover a set of communities with denser within-group connections than between-group connections. Three clustering techniques, including modularity maximization [275], spectral clustering [276], and edge clustering [277], are employed to discover latent social dimensions. Each social dimension describes the likelihood of a vertex belonging to a plausible affiliation. These methods preserve the global community structure, but neglect local structure properties, for example, the first-order and second-order proximities.

Modularized Nonnegative Matrix Factorization (M-NMF) [278] augments the second-order and high-order proximities with broader community structure to learn more informative vertex embeddings $U \in \mathbb{R}^{|V| \times d}$ has the following objective:

$$\min_{M,U,H,C} \left\| S - MU^{\mathrm{T}} \right\|_F^2 + \alpha \left\| H - UC^{\mathrm{T}} \right\|_F^2 - \beta tr\big(H^{\mathrm{T}}BH\big) \tag{7.207}$$

$$s.t., M \geq 0,\ U \geq 0,\ H \geq 0,\ C \geq 0,\ tr(H^{\mathrm{T}}H) = |V|,$$

where vertex embedding U is learned by minimizing $\left\| S - MU^{\mathrm{T}} \right\|_F^2$, with $S \in \mathbb{R}^{|V| \times |V|}$ being the vertex pairwise proximity matrix, which captures the second-order and the high-order proximities when taken as representations. The community-indicative vertex embedding H is learned by maximizing $r(H^{\mathrm{T}}BH)$, which is essentially the objective of modularity maximization with B being the modularity matrix. The minimization on $\left\| H - UC^{\mathrm{T}} \right\|_F^2$ makes these two embeddings consistent with each other by importing a community representation matrix C.

7.11.2.1.3 Macroscopic Structure Preserving NRL

Macroscopic structure preserving methods aim to preserve certain global network properties in a macroscopic view. Only very few recent studies have been performed on this topic.

Degree penalty principle (DP): Many real-world networks are characterized by the macroscopic scale-free property, in which the vertex degree follows a long-tailed distribution; that is, most vertices are sparsely connected, and only a few vertices have dense edges. To capture the scale-free property, [279] proposes the DP: penalizing the proximity between high-degree vertices. This principle is then coupled with two NRL algorithms (i.e., spectral embedding [281] and DeepWalk, discussed earlier) to learn scale-free property preserving vertex representations.

Hierarchical Representation Learning for Networks (HARP): To capture the global patterns in networks, HARP [280] samples small networks to approximate the global structure. The vertex representations learned from sampled networks are taken as the initialization for inferring the vertex representations of the original network. In this way, global structure is preserved in the final representations. To obtain smooth solutions, a series of smaller networks are successively sampled from the original network by coalescing edges and vertices, and the vertex representations are hierarchically inferred back from the smallest network to the original network. In HARP, DeepWalk and LINE, discussed earlier, are used to learn vertex representations.

7.11.2.2 Unsupervised Content Augmented NRL

Besides network structure, real-world networks are often attached with rich content as vertex attributes, such as web pages in web page networks, papers in citation networks, and user metadata in social networks. Vertex attributes provide direct evidence to measure content-level similarity between vertices. Therefore, NRL can be significantly improved if vertex attribute information is properly incorporated into the learning process. Recently, several content augmented NRL algorithms have been proposed to incorporate network structure and vertex attributes to reinforce the NRL.

7.11.2.2.1 Text-Associated DeepWalk (TADW)

[282] first proves the equivalence between DeepWalk and the following matrix factorization:

$$\min{}_{W,H} \left\| M - W^{\mathrm{T}}H \right\|_F^2 + \frac{\lambda}{2} \left(\|W\|_F^2 + \|H\|_F^2 \right), \tag{7.208}$$

where W and H are learned latent embeddings, and M is the vertex-context matrix carrying transition probability between each vertex pair within k steps. Then, textual features are imported through inductive matrix factorization [283]

$$\min{}_{W,H} \left\| M - W^{\mathrm{T}}HT \right\|_F^2 + \frac{\lambda}{2} \left(\|W\|_F^2 + \|H\|_F^2 \right), \tag{7.209}$$

where T is a vertex textual feature matrix. After Eq. (7.209) is solved, the final vertex representations are formed by taking the concatenation of W and HT.

7.11.2.2.2 Homophily, Structure, and Content Augmented Network Representation Learning (HSCA)

Despite its ability to incorporate textural features, TADW [282] only considers structural context of network vertices, i.e. the second-order and high-order proximity, but ignores the important homophily property (the first-order proximity) in its learning framework. HSCA [284] is proposed to simultaneously integrates homophily, structural context, and vertex content to learn effective network representations. For TADW, the learned representation for the i-th vertex v_i is $\left[W_i^{\mathrm{T}}, (HT_{i:})^{\mathrm{T}} \right]^{\mathrm{T}}$, where $W_{i:}$ and $T_{i:}$ is the i-th row of W and T, respectively. To enforce the first-order proximity, HSCA introduces a regularization term to enforce homophily between directly connected nodes in the embedding space, which is formulated as

$$\mathcal{R}(W,H) = \frac{1}{4} \sum_{i,j=1}^{|V|} S_{ij} \left\| \left\{ \begin{array}{c} W_{i:} \\ HT_{i:} \end{array} \right\} - \left\{ \begin{array}{c} W_{j:} \\ HT_{j:} \end{array} \right\} \right\|_2^2, \tag{7.210}$$

where S is the adjacent matrix. The objective of HSCA is

$$\min_{W,H} \left\| M - W^{\mathrm{T}} HT \right\|_F^2 + \frac{\lambda}{2} \left(\|W\|_F^2 + \|H\|_F^2 \right) + \mu \mathcal{R}(W,H), \tag{7.211}$$

where λ and μ are the trade-off parameters. After solving the above optimization problem, the concatenation of W and HT is taken as the final vertex representations.

7.11.2.2.3 Paired Restricted Boltzmann Machine (pRBM)

By leveraging the strength of the restricted Boltzmann machine (RBM) [285–287] designs, a novel model called Paired RBM (pRBM) learns vertex representations by combining vertex attributes and link information. The pRBM considers networks with vertices associated with binary attributes. For each edge $(v_i, v_j) \in E$, the attributes for v_i and v_j are $\mathrm{v}^{(i)}$ and $\mathrm{v}^{(j)} \in \{0, 1\}^m$, and their hidden representations are $\mathrm{h}^{(i)}$ and $\mathrm{h}^{(j)} \in \{0, 1\}^d$. Vertex hidden representations are learned by maximizing the joint probability of pRBM defined over $\mathrm{v}^{(i)}$, $\mathrm{v}^{(j)}$, $\mathrm{h}^{(i)}$ and $\mathrm{h}^{(j)}$:

$$\Pr\left(\mathrm{v}^{(i)}, \mathrm{v}^{(j)}, \mathrm{h}^{(i)}, \mathrm{h}^{(j)}, w_{ij}; \theta \right) = \exp\left(-E\left(\mathrm{v}^{(i)}, \mathrm{v}^{(j)}, \mathrm{h}^{(i)}, \mathrm{h}^{(j)}, w_{ij} \right) \right)/Z, \tag{7.212}$$

where $\theta = \{\mathrm{W} \in \mathbb{R}^{d \times m}, \mathrm{b} \in \mathbb{R}^{d \times 1}, \mathrm{c} \in \mathbb{R}^{m \times 1}, \mathrm{M} \in \mathbb{R}^{d \times d}\}$ is the parameter set, and Z is the normalization term. To model the joint probability, the energy function is defined as

$$E\left(\mathrm{v}^{(i)}, \mathrm{v}^{(j)}, \mathrm{h}^{(i)}, \mathrm{h}^{(j)}, w_{ij} \right) = -w_{ij} \left(\mathrm{h}^{(i)} \right)^{\mathrm{T}} \mathrm{Mh}^{(j)} - \left(\mathrm{h}^{(i)} \right)^{\mathrm{T}} \mathrm{Wv}^{(i)} - \mathrm{c}^{\mathrm{T}} \mathrm{v}^{(i)} - \mathrm{b}^{\mathrm{T}} \mathrm{h}^{(i)}$$
$$- \left(\mathrm{h}^{(j)} \right)^{\mathrm{T}} \mathrm{Wv}^{(j)} - \mathrm{c}^{\mathrm{T}} \mathrm{v}^{(i)} - \mathrm{b}^{\mathrm{T}} \mathrm{h}^{(j)}, \tag{7.213}$$

where $w_{ij}(\mathrm{h}^{(i)})^{\mathrm{T}} \mathrm{Mh}^{(j)}$ forces the latent representations of v_i and v_j to be close, and w_{ij} is the weight of edge (v_i, v_j) .

7.11.2.2.4 User Profile Preserving Social Network Embedding (UPP-SNE)

[288] leverages user profile features to enhance the embedding learning of users in social networks. Compared with textural content features, user profiles have two unique properties: (i) user profiles are noise, sparse, and incomplete and (ii) different dimensions of user profile features are topic

inconsistent. To filter out noise and extract useful information from user profiles, UPP-SNE constructs user representations by performing a nonlinear mapping on user profile features, which is guided by the network structure. The approximated kernel mapping [289] is used in UPP-SNE to construct user embedding from user profile features:

$$f(v_i) = \varphi(x_i) = \frac{1}{\sqrt{d}} \big[\cos\left(\mu_1^T x_i\right), ..., \cos\left(\mu_d^T x_i\right),$$

$$\sin\left(\mu_1^T x_i\right), \cdots, \sin\left(\mu_d^T x_i\right)\big]^T, \tag{7.214}$$

where x_i is the user profile feature vector of vertex v_i, and μ_i is the corresponding coefficient vector.

To supervise the learning of the nonlinear mapping and make user profiles and network structure complement each other, the objective of DeepWalk is used:

$$min_f - \log\Pr(\{v_{i-t}, \cdots, v_{i+t}\} \backslash v_i \mid f(v_i)), \tag{7.215}$$

where $\{v_{i-t}, \cdots, v_{i+t}\}/v_i$ is the context vertices of vertex v_i within the t-window size in the given random walk sequence.

7.11.2.2.5 Property Preserving Network Embedding (PPNE)

[290] jointly optimizes two objectives: (i) the structure-driven objective and (ii) the attribute-driven objective, to learn content augmented vertex representations. Following DeepWalk, the structure-driven objective aims to make the representation of vertices sharing similar context vertices close. For a given random walk sequence $\mathcal{S}$, the structure-driven objective is formulated as

$$\min D_T = \prod_{v \in \mathcal{S}} \prod_{u \in context(v)} \Pr(u \mid v) \tag{7.216}$$

The attribute-driven objective aims to make the vertex representations learned by Eq. (7.216) respect the vertex attribute similarity. A realization of the attribute-driven objective is

$$\min D_N = \sum_{v \in \mathcal{S}} \sum_{u \in pos(v) \cup neg(v)} P(v, u) d(v, u) \tag{7.217}$$

where $P(u, v)$ is the attribute similarity between u and v, $d(u, v)$ is the distance between u and v in the embedding space, and $pos(v)$ and $neg(v)$ are the top-k similar and dissimilar vertices according to $P(u, v)$, respectively.

7.11.3 Semi-Supervised NRL

Label information attached to vertices directly indicates vertices' group or class affiliation. Such labels have strong correlations, although they are not always consistent with the network structure and vertex attributes, and are always helpful in learning informative and discriminative network representations. Semi-supervised NRL algorithms are developed along these lines to utilize vertex labels available in the network for seeking more effective vertex representations.

7.11.3.1 Semi-Supervised Structure Preserving NRL

The first group consists of semi-supervised NRL algorithms that aim to simultaneously optimize the representation learning that preserves network structure and discriminative learning. As a result, the information derived from vertex labels can help improve the representative and discriminative power of the learned vertex representations.

7.11.3.1.1 Discriminative Deep Random Walk (DDRW)

[293] is inspired by discriminative representation learning [291, 292], and proposes to learn discriminative network representations by jointly optimizing the objective of DeepWalk together with the following L2-loss Support Vector Classification objective:

$$\mathcal{L}_c = C \sum_{i=1}^{|V|} \left(\sigma \left(1 - Y_{ik} \beta^T r_{v_i}\right) \right)^2 + \frac{1}{2} \beta^T \beta, \tag{7.218}$$

where $\sigma(x) = x$, if $x > 0$ and otherwise $\sigma(x) = 0$. The joint objective of DDRW is thus defined as

$$\mathcal{L} = \eta \mathcal{L}_{DW} + \mathcal{L}_c, \tag{7.219}$$

where $\mathcal{L}_{DW}$ is the objective function of DeepWalk. The objective (Eq. (7.219)) aims to learn discriminative vertex representations for binary classification for the k-th class. DDRW is generalized to handle multi-class classification by using the one-against-the-rest strategy [294].

7.11.3.1.2 Max-Margin DeepWalk (MMDW)

[295] couples similarly the objective of the matrix factorization version DeepWalk with the following multi-class support vector machine (SVM) objective and the $\{(r_{v_1}, Y_{1:}), \cdots, (r_{v_T}, Y_{T:})\}$ training set:

$$\min_{W,\xi} \mathcal{L}_{SVM} = \min_{W,\xi} \frac{1}{2} \|W\|_2^2 + C \sum_{i=1}^{T} \xi_i, \tag{7.220}$$

$$s.t. \ w_{l_i}^T r_{v_i} - w_j^T r_{v_i} \geq e_i^j - \xi_i, \ \forall i, j,$$

where $e_i^j = 1$, if $Y_{ij} = -1$. Otherwise, $e_i^j = 0$, if $Y_{ij} = 1$. The joint objective of MMDW is

$$\min_{U,H,W,\xi} \mathcal{L} = \min_{U,H,W,\xi} \mathcal{L}_{DW} + \frac{1}{2} \|W\|_2^2 + C \sum_{i=1}^{T} \xi_i, \tag{7.221}$$

$$s.t. \ w_{l_i}^T r_{v_i} - w_j^T r_{v_i} \geq e_i^j - \xi_i, \ \forall i, j.$$

where $\mathcal{L}_{DW}$ is the objective of the matrix factorization version of DeepWalk.

7.11.3.1.3 Transductive LINE (TLINE)

[296] is proposed as a semi-supervised extension of LINE that simultaneously learns LINE's vertex representations and an SVM classifier. Given a set of labeled vertices $\{v_1, v_2, \cdots, v_L\}$ and $\{v_{L+1}, \cdots, v_{|V|}\}$, TLINE trains a multi-class SVM classifier on $\{v_1, v_2, \cdots, v_L\}$ by optimizing the objective

$$\mathcal{O}_{svm} = \sum_{i=1}^{L} \sum_{k=1}^{K} \max\left(0, 1 - Y_{ik} w_k^T r_{v_i}\right) + \lambda \|w_k\|_2^2. \tag{7.222}$$

Based on LINE's formulations that preserve the first-order and second-order proximities, TLINE optimizes two objective functions:

$$\mathcal{O}_{TLINE} (1st) = \mathcal{O}_{line1} + \beta \mathcal{O}_{svm}, \text{and } \mathcal{O}_{TLINE} (2nd) = \mathcal{O}_{line2} + \beta \mathcal{O}_{svm}. \tag{7.223}$$

Inheriting LINE's ability to deal with large-scale networks, TLINE is claimed to be able to learn discriminative vertex representations for large-scale networks with low time and memory cost.

7.11.3.1.4 Group Enhanced Network Embedding (GENE)

[297] integrates group (label) information with network structure in a probabilistic manner. GENE assumes that vertices should be embedded closely in low-dimensional space, if they share similar neighbors or join similar groups. Inspired by DeepWalk and document modeling [298], the

mechanism of GENE for learning group label informed vertex representations is achieved by maximizing the following log probability:

$$\mathcal{L} = \sum_{g_i \in \mathcal{Y}} \left[\alpha \sum_{W \in W_{g_i}} \sum_{v_j \in W} \log\text{Pr}\left(v_j \mid v_{j-t}, \cdots, v_{j+t}, g_i\right) \right.$$

$$\left. + \beta \sum_{\hat{v}_j \in \hat{W}_{g_j}} \log\text{Pr}\left(\hat{v}_j \mid g_i\right) \right], \tag{7.224}$$

where $\mathcal{Y}$ is the set of different groups, W_{g_i} is the set of random walk sequences labeled with g_i, and $\hat{W}_{g_i}$ is the set of vertices randomly sampled from group g_i.

7.11.3.1.5 Semi-supervised Network Embedding (SemiNE)

[299] learns semi-supervised vertex representations in two stages. In the first stage, SemiNE exploits the DeepWalk framework to learn vertex representations in an unsupervised manner. Note that DeepWalk does not consider the order information of the context vertex, that is, the distance between the context vertex and the central vertex, when using the context vertex v_{i+j} to predict the central vertex v_i. Thus, SemiNE encodes the order information into DeepWalk by modeling the probability $\text{Pr}(v_{i+j} \mid v_i)$ with j-dependent parameters:

$$\text{Pr}\left(v_{i+j} \mid v_i\right) = \frac{\exp\left(\Phi(v_i) \cdot \Psi_j\left(v_{i+j}\right)\right)}{\sum\limits_{u \in V} \exp\left(\Phi(v_i) \cdot \Psi_j(u)\right)}, \tag{7.225}$$

where $\Phi(\cdot)$ is the vertex representation, and $\Psi_j(\cdot)$ is the parameter for calculating $\text{Pr}(v_{i+j} \mid v_i)$. In the second stage, SemiNE learns a neural network that tunes the learned unsupervised vertex representations to fit the vertex labels.

7.11.3.2 Semi-supervised Content Augmented NRL

Recently, more research efforts have shifted to the development of label- and content augmented NRL algorithms that investigate the use of vertex content and labels to assist network representation learning. With content information incorporated, the learned vertex representations are expected to be more informative, and with label information considered, the learned vertex representations can be highly customized for the underlying classification task.

7.11.3.2.1 Tri-Party Deep Network Representation (TriDNR)

[300] learns vertex representations from three information sources using a coupled neural network framework: network structure, vertex content, and vertex labels. To capture the vertex content and label information, TriDNR employs the Paragraph Vector model [301] to describe the vertex–word correlation and the label–word correspondence by maximizing the following objective:

$$\mathcal{L}_{PV} = \sum_{i \in L} \log\text{Pr}(w_{-b} : w_b \mid c_i) + \sum_{i=1}^{|V|} \log\text{Pr}(w_{-b} : w_b \mid v_i), \tag{7.226}$$

where $\{w_{-b} : w_b\}$ is a sequence of words inside a contextual window of length $2b$, c_i is the class label of vertex v_i, and L is the set of indices of labeled vertices. TriDNR is then realized by coupling the Paragraph Vector objective with the DeepWalk objective:

$$max(1-\alpha)\mathcal{L}_{DW} + \alpha\mathcal{L}_{PV}, \tag{7.227}$$

where $\mathcal{L}_{DW}$ is the DeepWalk maximization objective function, and α is the trade-off parameter.

7.11.3.2.2 Linked Document Embedding (LDE)

[302] is proposed to learn representations for linked documents, which are actually the vertices of citation or web page networks. Similar to TriDNR, LDE learns vertex representations by modeling three kinds of relations: word–word–document relations, document–document relations, and document–label relations. LDE is realized by solving the following optimization problem:

$$
min_{W,D,Y} - \frac{1}{|\mathcal{P}|} \sum_{(w_i, w_j, d_k) \in \mathcal{P}} \log\Pr(w_j \mid w_i, d_k)
$$

$$
- \frac{1}{|E|} \sum_i \sum_{j:(v_i, v_j) \in E} \log\Pr(d_j \mid d_i) \tag{7.228}
$$

$$
- \frac{1}{|\mathcal{Y}|} \sum_{i:y_i \in \mathcal{Y}} \log\Pr(y_i \mid d_i) + \gamma \left(\|W\|_F^2 + \|D\|_F^2 + \|Y\|_F^2 \right).
$$

Here, the probability $\Pr(w_j \mid w_i, d_k)$ is used to model word–word–document relations, and denotes the probability that word w_j is a neighboring word of w_i in document d_k. To capture word–word–document relations, triplets (w_i, w_j, d_k) are extracted, with the word–neighbor pair (w_i, w_j) occurring in document d_k. The set of triplets (w_i, w_j, d_k) is denoted by $\mathcal{P}$. The document–document relations are captured by the conditional probability between linked document pairs (d_i, d_j), $\Pr(d_j \mid d_i)$. The document–label relations are also considered by modeling $\Pr(y_i \mid d_i)$, the probability of the occurrence of class label y_i conditioned on document d_i. In Eq. (7.288), W, D, and Y are the embedding matrix for words, documents, and labels, respectively.

7.11.3.2.3 Discriminative Matrix Factorization (DMF)

[303] enforces the objective of TADW (Eq. (7.209)) to empower vertex representations with discriminative ability, with an empirical loss minimization for a linear classifier trained on labeled vertices:

$$
min_{W,H,\eta} \frac{1}{2} \sum_{i,j=1}^{|V|} \left(M_{ij} - w_i^T H t_j \right)^2 + \frac{\mu}{2} \sum_{n \in \mathcal{L}} \left(Y_{n1} - \eta^T x_n \right)^2 \tag{7.229}
$$

$$
+ \frac{\lambda_1}{2} \left(\|H\|_F^2 + \|\eta\|_2^2 \right) + \frac{\lambda_2}{2} \|W\|_F^2,
$$

where w_i is the i-th column of the vertex representation matrix W, t_j is the j-th column of the vertex textual feature matrix T, and $\mathcal{L}$ is the set of indices of labeled vertices. DMF considers binary-class classification, that is, $\mathcal{Y} = \{+1, -1\}$. Hence, Y_{n1} is used to denote the class label of vertex v_n. DMF constructs vertex representations from W rather than from W and HT. This is based on empirical findings that W contains sufficient information for vertex representations. In the objective of Eq. (7.229), x_n is set to $\left[w_n^T, 1 \right]^T$, which incorporates the intercept term b of the linear classifier into η. The optimization problem (Eq. (7.299)) is solved by optimizing W, H, and η alternately. Once the optimization problem is solved, the discriminative and informative vertex representations together with the linear classifier are learned, and work together to classify unlabeled vertices in networks.

7.11.3.2.4 Predictive Labels and Neighbors with Embeddings Transductively or Inductively from Data (Planetoid)

[304] leverages network embedding together with vertex attributes to carry out semi-supervised learning. Planetoid learns vertex embeddings by minimizing the loss for predicting structural context, which is formulated as

$$
\mathcal{L}_u = - \mathbb{E}_{(i,c,\gamma)} \log\sigma\left(\gamma w_c^T e_i \right), \tag{7.230}
$$

where (i, c) is the index for the vertex-context pair (v_i, v_c), e_i is the embedding of vertex v_i, w_c is the parameter vector for the context vertex v_c, and $\gamma \in \{+1, -1\}$ indicates whether the sampled vertex-context pair (i, c) is positive or negative. The triple (i, c, γ) is sampled according to both the network structure and the vertex labels.

Planetoid then maps the learned vertex representations e and vertex attributes x to the hidden layer space via a deep neural network, and concatenates these two hidden layer representations together to predict vertex labels, by minimizing the following classification loss:

$$\mathcal{L}_s = -\frac{1}{L}\sum_{i=1}^{L} \log p(y_i \mid x_i, e_i), \tag{7.231}$$

To integrate the network structure, vertex attributes, and vertex labels together, Planetoid jointly minimizes the two objectives, Eqs. (7.230) and (7.231), to learn vertex embedding e with deep neural networks.

7.11.3.2.5 *Label informed Attribute Network Embedding (LANE)*
[305] learns vertex representations by embedding the network structure proximity, attribute affinity, and label proximity into a unified latent representation. The learned representations are expected to capture both network structure and vertex attribute information, and label information if it is provided. The embedding learning in LANE is carried out in two stages. During the first stage, vertex proximity in network structure and attribute information are mapped into latent representations $U^{(G)}$ and $U^{(A)}$; then $U^{(A)}$ is incorporated into $U^{(G)}$ by maximizing their correlations. In the second stage, LANE employs the joint proximity (determined by $U^{(G)}$) to smooth label information and uniformly embeds them into another latent representation $U^{(Y)}$, and then embeds $U^{(A)}$, $U^{(G)}$, and $U^{(Y)}$ into a unified embedding representation H.

References

1 Eswaradass A, Sun XH, Wu M. Network bandwidth predictor (nbp): A system for online network performance forecasting. In: Proceedings of 6th IEEE International Symposium on Cluster Computing and the Grid (CCGRID). IEEE; 2006. p. 4.

2 Wolski, R. (1998). Dynamically forecasting network performance using the network weather service. *Clust. Comput.* **1** (1): 119–132.

3 Cortez P, Rio M, Rocha M, Sousa P. Internet traffic forecasting using neural networks. In: Proceedings of IEEE International Joint Conference on Neural Networks (IJCNN). IEEE; 2006. p. 2635–42.

4 Chabaa, S., Zeroual, A., and Antari, J. (2010). Identification and prediction of internet traffic using artificial neural networks. *J. Intell. Learn. Syst. Appl.* **2** (03): 147.

5 Zhu, Y., Zhang, G., and Qiu, J. (2013). Network traffic prediction based on particle swarm bp neural network. *JNW.* **8** (11): 2685–2691.

6 Bermolen, P. and Rossi, D. (2009). Support vector regression for link load prediction. *Comput. Netw.* **53** (2): 191–201.

7 Li Y, Liu H, Yang W, Hu D, Xu W. Inter-data-center network traffic prediction with elephant flows: IEEE; 2016, 2016 IEEE/IFIP Network Operations and Management Symposium (NOMS 2016) pp. 206–13.

8 Chen Z, Wen J, Geng Y. Predicting future traffic using hidden markov models. In: Proceddings of 24th IEEE International Conference on Network Protocols (ICNP). IEEE; 2016. p. 1–6.

9 Roughan M, Zhang Y, Ge Z, Greenberg A. Abilene network; 2004b. http://www.maths.adelaide.edu. au/matthew.roughan/data/Abilene.tar. gz. Accessed 28 Dec 2017.

10 Poupart P, Chen Z, Jaini P, Fung F, Susanto H, Geng Y, Chen L, Chen K, Jin H. Online flow size prediction for improved network routing. 2016 IEEE 24th International Conference on Network Protocols (ICNP), pp. 1–6.

11 Kotz D, Henderson T, Abyzov I, Yeo J. CRAWDAD dataset dartmouth/campus (v. 2009-09-09). 2009. https://crawdad.org dartmouth/campus/20090909. Accessed 28 Dec 2017.

12 Benson T. Data Set for IMC 2010 Data Center Measurement. 2010. http://pages.cs.wisc.edu/ tbenson/IMC10_Data.html. Accessed 28 Dec 2017.

13 Netflix Inc. Netflix. 2017. https://www.netflix.com. Accessed 01 Aug 2017.

14 Roughan M, Sen S, Spatscheck O, Duffield N. Class-of-service mapping for QoS: a statistical signature-based approach to ip traffic classification. In: Proceedings of the 4th ACM SIGCOMM conference on Internet measurement. ACM; 2004a. p. 135–148.

15 Microsoft Cor. Skype. 2017. https://www.skype.com. Acc. 01 Aug 2017.

16 YouTube LLC. YouTube. 2017. https://www.youtube.com. Acc. 01 Aug 2017.

17 Stratonovich, R.L. (1960). Conditional markov processes. *Theory Probab. Appl.* **5** (2): 156–178.

18 Bakhshi, T. and Ghita, B. On internet traffic classification: a two-phased machine learning approach. *Hindawi Limited in Journal of Computer Networks and Communications Journal of Computer Networks and Communications* **2016**: 1–21.

19 Hyunchul Kim, KC Claffy, Marina Fomenkov, et al. Internet traffic classification demystified: myths, caveats, and the best practices. ACMCoNEXT2008, December 10-12, 2008, Madrid,SPAIN, p. 11.

20 Internet Assigned Numbers Authority. IANA. 2017. https://www.iana.org/. Accessed 01 Aug 2017

21 Karagiannis T, Broido A, Brownlee N, Claffy KC, Faloutsos M. Is p2p dying or just hiding?[p2p traffic measurement]. In: IEEE Global Telecommunications Conference (GLOBECOM), vol. 3. 2004. p. 1532–8.

22 Dainotti, A., Pescape, A., and Claffy, K.C. (2012). Issues and future directions in traffic classification. *IEEE Netw.* **26** (1): 35–40.

23 Bernaille, L. and Teixeira, R. (2007). Implementation issues of early application identification. *Lect. Notes Comput. Sci.* **4866**: 156.

24 Erman J, Mahanti A, Arlitt M, Williamson C. Identifying and discriminating between web and peer-to-peer traffic in the network core. In: Proceedings of the 16th international conference on World Wide Web. ACM; 2007b. p. 883–92.

25 Schatzmann D, Mühlbauer W, Spyropoulos T, Dimitropoulos X. Digging into https: Flow-based classification of webmail traffic. In: Proceedings of the 10th ACM SIGCOMM Conference on Internet Measurement; 2010. p. 322–27.

26 Kim H, Fomenkov M, Claffy KC, Brownlee N, Barman D, Faloutsos M. Comparison of internet traffic classification tools. In: IMRG Workshop on Application Classification and Identification; 2007. p. 1–2.

27 Bermolen, P., Mellia, M., Meo, M. et al. (2011). Abacus: accurate behavioral classification of P2P-tv traffic. *Comput. Netw.* **55** (6): 1394–1411.

28 Karagiannis, T., Papagiannaki, K., and Faloutsos, M. (2005). BLINC: multilevel traffic classification in the dark. *ACM SIGCOMM Comput. Com. Rev.* **35** (4): 229–240.

29 Cisco Systems. Cisco IOS Netflow. 2012. http://www.cisco.com/go netflow. Accessed 01 Aug 2017.

30 Bakhshi, T. and Ghita, B. (2016). On internet traffic classification: a two-phased machine learning approach. *J. Comput. Netw. Commun.* **2016**: 2016.

31 Park J, Tyan HR, Kuo CCJ. Internet traffic classification for scalable qos provision. In: Multimedia and Expo, vol 2006 IEEE International Conference on. IEEE; 2006. p. 1221–4.

32 Roughan M, Sen S, Spatscheck O, Duffield N. Class-of-service mapping for QoS: a statistical signature-based approach to ip traffic classification. In: Proceedings of the 4th ACM SIGCOMM conference on Internet measurement. ACM; 2004a. p. 135–148.

33 Moore, A.W. and Zuev, D. (2005). Internet traffic classification using bayesian analysis techniques. *ACM SIGMETRICS PER, ACM* **33**: 50–60.

34 Machine Learning Group, University of Waikato. WEKA. 2017. http:// www.cs.waikato.ac.nz/ml/weka. Accessed 01 Aug 2017

35 McGregor, A., Hall, M., Lorier, P., and Brunskill, J. (2004). Flow clustering using machine learning techniques. *Passive and Active Net. Meas.*: 205–214.

36 Bernaille, L., Teixeira, R., Akodkenou, I. et al. (2006a). Traffic classification on the fly. *ACM SIGCOMM Comput. Commun. Rev.* **36** (2): 23–26.

37 Bernaille L, Teixeira R, Salamatian K. Early application identification. In: Proceedings of the 2006 ACM CoNEXT Conference. ACM; 2006b. p. 61–6:12.

38 Bonfiglio D, Mellia M, Meo M, Rossi D, Tofanelli P. Revealing skype traffic: when randomness plays with you. In: ACM SIGCOMM Computer Communication Review. ACM; 2007. p. 37–48.

39 Alshammari R, Zincir-Heywood AN. Machine learning based encrypted traffic classification: Identifying ssh and skype. In: Computational Intelligence for Security and Defense Applications, 2009. CISDA 2009. IEEE Symp. on. IEEE; 2009. p. 1–8.

40 Shbair WM, Cholez T, Francois J, Chrisment I. A multi-level framework to identify https services. In: IEEE/IFIP Network Operations and Management Symposium (NOMS) 2016. p. 240–8.

41 He L, Xu C, Luo Y. vtc: Machine learning based traffic classification as a virtual network function. In: Proceedings of the 2016 ACM International Workshop on Security in Software Defined Networks & Network Function Virtualization. ACM; 2016. p. 53–56.

42 Amaral P, Dinis J, Pinto P, Bernardo L, Tavares J, Mamede HS. Machine learning in software defined networks: Data collection and traffic classification. In: Network Protocols (ICNP), 2016 IEEE 24th International Conference on. IEEE; 2016. p. 1–5.

43 Wang P, Lin SC, Luo M. A framework for qos-aware traffic classification using semi-supervised machine learning in sdns. In: Services Computing (SCC), 2016 IEEE International Conference on. IEEE; 2016. p. 760–5.

44 Boyan JA, Littman ML. Packet routing in dynamically changing networks: A reinforcement learning approach. In: Advances in neural information processing systems; 1994. p. 671–8.

45 Littman M, Boyan J. A distributed reinforcement learning scheme for network routing. In: Proceedings of the international workshop on applications of neural networks to telecommunications. Psychology Press; 1993. p. 45–51.

46 Choi SP, Yeung DY. Predictive q-routing: A memory-based reinforcement learning approach to adaptive traffic control. In: Advances in Neural Information Processing Systems. 1996. p. 945–51.

47 Kumar S, Miikkulainen R. Dual reinforcement q-routing: An on-line adaptive routing algorithm. In: Proceedings of the artificial neural networks in engineering Conference. 1997. p. 231–8

48 Sun R, Tatsumi S, Zhao G. Q-map: A novel multicast routing method in wireless ad hoc networks with multiagent reinforcement learning. In: TENCON'02. Proceedings. 2002 IEEE Region 10 Conference on Computers, Communications, Control and Power Engineering, vol 1. IEEE; 2002. p. 667–670.

49 Goetz P, Kumar S, Miikkulainen R. On-line adaptation of a signal predistorter through dual reinforcement learning. In: ICML. 1996. p. 175–81.

50 Stone P. Tpot-rl applied to network routing. In: ICML. 2000. p. 935–42.

51 Stone P, Veloso M. Team-partitioned, opaque-transition reinforcement learning. In: Proceedings of the third annual conference on Autonomous Agents. ACM; 1999. p. 206–12.

52 Forster A, Murphy AL. Froms: Feedback routing for optimizing multiple sinks in wsn with reinforcement learning. In: Intelligent Sensors, Sensor Networks and Information, 2007. ISSNIP 2007. 3rd International, Conference on. IEEE; 2007. p. 371–6.

53 Intanagonwiwat, C., Govindan, R., Estrin, D. et al. (2003). Directed diffusion for wireless sensor networking. *IEEE/ACM Trans Netw. (ToN).* **11** (1): 2–16.

54 Wang P, Wang T. Adaptive routing for sensor networks using reinforcement learning. In: Computer and Information Technology, 2006. CIT'06. The Sixth IEEE International Conference on. IEEE; 2006. p. 219.

55 Lagoudakis MG, Parr R. Model-free least-squares policy iteration. In: Advances in neural information processing systems. 2002. p. 1547–54.

56 Lin SC, Akyildiz IF, Wang P, Luo M. Qos-aware adaptive routing in multi-layer hierarchical software defined networks: a reinforcement learning approach. In: Services Computing (SCC) 2016, IEEE International Conference on. IEEE; 2016. p. 25–33.

57 Braden B, et al Recommendations on queue management and congestion avoidance in the internet. RFC 2309, Internet Engineering Task Force. 1998. https://tools.ietf.org/html/rfc2309

58 Habib, I., Tarraf, A., and Saadawi, T. (1997). A neural network controller for congestion control in atm multiplexers. *Comput. Netw. ISDN Syst.* **29** (3): 325–334.

59 Lee, S.J. and Hou, C.L. (2000). A neural-fuzzy system for congestion control in ATM networks. *IEEE Trans. on Sys., Man, and Cyb. Part B (Cyb.)* **30** (1): 2–9.

60 Liu YC, Douligeris C. Static vs. adaptive feedback congestion controller for atm networks. In: Global Telecommunications Conference, 1995. GLOBECOM '95., vol 1. IEEE; 1995. p. 291–5.

61 Tarraf AA, Habib IW, Saadawi TN. Congestion control mechanism for atm networks using neural networks. In: Communications 1995. ICC '95 Seattle, 'Gateway to Globalization' 1995 IEEE Int. Conference on, vol 1. 1995. p. 206–10.

62 Fonseca N, Crovella M. Bayesian packet loss detection for tcp. In: Proceedings IEEE 24th Annual Joint Conference of the IEEE Computer and Communications Societies., vol 3. 2005. p. 1826–37.

63 El Khayat, I., Geurts, P., and Leduc, G. (2010). Enhancement of tcp over wired/wireless networks with packet loss classifiers inferred by supervised learning. *Wirel. Netw.* **16** (2): 273–290.

64 Jayaraj, A., Venkatesh, T., and Murthy, C.S.R. (2008). Loss classification in optical burst switching networks using machine learning techniques: improving the performance of tcp. *IEEE J. Sel. Areas Commun.* **26** (6): 45–54.

65 Barman D, Matta I. Model-based loss inference by tcp over heterogeneous networks. In: Proceedings of WiOpt 2004 Modeling and Optimization in Mobile, Ad Hoc and Wireless Networks. Cambridge; 2004. p. 364–73.

66 El Khayat I, Geurts P, Leduc G. Improving TCP in Wireless Networks with an Adaptive Machine-Learnt Classifier of Packet Loss Causes. Berlin, Heidelberg: Springer Berlin Heidelberg; 2005, pp. 549–60.

67 Geurts P, Khayat IE, Leduc G. A machine learning approach to improve congestion control over wireless computer networks. In: Data Mining, 2004. ICDM '04. Fourth IEEE International Conference on; 2004. p. 383–6.

68 Liu J, Matta I, Crovella M. End-to-End Inference of Loss Nature in a Hybrid Wired/Wireless Environment. 2003. https://citeseerx.ist.psu.edu/viewdoc/download?doi=10.1.1.15.878&rep=rep1&type=pdf

69 Brakmo LS, O'Malley SW, Peterson LL. Tcp vegas: New techniques for congestion detection and avoidance. In: Proceedings of the Conference on Communications Architectures, Protocols and Applications, ACM, New York, NY, USA, SIGCOMM '94. New York: ACM; 1994. p. 24–35.

70 Biaz S, Vaidya NH. Distinguishing congestion losses from wireless transmission losses: a negative result. In: Proceedings 7th International Conference on Computer Communications and Networks (Cat. No.98EX226). Piscataway: IEEE; 1998. p. 722–31.

71 Barman D, Matta I. Model-based loss inference by tcp over heterogeneous networks. In: Proceedings of WiOpt 2004 Modeling and Optimization in Mobile, Ad Hoc and Wireless Networks. Cambridge; 2004. p. 364–73.

72 El Khayat, I., Geurts, P., and Leduc, G. (2005). Improving TCP in Wireless Networks with an Adaptive Machine-Learnt Classifier of Packet Loss Causes, 549–560. Berlin, Heidelberg: Springer Berlin Heidelberg.

73 Bonald T, May M, Bolot JC. Analytic evaluation of red performance. In: Proceedings IEEE INFOCOM 2000. Conference on, Computer Communications. Nineteenth Annual Joint Conference of the IEEE Computer and Communications Societies (Cat. No.00CH37064), vol 3. 2000. p. 1415–24.

74 Gao Y, He G, Hou JC. On exploiting traffic predictability in active queue management. In: Proceedings. Twenty-First Annual Joint Conference of the IEEE Computer and Communications Soc., vol. 3. Piscataway: IEEE; 2002. p. 1630–9.

75 Hariri, B. and Sadati, N. (2007). Nn-red: an aqm mechanism based on neural networks. *Electron. Lett.* **43** (19): 1053–1055.

76 Jain A, Karandikar A, Verma R. An adaptive prediction based approach for congestion estimation in active queue management (apace). In: Global Telecommunications Conference, 2003. GLOBECOM '03. IEEE, vol. 7. Piscataway: IEEE; 2003. p. 4153–7.

77 Zhani MF, Elbiaze H, Kamoun F. α_snfaqm: an active queue management mechanism using neurofuzzy prediction. In: 2007 12th

78 Zhou C, Di D, Chen Q, Guo J. An adaptive aqm algorithm based on neuron reinforcement learning. In: 2009 IEEE International Conference on Control and Automation; 2009. p. 1342–6.

79 Yan Q, Lei Q. A new active queue management algorithm based on self-adaptive fuzzy neural-network pid controller. In: 2011 International Conference on, Internet Technology and Applications; 2011. p. 1–4.

80 Sun J, Zukerman M. An adaptive neuron aqm for a stable internet. In: Proceedings of the 6th International IFIP-TC6 Conference on Ad Hoc and Sensor Networks, Wireless Networks, Next Generation Internet, Springer-Verlag, Berlin, Heidelberg, NETWORKING'07. 2007. p. 844–54.

81 Sun J, Chan S, Ko Kt, Chen G, Zukerman M. Neuron pid: A robust aqm scheme. In: Proceedings of the Australian Telecommunication Networks and Applications Conference (ATNAC) 2006. 2006. p. 259–62.

82 Badarla, V. and Murthy, C.S.R. (2011). Learning-tcp: a stochastic approach for efficient update in tcp congestion window in ad hoc wireless networks. *J. Parallel Distrib. Comput.* **71** (6): 863–878.

83 Jiang, H., Luo, Y., Zhang, Q. et al. (2017). Tcp-gvegas with prediction and adaptation in multi-hop ad hoc networks. *Wirel. Netw.* **23** (5): 1535–1548.

84 Ramana BV, Murthy CSR. Learning-tcp: A novel learning automata based congestion window updating mechanism for ad hoc wireless networks. In: Proceedings of the 12th International Conference on High Performance Computing, Springer-Verlag, Berlin, Heidelberg, HiPC'05. 2005. p. 454–464.

85 Ramana BV, Manoj BS, Murthy CSR. Learning-tcp: a novel learning automata based reliable transport protocol for ad hoc wireless networks. In: 2nd International Conference on Broadband Networks 2005. 2005. p. 484–493. Vol. 1.

86 Li W, Zhou F, Meleis W, Chowdhury K. Learning-based and data-driven tcp design for memory-constrained iot. In: 2016 International Conference on Distributed Computing in Sensor Systems (DCOSS). 2016a. p. 199–205.

87 Badarla, V. and Murthy, S.R. (2010). A novel learning based solution for efficient data transport in heterogeneous wireless networks. *Wireless Networks* **16** (6): 1777–1798.

88 Dong M, Li Q, Zarchy D, Godfrey PB, Schapira M. Pcc: Re-architecting congestion control for consistent high performance. Proceedings of the 12th, USENIX Conf. on Networked Systems Design and Implementation, USENIX Ass., Berkeley, CA, USA, NSDI'15. Berkley: USENIX Association; 2015. p. 395–408.

89 Winstein K, Balakrishnan H. Tcp ex machina: Computer-generated congestion control. In: Proceedings of the ACM SIGCOMM 201 Conference on SIGCOMM, SIGCOMM '13. New York: ACM; 2013. p. 123–34.

90 Khayat, I.E., Geurts, P., and Leduc, G. (2007). Machine-learnt versus analytical models of TCP throughput. *Comput. Netw.* **51** (10): 2631–2644.

91 Mirza, M., Sommers, J., Barford, P., and Zhu, X. (2010). A machine learning approach to tcp throughput prediction. *IEEE/ACM Trans. Netw.* **18** (4): 1026–1039.

92 Quer G, Meenakshisundaram H, Tamma B, Manoj BS, Rao R, Zorzi M. Cognitive network inference through bayesian network analysis. 2010, pp. 1–6.

93 Arouche Nunes, B.A., Veenstra, K., Ballenthin, W. et al. (2014). A machine learning framework for tcp round-trip time estimation. *EURASIP J. Wirel. Commun. Netw.* **2014** (1): 47.

94 Edalat, Y., Ahn, J.S., and Obraczka, K. (2016). Smart experts for network state estimation. *IEEE Trans. Netw. Serv. Manag.* **13** (3): 622–635.

95 Mezzavilla M, Quer G, Zorzi M. On the effects of cognitive mobility prediction in wireless multi-hop ad hoc networks. In: 2014 IEEE International Conference on Communications (ICC); 2014. p. 1638–44.

96 Karami, A. (2015). Accpndn: adaptive congestion control protocol in named data networking by learning capacities using optimized time-lagged feedforward neural network. *J. Netw. Comput. Appl.* **56** (Supplement C): 1–18.

97 Silva AP, Obraczka K, Burleigh S, Hirata CM. Smart congestion control for delay- and disruption tolerant networks. In: 2016 13th Annual IEEE International Conference on Sensing, Communication, and Networking (SECON). 2016. p. 1–9.

98 Prevost JJ, Nagothu K, Kelley B, Jamshidi M. Prediction of cloud data center networks loads using stochastic and neural models. IEEE; 2011. p. 276–281.

99 Cheng, R.G. and Chang, C.J. (1997). Neural-network connection-admission control for atm networks. *IEE Proc-Commun.* **144** (2): 93–98.

100 Hiramatsu, A. (1990). Atm communications network control by neural networks. *IEEE Trans. Neural Netw.* **1** (1): 122–130.

101 Hiramatsu, A. (1991). Integration of atm call admission control and link capacity control by distributed neural networks. *IEEE J. Sel. Areas Com.* **9** (7): 1131–1138.

102 Ahn, C.W. and Ramakrishna, R.S. (2004). Qos provisioning dynamic connection-admission control for multimedia wireless networks using a hopfield neural network. *IEEE Trans. Veh. Technol.* **53** (1): 106–117.

103 Baldo N, Dini P, Nin-Guerrero J. User-driven call admission control for VoIP over ALAN with a neural network based cognitive engine. In: Cognitive Information Processing (CIP), 2010 2nd International Workshop on. IEEE; 2010. p. 52–6.

104 Piamrat K, Ksentini A, Viho C, Bonnin JM. Qoe-aware admission control for multimedia applications in ieee 802.11 wireless networks. In:Vehicular Technology Conference, 2008. VTC 2008-Fall. IEEE 68th. IEEE; 2008. p. 1–5.

105 Bojovic B, Baldo N, Nin-Guerrero J, Dini P. A supervised learning approach to cognitive access point selection. In: GLOBECOM Workshops (GC Wkshps), 2011 IEEE. Piscataway: IEEE; 2011. p. 1100–5.

106 Bojovic B, Baldo N, Dini P. A cognitive scheme for radio admission control in lte systems. In: Cognitive Information Processing (CIP), 2012 3rd International Workshop on. Piscataway: IEEE; 2012. p. 1–3.

107 Bojovic B, Quer G, Baldo N, Rao RR. Bayesian and neural network schemes for call admission control in lte systems. In: Global Communications Conference (GLOBECOM), 2013 IEEE. Piscataway: IEEE; 2013. p. 1246–52.

108 Liu, D., Zhang, Y., and Zhang, H. (2005). A self-learning call admission control scheme for cdma cellular networks. *IEEE Trans. Neural Netw.* **16** (5): 1219–1228.

109 Quer G, Baldo N, Zorzi M. Cognitive call admission control for voip over ieee 802.11 using bayesian networks. In: Global Telecommunications Conference (GLOBECOM 2011), 2011 IEEE. IEEE; 2011. p. 1–6.

110 Wang J, Qiu Y. A new call admission control strategy for lte femtocell networks. In: 2nd international conference on advances in computer science and engineering. 2013.

111 Vassis D, Kampouraki A, Belsis P, Skourlas C. Admission control of video sessions over ad hoc networks using neural classifiers. 2014 IEEE Military Communications Conference, 978-1-4799-6770-4/1 pp. 1015–20.

112 Mignanti S, Di Giorgio A, Suraci V. A model based RL admission control algorithm for next generation networks. In: Networks, 2009. ICN'09. Eighth International Conference on. IEEE; 2009. p. 191–6.

113 Tesauro G, Online resource allocation using decompositional reinforcement learning. American Association for Artificial Intelligence (www.aaai.org) 2005. pp. 886–91.also https://www.aaai.org/Papers/AAAI/2005/AAAI05-140.pdf.

114 Mijumbi, R., Gorricho, J.L., Serrat, J. et al. Design and evaluation of learning algorithms for dynamic resource management in virtual networks. *IEEE Network Operations and Management Symposium (NOMS)* **2014**: 1–9.

115 Mijumbi R, Hasija S, Davy S, Davy A, Jennings B, Boutaba R. A connectionist approach to dynamic resource management for virtualised network functions. In: Network and Service Management (CNSM) 2016 12th International Conference on. IEEE; 2016. p. 1–9.

116 Maxion RA. Anomaly detection for diagnosis. In: Fault-Tolerant Computing, 1990. FTCS-20. Digest of, Papers., 20th Int. Symposium. IEEE; 1990. p. 20–7.

117 Hood, C.S. and Ji, C. (1997). Proactive network-fault detection. *IEEE Trans. Reliab.* **46** (3): 333–341.

118 Kogeda, P. and Agbinya, J. (2006). Prediction of Faults in Cellular Networks Using Bayesian Network Model. UTS ePress.

119 Ding J, Kramer B, Xu S, Chen H, Bai Y. Predictive fault management in the dynamic environment of ip networks. In: IP Operations and Management, 2004. Proceedings IEEE Workshop on. Piscataway: IEEE; 2004. p. 233–9.

120 Rao, S. (2006). Operational fault detection in cellular wireless base-stations. *IEEE Trans. Netw. Serv. Manag.* **3** (2): 1–11.

121 Baras JS, Ball M, Gupta S, Viswanathan P, Shah P. Automated network fault management. In: MILCOM 97 Proceedings. IEEE; 1997. p. 1244–50.

122 Adda, M., Qader, K., and Al-Kasassbeh, M. (2017). Comparative analysis of clustering techniques in network traffic faults classification. *Int. J. Innov. Res. Comput. Commun. Eng.* **5** (4): 6551–6563.

123 Qader K, Adda M. Fault classification system for computer networks using fuzzy probabilistic neural network classifier (fpnnc) International Conference on Engineering Applications of Neural Networks. Springer; 2014. p. 217–26.

124 Moustapha, A.I. and Selmic, R.R. (2008). Wireless sensor network modeling using modified recurrent neural networks: application to fault detection. *IEEE Trans. Instrum. Meas.* **57** (5): 981–988.

125 Hashmi US, Darbandi A, Imran A. Enabling proactive self-healing by data mining network failure logs. In: Computing, Networking and Communications (ICNC), 2017 International Conference on. Piscataway: IEEE; 2017. p. 511–7.

126 Chen M, Zheng AX, Lloyd J, Jordan MI, Brewer E. Failure diagnosis using decision trees. In: Autonomic Computing, 2004. Proceedings. International Conference on. Piscataway: IEEE; 2004. p. 36–43.

127 Chen MY, Kiciman E, Fratkin E, Fox A, Brewer E. Pinpoint: Problem determination in large, dynamic internet services. In: Dependable Systems and Networks, 2002. DSN 2002. Proceedings. International Conference on. Piscataway: IEEE; 2002. p. 595–604.

128 eBay Inc. eBay. 2017. https://www.ebay.com. Accessed 01 Aug 2017.

129 Ruiz M, Fresi F, Vela AP, Meloni G, Sambo N, Cugini F, Poti L, Velasco L, Castoldi P. Service-triggered failure identification/localization through monitoring of multiple parameters. In: ECOC 2016; 42nd European Conference on Optical Communication: Proceedings of. VDE; 2016. p. 1–3.

130 Khanafer, R.M., Solana, B., Triola, J. et al. (2008). Automated diagnosis for umts networks using bayesian network approach. *IEEE Trans. Veh. Technol.* **57** (4): 2451–2461.

131 Kiciman, E. and Fox, A. (2005). Detecting application-level failures in component-based internet services. *IEEE Trans. Neural Netw.* **16** (5): 1027–1041.

132 Johnsson A, Meirosu C. Towards automatic network fault localization in real time using probabilistic inference. In: Integrated Network Management (IM 2013), 2013 IFIP/IEEE International Symposium on. Piscataway: IEEE; 2013. p. 1393–8.

133 Barreto, G.A., Mota, J.C.M., Souza, L.G.M. et al. (2005). Condition monitoring of 3g cellular networks through competitive neural models. *IEEE Trans. Neural Netw.* **16** (5): 1064–1075.

134 He Q, Shayman MA. Using reinforcement learning for proactive network fault management. In: Proceedings of the International Conference on Communication Technologies. 1999.

135 Watanabe, A., Ishibashi, K., Toyono, T. et al. (2016). Workflow extraction for service operation using multiple unstructured trouble tickets. *IEEE*: 652–658.

136 Fiedler, M., Hossfeld, T., and Tran-Gia, P. (2010). A generic quantitative relationship between quality of experience and quality of service. *IEEE Netw.* **24** (2): 36–41.

137 Khorsandroo, S., Md Noor, R., and Khorsandroo, S. (2013). A generic quantitative relationship to assess interdependency of QoE and QoS. *KSII Trans. Internet Inf. Syst.* **7** (2): 327–346.

138 Aroussi S, Bouabana-Tebibel T, Mellouk A. Empirical QoE/QoS correlation model based on multiple parameters for VoD flows. In: Global Communications Conference (GLOBECOM), 2012 IEEE;. p. 1963–8.

139 Shaikh, J., Fiedler, M., and Collange, D. (2010). Quality of experience from user and network perspectives. *Annals of Telecommun-Annales Des Telecommun.* **65** (1–2): 47–57.

140 Elkotob M, Grandlund D, Andersson K, Ahlund C. Multimedia qoe optimized management using prediction and statistical learning. In: Local Computer Networks (LCN), 2010 IEEE 35th Conference on. IEEE; 2010. p. 324–7.

141 Erman J, Arlitt M, Mahanti A. Traffic classification using clustering algorithms. In: Proceedings of the 2006 SIGCOMM workshop on Mining network data. ACM; 2006a. p. 281–6.

142 Erman J, Mahanti A, Arlitt M. Internet traffic identification using machine learning. In: Global Telecommunications Conference, 2006. GLOBECOM'06. IEEE. IEEE; 2006b. p. 1–6.

143 Vega, M.T., Mocanu, D.C., and Liotta, A. (May, 2017). Unsupervised deep learning for real-time assessment of video streaming services. *Multimed. Tools Appl.* **76** (4): 1–25.

144 Sun Y, Yin X, Jiang J, Sekar V, Lin F, Wang N, Liu T, Sinopoli B. Cs2p: Improving video bitrate selection and adaptation with data-driven throughput prediction. In: Proceedings of the 2016 conference on ACM SIGCOMM 2016 Conference. ACM; 2016. p. 272–85.

145 Claeys, M., Latre, S., Famaey, J., and De Turck, F. (2014a). Design and evaluation of a self-learning http adaptive video streaming client. *IEEE Com. Lett.* **18** (4): 716–719.

146 Cannady J. Artificial neural networks for misuse detection. In: Proceedings of the 21st National information systems security conference, vol. 26. Virginia; 1998. p. 368–81.

147 Amor NB, Benferhat S, Elouedi Z. Naive bayes vs decision trees in intrusion detection systems. In: Proceedings of the 2004 ACM symposium on Applied computing. ACM; 2004. p. 420–4.

148 Chebrolu, S., Abraham, A., and Thomas, J.P. (2005). Feature deduction and ensemble design of intrusion detection systems. *Comput. secur.* **24** (4): 295–307.

149 Kruegel, C. and Toth, T. (2003). Using decision trees to improve signature-based intrusion detection. In: Recent Advances in Intrusion Detection (ed. R. Lippmann), 173–191. Springer.

150 Moradi M, Zulkernine M. A neural network based system for intrusion detection and classification of attacks. In: Proceedings of the IEEE International Conference on Advances in Intelligent Systems-Theory and Applications. 2004. p. 15–8.

151 Pan ZS, Chen SC, Hu GB, Zhang DQ. Hybrid neural network and c4.5 for misuse detection. 2003, pp. 2463–7.

152 Peddabachigari, S., Abraham, A., Grosan, C., and Thomas, J. (2007). Modeling intrusion detection system using hybrid intelligent systems. *J. Netw. Comput. Appl.* **30** (1): 114–132.

153 Sangkatsanee, P., Wattanapongsakorn, N., and Charnsripinyo, C. (2011). Practical real-time intrusion detection using machine learning approaches. *Comput. Commun.* **34** (18): 2227–2235.

154 Stein G, Chen B, Wu AS, Hua KA. Decision tree classifier for network intrusion detection with ga-based feature selection. In: Proceedings of the 43rd annual Southeast regional conference-Volume 2. ACM; 2005. p. 136–41.

155 Ahmed T, Coates M, Lakhina A. Multivariate online anomaly detection using kernel recursive least squares. IEEE INFOCOM 2007 - 26th IEEE International Conference on Computer Communications. pp. 625–33.

156 Boero L, Marchese M, Zappatore S. Support vector machine meets software defined networking in ids domain. In: Proceedings of the 29th Int. Teletraffic Congress (ITC), vol. 3. New York: IEEE; 2017. p. 25–30.

157 Dump CM. Dde command execution malware samples. 2017. http://contagiodump.blogspot.it. Accessed 1 Mar 2017.

158 Malware-Traffic-Analysisnet. A source for pcap files and malware samples. 2017. http://www.malware-traffic-analysis.net. Accessed 15 Dec 2017

159 Parkour M. Pcap traffic patterns. 2013. http://www.mediafire.com? a49l965nlayad. Accessed 1 Mar 2017.

160 Pcap-Analysis. Malware. 2017. www.pcapanalysis.com. Accessed 1 Mar 2017.

161 Wang K, Stolfo SJ. Anomalous payload-based network intrusion detection. In: RAID, vol 4. Springer; 2004. p. 203–22.

162 Perdisci, R., Ariu, D., Fogla, P. et al. (2009). Mcpad: a multiple classifier system for accurate payload-based anomaly detection. *Comput. Netw.* **53** (6): 864–881.

163 Ingham, K.L. and Inoue, H. (2007). Comparing anomaly detection techniques for http. In: International Workshop on Recent Advances in Intrusion Detection (RAID) (eds. C. Kruegel, R. Lippmann and A. Clark), 42–62. Berlin: Springer.

164 Detristan T, Ulenspiegel T, Malcom Y, Underduk M. Polymorphic shellcode engine using spectrum analysis. 2003. http://www.phrack. org/show.php?p=61&a=9. Accessed 25 May 2018.

165 Zanero S, Savaresi SM. Unsupervised learning techniques for an intrusion detection system: ACM; 2004, pp. 412–9.

166 Beale, J., Deraison, R., Meer, H. et al. (2004). Nessus Network Auditing. Burlington: Syngress Publishing.

167 Tavallaee M, Bagheri E, Lu W, Ghorbani AA. A detailed analysis of the KDD cup 99 data set. IEEE; 2009, pp. 1–6.

168 Javaid A, Niyaz Q, Sun W, Alam M. A deep learning approach for network intrusion detection system. In: Proceedings of the 9th EAI International Conference on Bio-inspired Information and Communications Technologies (formerly BIONETICS), ICST, (Institute for Computer Sciences Social-Informatics and Telecommunications Engineering). Brussels; 2016. p. 21–6.

169 Li Y, Ma R, Jiao R. A hybrid malicious code detection method based on deep learning. Methods. 2015;9(5).

170 Kim J, Kim J, Thu HLT, Kim H. Long short term memory recurrent neural network classifier for intrusion detection. International Conference on. IEEE; 2016, pp. 1–5.

171 Servin A, Kudenko D. Multi-agent reinforcement learning for intrusion detection: A case study and evaluation. In: German Conference on Multiagent System Technologies. Springer; 2008. p. 159–70.

172 Mukkamala S, Janoski G, Sung A. Intrusion detection using neural networks and support vector machines. 2002, pp. 1702–7.

173 Bharath, B.N., Nagananda, K.G., and Poor, H.V. (April 2016). A learning-based approach to caching in heterogenous small cell networks. *IEEE Trans. Commun.* **64** (4): 1674.

174 Asheralieva, A. and Miyanaga, Y. (September 2016). An autonomous learning-based algorithm for joint channel and power level selection by D2D pairs in heterogeneous cellular networks. *IEEE Trans. Commun.* **64** (9): 3996.

175 Xiao, Y., Chen, K.-C., Yuen, C. et al. (Jul. 2015). A Bayesian overlapping coalition formation game for device-to-device spectrum sharing in cellular networks. *IEEE Trans. Wirel. Commun.* **14** (7): 4034–4051.

176 P.V. Klaine, et al, A Survey of Machine Learning Techniques Applied to Self-Organizing Cellular Networks, IEEE Communications Surveys & Tutorials · July 201.

177 Aliu, O.G., Imran, A., Imran, M.A., and Evans, B. (2013). A survey of self organisation in future cellular networks. *IEEE Commun. Surv. Tut.* **15**: 336–361, First.

178 "3rd generation partnership project; technical specification group services and system aspects; telecommunications management; selforganizing networks (SON); self-healing concepts and requirements (release 11), 3GPP TS 32.541, 2012–09, v11.0.0, https://arib.or.jp/english/html/overview/doc/STD-T63v11_00/5_Appendix/Rel11/32/32541-b00.pdf 2012,"

179 "3GPP TS 36.902 evolved universal terrestrial radio access network (E-UTRAN); self-configuring and self-optimizing network (SON) use cases and solutions," https://portal.3gpp.org/desktopmodules/Specifications/SpecificationDetails.aspx?specificationId=2581.

180 "3GPP TS 32.500 telecommunication management; self-organizing networks (SON); concepts and requirements," https://portal.3gpp.org/desktopmodules/Specifications/SpecificationDetails.aspx?specificationId=2031.

181 P. Wainio and K. Seppnen, "Self-optimizing last-mile backhaul network for 5G small cells," in 2016 IEEE International Conference on Communications Workshops (ICC), pp. 232–239, May 2016

182 Hu, H., Zhang, J., Zheng, X. et al. (2010). Self-configuration and self-optimization for LTE networks. *IEEE Commun. Mag.* **48** (2): 94–100.

183 A. Imran, E. Yaacoub, Z. Dawy, and A. Abu-Dayya, "Planning future cellular networks: A generic framework for performance quantification," in Wireless Conference (EW), Proceedings of the 2013 19th European, pp. 1–7 April 2013.

184 T. Binzer and F. M. Landstorfer, "Radio network planning with neural networks," in Vehicular Technology Conference, 2000. IEEE-VTS Fall VTC 2000. 52nd, vol. 2, pp. 811–817 vol.2, 2000.

185 P. Wainio and K. Seppnen, "Self-optimizing last-mile backhaul network for 5G small cells," in 2016 IEEE International Conference on Communications Workshops (ICC), pp. 232–239, May 2016.

186 Peng, M., Liang, D., Wei, Y. et al. (2013). Self-configuration and self-optimization in LTE-advanced heterogeneous networks. *IEEE Commun. Mag.* **51** (5): 36–45.

187 Hu, H., Zhang, J., Zheng, X. et al. (2010). Self-configuration and self-optimization for LTE networks. *IEEE Commun. Mag.* **48** (2): 94–100.

188 Iacoboaiea, O.-C., Sayrac, B., Jemaa, S.B., and Bianchi, P. (September 2016). SON coordination in heterogeneous networks: a reinforcement learning framework. *IEEE Trans. Wirel. Commun.* **15** (9): 5835.

189 Sutton, R.S. and Barto, A.G. (1998). Reinforcement Learning: An Introduction (A Bradford Book). Cambridge, MA, USA: MIT Press.

190 3GPP, "LTE; E-UTRA; physical layer; measurements," 3rd Generation. Partnership Project, Sophia Antipolis, France, Tech. Rep. TS 36.214, 2012.

191 3GPP, "LTE; E-UTRA and E-UTRAN; overall description," 3rd Generat. Partnership Project, Sophia Antipolis, France, Tech. Rep. TS 36.300, 2013.

192 SEMAFOUR Project Web Page, accessed on Sep. 1, 2015. [Online]. Available: http://fp7-semafour.eu.

193 A. Sadeghi, et al, Optimal and Scalable Caching for 5G Using Reinforcement Learning of Space-time Popularities, arXiv:1708.06698v2 [cs.NI] 18 Nov 2017, also in in IEEE Journal of Selected Topics in Signal Processing, vol. 12, no. 1, pp. 180–190, Feb. 2018, doi: 10.1109/JSTSP.2017.2787979.

194 L. Breslau, P. Cao, L. Fan, G. Phillips, and S. Shenker, "Web caching and zipf-like distributions: Evidence and implications," in Intl. Conf. on Computer Communications, New York, USA, March 1999, pp. 126–134.

195 M. G. Kibri et al, Big Data Analytics, Machine Learning, and Artificial Intelligence in Next-Generation Wireless Networks, IEEE Access, 2018.

196 Cheng, X., Fang, L., Yang, L., and Cui, S. (Oct. 2017). Mobile big data: the fuel for data-driven wireless. *IEEE Intenet Things J.* **4** (5): 1489–1516.

197 Cheng, X., Fang, L., Hong, X., and Yang, L. (2017). Exploiting mobile big data: sources, features, and applications. *IEEE Netw.* **31** (1): 72–79.

198 Kyriazakos, S.A. and Karetsos, G.T. (2004). Practical Radio Resource Management in Wireless Systems. Boston, MA, USA: Artech House.

199 Procera Networks. RAN Perspectives: RAN Analytics & Enforcement. Accessed: Oct. 13, 2017. [Online]. Available: https://www. http://proceranetworks.com/hubfs/Resource%20Downloads/Datasheets Procera_DS_RAN_Perspectives.pdf?t=1481193315415.

200 Lu, X., Wetter, E., Bharti, N. et al. (Nov. 2013). Approaching the limit of predictability in human mobility. *Sci. Rep.* **3**: 324.

201 R. Atawia, H. S. Hassanein, and A. Noureldin, "Fair robust predictive resource allocation for video streaming under rate uncertainties," in Proc. IEEE Globecom, Dec. 2016, pp. 1–6.

202 Oh, E., Krishnamachari, B., Liu, X., and Niu, Z. (Jun. 2011). Toward dynamic energyefficient operation of cellular network infrastructure. *IEEE Commun. Mag.* **49** (6): 56–61.

203 A. Banerjee, "Advanced predictive network analytics: Optimize your network investments & transform customer experience," Heavy Reading, New York, NY, USA, White Paper, Feb. 2014.

204 Hong, W., Jiang, Z.H., Yu, C. et al. (Dec. 2017). Multibeam antenna technologies for 5G wireless communications. *IEEE Trans. Antennas Propag.* **65** (12): 6231–6249.

205 Mijumbi, R., Hasija, S., Davy, S. et al. (March 2017). Topology-aware prediction of virtual network function resource requirements. *IEEE Trans. Netw. Serv. Manag.* **14** (1): 1–14.

206 Mijumbi, R., Serrat, J., Gorrich, J.-L. et al. (2016). Network function virtualization: state-of-the-art and research challenges. *IEEE Commun. Surveys Tuts.* **18** (1): 236–262, 1st Quart.

207 R. Guerzoni, "Network functions virtualisation: An introduction, benefits, enablers, challenges and call for action. Introductory white paper," in Proc. SDN OpenFlow World Congr., Jun. 2012, pp. 1–16.

208 Scarselli, F., Gori, M., Tsoi, A.C. et al. (Jan. 2009). The graph neural network model. *IEEE Trans. Neural Netw.* **20** (1): 61–80.

209 Khamsi, M.A. and Kirk, W.A. (2001). Banach Spaces: Introduction. New Jersey, USA: Wiley.

210 Metaswitch Networks. (Jun. 2016). Project Clearwater. Accessed on Aug. 29, 2020. [Online]. Available: https://clearwater.readthedocs.io/en/stable.

211 R. Day. (Jun. 2016). SIPp. Accessed on Nov. 16, 2016. [Online]. Available: http://sipp. sourceforge.net.

212 The Cacti Group Inc. (Jun. 2016). Cacti. Accessed on Nov. 16, 2016. [Online]. Available: http://www. cacti.net.

213 Internet Systems Consortium. (Jun. 2016). BIND. Accessed on Nov. 16, 2016. [Online]. Available: https://www.isc.org/downloads/bind.

214 OpenStack. (Jun. 2016). Heat Orchestration Templates. Accessed on Nov. 16, 2016. [Online]. Available: https://wiki.openstack.org/wiki/Heat.

215 TSTAT. (Jun. 2016). TCP STatistic and Analysis Tool: Skype Traces. Accessed on Nov. 16, 2016. [Online]. Available: http://tstat.polito.it/traces-skype.shtml.

216 Heaton, J. (2008). Introduction to Neural Networks for Java, 2e. St. Louis, MO, USA: Heaton Res.

217 Scarselli, F. and Tsoi, A.C. (1998). Universal approximation using feedforward neural networks: a survey of some existing methods, and some new results. *Neural Netw.* **11** (1): 15–37.

218 Chen, X., Zhao, Z., Wu, C. et al. (October 2019). Multi-tenant cross-slice resource orchestration: a deep reinforcement learning approach. *IEEE J. Sel. Areas Comm.* **37** (10): 2377. also arXiv:1807.09350v2 [cs.NI] 3 Jun 2019.

219 Berry, R.A. and Gallager, R.G. (May 2002). Communication over fading channels with delay constraints. *IEEE Trans. Inf. Theory* **48** (5): 1135–1149.

220 Fink, A.M. (1964). Equilibrium in a stochastic n-person game. *J. Sci. Hiroshima Univ. Ser. A-I* **28** (1): 89–93.

221 Chen, X., Han, Z., Zhang, H. et al. (Apr. 2018). Wireless resource scheduling in virtualized radio access networks using stochastic learning. *IEEE Trans. Mobile Comput.* **17** (4): 961–974.

222 C. Kroer and T. Sandholm, "Imperfect-recall abstractions with bounds in games," in Proc. ACM EC, Maastricht, The Netherlands, Jul. 2016, pp. 459–476.

223 D. Abel, D. Hershkowitz, and M. Littman, "Near optimal behavior via approximate state abstraction," in Proc. ICML, New York, NY, USA, Jun. 2016, pp. 1–18.

224 Fu, F. and Schaar, M.V.D. (May 2009). Learning to compete for resources in wireless stochastic games. *IEEE Trans. Veh. Technol.* **58** (4): 1904–1919.

225 Loève, M. (1977). Probability Theory I. Berlin, Germany: Springer-Verlag.

226 Sutton, R.S. and Barto, A.G. (1998). Reinforcement Learning: An Introduction. Cambridge, MA, USA: MIT Press.

227 Watkins, C.J.C.H. and Dayan, P. (1992). Q-learning. *Mach. Learn.* **8** (3–4): 279–292.

228 Chen, X., Wu, J., Cai, Y. et al. (Apr. 2015). Energy-efficiency oriented traffic offloading in wireless networks: a brief survey and a learning approach for heterogeneous cellular networks. *IEEE J. Sel. Areas Commun.* **33** (4): 627–640.

229 H. van Hasselt, A. Guez, and D. Silver, "Deep reinforcement learning with double Q-learning," in Proc. AAAI, Phoenix, AZ, Feb. 2016.

230 L.-J. Lin, "Reinforcement learning for robots using neural networks," Ph.D. dissertation, School Comput. Sci., Carnegie Mellon Univ., Pittsburgh, PA, USA, 1992.

231 Kaige Qu, et al, Dynamic Resource Scaling for VNF over Nonstationary Traffic: A Learning Approach IEEE Transactions on Cognitive Communications and Networking.

232 Liu, S., Yamada, M., Collier, N., and Sugiyama, M. (July 2013). Change-point detection in time-series data by relative density-ratio estimation. *Neural Netw.* **43**: 72–83.

233 Adams, R.P. and MacKay, D.J. (2007). Bayesian online changepoint detection. University of Cambridge, Cambridge, U.K: Tech. Rep.

234 Comert, G. and Bezuglov, A. (Sep. 2013). An online change-point-based model for traffic parameter prediction. *IEEE Trans. Intell. Transport. Syst.* **14** (3): 1360–1369.

235 C. Fraleigh, F. Tobagi, and C. Diot, "Provisioning IP backbone networks to support latency sensitive traffic," in Proc. IEEE INFOCOM'03 Apr. 2003, pp. 1871–1879.

236 Kim, J. and Hwang, G. (Oct. 2019). Adaptive bandwidth allocation based on sample path prediction with Gaussian process regression. *IEEE Trans. Wirel. Commun.* **18** (10): 4983–4996.

237 Cheng, Y., Zhuang, W., and Wang, L. (Aug. 2007). Calculation of loss probability in a finite size partitioned buffer for quantitative assured service. *IEEE Trans. Commun.* **55** (9): 1757–1771.

238 Qu, K., Zhuang, W., Ye, Q. et al. (Apr. 2020). Dynamic flow migration for embedded services in SDN/NFV-enabled 5G core networks. *IEEE Trans. Commun.* **68** (4): 2394–2408.

239 L. Guo, J. Pang, and A. Walid, "Dynamic service function chaining in SDN-enabled networks with middleboxes," in Proc. IEEE ICNP'16 Nov. 2016, pp. 1–10.

240 I. Kovacevic, A. S. Shafigh, S. Glisic, B. Lorenzo, and E. Hossain, Multi-Domain Network Slicing with Latency Equalization, IEEE Transactions on Network and Service Management, 2020.

241 Williams, C.K. and Rasmussen, C.E. (2006). Gaussian Processes for Machine Learning, vol. **2**. MIT press Cambridge, MA no. 3.

242 Mnih, V., Kavukcuoglu, K., Silver, D. et al. (Feb. 2015). Human level control through deep reinforcement learning. *Nature* **518** (7540): 529–533.

243 Z. Xu, J. Tang, J. Meng, W. Zhang, Y. Wang, C. H. Liu, and D. Yang, "Experience-driven networking: A deep reinforcement learning based approach," in Proc. IEEE INFOCOM'18 Apr. 2018, pp. 1871–1879.

244 T. Schaul, J. Quan, I. Antonoglou, and D. Silver, "Prioritized experience replay," in Proc. ICLR'16 May 2016, pp. 1–7.

245 Kobayashi, H. and Mark, B.L. (2009). System Modeling and Analysis: Foundations of System Performance Evaluation. Pearson Education India.

246 Wang, J. et al. (February 2020). Whittle index policy for dynamic multichannel allocation in remote state estimation. *IEEE Trans. Autom. Control* **65** (2): 591.

247 Fawzi, H., Tabuada, P., and Diggavi, S. (Jun. 2014). Secure estimation and control for cyber-physical systems under adversarial attacks. *IEEE Trans. Autom. Control* **59** (6): 1454–1467.

248 Jazwinski, A.H. (2007). Stochastic Processes and Filtering Theory. North Chelmsford, MA, USA: Courier Corporation.

249 Altman, E. (1999). Constrained Markov Decision Processes, vol. **7**. Boca Raton, FL, USA: CRC Press.

250 Whittle, P. (1988). Restless bandits: activity allocation in a changing world. *J. Appl. Probab.* **25** (A): 287–298.

251 Palomar, D.P. and Chiang, M. (Aug. 2006). A tutorial on decomposition methods for network utility maximization. *IEEE J. Sel. Areas Commun.* **24** (8): 1439–1451.

252 Verloop, I.M. (2016). Asymptotically optimal priority policies for indexable and nonindexable restless bandits. *Ann. Appl. Probab.* **26** (4): 1947–1995.

253 Liu, S., Fardad, M., Masazade, E., and Varshney, P.K. (Jun. 2014). Optimal periodic sensor scheduling in networks of dynamical systems. *IEEE Trans. Signal Process.* **62** (12): 3055–3068.

254 Cao, Z., Lu, J., Zhang, R., and Gao, F. (2016). Iterative learning Kalman filter for repetitive processes. *J. Process Control* **46**: 92–104.

255 Liu, K. and Zhao, Q. (Nov. 2010). Indexability of restless bandit problems and optimality of Whittle index for dynamic multichannel access. *IEEE Trans. Inf. Theory* **56** (11): 5547–5567.

256 C. Yang, Z. Liu, D. Zhao, M. Sun, and E. Y. Chang, "Network representation learning with rich text information," in Proceedings of the 24th International Joint Conference on Artificial Intelligence, 2015, pp. 2111–2117.

257 L. Tang and H. Liu, "Relational learning via latent social dimensions," in Proceedings of the 15th ACM SIGKDD International Conference on Knowledge Discovery and Data Mining. ACM, 2009, pp. 817–826.

258 J. Tang, M. Qu, M. Wang, M. Zhang, J. Yan, and Q. Mei, "LINE: Large-scale information network embedding," in Proceedings of the 24th International Conference on World Wide Web. ACM, 2015, pp. 1067–1077.

259 B. Perozzi, R. Al-Rfou, and S. Skiena, "DeepWalk: Online learning of social representations," in Proceedings of the 20th ACM SIGKDD International Conference on Knowledge Discovery and Data Mining. ACM, 2014, pp. 701–710.

260 J. Tang, M. Qu, M. Wang, M. Zhang, J. Yan, and Q. Mei, "LINE: Large-scale information network embedding," in Proceedings of the 24th International Conference on World Wide Web. ACM, 2015, pp. 1067–1077.

261 S. Cao, W. Lu, and Q. Xu, "GraRep: Learning graph representations with global structural information," in Proceedings of the 24th ACM International Conference on Information and Knowledge Management. ACM, 2015, pp. 891–900.

262 S. Cao, W. Lu, and Q. Xu, "Deep neural networks for learning graph representations," in Proceedings of the 30th AAAI Conference on Artificial Intelligence. AAAI Press, 2016, pp. 1145–1152.

263 D. Wang, P. Cui, and W. Zhu, "Structural deep network embedding," in Proceedings of the 22nd ACM SIGKDD International Conference on Knowledge Discovery and Data Mining. ACM, 2016, pp. 1225–1234.

264 A. Grover and J. Leskovec, "node2vec: Scalable feature learning for networks," in Proceedings of the 22nd ACM SIGKDD International Conference on Knowledge Discovery and Data Mining. ACM, 2016, pp. 855–864.

265 M. Ou, P. Cui, J. Pei, Z. Zhang, and W. Zhu, "Asymmetric transitivity preserving graph embedding," in Proceedings of the 22nd ACM SIGKDD International Conference on Knowledge Discovery and Data Mining. ACM, 2016, pp. 1105–1114.

266 C. Zhou, Y. Liu, X. Liu, Z. Liu, and J. Gao, "Scalable graph embedding for asymmetric proximity," in Proceedings of the 31st AAAI Conference on Artificial Intelligence, 2017, pp. 2942–2948.

267 H. H. Song, T. W. Cho, V. Dave, Y. Zhang, and L. Qiu, "Scalable proximity estimation and link prediction in online social networks," in Proceedings of the 9th ACM SIGCOMM Conference on Internet Measurement Conference. ACM, 2009, pp. 322–335.

268 T. Mikolov, K. Chen, G. Corrado, and J. Dean, "Efficient estimation of word representations in vector space," arXiv preprint arXiv:1301.3781, 2013.

269 Mikolov, T., Sutskever, I., Chen, K. et al. (2013). Distributed representations of words and phrases and their compositionality. In: Advances in Neural Information Processing Systems, 3111–3119. arXiv.org > cs > arXiv:1310.4546v1.

270 H. Wang, J. Wang, J. Wang, M. Zhao, W. Zhang, F. Zhang, X. Xie, and M. Guo, "GraphGAN: Graph representation learning with generative adversarial nets," in Proceedings of the 32nd AAAI Conference on Artificial Intelligence. AAAI Press, 2018.

271 Goodfellow, I., Pouget-Abadie, J., Mirza, M. et al. (2014). Generative adversarial nets. In: Advances in Neural Information Processing Systems, 2672–2680.also; arXiv:1406.2661v1 [stat.ML] 10 Jun 2014.

272 L. F. Ribeiro, P. H. Saverese, and D. R. Figueiredo, "struc2vec: Learning node representations from structural identity," in Proceedings of the 23rd ACM SIGKDD International Conference on Knowledge Discovery and Data Mining. ACM, 2017, pp. 385–394.

273 C. Donnat, M. Zitnik, D. Hallac, and J. Leskovec, "Spectral graph wavelets for structural role similarity in networks," arXiv preprint arXiv:1710.10321, 2017.

274 T. Lyu, Y. Zhang, and Y. Zhang, "Enhancing the network embedding quality with structural similarity," in Proceedings of the 2017 ACM on Conference on Information and Knowledge Management. ACM, 2017, pp. 147–156.

275 L. Tang and H. Liu, "Relational learning via latent social dimensions," in Proceedings of the 15th ACM SIGKDD International Conference on Knowledge Discovery and Data Mining. ACM, 2009, pp. 817–826.

276 Tang, L. and Liu, H. (2011). Leveraging social media networks for classification. *Data Min. Knowl. Disc.* **23** (3): 447–478.

277 L. Tang and H. Liu, "Scalable learning of collective behavior based on sparse social dimensions," in Proceedings of the 18th ACM International Conference on Information and Knowledge Management. ACM, 2009, pp. 1107–1116.

278 X. Wang, P. Cui, J. Wang, J. Pei, W. Zhu, and S. Yang, "Community preserving network embedding," in Proceedings of the 31st AAAI Conference on Artificial Intelligence, 2017, pp. 203–209.

279 R. Feng, Y. Yang, W. Hu, F. Wu, and Y. Zhuang, "Representation learning for scale-free networks," in Proceedings of the 32nd AAAI Conference on Artificial Intelligence. AAAI Press, 2018.

280 H. Chen, B. Perozzi, Y. Hu, and S. Skiena, "HARP: Hierarchical representation learning for networks," in Proceedings of the 32nd AAAI Conference on Artificial Intelligence. AAAI Press, 2018.

281 M. Belkin and P. Niyogi, "Laplacian eigenmaps and spectral techniques for embedding and clustering," in Advances in Neural Information Processing Systems, 2002, pp. 585–591 https://proceedings.neurips.cc/paper/2001/file/f106b7f99d2cb30c3db1c3cc0fde9ccb-Paper.pdf.

282 C. Yang, Z. Liu, D. Zhao, M. Sun, and E. Y. Chang, "Network representation learning with rich text information," in Proceedings of the 24th International Joint Conference on Artificial Intelligence, 2015, pp. 2111–2117.

283 Natarajan, N. and Dhillon, I.S. (2014). Inductive matrix completion for predicting gene–disease associations. *Bioinformatics* **30** (12): i60–i68.

284 D. Zhang, J. Yin, X. Zhu, and C. Zhang, "Homophily, structure, and content augmented network representation learning," in Proceedings of the 16th IEEE International Conference on Data Mining. IEEE, 2016, pp. 609–618.

285 Hinton, G.E. and Salakhutdinov, R.R. (2006). Reducing the dimensionality of data with neural networks. *Science* **313** (5786): 504–507.

286 Sik-Ho Tsang, Review — Autoencoder: Reducing the Dimensionality of Data with Neural Networks (Data Visualization), https://sh-tsang.medium.com/review-autoencoder-reducing-the-dimensionality-of-data-with-neural-networks-data-visualization-fc16446ae32d.

287 S. Wang, J. Tang, F. Morstatter, and H. Liu, "Paired restricted Boltzmann machine for linked data," in Proceedings of the 25th ACM International Conference on Information and Knowledge Management. ACM, 2016, pp. 1753–1762.

288 D. Zhang, J. Yin, X. Zhu, and C. Zhang, "User profile preserving social network embedding," in Proceedings of the 26th International Joint Conference on Artificial Intelligence, 2017, pp. 3378–3384.

289 A. Rahimi and B. Recht, "Random features for large-scale kernel machines," NIPS'07: Proceedings of the 20th International Conference on Neural Information Processing Systems December 2007 , pp. 1177–1184.

290 C. Li, S. Wang, D. Yang, Z. Li, Y. Yang, X. Zhang, and J. Zhou, "PPNE: Property preserving network embedding," in International Conference on Database Systems for Advanced Applications. Springer, 2017, pp. 163–179.

291 Zhu, J., Ahmed, A., and Xing, E.P. (2012). MedLDA: maximum margin supervised topic models. *J. Mach. Learn. Res.* **13** (Aug): 2237–2278.

292 J. Mairal, J. Ponce, G. Sapiro, A. Zisserman, and F. R. Bach, "Supervised dictionary learning," NIPS'08: Proceedings of the 21st International Conference on Neural Information Processing Systems, December 2008 , pp. 1033–1040.

293 J. Li, J. Zhu, and B. Zhang, "Discriminative deep random walk for network classification," in Proceedings of the 54th Annual Meeting of the Association for Computational Linguistics, vol. 1, 2016, pp. 1004–1013.

294 Fan, R.-E., Chang, K.-W., Hsieh, C.-J. et al. (2008). LIBLINEAR: a library for large linear classification. *J. Mach. Learn. Res.* **9** (Aug): 1871–1874.

295 C. Tu, W. Zhang, Z. Liu, and M. Sun, "Max-Margin DeepWalk: discriminative learning of network representation," in Proceedings of the 25th International Joint Conference on Artificial Intelligence, 2016, pp. 3889–3895.

296 Zhang, X., Chen, W., and Yan, H. (2016). TLINE: scalable transductive network embedding. In: Information Retrieval Technology. AIRS 2016. Lecture Notes in Computer Science, vol. **9994** (eds. S. Ma et al.), 98–110. Cham: Springer https://link.springer.com/chapter/10.1007/978-3-319-48051-0_8.

297 J. Chen, Q. Zhang, and X. Huang, "Incorporate group information to enhance network embedding," in Proceedings of the 25th ACM International Conference on Information and Knowledge Management. ACM, 2016, pp. 1901–1904.

298 N. Djuric, H. Wu, V. Radosavljevic, M. Grbovic, and N. Bhamidipati, "Hierarchical neural language models for joint representation of streaming documents and their content," in Proceedings of the 24th International Conference on World Wide Web. ACM, 2015, pp. 248–255.

299 C. Li, Z. Li, S. Wang, Y. Yang, X. Zhang, and J. Zhou, "Semisupervised network embedding," in International Conference on Database Systems for Advanced Applications. Springer, 2017, pp. 131–147.

300 S. Pan, J. Wu, X. Zhu, C. Zhang, and Y. Wang, "Tri-party deep network representation," in Proceedings of the 25th International Joint Conference on Artificial Intelligence, 2016, pp. 1895–1901.

301 Q. Le and T. Mikolov, "Distributed representations of sentences and documents," in Proceedings of the 31st International Conference on Machine Learning, 2014, pp. 1188–1196.

302 S. Wang, J. Tang, C. Aggarwal, and H. Liu, "Linked document embedding for classification," in Proceedings of the 25th ACM International Conference on Information and Knowledge Management. ACM, 2016, pp. 115–124.

303 D. Zhang, J. Yin, X. Zhu, and C. Zhang, "Collective classification via discriminative matrix factorization on sparsely labeled networks," in Proceedings of the 25th ACM International Conference on Information and Knowledge Management. ACM, 2016, pp. 1563–1572.

304 Z. Yang, W. W. Cohen, and R. Salakhutdinov, "Revisiting semisupervised learning with graph embeddings," in Proceedings of the 33rd International Conference on International Conference on Machine Learning (ICML), 2016, pp. 40–48.

305 X. Huang, J. Li, and X. Hu, "Label informed attributed network embedding," in Proceedings of the 10th ACM International Conference on Web Search and Data Mining. ACM, 2017, pp. 731–739.

306 D. Zhang, J. Yin, X. Zhu, and C. Zhang, *Network Representation Learning: A Survey*, arXiv:1801.05852v3 [cs.SI] 19 Jul 2018.

Part II

Quantum Computing

8

Fundamentals of Quantum Communications

8.1 Introduction

Quantum bits: Similar to the *bit*, the fundamental concept of classical computation and classical information, quantum computation and quantum information are built upon an analogous concept, the *quantum bit*, often referred to as *qubit*. In this section, we introduce the properties of single and multiple qubits, comparing and contrasting their properties to those of classical bits. For the most part, we treat qubits as abstract mathematical objects. This gives us the freedom to construct a general theory of quantum computation and quantum information that does not depend upon a specific system for its realization.

Just as a classical bit has a *state* – either 0 or 1 – a qubit also has a state. Two possible states for a qubit are the states $|0\rangle$ and $|1\rangle$, which as you might guess correspond to the states 0 and 1 for a classical bit. Notation like "$|\ \rangle$" is called the *Dirac notation*, and we will be seeing it often, as this is the standard notation for states in quantum mechanics. The difference between bits and qubits is that a qubit can be in a state *other* than $|0\rangle$ or $|1\rangle$. It is also possible to form *linear combinations* of states, often called *superpositions*:

$$|q\rangle = \alpha|0\rangle + \beta|1\rangle. \tag{8.1}$$

The parameters α and β are complex numbers, although for many purposes not much is lost by thinking of them as real numbers. In other words, the state of a qubit is a vector in a two-dimensional complex vector space. The special states $|0\rangle$ and $|1\rangle$ are known as *computational basis states*, and form an orthonormal basis for this vector space. Geometrically, we can interpret this as the condition that the qubit's state be normalized to length 1. Thus, in general, a qubit's state is a unit vector in a two-dimensional complex vector space.

If we choose $\alpha = \beta = 1/\sqrt{2}$, then we have

$$|q\rangle = (|0\rangle + |1\rangle)/\sqrt{2}. \tag{8.2}$$

This quantum state seems to exhibit a symmetry with respect to the orthogonal states $|0\rangle$ and $|1\rangle$, not favoring one over the other and is often used in the analysis. Assuming only real-valued amplitudes for a quantum state $\beta \in \mathbb{R}$, the resultant 2D geometrical representation of a qubit's state is shown in Figure 8.1, since its state may be written as $|q\rangle = \cos(\theta)|0\rangle + \sin(\theta)|1\rangle$. In the general case, the amplitudes of the quantum states are complex-valued, and therefore the state of a qubit is represented by the 3D Bloch sphere [1, 2] of Figure 8.2, since a qubit's state may always be written as $|q\rangle = \cos(\theta/2)|0\rangle + \exp(i\phi)\sin(\theta/2)|1\rangle$. In the following, we will be using both representations of the qubit depending on the algorithm we are discussing.

Artificial Intelligence and Quantum Computing for Advanced Wireless Networks, First Edition.
Savo G. Glisic and Beatriz Lorenzo.

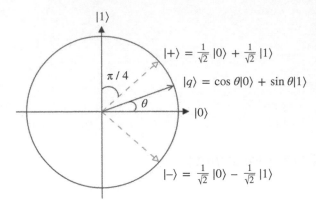

Figure 8.1 The 2D representation of a qubit, when the amplitudes of its quantum states are real-valued.

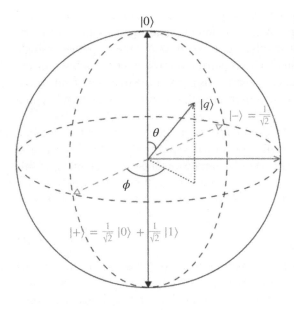

Figure 8.2 The generic 3D representation of a qubit using a Bloch sphere, when the amplitudes of its quantum states are complex-valued. *Sources:* Nielsen and Chuang [1]; Imre and Balázs [2].

Physics: To get a concrete feel for how a qubit can be realized, it may be helpful to list some of the ways this realization may occur: as the two different polarizations of a photon; as the alignment of a nuclear spin in a uniform magnetic field; or as two states of an electron orbiting a single atom such as shown in Figure 8.3. In the atom model, the electron can exist in either the so-called "ground" or "excited" states, which we will call $|0\rangle$ and $|1\rangle$, respectively. By shining light on the atom with appropriate energy and for an appropriate length of time, it is possible to move the electron from the $|0\rangle$ state to the $|1\rangle$ state, and vice versa. But more interestingly, by reducing the time we shine the light, an electron initially in the state $|0\rangle$ can be moved "halfway" between $|0\rangle$ and $|1\rangle$, into the $|+\rangle$ state.

Measurement of a qubit: We can examine a bit to determine whether it is in the state 0 or 1. For example, computers do this all the time when they retrieve the contents of their memory. On the other hand, even though a qubit may be in a superposition of two orthogonal states, if we desire to *observe*, or *measure*, its value, we will only obtain one of the two orthogonal states. The measurement of a quantum state may be considered as a quantum-to-classical (Q/C) conversion, since it

Figure 8.3 Qubit represented by two electronic levels in an atom. *Source: Based on Nielsen and Chuang [1].*

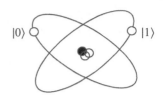

$|0\rangle$ $|1\rangle$

allows us to gain some insight into the quantum system. The measurement of a qubit's state may also be done in a basis different from that which the qubit was prepared in. For now, let us use the computational basis also for measuring a quantum state. According to the most widely adopted interpretation of a measurement's operation, a quantum state does not have specific properties before it is measured [3]. However, when it is observed, the probabilities of its superimposed states define not only the outcome of the measurement but also the new quantum state of the system. The amplitudes α and β of the quantum state $|q\rangle)$ uniquely define the probabilities of obtaining $|0\rangle$ or $|1\rangle$ when we measure the qubit's state $|q\rangle$ on the orthogonal basis $\{|0\rangle, |1\rangle\}$. More specifically, there is a $|\alpha|^2$ probability that we will obtain the quantum state $|0\rangle$ and a $|\beta|^2$ probability that $|1\rangle$ will be observed. This is also the reason why $|\alpha|^2 + |\beta|^2 = 1$ is always true. For example, for $\alpha = 0$ and $\alpha = 1$, since the system's state is already equal to one of the two states of the computational basis that was used for the measurement, we would always observe $|1\rangle$ and $|0\rangle$, respectively. However, when we measure the quantum state of $\alpha = \beta = 1/\sqrt{2}$, there is a $|\alpha|^2 = 1/2 = 50\%$ probability of obtaining the quantum state $|0\rangle$ and $|\beta|^2 = 1/2 = 50\%$ probability of obtaining the quantum state $|1\rangle$. Since the probability of observing either of the two states is the same, such a quantum system is said to be in an *equiprobable superposition* of states, always with respect to the computational orthogonal basis.

After the measurement, the quantum state *collapses* to the observed quantum state. For example, let us assume that the output of the quantum state's measurement in Eq. (8.2) was $|1\rangle$. As mentioned before, this event had a 50% probability of occurrence. Given that it has happened, however, the system's quantum state from that point onward *becomes identical to the observed quantum state*, and hence we have $|q'\rangle = |1\rangle$. This feature is termed *wave function collapse* in quantum mechanics, and it is irreversible. In other words, we are not able to reconstruct the system's quantum state to that before the measurement, unless we have knowledge about the pre-measurement amplitudes α and β of Eq. (8.1).

Experimentally, the phenomenon of quantum superposition can be demonstrated as follows. Consider Figure 8.4.

Figure 8.4 Beam splitting of light.

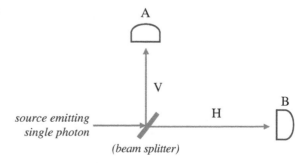

Here, a light source emits a photon along a path toward a half-silvered mirror. This mirror splits the light, reflecting half vertically toward detector A and transmitting half toward detector B. A photon, however, represents a single quantized energy state ($E = h\nu$) and hence cannot be split, so it is detected with equal probability at either A or B. This is verified by observation: if detector A registers the signal, then B does not; and vice versa. With this piece of information, one would like to think that any given photon travels either vertically or horizontally, randomly choosing between the two paths. Quantum mechanics, however, predicts that the photon actually travels both paths simultaneously, collapsing down to one path only upon measurement (collapse of the wave function). This effect is known as single-particle interference resulting from the linear superposition of the possible photon states of potential paths.

The phenomenon of single-particle interference can be better illustrated in a slightly more elaborate experiment, outlined in Figure 8.5. In this experiment, the photon first encounters a half-polished mirror (beam splitter), thus getting split into two parts: a reflected beam and a transmitted beam. The two beams are recombined with the half of the full-silvered mirrors, and finally another half-silvered mirror splits them before they reach a detector. Each half-silvered mirror introduces the probability of the photon taking one path or the other. Once a photon strikes the mirror along either of two paths after the first beam splitter, the arrangement is identical to that in Figure 8.5. Thus, a single photon traveling vertically, after striking the mirror, should – from the experiment in Figure 8.5 – strike either detector A or detector B with equal probability (50%). The same applies to a photon traveling down the horizontal path. However, the actual result is drastically different. If the two possible paths are exactly equal in length, then it turns out that there is 100% probability that photon reaches the detector A and 0% probability that it reaches the detector B, and thus the photon is certain to strike the detector A; it seems an inescapable conclusion that the photon must, in some sense, have actually traveled both routes simultaneously.

This can be demonstrated by placing an absorbing screen in the path of either of the routes; then it becomes equally probable that detector A or B is reached. Blocking one of the paths actually allows detector B to be reached; it is therefore perfectly legitimate to say that between the two half-silvered mirrors the photon took both the transmitted and reflected paths, or using more technical language, we can say that photon is in a coherent superposition of being in the transmitted beam and in the reflected beam. This quantum interference is the result of the linear superposition principle. This is one of those unique characteristics that make current research in quantum computing not merely a continuation of today's idea of the computer but rather an entirely new branch

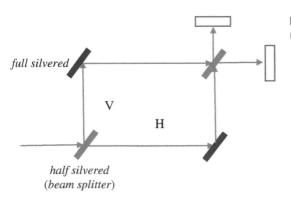

full silvered

V

H

half silvered
(beam splitter)

Figure 8.5 Wave and particle nature of light. (for more details see the color figure in the bins).

of thought and underlying concept, and it is because quantum computers harness those special characteristics that gives them the potential to be an incredibly powerful computational device.

Algebraic representation of a quantum state: A quantum state $|q\rangle$ may be fully described by its state vector [1]. The size of the state vector $|q\rangle$ is equal to the number of orthogonal states that the quantum state could be superimposed in. The values of the state vector $|q\rangle$ are the amplitudes of each orthogonal state. For example, when a qubit is in the state $|q\rangle = \alpha |0\rangle + \beta |1\rangle$ as in Eq. (8.1), the two-element state vector is

$$|q\rangle = \begin{bmatrix} \alpha \\ \beta \end{bmatrix} = \alpha |0\rangle + \beta |1\rangle, \tag{8.3}$$

implying that the first element corresponds to the amplitude of the state $|0\rangle$, while the second element corresponds to the amplitude of the state $|1\rangle$. As another example, the state vector of the equiprobable quantum state of Eq. (8.2) is

$$|q\rangle = \begin{bmatrix} 1/\sqrt{2} \\ 1/\sqrt{2} \end{bmatrix} = \left(1/\sqrt{2} \right) \begin{bmatrix} 1 \\ 1 \end{bmatrix}. \tag{8.4}$$

As expected, when more qubits are used, the system's state vector has more elements in order to accommodate the amplitudes of all legitimate state combinations.

Multi-qubit quantum registers: In a two-qubit register, there are four legitimate states that the composite quantum system can be superimposed in. If the first qubit of the register is in the state $|q_1\rangle = \alpha |0\rangle + \beta |1\rangle$ and the second qubit is in the state $|q_2\rangle = \gamma |0\rangle + \delta |1\rangle$, the state of the system is

$$\begin{aligned} |q\rangle = |q_1\rangle \otimes |q_2\rangle = |q_1 q_2\rangle &= (\alpha |0\rangle + \beta |1\rangle) \otimes (\gamma |0\rangle + \delta |1\rangle) \\ &= \alpha \cdot \gamma |00\rangle + \alpha \cdot \delta |01\rangle + \beta \cdot \gamma |10\rangle + \beta \cdot \delta |11\rangle \\ &= \begin{bmatrix} \alpha\gamma \\ \alpha\delta \\ \beta\gamma \\ \beta\delta \end{bmatrix}, \end{aligned} \tag{8.5}$$

where $\otimes$ is the tensor product operator, and the system's state vector includes the amplitudes of the four quantum states $|00\rangle, |01\rangle, |10\rangle$, and $|11\rangle$. In general, in an n-qubit register, the state vector will have 2^n entries, each corresponding to the amplitude of the respective orthogonal state.

Now let us consider a two-qubit register with the following quantum state:

$$|q\rangle = \sqrt{3}/2 |00\rangle + 1/2 |10\rangle = \begin{bmatrix} \alpha\gamma \\ 0 \\ \beta\gamma \\ 0 \end{bmatrix} = \begin{bmatrix} \sqrt{3}/2 \\ 0 \\ 1/2 \\ 0 \end{bmatrix} \tag{8.6}$$

After a potential measurement of that quantum register, there is a $\left(\sqrt{3}/2\right)^2 = 0.75$ probability of observing the state $|00\rangle$ and a $(1/2)^2 = 0.25$ probability of obtaining the state $|10\rangle$. *It is impossible to observe the states $|01\rangle$ or $|11\rangle$.* We may also observe that it is possible to rewrite its state as

$$|q\rangle = \left(\left(\sqrt{3}/2\right) |0\rangle + (1/2) |1\rangle \right) \otimes |0\rangle = \begin{bmatrix} \sqrt{3}/2 \\ 1/2 \end{bmatrix} \otimes \begin{bmatrix} 1 \\ 0 \end{bmatrix} = |q_1\rangle |q_2\rangle. \tag{8.7}$$

This means that the first qubit is in a superposition (not equiprobable) of its two possible states, while the second qubit is at the state $|q_2\rangle = |0\rangle$. Since the state of the quantum register may be written as a tensor product of the quantum states of the individual qubits, the two qubits $|q_1\rangle$ and $|q_2\rangle$ are *independent* of each other.

Entanglement: When the quantum states of two or more qubits may not be represented separately and independently of each other, the qubits are *entangled* with each other. For example, let us consider the state

$$|q\rangle = \frac{1}{\sqrt{2}}|00\rangle + \frac{1}{\sqrt{2}}|11\rangle = \begin{bmatrix} \frac{1}{\sqrt{2}} \\ 0 \\ 0 \\ \frac{1}{\sqrt{2}} \end{bmatrix} \tag{8.8}$$

This two-qubit register is in an equiprobable superposition of the states $|00\rangle$ and $|01\rangle$. It is impossible to describe the states of the two qubits individually as in Eq. (8.7). Therefore, the two qubits of the quantum register in Eq. (8.8) are entangled. The quantum state in Eq. (8.8) is one of the four *Bell states* [4, 5],

$$\frac{1}{\sqrt{2}}|00\rangle + \frac{1}{\sqrt{2}}|11\rangle, \quad \frac{1}{\sqrt{2}}|00\rangle - \frac{1}{\sqrt{2}}|11\rangle$$
$$\frac{1}{\sqrt{2}}|01\rangle + \frac{1}{\sqrt{2}}|10\rangle, \quad \frac{1}{\sqrt{2}}|01\rangle - \frac{1}{\sqrt{2}}|10\rangle \tag{8.9}$$

which are widely used, since they are the only four quantum states of a two-qubit register that provide an equiprobable entanglement between two qubits.

Partial measurement of a quantum register: In a multi-qubit quantum register, it is possible to observe only a subset of the qubits it consists of. Therefore, when we measure one of the qubits, its quantum state collapses to the observed state, while the quantum state of the rest of the *independent* qubits remains unaltered. However, this is not the case for the rest of the *entangled* qubits, whose state will also be affected by the observation of an entangled qubit.

As an example, let us try to observe only the second qubit of the quantum register in Eq. (8.7). The second qubit has a 100% probability of yielding the observation $|0\rangle$, and therefore this is the state we will obtain. At the same time, the state of the first qubit $|q_1\rangle = \sqrt{3}/2|0\rangle + 1/2|1\rangle$ will remain unaltered, because it is in a superposition of its own independent states.

Let us now try to measure the second qubit of the entangled two-qubit register of Eq. (8.8). There is a $\left(1/\sqrt{2}\right)^2 = 0.5 = 50\%$ chance of observing either the state $|0\rangle$ or the state $|1\rangle$. Let us assume that we observed the state $|0\rangle$. Therefore, the quantum state of the second qubit collapses to $|0\rangle$. Based on Eq. (8.8), we should note that the state of the first qubit also collapses to $|0\rangle$ instantaneously, upon obtaining the measurement output of the second qubit. This occurred because the whole quantum register could be observed either in the state $|00\rangle$ or in the state $|11\rangle$. Since we observed the second qubit in the state $|0\rangle$, the first qubit can only be in the state $|0\rangle$ from this point onward. Entanglement enables a plethora of applications, since it allows instantaneous information exchange between qubits. As will be discussed in the following, the quantum algorithms appropriately manipulate the available qubits in order to finally measure a quantum state, which has a desirable property.

Interpretation of the entanglement: Although the formal definition of the entanglement is straightforward, in practice there is still a lack of full understanding of the physical interpretation of the process. In his effort to explain the phenomenon of entanglement, Prashant has provided some interesting discussions on the analogies between real and quantum worlds in his manuscript *A Study on the Basics of Quantum Computing* [6]. The observation of correlation among various events is an everyday phenomenon. These correlations are well described with the help of the laws of classical physics. He uses the following example: Imagine the scene of a bank robbery. The bank robber is pointing a gun at the terrified teller. By looking at the teller, one can tell whether the gun has gone off or not: if the teller is alive and unharmed, one can be sure the gun has not been fired. If the teller is lying dead of a gunshot wound on the floor, one knows the gun has been fired. This is a simple case of detection. Thus, there is a direct correlation between the state of gun and the state of the teller: "gun fired" means "teller dead." In the event, it is presumed the robber only shoots to kill and he never misses.

In the world of microscopic objects described by quantum mechanics, correlation among events is not so simple. Consider a nucleus that might undergo a radioactive decay in a certain time or it might not. Thus, with respect to decay, the nucleus exists in two possible states only: "decayed" and "not decayed," just as we had two states, "fired" and "not fired" for the gun or "alive" and "dead" for the teller. However, in the quantum mechanical world, it is also possible for the atom to be in a combined state – decayed–not decayed – in which it is neither one nor the other but somewhere in between. This is due to the principle of linear superposition of two quantum mechanical states of the atom, and is not something we normally expect of classical objects like guns or tellers. Further, let us consider a system consisting of two nuclei. Two nuclei may be correlated so that if one has decayed, the other will also have decayed. And if one has not decayed, neither has the other. This is 100% correlation. However, the nuclei may also be correlated so that if one is in the superposition state – decayed–not decayed – the other will also be. Thus, quantum mechanically, we have one more correlation between nuclei than we would expect classically. This kind of quantum "super-correlation" is called *entanglement*.

Entanglement was, in fact, originally called "Verschrankung" (a German word) by Erwin Schrodinger, who was awarded the Nobel Prize in physics for his fundamental contributions to quantum mechanics. Schrodinger was the first to realize the strange character of entanglement. Imagine that it is not the robber but the nucleus that determines whether the gun fires. If the nucleus decays, it sets off a hair trigger that fires the gun. If it does not decay, the gun does not fire. But if the nucleus is in superposition it can be correlated to the gun in a superposition state fired–not fired. However, such a correlation leads to a catastrophic situation: in our bank robbery example, the teller is dead and alive at the same time! Schrodinger was worried about a similar situation where the victim of the quantum entanglement was a cat in a box (Schrodinger's cat: A paradox). For Schrodinger, a cat in a box with a decaying nucleus could trigger the release of lethal chemical. The basic problem is that in the everyday world we are not used to see anything like a dead–alive cat or a dead–alive teller. However, in principle, if quantum mechanics is to be a complete theory describing every level of our experience, such strange states should be possible. Where does the quantum world stop and the classical world begin? Does an interface really exist that separates quantum phenomena from the classical phenomena? And so on. These and allied problems have been described for a long time, and in the process a number of different interpretations of quantum theory have been suggested.

The problem was brought into focus in 1935 by Einstein, Podolsky, and Rosen (EPR), who argued that the strange behavior of entanglement showed that quantum mechanics is an incomplete theory, not a wrong theory. This is widely known as the EPR paradox. The concept of the EPR paradox

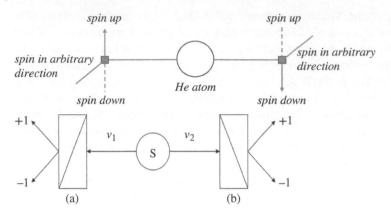

Figure 8.6 (a) Einstein–Podolsky–Rosen (EPR) paradox description using He atom, (b) graphical description of the EPR situation.

can be understood with the help of the following example (Figure 8.6a): consider a helium atom in the ground state. It has two electrons having the following quantum numbers: $n = 1, l = 0, s = 1/2$, $s_z = +1/2$ for one and $s_z = -1/2$ for another. Thus, we have $j = 0$ and 1; but $j_z = (s_z)_1 + (s_z)_2 = 0$. Hence, only the $j = 0$ state is allowed. Thus in a helium atom, two electrons are antiparallel to each other and hence form an entangled pair. The atom is provided sufficient energy (equal to the binding energy of the atom) so that it disintegrates at rest. Consequently, two electrons fly away in the opposite direction. Two electrons are taken apart. With the application of a magnetic field when the spin of one electron is flipped, the spin of other electron is also flipped instantaneously (communication with a speed faster than the speed of light). This is a real phenomenon that Einstein called spooky action at a distance, the mechanism of which cannot, as yet be explained by any theory – it simply must be taken as given, and this was Einstein's objection about the completeness of quantum theory. However, we know that further developments (the Bell inequality and its experimental verification) proved that quantum considerations are correct. Even more amazing is knowledge about the state of spin of another electron without measuring it. Quantum ENTANGLEM`ENT allows qubits that are separated by incredible distances to interact with each other instantaneously (not limited to the speed of light). No matter how large the distance between the correlated particles, they will remain entangled as long as they are isolated. Taken together, quantum superposition and entanglement create an enormously enhanced computing power.

Bell theorem: The critical examination of the paper "Is Quantum Mechanics Complete?" by EPR carried out by John Bell led to the following contradictory conclusion: (i) EPR correlations (usually referred to as quantum entanglement) predicted by quantum mechanics are so strong that one can hardly avoid the conclusion that quantum mechanics should be completed by some supplementary parameters (those so-called hidden variables). (ii) The elaboration of the above result demonstrates that the hidden variables' description in fact contradicts some predictions of quantum mechanics.

In the face of these two perfectly convincing and contradictory results, there is only one way out: ask Nature how it works. Until the end of 1970, there was no experimental result to answer this question. The contradiction discovered by Bell in the EPR paper is so subtle that it appears only in very peculiar situations that had not been investigated, and required designing and building specific experiments.

An EPR situation: Consider a source that emits a pair of photons v1 and v2 traveling in opposite directions (Figure 8.6b). Each photon impinges onto a polarizer, which measures the linear polarization along both of two directions (a and b) determined by the orientation of the corresponding polarizer.

There are two possible outcomes for each measurement: $+1$ and -1. Quantum mechanics allows for the existence of a two-photon state (EPR state) for which the polarization measurements taken separately appear random, but which are strongly correlated. More precisely, denoting $P_+(a)$ and $P(a)$ as the probabilities that the polarization of $\nu1$ along a is found equal to $+$ or $-$, these probabilities are predicted to be equal to 0.5; similarly the probabilities $P_+(b)$ and $P_-(b)$ for photon ν_2 are equal to 0.5 and independent of the orientation b. On the other hand, the joint probability $P_{++}(a)$ for observing $+$ for both the photons is equal to $0.5\ Cos^2(a.b)$. In the case of parallel polarizers $[(a.b) = 0]$, this joint probability is $P_{++}(0) = 0.5$; similarly $P_{--}(0) = 0.5$. For a cross-polarizer $[(a.b) = \pi/2]$, and the joint probability is $P_{-+}(\pi/2) = P_{+-}(\pi/2) = 0$. The results for the two photons of the same pair are thus always identical, both $+$ or $-$; that is, they are completely correlated. Such correlations between events – each of which appears to be random – may arise outside the physics world as well. Consider, for instance, the occurrence of some defined disease (say G), and let us assume that biologists have observed its development in 50% of the population aged 20, and its absence in the remaining half. Now, on investigating a specific pair of (true) twin brothers, a perfect correlation is found between the outcomes: if one brother is affected, the other is also found to be afflicted with the disease; but if one member of the pair has not developed the disease, then the other is also unaffected. In the face of such perfect correlation for twin brothers, the biologists will certainly conclude that the disease has a genetic origin. A simple scenario may be invoked: at the first step of conception of the embryo, a genetic process that is random in nature produced a pair of chromosome sequences, and the one that is responsible for the occurrence or absence of the disease has been duplicated and given to both brothers.

Thus, the two situations – the case of correlation between the polarized states of two photons and the case of twin brothers (a number of such situations can be described) – are exactly analogous. It therefore seems natural to link this correlation between the pairs of photons to some common property analogous to the common genome of the two twin brothers. This common property changes form pair to pair, which accounts for the random character of the single event. This is the basic conclusion drawn by John Bell regarding EPR states. *A natural generalization of the EPR reasoning leads to the conclusion that quantum mechanics is not a complete description of physical reality.* As a matter of fact, the introduction of "some common property" that changes from pair to pair invokes the idea that a complete description of a pair must include "something" in addition to the state vector that is the same for all pairs. This "something" can be called a supplementary parameter or hidden variables. Inclusion of hidden variables enables complete description of the polarized states of two photons, for any set (a, b) of orientations.

Bell inequalities: Bell critically examined the requirement for hidden variables to explain the expected correlation between the two polarized states of photons. It was shown that the expected correlations for the joint measurements of polarized states of photons, as mentioned above, cannot take any set of values, but are subject to certain constraints. More precisely, if we consider four possible sets of orientations – [(a.b), (a.b′), (a′.b), (a′.b′)] – the corresponding correlation coefficients (which measure the amount of correlation) are restricted by Bell inequalities, which states that a given combination of these four coefficients "s" lies between -2 and $+2$ for any reasonable hidden variable theory. Thus, Bell inequalities prescribe a test for the validity of hidden variable theory. However, quantum mechanics predicts the value of s as 2.8; that is, it violates Bell inequalities, and this has been confirmed by experiments. Thus, the hidden variable theories envisaged above are unable to describe the EPR correlation (quantum entanglement) predicted by quantum mechanics. As a matter of fact, quantum mechanical correlations are more difficult to understand than mutual correlations between twin brothers. The Bell inequality is based on the assumption of local hidden variable models. The assumption of locality states that the result of a measurement by a polarizer cannot be directly influenced by the choice of orientation of the other remotely located polarizer. Actually, this is nothing but the consequence of Einstein causality (no signal can move with a speed greater than the speed of light in vacuum). Nevertheless, Bell inequalities apply to wider class of theories than local hidden variable theories. Any theory in which each photon has a "physical reality" localized in space-time that determines the outcome of the corresponding measurement will lead to inequalities that (sometimes) conflict with quantum mechanics. Bell's theorem can thus be rephrased in the following way: some quantum mechanical predictions (EPR correlations-quantum entanglement) cannot be mimicked by any local realistic model in the spirit of Einstein's ideas regarding the theory of hidden variables.

No cloning theorem: The irreversible nature of a quantum measurement is exploited in quantum cryptography [7–9], a field that also exploits the no cloning theorem [10]. According to the no cloning theorem, it is impossible to copy the unknown quantum state of a qubit into the quantum state of another qubit while keeping their states independent of each other at the same time. In other words, it is impossible to make independent copies of qubits without entangling them with each other in the process. The rules of entanglement, the no cloning theorem, and the irreversible nature of measurements allow quantum-based communications to be very promising for sharing private keys between two parties. By exploiting these features in the available quantum key distribution (QKD) protocols, such as the Bennett-Brassard 1984 (BB84) protocol [11], one or both parties become capable of detecting whether an eavesdropper tampered with their communications or not, due to the imperfections that the eavesdropper would have left behind on the measured and retransmitted states, since the eavesdropper would have been unable to simply copy and forward the intercepted qubits. If the two parties determine that an eavesdropper was present during the transmission of the qubits, the whole process is aborted and restarted.

8.2 Quantum Gates and Quantum Computing

Evolution of a quantum state: The state of a quantum register may be changed by applying *unitary operators or gates* to its qubits [1]. Let us first investigate a single-qubit system. One of the most widely used single-qubit unitary operators is the *Hadamard operator H*, which creates equiprobable superpositions of the two states, given that the initial state was either $|0\rangle$ or $|1\rangle$, as encapsulated in

$$H \,|\, 0\rangle = \frac{1}{\sqrt{2}} \begin{bmatrix} 1 & 1 \\ 1 & -1 \end{bmatrix} \begin{bmatrix} 1 \\ 0 \end{bmatrix} = \frac{1}{\sqrt{2}} \begin{bmatrix} 1 \\ 1 \end{bmatrix} \rightarrow \frac{1}{\sqrt{2}} |\, 0\rangle + \frac{1}{\sqrt{2}} |\, 1\rangle = |\, +\,\rangle$$

$$H \,|\, 1\rangle = \frac{1}{\sqrt{2}} \begin{bmatrix} 1 & 1 \\ 1 & -1 \end{bmatrix} \begin{bmatrix} 0 \\ 1 \end{bmatrix} = \frac{1}{\sqrt{2}} \begin{bmatrix} 1 \\ -1 \end{bmatrix} \rightarrow \frac{1}{\sqrt{2}} |\, 0\rangle - \frac{1}{\sqrt{2}} |\, 1\rangle = |\, -\rangle. \tag{8.10}$$

The states $|+\rangle$ and $|-\rangle$ form the orthogonal Hadamard basis, as depicted in Figure 8.1. The matrix representation of the single-qubit Hadamard operator is

$$H = \frac{1}{\sqrt{2}} \begin{bmatrix} 1 & 1 \\ 1 & -1 \end{bmatrix} \tag{8.11}$$

Figure 8.7 Circuit representation of the Hadamard gate H, of the three Pauli gates X, Z, and Y, as well as of the Controlled-NOT (*CNOT*) operation, of the general controlled-U gate and of the Toffoli gate.

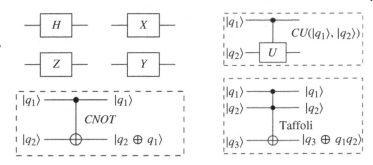

while that of the two-qubit Hadamard operator is

$$H^{\otimes 2} = \frac{1}{2} \begin{bmatrix} 1 & 1 & 1 & 1 \\ 1 & -1 & 1 & -1 \\ 1 & 1 & -1 & -1 \\ 1 & -1 & -1 & 1 \end{bmatrix} \tag{8.12}$$

An n-qubit Hadamard gate has to be employed for creating an equiprobable superposition of all legitimate states at the beginning of most quantum algorithms, which is achieved by applying it to an n-qubit quantum register in the all-zero state $|0\rangle^{\otimes n}$. The circuit representation of the Hadamard gate is shown in Figure 8.7.

The parallel evolution of the state of a quantum register that consists of multiple qubits is referred to as *quantum parallelism*. Quantum parallelism is one of the pivotal features of quantum computing, and is exploited in order to create quantum algorithms that solve problems by requiring, for example, fewer cost function (CF) evaluations than their classical counterparts.

Another popular set of single-qubit quantum gates is represented by the Pauli gates [1, 2]

$$X = \begin{bmatrix} 0 & 1 \\ 1 & 0 \end{bmatrix}, Z = \begin{bmatrix} 1 & 0 \\ 0 & -1 \end{bmatrix}, Y = \begin{bmatrix} 0 & -i \\ i & 0 \end{bmatrix}. \tag{8.13}$$

Explicitly, the X operator is the NOT gate, also known from classical logic circuits, since it swaps the amplitudes of the quantum states of a qubit as in

$$X(a \,|\, 0\rangle + b \,|\, 1\rangle) = \begin{bmatrix} 0 & 1 \\ 1 & 0 \end{bmatrix} \cdot \begin{bmatrix} a \\ b \end{bmatrix} = \begin{bmatrix} b \\ a \end{bmatrix} = b \,|\, 0\rangle + a \,|\, 1\rangle.$$

The Z operator is the gate imposing a *phase shift* by π radians, since it flips the sign of the amplitude of just the state $|1\rangle$, as described in

$$Z(a \,|\, 0\rangle + b \,|\, 1\rangle) = \begin{bmatrix} 1 & 0 \\ 0 & -1 \end{bmatrix} \cdot \begin{bmatrix} a \\ b \end{bmatrix} = \begin{bmatrix} a \\ -b \end{bmatrix} = a \,|\, 0\rangle - b \,|\, 1\rangle.$$

The Y operator may be considered as a combination of the X and Z gates, since it results in

$$Y(a \,|\, 0\rangle + b \,|\, 1\rangle) = \begin{bmatrix} 0 & -i \\ i & 0 \end{bmatrix} \cdot \begin{bmatrix} a \\ b \end{bmatrix} = \left\{ \begin{matrix} -ib \\ ia \end{matrix} \right\} \begin{bmatrix} -ib \\ ia \end{bmatrix}$$

$$= i(-b \,|\, 0\rangle + a \,|\, 1\rangle).$$

The circuit representation of the Pauli gates is also depicted in Figure 8.7. Other popular gates require the use of *control qubits*. For example, the CNOT gate applies the *NOT* operation to the qubit $|q_2\rangle$, only when the qubit $|q_1\rangle$ is in the state $|1\rangle$, as described by

$$CNOT = \begin{bmatrix} 1 & 0 & 0 & 0 \\ 0 & 1 & 0 & 0 \\ 0 & 0 & 0 & 1 \\ 0 & 0 & 1 & 0 \end{bmatrix} \tag{8.14}$$

For example, if the first (control) qubit was in the state $|q_1\rangle = a\,|\,0\rangle + b\,|\,1\rangle$ and the second (target) qubit was in the state $|q_2\rangle = c\,|\,0\rangle + d\,|\,1\rangle$, the *CNOT* gate would result in

$$CNOT\,(|\,q_1\rangle\,|\,q_2\rangle) = CNOT(a \cdot c\,|\,00\rangle + a \cdot d\,|\,01\rangle + b \cdot c\,|\,10\rangle + b \cdot d\,|\,11\rangle)$$

$$\begin{bmatrix} 1 & 0 & 0 & 0 \\ 0 & 1 & 0 & 0 \\ 0 & 0 & 0 & 1 \\ 0 & 0 & 1 & 0 \end{bmatrix} \begin{bmatrix} ac \\ ad \\ bc \\ bd \end{bmatrix}$$

$$= a \cdot c\,|\,00\rangle + a \cdot d\,|\,01\rangle + b \cdot d\,|\,10\rangle + b \cdot c\,|\,11\rangle.$$

We may observe that the amplitudes of the quantum states where the first qubit is equal to $|1\rangle$ have been swapped. In general, the *controlled-U* gate applies a general quantum gate U to a target qubit only when the control qubit is equal to $|1\rangle$, as described by

$$CU = \begin{bmatrix} 1 & 0 & 0 & 0 \\ 0 & 1 & 0 & 0 \\ 0 & 0 & u_{11} & u_{12} \\ 0 & 0 & u_{21} & u_{22} \end{bmatrix} \tag{8.15}$$

where the aforementioned general single-qubit unitary operator U is

$$U = \begin{bmatrix} u_{11} & u_{12} \\ u_{21} & u_{22} \end{bmatrix} \tag{8.16}$$

When the control qubits is equal to $|0\rangle$, the identity gate is applied to the target qubit, as stated in Eq. (8.15). Table 8.1 lists the operation that the *CU* gate would carry out based on the four possible

Table 8.1 Operation of a *CU* gate.

Before: $|q_1\rangle\,|q_2\rangle$	After: $CU\,|\,q_1\rangle\,|\,q_2\rangle$
$|0\rangle\,|\,0\rangle$	$|0\rangle\,|\,0\rangle$
$|0\rangle\,|\,1\rangle$	$|0\rangle\,|\,1\rangle$
$|1\rangle\,|\,0\rangle$	$|1\rangle U\,|\,0\rangle$
$|1\rangle\,|\,1\rangle$	$|1\rangle U\,|\,1\rangle$

quantum states of two qubits, where the first one is the control qubit and the second one is the target qubit. Finally, the Toffoli gate accepts two control qubits and flips the state of the target qubit if and only if both control qubits are in the state $|1\rangle$. The matrix representation of the Toffoli gate is [1]

$$CCNOT = \begin{bmatrix} 1 & 0 & 0 & 0 & 0 & 0 & 0 & 0 \\ 0 & 1 & 0 & 0 & 0 & 0 & 0 & 0 \\ 0 & 0 & 1 & 0 & 0 & 0 & 0 & 0 \\ 0 & 0 & 0 & 1 & 0 & 0 & 0 & 0 \\ 0 & 0 & 0 & 0 & 1 & 0 & 0 & 0 \\ 0 & 0 & 0 & 0 & 0 & 1 & 0 & 0 \\ 0 & 0 & 0 & 0 & 0 & 0 & 0 & 1 \\ 0 & 0 & 0 & 0 & 0 & 0 & 1 & 0 \end{bmatrix}. \tag{8.17}$$

The circuit representation of the controlled gates is also depicted in Figure 8.7. Table 8.2 describes the initial and resultant states of a three-qubit register when the Toffoli gate is applied to it, where the first two qubits are the control qubits and the last one is the target qubit.

Quantum teleportation and quantum theory of information: "Information is physical and any processing of information is always performed by physical means" is an innocent-sounding statement, but its consequences are anything but trivial. In the last few years, there has been an explosion of theoretical and experimental innovations leading to the creation of a fundamental new discipline: a *quantum theory of information.* Quantum physics allows the construction of qualitatively new types of logic gates, absolutely secure cryptosystems (systems that combine communications and cryptography), the cramming of two bits of information into one physical bit, and has redefined the concept of "teleportation."

Until recently, teleportation was not taken seriously by scientists. Usually, teleportation is the name given by science fiction writers to describe an object or person disintegrating in one place while a perfect replica appears somewhere else. Normally this is done by scanning the object in such a way as to extract all the information from it; then this information is transmitted to the receiving location and used to construct the replica, not necessarily from the actual material of the original, but probably from atoms of the same kinds, arranged in exactly the same pattern

Table 8.2 Operational of a Toffoli gate.

Before: $|q_1\rangle\,|q_2\rangle\,|q_3\rangle$	After: $CCNOT\,|q_1\rangle\,|q_2\rangle\,|q_3\rangle$
$|0\rangle\,|0\rangle\,|0\rangle$	$|0\rangle\,|0\rangle\,|0\rangle$
$|0\rangle\,|0\rangle\,|1\rangle$	$|0\rangle\,|0\rangle\,|1\rangle$
$|0\rangle\,|1\rangle\,|0\rangle$	$|0\rangle\,|1\rangle\,|0\rangle$
$|0\rangle\,|1\rangle\,|1\rangle$	$|0\rangle\,|1\rangle\,|1\rangle$
$|1\rangle\,|0\rangle\,|0\rangle$	$|1\rangle\,|0\rangle\,|0\rangle$
$|1\rangle\,|0\rangle\,|1\rangle$	$|1\rangle\,|0\rangle\,|1\rangle$
$|1\rangle\,|1\rangle\,|0\rangle$	$|1\rangle\,|1\rangle\,|1\rangle$
$|1\rangle\,|1\rangle\,|1\rangle$	$|1\rangle\,|1\rangle\,|0\rangle$

as the original. A teleportation machine would be like a fax machine, except that it would work on three-dimensional objects as well as documents, it would produce an exact copy rather an approximate facsimile, and it would destroy the original in the process of scanning it.

In classical physics, an object can be teleported, in principle by performing a measurement to completely characterize the properties of the object; that information can then be sent to another location, and this object reconstructed. Moreover, classical information theory agrees with everyday intuition: if a message is to be sent using an object that can be put into one of N distinguishable states, the maximum number of different messages that can be sent is N. For example, a single photon can have only two distinguishable polarization states: left handed and right handed. Thus, a single photon cannot transmit more than two distinguishable messages, that is, one bit of information. The basic question is: is it possible to provide a complete reconstruction of the original object? The answer is no. All the physical systems are ultimately quantum mechanical, and quantum mechanics tells us that it is impossible to completely determine the state of an unknown quantum system, making it impossible to use the classical measurement procedure to move a quantum system from one location to another. This is due to the Heisenberg uncertainty principle, which states that the more accurately an object is scanned, the more it is disturbed by the scanning process, until one reaches a point where the object's original state has been completely disrupted, still without having extracted enough information to make a perfect replica. This sounds like a solid argument against teleportation: if one cannot extract enough information from an object to make a perfect copy, it would be seen that a perfect copy cannot be made.

Charles H. Bennet with his group and *Stephen Wiesner* have suggested a remarkable procedure for teleporting quantum states using EPR states (entangled states). Quantum teleportation may be described abstractly in terms of two particles, A and B. A has in its possession an unknown state $|q\rangle$ represented as $|q\rangle = \alpha |0\rangle + \beta |1\rangle$.

This is a single quantum bit (qubit): a two-level quantum system. The aim of teleportation is to transport the state $|q\rangle$ from A to B. This is achieved by employing entangled states. A and B each posses one qubit of the following two-qubit entangled state: $|q\rangle(|0\rangle_A|0\rangle_B) + |1\rangle_A|1\rangle_B)$. The above state can be rewritten in the Bell basis $(|00\rangle \pm |11\rangle))$, $(|01\rangle \pm |10\rangle)$ for the first two qubits and as a conditional unitary transformation of the state $|q\rangle$ for the last one, that is

$$(|00\rangle \pm |11\rangle) |q\rangle + (|00\rangle - |11\rangle)\sigma_z |q\rangle + (|01\rangle + |10\rangle)\sigma_x |q\rangle$$
$$+ (|01\rangle - |10\rangle)(-i\sigma_y |q\rangle)$$

where σ_x, σ_y, σ_z are Pauli matrices in the $|0\rangle$, $|1\rangle$ basis. A measurement is preformed on A's qubits in the Bell basis. Depending on the outcomes of these measurements, B's respective states are $|q\rangle$, $\sigma_z |q\rangle$, $\sigma_x |q\rangle$, and $-i\sigma_y |q\rangle$ A sends the outcome of its measurement to B, who can then recover the original state $|q\rangle$ by applying the appropriate unitary transformation I, σ_z, σ_x or $i\sigma_y$ depending on A's measurement outcome. It may be noted that quantum state transmission has not been accomplished faster than light because B must wait for A's measurement result to arrive before he can recover the quantum state. The above process is presented in Figure 8.8.

8.2.1 Quantum Circuits

We have already met a few simple quantum circuits. Let us look in a little more detail at the elements of a quantum circuit. A simple quantum circuit containing three quantum gates is shown in the following figure.

Figure 8.8 Quantum teleportation using entanglement.

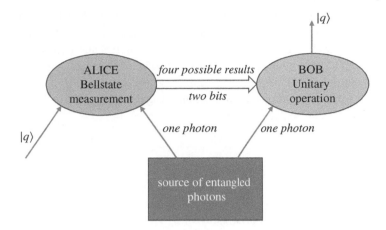

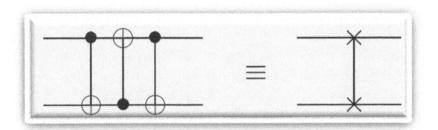

The circuit is to be read from left to right. Each line in the circuit represents a "wire" in the quantum circuit. This wire does not necessarily correspond to a physical wire; it may correspond instead to the passage of time, or perhaps to a physical particle such as a photon – a particle of light – moving from one location to another through space. It is conventional to assume that the state input to the circuit is a computational basis state, usually the state consisting of all $|0\rangle$s. This rule is broken frequently in the literature on quantum computation and quantum information, but it is considered polite to inform the reader when this is the case.

The circuit described in the following accomplishes a simple but useful task: it swaps the states of the two qubits. To see that this circuit accomplishes the swap operation, note that the sequence of gates has the following sequence of effects on a computational basis state $|a, b\rangle$:

$$
\begin{aligned}
|a,b\rangle &\to |a, a \oplus b\rangle \\
&\to |a \oplus (a \oplus b), a \oplus b\rangle = |b, a \oplus b\rangle \\
&\to |b, (a \oplus b) \oplus b\rangle = |b, a\rangle,
\end{aligned}
\tag{8.18}
$$

where all additions are done modulo 2. The effect of the circuit, therefore, is to interchange the state of the two qubits. An equivalent schematic symbol notation for this circuit is as follows:

As we proceed, we will introduce new quantum gates as needed. It is convenient to introduce another convention about quantum circuits at this point. This convention is illustrated as follows:

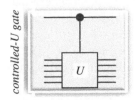

controlled-U gate

Suppose U is any unitary matrix acting on some number n of qubits, so that U can be regarded as a quantum gate on those qubits. Then we can define a controlled-U gate that is a natural extension of the controlled gate. Such a gate has a single control qubit, indicated by the line with the black dot, and n target qubits, indicated by the boxed U. If the control qubit is set to 0, then nothing happens to the target qubits. If the control qubit is set to 1, then the gate U is applied to the target qubits. The prototypical example of the controlled-U gate is the *CNOT* gate, which is a controlled-U gate with U = X, represented as follows:

two different representations
for the controlled-NOT

Another important operation is measurement, which we represent by a "meter" symbol:

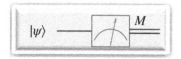

quantum circuit symbol for measurement

As previously described, this operation converts a single-qubit state $|q\rangle = \alpha|0\rangle + \beta|1\rangle$ into a probabilistic classical bit M (distinguished from a qubit by drawing it as a double-line wire), which is 0 with probability $|\alpha|^2$, or 1 with probability $|\beta|^2$. We shall find quantum circuits useful as models of all quantum processes, including but not limited to computation, communication, and even quantum noise. Several simple examples illustrate this below.

Qubit copying circuit: The gate is useful for demonstrating a particularly fundamental property of quantum information. Consider the task of *copying a classical bit*. This may be done using a classical gate, which takes in the bit to copy (in some unknown state x) and a "scratchpad" bit initialized to zero, as illustrated in following figure:

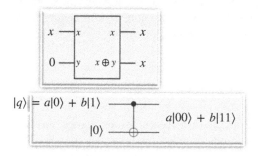

The output is two bits, both of which are in the same state x. Now, suppose we try to copy a qubit in the unknown state $|q\rangle = a|0\rangle + b|1\rangle$ in the same manner by using a gate. The input state of the two qubits may be written as $[a|0\rangle + b|1\rangle]|0\rangle = a|00\rangle + b|10\rangle$. The function of *CNOT* is to negate the second qubit when the first qubit is 1, and thus the output is simply $a|00\rangle + b|11\rangle$. Have we successfully copied $|q\rangle$? That is, have we created the state $|q\rangle|q\rangle$? In the case where $|q\rangle = |0\rangle$ or $|q\rangle = |1\rangle$, that is indeed what this circuit does: it is possible to use quantum circuits to

copy classical information encoded as a $|0\rangle$ or a $|1\rangle$. However, for a general state $|q\rangle$ we see that $|q\rangle$
$|q\rangle = a^2|00\rangle + ab|01\rangle + ab|10\rangle + b^2|11\rangle$.

Comparing with $a|00\rangle + b|11\rangle$, we see that unless $ab = 0$, the "copying circuit" above does not copy the quantum state input. In fact, it turns out to be impossible to make a copy of an unknown quantum state. This property – that qubits cannot be copied, which we already discussed earlier, and referred to as the no cloning theorem – is one of the chief differences between quantum and classical information.

There is another way of looking at the failure of the above circuit, based on the intuition that a qubit somehow contains "hidden" information not directly accessible to measurement. Consider what happens when we measure one of the qubits of the state $a|00\rangle + b|11\rangle$. As previously described, we obtain either 0 or 1 with probabilities $|a|^2$ and $|b|^2$. However, once a qubit is measured, the state of the other qubit is completely determined, and no additional information can be gained about a and b. In this sense, the extra hidden information carried in the original qubit $|q\rangle$ was lost in the first measurement, and cannot be regained. If, however, the qubit had been copied, then the state of the other qubit should still contain some of that hidden information. Therefore, a copy cannot have been created.

Bell states: Let us consider the slightly more complicated circuit shown in the following figure:

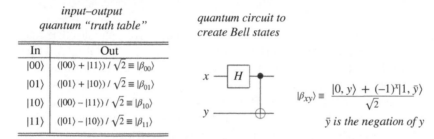

In	Out
$|00\rangle$	$(|00\rangle + |11\rangle)/\sqrt{2} \equiv |\beta_{00}\rangle$
$|01\rangle$	$(|01\rangle + |10\rangle)/\sqrt{2} \equiv |\beta_{01}\rangle$
$|10\rangle$	$(|00\rangle - |11\rangle)/\sqrt{2} \equiv |\beta_{10}\rangle$
$|11\rangle$	$(|01\rangle - |10\rangle)/\sqrt{2} \equiv |\beta_{11}\rangle$

input–output quantum "truth table"

quantum circuit to create Bell states

$$|\beta_{xy}\rangle \equiv \frac{|0, y\rangle + (-1)^x|1, \bar{y}\rangle}{\sqrt{2}}$$

$\bar{y}$ is the negation of y

It has a Hadamard gate followed by a *CNOT*, and transforms the four computational basis states according to the given table. As an explicit example, the Hadamard gate takes the input $|00\rangle$ to $(|0\rangle + |1\rangle)|0\rangle/\sqrt{2}$ and then the gives the output state $(|00\rangle + |11\rangle)/\sqrt{2}$. Note how this works: first, the Hadamard transform puts the top qubit in a superposition; this then acts as a control input to the *CNOT*, and the target gets inverted only when the control is 1. The output states, as we already discussed earlier, are known as the Bell states, or sometimes the EPR states or EPR pairs, after some of the people – Bell, and Einstein, Podolsky, and Rosen – who first pointed out the strange properties of states like these. The mnemonic notation $|\beta_{00}\rangle$, $|\beta_{01}\rangle$, $|\beta_{10}\rangle$, $|\beta_{11}\rangle$ are represented in the above figure.

Quantum teleportation: We will now revisit the problem of teleportation and apply the techniques of the last few pages to further elaborate the formal presentation of the process. As we mentioned earlier, quantum teleportation is a technique for moving quantum states around even in the absence of a quantum communications channel linking the sender of the quantum state to the recipient. Let us resume our description of how quantum teleportation works by adding a bit more of the narrative. Alice and Bob met long ago but now live far apart. While together, they generated an EPR pair, each taking one qubit of the EPR pair when they separated. Many years later, Bob is in hiding, and Alice's mission, should she choose to accept it, is to deliver a qubit $|q\rangle$ to Bob. She does not know the state of the qubit, and moreover can only send classical information to Bob. Should Alice accept the mission? Intuitively, things look pretty bad for Alice. She does not know the state $|q\rangle$ of the qubit she has to send to Bob, and the laws of quantum mechanics prevent her from determining the state when she only has a single copy of $|q\rangle$ in her possession. What is worse, even if she did know the state $|q\rangle$, describing it precisely takes an infinite amount of classical information since $|q\rangle$ takes values in a continuous space. So even if she did know $|q\rangle$, it would take forever for Alice to describe the state to Bob. It is not looking good for Alice. Fortunately for Alice, quantum teleportation is a way of utilizing the entangled EPR pair in order to send $|q\rangle$ to Bob, with only a small overhead of classical communication. In summary, the steps of the solution are as follows: Alice interacts the qubit $|q\rangle$ with her half of the EPR pair, and then measures the two qubits in her possession, obtaining one of four possible classical results, 00, 01, 10, and 11. She sends this information to Bob. Depending on Alice's classical message, Bob performs one of four operations on his half of the EPR pair. Amazingly, by doing this he can recover the original state $|q\rangle$! The quantum circuit shown in the following figure gives a more precise description of quantum teleportation:

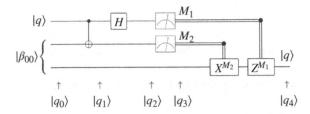

The state to be teleported is $|q\rangle = \alpha|0\rangle + \beta|1\rangle$, where α and β are unknown amplitudes. The state input into the circuit $|q_0\rangle$ is $|q_0\rangle = |q\rangle|\beta_{00}\rangle = [\alpha|0\rangle(|00\rangle + |11\rangle) + \beta|1\rangle(|00\rangle + |11\rangle)]/\sqrt{2}$, where we use the convention that the first two qubits (on the left) belong to Alice, and the third qubit to Bob. As we explained previously, Alice's second qubit and Bob's qubit start out in an EPR state. Alice sends her qubits through a *CNOT* gate, obtaining $|q_1\rangle = [\alpha|0\rangle(|00\rangle + |11\rangle) + \beta|1\rangle(|10\rangle + |01\rangle)]/\sqrt{2}$. She then sends the first qubit through a Hadamard gate, obtaining $|q_2\rangle = [\alpha(|0\rangle + |1\rangle)(|00\rangle + |11\rangle) + \beta(|0\rangle - |1\rangle)(|10\rangle + |01\rangle)]/2$. This state may be rewritten in the following way, simply by regrouping terms:

$$|q_2\rangle = [|00\rangle(\alpha|0\rangle + \beta|1\rangle) + |01\rangle(\alpha|1\rangle + \beta|0\rangle) + |10\rangle(\alpha|0\rangle - \beta|1\rangle) + |11\rangle(\alpha|1\rangle - \beta|0\rangle)]$$

This expression naturally breaks down into four terms. The first term has Alice's qubits in the state $|00\rangle$, and Bob's qubit in the state $\alpha|0\rangle + \beta|1\rangle$, which is the original state $|q\rangle$. If Alice performs a measurement and obtains the result 00, then Bob's system will be in the state $|q\rangle$. Similarly, from the previous expression, we can read off Bob's post-measurement state, given the result of Alice's measurement:

$$
\begin{aligned}
00 &\mapsto |q_3(00)\rangle \equiv [\alpha|0\rangle + \beta|1\rangle] \\
01 &\mapsto |q_3(01)\rangle \equiv [\alpha|1\rangle + \beta|0\rangle] \\
10 &\mapsto |q_3(10)\rangle \equiv [\alpha|0\rangle + \beta|1\rangle] \\
11 &\mapsto |q_3(11)\rangle \equiv [\alpha|1\rangle + \beta|0\rangle].
\end{aligned}
\tag{8.19}
$$

Depending on Alice's measurement outcome, Bob's qubit will end up in one of these four possible states. Of course, to know which state it is in, Bob must be told the result of Alice's measurement; it is this fact that prevents teleportation from being used to transmit information faster than light. Once Bob has learned the measurement outcome, Bob can "fix up" his state, recovering $|q\rangle$, by applying the appropriate quantum gate (see the previous discussion and Figure 8.8). For example, in the case where the measurement yields 00, Bob does not need to do anything. If the measurement is 01, then Bob can fix up his state by applying the X gate. If the measurement is 10, then Bob can fix up his state by applying the Z gate. If the measurement is 11, then Bob can fix up his state by applying first an X and then a Z gate. Summing up, Bob needs to apply the transformation $Z^{M1} X^{M2}$ (note how time goes from left to right in the circuit diagrams, but in matrix products terms on the right occur first) to his qubit, and he will recover the state $|q\rangle$.

There are many interesting features of teleportation, and for now we content ourselves with commenting on a couple of aspects. First, does not teleportation allow one to transmit quantum states faster than light? This would be rather peculiar, because the theory of relativity implies that faster than light information transfer could be used to send information backward in time.

Fortunately, quantum teleportation does not enable faster than light communication, because to complete the teleportation Alice must transmit her measurement result to Bob over a classical communication channel. Without this classical communication, teleportation does not convey any information at all. The classical channel is limited by the speed of light, so it follows that quantum teleportation cannot be accomplished faster than the speed of light, resolving the apparent paradox.

A second puzzle about teleportation is that it appears to create a copy of the quantum state being teleported, in apparent violation of the no cloning theorem discussed earlier. This violation is only illusory since after the teleportation process only the target qubit is left in the state $|q\rangle$, and the original data qubit ends up in one of the computational basis states $|0\rangle$ or $|1\rangle$, depending upon the measurement result on the first qubit. What can we learn from quantum teleportation? Quite a lot! It is much more than just a neat trick one can play with quantum states. Quantum teleportation emphasizes the interchangeability of different resources in quantum mechanics, showing that one shared EPR pair together with two classical bits of communication is a resource that is at least the equal to one qubit of communication. Quantum computation and quantum information have revealed a plethora of methods for interchanging resources, many built upon quantum teleportation. In particular, later in the book, we will explain how teleportation can be used to build quantum gates that are resistant to the effects of noise, and that teleportation is intimately connected with the properties of quantum error-correcting codes. Despite these connections with other subjects, it is fair to say that we are only beginning to understand why it is that quantum teleportation is possible in quantum mechanics; in later chapters, we endeavor to explain some of the insights that make such an understanding possible.

8.2.2 Quantum Algorithms

What class of computations can be performed using quantum circuits? How does that class compare with the computations that can be performed using classical logical circuits? Can we find a task that a quantum computer may perform better than a classical computer? In this section, we initially investigate these questions, explaining how to perform classical computations on quantum computers, giving some examples of problems for which quantum computers offer an advantage over classical computers, and summarizing the known quantum algorithms. This discussion will continue in Chapter 10 with additional details.

Quantum parallelism: This is a fundamental feature of many quantum algorithms. Heuristically, and at the risk of oversimplifying, quantum parallelism allows quantum computers to evaluate a function $f(x)$ for many different values of x simultaneously. In this section, we explain how quantum parallelism works, and some of its limitations.

Suppose $f(x)$: $\{0, 1\} \rightarrow \{0, 1\}$ is a function with a one-bit domain and range. A convenient way of computing this function on a quantum computer is to consider a two-qubit quantum computer that starts in the state $|x, y\rangle$. With an appropriate sequence of logic gates, it is possible to transform this state into $|x, y \oplus f(x)\rangle$, where $\oplus$ indicates addition modulo 2; the first register is called the "data" register, and the second register the "target" register. We give the transformation defined by the map $|x, y\rangle \rightarrow |x, y \oplus f(x)\rangle$ a name, U_f, and note that it is easily shown to be unitary. If $y = 0$, then the final state of the second qubit is just the value $f(x)$. (It can be shown that given a classical circuit for computing f, there is a quantum circuit of comparable efficiency that computes the transformation U_f on a quantum computer [1]. For our purposes, it can be considered to be a black box.) Consider the circuit shown in the figure, which applies U_f to an input not in the computational basis.

Instead, the data register is prepared in the superposition $(|0\rangle + |1\rangle)/\sqrt{2}$, which can be created with a Hadamard gate acting on $|0\rangle$. Then we apply U_f, resulting in the state $(|0, f(0)\rangle + |1, f(1)\rangle)/\sqrt{2}$. This is a remarkable state! The different terms contain information about both $f(0)$ and $f(1)$; it is almost as if we have evaluated $f(x)$ for two values of x simultaneously, a feature known as *quantum parallelism*. Unlike classical parallelism, where multiple circuits each built to compute $f(x)$ are executed simultaneously, here a single $f(x)$ circuit is employed to evaluate the function for multiple values of x simultaneously, by exploiting the ability of a quantum computer to be in superpositions of different states.

This procedure can easily be generalized to functions on an arbitrary number of bits, by using a general operation known as the Hadamard transform, or sometimes the Walsh–Hadamard transform. This operation is just n Hadamard gates acting in parallel on n qubits. For example,

$$\boxed{\begin{array}{c} -\boxed{H}- \\ -\boxed{H}- \end{array}}$$

is the case n = 2 with qubits initially prepared as $|0\rangle$, which gives

$$\left(\frac{|0\rangle + |1\rangle}{\sqrt{2}}\right)\left(\frac{|0\rangle + |1\rangle}{\sqrt{2}}\right) = \frac{|00\rangle + |01\rangle + |10\rangle + |11\rangle}{2}$$

as output. We write $H^{\otimes 2}$ to denote the parallel action of two Hadamard gates, and read "$\otimes$" as "tensor." More generally, the result of performing the Hadamard transform on n qubits initially in the all $|0\rangle$ state is

$$\frac{1}{\sqrt{2^n}}\sum_x |x\rangle \qquad (8.20)$$

where the sum is over all possible values of x, and we write $H^{\otimes n}$ to denote this action. That is, the Hadamard transform produces an equal superposition of all computational basis states. Moreover, it does this extremely efficiently, producing a superposition of 2^n states using just n gates. Quantum parallel evaluation of a function with an n-bit input x and 1-bit output, $f(x)$, can thus be performed in the following manner. Prepare the $n + 1$ qubit state $|0\rangle^{\otimes n}|0\rangle$, and then apply the Hadamard transform to the first n qubits, followed by the quantum circuit implementing U_f. This produces the state

$$\frac{1}{\sqrt{2^n}}\sum_x |x\rangle|f(x)\rangle \tag{8.21}$$

In some sense, quantum parallelism enables all possible values of the function f to be evaluated simultaneously, even though we apparently evaluated f only once. However, this parallelism is not immediately useful. In our single-qubit example, measurement of the state gives only either $|0, f(0)\rangle$ or $|1, f(1)\rangle$! Similarly, in the general case, measurement of the state $\sum_x |x, f(x)\rangle$ would give only $f(x)$ for a single value of x. Of course, a classical computer can do this easily! Quantum computation requires something more than just quantum parallelism to be useful; it requires the ability to extract information about more than one value of f(x) from superposition states like $\sum_x |x, f(x)\rangle$. Over the next two sections, we investigate examples of how this may be done.

Deutsch's algorithm: A simple modification of the U_f circuit demonstrates how quantum circuits can outperform classical ones by implementing Deutsch's algorithm (we actually present a simplified and improved version of the original algorithm). Deutsch's algorithm combines quantum parallelism with a property of quantum mechanics known as *interference*. As before, let us use the Hadamard gate to prepare the first qubit as the superposition $(|0\rangle + |1\rangle)/\sqrt{2}$, but now let us prepare the second qubit y as the superposition $(|0\rangle - |1\rangle)/\sqrt{2}$, using a Hadamard gate applied to the state $|1\rangle$. Let us follow the states along to see what happens in this circuit, shown in following figure:

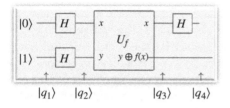

The input state $|q_0\rangle = |01\rangle$ is sent through two Hadamard gates to give

$$|q_1\rangle = \left[\frac{|0\rangle + |1\rangle}{\sqrt{2}}\right]\left[\frac{|0\rangle - |1\rangle}{\sqrt{2}}\right] \tag{8.22}$$

A little thought shows that if we apply U_f to the state $|x\rangle(|0\rangle - |1\rangle)/\sqrt{2}$, then we obtain the state $(-1)^{f(x)}|x\rangle(|0\rangle - |1\rangle)/\sqrt{2}$. Applying U_f to $|q_1\rangle$ therefore leaves us with one of two possibilities:

$$|q_2\rangle = \begin{cases} \pm\left[\dfrac{|0\rangle + |1\rangle}{\sqrt{2}}\right]\left[\dfrac{|0\rangle - |1\rangle}{\sqrt{2}}\right] & \text{if } f(0) = f(1) \\[4mm] \pm\left[\dfrac{|0\rangle - |1\rangle}{\sqrt{2}}\right]\left[\dfrac{|0\rangle - |1\rangle}{\sqrt{2}}\right] & \text{if } f(0) \neq f(1) \end{cases} \tag{8.23}$$

The final Hadamard gate on the first qubit thus gives us

$$|q_3\rangle = \begin{cases} \pm|0\rangle\left[\dfrac{|0\rangle - |1\rangle}{\sqrt{2}}\right] & \text{if } f(0) = f(1) \\[4mm] \pm|1\rangle\left[\dfrac{|0\rangle - |1\rangle}{\sqrt{2}}\right] & \text{if } f(0) \neq f(1) \end{cases} \tag{8.24}$$

Recalling that $f(0) \oplus f(1)$ is 0 if $f(0) = f(1)$ and 1 otherwise, we have

$$|q_3\rangle = \left\{ \pm \mid f(0) \oplus f(1)\rangle \left[\frac{|0\rangle - |1\rangle}{\sqrt{2}} \right] \right. \tag{8.25}$$

so by measuring the first qubit we may determine $f(0) \oplus f(1)$. This is very interesting indeed: the quantum circuit has given us the ability to determine a global property of $f(x)$, namely, $f(0) \oplus f(1)$, using only one evaluation of $f(x)$! This is faster than is possible with a classical apparatus, which would require at least two evaluations. This example highlights the difference between quantum parallelism and classical randomized algorithms. Naively, one might think that the state $|0\rangle|f(0)\rangle + |1\rangle|f(1)\rangle$ corresponds rather closely to a probabilistic classical computer that evaluates $f(0)$ with probability one-half, or $f(1)$ with probability one-half. The difference is that in a classical computer these two alternatives forever exclude one another; in a quantum computer, it is possible for the two alternatives to *interfere* with one another to yield some global property of the function f, by using something like the Hadamard gate to recombine the different alternatives, as was done in Deutsch's algorithm. The essence of the design of many quantum algorithms is that a clever choice of function and final transformation allows efficient determination of useful global information about the function – information that cannot be attained quickly on a classical computer.

The Deutsch–Jozsa algorithm: Deutsch's algorithm is a simple case of a more general quantum algorithm, which we shall refer to as the Deutsch–Jozsa algorithm. The application, known as Deutsch's problem, may be described as the following game.

Alice, in Amsterdam, selects a number x from 0 to $2n - 1$, and mails it in a letter to Bob, in Boston. Bob calculates some function $f(x)$ and replies with the result, which is either 0 or 1. Now, Bob has promised to use a function f that is of one of two kinds: either $f(x)$ is constant for all values of x, or else $f(x)$ is balanced, that is, equal to 1 for exactly half of all the possible x, and 0 for the other half. Alice's goal is to determine with certainty whether Bob has chosen a constant or a balanced function, corresponding with him as little as possible. How fast can she succeed?

In the classical case, Alice may only send Bob one value of x in each letter. At worst, Alice will need to query Bob at least $2^n/2 + 1$ times, since she may receive $2^n/2$ 0 s before finally getting a 1, telling her that Bob's function is balanced. The best deterministic classical algorithm she can use therefore requires $2^n/2 + 1$ queries. Note that in each letter, Alice sends Bob n bits of information. Furthermore, in this example, physical distance is being used to artificially elevate the cost of calculating $f(x)$, but this is not needed in the general problem, where $f(x)$ may be inherently difficult to calculate. If Bob and Alice were able to exchange qubits, instead of just classical bits, and if Bob agreed to calculate $f(x)$ using a unitary transform U_f, then Alice could achieve her goal in just one correspondence with Bob, using the following algorithm.

By analogy with Deutsch's algorithm, Alice has an n-qubit register to store her query in, and a single-qubit register that she will give to Bob, to store the answer in. She begins by preparing both her query and answer registers in a superposition state. Bob will evaluate $f(x)$ using quantum parallelism and leave the result in the answer register. Alice then interferes states in the superposition using a Hadamard transform on the query register, and finishes by performing a suitable measurement to determine whether f was constant or balanced. The specific steps of the algorithm are depicted in the following figure:

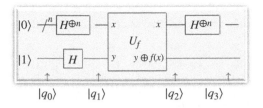

Let us follow the states through this circuit. The input state $|q_0\rangle = |0\rangle^{\otimes n}|1\rangle$ is similar to that of the previous case, but here the query register describes the state of n qubits all prepared in the $|0\rangle$ state. After the Hadamard transform on the query register and the Hadamard gate on the answer register, we have

$$|q_1\rangle = \sum_{x\in\{0,1\}^n} \frac{|x\rangle}{\sqrt{2^n}} \left[\frac{|0\rangle - |1\rangle}{\sqrt{2}}\right] \tag{8.26}$$

The query register is now a superposition of all values, and the answer register is in an evenly weighted superposition of 0 and 1. Next, the function f is evaluated (by Bob) using U_f: $|x, y\rangle \rightarrow |x, y \oplus f(x)\rangle$, giving

$$|q_2\rangle = \sum_{x} \frac{(-1)^{f(x)}|x\rangle}{\sqrt{2^n}} \left[\frac{|0\rangle - |1\rangle}{\sqrt{2}}\right] \tag{8.27}$$

Alice now has a set of qubits in which the result of Bob's function evaluation is stored in the amplitude of the qubit superposition state. She now interferes terms in the superposition using a Hadamard transform on the query register. To determine the result of the Hadamard transform, it helps to first calculate the effect of the Hadamard transform on a state $|x\rangle$. By checking the cases x = 0 and x = 1 separately, we see that for a single qubit $H|x\rangle = \sum_z(-1)^{xz}|z\rangle/\sqrt{2}$. Thus

$$H^{\otimes n}|x_1,...,x_n\rangle = \frac{\sum_{z_1,...,z_n}(-1)^{x_1 z_1 + ... + x_n z_n}|z_1,...,z_n\rangle}{\sqrt{2^n}} \tag{8.28}$$

This can be further simplify as

$$H^{\otimes n}|x\rangle = \frac{\sum_z(-1)^{xz}|z\rangle}{\sqrt{2^n}} \tag{8.29}$$

where $x \cdot z$ is the bitwise inner product of x and z, modulo 2. Using this equation and Eq. (8.27), we can now evaluate $|q_3\rangle$,

$$|q_3\rangle = \sum_z\sum_x \frac{(-1)^{xz + f(x)}|z\rangle}{2^n} \left[\frac{|0\rangle - |1\rangle}{\sqrt{2}}\right] \tag{8.30}$$

Alice now observes the query register. Note that the amplitude for the state $|0\rangle^{\otimes n}$ is $\sum_x(-1)^{f(x)}/2^n$. Let us look at the two possible cases, f constant and f balanced, to determine what happens. In the case where f is constant, the amplitude for $|0\rangle^{\otimes n}$ is +1 or −1, depending on the constant value $f(x)$ takes. Because $|q_3\rangle$ is of unit length, it follows that all the other amplitudes must be zero, and an observation will yield 0s for all qubits in the query register. If f is balanced, then the positive and negative contributions to the amplitude for $|0\rangle^{\otimes n}$ cancel, leaving an amplitude of zero, and a measurement must yield a result other than 0 on at least one qubit in the query register. Summarizing, if Alice measures all 0s, then the function is constant; otherwise the function is balanced. The Deutsch–Jozsa algorithm is summarized as follows:

Algorithm: Deutsch–Jozsa

Inputs: (1) A black box U_f which performs the transformation $|x\rangle|y\rangle \rightarrow |x\rangle|y \oplus f(x)\rangle$, for $x \in \{0, \ldots, 2^n - 1\}$ and $f(x) \in \{0, 1\}$. It is promised that $f(x)$ is either *constant* for all values of x, or else $f(x)$ is *balanced*, that is, equal to 1 for exactly half of all the possible x, and 0 for the other half.

Outputs: 0 if and only if f is constant.

Runtime: One evaluation of U_f. Always succeeds.

Procedure:

1. $|0\rangle^{\otimes n}|1\rangle$ initialize state

2. $\rightarrow \dfrac{1}{\sqrt{2^n}} \displaystyle\sum_{x=0}^{2^n-1} |x\rangle \left[\dfrac{|0\rangle - |1\rangle}{\sqrt{2}}\right]$ create superposition using Hadamard gates

3. $\rightarrow \displaystyle\sum_x (-1)^{f(x)}|x\rangle \left[\dfrac{|0\rangle - |1\rangle}{\sqrt{2}}\right]$ calculate function f using U_f

4. $\rightarrow \displaystyle\sum_z \sum_x \dfrac{(-1)^{x \cdot z + f(x)}|z\rangle}{\sqrt{2^n}} \left[\dfrac{|0\rangle - |1\rangle}{\sqrt{2}}\right]$ perform Hadamard transform

5. $\rightarrow z$ measure to obtain final output z

8.3 Quantum Fourier Transform (QFT)

The QFT is a *quantum* implementation of the discrete Fourier transform. In this section, we will present a quantum algorithm for computing the discrete Fourier transform that is *exponentially faster* than the famous fast Fourier transform (FFT) of classical computers. However, this algorithm is an example of the tension between exponentially faster quantum algorithms and the problems of measurement. Although we can carry out the QFT algorithm to transform the n–qubit state vector $|\alpha\rangle = \alpha_0|0\rangle + \alpha_1|1\rangle + \cdots + \alpha_n|n\rangle$ to its Fourier transform $|\beta\rangle = \beta_0|0\rangle + \beta_1|1\rangle + \cdots + \beta_n|n\rangle$, a measurement on $|\beta\rangle$ will only return one of its n components, and we are not able to recover all the information of the Fourier transform. For this reason, we describe this algorithm as a quantum Fourier *sampling*. The QFT is a generalization of the Hadamard transform. It is very similar, with the exception that QFT introduces phase. The specific kinds of phases introduced are what we call primitive roots of unity, ω. Before defining the Fourier transform, we will take a quick look at these primitive roots of unity.

Recall that in the complex numbers, there exist n solutions to the equation $z^n = 1$. For example, if $n = 2$, z could be 1 or -1. If $n = 4$, z could be 1, i, -1, or $-i$. You can easily check that these roots can be written as powers of $\omega = e^{2\pi i/n}$. This number ω is called a primitive n-th root of unity. In Figure 8.9, ω is drawn along with the other complex roots of unity for n = 5.

In this figure, we see that ω lies on the unit circle so $|\omega| = 1$, and the line from the origin to ω makes the angle $\phi = 2\pi/M$ with the real line. If we square ω, we double the angle. Furthermore, if

Figure 8.9 The five complex fifth roots of 1.

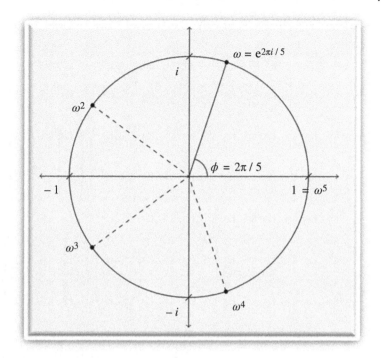

we raise ω to the j-th power, ω. has phase angle $\phi = 2j\pi/M$ and is still an M-th root of unity. Now, we can move in to the Fourier transform itself. The discreet Fourier transform is defined by

$$QFT_M = \frac{1}{\sqrt{M}} \begin{pmatrix} 1 & 1 & 1 & 1 & \cdots & 1 \\ 1 & \omega & \omega^2 & \omega^3 & \cdots & \omega^{M-1} \\ 1 & \omega^2 & \omega^4 & \omega^6 & \cdots & \omega^{2M-2} \\ 1 & \omega^3 & \omega^6 & \omega^9 & \cdots & \omega^{3M-3} \\ \vdots & \vdots & \vdots & \vdots & \ddots & \vdots \\ 1 & \omega^{M-1} & \omega^{2M-2} & \omega^{3M-3} & \cdots & \omega^{(M-1)(M-1)} \end{pmatrix}$$

Another way of writing this is to say that the jk-th entry of QFT_M is ω^{jk}. The transform takes the vector $(\alpha_0, \alpha_1, ..., \alpha_{n-1})^T$ to its Fourier transform $(\beta_0, \beta_1, ..., \beta_{n-1})^T$ as specified by the above matrix.

Design Example 8.1

Let us take a look at QFT_2. Because $M = 2$, $\omega = 2^\pi = -1$. Therefore, we have

$$QFT_2 = \frac{1}{\sqrt{2}} \begin{pmatrix} 1 & 1 \\ 1 & \omega \end{pmatrix} = \frac{1}{\sqrt{2}} \begin{pmatrix} 1 & 1 \\ 1 & -1 \end{pmatrix}$$

As you can see, QFT_2 is simply equal to the Hadamard gate H. For QFT_4 the primitive fourth root of unity is i, so that

$$QFT_4 = \frac{1}{2} \begin{pmatrix} 1 & 1 & 1 & 1 \\ 1 & i & -1 & -i \\ 1 & -1 & 1 & -1 \\ 1 & -i & -1 & i \end{pmatrix}$$

(Continued)

Design Example 8.1 (Continued)

Let us find the QFT for $M = 4$ of the functions $|f\rangle = \frac{1}{2}(|0\rangle + |1\rangle + |2\rangle + |3\rangle) = (1\ 1\ 1\ 1)^{\mathsf{T}}$; $|g\rangle = |0\rangle = (1\ 0\ 0\ 0)^{\mathsf{T}}$ and $|h\rangle = |1\rangle = (0\ 1\ 0\ 0)^{\mathsf{T}}$. The corresponding Fourier transforms are given by

QFT_4 to $|f\rangle$.

$$|\hat{f}\rangle = \frac{1}{4}\begin{pmatrix} 1 & 1 & 1 & 1 \\ 1 & i & -1 & -i \\ 1 & -1 & 1 & -1 \\ 1 & -i & -1 & i \end{pmatrix}\begin{pmatrix} 1 \\ 1 \\ 1 \\ 1 \end{pmatrix} = \begin{pmatrix} 1 \\ 0 \\ 0 \\ 0 \end{pmatrix}$$

QFT_4 on $|g\rangle$.

$$|\hat{g}\rangle = \frac{1}{2}\begin{pmatrix} 1 & 1 & 1 & 1 \\ 1 & i & -1 & -i \\ 1 & -1 & 1 & -1 \\ 1 & -i & -1 & i \end{pmatrix}\begin{pmatrix} 1 \\ 0 \\ 0 \\ 0 \end{pmatrix} = \frac{1}{2}\begin{pmatrix} 1 \\ 1 \\ 1 \\ 1 \end{pmatrix}$$

QFT_4 on $|h\rangle$.

$$|\hat{h}\rangle = \frac{1}{2}\begin{pmatrix} 1 & 1 & 1 & 1 \\ 1 & i & -1 & -i \\ 1 & -1 & 1 & -1 \\ 1 & -i & -1 & i \end{pmatrix}\begin{pmatrix} 0 \\ 1 \\ 0 \\ 0 \end{pmatrix} = \frac{1}{2}\begin{pmatrix} 1 \\ i \\ -1 \\ -i \end{pmatrix}$$

By analyzing these examples, we might notice that the columns of QFT_4 are orthogonal. For example, the inner product of the first column with the fourth column is $\frac{1}{2}[(1*1) + (1*-i) + (1*-1) + (1*i)] = \frac{1}{2}(1 - i - 1 + i) = 0$. You should also notice that, by design, the columns of QFT_4 have magnitude 1. Thus QFT_4 is unitary. Another thing you should notice is that vectors like $|f\rangle$ that had a lot of 1's (large spread) had Fourier transforms with few 1's (narrow spread), and vice versa. Finally, in Examples 2 and 3, note how the only difference between the Fourier transforms of $|g\rangle$ and $|h\rangle$ is a difference of relative phase shifts.

Classical fast Fourier transform: The FFT uses the symmetry of the Fourier transform to reduce the computation time. Simply put, we rewrite the Fourier transform of size M as two Fourier transforms of size $M/2$: the odd and the even terms. We then repeat this over and over again to exponentially reduce the time. To see how this works in detail, we turn to the matrix of the Fourier transform. While we go through this, it might be helpful to have QFT_8 in front of you to take a look at. Note that the exponents have been written modulo 8, since $\omega^8 = 1$.

$$\begin{pmatrix} 1 & 1 & 1 & 1 & 1 & 1 & 1 & 1 \\ 1 & \omega & \omega^2 & \omega^3 & \omega^4 & \omega^5 & \omega^6 & \omega^7 \\ 1 & \omega^2 & \omega^4 & \omega^6 & 1 & \omega^2 & \omega^4 & \omega^6 \\ 41 & \omega^3 & \omega^6 & \omega & \omega^4 & \omega^7 & \omega^2 & \omega^5 \\ 51 & \omega^4 & 1 & \omega^4 & 1 & \omega^4 & 1 & \omega^4 \\ 61 & \omega^5 & \omega^2 & \omega^7 & \omega^4 & \omega & \omega^6 & \omega^3 \\ 1 & \omega^6 & \omega^4 & \omega^2 & 1 & \omega^6 & \omega^4 & \omega^2 \\ 1 & \omega^7 & \omega^6 & \omega^5 & \omega^4 & \omega^3 & \omega^2 & \omega^1 \end{pmatrix}$$

Design Example 8.1 (Continued)

Note how row j is very similar to row $j + 4$. Also, note how column j is very similar to column j + 4. Motivated by this, we are going to split the Fourier transform into its even and odd columns.

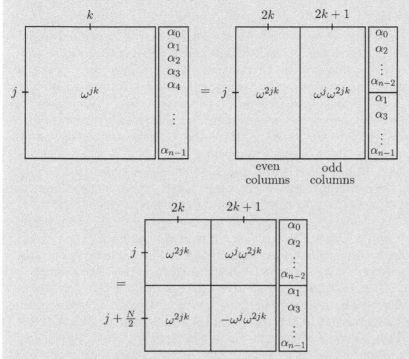

In the first frame, we have represented the whole Fourier transform matrix by describing the j-th row and k-th column: ω^{jk}. In the next frame, we separate the odd and even columns, and similarly separate the vector that is to be transformed. You should convince yourself that the first equality really is an equality. In the third frame, we add a little symmetry by noticing that $\omega^{j + N/2} = -\omega^{j}$ (since $\omega^{n/2} = -1$).

Note that both the odd side and even side contain the term ω^{2jk}. But if ω is the primitive N-th root of unity, then ω^2 is the primitive $N/2$nd root of unity. Therefore, the matrices whose j, k-th entry is ω^{2jk} are really just $QFT_{N/2}$! Now we can write QFT_N in a new way:

Now, suppose we are calculating the Fourier transform of the function (x) . We can write the above manipulations as an equation that computes the j-th term $\hat{f}(j)$.

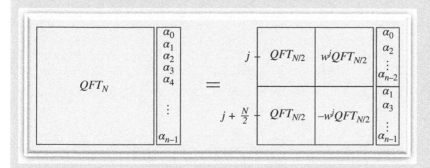

(*Continued*)

Design Example 8.1 (Continued)

$$\hat{f}(j) = \left(F_{M/2}\overrightarrow{f_{\text{even}}}\right)(j) + \omega^j\left(F_{M/2}\overrightarrow{f_{\text{odd}}}\right)(j)$$

This turns our calculation of QFT_N into two applications of $QFT_{N/2}$. We can turn this into four applications of $QFT/4$, and so forth. As long as $N = 2^n$ for some n, we can break down our calculation of QFT_N into N calculations of $QFT_1 = 1$. This greatly simplifies our calculation.

QFT with quantum gates: The strength of the FFT is that we are able to use the symmetry of the discrete Fourier transform to our advantage. The circuit application of QFT uses the same principle, but because of the power of superposition the QFT is even faster. The QFT is motivated by the FFT, so we will follow the same steps, but because this is a quantum algorithm the implementation of the steps will be different. That is, we first take the Fourier transform of the odd and even parts, and then multiply the odd terms by the phase ω^j.

In a quantum algorithm, the first step is fairly simple. The odd and even terms are together in superposition: the odd and even terms are those whose least significant bits are 1 and 0, respectively. Therefore, we can apply $QFT_{M/2}$ to both the odd and even terms together. We do this by applying simply $QFT_{M/2}$ to the $m - 1$ most significant bits, and recombine the odd and even appropriately by applying the Hadamard operation to the least significant bit.

Now, to carry out the phase multiplication, we need to multiply each odd term j by the phase ω^j. However, recall that an odd number in binary ends with a 1, whereas an even number ends with a 0. Thus, we can use the *controlled phase shift*, where the least significant bit is the control. Multiplying only the odd terms by the phase shift is similar to the *CNOT* gate in that it applies a phase to the target only if the control bit is 1. The phase associated with each controlled phase shift should be equal to ω^j, where j is associated with the k-th bit by $j = 2^k$. Thus, we apply the controlled phase shift to each of the first $m - 1$ qubits, with the least significant bit as the control. With the controlled phase shift and the Hadamard transform, QFT_M has been reduced to $QFT_M/2$.

This process is illustrated in Figures 8.10 and 8.11.

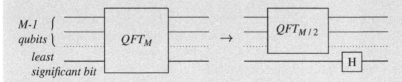

Figure 8.10 $QFT_{M/2}$ and a Hadamard gate correspond to $FFT_{M/2}$ on the odd and even terms.

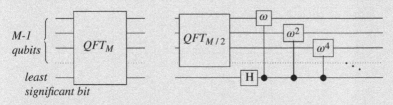

Figure 8.11 QFT_M is reduced to $QFT_{M/2}$ and M additional gates.

Design Example 8.2

Let us construct QFT_3. Following the algorithm, we will turn QFT_3 into QFT_2 and a few quantum gates. Then, continuing in this way, we turn QFT_2 into QFT_1 (which is just a Hadamard gate) and a few other gates. Controlled phase gates will be represented by $R\varphi$. Then, run through another iteration to get rid of QFT_2. The process is illustrated in Figure 8.12. You should now be able to visualize the circuit for QFT on more qubits easily. Furthermore, you can see that the number of gates necessary to carry out QFT_M is given exactly by $\sum_{i=1}^{\log M} i = \log M(\log M + 1)/2 = O(\log^2 M)$.

Figure 8.12 Quantum Fourier transform (QFT) iterations.

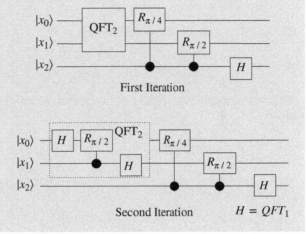

First Iteration

Second Iteration $H = QFT_1$

8.3.1 QFT Versus FFT Revisited

In the previous section, we introduced the concept of the QFT in a rather informal way with the goal of attracting the attention of the reader to the problem. In this section, we will revisit the same concept with more details by formulating tighter and more formal analogies with the FFT that should bring more insight into the physical interpretation of the QFT. We will also develop in a systematic way the general circuit from Figure 8.13 for arbitrary N.

Discrete Fourier transform: Suppose that we have a vector f of N complex numbers, f_k, $k \in \{0, 1, ..., N-1\}$. Then the discrete Fourier transform (DFT) is a map from these N complex numbers to N complex numbers, the Fourier-transformed coefficients $\tilde{f}_j$, given by

$$\tilde{f}_j = \frac{1}{\sqrt{N}} \sum_{k=0}^{N-1} \omega^{-jk} f_k$$

where $= \exp(2\pi i/N)$. The inverse DFT is given by

$$f_j = \frac{1}{\sqrt{N}} \sum_{k=0}^{N-1} \omega^{jk} \tilde{f}_k$$

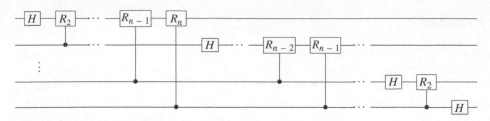

Figure 8.13 General block diagram of QFT processor.

To see this, consider how the basis vectors transform. If $f_k^l = \delta_{k,l}$, then

$$\widetilde{f}_j^{\,l} = \frac{1}{\sqrt{N}} \sum_{k=0}^{N-1} \omega^{-jk} \delta_{k,l} = \frac{1}{\sqrt{N}} \omega^{-jl}.$$

These DFT-ed vectors are orthonormal:

$$\sum_{j=0}^{N-1} \widetilde{f}_j^{\,l^*} \widetilde{f}_j^{\,m} = \frac{1}{N} \sum_{j=0}^{N-1} \omega^{jl} \omega^{-jm} = \frac{1}{N} \sum_{j=0}^{N-1} \omega^{j(l-m)}$$

This last sum can be evaluated as a geometric series – but be aware of the $(l - m) = 0$ term – and yields

$$\sum_{j=0}^{N-1} \widetilde{f}_j^{\,l^*} \widetilde{f}_j^{\,m} = \delta_{l,m}.$$

From this, we can check that the inverse DFT does indeed perform the inverse transform:

$$f_j = \frac{1}{\sqrt{N}} \sum_{k=0}^{N-1} \omega^{jk} \widetilde{f}_k = \frac{1}{\sqrt{N}} \sum_{k=0}^{N-1} \omega^{jk} \frac{1}{\sqrt{N}} \sum_{l=0}^{N-1} \omega^{-lk} f_l = \frac{1}{N} \sum_{k,l=0}^{N-1} \omega^{(j-l)k} f_l$$

$$= \sum_{l=0}^{N-1} \delta_{j,l} f_l = f_j$$

An important property of the DFT is the convolution theorem. The circular convolution of two vectors f and g is given by

$$(f*g)_i = \sum_{j=0}^{N-1} f_j g_{i-j}$$

where we define $g_{-m} = g_{N-m}$. The convolution theorem states that the DFT turns convolution into pointwise vector multiplication. In other words, if the components of the DFT of $(f * g)$ are $\widetilde{c}_k$, then $\widetilde{c}_k = \widetilde{f}_k \widetilde{g}_k$. What use is the convolution theorem? Well, this leads us nicely to our next topic, the FFT.

FFT: We start with the following question: how many math operations do we need to perform a DFT? Well, for each component of the new vector, we will need to perform N multiplications, and then we will need to add these components. Since we need to do this for each of the N different components, we see that N^2 complex multiplications and $N(N-1)$ complex additions are needed to compute the DFT. The goal of the FFT is to perform the DFT using fewer basic math operations. There are many ways to do this. As in the previous section, we will describe in more detail one particular method for $N = 2^n$, so assume $N = 2^n$ from here until indicated otherwise. The FFT we will consider is based on the observation that there are symmetries of the coefficients in the DFT:

$$\omega^{k + N/2} = -\omega^k$$

$$\omega^{k + N} = \omega^k.$$

Suppose we want to perform the DFT of the vector f. Split the components of f up into smaller vectors of size $N/2$, e, and o. The coefficients of e are the components of f that are even, and the coefficients of o are the components of f that are odd. The order of the coefficients is retained. Then it is easy to see that

$$\widetilde{f}_j = \frac{1}{\sqrt{N}} \sum_{i=0}^{N-1} \omega^{-ij} f_i = \frac{1}{\sqrt{N}} \sum_{i=0}^{N/2-1} \omega^{-2ij} e_i + \sum_{i=0}^{N/2-1} \omega^{-(2i+1)j} o_i$$

$$= \frac{1}{\sqrt{N}} \left(\sum_{i=0}^{N/2-1} \omega_{N/2}^{-ij} e_i + \omega_N^{-j} \sum_{i=0}^{N/2-1} \omega_{N/2}^{-ij} o_i \right)$$

where $\omega_{N/2} = \exp(2\pi i / N)$, and we have denoted ω by ω_N for clarity. We have thus obtained a formula for the DFT of f in terms of the DFT of e and o:

$$\widetilde{f}_j = \widetilde{e}_j + \omega_N^{-j} \widetilde{o}_j$$

Now recall that j runs from 0 to $N-1$, and the DFTs of e and f are periodic with period $N/2$. Using this and the above symmetry, we find that we can express our formula as

$$\sqrt{2} \widetilde{f}_j = \widetilde{e}_j + \omega_N^{-j} \widetilde{o}_j \qquad 0 \le j \le N/2 - 1$$
$$\sqrt{2} \widetilde{f}_j = \widetilde{e}_j - \omega_N^{-j} \widetilde{o}_j \qquad N/2 - 2 \le j \le N - 1$$

Suppose that we first compute the DFT over e and o and then use them in this formula to compute the full DFT of f. How many complex multiplications do we need to perform? Well, to compute e and o requires $2(N/2)^2 = N^2/2$ multiplications. We need another $N/2$ to compute $\omega_N^{-j} \widetilde{o}_j$. We can ignore the square root of two, as it can always be put in at the end as an extra N multiplications. Thus, we require $N^2/2 + N/2$ complex multiplications to compute the DFT as opposed to N^2 in the the previous method. This is a reduction of about a factor of 2 for large N. As indicated in the previous section, it is clear that for $N = 2^n$ we can use the above trick all the way down to $N = 2$. How many complex multiplications do we need to perform if we do this? Let T_n denote the number of multiplications at the $N = 2^n$–th level, such that $T_1 = 4$. Then $T_n = 2T_{n-1} + 2^{n-1}$, which can be bounded by $T_n \le 2T_{n-1} + 2^n$, yielding the solution $T_n \le 2^n n$. In other words, since $N = 2^n$ the running time is bounded by $N \log N$. Thus, we see that in the FFT we can compute the DFT in a complexity of $N \log N$ operations. This is a nice little improvement.

Here is an interesting application of the FFT. Suppose that you have two polynomials with complex coefficients: $f(x) = a_0 + a_1 x + \cdots + a_{N-1} x^{N-1}$ and $g(x) = b_0 + b_1 x + \cdots + b_{N-1} x^{N-1}$. If you multiply these two polynomials together, you get a new polynomial $f(x)g(x) = \sum_{i,j=0}^{N-1} a_i b_j x^{i+j} = \sum_{k=0}^{2(N-1)} c_k x^k$. The new coefficients for this polynomial are a function of the two polynomials:

$$c_k = \sum_{l=0}^{N-1} a_l b_{k-l}$$

where the sum is over all valid polynomial terms (i.e., when $k - l$ is negative, there is no term in the sum.) One sees that computing c_k requires N^2 multiplications.

Here, the expression for c_k looks a lot like convolution. Indeed, suppose that we form a $2N$–dimensional vector $a = (a_0, ..., a_{N-1}, 0, ..., 0)$ and $b = (b_0, ..., b_{N-1}, 0, ..., 0)$ from our original data. The vector c that will represent the coefficients of the new polynomial are then given by

$$c_k = \sum_{l=0}^{2N-1} a_l b_{k-l \bmod 2N}$$

Now, we do not need to condition this sum on their being valid terms. This is explicitly convolution! Thus, we can compute the coefficients c_k by the following algorithm. Compute the DFT of the vectors a and b. Pointwise multiply these two vectors, and inverse-DFT this new vector. The result will be c_k by the convolution theorem. If we use the FFT algorithm for this procedure, then we will require $O(N \log N)$ multiplications. This is nice: by using the FFT, we can multiply polynomials faster than with our naive grade school method for multiplying polynomials.

Quantum Fourier transform circuits: Now, let us turn to the QFT. We have already seen in the previous section that the QFT for $N = 2$ is the Hadamard transform:

$$H = \frac{1}{\sqrt{2}} \begin{Bmatrix} 1 & 1 \\ 1 & -1 \end{Bmatrix}$$

Why is this the QFT for $N = 2$? Well, suppose we have the single-qubit state $a_0 |0\rangle + a_1 |1\rangle$. If we apply the Hadamard operation to this state, we obtain the new state

$$\frac{1}{\sqrt{2}}(a_0 + a_1)|0\rangle + \frac{1}{\sqrt{2}}(a_0 - a_1)|1\rangle = \tilde{a}_0|0\rangle + \tilde{a}_1|1\rangle.$$

In other words, the Hadamard gate performs the DFT for $N = 2$ on the amplitudes of the state! Note that this is very different from computing the DFT for $N = 2$: recall that the amplitudes are not numbers which are accessible to us mere mortals; they just represent our description of the quantum system.

So, what is the full QFT? It is the transform that takes the amplitudes of an $N-$ dimensional state and computes the Fourier transform on these amplitudes (which are then the new amplitudes in the computational basis.) In other words, the QFT enacts the transform

$$\sum_{x=0}^{N-1} a_x|x\rangle \rightarrow \sum_{x=0}^{N-1} \tilde{a}_x|x\rangle = \sum_{x=0}^{N-1} \frac{1}{\sqrt{N}} \sum_{y=0}^{N-1} \omega_N^{-xy} a_y|x\rangle.$$

It is easy to see that this implies that the QFT performs the following transform on basis states:

$$|x\rangle \rightarrow \frac{1}{\sqrt{N}} \sum_{y=0}^{N-1} \omega_N^{-xy} |y\rangle$$

Thus, the QFT is given by the matrix

$$U_{QFT} = \frac{1}{\sqrt{N}} \sum_{x=0}^{N-1} \sum_{y=0}^{N-1} \omega_N^{-yx} |y\rangle\langle x|.$$

This matrix is unitary. Let us check this:

$$U_{QFT}U_{QFT}^\dagger = \frac{1}{N} \sum_{x=0}^{N-1} \sum_{y=0}^{N-1} \omega_N^{yx} |x\rangle\langle y| \sum_{x'=0}^{N-1} \sum_{y'=0}^{N-1} \omega_N^{-y'x'} |y'\rangle\langle x'|$$

$$= \frac{1}{N} \sum_{x,y,x',y'=0}^{N-1} \omega_N^{yx-y'x'} \delta_{y,y'} |x\rangle\langle x'| = \frac{1}{N} \sum_{x,y,x'=0}^{N-1} \omega_N^{y(x-x')} |x\rangle\langle x'|$$

$$= \sum_{x,x'=0}^{N-1} \delta_{x,x'} |x\rangle\langle x'| = I$$

Efficient implementation of the QFT with a quantum circuit is intimately related to the FFT. Let us derive a circuit for the QFT when $N = 2^n$. The QFT performs the transform

$$|x\rangle \rightarrow \frac{1}{\sqrt{2^n}} \sum_{y=0}^{2^n-1} \omega_N^{-xy} |y\rangle.$$

Then we can expand this sum

$$|x\rangle \rightarrow \frac{1}{\sqrt{2^n}} \sum_{y_1,y_2,\ldots,y_n \in \{0,1\}} \omega_N^{-x\sum_{k=1}^n 2^{n-k}y_k} |y_1,y_2,\ldots,y_n\rangle$$

Expanding the exponential of a sum to a product of exponentials and collecting these terms in from the appropriate terms, we can express this as

$$|x\rangle \rightarrow \frac{1}{\sqrt{2^n}} \sum_{y_1,y_2,\ldots,y_n \in \{0,1\}} \otimes_{k=1}^n \omega_N^{-x2^{n-k}y_k} |y_k\rangle$$

After rearranging, we get

$$|x\rangle \rightarrow \frac{1}{\sqrt{2^n}} \otimes_{k=1}^n \left[\sum_{y_k \in \{01\}} , \omega_N^{-x2^{n-k}y_k} |y_k\rangle \right]$$

Expanding this sum yields

$$|x\rangle \rightarrow \frac{1}{\sqrt{2^n}} \otimes_{k=1}^n \left[|0\rangle + \omega_N^{-x2^{n-k}} |1\rangle \right]$$

At this point, note that $\omega_N^{-x2^{n-k}}$ is not dependent on the higer-order bits of x. It is convenient to adopt the following expression for a binary fraction:

$$0.x_l x_{l+1} \ldots x_n = \frac{x_l}{2} + \frac{x_{l+1}}{4} + + \frac{x_n}{2^{n-l+1}}$$

Then we can see that

$$|x\rangle$$
$$\rightarrow \frac{1}{\sqrt{2^n}} \left[|0\rangle + e^{-2\pi i 0.x_n} |1\rangle \right] \otimes \left[|0\rangle + e^{-2\pi i 0.x_{n-1}x_n} |1\rangle \right] \otimes \cdots \otimes \left[|0\rangle + e^{-2\pi i 0.x_1 x_2 \cdots x_n} |1\rangle \right]$$

This is a very useful form of the QFT for $N = 2^n$. Why? Because we see that only the last qubit depends on the values of all the other input qubits, and each further bit depends less and less on the input qubits. Further, we note that $e^{-2\pi i 0. \, a}$ is either $+1$ or -1, which reminds us of the Hadamard transform.

So, how do we use this to derive a circuit for the QFT over $N = 2^n$?

Take the first qubit of $|x_1, \ldots, x_n\rangle$ and apply a Hadamard transform. This produces the transform

$$|x\rangle \rightarrow \frac{1}{\sqrt{2}} \left[|0\rangle + e^{-2\pi i 0.x_1} |1\rangle \right] \otimes |x_2, x_3, \ldots, x_n\rangle$$

Now define the rotation gate

$$R_k = \begin{bmatrix} 1 & 0 \\ 1 & \exp\left(\frac{-2\pi i}{2^k}\right) \end{bmatrix}$$

If we now apply controlled R_2, R_3, and so on, gates controlled on the appropriate bits, this enacts the transform

$$|x\rangle \rightarrow \frac{1}{\sqrt{2}}\left[|0\rangle + e^{-2\pi i 0.x_1 x_2 \ldots x_n} |1\rangle\right] \otimes |x_2, x_3, \ldots, x_n\rangle$$

Thus, we have reproduced the last term in the QFT-ed state. Of course, now we can proceed to the second qubit, perform a Hadamard, and the appropriate controlled R_k gates and get the second to last qubit. Thus, when we are finished we will have the transform

$$|x\rangle \rightarrow \frac{1}{\sqrt{2^n}}\left[|0\rangle + e^{-2\pi i 0.x_1 x_2 \cdots x_n} |1\rangle\right] \otimes \left[|0\rangle + e^{-2\pi i 0.x_1 x_2 \cdots x_{n-1}} |1\rangle\right] \otimes \cdots \otimes \left[|0\rangle + e^{-2\pi i 0.x_n} |1\rangle\right]$$

Reversing the order of these qubits will then produce the QFT! The circuit we have constructed on n qubits is

This circuit is polynomial size in n. In fact, we can count the number of quantum gates in it: $\sum_{i=1}^{n} i = n(n+1)/2$ Hadamards and controlled R_k gates plus $\left\lfloor \frac{n}{2} \right\rfloor$ swap gates. What was it that allowed us to construct an efficient circuit? Well, if you look at the factorization we used, you will see that we have basically used the same trick that we used for the FFT! But now, since we are working on amplitudes and not operating on the complex vectors themselves, we get an algorithm that scales nicely in the number of qubits. It is important to realize that the QFT cannot be used like the FFT on data. Thus, there is a tendency to want to port quantum computers over to signal processing. Currently, there are some preliminary ideas about how to do this, but the naive way you might expect this to work does not work.

References

1 Nielsen, M.A. and Chuang, I.L. (2011). *Quantum Computation and Quantum Information*, 10e. New York: Cambridge University Press.

2 Imre, S. and Balázs, F. (2005). *Quantum Computing and Communications: An Engineering Approach*. Chichester: Wiley.

3 Wimmel, H. (1992). *Quantum Physics & Observed Reality: A Critical Interpretation of Quantum Mechanics*. Singapore: World Scientific.

4 Bell, J.S. (Jul. 1966). On the problem of hidden variables in quantum mechanics. *Rev. Mod. Phys.* **38**: 447–452.

5 Chandra, N. and Ghosh, R. (2013). *Quantum Entanglement in Electron Optics: Generation, Characterization, and Applications*. Heidelberg: Springer.

6 Prashant, A Study on the basics of Quantum Computing, https://arxiv.org/vc/quant-ph/papers/0511/0511061v1.pdf

7 Gisin, N., Ribordy, G., Tittel, W., and Zbinden, H. (Jan. 2002). Quantum cryptography. *Rev. Mod. Phys.* **74**: 145–195.

8 Scarani, V., Scarani, V., Bechmann-Pasquinucci, H. et al. (2009). The security of practical quantum key distribution. *Rev. Mod. Phys.* **81**: 1301–1350.

9 Hughes, R. and Nordholt, J. (2011). Refining quantum cryptography. *Science* **333** (6049): 1584–1586.

10 Wootters, W.K. and Zurek, W.H. (1982). A single quantum cannot be cloned. *Nature* **299**: 802–803.

11 C. H. Bennett and G. Brassard, "Quantum cryptography: Public key distribution and coin tossing," in Proc. IEEE Int. Conf. Comput. Syst. Signal Process., 1984, pp. 175–179.

9

Quantum Channel Information Theory

Communication through a quantum channel cannot be described by the results of classical information theory; it requires the generalization of classical information theory by quantum perception of the world. In the general model of communication over a quantum channel $\mathcal{Q}$, the encoder encodes the message in some coded form, and the receiver decodes it. However, in this case, the whole communication is realized through a quantum system. The information sent through quantum channels is carried by quantum states, and hence the encoding $\mathcal{E}$ is fundamentally different from any classical encoder scheme. The encoding here means the preparation of a quantum system, according to the probability distribution of the classical message being encoded. Similarly, the decoding $\mathcal{D}$ process is also different: here, it means the measurement $\mathcal{M}$ of the received quantum state. The properties of the quantum communication channel, and the fundamental differences between the classical $\mathcal{N}$ channel and $\mathcal{Q}$ channel, cannot be described without the elements of quantum information theory.

The model of the quantum channel represents the physically allowed transformations that can occur on the sent quantum system. The result of the channel transformation is another quantum system, while the quantum states are represented by matrices. The physically allowed channel transformations could be very different; nevertheless, they are always *completely positive trace preserving* (CPTP) transformations (trace: the sum of the elements on the main diagonal of a matrix). The trace preserving property therefore means that the corresponding density matrices (density matrix: mathematical description of a quantum system) at the input and output of the channel have the same trace.

The input of a quantum channel is a quantum state $\mathcal{S}$, which encodes information into a physical property. The quantum state is sent through a quantum communication channel, which in practice can be implemented, for example, by an optical fiber channel, or by a wireless quantum communication channel. To extract any information from the quantum state, it has to be measured at the receiver's side. The outcome of the measurement of the quantum state (which might be perturbed) depends on the transformation of the quantum channel, since it can be either totally probabilistic or deterministic. In contrast to classical channels, a quantum channel transforms the information coded into quantum states, which can be, as indicated in Chapter 8, the spin state of the particle, the ground and excited state of an atom, or several other physical approaches. The classical capacity of a quantum channel is relevant if the goal is to transmit classical information in a quantum state, or to send classical information privately via quantum systems (private classical capacity). The quantum capacity is relevant if one would like to transmit quantum information such as superposed quantum states or quantum entanglement. We first discuss the process of transmission of

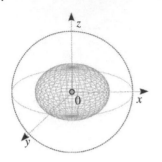

Figure 9.1 Geometrical picture of a noisy qubit quantum channel on the Bloch sphere. Sources: Gyongyosi et al. [1]; Imre and Gyongyosi [2].

information over a Q channel. Then, the interaction between the Q channel output and the environment will be described.

The Q channel map: From the algebraic point of view, Q channels are linear CPTP maps, while from a geometrical viewpoint, the quantum channel Q is an affine transformation. Although from the algebraic view the transformations are defined on density matrices, in the geometrical approach, the qubit transformations are also interpretable via the Bloch sphere (as discussed in Chapter 8). Since density matrices can be expressed in terms of Bloch vectors, the map of a Q channel also can be analyzed in the geometrical picture. To preserve the condition for a density matrix ρ, the noise on the quantum channel Q must be trace preserving, that is, $Tr(\rho) = Tr(Q(\rho))$ and it must be completely positive (CP); that is, for any identity map I, the map $I \otimes Q$ maps a semi-positive Hermitian matrix to a semi-positive Hermitian matrix. For a unital quantum channel Q, the channel map transforms the I identity transformation to the I identity transformation, but this condition does not hold for a non-unital channel. To express it for a unital quantum channel, we have $Q(I) = I$, and for a non-unital quantum channel, $Q(I) \neq I$.

Focusing on a qubit channel, the image of the quantum channel's linear transform is an *ellipsoid* on the Bloch sphere, as it is depicted in Figure 9.1 [1, 2]. For a unital quantum channel, the center of the geometrical interpretation of the channel ellipsoid is equal to the center of the Bloch sphere. This means that a unital quantum channel preserves the average of the system states. On the other hand, for a non-unital quantum channel, the center of the channel ellipsoid will differ from the center of the Bloch sphere. The main difference between unital and non-unital channels is that the latter do not preserve the average state in the center of the Bloch sphere.

It follows from this that the numerical and algebraic analysis of non-unital quantum channels is more complicated than in the case of unital ones. While unital channels shrink the Bloch sphere in different directions with the center preserved, non-unital quantum channels shrink both the original Bloch sphere and move the center from the origin of the Bloch sphere. This fact makes our analysis more complex; however, in many cases, the physical systems cannot be described with unital quantum channel maps. Since the unital channel maps can be expressed as the convex combination of the basic unitary transformations, the unital channel maps can be represented in the Bloch sphere as different rotations with shrinking parameters. On the other hand, for a non-unital quantum map, the map cannot be decomposed into a convex combination of unitary rotations [2].

9.1 Communication Over a Q Channel

The transmission of information through $\mathcal{N}$ and Q channels differs in many ways. To describe the process of information transmission through a Q channel, we have to introduce the three main phases of quantum communication. (i) The sender, Alice, has to encode her information to compensate for the noise of the channel Q (i.e. for error correction), according to the properties of the physical channel – this step is called *channel coding*. (ii) After the sender has encoded the information into the appropriate form, it has to be put on the Q channel, which transforms it according to its channel map – this second phase is called *channel evolution*. The quantum channel Q conveys the quantum state to the receiver, Bob; however, this state is still a superposed and probably *mixed* (according to the noise of the channel) quantum state. (iii) To extract the information that is encoded in the state, the receiver has to make a measurement – this *decoding process* (with the error correction procedure) is the third phase of the communication over a quantum channel.

The channel transformation represents the noise of the quantum channel. Physically, the $\mathcal{Q}$ channel is the medium that moves the particle from the sender to the receiver. The noise disturbs the state of the particle, and in the case of a half-spin particle, it causes spin precession. The channel evolution phase is illustrated in Figure 9.2

Finally, the measurement process is responsible for the decoding and the extraction of the encoded information. The previous phase determines the success probability of the recovery of the original information. If the channel $\mathcal{Q}$ is completely noisy, then the receiver will get a maximally mixed quantum state. The output of the measurement of a maximally mixed state is completely undeterministic: it tells us nothing about the original information encoded by the sender. On the other hand, if the quantum channel $\mathcal{Q}$ is completely noiseless, then the information encoded by the sender can be recovered with probability 1: the result of the measurement will be completely deterministic and completely correlated with the original message. In practice, a $\mathcal{Q}$ channel realizes a map that is in between these two extreme cases. A general $\mathcal{Q}$ channel transforms the original pure quantum state into a mixed quantum state – but not into a maximally mixed state – which makes it possible to recover the original message with a high – or low – probability, depending on the level of the noise of the quantum channel $\mathcal{Q}$.

The *general model* in Figure 9.3, shows the information transmission through the quantum channel $\mathcal{Q}$ defined by the ρ_{in} input quantum state and the initial state of the environment $\rho_E = |0\rangle\langle 0|$. In the initial phase, the environment is assumed to be in the pure state $|0\rangle$. The system state, which consists of the input quantum state ρ_{in} and the environment $\rho_E = |0\rangle\langle 0|$, is called the *composite state* $\rho_{in} \otimes \rho_E$.

If the quantum channel $\mathcal{Q}$ is used for information transmission, then the state of the composite system changes unitarily as follows: $U(\rho_{in} \otimes \rho_E)U^\dagger$, where U is a unitary transformation, and $U^\dagger U = I$. After the quantum state has been sent over the quantum channel $\mathcal{Q}$, the ρ_{out} output state can be expressed as $\mathcal{Q}(\rho_{in}) = \rho_{out} = Tr_E[U(\rho_{in} \otimes \rho_E)U^\dagger]$, where Tr_E traces out the environment E from the joint state. Assuming the environment E in the pure state $|0\rangle$, $\rho_E = |0\rangle\langle 0|$, the $\mathcal{N}(\rho_{in})$ noisy evolution of the channel $\mathcal{Q}$ can be expressed as

$$\mathcal{Q}(\rho_{in}) = \rho_{out} = Tr_E U \rho_{in} \otimes |0\rangle\langle 0| U^\dagger, \tag{9.1}$$

Figure 9.2 The channel evolution phase.

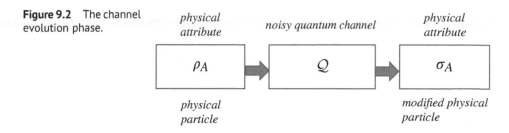

physical attribute

noisy quantum channel

physical attribute

ρ_A $\mathcal{Q}$ σ_A

physical particle

modified physical particle

Figure 9.3 The general model of transmission of information over a noisy $\mathcal{Q}$ channel.

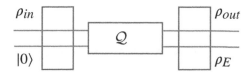

ρ_{in} $\mathcal{Q}$ ρ_{out}

$|0\rangle$ ρ_E

while the post state ρ_E of the environment after the transmission is

$$\rho_E = Tr_B U \rho_{in} \otimes |0\rangle \langle 0| U^\dagger, \tag{9.2}$$

where Tr_B traces out the output system B. In general, the i-th input quantum state ρ_i is prepared with probability p_i, which describes the ensemble $\{p_i, \rho_i\}$. The average of the *input* quantum system is

$$\sigma_{in} = \sum_i p_i \rho_i, \tag{9.3}$$

The average (or the mixture) of the *output* of the quantum channel is denoted by

$$\sigma_{out} = \mathcal{Q}(\sigma_{in}) = \sum_i p_i \mathcal{Q}(\rho_i). \tag{9.4}$$

$\mathcal{Q}$ *Channel capacity:* The capacity of a communication channel describes the capability of the channel for sending information from the sender to the receiver in a faithful and recoverable way. The perfect ideal communication channel realizes an identity map. For a $\mathcal{Q}$ channel, it means that the channel can transmit the quantum states perfectly. Clearly speaking, the capacity of the $\mathcal{Q}$ channel measures the closeness to the ideal identity transformation I. To describe the information transmission capability of the quantum channel $\mathcal{Q}$, we have to make a distinction between the various capacities of a quantum channel. The encoded quantum states can carry classical messages or quantum messages. In the case of classical messages, the quantum states encode the output from a classical information source, whereas in the latter the source is a quantum information source.

On the one hand, for a classical communication channel $\mathcal{Q}$, only one type of capacity measure can be defined; on the other hand, for a $\mathcal{Q}$ channel, a number of different types of $\mathcal{Q}$ channel capacities can be applied, with different characteristics. There are plenty of open questions regarding these various capacities. In general, the *single-use* capacity of a quantum channel is not equal to the *asymptotic* capacity of the quantum channel (as we will see later, it also depends on the type of $\mathcal{Q}$ channel). The asymptotic capacity gives us the amount of information that can be transmitted in a reliable form using the $\mathcal{Q}$ channel infinitely many times. The encoding and the decoding functions can be mathematically described by the operators $\mathcal{E}$ and $\mathcal{D}$, realized on the blocks of quantum states. These superoperators describe unitary transformations on the input states together with the environment of the quantum system. The model of communication through a noisy $\mathcal{Q}$ channel with encoding, delivery, and decoding phases is illustrated in Figure 9.4.

In the following, we will use the terms *classical* and *quantum quantity* as a measure of the classical or quantum transmission capabilities of a $\mathcal{Q}$ channel, respectively. *Quantum information theory* also is relevant to the discussion of the capacity of $\mathcal{Q}$ channels and to information transmission and storage in quantum systems. As we will see in this section, although the transmission of product states can be described similar to classical information, on the other hand, the properties of quantum entanglement cannot be handled by the elements of classical information theory.

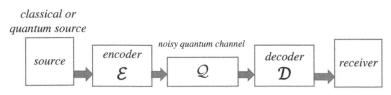

Figure 9.4 Communication over a noisy $\mathcal{Q}$ channel.

9.2   Quantum Information Theory

In this section, we introduce a basic concept of quantum information theory.

9.2.1   Density Matrix and Trace Operator

Let us first revisit some of the basic terms in matrix theory. An $n \times n$ square matrix A is called *positive-semidefinite* if $\langle \psi | A | \psi \rangle$ is a nonnegative real number for every vector $|\psi\rangle$. If $A = A^\dagger$, that is, A is a Hermitian matrix and the $\{\lambda_1, \lambda_2, ...\lambda_n\}$ eigenvalues of A are all nonnegative real numbers, then it is positive-semidefinite. This definition has an important role in quantum information theory, since *every density matrix is positive-semidefinite*. It means, for any vector $|\varphi\rangle$ the positive-semidefinite property says that

$$\langle \varphi | \rho | \varphi \rangle = \sum_{i=1}^{n} p_i \langle \varphi | \psi_i \rangle \langle \psi_i | \varphi \rangle = \sum_{i=1}^{n} p_i |\langle \varphi | \psi_i \rangle|^2 \geq 0. \tag{9.5}$$

In Eq. (9.5), the density matrix is denoted by ρ, and it describes the system by the classical-probability-weighted sum of possible states

$$\rho = \sum_i p_i |\psi_i\rangle \langle \psi_i|, \tag{9.6}$$

where $|\psi_i\rangle$ is the i-th system state occurring with classical probability p_i. As can be seen, this density matrix describes the system as a probabilistic mixture of the possible known states, the so-called *pure states*. For the pure state $|\psi\rangle$ the density matrix is $\rho = |\psi\rangle\langle\psi|$ and the rank of the matrix is equal to one. Trivially, classical states, for example, $|0\rangle$ and $|1\rangle$ are pure; however, if we know that our system is prepared to the *superposition* $\frac{1}{\sqrt{2}}(|0\rangle + |1\rangle)$ then this state is pure, too. Clearly speaking, whereas the superposition is a quantum linear combination of orthonormal basis states weighted by probability amplitudes, mixed states are a classical linear combination of pure superpositions (quantum states) weighted by classical probabilities.

The density matrix contains all the possible information that can be extracted from the quantum system. It is possible that two quantum systems possess the same density matrices: in this case, these quantum systems are called indistinguishable, since it is not possible to construct a measurement setting that can distinguish between the two systems.

The density matrix ρ of a simple pure quantum system that can be given in the state vector representation $|\psi\rangle = \alpha |0\rangle + \beta |1\rangle$ can be expressed as the outer product of the *ket* and *bra* vectors, where bra is the transposed complex conjugate of ket, and hence for $|\psi\rangle = \begin{bmatrix} \alpha \\ \beta \end{bmatrix}$, $\langle\psi| = [\alpha^* \ \beta^*]$ the density matrix is

$$\rho = |\psi\rangle\langle\psi| = \begin{bmatrix} \alpha \\ \beta \end{bmatrix} [\alpha^* \ \beta^*] = \begin{bmatrix} \alpha\alpha^* & \alpha\beta^* \\ \alpha^*\beta & \beta\beta^* \end{bmatrix} = \begin{bmatrix} |\alpha|^2 & \alpha\beta^* \\ \alpha^*\beta & |\beta|^2 \end{bmatrix} \tag{9.7}$$

The density matrix $\rho = \sum_{i=1}^{n} p_i |\psi_i\rangle\langle\psi_i|$ contains the probabilistic mixture of different pure states, which representation is based on the fact that the mixed states can be decomposed into the weighted sum of pure states [3].

The trace of a density matrix is equal to the sum of its diagonal entries. For an $n \times n$ square matrix A, the *Tr* trace operator is defined as $Tr(A) = a_{11} + a_{22} + \cdots + a_{nn} = \sum_{i=1}^{n} a_{ii}$, where a_{ii} are the elements of the main diagonal. The trace of the matrix A is also equal to the sum of the *eigenvalues* of its matrix. The eigenvalue is the factor by which the *eigenvector* changes if it is multiplied by the matrix A, for each eigenvector. The *eigenvectors* of the square matrix A are those nonzero vectors whose directions relative to the original vector remain the same after multiplication by the matrix A. This means the eigenvectors remain proportional to the original vector. For square matrix A, the nonzero vector v is called the *eigenvector* of A if there is a scalar λ for which $Av = \lambda v$, where λ is the *eigenvalue* of A corresponding to the eigenvector v. The trace operation gives us the sum of the eigenvalues of positive-semidefinite A, for each eigenvector, and hence $Tr(A) = \sum_{i=1}^{n} \lambda_i$, and $Tr(A^k) = \sum_{i=1}^{n} \lambda_i^k$. Using the eigenvalues, the *spectral decomposition* of density matrix ρ can be expressed as

$$\rho = \sum_i \lambda_i |\varphi_i\rangle\langle\varphi_i|, \tag{9.8}$$

where $|\varphi_i\rangle$ are orthonormal vectors. The trace is a linear map, and hence for square matrices A and B, $Tr(A + B) = Tr(A) + Tr(B)$, and $Tr(sA) = sTr(A)$, where s is a scalar. Another useful formula is that for an $m \times n$ matrix A and an $n \times m$ matrix B, $Tr(AB) = Tr(BA)$, which holds for any matrices A and B for which the product matrix AB is a square matrix, since $Tr(AB) = \sum_{i=1}^{m} \sum_{j=1}^{n} A_{ij}B_{ji} = Tr(BA)$.

Finally, we mention that the trace of a matrix A and the trace of its transpose A^T are equal, and hence $Tr(A) = Tr(A^T)$. If we take the conjugate transpose A^* of the $m \times n$ matrix A, then we will find that $Tr(A^*A) \geq 0$, which will be denoted by $\langle A, A \rangle$ and is called the *inner product*. For matrices A and B, the inner product $\langle A, B \rangle = Tr(B^*A)$, which can be used to define the angle between the two vectors. The inner product of two vectors will be zero if and only if the vectors are orthogonal. As we have seen, the trace operation gives the sum of the eigenvalues of matrix A, and this property can be extended to the density matrix; hence, for each eigenvectors λ_i of density matrix ρ

$$Tr(\rho) = \sum_{i=1}^{n} \lambda_i. \tag{9.9}$$

Now, we apply the trace operation to a density matrix. If we have an n-qubit system in the state $\rho = \sum_{i=1}^{n} p_i |\psi_i\rangle\langle\psi_i|$, then with notation

$$Tr\left(\sum_{i=1}^{n} p_i |\psi_i\rangle\langle\psi_i|\right) = \sum_{i=1}^{n} p_i Tr(|\psi_i\rangle\langle\psi_i|) = \sum_{i=1}^{n} p_i(\langle\psi_i|\psi_i\rangle) = 1, \tag{9.10}$$

where we exploited the relation for unit-length vectors $|\psi_i\rangle$ giving $\langle\psi_i|\psi_i\rangle \equiv 1$.

Thus, the trace of any density matrix is equal to one $Tr(\rho) = 1$. The trace operation can help to distinguish *pure* and *mixed* states since for a given *pure state* ρ, $Tr(\rho^2) = 1$, whereas for a *mixed* state σ, $Tr(\sigma^2) < 1$, where $Tr(\rho^2) = \sum_{i=1}^{n} \lambda_i^2$ and $Tr(\sigma^2) = \sum_{i=1}^{n} \omega_i^2$, where ω_i are the eigenvalues of density matrix σ.

Similarly, for a pure *entangled* system ρ_{EPR}, $Tr(\rho_{EPR}^2) = 1$, whereas for any mixed subsystem σ_{EPR} of the entangled state (i.e. for a half-pair of the entangled state), we will have $Tr(\sigma_{EPR}^2) < 1$.

The density matrix also can be used to describe the effect of a unitary transform on the probability distribution of the system. The probability that the whole quantum system is in $|\psi_i\rangle$ can be calculated by the trace operation. If we apply unitary transform U to the state $\rho = \sum_{i=1}^{n} p_i |\psi_i\rangle\langle\psi_i|$, the effect can be expressed as follows:

$$\sum_{i=1}^{n} p_i(U|\psi_i\rangle)(\langle\psi_i|U^\dagger) = U\left(\sum_{i=1}^{n} p_i |\psi_i\rangle\langle\psi_i|\right)U^\dagger = U\rho U^\dagger. \tag{9.11}$$

If the applied transformation is not unitary, a more general operator denoted by G is introduced, and with the help of this operator the transform can be written as

$$G(\rho) = \sum_{i=1}^{n} A_i\rho A_i^\dagger = \sum_{i=1}^{n} A_i(p_i |\psi_i\rangle\langle\psi_i|)A_i^\dagger, \tag{9.12}$$

where $\sum_{i=1}^{n} A_i A_i^{\dagger} = I$, for every matrices A_i. In this sense, operator G describes the physically admissible or CPTP operations. The application of a CPTP operator G on the density matrix ρ will result in a matrix (ρ), which in this case is still a density matrix.

In summary: (i) The density matrix ρ is a positive-semidefinite matrix; see Eq. (9.5). (ii) The trace of any density matrix ρ is equal to 1; see Eq. (9.10).

Geometrical interpretation of the density matrices: The geometrical representation can be extended to analyze the geometrical structure of the transmission of information though a quantum channel, and it provides a very useful tool to analyze the capacities of different quantum channel models. As has been mentioned (see Chapter 8), the Bloch sphere is a geometrical conception, constructed to represent two-level quantum systems in a more expressive way than is possible with algebraic tools. The Bloch sphere has unit radius and is defined in a three-dimensional real vector space. The pure states are on the surface of the Bloch sphere, whereas the mixed states are inside the original sphere. In the Bloch sphere representation, the state of a single qubit $|\psi\rangle = \alpha|0\rangle + \beta|1\rangle$ can be expressed as

$$|\psi\rangle = e^{i\delta} \left(\cos \frac{\theta}{2}|0\rangle + e^{i\varphi} \sin \frac{\theta}{2}|1\rangle \right),$$

where δ is the global phase factor, which can be ignored from the computations, and hence the state $|\psi\rangle$ in the terms of the angle θ and φ can be expressed as

$$|\psi\rangle = \cos \frac{\theta}{2}|0\rangle + e^{i\varphi} \sin \frac{\theta}{2}|1\rangle.$$

The Bloch sphere is a very useful tool, since it makes possible to describe various physically realized one-qubit quantum systems, such as photon polarization, spins, or the energy levels of an atom. Moreover, if we would like to compute the various channel capacities of the quantum channel, the geometrical expression of the channel capacity also can be represented by the Bloch sphere. Before we introduce the geometrical calculation of the channel capacities, we have to mention the geometrical interpretation of density matrices. The density matrix ρ can then be expressed using the Pauli matrices (see Chapter 8) σ_X, σ_Y, and σ_Z as $\rho = (1 + r_X\sigma_X + r_Y\sigma_Y + r_Z\sigma_Z)/2$, where $r = (r_X, r_Y, r_Z) = (\sin\theta\cos\varphi, \sin\theta \sin\varphi, \cos\theta)$ is the Bloch vector, $\|(r_X, r_Z, r_Y)\| \leq 1$, and $\sigma = (\sigma_X, \sigma_Y, \sigma_Z)^T$. In vector representation, the previously shown formula can be expressed as $\rho = (1 + r\sigma)/2$.

In conclusion, every state can be expressed as linear combinations of the Pauli matrices, and according to these Pauli matrices every state can be interpreted as a point in the three-dimensional real vector space. If we apply a unitary transformation U to the density matrix ρ, then it can be expressed as

$$\rho \rightarrow \rho' = U\rho U^{\dagger} = \left(1 + U r\sigma U^{\dagger}\right)/2 = \left(1 + U r U^{\dagger}\sigma\right)/2,$$

and $r' = U r U^{\dagger}$ realizes a unitary transformation on r as a rotation. A density matrix ρ can be expressed in a weighted form of density matrices ρ_1 and ρ_2 as $\rho = \gamma\rho_1 + (1 - \gamma)\rho_2$, where $0 \leq \gamma \leq 1$, and ρ_1 and ρ_2 are pure states and lie on a line segment connecting the density matrices in the Bloch sphere representation. Using probabilistic mixtures of the pure density matrices, any quantum state that lies between the two states can be expressed as a convex combination

$$\rho = p\rho_1 + (1-p)\rho_2, 0 \leq p \leq 1.$$

This remains true for an arbitrary number of quantum states, and hence this result can be expressed for an arbitrary number of density matrices. Mixed quantum states can be represented as *statistical mixtures* of pure quantum states. The statistical representation of a pure state is unique. On the other hand, the decomposition of a mixed quantum state is not unique. In the geometrical interpretation, a pure state ρ is on the surface of the Bloch sphere, whereas the mixed state σ is inside it. A maximally mixed quantum state, $\sigma = I/2$, can be found in the center of the Bloch sphere. The mixed state can be expressed as a probabilistic mixture of pure states $\{\rho_1, \rho_2\}$ and $\{\rho_3, \rho_4\}$. As has been stated by von Neumann, the *decomposition of a mixed state is not unique*, since it can be expressed as a mixture of $\{\rho_1, \rho_2\}$ or equivalently of $\{\rho_3, \rho_4\}$.

One can use a pure state ρ to recover a mixed state σ from it, after the effects of the environment (E) are traced out. With the help of the partial trace operator, the receiver can decouple the environment from his mixed state, and the original state can be recovered by discarding the effects of the environment. If receiver's state is a *probabilistic mixture* $\sigma = \sum_i p_i |\varphi_i\rangle\langle\varphi_i|$, then a global pure *purification* state $|\Psi\rangle$ exists, which from the receiver's state can be expressed as $\sigma = Tr_E |\Psi\rangle\langle\Psi|$.

Note that the density matrix σ can be recovered from $|\Psi\rangle$ after discarding the environment. The decoupling of the environment can be achieved with the Tr_E operator. For any unitary transformation of the environment, the pure state $|\Psi\rangle$ is a unique state. We have seen that the decomposition of mixed quantum states into pure quantum states is not unique, and hence for example, it can be easily verified that the decomposition of a mixed state $\sigma = \frac{1}{2}(|0\rangle\langle0| + |1\rangle\langle1|)$ can be made with pure states $\{|0\rangle, |1\rangle\}$, and also can be given with pure states $\left\{ \frac{1}{\sqrt{2}}(|0\rangle + |1\rangle), \frac{1}{\sqrt{2}}(|0\rangle - |1\rangle) \right\}$. Here, we have just changed the basis from rectilinear to diagonal, and we have used just pure states – and it resulted in the same mixed quantum state.

9.2.2 Quantum Measurement

Now, let us turn to measurements and their relation to the density matrices discussed in the previous section. Assuming a projective measurement device, defined by measurement operators – that is, projectors $\{P_j\}$. The projector P_j is a Hermitian matrix, for which $P_j = P_j^\dagger$ and $P_j^2 = P_j$. According to the third *postulate of quantum mechanics* the trace operator can be used to give the probability of the outcome j belonging to the operator P_j in the following way [1]:

$$Pr[j|P_j\rho] = Tr\left(P_j\rho P_j^\dagger\right) = Tr\left(P_j^\dagger P_j\rho\right) = Tr\left(P_j\rho\right). \tag{9.13}$$

After the measurement, the measurement operator P_j leaves the system in a post-measurement state:

$$\rho_j = \frac{P_j\left[\sum_{i=1}^n p_i |\psi_i\rangle\langle\psi_i|\right]P_j}{Tr\left(P_j\left[\sum_{i=1}^n p_i |\psi_i\rangle\langle\psi_i|\right]P_j\right)} = \frac{P_j\rho P_j}{Tr\left(P_j\rho P_j\right)} = \frac{P_j\rho P_j}{Tr\left(P_j\rho\right)}. \tag{9.14}$$

If we have a pure quantum state, $|\psi\rangle = \alpha|0\rangle + \beta|1\rangle$, where $\alpha = \langle0|\psi\rangle$ and $\beta = \langle1|\psi\rangle$. Using the trace operator and the notation $\langle0||\psi\rangle = \langle0|\psi\rangle$, the measurement probabilities of $|0\rangle$ and $|1\rangle$ can be expressed as

$$\begin{aligned} Pr[j = 0|\psi] = Tr(P_j\rho) &= Tr(|0\rangle\langle0||\psi\rangle\langle\psi|) = \langle0|\psi\rangle Tr(|0\rangle\langle\psi|) \\ &= \langle0|\psi\rangle\langle\psi|0\rangle = \langle0|\psi\rangle(\langle0|\psi\rangle)^* = \alpha\cdot\alpha^* = |\alpha|^2, \end{aligned} \tag{9.15}$$

And with $\langle1||\psi\rangle = \langle1|\psi\rangle$

$$\begin{aligned} Pr[j = 1|\psi] = Tr(P_j\rho) &= Tr(|1\rangle\langle1||\psi\rangle\langle\psi|) = \langle1|\psi\rangle Tr(|1\rangle\langle\psi|) \\ &= \langle1|\psi\rangle\langle\psi|1\rangle = \langle1|\psi\rangle(\langle1|\psi\rangle)^* = \beta\cdot\beta^* = |\beta|^2, \end{aligned} \tag{9.16}$$

as it was expected.

Let us assume we have an *orthonormal* basis $M = \{ | x_1 \rangle \langle x_1 |, ..., | x_n \rangle \langle x_n | \}$ and an arbitrary (i.e. non-diagonal) density matrix ρ. The set of Hermitian operators $P_i = \{|x_i\rangle\langle x_i|\}$ satisfies the *completeness relation*, where $P_i = | x_i \rangle \langle x_i |$ is the projector over $|x_i\rangle$; that is, the quantum measurement operator $M_i = | x_i \rangle \langle x_i |$ is a valid measurement operator. The measurement operator M_i projects the input quantum system $|\psi\rangle$ to the pure state $|x_i\rangle$ from the orthonormal basis $M = \{ | x_1 \rangle \langle x_1 |, ..., | x_n \rangle \langle x_n | \}$. Now, the probability that after the measurement the quantum state $|\psi\rangle$ is in basis state $|x_i\rangle$ can be expressed as

$$\langle \psi | M_i^\dagger M_i | \psi \rangle = \langle \psi | P_i | \psi \rangle$$
$$= \left(\sum_{j=1}^{n} x_j^* \langle x_j | \right) | x_i \rangle \langle x_i | \left(\sum_{l=1}^{n} |x_i\rangle x_l \right) = |x_i|^2. \tag{9.17}$$

In the computational basis $\{|x1\rangle, ..., | x_n \rangle\}$, the state of the quantum system after the measurement can be expressed as

$$\rho' = \sum_{i=1}^{n} p_i |x_i\rangle \langle x_i|, \tag{9.18}$$

and the matrix of the quantum state ρ' will be *diagonal* in the computational basis $\{|x_i\rangle\}$, and can be given by

$$\rho' = \begin{bmatrix} p_1 & 0 & \cdots & 0 \\ 0 & p_2 & 0 & \vdots \\ \vdots & \vdots & \ddots & 0 \\ 0 & 0 & 0 & p_n \end{bmatrix}. \tag{9.19}$$

Design Example 9.1 [1]

Let us assume we have an initial (not diagonal) density matrix in the computational basis $\{|0\rangle, |1\rangle\}$, for example, $|\psi\rangle = \alpha | 0 \rangle + \beta | 1 \rangle$ with $p = |\alpha|^2$ and $1 - p = |\beta|^2$ as [1]

$$\rho = |\psi\rangle\langle\psi| = \left\{ \begin{matrix} |\alpha|^2 & \alpha\beta^* \\ \alpha^*\beta & |\beta|^2 \end{matrix} \right\},$$

where $\{\}$ denotes a matrix, and we have an orthonormal basis $M = \{ | 0 \rangle \langle 0 |, | 1 \rangle \langle 1 | \}$. In this case, the after-measurement state can be expressed as

$$\rho' = p|0\rangle\langle 0| + (1-p)|1\rangle\langle 1| = \left\{ \begin{matrix} |\alpha|^2 & 0 \\ 0 & |\beta|^2 \end{matrix} \right\} = \left\{ \begin{matrix} p & 0 \\ 0 & 1-p \end{matrix} \right\}.$$

As can be seen, the matrix of ρ' is a diagonal matrix in the computational basis $\{|0\rangle, |1\rangle\}$. The previous two equations highlight the difference between quantum superpositions (probability-amplitude-weighted sum) and classical probabilistic mixtures of quantum states.

Now, let us see the result of the measurement on the input quantum system ρ

$$M(\rho) = \sum_{j=0}^{1} M_j \rho M_j^\dagger = M_0 \rho M_0^\dagger + M_1 \rho M_1^\dagger.$$

For the measurement operators $M_0 = | 0 \rangle \langle 0|$ and $M_1 = | 1 \rangle \langle 1|$, the completeness relation holds:

$$\sum_{j=0}^{1} M_j M_j^\dagger = |0\rangle \langle 0||0\rangle\langle 0| + |1\rangle \langle 1||1\rangle \langle 1|$$

$$= |0\rangle\langle 0| + |1\rangle\langle 1| = \left\{ \begin{matrix} 1 & 0 \\ 0 & 1 \end{matrix} \right\} = I.$$

(Continued)

Design Example 9.1 (Continued)

Using the input system $\rho = |\psi\rangle\langle\psi|$, where $|\psi\rangle = \alpha|0\rangle + \beta|1\rangle$, the state after the measurement operation is

$$M(\rho) = \sum_{j=0}^{1} M_j\rho M_j^\dagger = |0\rangle\langle 0|\rho|0\rangle\langle 0| + |1\rangle\langle 1|\rho|1\rangle\langle 1|$$

$$= |0\rangle\langle 0||\psi\rangle\langle\psi||0\rangle\langle 0| + |1\rangle\langle 1||\psi\rangle\langle\psi||1\rangle\langle 1|$$

$$= |0\rangle\langle 0|\psi\rangle\langle 0|\psi\rangle\langle 0| + |1\rangle\langle 1|\psi\rangle\langle 1|\psi\rangle\langle 1|$$

$$= |\langle 0|\psi\rangle|^2|0\rangle\langle 0| + |\langle 1|\psi\rangle|^2|1\rangle\langle 1|$$

$$= |\alpha|^2|0\rangle\langle 0| + |\beta|^2|1\rangle\langle 1| = p|0\rangle\langle 0| + 1 - p|1\rangle\langle 1|.$$

As we have found, after the measurement operation (ρ), the *off-diagonal* entries will have zero values, and they *have no relevance*. It follows that the initial input system $\rho = |\psi\rangle\langle\psi|$ after operation M becomes

$$\rho = \left\{ \begin{matrix} |\alpha|^2 & \alpha\beta^* \\ \alpha^*\beta & |\beta|^2 \end{matrix} \right\} \xrightarrow{M} \rho' = \left\{ \begin{matrix} |\alpha|^2 & 0 \\ 0 & |\beta|^2 \end{matrix} \right\}. \tag{9.20}$$

Orthonormal basis decomposition: Let assume we have an orthonormal basis $\{|b_1\rangle, |b_2\rangle, \ldots, |b_n\rangle\}$ that can be used to rewrite the quantum system $|\psi\rangle$ in a unique decomposition

$$|\psi\rangle = b_1|b_1\rangle + b_2|b_2\rangle + \cdots + b_n|b_n\rangle = \sum_{i=1}^{n} b_i|b_i\rangle, \tag{9.21}$$

with complex b_i. Since $\langle\psi|\psi\rangle = 1$, we can express it in the form

$$\langle\psi|\psi\rangle = \sum_{i=1}^{n}\sum_{j=1}^{n} b_i^* b_j\langle b_i|b_j\rangle = \sum_{i=1}^{n} |b_i|^2 = 1, \tag{9.22}$$

where b_i^* is the complex conjugate of the *probability amplitude* b_i, thus, $|b_i|^2$ is the *probability p_i* of measuring the quantum system $|\psi\rangle$ in the given basis state $|b_i\rangle$, that is, $p_i = |b_i|^2$.

Using Eqs. (9.6), (9.21), and (9.22), the density matrix of quantum system $|\psi\rangle$ can be expressed as

$$\rho = |b_1|^2|b_1\rangle\langle b_1| + |b_2|^2|b_2\rangle\langle b_2| + \cdots + |b_n|^2|b_n\rangle\langle b_n|$$

$$= \sum_{i=1}^{n} |b_i|^2|b_i\rangle\langle b_i| = \sum_{i=1}^{n} p_i|b_i\rangle\langle b_i|. \tag{9.23}$$

This density matrix is a diagonal matrix with the probabilities in the diagonal entries in the same form as given in Eq. (9.19). The diagonal property of the density matrix Eq. (9.23) in Eq. (9.19) can be checked, since the elements of the matrix can be expressed as

$$\rho_{ij} = \langle b_i|\rho|b_j\rangle$$

$$= \langle b_i|\left(\sum_{l=1}^{n} p_l|b_l\rangle\langle b_l|\right)|b_j\rangle = \sum_{l=1}^{n} p_l\langle b_i|b_l\rangle\langle b_l|b_j\rangle, \tag{9.24}$$

where $\sum_{l=1}^{n} p_l = 1$.

The projective and positive operator valued measurement (POVM) measurement: The projective measurement, also known as the von Neumann measurement, can formally be described by the Hermitian operator $\mathcal{Z}$, which has the spectral decomposition $\mathcal{Z} = \sum_m \lambda_m P_m$, where P_m is a projector to the eigenspace of $\mathcal{Z}$ with eigenvalue λ_m. For the projectors, $\sum_m P_m = I$, and they are pairwise orthogonal. The measurement outcome m corresponds to the eigenvalue λ_m, with measurement probability $Pr[m \mid \psi)] = \langle \psi \mid P_m \mid \psi \rangle$. When a quantum system is measured in an orthonormal basis $|m\rangle$, then we make a projective measurement with projector $P_m = |m\rangle\langle m|$; thus, $\mathcal{Z}$ can be expressed as $\mathcal{Z} = \sum_m m P_m$. The $\mathcal{P}$ POVM (positive operator valued measurement) is intended to select from among the non-orthogonal states $\{|\psi_i\rangle\}_{i=1}^m$ and is defined by a set of POVM operators $\{\mathcal{M}_i\}_{i=1}^{m+1}$, where $\mathcal{M}_i = \mathcal{Q}_i^\dagger \mathcal{Q}_i$, and since we are not interested in the post-measurement state, exact knowledge about the measurement operator $\mathcal{Q}_i$ is not required. For POVM operators $\mathcal{M}_i$, the completeness relation holds: $\sum_i \mathcal{M}_i = I$. For the POVM, the probability of a given outcome n for the state $|\psi\rangle$ can be expressed as $Pr[i \mid \psi)] = \langle \psi \mid \mathcal{M}_i \mid \psi \rangle$.

The POVM also can be imagined as a black box that outputs a number from 1 to m for the given input quantum state ψ, using the set of operators $\{\mathcal{M}_1, \ldots \mathcal{M}_m, \mathcal{M}_{m+1}\}$, where $\{\mathcal{M}_1, \ldots, \mathcal{M}_m\}$ are responsible for distinguishing m different typically non-orthogonal states; that is, if we observe $i \in [1, m]$ on the display of the measurement device, we can be sure that the result is correct. However, because unknown non-orthogonal states cannot be distinguished with probability 1, we have to introduce an extra measurement operator, $\mathcal{M}_{m+1}$, as the price of the distinguishability of the m different states, and if we obtain $m+1$ as the measurement results, we can say nothing about $|\psi\rangle$. This operator can be expressed as $\mathcal{M}_{m+1} = I - \sum_{i=1}^m \mathcal{M}_i$. Such an $\mathcal{M}_{m+1}$ can be always constructed if the states in $\{|\psi_n\rangle\}_{n=1}^m$ are linearly independent. We will not list the operator $\mathcal{M}_{m+1}$ hereafter. The POVM measurement apparatus will be a key ingredient to distinguish quantum codewords with zero error, and to reach the zero-error capacity of quantum channels. The POVM can be viewed as the most general formula from among any of the possible measurements in quantum mechanics. Therefore, the effect of a projective measurement can be described by POVM operators, too. Or in other words, the projective measurements are a special case of POVM measurement. The elements of the POVM are not necessarily orthogonal, and the number of elements can be larger than the dimensions of the Hilbert space that they are originally used in.

9.3 Q Channel Description

If we are interested in the origin of noise (randomness) in the $\mathcal{Q}$ channel, the model should be refined in the following way: the transmitter's register X, the purification state P, channel input A, channel output B, and the environment state E. The input system A is described by a quantum system ρ_x, which occurs on the input with probability $p_X(x)$. They together form an ensemble denoted by $\{p_X(x), \rho_x\}_{x \in X}$, where x is a classical variable from the register X. In the preparation process, the transmitter generates pure states ρ_x according to the random variable x; that is, the input density operator can be expressed as $\rho_x = |x\rangle\langle x|$, where the classical states $\{|x\rangle\}_{x \in X}$ form an orthonormal basis. According to the elements of the transmitter's register X, the input system can be characterized by the quantum system $\rho_A = \sum_{x \in X} p_X(x)\rho_x = \sum_{x \in X} p_X(x)|x\rangle\langle x|$. The system description is illustrated in Figure 9.5.

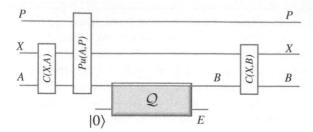

Figure 9.5 Detailed model of Q channel: P purification state, X transmitter register, A channel input state, B channel output state, E environment, $C(X,A)$ correlation between X and A, $Pu(A,P)$ purification of A with P, and $C(X,B)$ correlation between X and B.

The system state ρ_x with the corresponding probability distribution $p_X(x)$ can be identified by a set of measurement operators $\mathcal{M} = \{|x\rangle\langle x|\}_{x \in X}$. If the density operators ρ_x in ρ_A are mixed, the probability distribution $p_X(x)$ and the classical variable x from the register X cannot be identified by the measurement operators $\mathcal{M} = \{|x\rangle\langle x|\}_{x \in X}$, since the system state ρ_x is assumed to be a mixed or in a non-orthonormal state. The transmitter's register X and the quantum system A can be viewed as the tensor product system $\{p_X(x), |x\rangle\langle x|_X \otimes \rho_A^x\}_{x \in X}$, where the classical variable x is correlated with the quantum system ρ_x, using the orthonormal basis $\{|x\rangle\}_{x \in X}$. The transmitter's register X represents a classical variable, the channel input system is generated corresponding to the register X in the form of a quantum state, and it is described by the density operator ρ_A^x. The input system A with respect to the register X is described by the density operator $\rho_{XA} = \sum_{x \in X} p_X(x) |x\rangle\langle x|_X \otimes \rho_A^x$, where $\rho_A^x = |\psi_x\rangle\langle\psi_x|_A$ is the density matrix representation of the transmitter's input state $|\psi_x\rangle_A$.

The purification gives us a new viewpoint on the noise of the quantum channel. Assuming the transmitter's side A and the transmitter's register X, the spectral decomposition of the density operator ρ_A can be expressed as $\rho_A = \sum_x p_X(x)|x\rangle\langle x|_A$, where $p_X(x)$ is the probability of the variable x in the transmitter's register X. The $\{p_X(x), |x\rangle\}$ together is called an ensemble, where $|x\rangle$ is a quantum state according to the classical variable x. Using the set of orthonormal basis vectors $\{|x\rangle_P\}_{x \in X}$ of the purification system P, the purification of ρ_A can be given in the following way:

$$|\varphi\rangle_{PA} = \sum_x \sqrt{p_X(x)}|x\rangle_P|x\rangle_A. \tag{9.25}$$

From the purified system state $|\varphi\rangle_{PA}$, the original system state ρ_A can be expressed with the partial trace operator (see Design Example 9.2) $Tr_P(\cdot)$, which traces out the purification state from the system $\rho_A = Tr_P(|\varphi\rangle\langle\varphi|_{PA})$

From the joint system (Eq. 9.24) and the purified state, one can introduce a new definition. The *extension* of ρ_A can be given as $\rho_A = Tr_P(\omega_{PA})$, where ω_{PA} is the joint system of the purification state P and the channel input A [4], which represents a noisy state.

Isometric extension is of utmost importance, because it helps us understand what happens between the quantum channel and its environment whenever a quantum state is transmitted from A (transmitter) to B (receiver). Since the channel and the environment together form a closed physical system, the isometric extension of the quantum channel Q is the *unitary representation* of the channel $Q : U_{A \to BE}$, enabling the one-sender and two-receiver view: apart from A, the sender, both receiver B and the environment of the channel are playing the role of receivers $r(B,E)$. In other words, the output of the noisy quantum channel Q can be described only after the environment of the channel is traced out

$$\rho_B = Tr_E(U_{A \to BE}(\rho_A)) = Q(\rho_A).$$

Kraus representation: The map of the quantum channel can also be expressed by means of a special tool called the Kraus representation. For a given input system ρ_A and quantum channel $\mathcal{N}$, this representation can be expressed as

$$\mathcal{Q}(\rho_A) = \sum_i Q_i \rho_A Q_i^\dagger, \tag{9.26}$$

where Q_i are the Kraus operators, and $\sum_i Q_i^\dagger Q_i = I$. The isometric extension of $\mathcal{Q}$ by means of the Kraus representation can be expressed as

$$\rho_B = \mathcal{Q}(\rho_A) = \sum_i Q_i \rho_A Q_i^\dagger \rightarrow U_{A \rightarrow BE}(\rho_A) = \sum_i Q_i \otimes |i\rangle_E. \tag{9.27}$$

The action of the quantum channel $\mathcal{Q}$ on an operator $|k\rangle\langle l|$, where $\{|k\rangle\}$ form an orthonormal basis can also be given in operator form using the Kraus operator $Q_{kl} = \mathcal{Q}(|k\rangle\langle l|)$. By exploiting the property $UU^\dagger = P_{BE}$, for the input quantum system ρ_A

$$\rho_B = U_{A \rightarrow BE}(\rho_A) = U\rho_A U^\dagger = \left(\sum_i Q_i \otimes |i\rangle_E\right)\rho_A\left(\sum_j Q_j^\dagger \otimes \langle j|_E\right)$$
$$= \sum_{i,j} Q_i \rho_A Q_j^\dagger \otimes |i\rangle\langle j|_E. \tag{9.28}$$

If we trace out the environment, we get the equivalence of the two representations

$$\rho_B = Tr_E(U_{A \rightarrow BE}(\rho_A)) = \sum_i Q_i \rho_A Q_i^\dagger. \tag{9.29}$$

Design Example 9.2   Partial Trace

A density matrix that describes only a subset of a larger quantum space is referred to as a reduced density matrix. The larger quantum system can be expressed as the tensor product of the reduced density matrices of the subsystems if there is no correlation (entanglement) between the subsystems. On the other hand, if we have two subsystems with reduced density matrices ρ_A and ρ_B, then from the overall density matrix denoted by ρ_{AB} the subsystems can be expressed as $\rho_A = Tr_B(\rho_{AB})$ and $\rho_B = Tr_A(\rho_{AB})$, where Tr_B and Tr_A refer to the partial trace operators. So, this partial trace operator can be used to generate one of the subsystems from the joint state $\rho_{AB} = |\psi_A\rangle\langle\psi_A| \otimes |\psi_B\rangle\langle\psi_B|$, which can be represented as

$$\rho_A = Tr_B(\rho_{AB}) = Tr_B(|\psi_A\langle\psi_A|\otimes|\psi_B\rangle\langle\psi_B|)$$
$$= |\psi_A\rangle\langle\psi_A|Tr(|\psi_B\rangle\langle\psi_B|) = |\psi_A\rangle\langle\psi_A|\langle\psi_B|\psi_B\rangle.$$

Since the inner product is trivially $\langle\psi_B|\psi_B\rangle = 1$, it follows that $Tr_B(\rho_{AB}) = \langle\psi_B|\psi_B\rangle|\psi_A\rangle\langle\psi_A| = |\psi_A\rangle\langle\psi_A| = \rho_A$.

In the calculation, we used the fact that $Tr(|\psi_1\rangle\langle\psi_2|) = \langle\psi_2|\psi_1\rangle$. In general, if we have two systems $A = |i\rangle\langle k|$ and $B = |j\rangle\langle l|$, then the partial trace can be calculated as $Tr_B(A \otimes B) = ATr(B)$, Since $Tr_2(|i\rangle\langle k| \otimes |j\rangle\langle l|) = |i\rangle\langle k| \otimes Tr(|j\rangle\langle l|) = |i\rangle\langle k| \otimes \langle l|j\rangle = \langle l|j\rangle|i\rangle\langle k|$, where $|i\rangle\langle k| \otimes |j\rangle\langle l| = |i\rangle|j\rangle(|k\rangle|l\rangle)^T$. In this expression, we have used the fact that $(AB^T) \otimes (CD^T) = (A \otimes C)(B^T \otimes D^T) = (A \otimes C)(B \otimes D)^T$.

9.3.1 $\mathcal{Q}$ Channel Entropy

The von Neumann entropy: Quantum information processing exploits the quantum nature of information. It offers fundamentally new solutions in the field of computer science and extends the possibilities to a level that cannot be imagined in classical communication systems. On the other hand, it requires the generalization of classical information theory through a quantum perception of the world. As Shannon entropy plays a fundamental role in classical information theory, von Neumann entropy does the same for quantum information. The von Neumann entropy $S(\rho)$ of quantum state ρ can be viewed as an extension of classical entropy for quantum systems. It measures the information of quantum states in the form of the uncertainty of a quantum state.

The classical *Shannon entropy* $H(X)$ of a variable X with probability distribution $p(X)$ can be defined as

$$H(X) = -\sum_{x \in X} p(x) \, log \, (p(x)), \tag{9.30}$$

with $1 \leq H(X) \leq log(|X|)$, where $|X|$ is the cardinality of the set X.

The *von Neumann entropy*

$$S(\rho) = - Tr(\rho \, log \, (\rho)) \tag{9.31}$$

measures the information contained in the quantum system ρ. Furthermore $S(\rho)$ can be expressed by means of the Shannon entropy for the eigenvalue distribution

$$S(\rho) = H(\lambda) = -\sum_{i=1}^{d} \lambda_i \, log \, (\lambda_i), \tag{9.32}$$

where d is the level of the quantum system, and λ_i are the eigenvalues of density matrix ρ.

The Holevo quantity: The *Holevo bound* determines the amount of information that can be extracted from a single-qubit state. If transmitter A sends a quantum state ρ_i with probability p_i over an ideal quantum channel, then at receiver B a mixed state $\rho_B = \rho_A = \sum_i p_i \rho_i$ appears. Receiver B constructs a measurement $\{M_i\}$ to extract the information encoded in the quantum states. If he applies the measurement to ρ_A, the probability distribution of B's classical symbol B will be $\Pr[b \mid \rho_A] = Tr(M_b^\dagger M_b \rho_A)$. As had been shown by Holevo [5], the bound for the maximal classical mutual information between A and B is

$$I(A : B) \leq S(\rho_A) - \sum_i p_i S(\rho_i) \equiv \chi, \tag{9.33}$$

where χ is called the *Holevo quantity*, and Eq. (9.33) is known as the *Holevo bound*.

In classical information theory and classical communication systems, the mutual information I $(A : B)$ is bounded only by the classical entropy of (A), and hence $I(A : B) \leq H(A)$. The mutual information $I(A : B)$ is bounded by the classical entropy of (A), and hence $I(A : B) \leq H(A)$. On the other hand, for mixed states and pure non-orthogonal states, the Holevo quantity χ can be greater than the mutual information $(A : B)$; however, it is still bounded by $H(A)$, which is the bound for the pure orthogonal states

$$I(A : B) \leq \chi \leq H(A). \tag{9.34}$$

The *Holevo bound* highlights the important fact that one qubit can contain at most one classical bit, that is, one cbit of information.

Quantum conditional entropy: Although the classical conditional entropy function always takes a nonnegative value, the *quantum conditional entropy can be negative*. The quantum conditional entropy between quantum systems A and B is given by $S(A \mid B) = S(\rho_{AB}) - S(\rho_B)$. If we have two uncorrelated subsystems ρ_A and ρ_B, then the information of the quantum system ρ_A does not contain any information about ρ_B, and conversely; thus, $S(\rho_{AB}) = S(\rho_A) + S(\rho_B)$, and hence we get $S(A \mid B) = S(\rho_A)$, and similarly $S(B \mid A) = S(\rho_B)$. The negative property of conditional entropy $S(A \mid B)$ can be demonstrated with an *entangled* state, since in this case, the joint quantum entropy of the joint state is less than the sum of the von Neumann entropies of its individual components. For a pure entangled state, $S(\rho_{AB}) = 0$, while $S(\rho_A) = S(\rho_B) = 1$ since the two qubits are in the *maximally mixed* $I/2$ state, which is classically totally unimaginable. Thus, in this case, $S(A \mid B) = -S(\rho_B) \leq 0$, and $S(B \mid A) = -S(\rho_A) \leq 0$ and $S(\rho_A) = S(\rho_B)$.

Quantum mutual information: The classical mutual information $I(\cdot)$ measures the information correlation between random variables A and B. By analogy with classical information theory, $I(A:B)$ can be described by the quantum entropies of individual states and the von Neumann entropy of the joint state as follows:

$$I(A:B) = S(\rho_A) + S(\rho_B) - S(\rho_{AB}) \geq 0, \tag{9.35}$$

that is, the quantum mutual information is always a nonnegative function. However, there is a distinction between classical and quantum systems, since the quantum mutual information can take a value above the maximum of the classical mutual information. This statement can be confirmed if we take into account that for a pure entangled quantum system, the quantum mutual information is $I(A:B) = S(\rho_A) + S(\rho_B) - S(\rho_{AB}) = 1 + 1 - 0 = 2$, and we can rewrite this equation as

$$I(A:B) = 2S(\rho_A) = 2S(\rho_B). \tag{9.36}$$

For some pure joint system ρ_{AB}, Eq. (9.36) can be satisfied such that $S(\rho_A) = S(\rho_B)$ and $S(\rho_{AB}) = 0$. If we use entangled states, the quantum mutual information could be 2, and the quantum conditional entropies could also be 2. In classical information theory, negative entropies can be obtained only in the case of mutual information of three or more systems. An important property of maximized quantum mutual information is that *it is always additive for a quantum channel*. Classical information and quantum information are significantly different in nature. There are many phenomena in quantum systems that cannot be described classically, such as entanglement, which makes it possible to store quantum information in the correlation of quantum states. Similarly, n quantum channel can be used with pure orthogonal states to realize classical information transmission, or it can be used to transmit non-orthogonal states or even quantum entanglement. Information transmission also can be approached using the question of whether the input consists of unentangled or entangled quantum states. This leads us to state that for quantum channels many new capacity definitions exist in comparison to a classical communication channel. With the general communication model and the quantities that are able to represent the information content of quantum states, we can begin to investigate the possibilities and limitations of information transmission through quantum channels [6].

The *quantum relative entropy* measures the informational distance between quantum states, and introduces a deeper characterization of quantum states than the von Neumann entropy. Like the classical relative entropy, this quantity measures the distinguishability of the quantum states; in practice, it can be realized by POVM measurements. The relative entropy classically is a measure that quantifies how close a probability distribution p is to a model or candidate probability distribution q.

For probability distributions p and q, the classical relative entropy is given by

$$D(p\|q) = \sum_i p_i \ log \ \left(\frac{p_i}{q_i}\right), \tag{9.37}$$

while the quantum relative entropy between quantum states ρ and σ is

$$\begin{aligned} D(\rho\|\sigma) &= Tr(\rho \ log \ (\rho)) - Tr(\rho \ log \ (\sigma)) \\ &= Tr[\rho(log \ (\rho) - log \ (\sigma))]. \end{aligned} \tag{9.38}$$

In the box above, the term $Tr(\rho \log (\sigma))$ is finite only if $\rho \log (\sigma) \geq 0$ for all diagonal matrix elements. If this condition is not satisfied, then $D(\rho\|\sigma)$ could be infinite, since the trace of the second term could go to infinity.

The *quantum informational distance* (i.e. the quantum relative entropy) has some distance-like properties (for example, the quantum relative entropy function between a maximally mixed state and an arbitrary quantum state is symmetric, and hence in this case it is not just a pseudo-distance); however, it is *not commutative*, and thus $D(\rho\|\sigma) \neq D(\sigma\|\rho)$, and $D(\rho\|\sigma) \geq 0$ iff $\rho \neq \sigma$, and $D(\rho\|\sigma) = 0$ iff $\rho = \sigma$. Note that if σ has zero eigenvalues, $D(\rho\|\sigma)$ may diverge, otherwise it is a finite and continuous function. Furthermore, the quantum relative entropy function has another interesting property: if we have two density matrices ρ and σ, the following property holds for the traces used in the expression of $D(\rho\|\sigma)$: $Tr(\rho \log (\rho)) \geq Tr(\rho \log (\sigma))$.

The symmetric Kullback–Leibler distance is widely used in classical systems, for example, in computer vision and sound processing. Quantum relative entropy reduces to the classical Kullback–Leibler relative entropy for simultaneously diagonalizable matrices. We note that the quantum mutual information can be defined by quantum relative entropy $(\cdot\|\cdot)$. This quantity can be regarded as the informational distance between the tensor product of the individual subsystems $\rho_A \otimes \rho_B$, and the joint state ρ_{AB} as follows:

$$I(A:B) = D(\rho_{AB}\|\rho_A \otimes \rho_B) = S(\rho_A) + S(\rho_B) - S(\rho_{AB}). \tag{9.39}$$

Quantum Rényi entropy: As we have seen, quantum informational entropy can be defined by the S(ρ) von Neumann entropy function. On the other hand, another entropy function can also be defined in the quantum domain: it is called the Rényi entropy and is denoted by R(ρ). This function is important mainly for the description of quantum entanglement. The Rényi entropy function is defined as follows:

$$R(\rho) = \frac{1}{1-r} Tr(\rho^r), \tag{9.40}$$

where $r \geq 0$, while R(ρ) is equal to the von Neumann entropy function S(ρ) if $\lim_{r \to 1} R(\rho) = S(\rho)$. If parameter r converges to infinity, then we have $\lim_{r \to \infty} R(\rho) = -\log (\|\rho\|)$. On the other hand, if $r = 0$ then R(ρ) can be expressed from the rank of the density matrix R$(\rho) = \log (rank(\rho))$.

9.3.2 Some History

The field of quantum information processing is a rapidly growing field of science, and will continue to attract the attention of the researchers since there are still many challenging questions and problems.

Beginnings of quantum information theory: Quantum information theory extends the possibilities of classical information theory; however, for some questions, it gives extremely different answers. It is expected that the advanced communications and quantum networking technologies offered by quantum information processing will revolutionize traditional communication and networking methods. Classical information theory was founded by Claude Shannon in 1948 [7]. In Shannon's paper, the mathematical framework of communication was invented, and the main definitions and theorems of classical information theory were laid down. On the other hand, classical information theory is just one part of quantum information theory. The other, missing part is quantum theory, which was completely finalized in 1926. The results of quantum information theory are mainly based on the results of von Neumann, who constructed the mathematical background of quantum mechanics [8]. Further details about the history of quantum theory, and the main results of physicists from the first half of the twentieth century such as Planck, Einstein, Schrödinger, Heisenberg, or Dirac, can be found in [9–13].

An interesting work about the importance of quantum mechanical processes was published by Dowling and Milburn [14]. Some fundamental results from the very early days of quantum mechanics can be found in [14–24]. About the early days of information theory, see the work of Pierce [25]. A good introduction to information theory can be found in the work of Yeung [26]. More information about the connection between information theory and statistical mechanics can be found in work of Aspect from 1981 [27] and in the books of Jaynes [28] or Petz [29]. The elements of classical information theory and its mathematical background were summarized in a very good book by Cover and Thomas [30]. On matrix analysis, a great work was published by Horn and Johnson [31].

A very good introduction to quantum information theory was published by Bennett and Shor [32]. The idea that the results of quantum information theory can be used to solve computational problems was first claimed by Deutsch in 1985 [33].

Later, in the 1990s, the answers to the most important questions of quantum information theory were answered, and the main elements and the fundamentals of this field were discovered. Details about the simulation of quantum systems and the possibility of encoding quantum information in physical particles can be found in Feynman's work from 1982 [34]. Further information on quantum simulators and continuous-time automata can be found in the work of Vollbrecht and Cirac [35]. For the work on quantum coding and quantum compression, mainly by Schumacher, see [32, 36–46].

Quantum entanglement is one of the most important differences between the classical and the quantum worlds. An interesting paper on communication via one- and two-particle operators on Einstein–Podolsky–Rosen states was published in 1992, by Bennett and Wiesner [47]. About the history of entanglement, see the paper of Einstein et al. from 1935 [18]. A complete mathematical background of quantum entanglement can be found in Nielsen's book [48] or the one by Hayashi [49], or in a very good article published by the four Horodeckis in 2009 [50]. We have seen that entanglement concentration can be applied to generate maximally mixed entangled states. We also gave the asymptotic rate at which entanglement concentration can be made; it is called the entropy of entanglement, and we have expressed it in an explicit form. A very important paper on the communication cost of entanglement transformations was published by Hayden and Winter; for details, see [51–53].

Quantum channels: About the statistical properties of the HSW (Holevo, Schumacher, and Westmoreland) theory and the general HSW capacity, a very interesting paper was published by Hayashi and Nagaoka in 2003 [54]. As we have seen, some results of quantum information theory are similar to the results of classical information theory; however, many concepts have no classical analogue.

As we have seen in this section, the Holevo theorem gives an information-theoretic meaning to the von Neumann entropy; however, it cannot be used to interpret the von Neumann entropy of physical macrosystems. Further properties of the von Neumann entropy function were studied by Audenaert in 2007 [55].

The concept of quantum mutual information measures the classical information that can be transmitted through a noisy quantum channel (originally introduced by Adami and Cerf [56]); however, it cannot be used to measure the maximum transmittable quantum information. The maximized quantum mutual information is always additive; however, this is not true for the Holevo information. In this case, the entanglement makes the Holevo information non-additive, but it has no effect on the quantum mutual information.

For research on satellite quantum communications, see [57–60]. For research results on quantum repeaters, see [61–67]. For further research topics on quantum channels, see [68–80].

9.4 $\mathcal{Q}$ Channel Classical Capacities

Communication over quantum channels is limited by the corresponding capacities. Now, we lay down the fundamental theoretic results on the *classical capacities of quantum channels*. These results are required to analyze the advanced and more promising properties of quantum communications.

Extended Formal Model: The discussed model is general enough to analyze the limitations of information transfer over $\mathcal{Q}$ channels. However, later we will investigate special $\mathcal{Q}$ channels that model specific physical environments. Each $\mathcal{Q}$ channel can be represented as a CPTP map (*completely positive trace preserving*), and hence the process of information transmission through a quantum communication channel can be described as a quantum operation.

The general model of a $\mathcal{Q}$ channel describes the transmission of an input quantum bit, and its interaction with the environment as shown in Figure 9.6.

Assuming transmitter A sends quantum state ρ_A into the channel, this state becomes entangled with the environment ρ_E, which is initially in a pure state $|0\rangle$. For a mixed input state, a so-called *purification state P* can be defined, from which the original mixed state can be restored by a partial trace (see Design Example 9.2) of the pure system $\rho_A P$. The unitary operation U_{AE} of a quantum channel $\mathcal{N}$ entangles $\rho_A P$ with the environment ρ_E, and outputs receiver B's mixed state as ρ_B (and the purification state as P). The purification state is a reference system, it cannot be accessed, and it remains the same after the transmission.

The output of the noisy quantum channel is denoted by ρ_B and the post state of the environment by ρ_E, while the postpurification state after the output realized on the channel output is depicted by P.

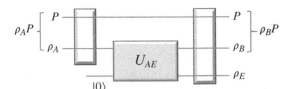

Figure 9.6 The formal model of a noisy quantum communication channel. The output of the channel is a mixed state.

9.4.1 Capacity of Classical Channels

Before we start to investigate quantum channels, we survey the results of transmitting information over classical noisy channels. In order to achieve reliable (error-free) information transfer, we use the so-called *channel coding*, which extends the payload (useful) information bits with redundancy bits so that at the receiver B will be able to correct some amount of error by means of this redundancy.

The channel is given an input A, and maps it probabilistically (it is a *stochastic* mapping, not a unitary or deterministic transformation) to an output B, and the probability of this mapping is denoted by $p(B|A)$.

The *channel capacity* $C(N)$ of a *classical* memoryless communication channel N gives an upper bound on the number of classical bits that can be transmitted per channel use, in a reliable manner, that is, with an arbitrarily small error at the receiver. As has been proved by Shannon, the capacity C (N) of a noisy classical memoryless communication channel N can be expressed by means of the maximum of the mutual information $I(A:B)$ over all possible input distributions $p(x)$ of random variable X:

$$C(N) = \max\ I(A:B)p(x).$$

In order to make the capacity definition more plausible, let us consider Figure 9.7. Here, the effect of the environment E is represented by the classical conditional entropies $H(A:E|B) > 0$ and $H(B:E|A) > 0$.

Shannon's noisy coding theorem claims that forming K different codewords $m = \log K$ of length from the source bits and transmitting each of them using the channel n times (m to n coding) the rate at which information can be transmitted through the channel is $R = \log(K)/n$, and an exponentially small probability of error at this rate can be achieved only if $R \le C(N)$, otherwise the probability of a successful decoding exponentially tends to zero, as the number of channel users increases. Now, having introduced the capacity of a classical channel, it is important to highlight the following distinction. The asymptotic capacity of any channel describes that rate that can be achieved if the channel can be used n times (denoted by $N^{\otimes n}$), where $n \to \infty$. Without loss of generality, in the case of $n = 1$ we speak about single-use capacity. Multiple-channel uses can be implemented in consecutive or parallel ways; however, for practical reasons, we will prefer the latter method.

Transmission of classical information over noisy Q channels: As the next step, we are leaving the well-known classical (macro) world and just entering the border zone. By this, we mean that we remain classical in terms of inputs and outputs but allow the channel to operate in a quantum manner.

Q channels can be used in many different ways to transmit information from A to B. Transmitter A can send classical bits to B, but she can also transmit quantum bits. In the first case, we talk about

Figure 9.7 Effects of the environment on the transmittable information and on the receiver's uncertainty.

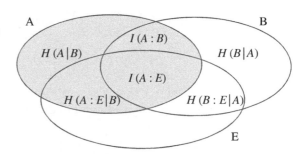

the classical capacity of the quantum channel, whereas in the latter case, we have a different measure: the quantum capacity. The map of the channel is denoted by $\mathcal{Q}$, which is trace preserving if $Tr(\mathcal{Q}(\rho)) = Tr(\rho)$ for all density matrices ρ, and positive if the eigenvalues of $\mathcal{Q}(\rho)$ are nonnegative whenever the eigenvalues of ρ are nonnegative.

Compared to classical channels, which have only one definition of capacity, the transmittable classical information and thus the corresponding capacity definition can be different when one considers $\mathcal{Q}$ channels. This fact splits the classical capacity of $\mathcal{Q}$ channels into three categories, namely, the (*unentangled*) *classical* (also known as the *product-state* classical capacity, or the HSW [Holevo–Schumacher–Westmoreland] capacity) *capacity* ($\mathcal{N}$), *private classical capacity* $P(\mathcal{Q})$, and *entanglement-assisted classical capacity* $C_E(\mathcal{Q})$.

The (*unentangled*) *classical capacity* $C(\mathcal{Q})$ is a natural extension of the capacity definition from classical channels to the quantum world. For the sake of simplicity, the term *classical capacity* will refer to the *unentangled* version in the sequel. (The entangled version will be referred as the entanglement-assisted classical capacity. As we will see, the HSW capacity is defined for product-state inputs; however, it is possible to extend it for entangled input states).

The *private classical capacity* $P(\mathcal{Q})$ has deep relevance in secret quantum communications and quantum cryptography. It describes the rate at which A is able to send classical information through the channel in a secure manner. Security here means that an eavesdropper will not be able to access the encoded information without revealing herself/himself.

The *entanglement-assisted classical capacity* $C_E(\mathcal{Q})$ measures the classical information that can be transmitted through the channel if A and B have already shared entanglement before the transmission. A well-known example of such protocols is *superdense coding* [81]. Next, we discuss the aforementioned classical capacities of quantum channels in detail.

As the first obvious generalization of the classical channel capacity definition, we maximize the quantum mutual information over all possible input ensembles $C(\mathcal{Q}) = \max I(A:B)$. Next, we begin a discussion of the classical information transmission capability of a noisy $\mathcal{Q}$ channel.

The Holevo–Schumacher–Westmoreland capacity: The HSW theorem defines the maximum classical information that can be transmitted through a noisy quantum channel $\mathcal{Q}$ if the input contains product states (i.e. entanglement is not allowed, also known as the product-state classical capacity) and the output is measured by a joint measurement setting. In this setting, for the quantum noisy communication channel $\mathcal{Q}$, the classical capacity can be expressed as follows:

$$
\begin{aligned}
C(\mathcal{Q}) &= \max\nolimits_{all\ \rho_i, p_i} \chi = \max\nolimits_{all\ \rho_i, p_i} \left[S(\sigma_{out}) - \sum_i p_i S(\sigma_i) \right] \\
&= \max \left[S\left(\mathcal{Q}\left(\sum_i p_i \rho_i \right) \right) - \sum_i p_i S(\mathcal{Q}(\rho_i)) \right] = \chi(\mathcal{Q}),
\end{aligned}
\tag{9.41}
$$

If A chooses among a set of quantum codewords, then is it possible to transmit these codewords through the noisy quantum channel $\mathcal{Q}$ to B with an arbitrary small error? If

$$
R < C(\mathcal{Q}) = \max \left[S\left(\mathcal{Q}\left(\sum_i p_i \rho_i \right) \right) - \sum_i p_i S(\mathcal{Q}(\rho_i)) \right];
\tag{9.42}
$$

and if A adjusts R to be under $\max_{all\ p_i, \rho_i} \chi$, then she can transmit her codewords with an arbitrarily small error. If A chooses $R > C(Q)$, then she cannot select a quantum code of arbitrary size, which was needed for her to achieve error-free communication. The HSW channel capacity guarantees error-free quantum communication only if $R < C(\mathcal{Q}) = \max_{all\ p_i, \rho_i} \chi$ is satisfied for her code rate R.

Classical capacities of a Q channel: The asymptotic channel capacity is the true measure" of the various channel capacities, rather than the single-use capacity, which characterizes the capacity only in a very special case. In the following, the three classical capacities of the $\mathcal{Q}$ channel will be discussed.

As an illustration, let us look in an example allowing the comparison of the classical capacity of a simple channel model in the classical and quantum contexts. The binary symmetric channel inverts the input *cbits* with probability p and leaves it unchanged with $(1 - p)$. The equivalent quantum bit-flip channel (see Chapter 8) applies the Pauli X and the identity transform I.

Considering the worst case $p = 0.5$, all the sent information vanishes in the classical channel C $(N) = 1 - H(p) = 0$. However, the HSW theorem enables optimization not only over the input probabilities but also over input ensembles $\{p_i, \rho_i\}$. If we set ρ_i to the eigenvectors of Pauli X, deriving them from its spectral decomposition $X = 1 \mid + \rangle \langle + \mid + (-1) \mid - \rangle \langle - \mid$, where $\mid \pm \rangle = (\mid 0 \rangle \pm \mid 1 \rangle)/\sqrt{2}$, $C(\mathcal{N}) = 1$ can be achieved. This result is more than surprising; encoding into quantum states in certain cases may improve the transfer of classical information between distant points. That is, the increased degree of freedom enables the uncertainty introduced by the channel to be reduced.

Measurement settings: Similar to classical channel encoding, the quantum states can be transmitted in codewords n qubit of length using the quantum channel consecutively n times or, equivalently, we can send codewords over n copies of quantum channel $\mathcal{Q}$ denoted by $\mathcal{Q}^{\otimes n}$. For the sake of simplicity, we use $n = 2$ in the figures illustrating the following explanation. In order to make the transient smoother between the single-shot and the asymptotic approaches, we depicted the scenario using *product input states* and *single* (or independent) measurement devices at the output of the channel in Figure 9.8. In that case, the $C(\mathcal{Q})$ classical capacity of quantum channel $\mathcal{Q}$ with input A and output B can be expressed by the maximization of the $I(A : B)$ quantum mutual information as follows:

$$C(\mathcal{Q}) = \max\nolimits_{all\ p_i, \rho_i} I(A:B). \qquad (9.43)$$

From this relation, it also follows that for this setting the single-use $C^{(1)}(\mathcal{Q})$ and the asymptotic $C(\mathcal{Q})$ classical capacities are equal: $C^{(1)}(\mathcal{Q}) = C(\mathcal{Q}) = \max\nolimits_{all\ p_i, \rho_i} I(A : B)$.

On the other hand, if we have *product-state inputs* but we change the measurement setting from the single measurement setting to the *joint measurement* setting, then the classical channel capacity cannot be given by Eq. (9.43), and hence $C(\mathcal{Q}) \neq \max\nolimits_{all\ p_i, \rho_i} I(A : B)$.

If we would like to step forward, we have to accept the fact that the quantum mutual information cannot be used to express the asymptotic version: the *maximized* quantum mutual information is *always additive*, but not the Holevo information. It follows that if we use the regularized form of quantum mutual information to express the capacity, we will find that the asymptotic version is equal to the single-use version: since: $\lim\nolimits_{n \to \infty} \max\nolimits_{all\ p_i, \rho_i} I(A : B)/n = \max\nolimits_{all\ p_i, \rho_i} I(A : B)$.

From this, it follows that if we have *product inputs* and *joint measurement* at the outputs, we cannot use the $\max\nolimits_{all\ p_i, \rho_i} I(A : B)$ maximized quantum mutual information function to express $C(\mathcal{Q})$.

Figure 9.8 Transmission of classical information over quantum channel with product-state inputs and single measurements. The environment is not depicted.

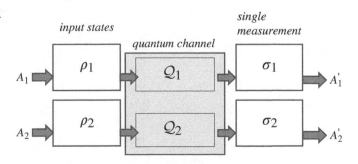

If we would like to compute the classical capacity $C(\mathcal{Q})$ for that case, we have to leave the quantum mutual information function, and instead use the maximized Holevo information $\max_{all\, p_i, \rho_i} \chi$. This new $C(\mathcal{Q})$ capacity (according to the *HSW* theorem) can be expressed by the Holevo capacity $\chi(\mathcal{Q})$, which will be equal to the maximization of the Holevo information of channel $\mathcal{Q}$: given as $C(\mathcal{Q}) = \chi(\mathcal{Q}) = \max_{all\, p_i, \rho_i} \chi$. The Holevo capacity and the asymptotic channel capacity will be equal in this case.

The HSW theorem gives an explicit answer for the classical capacity of the *product-state input* with the *joint measurement* setting, and expresses $C(\mathcal{Q})$ as follows:

$$C(\mathcal{Q}) = \chi(\mathcal{Q}) = \max_{all\, p_i, \rho_i} \left[S\left(\mathcal{Q}\left(\sum_i p_i \rho_i \right) \right) - \sum_i p_i S(\mathcal{Q}(\rho_i)) \right]. \tag{9.44}$$

The relation discussed above holds for the restricted channel setting illustrated in Figure 9.9, where the input consists of product states, and the output is measured by a joint measurement setting.

However, if *entangled inputs* are allowed with the *joint measurement setting* – then this equality does not hold anymore. In conclusion, the relation between the maximized Holevo information $\chi(\mathcal{Q})$ of the channel and the asymptotic classical channel capacity $C(\mathcal{Q})$ is $\chi(\mathcal{Q}) \leq C(\mathcal{Q})$.

This means that we have to redefine the asymptotic formula of $C(\mathcal{Q})$ for entangled inputs and the joint measurement setting to measure the maximum transmittable classical information through a quantum channel. In the 1990s, it was conjectured that the formula of Eq. (9.44) can be applied to describe the channel capacity for entangled inputs with the *single measurement* setting; however, it was an open question for a long time. Single measurement *destroys* the possible benefits arising from the entangled inputs, and joint measurement is required to achieve the benefits of entangled inputs [82].

In 2009, Hastings used *entangled input states* and showed that the entangled inputs (with the *joint measurement*) can increase the amount of classical information that can be transmitted over a noisy quantum channel. In this case, $C(\mathcal{Q}) \neq \chi(\mathcal{Q})$ and the $C(\mathcal{Q})$ can be expressed with the help of the Holevo capacity as follows: using the asymptotic formula of $\chi(\mathcal{Q})$ we have $C(\mathcal{Q}) = \lim_{n \to \infty} \chi(\mathcal{Q}^{\otimes n})/n$.

The channel construction for this relation is illustrated in Figure 9.10. The entangled input is formally denoted by Ψ_{12}. We also show the channel construction of the fourth possible construction to measure the classical capacity of a quantum channel. In this case, we have entangled input states; however, we use a single measurement setting instead of a joint measurement setting. Currently, there is no quantum channel model where the channel capacity can be increased with this setting since in this case the benefits of entanglement vanish because the joint measurement setting has been changed into the single measurement setting. We illustrate this setting in Figure 9.11.

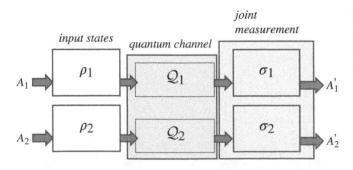

Figure 9.9 Transmission of classical information over quantum channel with product-state inputs and joint measurements. The environment is not depicted.

Figure 9.10 Transmission of classical information over quantum channel with entangled inputs Ψ_{12} and joint measurements. The environment is not depicted.

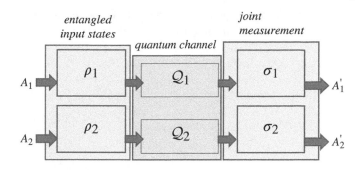

Figure 9.11 Transmission of classical information over quantum channel with entangled inputs and single measurements. The environment is not depicted.

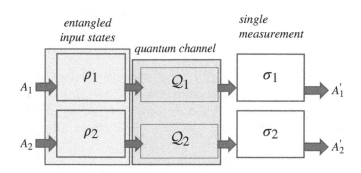

We have seen in Eq. (9.44) that if we have *product input states* and we change from a single to a *joint measurement* setting, then the classical capacity of Q cannot be expressed by the maximized quantum mutual information function, because it is always additive, and hence $C(Q) \neq \lim_{n\to\infty} \max_{all\, p_i, \rho_i} I(A:B)/n$.

If we allow *entangled input states* and *joint measurement*, then we have to use the $C(Q)$ asymptotic formula of the previously derived Holevo capacity, $\chi(Q)$, which yields $C(Q) = \lim_{n\to\infty} \chi(Q^{\otimes n})/n \neq \chi(Q)$.

9.4.2 The Private Classical Capacity

The private classical capacity $P(Q)$ of a quantum channel Q describes the maximum rate at which the channel is able to send *classical information* through the channel reliably and *privately* (i.e. without any information leaked about the original message to an eavesdropper). "Privately" here means that an eavesdropper will not be able to access the encoded information without revealing her/himself; that is, the private classical capacity describes the maximal secure information that can be obtained by receiver B on an eavesdropped quantum communication channel Q.

The generalized model of private communication over quantum channels is illustrated in Figure 9.12. The first output of the channel is denoted by $\sigma_B = Q(\rho_A)$, and the second "receiver" is the eavesdropper E, with state σ_E. The single-use private classical capacity from these quantities can be expressed as the maximum of the difference between two mutual information quantities. The eavesdropper, E, attacks the Q channel, and she steals $I(A:E)$

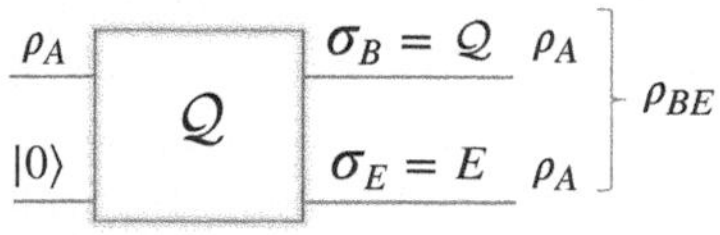

Figure 9.12 Model of private classical communication of a Q channel.

from the information $I(A:B)$ sent by A to B, and therefore the *single-use* private classical capacity (or *private information*) of $\mathcal{Q}$ can be determined as

$$P^{(1)}(\mathcal{Q}) = \max{}_{all\, p_i, \rho_i} (I(A:B) - I(A:E)). \tag{9.45}$$

while the *asymptotic* private classical capacity is

$$
\begin{aligned}
P(\mathcal{Q}) &= \lim{}_{n \to \infty} P^{(1)}\big(\mathcal{Q}^{\otimes n}\big)/n \\
&= \lim{}_{n \to \infty} \max{}_{all\, p_i, \rho_i} (I(A:B) - I(A:E))/n.
\end{aligned} \tag{9.46}
$$

The private classical capacity can be expressed as the difference of two quantum mutual information functions; see Eq. (9.46). Here, we give an equivalent definition for the private classical capacity $P(\mathcal{Q})$ and show that it also can be rewritten using the Holevo quantity $\mathcal{X}$ as follows:

$$P(\mathcal{Q}) = \lim{}_{n \to \infty} \max{}_{all\, p_i, \rho_i} (\mathcal{X}_{AB} - \mathcal{X}_{AE}), \tag{9.47}$$

where $\mathcal{X}_{AB} = S(\mathcal{Q}_{AB}(\rho_{AB})) - \sum_i p_i S(\mathcal{Q}_{AB}(\rho_i))$ and $\mathcal{X}_{AE} = S(\mathcal{Q}_{AE}(\rho_{AE})) - \sum_i p_i S(\mathcal{Q}_{AE}(\rho_i))$ measure the Holevo quantities between A and B, and A and the eavesdropper E, respectively, while $\rho_{AB} = \sum_i p_i \rho_i$ and $\rho_{AE} = \sum_i p_i \rho_i$. An important corollary from Eq. (9.46) is that although the quantum mutual information itself is additive, the difference of two quantum mutual information functions is not (i.e. we need the asymptotic version to compute the true private classical capacity of a $\mathcal{Q}$ channel.)

9.4.3 The Entanglement-Assisted Classical Capacity

The last capacity regarding classical communication over $\mathcal{Q}$ channels is referred to as *entanglement-assisted classical capacity* $C_E(\mathcal{Q})$, which measures the classical information that can be transmitted through the channel if transmitter A and receiver B have shared entanglement before the transmission; that is, entanglement is applied not between the input states as in the case of the HSW (i.e. the product-state capacity) theorem. This capacity measures classical information, and it can be expressed with the help of the *quantum mutual information function* as

$$C_E(\mathcal{Q}) = \max{}_{all\, p_i, \rho_i} I(A:B). \tag{9.48}$$

The main difference between the classical capacity $C(\mathcal{Q})$ and the entanglement-assisted classical capacity $C_E(\mathcal{Q})$, is that in the latter case the maximum of the transmittable classical information is equal to the maximized quantum mutual information; hence, the entanglement-assisted classical capacity $C_E(\mathcal{Q})$ can be derived from the *single-use* version $C_E^{(1)}(\mathcal{Q})$. From Eq. (9.48) one can see there is no need for the asymptotic version to express the entanglement-assisted classical capacity, that is, $C_E(\mathcal{Q}) = C_E^{(1)}(\mathcal{Q}) = \max{}_{all\, p_i, \rho_i} I(A:B)$. It also can be concluded that shared entanglement does not change the additivity of the maximized quantum mutual information; in other words, additivity holds if the parties use shared entanglement for the transmission of classical information over $\mathcal{Q}$. Figure 9.13 illustrates the general model of entanglement-assisted classical capacity $C_E(\mathcal{Q})$.

We note an important property of shared entanglement: although it does not improve the classical capacity of the quantum channel, (see Eq. 9.48), it can be used to increase the single-use classical capacity. It was shown that with the help of shared entanglement the transmission of a single quantum bit can be realized with a higher probability of success; this strategy is known as the CHSH (*Clauser–Horne–Shimony–Holt*) game. For details, see [81].

Figure 9.13 Entanglement-assisted capacity of a $\mathcal{Q}$ channel.

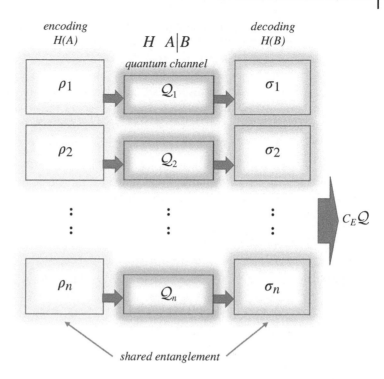

9.4.4 The Classical Zero-Error Capacity

In this subsection, we give the exact definitions required for the characterization of a quantum zero-error communication system. We will discuss the classical and quantum zero-error capacities and give the connection between zero-error quantum codes and the elements of graph theory.

Classical zero-error capacities of $\mathcal{Q}$ channels: In this section, we review the background of the zero-error capacity $C_0(\mathcal{N})$ of a quantum channel $\mathcal{Q}$. Let us assume that A has information source $\{X_i\}$ encoded into quantum states $\{\rho_i\}$ that will be transmitted through a quantum channel $\mathcal{Q}$ (see Figure 9.14). The quantum states will be measured by a set of POVM operators $\mathcal{P} = \{\mathcal{M}_1, ..., \mathcal{M}_k\}$ at the receiver. The classical zero-error quantum capacity $C_0(\mathcal{Q})$ for product input states can be reached if and only if the input states are *pure* states, similar to the HSW capacity $C(\mathcal{Q})$.

The zero-error transmission of quantum states requires perfect distinguishability. To achieve this perfect distinguishability of the zero-error quantum codewords, they have to be *pairwise orthogonal*. Non-adjacent codewords can be distinguished perfectly. Two inputs are called *adjacent* if they

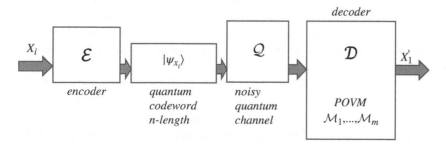

Figure 9.14 Quantum zero-error communication system.

can result in the same output. The number of possible non-adjacent codewords determines the rate of maximal transmittable classical information through Q.

In the $d-$dimensional Hilbert space (e.g. $d = 2$ for qubits) at most d pairwise distinguishable quantum states exist; thus, for a quantum system that consists of n pieces of $d-$dimensional quantum states at most d^n pairwise distinguishable n-length quantum codewords are available. Obviously if two quantum codewords are not orthogonal, then they cannot be distinguished perfectly. Note that if we would like to distinguish between K *pairwise orthogonal* quantum codewords (the length of each codeword is n) in the d^n-dimensional Hilbert space, then we have to define the POVM set $\mathcal{P} = \left\{ \mathcal{M}^{(1)}, ..., \mathcal{M}^{(K)} \right\}$, where $\mathcal{M}^{(i)}$ are sets of d-dimensional projectors on the individual quantum systems (e.g. qubits) that distinguish the n-length codewords $\mathcal{M}^{(i)} = \{ \mathcal{M}_1, ..., \mathcal{M}_m \}$ where $m = d^n$. The probability that B gives measurement outcome j from quantum state ρ_i is

$$Pr[j | \rho_i] = Tr(\mathcal{M}_j \, Q(\rho_i)). \tag{9.49}$$

The i-th *codeword* $| \psi_{X_i} \rangle$ encodes the n-length classical codeword $X_i = \{ x_{i,1}, x_{i,2}, ..., x_{i,n} \}$ consisting of n product input quantum states: $| \psi_{x_i} \rangle = \left[| \psi_{i,1} \rangle \otimes | \psi_{i,2} \rangle \otimes | \psi_{i,3} \rangle \otimes | \psi_{i,n} \rangle \right]$, $i = 1 \cdots K$, where $\rho_i = | \psi_{X_i} \rangle \langle \psi_{X_i} |$. The quantum block code consist of codewords

$$| \psi_{X_1} \rangle = \left[| \psi_{1,1} \rangle \otimes | \psi_{1,2} \rangle \otimes | \psi_{1,3} \rangle \cdots \otimes | \psi_{1,n} \rangle \right]$$
$$\vdots$$
$$\vdots \tag{9.50}$$
$$| \psi_{X_K} \rangle = \left[| \psi_{K,1} \rangle \otimes | \psi_{K,2} \rangle \otimes | \psi_{K,3} \rangle \cdots \otimes | \psi_{K,n} \rangle \right],$$

where K is the number of classical (n length) messages. The decoder will produce the output codeword $X_i' = \{ x_{i,1}', x_{i,2}', ..., x_{i,n}' \}$ generated by the POVM measurement operators, where the POVM $\mathcal{M}^{(i)}$ can distinguish m messages $\{ X_1', X_2', ... X_m' \}$ (n-length) at the output. Receiver B would like to determine each message $i \in [1, K]$ with unit probability. The zero probability of error means that for the input code $| \psi_{X_i} \rangle$ the decoder has to identify the classical output codeword X_i' with the classical input codeword X_i perfectly for each possible i, otherwise the quantum channel has no zero-error capacity; that is, for the zero-error quantum communication system: $Pr[X_i | X_i] = 1$.

The *non-adjacent* elements are important for zero-error capacity, since *only non-adjacent codewords can be distinguished perfectly*. Two inputs are called *adjacent* if they can result in the same output, while for *non-adjacent* inputs, the output of the encoder is unique. The number of possible non-adjacent codewords determines the rate of maximal transmittable classical information through quantum channels. Formally, the *non-adjacent* property of two quantum states ρ_1 and ρ_2 can be given as $Set_1 \cap Set_2 = \emptyset$, where $Set_i = \left\{ Pr \left[X_j' | X_i \right] = Tr(\mathcal{M}_j Q(| \psi_{X_i} \rangle \langle \psi_{X_i} |)) > 0 \right\}, j \in \{ 1, ..., m \}, i = 1, 2$, and $\mathcal{P} = \{ \mathcal{M}_1, ..., \mathcal{M}_m \}$ is a POVM measurement operator. For a noisy quantum channel Q, the non-adjacent property can be rephrased as follows. Two input quantum states ρ_1 and ρ_2 are non-adjacent with relation to Q if $Q(\rho_1)$ and $Q(\rho_2)$ are *perfectly distinguishable*. The notation $\rho_1 (\perp Q) \rho_2$ also can be used to denote the non-adjacent inputs of quantum channel Q. We will simplify this notation to $\rho_1 \perp \rho_2$

A quantum channel Q has positive zero-error capacity if and only if a subset of quantum states $\Omega = \{ \rho_i \}_{i=1}^l$ and POVM $\mathcal{P} = \{ \mathcal{M}_1, ..., \mathcal{M}_m \}$ exists where for *at least two states* ρ_1 and ρ_2 from subset Ω, the relation $Set_1 \cap Set_2 = \emptyset$, holds; that is, the non-adjacent property with relation to the POVM measurement is satisfied. For the quantum channel Q, the two inputs ρ_1 and ρ_2 are non-adjacent if and only if the quantum channel takes the input states ρ_1 and ρ_2 into orthogonal subspaces

$Q(\rho_1) \perp Q(\rho_2)$; that is, the quantum channel has positive classical zero-error capacity $C_0(Q)$ iff this property holds for the output of the channel for a given POVM $P = \{\mathcal{M}_1, ..., \mathcal{M}_m\}$. The previous result can be rephrased as follows. Using the trace preserving property of the Q channel, the two quantum states ρ_1 and ρ_2 are non-adjacent if and only if for the channel output states $Q(\rho_1)$, $Q(\rho_2)$ we have $Tr(Q(\rho_1)Q(\rho_2)) = 0$, and if ρ_1 and ρ_2 are non-adjacent input states then $Tr(\rho_1\rho_2) = 0$.

Let the two *non-adjacent* input codewords of the Q be denoted by $| \psi_{X_1} \rangle$ and $| \psi_{X_2} \rangle$. These quantum codewords encode messages $X_1 = \{x_{1, 1}, x_{1, 2}, ..., x_{1, n}\}$ and $X_2 = \{x_{2, 1}, x_{2, 2}, ..., x_{2, n}\}$. For this setting, we construct the following POVM operators for the given complete set of POVM $P = \{\mathcal{M}_1, ..., \mathcal{M}_m\}$ and the two input codewords $| \psi_{X_1} \rangle$ and $| \psi_{X_2} \rangle$ as follows: $\mathcal{M}^{(1)} = \{\mathcal{M}_1, ..., \mathcal{M}_k\}$ and $\mathcal{M}^{(2)} = \{\mathcal{M}_{k+1}, ... \mathcal{M}_m\}$.

The groups of operators $\mathcal{M}^{(1)}$ and $\mathcal{M}^{(2)}$ will identify and distinguish the input codewords $| \psi_{X_1} \rangle$ and $| \psi_{X_2} \rangle$. Using this setting the two non-adjacent codewords, $| \psi_{X_1} \rangle$ and $| \psi_{X_2} \rangle$ can be distinguished with probability 1 at the output since

$$Pr[X_i'|X_1] = 1, i = 1, ..., k,$$
$$Pr[X_i'|X_2] = 1, i = k + 1, ..., m,$$

$$(9.51)$$

where X_i' is a number between 1 and m (according to the possible number of POVM operators) that identifies the measured unknown quantum codeword and consequently

$$Pr[X_i'|X_1] = 0, i = k + 1, ..., m,$$
$$Pr[X_i'|X_2] = 0, i = 1, ..., k.$$

$$(9.52)$$

For input message $| \psi_{X_1} \rangle$ and $| \psi_{X_2} \rangle$ with the help of set $\mathcal{M}^{(1)}$ and $\mathcal{M}^{(2)}$, these probabilities are

$$Pr[X_1'|X_1] = Tr(\mathcal{M}^{(1)}Q(|\psi_{X_1}\rangle\langle\psi_{X_1}|)) = 1,$$
$$Pr[X_2'|X_2] = Tr(\mathcal{M}^{(2)}Q(|\psi_{X_2}\rangle\langle\psi_{X_2}|)) = 1,$$

$$(9.53)$$

where $\mathcal{M}^{(1)}$ and $\mathcal{M}^{(2)}$ are orthogonal projectors, $\mathcal{M}^{(1)}$ and $\mathcal{M}^{(2)}$ were defined earlier, and $\mathcal{M}^{(1)} + \mathcal{M}^{(2)} + \mathcal{M}^{(2+1)} = I$ to make it possible for the quantum channel to take the input states into orthogonal subspaces; that is, $Q(| \psi_{X_1} \rangle\langle\psi_{X_1} |) \perp Q(| \psi_{X_2} \rangle\langle\psi_{X_2} |)$ has to be satisfied. The POVM measurement has to be restricted to projective measurement. As follows, the $P = \{\mathcal{M}^{(1)}, \mathcal{M}^{(2)}\}$ POVM measurement can be replaced with the set of *von Neumann* operators $Z = \{\mathcal{P}^{(1)}, \mathcal{P}^{(2)}\}$, where $\mathcal{P}^{(1)} + \mathcal{P}^{(2)} = I$. This result can also be extended for an arbitrary number of operators, depending on the actual system. The non-adjacent property can also be interpreted for an arbitrary length of quantum codewords. For a given quantum channel Q, the two n-length input quantum codewords $| \psi_{X_1} \rangle$ and $| \psi_{X_2} \rangle$, which are tensor products of n quantum states, are non-adjacent in relation with Q if and only if *at least one* pair of quantum states $\{|\psi_{1, i}\rangle, | \psi_{2, i}\rangle\}$ from the two n-length sequences is perfectly distinguishable. Formally, at least one *input* quantum state pair $\{|\psi_{1, i}\rangle, | \psi_{2, i}\rangle\}$ with i, $1 \leq i \leq n$, exists in $| \psi_{X_1} \rangle$ and $| \psi_{X_2} \rangle$, for which $Q(| \psi_{1,i}\rangle\langle.\psi_{1,i} |)$ is non-adjacent to $Q(| \psi_{2,i}\rangle\langle\psi_{2,i} |)$. Because we have stated that the two codewords can be distinguished at the channel output, the following relation has to hold for their trace, and their non-adjacency can be verified as follows:

$$Tr(Q(|\psi_{X_1}\rangle\langle\psi_{X_1}|) Q(|\psi_{X_2}\rangle\langle\psi_{X_2}|))$$
$$= Tr((\otimes_{i=1}^n Q(|\psi_{1,i}\rangle\langle\psi_{1,i}|)) (\otimes_{i=1}^n Q(|\psi_{2,i}\rangle\langle\psi_{2,i}|)))$$
$$= \prod_{i=1}^n Tr(Q(|\psi_{1,i}\rangle\langle\psi_{1,i}|) Q(|\psi_{2,i}\rangle\langle\psi_{2,i}|)) = 0.$$

$$(9.54)$$

As follows from Eq. (9.54), a quantum channel Q has a positive zero-error capacity if and only if there exist at least two non-adjacent input quantum states ρ_1 and ρ_2. These two non-adjacent quantum states make the two n-length quantum codewords at the output of quantum channel Q distinguishable , and these input codewords will be called *non-adjacent quantum codewords*. The joint measurement of the quantum states of an output codeword is *necessary* and *sufficient* to distinguish the input codewords with zero error: *necessary*, because the joint measurement is required to distinguish orthogonal general (i.e. nonzero-error code) tensor product states [83], and sufficient, because the non-adjacent quantum states have orthogonal *supports* at the output of the noisy quantum channel; that is, $Tr(\rho_i\rho_j) = 0$ [84]. (The *support* of a matrix A is the orthogonal complement of the kernel of the matrix. The *kernel* of A is the set of all vectors v for which $Av = 0$.) In the joint measurement, the $\{\mathcal{M}_i\}$, $i = 1, ..., m$ projectors are $d^n \times d^n$ matrices, while if we were to use a single measurement then the size of these matrices would be $d \times d$.

In Figure 9.15, we compare the difference between single and joint measurement settings for a given n-length quantum codeword $|\psi_X\rangle =[|\psi_1\rangle \otimes |\psi_2\rangle \otimes |\psi_3\rangle\cdots \otimes |\psi_n\rangle]$. In the case of single measurement, B measures each of the n quantum states of the i-th codeword states individually. In the case of the joint measurement, B waits until he receives the n quantum states, and then measures them together.

Achievable zero-error rates in quantum systems: Theoretically (without making any assumptions about the physical attributes of the transmission), the *classical single-use zero-error capacity* $C_0^{(1)}(Q)$ of the noisy quantum channel can be expressed as

$$C_0^{(1)}(Q) = \log\,(K(Q)), \tag{9.55}$$

where $K(Q)$ is the maximum number of different messages that can be sent over the channel with a *single use* of Q (or, in other words, the maximum size of the set of *mutually non-adjacent* inputs). The asymptotic *zero-error capacity* of the noisy quantum channel Q can be expressed as

$$C_0(\mathcal{N}) = \lim_{n\to\infty}\,\log\frac{\left(K(Q^{\otimes n})\right)}{n}, \tag{9.56}$$

where $K(Q^{\otimes n})$ is the maximum number of n-length classical messages that the quantum channel can transmit with zero error, and $Q^{\otimes n}$ denotes the n-uses of the channel. The $C_0(Q)$ asymptotic classical zero-error capacity of a quantum channel is *upper-bounded* by the HSW capacity; that is, $C_0^{(1)}(Q) \leq C_0(Q) \leq C(Q)$.

Connection with graph theory: The problem of finding *non-adjacent* codewords for the zero-error information transmission can be rephrased in terms of graph theory. The adjacent codewords are also called *confusable*, since these codewords can generate the same output with a given nonzero probability. The two input codewords $| \psi_{X_1}\rangle$ and $| \psi_{X_2}\rangle$ are *adjacent* if there is a channel output codeword $| \psi_{X'}\rangle$ that can be produced by either of these two, $\Pr[X' \,|\, X_1] > 0$ and $\Pr[X' \,|\, X_2] > 0$.

The non-adjacent property of two quantum codewords can be analyzed by the *confusability graph* $\mathcal{G}_n$, where n denotes the *length of the block code*.

Let us take as many vertices as the number of input messages K, and connect two vertices if these input messages are adjacent. For example, using the quantum version of the famous *pentagon graph*, we show how the classical zero-error capacity $C_0(Q)$ of the quantum channel Q changes if we use block codes of length $n = 1$ and $n = 2$. In the pentagon graph, an input codeword from the set of non-orthogonal qubits $\{|0\rangle, | 1\rangle, | 2\rangle, | 3\rangle, | 4\rangle\}$ is connected with two other adjacent input codewords, and the number of total codewords is 5 [85].

Figure 9.15 Comparison of single (a) and joint (b) measurement settings. The joint measurement is necessary to achieve quantum zero-error communication.

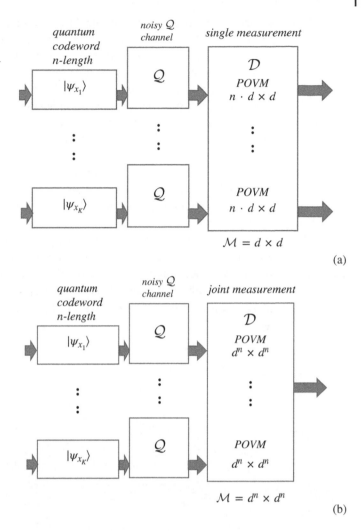

The $\mathcal{G}_1$ *confusability* graph of the pentagon structure for block codes of length $n = 1$ is shown in Figure 9.16. The vertices of the graph are the possible input messages, where $K = 5$. The *adjacent* input messages are connected by a line. The non-adjacent inputs $|2\rangle$ and $|4\rangle$ are denoted by gray circles, and there is no connection between these two input codewords.

Figure 9.16 Confusability graph of a zero-error code for one channel use. The two possible non-adjacent codewords are denoted by the large green circles.

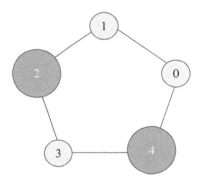

For the block codes of length $n = 1$, the maximal transmittable classical information with zero error is $C_0(\mathcal{Q}) = \log(2) = 1$, since only two non-adjacent vertices can be found in the graph. We note that other possible codeword combinations also can be used to achieve zero-error transmission, in comparison with the confusability graph; for example, $|1\rangle$ and $|3\rangle$ also non-adjacent, and so on. On the other hand, the maximum number of non-adjacent vertices (two in this case) cannot be exceeded, and thus $C_0(\mathcal{Q}) = 1$ holds in all other possible cases, too.

Let assume that we use $n = 2$ length of block codes. First, let us see how the graph changes. The non-adjacent inputs are denoted by the large gray shaded circles. The connections between the possible codewords (which can be used as a block code) are denoted by the thick line and the dashed circle. The confusability graph $\mathcal{G}_2$ for $n = 2$ length of block codes is shown in Figure 9.17. The two half-empty circles together on the left and right sides represent one full circle, and the two half-empty circles at the top and bottom of the figure also represent one full circle; thus, there are five dashed circles in the figure.

It can be seen that the complexity of the structure of the graph has changed, although we have made only a small modification: we increased the lengths of the block codes from $n = 1$ to $n = 2$. The five two-length codewords and zero-error quantum block codes that can achieve zero-error transmission can be defined using the computational basis $\{|0\rangle, |1\rangle, |2\rangle, |3\rangle, |4\rangle\}$. The classical zero-error capacity that can be achieved by $n = 2$ length block codes is $C_0(\mathcal{Q}^{\otimes 2}) = \log(5)/2 = 1.1609$.

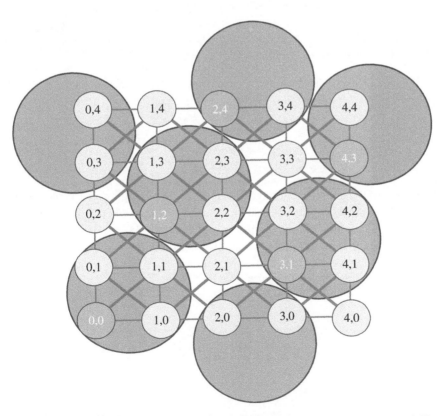

Figure 9.17 Graph of a zero-error code for two channel uses of a quantum channel. The possible zero-error codewords are depicted by the thick lines and blue circles.

From an engineering point of view, this result means that for the pentagon graph, the maximum rate at which classical information can be transmitted over a noisy quantum channel Q with zero-error probability can be achieved with a quantum block code length of two.

9.4.5 Entanglement-Assisted Classical Zero-Error Capacity

In the previous subsection, we discussed the main properties of zero-error capacity using product input states. Now, we add the entanglement to the picture. Here, we discuss how the encoding and the decoding setting will change if we bring entanglement to the system and how it affects the classical zero-error capacity of a quantum channel.

If entanglement is allowed between the communicating parties, then the single-use and asymptotic *entanglement-assisted* classical zero-error capacities are defined as

$$C_0^{E(1)}(Q) = \log\left(K^E(Q)\right) \tag{9.57}$$

and

$$C_0^E(Q) = \lim_{n \to \infty} \log \frac{\left(K^E\left(Q^{\otimes n}\right)\right)}{n}. \tag{9.58}$$

where $K^E\left(Q^{\otimes n}\right)$ is the maximum number of n-length mutually non-adjacent classical messages that the quantum channel can transmit with zero error using *shared entanglement*.

Before we start to discuss the properties of the entanglement-assisted zero-error quantum communication, we introduce a new type of graph, called the *hypergraph G_H*. The hypergraph is very similar to our previously shown *confusability* graph G_n. The hypergraph contains a set of vertices and hyperedges. The vertices represent the *inputs* of the quantum channel Q, while the hyperedges contain all the channel inputs that could produce the same channel output with nonzero probability. We will use some new terms from graph theory in this subsection; hence, we briefly summarize these definitions:

1) Maximum independent set of G_n: The maximum number of non-adjacent inputs (K)
2) Clique of G_n : κ_i, the set of possible inputs of a given output in a confusability graph (inputs that could produce the same output with nonzero probability)
3) Complete graph: If all the vertices are connected with one another in the graph; in this case, there are no non-adjacent inputs: that is, the channel has no zero-error capacity.

In Figure 9.18a, we show a hypergraph G_H where the inputs of the channel are the vertices and the hyperedges represent the channel outputs. Two inputs are non-adjacent if they are in a different loop. The two non-adjacent inputs are depicted by the larger gray-shaded vertices. In Figure 9.18b, we give the confusability graph G_n for single-channel use ($n = 1$), for the same input set. The cliques in the G_n confusability graph are depicted by κ_i.

Both the hypergraph and the confusability graph can be used to determine the non-adjacent inputs. However, if the number of inputs starts to increase, the number of hyperedges in the hypergraph will be significantly lower than the number of edges in the confusability graph of the same system.

In short, the entanglement-assisted zero-error quantum communication protocol works as follows according to Figure 9.19 [86]. Before the communication, transmitter A and receiver B share

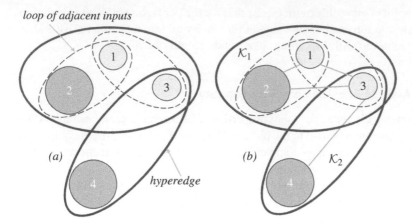

loop of adjacent inputs

(a)

(b)

hyperedge

Figure 9.18 Hypergraph and the confusability graph of a given input system with four inputs. The hyperedges of the hypergraph are labeled by the output. The number of non-adjacent inputs is two [1].

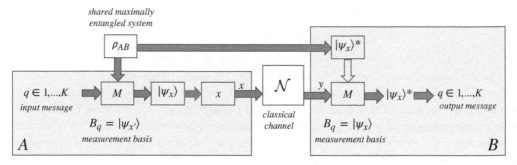

Figure 9.19 Steps of the entanglement-assisted zero-error quantum communication protocol. *Source:* Based on Chen et al. adapted from [1].

entanglement between themselves. The d-dimensional shared system between A and B will be denoted by $\rho_{AB} = |\Phi_{AB}\rangle\langle\Phi_{AB}|$, where

$$|\Phi_{AB}\rangle = \frac{1}{\sqrt{d}}\sum_{i=0}^{d-1} |i\rangle_A |i\rangle_B \tag{9.59}$$

is a rank-d maximally entangled qudit state (also called *edit*). If A would like to send a message $q \in \{1, ..., K\}$, where K is the number of messages, to B, she has to measure her half of the entangled system using a complete orthogonal basis $B_q = \{|\psi_{x'}\rangle\}$, $x' \in \kappa_q$, where x' is a vertex in the hypergraph $\mathcal{G}_H$ from clique κ_q.

The *orthonormal representation of a graph is a map*: the vertex x' represents the unit vector $|\psi_{x'}\rangle$ such that if x and x' are *adjacent*, then $\langle\psi_x | \psi_{x'}\rangle = 0$ (i.e. *they are orthogonal in the orthonormal representation*) and κ_q is the clique corresponding to message q in the hypergraph $\mathcal{G}_H$. The hypergraph has K cliques of size d, $\{\kappa_1, ..., \kappa_K\}$ (i.e. each message $q \in \{1, ..., K\}$ is represented by a d-size clique in the hypergraph $\mathcal{G}_H$.) After the measurement, B's state will collapse to $|\psi_x\rangle^*$. B will measure his state in $B_q = \{|\psi_x\rangle\}$ to get the final state $|\psi_{x'}\rangle^*$. B's output is denoted by y. B's possible states are determined by those vertices x' for which $p(y | x') > 0$, and these *adjacent* states are *mutually orthogonal*; that is, for any two x'_1 and x'_2, $\langle\psi_{x'_1} | \psi_{x'_2}\rangle = 0$. Finally, A makes her measurement using $B_q = \{|\psi_x\rangle\}$, and then B measures his state $|\psi_x\rangle^*$ in $B_q = \{|\psi_x\rangle\}$ to produce $|\psi_{x'}\rangle^*$.

Design Example 9.3

Supposed A's set contains $K = 6$ codewords, and she shares a rank-four (i. e. $d = 4$) maximally entangled qudit state with B

$$\Phi_{AB} = \frac{1}{\sqrt{4}}\sum_{i=0}^{3}|i\rangle_A|i\rangle_B, \tag{9.60}$$

however, in the general case, d can be chosen as large as A and B would like to use. A measures her system from the maximally entangled state, and she chooses a basis among the K possible states, according to which message q she wants to send B. A's measurement outcome is denoted by x, which is a random value. A sends q and x to the classical channel $\mathcal{N}$. In the next phase, B performs a projective measurement to decide which x value was sent to the classical channel by A. After B has determined it, he can answer which one of the possible K messages was sent by A with the help of the maximally entangled system. Alice makes her measurement on her side using one of the six possible bases $B_q = \{|\psi_{x'}\rangle\}$ on her half of the state ρ_{AB}. Her system collapses to $|\psi_x\rangle \in B_q$, while B's system collapses to $|\psi_x\rangle^*$, conditioned on x. Alice sends x to the classical channel $\mathcal{N}$; B will receive classical message y. From the channel output $= \mathcal{N}(x)$, where $\mathcal{N}$ is the classical channel between A and B, B can determine the mutually adjacent inputs (i.e. those inputs that could produce the given output). If B makes a measurement in basis $B_q = \{|\psi_x\rangle\}$, then he will get $|\psi_{x'}\rangle^*$, where these states for a given set of x' corresponding to possible x are orthogonal states, so he can determine x and the original message q. The channel output gives B the information that some set of mutually adjacent inputs were used on A's side. On his half of the entangled system, the states will be mutually orthogonal.

A measurement on these mutually orthogonal states will determine B's state, and he can tell A's input with certainty. Using this protocol, the number of mutually non-adjacent input messages is $K^E \geq 6$, while if A and B would like to communicate with zero error but without shared entanglement, then $K = 5$. It follows that for the single-use classical zero-error capacities, we get $C_0^{(1)} = log\,(5)$ and $C_0^{E(1)} = log\,(K^E) = log\,(6)$, while for the asymptotic entanglement-assisted classical zero-error capacity, we get $C_0^E \geq log\,(K^E) = log\,(6)$. According to A's $K^E = 6$ messages, the hypergraph can be partitioned into six cliques of size $d = 4$. The adjacent vertices are denoted by a common loop. The overall system contains $6 \times 4 = 24$ basis vectors. These vectors are grouped into $K^E = 6$ orthogonal bases. Two input vectors are connected in the graph if they are adjacent vectors; that is, they can produce the same output.

The hypergraph $\mathcal{G}_H$ of this system is shown in Figure 9.20. The mutually non-adjacent inputs are denoted by the great shaded circles. An important property of the entanglement-assisted classical zero-error capacity is that the number of maximally transmittable messages is not equal to the number of non-adjacent inputs. Whereas the hypergraph has five independent vertices, the maximally transmittable messages are greater than or equal to six.

The confusability graph of this system for a single use of quantum channel $\mathcal{Q}$ would consist of $6 \times 4 \times 9 = 216$ connections, while the hypergraph has a significantly lower number ($6 \times 6 = 36$) of hyperedges. The adjacent vertices are depicted by the loops connected by the thick lines. The six possible messages are denoted by the six four-dimensional (i.e. each contains four vertices) cliques $\{\kappa_1, ..., \kappa_K\}$. The cliques (dashed circles) show the set of those input messages that could result in the same output with a given probability $p > 0$.

(Continued)

Design Example 9.3 (Continued)

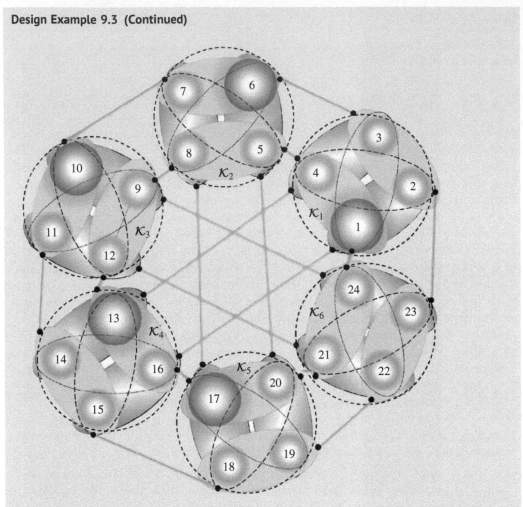

Figure 9.20 Hypergraph of an entanglement-assisted zero-error quantum code. The non-adjacent inputs are depicted by the large shaded circles. The adjacent vertices are depicted by loops connected by the thick lines. *Source:* Gyongyosi et al. [1].

We note that the cliques are defined in the $\mathcal{G}_n$ confusability graph representation, but we also included them on the hypergraph $\mathcal{G}_H$. The adjacent vertices that share a loop represent mutually orthogonal input states. For these mutually orthogonal inputs, the output will be the same.

The complete theoretical background of this example, that is, the proof of the fact that entanglement can increase the asymptotic classical zero-error capacity $C_0(\mathcal{Q})$ of a quantum channel was described in [87].

Source: Based on Cubitt et al. [87].

We have seen in this subsection that shared entanglement between transmitter A and receiver B can help to increase the maximally transmittable classical messages using noisy quantum channels with zero-error probability. It was shown in [87] that there exists an entanglement-assisted quantum communication protocol that can send one of K messages with *zero error*, and hence for the entanglement-assisted asymptotic classical zero-error capacity

$$\log (K) \leq C_0 = \lim_{n \to \infty} \log \left(K(\mathcal{Q}^{\otimes n})\right)/n$$
$$< C_0^E = \lim_{n \to \infty} \log K^E(\mathcal{Q}^{\otimes n})/n \geq \log (K^E). \tag{9.61}$$

Entanglement is very useful in zero-error quantum communication, since with the help of entanglement the maximum amount of perfectly transmittable information can be achieved.

As was show in [88], using special input codewords (based on a special Pauli graph), entanglement can help to increase the classical zero-error capacity to the maximum achievable HSW capacity; that is, there exists a special combination for which the entanglement-assisted classical zero-error capacity $C_0^E(\mathcal{Q})$ is $C_0^E(\mathcal{Q}) = \log (9)$, while the classical zero-error capacity is $C_0(\mathcal{Q}) = \log (7)$; that is, with the help of entanglement assistance the number of possible input messages (K) can be increased.

Another important discovery is that for this special input system, the entanglement-assisted classical zero-error capacity, $C_0^E(\mathcal{Q})$, is equal to the maximal transmittable classical information over $\mathcal{Q}$; that is, $C_0^E(\mathcal{Q}) = C(\mathcal{Q}) = \log (9)$.

9.5 *Q* Channel Quantum Capacity

Having discussed the general model of quantum channels and introduced various classical capacities in this section, we focus on the *quantum information* transfer over quantum channels. Two new quantities will be explained. By using the *fidelity F*, one can describe the differences between two quantum states, for example, between the input and output states of a quantum channel. On the other hand, *quantum coherent information* represents the quantum information loss to the environment during quantum communication as mutual information did for a classical channel $\mathcal{N}$. Exploiting this latter quantity, we can define the maximal quantum information transmission rate through quantum channels – the quantum capacity $Q(\mathcal{Q})$ by analogy with Shannon's noisy channel theorem. At this point, one must be aware of the difference in notation for quantum channel $\mathcal{Q}$ and the quantum capacity Q. As we have seen in Section 9.3, the classical capacity C of a quantum channel is described by the maximum of quantum mutual information and the Holevo information. The quantum capacity of the quantum channels is described by the maximum of *quantum coherent information*. The concept of quantum coherent information plays a fundamental role in the computation of the *LSD (Lloyd–Shor–Devetak)* channel capacity [89–91], which measures the asymptotic quantum capacity of the quantum capacity in general.

9.5.1 Preserving Quantum Information

The encoding and decoding quantum information have many similarities to the classical case; however, there are some fundamental differences, as we will reveal in this section. In the case of quantum communication, the source is a quantum information source, and the *quantum information* is encoded into quantum states. When transmitting quantum information, the information is encoded into non-orthogonal superposed or entangled quantum states chosen from the ensemble $\{\rho_k\}$ according to a given probability $\{p_k\}$. If the states $\{\rho_k\}$ are pure and mutually orthogonal, we talk about classical information; that is, in this case the quantum information reduces to classical information.

As shown in Figure 9.21, the encoding and the decoding can mathematically be described by the operators $\mathcal{E}$ and $\mathcal{D}$ realized on the blocks of quantum states. The input of the encoder consists of m pure quantum states, and the encoder maps the m quantum states into the joint state of n

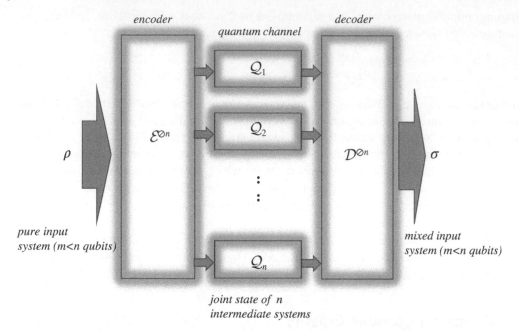

Figure 9.21 Transmission of quantum information through the quantum channel. The encoder produces a joint state of n intermediate systems. The encoded qubits are passed through the independent instances of the quantum channel.

intermediate systems. Each of them is sent through an independent instance of the quantum channel $\mathcal{Q}$ and decoded by the decoder $\mathcal{D}$, which results in m quantum states again. The output of the decoder $\mathcal{D}$ is typically mixed, according to the noise of the $\mathcal{Q}$ channel. The rate of the code is equal to m/n.

Theoretically, quantum states have to preserve their original superposition during the whole transmission, without affecting their actual properties. Practically, $\mathcal{Q}$ channels are entangled with the environment, which results in mixed states at the output. Mixed states are classical-probability-weighted sums of pure states where these probabilities appear due to the interaction with the environment (i.e. noise). So, we introduce a new quantity that is able to describe the quality of the transmission of the superposed states through the quantum channel.

The fidelity for two pure quantum states is defined as

$$F(|\varphi\rangle, |\psi\rangle) = |\langle\varphi|\psi\rangle|^2. \tag{9.62}$$

The fidelity of quantum states can describe the relation of Alice pure channel input state $|\psi\rangle$ and the received mixed quantum system $\sigma = \sum_{i=0}^{n-1} p_i \rho_i = \sum_{i=0}^{n-1} p_i |\psi_i\rangle\langle\psi_i|$ at the channel output as

$$F(|\psi\rangle, \sigma) = \langle\psi|\sigma|\psi\rangle = \sum_{i=0}^{n-1} p_i |\langle\psi|\psi_i\rangle|^2. \tag{9.63}$$

Fidelity can also be defined for *mixed* states σ and ρ:

$$F(\rho, \sigma) = \left[Tr\left(\sqrt{\sqrt{\sigma}\rho\sqrt{\sigma}} \right) \right]^2 = \sum_i p_i \left[Tr\left(\sqrt{\sqrt{\sigma_i}\rho_i\sqrt{\sigma_i}} \right) \right]^2 \tag{9.64}$$

Figure 9.22 (a) Initially, the quantum system and the reference system are in a pure entangled state. (b) After system A is sent through the quantum channel N, both the quantum system A and the entanglement between A and P are affected.

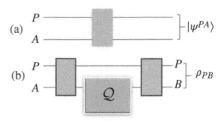

Let us assume that we have a quantum system denoted by A and a reference system P. Initially, the quantum system A and the reference system P are in a *pure entangled* state, denoted by $|\psi^{PA}\rangle$. The density matrix ρ_A of system A can be expressed by a partial trace over P, as follows:

$$\rho_A = Tr_P\big(|\psi^{PA}\rangle\langle\psi^{PA}|\big). \tag{9.65}$$

The entanglement between the initial quantum system and the reference state is illustrated in Figure 9.22a.

In the next step, ρ_A will be transmitted through the quantum channel $\mathcal{Q}$, while the reference state P is *isolated from the environment*, and hence it has not been modified during the transmission. After the quantum system ρ_A is transmitted through the quantum channel, the final state will be

$$\rho^{PB} = \big(\mathcal{I}^P \otimes \mathcal{Q}^A\big)\big(|\psi^{PA}\rangle\langle\psi^{PA}|\big), \tag{9.66}$$

where $\mathcal{I}^P$ is the identity transformation realized on the reference system P. After the system A is sent through the quantum channel, both the quantum system A and the entanglement between A and P are affected, as illustrated in Figure 9.22b. The resultant output system is denoted by B.

Now, we can study the preserved entanglement between the two systems A and P. The entanglement fidelity F_E measures the fidelity between the initial pure system $|\psi^{PA}\rangle$ and the mixed output quantum system ρ_{PB} as follows:

$$F_E = F_E(\rho_A, \mathcal{Q}) = F\big(|\psi^{PA}\rangle, \rho_{PB}\big) = \langle\psi^{PA}|\big(\mathcal{I}^P \otimes \mathcal{Q}^A\big)\big(|\psi^{PA}\rangle\{\psi^{PA}|\big)|\psi^{PA}\rangle.$$

It is important to point out the fact that F_E depends on $|\psi^{PA}\rangle$, that is, on the reference system. The sender's goal is to transmit quantum information, that is, to preserve entanglement between A and the inaccessible reference system P. Transmitter A can apply many independent channel uses of the same noisy quantum channel $\mathcal{Q}$ to transmit the quantum information. Similar to encoding classical information into the quantum states, the quantum messages can be transmitted over copies of a $\mathcal{Q}$ channel. In this case, we have n copies of a quantum channel $\mathcal{Q}$.

9.5.2 Quantum Coherent Information

In the case of the classical capacity $C(\mathcal{Q})$, the correlation between the input and the output is measured by the Holevo information and the quantum mutual information function. In case of the quantum capacity $Q(\mathcal{Q})$, we have a completely different correlation measure with completely different behaviors: it is called the *quantum coherent information*. There is a *very important distinction* between the maximized quantum mutual information and the maximized quantum coherent information: *the maximized quantum mutual information of a quantum channel $\mathcal{Q}$ is always additive, but the quantum coherent information is not*.

The S_E *entropy exchange* between the initial system PA and the output system PB is defined as follows. The entropy that is acquired by PA when input system A is transmitted through the quantum channel $\mathcal{Q}$ can be expressed with the help of the von Neumann entropy function as follows:

$$S_E = S_E(\rho_A : \mathcal{Q}(\rho_A)) = S(\rho_{PB}), \tag{9.67}$$

or in other words the von Neumann entropy of the output system ρ_{PB}. As can be observed, the value of the entropy exchange depends on ρ_A and $\mathcal{Q}$, and is independent of the purification system P. Now, we introduce the environment state E, and we will describe the map of the quantum channel as a unitary transformation. The environment is initially in a pure state $|0\rangle$. After the unitary transformation $U_{A \to BE}$ has been applied to the initial system $A |0\rangle$, it becomes $U_{A \to BE}(A |0\rangle) = BE$. From the entropy of the *final state* of the environment ρ_E, the *entropy exchange* S_E can be expressed as

$$S(\rho_{PB}) = S(\rho_E) = S_E. \tag{9.68}$$

S_E measures the increase in entropy of the environment E, or in other words, the entanglement between PA and E, after the unitary transformation $U_{A \to BE}$ had been applied to the system. This entropy exchange S_E is analogous to the classical conditional entropy; however, in this case we talk about quantum instead of classical information. Using the notations of Figure 9.22b, the quantum coherent information can be expressed as

$$\begin{aligned} I_{coh}(\rho_A : \mathcal{Q}(\rho_A)) &= S(\mathcal{Q}(\rho_A)) - S_E(\rho_A : \mathcal{Q}(\rho_A)) \\ &= S(\rho_B) - S(\rho_{PB}) = S(\rho_B) - S(\rho_E), \end{aligned} \tag{9.69}$$

where $S_E(\rho_A : \mathcal{Q}(\rho_A))$ is the entropy exchange as defined in Eq. (9.67).

Using the definition of quantum coherent information (Eq. 9.69), it can be verified that quantum coherent information takes its maximum value if systems A and P are *maximally entangled* and the quantum channel $\mathcal{Q}$ is *completely noiseless*. This can be presented easily: $S(\rho_B) = S(\rho_A)$, since the input state ρ_A is maximally mixed, and $S(\rho_{PB}) = 0$, because $|\psi^{PA}\rangle \langle \psi^{PA}|$ will remain pure after the state has been transmitted through the ideal quantum channel. If the input system $|\psi^{PA}\rangle \langle \psi^{PA}|$ is not a maximally entangled state, or the quantum channel $\mathcal{Q}$ is not ideal, then the value of quantum coherent information will decrease.

Considering another interpretation, quantum coherent information measures the quantum capacity as the difference between the von Neumann entropies of two channel output states. The first state is received by B, while the second one is received by a second receiver called the environment. If we express the transformation of a quantum channel as the partial trace of the overall system, then $\mathcal{Q}(\rho_A) = Tr_E(U\rho_A U^\dagger)$, and similarly, for the effect of the environment E, we will get $E(\rho_A) = \rho_E = Tr_B(U\rho_A U^\dagger)$. These results are summarized in Figure 9.23.

9.5.3 Connection Between Classical and Quantum Information

As has been shown in [92], the I_{coh} quantum coherent information also can be expressed with the help of the Holevo information, as follows:

$$I_{coh}(\rho_A : \mathcal{Q}(\rho_A)) = (\mathcal{X}_{AB} - \mathcal{X}_{AE}), \tag{9.70}$$

where

$$\mathcal{X}_{AB} = S(\mathcal{Q}_{AB}(\rho_{AB})) - \sum_i p_i S(\mathcal{Q}_{AB}(\rho_i)) \tag{9.71}$$

and

Figure 9.23 The conceptual meaning of quantum coherent information. The unitary transformation represents the channel and the environment. The first receiver is Bob, and the second receiver is the environment. The state of the environment belonging to the unitary transformation is represented by the lowest line. The outputs can be computed as the partial traces of the joint system.

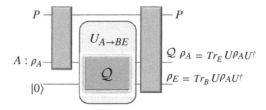

$$\mathcal{X}_{AE} = S(\mathcal{Q}_{AE}(\rho_{AE})) - \sum_i p_i S(\mathcal{Q}_{AE}(\rho_i)) \tag{9.72}$$

measure the Holevo quantities between A and B, and between and environment E, where $\rho_{AB} = \sum_i p_i \rho_i$ and $\rho_{AE} = \sum_i p_i \rho_i$ are the average states. The definition of Eq. (9.70) also draws a very important connection: *the amount of transmittable quantum information can be derived by the Holevo information*, which measures classical information.

It follows that the *single-use* quantum capacity $Q^{(1)}(\mathcal{Q})$ can be expressed as

$$
\begin{aligned}
Q^{(1)}(\mathcal{Q}) &= max_{\text{all } p_i, \rho_i} (\mathcal{X}_{AB} - \mathcal{X}_{AE}) \\
&= max_{\text{all } p_i, \rho_i} S\left(\mathcal{Q}_{AB}\left(\sum_{i=1}^n p_i(\rho_i)\right)\right) - \sum_{i=1}^n p_i S(\mathcal{N}\mathcal{Q}_{AB}(\rho_i)) \\
&\quad - S\left(\mathcal{Q}_{AE}\left(\sum_{i=1}^n p_i(\rho_i)\right)\right) + \sum_{i=1}^n p_i S(\mathcal{Q}_{AE}(\rho_i)),
\end{aligned}
\tag{9.73}
$$

where $\mathcal{Q}(\rho_i)$ represents the i-th output density matrix obtained from the $\mathcal{Q}$ channel input density matrix ρ_i. The *asymptotic* quantum capacity $Q(\mathcal{Q})$ can be expressed by

$$
\begin{aligned}
Q(\mathcal{Q}) &= \lim_{n\to\infty} Q^{(1)}(\mathcal{N}^{\otimes n})/n \\
&= \lim_{n\to\infty} max_{\text{all } p_i, \rho_i} I_{coh}(\rho_A : \mathcal{N}^{\otimes n}(\rho_A)) \\
&= \lim_{n\to\infty} max_{\text{all } p_i, \rho_i} (\mathcal{X}_{AB} - \mathcal{X}_{AE})/n.
\end{aligned}
\tag{9.74}
$$

The quantum capacity $Q(\mathcal{Q})$ of a quantum channel $\mathcal{Q}$ can also be expressed by $\mathcal{X}_{AB}$, the *Holevo quantity* of B's output and by $\mathcal{X}_{AE}$, the information leaked to the environment during the transmission.

Quantum coherent information and quantum mutual information: Let us now make an interesting comparison between quantum coherent information and quantum mutual information. For classical information transmission, the *quantum mutual information* can be expressed as $I(A:B) = S(\rho_A) + S(\rho_B) - S(\rho_{AB})$. However, in the case of *quantum coherent information* (Eq. 9.69), the term $S(\rho_A)$ vanishes. The channel transformation $\mathcal{Q}$ modifies A's original state ρ_A, and hence A's original density matrix cannot be used to express $S(\rho_A)$ *after A's qubit has been sent through* the quantum channel $\mathcal{Q}$. After the channel has modified A's quantum state, the initially sent qubit vanishes from the system, and we will have a different density matrix, denoted by $\rho_B = \mathcal{Q}(\rho_A)$. The coherent information can be expressed as $S(\rho_B) - S(\rho_{AB})$, where ρ_B is the transformed state of B, and $S(\rho_{AB})$ is the joint von Neumann entropy. It follows that we will have $S(\rho_B) - S(\rho_{AB})$, which is equal to the *negative conditional entropy* $S(A|B)$, and thus $I_{coh}(\rho_A : \mathcal{Q}(\rho_A)) = S(\rho_B) - S(\rho_{AB}) = -S(A|B)$. This result is summarized in Figure 9.24.

So, there is a *very important difference* between the maximized quantum *mutual information* and the maximized *quantum coherent information* of a $\mathcal{Q}$ channel. Whereas the former is always additive, this does not remain true for the latter. *The quantum coherent information* is defined as follows:

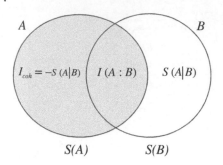

Figure 9.24 Expression of quantum coherent information. The source entropy of A's state vanishes after the state is passed to B.

$I_{coh}(\mathcal{Q}) = S(\rho_B) - S(\rho_E)$, where ρ_B refers to the output of the quantum channel $\mathcal{Q}$, while ρ_E is the state of the environment. The term $S(\rho_B)$ measures how much information B has, while $S(\rho_E)$ measures how much information environment has. It follows that the quantum coherent information $I_{coh}(\mathcal{Q})$ measures *how much more information B has than the environment* about the original input quantum state.

Quantum coherent information of an ideal channel: Now, we have arrived at the question of whether the $Q(\mathcal{Q})$ quantum capacity of $\mathcal{Q}$, as defined previously by the I_{coh} quantum coherent information, is an appropriate measure to describe the whole quantum capacity of a $\mathcal{Q}$ channel. The answer is yes for an ideal channel. If we have a completely noiseless channel, then channel $\mathcal{Q}_{AB} = I$ leads us to coherent information $Q(I) = I_{coh}(I) = S(\mathcal{Q}_{AB}(\rho)) - S(\mathcal{Q}_E(|\,0\rangle\langle 0\,|)) = S(\rho)$.

This equation can be used to calculate the $Q(\mathcal{Q}_{AB})$ quantum capacity of a $\mathcal{Q}$ channel (i.e. without maximization) only when we have a completely noiseless idealistic channel $\mathcal{Q}_{AB} = I$. It also implies the following: to achieve the maximal coherent information for an idealistic quantum channel $\mathcal{Q}_{AB} = I$, the input quantum states have to be maximally mixed states or one half of an Einstein–Podolsky–Rosen (EPR) state, since in these cases the von Neumann entropies will be maximum.

On the other hand, if the environment of the communication system interacts with the quantum state, the quantum capacity could vanish, but not the classical capacity of the channel. In this case, the quantum channel $\mathcal{Q}_{AB} = I$ can transmit pure orthogonal states faithfully, but it cannot transmit the superposed or entangled states. Furthermore, if the interaction is more significant, it could result in an extremely noisy quantum channel for which the $C(\mathcal{Q}_{AB})$ classical capacity of $\mathcal{Q}_{AB}$ could also vanish.

The concept of quantum coherent information can be used to express the *asymptotic* quantum capacity $Q(\mathcal{Q})$ of quantum channel $\mathcal{Q}$ called the *LSD* capacity as follows:

$$Q(\mathcal{Q}) = \lim_{n \to \infty} Q^{(1)}\left(\mathcal{Q}^{\otimes n}\right)/n = \lim_{n \to \infty} max_{all\ p_i, \rho_i} I_{coh}\left(\rho_A : \mathcal{Q}^{\otimes n}(\rho_A)\right)/n$$
$$= \lim_{n \to \infty} max_{all\ p_i, \rho_i} \left(S(\rho_B) - S(\rho_E)\right)/n, \tag{9.75}$$

where $Q^{(1)}(\mathcal{Q})$ represents the *single-use* quantum capacity. The asymptotic quantum capacity can also be expressed using the Holevo information, since as we have seen previously, the quantum coherent information can be derived from the Holevo information:

$$Q(\mathcal{Q}) = \lim_{n \to \infty} max_{all\ p_i, \rho_i} \frac{(\mathcal{X}_{AB} - \mathcal{X}_{AE})}{n}, \tag{9.76}$$

where $\mathcal{X}_{AB}$ denotes the classical information sent from A to B, and $\mathcal{X}_{AE}$ describes the classical information passed from A to the environment during the transmission.

Quantum coherent information plays a fundamental role in describing the maximum amount of transmittable quantum information through a quantum channel $\mathcal{Q}$, and – as the Holevo quantity has deep relevance in the classical HSW capacity of a quantum channel – the quantum coherent information will play a crucial role in the LSD capacity of Q.

The assisted quantum capacity: This measures the quantum capacity for a channel pair that contains different channel models – and it will have relevance in the *superactivation* of quantum channels [93]. If we have a quantum channel Q, then we can find a symmetric channel A that results in the following assisted quantum capacity: $Q_A(Q) = Q(Q \otimes A)$. We note that the symmetric channel has an unbounded dimension in the strongest case, and this quantity cannot be evaluated in general. $Q_A(Q)$ makes it possible to realize the superactivation of zero-capacity (in terms of LSD capacity) Q channels. For example, if we have a zero-capacity *Horodecki channel* and a zero-capacity symmetric channel, then their combination can result in positive joint capacity [93].

The zero-error quantum capacity: In this case, $Q_0^{(1)}(Q)$ and $Q_0(Q)$, the encoding and decoding processes, differ from the classical zero-error capacity: the encoding and decoding are carried out by the *coherent* encoder and *coherent* POVM decoder, whose special techniques make it possible to preserve the quantum information during the transmission [94, 95].

The *single-use* and *asymptotic* quantum zero-error capacity are defined similarly as $Q_0^{(1)}(Q) = \log(K(Q))$ and $Q_0(Q) = \lim_{n \to \infty} \log(K(Q^{\otimes n}))/n$, where $K(Q^{\otimes n})$ is the maximum number of n-length mutually non-adjacent quantum messages that the quantum channel can transmit with zero error. The quantum zero-error capacity is upper-bounded by LSD channel capacity $Q(Q)$; that is, the following relation holds between the quantum zero-error capacities: $Q_0(Q) \leq Q(Q)$.

In summary: The quantum capacity of Q cannot exceed the maximum classical capacity that can be measured with entangled inputs and joint measurement; at least, it is not possible in general. On the other hand, for some Q channels, it is conjectured that the maximal *single-use* classical capacity – hence the capacity that can be reached with *product* inputs and a *single* measurement setting – is lower than the *quantum capacity* for the same quantum channel. For all quantum channels, $C(Q) \geq Q(Q)$, where $C(Q)$ is the classical capacity of the quantum channel that can be achieved with entangled input states and a joint measurement setting. On the other hand, it is conjectured that for some quantum channels, $C(Q) < Q(Q)$ holds as long as the classical capacity $C(Q)$ of the Q channel is measured by a classical encoder and a single measurement setting. (As we have seen, the classical capacities of a quantum channel can be measured in different settings, and the strongest version can be achieved with the combination of entangled inputs and joint measurement decoding.)

9.6 Quantum Channel Examples

Here, we give a brief survey of some important quantum channel maps and study some capacity formulas.

9.6.1 Channel Maps

The Pauli Channel: A model having an input state ρ can be formulated as

$$\rho \to C_P(\rho) = (1-p)\rho + p_x X\rho X + p_y Y\rho Y + p_x Z\rho Z,$$

where X, Y, and Z are single-qubit Pauli determined by (see Chapter 8)

$$X = \begin{pmatrix} 0 & 1 \\ 1 & 0 \end{pmatrix}, \ Y = \begin{pmatrix} 0 & -i \\ i & 0 \end{pmatrix}, \ Z = \begin{pmatrix} 1 & 0 \\ 0 & -1 \end{pmatrix}.$$

Note that the depolarizing probability $p = p_x + p_y + p_z$ is the sum of p_x, p_y, and p_z representing the depolarizing probability of Pauli X, Y, and Z errors, respectively. The probabilities of the errors at time instant t are dependent on the relaxation time T_1 and dephasing time T_2 as

$$p_x = p_y = \left(1 - e^{-t/T_2} \right)/4, p_z = \left(1 + e^{-t/T_1} - 2e^{-t/T_2} \right)/4.$$

The depolarizing channel: It performs the following transformation:

$$\mathcal{Q}(\rho_i) = \frac{pI}{2} + (1-p)\rho_i,$$

where p is the *depolarizing parameter* of the channel, and if A uses two orthogonal states ρ_0 and ρ_1 for the encoding then the mixed input state is

$$\rho = \left(\sum_i p_i \rho_i \right) = p_0 \rho_0 + (1-p_0)\rho_1.$$

After the unital channel has realized the transformation $\mathcal{Q}$ on state ρ, we will get the following result:

$$\mathcal{Q}\left(\sum_i p_i \rho_i \right) = \mathcal{Q}(p_0 \rho_0 + (1-p_0)\rho_1)$$
$$= pI/2 + (1-p)(p_0 \rho_0 + (1-p_0)\rho_1).$$

The damping channel: Let us consider the influences of the environment on a single qubit of a quantum system, where, for example, the qubit is realized by using a two-level atom having the ground state $|0\rangle$ and the excited state $|1\rangle$. The atom may undergo a spontaneous dissipation/absorption of energy to/from the environment, which makes the atom change its state from the ground state $|0\rangle$ to the excited state $|1\rangle$, or vice versa. The transition of the state is referred to as the decoherence process. As a result, the state of the qubit when there is no interaction with the environment is as follows [96]: $|0\rangle |0\rangle_E \rightarrow |0\rangle |0\rangle_E, |0\rangle |1\rangle_E \rightarrow |0\rangle |1\rangle_E, |1\rangle |0\rangle_E \rightarrow |1\rangle |0\rangle_E, |1\rangle |1\rangle_E \rightarrow |1\rangle |1\rangle_E$, where $|0\rangle_E$ and $|1\rangle_E$ represent the low and high basis states of the environment. On the other hand, if the dissipation/absorption occurs, we have $|1\rangle |0\rangle_E \rightarrow |0\rangle |1\rangle_E, |0\rangle |1\rangle_E \rightarrow |1\rangle |0\rangle_E$. This transition may be formulated as

$$|1\rangle |0\rangle_E \rightarrow \sqrt{1-p_l}|1\rangle |0\rangle_E + \sqrt{p_l}|0\rangle |1\rangle_E,$$
$$|0\rangle |1\rangle_E \rightarrow \sqrt{1-p_o}|0\rangle |1\rangle_E + \sqrt{p_o}|1\rangle |0\rangle_E,$$

where p_l and p_o are the probability of the atom losing its energy to the environment or obtaining its energy from the environment, respectively. We may generalize the above channel model by alternating the basis states by the superposition states to lead to

$$(\alpha|0\rangle + \beta|1\rangle)|0\rangle_E \rightarrow (\alpha|0\rangle + \beta\sqrt{1-p_l}|1\rangle)|0\rangle_E + \beta\sqrt{p_l}|0\rangle |1\rangle_E,$$
$$(\alpha|0\rangle + \beta|1\rangle)|1\rangle_E \rightarrow \alpha\sqrt{p_o}|1\rangle |0\rangle_E + (\alpha\sqrt{1-p_o}|0\rangle + \beta|1\rangle)|1\rangle_E.$$

It should be noted that the coefficients α and β may be used to represent the $(N-1)$ qubit states orthogonal to the states $|0\rangle$ and $|1\rangle$ of the considered qubit. Moreover, if it can be assumed that each qubit interacts independently with the environment, the associated decoherence process in the N-qubit system may be considered to be temporally and spatially uncorrelated. Accordingly, the process where the qubit loses its energy can be modeled by an amplitude damping channel C_{AD} having an input state ρ: $\rho \rightarrow C_{AD}(\rho) = E_{AD1}\rho E_{AD1}^{\dagger} + E_{AD2}\rho E_{AD2}^{\dagger}$ [97], where Kraus matrices E_{AD} used for characterizing the amplitude damping channel are as follows:

$$E_{AD1} = \begin{pmatrix} 1 & 0 \\ 0 & \sqrt{1-p_l} \end{pmatrix}, \quad E_{AD2} = \begin{pmatrix} 0 & \sqrt{p_l} \\ 0 & 0 \end{pmatrix}.$$

Influences from the environment may results in random phase kicks on a single qubit. In such a scenario, the decoherence process reflecting phase changes of the qubit is modeled as the phase damping channel $C_{PD}(\rho)$ as $\rho \rightarrow C_{PD}(\rho) = E_{PD1}\rho E_{PD1}^{\dagger} + E_{PD2}\rho E_{PD2}^{\dagger}$, where we have the corresponding Kraus matrices as

$$E_{PD1} = \begin{pmatrix} 1 & 0 \\ 0 & \sqrt{1-p_l} \end{pmatrix}, \quad E_{PD2} = \begin{pmatrix} 0 & \sqrt{p_l} \\ 0 & 0 \end{pmatrix}.$$

In order to reflect changes of the qubit in both phase and amplitude, the combination of amplitude and phase damping channels may be used. However, in general, it is not affordable to classically simulate an N-qubit combined channel, which requires a $2N$-dimensional Hilbert space. For the sake of facilitating efficient classical simulations, the combined amplitude and phase damping channel may be approximated using a Pauli channel model.

The dephasing channel model: Another type of decoherence map is unitary and results in relative phase differences between the computational basis states: the channel map that realizes it is called the *dephasing* map. In contrast to the amplitude damping map, it realizes a unitary transformation. The unitary representation of the dephasing $\mathcal{Q}$ channel for a given input $\rho = \sum_{i,j} \rho_{ij} |i\rangle\langle j|$ can be expressed as $\mathcal{Q}(\rho) = \sum_i \rho_{ii} |E_i\rangle\langle E_i|$, where $|E_i\rangle$ are the environment states. The dephasing $\mathcal{Q}$ channel acts on the density operator ρ as follows: $\mathcal{Q}(\rho_i) = p\sigma_Z \rho \sigma_Z + (1-p)\rho_i$, where σ_Z is the Pauli Z-operator. The image of the dephasing channel map is similar to that of the phase-flip channel map; however, the shrinkage of the original Bloch sphere is greater. The dephasing channel transforms an arbitrary superposed pure quantum state $\alpha|0\rangle + \beta|1\rangle$ into a mixture

$$\mathcal{Q}(\rho) \rightarrow \rho' = \begin{bmatrix} |\alpha|^2 & \alpha\beta^* e^{-y(t)} \\ \alpha^*\beta e^{-y(t)} & |\beta|^2 \end{bmatrix},$$

where $\gamma(t)$ is a positive real parameter, which characterizes the coupling to the environment using the time parameter t.

The pancake map: To give an example of physically not-allowed (nonphysical, non-CP) transformations, we discuss the *pancake map*. The non-CP property means that there exists no CPTP map that preserves some information along the equatorial spanned by the x and y axes of the Bloch sphere, while it completely demolishes any information along the z axis. This map is called the pancake map, and it realizes a physically not-allowed (non-CP) transformation. The effect of the pancake map is similar to the bit-phase-flip channel; however, this channel defines a non-CP transform: it "smears" the original Bloch sphere along the equatorial spanned by the x and y axes. On the other hand, the pancake map – besides the fact that is a nonphysical map – can be used theoretically to transfer some information, and some information can be transmitted through these kinds of channel maps. The reason behind decoherence is Nature. She cannot be perfectly eliminated from quantum systems in practice. The reduction of decoherence is also a very complex task, and hence it brings us on the engineering side of the problem: the quantum systems have to be designed in such a way that the unwanted interaction between the quantum states and the environment has to be minimum [98, 99]. Currently – despite the efficiency of these schemes – the most important tools to reduce decoherence are quantum error-correcting codes and decoupling methods.

9.6.2 Capacities

Next, we study the classical and quantum capacities of the following quantum channels: the erasure quantum channel, phase-erasure quantum channel, mixed erasure/phase-erasure quantum channel, and amplitude damping channel.

Erasure quantum channel: Q_p erases the input state ρ with probability p or transmits the state unchanged with probability $(1-p)$, so we have $Q_p(\rho) \to (1-p)\rho + (p \mid e\rangle\langle e \mid)$, where $|e\rangle$ is the erasure state. The classical capacity of the erasure quantum channel Q_p can be expressed as $(Q_p) = (1-p)\log(d)$, where d is the dimension of the input system ρ. It follows from this equation that the classical capacity of Q_p vanishes at $p = 1$, whereas if $0 \leq p < 1$, then the channel Q_p can transmit some classical information.

The quantum capacity of the erasure quantum channel Q_p is $Q(Q_p) = (1-2p)\log(d)$, and $Q(Q_p)$ vanishes at $p = 1/2$, but it can transmit some quantum information if $0 \leq p < 1/2$.

Phase-erasure quantum channel: Q_δ erases the phase of the input quantum state with probability p without disturbing the amplitude. Using the input density matrix ρ, the map of the phase-erasure quantum channel can be expressed as

$$Q(\rho) \to (1-p)\rho \otimes |0\rangle\langle 0| + p\frac{\rho + Z\rho Z^\dagger}{2} \otimes |1\rangle\langle 1|,$$

where Z realizes the phase transformation on the input quantum system ρ, while the second qubit is used as a flag qubit.

The classical capacity of the Q_δ phase-erasure quantum channel using the phase erasing probability q is $C(Q_\delta) = 1$, since the phase error has no effect on the distinguishability of orthogonal input quantum states $|0\rangle$ and $|1\rangle$. On the other hand, if we talk about the quantum capacity $Q(Q_\delta)$ of Q_δ, the picture changes: $Q(Q_\delta) = (1-q)\log(d)$.

Mixed erasure/phase-erasure quantum channel: This channel erases the input quantum system with probability p, erases the phase with probability q, and leaves the input unchanged with probability $1 - p - q \geq 0$. Using the previous equations, the classical capacity of the mixed erasure/phase-erasure quantum channel, Q_{p+q}, can be expressed as $C(Q_{p+q}) = (1-p)\log(d) = C(Q_p)$. By combining the previous expressions for the quantum capacity of the mixed erasure/phase-erasure quantum channel, Q_{p+q}, we get $Q(Q_{p+q}) = (1-q-2p)\log(d)$.

Amplitude damping quantum channel: The classical capacity can be expressed as

$$C(A_\gamma) = \max_\tau H(\tau) + [-H(\tau(\gamma)) + H(\tau(1-\gamma))],$$

where $\tau \in [0, 1]$ is a special parameter called the *population* parameter, H is the Shannon entropy function, and $H(\tau) = -\tau\log(\tau) - (1-\tau)\log(1-\tau)$. It follows from the previous equation that the classical capacity $C(A_\gamma)$ of the amplitude damping channel completely vanishes if $\gamma = 1$, otherwise (if $0 \leq \gamma < 1$) the channel can transmit classical information. On the other hand, for the quantum capacity $Q(A_\gamma)$, the capacity behaves differently. The quantum capacity of this channel can be expressed as a maximization: $Q(A_\gamma) = \max_\tau [H(\tau(\gamma)) - H(\tau(1-\gamma))]$.

9.6.3 Q Channel Parameters

The *asymmetric depolarizing channel*, characterized by the probabilities p_x, p_y, and p_z, is used for modeling quantum systems employing diverse materials. In other words, the quantum depolarizing channel can be used for modeling the imperfections in quantum hardware, namely, qubit flips resulting from quantum decoherence and quantum gates. Furthermore, a quantum depolarizing channel can also be invoked for modeling quantum state flips imposed by the real transmission medium, including free-space wireless channels and optical fiber links, when qubits are transmitted across these media. For the sake of simplicity, most recent studies of the quantum channel capacity [100, 101], as well as of quantum error correction (QEC) schemes, considered the symmetric polarizing channel [101], where the constituent flip probabilities obey $p_x = p_y = p_z = p/3$. By contrast, popular materials employed for producing quantum devices often exhibit asymmetric behavior, where a phase flip is orders of magnitude more likely than a bit flip [102], which can be modeled by an asymmetric quantum depolarizing channel [103–105]. In such asymmetric depolarizing channels, an extra parameter α called the channel's ratio of asymmetry is introduced to reflect the ratio of the phase-flip probability p_z and the bit-flip probability p_x as [106]

$$\alpha = \frac{p_z}{p_x} = 1 + 2\frac{e^{\frac{-t}{T_1}} - e\left(\frac{-t}{2T_1} - \frac{2t}{T_2}\right)}{1 - e^{\frac{-t}{T_1}}}.$$

Note that the bit-flip probability p_x as well as the simultaneous bit-and-phase-flip probability p_y may be considered to be equal [106], while time instant t may be interpreted as the coherent operation duration of a physical quantum gate [107]. If the coherent operation duration t is relatively short, formulated as $t << T_1$, we can invoke the approximation of $\alpha \approx 2T_2/T_1 - 1$. As a result, the phase-flip probability p_z can be directly determined from the values of α and p_x. Note that in the case of $\alpha = 1$, the depolarizing channel is the symmetric depolarizing channel, where the condition of $p_x = p_y = p_z = p/3$ is satisfied. In practice the channel's ratio of asymmetry has popular values of $\alpha = 10^2$, 10^4, and 10^6 [108], which correspond to the typical materials of Table 9.1, which are used for producing quantum devices. There is currently no preferred qubit technology; a variety of physical systems are being explored for use as qubits, including photons [111, 112], trapped ions [113–116], superconducting circuits [117–119], and spins in semiconductors [120–122].

Acting time in asymmetric channels: In the asymmetric depolarizing channel, when the acting time t (evolution time of the quantum system with the presence of decoherence, which can be considered to be equal to the duration of a physical quantum gate) of the channels under investigation is small, the value of α in the previous equation may be calculated by

$$\alpha = 1 + 2\frac{1 - e^{t/T_1(1 - T_1/T_2)}}{e^{t/(T_1 - 1)}},$$

Then, the bit-flip probability p_x is calculated upon the asymmetric level α and the depolarizing probability of p as $p_x = p/(\alpha + 2)$. As a result, the phase-flip probability p_z can be determined from the values of α and p_x. Since the phase-flip probability dominates the bit-flip one, the bit-flip probability p_x and the bit-and-phase flip probability p_y may be considered to be equal. We may use the pre-calculated α values in Table 9.1 for characterizing the quantum channel.

Since this method does not take into consideration the absolute values of t, T_1, and T_2, it may not closely characterize different systems manufactured by different materials in Table 9.1 that are associated with the same value of α. The absolute values of t, T_1, and T_2 may be used for calculating the depolarizing probabilities of p_x, p_z, and p_y as follows [106]:

$$p_z(t) = \frac{1}{4\left[1 + e^{\frac{-t}{T_1}} - 2e^{\left(\frac{-t}{2T_1} - \frac{2t}{T_2}\right)}\right]}; \; p_x(t) = p_y(t) = \frac{1}{4\left(1 - e^{\frac{-t}{T_1}}\right)}.$$

Accordingly, the encoding and decoding gate operation times pertaining to different materials are listed in Table 9.2.

Table 9.1 Quantum depolarizing channels.

System (Material)	T_1	T_2	α
P:Si [103]	1 h	1 ms	10^6
GaAs Quantum dots [104]	10 ms	$>1\,\mu s$	10^4
Super conducting (flux qubits) [109]	$1\,\mu s$	100 ns	10^2
Trapped ions [110]	100 ms	1 ms	10^2
Solid state nuclear magnetic resonance (NMR) [105]	>1 min	>1 s	10^2

Table 9.2 Maximum number of computational steps that can be performed without losing coherence.

Quantum systems	Time per gate operation (s)	Coherence time
Electrons from a gold atom	10^{-14}	10^{-8}
Trapped indium atoms	10^{-14}	10^{-1}
Optical micro cavity	10^{-14}	10^{-5}
Electron spin	10^{-7}	10^{-3}
Electron quantum dot	10^{-6}	10^{-3}
Nuclear spin	10^{-3}	10^4

Quantum systems	Maximal number of coherence steps
Electrons from a gold atom	10^6
Trapped indium atoms	10^{13}
Optical micro cavity	10^9
Electron spin	10^4
Electron quantum dot	10^3
Nuclear spin	10^7

Design Example 9.4

In this section, we discuss the design parameters for implementation of quantum key distribution (QKD) in the quantum free-space optical (FSO) channel. Depending on the specific form of the electromagnetic plane wave pertaining to the monochromatic laser signal generating photons, photons may be linearly polarized (LP) or elliptically polarized (EP) [123]. In the context of QKD systems, we consider only LP photons having polarizations of, say, $0^0, 90^0, -45^0$, and 45^0 [124]. Accordingly, the basis associated with the polarization of $0^0, 90^0$ can be characterized by

$$|0^0\rangle = 1|0^0\rangle + 0i|90^0\rangle \text{ and } |90^0\rangle = 0|0^0\rangle + i|90^0\rangle.$$

The relationship between the two bases can also be expressed by

$$|0^0\rangle = \frac{1}{\sqrt{2}}|45^0\rangle + \frac{i}{\sqrt{2}}|-45^0\rangle \text{ and } |90^0\rangle = \frac{1}{\sqrt{2}}|45^0\rangle - \frac{i}{\sqrt{2}}|-45^0\rangle.$$

Design Example 9.4 (Continued)

An FSO quantum transmission channel is used for carrying the photon stream from the source (S) to the destination (D). Since the FSO channel imposes deleterious effects, such as diffraction, atmospheric turbulence, and extinction [125], only a certain fraction γ of the photon stream transmitted by S arrives at D. In other words, the term γ invoked for characterizing the power transfer properties of the FSO channel over a distance L imposed on the QKD system's performance is approximated by $\gamma = \mu exp(-\alpha L)$ [126], where μ represents the diffraction losses or the normalized version of the fraction γ, and α is the extinction coefficient. The value of μ depends on the Fresnel number $D_f^0 = (\pi d_1 d_2 / 4\lambda L)^2$, where d_1 is the transmit aperture diameter and d_2 is the receiver's aperture diameter, and λ is the wavelength of the optical signal. In the near-field region with $D_f^0 >> 1$, the parameter μ is bounded by [126] $\mu_{NF, LB} \leq \mu \leq \mu_{NF, UB}$, where the upper bound $\mu_{NF, UB}$ can be calculated by [126] $\mu_{NF,UB} = min\left(D_f^0, 1\right)$, and the lower bound $\mu_{NF, LB}$ is given by [126]

$$\mu_{NF,LB} = \left(8\sqrt{D_f^0/\pi^2}\right)\int_0^1 exp\left(-D(d_2 x)/2\right)$$
$$\times \left(arccos\,(x) - x\sqrt{1-x^2}\right) J_1\left(4x\sqrt{D_f^0}\right) dx,$$

where $J_1(.)$ is the first-order Bessel function. The spherical-wave structure function $D(\rho)$ of the above equation is calculated for the worse-case scenario of having $d_1 = d_2$ as [126]: $D(\rho) = 51\sigma_R^2\left(D_f^0\right)^{5/12}\rho^{5/3}$, where σ_R^2 is the Rytov variance [127] of $\sigma_R^2 = 1.24(2\pi/\lambda)^{7/6}C_n^2 L^{11/6}$, with C_n^2 ranging from 10^{-13} to 10^{-17} representing the altitude-dependent index of the refractive structure parameter [128]. By contrast, in the far-field region with $D_f^0 << 1$, the value of μ can be calculated by [129]

$$\mu_{FF} = \left(8\sqrt{D_f^0/\pi^2}\right)\int_0^1 exp\left(-D(d_2 x)/2\right)$$
$$\times \left(arcos^{-1}(x) - x\sqrt{1-x^2}\right) J_1\left(4x\sqrt{D_f^0}\right) dx,$$

where the spherical-wave structure function $D(\rho)$ in the previous equation can be calculated by $D(\rho) = 1.09(2\pi/\lambda)^2 C_n^2 L\rho^{5/3}$.

As a result, when a more accurate value range of γ is sought, the following bounds should be used: $\gamma_{LB} \leq \gamma \leq \gamma_{UB}$, where the upper bound γ_{UB} is determined by

$$\gamma_{UB} = \begin{cases} \gamma_{NF,UB}: & if\ D_f^0 > T_{near} \\ (\gamma_{NF,UB} + \gamma_{FF})/2: & if\ T_{far} \leq D_f^0 \leq T_{near}, \\ \gamma_{FF}: & if\ D_f^0 < T_{far} \end{cases}$$

(Continued)

Design Example 9.4 (Continued)

and the lower bound γ_{LB} is calculated by

$$
\gamma_{LB} = \begin{cases}
\gamma_{NF,LB}: & \text{if } D_f^0 > T_{near} \\
\dfrac{(\gamma_{NF,LB} + \gamma_{FF})}{2}: & \text{if } T_{far} \leq D_f^0 \leq T_{near}, \\
\gamma_{FF}: & \text{if } D_f^0 < T_{far}
\end{cases}
$$

where the region with $T_{far} \leq D_f^0 \leq T_{near}$ is the transition region between the near-field and far-field regimes. The polarization optics of the QKD transmitter and receiver is shown in Figure 9.25 [130]. In the scheme, the outputs of the data lasers (DL) in A are attenuated (average photon number $\mu < 1$), their polarizations set to the BB84 values (shown as two-headed arrows) by linear polarizers (P), combined using beam splitters (BS), passed through a spatial filter to erase spatial mode information (not shown), constrained by an interference filter (IF) to remove spectral information, and then directed onto a BS. Photons transmitted through the BS are launched toward B, whereas those reflected are directed onto a single-photon detector (SPD) with a ~20 ns timing window, to monitor the μ-value of the launched data pulses. The relative timings of the DLs are matched to within the SPD timing jitter. At Bob's end, data pulses pass through an IF and onto a BS, where they are randomly transmitted or reflected. Along the reflected path, a data pulse's polarization is analyzed in the rectilinear basis, using a polarization controller (PC) and a polarizing beam splitter (PBS). If one of the SPDs in the PBS output ports fires within the timing window (and no other SPD fires), Bob assigns a bit value to the data pulse. An analogous procedure occurs for data pulses taking the transmitted path, where their polarization is analyzed according to B's conjugate (diagonal) basis. (It was estimated that the probability for a photon produced in the SPD breakdown "flash" to emerge from the receiver telescope is $<10^{-9}$.) Multi-detection events, in which more than one SPD fires, are recorded but not used for key generation [130].

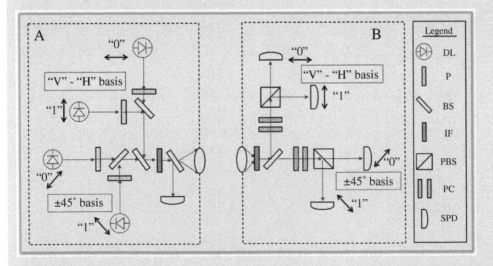

Figure 9.25 Polarization optics of the QKD transmitter and receiver. *Source:* Hughes et al. [130].

References

1 Gyongyosi, L., Imre, S., and Nguyen, H.V. (2018). A survey on quantum channel capacities. *IEEE Commun. Surv. Tutorials* **20** (2) Second Quarter: 1149.

2 Imre, S. and Gyongyosi, L. (2013). *Advanced Quantum Communications – An Engineering Approach.* Hoboken, NJ: Wiley.

3 Watrous, J. (2006). *Lecture Notes in Quantum Computation.* Calgary, AB: University of Calgary.

4 Wilde, M.M. (2013). *Quantum Information Theory.* Cambridge: Cambridge University Press.

5 Holevo, A.S. (1975). Bounds for the quantity of information transmitted by a quantum communication channel. *Probl. Inf. Trans.* **9** (3): 177–183.

6 Lloyd, S., Shapiro, J.H., Wong, F.N.C. et al. (2004). Infrastructure for the quantum internet. *ACM SIGCOMM Comput. Commun. Rev.* **34** (5): 9–20.

7 Shannon, C.E. (1948). A mathematical theory of communication. *Bell Syst. Tech. J.* **27**: 379–423, 623–656. Also available at http://people.math.harvard.edu/~ctm/home/text/others/shannon/entropy/entropy.pdf.

8 von Neumann, J. (1996). *Mathematical Foundations of Quantum Mechanics.* Princeton, NJ: Princeton University Press.

9 Misner, C., Thorne, K., Zurek, W., and Wheeler, J. (2009). Relativity, and quantum information. *Phys. Today* **62** (4): 40–46.

10 McEvoy, J.P. and Zarate, O. (2004). *Introducing Quantum Theory*, 3e. Royston: Totem Books.

11 Sakurai, J. (1994). *Modern Quantum Mechanics.* Reading, MA: Addison-Wesley.

12 Griffiths, D.J. (1995). *Introduction to Quantum Mechanics.* Englewood Cliffs, NJ: Prentice-Hall.

13 Bohm, D. (1989). *Quantum Theory.* New York, NY: Courier Dover.

14 Dowling, J.P. and Milburn, G.J. (2003). Quantum technology: the second quantum revolution. *Philos. Trans. R. Soc. London Ser. A* **361** (1809): 1655–1674.

15 de Broglie, L. (1925). Recherches sur la théorie des quanta. *Ann. Phys.* **2**: 22–128.

16 Dirac, P.A.M. (1982). *The Principles of Quantum Mechanics (International Series of Monographs on Physics).* Oxford: Oxford University Press.

17 Einstein, A. (1905). Über einen die erzeugung und verwandlung des lichtes betreenden heuristischen gesichtspunkt. *Ann. Phys.* **17**: 132–148.

18 Einstein, A., Podolsky, B., and Rosen, N. (1935). Can quantum-mechanical description of physical reality be considered complete? *Phys. Rev.* **47** (10): 777–780.

19 Kelvin, W.T.B. (1901). Nineteenth-century clouds over the dynamical theory of heat and light. *London Edinburgh Dublin Philos. Mag. J. Sci.* **2** (7): 10–20.

20 Schrödinger, E. (1926). Quantisierung als eigenwertproblem. *Ann. Phys.* **79** (4): 361–376.

21 Schrödinger, E. (1935). Discussion of probability relations between separated systems. *Proc. Cambridge Philos. Soc.* **31** (4): 555–563.

22 Planck, M. (1901). Ueber das gesetz der energieverteilung im normalspectrum. *Ann. Phys.* **309** (3): 553–563.

23 Heisenberg, W. (1925). Über quantentheoretische umdeutung kinematischer und mechanischer Beziehungen. *Z. Phys.* **33** (1): 879–893.

24 Gerlach, W. and Stern, O. (1922). Das magnetische moment des silberatoms. *Z. Phys.* **9** (1): 353–355.

25 Pierce, J. (1973). The early days of information theory. *IEEE Trans. Inf. Theory* **IT-19** (1): 3–8.

26 Yeung, R.W. (2002). A first course in information theory. In: *Information Technology: Transmission, Processing, and Storage* (ed. R.W. Yeung). New York, NY: Kluwer Academic Plenum Publishers.

27 Aspect, A., Grangier, P., and Roger, G. (1981). Experimental tests of realistic local theories via Bell's theorem. *Phys. Rev. Lett.* **47** (7): 460–463.

28 Jaynes, E.T. (2003). *Probability Theory: The Logic of Science*. Cambridge: Cambridge University Press.

29 Petz, D. (2008). *Quantum Information Theory and Quantum Statistics*. Heidelberg: Springer-Verlag.

30 Cover, T.M. and Thomas, J.A. (1991). *Elements of Information Theory*. New York, NY: Wiley.

31 Horn, R. and Johnson, C. (1986). *Matrix Analysis*. Cambridge: Cambridge University Press.

32 Bennett, C.H. and Shor, P.W. (1998). Quantum information theory. *IEEE Trans. Inf. Theory* **44** (6): 2724–2742.

33 Deutsch, D. (1985). Quantum theory, the church–turing principle and the universal quantum computer. *Proc. R. Soc. London Ser. A* **400** (1818): 97–117.

34 Feynman, R.P. (1982). Simulating physics with computers. *Int. J. Theor. Phys.* **21** (6–7): 467–488.

35 Vollbrecht, K.G.H. and Cirac, J.I. (2008). Quantum simulators, continuoustime automata, and translationally invariant systems. *Phys. Rev. Lett.* **100**: 010501.

36 Jozsa, R. and Schumacher, B. (1994). A new proof of the quantum noiseless coding theorem. *J. Mod. Opt.* **41** (12): 2343–2349.

37 Schumacher, B., Hausladen, P., Westmoreland, M.D., and Wootters, W.K. (1995). Sending classical bits via quantum bits. *Ann. New York Acad. Sci.* **755**: 698–705.

38 Schumacher, B. (1995). Quantum coding. *Phys. Rev. A* **51** (4): 2738–2747.

39 Schumacher, B. (1996). Sending entanglement through noisy quantum channels. *Phys. Rev. A* **54** (4): 2614–2628.

40 Schumacher, B. and Nielsen, M.A. (1996). Quantum data processing and error correction. *Phys. Rev. A* **54** (4): 2629–2635.

41 Schumacher, B. and Westmoreland, M.D. (1997). Sending classical information via noisy quantum channels. *Phys. Rev. A* **56** (1): 131–138.

42 Schumacher, B. and Westmoreland, M.D. (1998). Quantum privacy and quantum coherence. *Phys. Rev. Lett.* **80**: 5695–5697.

43 Barnum, H., Nielsen, M.A., and Schumacher, B. (1998). Information transmission through a noisy quantum channel. *Phys. Rev. A* **57** (6): 4153–4175.

44 Schumacher, B., Caves, C.M., Nielsen, M.A., and Barnum, H. (1998). Information theoretic approach to quantum error correction and reversible measurement. *Proc. R. Soc. London Ser. A* **454**: 277–304.

45 Schumacher, B. and Westmoreland, M.D. (1999). Optimal signal ensembles. eprint quant-ph/9912122.

46 Schumacher, B. and Westmoreland, M.D. (1999). Characterizations of classical and quantum communication processes. *Chaos Solitons Fractals* **10** (1): 1719–1736.

47 Bennett, C.H. and Wiesner, S.J. (1992). Communication via one- and twoparticle operators on Einstein–Podolsky–Rosen states. *Phys. Rev. Lett.* **69** (20): 2881–2884.

48 Nielsen, M.A. and Chuang, I.L. (2000). *Quantum Computation and Quantum Information*. Cambridge: Cambridge University Press.

49 Hayashi, M. (2006). *Quantum Information: An Introduction*. Heidelberg: Springer-Verlag.

50 Horodecki, R., Horodecki, P., Horodecki, M., and Horodecki, K. (2009). Quantum entanglement. *Rev. Mod. Phys.* **81** (2): 865–942.

51 Hayden, P. and Winter, A. (2003). Communication cost of entanglement transformations. *Phys. Rev. A* **67** (1): 012326.

52 Yard, J. (2005). Simultaneous classical-quantum capacities of quantum multiple access channels, Ph.D. dissertation. Dept. Elect. Eng., Stanford Univ., Stanford, CA, USA.

53 Yard, J., Devetak, I., and Hayden, P. (2005). Capacity theorems for quantum multiple access channels. In *Proceedings of the International Symposium on Information Theory*, Adelaide, SA, Australia, pp. 884–888.

54 Hayashi, M. and Nagaoka, H. (2003). General formulas for capacity of classical-quantum channels. *IEEE Trans. Inf. Theory* **49** (7): 1753–1768.

55 Audenaert, K.M.R. (2007). A sharp continuity estimate for the von Neumann entropy. *J. Phys. A Math. Theor.* **40** (28): 8127–8136.

56 Adami, C. and Cerf, N.J. (1996). On the von Neumann capacity of noisy quantum channels. *Phys. Rev. A* **56** (5): 3470–3483.

57 Bacsardi, L. (2005). Using quantum computing algorithms in future satellite communication. *Acta Astronaut.* **57** (2–8): 224–229.

58 Bacsardi, L. (2007). Satellite communication over quantum channel. *Acta Astronaut.* **61** (1–6): 151–159.

59 Bacsardi, L. and Imre, S. (2010). Quantum based information transfer in satellite communication. In: *Satellite Communications*, 421–436. Rijeka: Sciyo https://pdfs.semanticscholar.org/59a9/7ad5e55c8fd77bb93bd341a54690261035f7.pdf.

60 Bacsardi, L. (2013). On the way to quantum-based satellite communication. *IEEE Commun. Mag.* **51** (8): 50–55.

61 Munro, W.J., Van Meter, R., Louis, S.G.R., and Nemoto, K. (2008). Highbandwidth hybrid quantum repeater. *Phys. Rev. Lett.* **101** (4): 040502.

62 Munro, W.J., Harrison, K.A., Stephens, A.M. et al. (2010). From quantum fusiliers to high-performance networks. *Nat. Photon.* **4** (1): 792–796.

63 Munro, W.J., Harrison, K.A., Stephens, A.M. et al. (2010). From quantum multiplexing to high-performance quantum networking. *Nat. Photon.* **4**: 792–796. https://doi.org/10.1038/nphoton.2010.213.

64 Van Meter, R., Ladd, T., Munro, W.J., and Nemoto, K. (2007). Communication links for distributed quantum computation. *IEEE Trans. Comput.* **56** (12): 1643–1653.

65 Van Meter, R., Ladd, T.D., Munro, W.J., and Nemoto, K. (2009). System design for a long-line quantum repeater. *IEEE/ACM Trans. Netw.* **17** (3): 1002–1013.

66 Van Meter, R., Satoh, T., Ladd, T.D. et al. (2013). Path selection for quantum repeater networks. *Netw. Sci.* **3** (1–4): 82–95.

67 Van Meter, R. (2014). *Quantum Networking*. London: Wiley.

68 Gyongyosi, L. and Imre, S. (2013). Algorithmic superactivation of asymptotic quantum capacity of zero-capacity quantum channels. *Inf. Sci.* **222**: 737–753.

69 Gyongyosi, L. and Imre, S. (2011). Quantum cryptographic protocols and quantum security. In: *Cryptography: Protocols, Design and Applications* (eds. K. Lek and N. Rajapakse). Hauppauge, NY: Nova Science.

70 Gyongyosi, L. and Imre, S. (2011). Cellular automata. In: *Quantum Cellular Automata Controlled Self-Organizing Networks* (ed. A. Salcido), 113–153. New York, NY: INTECH.

71 Gyongyosi, L. and Imre, S. (2012). Quasi-superactivation of classical capacity of zero-capacity quantum channels. *J. Mod. Opt.* **59** (14): 1243–1264.

72 Gyongyosi, L. and Imre, S. (2013). Superactivation of quantum channels is limited by the quantum relative entropy function. *Quantum Inf. Process.* **12** (2): 1011–1021.

73 Gyongyosi, L. (2013). Information geometric superactivation of asymptotic quantum capacity and classical zero-error capacity of zero-capacity quantum channels, Ph.D. dissertation. Dept. Telecommun., Budapest Univ. Technol. Econ., Budapest, Hungary.

74 Gyongyosi, L. (2014). The correlation conversion property of quantum channels. *Quantum Inf. Process.* **13** (2): 467–473.

75 Gyongyosi, L. (2014). A statistical model of information evaporation of perfectly reflecting black holes. *Int. J. Quantum Inf.* **12**: 1560025.

76 Gyongyosi, L. (2014). The private classical capacity of a partially degradable quantum channel. *Physica Scripta Int. J. Exp. Theor. Phys.* **10**: 11–20.

77 Gyongyosi, L. (2014). The structure and quantum capacity of a partially degradable quantum channel. *IEEE Access* **2**: 333–355.

78 Gyongyosi, L. (2014). Quantum information transmission over a partially degradable channel. *IEEE Access* **2**: 195–198.

79 Gyongyosi, L. (2017). Quantum imaging of high-dimensional Hilbert spaces with radon transform. *Int. J. Circuit Theory Appl.* **45** (7): 1029–1046.

80 Gyongyosi, L. and Imre, S. (2011). Information geometric superactivation of classical zero-error capacity of quantum channels. *Progr. Informat.* **8** (4): 89–109.

81 Imre, S. and Balázs, F. (2005). *Quantum Computing and Communications – An Engineering Approach*. Hoboken, NJ: Wiley.

82 King, C. and Ruskai, M.B. (2001). Capacity of quantum channels using product measurements. *J. Math. Phys.* **42** (5): 87–98.

83 Bennett, C.H., DiVincenzo, D.P., Fuchs, C.A. et al. (1999). Quantum nonlocality without entanglement. *Phys. Rev. A* **59** (2): 1070–1091.

84 Medeiros, R.A.C. and de Assis, F.M. (2005). Quantum zero-error capacity. *Int. J. Quantum Inf.* **3** (1): 135.

85 Lovász, L. (1979). On the Shannon capacity of a graph. *IEEE Trans. Inf. Theory* **IT-25** (1): 1–7.

86 Chen, J., Cubitt, T.S., Harrow, A.W., and Smith, G. (2010). Super-duperactivation of the zero-error quantum capacity. In *Proceedings of the IEEE International Symposium Information Theory (ISIT)*, Austin, TX, USA, pp. 2695–2697.

87 Cubitt, T.S., Leung, D., Matthews, W., and Winter, A. (2010). Improving zero-error classical communication with entanglement. *Phys. Rev. Lett.* **104**: 230503.

88 Leung, D., Mancinska, L., Matthews, W. et al. (2012). Entanglement can increase asymptotic rates of zero-error classical communication over classical channels. *Commun. Math. Phys.* **311** (2): 97–111.

89 Devetak, I. and Winter, A. (2003). Classical data compression with quantum side information. *Phys. Rev. A* **68** (4): 042301.

90 Lloyd, S. (1997). Capacity of the noisy quantum channel. *Phys. Rev. A* **55**: 1613–1622.

91 Shor, P.W. (2002). The quantum channel capacity and coherent information. In *Proceeding of the Lecture Notes MSRI Workshop in Quantum Computing*, San Francisco, CA, USA, pp. 10–50. http://www.msri.org/publications/ln/msri/2002/quantumcrypto/shor/1

92 Schumacher, B. and Westmoreland, M.D. (2000). Relative entropy in quantum information theory. In: *Quantum Computation and Quantum Information: A Millenium Volume*, American Mathematical Society Contemporary Mathematics (ed. S. Lomonaco). Boston, MA: American Mathematical Society.

93 Smith, G. and Yard, J. (2008). Quantum communication with zero-capacity channels. *Science* **321** (5897): 1812–1815.

94 Harrow, A.W. (2004). Coherent communication of classical messages. *Phys. Rev. Lett.* **92** (3): 097902.

95 Hsieh, M.-H., Devetak, I., and Winter, A. (2008). Entanglement-assisted capacity of quantum multiple-access channels. *IEEE Trans. Inf. Theory* **54** (7): 3078–3090.

96 Preskill, J. (2015). *Lecture Notes for Physics 229: Quantum Information and Computation*. CreateSpace Independent Publishing Platform.

97 Ghosh, J., Fowler, A.G., and Geller, M.R. (2012). Surface code with decoherence: an analysis of three superconducting architectures. *Phys. Rev. A* **86**: 062318.

98 Shor, P.W. (1995). Scheme for reducing decoherence in quantum computer memory. *Phys. Rev. A* **52** (4): R2493–R2496.

99 Shor, P.W. (1996). Fault-tolerant quantum computation. In *Proceedings of the IEEE Annual Symposium on Foundation of Computer Science*, pp. 56–65.

100 Wilde, M.M. and Hsieh, M.-H. (2012). The quantum dynamic capacity formula of a quantum channel. *Quantum Inf. Process.* **11** (6): 1431–1463.

101 Wilde, M.M., Hsieh, M.-H., and Babar, Z. (2014). Entanglement-assisted quantum turbo codes. *IEEE Trans. Inf. Theory* **60** (2): 1203–1222.

102 Ioffe, L. and Mezard, M. (2007). Asymmetric quantum error-correcting codes. *Phys. Rev. A* **75** (3): 032345.

103 Tyryshkin, A.M., Morton, J.J.L., Benjamin, S.C. et al. (2006). Coherence of spin qubits in silicon. *J. Phys. Condens. Matter* **18** (21): S783–S794.

104 Petta, J.R., Johnson, A.C., Taylor, J.M. et al. (2005). Coherent manipulation of coupled electron spins in semiconductor quantum dots. *Science* **309** (5744): 2180–2184.

105 Vandersypen, L.M.K., Steffen, M., Breyta, G. et al. (2001). Experimental realization of Shor's quantum factoring algorithm using nuclear magnetic resonance. *Nature* **414**: 883–887.

106 Evans, Z.W.E., Stephens, A.M., Cole, J.H., and Hollenberg, L.C.L. (2007). Error correction optimisation in the presence of X/Z asymmetry. ArXiv.

107 Williams, C.P. and Clearwater, S.H. (2000). *Ultimate Zero and One Computing at the Quantum Frontier*. New York, NY: Springer-Verlag.

108 Poulin, D., Tillich, J., and Ollivier, H. (2009). Quantum serial turbo codes. *IEEE Trans. Inf. Theory* **55** (6): 2776–2798.

109 Bertet, P., Chiorescu, I., Burkard, G. et al. (2005). Dephasing of a superconducting qubit induced by photon noise. *Phys. Rev. Lett.* **95**: 257002.

110 Schmidt-Kaler, F., Gulde, S., Riebe, M. et al. (2003). The coherence of qubits based on single ca+ ions. *J. Phys. B Atomic Mol. Opt. Phys.* **36** (3): 623–636.

111 Wang, X.L., Chen, L.K., Li, W. et al. (2016). Experimental ten-photon entanglement. *Phys. Rev. Lett.* **117** (21) https://doi.org/10.1103/physrevlett.117.210502.

112 Qiang, X., Zhou, X., Wang, J. et al. (2018). Large-scale silicon quantum photonics implementing arbitrary two-qubit processing. *Nat. Photon.* **12** (9): 534–539. https://doi.org/10.1038/s41566-018-0236-y.

113 Randall, J., Weidt, S., Standing, E.D. et al. (2015). Efficient preparation and detection of microwave dressed-state qubits and qutrits with trapped ions. *Phys. Rev. A* **91** (1) https://core.ac.uk/download/pdf/30610435.pdf.

114 Ballance, C., Harty, T., Linke, N. et al. (2016). High-fidelity quantum logic gates using trapped-ion hyperfine qubits. *Phys. Rev. Lett.* **117** (6) https://arxiv.org/pdf/1512.04600.pdf.

115 Brandl, M.F., van Mourik, M.W., Postler, L. et al. (2016). Cryogenic setup for trapped ion quantum computing. *Rev. Sci. Instrum.* **87** (11): 113103.

116 Debnath, S., Linke, N.M., Figgatt, C. et al. (2016). Demonstration of a small programmable quantum computer with atomic qubits. *Nature* **536** (7614): 63.

117 Chow, J.M., Gambetta, J.M., C'orcoles, A.D. et al. (2012). Universal quantum gate set approaching fault23 July 26, 2019 tolerant thresholds with superconducting qubits. *Phys. Rev. Lett.* **109** (6) https://doi.org/10.1103/physrevlett.109.060501.

118 Chen, Y., Neill, C., Roushan, P. et al. (2014). Qubit architecture with high coherence and fast tunable coupling. *Phys Rev Lett.* **113**: 220502. https://doi.org/10.1103/PhysRevLett.113.220502.

119 Wendin, G. (2017). Quantum information processing with superconducting circuits: a review. *Rep. Progress Phys.* **80** (10): 106001. https://doi.org/10.1088/1361-6633/aa7e1a.

120 Kane, B.E. (1998). A silicon-based nuclear spin quantum computer. *Nature* **393** (6681): 133–137. https://doi.org/10.1038/30156.

121 Hill, C.D., Peretz, E., Hile, S.J. et al. (2015). A surface code quantum computer in silicon. *Sci. Adv.* **1** (9): e1500707. https://doi.org/10.1126/sciadv.1500707.

122 van der Heijden, J., Kobayashi, T., House, M.G. et al. (2018). Readout and control of the spin-orbit states of two coupled acceptor atoms in a silicon transistor. *Sci. Adv.* **4** (12): eaat9199. https://doi.org/10.1126/sciadv.aat9199.

123 Pade, J. (2014). *Quantum Mechanics for Pedestrians 1: Fundamentals. Undergraduate Lecture Notes in Physics*, 1e. Cham, Switzerland: Springer.

124 Zeilinger, A. (1999). Experiment and the foundations of quantum physics. *Rev. Mod. Phys.* **71**: S288–S297.

125 Trinh, P.V., Dang, N.T., and Pham, A.T. (2015). All-optical relaying FSO systems using EDFA combined with optical hard-limiter over atmospheric turbulence channels. *J. Lightw. Technol.* **33** (19): 4132–4144.

126 Shapiro, J.H. (2003). Near-field turbulence effects on quantum-key distribution. *Phys. Rev. A* **67**: 022309.

127 Karp, S., Gagliardi, R.M., Moran, S.E., and Stotts, L.B. (eds.) (1988). *Optical Channels: Fibers, Clouds, Water and the Atmosphere*. New York, NY: Plenum Press.

128 Zhang, W., Hranilovic, S., and Shi, C. (2009). Soft-switching hybrid FSO/RF links using short-length raptor codes: design and implementation. *IEEE J. Sel. Areas Commun.* **27** (9): 1698–1708.

129 Shapiro, J.H. (1974). Normal-mode approach to wave propagation in the turbulent atmosphere. *Appl. Opt.* **13** (11): 2614–2619.

130 Hughes, R.J., Nordholt, J.E., Derkacs, D., and Peterson, C.G. Practical free-space quantum key distribution over 10 km in daylight and at night. https://iopscience.iop.org/article/10.1088/1367-2630/4/1/343

10

Quantum Error Correction

Classical information technologies employ b9inary encodings in which data are represented as sequences of bits taking values of "0" or "1." The basic principle behind error correction is that the number of bits used to encode a given amount of information is increased. The exact way in which this *redundant* encoding is achieved is specified by a set of instructions known as an *error correction code* [1, 2]. The simplest example of an error correction code is the three-bit repetition code, in which the encoder duplicates each bit value $0 \rightarrow 000$ and $1 \rightarrow 111$. More formally, we can define the three-bit encoder as a mapping from a "raw" binary alphabet B to a code alphabet C_3, that is, $B = \{0, 1\}$ (*three-bit encoding*) $\rightarrow C_3 = \{000,111\}$, where the encoded bit-strings "000" and "111" are referred to as the *logical codewords* of the code C_3.

> **Design Example 10.1**
>
> Consider the simple case where we wish to communicate a single-bit message ("0" to a recipient in a different location. Using the three-bit encoding, the message that we would send would be the "000" codeword. If the message is subject to a single bit-flip error during transmission so that the bit string the recipient receives is (010'. In this scenario, the recipient will be able to infer that the intended codeword is "000" by a majority vote. The same will be true for all cases where the codeword is subject to only a single error. However, if the codeword is subject to two bit-flip errors, the majority vote will lead to the incorrect codeword. The final scenario to consider is when all three bits are flipped so that the codeword "000" becomes "111." In this case, the corrupted message is also a codeword: the recipient will therefore have no way of knowing that an error has occurred. The distance of a code is defined as the minimum number of errors that will change one codeword to another in this way. We can relate the distance d of a code to the number of errors it can correct as $d = 2t + 1$, where t is the number of errors the code can correct. It is clear that the above equation is satisfied for the three-bit code where $t = 1$ and $d = 3$. In general, error correction codes are described in terms of the [n, k, d] notation, where n is the total number of bits per codeword, k is the number of encoded bits (the length of the original bit string), and d is the code distance. Under this notation, the three-bit repetition code is labeled [3, 1, 3].

What is now different when we move from bits to qubits? In place of bits in classical systems, the fundamental unit of quantum information is the qubit. The general qubit state can be written as $|\psi\rangle = \alpha |0\rangle + \beta |1\rangle$, where α and β are complex numbers that satisfy the condition $|\alpha|^2 + |\beta|^2 = 1$.

Artificial Intelligence and Quantum Computing for Advanced Wireless Networks, First Edition.
Savo G. Glisic and Beatriz Lorenzo.
© 2022 John Wiley & Sons Ltd. Published 2022 by John Wiley & Sons Ltd.

Details regarding the notation we use to represent quantum states are covered in the previous chapters of the book. Qubits can encode information in a superposition of their basis states, meaning quantum computers have access to a computational space that scales as 2^n, where n is the total number of qubits. It is by exploiting superposition, in combination with other quantum effects such as entanglement, that it is possible to construct algorithms that provide a quantum advantage. However, if such algorithms are ever to be realized on current or future quantum hardware, it will be necessary for the qubits to be error corrected.

The digitization of quantum errors: In classical information, bits are either in the "0" or "1" state. Therefore, the only error type to be considered is the bit flip that takes $0 \to 1$ and vice versa. By contrast, the general qubit state can assume a continuum of values between its basis states. From the perspective of developing error correction codes, this property is problematic as it means the qubit is subject to an infinite number of different errors.

Design Example 10.2

To illustrate this more clearly, it is useful to rewrite the general qubit state in terms of a geometric representation given by

$$|\psi\rangle = \cos\frac{\theta}{2}\,|0\rangle + e^{i\varphi}\sin\frac{\theta}{2}\,|1\rangle,$$

where the probability amplitudes maintain the condition that $\left|\cos\frac{\theta}{2}\right|^2 + \left|e^{i\varphi}\sin\frac{\theta}{2}\right|^2 = 1$. In this form, the qubit state corresponds to a point, specified by the angles θ and φ, on the surface of a Bloch sphere (see Chapter 8). Qubit errors can occur by a variety of physical processes. The simplest case to examine is errors that cause the qubit to coherently rotate from one point on the Bloch sphere to another. Such qubit errors could, for example, arise from systematic control faults in the hardware with which the qubits are realized. Mathematically, coherent errors are described by a unitary operation $U(\delta\theta, \delta\varphi)$ that evolves the qubit state as follows:

$$U(\delta\theta, \delta\varphi)\,|\psi\rangle = \cos\frac{\theta + \delta\theta}{2}\,|0\rangle + \exp[ei(\varphi + \delta\varphi)]\sin\frac{\theta + \delta\theta}{2}\,|1\rangle, \tag{10.1}$$

where $\theta + \delta\theta$ and $\varphi + \delta\varphi$ are the new coordinates on the Bloch sphere. From this, we see that qubits are susceptible to a continuum of coherent errors obtained by varying the parameters $\delta\theta$ and $\delta\varphi$. It would therefore seem, at first glance, that quantum error correction (QEC) protocols will have to be based on techniques from classical analogue computation for which the theory of error correction is not well developed. Luckily, however, it turns out that quantum errors can be digitized, so that the ability to correct for a finite set of errors is sufficient to correct for any error [3]. To see how this is possible, we first note that coherent noise processes are described by matrices that can be expanded terms of a Pauli basis. For example, the Pauli basis for two-dimensional matrices is given by

$$I = \begin{pmatrix} 1 & 0 \\ 0 & 1 \end{pmatrix}, X = \begin{pmatrix} 0 & 1 \\ 1 & 0 \end{pmatrix}, Y = \begin{pmatrix} 0 & -i \\ i & 0 \end{pmatrix}, Z = \begin{pmatrix} 1 & 0 \\ 0 & -1 \end{pmatrix}$$

The single-qubit coherent error process described in Eq. (10.1) can be expanded in the above basis as follows:

$$U(\delta\theta, \delta\varphi)\,|\psi\rangle = \alpha_I I\,|\psi\rangle + \alpha_X X\,|\psi\rangle + \alpha_Z Z\,|\psi\rangle + \alpha_Y Y\,|\psi\rangle, \tag{10.2}$$

Design Example 10.2 (Continued)

where $\alpha_{I, X, Y, Z}$ are the expansion coefficients. By noting that the Pauli Y-matrix is equivalent (up to a phase) to the product XZ, this expression can be further simplified to

$$U(\delta\theta, \delta\varphi) \mid \psi\rangle = \alpha_I I \mid \psi\rangle + \alpha_X X \mid \psi\rangle + \alpha_Z Z \mid \psi\rangle + \alpha_{XZ} XZ \mid \psi\rangle, \tag{10.3}$$

The above expression shows that any coherent error process can be decomposed into a sum from the Pauli set $\{I, X, Z, XZ\}$. In the following sections, we will see that the error correction process itself involves performing projective measurements that cause the above superposition to collapse to a subset of its terms. As a result, a QEC code with the ability to correct errors described by the X- and Z-Pauli matrices will be able to correct any coherent error. This effect, referred to as the digitization of the error, is crucial to the success of QEC codes.

Quantum error types: As a result of the digitization of the error, there are two fundamental quantum error types that need to be accounted for by quantum codes. Pauli X-type errors can be thought of as quantum *bit flips* that map $X \mid 0\rangle = \mid 1\rangle$ and $X \mid 1\rangle = \mid 0\rangle$. The action of an X-error on the general qubit state is

$$X \mid \psi\rangle = \alpha X \mid 0\rangle + \beta X \mid 1\rangle = \alpha \mid 1\rangle + \beta \mid 0\rangle. \tag{10.4}$$

The second quantum error type, the Z-error, is often referred to as a phase flip and has no classical analogue. Phase flips map the qubit basis states $Z \mid 0\rangle = \mid 0\rangle$ and $Z \mid 1\rangle = - \mid 1\rangle$, and therefore have the following action on the general qubit state:

$$Z \mid \psi\rangle = \alpha Z \mid 0\rangle + \beta Z \mid 1\rangle = \alpha \mid 0\rangle - \beta \mid 1\rangle. \tag{10.5}$$

So far, for simplicity, we have restricted discussion to coherent errors acting on single qubits. However, the digitization of the error result generalizes to arbitrary quantum error processes, including those that describe incoherent evolution of the quantum state as a result of the qubits' interaction with their environment [3].

The challenges of QEC: The digitization of quantum errors makes it possible to reuse certain techniques from classical coding theory in QEC. However, there remain a number of problems that prevent the straightforward translation of classical codes to quantum codes. (i) The first problem is the no-cloning theorem for quantum states (see Chapter 8), which asserts that it is not possible to construct a unitary operator U_{clone} that performs the following operation: $U_{\text{clone}}(\mid \psi\rangle \otimes \mid 0\rangle) \rightarrow \mid \psi\rangle \otimes \mid \psi\rangle$, where $\mid \psi\rangle$ is the state to be cloned. By contrast, classical codes work under the assumption that data can be arbitrarily duplicated. For quantum coding, it is therefore necessary to find alternative ways of adding redundancy to the system. (ii) The second problem in quantum coding arises from the fact that qubits are susceptible to both bit flips (X-errors) and phase flips (Z-errors). QEC codes must therefore be designed with the ability to detect both error types simultaneously, whereas, in classical coding, only bit-flip errors need to be considered. (iii) The final problem specific to QEC is the problem of wave function collapse. In a classical system, it is possible to measure arbitrary properties of the bit register without the risk of compromising the encoded information. For quantum codes, however, any measurements of the qubits performed as part of the error correction procedure must be carefully chosen so as not to cause the wave function to collapse and erase the encoded information. In the next section, we will see how this is achieved by using a special type of projective measurement referred to as a *stabilizer measurement* [4].

Quantum redundancy and stabilizer measurement: As pointed out in the previous section, QEC is complicated by the no-cloning theorem, wave function collapse at qubit measurement, and the existence of a characteristic quantum error type: the phase flip. So, given these challenges, how is redundancy added to a quantum system to allow errors to be detected in real time? Classical repetition codes work by increasing the resources used to encode the data beyond the theoretical minimum. Analogously, in quantum codes, redundancy is added by expanding the Hilbert space in which the qubits are encoded [5].

Design Example 10.3

To see how this is achieved in practice, we now describe the two-qubit code, a prototypical quantum code designed to detect a single bit-flip error. The encode stage of the two-qubit code, acting on the general state $|\psi\rangle$, has the following action:

$$|\psi\rangle = \alpha\,|\,0\rangle + \beta\,|\,1\rangle\,(two-qubit\ encoder)$$
$$\rightarrow|\,\psi\rangle_L = \alpha\,|\,00\rangle + \beta\,|\,11\rangle = \alpha\,|\,0\rangle_L + \beta\,|\,1\rangle_L, \tag{10.6}$$

where, after encoding, the logical codewords are $|0\rangle_L = |\,00\rangle$ *and* $|1\rangle_L = |\,11\rangle$. Note that this does not correspond to cloning the state as $|\psi\rangle_L = \alpha\,|\,00\rangle + \beta\,|\,11\rangle \neq |\psi\rangle \otimes |\psi\rangle$. The effect of the encoding operation is to distribute the quantum information in the initial state $|\psi\rangle$ across the entangled two-party logical state $|\psi\rangle_L$. This introduces redundancy to the encoding that can be exploited for error detection. To understand exactly how this works, it is instructive to consider the computational Hilbert spaces before and after encoding. Prior to encoding, the single qubit is parametrized within a two-dimensional Hilbert space $|\psi\rangle \in \mathcal{H}_2 =$ span $\{|0\rangle, |1\rangle\}$. After encoding, the logical qubit occupies a four-dimensional Hilbert space $|\psi\rangle \in \mathcal{H}_4 =$ span $\{|00\rangle, |01\rangle, |10\rangle, |11\rangle\}$.

More specifically the logical qubit is defined within a two-dimensional subspace of this expanded Hilbert space $|\psi\rangle_L \in \mathcal{C} =$ span $\{|\,00\rangle, |\,11\rangle\} \subset \mathcal{H}_4$, where $\mathcal{C}$ is called the codespace. Now, imagine that the logical qubit is subject to a bit-flip error on the first qubit resulting in the state $X_1\,|\,\psi\rangle_L = \alpha\,|\,10\rangle + \beta\,|\,01\rangle$, where X_1 is a bit-flip error acting on the first qubit. The resultant state is rotated into a new subspace $X_1\,|\,\psi\rangle_L \in \mathcal{F} \subset \mathcal{H}_4$, where we call $\mathcal{F}$ the error subspace. Note that an X_2-error will also rotate the logical state into the $\mathcal{F}$ subspace. If the logical state $|\psi\rangle_L$ is uncorrupted, it occupies the codespace $\mathcal{C}$, whereas if it was subject to a single-qubit bit-flip, it occupies the error space $\mathcal{F}$. As the $\mathcal{C}$ and $\mathcal{F}$ subspaces are mutually orthogonal, it is possible to distinguish which subspace the logical qubit occupies via a projective measurement without compromising the encoded quantum information. In the context of quantum coding, measurements of this type are called stabilizer measurements.

For the purposes of differentiating between the codespace $\mathcal{C}$ and the error space $\mathcal{F}$, a projective measurement of the form Z_1Z_2 is performed. The Z_1Z_2 operator yields a $(+1)$ eigenvalue when applied to the logical state $Z_1Z_2\,|\,\psi\rangle_L = Z_1Z_2(\alpha\,|\,00\rangle + \beta\,|\,11\rangle) = (+1)\,|\,\psi\rangle_L$. The Z_1Z_2 operator is said to *stabilize* the logical qubit $|\psi\rangle_L$ as it leaves it unchanged [6]. Conversely, the Z_1Z_2 operator projects the errored states, $X_1\,|\,\psi\rangle_L$ and $X_2\,|\,\psi\rangle_L$, onto the (-1) eigenspace. Note that for either outcome, the information encoded in the α and β coefficients of the logical state remains undisturbed.

Figure 10.1 Circuit diagram for the two-qubit code.

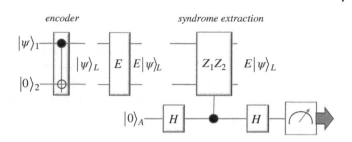

Figure 10.1 shows the circuit implementation of the two-qubit code. In the encode stage, a controlled-NOT (CNOT) gate is used to entangle the $|\psi\rangle$ state with a redundancy qubit to create the logical state $|\psi\rangle_L$. Following this, we assume the logical qubit is subject to a bit-flip error E, applied during the stage of the circuit labeled "E." Following the error stage, an ancilla qubit $|0\rangle_A$ is introduced to perform the measurement of the $Z_1 Z_2$ stabilizer. The syndrome extraction stage of the circuit transforms the quantum state as follows

$$E \mid \psi\rangle_L \mid 0\rangle_A \left(\underset{\Rightarrow}{se} \right) \frac{1}{2}(I_1 I_2 + Z_1 Z_2)E \mid \psi\rangle_L \mid 0\rangle_A + \frac{1}{2}(I_1 I_2 - Z_1 Z_2)E \mid \psi\rangle_L \mid 1\rangle_A, \tag{10.7}$$

where $\left(\underset{\Rightarrow}{se} \right)$ stands for (syndrome extraction), and E is an error from the set $\{I, X_1, X_2, X_1 X_2\}$. Now, consider the case where $E = X_1$ so that the logical state occupies the error space $E \mid \psi\rangle_L \in \mathcal{F}$. In this scenario, it can be seen that the first term in Eq. (10.7) goes to zero. The ancilla qubit is therefore measured deterministically as "1."

Considering the other error patterns, we see that if the logical state is in the codespace (i.e., if $E = \{I, X_1 X_2\}$), then the ancilla is measured as "0." Likewise, if the logical state is in the error subspace (i.e., if $E = \{X_1, X_2\}$), then the ancilla is measured as "1." The outcome of the ancilla qubit measurement is referred to as a syndrome, and tells us whether or not the logical state was subject to an error. The syndromes for all bit-flip error types in the two-qubit code are shown in Table 10.1.

Up to this point, we have assumed that the error introduced by the circuit element labeled "E" is deterministic. We now demonstrate how the two-qubit code works under a more general probabilistic error of the type discussed earlier.

Table 10.1 The syndrome table for the two-qubit code.

Error	Syndrome S
$I_1 I_2$	0
$X_1 I_2$	1
$I_1 X_2$	1
$X_1 X_2$	0

Design Example 10.4

For the purposes of this example, we will assume that each qubit in the two-qubit code is subject to a coherent error of the form $\mathcal{E} = \alpha_I I + \alpha_X X$, where $|\alpha_I|^2 + |\alpha_X|^2 = 1$. Here we see that $|\alpha_X|^2 = p_X$ is the probability of an X-error occurring on the qubit. The probability of no error occurring is therefore equal to $|\alpha_I|^2 = 1 - p_X$. The combined action of the error operator $\mathcal{E}$ acting on both qubits is given by

$$E = \mathcal{E}_1 \otimes \mathcal{E}_2 = \alpha_I^2 I_1 I_2 + \alpha_I \alpha_X (X_1 + X_2) + \alpha_X^2 X_1 X_2. \tag{10.8}$$

With the above error operator E, the syndrome extraction stage shown in Figure 10.1 transforms the quantum state as follows:

$$E \,|\, \psi \rangle_L \,|\, 0 \rangle_A \left(\underset{\Rightarrow}{se} \right) (\alpha_I^2 I_1 I_2 + \alpha_X^2 X_1 X_2) \,|\, \psi \rangle_L \,|\, 0 \rangle_A + \alpha_I \alpha_X (X_1 + X_2) \,|\, \psi \rangle_L \,|\, 1 \rangle_A. \tag{10.9}$$

where $\left(\underset{\Rightarrow}{se} \right)$ stands for (syndrome extraction). If the syndrome is measured as "0," the state collapses to a subset of its terms

$$\frac{(\alpha_I^2 I_1 I_2 + \alpha_X^2 X_1 X_2)}{\sqrt{\left|\alpha_I^2\right|^2 + \left|\alpha_X^2\right|^2}} \,|\psi\rangle_L |0\rangle_A, \tag{10.10}$$

where the denominator ensures normalization. By calculating the square-norm in the first term in the above, we can calculate the probability p_L that the logical state is subject to an error

$$p_L = \left| \frac{\alpha_X^2}{\sqrt{\left|\alpha_I^2\right|^2 + \left|\alpha_X^2\right|^2}} \right|^2 = \frac{p_x^2}{(1 - p_x)^2 + p_x^2} \approx p_x^2 \tag{10.11}$$

where the above approximation is made under the assumption that p_x is small. For the single-qubit $|\psi\rangle$, the probability of error is p_x when it is subject to the error operator $\mathcal{E}$. For the logical qubit $|\psi\rangle_L$ subject to the error operator $\mathcal{E}_1 \otimes \mathcal{E}_2$, the logical error rate is $p_L = p_x^2$. From this, we see that the two-qubit code reduces the error rate relative to the unencoded case.

The syndrome produced by the two-qubit code informs us of the presence of an error, but does not provide enough information to allow us to infer which qubit the error occurred on. It is therefore a detection code. In order to create an error correction code with the ability to both detect and localize errors, multiple stabilizer measurements need to be performed.

Design Example 10.5

Here we describe the three-qubit code, the natural extension of the two-qubit code in which the encoding operation distributes the quantum information across an entangled three-party state to give a logical state of the form $|\psi\rangle_L = \alpha \,|\, 000 \rangle + \beta \,|\, 111 \rangle$. This logical state occupies an eight-dimensional Hilbert space that can be partitioned into four two-dimensional subspaces as follows:

$$\begin{aligned} \mathcal{C} &= span \,\{|\, 000 \rangle, \,|\, 111 \rangle\}, \mathcal{F}_1 = span \,\{|\, 100 \rangle, \,|\, 110 \rangle\}, \\ \mathcal{F}_2 &= span \,\{|\, 010 \rangle, \,|\, 101 \rangle\}, \mathcal{F}_3 = span \,\{|\, 001 \rangle, \,|\, 110 \rangle\}, \end{aligned} \tag{10.12}$$

Design Example 10.5 (Continued)

where $\mathcal{C}$ is the logical codespace, and $\mathcal{F}_{\{1,2,3\}}$ are the logical error spaces. We see that each single-qubit error from the set $E = \{X_1, X_2, X_3\}$ will rotate the codespace to a unique error space so that $X_i \mid \psi \rangle_L \in \mathcal{F}_i$. In order to differentiate between these subspaces, we perform two stabilizer measurements $Z_1 Z_2$ and $Z_2 Z_3$ using the circuit shown in Figure 10.2. The resultant syndrome table for single-qubit errors is given in Table 10.2. From this, we see that each single-qubit error produces a unique two-bit syndrome $S = s_1 s_2$, enabling us to choose a suitable recovery operation.

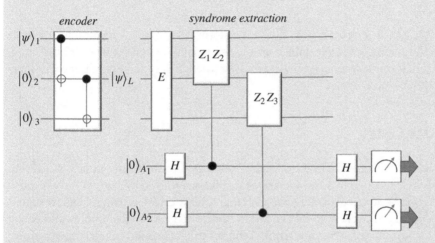

Figure 10.2 The circuit diagram of the three-qubit code.

Table 10.2 The syndrome table for all bit-flip errors on the three-qubit code.

Error	Syndrome S	Error	Syndrome S
$I_1 I_2 I_3$	00	$X_1 X_2 I_3$	01
$X_1 I_2 I_3$	10	$I_1 X_2 X_3$	10
$I_1 X_2 I_3$	11	$X_1 I_2 X_3$	11
$I_1 I_2 X_3$	01	$X_1 X_2 X_3$	00

Quantum code distance: As in classical codes, the distance of a quantum code is defined as the minimum size error that will go undetected. Alternatively, this minimum size error can be viewed as a logical Pauli operator that transforms one codeword state to another. For the three-qubit code described earlier in the section, we see that the logical Pauli-X operator is given by $\bar{X} = X_1 X_2 X_3$, so that

$$\bar{X} \mid 0 \rangle_L = \mid 1 \rangle_L \text{ and } \bar{X} \mid 1 \rangle_L = \mid 0 \rangle_L, \tag{10.13}$$

where $|0\rangle_L = |000\rangle$ and $|1\rangle_L = |111\rangle$ are the logical codewords for the three-qubit code. If it were the case that qubits were susceptible only to X-errors, then the three-qubit code would have distance $d = 3$. However, as qubits are also susceptible to phase-flip errors, it is also necessary to consider the logical Pauli-Z operator $\bar{Z}$ when determining the code distance. To do this, it is useful to switch from the computational basis, $\{|0\rangle, |1\rangle\}$, to the conjugate basis, $\{|+\rangle, |-\rangle\}$, where we define

$$|+\rangle = \frac{1}{\sqrt{2}}(|0\rangle + |1\rangle) \text{ and } |-\rangle = \frac{1}{\sqrt{2}}(|0\rangle - |1\rangle). \tag{10.14}$$

A Z-error maps the conjugate basis states as follows $Z|+\rangle = |-\rangle$ and $Z|-\rangle = |+\rangle$. Now, encoding the conjugate basis states with the three-qubit code gives the logical states

$$|+\rangle_L = \frac{1}{\sqrt{2}}(|000\rangle + |111\rangle) \text{ and } |-\rangle_L = \frac{1}{\sqrt{2}}(|000\rangle - |111\rangle). \tag{10.15}$$

A weight-one logical Pauli-Z operator $\bar{Z} = Z_1$ will transform $Z|+\rangle_L = |-\rangle_L$, meaning the code is unable to detect the presence of single-qubit Z-errors. As a result, the three-qubit code has a quantum distance $d = 1$. In the next section, we outline the construction of general stabilizer codes capable of detecting both X- and Z-errors.

10.1 Stabilizer Codes

The three-qubit code de-localizes the information in a single-qubit across three qubits. The resultant logical state is then encoded in a two-dimensional subspace (the codespace) of the expanded Hilbert space. The three-qubit code is designed such that if an X-error occurs, the logical state is rotated to an orthogonal error space, an event that can be detected via a sequence of two stabilizer measurements. This section describes how the procedure can be generalized to create $[[n, k, d]]$ stabilizer codes, where n is the total number of qubits, k is the number of logical qubits, and d is the code distance. Note the use of double brackets to differentiate quantum codes from classical codes, which are labeled with single brackets.

The circuit in Figure 10.3 shows the basic structure of an $[[n, k, d]]$ stabilizer code. A register of k data qubits, $|\psi\rangle_D$, is entangled with $m = n - k$ redundancy qubits $|0\rangle_R$ via an encoding operation to create a logical qubit $|\psi\rangle_L$. At this stage, the data previously stored solely in $|\psi\rangle_D$ is distributed across the expanded Hilbert space. Errors can then be detected by performing m stabilizer measurements P_i as shown to the right of Figure 10.3.

In the circuit in Figure 10.3, each of the stabilizers is measured using the same syndrome extraction method that was used for the two-qubit code in Figure 10.1. For each stabilizer P_i, the syndrome extraction circuit maps the logical state as follows:

$$E|\psi\rangle_L|0\rangle_{A_i} \left(\underset{\Rightarrow}{se}\right) \frac{1}{2}(I^{\otimes n} + P_i)E|\psi\rangle_L|0\rangle_{A_i} + \frac{1}{2}(I^{\otimes n} - P_i)E|\psi\rangle_L|1\rangle_{A_i}. \tag{10.16}$$

where $\left(\underset{\Rightarrow}{se}\right)$ stands for (*syndrome extraction*). From the above, we see that if the stabilizer P_i commutes with an error E the measurement of ancilla qubit A_i returns "0." If the stabilizer P_i anti-commutes with an error E, the measurement returns "1." The task of constructing a good code therefore involves finding stabilizers that anti-commute with the errors to be detected. In general, two Pauli operators will commute with one another if they intersect non-trivially on an even number of qubits, and anti-commute otherwise. The results of the m stabilizer measurements are

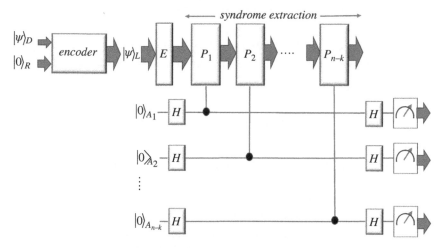

Figure 10.3 Circuit illustrating the structure of an [[n, k, d]] stabilizer code.

combined to give an m-bit syndrome. For a well-designed code, the syndrome allows us to deduce the best recovery operation to restore the logical state to the codespace.

Design Example 10.6 COMMUTATION PROPERTIES FOR PAULI OPERATORS

The elements of the Pauli group have eigenvalues $\{\pm 1, \pm i\}$. As a result, Pauli errors either commute or anti-commute with one another. In this example, we outline how to determine whether Pauli operators commute with one another. First, recall that two operators, F_i and F_j, commute if $F_iF_j = F_jF_i$, and anti-commute if $F_iF_j = (-1)F_jF_i$. For single-qubit Pauli operators, we see that all pairs of distinct operators anti-commute $X_1Z_1 = -Z_1X_1, X_1Y_1 = -Y_1X_1, Z_1Y_1 = -Y_1Z_1$. Now consider the operators Z_1Z_2 and X_1X_2. These multi-qubit operators commute as $Z_1Z_2X_1X_2 = Z_1X_1Z_2X_2 = (-1)X_1Z_1(-1)X_2Z_2 = X_1X_2Z_1Z_2$. In general, two Pauli operators will commute with one another if they intersect non-trivially on an even number of qubits as above. Conversely, if the number of non-trivial intersections is odd, then the two operators anti-commute. As an example, consider the two operators $X_1Z_2Z_3Z_5X_7$ and $X_1X_2X_5Z_7$. These operators intersect on the qubits 1, 2, 5, and 7. However, the intersection on qubit 1 is trivial as both operators apply the same X-gate to that qubit. The number of nontrivial intersections that remain is therefore three. As the two operators intersect non-trivially an odd number of times, the two operators anti-commute.

Properties of the code stabilizers: The stabilizers P_i of an [[n, k, d]] code must satisfy the following properties:

1) They must be Pauli group elements, $P_i \in \mathcal{G}_n$. Here, $\mathcal{G}_n$ is the Pauli group over n-qubits (see the following box for the definition of the Pauli group).
2) They must stabilize all logical states $|\psi\rangle_L$ of the code. This means that each P_i has the action $P_i |\psi\rangle_L = (+1)$ for all possible values of $|\psi\rangle_L$.
3) All the stabilizers of a code must commute with one another, so that $[P_i, P_j] = 0$ for all i and j. This property is necessary so that the stabilizers can be measured simultaneously (or in a way independent of their ordering) as depicted in Figure 10.3.

Pauli Operator Notation

The Pauli group on a single-qubit, $\mathcal{G}_1$, is defined as the set of Pauli operators $\mathcal{G}_1 = \{ \pm 11, \pm i11, \pm X, \pm iX, \pm Y, \pm iY, \pm Z, \pm iZ \}$, where the ± 1 and $\pm i$ terms are included to ensure $\mathcal{G}_1$ is closed under multiplication and thus forms a legitimate group. In matrix form, the four Pauli operators are given by

$$1 = \begin{pmatrix} 1 & 0 \\ 0 & 1 \end{pmatrix}, X = \begin{pmatrix} 0 & 1 \\ 1 & 0 \end{pmatrix}, Y = \begin{pmatrix} 0 & -i \\ i & 0 \end{pmatrix}, Z = \begin{pmatrix} 1 & 0 \\ 0 & -1 \end{pmatrix}$$

The general Pauli group, $\mathcal{G}$, consists of the set of all operators that are formed from tensor products of the matrices in $\mathcal{G}_1$. For example, the operator $I \otimes X \otimes I \otimes Y \in \mathcal{G}$ is an element of the four-qubit Pauli group. The support of a Pauli operator is given by the list of its non-identity elements. For example, the support of the Pauli operator in the last equation is $X_2 Y_4$ where the indices point to the qubit each element acts on. In this chapter, Pauli errors are always written in terms of their support. As an example, we would say that the bit-flip error X_2 acts on the two-qubit basis element $|00\rangle$ as follows: $X_2 |00\rangle = |01\rangle$.

In the language of group theory, the stabilizers P_i of an $[[n, k, d]]$ code form an Abelian subgroup $\mathcal{S}$ of the Pauli group. The stabilizer requirements listed above are incorporated into the definition of $\mathcal{S}$ as follows: $\mathcal{S} = \{ P_i \in \mathcal{G}_n \mid P_i |\psi\rangle_L = (+ 1) |\psi\rangle_L \forall |\psi\rangle_L \wedge [P_i, P_j] = 0 \forall (i, j) \}$. An important point to note is that any product of the stabilizers $P_i P_j$ will also be a stabilizer, as $P_i P_j |\psi\rangle_L = P_i(+1) |\psi\rangle_L = (+1) |\psi\rangle_L$. Given this, it is important to ensure that the set of $m = n - k$ stabilizers that are actually measured in the syndrome extraction process form a minimal set of the stabilizer group $\mathcal{S} = \langle G_1, G_2, ..., G_m \rangle$. In a minimal set, it is not possible to obtain one stabilizer G_i as a product of any of the other elements G_j. As a simple example, consider the following set of stabilizers for the three-qubit code: $\mathcal{S} = \{ Z_1 Z_2, Z_2 Z_3, Z_1 Z_3 \}$. This is not a minimal set, as it is possible to obtain the third stabilizer as a product of the first two. A possible minimal set is $\mathcal{S} = \langle Z_1 Z_2, Z_2 Z_3 \rangle$, which are the two stabilizers measured in the example from Figure 10.2.

The logical operators of stabilizer codes: An $[[n, k, d]]$ stabilizer code has $2k$ logical Pauli operators that allow for logical states to be modified without having to decode/re-encode. For each logical qubit i, there is a logical Pauli-X operator $\bar{X}_i$ and a logical Pauli-Z operator $\bar{Z}_i$. Each pair of logical operators, $\bar{X}_i$ and $\bar{Z}_i$, satisfy the following properties: (i) They commute with all the code stabilizers in $\mathcal{S}$. (ii) They anti-commute with one another, so that $[\bar{X}_i, \bar{Z}_i]_+ = \bar{X}_i \bar{Z}_i + \bar{Z}_i \bar{X}_i = 0$ for all qubits i. Any product of a logical operator $\bar{L}_i$ and stabilizer P_j will also be a logical operator. This is clear from the fact that the stabilizer maps the logical state onto its $(+1)$ eigenspace. Any product $\bar{L}_i P_j$ therefore has the following action on the logical state $\bar{L}_i P_j |\psi\rangle_L = \bar{L}_i |\psi\rangle_L$.

Design Example 10.7 THE [[4, 2, 2]] DETECTION CODE

The [[4, 2, 2]] error detection code is the smallest stabilizer code to offer protection against a quantum noise model in which the qubits are susceptible to both X- and Z-errors [7, 8]. As such, it provides a useful demonstration of the structure and properties of a stabilizer code. An encoder for the [[4, 2, 2]] code is shown in Figure 10.4. A two-qubit register $|\psi\rangle_1 |\psi\rangle_2$ is entangled across four qubits to give the code state $|\psi_1 \psi_2\rangle_L$. As there are two encoded logical qubits in the [[4, 2, 2]] code, its codespace is four dimensional and is spanned by

Design Example 10.7 (Continued)

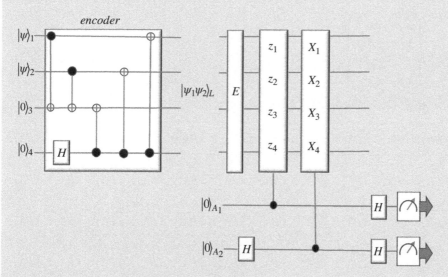

Figure 10.4 Circuit diagram for the four-qubit code.

$$
\mathcal{C}_{[[4,2,2]]} = \text{span}
\left\{
\begin{aligned}
|00\rangle_L &= \frac{1}{\sqrt{2}}(|0000\rangle + |1111\rangle) \\
|01\rangle_L &= \frac{1}{\sqrt{2}}(|0110\rangle + |1001\rangle), \\
|10\rangle_L &= \frac{1}{\sqrt{2}}(|1010\rangle + |0101\rangle) \\
|11\rangle_L &= \frac{1}{\sqrt{2}}(|1100\rangle + |0011\rangle)
\end{aligned}
\right\}.
$$

The stabilizers of the above logical basis states are $\mathcal{S}_{[[4,2,2]]} = \langle X_1 X_2 X_3 X_4, Z_1 Z_2 Z_3 Z_4 \rangle$. It is clear that these stabilizers commute with one another, as required by the definition. These stabilizers can be measured using the syndrome extraction circuit shown to the right of Figure 10.4.

In the encode stage, the information contained in the two-qubit register $|\psi\rangle_1 | \psi\rangle_2$ is distributed across two redundancy qubits, $|0\rangle_3$ and $|0\rangle_4$, to create a logical state $|\psi_1\psi_2\rangle_L$ that encodes two qubits. In the syndrome extraction stage, the code stabilizers, $Z_1 Z_2 Z_3 Z_4$ and $X_1 X_2 X_3 X_4$, are measured on the code qubits, and the results are copied to the ancilla qubits. The subsequent measurement of the ancilla qubits provides a two-bit syndrome S that informs of the occurrence of an error.

From Eq. (10.16), we know that for a syndrome measurement to be nonzero, the error E has to anti-commute with the stabilizer being measured. Considering first the single-qubit X-errors ($E = \{X_1, X_2, X_3, X_4\}$), we see that they all anti-commute with the $Z_1 Z_2 Z_3 Z_4$ stabilizer. Likewise, the single-qubit Z-errors ($E = \{Z_1, Z_2, Z_3, Z_4\}$) anti-commute with the $X_1 X_2 X_3 X_4$ stabilizer. Any single-qubit error on the [[4, 2, 2]] code will therefore trigger a nonzero syndrome. The syndrome table for all single-qubit errors in the [[4, 2, 2]] code is shown in Table 10.3. For completeness, the table also includes the syndromes for single-qubit Y-errors, which are equivalent to the simultaneous occurrence of an X- and Z-error.

The [[4, 2, 2]] code has Pauli-X and Pauli-Z logical operators for each of its encoded logical qubits. A possible choice of these logical operators is given by

(Continued)

Design Example 10.7 (Continued)

$$\mathcal{L}_{[[4,2,2]]} = \begin{cases} \bar{X}_1 = X_1 X_3 \\ \bar{Z}_1 = Z_1 Z_4 \\ \bar{X}_2 = X_2 X_3 \\ \bar{Z}_2 = Z_2 Z_4 \end{cases}. \tag{10.17}$$

Table 10.3 The syndrome table for the [[4, 2, 2]] code for all single-qubit X-, Z-, and Y-errors.

Error	Syndrome S	Error	Syndrome S	Error	Syndrome S
X_1	10	Z_1	01	Y_1	11
X_2	10	Z_2	01	Y_2	11
X_3	10	Z_3	01	Y_3	11
X_4	10	Z_4	01	Y_4	11

Each logical operator commutes with the two stabilizers of the code so that $[L_i, P_i] = 0$ for all $L_i \in \mathcal{L}_{[[4,2,2]]}$ and $P_i \in \mathcal{S}$. Furthermore, it can be checked that the requirement $[\bar{X}_i, \bar{Z}_i]_+ = 0$ is satisfied for each pair of logical operators. The minimum weight logical operator in $\mathcal{L}_{[[4,2,2]]}$ is two, which sets the code distance to $d = 2$. As the distance of the [[4, 2, 2]] code is less than three, it is a detection code rather than a full correction code. Later in this chapter, we introduce the Shor [[9, 1, 3]] code as an example of a code that is capable of both detecting and correcting errors.

A general encoding circuit for stabilizer codes: The quantum codes presented in this chapter have included bespoke encoding circuits to prepare the logical states. Special methods exist for constructing such circuits given a set of stabilizers [9, 10]. In this section, we describe a general method for preparing the logical states of stabilizer code using the same circuits that are used for syndrome extraction. The $|0\rangle_L$ codeword of any [[n, k, d]] stabilizer can be obtained via a projection onto the (+1) eigenspace of all of its stabilizers:

$$|0\rangle_L = \frac{1}{N} \prod_{P_i \in \langle \mathcal{S} \rangle} (I^{\otimes n} + P_i) |0^{\otimes n}\rangle, \tag{10.18}$$

where $\langle \mathcal{S} \rangle$ is the minimal set of the code stabilizers, and the $1/N$ term is a factor that ensures normalization. For example, the $|00\rangle_L$ codeword of the four-qubit code defined in the previous section is given by

$$\begin{aligned} |00\rangle_L &= \frac{1}{\sqrt{2}} (I^{\otimes 4} + X_1 X_2 X_3 X_4)(I^{\otimes 4} + Z_1 Z_2 Z_3 Z_4) |0000\rangle \\ &= \frac{1}{\sqrt{2}} (|0000\rangle + |1111\rangle). \end{aligned} \tag{10.19}$$

The remaining codewords of the code can be obtained by applying logical operators to the $|0\rangle_L$ codeword. The $|0\rangle_L$ codeword of any stabilizer code can be prepared via the projection in Eq. (10.18) by applying the general syndrome extraction circuit (shown on the right-hand side of Figure 10.3) to a $|0\rangle^{\otimes n}$ state. As an example, consider the case where we apply the syndrome extraction circuit to the state $|0\rangle^{\otimes 4}$ to prepare the $|0\rangle_L$ codeword of the four-qubit code. The intermediary state immediately after the extraction of the $X_1 X_2 X_3 X_4$ stabilizer is given by

$$\frac{1}{2} (I^{\otimes 4} + X_1 X_2 X_3 X_4) |0000\rangle |0\rangle_A + \frac{1}{2} (I^{\otimes 4} - X_1 X_2 X_3 X_4) |0000\rangle |1\rangle_A. \tag{10.20}$$

Figure 10.5 The general procedure for active recovery in a quantum error correction (QEC) code.

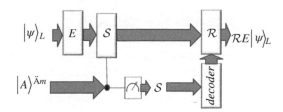

When the ancilla is measured, the above state collapses to either the $(+1)$ or (-1) projection with equal probability. In the case where the "1" syndrome is measured, a correction needs to be applied to transform the state back onto the $(+1)$ eigenspace of the stabilizer. Repeating this procedure for the remaining stabilizers leads to the preparation of the $|0\rangle_L$ codeword.

QEC with stabilizer codes: As for classical codes, the distance of a quantum code is related to the number of correctable errors t via the relation $d = 2t + 1$. As a result, stabilizer codes with $d \geq 3$ are error correction codes for which active recovery operations can be applied. By contrast, detection protocols such as the $[[4, 2, 2]]$ code require a repeat-until-success approach.

Figure 10.5 shows the general error correction procedure for a single cycle of an $[[n, k, d \geq 3]]$ stabilizer code. The encoded logical state $|\psi\rangle_L$ is subject to an error process described by the circuit element E. Next, the code stabilizers are measured (using the syndrome extraction method illustrated in Figure 10.3), and the results copied to a register of $m = n - k$ ancilla qubits $|A\rangle^{\otimes m}$. The ancilla qubits are then read out to give an m-bit syndrome S.

The next step in the error correction procedure is referred to as decoding, and involves processing the syndrome to determine the best unitary operation $\mathcal{R}$ to return the logical state to the codespace. After this recovery operation has been applied, the output of the code cycle is given by $\mathcal{R}E \mid \psi\rangle_L \in \mathcal{C}_{[[n,k,d]]}$. The decoding step is a success if the combined action of $\mathcal{R}E$ on the code state is as follows:

$$\mathcal{R}E \mid \psi\rangle_L = (\,+1)\mid \psi\rangle_L. \tag{10.21}$$

The above condition is trivially satisfied if $\mathcal{R} = E^\dagger$ so that $\mathcal{R}E = \mathrm{I}$. However, this is not the only solution. Eq. (10.21) is also satisfied for any product $\mathcal{R}E$ that is an element of the code stabilizer such that $\mathcal{R}E = P \in \mathcal{S}$. In the next section, we will see that the fact that the solution for $\mathcal{R}$ is not unique means it is possible to design *degenerate* quantum codes for which multiple errors can map to the same syndrome. The decoding step fails if the recovery operation maps the code state as follows:

$$\mathcal{R}E \mid \psi\rangle_L = L \mid \psi\rangle_L, \tag{10.22}$$

where L is a logical operator of the code. In this case, the state is returned to the codespace, but the recovery operation leads to a change in the encoded information.

Design Example 10.8 THE SHOR [[9, 1, 3]] CODE

The Shor nine-qubit code was the first QEC scheme to be proposed. It is an example of a distance-three degenerate code for which it is possible to apply a successful recovery operation for any single-qubit error [5]. We now outline how the Shor code can be constructed via a method known as code concatenation. The method involves embedding the output of one code into the input of another. In the construction of the Shor nine-qubit code, the two codes that are

(Continued)

Design Example 10.8 (Continued)

concatenated are the three-qubit code for bit flips and the three-qubit code for phase flips [11]. The three-qubit code for bit flips, C_{3b}, was described in Eq. (10.12) and is defined as follows:

$$C_{3b} = span\{|\,0\rangle_{3b} = |\,000\rangle, |\,1\rangle_{3b} = |\,111\rangle\},$$
$$S_{3b} = \langle Z_1 Z_2, Z_2 Z_3\rangle,$$

(10.23)

where S_{3b} are the code stabilizers. Similarly, the three-qubit code for phase flips C_{3p} is defined as

$$C_{3p} = span\{|\,0\rangle_{3p} = |+++\rangle, |\,1\rangle_{3p} = |---\rangle\},$$
$$S_{3p} = \langle X_1 X_2, X_2 X_3\rangle,$$

(10.24)

To construct the nine-qubit code, the bit-flip code is embedded into the codewords of the phase-flip code. This concatenation maps the $|0\rangle_{3p}$ codeword of the phase-flip code to a nine-qubit codeword $|0\rangle_9$ as follows:

$$|\,0\rangle_{3p} = |+++\rangle\left(\overset{con}{\Rightarrow}\right)|\,0\rangle_9 = |+\rangle_{3b}\,|+\rangle_{3b}\,|+\rangle_{3b},$$

(10.25)

where $\left(\overset{con}{\Rightarrow}\right)$ stands for concatenation, and $|+\rangle_{3b} = \frac{1}{\sqrt{2}}(|\,000\rangle + |\,111\rangle)$ is a logical state of the bit-flip code. Similarly, the concatenation maps the $|1\rangle_{3p}$ codeword of the phase-flip code to

$$|\,1\rangle_{3p} = |---\rangle\left(\overset{con}{\Rightarrow}\right)|\,1\rangle_9 = |-\rangle_{3b}\,|-\rangle_{3b}\,|-\rangle_{3b},$$

(10.26)

where $|-\rangle_{3b} = \frac{1}{\sqrt{2}}(|000\rangle - |111\rangle)$. The code defined by the codewords $|0\rangle_9$ *and* $|1\rangle_9$ is the nine-qubit Shor code with parameters [[9, 1, 3]]. Rewriting the right-hand sides of Eqs. (10.25) and (10.26) in the computational basis, we get the following codespace for the Shor code

$$C_{[[9,1,3]]} = span\left\{\begin{array}{l}|\,0\rangle_9 = \dfrac{1}{\sqrt{8}}(|\,000\rangle + |\,111\rangle)(|\,000\rangle + |\,111\rangle)(|\,000\rangle + |\,111\rangle)\\[2mm]|\,1\rangle_9 = \dfrac{1}{\sqrt{8}}(|\,000\rangle - |\,111\rangle)(|\,000\rangle - |\,111\rangle)(|\,000\rangle - |\,111\rangle)\end{array}\right\}.$$

(10.27)

The stabilizers of the above code are given by

$$S_{[[9,3,3]]} = \langle Z_1 Z_2, Z_2 Z_3, Z_4 Z_5, Z_5 Z_6, Z_7 Z_8, Z_8 Z_9,$$
$$X_1 X_2 X_3 X_4 X_5 X_6, X_4 X_5 X_6 X_7 X_8 X_9\rangle.$$

(10.28)

The first six terms are the stabilizers of the bit-flip codes in the three blocks of the code. The final two stabilizers are derived from the stabilizers of the phase-flip code. Table 10.4 shows the syndromes for all single-qubit errors in the nine-qubit code.

Each of the X-errors produces unique syndromes. By contrast, Z-errors that occur in the same block of the code have the same syndrome. Fortunately, this degeneracy in the code syndromes does not reduce the code distance. To see why this is the case, consider the single-qubit errors Z_1 and Z_2, both of which map to the syndrome "00000010." The decoder therefore has insufficient information to differentiate between the two errors and will output the same recovery operation for both. For the purposes of this example, we will assume that the recovery operation the decoder outputs is $\mathcal{R} = Z_1$. For the case where the error is $E = Z_1$, the recovery operation trivially restores the logical state as $\mathcal{R}E\,|\,\psi\rangle_9 = Z_1 Z_1\,|\,\psi\rangle_9 = |\,\psi\rangle_9$. In the event where $E = Z_2$, the recovery operation still restores the logical state as $\mathcal{R}E = Z_1 Z_2$ is in the stabilizer

Design Example 10.8 (Continued)

of $\mathcal{C}_{[[9,1,3]]}$, and therefore acts on the logical state as follows $Z_1 Z_2 |\psi\rangle_9 = |\psi\rangle_9$. The same arguments can be applied to the remaining degenerate errors of the code. As a result, the nine-qubit code has the ability to correct all single-qubit errors and has distance $d = 3$.

Table 10.4 The syndrome table for single-qubit X- and Z-errors on the nine-qubit code.

Error	Syndrome S	Error	syndrome S
X_1	10 000 000	Z_1	00000010
X_2	11 000 000	Z_2	00000010
X_3	01000000	Z_3	00000010
X_4	00100000	Z_4	00000011
X_5	00110000	Z_5	00000011
X_6	00010000	Z_6	00000011
X_7	00001000	Z_7	00000001
X_8	00001100	Z_8	00000001
X_9	00000100	Z_9	00000001

The nine-qubit code is a degenerate code, as certain Z-errors share the same syndrome.

10.2 Surface Code

The challenge in creating QEC codes lies in finding commuting sets of stabilizers that enable errors to be detected without disturbing the encoded information. Finding such sets is nontrivial, and special code constructions are required to find stabilizers with the desired properties. In the previous section, we discussed how a code can be constructed by concatenating two smaller codes. Other constructions include methods for repurposing classical codes to obtain commuting stabilizer checks [12–15]. In this section, we outline a construction known as the surface code [16, 17].

The realization of a surface code logical qubit is a key goal for many quantum computing hardware efforts [18–22]. The codes belong to a broader family of so-called *topological* codes [23]. The general design principle underlying topological codes is that the code is built up by "patching together" repeated elements. We will see that this modular approach ensures that the surface code can be straightforwardly scaled in size while ensuring stabilizer commutativity. In terms of actual implementation, the specific advantage of a surface code for current hardware platforms is that it requires only nearest-neighbor interactions. This is advantageous as many quantum computing platforms are unable to perform high-fidelity long-range interactions between qubits.

The surface code four cycle: When it comes to surface codes, it is beneficial to adopt a graphical representation of the code qubits instead of the circuit notation we have used up to this point. Figure 10.6a shows a surface code four cycle, the fundamental building block around which surface codes are constructed. The circles in the graph in Figure 10.6a represent the code qubits and the squares the ancilla qubits. The red edges represent controlled-X gates, each controlled on an ancilla

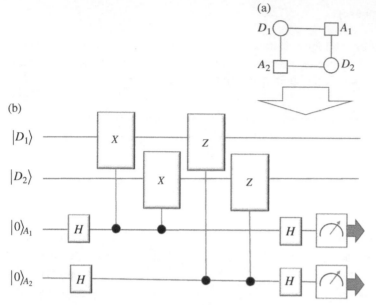

(a)

Figure 10.6 The surface code four cycle. (a) Graphical representation. (b) An equivalent surface code four cycle in circuit notation.

(b)

qubit A and acting on a data qubit D. Likewise, the blue edges represent controlled-Z operations, each controlled by an ancilla qubit and acting on a data qubit. These controlled operations are the gates with which the stabilizers of the four cycle are measured. Ancilla qubit A_1 connects to data qubits D_1 and D_2 via red edges, and therefore measures the stabilizer $X_{D_1}X_{D_2}$. Similarly, ancilla qubit A_2 measures the stabilizer $Z_{D_1}Z_{D_2}$. For comparison, the four cycle is shown in quantum circuit notation in Figure 10.6b. The stabilizers of the four cycle, $X_{D_1}X_{D_2}$ and $Z_{D_1}Z_{D_2}$, commute with one another as they intersect non-trivially on an even number of code qubits. This can easily be verified by inspection of Figure 10.6b.

The $|0\rangle_L$ codeword of the four cycle can be prepared by setting the initial state of the code qubits to $|D_1D_2\rangle = |00\rangle$, and following the general encoding procedure outlined earlier in this chapter. However, as the four cycle has two code qubits $n = 2$ and two stabilizers $m = 2$, the number of logical qubits it encodes is equal to $k = n - m = 0$. As a result, the four cycle is not in itself a useful code. However, we will see that working detection and correction codes can be formed by interconnecting together multiple four cycles to form square lattices.

Design Example 10.9 THE [[5,1,2]] SURFACE CODE

The [[5, 1, 2]] surface code: Figure 10.7a shows the five-qubit surface code formed by putting together four four cycles in a square lattice [24]. By inspecting which data qubits each ancilla qubit connects to, the stabilizers of the code in Figure 10.7 can be read off to give

$$\mathcal{S}_{[[5,1,2]]} = \langle X_{D_1}X_{D_2}X_{D_3}, Z_{D_1}Z_{D_3}Z_{D_4}, Z_{D_2}Z_{D_3}Z_{D_5}, X_{D_3}X_{D_4}X_{D_5}\rangle. \tag{10.29}$$

The first term in the above is the stabilizer measured by ancilla qubit, the second by ancilla etc. The stabilizers in commute with one another, as the X- and -type stabilizers all intersect on an even number of code qubits. From Fig.10., we see that there are five code qubits and four stabilizers meaning the code encodes one logical qubit. Figure 10.7b shows two examples

Design Example 10.9 (Continued)

of errors on the surface code and how they are detected. The Z_{D_1}-error on qubit D_1 anti-commutes with the $X_{D_1} X_{D_2} X_{D_3}$ stabilizer, and therefore triggers a "1" syndrome. This is depicted by the red filling in the ancilla qubit A_1. Similarly, the X_{D_5}-error anti-commutes with the $Z_{D_2} Z_{D_3} Z_{D_5}$ stabilizer and triggers a "1" syndrome measurement in ancilla qubit A_4. From Figure 10.7, it can be seen that the surface code is a square lattice with two types of boundaries. The vertical boundaries are formed of blue edges representing Z-type stabilizer measurements. The horizontal boundaries are formed of red edges representing X-type stabilizer measurements. The logical operators of the surface code can be defined as chains of Pauli operators along the edges of these boundaries.

Figure 10.7c shows a two-qubit Pauli chain $X_{D_1} X_{D_4}$ along the left-hand boundary of the five-qubit surface code. The $X_{D_1} X_{D_4}$ operator commutes with all the stabilizers in $\mathcal{S}_{[[5,1,2]]}$, in particular the stabilizer $Z_{D_1} Z_{D_3} Z_{D_4}$ with which it shares two qubits. Similarly, Figure 10.7d shows an operator $Z_{D_1} Z_{D_2}$, which acts across the top of the lattice. It can easily be checked that this operator also commutes with all the code stabilizers. Finally, we note that the operators $X_{D_1} X_{D_4}$ and $Z_{D_1} Z_{D_2}$ anti-commute. As outlined earlier in this chapter, the Pauli-X and Pauli-Z logical operators for each encoded qubit are pairs of operators that commute with all the code stabilizers but anti-commute with one another. A suitable choice for the logical operators of the [[5, 1, 2]] surface code would therefore be $\bar{X} = X_{D_1} X_{D_4}$ and $\bar{Z} = Z_{D_1} Z_{D_2}$. From the above, we see that the minimum weight of the logical operators is 2, meaning the [[5, 1, 2]] code is a detection code with $d = 2$.

Figure 10.7 [50] (a) The [[5, 1, 2]] surface code formed by putting together 4 four cycles in a square lattice. (b) Examples of error detection in the [[5, 1, 2]] surface code. (c) The Pauli-X logical operator $\bar{X} = X_{D_1} X_{D_4}$ acts along the boundary along which Z-type stabilizers are measured. (d) The Pauli-Z logical operator $\bar{Z} = Z_{D_1} Z_{D_2}$ acts along the boundary along which X-type stabilizers are measured. The two logical operators anti-commute with one another. (For more details see color figure in bins).

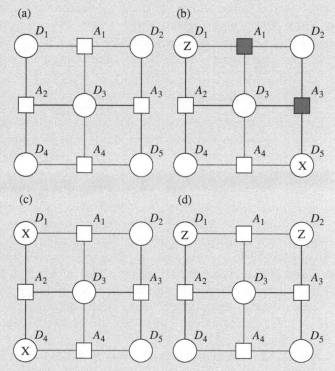

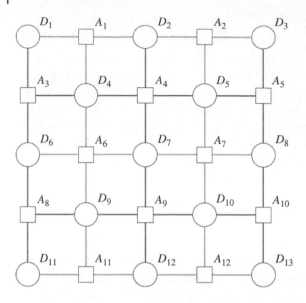

Figure 10.8 A distance-three surface code with parameters [13, 1, 3]. (For more details see color figure in bins).

Scaling the surface code: The distance of a surface code can be increased simply by scaling the size of the lattice. In general, a surface code with distance $d = \lambda$ will encode a *single* logical qubit and have code parameters given by $[[n = \lambda^2 + (\lambda - 1)^2, k = 1, d = \lambda]]$. For example, the distance-three $[[13, 1, 3]]$ surface code is depicted in Figure 10.8 The Pauli-X logical operator of a surface code can be defined as a chain of X-Pauli operators along the boundary of the code along which the Z-stabilizers are applied (the blue boundary in the graph representation). Similarly, the Z-Pauli logical operator can be defined as a chain of Z-operators across the adjacent boundary along which the X-type stabilizers are applied (the red edges in the graph representation). For the distance-three code, a choice of logical operators would be $\bar{X} = X_{D_1} X_{D_6} X_{D_{11}}$ and $\bar{Z} = Z_{D_1} Z_{D_2} Z_{D_3}$. The $[[13, 1, 3]]$ code is the smallest surface code capable of detecting and correcting errors.

10.2.1 The Rotated Lattice

The standard method for creating planar encoded qubits uses the square lattice with regular boundaries, as in Figure 10.8. However, it is possible to reduce the number of physical qubits required for a single planar surface of a given distance by considering a "rotated" form of the lattice used. This removes physical qubits from the edges of the lattice, creating irregular boundaries. The shortest string of operators creating a logical operator is more frequently then not a straight line; however, as we shall see, it never goes below the code distance of the original surface.

Let us consider the distance 5 code surface shown in Figure 10.9a. We now create a "rotated" lattice form by removing all the qubits outside the red box, and rotating (for clarity) 45° clockwise. This now has the logical operators and boundaries as shown in Figure 10.9b. If we now color in the stabilizers in this new rotated form, we have the lattice in Figure 10.9c, with 25 physical qubits and 24 independent stabilizers. The boundaries are now no longer "rough" or "smooth." Instead we use *X-boundaries* and *Z-boundaries*: X-boundaries have X syndrome measurements along the boundary (shown in the figures as brown), and Z-boundaries have Z-syndrome measurements along the edge (shown as yellow) [25].

There are now more possible paths across the lattice area for a logical operator to take; the smallest paths do, however, stay the same length as before the rotation, so the rotated and unrotated lattices have the same error correction strength. Figure 10.9c shows several example logical operators; note that, in the rotated form, logical operator chain paths can go diagonally through

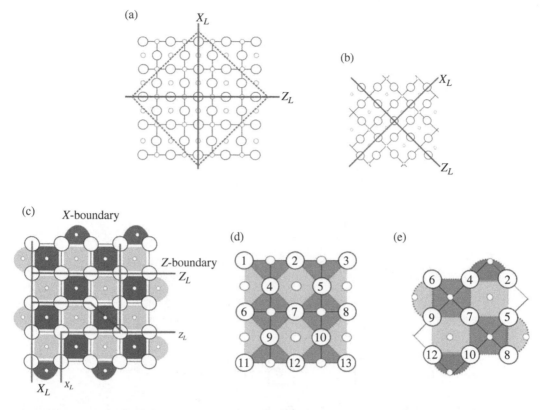

Figure 10.9 (a),(b),(c) Rotating a distance 5 lattice to produce another distance 5 encoded qubit. (a) The original surface. The red square shows the area of the rotated surface. (b) The rotated surface. (c) The rotated plaquettes (vertex plaquettes are marked brown, face plaquettes as yellow), new example logical operators, and boundaries. X(Z) logical operators are shown as red(blue) lines. (d), (e) Two lattices encoding a single qubit with distance 3: (d) standard planar lattice; (e) the rotated lattice. Light (dark) plaquettes show Z(X) syndrome measurements. *Source:* Horsman et al. [24]. (For more details see color figure in bins).

plaquettes of the opposite type (i.e., X-chains can go vertically through Z-plaquettes, and vice versa). Not all such paths are possible logical operators: care must be taken to ensure that each face (vertex) plaquette is touched an even number of times for an $X(Z)$ operator. This maintains the commutation of the operator with the lattice stabilizers, and the logical operator operations are undetectable by syndrome measurements. The code distance of the logical qubit remains unchanged, and we have reduced the number of lattice data qubits from $d^2 + (d-1)^2$ to d^2 for a distance d code.

The smallest code that detects and corrects one error is the distance 3 code (Figure 10.10). The rotated lattice is shown in Figure 10.10. Note that measuring all the boundary syndromes is unnecessary as the stabilizers are not independent; only the marked syndromes are measured. We can explicitly demonstrate the action of creating the rotated lattice by considering all the stabilizers of the surface, choosing the logical state to be the +1 eigenstate of the X_L logical operator. The left-hand column of Table 10.5 shows the surface stabilizers of the standard lattice in this case, and the right-hand column gives the corresponding stabilizers in the rotated case. The "rotated" encoding allows us to produce a distance 3 planar qubit with 9 data qubits and 8 syndromes that require measurement. This can be done with either 8 syndrome qubits, or else the 4 central syndrome qubits can be used twice (while still requiring only neighboring qubits to interact). The rotated encoding therefore reduces the number of physical qubits for the smallest code distance from 25 to 13.

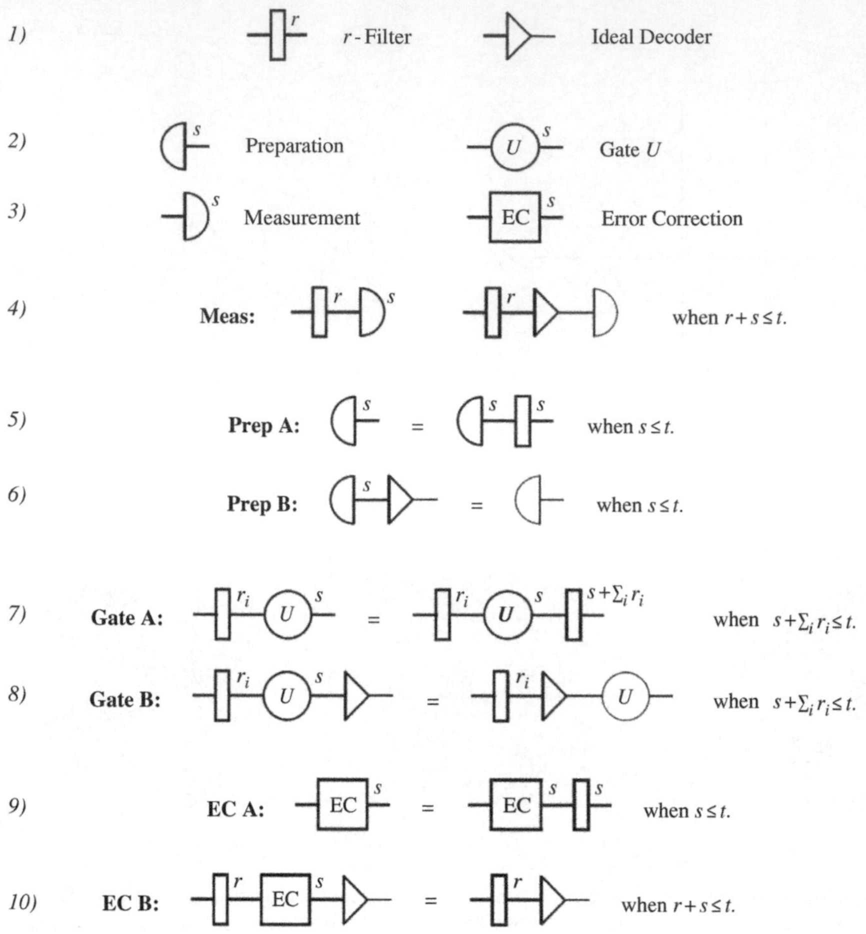
1)
r
r-Filter
Ideal Decoder
2)
s
Preparation
U
s
Gate U
3)
s
Measurement
EC
s
Error Correction
4)
Meas:
r
s
r
when r+s≤t.
5)
Prep A:
s
=
s
s
when s≤t.
6)
Prep B:
s
=
when s≤t.
7)
Gate A:
r_i
U
s
=
r_i
U
s
s+Σ_i r_i
when s+Σ_i r_i≤t.
8)
Gate B:
r_i
U
s
=
r_i
U
when s+Σ_i r_i≤t.
9)
EC A:
EC
s
=
EC
s
s
when s≤t.
10)
EC B:
r
EC
s
=
r
when r+s≤t.

Figure 10.10 Notation for fault-tolerant circuits.

Table 10.5 Stabilizers for the distance 3 planar qubit of Figures 10.9d and e, encoding the state $|+\rangle$, for the standard and rotated lattices. Note that the vertical chain $X_4X_7X_{10}$ is also a valid logical X_L operator.

Standard lattice stabilizers	Rotated lattice stabilizers
$X_2X_7X_{12}(=X_L)$	$X_2X_7X_{12}(=X_L)$
$X_1X_2X_4$	
$X_2X_3X_4$	X_2X_4
$X_4X_6X_7X_9$	$X_4X_6X_7X_9$
$X_5X_7X_8X_10$	$X_5X_7X_8X_{10}$
$X_9X_{11}X_{12}$	
$X_{10}X_{12}X_{13}$	$X_{10}X_{12}$
$Z_1Z_4Z_6$	
$Z_2Z_4Z_5Z_7$	$Z_2Z_4Z_5Z_7$
$Z_3Z_5Z_8$	Z_5Z_8
$Z_6Z_9Z_{11}$	Z_6Z_9
$Z_7Z_9Z_{10}Z_{12}$	$Z_7Z_9Z_{10}Z_{12}$
$Z_8Z_{10}Z_{13}$	

10.3   Fault-Tolerant Gates

There is still a major hurdle before we reach the goal of making quantum computers resistant to errors. We must also understand how to perform operations on a state encoded in a quantum code without losing the code's protection against errors, and how to safely perform error correction when the gates used are themselves noisy. A protocol that performs these tasks is called *fault tolerant* (*FT* for short). Shor presented the first protocols for fault-tolerant quantum computation [26], but there have been some substantial improvements since then. Now we know that, provided that the physical error rates per gate and per time step are below some constant threshold value, it is possible to make the logical quantum computation we wish to perform arbitrarily close to correct with overhead that is polylogarithmic in the length of the computation [27–29]. The goal is to produce protocols that continue to produce the correct answer even though any individual component of the circuit may fail. The basic components we need to create a universal quantum computer are the following:

1) Preparation: Operations that prepare a new qubit in some standard state. It is sufficient to have just one type of preparation that prepares a $|0\rangle$ state, although we will actually use a number of different prepared states.
2) Quantum gates: A universal set of quantum gates. To have a universal set, it is sufficient to use the gates H, CNOT, and the $\pi/8$ phase rotation $R_{\pi/8} = \begin{pmatrix} 1 & 0 \\ 0 & e^{i\pi/4} \end{pmatrix}$. This set of gates generates a group dense in $U(2^n)$ [30].
3) Measurement: Measurement of qubits. It is sufficient to be able to measure individual qubits in the standard basis $|0\rangle$, $|1\rangle$.
4) Wait: In order to synchronize the operation of gates, we may sometimes need to have qubits wait around without performing any action on them.

The individual qubits making up our quantum error correcting code are called *physical qubits*, and each of these actions is a *physical* action (e.g., a physical gate). Each instantiation of one of these components is called a *physical location* (or more often just *location*). The number of locations in a circuit is then at most the total number of qubits used times the total number of time steps used. The number of locations will frequently be less than the maximum, as we will often prepare new qubits during the computation and measure qubits, which can then be discarded, before the computation is completed. Note that wait steps count as locations, but that operations on classical data (in particular, measurement results) do not, as we will assume that classical computation is perfect. Depending on the precise model we are using, we may wish to simplify by assuming that modest amounts of classical computation take no time, but this is not essential.

Any location can fail, including a wait step. We assume that when a location fails, it results in an error that can affect all of the qubits involved in the action. In the case of preparation, a single-qubit quantum gate, measurement, or wait, that is just a single qubit. For a two-qubit quantum gate such as CNOT, we allow an arbitrary error acting on the two qubits involved in the gate, including errors that entangle the two qubits. The actual error should be considered to be the action of the failed component times the inverse of the desired component in that location. Thus, if we wish to use Z, but instead use Y, the error is $YZ = iX$. The goal of fault tolerance is to take a quantum circuit that is designed to work in the absence of errors and modify it to produce a new circuit which produces the same output as the original circuit, but with the weaker assumption that the number of failed locations is not too large. The precise rules for the probability of locations failing and the type of errors produced when a location fails will be discussed in the following. We will sometimes refer to a location with an error in it as a *faulty location*. The biggest obstacle that we must overcome in order to create a fault-tolerant protocol is that of error propagation. Even if the gates we use are themselves perfect, the action of those gates on the state can alter any errors that have already occurred and cause them to spread: $UE|\psi\rangle = (UEU^{\dagger})U|\psi\rangle$.

That is, a preexisting error E on a state $|\psi\rangle$ followed by a correct gate U is equivalent to the correct state $(U|\psi\rangle)$, but with an error $UEU^{\dagger}$. When U is a single-qubit gate, this is not a very serious problem, since the weight of E does not change, although the exact type of error may now be different. For instance, an X error will become a Z error under the action of a Hadamard gate. The troublesome case is when U is a two-qubit gate, in which case a single-qubit error E will often become a two-qubit error. For instance, note that CNOT can propagate an X error from the first qubit to the second, and can propagate Z from the second qubit to the first: $CNOT: X \otimes I \mapsto X \otimes X, I \otimes Z \mapsto Z \otimes Z$.

This is a problem because it can increase the weight of an error. For instance, if we are using a distance 3 code, it can handle a single-qubit error, but if we then use a CNOT, even if the CNOT itself is perfect, that single-qubit error can become a two-qubit error, and our distance 3 code cannot necessarily correct that. Since we are not going to be able to make a universal quantum computer using only single-qubit gates, clearly we are going to have to be very careful as to how we use two-qubit gates.

There is, of course, a solution to this problem, which we will discuss in the remainder of the chapter. Fault-tolerant circuits will be designed in such a way as to ensure error propagation does not get out of hand. Even though errors may spread somewhat, we can still correct the resulting errors, provided there are not too many to start with. Our eventual goal is to produce fault-tolerant versions of all the types of physical location. We will refer to each such construction as a *gadget* for the particular operation. For instance, we will have fault-tolerant gates for each member of a universal set of quantum gates. Each of these gadgets will simulate the behavior of the corresponding non-fault-tolerant action, but instead of doing so on one or two physical qubits, it will perform the action on the logical qubits encoded in a quantum error correcting code. When we are given a quantum circuit that we would like to use, we replace each of the locations in the original circuit with the corresponding fault-tolerant gadget.

Generally, we assume that the original circuit takes no input: all qubits used in it must be prepared using preparation locations. This still allows us to perform arbitrary quantum computations, since we can modify the quantum circuit based on the classical description of the problem we wish to solve. (For instance, if we wish to factor a number N, we could tailor the exact quantum circuit to work with N.) Then the final fault-tolerant measurement gadgets will produce classical information that should, if the fault-tolerant circuit has done its work properly, give the same outcome as the original circuit would have if we could have implemented it without error.

10.3.1 Fault Tolerance

A fault-tolerant gadget should have two basic properties: when the input state to the gadget does not have too many errors in it, and there are not too many errors on the physical locations in the gadget, the output state should also not have too many errors; and, when there are not too many errors in the input state or during the course of the gadget, the gadget should perform the correct logical operation on the encoded state. To define these properties rigorously, we need to first introduce the notions of an r-filter and an ideal decoder [31, 32].

An r-filter is a projector onto the subspace spanned by all states of the form $Q|\psi\rangle$, where $|\psi\rangle$ is an arbitrary codeword and Q is a Pauli error of weight at most r.

An *ideal decoder* is a map constructed by taking the input state and performing a decoding operation (including error correction) consisting of a circuit with no faulty locations.

That is, the *r*-filter projects onto states with at most *r* errors. Of course, the *r*-filter has no way of knowing what the correct codeword is at this point of the computation, so even a 0-filter might project on the wrong state. The point is that the only states that can pass through the *r*-filter are those that could possibly be created from a valid codeword with at most *r* single-qubit errors. The ideal decoder takes the encoded state, corrects any errors, and gives us an unencoded state. The ideal decoder gives us a way of talking about the logical state of the quantum computer at any point during the computation, and the *r*-filter makes precise the notion of a state having "at most *r* errors." We use the notations in line 1) of Figure 10.10, for these components:

The thick horizontal lines represent a single block of a quantum error correcting code (QECC), except for the thin one on the right end of the ideal decoder symbol, which is a single unencoded qubit. We will focus on the case where the code we use is an $[[n, 1, 2t + 1]]$ code. That is, there is just one encoded qubit per block, the code can correct *t* errors, and the thick horizontal lines in the diagrams represent *n* qubits. It is also possible to achieve fault tolerance with multiple qubits encoded per block [21], but matters are somewhat more complicated then.

We are going to need fault-tolerant gadgets representing state preparation, measurement, and gates. (The fault-tolerant "wait" gadget just consists of having all the encoded qubits wait.) In addition, we will need to correct errors during the course of the computation so that they do not build up to an unacceptable level. Naturally, our error correction step also needs to be fault tolerant, since otherwise performing error correction would incur a substantial risk of creating more errors than it fixes. This may still happen if the error rate is too high, but at least by designing the error correction step properly, we have a fighting chance of improving matters by doing error correction. We will represent all of these gadgets graphically as well as lines 2) and 3) of Figure 10.10.

As before, the thick horizontal lines represent a block of an $[[n, 1, 2t + 1]]$ QECC. In the case of the encoded gate, if it is a two-qubit logical gate, the horizontal lines represent *two* blocks of the QECC, each containing one logical qubit involved in the gate. The *s* in each diagram represents the maximum number of faulty locations that may be involved in the circuit represented by the graphic. For simplicity, let us restrict our attention to cases where the error associated with each fault is a Pauli operator. A slight generalization will allow us to consider other sorts of errors by looking at linear combinations of diagrams with specific Pauli errors. If we draw a similar diagram but with thin lines and no indication of the number of errors, that means the diagram represents an idealized unencoded version of the same operation.

Now we can say rigorously what it means for these gadgets to be fault tolerant. The following definitions will involve *t*, the number of errors the code can correct, and the ideal decoder for the code. We need guarantee the behavior of the system only when the total number of errors involved is less than *t*, since we expect the constructions to fail no matter what we do when there are more errors than the code can correct.

Fault-tolerant measurement: A measurement gadget is *fault tolerant* if it satisfies the property defined by line 4) of Figure 10.10. In other words, if the total number of errors in the incoming state and measurement gadget is at most *t*, then we should get the same result from the real gadget as if we had performed ideal decoding on the incoming state and measured the decoded qubit. By "the same result" we mean not only that the various measurement outcomes have the same probability in both cases, but that the remainder of the computer is left in the same relative state, conditioned on the measurement outcome, for either diagram. In fact, we are comparing two operations, each of which transforms a quantum state of the whole computer into a quantum state for the computer minus one encoded block, plus a classical measurement outcome. The two operations are the same when the measurement gadget is fault tolerant.

Fault-tolerant preparation: A preparation gadget is *fault tolerant* if it satisfies the two properties defined by lines 5) and 6) of Figure 10.10. In other words, a fault-tolerant preparation step with $s \leq t$ errors should output a state that is within s errors of a properly encoded state, and that furthermore, the state should decode to the correct state under an ideal decoder. In the diagram, the equation for Prep A, and in many of the equations below, when we have a fault-tolerant gadget on both the left-hand and right-hand sides of the equation, assume that the faults on both sides are in the same locations and of the same type. The definitions for a fault-tolerant gate are slightly more complicated, but have much the same form.

A gate gadget is fault tolerant if it satisfies the properties defined by lines 7) and 8) of Figure 10.10. In all of these diagrams, a separate filter is applied to each input block when U is a multiple-qubit gate. Input block i gets an r_i-filter. In property 7), a separate filter is applied to each output block, but in all cases it is an $s + \sum_i r_i$-filter. In property 8), an ideal decoder is applied separately to each block. Property 7) states that errors should not propagate too badly: it is acceptable (and unavoidable) for errors to propagate from one block to another, but they should not spread within a block. Thus, the final number of errors on the outgoing state of each block should be no more than the total number of errors on the incoming states, plus the number of errors that occurred on the gate gadget. As before, this needs to apply only when the total number of errors is less than t. Property 8) states that if there are not too many errors in the incoming blocks and gadget combined, then the fault-tolerant gate gadget should use the right encoded gate. Line 8) almost states that we can create a commutative diagram with the ideal decoder, the *FT* gate gadget, and the unencoded ideal gate gadget, but the commutation need hold only when the incoming states have few total errors. Finally, we must define fault-tolerant error correction.

An error correction (EC) gadget is fault tolerant if it satisfies the two properties defined by lines 9) and 10) in Figure 10.10. In other words, after an EC step with at most s faulty locations, the state is at most s errors away from some encoded state. Note that this must apply no matter how many errors were in the incoming state. This does not necessarily mean those errors were dealt with properly; it only means that the final state is near a codeword. It might be the *wrong* codeword, but it is still a valid codeword. Property 10) does state that if the total number of incoming errors and errors during the *FT* EC step is less than t, the state has been corrected, in the sense that the logical state after the EC step is the same as the logical state before it.

10.4 Theoretical Framework

In this section, we will revisit the problems discussed so far by introducing a more rigorous mathematical framework in analogy with classical EC theory. This analogy may help readers with a background in the field of EC coding understand the same problem in the quantum world more easily.

10.4.1 Classical EC

Classical EC is a well-established subject, and a full introduction may be found in many readily available textbooks [33–36]. In order to keep the present discussion reasonably self-contained, a minimal set of ideas is given here. These will be sufficient to guide us in the construction of QECCs. Classical communication can be considered without loss of generality to consist in the communication of strings of binary digits, that is, the binary vectors introduced in the previous sections.

A given binary vector, also called a binary *word*, which we wish to send from A to B, is called a *message*. A noisy communication channel will corrupt the message, but since the message u is a binary vector, the only effect the noise can have is to change it to some other binary vector u'. The difference $e = u' - u$ is called the *error vector*. EC consists in deducing u from u'.

A *classical error correcting code* is a set of words, that is, a binary vector space. It need not necessarily be linear – for example, if cryptography is included – though here we will be concerned almost exclusively with linear codes. Each error correcting code C allows correction of a certain set $\mathcal{S} \equiv \{e_i\}$ of error vectors. The correctable errors are those that satisfy

$$u + e_i \neq v + e_j \forall u, v \in C(u \neq v). \tag{10.30}$$

The case of no error, $e = 0$, is included in $\mathcal{S}$, so that error-free messages are "correctable." To achieve EC, we use the fact that each message u is corrupted to $u' = u + e$ for some $e \in \mathcal{S}$. However, the receiver can deduce u unambiguously from $u + e$ since by condition (10.30), no other message v could have been corrupted to $u + e$, as long as the channel generates only correctable error vectors. In practice a noisy channel causes both correctable and uncorrectable errors, and the problem is to match the code to the channel, so that the errors *most likely* to be generated by the channel are those the code can correct.

Design Example 10.10 ERROR CORRECTION

First, suppose the channel is highly noisy, but noise occurs in bursts, always affecting pairs of bits rather than one bit at a time. In this case, we use the simple code $C = \{00, 01\}$. Longer messages are sent bit by bit using the code, by sending 00 for 0 and 01 for 1. The possible error vectors (those that the channel can produce) are $\{00, 11\}$, and in this example, this is also a set of correctable errors: the receiver interprets 00 or 11 as the message 00, and 01 or 10 as the message 01. Therefore, error correction always works perfectly! This illustrates the fact that we can always take advantage of structure in the noise (here, pairs of bits being equally affected) in order to circumvent it. In the quantum case, the corresponding situation is called a "noise-free (or decoherence-free) subspace" [37], where parts of the state space of the quantum system are unaffected by environmental coupling, so they can be used to store information that will not be influenced by the noise.

Next, suppose the noise affects each bit independently, with a fixed error probability $p < 1/2$. This noise has less structure than that we just considered, but it still has some predictable features, the most important being that the most likely error vectors are those with the smallest weight. We use the code $C = \{000, 111\}$. The errors that the channel can produce are, in order of decreasing probability, $\{000, 001, 010, 100, 011, 101, 011, 111\}$. With $n = 3$ and $m = 2$, the set of correctable errors can have at most $2^3/2 = 4$ members, and these are $\{000, 001, 010, 100\}$.

Minimum distance coding: The noisy channel just described is called the binary symmetric channel. The noise affects each bit sent down the channel independently in this binary channel (the only kind we are considering). It is furthermore symmetric, meaning that the channel causes errors $0 \rightarrow 1$ and $1 \rightarrow 0$ with equal probability. If n bits are sent down a binary symmetric channel, the probability that m of them are flipped ($0 \leftrightarrow 1$) is the probability for m independent events in n opportunities: $C(n, m)p^m(1 - p)^{n-m}$, where the binomial coefficient $C(n, m) = n!/(m!(n-m)!)$.

The binary symmetric channel is important because other types of noise can be treated as a combination of a structured component and a random component. The structured component can be tackled in more efficient ways – for example, burst-error correcting codes – and then the remaining random component forms a problem equivalent to that of the binary symmetric channel.

To code for the binary symmetric channel, we clearly need a code in which error vectors of small weight are correctable, since these are the most likely ones. A code that corrects all error vectors of weight up to and including t is called a t-error correcting code. A simple but important observation is the following: a code of minimum distance d can correct all error vectors of weight less than or equal to t if and only if $d > 2t$.

Proof: If $d > 2t$, then $\text{wt}(u+v) > 2t$ for all u, v in the code, and therefore $\text{wt}(u+v+e_1+e_2) \neq 0$ for all error vectors e_1, e_2 of weight $\leq t$. This implies $u + e_1 \neq v + e_2$, so condition (10.30) is satisfied. Also, if $d = \text{wt}(u+v) \leq 2t$, then there exist error vectors e_1, e_2 of weight $\leq t$ such that $\text{wt}(u+v+e_1+e_2) = 0$, which implies $u + e_1 = v + e_2$, so correction is impossible. This argument shows that a good set of codes for the binary symmetric channel are those of high minimum distance.

Bounds on the size of codes: In order to communicate k bits of information using an error correcting code, $n > k$ bits must be sent down the channel. The ratio k/n, called the *rate* of the code, gives a measure of the cost of EC. Various bounds on k/n can be deduced.

In a Hamming space of n dimensions, that is, one consisting of n-bit vectors, there are $C(n, t)$ error vectors of weight t. Any member of a t-error correcting code has $\sum_{i=0}^{t} C(n, i)$ erroneous versions (including the error-free version) which must all be distinct from the other members of the code and their erroneous versions if correction is to be possible. They are also distinct from each other because

$$e_1 \neq e_2 \Rightarrow u + e_1 \neq u + e_2. \tag{10.31}$$

However, there are only 2^n possible vectors in the whole Hamming space, therefore the number of vectors m in n-bit t-error correcting codes is limited by the *Hamming bound* [1, 33]:

$$m \sum_{i=0}^{t} C(n, i) \leq 2^n \tag{10.32}$$

This is also called the *sphere packing bound* because the problem is equivalent to that of packing as many spheres as possible in the n-dimensional rectangular space, where each sphere has radius t. For linear codes $m = 2^k$, so the Hamming bound becomes

$$k \leq n - \log_2 \left(\sum_{i=0}^{t} C(n, i) \right). \tag{10.33}$$

From this, one may deduce in the limit of large n, k, t:

$$\frac{k}{n} \leq \left(1 - H\left(\frac{t}{n}\right)\right)(1 - \eta) \tag{10.34}$$

where $\eta \to 0$ as $n \to \infty$, and $H(x)$ is the entropy function

$$H(x) \equiv -x \log_2 x - (1-x) \log_2(1-x). \tag{10.35}$$

The Hamming bound makes precise the intuitively obvious fact that error correcting codes cannot achieve an arbitrarily high rate k/n while still retaining their correction ability. As yet we have no definite guide as to whether good codes exist in general. A very useful result is the Gilbert–Varshamov bound: it can be shown [34] that for given d, there exists a linear $[n, k, d]$ code provided

$$2^k \sum_{i=0}^{d-2} C(n-1, i) < 2^n \tag{10.36}$$

In the limit of large n, k, d, and putting $t = d/2$, this becomes

$$\frac{k}{n} \geq \left(1 - H\left(\frac{2t}{n}\right)\right)(1 - \eta) \tag{10.37}$$

where $\eta \to 0$ as $n \to \infty$. It can be shown that there exists an infinite sequence of $[n, k, d]$ codes satisfying Eq. (10.37) with $d/n \geq \delta$ if $0 \leq \delta < 1/2$. The Gilbert–Varshamov bound necessarily lies below the Hamming bound, but it is an important result because it shows that EC can be very powerful. In the binary symmetric channel, for large n the probability distribution of all the possible error vectors is strongly peaked around error vectors of weight close to the mean np, where p is the error probability per bit. This is an example of the law of large numbers. Therefore, as long as $> np(1 + \eta)$, where $\eta < < 1$, EC is almost certain to succeed in the limit $n \to \infty$. The Gilbert–Varshamov bound tells us that this can be achieved without the need for codes of vanishingly small rate.

Another result on coding limitations is Shannon's theorem [33, 34], which states that codes exist whose average performance is close to that of the Hamming bound:

Shannon's theorem: If the rate k/n is less than the channel capacity, and n is sufficiently large, then there exists a binary code allowing transmission with arbitrarily low failure probability.

The failure probability is the probability that an uncorrectable error will occur; the capacity of the binary symmetric channel is $1 - H(p)$. Shannon's theorem is "close to" the Hamming bound in the sense that we would expect a correction ability $t > np$ to be required to ensure success in a binary symmetric channel, which implies $k/n < 1 - H(p)$ in the Hamming bound; Shannon's theorem assures us that codes exist that get arbitrarily close to this. However, the codes whose existence is implied by Shannon's theorem are not necessarily convenient to use.

Linear codes, error syndrome: The importance of linear codes is mainly in their convenience, especially the speed with which any erroneous received word can be corrected. They are also highly significant when it comes to generalizing classical EC to QEC. So far the only EC method we have mentioned is the simple idea of a lookup table, in which a received vector w is compared with all the code vectors $u \in C$ and their erroneous versions $u + e$, $e \in S$, until a match $w = u + e$ is found, in which case the vector is corrected to u. This method makes inefficient use of either time or memory resources since there are 2^n vectors $u + e$. For linear codes, a great improvement is to calculate the *error syndrome s* given by

$$s = Hw^T. \tag{10.38}$$

where H is the parity check matrix. Since H is an $(n - k) \times n$ matrix, and w is an n-bit row vector, the syndrome s is an $n - k$ bit column vector. The transpose of w is needed to allow the normal rules of matrix multiplication, though the notation $H \cdot w$ is sometimes also used. Consider

$$s = H(u + e)^T = Hu^T + He^T = He^T \tag{10.39}$$

where we used Eq. (10.A.2) (see Appendix 10.A) for the second step. This shows that *the syndrome depends only on the error vector, and not on the transmitted word*. If we could deduce the error from the syndrome, which will be shown next, then we only have 2^{n-k} syndromes to look up, instead of 2^n erroneous words. Furthermore, many codes can be constructed in such a way that the error vector can be deduced from the syndrome by analytical methods, such as the solution of a set of simultaneous equations.

Proof that the error can be deduced from the syndrome: The parity check matrix consists of $n - k$ linearly independent parity check vectors. Each check vector divides the Hamming space in half, into those vectors that satisfy the check and those that do not. Hence, there are exactly 2^k vectors in Hamming space that have any given syndrome s. Using Eq. (10.39), these vectors must be the vectors $u + e_s$ where $u \in C$ is one of the 2^k members of the code C. Hence, the only error vectors that give the syndrome s are the members of the set $\{e_s + u\}$, $u \in C$. Such a set is called a *coset*. The syndrome cannot distinguish among errors in a given coset. In choosing which errors are correctable by the code, we can choose at most one from each coset. Then, we have proved that each correctable error is uniquely determined by its syndrome.

Design Example 10.11

We assume that the Hamming code [7, 4, 3] given by Eqs. (10.A.4)–(10.A.6) (see Appendix 10.A) is used. Since this code has minimum distance 3, it is a single-error correcting code. The number of code vectors is limited by the Hamming bound to $2^7/(C(7, 0) + C(7, 1)) = 2^7/(1 + 7) = 2^4$. Since there are indeed 2^4 vectors, the code saturates the bound; such codes are called perfect. The set of correctable errors is {0000000, 0000001, 0000010, 0000100, 0001000, 0010000, 0100000, 1000000}. Suppose the message is 0110011 and the error is 0100000. The received word is 0110011 + 0100000 = 0010011. The syndrome, using Eq. (10.A.6) (see Appendix 10.A), is $H(0010011)^T = (010)^T$. The only word of weight ≤ 1 that fails the second parity check and passes the others is 0100000, so this is the deduced error. We thus deduce the message to be 0010011 − 0100000 = 0110011.

10.4.2 Theory of QEC

10.4.2.1 Preliminaries

We will now go back to our toy three-bit code example, introduced at the very beginning of the chapter. For this introductory section, the following properties will be assumed: the noise acts on each qubit independently, and for a given qubit has an effect chosen at random between leaving the qubit's state unchanged (probability $1 - p$) and applying a Pauli σ_x operator (probability $p < 1/2$). This is a very artificial type of noise, but once we can correct it, as we saw in the first part of the chapter, we will find that our correction can also offer useful results for much more realistic types of noise.

The simplest QEC method is summarized in Figure 10.11. The state of any qubit that transmitter A wishes to transmit can be written without loss of generality as $a \,|\, 0\rangle + b \,|\, 1\rangle$. A prepares two further qubits in the state $|0\rangle$, so the initial state of all three qubits is $a \,|\, 000\rangle + b \,|\, 100\rangle$. A now operates a CNOT gate from the first qubit to the second, producing $a \,|\, 000\rangle + b \,|\, 110\rangle$, followed by a CNOT gate from the first qubit to the third, producing $a \,|\, 000\rangle + b \,|\, 111\rangle$. Finally, A sends all three qubits down the channel.

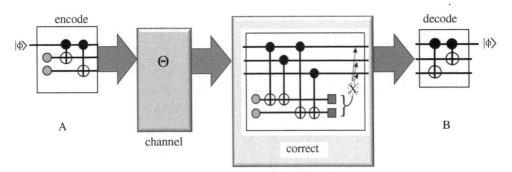

Figure 10.11 Simple example illustrating the principles of quantum error correction (QEC).

The receiver B receives the three qubits, but they have been acted on by the noise in the channel. Their state is one of the following:

$$
\begin{array}{cc}
\text{state} & \textit{probability} \\
a|000\rangle + b|111\rangle & (1-p)^3 \\
a|100\rangle + b|011\rangle & p(1-p)^2 \\
a|010\rangle + b|101\rangle & p(1-p)^2 \\
a|001\rangle + b|110\rangle & p(1-p)^2 \\
a|110\rangle + b|001\rangle & p^2(1-p) \\
a|101\rangle + b|010\rangle & p^2(1-p) \\
a|011\rangle + b|100\rangle & p^2(1-p) \\
a|111\rangle + b|000\rangle & p^3
\end{array}
\tag{10.40}
$$

B now introduces two more qubits of his own, prepared in the state $|00\rangle$. This extra pair of qubits, referred to as an *ancilla*, is not strictly necessary, but makes EC easier to understand and becomes necessary when fault-tolerant methods are needed. B uses the ancilla to gather information about the noise. He first carries out CNOTs from the first and second received qubits to the first ancilla qubit, then from the first and third received qubits to the second ancilla bit. The total state of all five qubits is now

$$
\begin{array}{cc}
\text{state} & \textit{probability} \\
(a|000\rangle + b|111\rangle)|00\rangle & (1-p)^3 \\
(a|100\rangle + b|011\rangle)|11\rangle & p(1-p)^2 \\
(a|010\rangle + b|101\rangle)|10\rangle & p(1-p)^2 \\
(a|001\rangle + b|110\rangle)|01\rangle & p(1-p)^2 \\
(a|110\rangle + b|001\rangle)|01\rangle & p^2(1-p) \\
(a|101\rangle + b|010\rangle)|10\rangle & p^2(1-p) \\
(a|011\rangle + b|100\rangle)|11\rangle & p^2(1-p) \\
(a|111\rangle + b|000\rangle)|00\rangle & p^3
\end{array}
\tag{10.41}
$$

Bob measures the two ancilla bits in the basis $\{|0\rangle, |1\rangle\}$. This gives him two classical bits of information. This information is called the *error syndrome*, since it helps to diagnose the errors in the received qubits. Bob's next action is as follows:

Measured Syndrome	Action
00	*do nothing*
01	*apply σ_x to third qubit*
10	*apply σ_x to second qubi*
11	*apply σ_x to first qubit*

Suppose, for example, that B's measurements give 10 (i.e., the ancilla state is projected onto $|10\rangle$). Examining Eq. (10.41), we see that the state of the received qubits must be either $a|010\rangle + b|101\rangle$ (probability $p(1-p)^2$) or $a|101\rangle + b|010\rangle$ (probability $p^2(1-p)$). Since the former is more likely, B corrects the state by applying a Pauli σ_x operator to the second qubit. He thus obtains either $a|000\rangle + b|111\rangle$ (most likely) or $a|111\rangle + b|000\rangle$. Finally, to extract the qubit that A sent, Bob applies CNOT from the first qubit to the second and third qubits, obtaining either $(a|0\rangle + b|1\rangle)|00\rangle$ or $(a|1\rangle + b|0\rangle)|00\rangle$. Therefore, B has either the exact qubit sent by A, or A's qubit operated on by σ_x. Bob does not know which he has, but the important point is that the method has a probability of success greater than $1 - p$. The correction is designed to succeed whenever either no qubit or just one qubit is corrupted by the channel, which are the most likely possibilities. The failure probability is the probability that at least two qubits are corrupted by the channel, which is $3p^2(1 - p) + p^3 = 3p^2 - 2p^3$, that is, less than p (as long as $p < 1/2$). In summary, A communicates a single general qubit by expressing its state as a joint state of three qubits, which are then sent to B. On his side, B first applies EC, then extracts a single qubit state. The probability that he fails to obtain A's original state is (p^2), whereas it would have been $O(p)$ if no EC method had been used. We will see later that with more qubits the same basic ideas lead to much more powerful noise suppression, but it is worth noting that we already have quite an impressive result: by using just three times as many qubits, we reduce the error probability by a factor $\sim 1/3p$, that is, a factor ~ 30 for $p = 0.01$, ~ 300 for $p = 0.001$, and so on.

10.4.2.2 Basics of QEC Theory

The introductory example of QEC that was given in the previous section was in fact based on the most simple classical error correcting code, the [3, 1, 3] repetition code, whose parity check matrix has two rows: 110 and 011. It illustrates the basic idea of using parity checks to acquire an error syndrome in the quantum case, but it cannot correct the more general type of noise that can affect qubits. In order to generalize to full QEC, we will need to introduce further concepts. The simplest aspects of this more general theory, which were initially introduced in the previous sections of this chapter, will be now summarized using a theoretical framework and analogy with classical EC. As already discussed earlier, QEC is based on three central ideas: digitization of noise, the manipulation of error operators and syndromes, and QECC construction. The degree of success of QEC relies on the physics of noise; we will turn to this after discussing the three central ideas.

Digitization of noise is based on the observation that *any* interaction between a set of qubits and another system (such as the environment) can be expressed in the form

$$| \varphi \rangle \, | \psi_0 \rangle_e \rightarrow \sum_i (E_i \, | \varphi \rangle) \, | \psi_i \rangle_e \qquad (10.42)$$

where each "error operator" E_i is a tensor product of Pauli operators acting on the qubits, $| \varphi \rangle$ is the initial state of the qubits, and $| \psi_i \rangle_e$ are states of the environment, not necessarily orthogonal or normalized. We thus express general noise and/or decoherence in terms of Pauli operators σ_x, σ_y, σ_z acting on the qubits. As before, these will be written $X \equiv \sigma_x$, $Z \equiv \sigma_z$, $Y \equiv -i\sigma_y = XZ$. The statement Eq. (10.42) is true because the Pauli matrices are a complete set: they can describe any transformation of the qubits, because we allow any sort of entanglement with the environment. Physicists often consider coupling to the environment by starting from a Hamiltonian, or through a density matrix approach; it is important to see that we are being completely general here, so those other methods can be completely encompassed by Eq. (10.42).

To write tensor products of Pauli matrices acting on n qubits, we introduce the notation $X_u Z_v$ where u and v are n-bit binary vectors. The nonzero coordinates of u and v indicate where X and Z operators appear in the product. For example,

$$X \otimes I \otimes Z \otimes Y \otimes X \equiv X_{10011} Z_{00110} \qquad (10.43)$$

EC is a process that takes a state such as $E_i | \varphi \rangle$ to $| \varphi \rangle$. Correction of X errors takes $X_u Z_v | \varphi \rangle$ to $Z_v | \varphi \rangle$; correction of Z errors takes $X_u Z_v | \varphi \rangle$ to $X_u | \varphi \rangle$. Putting all this together, we discover the highly significant fact that to correct *the most general possible* noise (Eq. (10.42)), it is sufficient to correct just X and Z errors. See Eq. (10.49) and following for a proof. It may look as though we are correcting only unitary bit-flip and phase-flip rotations, but this is a false impression: actually, we will correct everything, including nonunitary relaxation processes!

Error operators, stabilizer, and syndrome extraction: We will now examine the mathematics of error operators and syndromes, using the insightful approach put forward by Gottesman [38] and Calderbank et al. [39, 40]. These works introduced the concept of the stabilizer, which yielded important insights into the first discoveries, and enabled significant generalizations to be written down simply.

Consider the set $\{I, X, Y, Z\}$ consisting of the identity operator plus the three Pauli operators. The Pauli operators all square to $I : X^2 = Y^2 = Z^2 = I$, and have eigenvalues ± 1. Two members of the set only ever commute ($XI = IX$) or anti-commute: $XZ = -ZX$. Tensor products of Pauli operators, that is, error operators, also square to one and either commute or anti-commute. The term "error operator" is here just a shorthand for "product of Pauli operators"; such an operator will sometimes play the role of an error, sometimes of a parity check, analogous with classical coding theory.

If there are n qubits in the quantum system, then the error operators will be of *length n*. The *weight* of an error operator is the number of terms not equal to I. For example, $X_{10011}Z_{00110}$ has length 5 and weight 4.

Let $\mathcal{H} = \{M\}$ be a set of commuting error operators. Since the operators all commute, they can have simultaneous eigenstates. Let $\mathcal{C} = \{|u\rangle\}$ be an orthonormal set of simultaneous eigenstates all having eigenvalue +1:

$$M \mid u\rangle = \mid u\rangle \forall u \in \mathcal{C}, \forall M \in \mathcal{H}. \tag{10.44}$$

The set $\mathcal{C}$ is a QECC, and $\mathcal{H}$ is its *stabilizer*. The orthonormal states $|u\rangle$ are referred to as *code vectors* or *quantum codewords*. In what follows, we will restrict our attention to the case that $\mathcal{H}$ is a group. Its size is 2^{n-k}, and it is spanned by $n - k$ linearly independent members of $\mathcal{H}$. In this case, $\mathcal{C}$ has 2^k members, so it encodes k qubits, since its members span a 2^k dimensional subspace of the 2^n dimensional Hilbert space of the whole system. A general state in this subspace, called an *encoded state* or *logical state*, can be expressed as a superposition of the code vectors:

$$\mid \varphi\rangle_L = \sum_{u \in \mathcal{C}} a_u \mid u\rangle \tag{10.45}$$

Naturally, a given QECC does not allow correction of all possible errors. Each code allows correction of a particular set $\mathcal{S} = \{E\}$ of *correctable errors*. The task of code construction consists of finding codes whose correctable set includes the errors most likely to occur in a given physical situation. We will turn to this important topic in the next section. First, let us show how the correctable set is related to the stabilizer, and demonstrate how the EC is actually achieved.

First, error operators in the stabilizer are all correctable, $E \in \mathcal{S} \forall E \in \mathcal{H}$, since these operators actually have no effect on a general logical state (Eq. (10.45)). If these error operators are themselves the only terms in the noise of the system under consideration, then the QECC is a noise-free subspace, also called the decoherence-free subspace of the system.

There is a large set of further errors that do change encoded states but are nevertheless correctable by a process of extracting an error syndrome, and then acting on the system depending on what syndrome is obtained. We will show that $\mathcal{S}$ can be any set of errors $\{E_i\}$ such that every product $E_1 E_2$ of two members is either in $\mathcal{H}$, or anti-commutes with a member of $\mathcal{H}$. To see this, take the second case first:

$$E_1 E_2 M = -M E_1 E_2 \text{ for some } M \in \mathcal{H}. \tag{10.46}$$

We say that the combined error operator $E_1 E_2$ is *detectable*. This can only happen if

$$\text{either } \{ M E_1 = -E_1 M; \quad M E_2 = E_2 M \}$$
$$\text{or } \{ M E_1 = E_1 M, \quad M E_2 = -E_2 M \}. \tag{10.47}$$

To extract the syndrome, we measure all the observables in the stabilizer. To do this, it is sufficient to measure any set of $n - k$ linearly independent M in $\mathcal{H}$. Note that such a measurement has no effect on a state in the encoded subspace, since such a state is already an eigenstate of all these observables. The measurement projects a noisy state onto an eigenstate of each M, with eigenvalue ± 1. The string of $n - k$ eigenvalues is the syndrome. Equation (10.47) guarantee that E_1 and E_2 have different syndromes, and so can be distinguished from each other, for when the observable M is measured on the corrupted state $E \, |\varphi\rangle_L$, Eq. (10.47) means that a different eigenvalue will be obtained when $E = E_1$ than when $E = E_2$. Therefore, the error can be deduced from the syndrome, and reversed by re-applying the deduced error to the system (taking advantage of the fact that error operators square to 1).

Let us see how this whole process looks when applied to a general noisy encoded state. The noisy state is

$$\sum_i (E_i \, | \, \varphi \rangle_L) \, | \, \psi_i \rangle_e. \tag{10.48}$$

The syndrome extraction can be done most simply by attaching an $n - k$ qubit ancilla a to the system, and storing in it the eigenvalues by a sequence of CNOT gates and Hadamard rotations. The exact network can be constructed either by thinking in terms of parity check information stored into the ancilla (discussed in the sequel), or by the following standard eigenvalue measurement method.

To extract the $\lambda = \pm 1$ eigenvalue of operator M, prepare an ancilla in $(| \, 0 \rangle + | \, 1 \rangle)/\sqrt{2}$. Operate controlled-$M$ with the ancilla as control and the system as target; then Hadamard-rotate the ancilla. The final state of the ancilla is $[(1 + \lambda) | \, 0 \rangle + (1 - \lambda) | \, 1 \rangle]/2$. Carrying out this process for the $n - k$ operators M that span $\mathcal{H}$, the effect is to couple system and environment with the ancilla as follows:

$$| \, 0 \rangle_a \sum_i (E_i \, | \, \varphi \rangle_L) \, | \, \psi_i \rangle_e \rightarrow \sum_i | \, s_i \rangle_a (E_i \, | \, \varphi \rangle_L) \, | \, \psi_i \rangle_e. \tag{10.49}$$

The syndromes s_i are $(n - k)$-bit binary strings. Thus far, the treatment has been completely general.

Now suppose the E_i all have different syndromes. Then a projective measurement of the ancilla will collapse the sum to a single term taken at random: $| s_i \rangle_a (E_i \, | \, \varphi \rangle_L) \, | \, \psi_i \rangle_e$, and will yield s_i as the measurement result. Since there is only one E_i with this syndrome, we can deduce the operator E_i, which should now be applied to correct the error. The system is therefore "magically" disentangled from its environment, and perfectly restored to $| \varphi \rangle_L$!

This process can be understood as first forcing the general noisy state to "choose" among a discrete set of errors, via a projective measurement, and then reversing the particular discrete error "chosen" using the fact that the measurement result tells us which one it was. Alternatively, the correction can be accomplished by a unitary evolution consisting of controlled gates with the ancilla as control and the system as target, effectively transferring the noise (including entanglement with the environment) from the system to the ancilla.

In practice, the supposition that all errors generated by the noise have different syndromes will not be true. Usually there will be more than one error E having a given syndrome s_i, just as in the classical case, and we must choose one error per coset (i.e., the set having the same syndrome) to be correctable, except in a special case. This is the case mentioned just before Eq. (10.46), namely, when $E_1E_2 \in \mathcal{H}$.

In this case, E_1 and E_2 will have the same syndrome, and so are indistinguishable in the syndrome extraction process, but both are correctable because we may simply interpret the common syndrome of these two errors as an indication that the corrective operation E_1 should be applied. If it was E_1 that occurred, this is obviously fine, whereas if in fact E_2 occurred, the final state is E_1E_2 $|\varphi\rangle_L$, which is also correct! This situation has no analogue in classical coding theory. The quantum codes that take advantage of it are referred to as *degenerate* and are not constrained by the quantum Hamming bound.

Conditions for QECCs: The previous discussion based on the stabilizer is useful because it focuses attention on operators rather than states. Quantum codewords are nevertheless very interesting states, having a lot of symmetry and interesting forms of entanglement. The codewords in the QECC can readily be shown to allow correction of the set $\mathcal{S}$ if and only if [3, 41]

$$\langle u \mid E_1E_2 \mid v \rangle = 0, \langle u \mid E_1E_2 \mid u \rangle = \langle v \mid E_1E_2 \mid v \rangle \tag{10.50}$$

for all $E_1, E_2 \in \mathcal{S}$ and $|u\rangle, |v\rangle \in \mathcal{C}$, $|u\rangle \neq |v\rangle$. These are the requirements for quantum codewords that correspond to the requirement Eq. (10.30) for classical codes. In the case that E_1E_2 always anticommutes with a member of the stabilizer, we have $\langle u \mid E_1E_2 \mid u \rangle = \langle u \mid E_1E_2M \mid u \rangle = -\langle u \mid ME_1E_2 \mid u \rangle = -\langle u \mid E_1E_2 \mid u \rangle$, and therefore $\langle u \mid E_1E_2 \mid u \rangle = 0$. This is a nondegenerate code; all the code vectors and their erroneous versions are mutually orthogonal, and the quantum Hamming bound (see next section) must be satisfied.

The first condition says that to be correctable, an error acting on one codeword must not produce a state that overlaps with another codeword, or with an erroneous version of another codeword. This is what we would expect intuitively.

Proof. Let the unitary operator $\mathcal{R}$ describe the whole recovery operation (e.g., syndrome extraction followed by correction), then

$$\left.\begin{array}{r} \mathcal{R} \mid \alpha_j \rangle E_j \mid v \rangle = \mid \alpha_j' \rangle \mid v \rangle \\ \mathcal{R}|\alpha_i\rangle E_i|u\rangle = |\alpha_i'\rangle|u\rangle \end{array}\right\}$$

$$\Rightarrow \langle u \mid E_i^\dagger \langle \alpha_i \mid \mathcal{R}^\dagger \mathcal{R} \mid \alpha_j \rangle E_j \mid v \rangle = \langle \alpha_i' \mid \alpha_j' \rangle \langle u \mid v \rangle$$

$$\Rightarrow \langle u \mid E_i^\dagger E_j \mid v \rangle = 0.$$

where $|\alpha\rangle$ are states of the ancilla, environment, and any other systems used during recovery. The last step uses the fact that the recovery must work when $|\alpha_i\rangle = |\alpha_j\rangle$ (as well as when $|\alpha_i\rangle \neq |\alpha_j\rangle$).

The second condition in Eq. (10.50) is surprising since it permits one erroneous version of a codeword $|u\rangle$ to overlap with another, as long as all the other codewords subject to the same error have the same overlap with their respective other erroneous versions. This is not possible in classical EC because of Eq. (10.31).

Proof of Eq. (10.50):

$$\mathcal{R} \mid \alpha \rangle E_i \mid u \rangle = |\alpha_i'|u$$

$$\Rightarrow \langle u \mid E_i^\dagger \langle \alpha \mid \mathcal{R}^\dagger \mathcal{R} \mid \alpha \rangle E_j \mid u \rangle = \langle \alpha_i' \mid \alpha_j' \rangle$$

$$\Rightarrow \langle u \mid E_i^\dagger E_j \mid u \rangle = \langle \alpha_i' \mid \alpha_j' \rangle.$$

The same result is obtained starting from $|v\rangle$, from which Eq. (10.50) is derived. For further details, see [37].

Quantum Hamming bound: A t-error correcting quantum code is defined to be a code for which all errors of weight less than or equal to t are correctable. Since there are three possible single-qubit errors, the number of error operators of weight t acting on n qubits is $3^t C(n, t)$. Therefore, a t-error correcting code must be able to correct $\sum_{i=1}^{t} 3^i C(n, i)$ error operators. For nondegenerate codes, $\langle u | E_1 E_2 | u \rangle = 0$ in Eq. (10.50), every codeword $|u\rangle$ and all its erroneous versions $M | u \rangle$ must be orthogonal to every other codeword and all its erroneous versions. All these orthogonal states can only fit into the 2^n-dimensional Hilbert space of n qubits if

$$m \sum_{i=0}^{t} 3^i C(n, i) \leq 2^n. \tag{10.51}$$

This bound is known as the quantum Hamming bound [13–16]. For $m = 2^k$ and large n, t it becomes

$$\frac{k}{n} \leq 1 - \frac{t}{n} \log_2 3 - H(t/n). \tag{10.52}$$

What is the smallest single-error correcting orthogonal quantum code? A code with $m = 2$ codewords represents a Hilbert space of one qubit (it "encodes" a single qubit). Putting $m = 2$ and $t = 1$ in the quantum Hamming bound, we have $1 + 3n \leq 2^{n-1}$, which is saturated by $n = 5$, and indeed a 5-qubit code exists; see Eq. (10.62).

10.4.2.3 Code Construction

The power of QEC results from the physical insights and mathematical techniques already discussed, combined with the fact that useful QECCs can actually be found. Code construction is itself a subtle and interesting area, which we will merely introduce here. We will first present a general description of stabilizer codes; this will connect the mathematics of error operators to that of binary vector spaces, which has been studied in classical coding theory. The subsequent sections will then examine examples in more detail.

First, recall that we require all members of the stabilizer to commute. It is easy to show that $X_u Z_v = (-1)^{u \cdot v} Z_v X_u$, where $u \cdot v$ is the binary parity check operation, or inner product between binary vectors, evaluated in $GF(2)$. From this, $M = X_u Z_v$ and $M' = X_{u'} Z_{v'}$ commute if and only if

$$u \cdot v' + v \cdot u' = 0 \tag{10.53}$$

The stabilizer is completely specified by writing down any $n - k$ linearly independent error operators that span it. It is convenient to write these error operators by giving the binary strings u and v, which indicate the X and Z parts, in the form of two $(n - k) \times n$ binary matrices H_x, H_z. The whole stabilizer is then uniquely specified by the $(n - k) \times 2n$ binary matrix

$$H = (H_x \mid H_z) \tag{10.54}$$

and the requirement that the operators all commute (i.e., $\mathcal{H}$ is an Abelian group) is expressed by

$$H_x H_z^T + H_z H_x^T = 0 \tag{10.55}$$

where T indicates the matrix transpose.

The matrix H is the analogue of the parity check matrix for a classical error correcting code. The analogue of the generator matrix is the matrix $G = (G_x \mid G_z)$ satisfying

$$H_x G_z^T + H_z G_x^T = 0. \tag{10.56}$$

In other words, H and G are duals with respect to the inner product defined by Eq. (10.53). G has $n + k$ rows. H may be obtained directly from G by swapping the X and Z parts and extracting the usual binary dual of the resulting $(n + k) \times 2n$ binary matrix. Note that Eqs. (10.56) and (10.55) imply that G contains H. Let $\mathcal{G}$ be the set of error operators generated by G; then also $\mathcal{G}$ contains $\mathcal{H}$.

Since by definition (10.56), all the members of $\mathcal{G}$ commute with all the members of $\mathcal{H}$, and since (by counting) there can be no further error operators that commute with all of $\mathcal{H}$, we deduce that all error operators not in $\mathcal{G}$ anti-commute with at least one member of H. This leads us to a powerful observation: if all members of $\mathcal{G}$ (other than the identity) have a weight of at least d, then all error operators (other than the identity) of weight less than d anti-commute with a member of $\mathcal{H}$, and so are detectable. Such a code can therefore correct all error operators of weight less than $d/2$.

What if the only members of $\mathcal{G}$ having weight less than d are also members of $\mathcal{H}$? Then the code can still correct all error operators of weight less than $d/2$, using property $E_1 E_2 \in \mathcal{H}$ (a degenerate code). The weight d is called the minimum distance of the code. We use the notation $[[n, k, d]]$ to indicate the main properties of the quantum code.

The problem of code construction is thus reduced to a problem of finding binary matrices H that satisfy Eq. (10.55), and whose duals G, defined by Eq. (10.56), have large weights. We will now write down such a code by combining well-chosen classical binary error correcting codes

$$H = \begin{pmatrix} H_2 & 0 \\ 0 & H_1 \end{pmatrix}, \qquad G = \begin{pmatrix} G_1 & 0 \\ 0 & G_2 \end{pmatrix}. \tag{10.57}$$

Here H_i, $i = 1, 2$, is the check matrix of the classical code C_i generated by G_i. Therefore $H_i G_i^T = 0$ (Eqs. (10.A.2) (see Appendix 10.A) and (10.56)) is satisfied. To satisfy commutativity, Eq. (10.55), we force $H_1 H_2^T = 0$, in other words, $C_2^\perp \subset C_1$. These are the CSS (Calderbank–Shor–Steane) codes. Their significance is, first, that they can be efficient (see below) and, second, that they are useful in fault-tolerant computing.

By construction, if the classical codes underlying a CSS code have parameters $[n, k_1, d_1]$, $[n, k_2, d_2]$, then the quantum code has size $k = k_1 + k_2 - n$. Also, the (nonzero) members of $\mathcal{G}$ have weights of at least $min (d_1, d_2)$, so we have a quantum code of minimum distance = min (d_1, d_2). One way to form the quantum codewords is

$$|u\rangle_L = \sum_{x \in C_2^\perp} |x + u \cdot D\rangle \tag{10.58}$$

where u is a k-bit binary word, x is an n-bit binary word, and D is a $(k \times n)$ matrix of coset leaders. We can understand the structure of these codewords as follows.

Start with the case $u = 0$: $|0\rangle_L$ is an equal superposition of all the members of $C_2^\perp$. The next encoded state is found by displacing all the members of $C_2^\perp$ by the same vector (the first row of D): in other words, we have a superposition of all the members of a coset. We choose the vector (the coset leader) so that this coset is still in C_1. The other quantum codewords are formed similarly by further cosets of $C_2^\perp$, all within C_1. Bit-flip correction follows from the use of product states all in C_1. Phase-flip correction follows from the fact that the Hadamard transform of an equal superposition of members of $C_2^\perp$, or of one of its cosets, will produce only members of C_2 (this is discussed later in this section).

By "efficient," we mean that there exist codes of given d/n whose rate k/n remains above a finite lower bound, as $k, n, d \to \infty$. The CSS codes have = min (d_1, d_2). If we choose the pair of classical codes in the construction to be the same, $C_1 = C_2 = C$, then we are considering a classical code that contains its dual. A finite lower bound for the rate of such codes can be shown to exist [11]. This is highly significant: it means there exist codes of useful rate and large minimum distance, and therefore QEC can be a very powerful method to suppress noise, because all the most likely errors from random noise can be in the correctable set. Specifically, it can be shown [42] that there exists an infinite sequence of classical codes that contain their dual and satisfy the Gilbert–Varshamov bound (Eq. (10.36)). Therefore, there exists an infinite sequence of quantum $[[n, K, d]]$ CSS codes provided Eq. (10.36) is satisfied with $k = (K + n)/2$. In the limit of large n, k, t this becomes [42, 43]

$$\frac{K}{n} \geq 1 - 2H(2t/n) \tag{10.59}$$

where the usual factor $(1 - \eta)$ has been suppressed.

Design Example 10.12 CODES

The simplest CSS code is the 7-bit code discovered by Steane. It uses the CSS construction (Eq. (10.57)) with $H_1 = H_2 = H$ as given in Eq. (10.A.6). This is the [7, 4, 3] Hamming code; it is single-error correcting and contains its dual, and so leads to a single-error correcting quantum code of parameters $[[n, k, d]] = [[7, 1, 3]]$, that is, a single qubit stored in 7, with minimum distance 3. The two codewords are

$$| 0 \rangle_L = | 0000000 \rangle + | 1010101 \rangle + | 0110011 \rangle + | 1100110 \rangle$$
$$+ | 0001111 \rangle + | 1011010 \rangle + | 0111100 \rangle + | 1101001 \rangle, \tag{10.60}$$

$$| 1 \rangle_L = X_{1111111} | 0 \rangle_L \tag{10.61}$$

The syndrome extraction operation for this code is illustrated in Figure 10.12.

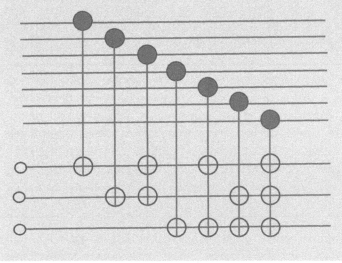

Figure 10.12 Syndrome extraction operation for [[7, 1, 3]] CSS code.

There exist QECCs more efficient than CSS codes. Good codes can be found by extending CSS codes, and by other methods. The $[[n, k, d]] = [[5, 1, 3]]$ perfect code encodes a single qubit ($k = 1$), and corrects all errors of weight 1. The stabilizer and generator are given by

$$H = \begin{pmatrix} 11000 & 00101 \\ 01100 & 10010 \\ 00110 & 01001 \\ 00011 & 10100 \end{pmatrix}, \quad G = \begin{pmatrix} H_x & H_z \\ 11111 & 00000 \\ 00000 & 11111 \end{pmatrix}. \tag{10.62}$$

One possible choice of the two codewords is

$$| 0 \rangle_L = | 00000 \rangle + | 11000 \rangle + | 01100 \rangle - | 10100 \rangle$$
$$+ | 00110 \rangle - | 11110 \rangle - | 01010 \rangle - | 10010 \rangle$$
$$+ | 00011 \rangle - | 11011 \rangle - | 01111 \rangle - | 10111 \rangle$$
$$- | 00101 \rangle - | 11101 \rangle - | 01001 \rangle + | 10001 \rangle$$

and

$$| 1 \rangle_L = X_{11111} | 0 \rangle_L.$$

The expression for $| 0 \rangle_L$ follows from combining the rows H. The combination $|00000\rangle + | 11000 \rangle$ is obviously unaffected by the operator $X_{11000} Z_{00101}$ (first row of H) since this operator converts each of the two product states into the other. We then add the state $|01100\rangle$ with the second row of H in mind, and its partner must be $- | 10100 \rangle$ so that the result is still an eigenstate of the first row of H. It is seen that the combination is then also an eigenstate of $X_{01100} Z_{10010}$ (second row of H). The rest follows similarly. The final two rows of G can be regarded as logical X and Z operators in the encoded subspace, and hence we obtain the expression for $| 1 \rangle_L$. (The choice is not unique: we could equally regard X_{11111} as logical Z and Z_{11111} as logical X, and then the expression for $| 1 \rangle_L$ would be $Z_{11111} | 0 \rangle_L$.)

To bring out the cyclic structure evident in the matrices, we can also write the state

$$| 0 \rangle_L = | 00000 \rangle$$
$$+ | 11000 \rangle + | 01100 \rangle + | 00110 \rangle + | 00011 \rangle + | 10001 \rangle$$
$$- | 10100 \rangle - | 01010 \rangle - | 00101 \rangle - | 10010 \rangle - | 01001 \rangle$$
$$- | 11110 \rangle - | 01111 \rangle - | 10111 \rangle - | 11011 \rangle - | 11101 \rangle.$$

By construction, the codewords are eigenstates of the stabilizer. It is also simple to check this by explicit calculation. To show that the code is a single-error correcting code, one can either [44] examine the syndrome for every error vector of weight ≤ 1, or confirm that G generates operators of minimum weight 3.

An example degenerate code is the 9-bit code discovered by Shor (this was in fact the first QECC to be discovered):

$$| 0 \rangle_L = (| 000 \rangle + | 111 \rangle)(| 000 \rangle + | 111 \rangle)(| 000 \rangle + | 111 \rangle),$$
$$| 1 \rangle_L = (| 000 \rangle - | 111 \rangle)(| 000 \rangle - | 111 \rangle)(| 000 \rangle - | 111 \rangle).$$

The stabilizer and generator are

$$
H = \begin{pmatrix}
111111000 & 000000000 \\
111000111 & 000000000 \\
000000000 & 110000000 \\
000000000 & 101000000 \\
000000000 & 000110000 \\
000000000 & 000101000 \\
000000000 & 000000110 \\
000000000 & 000000101
\end{pmatrix},
\tag{10.63}
$$

$$
G = \begin{pmatrix}
H_x & H_z \\
111111111 & 000000000 \\
000000000 & 111111111
\end{pmatrix}.
$$

The degeneracy of the code is evidenced by the fact that it corrects all single-qubit errors, even though some different single-qubit errors have the same syndrome (for example, a Z error on any of the first three bits). The correction still works because the product of any pair of such errors is in the stabilizer. The degenerate nature of the code is also seen by the fact that the minimum distance of $\mathcal{G}/\mathcal{H}$ is greater than the minimum distance of $\mathcal{G}$. The 7-bit and 9-bit codes are both CSS codes, whereas the 5-bit code is not. A method to enlarge many CSS codes, producing a higher-rate code that is not CSS, is described in [45].

Finally, a[[8, 3, 3]] code [38, 39, 46, 47] is given by Eq. (10.64). Each codeword can be written as a superposition of 16 states; further details are given by Gottesman [38] and Steane [46, 47]. This code is the first of an infinite set of quantum codes based on classical Reed–Muller codes [34, 47].

$$
H = \begin{pmatrix}
11111111 & 00000000 \\
00000000 & 11111111 \\
00001111 & 00110011 \\
00110011 & 01010101 \\
01010101 & 00111100
\end{pmatrix},
$$

$$
G = \begin{pmatrix}
11111111 & 00000000 \\
00001111 & 00000000 \\
00110011 & 00000000 \\
01010101 & 00000000 \\
00000000 & 11111111 \\
00000000 & 00001111 \\
00000000 & 00110011 \\
00000000 & 01010101 \\
00000011 & 00000101 \\
00000101 & 00010001 \\
00010001 & 00000110
\end{pmatrix}.
\tag{10.64}
$$

10.4.2.4 More on Coding and Syndrome Extractions

We will now examine some of the simplest codes in more detail, with the aim of making both the form of the codewords and the extraction of the syndrome physically intuitive.

Quasi-classical codes: Suppose first of all that the noise includes only error operators composed of tensor products of I and X, so $E_i = X_e$. This mimics the errors occurring in the binary vector spaces of classical EC. A suitable QECC in this situation is the set of codewords $\{|u \in C\rangle\}$, where C is a classical t-error correcting code, and we use the standard notation $|00101\rangle \equiv |0\rangle|0\rangle|1\rangle|0\rangle|1\rangle$. It is easy to see that the conditions defined by (Eq. (10.50) are satisfied for all error operators of weight $\leq t$, since $X_e|u\rangle = |u + e\rangle$, in which u, e, and $u + e$ are binary vectors.

Earlier we described the general method to extract syndromes as essentially a measurement of the members M of the stabilizer, using ancillary bits and controlled gates where the ancilla is the control bit. The same measurement can also be understood as a measurement of parity checks, with the ancillary bit acting as the target. This is the method of extracting the syndrome that was illustrated earlier. It can be generalized as follows. Suppose C is an $[n, k, d]$ linear code. We introduce an ancilla of $n - k$ qubits, prepared in $|0\rangle$. To evaluate each classical parity check, we perform a sequence of CNOT ($\equiv$xor) operations from qubits in q to a single qubit in a. The single qubit in a is the target, and the qubits in q that act as control bits are those specified by the 1's in the n-bit parity check vector. The $n - k$ parity checks specified by the classical parity check matrix H are thus evaluated on the $n - k$ qubits in a. The notation $XOR_{q,a}^{(H)}$ will be used for this unitary interaction between q and a; an example is shown in Figure 10.12.

The syndrome extraction operation is

$$\mathrm{xor}_{q,a}^{(H)}(|0\rangle_a |u + e\rangle) = |He^T\rangle_a |u + e\rangle \tag{10.65}$$

where we used Eq. (10.39). The fact that the classical syndrome is independent of the message is now highly significant, for if the initial state of q is any superposition $\sum_{u \in C} a_u |u\rangle$, the syndrome extraction does not leave q and a entangled:

$$\mathrm{xor}_{q,a}^{(H)} |0\rangle_a X_e \sum_{u \in C} a_u |u\rangle = |He^T\rangle_a \sum_{u \in C} a_u |u + e\rangle \tag{10.66}$$

Recovery is completed by measuring a, deducing e from He^T, and applying $X_e^{-1} = X_e$ to q.

Phase decoherence: The noise process just considered is quite unusual in practice. However, it is closely related to a common type of noise, namely phase decoherence. As we already discuss it in the chapter, this is the situation where the channel generates random rotations of the qubits about the z axis. Such a rotation is given by the operator

$$P(\varepsilon\varphi) = \begin{pmatrix} e^{i\varepsilon\varphi} & 0 \\ 0 & e^{-i\varepsilon\varphi} \end{pmatrix} \equiv \cos(\varepsilon\varphi)I + i\sin(\varepsilon\varphi)Z \tag{10.67}$$

where I is the identity, ε is a fixed quantity indicating the typical size of the rotations, and $-\pi < \varphi < \pi$ is a random angle. We may consider such an error as a combination of no error (I) and a phase flip error (Z). Therefore, phase decoherence takes the form Eq. (10.42) with error operators consisting of tensor products of I and Z, so $E_i = Z_e$.

The QECC for this case is now simple to find because $Z = RXR$, where R is the Hadamard or basis change operation:

$$R = \frac{1}{\sqrt{2}} \begin{pmatrix} 1 & 1 \\ 1 & -1 \end{pmatrix}. \tag{10.68}$$

The letter H is often used for this operator, but R is adopted here to avoid confusion with the parity check matrix. We will use $R = R_1R_2 \dots R_n$ to denote Hadamard rotation of all the n qubits in q. Apply R at the two ends of the channel. The combined effect of phase error and these Hadamard rotations on any given qubit is

$$RPR = \cos(\varepsilon\varphi)I + i\sin(\varepsilon\varphi)X \qquad (10.69)$$

Thus, we can convert a channel creating phase noise to one creating bit-flip noise.

In the formal analysis, the quantum codewords are $|c_u\rangle = R \mid u \in C\rangle$ where C is a classical error correcting code. An ancilla is prepared in the state $|0\rangle_a$, and the syndrome extraction operation is $\mathrm{Rxor}_{q,a}^{(H)}R$, where H is the parity check matrix of C. This can be considered as exactly the same code extraction as in the previous example, except that now all operations are carried out in the basis $\{R\mid 0\rangle, R\mid 1\rangle\}$ instead of $\{|0\rangle, |1\rangle\}$. An error acting on a codeword produces

$$Z_e(R \mid u\rangle) = RX_e \mid u\rangle = R \mid u + e\rangle. \qquad (10.70)$$

Now introduce the ancilla and perform syndrome extraction:

$$\begin{aligned}(\mathrm{Rxor}_{q,a}^{(H)}R) \mid 0\rangle_a R \mid u + e\rangle &= \mathrm{Rxor}_{q,a}^{(H)} \mid 0\rangle_a \mid u + e\rangle \\ &= \mid He^T\rangle_a R \mid u + e\rangle\end{aligned} \qquad (10.71)$$

where we use the fact that R does not operate on a. The error vector e is deduced from He^T, and the corrective operation Z_e is applied, returning q to $R\mid u\rangle$.

The simplest example of a phase error correcting code is a single-error correcting code using three qubits. The two quantum codewords are

$$R \mid 000\rangle = \mid 000\rangle + \mid 001\rangle + \mid 010\rangle + \mid 011\rangle + \mid 100\rangle + \mid 101\rangle + \mid 110\rangle + \mid 111\rangle,$$
$$R \mid 111\rangle = \mid 000\rangle - \mid 001\rangle - \mid 010\rangle + \mid 011\rangle - \mid 100\rangle + \mid 101\rangle + \mid 110\rangle - \mid 111\rangle.$$

where the normalization factor $1/\sqrt{8}$ has been omitted. An equivalent code is one using codewords $R(|000\rangle \pm \mid 111\rangle)$, which are slightly simpler (they are the sets of even and odd parity words).

Let us now find the fidelity for this three-bit code example. In the channel under discussion, instead of an X bit flip being applied randomly with probability p to each qubit, every qubit certainly experiences an error that is a combination of the identity and Z. An analysis as in Section A of Figure 10.11, modeling the measurements on the ancilla qubits as standard von Neumann projective measurements, gives exactly the same outcome as before, with the quantity p equal to the average of the squared coefficients of the terms in the quantum state that have single bit-flip errors (before correction). This average is over the random variable φ, and thus $p = \langle \sin^2\varepsilon\varphi \rangle \simeq (\pi\varepsilon)^2/3$ for $\varepsilon \ll 1$, where we have considered the worst case, in which the states being transmitted are taken to orthogonal states by the action of Z. The fidelity of the final corrected state is found to be $f \simeq 1 - 3p^2$ for small p. For further details, see [43].

Projective errors: It is well known that a set of particles where each is in an equal superposition of two states $(|0\rangle + \exp[i\varphi] |1\rangle)/\sqrt{2}$, with the relative phase φ of the two terms random, is indistinguishable from a statistical mixture, that is, a set of particles where each is randomly either in the state $|0\rangle$ or in $|1\rangle$. This follows immediately from the fact that these two cases have the same density matrix. With this in mind, it should not be surprising that another type of error that a quasi-classical code such as the three-bit code can correct is an error process that projects the qubit onto the $|0\rangle, |1\rangle$ basis. In other words, imagine that the channel acts as follows: for each qubit passing through, either no change occurs (probability $1 - 2p$) or a projection onto the $|0\rangle, |1\rangle$ basis occurs (probability

$2p$). The projection is $|0\rangle\langle 0| = (I + Z)/2$ and $|1\rangle\langle 1| = (I - Z)/2$. Such errors are identical to phase errors (Eq. (10.67)), except for the absence of the factor i before the Z term. However, this factor does not affect the argument, and once again the analysis in Eq. (10.41) applies (once we have used the Hadamard trick to convert phase errors to bit-flip errors) in the limit of small p. Note that we define p in terms of the effect of the noise on the state: it is not the probability that a projection occurs, but the probability that a Z error is produced in the state of any single qubit when quantum codewords are sent down the channel.

Another method of modeling projective errors is to consider that the projected qubit is first coupled to some other system, and then we ignore the state of the other system. Let another such system have, among its possible states, two states $|\alpha\rangle_e$ and $|\beta\rangle_e$ that are close to one another, $\langle\alpha|\beta\rangle = 1 - \varepsilon$. The error consists in the following coupling between qubit and extra system:

$$(a\,|\,0\rangle + b\,|\,1\rangle)\,|\,\alpha\rangle_e \rightarrow a\,|\,0\rangle\,|\,\alpha\rangle_e + b\,|\,1\rangle\,|\,\beta\rangle_e, \tag{10.72}$$

which is an entanglement between the qubit and the extra system. A useful insight is to express the entangled state in the following way:

$$a\,|\,0\rangle\,|\,\alpha\rangle_e + b\,|\,1\rangle\,|\,\beta\rangle_e \equiv [(a\,|\,0\rangle + b\,|\,1\rangle)\,|\,+\,\rangle_e + (a\,|\,0\rangle - b\,|\,1\rangle)\,|\,-\,\rangle_e]/\sqrt{2}$$

where $|\pm\rangle_e = (|\alpha\rangle_e \pm |\beta\rangle_e)/\sqrt{2}$. Hence, the error on the qubit is seen to be a combination of identity and Z, and is correctable as before. The probability that the Z error is produced is calculated by finding the weights of the different possibilities in Eq. (10.41) after tracing over the extra system. We thus obtain $p = (1 - \mathrm{Re}\,(\langle\alpha|\beta\rangle))^2/2 = \varepsilon^2/2$.

CSS Codes: We now turn to quite general types of noise, where the error operators include X, Y, and Z terms. The code construction and correction method discovered by Calderbank, Shor [42], and Steane [43, 48] works by separately correcting the X and Z errors contained in a general error operator

$E_s = X_x Z_z$. The key to the code construction is the "dual code theorem" [48]:

$$R \sum_{i \in C} |\,i\rangle = \sum_{i \in C^\perp} |\,i\rangle. \tag{10.73}$$

The normalization has been omitted from this expression in order to make apparent the significant features; normalization factors will be dropped hereafter since they do not affect the argument. Equation (10.73) implies that if we form a state by superposing all the members of a linear classical code, then the Hadamard-transformed state is a superposition of all the members of the dual code. We can correct both X and Z errors by using states like those in Eq. (10.73), as long as both C and $C^\perp$ have good EC abilities.

The codewords of a CSS code can be chosen as in Eq. (10.58). For brevity, we will consider $C_2 = C_1 = C$, with $C^\perp \subset C$; the generalization to $C_1 \neq C_2$ is straightforward. If $C = [n, k, d]$, then $C^\perp = [n, n - k, d^\perp]$. The number of linearly independent u that generate new states is therefore $k - (n - k) = 2k - n$. We can construct 2^{2k-n} orthonormal quantum codewords, which represents a Hilbert space large enough to store $2k - n$ qubits. We will show that the resulting code can correct all errors of weight less than $d/2$. The parameters of the quantum code are thus $[[n, 2k - n, d]]$.

To correct a CSS code obtained from a classical code $C = [n, k, d]$, $C^\perp \subset C$, we introduce two ancillas $a(x)$ and $a(z)$, each of $n - k$ qubits, prepared in the state $|0\rangle$. The syndrome extraction operation is

$$\left(\mathrm{Rxor}_{q,a(z)}^{(H)} R\right) \mathrm{xor}_{q,a(x)}^{(H)} \tag{10.74}$$

where H is the check matrix of C. The proof that this works correctly for all errors $M_s = X_x Z_z$ of weight less than $d/2$ is left as an exercise for the reader. It is straightforward through use of the relations $X_x Z_z = (-1)^{x \cdot z} Z_z X_z$; $\mathrm{xor}_{q,a}^{(H)} Z_z = Z_z \mathrm{xor}_{q,a}^{(H)}$; $RX_s = Z_s R$ and $R \sum_{i \in C^\perp} | i + u \rangle = \sum_{i \in C} (-1)^{i \cdot u} | i \rangle$, where the latter follows from Eq. (10.73).

The syndrome extraction operation is illustrated in Figure 10.12 for the 7-bit CSS code given in Eq. (10.60). For a general stabilizer code (not necessarily CSS), the syndrome extraction can always be carried out by a network of the form

$$\left(\mathrm{Rxor}_{q,a}^{(H_x)} R \right) \mathrm{xor}_{q,a}^{(H_z)} \tag{10.75}$$

where we use an $n - K$ bit ancilla prepared in $|0\rangle_a$. The relationship between this network and the one described after Eq. (10.48), based on the concept of measuring eigenvalues of operators in the stabilizer, is simply in the direction of the CNOT operations: we can always replace a CNOT from system to ancilla by a CNOT going in the other direction and surrounded by Hadamard rotations.

10.A Binary Fields and Discrete Vector Spaces

Classical EC is concerned with classical bits, not quantum states. The mathematical treatment is based on the fact that linear algebraic operations such as addition and multiplication can be consistently defined using finite rather than infinite sets of integers, by using modular arithmetic. The simplest case, of modulo 2 arithmetic, will cover almost everything in this article. The addition operation is defined by $0 + 0 = 0$, $0 + 1 = 1 + 0 = 1$, $1 + 1 = 0$. The set $\{0, 1\}$ is a group under this operation, since 0 is the identity element, both elements are their own inverse, and the operation is associative. The set $\{0, 1\}$ is also a group under multiplication, with identity element 1. Furthermore, we can also define division (except division by zero) and subtraction, and the commutative and distributive laws hold. These properties together define a *finite field*, also called a *Galois field*. Thus, the set $\{0, 1\}$ is referred to as the field GF(2), where addition and multiplication are as defined.

A string of n bits is considered to be a vector of n components; for example, 011 is the vector $(0, 1, 1)$. Vector addition is carried out by the standard method of adding components; for example, $(0, 1, 1) + (1, 0, 1) = (0 + 1, 1 + 0, 1 + 1) = (1, 1, 0)$. It is easy to see that this operation is equivalent to the exclusive-or operation $\oplus$ carried out bitwise between the binary strings: $011 \oplus 101 = 110$. Note that $u + u \equiv 0$ and $u - v = u + v$ (prove this by adding v to both sides).

We can define the inner product (or scalar product) by the standard rule of multiplying corresponding components, and summing the results: $(1, 1, 0, 1) \cdot (1, 0, 0, 1) = 1 + 0 + 0 + 1 = 0$. Note that all the arithmetic is done by the rules of the Galois field, so the final answer is only 0 or 1. The inner product is also called a *parity check* or *check sum* since it indicates whether the second vector satisfies the parity check specified by the first vector (or equivalently whether the first vector satisfies the parity check specified by the second). To satisfy a parity check u, a vector v must have an even number of 1's at the positions (coordinates) specified by the 1's in u. If u and v are row vectors, then $u \cdot v = u v^T$, where T is the transpose operation.

The number of nonzero components of a binary vector u is important in what follows, and is called the *weight* (or Hamming weight), written s wt(u). For example, wt(0001101) = 3. The number of places (coordinates) where two vectors differ is called the *Hamming distance* between the vectors; the distance between u and v is equal to wt($u + v$).

There are 2^n vectors of n components (stated in other language, there are 2^n n-bit words). This set of vectors forms a linear vector space, sometimes called the Hamming space. It is a discrete vector space since vector components are only equal to 0 or 1. The vectors point to the vertices of a square lattice in n dimensions. The space is spanned by any set of n linearly independent vectors. The most obvious set that spans the space is $\{1000\cdots00, 0100\cdots00, 0010\cdots00, \ldots ,0000\cdots01\}$.

There are subspaces within a Hamming space. A *linear* subspace C is any set of vectors that is closed under addition, that is, $u + v \in C \, \forall \, u, \, v \in C$. For example, the set 0000,0011,1100,1111 is a 2^2 linear subspace of the 2^4 Hamming space. A linear subspace containing 2^k vectors is spanned by k linearly independent vectors (for example, 0011 and 1100 in the case just given). Any linear subspace is thus completely specified by its *generator matrix G*, which is just the matrix whose k rows are any k vectors that span the space. We can always linearly combine rows to get an equivalent generator matrix, for example

$$G = \begin{pmatrix} 0011 \\ 1100 \end{pmatrix} = \begin{pmatrix} 0011 \\ 1111 \end{pmatrix} \tag{10.A.1}$$

The *minimum distance d* of a subspace is the smallest Hamming distance between any two members of the subspace. If the two closest vectors are u and v, then $d = \text{wt}(u + v)$. For the case of a linear space, $w = u + v$ is also a member of the space. From this we deduce that the minimum distance of a linear space is equal to the smallest weight of a nonzero member of the space. This fact is useful in calculating the value of d, since it is much easier to find the minimum weight than to evaluate all the distances in the space.

Now, if $u \cdot v = 0$ and $u \cdot w = 0$, then $u \cdot (v + w) = 0$. From this it follows that if all the rows of a generator satisfy the parity check u, then so do all the vectors in the subspace. Any given parity check u divides the Hamming space exactly in half, into those vectors that satisfy u and those that do not. Therefore, the 2^k vectors of a linear subspace in 2^n Hamming space can satisfy at most $n - k$ linearly independent parity checks. These parity checks together form the *parity check matrix H*, which is another way to define the linear subspace. H has n columns and $n - k$ rows. For any given subspace, the check and generator matrices are related by

$$HG^T = 0 \tag{10.A.2}$$

where G^T is the transpose of G, and 0 is the $(n - k) \times k$ zero matrix.

The simple EC method described in the chapter is based around the very simple binary vector space 000, 111. Its generator matrix is $G = (111)$, and the parity check matrix is

$$H = \begin{pmatrix} 110 \\ 101 \end{pmatrix} \tag{10.A.3}$$

A useful relationship enables us to derive each of H and G from the other. It is always possible to convert G to the form $G = (I_k, A)$, where I_k is the $k \times k$ identity matrix, and A is the rest of G (so A is $k \times n - k$). To perform the conversion, we can linearly combine rows of G, and if necessary swap columns of G. Once we have the right form for G, then H can be written down immediately, as $H = (A^T, I_{n-k})$.

The last concept that we will need in the sequel is that of the *dual*. The dual space $C^\perp$ is the set of all vectors u that have zero inner product with all vectors in C, $u \cdot v = 0 \, \forall \, v \in C$. It is simple to deduce that the parity check matrix of C is the generator matrix of $C^\perp$, and vice versa. If $H = G$, then $C = C^\perp$; such spaces are referred to as self-dual.

The notation (n, m, d) is a shorthand for a set of m n-bit vectors having minimum distance d. For linear vector spaces, the notation $[n, k, d]$ is used, where k is now the dimension of the vector space, so it contains 2^k vectors.

Let us conclude this Appendix with another example of a linear binary vector space that is important in this chapter. It is a $[7, 4, 3]$ space discovered by Hamming [1]. The generator matrix is

$$G = \begin{pmatrix} 1010101 \\ 0110011 \\ 0001111 \\ 1110000 \end{pmatrix}, \tag{10.A.4}$$

and so the 16 members of the space are

$$
\begin{array}{cccc}
0000000 & 1010101 & 0110011 & 1100110 \\
0001111 & 1011010 & 0111100 & 1101001 \\
1110000 & 0100101 & 1000011 & 0010110 \\
1111111 & 0101010 & 1001100 & 0011001
\end{array}
\tag{10.A.5}
$$

These have been written in the following order: first the zero vector, then the first row of G. Next add the second row of G to the two vectors thus far obtained, then add the third row to the four vectors previously obtained, and so on. We can see at a glance that the minimum distance is 3, since the minimum nonzero weight is 3. The parity check matrix is

$$H = \begin{pmatrix} 1010101 \\ 0110011 \\ 0001111 \end{pmatrix}. \tag{10.A.6}$$

It is simple to confirm that $HG^T = 0$. Note also that since H is made of up rows of G, this code contains its dual: $C^\perp \in C$.

10.B Some Noise Physics

Noise and decoherence is itself a complex subject. Here, we will simply introduce a few basic ideas in order to clarify what QEC can and cannot do. By "noise" we mean any unknown or unwanted change in the density matrix of our system.

The statement Eq. (10.42) about digitization of noise is equivalent to the statement that any interaction between a system of qubits and its environment has the form

$$H_I = \sum_i E_i \otimes H_i^e \tag{10.B.1}$$

where the operators H_i^e act on the environment. Under the action of this coupling, the density matrix of the system (after tracing over the environment) evolves from ρ_0 to $\sum_i a_i E_i \rho_0 E_i$. QEC returns all terms of this sum having correctable E_i to ρ_0. Therefore, the fidelity of the corrected state, compared to the noise-free state ρ_0, is determined by the sum of all coefficients a_i associated with uncorrectable errors.

For a mathematically thorough analysis of this problem, see [3, 37, 49]. The essential ideas are as follows. Noise is typically a continuous process affecting all qubits all the time. However, when we discuss QEC, we can always adopt the model in which the syndrome is extracted by a projective measurement. Any statement such as "the probability that error E_i occurs" is just a shorthand for "the probability that the syndrome extraction projects the state onto one that differs from the noise-free state by error operator E_i." We would like to calculate such probabilities.

To do so, it is useful to split Eq. (10.B.1) into a sum of terms having error operators of different weight:

$$H_I = \sum_{\text{wt}(E) = 1} E \otimes H_E^e + \sum_{\text{wt}(E) = 2} E \otimes H_E^e + \sum_{\text{wt}(E) = 3} E \otimes H_E^e + \dots. \tag{10.B.2}$$

There are $3n$ terms in the first sum, $3^2 n! / (2! (n - 2)!)$ terms in the second, and so on. The strength of the system-environment coupling is expressed by coupling constants that appear in the H_E^e operators. If only the weight 1 terms are present, we say that the environment acts independently on the qubits: it does not directly produce correlated errors across two or more qubits. In this case, errors of all weights will still appear in the density matrix of the noisy system, but the size of the terms corresponding to the errors of weight w will be $O(\varepsilon^{2w})$, where ε is a parameter giving the system-environment coupling strength.

Since QEC restores all terms in the density matrix whose errors are of weight $\leq t = (d - 1)/2$, the fidelity of the corrected state, in the uncorrelated noise model, can be estimated as one minus the probability $P(t + 1)$ for the noise to generate an error of weight $t + 1$. This is approximately

$$P(t + 1) \simeq \left(3^{t + 1} \binom{n}{t + 1} \varepsilon^{t + 1} \right)^2 \tag{10.B.3}$$

when all the single-qubit error amplitudes can add coherently (i.e., the qubits share a common environment), or

$$P(t + 1) \simeq 3^{t + 1} \binom{n}{t + 1} \varepsilon^{2(t + 1)} \tag{10.B.4}$$

when the errors add incoherently (i.e., either separate environments, or a common environment with couplings of randomly changing phase). The significance of Eqs. (10.B.3) and (10.B.4) is that they imply that QEC works extremely well when t is large and $\varepsilon^2 < t/3n$. Since good codes exist, t can tend to infinity while t/n and k/n remain fixed. Therefore, as long as the noise per qubit is below a threshold of around $t/3n$, almost perfect recovery of the state is possible. The ratio t/n constrains the rate of the code through the quantum Hamming bound or its cousins.

Such uncorrelated noise is a reasonable approximation in many physical situations, but we need to be careful about the degree of approximation, since we are concerned with very small terms of order ε^d. If we relax the approximation of completely uncorrelated noise, Eqs. (10.B.3) and (10.B.4) remain approximately unchanged, if and only if the coupling constants in Eq. (10.B.2) for errors of weight t are themselves of order $\varepsilon^t/t!$.

A very different case in which QEC is also highly successful is when a set of correlated errors, also called burst errors, dominate the system-environment coupling, but we can find a QEC whose stabilizer includes all these correlated errors. This is sometimes called "error avoiding" rather than "EC" since by using such a code, we do not even need to correct the logical state: it is already decoupled from the environment. The general lesson is that the more we know about the environment, and the more structure there exists in the system-environment coupling, the better able we are to find good codes.

The obvious approach to take in practice is a combined one, in which we first discover the correlated contributions to the noise in our system, and design a first layer of encoding accordingly, and then overlay a second layer optimized for minimum distance coding. Such ideas have been studied in classical coding theory, where sometimes many layers of encoding are combined, including tricks such as not placing adjacent physical bits in the same logical block when the code is not designed for burst errors.

The process of encoding one bit in several, and then encoding each of those bits, and so on, is referred to as code *concatenation*. When used recursively, we obtain a powerful code whose behavior is relatively simple to analyze. This is the structure that underlies the "threshold result," which states that arbitrarily long quantum computations can be made reliable by introducing more and more layers of concatenation, provided the level of noise per time step and per elementary operation on the physical hardware is below a finite threshold. In other words, we do not require a more and more precise and noiseless computer if we want to evolve longer and longer computations. However, we do need a bigger one.

References

1 Hamming, R.W. (1950). Error detecting and error correcting codes. *Bell Syst. Tech. J.* **29** (2): 147–160. https://doi.org/10.1002/j.1538-7305.1950.tb00463.x.

2 MacKay, D.J. (2003). *Information Theory, Inference and Learning Algorithms.* Cambridge University Press.

3 Knill, E. and Laflamme, R. (1997). Theory of quantum error-correcting codes. *Phys. Rev. A* **55** (2): 900–911.

4 Gottesman D. (1999) The Heisenberg representation of quantum computers. *Group22: Proceedings of the XXII International Colloquium on Group Theoretical Methods in Physics*, pp 32–43, Cambridge, MA, International Press.

5 Shor, P.W. (1995). Scheme for reducing decoherence in quantum computer memory. *Phys. Rev. A* **52**: R2493.

6 Gottesman D. An introduction to quantum error correction and fault-tolerant quantum computation. arXiv:09042557. 2009;.

7 Vaidman, L., Goldenberg, L., and Wiesner, S. (1996). Error prevention scheme with four particles. *Phys. Rev. A* **54** (3): R1745–R1748.

8 Grassl, M., Beth, T., and Pellizzari, T. (1997). Codes for the quantum erasure channel. *Phys. Rev. A* **56** (1): 33–38.

9 Gottesman DE. Stabilizer codes and quantum error correction [dissertation]; 1997. Available from: http://resolver.caltech.edu/CaltechETD:etd-07162004-113028.

10 Roffe, J., Headley, D., Chancellor, N. et al. (2018). Protecting quantum memories using coherent parity check codes. *Quantum Sci. Technol.* **3** (3): 035010.

11 Terhal, B.M. (2015). Quantum error correction for quantum memories. *Rev. Mod. Phys.* **87** (2): 307–346. Available from: https://doi.org/10.1103/revmodphys.87.307.

12 Calderbank, A.R. and Shor, P.W. (1996). Good quantum error-correcting codes exist. *Phys. Rev. A* **54**: 1098–1106.

13 Steane, A. (1996). Error correcting codes in quantum theory. *Phys. Rev. Lett.* **77**: 793–797.

14 Kovalev, A.A. and Pryadko, L.P. (2013). Quantum kronecker sum-product low-density paritycheck codes with finite rate. *Phys. Rev. A* **88** (1) Available from: https://doi.org/10.1103/physreva.88.012311.

15 Tillich, J.P. and Zemor, G. (2014). Quantum LDPC codes with positive rate and minimum distance proportional to the square root of the blocklength. *IEEE Trans. Inf. Theory* **60** (2): 1193.

16 Bravyi SB, Kitaev AY. Quantum codes on a lattice with boundary. https://arxiv.org/pdf/quant-ph/9811052.pdf. 1998;.

17 Freedman MH, Meyer DA. Projective plane and planar quantum codes; 1998 arXiv:quant-ph/9810055v1 18 Oct 1998.

18 Nickerson, N.H., Fitzsimons, J.F., and Benjamin, S.C. (2014). Freely scalable quantum technologies using cells of 5-to-50 qubits with very lossy and noisy photonic links. *Phys. Rev. X.* **4** (4): 041041.

19 Kelly, J., Barends, R., Fowler, A.G. et al. (2016). Scalablein situqubit calibration during repetitive error detection. *Phys. Rev. A* **94** (3).

20 Sete EA, Zeng WJ, Rigetti CT. A functional architecture for scalable quantum computing. In: 2016 IEEE International Conference on Rebooting Computing (ICRC). IEEE; 2016.

21 O'Gorman, J., Nickerson, N.H., Ross, P. et al. (2016). A silicon-based surface code quantum computer. *npj Quantum Inf.* **2** (1) Available from: https://doi.org/10.1038/npjqi.2015.19.

22 Takita, M., Cross, A.W., Córcoles, A. et al. (2017). Experimental demonstration of fault-tolerant state preparation with superconducting qubits. *Phys. Rev. Lett.* **119** (18).

23 Kitaev, A. (2003). Fault-tolerant quantum computation by anyons. *Ann. Phys. Rehabil. Med.* **303** (1): 2–30. Available from: https://doi.org/10.1016/s0003-4916(02)00018-0.

24 Horsman, C., Fowler, A., Devitt, S. et al. (2012). Surface code quantum computing by lattice surgery. *New J. Phys.* **14** (12): 123011.

25 Bravyi, S.B. and Kitaev, A.Y. (1998). Quantum codes on a lattice with boundary. quant-ph/9811052. *Transl. Quantum Computers Comput.* **2** (1): 43–48. (2001).

26 P. W. Shor, Fault-tolerant quantum computation, Proc. 35th Ann. Symp. on Foundations of Computer Science (IEEE Press, Los Alamitos, 1996), pp. 56–65; arXiv:quant-ph/9605011.

27 D. Aharonov and M. Ben-Or, Fault-tolerant quantum computation with constant error, Proc. 29th Ann. ACM Symp. on Theory of Computation (ACM, New York, 1998), 176–188; arXiv:quant-ph/9611025; D. Aharonov and M. Ben-Or, Fault-tolerant quantum computation with constant error rate, SIAM J. Comput. 38 (2008), 1207–1282; arXiv:quant-ph/9906129.

28 Kitaev, A.Y., gates, Q.e.c.w.i., and Communication, Q. (1997). *Computing, and Measurement (Proc. 3rd Int. Conf. Of Quantum Communication and Measurement)*, 181–188. New York: Plenum Press.

29 E. Knill, R. Laflamme, and W. H. Zurek, Threshold accuracy for quantum computation, arXiv:quant-ph/9610011; E. Knill, R. Laflamme, and W. H. Zurek, Resilient quantum computation, Science 279 (1998), 342–345; E. Knill, R. Laflamme, and W. H. Zurek, Resilient quantum computation: error models and thresholds, Proc. Royal Soc. London A 454 (1998), 365–384, arXiv:quant-ph/9702058

30 P. O. Boykin, T. Mor, M. Pulver, V. Roychowdhury, and F. Vatan, On Universal and FaultTolerant Quantum Computing, Proc. 40th Ann. Symp. on Found. of Comp. Sci. (IEEE, New York, 1999), 486–494; arXiv:quant-ph/9906054.

31 Aliferis, P., Gottesman, D., and Preskill, J. (2006). Quantum accuracy threshold for concatenated distance-3 codes. *Quant. Info. Comp.* **6**: 97–165; arXiv:quant-ph/0504218.

32 Gottesman, D. (1998). Theory of fault-tolerant quantum computation. *Phys. Rev. A* **57**: 127–137; arXiv: quant-ph/9702029.

33 Hamming, R.W. (1986. A Tutorial on Quantum Error Correction). *Coding and Information Theory*, 2e, 24. Englewood Cliffs: Prentice-Hall.

34 MacWilliams, F.J. and Sloane, N.J.A. (1977). *The Theory of Error Correcting Codes*. Amsterdam: Elsevier Science.

35 Jones, D.S. (1979). *Elementary Information Theory*. Oxford: Clarendon Press.

36 Hill, R. (1986). *A First Course in Coding Theory*. Oxford: Clarendon Press.

37 Nielsen, M.A. and Chuang, I.L. (2000). *Quantum Computation and Quantum Information*. Cambridge: Cambridge University Press.

38 Gottesman, D. (1996). Class of quantum error-correcting codes saturating the quantum Hamming bound. *Phys. Rev. A* **54**: 1862–1868.

39 Calderbank, A.R., Rains, E.M., Shor, P.W., and Sloane, N.J.A. (1997). Quantum error correction and orthogonal geometry. *Phys. Rev. Lett.* **78**: 405.

40 Calderbank, A.R., Rains, E.M., Shor, P.W., and Sloane, N.J.A. (1998). Quantum error correction via codes Over GF(4). *IEEE Trans. Inf. Theory* **44**: 1369–1387.

41 Bennett, C.H., DiVincenzo, D.P., Smolin, J.A., and Wootters, W.K. (1996). Mixed state entanglement and quantum error correction. *Phys. Rev. A* **54**: 3824.

42 Calderbank, A.R. and Shor, P.W. (1996). Good quantum error-correcting codes exist. *Phys. Rev. A* **54**: 1098–1105.

43 Steane, A.M. (1996). Multiple-particle interference and quantum error correction. *Proc. Roy. Soc. Lond. A* **452**: 2551–2577.

44 Laflamme, R., Miquel, C., Paz, J.P., and Zurek, W.H. (1996). Perfect quantum error correcting code. *Phys. Rev. Lett.* **77**: 198.

45 Steane, A.M. (1999). Enlargement of Calderbank Shor Steane quantum codes. *IEEE Trans. Inf. Theory* **45**: 2492–2495.

46 Steane, A.M. (1996). Simple quantum error-correcting codes. *Phys. Rev. A* **54**: 4741–4751.

47 Steane, A.M. (1999). Quantum Reed-Muller Codes. *IEEE Trans. Inf. Theory* **45**: 1701–1703; (quant-ph/9608026).

48 Steane, A.M. (1996). Error correcting codes in quantum theory. *Phys. Rev. Lett.* **77**: 793–767.

49 Knill E. and Laflamme R., (quant-ph/9608012).

50 J. Roffe, Quantum Error Correction: An Introductory Guide, https://arxiv.org/abs/1907.11157v1.

11

Quantum Search Algorithms

In this section, we first briefly review the general problems and the high-level operation of the major quantum algorithms, after which we describe some of them in more detail [1].

11.1 Quantum Search Algorithms

11.1.1 The Deutsch Algorithm [2]

The algorithm was published in 1985 and can be used to solve the black-box problem. The problem involves a function f whose operation is unknown. We have to determine the features of the function by evaluating it with only the aid of different input arguments and then observing its corresponding outputs. Here, we have to determine whether the binary function $f: \{0, 1\} \rightarrow \{0, 1\}$ does or does not have a one-to-one mapping. When the function f has a one-to-one mapping, we would expect $f(0) \oplus f(1) = 1$, otherwise it would be $f(0) \oplus f(1) = 0$, since that would mean $f(0) = f(1)$, where $\oplus$ is the modulo-2 addition. In classical computing, a single evaluation for each of the legitimate inputs would be required, bringing the total number of function evaluations to two. The Deutsch algorithm [2] succeeds in determining whether the function f has a one-to-one mapping by using only a single function evaluation. In Section 11.1, we will discuss the algorithm in greater detail.

11.1.2 The Deutsch–Jozsa Algorithm

An extension of the previous algorithm, referred to as the Deutsch–Jozsa algorithm [3], was formulated to determine whether a function $f: \{0, 1\}^n \rightarrow \{0, 1\}$ is balanced or constant. A function f is constant if it yields the same value at its output regardless of the input argument. On the other hand, a function f is balanced if it yields one value (e.g., 0) for half of the input arguments and another value (e.g., 1) for the other half of the input arguments. Let us consider the problem in a real scenario, where transmitter A and receiver B communicate with each other. A sends an n-bit number to B, who uses it as the input argument of his function f. B then transmits back the output bit. A has to determine whether the function that B used was balanced or constant. In classical computing, the best-case scenario would only be achieved if the function were balanced, A transmitted two different numbers, and these two numbers happened to yield the two different outputs. The worst-case scenario is always encountered when the function is constant, since Alice has to transmit $(2^{n-1} + 1)$ different input arguments (one more than half the set of inputs) before she realizes that the function

Artificial Intelligence and Quantum Computing for Advanced Wireless Networks, First Edition.
Savo G. Glisic and Beatriz Lorenzo.
© 2022 John Wiley & Sons Ltd. Published 2022 by John Wiley & Sons Ltd.

Bob is using is constant. By using the Deutsch–Jozsa algorithm, A is able to determine whether the function f used by B is balanced or constant, with just a single transmission of n qubits in an equiprobable superposition of all possible inputs. B uses an extra auxiliary qubit, Hadamard gates, and a quantum gate U_f that performs the same operation as f, but accepts qubits as its inputs. Finally, B measures the quantum state of the n qubits at the output of his quantum circuit. If the observed state is the all-zero state $|0\rangle^{\otimes n}$, the function f is constant, otherwise it is balanced.

The Deutsch–Jozsa algorithm solves the generalized black-box problem of the previous section. Indeed, if the function f allows only 0 or 1 as its legitimate inputs, determining whether the function has a one-to-one mapping or if it is balanced answers exactly the same question. The algorithm was later improved by Cleve et al. [4] for achieving a 100% probability of success. The Deutsch–Jozsa algorithm laid the foundations for the development of the so-called quantum oracle gates [5], which are quantum circuits implementing a generic function $f\colon \{0, 1\}^N \to \{0, 1\}^M$ that are capable of calculating all the pairs of possible inputs-outputs of f using a single call to f by exploiting quantum parallelism.

11.1.3 Simon's Algorithm

In 1994, Simon managed to solve a black-box problem by using on the order of $O(n)$ queries addressed to the black box, while the optimal classical algorithm has to use $\Omega(2^{n/2})$ queries for the same task [6]. The black box U_f implements a function $f\colon \{0, 1\}^n \to \{0, 1\}^n$ and has the property that $f(x) = f(y)$ if and only if $x = y$ or if $x \oplus y = s$, for some unknown $s \in \{0, 1\}^n$, where $x, y \in \{0, 1\}^n$. Simon's algorithm succeeds in finding the value s that satisfies the function's abovementioned property.

11.1.4 Shor's Algorithm

Shor has proposed a quantum algorithm [7, 8] for efficiently solving the problem of factoring a given integer N. The best classical algorithm is the general number field sieve (GNFS) [9]. Shor's algorithm requires an exponentially lower complexity than the GNFS, which is achieved by combining classical and quantum processing. It first reduces the factoring problem to the so-called order-finding problem addressed below using a classical algorithm. Initially, it randomly picks a number $a < N$. Let us assume that the greatest common divisor between a and N is equal to 1. (If the greatest common divisor between a and N was not equal to 1, then a would be a nontrivial factor of N and the algorithm ends, since N can be factored in a and N/a. Then we have the problem of factoring i and N/a, if they are not prime numbers, and so on.) Then a quantum circuit is employed for finding the period r of the function $f(x) = a^x mod\ N$.

(The period of a function $f(x)$ is the smallest positive integer r so that $f(x + r) = f(x)$ for all values of x.) If the estimated period r is even and $a^{r/2} = -1$ mod N is false, then $gcd(a^{r/2} + 1,\ N)$ and $gcd(a^{r/2} - 1,\ N)$ are two nontrivial factors of N and the algorithm ends. The order-finding quantum algorithm initially creates an equiprobable superposition of $C = 2^c$ states, using an appropriate number of c qubits, as shown in Figure 11.1.

Any number of qubits c that results in $C = 2^c$ states such that $N^2 \le C < 2 N^2$ would suffice. It then employs controlled-U_f operators, where each of the c qubits controls the operation of a quantum gate that performs the function $f(x)$ of (11.1) on $n = \log_2 N$ auxiliary qubits. One should remember that a controlled-U_f gate performs the U_f gate to the input target qubits only if the control qubits are in the state $|1\rangle$. When the control qubits are in the state $|0\rangle$, the identity operator is applied instead. All n auxiliary qubits should initially be in the quantum state $|1\rangle^{\otimes n}$. This part is the bottleneck of Shor's algorithm, since it requires the operation of multiple controlled-U_f gates and $n = \log_2$

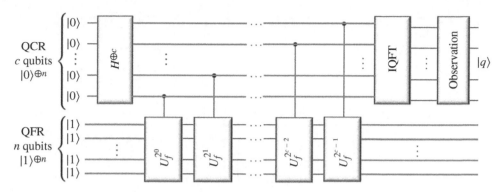

Figure 11.1 The quantum circuit employed in Shor's algorithm for finding the period of the function $f(x) = a^x \bmod N$. *Source:* Based on Shor [7].

N auxiliary qubits. Therefore, when N is high, more gates are required for a single U_f operation. At the same time, when C is high, the estimation of the period will be more accurate, but more controlled-U_f operations are required, hence increasing the complexity.

After the operation of the controlled-Uf gates in Figure 11.1, the c qubits pass through an inverse quantum Fourier transform (IQFT) (see Chapter 8) operator. The IQFT has the same effect as a classical inverse discrete Fourier transform (IDFT), where the amplitude of each of the superimposed states is equally spread over the amplitudes of the resultant superimposed state. At the output of the IQFT, if we measure the resultant state of the c-qubit register, we will obtain a value $|q\rangle$, which may then be classically processed to approximate the period r. As mentioned earlier, after finding the period i, classical processing is employed for the rest of Shor's algorithm.

11.1.5 Quantum Phase Estimation Algorithm

A few years after Shor's algorithm was introduced, the order-finding quantum algorithm of Figure 11.1 used in Shor's algorithm was found in [4] to be just a specific application of a general quantum circuit and algorithm, which is referred to as the quantum phase estimation algorithm (QPEA). The QPEA follows exactly the same procedure as the period-finding quantum algorithm. More specifically, given a unitary operator U that operates on n qubits and an eigenvector $|\varphi\rangle$, such that $U|\varphi\rangle = 2^{i\pi\theta}|\varphi\rangle$, the QPEA estimates the period θ, which means that it can find the eigenvalue of a unitary operator. The quantum circuit of the QPEA is given in Figure 11.2. The upper c qubits are referred to as the *quantum control register* (QCR), while the bottom n qubits represent the *quantum function register* (QFR).

The QPEA is used as a building block for multiple quantum algorithms. As an example, let us now revisit Shor's algorithm in order to relate it to the operation of the QPEA. In Shor's algorithm, the factoring problem was reduced to finding the period r of the function $f(x) = a^x \bmod N$. In order to solve this problem, we have $U = f(x)$ and $\theta = r$ in $U|\varphi\rangle = 2^{i\pi\theta}|\varphi\rangle$. Comparing the quantum circuits of Figure 11.1 and Figure 11.2, we observe that in the former, the n qubits of the function register are initialized to the all-one state $|1\rangle^{\otimes n}$, because it is one of the eigenvectors of $f(x) = a^x \bmod N$. Essentially, since we force a controlled function CU to operate on its eigenvectors, instead of altering the quantum states of the function register, we manage to rotate the states of the c-qubit control register. By applying the quantum Fourier transform (QFT) to that control register, we are able to estimate the phase, eigenvalue, or period of the unitary transform U, upon its measurement.

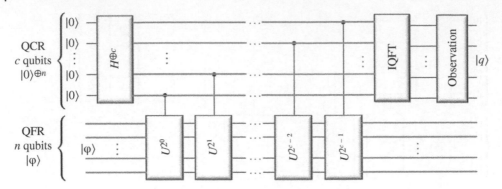

Figure 11.2 The quantum circuit of the quantum phase estimation algorithm, which estimates the eigenvalues of a unitary operator U, which corresponds to its eigenvector $|\varphi\rangle$, as $U|\varphi\rangle = 2^{i\pi\theta}|\varphi\rangle$. *Source:* Modified from Cleve et al. [4].

11.1.6 Grover's Quantum Search Algorithm

Network optimization problems are becoming more and more complex due to both the unprecedented increase in the scale of the networks and our ambition to optimize more and more sophisticated algorithms [45]. As a result, the size of the set of data that should be searched for finding optimal solutions is constantly increasing. Grover [10, 11] proposed a quantum search algorithm (QSA) that solves a specific search problem: find a desired value δ in a database of N entries. We aim to find which of the N entries is equal to δ; that is, we are interested in finding the position of δ in the database. If the database is sorted from the lowest to the highest values, the classical iterative halving-based search algorithm [12] is indeed optimal. On the other hand, if the database is unsorted, the optimal classical algorithm relies on a full search of the database. The average complexity of the full search would be on the order of O(N) database queries. The worst-case scenario occurs when the desired value is found at the entry that is checked last.

By contrast, Grover's QSA succeeds in finding the desired entry with 100% probability of success after querying the database on the order of $O(\sqrt{N})$ times [10]. This provides a quadratic reduction in complexity over the classical full search. Grover's QSA has been shown to be optimal by Zalka [13]. However, Grover's QSA requires some additional knowledge about the database. More explicitly, Grover's QSA employs the Grover operator $\mathcal{G}$ depicted in Figure 11.3 L_{opt} number of consecutive times. Apart from knowing N and (obviously) the desired value δ, Grover's QSA also requires knowledge of how many times the entry δ appears in the database, which is referred to as the number of solutions S. For example, when we have $\delta = 2$ and $N = 16$, if $S = 3$ entries out of $N = 16$ are equal to $\delta = 2$, a different number of iterations L_{opt} is used in Grover's QSA, compared to the scenario where only $S = 1$ out of $N = 16$ entries is equal to $\delta = 2$. However, in both examples, the same procedure is followed at each iteration. Using fewer or more Grover iterations than L_{opt} may reduce the success probability, which might even approach 0%. Grover's QSA relies on the generic amplitude amplification process of Brassard et al. [14]. Explicitly, the optimal number of Grover operator applications is $L_{opt} = \lfloor 0.25\pi\sqrt{(N/S)} \rfloor$.

In Figure 11.3, the $n = \log_2 N$ qubits in the register $|x\rangle_1$ are initialized to an equiprobable superposition of N states, each corresponding to the index of an entry in the database. The unitary operator O is referred to as the oracle (see Chapter 8), which marks the indices of the specific entries in the database that are equal to the sought value δ. Specifically, the oracle marks an index by changing its sign in the superposition of states. In order to achieve this, an auxiliary qubit $|\omega\rangle_1$ initialized

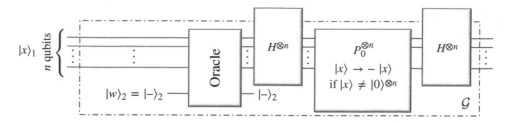

Figure 11.3 Grover operator's quantum circuit including an oracle, two n-qubit Hadamard gates H, and an n-qubit phase shift gate P_0. The HP_0H operator forms the diffusion operator of the Grover operator $\mathcal{G} = HP_0H \cdot O$. *Source:* Based on Grover [10].

to the $|-\rangle$ state is used, along with the value δ represented in form of a quantum state. The two Hadamard gates H and a phase rotation gate P_0 that follow the oracle in Figure 11.3 constitute the diffusion operator of Grover's circuit, which essentially changes the amplitude of each state by reflecting it with respect to the average amplitude of the current superposition of the states. This has been proved in [10] to result in an amplitude closer to $\sqrt{(1/S)}$ for each of the specific S states that correspond to the solution entries, while yielding a lower amplitude for the rest of the states that do not correspond to solutions. By repeating this process L_{opt} number of times, the amplitudes of the S quantum states in the superposition that correspond to solution entries gradually approach $\sqrt{(1/S)}$, resulting in an $S \cdot \left(\sqrt{(1/S)}\right)^2 = 100\%$ probability of observing a state that is indeed the solution state. The resultant amplitude of each solution state prior to measurement is equal to $\sqrt{(1/S)}$ because all solution states are treated in the same way in Grover's QSA and hence have the same probability $\left(\sqrt{(1/S)}\right)^2 = 1/S$ of being observed at the output.

Design Example 11.1

Let us assume that a database has a size of $N = 32$ entries and that the sought value δ is stored only in a single entry of the database, but we do not know in which portion exactly. Therefore, we have a single solution $S = 1$, leading us to apply the Grover operator $L_{opt} = \lfloor 0.25\pi\sqrt{(N/S)} \rfloor = 4$ times. As shown in Figure 11.4a, we commence with an equiprobable superposition of all indices, since we do not have a particular preference as to which index may be associated with the desired entry. After applying the oracle operator in Figure 11.4b, the sign of the amplitude of index 18 is flipped. In practice, we will not be aware of that, since we have not observed the quantum system yet. However, for the sake of clarity, we show the intermediate steps of Grover's QSA. The red dashed horizontal line in Figure 11.4 indicates the mean value of the amplitudes of all superimposed states after the application of the oracle. In Figure 11.4c, the diffusion operator reflects the amplitudes of each state with respect to the mean value of the amplitudes. This concludes the first iteration of Grover's QSA. We can see that, even at this stage, the index 18 has a higher probability of being observed than the rest of the superimposed states. However, we may increase the probability of observing the solution state 18 even further by applying three more Grover iterations. Following the same approach, Figures 11.4d and e characterize the second Grover iteration, Figures 11.4f and g the third Grover iteration, while Figures 11.4h

(Continued)

Design Example 11.1 (Continued)

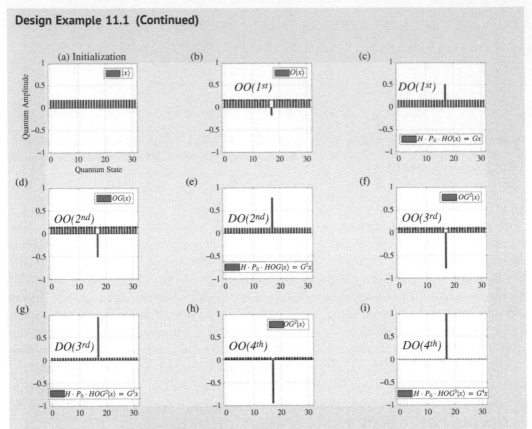

Figure 11.4 Example of Grover's QSA, OO-Oracle Operator, and DO-Diffusion Operator in the *i*-th iteration.

and i illustrate the fourth and final Grover iteration. In Figure 11.4i, the probability of observing the solution state 18 after the fourth Grover iteration is equal to 99.92%. Again, these intermediate steps of Grover's QSA are not readily accessible to us, and therefore we have to find another way of determining when to stop the iterations and observe the resultant state. For that, we have to know both the number of solutions in the database and the size of the database. If there are no solutions in a search problem corresponding to S = 0, the oracle in Figure 11.3 will not mark any quantum state, and hence the diffusion operator will leave the amplitudes of the quantum states unaltered, since the amplitude of each of the states found in an equiprobable superposition of states is equal to the average amplitude; and hence, a reflection with respect to the average amplitude will not affect the system. Therefore, regardless of the number of Grover iterations, the initial superposition will not change, and a potential measurement at the end will result in any of the N states with equal probability. We can then classically check that the observed index does not correspond to a solution in the database, and hence conclude that no solution exists for the search problem.

11.1.7 Boyer–Brassard–Høyer–Tapp QSA

Nevertheless, requiring a priori knowledge of the number of solutions that exist in the system may not always be viable in practical engineering problems. A beneficial extension of Grover's QSA has been introduced by Boyer et al. [15] in the form of the so-called Boyer–Brassard–Høyer–Tap

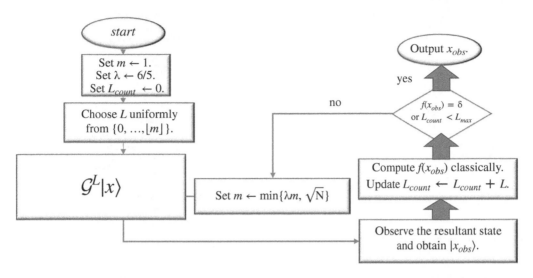

Figure 11.5 Flowchart of the Boyer–Brassard–Høyer–Tapp (BBHT) quantum search algorithm (QSA).

(BBHT) QSA, which is applicable in the specific scenario where the actual number S of valid solutions is unknown, while imposing the same order of complexity as Grover's QSA, namely, $O(\sqrt{N})$ in a database having N entries. The BBHT QSA solves the same problem as Grover's QSA, while assuming less knowledge about the database. Therefore, it may be employed in a larger number of engineering problems, where no information is available about the entries of the database. Since the number of solutions S is unknown, we are unable to find the optimal number of Grover iterations L_{opt} that we should apply to the initial equiprobable superposition of states in Figure 11.3. Hence, it employs classical processing and a "trial-and-error" approach for finding L_{opt}, proved to eventually lead to a 100% probability of success in [15]. The flowchart of the BBHT QSA is depicted in Figure 11.5, where $\lambda = 6/5$ is a constant that should be chosen to be in the range [6/5, 4/3] [15]. If the BBHT QSA is not terminated after $4.5\sqrt{N}$ applications of Grover's operator, we may conclude that no solution exists for this search problem.

11.1.8 Dürr–Høyer QSA

A QSA that solves a different search problem was conceived by Dürr and Høyer [16]. More specifically, the Dürr–Høyer (DH) QSA is employed for identifying the extreme values of an unsorted database having N entries, while imposing a low complexity that is on the order of $O(\sqrt{N})$. In this problem, either the minimum or the maximum entry of a database is sought, without knowing the specific value of that minimum or maximum entry. Therefore, the sought value δ is unknown. Let us describe the problem when the minimum entry of the database is desired, without any loss of generality, as described in the flowchart of Figure 11.6. The DH QSA starts by randomly picking one of the N entries in the database. Let us assume that the randomly selected entry has a value δ_i and an index i. It then invokes the BBHT QSA for finding any entry that has a lower value than the randomly picked one. Since there is no knowledge about the database, it is not possible to know how many entries have a value lower than δ_i, and therefore only the BBHT QSA can be used. If we somehow were aware of the number of entries that have a value lower than δ_i, then Grover's QSA could also be used. Once an entry with a lower value than δ_i is found, corresponding to the index x_s and hence $f(x_s) < \delta_i$, we update the value δ_i with the newly found entry's value $\delta_i = f(x_s)$. Then another

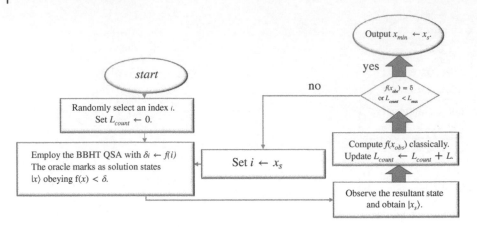

Figure 11.6 Flowchart of the Dürr–Høyer (DH) quantum search algorithm (QSA).

BBHT QSA iteration is employed for finding an entry that has a lower value than the updated δ_i. This process is repeated until no better value is found.

Since the DH QSA uses the BBHT QSA, its minimum complexity is equal to $4.5\sqrt{N}$ Grover iterations, referring to the case where the initially selected entry δ_i was indeed the minimum entry in the database. That would result in the BBHT QSA not being able to find an entry with a lower value, causing it to terminate after $4.5\sqrt{N}$ applications of Grover's operator. The maximum number of Grover iterations required for finding the minimum of the database was proved by Dürr and Høyer to be equal to $22.5\sqrt{N}$ Grover iterations [16]. In [17], it was shown that if the initial entry is carefully chosen instead of being randomly chosen, the average complexity of the DH QSA is further reduced. At the same time, if offline statistics are available about the database of the specific engineering problem, a one-to-one relationship between the number of Grover iterations used and the success probability may be found [17].

11.1.9 Quantum Counting Algorithm

Brassard et al. proposed the quantum counting algorithm (QCA) [14], by combining Grover's QSA [10] and the QPEA [4]. The problem that is solved by using the QCA is the search for the number of solutions S in a search problem. Given a database having N entries, we are interested in finding how many times a known value δ appears in the database, without aiming to find its position in the database. In order to achieve this, the controlled-U_f gates of Figure 11.2 are replaced by controlled-Grover operators. Explicitly, the Grover operators of Figure 11.3, are used in the quantum circuit of Figure 11.7. Furthermore, the function register consists of $n = \log_2 N$ qubits initialized in an equiprobable superposition of $2^n = N$ states. The eigenvector of Grover's QSA consists of a superposition of the specific states that do correspond to solutions in the database and a superposition of the states that do not correspond to solutions in the database. By creating an equiprobable superposition of all states at the beginning of the circuit, we essentially feed the controlled-Grover operators with their eigenvector. Therefore, an application of Grover's operator to such a superimposed state will result in a rotation of their amplitudes [14]. The rotation angle depends on the ratio between the number of solutions S and the size of the database N. Therefore, by applying the QPEA using Grover's QSA, the QCA obtains the number of solutions S upon observing the control register at the output of the QFT seen in Figure 11.7, followed by classical processing.

Figure 11.7 Quantum circuit of the quantum counting algorithm (QCA). *Source:* Based on Brassard et al. [18].

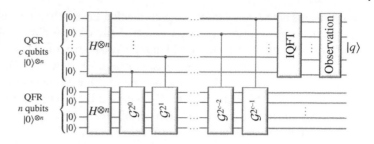

The QCA's accuracy depends on the number of qubits in the control register c. Its complexity depends on both the number of qubits in the control register c and in the function register n. In other words, the complexity to be invested depends on the required accuracy in terms of the number of solutions, as well as on the size of the database. Again, the optimal classical algorithm is the full search, since all entries in the unsorted database have to be checked in order to count the number of solutions. This results in a complexity on the order of $O(N)$ for the full search. The QCA achieves a quadratic speedup compared to the full search, with the specific complexity required depending on both the estimation error margin and on the size of the database [14].

11.1.10 Quantum Heuristic Algorithm

Hogg has proposed a quantum heuristic algorithm (QHA) [19, 20] that relies on Grover's QSA's circuit. The aim of the QHA is to solve the particular optimization problem of finding either the minimum or the maximum of a database by requiring fewer cost function evaluations (CFEs) than the DH QSA, when the database has some form of correlation. To be more specific, Grover's QSA, the BBHT QSA, and the DH QSA are optimal when they perform search in an unsorted database. When the entries of a database are inherently correlated to each other, heuristic algorithms may succeed in solving the optimization problem while requiring fewer queries to the database. In order to achieve this, Hogg changed both the oracle and the diffusion operator used in Grover's QSA. Recall that in Grover's QSA, where δ is known, the oracle marks the quantum states that correspond to solutions by flipping the sign of their amplitudes. This may be interpreted as a rotation by π for the amplitudes of the solution states and no rotation for the rest of the states. Since in the optimization problem the minimum value δ is unknown, Hogg conceived a different oracle, where the rotation angle of the amplitudes of each state depends on the value of the entry it corresponds to. The QHA has been demonstrated to outperform Hogg QSA [19], but it needs fine-tuning for each specific system and scenario, since the exact rotation angles applied by the oracle and the diffusion operator have to be appropriately chosen. This is reminiscent of the employment of classical heuristic algorithms, like the genetic algorithm (GA) [21, 22, 46], where the algorithm's parameters have to be carefully selected for a heuristic algorithm to converge to the solution.

11.1.11 Quantum GA

In order to solve the same optimization problem of finding either the minimum or maximum of a database, Malossini et al. proposed the quantum genetic algorithm (QGA) [23], which is an amalgam of the classical GA [21, 22] and the DH QSA. Please note that as with the QHA, the QGA may be employed in particular problems where there is correlation between the entries of the database. More specifically, in the classical GA, a population of P agents or chromosomes is generated where each agent represents an index of the database. The database is then queried P times, once for each of the agents of the population. After combining the two best agents found thus far, the next generation of the population is created based on them, with the aim of having agents representing even smaller values. By "best agents found thus far" we refer to the agents that correspond to the smallest entries in the database in that population. Eventually, after a sufficiently high number of generations, an agent corresponding to the minimum value of the database is found. Since it cannot be mathematically predicted when the GA will find the minimum of the database, the algorithm is terminated after a predetermined number of generations.

In the QGA, the same procedure is followed as in the GA – with one difference. The DH QSA is invoked for searching through the population of each generation for finding the best agents. In other words, the DHA QSA in the QGA is employed for reducing the complexity imposed by the GA while querying the database during each generation. Since only the two best agents have to be found in order to create the subsequent generation's population, the DH QSA may be employed twice. The QGA was demonstrated to outperform the GA for the same complexity, or to require a lower complexity for the same success probability.

11.1.12 Harrow–Hassidim–Lloyd Algorithm

The Harrow–Hassidim–Lloyd (HHL) algorithm [24] is a quantum algorithm that relies on the QPEA and solves linear systems of equations at an exponential reduction of the computational complexity required. The problem of solving a linear system of equations may be formulated as follows. Given an $(N \times N)$-element matrix A and an $(N \times 1)$-element vector b, find an $(N \times 1)$-element vector x, so that we have $A \cdot x = b$.

For the HHL algorithm to be practically applicable, the goal of the problem should be a bit different from the aforementioned one. The linear system of equations has to exhibit a few specific features. First, the output is a superposition of N states $|x\rangle$, where the values of the solution vector are encoded in the amplitudes of that superposition of states. Therefore, it cannot provide all values of the solution vector x for further classical processing. Alternatively, it may result in specific properties for the solution vector, for example, for its moments. Moreover, both the solution vector x' and the vector b' should be unit vectors. Furthermore, the matrix A should be sparse.

The HHL algorithm estimates the eigenvalues of the matrix A, using an appropriately modified version of the QPEA. The QPEA circuit is employed as a subroutine of an amplitude amplification procedure in the HHL algorithm, in order to further reduce its complexity of obtaining the solution quantum state $|x\rangle$. The HHL algorithm's complexity was further reduced by Ambainis in [25], while the precision of the estimated solution was exponentially increased by Childs et al. in [26].

11.1.13 Quantum Mean Algorithm

Brassard et al. [27] proposed the quantum mean algorithm (QMA), which finds the mean value $a = \sum_{x=0}^{N} f(x)/N$ of a function f requiring an exponentially reduced number of evaluations of the function than the optimal classical algorithm, since the latter would require access to all legitimate evaluations of the function. In order to achieve this, a modified QPEA is used, where the controlled-U_f operation evaluates the output of the function f to its inputs, as illustrated in Figure 11.8. One of the main differences between the QMA and the QPEA is that even though there are N legitimate inputs for the function f, $\log_2(N) + 1 = n + 1$ qubits are employed in the function register, instead of $n = \log_2(N)$, which would have been the case in the QPEA. The abovementioned extra qubit is required because the function register is initialized using a unitary operator A, which

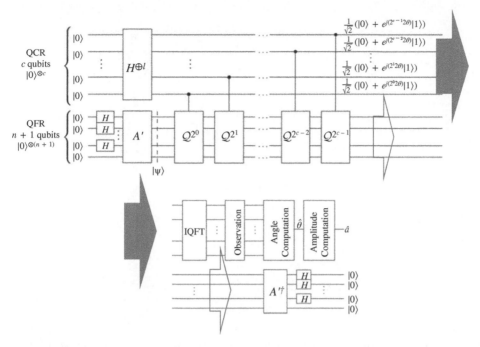

Figure 11.8 Quantum circuit of the quantum mean algorithm (QMA). *Source:* Botsinis et al. [28].

relies on the function f, and it performs controlled rotations on the extra qubit [27, 28]. At the output of the unitary operator A, there is a superposition of states $|\Psi\rangle$. Each state of Ψ was used for evaluating U_f in the unitary operator A. Based on the U_f and the controlled rotations imposed on the auxiliary qubit, the amplitudes of half of the states in $|\Psi\rangle$ are equal to their respective function's output. In fact, this is true for the specific states, for which the auxiliary qubit is equal to $|1\rangle$. The size of the control register determines the precision of the estimated mean value, as in the QPEA. The unitary operator Q may be considered as a generalized Grover operator, since it is constructed in a similar way as the generalized Grover operators in [29], by replacing the Hadamard operators H with the unitary operators A, as well as the oracle O by B and leaving the controlled phase shift operator P0 unaltered.

11.1.14 Quantum Weighted Sum Algorithm

The Quantum weighted sum algorithm (QWSA) [28] is based on the QMA and finds the weighted sum of the values of a function f with N inputs, again requiring $O(\sqrt{N})$ evaluations of the function f. The difference between the QWSA and the QMA is the initialization of the function register, as seen in Figure 11.9.

Instead of initializing it in an equiprobable superposition of states, the inputs of the function f are initialized in a superposition of states, where each state's amplitude is the weight of the desired weighted sum. Therefore, the QWSA may be considered as a generalization of the QMA, since in the latter all weights are the same and equal to $1/N$ in an N-element database, resulting in the use of Hadamard gates instead of general unitary rotation gates, as shown in Figure 11.8.

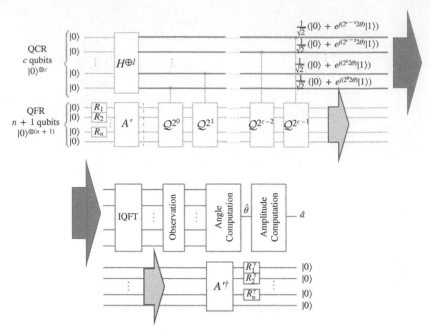

Figure 11.9 Quantum circuit of the quantum weighted sum algorithm (QWSA). *Source:* Botsinis et al. [28].

11.2 Physics of Quantum Algorithms

In this section, we provide more physical insights into some of the algorithms described in the previous section. Quantum computation is based on quantum interference, which is a *dynamical process* that allows one to evolve initial quantum states (inputs) into final states (outputs) by modifying intermediate multi-particle superpositions in some prescribed way. Multi-particle quantum interference, unlike single particle interference, does not have any classical analogue and can be viewed as an inherently quantum process.

We may think of quantum computations as multi-particle processes (just as classical computations are processes involving several "particles" or bits). It turns out that viewing quantum computation as multi-particle interferometry leads to a simple and unifying picture of the known quantum algorithms. In this language, quantum computers are basically multi-particle interferometers with phase shifts that result from operations of some quantum logic gates. To illustrate this point, consider, for example, an interferometer (Figure 11.10a).

A particle, say a photon, impinges on a half-silvered mirror, and, with some probability amplitudes, propagates via two different paths to another half-silvered mirror that directs the particle to one of the two detectors. Along each path between the two half-silvered mirrors, is a phase shifter. If the lower path is labeled as state $|0\rangle$ and the upper one as state $|1\rangle$, then the state of the particle between the half-silvered mirrors and after passing through the phase shifters is a superposition of the type $(|0\rangle + e^{i(\varphi_1 - \varphi_0)}|1\rangle)/\sqrt{2}$, where φ_0 and φ_1 are the settings of the two phase shifters. The phase shifters in the two paths can be tuned to effect any prescribed relative phase shift $\phi = \varphi_1 - \varphi_0$ and to direct the particle with probabilities $(1 + \cos\phi)/2$ and $(1 - \cos\phi)/2$, respectively, to detectors "0" and "1." The second half-silvered mirror effectively erases all information about

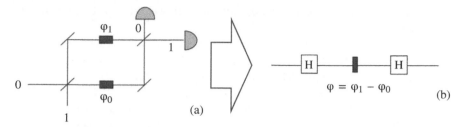

Figure 11.10 Interferometer with two phase shifters. *Source:* Cleve et al. [4].

the path taken by the particle (path $|0\rangle$ or path $|1\rangle$), which is essential for observing quantum interference in the experiment.

Let us now rephrase the experiment in terms of quantum logic gates. We identify the half-silvered mirrors with the single qubit *Hadamard transform* (*H*), defined as $|0\rangle \rightarrow^H (|0\rangle + |1\rangle)/\sqrt{2}$; $|1\rangle \rightarrow^H (|0\rangle - |1\rangle)/\sqrt{2}$. We view the phase shifter as a single qubit gate. The resulting network corresponding to the interferometer from Figure 11.10a is shown in Figure 11.10b. The phase shift can be "computed" with the help of an auxiliary qubit (or a set of qubits) in a prescribed state $|u\rangle$ and some controlled-*U* transformation

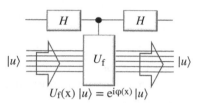

Figure 11.11 Network representation for the phase shift transformation of Eq. (11.1). Here x is a label for the state of the first qubit. *Source:* Cleve et al. [4].

where $U|u\rangle = e^{i\varphi}|u\rangle$ (Figure 11.11). As already discussed earlier in Chapter 8, the controlled-*U* means that the form of *U* depends on the logical value of the control qubit; for example, we can apply the identity transformation to the auxiliary qubits (i.e., do nothing) when the control qubit is in state $|0\rangle$ and apply a prescribed *U* when the control qubit is in state $|1\rangle$. The controlled-*U* operation must be followed by a transformation that brings all the computational paths together, like the second half-silvered mirror in the interferometer. This last step is essential to enable the interference of different computational paths to occur – for example, by applying a Hadamard transform. In our example, we can obtain the following sequence of transformations on the two qubits

$$|0\rangle|u\rangle \rightarrow^H \frac{1}{\sqrt{2}}(|0\rangle + |1\rangle)|u\rangle \rightarrow^{C-U} \frac{1}{\sqrt{2}}(|0\rangle + e^{i\phi}|1\rangle)|u\rangle$$
$$\rightarrow^H \left(\cos\frac{\phi}{2}|0\rangle - i\sin\frac{\phi}{2}|1\rangle\right)e^{i\frac{\phi}{2}}|u\rangle. \tag{11.1}$$

We note that the state of the auxiliary register $|u\rangle$, being an eigenstate of *U*, is not altered along this network, but its eigenvalue $e^{i\varphi}$ is "kicked back" in front of the $|1\rangle$ component in the first qubit. The sequence Eq. (11.1) is the exact simulation of the interferometer (Figure 11.10) and, as we will illustrate in the following sections, the kernel of quantum algorithms.

11.2.1 Implementation of Deutsch's Algorithm

Since quantum phases in the interferometers can be introduced by some controlled-*U* operations, it is natural to ask whether influencing these operations can be described as an interesting computational problem. In this section, we illustrate how interference patterns lead to computational problems that are well suited to quantum computations, by presenting the first such problem that was proposed by David Deutsch.

To begin with, suppose that the phase shifter in the interferometer example is set either to $\varphi = 0$ or to $\varphi = \pi$. Can we tell the difference? Of course we can. In fact, a single instance of the experiment determines the difference: for $\varphi = 0$, the particle *always* ends up in detector "0," and for $\varphi = \pi$, it *always* ends up in detector "1." Deutsch's problem is related to this effect.

Consider the Boolean functions f that map $\{0, 1\}$ to $\{0, 1\}$. There are exactly four such functions: two constant functions ($f(0) = f(1) = 0$ and $f(0) = f(1) = 1$) and two "balanced" functions ($f(0) = 0$, $f(1) = 1$ and $(0) = 1, f(1) = 0$). Informally, in Deutsch's problem, one is allowed to evaluate the function f *only once* and required to deduce from the result whether f is constant or balanced (in other words, whether the binary numbers $f(0)$ and $f(1)$ are the same or different).

Note that we are not asked for the particular values $f(0)$ and $f(1)$ but for a global property of f. Classical intuition tells us that to determine this global property of f, we have to evaluate both $f(0)$ and $f(1)$ anyway, which involves evaluating f twice. We shall see that this is not so in the setting of quantum information, where we can solve Deutsch's problem with a single function evaluation, by employing an algorithm that has the same mathematical structure as the example interferometer.

Let us formally define the operation of "evaluating" f in terms of the f *controlled NOT (CNOT)* operation on two bits: the first contains the input value, and the second contains the output value. If the second bit is initialized to 0, the f-CNOT maps $(x, 0)$ to $(x, f(x))$. This is clearly just a formalization of the operation of computing f. In order to make the operation reversible, the mapping is defined for *all* initial settings of the two bits, taking (x, y) to $(x, y \oplus f(x))$. Note that this operation is similar to the CNOT (see Chapter 8), except that the second bit is negated when $f(x) = 1$, rather than when $x = 1$.

If one is allowed to perform the classical f-CNOT operation only once, on any input from $\{0, 1\}^2$, then it is *impossible* to distinguish between balanced and constant functions in the following sense. Whatever the outcome, both possibilities (balanced and constant) remain for f. However, if quantum mechanical superpositions are allowed, then a single evaluation of the f-CNOT suffices to classify f. Our quantum algorithm that accomplishes this is best represented as the quantum network shown in Figure 11.12b, where the middle operation is the f-CNOT, whose semantics in quantum mechanical notation are $|x\rangle|y\rangle \xrightarrow{f-c-N} |x\rangle|y \oplus f(x)\rangle$.

The initial state of the qubits in the quantum network is $|0\rangle(|0\rangle - |1\rangle)$ (apart from a normalization factor, which will be omitted in the following). After the first Hadamard transform, the state of the two qubits has the form $(|0\rangle + |1\rangle)(|0\rangle - |1\rangle)$. To determine the effect of the f-CNOT on this state, first note that, for each $x \in \{0, 1\}$, $|x\rangle(|0\rangle - |1\rangle) \xrightarrow{f-c-N} |x\rangle(|0 \oplus f(x)\rangle - |1 \oplus f(x)\rangle) = (-1)^{f(x)} |x\rangle$ $(|0\rangle - |1\rangle)$. Therefore, the state after the f-CNOT is $((-1)^{f(0)} |0\rangle + (-1)^{f(1)} |1\rangle)(|0\rangle - |1\rangle)$.

That is, for each x, the $|x\rangle$ term acquires a phase factor of $(-1)^{f(x)}$, which corresponds to the eigenvalue of the state of the auxiliary qubit under the action of the operator that sends $|y\rangle$ to $|y \oplus f(x)\rangle$. This state can also be written as $(-1)^{f(0)}(|0\rangle + (-1)^{f(0) \oplus f(1)} |1\rangle)$, which, after applying the second Hadamard transform, becomes $(-1)^{f(0)} |f(0) \oplus f(1)\rangle$.

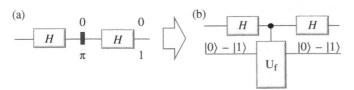

(a) ... (b) ...

Figure 11.12 Network representation of Deutsch's algorithm. *Source:* Cleve et al. [4].

Therefore, the first qubit is finally in state $|0\rangle$ if the function f is constant and in state $|1\rangle$ if the function is balanced, and a measurement of this qubit distinguishes these cases with certainty.

This algorithm is an improved version of the first quantum algorithm for this problem proposed by Deutsch [2], which accomplishes the following. There are three possible outcomes: "balanced," "constant," and "inconclusive." For any f, the algorithm has the property that: with probability 0.5, it outputs "balanced" or "constant" (correctly corresponding to f); and, with probability 0.5, it outputs "inconclusive" (in which case no information is determined about f). This is a task that no classical computation can accomplish (with a single evaluation of the f-CNOT gate). In comparison, our algorithm can be described as *always* producing the output "balanced" or "constant" (correctly).

11.2.2 Implementation of Deutsch–Jozsa Algorithm

As already discussed in the previous section, Deutsch's original problem was subsequently generalized by Deutsch and Jozsa [3] for Boolean functions $f: \{0, 1\}^n \to \{0, 1\}$ in the following way. Assume that, for one of these functions, it is "promised" that it is either constant or balanced (i.e., has an equal number of 0 and 1 outputs), and consider the goal of determining which of the two properties the function actually has.

How many evaluations of f are required to do this? Any classical algorithm for this problem would, in the worst case, require $2^{n-1} + 1$ evaluations of f before determining the answer with certainty. There is a quantum algorithm that solves this problem with a single evaluation of f. It is presented in Figure 11.13, where the control register is now composed of n qubits, all initially in state $|0\rangle$, denoted as $|00\cdots0\rangle$, and, as in the quantum algorithm for Deutsch's simple problem, an auxiliary qubit is employed, which is initially set to state $|0\rangle - |1\rangle$ and is not altered during the computation. Also, the n-qubit Hadamard transform H is defined as $|x\rangle \xrightarrow{H} \sum_{y\in\{0,1\}^n} (-1)^{x\cdot y} |y\rangle$ for all $x \in \{0, 1\}^n$, where $x \cdot y = (x_1 \wedge y_1) \oplus \cdots \oplus (x_n \wedge y_n)$ (i.e., the scalar product modulo two).

This is equivalent to performing a one-qubit Hadamard transform on each of the n qubits individually. The actual computation of the function f is by means of an f-CNOT gate (the middle gate in Figure 11.13), which acts as $|x\rangle |y\rangle \xrightarrow{f-c-N} |x\rangle |y \oplus f(x)\rangle$. This is similar to the relation we had in the previous session, except that now $x \in \{0, 1\}^n$.

Stepping through the execution of the network, the state after the first n-qubit Hadamard transform is applied is

$$\sum_{x\in\{0,1\}^n} |x\rangle(|0\rangle - |1\rangle), \tag{11.2}$$

which, after the f-CNOT gate, is

Figure 11.13 Network representation of Deutsch–Jozsa and Bernstein–Vazirani algorithms. *Source:* Cleve et al. [4].

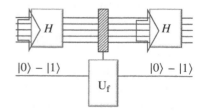

$$\sum_{x\in\{0,1\}^n}(-1)^{f(x)}|x\rangle(|0\rangle - |1\rangle).\tag{11.3}$$

Finally, after the last Hadamard transform, the state is

$$\sum_{x,y\in\{0,1\}^n}(-1)^{f(x)\oplus(x\cdot y)}|y\rangle(|0\rangle - |1\rangle).\tag{11.4}$$

Note that the amplitude of $|00\cdots0\rangle$ is $\sum_{x\in\{0,1\}^n}(-1)^{f(x)}/2^n$; so if f is constant, then this state is $(-1)^{f(00...0)}|00\cdots0\rangle(|0\rangle - |1\rangle)$; whereas, if f is balanced, then for the state of the first n qubits, the amplitude of $|00\cdots0\rangle$ is zero. Therefore, by measuring the first n qubits, it can be determined with certainty whether f is constant or balanced. Note that, as in Deutsch's simple example, this entails a single f-CNOT operation. (This is a slight improvement of Deutsch and Jozsa's original algorithm, which involves two f-CNOT operations.)

11.2.3 Bernstein and Vazirani's Implementation

They formulated a variation of the above problem that can be solved with the same network. Suppose that: $\{0,1\}^n \to \{0,1\}$ is of the form

$$f(x) = (a_1 \wedge x_1)\oplus\cdots\oplus(a_n \wedge x_n)\oplus b = (a \cdot x)\oplus b,\tag{11.5}$$

where $a \in \{0,1\}^n$ and $b \in \{0,1\}$, and consider the goal of determining a. Note that such a function is constant if $a = 00\cdots0$ and balanced otherwise (though a balanced function need not be of this form). Furthermore, the classical determination of a requires at least n f-CNOT operations (since a contains n bits of information, and each classical evaluation of f yields a single bit of information). Nevertheless, by running the quantum network given in Figure 11.13, it is possible to determine a with a single f-CNOT operation.

The initial conditions are the same as above. In this case, Eq. (11.3) takes the simple form

$$\sum_{x\in\{0,1\}^n}(-1)^{(a\cdot x)\oplus b}|x\rangle(|0\rangle - |1\rangle),\tag{11.6}$$

which, after the final Hadamard transform, becomes

$$(-1)^b\sum_{x,y\in\{0,1\}^n}(-1)^{x\cdot(a\oplus y)}|y\rangle(|0\rangle - |1\rangle),\tag{11.7}$$

which is equivalent to $(-1)^b|a\rangle(|0\rangle - |1\rangle)$. Thus, a measurement of the control register yields the value of a. (Bernstein and Vazirani's algorithm is similar to the above, except that it employs two f-CNOT operations instead of one. Also, this problem, and its solution, is very similar to the search problems considered by Barbara Terhal and John Smolin [30].)

The network construction presented in this section (Figure 11.13) can be generalized to the case of a Boolean function $f: \{0,1\}^n \to \{0,1\}^m$ (with $m \le n$), with the promise that the parity of the elements in the range of f is either constant or evenly balanced (i.e., its output values all have the same parity, or half of them have parity 0 and half have parity 1). In this case, by choosing an auxiliary register composed of m qubits, and setting all of them in the initial state $(|0\rangle - |1\rangle)$, it is possible to solve the problem with certainty in one run of the network. As in the above case, the function is constant when the n qubits of the first register are detected in state $|00\cdots0\rangle$, and evenly balanced otherwise.

A particular subclass of the above functions consists of those that are of the form $f(x) = (A \cdot x) \oplus b$, where A is an $m \times n$ binary matrix, b is a binary m-tuple, and $\oplus$ is applied bitwise (this can be thought of as an affine linear function in modulo-two arithmetic). The output string of f has constant parity if $(11\cdots1)\cdot A = (00\cdots0)$ and has balanced parity otherwise. It is possible to determine all the entries of A by evaluating the function f only m times, via a suitable multi-qubit f-CNOT gate of the form

$$|x\rangle|y\rangle \xrightarrow{f-c-N} |x\rangle|y\oplus f(x)\rangle, \tag{11.8}$$

where $x \in \{0, 1\}^n$ and $y \in \{0, 1\}^m$. The network described below is a generalization of that in Figure 11.13, and determines the n-tuple $c \cdot A$, where c is any binary m-tuple. The auxiliary register is composed of m qubits, which are initialized to the state

$$\left(|\,0\rangle + (-1)^{c1}\,|\,1\rangle\right)\left(|\,0\rangle + (-1)^{c2}\,|\,1\rangle\right)\cdots\left(|0\rangle + (-1)^{cm}|1\rangle\right). \tag{11.9}$$

(This state can be "computed" by first setting the auxiliary register to the state $|c_1c_2\cdots c_m\rangle$ and then applying a Hadamard transform to it.) The n-qubit control register is initialized in state $|00\cdots0\rangle$, and then a Hadamard transform is applied to it. Then the f-CNOT operation is performed, and is followed by another Hadamard transform to the control register. It is straightforward to show that the control register will then reside in the state $|c\cdot A\rangle$. By running the network m times with suitable choices for c, all the entries of A can be determined. Peter Høyer [31] independently solved a problem that is similar to the above, except that f is an Abelian group homomorphism, rather than an affine linear function.

11.2.4 Implementation of QFT

The QFT on the additive group of integers modulo 2^m is the mapping

$$|a\rangle \xrightarrow{F_{2m}} \sum\nolimits_{y=0}^{2^m-1} e^{\frac{2\pi iay}{2^m}}|y\rangle, \tag{11.10}$$

where $a \in \{0, ..., 2^m - 1\}$ (see Chapter 8). Let a be represented in binary as $a_1 ... a_m \in \{0, 1\}^m$, where $a = 2^{m-1}a_1 + 2^{m-2}a_2 + \cdots + 2^1 a_{m-1} + 2^0 a_m$ (and similarly for y). It is interesting to note that the state Eq. (11.10) is unentangled, and can in fact be factorized as

$$\left(|\,0\rangle + e^{2\pi i(0.a_m)}\,|\,1\rangle\right)\left(|\,0\rangle + e^{2\pi i(0.a_{m-1}a_m)}\,|\,1\rangle\right)\cdots\left(|0\rangle + e^{2\pi i(0.a_1a_2...a_m)}|1\rangle\right). \tag{11.11}$$

This follows from the fact that

$$\begin{aligned}
&e^{\frac{2\pi iay}{2^m}}\,|\,y_1\cdots y_m\rangle \\
&= e^{2\pi i(0.a_m)y_1}|y_1\rangle e^{2\pi i(0.a_{m-1}a_m)y_2}|y_2\rangle\cdots \\
&\cdots e^{2\pi i(0.a_1a_2\cdots am)y_m}|y_m\rangle,
\end{aligned} \tag{11.12}$$

so the coefficient of $|y_1y_2\cdots y_m\rangle$ in Eq. (11.10) matches that in Eq. (11.11). A network for computing F_{2^n} is shown in Figure 11.14.

In the above network, R_k denotes the unitary transformation

$$R_k = \begin{bmatrix} 1 & 0 \\ 0 & e^{2\pi i/2^k} \end{bmatrix} \tag{11.13}$$

We now show that the network shown in Figure 11.14 produces the state (11.10). The initial state is $|a\rangle = |\,a_1a_2\cdots a_m\rangle$ (and $a/2^m = 0.\,a_1a_2 ... a_m$ in binary). Applying H to the first qubit in $|a_1\cdots a_m\rangle$

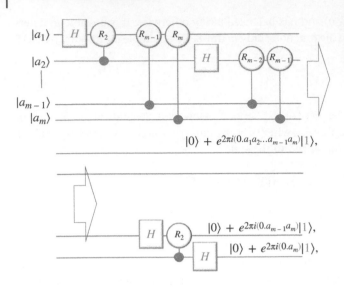

Figure 11.14 Network for F_{2^m} shown acting on the basis state $|a_1 a_2 \cdots a_m\rangle$. At the end, the order of the output qubits is reversed (not shown in diagram). *Source:* Cleve et al. [4].

produces the state $(|0\rangle + e^{2\pi i(0.\,a1)}|1\rangle)\,|a_2 \cdots a_m\rangle$. Then applying the controlled- R_2 changes the state to $(|0\rangle + e^{2\pi i(a1a20.)}|1\rangle)\,|a_2 \cdots a_m\rangle$. Next, the controlled -$R_3$ produces $(|0\rangle + e^{2\pi i(3)}0.\,a1a2a\,|1\rangle)$ $|a_2 \cdots a_m\rangle$, and so on, until the state is $(|0\rangle + e^{2\pi i(0.a1\cdots a_m)}\,|1\rangle)\,|a_2 \cdots a_m\rangle$. The next H yields

$$\left(|0\rangle + e^{2\pi i(0.a1\cdots a_m)}\,|1\rangle\right)\left(|0\rangle + e^{2\pi i(0.a)2}\,|1\rangle\right)\,|a_3 \cdots a_m\rangle$$

and the controlled -R_2 to -R_{m-1} yields

$$\left(|0\rangle + e^{2\pi i(0.a1\cdots a_m)}\,|1\rangle\right)\left(|0\rangle + e^{2\pi i(0.a2\cdots a_m)}\,|1\rangle\right)|a_3 \cdots a_m\rangle. \tag{11.14}$$

Continuing in this manner, the state eventually becomes

$$\left(|0\rangle + e^{2\pi i(0.a1\cdots a_m)}\,|1\rangle\right)\left(|0\rangle + e^{2\pi i(0.a2\cdots a_m)}\,|1\rangle\right)\cdots\left(|0\rangle + e^{2\pi i(0.a_m)}|1\rangle\right),$$

which, when the order of the qubits is reversed, is state Eq. (11.11). Note that, if we do not know $a_1 \cdots a_m$, but are given a state of the form Eq. (11.11), then $a_1 \cdots a_m$ can be easily extracted by applying the inverse of the QFT to the state, which will yield the state $|a_1 \cdots a_m\rangle$.

11.2.5 Estimating Arbitrary Phases

At the beginning of the section, we noted that differences in phase shifts by π can, in principle, be precisely detected by interferometry, and by quantum computations. Then, we reviewed powerful computational tasks that can be performed by quantum computers, based on the mathematical structure used to detect these phase differences. In this section, we consider the case of *arbitrary* phase differences, and show in simple terms how to obtain good estimators for them, via the QFT. This phase estimation plays a central role in the fast quantum algorithms for factoring and for finding discrete logarithms.

Suppose that U is any unitary transformation on n qubits, and $|\psi\rangle$ is an eigenvector of U with eigenvalue $e^{2\pi i\varphi}$, where $0 \le \varphi < 1$. Consider the following scenario. We do not explicitly know U or $|\psi\rangle$ or $e^{2\pi i\varphi}$, but instead are given devices that perform controlled-U, controlled-U^{2^1}, controlled-U^{2^2} (and so on) operations. Also, assume that we are given a single preparation of

Figure 11.15 Network illustrating estimation of phase φ with *j*-bit precision. The same network forms the kernel of the order-finding algorithm discussed in the next section. *Source:* Cleve et al. [4].

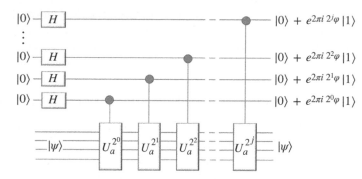

the state $|\psi\rangle$. Now, our goal is to obtain an m-bit estimator of φ. To solve this, we first apply the network of Figure 11.15. This network produces the state

$$\left(|0\rangle + e^{2\pi i 2^{m-1}\varphi}|1\rangle\right)\left(|0\rangle + e^{2\pi i 2^{m-2}\varphi}|1\rangle\right)\cdots$$
$$\cdots\left(|0\rangle + e^{2\pi i 2^{0}\varphi}|1\rangle\right) = \sum_{y=0}^{2^m-1} e^{2\pi i \varphi y} \tag{11.15}$$

As noted in the last section, in the special case where $\varphi = 0. a_1 \ldots a_m$, the state $|a_1 \cdots a_m\rangle$ (and hence φ) can be obtained by just applying the inverse of the QFT (which is the network of Figure 11.14 in the backward direction). This will produce the state $|a_1 \cdots a_m\rangle$ exactly (and hence φ).

However, φ is not in general a fraction of a power of two (and may not even be a rational number). For such a φ, it turns out that applying the inverse of the QFT produces the best m-bit approximation of φ with a probability of at least $4/\pi^2 = 0.405 \ldots$ To see why this is so, let $a/2^m = 0. a_1 \ldots a_m$ be the best m-bit estimate of φ. Then $\varphi = a/2^m + \delta$, where $0 < |\delta| \leq 1/2^{m+1}$. Applying the inverse QFT to state Eq. (11.15) yields the state

$$\frac{1}{2^m}\sum_{x=0}^{2^m-1}\sum_{y=0}^{2^m-1} exp\left(\frac{-2\pi ixy}{2^m}\right) exp\left(2\pi i\varphi y\right) |x\rangle$$
$$= \frac{1}{2^m}\sum_{x=0}^{2^m-1}\sum_{y=0}^{2^m-1} exp\left(\frac{-2\pi ixy}{2^m}\right) e^{2\pi i\left(\frac{a}{2^m} + \delta\right)} |x\rangle \tag{11.16}$$
$$= \frac{1}{2^m}\sum_{x=0}^{2^m-1}\sum_{y=0}^{2^m-1} e^{\frac{2\pi i(a-x)y}{2^m}} e^{2\pi i\delta y} |x\rangle$$

(for clarity, we are now including the normalization factors) and the coefficient of $|a_1 \cdots a_m\rangle$ in the above is the geometric series

$$\frac{1}{2^m}\sum_{y=0}^{2^m-1}\left(e^{2\pi i\delta}\right)^y = \frac{1}{2^m}\left(\frac{1-\left(e^{2\pi i\delta}\right)^{2^m}}{1-e^{2\pi i\delta}}\right). \tag{11.17}$$

Since $|\delta| \leq 1/2^{m+1}$, it follows that $2\pi\delta 2^m \leq \pi$, and thus $|1 - e^{2\pi i\delta 2^m}| \geq 2\pi\delta 2^m/(\pi/2) = 4\delta 2^m$. Also, $|1 - e^{2\pi i\delta}| \leq 2\pi\delta$. Therefore, the probability of observing $a_1 \cdots a_m$ when measuring the state is

$$\left|\frac{1}{2^m}\left(\frac{1-\left(e^{2\pi i\delta}\right)^{2^m}}{1-e^{2\pi i\delta}}\right)\right|^2 \geq \left(\frac{1}{2^m}\left(\frac{4\delta 2^m}{2\pi\delta}\right)\right)^2 = \frac{4}{\pi^2}. \tag{11.18}$$

Note that the above algorithm (described by networks in Figures 11.14 and 11.15 consists of m controlled $-U^{2^k}$ operations, and $O(m^2)$ other operations.

In many contexts (such as that of the factoring Shor's algorithm), the above positive probability of success is sufficient to be useful; however, in other contexts, a higher probability of success may be desirable. The success probability can be amplified to $1 - \varepsilon$ for any $\varepsilon > 0$ by increasing m to $m' = m + O(\log(1/\varepsilon))$, and rounding off the resulting m'-bit string to its most significant m bits.

11.2.6 Improving Success Probability When Estimating Phases

Let φ be a real number satisfying $0 \le \varphi < 1$ that is not a fraction of 2^m, and let $a/2^m = 0. a_1 a_2 \ldots a_m$ be the closest m-bit approximation to φ so that $\varphi = q/2^m + \delta 2^m$ where $0 < |\delta| \le 1/2^{m+1}$. For such a φ, we have already shown that applying the inverse of the QFT to Eq. (11.15) and then measuring yields the state $|a\rangle$ with a probability of at least $4/\pi^2 = 0.405$ ....

Without lost of generality, assume $0 < \delta \le \frac{1}{2^{m+1}}$. For t satisfying $-2^{m-1} \le t < 2^{m-1}$ let α_t denote the amplitude of $|a - t \bmod 2^m\rangle$. It follows from Eq. (11.15) that

$$\alpha_t = \frac{1}{2^m} \left(\frac{1 - \left(e^{2\pi i \left(\delta + \frac{t}{2^m}\right)}\right)^{2^m}}{1 - e^{2\pi i \left(\delta + \frac{t}{2^m}\right)}} \right). \tag{11.19}$$

Since

$$\left| 1 - e^{2\pi i \left(\delta + \frac{t}{2^m}\right)} \right| \le \frac{2\pi \left(\delta + \frac{t}{2^m}\right)}{\pi/2} = 4\left(\delta + \frac{t}{2^m}\right)$$

then

$$|\alpha_t| \le \left| \frac{2}{2^m 4 \left(\delta + \frac{t}{2^m}\right)} \right| \le \frac{1}{2^{m+1} \left(\delta + \frac{t}{2^m}\right)}.$$

The probability of getting an error greater than $\frac{k}{2^m}$ is

$$\begin{aligned}
&\sum_{k \le t < 2^{m-1}} |\alpha_t|^2 + \sum_{-2^{m-1} \le t < -k} |\alpha_t|^2 \\
&\le \sum_{t=k}^{2^{m-1}-1} \frac{1}{4(t + 2^m \delta)^2} + \sum_{t=-2^{m-1}}^{-(k+1)} \frac{1}{4(t + 2^m \delta)^2} \\
&\le \sum_{t=k}^{2^{m-1}-1} \frac{1}{4t^2} + \sum_{t=k+1}^{2^{m-1}} \frac{1}{4\left(t - \frac{1}{2}\right)^2} \\
&\le \sum_{t=2k}^{2^m-1} \frac{1}{4\left(\frac{t}{2}\right)^2} < \int_{2k-1}^{2^m-1} \frac{1}{t^2} < \frac{1}{2k-1}.
\end{aligned} \tag{11.20}$$

So, for example, if we wish to have an estimate that is within $1/2^{n+1}$ of the value φ with a probability of at least $1 - \varepsilon$, it suffices to use this technique with $m = n + \left\lceil \log_2\left(\frac{1}{2\varepsilon} + \frac{1}{2}\right) \right\rceil$ bits.

11.2.7 The Order-Finding Problem

In this section, we show how the scheme from the previous section can be applied to solve the order-finding problem, where one is given positive integers a and N that are relatively prime and such that $a < N$, and the goal is to find the minimum positive integer r such that $a^r \bmod N = 1$. There is no known classical procedure for doing this in time polynomial in n, where n is the number of bits of N.

Shor [32] presented a polynomial-time quantum algorithm for this problem, and noted that since there is an efficient classical randomized reduction from the factoring problem to order finding, there is a polynomial-time quantum algorithm for factoring. Also, the quantum order-finding algorithm can be used directly to break the RSA cryptosystem (see the design example in the following text).

Let us begin by assuming that we are also supplied with a prepared state of the form

$$| \psi_1 \rangle = \sum_{j=0}^{r-1} \exp\left(\frac{-2\pi ij}{r}\right) | a^j \bmod N \rangle. \tag{11.21}$$

Such a state is not at all trivial to fabricate; we shall see how this difficulty is circumvented later. Consider the unitary transformation U that maps $|x\rangle$ to $|axmodN\rangle$. Note that $|\psi_1\rangle$ is an eigenvector of U with eigenvalue $\exp(2\pi i/r)$. Also, for any j, it is possible to implement a controlled -U^{2^j} gate in terms of $O(n^2)$ elementary gates. Thus, using the state $|\psi_1\rangle$ and the implementation of controlled-U^{2^j} gates, we can directly apply the method of the previous section to efficiently obtain an estimator of $1/r$ that has $2n$ bits of precision with high probability. This is sufficient precision to extract r.

The problem with the above method is that we are aware of no straightforward efficient method to prepare state $|\psi_1\rangle$. Let us now suppose that we have a device for the following kind of state preparation. When executed, the device produces a state of the form

$$| \psi_k \rangle = \sum_{j=0}^{r-1} \exp\left(-\frac{2\pi ikj}{r}\right) |a^j \bmod N \rangle, \tag{11.22}$$

where k is randomly chosen (according to the uniform distribution) from $\{1, ..., r\}$. We shall first show that this is also sufficient to efficiently compute r, and then later address the issue of preparing such states. For each $k \in \{1, ..., r\}$, the eigenvalue of state $|\psi_k\rangle$ is $e^{2\pi i(k/r)}$, and we can again use the technique from the previous section to efficiently determine k/r with $2n$ bits of precision. From this, we can extract the quantity k/r exactly by the method of continued fractions. If k and r happen to be coprime, then this yields r; otherwise, we might obtain only a divisor of r.

Note that we can efficiently verify whether or not we happen to have obtained r, by checking if $a^r \bmod N = 1$. If verification fails, then the device can be used again to produce another $|\psi_k\rangle$. The expected number of random trials until k is coprime to r is $(\log \log (N)) = O(\log n)$.

The expected number of trials for the above procedure can be improved to a constant. This is because given any two independent trials that yield k_1/r and k_2/r, it suffices for k_1 and k_2 to be coprime to extract r (which is then the least common denominator of the two quotients). The probability that k_1 and k_2 are coprime is bounded below by

$$1 - \sum_{p \, prime} \Pr[p \text{ divides } k_1] \Pr[p \text{ divides } k_2] \geq$$
$$1 - \sum_{p \, prime} 1/p^2 > 0.54. \tag{11.23}$$

Now, returning to our actual setting, where we have no special devices that produce random eigenvectors, the important observation is that $| 1 \rangle = \sum_{k=1}^{r} | \psi_k \rangle$, and $|1\rangle$ *is* an easy state to prepare. Consider what happens if we use the previous quantum algorithm, but with state $|1\rangle$ substituted in place of a random $|\psi_k\rangle$. In order to understand the resulting behavior, imagine if, initially, the control register were measured with respect to the orthonormal basis consisting of $|\psi_1\rangle, ..., |\psi_r\rangle$. This would yield a uniform sampling of these r eigenvectors, so the algorithm would behave exactly like the previous one. Also, since this imagined measurement operation is with respect to an orthonormal set of eigenvectors of U, it commutes with all the controlled -U^{2^j} operations, and hence will have the same effect if it is performed at the *end* rather than at the beginning of the computation. Now, if the measurement were performed at the end of the computation, then it would have no effect on the outcome of the measurement of the control register. This implies that state $|1\rangle$ can in fact be used in place of a random $|\psi_k\rangle$, because the relevant information that the resulting algorithm yields is *equivalent*. This completes the description of the algorithm for the order-finding problem.

It is interesting to note that the algorithm that we have described for the order-finding problem, which follows Kitaev's methodology, results in a network (Figure 11.15 followed by Figure 11.14 backward) that is identical to the network for Shor's algorithm, although the latter algorithm was derived by an apparently different methodology. The sequence of controlled $-U^{2^j}$ operations is equivalent to the implementation (via repeated squarings) of the modular exponentiation function in Shor's algorithm. This demonstrates that Shor's algorithm, in effect, estimates the eigenvalue corresponding to an eigenstate of the operation U that maps $|x\rangle$ to $|ax mod\ N\rangle$.

Design Example 11.2

Cracking RSA: What we seek is a way to compute $P modulo N$ given P^e, e, and N, that is, a method of finding e-th roots in the multiplicative group of integers *modulo N* (this group is often denoted by Z_{N^*} and contains the integers coprime to N). It is still an open question whether a solution to this problem necessarily gives us a polynomial-time randomized algorithm for factoring. However, factoring does give a polynomial-time algorithm for finding e-th roots for any e relatively prime to $\varphi(N)$ and thus for cracking RSA. Knowing the prime factorization of N, say $\prod_i^k p_i^{a_i}$, we can easily compute $\varphi(N) = N\prod_{i=1}^n (1 - 1/p_i)$. Then we can compute d such that $ed \equiv 1 mod\ \varphi(N)$, which implies $P^{ed} \equiv P modulo N$.

However, to crack a particular instance of RSA, it suffices to find an integer d such that $ed \equiv 1 modulo\ ord(P)$, that is $ed = ord(P)k + 1$ for some integer k. We would then have $C^d \equiv P^{ed} \equiv P^{ord(P)k+1} \equiv P\ modulo\ N$.

Since e is relatively prime to $\varphi(N)$, it is easy to see that $ord(P) = ord(P^e) = ord(C)$. So, given $C = P^e$, we can compute $ord(P)$ using Shor's algorithm and then compute d satisfying $de \equiv 1\ modulo\ ord(P)$ using the extended Euclidean algorithm. Thus, we do not need several repetitions of Shor's algorithm to find the order of a for various random a; we just find the order of C and solve for P regardless of whether or not this permits us to factor N.

Generating arbitrary interference (transformation) patterns: We will show in this section how to generate specific interference patterns with arbitrary precision via some function evaluations. The interference plays a key role in creating a pattern of measurements to calculate the final results. A simple demonstration will be presented in the next design example. Here we require two registers. The first we call the control register; it contains the states we wish to interfere with. The second we call the auxiliary register, and it is used solely to induce relative phase changes in the first register.

Suppose the first register contains n bits. For each n-bit string $|x\rangle$, we require a unitary operator U_x. All of these operators U_x should share an eigenvector $|\Psi\rangle$ that will be the state of the auxiliary register. Suppose the eigenvalue of $|\Psi\rangle$ for x is denoted by $\exp(2\pi i\varphi(x))$. By applying a unitary operator to the auxiliary register conditioned upon the value of the first register, we will get the following interference pattern:

$$\sum_{x=0}^{2^n-1} |x\rangle |\Psi\rangle \rightarrow \sum_{x=0}^{2^n-1} |x\rangle U_x(|\Psi\rangle) = \sum_{x=0}^{2^n-1} \exp(2\pi i \varphi(x)) |x\rangle |\Psi\rangle. \tag{11.24}$$

The conditional U_f gate that was described in the previous sections can be viewed in this way. That is, the operator $U_{f(0)}$ that maps $|y\rangle$ to $|y \oplus f(0)\rangle$ and the operator $U_{f(1)}$ that maps $|y\rangle$ to $|y \oplus f(1)\rangle$ have a common eigenstate $|0\rangle - |1\rangle$. The operator $U_{f(j)}$ has the eigenvalue $\exp(2\pi i f(j)/2)$ for $j = 0, 1$.

In general, the family of unitary operators on m qubits that simply adds a constant integer k modulo 2^m shares the eigenstates

$$\sum_{y=0}^{2^m-1} \exp(-2\pi i l y/2^m) |y\rangle, \tag{11.25}$$

and compensates a phase change of $\exp(-2\pi i l y/2^m)$. For example, let us suppose we wish to create the state $|0\rangle + \exp(2\pi i \varphi)|1\rangle$ where $\varphi = 0. a_1 a_2 a_3 \dots a_m$. We could set up an auxiliary register with m qubits and set it to the state

$$\sum_{y=0}^{2^m-1} \exp(-2\pi i \varphi y)|y\rangle. \tag{11.26}$$

By applying the identity operator when the control bit is $|0\rangle$ and the add 1 modulo 2^m operator, U_1, when the control bit is $|1\rangle$, we see that $|0\rangle \sum_{y=0}^{2^m-1} e(-2\pi i \varphi y) |y\rangle$ gets mapped to itself and $|1\rangle \sum_{y=0}^{2^m-1} e(-2\pi i \varphi y) |y\rangle$ goes to

$$|1\rangle \sum_{y=0}^{2^m-1} \exp(-2\pi i \varphi y) |y + 1 \bmod 2^m\rangle$$

$$= \exp(2\pi i \varphi)|1\rangle \sum_{y=0}^{2^m-1} \exp(-2\pi i \varphi(y+1)) |y + 1 \bmod 2^m\rangle \tag{11.27}$$

$$= \exp(2\pi i \varphi)|1\rangle \sum_{y=0}^{2^m-1} \exp(-2\pi i \varphi y) |y\rangle.$$

An alternative is to set the m-bit auxiliary register to the eigenstate $\sum_{y=0}^{2^m-1} e^{-2\pi i y/2^m} |y\rangle$ and conditionally apply $U\varphi$, which adds $a = a_1 a_2 \dots a_m$ to the auxiliary register. Similarly, the state $|1\rangle \sum_{y=0}^{2^m-1} e^{-2\pi i y/2^m} |y\rangle$ goes to

$$|1\rangle \sum_{y=0}^{2^m-1} e^{-\frac{2\pi i}{2^m}y} |y + a \bmod 2^m\rangle$$

$$= \exp(2\pi i \varphi) |1\rangle \sum_{y=0}^{2^m-1} e^{-\frac{2\pi i}{2^m}(y+a)} |y + a \bmod 2^m\rangle \tag{11.28}$$

$$= \exp(2\pi i \varphi) |1\rangle \sum_{y=0}^{2^m-1} e^{-\frac{2\pi i}{2^m}y} |y\rangle.$$

Similarly, if $\varphi = ab/2^m$ for some integers a and b, we could also obtain the same phase "kick-back" by starting with state $\sum_{y=0}^{2^m-1} e^{-2\pi i a y/2^m} |y\rangle$ and conditionally adding b to the second register.

The method using eigenstate $\sum_{y=0}^{2^m-1} e^{-2\pi i y/2^m} |y\rangle$ has the advantage that we can use the same eigenstate in the auxiliary register for any φ. So in the case of an n-qubit control register where we want phase change $\exp(2\pi i \varphi(x))$ for state $|x\rangle$ and if we have a reversible network for adding $\varphi(x)$ to the auxiliary register when we have $|x\rangle$ in the first register, we can use it on a superposition of control inputs to produce the desired phase "kick-back" $\exp(2\pi i \varphi(x))$ in front of $|x\rangle$. Functions $\varphi(x)$ that will produce a useful result, and their method of computation, depend on the problems we are trying to solve.

11.2.8 Concatenated Interference

The generic sequence, a Hadamard/Fourier transform, followed by an f controlled-U, followed by another Hadamard/Fourier transform can be repeated several times. This can be illustrated, for example, with Grover's database search algorithm. Suppose we are given (as an oracle) a function f_k that maps $\{0, 1\}^n$ to $\{0, 1\}$ such that $f_k(x) = \delta_{xk}$ for some k. Our task is to find k. Thus, in a set of numbers from 0 to $2^n - 1$ one element has been "tagged," and by evaluating f_k we have to find which one. To find k with probability of 50%, any classical algorithm, be it deterministic or randomized, will need to evaluate f_k a minimum of 2^{n-1} times. By contrast, a quantum algorithm needs only $O(2^{n/2})$ evaluations. Grover's algorithm can be presented as a network, as shown in Figure 11.16.

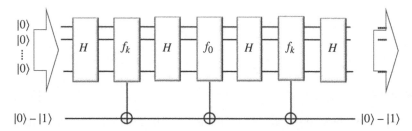

Figure 11.16 Network representation of Grover's algorithms. By repeating the basic sequence $2^{n/2}$ times, the value k is obtained at the output with probability greater than 0.5. *Source:* Cleve et al. [4].

Design Example 11.3

In this example, we will demonstrate ways to build a quantum program, in particular, how quantum parallelism and interference work. Interference plays a key role in creating a pattern of measurements $\mathcal{M}$ to calculate the final results. Let us go back to the Deutsch–Jozsa algorithm with additional details of implementation. The algorithm considers a function f that takes 0 or 1 as input and outputs either 0 or 1 represented as $f: \{0,1\} \rightarrow \{0,1\}$. The functions we have in mind are either balanced or constant. A function f is called balanced if it outputs 0 half the time and 1 the other half. It is a constant function if its output is a constant (1 or 0) regardless of input. Here is an example with a single-bit input: *balanced $f(0) = 0$, $f(1) = 1$, balanced $f(0) = 1$, $f(1) = 0$, constant $f(0) = 1$, $f(1) = 1$, constant $f(0) = 0$, $f(1) = 0$.* Our task is given a function: determine if it is constant or balanced. The problem is simple, but involves a few cool quantum concepts. But before we develop the math, let us conceptualize a possible solution. For classical computing, we can query the function twice and aggregate $\mathcal{A}$ the result with some if-then-else statements.

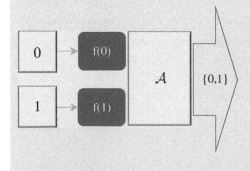

Design Example 11.3 (Continued)

If the number of input bits is increased to n, to verify that a function is balanced, the number of times we query f is $(2^{n-1} + 1)$ in the worst case. Therefore, we have a problem with query complexity, which can grow exponentially in the worst case. Let us expand n to two qubits. We can use Hadamard gates to prepare a superposition representing all four possible bit combinations. We assume that we have an oracle function (see Chapter 8). It uses the quantum parallelism concept to compute all values of $f(x)$ from the superposition in polynomial time, instead of growing exponentially with the number of bases. We will provide additional discussion on the implementation of the oracle function later. By creating a superposition, we allow an oracle function to work on all possible configurations all at once: $2|\alpha\rangle = |00\rangle + |01\rangle + |10\rangle + |11\rangle$. The key idea is that the oracle function $\mathcal{O}$ will output values that, after applying interference (a transformation), we will measure as 0 for all constant functions or 1 for balanced functions (the output of the measurement block $\mathcal{M}$).

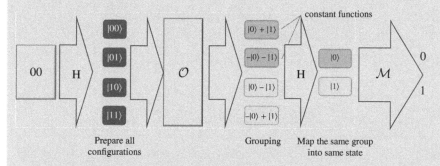

For simplicity, our function f will take 0 or 1 only. Below is the quantum circuit. Steps a) and b) prepare the superposition, step c) is the oracle, and step d) is the interference.

The signal transformations in each step can be represented as

$$|0\rangle|0\rangle \Rightarrow I \otimes X \rightarrow \ |0\rangle|1\rangle \qquad\qquad a)$$

$$\Rightarrow H \otimes H \rightarrow \frac{|0\rangle + |1\rangle}{\sqrt{2}} \otimes \frac{|0\rangle - |1\rangle}{\sqrt{2}} \qquad\qquad b)$$

$$\Rightarrow \mathcal{O}_f \rightarrow \frac{(-1)^{f(0)}|0\rangle + (-1)^{f(1)}|1\rangle}{\sqrt{2}} \otimes \frac{|0\rangle - |1\rangle}{\sqrt{2}} \qquad\qquad c)$$

$$\Rightarrow H \otimes I \rightarrow \ \pm|f(0) \otimes f(1)\rangle \otimes \frac{|0\rangle - |1\rangle}{\sqrt{2}} \qquad\qquad d)$$

(Continued)

Design Example 11.3 (Continued)

Steps a) and b) are straightforward, so let us look at step c) more closely. By dropping $1/\sqrt{2}$ for simplicity, we have $x = |0\rangle + |1\rangle$ *and* $y = |0\rangle - |1\rangle$, and the oracle function will produce by definition $(x, y) \rightarrow (x, y \oplus f(x))$

For $f(x) = 0$, the second qubit is simply y, and we have

$$f(x) = 0 :$$
$$(x, y) \rightarrow (x, y \oplus 0) = (x, y)$$
$$|x\rangle = (|0\rangle - |1\rangle) \rightarrow |x\rangle (|0\rangle - |1\rangle)$$

For $f(x) = 1$, we flip the sign

$$f(x) = 1 :$$
$$(x, y) \rightarrow (x, y \oplus 1)$$
$$|x\rangle (|0\rangle - |1\rangle) \rightarrow |x\rangle (|1\rangle - |0\rangle)$$

By examining both outputs, we can jointly write them as $(-1)^{f(x)}|x\rangle (|0\rangle - |1\rangle)$.
Replacing $|x\rangle$ in $(-1)^{f(x)}|x\rangle$ by $|0\rangle + |1\rangle$, we get

$$(-1)^{f(x)}|x\rangle = (-1)^{f(x)}(|0\rangle + |1\rangle) = (-1)^{f(0)}|0\rangle + (-1)^{f(1)}|1\rangle$$

and

$$\frac{|0\rangle + |1\rangle}{\sqrt{2}} \otimes \frac{|0\rangle - |1\rangle}{\sqrt{2}} \Rightarrow \mathcal{O}_f \rightarrow \frac{(-1)^{f(0)}|0\rangle + (-1)^{f(1)}|1\rangle}{\sqrt{2}} \otimes \frac{|0\rangle - |1\rangle}{\sqrt{2}}$$

We can go through all possible combination of f and compute the superposition of the first qubit for each scenario.

first qubit

$balanced\, f(0) = 0, f(1) = 1,$

$balanced\, f(0) = 1, f(1) = 0,$ $\pm \dfrac{|0\rangle - |1\rangle}{\sqrt{2}}$

$constant\, f(0) = 1, f(1) = 1,$

$constant\, f(0) = 0, f(1) = 0$ $\pm \dfrac{|0\rangle - |1\rangle}{\sqrt{2}}$

We find that for the same function type, the values differ by a sign only, that is, by a global phase with $\Delta\gamma$ equal to π. So, in the general representation we have

$$|\psi\rangle = e^{i\gamma}\left(\cos\frac{\theta}{2}|0\rangle + \sin\frac{\theta}{2}|1\rangle \right)$$

Superpositions that differ by a constant global phase are indistinguishable in the real word. They always have the same probability of measurements regardless of how they are measured. This does not change as long as no operations or the same operations are applied to both.

This is excellent news! Within the same function type, they will always produce the same measurement result. So, our focus is applying a transformation so that different groups produce

Design Example 11.3 (Continued)

different measurement results. Therefore, step d) (interference) applies the Hadamard gate, and a constant function will be measured as $|0\rangle$ and a balanced function as $|1\rangle$:

$$H\left[\frac{|0\rangle + |1\rangle}{\sqrt{2}}\right] = |0\rangle; H\left[\frac{|0\rangle - |1\rangle}{\sqrt{2}}\right] = |1\rangle$$

Let us expand our solution for an input with n bits. We can apply n Hadamard gates to prepare the superposition $H^{\otimes n}$. And apply the oracle function $\mathcal{O} \Rightarrow (x, y) \rightarrow (x, y \oplus f(x)): |x\rangle|y\rangle \rightarrow |x\rangle|y \oplus f(x)\rangle$ again. If we work out the case where $f(x) = 0$ and $f(x) = 1$, as we did earlier, we will end up with the same equation in the last step as below. The equiprobable superposition and $H^{\otimes n}$ operation gives

$$\frac{1}{\sqrt{2^n}}\sum_{x=0}^{2^n-1}|x\rangle(|0\rangle - |1\rangle)$$

$$\Rightarrow \mathcal{O} \rightarrow \frac{1}{\sqrt{2^n}}\sum_{x=0}^{2^n-1}|x\rangle(|0 \oplus f(x)\rangle - |1 \oplus f(x)\rangle)$$

$$\frac{1}{\sqrt{2^n}}\sum_{x=0}^{2^n-1}|x\rangle(|f(x)\rangle - |1 \oplus f(x)\rangle)$$

$$\frac{1}{\sqrt{2^n}}\sum_{x=0}^{2^n-1}(-1)^{f(x)}|x\rangle(|0\rangle - |1\rangle)$$

As before, the second qubit above will remain the same for the rest of the circuit. So, for simplicity, we focus only on the first qubit:

$$\frac{1}{\sqrt{2^n}}\sum_{x=0}^{2^n-1}(-1)^{f(x)}|x\rangle$$

Then, we apply n Hadamard gates again. The general equation for the Hadamard gate transformation on multiple qubits is

$$H^{\otimes n} \rightarrow \frac{1}{\sqrt{2^n}}\sum_{z \in \{0,1\}}(-1)^{\langle x,z\rangle}|z\rangle$$

where $\langle x, z\rangle$ is the bitwise dot product of the binary representation of x and y. For example,

$$(H_n)_{3.2} = (-1)^{(1,1)\cdot(1,0)} = (-1)^{1+0} = -1$$

So, after applying the Hadamard gates, the qubits become

$$\frac{1}{\sqrt{2^n}}\sum_{x=0}^{2^n-1}(-1)^{f(x)}|x\rangle(|0\rangle - |1\rangle)$$

$$\Rightarrow H^{\otimes n} \rightarrow \frac{1}{2^n}\sum_{x=0}^{2^n-1}(-1)^{f(x)}\left[\sum_{y=0}^{2^n-1}(-1)^{xy}|y\rangle\right]$$

$$\frac{1}{2^n}\sum_{y=0}^{2^n-1}\left[\sum_{x=0}^{2^n-1}(-1)^{f(x)}(-1)^{xy}\right]|y\rangle$$

where $xy = x_0y_0 \oplus x_1y_1 \oplus \cdots \oplus x_{n-1}y_{n-1}$ is the sum of the bitwise products. Suppose $y = |000...00\rangle$; then $xy = 0$ and

(Continued)

Design Example 11.3 (Continued)

$$(-1)^0 = 1$$

$$\frac{1}{2^n} \sum_{y=0}^{2^n-1} \left[\sum_{x=0}^{2^n-1} (-1)^{f(x)} (-1)^{xy} \right] |y\rangle$$

becomes $\frac{1}{2^n} \left[\sum_{x=0}^{2^n-1} (-1)^{f(x)} \right] |000...00\rangle$. When $f(x)$ is balanced, half of the inner summation terms above will destructively cancel each other. If $f(x)$ is a constant, the sum of all the inner summation terms will give

$$\frac{1}{2^n} 2^n |000...0\rangle = |000...0\rangle$$

So, for the former case, no measurement should be made for $|00000...00\rangle$, whereas in the second case, all the measurements are $|00000...00\rangle$. In short, the measurement of the superposition depends on the interference created by $f(x)$.

Design Example 11.4 Grover's Algorithm

We have initially described Grover's algorithm in the previous section of the chapter, and here we discuss its design aspects in greater detail. Consider a function that is always equal to 0 except for a single value u. How are we going to find u? f(x) = 0 if $x \neq u$ and f(x) = 0 if $x = u$. As we already indicated earlier, a classical algorithm requires $O(N)$ queries to find u in the worst case. But Grover's algorithm can complete the task in $O(\sqrt{N})$. But that assumes Gover's algorithm has access to an oracle function that can compute $f(x)$ simultaneously. (For a classical computer, such a function may require an N core computer. So the complexity remains $O(N)$.) Next, you may want to know how the oracle function is implemented. In practice, if you want an oracle that handles all possible functions f, quantum computing will unlikely have any competitive edge. But for some specific domain, if you can identify some specific pattern to load the desired superposition in polynomial time, you can win. But in reality, it is one of the milestones in quantum computing. We demonstrate that quantum computing may be superior even we do not demonstrate a practical oracle function. As advances are being made in quantum algorithms today, we may put different techniques together for commercial applications. So, let us treat this oracle function as a black box and study Grover's algorithm. As the first step, we prepare a superposition as

$$|\psi\rangle = H^{\otimes n} |0\rangle^{\otimes n} = \frac{1}{\sqrt{2^n}} \sum_{x=0}^{2^n-1} |x\rangle$$

If we use three qubits, we have

$$H^3 |000\rangle = \frac{1}{2\sqrt{2}} |000\rangle + \frac{1}{2\sqrt{2}} |001\rangle + ... + \frac{1}{2\sqrt{2}} |111\rangle$$

$$= \frac{1}{2\sqrt{2}} \sum_{x=0}^{7} |x\rangle = |\psi\rangle$$

After the state preparation, Grover's algorithm turns into an iterative process comprising multiple iterations of the oracle function and the Grover operator as shown in the following figure:

Design Example 11.4 Grover's Algorithm (Continued)

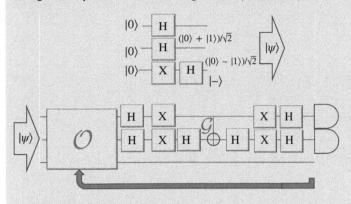

In block $\mathcal{O}$ we apply the oracle function:

$$|x\rangle|q\rangle \Rightarrow \mathcal{O} \rightarrow |x\rangle|\,f(x)\oplus q\rangle$$

$$f(x) = \begin{cases} 0 \text{ if } x \neq u \\ 1 \text{ if } x \neq u \end{cases}$$

$$|q\rangle = \frac{|0\rangle - |1\rangle}{\sqrt{2}}$$

Let us substitute the state we prepared and check its output for different value of $f(x)$:

$$\mathcal{O}|x\rangle\frac{|0\rangle - |1\rangle}{\sqrt{2}} \rightarrow |x\rangle\frac{|\,f(x)\oplus 0\rangle - |\,f(x)\oplus 1\rangle}{\sqrt{2}}$$

amplitude change

$$\text{if } f(x) = 1 \rightarrow |x\rangle\frac{|1\oplus 0\rangle - |1\oplus 1\rangle}{\sqrt{2}} = -|x\rangle\frac{|0\rangle - |1\rangle}{\sqrt{2}}$$

$$\text{if } f(x) = 0 \rightarrow |x\rangle\frac{|0\oplus 0\rangle - |0\oplus 1\rangle}{\sqrt{2}} = |x\rangle\frac{|0\rangle - |1\rangle}{\sqrt{2}}$$

no change

So, for any $|x\rangle$ with *f(x) = 0*, its amplitude does not change; otherwise, the amplitude becomes negative. In our example, *f(011) = 1* and after applying the oracle function, the superposition state turns into

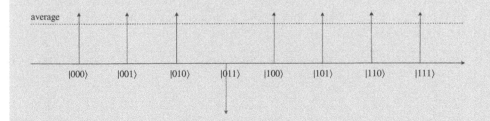

The average of the amplitudes (the dotted line) will decrease because of the negative amplitude of $|011\rangle$. Now we apply the Grover operator $\mathcal{G}$:

(Continued)

Design Example 11.4 Grover's Algorithm (Continued)

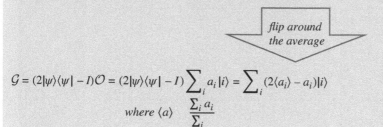

flip around the average

$$\mathcal{G} = (2|\psi\rangle\langle\psi| - I)\mathcal{O} = (2|\psi\rangle\langle\psi| - I) \sum_i a_i |i\rangle = \sum_i (2\langle a_i \rangle - a_i)|i\rangle$$

$$where \; \langle a \rangle \quad \frac{\Sigma_i a_i}{\Sigma_i}$$

It flips every amplitude around the average; see the horizontal dotted line below.

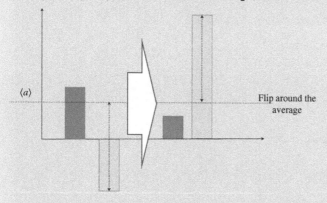

$\langle a \rangle$

Flip around the average

So, after applying the Grover operator, the superposition becomes

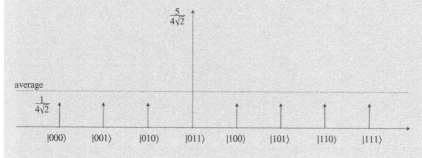

$\frac{5}{4\sqrt{2}}$

average

$\frac{1}{4\sqrt{2}}$

|000⟩ |001⟩ |010⟩ |011⟩ |100⟩ |101⟩ |110⟩ |111⟩

So, if we make any measurement, the probability that the measured state equals the correct answer increases. If we measure the qubits now, we still have a reasonable chance of selecting the wrong answer. So, we repeat this process $\sqrt{N}$ times to amplify the amplitude of the right answer. Let us go through the math in detail again. After applying the oracle function in the first iteration, the superposition is

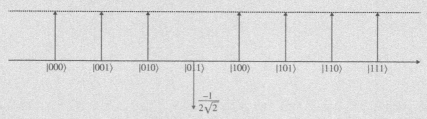

|000⟩ |001⟩ |010⟩ |011⟩ |100⟩ |101⟩ |110⟩ |111⟩

$\frac{-1}{2\sqrt{2}}$

Design Example 11.4 Grover's Algorithm (Continued)

With the original state, $|\psi\rangle$ equals

$$|\psi\rangle = \left[\frac{1}{2\sqrt{2}}\sum_{x=0}^{7}|x\rangle\right]$$

The state after the Grover operation becomes

$$[2|\psi\rangle\langle\psi| - I]|x\rangle = [2|\psi\rangle\langle\psi| - I]\left[|\psi\rangle - \frac{2}{2\sqrt{2}}|011\rangle\right]$$

$$= 2|\psi\rangle\langle\psi|\psi\rangle - |\psi\rangle - \frac{2}{\sqrt{2}}|\psi\rangle\langle\psi|011\rangle + \frac{1}{\sqrt{2}}|011\rangle$$

Recalling that $\langle\psi|011\rangle = \langle011|\psi\rangle = 1/2\sqrt{2}$, we have

$$2|\psi\rangle - |\psi\rangle - \frac{2}{\sqrt{2}}\left(\frac{1}{2\sqrt{2}}\right)|\psi\rangle + \frac{1}{\sqrt{2}}|011\rangle =$$

$$|\psi\rangle - \frac{1}{2}|\psi\rangle + \frac{1}{\sqrt{2}}|011\rangle = \frac{1}{2}|\psi\rangle + \frac{1}{\sqrt{2}}|011\rangle$$

and substituting $|\psi\rangle$ gives us

$$\frac{1}{2}\left[\frac{1}{2\sqrt{2}}\sum_{x=0}^{7}|x\rangle\right] + \frac{1}{\sqrt{2}}|011\rangle =$$

$$\frac{1}{4\sqrt{2}}\sum_{\substack{x=0\\x\neq3}}^{7}|x\rangle + \frac{1}{4\sqrt{2}}|011\rangle + \frac{1}{\sqrt{2}}|011\rangle =$$

$$\frac{1}{4\sqrt{2}}\sum_{\substack{x=0\\x\neq3}}^{7}|x\rangle + \frac{5}{4\sqrt{2}}|011\rangle$$

which is the result after the first iteration.

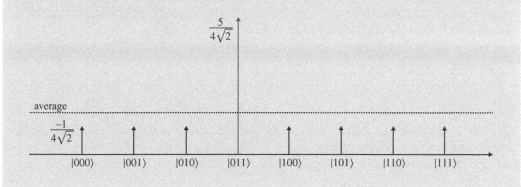

Design Example 11.5 Simon's Algorithm

Let us now revisit Simon's algorithm by looking into details of the mathematical operations within the QC (quantum computing) circuitry and start by considering a function $f(x) = f(x \oplus a)$. For example, for $a = 011$, f listed below fulfills this requirement:

$$f(000) = f(011) = 010; \; f(001) = f(010) = 101;$$
$$f(100) = f(111) = 110; \; f(101) = f(110) = 001$$

How do we find a given f? Let us define a six-qubit system as follows: The first three qubits form a register to store x, and the last three qubits from a second register to store $f(x)$. First, we prepare the superposition of the first register below using the Hadamard gates:

$$|000000\rangle \Rightarrow H \to \frac{1}{\sqrt{8}} (|000000\rangle + |001000\rangle + |010000\rangle + |011000\rangle$$
$$|100000\rangle + |101000\rangle + |110000\rangle + |111000\rangle)$$

We apply a controlled NOT U (CNOT U) gate with the first three qubits as controls and the last three qubits as targets. Therefore, the last three qubits become $f(x)$.

With our example f, the qubits are transformed to

$$\frac{1}{\sqrt{2^n}} \sum_{x\in[0,1]^n} |xf(x)\rangle \xrightarrow{} \frac{1}{\sqrt{8}} (|000010\rangle + |001101\rangle + |010101\rangle + |011010\rangle$$

$$|100110\rangle + |101001\rangle + |110001\rangle + |111110\rangle)$$

As one can see, there are four possible outputs for the second register: 010, 101, 110, or 001. Let us measure the second register. Say, our measurement is 110. This corresponds to the fifth and eighth terms of the previous equation. With this measure, the superposition of the first register (on the fifth and eighth positions) becomes $(|100\rangle + |111\rangle)/\sqrt{2}$. Applying three Hadamard gates again results in

$$\xrightarrow{H^{\otimes n}} \frac{1}{\sqrt{2^n}} \sum_{z\in[0,1]^n} (-1)^{\langle x,z \rangle} |z\rangle$$

where $\langle x, z \rangle$ is the bitwise addition modulo 2 – we perform a bitwise multiplication of x and z and "exclusive or $\oplus$" all the results ($\langle x, z \rangle = x_1 z_1 \oplus \ldots \oplus x_n z_n$. Below, we can see how the first qubit is transformed under a Hadamard gate:

$$\frac{1}{\sqrt{2}} (|100\rangle + |111\rangle) \xrightarrow{H} \frac{1}{2} (|000\rangle - |100\rangle + |011\rangle - |111\rangle)$$

Design Example 11.5 Simon's Algorithm (Continued)

Some of the signs of the amplitude have changed due to $(-1)^{\langle x,\, z\rangle}|z\rangle$. For example, $(H_n)_{3,\,2} = (-1)^{3 \cdot 2} = (-1)^{(1,\,1)\cdot(1,\,0)} = (-1)^{1+0} = (-1)^1 = -1$. We repeat the gates two more times. After Hadamard is applied on the second qubit, we obtain

$$(|000\rangle + |010\rangle - |100\rangle - |110\rangle + |001\rangle - |011\rangle - |101\rangle + |111\rangle)/\sqrt{8} \text{ and on the third}$$
$$(|000\rangle + |001\rangle + |010\rangle + |011\rangle - |100\rangle - |101\rangle - |110\rangle - |111\rangle$$
$$|000\rangle - |001\rangle - |010\rangle + |011\rangle - |100\rangle + |101\rangle + |110\rangle - |111\rangle)/4 =$$
$$(|000\rangle + |011\rangle - |100\rangle - |111\rangle)/2$$

Before applying the Hadamard gates as above, the superposition is $(|100\rangle + |111\rangle)/\sqrt{2}$, which can be rewritten as $(|x_0\rangle + |x_0 \oplus a\rangle)/\sqrt{2}$. After applying the Hadamard gates, we make a measurement. This measurement $\mathbf{z}$ will fulfill the following relation (the proof is given later) $a_1 z_1 \oplus \cdots \oplus a_n z_n = 0$, where z_i is the corresponding qubit of z. As shown in our previous calculation, our measurements will produce one of the following values: 000, 011, 100, or 111. Next, we use these measurements z to solve a. The measurement $|000\rangle$ gives us no useful information for solving the problem, but the last three measurements produce three equations with three unknowns. The second measurement 011 gives us $a_1 \cdot 0 \oplus a_2 \cdot 1 \oplus a_3 \cdot 1 \rightarrow a_2 \oplus a_3$ = 0 mod 2, the third measurement 100 gives us $a_1 \cdot 1 = a_1 = 0$ mod 2, and the forth measurement 111 gives us $a_1 \oplus a_2 \oplus a_3 = 0$ mod 2. Therefore, it can be solved, and the solution for a is either 011 or 000. We know $a = 0$ is not the solution we are looking for. Therefore, $a = 011$. Here is the quantum circuit we need to do it:

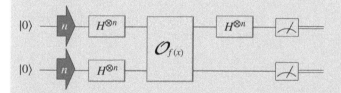

Let us work a bit more to show $a_1 z_1 \oplus \cdots \oplus a_n z_n = 0$. After the oracle function, the two registers become $\sum_{x\in\{0,1\}^n} |x\rangle\, |f(x)\rangle / \sqrt{2^n}$. Next, we measure the second register, and the first register becomes $(|z\rangle + |z \oplus a\rangle)/\sqrt{2}$.

$y = z;\ z = x$

$$H^{\otimes n}[|x\rangle + |x\oplus a\rangle]/\sqrt{2}$$
$$= [H^{\otimes n}|x\rangle + H^{\otimes n}|x\oplus a\rangle]/\sqrt{2}$$
$$= \left\{ \sum_{z\in\{0,1\}^n} (-1)^{xz}|z\rangle + \sum_{z\in\{0,1\}^n} (-1)^{(x\oplus a)z}|z\rangle \right\}/\sqrt{2}\sqrt{2^n}$$
$$= \left\{ \sum_{z\in\{0,1\}^n} [(-1)^{xz} + (-1)^{(x\oplus a)z}]|z\rangle \right\}/\sqrt{2^{n+1}}$$
$$= \left\{ \sum_{z\in\{0,1\}^n} [(-1)^{xz} + (-1)^{(xz\oplus az)}]|z\rangle \right\}/\sqrt{2^{n+1}}$$
$$= \left\{ \sum_{z\in\{0,1\}^n} (-1)^{xz}[1 + (-1)^{az}]|z\rangle \right\}/\sqrt{2^{n+1}}$$

Let us look first at the case where $\langle a,\, z\rangle = 1$. It turns out it will produce destructive interferences that cancel each other out; that is, there is no chance our measurement will have $\langle a,\, z\rangle = 1$. This comes from

(Continued)

Design Example 11.5 Simon's Algorithm (Continued)

$$\left\{ \sum_{z \in \{0,1\}^n} (-1)^{xz} [1 + (-1)^1] |z\rangle \right\} / \sqrt{2^{n+1}} =$$
$$\left\{ \sum_{z \in \{0,1\}^n} (-1)^{xz} [0] |z\rangle \right\} / \sqrt{2^{n+1}} = 0|z\rangle$$

If $\langle a, y \rangle = 0$.

$$\left\{ \sum_{z \in \{0,1\}^n} (-1)^{xz} [1 + (-1)^0] |z\rangle \right\} / \sqrt{2^{n+1}} = \left\{ \sum_{z \in \{0,1\}^n} (-1)^{xz} |z\rangle \right\} / \sqrt{2^{n-1}}$$

Even though the coefficient above may have a different sign, they all have the same probability of measurement equal to $1/2^{n-1}$. With enough measurements, we can find all the n measurements needed to solve a.

$$z_1 a = z_{11} a_1 + z_{12} a_2 + \ldots + z_{1n} a_n = 0$$
$$z_2 a = z_{21} a_1 + z_{22} a_2 + \ldots + z_{2n} a_n = 0$$
$$\vdots$$
$$z_{n-1} a = z_{(n-1)1} a_1 + z_{(n-1)2} a_2 + \ldots + z_{(n-1)n} a_n = 0$$

Design Example 11.6 Shor's Algorithm

RSA (Rivest–Shamir–Adleman) [33] is the standard cryptographic algorithm on the Internet. RSA encryption is based on the simple idea of prime factorization. The encryption/decryption process is illustrated below [34]:

Key generation
Select p,q   (p,q prime)
Calculate n=pq
Calculate $\phi(n)=(p-1)(q-1)$
Select integer e   (gcd $(\phi(n),e)=1$, $1<e< \phi(n)$)
Calculate d $(d=e^{-1} \bmod \phi(n))$
Public key KU=[e,n]
Private key KR=[d,n]
Encription
Plaintext M<n
Ciphertext $C= M^e (\bmod n)$
Decription
Ciphertext C
Plaintext $M=C^d (\bmod n)$

Operation of public key encryption system [34]. *Source:* Glisic [34].

Design Example 11.6 Shor's Algorithm (Continued)

$p=17$

$q=11$

$n=pq=187$

$\phi(n)=(p-1)(q-1)=160$

$e=7$

$d=23(de \bmod 160=1)$

$KU=[7,187]$

$KR=[23,187]$

$M=88$

Ciphertext

$C = 88^7 \bmod 187 = 11$

Pla int *ext*

$M = 11^{23} \bmod 187 = 88$

Numerical example of operation of public key encryption system [34]. *Source:* Glisic [34].

Multiplying two prime numbers is simple, but it is hard to factorize the result. For example, what are the factors of N = 507 906 452 803? Answer: P_1 = 566 557× P_2 = 896 479. By the way, N is a 32-bit integer. Nowadays, we can break a 1024-bit key with a sizable budget within months or a year. This is devastating, because Secure Sockets Layer (SSL) certificates holding the public key have a life span of 28 months. Fortunately, the complexity of the prime factorization problem grows exponentially with the key length. So, we are pretty safe since we have switched to 2048-bit keys already. But as we already pointed out earlier, the issue of its complexity has been solved by Shor's algorithm. Shor's algorithm was published in 1994. It solves a real problem that cannot be solved efficiently by classical computers. It is the kind of paradigm shift that attracts investments. For this reason, we look into the problem in greater detail.

In spite of the intensive efforts over many centuries of the best minds to find a polynomial-time factoring algorithm, no one has succeeded, and until recently, the most asymptotically efficient *classical* algorithm was the number-theoretic sieve [35, 36], which factors an integer N in time $O(\exp [(lgN)^{1/3} (lglg\ N)^{2/3}])$. Thus, this is a super-polynomial-time algorithm in the number $O(lgN)$ of digits in N. However, as already indicated in Chapter 8, Peter Shor suddenly changed the rules of the game.

Hidden in the above conjecture is the unstated, but implicitly understood, assumption that all algorithms run on computers based on the principles of classical mechanics, that is, on classical computers. But what if a computer could be built that is based not only on classical mechanics, but on quantum mechanics as well? That is, what if we could build a quantum computer? Shor, starting from the works of Benioff, Bennett, Deutsch, Feynman, Simon, and others, created an algorithm to be run on a quantum computer, that is, a quantum algorithm that factors integers in polynomial time! Shor's algorithm takes asymptotically $O((lgN)^2\ (lg\ lg\ N)(lglglgN))$ steps on a quantum computer, which is polynomial time in the number of digits $O(lgN)$ of N.

Number-theoretic preliminaries: It is a computationally easy (polynomial time) task to determine whether or not N is a prime or composite number. The primality testing algorithm of

(Continued)

Design Example 11.6 Shor's Algorithm (Continued)

Miller-Rabin [37] makes such a determination at the cost of $O(slgN)$ arithmetic operations [$O(slg^3N)$ bit operations] with probability of error $P(e) \leq 2^{-s}$.

However, once an odd positive integer N is known to be composite, it does not appear to be an easy (polynomial time) task on a classical computer to determine its prime factors. As mentioned earlier, so far the most asymptotically efficient *classical* algorithm known is the number-theoretic sieve.

It is well known [37] that factoring N can be reduced to the task of choosing at random an integer m relatively prime to N, and then determining its modulo N multiplicative order p, that is, to finding the smallest positive integer p such that $m^p = 1 \bmod N$. It was precisely this approach to factoring that enabled Shor to construct his factoring algorithm.

Shor's algorithm: Let N = {0, 1, 2, 3, ...} denote the set of natural numbers. Shor's algorithm provides a solution to the above problem. His algorithm consists of five steps (steps 1 through 5), with only STEP 2 requiring the use of a quantum computer. The remaining four other steps of the algorithm are to be performed on a classical computer. We begin by briefly describing all five steps. After that, we will then focus in on the quantum part of the algorithm, that is, STEP 2.

Step 1. Choose a random positive integer m. Use the polynomial-time Euclidean algorithm to compute the greatest common divisor $gcd(m, N)$ of m and N [38, 39]. If the greatest common divisor $gcd(m, N) \neq 1$, then we have found a nontrivial factor of N, and we are done. If, on the other hand, $gcd(m, N) = 1$, then proceed to STEP 2.

STEP 2. Use a quantum computer to determine the unknown period P of the function

$$\mathbb{N} \xrightarrow{f_N} \mathbb{N}$$

$$a \to m^a \bmod N$$

Step 3. If P is an odd integer, then go to Step 1. [The probability of P being odd is $(1/2)^k$, where k is the number of distinct prime factors of N.] If P is even, then proceed to Step 4.

Step 4. Since P is even, $(m^{P/2} - 1)(m^{P/2} + 1) = m^P - 1 = 0 \bmod N$.

If $m^{P/2} + 1 = 0 \bmod N$, then go to Step 1. If $m^{P/2} + 1 \neq 0 \bmod N$, then proceed to Step 5. It can be shown that the probability that $m^{P/2} + 1 = 0 \bmod N$ is less than $(1/2)^{k-1}$, where k denotes the number of distinct prime factors of N.

Step 5. Use the Euclidean algorithm to compute $gcd(m^{P/2} - 1, N)$. Since $m^{P/2} + 1 \neq 0 \bmod N$, it can easily be shown that d is a nontrivial factor of N. Exit with the answer d.

Thus, the task of factoring an odd positive integer N reduces to the following problem: Given a periodic function $f: \mathbb{N} \to \mathbb{N}$ find the period P of f.

Preparations for the quantum part of Shor's algorithm: Choose $Q = 2^L$ such that $N^2 \leq Q = 2^L < 2N^2$ and consider f restricted to the set $S_Q = \{0, 1, ... Q - 1\}$, which we also denote by f, that is, $f: S_Q \to S_Q$. In preparation for a discussion of STEP 2 of Shor's algorithm, we construct two L-qubit quantum registers, Register1 and Register2, to hold respectively the arguments and the values of the function f; that is,

$$| \text{Reg1} \rangle | \text{Reg2} \rangle = | a \rangle | f(a) \rangle = | a \rangle | b \rangle = | a_0 a_1 \cdots a_{L-1} \rangle | b_0 b_1 \cdots b_{L-1} \rangle$$

In doing so, we have adopted the following convention for representing integers in these registers: In a quantum computer, we represent an integer a with radix 2 representation

$$a = \sum_{j=0}^{L-1} a_j 2^j,$$

as a quantum register consisting of the 2^n qubits

$$|a\rangle = |a_0 a_1 \cdots a_{L-1}\rangle = \bigotimes_{j=0}^{L-1} |a_j\rangle$$

Before continuing, we remind the reader of the classical definition of the Q-point Fourier transform.

Definition 1 Let ω be a primitive Q-th root of unity, for example, $\omega = e^{2\pi i/Q}$. Then the Q-point Fourier transform is the map

$$Map(S_Q, \mathbb{C}) \xrightarrow{\mathcal{F}} Map(S_Q, \mathbb{C})$$
$$[f : S_Q \to \mathbb{C}] \to \left[\hat{f} : S_Q \to \mathbb{C}\right]$$

where

$$\hat{f}(y) = \frac{1}{\sqrt{Q}} \sum_{x \in S_Q} f(x) \omega^{xy}$$

We implement the Fourier transform $\mathcal{F}$ as a unitary transformation, which in the standard basis $|0\rangle, |1\rangle, \dots |Q-1\rangle$ is given by the $Q \times Q$ unitary matrix $\mathcal{F} = (\omega^{xy})/\sqrt{Q}$. This unitary transformation can be factored into the product of $O(\lg^2 Q) = O(\lg^2 N)$ sufficiently local unitary transformations [8, 40].

The quantum part of Shor's algorithm: The quantum part of Shor's algorithm, that is, STEP 2, is the following:

STEP 2.0 Initialize registers 1 and 2; that is,

$$|\psi_0\rangle = |Reg1\rangle |Reg2\rangle = |0\rangle |0\rangle = |00\cdots 0\rangle |0\cdots 0\rangle$$

STEP 2.1 Apply the Q-point Fourier transform $\mathcal{F}$ to Register1 $\xrightarrow{U_f}$

$$|\psi_0\rangle = |0\rangle |0\rangle \xrightarrow{\mathcal{F} \otimes I} |\psi_1\rangle = \frac{1}{\sqrt{Q}} \sum_{x=0}^{Q-1} \omega^{0 \cdot x} |x\rangle |0\rangle = \frac{1}{\sqrt{Q}} \sum_{x=0}^{Q-1} |x\rangle |0\rangle$$

Hence, Register1 now holds all the integers 0, 1, 2, ... $Q-1$ in superposition.

STEP 2.2 Let U_f be the unitary transformation that takes $|x\rangle |0\rangle$ to $|x\rangle |f(x)\rangle$. Apply the linear transformation U_f to the two registers. The result is

$$|\psi_1\rangle = \frac{1}{\sqrt{Q}} \sum_{x=0}^{Q-1} |x\rangle |0\rangle \xrightarrow{U_f} |\psi_2\rangle = \frac{1}{\sqrt{Q}} \sum_{x=0}^{Q-1} |x\rangle |f(x)\rangle$$

The state of the two registers is now more than a superposition of states. In this step, we have quantum-entangled the two registers.

STEP 2.3. Apply the Q-point Fourier transform $\mathcal{F}$ to Reg1 to get

$$|\psi_2\rangle = \frac{1}{\sqrt{Q}} \sum_{x=0}^{Q-1} |x\rangle |f(x)\rangle \xrightarrow{\mathcal{F} \otimes I} |\psi_3\rangle = \frac{1}{Q} \sum_{x=0}^{Q-1} \sum_{y=0}^{Q-1} \omega^{xy} |y\rangle |f(x)\rangle$$

$$= \frac{1}{Q} \sum_{y=0}^{Q-1} |||\mathcal{J}(y)\rangle\rangle y) \frac{|\mathcal{J}(y)\rangle}{|||\mathcal{J}(y)\rangle||},$$

where $|\mathcal{J}(y)\rangle = \sum_{x=0}^{Q-1} \omega^{xy} |f(x)\rangle$.

STEP 2.4. Measure Reg1; that is, perform a measurement with respect to the orthogonal projections

$$|0\rangle\langle0|\otimes I,\ |1\rangle\langle1|\otimes I,\ |2\rangle\langle2|\otimes I, ...,\ |Q-1\rangle\langle Q-1|\otimes I,$$

where I is the identity operator on the Hilbert space of the second register Reg2.

As a result of this measurement, we have, with probability $P(y_0) = \||\mathcal{J}(y)\rangle\|^2/Q^2$, *moved to the state* $|y_0\rangle|\mathcal{J}(y)\rangle/\||\mathcal{J}(y)\rangle\|$ and measured the value $y_0 \in \{0, 1, 2, ...Q-1\}$. If after this computation we ignore the two registers Reg1 and Reg2, we see that what we have created is nothing more than a classical probability distribution $\mathcal{S}$ on the sample space $\{0, 1, 2, ...Q-1\}$.

In other words, the sole purpose of executing STEPS 2.1 to 2.4 is to create a classical finite memoryless stochastic source $\mathcal{S}$ that outputs a symbol $y_0 \in \{0, 1, 2, ..., Q-1\}$ with probability $P(y_0) = \||\mathcal{J}(y)\rangle\|^2/Q^2$. As we shall see, the objective of the rest of Shor's algorithm is to glean information about the period P of f from the just-created stochastic source $\mathcal{S}$. The stochastic source was created precisely for that reason.

Shor's stochastic source $\mathcal{S}$: Before continuing to the final part of Shor's algorithm, we need to analyze the probability distribution $P(y)$ a little more carefully. It can be shown [41] that if q and r are the unique non-negative integers such that $Q = Pq + r$, where $0 \le r < P$; and let $Q_0 = Pq$, then

$$P(y) = \begin{cases} \dfrac{r\sin^2\left(\dfrac{\pi Py}{Q}\cdot\left(\dfrac{Q_0}{P}+1\right)\right) + (P-r)\sin^2\left(\dfrac{\pi Py}{Q}\cdot\dfrac{Q_0}{P}\right)}{Q^2\sin^2\left(\dfrac{\pi Py}{Q}\right)} & \text{if } Py \ne 0\bmod Q \\[4ex] \dfrac{r(Q_0+P)^2 + (P-r)Q_0^2}{Q^2P^2} & \text{if } Py = 0\bmod Q \end{cases}$$

And if P is an exact divisor of Q, then

$$P(y) = \begin{cases} 0 & \text{if } Py \ne 0 \bmod Q \\ 1/P & \text{if } Py = 0 \bmod Q \end{cases}$$

Continued fractions: We digress for a moment to review the theory of continued fractions [43, 44]. Every positive rational number ξ can be written as an expression in the form

$$\xi = a_0 + \cfrac{1}{a_1 + \cfrac{1}{a_2 + \cfrac{1}{a_3 + \cfrac{1}{\cdots + \cfrac{1}{a_N}}}}}, \qquad \begin{aligned} 8/3 &= 2 + \frac{2}{3} = 2 + \cfrac{1}{\frac{3}{2}} = 2 + \cfrac{1}{1 + \frac{1}{2}} \\[2ex] &= 2(a_0) + \cfrac{1}{1(a_1) + \cfrac{1}{2(a_2)}} \end{aligned}$$

where a_0 is a non-negative integer, and where $a_1, ..., a_N$ are positive integers. Such an expression is called a (finite, simple) continued fraction, and is uniquely determined by ξ provided we impose the condition $a_N > 1$. For typographical simplicity, we denote the above continued fraction by $[a_0, a_1, ... a_N]$. The continued fraction expansion of ξ can be computed with the following recurrence relation, which always terminates if ξ is rational:

$$
\begin{cases}
a_0 = |\xi| \\
\xi_0 = \xi - a_0
\end{cases}
\quad , \text{ and if } \xi_n \neq 0, \text{ then} \quad
\begin{cases}
a_{n+1} = |1/\xi_n| \\
\xi_{n+1} = \frac{1}{\xi_n} - a_{n+1}
\end{cases}
$$

The n-th convergent ($0 \leq n \leq N$) of the above continued fraction is defined as the rational number ξ_n given by $\xi_n = [a_0, a_1, ... a_n]$. Each convergent ξ_n can be written in the form, $\xi_n = p_n/q_n$, where p_n and q_n are relatively prime integers ($\gcd(p_n, q_n) = 1$). The integers p_n and q_n are determined by the recurrence relation $p_0 = a_0$, $p_1 = a_1 a_0 + 1$, $p_n = a_n p_{n-1} + p_{n-2}$, $q_0 = 1$, $q_1 = a_1$, $q_n = a_n q_{n-1} + q_{n-2}$.

Preparation for the final part of Shor's algorithm: For each integer a, let $\{a\}_Q = a - Q \cdot round\ (a/Q) = a - Q \cdot \lfloor a/Q + 1/2 \rfloor$ denote the residue of a modulo Q of smallest magnitude. In other words, $\{a\}_Q$ is the unique integer such that

$$
\begin{cases}
a = \{a\}_Q \bmod Q \\
-Q/2 < \{a\}_Q \leq Q/2
\end{cases}
$$

Let y be an integer lying in S_Q. Then [41]

$$
Prob(y) \geq
\begin{cases}
\dfrac{4}{\pi^2} \cdot \dfrac{1}{P} \cdot \left(1 - \dfrac{1}{N}\right)^2 & \text{if } 0 < |\{Py\}_Q| \leq \dfrac{P}{2} \cdot \left(1 - \dfrac{1}{N}\right) \\[4mm]
\dfrac{1}{P} \cdot \left(1 - \dfrac{1}{N}\right)^2 & \text{if } \{Py\}_Q = 0
\end{cases}
$$

Now, let $Y = \left\{ y \in S_Q \,\middle\|\, |\{Py\}_Q| \leq \frac{P}{2} \right\}$ and $S_P = \{d \in S_Q \,|\, 0 \leq d < P\}$ then the map

$$
Y \rightarrow S_P
$$

$$
y \rightarrow d = d(y) = round\left(\frac{P}{Q} \cdot y\right)
$$

is a bijection with inverse

$$
y = y(d) = round\left(\frac{Q}{P} \cdot d\right).
$$

Hence, Y and S_P are in one-to-one correspondence [41]. Moreover, $\{Py\}_Q = P \cdot y - Q \cdot d(y)$). In addition the following two sets of rationals are in one-to-one correspondence:

$$
\left\{ \frac{y}{Q} \,\middle|\, y \in Y \right\} \longleftrightarrow \left\{ \frac{d}{P} \,\middle|\, 0 \leq d < P \right\}
$$

As a result of the measurement performed in STEP 2.4, we have in our possession an integer $y \in Y$. We now show how y can be used to determine the unknown period P. We now need the following theorem [42] from the theory of continued fractions:

Theorem 1   Let ξ be a real number, and let a and b be integers with b > 0. If $|\xi - a/b| \leq 1/2b^2$, then the rational number a/b is a convergent of the continued fraction expansion of ξ.

As a corollary, we have If $|\{Py\}_Q| \leq P/2$, then the rational number $d(y)/P$ is a convergent of the continued fraction expansion of y/Q [41].

Since $d(y)/P$ is a convergent of the continued fraction expansion of y/Q, it follows that, for some n, $d(y)/P = p_n/q_n$, where p_n and q_n are relatively prime positive integers given by a recurrence relation found in the previous subsection. So it would seem that we have found a way of deducing the period P from the output y of STEP2.4, and so we are done; or maybe not yet!

We can determine P from the measured y produced by STEP 2.4, only if $p_n = d(y)$, $q_n = P$ which is true only when $d(y)$ and P are relatively prime. So what is the probability that the $y \in Y$ produced by STEP 2.4 satisfies the additional condition that $\gcd(P, d(y)) = 1$?

The probability that the random y produced by STEP 2.4 is such that $d(y)$ and P are relatively prime is bounded below by the following expression [41]:

$$Prob\{y \in Y \mid \gcd(d(y), P) = 1\} \geq \frac{4}{\pi^2} \cdot \frac{\varphi(P)}{P} \cdot \left(1 - \frac{1}{N}\right)^2,$$

where $\varphi(P)$ denotes Euler's totient function; that is, $\varphi(P)$ is the number of positive integers less than P that are relatively prime to P. The following theorem can be found in ([30], Theorem 328, Section 18.4):

Theorem 2

$$\lim \inf \frac{\varphi(N)}{N/\ln \ln N} = e^{-\gamma},$$

where γ denotes Euler's constant $\gamma = 0.57721566490153286061 \ldots$, and where $e^{-\gamma} = 0.5614594836 \ldots$

As a corollary, we have

$$Prob\{y \in Y \mid \gcd(d(y), P) = 1\} \geq \frac{4}{\pi^2 \ln 2} \cdot \frac{e^{-\gamma} - \varepsilon(P)}{\lg\lg N} \cdot \left(1 - \frac{1}{N}\right)^2,$$

where $\varepsilon(P)$ is a monotone decreasing sequence converging to zero. In terms of asymptotic notation,

$$Prob\{y \in Y \mid \gcd(d(y), P) = 1\} = \Omega\left(\frac{1}{\lg\lg N}\right).$$

Thus, if STEP 2.4 is repeated $O(\lg\lg N)$ times, then the probability of success is (1) [41].

The final part of Shor's algorithm: We are now prepared to give the last step in Shor's algorithm. This step can be performed on a classical computer.

Step 2.5 Compute the period P from the integer y produced by STEP 2.4.

- LOOP FOR EACH n FROM $n = 1$ *UNTIL* $\xi_n = 0$.
  - Use the recurrence relations

    $$p_0 = a_0, \quad p_1 = a_1 a_0 + 1, \quad p_n = a_n p_{n-1} + p_{n-2},$$
    $$q_0 = 1, q_1 = a_1, q_n = a_n q_{n-1} + q_{n-2}.$$

  to compute the p_n and q_n of the n-th convergent p_n/q_n of y/Q.
    Test to see if $q_n = P$ by computing

    $$m^{q_n} = \prod_i \left(m^{2^i}\right)^{q_{nj}} \mod N,$$

  where $q_n = \sum_i q_{n, i} 2^i$ is the binary expansion of q_n.
    If $m^{q_n} = 1 \mod N$, then exit with the answer $P = q_n$, and proceed to Step 3.
    If not, then continue the loop.
  - END OF LOOP

The probability that the integer y produced by STEP 2.4 will lead to a successful completion of Step 2.5 is bounded below by

$$\frac{4}{\pi^2 \ln 2} \cdot \frac{e^{-\gamma} - \varepsilon(P)}{\lg\lg N} \cdot \left(1 - \frac{1}{N}\right)^2 > \frac{0.232}{\lg\lg N} \cdot \left(1 - \frac{1}{N}\right)^2,$$

provided the period P is greater than 3 (denotes Euler's constant).

Design Example 11.7 QC Implementation of Shor's Algorithm

Let us now show how $N = 91(=7 \cdot 13)$ can be factored using Shor's algorithm. In [41] $Q = 2^{14} = 16\,384$ was chosen so that $N^2 \leq Q < 2N^2$. Based on this we have

STEP 1 Choose a random positive integer m, say $m = 3$. Since $\gcd(91, 3) = 1$, we proceed to STEP 2 to find the period of the function f given by $f(a) = 3^a \bmod 91$

Unknown to us, f has period $P = 6$. For,

$$a \quad 0 \quad 1 \quad 2 \quad 3 \quad 4 \quad 5 \quad 6 \quad 7 \cdots$$

$$f(a) \quad 1 \quad 3 \quad 9 \quad 27 \quad 81 \quad 61 \quad 1 \quad 3$$

Unknown period $P = 6$

STEP 2.0 Initialize registers 1 and 2. Thus, the state of the two registers becomes $|\psi_0\rangle = |0\rangle|0\rangle$.

STEP 2.1 Apply the Q-point Fourier transform $\mathcal{F}$ to register #1, where

$$\mathcal{F} \, | \, k \rangle = \frac{1}{\sqrt{16384}} \sum_{x=0}^{16\,383} \omega^{0 \cdot x} \, | \, x \rangle,$$

and where ω is a primitive Q-th root of unity, e.g. $\omega = e^{\frac{2\pi i}{16\,384}}$. Thus the state of the two registers becomes:

$$| \, \psi_1 \rangle = \frac{1}{\sqrt{16384}} \sum_{x=0}^{16\,383} | \, x \rangle \, | \, 0 \rangle$$

STEP 2.2 Apply the unitary transformation U_f to registers #1 and #2, where $U_f | \, x \rangle \, | \, \ell \rangle = | \, x \rangle \, | \, f(x) - \ell \bmod 91 \rangle$. (Recall that $U_f^2 = I$.) Thus, the state of the two registers becomes

$$| \psi_2 \rangle = \frac{1}{\sqrt{16384}} \sum_{x=0}^{16383} |k\rangle \, | \, 3^x \bmod 91 \rangle$$

$$= \frac{1}{\sqrt{16384}} (|0\rangle|1\rangle + |1\rangle|3\rangle + |2\rangle|9\rangle + |3\rangle|27\rangle + |4\rangle|81\rangle + |5\rangle|61\rangle$$

$$+ |6\rangle|1\rangle + |7\rangle|3\rangle + |8\rangle|9\rangle + |9\rangle|27\rangle + |10\rangle|81\rangle + |11\rangle|61\rangle$$

$$+ |12\rangle|1\rangle + |13\rangle|3\rangle + |14\rangle|9\rangle + |15\rangle|27\rangle + |16\rangle|81\rangle + |17\rangle|61\rangle + \ldots +$$

$$+ |16380\rangle|1\rangle + |16381\rangle|3\rangle + |16382\rangle|9\rangle + |16383\rangle|27\rangle)$$

The state of the two registers is now more than a superposition of states. We have in the above step quantum-entangled the two registers.

(Continued)

Design Example 11.7 QC Implementation of Shor's Algorithm (Continued)

STEP 2.3 Apply the Q-point $\mathcal{F}$ again to register #1. Thus, the state of the system becomes

$$|\psi_3\rangle = \frac{1}{\sqrt{16384}} \sum_{x=0}^{16383} \frac{1}{\sqrt{16384}} \sum_{y=0}^{16383} \omega^{xy} \, |y\rangle \, |3^x \bmod 91\rangle$$

$$= \frac{1}{16384} \sum_{x=0}^{16383} |y\rangle \sum_{x=0}^{16383} \omega^{xy} \, |3^x \bmod 91\rangle = \frac{1}{16384} \sum_{x=0}^{16383} |y\rangle \, |\mathcal{J}(y)\rangle,$$

where $|\mathcal{J}(y)\rangle = \sum_{x=0}^{16383} \omega^{xy} \, |3^x \bmod 91\rangle$. Thus,

$$\begin{aligned}
|\mathcal{J}(y)\rangle = \; & |1\rangle + \omega^{y}\,|3\rangle + \omega^{2y}\,|9\rangle + \omega^{3y}\,|27\rangle + \omega^{4y}\,|81\rangle + \omega^{5y}\,|61\rangle \\
& + \omega^{6y}\,|1\rangle + \omega^{7y}\,|3\rangle + \omega^{8y}\,|9\rangle + \omega^{9y}\,|27\rangle + \omega^{10y}\,|81\rangle + \omega^{11y}\,|61\rangle \\
& + \omega^{12y}\,|1\rangle + \omega^{13y}\,|3\rangle + \omega^{14y}\,|9\rangle + \omega^{15y}\,|27\rangle + \omega^{16y}\,|81\rangle + \omega^{17y}\,|61\rangle \\
& + \ldots + \\
& + \omega^{16380y}\,|1\rangle + \omega^{16381y}\,|3\rangle + \omega^{16382y}\,|9\rangle + \omega^{16383y}\,|27\rangle
\end{aligned}$$

STEP 2.4 Measure Reg1. The result of our measurement just happens to turn out to be $y = 13\,453$. Unknown to us, the probability of obtaining this particular y is $0.3189335551 \times 10^{-6}$. Moreover, unknown to us, the corresponding d is relatively prime to P; that is, $d = d(y) = \text{round}(Py/Q) = 5$. However, we do know that the probability of $d(y)$ being relatively prime to P is greater than

$$\frac{0.232}{\lg\lg N}\left(1 - \frac{1}{N}\right)^2 \approx 8.4\% \text{ (provided } P > 3\text{)},$$

and we also know that $d(y)/P$ is a convergent of the continued fraction expansion of $\xi = y/Q = 13453/16384$. So, with a reasonable amount of confidence, we proceed to STEP 2.5.

STEP 2.5 Using the recurrence relations, $p_0 = a_0$, $p_1 = a_1 a_0 + 1$, $p_n = a_n p_{n-1} + p_{n-2}$, $q_0 = 1$, $q_1 = a_1$, $q_n = a_n q_{n-1} + q_{n-2}$ we successively compute (beginning with $n = 0$) the a_n's and q_n's for the continued fraction expansion of $\xi = y/Q = 13453/16384$. For each nontrivial n in succession, we check to see if $3^{q_n} = 1 \bmod 91$. If this is the case, then we know $q_n = P$, and we immediately exit from STEP 2.5 and proceed to STEP 3.

- In this example, $n = 0$ and $n = 1$ are trivial cases.
- For $n = 2$, $a_2 = 4$, and $q_2 = 5$. We test q_2 by computing

$$3^{q_2} = 3^5 = \left(3^{2^0}\right)^1 \cdot \left(3^{2^1}\right)^0 \cdot \left(3^{2^2}\right)^1 = 61 \neq 1 \bmod 91.$$

Hence, $q_2 \neq P$.

- We proceed to $n = 3$, and compute $a_3 = 1$ and $q_3 = 6$.

We then test q_3 by computing

$$3^{q_3} = 3^6 = \left(3^{2^0}\right)^0 \cdot \left(3^{2^1}\right)^1 \cdot \left(3^{2^2}\right)^1 = 1 \bmod 91.$$

Hence, $q_3 = P$. Since we now know the period P, there is no need to continue to compute the remaining a_n's and q_n's. We proceed immediately to Step 3.

STEP 3. Since $P = 6$ is even, we proceed to Step 4.

STEP 4. Since $3^{P/2} = 3^3 = 27 \neq -1 \bmod 91$, we goto Step 5.

STEP 5. With the Euclidean algorithm, we compute

$$\gcd\left(3^{P/2} - 1, 91\right) = \gcd(3^3 - 1, 91) = \gcd(26, 91) = 13.$$

We have succeeded in finding a nontrivial factor of $N = 91$, namely, 13.

References

1 Botsinis, P. et al. Quantum search algorithms for wireless communications. *IEEE Communications Surveys & Tutorials* **21** (2) Second Quarter 2019: 1209.

2 Deutsch, D. (1985). Quantum theory, the church-turing principle and the universal quantum computer. *Proc. Roy. Soc. London A Math. Phys. Sci.* **400** (1818): 97–117.

3 Deutsch, D. and Jozsa, R. (1992). Rapid solution of problems by quantum computation. *Proc. Roy. Soc. A Math. Phys. Sci.* **439** (1907): 553–558.

4 Cleve, R., Ekert, A., Macchiavello, C., and Mosca, M. (1998). Quantum algorithms revisited. *Proc. Roy. Soc. London A* **454**: 339–357.

5 Nielsen, M.A. and Chuang, I.L. (2011). *Quantum Computation and Quantum Information*, 10e. New York, NY, USA: Cambridge UniversityPress.

6 Simon, D.R. (1997). On the power of quantum computation. *SIAM J. Comput.* **26** (5): 1474–1483.

7 P. W. Shor, "Algorithms for quantum computation: Discrete logarithms and factoring," in Proc. 35th Annu. Symp. Found. Comput. Sci., Nov. 1994, pp. 124–134.

8 Shor, P.W. (1997). Polynomial-time algorithms for prime factorization and discrete logarithms on a quantum computer. *SIAM J. Comput.* **26** (5): 1484–1509.

9 Pomerance, C. (1996). A tale of two sieves. *Notices Amer. Math. Soc* **43**: 1473–1485.

10 L. K. Grover, "A fast quantum mechanical algorithm for database search," in Proc. 28th Annu. ACM Symp. Theory Comput., May 1996, pp. 212–219.

11 Grover, L.K. (1997). Quantum mechanics helps in searching for a needle in a haystack. *Phys. Rev. Lett.* **79** (2): 325–328.

12 Knuth, D.E. (1998). *The Art of Computer Programming, Volume 3: Sorting and Searching*, 2e. Redwood City, CA, USA: Addison-Wesley.

13 Zalka, C. (1999). Grover's quantum searching algorithm is optimal. *Phys. Rev. A* **60**: 2746–2751.

14 G. Brassard, P. Høyer, M. Mosca, and A. Tapp, "Quantum amplitude amplification and estimation," eprint arXiv:quant-ph/0005055, May 2000.

15 Boyer, M., Brassard, G., Høyer, P., and Tapp, A. (1998). Tight bounds on quantum searching. *Fortschritte der Physik* **46** (4–5): 493–506.

16 C. Dürr and P. Høyer, "A quantum algorithm for finding the minimum," eprint arXiv:quant-ph/9607014, Jul. 1996.

17 Botsinis, P., Ng, S.X., and Hanzo, L. (2014). Fixed-complexity quantumassisted multi-user detection for CDMA and SDMA. *IEEE Trans. Commun.* **62** (3): 990–1000.

18 G. Brassard, P. Hoyer, and A. Tapp, "Quantum counting," eprint arXiv:quant-ph/9805082, May 1998. Also 25th Intl. Colloquium on Automata, Languages, and Programming (ICALP), LNCS 1443, pp. 820–831, 1998

19 Hogg, T. (2000). Quantum search heuristics. *Phys. Rev. A* **61**: 052311.

20 Hogg, T. and Portnov, D. (2000). Quantum optimization. *Inform. Sci.* **128** (3–4): 181–197.

21 Goldberg, D.E. (1989). *Genetic Algorithms in Search, Optimization and Machine Learning*, 1e. Boston, MA, USA: Addison-Wesley.

22 Syswerda, G. (1991). A study of reproduction in generational and steadystate genetic algorithms. *Found. Genet. Algorithms* **1**: 94–101.

23 Malossini, A., Blanzieri, E., and Calarco, T. (2008). Quantum genetic optimization. *IEEE Trans. Evol. Comput.* **12** (2): 231–241.

24 Harrow, A.W., Hassidim, A., and Lloyd, S. (2009). Quantum algorithm for linear systems of equations. *Phys. Rev. Lett.* **103** (15): 150502.

25 A. Ambainis, "Variable time amplitude amplification and a faster quantum algorithm for solving systems of linear equations," arXiv: 1010/4458v2, Oct. 2010.

26 A. M. Childs, R. Kothari, and R. D. Somma, "Quantum algorithm for systems of linear equations with exponentially improved dependence on precision," ArXiv e-prints, Nov. 2015

27 G. Brassard, F. Dupuis, S. Gambs, and A. Tapp, "An optimal quantum algorithm to approximate the mean and its application for approximating the median of a set of points over an arbitrary distance," eprint arXiv:quant-ph/1106.4267v1, Jun. 2011.

28 Botsinis, P., Ng, S.X., and Hanzo, L. (2013). Quantum search algorithms, quantum wireless, and a low-complexity maximum likelihood iterative quantum multi-user detector design. *IEEE Access* **1**: 94–122.

29 Imre, S. and Balázs, F. (2004). The generalized quantum database search algorithm. *Comput. Secur.* **73** (3): 245–269.

30 Terhal, B.M. and John, A. (1997). Smolin, Single quantum querying of a data base, arXiv:quant-ph/ 9705041v4 14 Nov 1997

31 Høyer, P. (1997). Efficient Quantum Transforms, arXiv:quant-ph/9702028v1 12 Feb 1997.

32 Shor, P.W. (1994). Algorithms for Quantum Computation: Discrete Logarithms and Factoring. Proceedings of the 35th Annual Symposium on Foundations of Computer Science, Santa Fe, 20–22 November 1994, 124–134. http://dx.doi.org/10.1109/SFCS.1994.365700.

33 Stinson, D.R. (1995). *Cryptography: Theory and Practice*. Boca Raton: CRC Press.

34 Glisic, S. (2016). *Advanced Wireless Networks: Technology and Business Models*. Wiley.

35 Lenstra, A.K. and Lenstra, H.W. Jr. (eds.) (1993). *The Development of the Number Field Sieve*," Lecture Notes in Mathematics, vol. **1554**. Springer-Velag.

36 Lenstra, A.K., H.W. Lenstra, Jr., M.S. Manasse, and J.M. Pollard, The number field sieve. Proc. 22nd Annual ACM Symposium on Theory of ComputingACM, New York, (1990), pp 564–572. (See exanded version in Lenstra & Lenstra, (1993), pp pp. 11–42.

37 Miller, G.L. (1976). Riemann's hypothesis and tests for primality. *J. Comput. Syst. Sci.* **13**: 300–317.

38 Cox, D., Little, J., and O'Shea, D. (1996). *Ideals, Varieties, and Algorithms*, 2e. Springer-Verlag.

39 Cormen, T.H., Leiserson, C.E., and Rivest, R.L. (1990). *Introduction to Algorithms*. McGraw-Hill.

40 Hoyer, Peter, Efficient quantum transforms, quant-ph/970202

41 S. J. Lomonaco, A lecture on Shor's quantum factoring algorithm https://arxiv.org/pdf/quant-ph/0010034.pdf

42 Hardy, G.H. and Wright, E.M. (1965). *An Introduction to the Theory of Numbers*. Oxford Press.

43 LeVeque, W.J. (1958). *Topics in Number Theory: Volume I*. Addison-Wesley.

44 P. Botsinis, S. X. Ng, and L. Hanzo, "Low-complexity iterative quantum multi-user detection in SDMA systems," in Proc. IEEE Int. Conf. Commun. (ICC), Jun. 2014, pp. 5592–5597.

45 B. Lorenzo and S. Glisic, "Compressed Control of Complex Wireless Networks," in IEEE Transactions on Wireless Communications, vol. 15, no. 8, pp. 5775–5788, Aug. 2016.

46 B. Lorenzo and S. Glisic, "Optimal Routing and Traffic Scheduling for Multihop Cellular Networks Using Genetic Algorithm," in IEEE Transactions on Mobile Computing, vol. 12, no. 11, pp. 2274–2288, Nov. 2013.

12

Quantum Machine Learning

In this chapter, we provide a brief description of quantum machine learning (QML) and its correlation with artificial intelligence (AI). We will see how the quantum counterpart of ML is much faster and more efficient than classical ML. Training the machine to learn from the algorithms implemented to handle data is the core of ML. The fields of computer science and statistics employ AI and computational statistics. The classical ML method, through its subsets of deep learning (supervised and unsupervised), helps to classify images, recognize patterns and speech, handle big data, and so on. For this reason, classical ML received great attention and investments from the industry. Nowadays, due to the huge quantities of data with which we deal every day, new approaches are needed to automatically manage, organize, and classify these data. Classical ML, which is a flexible and adaptable procedure, can recognize patterns efficiently, but some of these problems cannot be efficiently solved by these algorithms. The companies that specialize in the management of big databases are aware of these limitations and are very interested in new approaches to accomplish this. They have found one of these approaches in QML. However, the interest in implementing these techniques through quantum computation paves the way for QML, which aims to implement ML algorithms in quantum systems, by using quantum properties such as superposition and entanglement to solve these problems efficiently. This gives QML an edge over the classical ML technique in terms of speed of functioning and data handling. In the QML techniques, we develop quantum algorithms to operate the classical algorithms on a quantum computer. Thus, data can be classified, sorted, and analyzed using the quantum algorithms of supervised and unsupervised learning methods. These methods are again implemented through models of a quantum neural network (QNN) or support vector machine. We have now reached the point where we merge the algorithms discussed in Parts I and II of this book.

12.1 QML Algorithms

Here, we broadly discuss the two major learning processes: supervised and unsupervised learning. The pattern is learned observing the given set of training examples in the case of supervised learning, whereas structure is found in a clustered dataset in unsupervised learning. The chapter is structured in the same way as the previous ones. We start with a survey of the work and main results, and then go back and revisit some of the problems in greater detail.

The quantum clustering technique [1] uses the quantum Lloyd's algorithm to solve the k-means clustering problem. It basically uses a repetitive procedure to obtain the distance of the centroid of

Artificial Intelligence and Quantum Computing for Advanced Wireless Networks, First Edition.
Savo G. Glisic and Beatriz Lorenzo.
© 2022 John Wiley & Sons Ltd. Published 2022 by John Wiley & Sons Ltd.

the cluster. The basic methods involve randomly choosing an initial centroid and assigning every vector to the cluster with the closest mean. Repetitive calculation and updating of the centroid of the cluster should be done until a stationary value is obtained. The quantum algorithm speeds up the process in comparison to the classical algorithm. For an

N-dimensional space, it requires O(Mlog(MN)) time steps to run a quantum algorithm.

The QNN [2] model is the technique of deep supervised learning to train the machine to classify data and recognize patterns or images. It is a feedforward network. The basic principle is to design the circuits with qubits and rotation gates to operate the network in analogy with the neurons and weights as used in a classical neural network. The network learns from a set of training examples. Every input string comes with a label value. The function of the network is to obtain the label value of the dataset and minimize the deviation of the obtained label from the true label. The focus is to obtain the training parameter that gives the minimum error. The training parameter is updated at every iteration. Error minimization is done by the backpropagation technique, which is based on the gradient descent principle. All these techniques have been covered in Part I of the book.

The quantum decision tree [3] employs quantum states to create the classifiers used in ML. Decision trees generally consist of one starting node with outgoing edges but no incoming edges, that is, the root, which leads to several other leaves. In these structures, the answer to a question is classified as we move down the tree. The node contains a decision function that decides the direction of movement of the input vector along the branches and leaves. The quantum decision tree learns from a set of training data. In the quantum decision tree, each node basically splits the training data set into subsets based on a discrete function. The leaf is assigned to a class based on the target attribute state. Thus, the quantum decision tree classifies the data from the root to the final required leaf.

QML provides enormous scope in computing the techniques used in classical ML, covered in Part I of the book, on a quantum computer. The entanglement and superposition of the basic qubit states provides an edge over classical ML. Apart from neural networks, clustering methods, and decision trees, quantum machine algorithms have been proposed for several other applications of image and pattern classification, and data handling. Further implications of the algorithms will be discussed later in the chapter.

The quantum HHL algorithm for solving linear systems of equations was presented in [4]. The name comes from the authors' names: Aram Harrow, Avinatan Hassidim, and Seth Lloyd. More specifically, the algorithm can estimate the result of a scalar measurement on the solution vector b to a given linear system of equations Ax = b. In this context, A is an N × N Hermitian matrix with a spectral norm bounded by 1 and a finite condition number $\kappa = |\lambda_{max}/\lambda_{min}|$. The HHL algorithm can be efficiently implemented only when the matrix A is sparse (at most poly[log N] entries per row) and well conditioned (that is, its singular values lie between $1/\kappa$ and 1). We also emphasize the term "scalar measurement" here: the solution vector x produced by the HHL subroutine is actually (approximately) encoded in a quantum state $|\tilde{x}\rangle$ of $\lceil \log_2 N \rceil$ qubits, and it cannot be directly read out; in one run of the algorithm, we can at most determine some statistical properties of $|x\rangle$ by measuring it in some basis or rather sampling using some quantum mechanical operator M, that is, $\langle \tilde{x}|M|\tilde{x}\rangle$. Even determining a specific entry of the solution vector would take approximately N iterations of the algorithm. Furthermore, the HHL requires a quantum RAM (in theory): that is, a memory that can create the superposition state $|b\rangle$ (encoded b) all at once, from the entries $\{b_i\}$ of b without using parallel processing elements for each individual entry. Only if all these conditions are satisfied does the HHL run in the claimed O(log N$s^2\kappa^2/\varepsilon$) time, where s is the sparsity parameter of the matrix A (i.e., the maximum number of nonzero elements in a row), and ε is the desired/allowed error [5–7]. The HHL algorithm comprises three steps: phase estimation, controlled rotation, and *uncomputation* [8, 9]. We will discuss these steps in details later on in this chapter.

Quantum support vector machine (SVM): Data classification is one of the most important tools of ML today. It can used to identify, group, and study new data. As already discussed in Part I of the book, these machines learning classification tools have been used in traffic recognition, computer vision problems, medical imaging, drug discovery, handwriting recognition, geostatistics, and many other fields. Classification tools enable machines to identify data and therefore know how to react to a particular data. In ML, one of the most common methods of data classification is SVMs. An SVM is particularly useful because it allows us to classify an input set of data into one of two categories by drawing a hyperplane between the two categories. Quantum SVM machines have been recreated both theoretically [10] and experimentally [11]. These machines use qubits instead of classical bits to solve our problems. Many such quantum SVM [12–14] and quantum-inspired SVM [15–17] algorithms have been developed. We will revisit this problem later on in the chapter with all the necessary details.

A quantum classifier is a quantum computing algorithm that uses the quantum states of existing data to determine or categorize new data into their respective classes. A recent paper by Microsoft presented a quantum framework for supervised learning based on variational approaches [18]. Inference with the model $f(x, \theta) = y$ is executed by a quantum device that consists of a state preparation circuit S_x encoding the input x into the amplitudes of a quantum system, a model circuit U_θ, and a single-qubit measurement. The measurement retrieves the probability that the model will predict 0 or 1, from which in turn the binary prediction can be inferred. The classification circuit parameters θ are learnable and can be trained by a variational scheme. Given an encoded feature vector ψ_x which is now a ket vector in the Hilbert space of a n qubit system, the model circuit maps this ket vector to another ket vector $\psi' = U_\theta \psi(x)$ by a unitary operation U_θ that is parametrized by a set of variables θ. We will revisit this problem in greater detail later in the chapter.

Later that year, Farhi and Neven's [2] paper discussed a QNN that could represent labeled data, classical or quantum, and be trained by supervised learning. Imagine that a dataset consists of strings $z = z_1 z_2 \dots z_n$, where each z_i is a bit taking the value $+1$ or -1 and a binary label $l(z)$ chosen as $+1$ or -1. We have a quantum processor that acts on $n + 1$ qubits, and we ignore the possible need for ancilla qubits. The last qubit will serve as a readout. The quantum processor implements unitary transformations on input states. The unitaries that we have come from some toolbox of unitaries, perhaps determined by experimental considerations [19]. So we have a set of basic unitaries. The input state $|\Psi, 1\rangle$ is prepared and then transformed via a sequence of few qubit unitaries $U_i(\Theta_i)$ that depend on parameters Θ_i. These get adjusted during learning such that the measurement of Y_{n+1} on the readout qubit tends to produce the desired label for $|\Psi\rangle$.

A paper by Grant et al. [20] discusses how quantum circuits with a hierarchical structure have been used to perform binary classification of classical data encoded in a quantum state. They demonstrate more expressive circuits that can be used to classify highly entangled quantum states. The circuits used here are tree-like and can be parameterized with a simple gate set that is compatible with currently available quantum computers. The first of these circuits is known as a tree tensor network (TTN) [21]. We then consider a more complex circuit layout known as the multi-scale entanglement renormalization ansatz (MERA) [22]. MERAs are similar to TTNs, but make use of additional unitary transformations to effectively capture a broader range of quantum correlations. Both one-dimensional (1D) and two-dimensional (2D) versions of TTN and MERA circuits have been proposed in the literature [23, 24].

A paper by Turkpence *et al.* [25] on a steady-state quantum classifier exploits the additivity and the divisibility properties of completely positive (CP) quantum dynamical maps in order to obtain an open system classifier. He also numerically demonstrates that a steady state of a quantum unit subjected to different information environments acts as a quantum data classifier. The influence of a dissipative environment on the reduced system dynamics is the evolution of pure states into mixed steady states [26]. Mixed quantum states are a mixture of classical probability distributions that carry no quantum signature. The theoretical modeling of the proposed classifier without accounting for the imperfections or physical decay mechanisms. The objective of this model was to demonstrate that a small quantum system weakly in contact with different quantum environments can be used for classifying the data the environments contain.

Entanglement in QML: We have discussed the phenomenon of entanglement in Chapter 8. This feature is extensively used in ML as it reduces the number of qubits required to perform the same task in classical ML. However, there are some disadvantages of using *QML* as well, which is discussed in the work of Cristian [27].

In 2015, Cai [28] and his group demonstrated that the manipulation of high-dimensional vectors and the estimation of the distance and inner product between vectors, a ubiquitous task in ML, can be naturally done with quantum computers, thus proving the suitability and potential power of QML. They reported the first experimental entanglement-based classification of two-, four-, and eight-dimensional vectors to different clusters using a small-scale photonic quantum computer, which are then used to implement supervised and unsupervised ML. The method can in principle be scaled to larger number of qubits, and may provide a new route to accelerate ML.

In [29], simple numerical experiments related to pattern/images classification were implemented in which the classifiers are represented by many-qubit quantum states written in the matrix product states (MPS). Classical ML algorithm is applied to these quantum states to learn the classical data. They explicitly show how quantum entanglement (i.e., single-site and bipartite entanglement) can emerge in such represented images. Entanglement here characterizes the importance of data, and such information is used practically to guide the architecture of MPS and improve its efficiency. The number of needed qubits can be reduced to less than 1/10 of the original number, which is within the reach of the state-of-the-art quantum computers.

Work in [30] establishes contemporary deep learning architectures, in the form of deep convolution and recurrent networks, that can efficiently represent highly entangled quantum systems. By constructing tensor network equivalents of these architectures, they identified an inherent reuse of information in the network operation as a key trait that distinguishes them from standard tensor-network-based representations, and which enhances their entanglement capacity. Their results show that such architectures can support volume-law entanglement scaling that is polynomially more efficiently than the presently employed restricted Boltzmann machines (RBMs). Thus, beyond a quantification of the entanglement capacity of leading deep learning architectures, their analysis formally motivates a shift of trending neural-network-based wave function representations closer to the state of the art in ML.

The neural network is one of the most significant aspects of ML and AI. To make machines learn from the data patterns and analyze the data on their own, scientists devised algorithms to simulate our natural neural network. The first neural network for pattern recognition skills was presented in [31]. In this context, we see that as the demand of ML is increasing day by day, understanding the physical aspects of neural network has to be increased, and this is one of the areas where entanglement properties have to be studied. It was found that for short RBM states, entanglement entropy follows the area law, which is also inspired by the holographic principle that states all the information resides on the surface of a black hole, and hence the entropy depends on its surface area and not on its volume [32–34]. For any dimension and arbitrary bipartition geometric R-range RBM states, entanglement entropy becomes $\leq 2a(A)R \log 2$, where a(A) is the surface area of subsystem A.

Supervised learning can be enhanced by the entangled sensor network (SLEEN) as shown in [35]. Currently, the existing quantum supervised learning schemes depend on quantum random access memories (qRAM) to store quantum-encoded data given a priori in a classical description. However, the data acquisition process has not been used although this process makes the maximum usage of input data for different supervised ML tasks, as constrained by the quantum Cramér–Rao bound. The authors of [35] introduced the SLEEN. The entanglement states become useful in quantum data classification and data compression. They used SLEEN to construct entanglement-enhanced SVM and entangled-enhanced principal component analysis (PCA). In both cases they were able to take advantage of entangled states–data classification and data compression, respectively.

In the case of SVMs, whereas separable-state SVM becomes inaccurate due to measurement uncertainty making the data classification less contrasting, entangled-state SVM is not affected by the uncertainty and maintains the output as expected.

12.2 QNN Preliminaries

In [36], attempts were made to model a neural network in quantum computing, and discussions were presented on the versatility of the quantum neural computer in comparison with classical computers. In [37], a method based on the multi-universe interpretation of quantum theory was introduced that made neural network training more powerful than ever before by superposition of several single-layered neural networks to form a bigger QNN. Work in [38] is based on using the quantum version of classical gradient descent, coupled with controlled NOT (CNOT) gates, to demonstrate the use of parallelism in quantum neural architectures. Reference [39] features a comprehensive study of contemporary neural network (NN) architectures in a PhD thesis. Reference [40] addressed the question of implementation of an artificial NN architecture on quantum hardware. Reference [41] gave guidelines for QNN models: the ability of the network to (i) produce binary output with a length independent of the length of the binary input by some distance measure, (ii) reflect some neural computing mechanisms, and (iii) utilize quantum phenomena and be fully consistent with quantum theory.

In the recent past, several advancements have been made to bridge the gap between classical and quantum deep learning. In [42], the power of quantum computing over classical computing in deep learning and objective function optimization was demonstrated.

Other notable works include the quantum perception model [43], QNNs based on Deutsch's model of quantum computational network [44], a quantum classification algorithm based on a competitive learning NN and the entanglement measure [45], a novel autonomous perceptron model for pattern classification applications [46], and the quantum version of generative adversarial networks [47].

Quantum neuron: The current problem in QNNs is the problem of introducing nonlinearity, as is the case in classical NNs. Nonlinearity is central to learning complex functions, and thus efforts have been made to resolve this: for example, by using quantum measurements [48, 49], using dissipative quantum gates [48], and exploiting the idea that a QNN based on the time evolution of the system is intrinsically nonlinear.

A quantum neuron is strongly correlated to the actual neuron of the human system. The latter, based on the electrochemical signals received, either fires or not; this is similar to the model of the classical neuron in deep learning. An input vector x (corresponding to the stimulus in humans) is combined with a set of weights θ (corresponding to the neurotransmitters), and the result of this combination determines whether the neuron fires or not. Mathematically, an n-dimensional input vector $X = x_1, x_2, \ldots x_n$ is combined with weights $\theta = \theta_1, \theta_2, \ldots \theta_n$ to yield the combination $x_1\theta_1 + x_2\theta_2 + \ldots + x_n\theta_n + b$, where b is the *bias* added to the computation to incorporate functions not passing through the origin of the n-dimensional space considered here [50]. To introduce non-linearity in the same model, several activation functions are used that have been shown to benefit NN training [51]. Recent advances have explored learning activation functions for separate neurons using gradient descent [52], approximation of NNs using the Rectified Linear Unit (ReLU) as the activation function [53], and other conventional functions like the sigmoid function and the step function.

The quantum equivalent of the classical neuron, the quantum neuron, is used to build the QNNs, which benefit from the intrinsic property of quantum mechanics of storing co-matrices and performing linear algebraic operations on those matrices conveniently [54–60]. To implement a quantum neuron, a set of n qubits is prepared and operated upon by some unitary transformation, and the result is prepared in a separate ancilla qubit that is then measured – the measurement being the decision as to whether the quantum neuron fires or not. More specifically, to encode an m−dimensional classical input vector x, n qubits are used such that $m = 2^n$, $n < m$, thereby exploiting the advantage of quantum information storage that allows an exponential reduction in the number of input nodes required. The following transformation is done on the input qubits: $U | 0 \rangle^{\otimes n} = | \psi \rangle$.

Assuming the computational basis of the already defined n-dimensional Hilbert space is $|1\rangle$, $|2\rangle, |3\rangle, \ldots |n\rangle$, the input vector x and the weight vector θ can be defined in quantum terms as

$$|\psi\rangle = \frac{1}{n^{1/2}} \sum_{j=1}^{n} x_j |j\rangle \qquad (12.1)$$

where x_j represents the usual j-th component of the classical input vector x. Likewise, the weight vector θ can be encoded in the quantum realm as

$$|\varphi\rangle = \frac{1}{n^{1/2}} \sum_{j=1}^{n} \theta_j |j\rangle \qquad (12.2)$$

where θ_j represents the usual j-th component of the classical weight vector θ. Reference [61] defines a unitary operation that performs the inner product of the two terms defined above, and updates an ancilla qubit based on a multi-controlled NOT gate. The authors introduce a nonlinearity by performing a quantum measurement on the ancilla qubit.

Quantum convolutional N: CNNs provide great power over a variety of tasks: object tracking [62, 63], text detection and recognition [64], pose estimation [65], action recognition [66] scene labeling [67], and saliency detection using multi-context deep learning [68]. An additional review of convolutional deep learning is presented in [69]. The power of CNNs arises from the several convolutional layers and pooling layers, followed by a few densely and fully connected layers that help to reduce the huge size of various matrices of images to few hundred nodes, which can then be used for the final output layer of a few nodes (for instance, equal to the number of classes in a multi-classification problem). The weights are optimized by training on huge datasets fed into the network through multiple passes. CNNs also involve parameters that directly affect the parameters/weights, which are called the hyperparameters. Hyperparameters are fixed for specific networks based on experiments and comparisons across several models.

On the quantum side, NNs have been used to study the properties of quantum many-body systems [30, 70–75]. The use of quantum computers to enhance conventional ML tasks has gained attention in the modern world [76–79]. A QCNN circuit model has been proposed in [80]. The proposed model upper-bounds the n input parameters by $O(\log(n))$. Like conventional CNN, the authors continued the training on the quantum version of the *mean squared error*: $\text{MSE} = \sum_{i=0}^{m}(y_i - h(\psi))^2/2M$, where y_i is the actual output of the input state ψ, and $h(\psi)$ is the computation done by the quantum network. The *mean squared error* tends to reduce the distance between the actual output and the value predicted by the network. The authors discuss efficient implementation on experimental platforms: efficient preparation of quantum many-body input states, two-qubit gates application, and projective measurements. With the success of quantum convolutional NNs, it is hoped that other conventional deep learning networks will soon be converted, thus increasing the range of QNNs. To solve highly complex problems – like quantum phase recognition (QPR), which asks whether a given input quantum state ρ_{in} belongs to a particular quantum phase of matter; and quantum error correction (QEC) optimization, which asks for an optimal QEC code for a given a priori unknown error model such as dephasing or potentially correlated depolarization in realistic experimental settings – quantum convolution NNs have stood out as the best possible solution. The highly intrinsic quantum nature of these problems makes them difficult to solve using existing classical and QML techniques. Although conventional ML with large-scale NNs can successfully solve analogous classical problems such as image recognition or classical error correction improvement, the exponentially large many-body Hilbert space hinders efficiently translating such quantum problems into a classical framework without performing exponentially difficult quantum state or process tomography. Quantum algorithms avoid this overhead, but the limited size and coherence times of near-term quantum devices prevent the use of large-scale networks; thus, it is vital to first theoretically understand the most important ML mechanisms that must be implemented.

Many-body quantum systems and artificial neural network (ANN): Studying many-body quantum systems remains one of the most challenging areas of physics. It is mainly due to the exponential complexity of the many-body wave function and the difficulty in describing the nontrivial correlations encoded in its wave function [70]. However, recently the use of NNs for the variational representation of the quantum many-body states has generated enormous interest in this field [81–86]. This representation, first introduced by Carleo and Troyer in 2016, used the RBM architecture with a variable number of hidden neurons. Using this procedure, they could find the ground state of the transverse field Ising (TFI) and the antiferromagnetic Heisenberg (AFH) models with high accuracy [70]. Moreover, they could also describe the unitary time evolution of complex interacting quantum systems. Since then, NNs have been extensively used to study various physical systems. The representational power and the entanglement properties of the RBM states have been investigated, and the RBM representation of different systems such as the Ising model, toric code, graph states, and stabilizer codes have been constructed [81]. Also, the representational power of the other NN architectures such as the deep Boltzmann machine (DBM) are under active investigation.

Variational representation: An NN can represent a quantum state of a physical system in terms of its network parameters [70]. The RBM architecture consists of a visible layer of N neurons and a hidden layer of M neurons. The neurons of the visible layer and hidden layers are connected, but there are no intra-layer connections. As the spin of the neurons in the RBM network can have the values ± 1, the spins of the neurons of the visible layer can be mapped to the spins of the physical system they represent. Moreover, a set of weights is assigned to the visible (a_i for the i_{th} visible neuron) and hidden (b_i for the i_{th} hidden neuron) neurons and to the couplers connecting them (W_{ij} for the coupler connecting the $i - th$ visible neuron with the $j - th$ hidden neuron) [85]. Then, wave function ansatz (initialization) for the N-dimensional quantum state of spin variable configuration $\mathcal{S} = \{s_i\}_{i=1}^{N}$ would be given by $\psi_M(\mathcal{S}, \mathcal{W}) = \sum_{\{h_i\}} e^{\Sigma_i a_i s_i + \Sigma_j b_j h_j + \Sigma_{ij} W_{ij} s_i h_j}$, where s_i and h_i denote the spins of the visible and hidden neurons, respectively, and the whole state is given by the superposition of all the spin configuration states with $\psi(\mathcal{S})$ as the amplitude of the $|\mathcal{S}\rangle$ state $|\psi\rangle = \sum_S \psi(\mathcal{S})|\mathcal{S}\rangle$.

12.3 Quantum Classifiers with ML: Near-Term Solutions

The current generation of quantum computing technologies calls for quantum algorithms that require a limited number of qubits and quantum gates, and that are robust against errors. A suitable design approach is variational circuits where the parameters of gates are learned, an approach that is particularly fruitful for applications in ML. We will address variational quantum algorithms in more detail in the next section. Here, we discuss a low-depth variational quantum algorithm for supervised learning. The input feature vectors are encoded into the amplitudes of a quantum system, and a quantum circuit of parametrized single and two-qubit gates together with a single-qubit measurement is used to classify the inputs. This circuit architecture ensures that the number of learnable parameters is polylogarithmic in the input dimension. A quantum-classical training scheme is used where the analytical gradients of the model can be estimated by running several slightly adapted versions of the variational circuit. A design example shows that the classifier performs well on standard classical benchmark datasets while requiring dramatically fewer parameters than other methods. The sensitivity of the classification to state preparation and parameter noise is evaluated. A quantum version of dropout regularization and a graphical representation of quantum gates as highly symmetric linear layers of an NN are introduced.

Quantum computing – information processing with devices that are based on the principles of quantum theory – is currently undergoing a transition from a purely academic discipline to an industrial technology. So-called "small-scale" or "near-term" quantum devices are being developed on a variety of hardware platforms, and offer for the first time a test bed for quantum algorithms. However, allowing for only on the order of 1000–10 000 elementary operations on 50–100 qubits [87] and without the costly feature of error correction, these early devices are not yet suitable for implementing the algorithms that made quantum computing famous. A new generation of quantum routines that use only very limited resources and are robust against errors has therefore been created in recent years [88]. Although many of these small-scale algorithms have the sole purpose of demonstrating the power of quantum computing over classical information processing [89], an important goal is to find quantum solutions to useful applications.

One increasingly popular candidate application for near-term quantum computing is ML [90]. ML is data-driven decision making in which a computer fits a mathematical model to data (training) and uses the model to derive decisions (inference). Numerous quantum algorithms for ML have been proposed in the past few years [76, 91]. A possible strategy [10, 92–94] is to encode data into the amplitudes of a quantum state (here referred to as *amplitude encoding*), and use quantum circuits to manipulate these amplitudes. Quantum algorithms that are only polynomial in the number n of qubits can perform computations on 2^n amplitudes. If these 2^n amplitudes are used to encode the data, one can therefore process data inputs in polylogarithmic time. However, most of the existing literature on amplitude-encoded QML translates known ML models into nontrivial quantum subroutines that lead to resource-intensive algorithms that cannot be implemented on small-scale devices. Furthermore, quantum versions of training algorithms are limited to specific, mostly convex optimization problems. Hybrid approaches called "variational algorithms" [88, 95, 96] are much more suited to near-term quantum computing and have been rapidly gaining popularity lately in the quantum research community. A general picture of variational circuits for ML is introduced in [97]. An emphasis on low-depth circuits for QML is seen in [98], where the importance of entanglement as a resource has been analyzed for low-depth architectures in the context of Boltzmann machines. A solution that comes closest to the designs presented here, and will be described in Section 12.5, is based on [2]. The latter focuses mostly on the classification of discrete and discretized data that are encoded into qubits rather than into amplitudes, which requires an exponentially larger number of qubits for a given input dimension. The circuit architectures proposed in the work are of a more general nature compared to the focus here on a slim parameter count through the systematic use of entanglement.

Here, we present a quantum framework for supervised learning that exploits the advantages of amplitude encoding, but is based on a variational approach and therefore particularly designed for small-scale quantum devices (see Figure 12.1). To achieve low algorithmic depth, *circuit-centric* design is used, with a generic strongly entangling quantum circuit U_θ as the core of the ML model $f(x; \theta) = y$, where x is an input, θ a set of parameters, and y the prediction or output of the model. We call this circuit the *model circuit*. The model circuit consists of parameterized single and controlled single-qubit gates, with learnable (classical) parameters. The number of parameterized gates in the family of model circuits discussed here grows only polynomially with the number of qubits, which means that the QML algorithm has a number of parameters that are overall polylogarithmic in the input dimension. The model circuit acts on a quantum state that represents the input x via amplitude encoding. To prepare such a quantum state, a static *state preparation circuit* S_x has to be applied to the initial ground state. After applying the state preparation as well as the model circuit, the prediction is retrieved from the measurement of a single qubit. If the data is sufficiently low-dimensional or its structure allows for efficient approximation preparation, this yields a compact circuit that can be understood as a black box routine that executes the inference step of the ML algorithm on a small-scale quantum computer.

A hybrid quantum-classical gradient descent training algorithm is used. On the analytical side, we show how the exact gradients of the circuit can be retrieved by running slight variations of the inference algorithm (and for now assuming perfect precision in the prediction) a small, constant number of times and adding up the results, a strategy called *classical linear combination of unitaries*.

Figure 12.1 Circuit-centric quantum classifier.

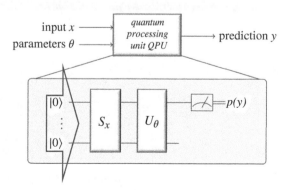

The parameter updates are then calculated on a classical computer. Keeping the model parameters as a classical quantity allows us not only to implement a large number of iterations without worrying about growing coherence times, but also to store and reuse learned parameters at will. Using single-batch gradient descent only requires the state preparation circuit S_x to encode one input at a time. In addition to that, the gradient descent scheme can be easily improved by standard methods such as adaptive learning rate.

12.3.1 The Circuit-Centric Quantum Classifier

The task our model intends to solve is that of supervised pattern recognition, and is a standard problem in ML with applications in image recognition, fraud detection, medical diagnosis, and many other areas. To formalize the problem, let $\mathcal{X}$ be a set of inputs and $\mathcal{Y}$ a set of outputs. Given a dataset $\mathcal{D} = \{(x^1, y^1), ...(x^M, y^M)\}$ of pairs of so-called training inputs $x^m \in \mathcal{X}$ and target outputs $y^m \in \mathcal{Y}$ for m = 1, ... M, our goal is to predict the output $y \in \mathcal{Y}$ of a new input $x \in \mathcal{X}$. For simplicity, we will assume in the following that $\mathcal{X} = \mathbb{R}^N$ and $\mathcal{Y} = \{0, 1\}$, which is a binary classification task on a N-dimensional real input space. Most ML algorithms solve this task in two steps: They first *train* a model $f(x, \theta)$ with the data by adjusting a set of parameters θ, and then use the trained model to *infer* the prediction y.

The main idea of the circuit-centric design is to turn a generic quantum circuit of single-qubit and two-qubit quantum gates into a model for classification. One can divide the full inference algorithm into four steps. As shown in Figure 12.2 [18], these four steps can be described using the language of

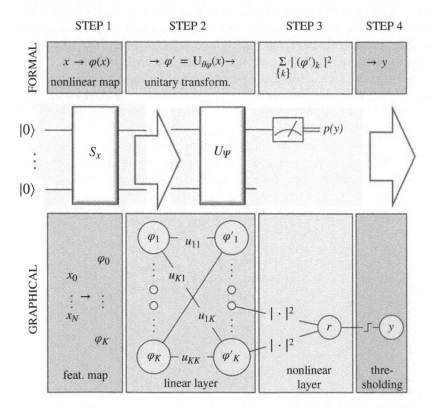

Figure 12.2 The circuit-centric quantum classifier representation. *Source:* Modified from Schuld et al. [18].

quantum circuits, but also as a formal mathematical model, and finally, using the idea of graphical representation for NNs, as a graphical model.

From a quantum circuit point of view:

1) We use the state preparation circuit S_x to encode the data into the state of a $n-$ qubit quantum system, which effectively maps an input $x \in \mathbb{R}^N$ to the 2^n-dimensional amplitude vector $\varphi(x)$ that describes the initial quantum state $|\varphi(x)\rangle$.
2) The model circuit U_θ is applied to the quantum state.
3) The prediction is read out from the final state $|\varphi'\rangle = U_\theta |\varphi(x)\rangle$. For this purpose, we measure the first of the n qubits. Repeated applications of the overall circuit and measurements resolve the probability of measuring the qubit in state 1.
4) The result is postprocessed by adding a learnable bias parameter b and mapping the result through a step function to the output $y \in \{0, 1\}$.

From a purely mathematical point of view, this procedure (that is, if we could perfectly resolve the probability of the first qubit by measurements) formally defines a classifier that takes decisions according to

$$
f(x; \theta, b) = \begin{cases} 1 & \text{if } \sum_{k = 2^{n-1} + 1}^{2^n} \left| (U_\theta \varphi(X))_k \right|^2 + b > 0.5, \\ 0 & \text{else.} \end{cases}
\tag{12.3}
$$

In Eq. (12.3), $\varphi: \mathbb{R}^N \to \mathbb{C}^{2^N}$ is a map that describes the procedure of information encoding via the state preparation routine (n is an integer such that $2^n \geq N$), U_θ is the parameterized unitary matrix describing the model circuit, and $(U_\theta \varphi(x))_k$ is the k-th entry of the result after we applied this matrix to $\varphi(x)$. The sum over the second half of the resulting vector corresponds to the single-qubit measurement resulting in state 1. Postprocessing adds the bias b and thresholds to compute a binary prediction. Now, if we formulate the four steps in the language of NNs and their graphical representation, state preparation corresponds to a feature map on the input space, while the unitary circuit resembles an NN of several parametrized linear layers. This is followed by two nonlinear layers, one simulating the readout via measurement (adding the squares of some units from the previous layer) and one that maps the output to the final binary decision. We will go through the four different steps in more detail and discuss the specific design decisions for the model.

State preparation: There are various strategies to encode input vectors into the n-qubit system of a quantum computer. In the most general terms, state preparation implements a feature map φ: $\mathbb{R}^N \to \mathbb{C}^{2^N}$, where n is the total number of qubits used to represent the features. In the following, we focus on *amplitude encoding*, where an input vector $x \in \mathbb{R}^N-$ possibly with some further preprocessing to bring it into a suitable form – is directly associated with the amplitudes of the 2^n-dimensional ket vector of the quantum system written in the computational basis. This option can be extended by preparing a set of copies of the initial quantum state, which effectively implements a tensor product of copies of the input, mapping it to much higher-dimensional spaces.

To directly associate an amplitude vector in the computational basis with a data input, we require that N be a power of 2 (so that we can use all 2^n amplitudes of a n-qubit system), and that the input is normalized to unit length: $x^T x = 1$.

The model circuit: Given an encoded feature vector $\varphi(x)$ that is now a "ket" vector in the Hilbert space of an n-qubit system, the model circuit maps this ket vector to another ket vector $\varphi' = U_\theta \varphi(x)$ by a unitary operation U_θ that is parametrized by a set of variables θ.

Decomposition into (controlled) single-qubit gates: As described before, we decompose U into $U = U_L \dots U_\ell \dots U_1$, where each U_l is either a single-qubit or a two-qubit quantum gate. As a reminder, a single-qubit gate G_k acting on the k-th of n qubits can be expressed as $U_l = \mathbb{I}_0 \otimes \cdots \otimes G_k \otimes \cdots \otimes \mathbb{I}_{n-1}$.

If the circuit depth L is in $\Omega(4^n)$, this decomposition allows us to represent general unitary transformations. Remember that unitary operators are linear transformations that preserve the length of a vector, a fact that holds a number of advantages for the classifier as we will discuss later. We further restrict the type of 2-qubit gate to simplify our "elementary parametrized gate set." A two-qubit unitary gate is called *imprimitive* if it can map a two-qubit product state into a non-product state. A common case of an imprimitive two-qubit gate is a singly controlled single-qubit gate $C(G)$ that in a standard computational basis can be written as

$$C_a(G_b)|x\rangle|y\rangle = |x\rangle \otimes G^x|y\rangle, \tag{12.4}$$

where G is a single-qubit gate other than a global phase factor on the qubit b and the state x of qubit a is either 0 or 1 (G^0 is the identity). For example, G could be a NOT gate, in which case $C(G)$ is simply the frequently used CNOT gate. It is known that circuits of the form $U = U_L \dots U_\ell \dots U_1$, composed of single-qubit gates and at least one type of imprimitive two-qubit gates generate the entire unitary group $U(2^n)$ in a topological sense. That is, for any $\varepsilon > 0$ and any unitary $V \in U(2^n)$ there is a circuit of the form $U = U_L \dots U_\ell \dots U_1$, the value of which is ε-close to V [99].

To make the single-qubit gates trainable, we need to formulate them in terms of parameters that can be learned. The way the parameterization is defined can have a significant impact on training, since it defines the shape of the cost function. A single-qubit gate G is a 2×2 unitary, which can always be written [100] as

$$G(\alpha, \beta, \gamma, \phi) = e^{i\phi} \begin{pmatrix} e^{i\beta} \cos\alpha & e^{-i\gamma} \sin\alpha \\ -e^{-i\gamma} \sin\alpha & e^{i\beta} \cos\alpha \end{pmatrix} \tag{12.5}$$

and is fully defined by four parameters $\{\alpha, \beta, \gamma, \phi\}$. For quantum gates – where we cannot physically measure the overall phase factors – we may neglect the prefactor $e^{i\phi}$ and consider only three learnable parameters per gate. The advantage in using angles (instead of, for example, a parameterization with Pauli matrices) is that training does not need an additional condition on the model parameters. A disadvantage: it might have unfavorable convergence properties of trigonometric functions close to their optima.

Read out and postprocessing: After executing the quantum circuit $U_\theta \varphi(x)$ in Step 2, the measurement of the first qubit (Step 3) results in state 1 with probability [101]

$$p(q_0 = 1, x; \theta) = \sum_{k = 2^{n-1} + 1}^{2^n} \left| (U_\theta \varphi(x))_k \right|^2 \tag{12.6}$$

To resolve these statistics, we have to run the entire circuit S times and measure the first qubit. We estimate $p(q_0 = 1)$ from these samples $s_1, \dots s_S$. This is a Bernoulli parameter estimation problem that we discuss later. The classical postprocessing (Step 4) consists of adding a learnable bias term b to produce the continuous output of the model,

$$\pi(x; \theta, b) = p(q_0 = 1, x, \theta) + b. \tag{12.7}$$

Thresholding the value finally yields the binary output that is the overall prediction of the model:

$$f(x; \theta) = \begin{cases} 1 & \text{if } \pi(x; \theta) > 0.5 \\ 0 & \text{else} \end{cases}$$

In Dirac notation, the measurement result can be written as the expectation value of a σ_z operator acting on the first qubit, measured after applying U to the initial state $|\varphi(x)\rangle$. In absence of nonlinear activation, the expectation value of the σ_z operator on the subspace of the first qubit is given by

$$\mathbb{E}(\sigma_z) = \langle \varphi(x) | U^\dagger (\sigma_z \otimes \mathbb{I} \otimes \ldots \otimes \mathbb{I}) U | \varphi(x) \rangle,$$

and we can retrieve the continuous output via

$$\pi(x; \theta) = \left(\frac{\mathbb{E}(\sigma_z)}{2} + \frac{1}{2} \right) + b. \tag{12.8}$$

Circuit architectures: Our initial goal was to build a classifier that at its core has a low-depth quantum circuit. With the circuit decomposed into L single or controlled single-qubit gates, we therefore want to constrain L to be polynomial in n, which will allow us to draw inferences with a number of elementary quantum operations that grows only polylogarithmically in the dimension of the data set. However, this obviously comes at a price. The vectors of the form $U_\theta | 0 \ldots 0 \rangle$ exhaust only a small subset of the Hilbert space of n qubits. In other words, the set of amplitude vectors $\varphi' = U_\theta \varphi(x)$ that the circuit can handle is limited. In ML terms, this limits the flexibility of the classifier.

Strongly entangling circuits: A natural approach to the problem of circuit design is to consider circuits that prepare strongly entangled quantum states. For one, such circuits can reach wide corners of the Hilbert space with $U_\theta | 0, 0 \rangle$. They have a better chance to project input data state $|\varphi(x)\rangle$ with the class label y onto the subspace $|y\rangle \otimes |\eta\rangle, \eta \in \mathbb{C}^{2^{n-1}}$, which corresponds to a decision of p $(q_0) = 0, 1$ in our classifier (for a zero bias). Moreover, from a theoretical point of view, a classifier has to capture both short- and long-range correlations in the input data, and there is mounting evidence [102, 103] that shallow circuits may be suitable for the purpose when they are strongly entangling.

More specifically, we compose the circuit $U = U_L \ldots U_\ell \ldots U_1$ out of several *code blocks* B (see dotted boxes in the example in Figure 12.3). A code block consists of a layer of single-qubit gates $G = G(\alpha, \beta, \gamma)$ applied to each of the n qubits, followed by a layer of $n/\gcd(n, r)$ controlled gates, where r is the "range" of the control, and $\gcd(n, r)$ is the greatest common denominator of n and r. For $j \in [1 .. n/\gcd(n, r)]$ the j-th two-qubit gate $C_{c_j}(G_{t_j})$ of a block has qubit number $t_j = (jr - r)$ mod n as the target, qubit number $c_j = jr$ mod n as control. A full block has the following composition:

$$B = \prod_{k=0}^{n-1} C_{c_k}(G_{t_k}) \prod_{j=0}^{n-1} G_j. \tag{12.9}$$

We observe that such code block is capable of entangling/unentangling all the qubits with numbers that are a multiple of $\gcd(n, r)$. In particular, assuming r is relatively prime with n, all n qubits can be entangled/unentangled. In the case of Figure 12.3, the circuit consists of two "code blocks" B1 and B3 with a range of controls of $r = 1$ and $r = 3$, respectively. The circuit consists of 17 trainable single-qubit gates $G = G(\alpha, \beta, \gamma)$, as well as 16 trainable controlled single-qubit gates C(G), which in

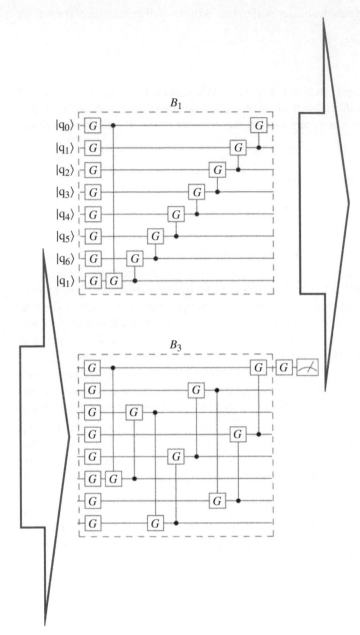

Figure 12.3 Generic model circuit architecture for eight qubits.

turn have to be decomposed into the elementary constant gate set used by the quantum computer on which to implement it. If optimization methods are used to reduce the controlled gates to a single parameter, we have a total of $(3 \times 33) + 1 = 100$ parameters to learn for this model circuit. These 100 parameters are used to classify inputs of $2^8 = 256$ dimensions, which shows that the circuit-centric classifier is a much more compact model than a conventional feedforward NN.

Design Example 12.1

This example demonstrates the entangling power of the circuit. Select a block with $n = 4$, $r = 1$. Let all controlled gates be CNOTs, and let all single-qubit gates be identities, except from $G_0 = G_2 = H$, which are Hadamard gates. Applying the circuit to the basis product state $|0000\rangle$, we get the state $|\psi\rangle = (|00\rangle|00\rangle + |01\rangle|11\rangle + |10\rangle|01\rangle + |11\rangle|10\rangle)/2$. If A is the subsystem consisting of qubits 0, 1 and B is the subsystem consisting of qubits 2, 3, then the marginal density matrix, corresponding to the state $|\psi\rangle$ and the partitioning $A \otimes B$, is completely mixed. Therefore, the state $|\psi\rangle$ strongly entangles the two subsystems.

Optimizing the architecture: The definition of the code block as Eq. (12.9) is redundant. It turns out that the parameter space of the circuit of Eq. (12.9) can for practical purposes be reduced to roughly 5n parameters. For this we need to introduce a controlled phase gate $C_j(P_k(\phi))$, $\phi \in \mathbb{R}$ that applies the phase shift $e^{i\phi}$ to a standard basis vector if and only if both the j-th and k-th qubits are in state $|1\rangle$. (Note the symmetry of the definition, which means that it does not matter which of the qubits is the control and which is the target.)

A block of the form Eq. (12.9) can, up to global phase, be uniquely rewritten as

$$B = \prod_{k=0}^{n-1} R_k^X C_{c_K}(P_{t_K}) \prod_{j=0}^{n-1} G_j. \tag{12.10}$$

where $\forall j$, $G_j \in SU(2)$ are single-qubit gates with the usual three parameters (and, moreover, G_j is an axial rotation for $j > 0$), P is a single-parameter phase gate, and R^X is a single-parameter X-rotation [18].

Graphical representation of gates: As a product of elementary gates, the model circuit U_x can be understood as a sequence of linear layers of an NN with the same number of units in each "hidden layer." This perspective facilitates a comparison of the circuit-centric quantum classifier with the widely studied NN models, and helps visualize the connectivity power of (controlled) single-qubit gates. The position of the qubit (as well as the control) determines the architecture of each layer, that is, which units are connected and which "weights" are tied in a "gate layer."

To show an example, consider a Hilbert space of dimension 2^n with $n = 2$ qubits $|q_0 q_1\rangle$. A single-qubit unitary G applied to q_0 would have the following matrix representation:

$$G_0 = \begin{pmatrix} e^{i\beta}\cos\alpha & 0 & e^{i\gamma}\sin\alpha & 0 \\ 0 & e^{i\beta}\cos\alpha & 0 & e^{i\gamma}\sin\alpha \\ -e^{-i\gamma}\sin\alpha & 0 & e^{-i\beta}\cos\alpha & 0 \\ 0 & -e^{-i\gamma}\sin\alpha & 0 & e^{-i\beta}\cos\alpha \end{pmatrix},$$

whereas the same unitary except that it is controlled by qubit q_1, $C_1(G_0)$, has matrix representation

$$C_1(G_0) = \begin{pmatrix} 1 & 0 & 0 & 0 \\ 0 & e^{i\beta}\cos\alpha & 0 & e^{i\gamma}\sin\alpha \\ 0 & 0 & 1 & 0 \\ 0 & -e^{-i\gamma}\sin\alpha & 0 & e^{-i\beta}\cos\alpha \end{pmatrix}$$

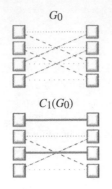

G_0

$C_1(G_0)$

Figure 12.4 Graphical representation of quantum gates.

At the same time, these two gates can be understood as layers with connections displayed in Figure 12.4. It becomes obvious that a single-qubit gate connects two sets of two variables with the same weights; in other words, it ties the parameters of these connections. The control removes half of the ties and replaces them with identities.

A quantum circuit can therefore be understood as an analogue of an NN architecture with highly symmetric, unitary linear layers, and controls break some of the symmetry. Note that although we speak of linear layers here, the weights (i.e., the entries of the weight matrix representing a gate) have a nonlinear dependency on the model parameters θ, a circumstance that plays a role in the convergence of the hybrid training method.

12.3.2 Training

We consider a specific stochastic gradient descent method for training. In Section 12.4, we will revisit the general problem of the quantum gradient descent algorithm in more detail. The parameters that define every single-qubit gate of the quantum circuit are at every stage of the quantum algorithm classical values. However, we are computing the model function on a quantum device, and therefore have no "classical" access to its gradients. This means that the training procedure has to be a hybrid scheme that combines classical processing to update the parameters and quantum information processing to extract the gradients. We will show how to use the quantum circuit to extract estimates of the analytical gradients, as opposed to other proposals for variational algorithms based on derivative – free or finite – difference gradients (see [104]). A related approach, but for a different gate representation, has been proposed in [2].

Cost function: We choose a standard least-squares objective to evaluate the cost of a parameter configuration θ and a bias b given a training set, $\mathcal{D} = \{(x^1, y^1), ..., (x^M, y^M)\}$,

$$C(\theta, b; \mathcal{D}) = \frac{1}{2} \sum_{m=1}^{M} |\pi(x^m; \theta, b) - y^m|^2,$$

where π is the continuous output of the model defined in Eq. (12.7). Note that we can easily add a regularization term (i.e., an L_1 or L_2 regularizer) to this objective, since it does not require any additional quantum information processing. For the sake of simplicity, we do not consider regularization in this section. Gradient descent updates each parameter μ from the set of circuit parameters θ via

$$\mu^{(t)} = \mu^{(t-1)} - \eta \frac{C(\theta, b; \mathcal{D})}{\partial \theta},$$

and similarly for the bias,

$$b^{(t)} = b^{(t-1)} - \eta \frac{\partial C(\theta, b; \mathcal{D})}{\partial b}.$$

The learning rate η can be adapted during training, and we can also add momenta to the updates, which can significantly decrease the convergence time.

In stochastic gradient descent, we do not consider the entire training set $\mathcal{D}$ in every iteration, but only a subset or batch $\mathcal{B} \subset \mathcal{D}$ [105]. The derivatives in the parameter updates are therefore taken with respect to $C(\theta, b; \mathcal{B})$ instead of $C(\theta, b; \mathcal{D})$. In principle, quantum computing allows us to encode a batch of B training inputs into a quantum state in superposition and feed it into the classifier, which can be used to extract gradients for the updates from the quantum device. However, guided by the design principle of a low-depth circuit, this would extend the state preparation routine to be in $\mathcal{O}(BN)$ for general cases, where N is the size of each input in the batch (which becomes even worse for more sophisticated feature maps in Step 1). We therefore consider single-batch gradient descent here (i.e., $B = 1$), where only one randomly sampled training input is considered in each iteration. Single-batch stochastic gradient descent can have favorable convergence properties, for example, in cases where there is a lot of data available [106].

Hybrid gradient descent scheme: The derivative of the objective function with respect to a model parameter $v = b, \mu$ (where $\mu \in \theta$ is a circuit parameter) for a single data sample $\{(x^m, y^m)\}$ is calculated as $\partial C/\partial v = (A\,(x^m; v) - y^m)\partial_v \pi(x^m; v)$. Note that $\pi\,(x^m; v)$ is a real-valued function, and the y^m and the parameters are also real-valued. Hence $\partial C/\partial v \in \mathbb{R}$. Although $\pi\,(x^m; v)$ is a simple prediction we can get from the quantum device, and y^m is a target from the classical training set, we have to look closer at how to compute the gradient $\partial_v \pi$. For $v = b$ this is, in fact, trivial, since $\partial_b \pi(x^m; b) = 1$.

In the case of $v = \mu$, the gradient forces us to compute derivatives of the unitary operator. In the following, we will calculate the gradients in vector as well as in Dirac notation and show how a trick allows us to estimate these gradients using a slight variation of the model circuit S_x. The derivative of the continuous output of the model with respect to the circuit parameter μ is formally given by

$$\partial_\mu \pi(x^m; \mu) = \partial_\mu p(q_0 = 1; x^m, \theta)$$

$$= \partial_\mu \sum_{k=2^{n-1}+1}^{2^n} (U_\theta \varphi(x))_k^\dagger (U_\theta \varphi(x))_k$$

$$= 2\,\mathrm{Re} \left\{ \sum_{k=2^{n-1}+1}^{2^n} \left(\partial_\mu U_\theta \varphi(x)\right)_k^\dagger (U_\theta \varphi(x))_k \right\}.$$

The last expression contains the "derivative of the circuit," $\partial_\mu U_\theta$, which is given by $\partial_\mu U_\theta = U_L \ldots (\partial_\mu U_i) \ldots U_1$, where we assume for simplicity that only the parameterized gate U_i depends on parameter μ. If the parameters of different unitary matrices are tied, then the derivative can simply be found by applying the product rule.

In Dirac notation, we have expressed the probability of measuring the first qubit in state 1 through the expectation value of a σ_z operator acting on the same qubit, $p(q_0 = 1; x^m, \theta) = \frac{1}{2}(\langle U_\theta \varphi(x) | \sigma_z | U_\theta \varphi(x) \rangle + 1)$ (see Eq. 12.8). We can use this expression to write the gradient in Dirac notation:

$$\partial_\mu \pi(x^m; \theta, b) = \mathrm{Re}\left\{ \langle (\partial_\mu U_\theta) \varphi(x^m) | \sigma_z | U_\theta \varphi(x) \rangle \right\} \tag{12.11}$$

This notation reveals the challenge in computing the gradients using the quantum device. The gradient of a unitary is not necessarily a unitary, which means that $|(\partial_\mu U_\theta)\varphi(x^m)\rangle$ is not a quantum state that can arise from a quantum evolution. How can we still estimate gradients using the quantum device?

Classical linear combinations of unitaries

It turns out that in our architecture we can always represent $\partial_\mu U_\theta$ as a linear combination of unitaries. Linear combination of unitaries is a known technique in quantum mechanics [107], where the sum is implemented in a coherent fashion. In our case, where we allow for classical postprocessing, we do not have to apply unitaries in superposition, but can simply run the quantum circuit several times and collect the output. This is what we will call *classical linear combinations of unitaries* here. Consider the derivative of U_i for the single-qubit gate. Given $U_l = \mathbb{I}_0 \otimes \cdots \otimes G_k \otimes \cdots \otimes \mathbb{I}_{n-1}$ we have $\partial_\mu U_i = \mathbb{I} \otimes \cdots \otimes \partial_\mu G(\alpha, \beta, \gamma) \otimes \cdots \otimes \mathbb{I}$, where $G(\alpha, \beta, \gamma)$ is given in the parameterization introduced in Eq. (12.5) and discounting the global phase. The derivatives of the single-qubit gate $G(\alpha, \beta, \gamma)$ witd respect to the parameters $\mu = \alpha, \beta, \gamma$ are as follows:

$$\partial_\alpha G = G\left(\alpha + \frac{\pi}{2}, \beta, \gamma\right), \partial_\beta G = \frac{1}{2}G\left(\alpha, \beta + \frac{\pi}{2}, 0\right) + \frac{1}{2}G\left(\alpha, \beta + \frac{\pi}{2}, \pi\right)$$
$$\partial_\gamma G = \frac{1}{2}G\left(\alpha, 0, \gamma + \frac{\pi}{2}\right) + \frac{1}{2}G\left(\alpha, \pi, \gamma + \frac{\pi}{2}\right) \tag{12.12}$$

One can see that although the derivative with respect to α requires us to implement the same gate but with the first parameter shifted by $\pi/2$, the derivative with respect to $\mu = \beta[\mu = \gamma]$ is a linear combination of single-qubit gates where the original parameter $\beta[\gamma]$ is shifted by $\pi/2$, while $\gamma[\beta]$ is replaced by 0 or π. Differentiating a controlled single-qubit gate is not that immediate, but fortunately we have $\partial_\mu C(G) = (C(\partial_\mu G) - C(-\partial_\mu G))/2$, which means that the derivative of the controlled single-qubit gate is half of the difference between a controlled derivative gate and the controlled negative version of that gate. In our design, when $\mu = \alpha$, each of the two controlled gates is unitary, while $\mu = \beta, \gamma$ requires us to use the linear combinations in Eq. (12.12).

If we plug the gate derivatives back into the expressions for the gradient in Eq. (12.11), we see that the gradients, irrespective of the gate or parameter, can be computed as "classical" linear combinations of the form

$$\partial_\mu \pi(x^m; \theta, b) = \sum_{j=1}^{J} a_j \, \text{Re} \, \left\{\langle U_{\theta^{[j]}} \varphi(x^m) | \sigma_z | U_\theta \, \varphi(x^m) \rangle\right\}$$

where $\theta^{[j]}$ is a modified vector of parameters corresponding to a term appearing in Eq. (12.12), and a_j is the corresponding coefficient, also stemming from Eq. (12.12). If there is no parameter tying between the constituent gates, for example, then J is either 2 or 4 depending on whether the gate with parameter μ is a one- or two-qubit gate. For each circuit, the eventual derivative has to be estimated by repeated measurements, and we will discuss the number of repetitions in the following section. The last thing to show is that we can compute the terms $\text{Re} \, \left\{\langle U_{\theta^{[j]}} \varphi(x^m) | \sigma_z | U_\theta \, \varphi(x^m) \rangle\right\}$ with the quantum device, so that classical multiplication and summation can deliver estimates of the desired gradients. It can be shown that given two unitary quantum circuits A and B that act on a n qubit register to prepare the two quantum states $|A\rangle, |B\rangle$, and which can be applied conditioned on the state of an ancilla qubit, we can use the quantum device to sample from the probability distribution $p = (1 + \text{Re} \, \langle A | B \rangle)/2$ [18]. To use this interference routine, we have to add an extra qubit and implement U_θ and $U_{\theta^{[j]}}$ conditioned on the state of the ancilla. Since these two circuits differ in only one gate, we do in fact need to apply only the differing gate in conditional mode. This turns a single-qubit gate into a singly controlled single-qubit gate, and a controlled gate into a double controlled gate. The desired value $\text{Re} \, \langle A | B \rangle$ can be derived by resolving $p(a = 0)$ through measurements and computing $\text{Re} \, \langle A | B \rangle = 2p(a = 0) - 1$.

12.4 Gradients of Parameterized Quantum Gates

In the previous section, we considered a specific stochastic gradient descent method for training. Here, we address the problem in greater detail. The parameter-shift rule is an approach to evaluating gradients of parameterized quantum circuits on quantum hardware [97, 108–111]. Suppose we have some objective function $f(\theta)$ of a quantum circuit,

$$f(\theta) = \langle \psi | U_G^\dagger(\theta) A \, U_G(\theta) | \psi \rangle \tag{12.13}$$

where the parameterized gate is

$$U_G(\theta) = e^{-ia\theta G}. \tag{12.14}$$

Here, G is the Hermitian generator of the gate, and a is a real constant. For the ways to compute the exponential of a matrix, see the Appendix at the end of this chapter and [112–115]. The parameter-shift rule states that if the generator of the gate G has only two unique eigenvalues, e_0 and e_1, then the derivative of this circuit expectation (Eq. (12.13)) with respect to the gate parameter is proportional to the difference in expectation of two circuits with shifted parameters,

$$\frac{d}{d\theta}f(\theta) = r\left[f\left(\theta + \frac{\pi}{4r}\right) - f\left(\theta - \frac{\pi}{4r}\right)\right], \tag{12.15}$$

where the shift constant is $r = \dfrac{a}{2}(e_1 - e_0)$. Compared to other approaches for evaluating circuit gradients [116], the parameter-shift rule has the advantage that it requires the performance of two circuits each of which has the same number of gates as the original circuit, and does not require ancilla qubits. Gradients of such quantum circuits are useful in the optimization step of variational quantum algorithms. In these hybrid quantum-classical approaches, we construct a quantum circuit, and then vary the parameters to minimize some objective function of interest. The parameter-shift approach to quantum gradients can be directly applied only to gates with two unique eigenvalues. However, we will next discuss how parameter-shift gradients can be evaluated for a much wider range of parameterized gates using the product rule of calculus, provided we can decompose our gate of interest into a product of gates, each of which is parameter-shift rule differentiable. We will demonstrate this idea for two-qubit gates and discuss several gate decompositions in detail. In classical simulations of quantum circuits, we do not need to resort to the parameter-shift rule, since we can apply non-unitary operators to quantum states. We will conclude the section with a discussion of how to efficiently calculate gradients of quantum circuits on classical hardware.

Parameter-shift rule gradients – Let us review why the parameter shift works. Suppose that the generator of the gate $G(2)$ is unitary as well as Hermitian, and the prefactor $a = 1$. Then G is also idempotent $GG = I$, and with Euler's identity we can express the gate as

$$U_G(\theta) = e^{-i\theta G} = I \cos(\theta) - iG \sin(\theta). \tag{12.16}$$

The key insight is that even if G is not unitary, if it has only two unique eigenvalues, e_0 and e_1, then we can always convert the generator aG to a unitary operator by adding and multiplying by real constants, $a(G - s)/r$, where $r = a(e_1 - e_0)/2$, and $s = (e_1 + e_0)/2$. The additive shift can be neglected since it only adds an irrelevant phase. Therefore, for any real constant a, and Hermitian operator G with two unique eigenvalues, we have

$$U_G(\theta) = e^{-ia\theta G} = I \cos(r\theta) - i\frac{a}{r}G \sin(r\theta) \tag{12.17}$$

up to phase. And as a special case of Eq. (12.17) we have

$$U_G\left(\pm\frac{\pi}{4r}\right) = \frac{1}{\sqrt{2}}\left(I \mp i\frac{a}{r}G\right). \tag{12.18}$$

Note that the derivative of the gate Eq. (12.17) is

$$\frac{\partial}{\partial\theta}U_G(\theta) = -iaGe^{-ia\theta G}. \tag{12.19}$$

We can now derive the parameter-shift rule, Eq. (12.15).

$$\frac{\partial}{\partial\theta}f(\theta) = \langle\psi|[+ iaG]U_G^\dagger(\theta)AU_G(\theta)|\psi\rangle \tag{12.20a}$$

$$+ \langle\psi|U_G^\dagger(\theta)A[- iaG]U_G(\theta)|\psi\rangle$$

$$= \frac{r}{2}\langle\psi|U_G^\dagger(\theta)\left(I + i\frac{a}{r}G\right)A\left(I - i\frac{a}{r}G\right)U_G(\theta)|\psi\rangle \tag{12.20b}$$

$$- \frac{r}{2}\langle\psi|U_G^\dagger(\theta)\left(I - i\frac{a}{r}G\right)A\left(I + i\frac{a}{r}G\right)U_G(\theta)|\psi\rangle \tag{12.20}$$

$$= r\langle\psi|U_G^\dagger\left(\theta + \frac{\pi}{4r}\right)A\,U_G\left(\theta + \frac{\pi}{4r}\right)|\psi\rangle \tag{12.20c}$$

$$- r\langle\psi|U_G^\dagger\left(\theta - \frac{\pi}{4r}\right)A\,U_G\left(\theta - \frac{A}{4r}\right)|\psi\rangle$$

$$= r\left[f\left(\theta + \frac{\pi}{4r}\right) - f\left(\theta - \frac{\pi}{4r}\right)\right] \tag{12.20d}$$

(i) We write out the gradient using Eq. (12.19) and the product rule; (ii) and then rearrange and gather terms so that the Hermitian measurement operators are acted upon by conjugate unitary operators; (iii) we recognize from Eq. (12.18) that these unitaries represent instances of the initial gate, and thus shift the gate's parameter; and (iv) this leads to the parameter-shift rule for circuit gradients.

Note that the value of the shift constant r depends upon the parameterization. For instance, the one-qubit Pauli rotation gates are all parameter-shift differentiable with $= \frac{1}{2}$:

$$R_X(\theta) = e^{-i\frac{1}{2}\theta X}\ r = \frac{1}{2} \tag{12.21a}$$

$$R_Y(\theta) = e^{-i\frac{1}{2}\theta Y}\ r = \frac{1}{2} \tag{12.21b}$$

$$R_Z(\theta) = e^{-i\frac{1}{2}\theta Z}\ r = \frac{1}{2} \tag{12.21c}$$

As a reminder from Chapter 8, the Pauli matrices are $X = \begin{pmatrix} 0 & 1 \\ 1 & 0 \end{pmatrix}, Y = \begin{pmatrix} 0 & -i \\ i & 0 \end{pmatrix}$ and $Z = \begin{pmatrix} 1 & 0 \\ 0 & -1 \end{pmatrix}$. On the other hand, it can be more convenient to represent the same gates as powers of the Pauli operators, but in that case the shift constant is $r = \frac{\pi}{2}$:

$$X^t \simeq R_X(\pi t) = e^{-i\frac{\pi}{2}tX}\ r = \frac{\pi}{2} \tag{12.22a}$$

$$Y^t \simeq R_Y(\pi t) = e^{-i\frac{\pi}{2}tY}\ r = \frac{\pi}{2} \tag{12.22b}$$

$$Z^t \simeq R_Z(\pi t) = e^{-i\frac{\pi}{2}tZ}\ r = \frac{\pi}{2} \tag{12.22c}$$

Here, we use $\simeq$ to indicate that the unitaries are equal up to a phase factor.

Parameter-shift gradients via gate decomposition – A direct application of the parameter-shift rule requires that the generator of the gate have only two eigenvalues. However, we can evaluate gradients for gates that do not meet this requirement by decomposing the dynamics into a sequence of gates, each of which has a generator of the requisite form. As a trivial example, consider the two-qubit canonical gate

$$U_{\text{CAN}} = \exp\left(-i\frac{\pi}{2}\left(t_x X \otimes X + t_y Y \otimes Y + t_z Z \otimes Z\right)\right). \tag{12.23}$$

This gate is of interest because it is, in a sense, the elementary two-qubit gate. Any other two-qubit gate can be constructed by prepending or appending local one-qubit rotations [117].

The Hamiltonian of the canonical gate has more than two unique eigenvalues in general, yet we can evaluate gradients with respect to any of the three parameters using the parameter-shift rule, with $r = \pi/2$. This is because the $X \otimes X$, $Y \otimes Y$, and $Z \otimes Z$ terms in the Hamiltonian all commute, and the canonical gate can be decomposed into a sequence of XX, YY, and ZZ gates (in arbitrary order).

$$
\boxed{CAN\,(t_x, t_y, t_z)} \;\Rightarrow\; \boxed{XX^{t_x}}\;\boxed{YY^{t_y}}\;\boxed{ZZ^{t_z}} \tag{12.24}
$$

$$
U_{XX}(t) \simeq e^{-\frac{i\pi t}{2}X \otimes X};\; U_{YY}(t) \simeq e^{-\frac{i\pi t}{2}Y \otimes Y};\; U_{ZZ}(t) \simeq e^{-\frac{i\pi t}{2}Z \otimes Z} \tag{12.25}
$$

For these parameterizations of the XX, YY, and ZZ gates, we have $r = \pi/2$. More generally, we can decompose any two-qubit gate into a canonical gate plus one-qubit gates [117–122] $CAN(t_7, t_8, t_9)$

$$
\boxed{X^{t_1}}\boxed{Y^{t_2}}\boxed{X^{t_3}}\;\boxed{CAN(t_7,t_8,t_9)}\;\boxed{X^{t_{10}}}\boxed{Y^{t_{11}}}\boxed{X^{t_{12}}} \\
\boxed{X^{t_4}}\boxed{Y^{t_5}}\boxed{X^{t_6}}\quad\quad\quad\quad\;\boxed{X^{t_{13}}}\boxed{Y^{t_{14}}}\boxed{X^{t_{15}}} \tag{12.26}
$$

Provided we can determine the functional relation between the original gate parameter θ and the parameters of the decomposition, we can evaluate gradients with the product rule:

$$
\frac{d}{d\theta}f(\theta) = \sum_{i=1}^{15} \frac{\partial}{\partial t_i} f_{CAN}(t_1, t_2, ..., t_{15}) \frac{dt_i}{d\theta} \tag{12.27}
$$

Since an arbitrary two-qubit gate has 15 parameters, we may need up to 30 expectation evaluations to evaluate one gradient of a two-qubit gate. Note that there are many essentially equivalent choices as to how to parameterize the local one-qubit rotations in Eq. (12.26). Here, we have used the X-Y-X Euler angle decomposition rather than the more common Z-Y-Z decomposition [123]. The canonical gate has many symmetries under local transformations, such that different coordinates can represent gates that differ only by one-qubit rotations. In particular CAN $(t, 0, 0)$, CAN(0, $t, 0$), and CAN $(0, 0, t)$ are all locally equivalent. To avoid redundancy, the canonical parameters can be restricted to a particular Weyl chamber ⌊124⌋, and traditionally this means that when the canonical gate has only one nonzero parameter we restrict it to the XX-gate class, CAN $(t, 0, 0)$. By choosing an X-Y-X decomposition, the inner X-gates can be readily commuted with the XX-gate, which may simplify the decomposition. On the other hand, when decomposing gates in the parametric swap (PSWAP) class [124], CAN$\left(\frac{1}{2}, \frac{1}{2}, t\right)$, it is advantageous to use a Z-Y-Z decomposition, since a PSWAP gate can be decomposed as a SWAP, CAN $\left(\frac{1}{2}, \frac{1}{2}, \frac{1}{2}\right)$, followed by a ZZ-gate, CAN $\left(0, 0, t - \frac{1}{2}\right)$. A Z-gate can therefore commute past a PSWAP while switching qubits.

Decomposition of the cross-resonance gate: As another illustration of differentiation via gate decomposition, we will consider a trickier example [109, 111] in the cross-resonance gate family:

$$
G_{CR} = X \otimes I - bZ \otimes X + cI \otimes X \tag{12.28}
$$

$$U_{CR} = \exp\left(-i\frac{\pi}{2}sG_{CR}\right) \tag{12.29}$$

The controlled rotation (CR) gate is a natural gate for certain microwave-controlled transmon superconducting qubit architectures [125–127].

Defined by 12.28 and 12.29

$$CR = \begin{pmatrix} 1 & 0 & 0 & 0 \\ 0 & 1 & 0 & 0 \\ 0 & 0 & 1 & 0 \\ 1 & 0 & 0 & e^{\theta i} \end{pmatrix}$$

This CR gate can be represented by the following circuit diagram:

$$\tag{12.30}$$

which can be canonically decomposed as a circuit of one-qubit gates and an XX-gate:

$$\tag{12.31}$$

An equivalent decomposition, using CNOTs as the two-qubit interaction, is

$$\tag{12.32}$$

The three nontrivial parameters of this circuit can be expressed using elementary functions of the CR gate parameters:

$$t_1 = \frac{1}{\pi} \arccos\left(\frac{\cos\left(\frac{\pi}{2}\sqrt{1+b^2}s\right)}{\cos\left(\frac{\pi}{2}t_7\right)} \right) \tag{12.33}$$

$$t_4 = cs \tag{12.34}$$

$$t_7 = \frac{1}{\pi} \arccos\left(\frac{1 + b^2 \cos\left(\pi\sqrt{1+b^2}s\right)}{1 + b^2} \right) \tag{12.35}$$

The procedure to decompose the CR gate is as follows: We first guess the circuit ansatz (Eq. (12.31)) by examining numerical decompositions of the CR gate [128]. We are left with three undetermined parameters. Since the CR gate is equivalent to an XX-gate up to one-qubit rotations, the t_7 parameter can be derived using Equation 25 of [128]:

$$t_7 = \frac{1}{\pi} \arccos\left(\frac{1}{4} \mathrm{Tr}\left[\left(M^\dagger U_{CR}M\right)^T \left(M^\dagger U_{CR}M\right) \right] \right) \tag{12.35a}$$

Here, M is the magic gate, which transforms to a magic basis [30, 31]. (In a magic basis, the Kronecker products of two one-qubit gates are orthogonal matrices.)

$$M = \frac{1}{\sqrt{2}} \begin{pmatrix} 1 & 0 & 0 & i \\ 0 & i & 1 & 0 \\ 0 & i & -1 & 0 \\ 1 & 0 & 0 & -i \end{pmatrix} \tag{12.36}$$

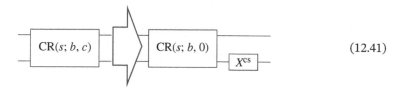

$$\tag{12.37}$$

The $I \otimes X$ term in the Hamiltonian commutes with the other two terms, and can be separated out as an X rotation on the second qubit, which gives the t_4 parameter. The final parameter, t_1, can then be solved for analytically. We can therefore calculate the gradients of the CR gate using the product rule, eight expectation evaluations using the parameter-shift rule, and the following derivatives:

$$\frac{dt_1}{ds} = \frac{\sqrt{1+b^2} \, \sec\left(\frac{\pi}{2}t_7\right) \, \sin\left(\sqrt{1+b^2}\frac{\pi}{2}s\right)}{2\sqrt{1 - \cos^2\left(\sqrt{1+b^2}\frac{\pi}{2}s\right)\sec^2\left(\frac{\pi}{2}t_7\right)}} \frac{dt_7}{ds} \tag{12.38}$$

$$\frac{dt_4}{ds} = c \tag{12.39}$$

$$\frac{dt_7}{ds} = \frac{b^2 \, \sin\left(\pi\left(\sqrt{b^2+1}\right)s\right)}{\sqrt{b^2+1}\sqrt{1 - \frac{\left(b^2 \cos\left(\pi\sqrt{b^2+1})s\right) + 1\right)^2}{\left(b^2+1\right)^2}}} \tag{12.40}$$

Parameters t_1 and t_7 and their derivatives are shown in Figure 12.5a and b, respectively.

Binary decomposition of the cross-resonance gate: As it happens, we do not need to resort to a full decomposition of the CR gate to evaluate the gradient. The CR Hamiltonian (Eq. (12.28)) has four unique eigenvalues in general, $\pm c \pm \sqrt{b^2+1}$ [111]. However, if c is zero, there are only two unique eigenvalues, and the parameter-shift rule applies. Since the $I \otimes X$ component of the Hamiltonian (Eq. (12.28)) commutes, we can separate out the c parameter onto a separate X rotation of the second qubit, as we did for the full canonical decomposition. Thus, we can decompose the full CR gate into just two components, each of which is parameter-shift rule differentiable with respect to s.

$$\tag{12.41}$$

The shift parameters for this circuit are $r = \frac{\pi}{2}\sqrt{b^2+1}$ and $r = \frac{\pi c}{2}$, respectively.

Middle-out quantum gradients on classical hardware: In a classical simulation of a quantum computer, we can apply arbitrary operators to quantum states, and therefore we can efficiently calculate

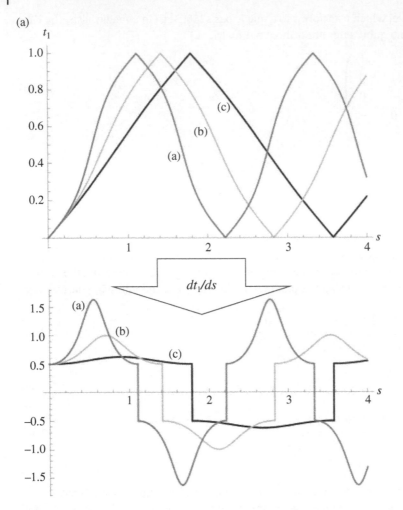

Figure 12.5 (a) Parameter t_1 and its derivative. (For more details see color figure in bins).

the gradients of quantum circuits without resorting to the parameter-shift rule. We could backpropagate the gradients using the chain rule Chapter 8. However, this requires storing the intermediate states during the forward propagation, resulting in a memory demand that scales as $O(2^M N)$ for M qubits and N gates. Fortunately, we can simplify the procedure and reduce the memory requirements by taking advantage of the time reversibility of quantum mechanics [129, 130]. Suppose we have a quantum circuit composed of N parameterized gates:

$$U(\theta) = U_N(\theta_N)...U_k(\theta_k)...U_2(\theta_2)U_1(\theta_1) \tag{12.42}$$

Then the derivative of our observable (Eq. (12.13)) with respect to one of the parameters is

$$\frac{df(\theta)}{d\theta_k} = \langle \psi | U_1^\dagger(\theta_1)...U_k^\dagger(\theta_k)...U_N^\dagger(\theta_N) \cdot A \cdot$$
$$U_N(\theta_N)...[-ia_k G_k]U_k(\theta_k)...U_1(\theta_1)|\psi\rangle + h.c. \tag{12.43}$$

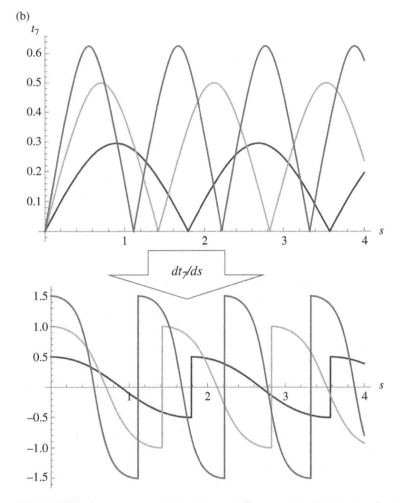

Figure 12.5b Parameter t_7 and its derivative. (For more details see color figure in bins).

Here, a_k and G_k are the scaling constant and Hermitian generator of the kth gate (Eq. (12.14)). We can rewrite this expression in a more compact form:

$$
\begin{aligned}
df(\theta)/d\theta_k &= -2a_k \, \text{Im} \, \langle B_k | G_k | F_k \rangle \\
|F_k\rangle &= U_k(\theta_k)...U_2(\theta_2)U_1(\theta_1)|\psi\rangle \\
|B_k\rangle &= U_{k+1}^\dagger(\theta_{k+1})...U_N^\dagger(\theta_N) \cdot A \cdot \\
&\quad U_N(\theta_N)...U_2(\theta_2)U_1(\theta_1)|\psi\rangle
\end{aligned}
\tag{12.44}
$$

Here, $|F_k\rangle$ is the initial state propagated forward in time up to the kth gate, and $|B_k\rangle$ is the initial state propagated forward in time through the entire circuit, followed by an application of the Hermitian observable, followed by a reversed time propagation backward to the $(k+1)$th gate. Note that $|B_k\rangle$ is not normalized due to the application of the Hermitian operator.

The trick is that if we are evaluating all of the gradients, we can recursively evaluate the forward and backward states, which requires only one additional gate application each per step:

$$|F_{k+1}\rangle = U_{k+1}(\theta_{k+1})|F_k\rangle$$
$$|B_{k+1}\rangle = U_{k+1}(\theta_{k+1})|B_k\rangle \tag{12.45}$$

Evaluating the original circuit of N gates requires storage of one state, N gate applications, and one inner product evaluation of the observable. Evaluating all N gradients using the middle-out approach requires $4N$ gates.

12.5 Classification with QNNs

In this section, we introduce a QNN that can represent labeled data – classical or quantum – and be trained by supervised learning. The quantum circuit consists of a sequence of parameter-dependent unitary transformations that acts on an input quantum state. For binary classification, a single Pauli operator is measured on a designated readout qubit. The measured output is the QNN's predictor of the binary label of the input state (Figure 12.6).

Here, we imagine a large dataset consisting of strings where each string comes with a binary label. For simplicity, we imagine that there is no label noise so that we can be confident that the label attached to each string is correct. We are given a training set comprising a set of S samples of strings with their labels. The goal is to use this information to be able to correctly predict the labels of unseen examples. Clearly, this can only be done if the label function has an underlying structure. If the label function is random, we may be able to learn (or fit with S parameters) the labels from the training set, but we will not be able to say anything about the label of a previously unseen example. Now imagine a real-world example where the dataset consists of pixilated images each of which has been correctly labeled to say if there is a dog or a cat in the image. In this case, classical NNs can learn to correctly classify new images as dog or cat. In Part I of the book, we have reviewed how this is done in the classical setting; here, we turn immediately to a QNN capable of learning to classify data. We continue to use the word *neural* to describe our network since the term has been adopted by the ML community, recognizing that the connection to neuroscience is now only historical.

To be concrete, imagine that the dataset consists of strings $z = z_1 z_2 \ldots z_n$ where each z_i is a bit taking the value $+1$ or -1 and a binary label $l(z)$ chosen as $+1$ or -1. For simplicity, imagine that the dataset consists of all 2^n strings. We have a quantum processor that acts on $n + 1$ qubits, and we ignore the possible need for ancilla qubits. The last qubit will serve as a readout. The quantum

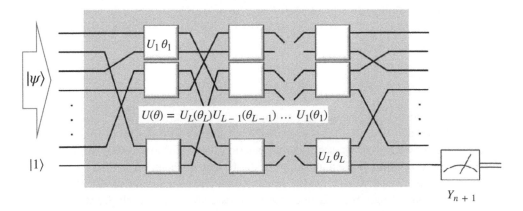

Figure 12.6 Schematic of the quantum neural network (QNN) on a quantum processor.

processor implements unitary transformations $\{U_a(\theta)\}$ on input states each of which acts on a subset of the qubits and depends on a continuous parameter θ, where for simplicity we have only one control parameter per unitary. Now we pick a set of L of these and make the unitary $U\left(\vec{\theta}\right) = U_L(\theta_L)U_{L-1}(\theta_{L-1}) \; ... \; U_1(\theta_1)$, which depends on the L parameters $\vec{\theta} = \theta_L, \theta_{L-1}, \; ... \; \theta_1$. For each z, we construct the computational basis state $|z, 1\rangle = |z_1 z_2 \; ... \; z_n, 1\rangle$ where the readout bit has been set to 1. Acting with the unitary on the input state gives the state

$$U\left(\vec{\theta}\right)|z,1\rangle. \tag{12.46}$$

On the readout qubit we measure a Pauli operator, say σ_y, which we call Y_{n+1}. This gives a $+1$ or a -1. Our goal is to make the measurement outcome correspond to the correct label of the input string, that is, $l(z)$. Typically, the measurement outcome is not certain. Our predicted label value is the real number between -1 and 1,

$$\langle z, 1|U^\dagger\left(\vec{\theta}\right)Y_{n+1}U\left(\vec{\theta}\right)|z,1\rangle \tag{12.47}$$

which is the average of the observed outcomes if Y_{n+1} is measured in multiple copies of Eq. (12.46). Our goal is to find parameters $\vec{\theta}$ so that the predicted label is near the true label. We will address the question of whether such parameters even exist (representation) as well as the question of whether such optimal parameters can then be efficiently found (learning). For a given circuit, that is, a choice of L unitaries, and a set of parameters $\vec{\theta}$, and an input string z, consider the sample loss

$$loss\left(\vec{\theta}, z\right) = 1 - l(z)\langle z, 1|U^\dagger\left(\vec{\theta}\right)Y_{n+1}U\left(\vec{\theta}\right)|z,1\rangle. \tag{12.48}$$

Note that the sample loss we use is linear in the margin (the product of the label and the predicted label value) and its minimum is at 0 (not minus infinity) because the predicted label value is automatically bounded to lie between -1 and 1. Suppose that the QNN is working perfectly, so that for each input z, the measurement always gives the correct label. This would mean that parameters $\vec{\theta}$ exist and have been found such that the sample loss is 0 for all inputs z.

Given a training set of S strings with their labels, we now describe how to use the quantum processor to find the parameters $\vec{\theta}$ that fulfill the learning task, that is, we describe supervised learning on a QNN. For now, we are assuming that our circuit is rich enough that there exist parameters that allow us to represent the label. Start with, say, random parameters $\vec{\theta}$ or perhaps an inspired choice. Pick a string z^1 from the training set. Use the quantum processor to construct

$$U\left(\vec{\theta}\right)|z^1,1\rangle$$

and measure σ_y on the last qubit. Do this enough times to get a good estimate of the expected value of Y_{n+1} and then compute loss $\left(\vec{\theta}, z^1\right)$ via Eq. (12.48). Now we want to make a small change in the parameters $\vec{\theta}$ to reduce the loss on training example z^1. We might do this by randomly sampling from nearby $\vec{\theta}$'s. Or we could compute the gradient with respect to $\vec{\theta}$ of loss $\left(\vec{\theta}, z^1\right)$ and then take a small step in the direction that reduces the loss (more on how to get the gradient later). This gives us new parameters $\theta^1 \rightarrow$. We now take a new training example z^2 and with quantum measurements estimate loss $\left(\vec{\theta}^1, z^2\right)$. Now change $\vec{\theta}^1$ by a small amount to slightly reduce this loss. Call the new parameters $\vec{\theta}^2$. We can continue in this fashion on, say, the whole set of training samples generating a sequence $\vec{\theta}^1, \vec{\theta}^2 \ldots \vec{\theta}^S$. If the learning has been successful, we would find that with the parameters $\vec{\theta}^S$, the operator $U\left(\vec{\theta}^S\right)$ acting on the state $|z, 1\rangle$ will produce a state that when the output qubit is measured will give the correct label $l(z)$. If z is from the training set, we could claim that we have fit the training data. If z is outside the training set, say, from a specified test set, we would conclude that the learning has generalized to unseen examples.

What we have just described is an implementation of what in classical ML is called "stochastic gradient descent." The stochasticity arises from the fact that the training examples are drawn randomly from the training set. When learning is successful, after enough training examples are processed, the parameters settle into a place where labels can be correctly predicted. There may be many values of the parameters that result in success, and for this reason even if the number of parameters is very large, starting from a random point may lead to a good solution. In traditional ML with an NN, the parameters (called weights) appear as entries in matrices that act linearly on internal vectors. The components of these vectors are acted on nonlinearly before the vector is multiplied by other weight-dependent matrices. Part of the art of building a successful ML implementation is the introduction of the right nonlinearity. In our setup, each unitary acts on the output of the previous unitary, and no nonlinearities are explicitly introduced. What we specify is the set of parameterized unitaries and the operator to be measured after the quantum evolution. Imagine that the individual unitaries in the set $\{U_a(\theta)\}$ are all of the form $\exp(i\theta\Sigma)$, where Σ is a generalized Pauli acting on a few qubits; that is, Σ is a tensor product of operators from the set $\{\sigma_x, \sigma_y, \sigma_z\}$ acting on a few qubits. The derivative with respect to θ gives an operator whose norm is bounded by 1. Therefore, the gradient of the loss function with respect to $\vec{\theta}$ is bounded by L, the number of parameters. This means that the gradient cannot blow up, and in this way we avoid a well-known problem that can occur when computing gradients in classical NNs. Researchers in classical ML have recently started to investigate the advantage of using unitary transformations to control gradient blowup [131–134]. Note that in our case this advantage comes for free.

12.5.1 Representation

Before discussing learning, we want to establish that our QNN is capable of expressing any two-valued label function, although – as we will see – at a possibly high cost in circuit depth (see also [135]). There are 2^n n-bit strings, and accordingly there are $2^{(2^n)}$ possible label functions $l(z)$. Given a label function, consider the operator whose action is defined on computational basis states as

$$U_l|z, z_{n+1}\rangle = \exp\left(i\frac{\pi}{4}l(z)X_{n+1}\right)|z, z_{n+1}\rangle. \tag{12.49}$$

In other words, it acts by rotating the output qubit about its x-axis by $\frac{\pi}{4}$ times the label of the string z. Correspondingly,

$$U_l^\dagger Y_{n+1}U_l = \cos\left(\frac{\pi}{2}l(Z)\right)Y_{n+1} + \sin\left(\frac{\pi}{2}l(Z)\right)Z_{n+1} \tag{12.50}$$

where in this formula $l(Z)$ is interpreted as an operator diagonal in the computational basis. Note that since $l(z)$ can only be $+1$ or -1, we have that

$$\langle z, 1|U_l^\dagger Y_{n+1}U_l|z, 1\rangle = l(z). \tag{12.51}$$

This shows that at least at some abstract level we have a way of representing any label function with a quantum circuit.

We now show how to write U_l as a product of two-qubit unitaries. For this discussion, it is convenient to switch to Boolean variables $b_i = \frac{1}{2}(1 - z_i)$ and think of our label function l as $1 - 2b$, where b is 0, 1 valued. Now we can use the Reed–Muller (RM) representation of any Boolean function in terms of the bits b_1 through b_n:

$$b = a_0 \oplus (a_1 b_1 \oplus a_2 b_2 \oplus ...a_n b_n) \oplus (a_{12} b_1 b_2 \oplus a_{13} b_1 b_3 + ..) \oplus ...$$
$$... \oplus a_{123...} b_1 b_2...b_n. \tag{12.52}$$

The addition is mod2, and the coefficients a are all 0 or 1. Note that there are 2^n coefficients, and since they are each 0 or 1 we see that there are indeed $2^{(2^n)}$ Boolean functions being represented. The formula can be exponentially long. Now we can write the label-dependent unitary U_l in Eq. (12.49) as

$$U_l = \exp\left(i\frac{A}{4}X_{n+1}\right) \exp\left(-i\frac{\pi}{2}BX_{n+1}\right) \tag{12.53}$$

where B is the operator, diagonal in the computational basis, corresponding to b. Each term in B in Eq. (12.53) is multiplied by X_{n+1}, and so each term commutes with the others. Each non-vanishing term in the RM formula gives rise in U_l to a controlled bit flip on the output qubit. To see this, consider, say, the three bit term involving bits 2, 7, and 9. This corresponds to the operator

$$\exp\left(-i\frac{\pi}{2}B_2 B_7 B_9 X_{n+1}\right) \tag{12.54}$$

which, acting on a computational basis state on the first n qubits, is the identity operator unless $b_2 = b_7 = b_9 = 1$, in which case it is $-iX_{n+1}$. We know from early work [100] that any controlled one-qubit unitary acting on qubit $n+1$ where the control is on the first n bits can be written as a product of n^2 two-qubit unitaries. So, any label function expressed in terms of the RM formula with, say, RM terms can be written as a product of RM commuting $n+1$ qubit operators, and each of these can be written as n^2 two-qubit unitaries.

Our quantum representation result is analogous to the classical representation theorem [136, 137]. This states that any Boolean label function can be represented on a depth-3 NN with the inner layer having size 2^n. Of course, such gigantic matrices cannot be represented on a conventional computer. In our case, we naturally work in a Hilbert space of exponential dimension, but we may need exponential circuit depth to express certain functions. The question of which functions can be compactly represented on a quantum circuit but cannot on a classical network is an open area of investigation. To this end, we now explore some examples.

Representing subset parity and subset majority: Consider the label function, which is the parity of a subset of the bits. Call the subset S, and let $a_j = 1$ if j is in the subset and $a_j = 0$ if j is not in the subset. The RM formula for the subset parity label is

$$P_S(z) = \sum_j \oplus a_j b_j \tag{12.55}$$

which is just the linear part of Eq. (12.52), where again the addition is mod2. This gives rise to the unitary that implements subset parity:

$$U_{P_S} = \exp\left(i\frac{\pi}{4}X_{n+1}\right) \exp\left(-i\frac{\pi}{2}\sum_j a_j B_j X_{n+1}\right) \tag{12.56}$$

Note that in the exponent the addition is automatically mod2 because of the $\frac{\pi}{2}$ and the properties of X_{n+1}. The circuit consists of (at most) n commuting two-qubit operators with the readout qubit in all the two-qubit gates. Classically, representing subset parity on a standard NN requires three layers.

Now consider the label function that is subset majority. The label is 1 if the majority of the bits in the subset are 1 and -1 otherwise. It is easiest to represent subset majority using the z variables. Then the subset majority label can be written as

$$M_S(z) = \text{sign}\left(\sum_j a_j z_j\right) \tag{12.57}$$

where we assume that the size of the subset is odd to avoid an ambiguity that occurs in the even case if the sum is 0. Although this is a compact way of writing subset majority, it is not in the RM form. We can write subset majority in the form Eq. (12.52), but Eq. (12.57) is more convenient for our current discussion. Now consider the unitary

$$U_{M_S} = \exp\left(i\frac{\beta}{2}\sum_j a_j Z_j X_{n+1}\right) \tag{12.58}$$

where we will specify β momentarily. Conjugating Y_{n+1} gives

$$U_{M_S}^\dagger Y_{n+1} U_{M_S} = \cos\left(\beta\sum_j a_j Z_j\right)Y_{n+1} + \sin\left(\beta\sum_j a_j Z_j\right)Z_{n+1} \tag{12.59}$$

so we have that

$$\langle z,1|U_{M_S}^\dagger Y_{n+1} U_{M_S}|z,1\rangle = \sin\left(\beta\sum_j a_j Z_j\right). \tag{12.60}$$

The largest possible value of $\sum_j a_j z_j$ is n, so if we set β equal to say $.9\pi/n$, we have that

$$\text{sign}\left(\sin\left(\frac{.9\pi}{n}\sum_j a_j z_j\right)\right) = M_S(z). \tag{12.61}$$

This means that if we make repeated measurements of Y_{n+1} and round the expected value up to 1 or down to -1, we can obtain perfect categorical error although the individual sample loss values are not 1 or -1. In classical ML, subset majority is an easy label to express because with one layer the labels on the whole data set can be separated with a single hyperplane.

12.5.2 Learning

We have already discussed earlier how with each new training example we need to modify the $\vec{\theta}$'s so that the sample loss decreases. We will now be explicit about two strategies to accomplish this, although other strategies may do better. With the parameters $\vec{\theta}$ and a given training example z, we first estimate the sample loss given (Eq. (12.48)). To do this, we make repeated measurements of Y_{n+1} in the state Eq. (12.46). To achieve, with probability greater than 99%, an estimate of the sample loss that is within δ of the true sample loss, we need to make at least $2/\delta^2$ measurements.

Once the sample loss is well estimated, we want to calculate the gradient of the sample loss with respect to $\vec{\theta}$. A straightforward way to proceed is to vary the components of $\vec{\theta}$ one at a time. With each changed component, we need to recalculate $\text{loss}\left(\vec{\theta'},z\right)$, where $\vec{\theta'}$ differs from $\vec{\theta}$ by a small amount in one component. Recall that one can get a second-order accurate estimate of the derivative of a function by taking the symmetric difference,

$$\frac{df}{dx}(x) = (f(x + \varepsilon) - f(x - \varepsilon))/(2\varepsilon) + O(\varepsilon^2).$$ (12.62)

To achieve this, you need to know that your error in the estimate of f at each x is no worse than $O(\varepsilon^3)$. To estimate loss $\left(\vec{\theta}, z\right)$ to order ε^3, we need order $1/\varepsilon^6$ measurements. So, for instance, using the symmetric difference we can get each component of the gradient accurate to order η by making measurements of order $1/\eta^3$. This needs to be repeated L times to get the full gradient.

There is an alternative strategy for computing each component of the gradient [138] that works when the individual unitaries are all of the form $\exp(i\theta\Sigma)$. Consider the derivative of the sample loss (Eq. (12.48)) with respect to θ_k which is associated with the unitary $U_k(\theta_k)$, which has the generalized Pauli operator Σ_k. Now

$$\frac{d\mathrm{loss}\left(\vec{\theta}, z\right)}{d\theta_k} = 2\,\mathrm{Im}\left(\langle z, 1 | U_1^\dagger ... U_L^\dagger Y_{n+1} U_L ... U_{k+1} \Sigma_k U_k ... U_1 | z, 1\rangle\right)$$ (12.63)

Note that Y_{n+1} and Σ_k are both unitary operators. Define the unitary operator

$$\mathcal{U}\left(\vec{\theta}\right) = U_1^\dagger ... U_L^\dagger Y_{n+1} U_L ... U_{k+1} \Sigma_k U_k ... U_1$$ (12.64)

so we re-express Eq. (12.48) as

$$\frac{d\mathrm{loss}(\theta, z)}{d\theta_k} \overrightarrow{} = 2\,\mathrm{Im}\left(\langle z, 1 | \mathcal{U} | z, 1\rangle\right).$$ (12.65)

$\mathcal{U}\left(\vec{\theta}\right)$ can be viewed as a quantum circuit composed of $2L + 2$ unitaries each of which depends on only a few qubits. We can use our quantum device to let $\mathcal{U}\left(\vec{\theta}\right)$ act on $|z, 1\rangle$. Using an auxiliary qubit, we can measure the right-hand side of Eq. (12.65). To see how this is done, start with

$$|z, 1\rangle \frac{1}{\sqrt{2}}(|0\rangle + |1\rangle)$$ (12.66)

and act with $i\mathcal{U}\left(\vec{\theta}\right)$ conditioned on the auxiliary qubit being 1. This produces

$$\frac{1}{\sqrt{2}}\left(|z, 1\rangle|0\rangle + i\mathcal{U}\left(\vec{\theta}\right)|z, 1\rangle|1\rangle\right)$$ (12.67)

Performing a Hadamard on the auxiliary qubit gives

$$\frac{1}{2}\left(|z, 1\rangle + i\mathcal{U}\left(\vec{\theta}\right)|z, 1\rangle|0\rangle\right) + \frac{1}{2}\left(|z, 1\rangle - i\mathcal{U}\left(\vec{\theta}\right)|z, 1\rangle|1\rangle\right).$$ (12.68)

Now measure the auxiliary qubit. The probability of getting 0 is

$$\frac{1}{2} - \frac{1}{2}\,\mathrm{Im}\left(\langle z, 1 | \mathcal{U}\left(\vec{\theta}\right)|z, 1\rangle\right)$$ (12.69)

so by making repeated measurements we can get a good estimate of the imaginary part which turns into an estimate of the k-th component of the gradient. This method avoids the numerical accuracy problem that accompanies the gradient approximation outlined in the previous paragraph. The cost is that we need to add an auxiliary qubit and run a circuit whose depth is $2L + 2$.

Given an accurate estimate of the gradient, we need a strategy for how to update $\vec{\theta}$. Let $\vec{g}$ be the gradient of loss $\left(\vec{\theta}z\right) \rightarrow$, with respect to $\vec{\theta}$. Now we want to change $\vec{\theta}$ in the direction of $\vec{g}$. To the lowest order in γ, we have that

$$\text{loss}\left(\vec{\theta} + \gamma\vec{g}, z\right) = \text{loss}\left(\vec{\theta}, z\right) + \gamma\vec{g}^2 + \mathcal{O}(\gamma^2). \tag{12.70}$$

We want to move the loss to its minimum at 0, so the first thought is to make

$$\gamma = -\frac{\text{loss}\left(\vec{\theta}, z\right)}{\vec{g}^2} \tag{12.71}$$

Doing this might drive the loss near 0 for the current training example, but in doing so it might have the undesirable effect of making the loss for other examples much worse. The usual ML technique is to introduce a learning rate r that is small and then set

$$\vec{\theta} \rightarrow \vec{\theta} - r\left(\frac{\text{loss}\left(\vec{\theta}, z\right)}{\vec{g}^2}\right)\vec{g}. \tag{12.72}$$

Part of the art of successful ML is to judiciously set the learning rate, which may vary as the learning proceeds. We do not yet have a quantum computer at our disposal, but we can simulate the quantum process using a conventional computer. Of course, this is only possible at a small number of bits because the Hilbert space dimension is $2^{(n+1)}$. The simulation has the nice feature that once the quantum state Eq. (12.46) is computed, we can evaluate the expected value of Y_{n+1} directly without doing any measurements. Also, for the systems that we simulate, the individual unitaries are of the form $\exp(i\theta\Sigma)$, and we can directly evaluate the expression Eq. (12.63). So, in our simulations, we evaluate the gradient exactly without resorting to finite difference methods.

Learning subset parity: As our first example, we consider learning subset parity. Recall that given a subset S the unitary U_{P_S} given by Eq. (12.56) will express subset parity on all input strings with zero sample loss. To learn, we need a set of unitaries that depend on parameters with the property that for each subset S there is a parameter setting that produces U_{P_S}. A simple way to achieve this is to use n parameters

$$U\left(\vec{\theta}\right) = \exp\left(i\frac{\pi}{4}X_{n+1}\right) \exp\left(-i\sum_j \theta_j B_j X_{n+1}\right) \tag{12.73}$$

and we see that the representation is perfect with $\theta_j = \frac{\pi}{2}$ if j is in the subset and $\theta_j = 0$ if j is not in the subset. Working from 6 to 16 bits and starting with a random $\vec{\theta}$, it was found [2] that with stochastic gradient descent we could learn the subset parity label function with far fewer than 2^n samples and therefore could successfully predict the label of unseen examples. It was also found that introducing 10% label noise did not impede the learning.

Note: What we just described is success at a low bit number, and as the number of bits increases, subset parity becomes impossible to learn.

Learning subset majority: Recall that we can represent subset majority with the unitary operator (Eq. (12.58)) with β set to $0.9\pi/n$. By thresholding the expected value of Y_{n+1}, according to Eq. (12.61), we can achieve zero categorical error. We are interested in having a parameter-dependent unitary for which there are parameter settings corresponding to the different subsets. Consider the unitary

$$U(\vec{\theta}) = \exp\left(i\frac{\beta}{2}\sum_j \theta_j Z_j X_{n+1}\right) \tag{12.74}$$

Now with $\theta_j = 1$ if j is in the subset and $\theta_j = 0$ if j is not in the subset, $U(\vec{\theta})$ represents subset majority on the selected subset. We now ask if we can learn the correct θ's given a training set labeled according to the majority of a selected subset. Note that the predicted label value on a training sample z is

$$\sin\left(\beta\sum_j \theta_j z_j\right) \tag{12.75}$$

and so rounding up or down gives the predicted label as

$$\text{sign}\left(\sum_j \theta_j z_j\right). \tag{12.76}$$

This result has a direct interpretation in terms of a classical NN with a single neuron that depends on the weights $\vec{\theta}$. The $\sum_j \theta_j z_j$ is the result of the neuron acting on the input. The nonlinearity comes from applying the sign function. But we know that since the data can be separated with one hyperplane, this is an easy label to learn with a single neuron. The same reasoning leads us to the conclusion that our QNN can efficiently be trained to represent subset majority. It was confirmed also in [2] in small-scale numerical simulations that the QNN was able to learn subset majority with low sample complexity.

12.6 Quantum Decision Tree Classifier

Formally, the problem can be stated as follows: given a set of classes containing m values: $C = \{c_1, \dots c_m\}$, a set of training data containing n objects is described as $\{(x_1, y_1), (x_2, y_2), \dots, (x_i, y_i), \dots, (x_n, y_n)\}$, where x_i is a vector of d attributes and $y_i \in C$ is the class label corresponding to the object x_i. The attribute set of the input objects can be denoted by $A = \{a_1, a_2, \dots, a_i, \dots, a_d\}$. For each attribute $a_i \in A$, its domain values set is described by $V_{a_i} = \{v_{i,1}, v_{i,2}, \dots, v_{i,m_i}\}$, where m_i is the cardinality of V_{a_i}. The goal of classification is to develop an optimal classification rule that can determine the class of any object from its values of the attributes. According to the classifier, we can find the class $y \in C$ for a new object x.

12.6.1 Model of the Classifier

A decision tree classifier learns from a training dataset that contains observations about objects, which are either obtained empirically or acquired from experts. In a quantum world, the training data consist of quantum objects instead of classical observations on classical data.

A *quantum training dataset* with n quantum data pairs can be described as $D = \{(|x_1\rangle, |y_1\rangle), (|x_2\rangle, |y_2\rangle), \dots, (|x_n\rangle, |y_n\rangle)\}$, where $|x_i\rangle$ is the i-th quantum object of the training dataset, and $|y_i\rangle$ is the known class state corresponding to the quantum state $|x_i\rangle$. We call the set of all example quantum states $X = \{|x_1\rangle, |x_2\rangle, \dots, |x_i\rangle, \dots, |x_n\rangle\}$ the *sample set*, and the set of all quantum class states $Y = \{|y_1\rangle, |y_2\rangle, \dots, |y_i\rangle, \dots, |y_n\rangle\}$ is called the *class sample set*. We also call a class state $|y_i\rangle$ the *target attribute state*.

A quantum state, $|x_i\rangle$, is represented by a d-dimensional attribute vector (or *attribute state*), $|x_i\rangle = (|x_{1,i}\rangle, |x_{2,i}\rangle, \dots, |x_{d,i}\rangle)$, depicting d measurements made on the tuple from d attributes, respectively, $a_1, a_2, ..., a_d$. For attribute a_i, where $i = 1, 2, ..., d$, its domain value set V_{a_i} is described as $\{|v_{i,1}\rangle, |v_{i,2}\rangle, ..., |v_{i,m_i}\rangle\}$, where $|v_{i,j}\rangle$ is the j-th basis state, and m_i stands for its cardinality. These basis states span a Hilbert space S_i. Any quantum state $|\varphi\rangle$ belongs to the space S_i and can be described by a superposition of the basis states:

$$|\varphi\rangle = \sum_{j=1}^{m_i} \alpha_{i,j} |v_{i,j}\rangle \tag{12.77}$$

The coefficients $\alpha_{i,j}$ may be complex with $\sum_j |\alpha_{i,j}|^2 = 1$. The set of all possible input objects is called the *instance space*, which is defined as a tensor product of all input attributes' quantum systems: $S = S_1 \otimes S_2 \otimes ... \otimes S_d$.

We assume that $C_b = \{|c_{b1}\rangle, |c_{b2}\rangle, ... |c_{bm}\rangle\}$ is the set of m basis states that describe the class state. $|c_{bi}\rangle$ is called the *class basis state*, where $i = 1, 2, ..., m$. These class basis states span a Hilbert space S_c (called *class space*). A class state $|y_j\rangle$ can be described by a superposition of these class basis states: $|y_j\rangle = \sum_{i=1}^m \alpha_i |c_{bi}\rangle$, where $\sum_i |\alpha_i|^2 = 1$, provided the universal set of distinct class states is described as $C = \{|c_1\rangle, |c_2\rangle, ..., |c_i\rangle, ..., |c_M\rangle\}$, where $|c_i\rangle \in S_c$. For arbitrary class state $|c_i\rangle \in C$ and $|c_j\rangle \in C$, we have $|c_i\rangle \neq |c_j\rangle$ if $i \neq j$.

Obviously, the *sample set* belongs to the *instance space*; that is, $X \subset S$. We also have $Y \subset S_c$. In this paper, we restrict the arbitrary *attribute state* $|x_{i,j}\rangle$ and class state $|y_k\rangle$ to pure states. Given a training dataset D with attribute set $A = \{a_1, a_2, ..., a_i, ..., a_d\}$, for each attribute $a_i \in A$, we denote the set of its attribute states by D_i, where $D_i = \{|x_{i,1}\rangle, |x_{i,2}\rangle, ..., |x_{i,n}\rangle\}$. The training dataset D can then be rewritten as $D = \{D_1^T, D_2^T, ...D_d^T, Y^T\}$.

The goal is to form a decision tree classifier that can be used to predict a previously unseen object by explicitly assigning it to a specific class state. More accurately, using the training quantum states and the corresponding class states, a decision tree classifier t is designed, provided we are given finite copies of a new pure state $|x_{new}\rangle \in S$. By searching over the quantum decision tree t, we can obtain a precise class state $|y_{new}\rangle \in C$ corresponding to the quantum state $|x_{new}\rangle$.

In a quantum world, learning is more difficult for a classification algorithm than in a classical world. The reason is that the quantum mechanics forbids us to obtain two or more identical copies of unknown quantum state. In this section, the constraint can be relaxed by considering the case of multiple copies of the state either to be learned or to be classified (see the quantum template matching problem of [139]). So, in the remainder of the section, both the training state $|x_{i,j}\rangle$ and the state to be classified $|x_{new}\rangle$ have multiple copies.

Quantum decision trees: Consider a quantum decision tree R derived from the training dataset $D = \{(|x_1\rangle, |y_1\rangle), (|x_2\rangle, |y_2\rangle), ..., (|x_n\rangle, |y_n\rangle)\} = \{D_1^T, D_2^T, ..., D_d^T, Y^T\}$. Each node in R is also a tree. Any node t in R is described as $t = \{D^{(t)}, a_i, \{t_{c1}, t_{c2}, ..., t_{ct_i}\}\}$, where $D^{(t)}$ is the set of training data in the node t, $a_i \in A$, and $\{t_{c1}, t_{c2}, ..., t_{ct_i}\}$ is the set of its t_i subnodes. The tree t is split into t_i subtrees according to the attribute a_i. Let $t.\,attribute$ denote the attribute of the node t; then $t.\,attribute = a_i$. For the root R, $D^{(R)} = D$.

For a node t, $D^{(t)} = \{D_1^{(t)}, D_2^{(t)}, ..., D_d^{(t)}, Y^{(t)}\}$. Let $t.\,attribute = a_i$; we divide $D_i^{(t)}$ into t_i clusters: $D_{i,1}^{(t)}, D_{i,2}^{(t)}, ..., D_{i,t_i}^{(t)}$, where $D_{i,j}^{(t)} \subseteq D_i^{(t)}$. Each cluster $D_{i,j}^{(t)}$ has a centroid denoted by $|xc_{i,j}^{(t)}\rangle$; then the set of centroids for attribute a_i at node t is described by $XC_i^{(t)} = \{|xc_{i,1}^{(t)}\rangle, |xc_{i,2}^{(t)}\rangle, ..., |xc_{i,t_i}^{(t)}\rangle\}$.

Then, each item $D_j^{(t)} \in D^{(t)}$ is divided into t_i clusters: $D_{j,1}^{(t)}, D_{j,2}^{(t)}, ..., D_{j,t_i}^{(t)}$, where $j \neq i$. The partitioning method is as follows:

- If a state $|x_{i,k}\rangle \in D_i^{(t)}$ is divided into the set $D_{i,l}^{(t)}$, then we assign the state $|x_{j,k}\rangle \in D_j^{(t)}$ into the cluster $D_{j,l}^{(t)}$, where $1 \leq l \leq t_i$.
- The training dataset $D^{(t)}$ then is partitioned into t_i subsets according to the set of centroids, $XC_i^{(t)}$. That is to say, the node t is split into t_i descendant nodes: $t_{c1}, t_{c2}, ..., t_{cj}, ..., t_{ct_i}$.
- In the meantime, the set of target attribute states, $Y^{(t)}$, is also partitioned into t_i subsets described by $Y^{(t)} = \left\{ Y_1^{(t)}, Y_2^{(t)}, ..., Y_{t_i}^{(t)} \right\}$, where t and i mean that the class states is partitioned by attribute a_i at node t.
- For a descendant node t_{cj}, we generate an edge with a label $|xc_{i,t_i}^{(t)}\rangle$ by linking node t to node t_{cj}. This process is then repeated for each subtree of t.

To construct a quantum decision tree, we need to (i) decide which attribute to test at each node in the tree. We would like to select the attribute that is most useful for classifying objects. We discuss the details of the node splitting criterion in the next section. We then need to (ii) cluster the attribute states of the expected attributes into appropriate clusters. The problem is discussed after that.

Node splitting criterion: Much of the research in designing decision trees focuses on assigning which attribute test should be performed at each node. The fundamental principle underlying tree creation is that of simplicity: We prefer decisions that lead to a simple, compact tree with few nodes. The simplest model that explains data is the one to be preferred. To this end, we look for an attribute test at each node that makes the subsidiary decision trees as simple as possible. In classical algorithms, the most popular criterion is the *entropy impurity*: $E(t) = \sum_{i=1}^{m} - p_i log_2 p_i$, where p_i is the proportion of node t belonging to class i, m_t is the total number of classes of node t. Classical node splitting criteria are not working in the quantum world since the classes can be in superposition states. We present a new criterion, *quantum entropy impurity*, to measure the attributes. Given a quantum decision tree or subtree t and the set of class states $Y^{(t)} = \left\{ |y_1^{(t)}\rangle, |y_2^{(t)}\rangle, ..., |y_{n_t}^{(t)}\rangle \right\}$ that belongs to t, where $Y^{(t)} \subseteq Y$, and n_t is the cardinality of $Y^{(t)}$, let $Y^{(dt)} = \left\{ |y_1^{(dt)}\rangle, |y_2^{(dt)}\rangle, ..., |y_{n_{dt}}^{(dt)}\rangle \right\}$ denote the set of distinct class states of $Y^{(t)}$, where n_{dt} is the cardinality of $Y^{(dt)}$, then $Y^{(dt)} \subseteq Y^{(t)}$, $Y^{(dt)} \subseteq C$, and $n_t \geq n_{dt}$. For any class states $|y_i^{(dt)}\rangle \in Y^{(dt)}$ and $|y_j^{(dt)}\rangle \in Y^{(dt)}$, we have $|y_i^{(dt)}\rangle \neq |y_j^{(dt)}\rangle$ if $i \neq j$. The *quantum entropy impurity* of node t can be defined by the following:

$$S(\rho) = - tr(\rho \log \rho) \tag{12.78}$$

where $\rho = \sum_{i=1}^{m} p_i^{(dt)} |y_i^{(dt)}\rangle \langle y_i^{(dt)}|$ is the average state of $Y^{(t)}$ or the *density operator* of $Y^{(t)}$, where $p_i^{(dt)}$ is the fraction of states $|y_i^{(dt)}\rangle$ at node t that are in $Y^{(t)}$. Equation (12.78) defines the *quantum entropy* or *von Neumann entropy* of quantum state ρ. When the target attribute states in $Y^{(dt)}$ are all orthogonal, the definition coincides with the classical case.

Given a partial quantum tree down to node t with the set of class states $Y^{(t)} = \left\{ |y_1^{(t)}\rangle, |y_2^{(t)}\rangle, ..., |y_{n_t}^{(t)}\rangle \right\}$, the key problem is what attribute value we should choose for the attribute test. If the expected splitting attribute is a_i at node t, and then the attribute states belonging to set $D_i^{(t)}$ are partitioned into t_i subsets $D_{i,1}^{(t)}, D_{i,2}^{(t)}, ..., D_{i,t_i}^{(t)}$, the set of class states $Y^{(t)}$ will then be partitioned into $Y_i^{(t)} = \left\{ Y_{i,1}^{(t)}, Y_{i,2}^{(t)}, ..., Y_{i,j}^{(t)}, ..., Y_{i,t_i}^{(t)} \right\}$, where $Y_i^{(t)} = Y^{(t)}$, $Y_{i,j}^{(t)}$ contains those target attribute states in $Y^{(t)}$ that have attribute states belonging to $D_{i,j}^{(t)}$. The quantum entropy of $Y_{i,j}^{(t)}$ is denoted by $S\left(\rho_{i,j}^{(t)}\right)$. Then, the expected quantum entropy of the system after node t is split using attribute a_i is

$$S_e\left(\rho_i^{(t)}\right) = \sum_{j=1}^{t_i} p_j S\left(\rho_{i,j}^{(t)}\right) \tag{12.79}$$

where $\rho^{(t)}$ is the density operator of $Y_{i,j}^{(t)}$, which represents the set of class states of the j-th expected subnode t_{ci_j} of attribute a_i in node t, and $p_j = |Y_{i,j}^{(t)}|/n_t$ is the probability of state $\rho_j^{(t)}$. The sum of the probabilities is equal to 1; that is, $\sum_{j=1}^{t_i} = 1$.

Quantum entropy specifies the minimum number of qubits of information needed to encode the classification of an arbitrary member of $Y^{(t)}$. The smaller the value of quantum entropy, the fewer the number of qubits required, and then the smaller or simpler the quantum decision tree is. For each attribute, we calculate its expected quantum entropy for node t, and then we get d expected quantum entropies for node t: $S_e\left(\rho_1^{(t)}\right), S_e\left(\rho_2^{(t)}\right), ..., S_e(\rho^{(t)}), ..., S_e\left(\rho_d^{(t)}\right)$. We choose the attribute a_i whose expected quantum entropy $S_e\left(\rho_i^{(t)}\right)$ is the minimum among above values of quantum entropies as the splitting attribute for node t.

Attribute data partition: In a quantum decision tree, each decision outcome at a node is called a partition, since it corresponds to splitting a subset of the training data. The root node splits the full training dataset, and each successive decision splits a proper subset of the data. The number of splits at a node is closely related to the type of the attribute and could vary throughout the tree.

Here we present a specific attribute data partition method as an example [140]. Suppose we are given the training dataset $D^{(t)}$ at node t and the set of attribute states for attribute $a_i \in A$: $D_i^{(t)} = \left\{ |x_{i,1}^{(t)}\rangle, |x_{i,2}^{(t)}\rangle, ..., |x_{i,n_t}^{(t)}\rangle \right\}$, where n_t is the number of attribute states for tree t. We have $D^{(t)} = \left\{ \left(D_1^{(t)}\right)^T, \left(D_2^{(t)}\right)^T, ..., \left(D_d^{(t)}\right)^T, \left(Y^{(t)}\right)^T \right\}$. Let $D_i^{(dt)} = \left\{ |x_{i,1}^{(dt)}\rangle, |x_{i,2}^{(dt)}\rangle, ..., |x_{i,n_{dt}}^{(dt)}\rangle \right\}$ denote the set of distinct attribute states of $D_i^{(t)}$, where n_{dt} is the cardinality of $D_i^{(dt)}$; then $D_i^{(dt)} \subseteq D_i^{(t)}, D_i^{(dt)} \subseteq D_i$. For any attribute state $|x_{i,j}^{(dt)}\rangle \in D_i^{(dt)}$ and $|x_{i,k}^{(dt)}\rangle \in D_i^{(dt)}$, we have $|x_{i,j}^{(dt)}\rangle \neq |x_{i,k}^{(dt)}\rangle$ if $j \neq k$. We partition the set $D_i^{(t)}$ into t_i subclasses: $D_{i,1}^{(t)}, D_{i,2}^{(t)}, ..., D_{i,j}^{(t)}, ..., D_{i,t_i}^{(t)}$, where $D_{i,j}^{(t)} \subseteq D_i^{(t)}, \bigcap_{k=1}^{t_i} D_{i,k}^{(t)} = D_i^{(t)}$. For any $D_{i,j}^{(t)} \subseteq D_i^{(t)}$ and $D_{i,k}^{(t)} \subseteq D_i^{(t)}, D_{i,j}^{(t)} \cap D_{i,k}^{(t)} = \emptyset$ if $j \neq k$. For each $|x_j^{(t)}\rangle \in D_i^{(t)t}$, we can find one and only one subclass $D_{i,k}^{(t)}$ that contains $|x_{i,j}^{(t)}\rangle$, that is, $|x_{i,j}^{(t)}\rangle \in D_{i,k}^{(t)}$, where $D_{i,k}^{(t)} \subseteq D_i^{(t)}$. For each subclass $D_{i,j}^{(t)'}$ we calculate its centroid $|xc_{i,j}^{(t)}\rangle$, which represents the subclass, and the set of the centroids is described by $XC_i^{(t)} = \left\{ |xc_{i,1}^{(t)}\rangle, |xc_{i,2}^{(t)}\rangle, ..., |xc_{i,t_i}^{(t)}\rangle \right\}$. In the meantime, the class states set $Y^{(t)}$ is also split into t_i subset $Y_{i'}^{(t)} = \left\{ Y_{i,1}^{(t)}, Y_{i,2}^{(t)}, ..., Y_{i,t_i}^{(t)} \right\}$, where $Y_i^{(t)} = Y^{(t)}$. For each $|y_j^{(t)}\rangle \in Y^{(t)}$, we can find one and only one subset $Y_{i,k}^{(t)}$ that contains $|y_j^{(t)}\rangle$, that is, $|y_{o,j}\rangle \in Y_{i,k}^{(t)}$, where $Y_{i,k}^{(t)} \in Y_i^{(t)}$. Next, the training dataset $D^{(t)}$ is also partitioned into t_i subsets: $D^{(t_{c1})}, D^{(t_{c2})}, ..., D^{(t_{cj})}, ..., D^{(t_{ci})}$, and the j-th partition is described by $D^{(t_{cj})} = \left\{ \left(D_{1,j}^{(t)}\right)^T, \left(D_{2,j}^{(t)}\right)^T, ..., \left(D_{d,j}^{(t)}\right)^T, \left(Y_{i,j}^{(t)}\right)^T \right\}$.

Before partitioning an attribute, its data distribution pattern is discriminated in advance. Given the attribute $a_i \in A$ and its attribute states set $D_i^{(t)}$ at node t, for an attribute state $|x_{i,j}^{(t)}\rangle$, we call the multiplicity of the state to the cardinality of the set the *multiplicity ratio*, denoted by $mr_{i,j}^{(t)} = m_{i,j}^{(t)}/t_i$, where $m_{i,j}^{(t)}$ is the multiplicity of $|x_{i,j}^{(t)}\rangle$ in set $D_i^{(t)}$. We say that an attribute state $|x_{i,j}^{(t)}\rangle$ is *large state* if its *multiplicity ratio* is not smaller than the user-specified minimum multiplicity ratio (called *minmr*). The ratio of the number of *large states* to the number of distinct attribute states in the set is called the *simple pattern ratio* of the attribute a_i at node t, defined by $spr_i^{(t)}$. The data pattern of an attribute at a node is a *simple pattern* if its *simple pattern ratio* is equal or greater than the user-specified minimum simple pattern ratio (called *minspr*); otherwise, it is called a *complex pattern*.

Constructing quantum decision tree: We now construct the quantum decision tree. At first, for each attribute a_i, we cluster the data into t_i clusters $D_{i,1}^{(t)}, D_{i,2}^{(t)}, ..., D_{i,t_i}^{(t)}$, and these clusters have mutually exclusive centroids $|xc_{i,1}^{(t)}\rangle, |xc_{i,2}^{(t)}\rangle, ..., |xc_{i,t_i}^{(t)}\rangle$ that represent the t_i clusters, respectively. The set of the clusters is denoted by $D_i^{(t)}$; we then have a set of d clusters: $D_1^{(t)}, D_2^{(t)}, ..., D_d^{(t)}$. Second, from Eq. (12.79), we calculate the expected quantum entropy after t is split for each attribute, and then we choose the attribute with the smallest expected quantum entropy as the splitting node. Suppose the splitting attribute is a_i; we then split t into t_i descendant nodes and label the edges from node t to each descendant node $|xc_{i,1}^{(t)}\rangle, |xc_{i,2}^{(t)}\rangle, ..., |xc_{i,t_i}^{(t)}\rangle$, respectively.

The process of choosing a new attribute and dividing the training data is then repeated for each internal child node. In the process, only the attribute states associated with the child node is used. This process continues until any of two stopping criteria is met: (i) Every attribute has already been included along this path through the tree, or (ii) the attribute states associated with the current node all have the same target attribute state (i.e., their quantum entropy is zero). We then come to a leaf node. A class label is assigned to the node; this is the simplest step in tree construction.

Appendix 12.7   Matrix Exponential

Objective: Solve

$$\frac{d\vec{x}}{dt} = A\vec{x}$$

with an $n \times n$ constant coefficient matrix A.

Here, the unknown is the vector function $\vec{x}(t) = \left\{ \begin{array}{c} x_1(t) \\ \cdot \\ \cdot \\ \cdot \\ x_n(t) \end{array} \right\}$

General solution formula in matrix exponential form:

$$\vec{x}(t) = e^{tA}\vec{C} = e^{tA} \left\{ \begin{array}{c} C_1 \\ \cdot \\ \cdot \\ \cdot \\ C_n \end{array} \right\}$$

where $C_1, \cdots, C_n$ are arbitrary constants.

The solution of the initial value problem

$$\frac{d\vec{x}}{dt} = A\vec{x}, \vec{x}(t_0) = \vec{x}_0$$

is given by

$$\vec{x}(t) = e^{(t-t_0)A}\vec{x}_0.$$

Definition (matrix exponential): For a square matrix A,

$$e^{tA} = \sum_{k=0}^{\infty} \frac{t^k}{k!} A^k = I + tA + \frac{t^2}{2!}A^2 + \frac{t^3}{3!}A^3 + \cdots.$$

Evaluation of matrix exponential in the diagonalizable case: Suppose that A is diagonalizable; that is, there are an invertible matrix P and a diagonal matrix $D = \left\{ \begin{matrix} \lambda_1 & & \\ & \ddots & \\ & & \lambda_n \end{matrix} \right\}$ such that $A = PDP^{-1}$. In this case, we have

$$e^{tA} = Pe^{tD}P^{-1} = P \left\{ \begin{matrix} e^{\lambda_1 t} & & \\ & \ddots & \\ & & e^{\lambda_n t} \end{matrix} \right\} P^{-1}$$

Design Example 12.2

Let $A = \left\{ \begin{matrix} 6 & 3 & -2 \\ -4 & -1 & 2 \\ 13 & 9 & -3 \end{matrix} \right\}$

(a) Evaluate e^{tA}.

(b) Find the general solutions of $\frac{d\vec{x}}{dt} = A\vec{x}$.

(c) Solve the initial value problem $\frac{d\vec{x}}{dt} = A\vec{x}$, $\vec{x}(0) = \left\{ \begin{matrix} -2 \\ 1 \\ 4 \end{matrix} \right\}$

Solution

The given matrix A is diagonalized: $A = PDP^{-1}$ with

$$P = \left\{ \begin{matrix} 1 & -1 & 1/2 \\ -1 & 2 & -1/2 \\ 1 & 1 & 1 \end{matrix} \right\}, D = \left\{ \begin{matrix} 1 & 0 & 0 \\ 0 & 2 & 0 \\ 0 & 0 & -1 \end{matrix} \right\}.$$

Design Example 12.2 (Continued)

Part (a): We have

$$e^{tA} = Pe^{tD}P^{-1}$$

$$= \left\{ \begin{array}{ccc} 1 & -1 & 1/2 \\ -1 & 2 & -1/2 \\ 1 & 1 & 1 \end{array} \right\} \left\{ \begin{array}{ccc} e^t & 0 & 0 \\ 0 & e^{2t} & 0 \\ 0 & 0 & e^{-t} \end{array} \right\} \left\{ \begin{array}{ccc} 5 & 3 & -1 \\ 1 & 1 & 0 \\ -6 & -4 & 2 \end{array} \right\}$$

$$= \left\{ \begin{array}{ccc} 5e^t - e^{2t} - 3e^{-t} & 3e^t - e^{2t} - 2e^{-t} & -e^t + e^{-t} \\ -5e^t + 2e^{2t} + 3e^{-t} & -3e^t + 2e^{2t} + 2e^{-t} & e^t - e^{-t} \\ 5e^t + e^{2t} - 6e^{-t} & 3e^t + e^{2t} - 4e^{-t} & -e^t + 2e^{-t} \end{array} \right\}.$$

Part (b): The general solutions to the given system are

$$\vec{x}(t) = e^{tA} \left\{ \begin{array}{c} C_1 \\ C_2 \\ C_3 \end{array} \right\},$$

where C_1, C_2, C_3 are free parameters.

Part (c): The solution to the initial value problem is

$$\vec{x}(t) = e^{tA} \left\{ \begin{array}{c} -2 \\ 1 \\ 4 \end{array} \right\} = \left\{ \begin{array}{c} -11e^t + e^{2t} + 8e^{-t} \\ 11e^t - 2e^{2t} - 8e^{-t} \\ -11e^t - e^{2t} + 16e^{-t} \end{array} \right\}.$$

Evaluation of matrix exponential using fundamental matrix: In the case, A is not diagonalizable; one approach to obtaining the matrix exponential is to use Jordan forms. Here, we use another approach. We have already learned how to solve the initial value problem

$$\frac{d\vec{x}}{dt} = A\vec{x}, \vec{x}(0) = \vec{x}_0.$$

We shall compare the solution formula with $\vec{x}(t) = e^{tA}\vec{x}_0$ to find out what e^{tA} is. We know the general solutions of $d\vec{x}/dt = A\vec{x}$ have the following structure: $\vec{x}(t) = C_1\vec{x}_1(t) + \cdots + C_n\vec{x}_n(t)$, where $\vec{x}_1(t), \cdots, \vec{x}_n(t)$ are n linearly independent particular solutions. The formula can be rewritten as $\vec{x}(t) = \left[\vec{x}_1(t)...\vec{x}_n(t) \right]\vec{C}$ with $\vec{C} = (C_1,..., C_n)^T$. For the initial value problem, $\vec{C}$ is determined by the initial condition $\left[\vec{x}_1(0)\ \vec{x}_n(0)\right]\vec{C} = \vec{x}_0 \Rightarrow$ $\vec{C} = \left[\vec{x}_1(0)\ \vec{x}_n(0)\right]^{-1}\vec{x}_0$. Thus, the solution of the initial value problem is given by $\vec{x}(t) = \left[\vec{x}_1(t)...\vec{x}_n(t)\right]\left[\vec{x}_1(0)...\vec{x}_n(0)\right]^{-1}\vec{x}_0$. Comparing this with $\vec{x}(t) = e^{tA}\vec{x}_0$, we obtain $e^{tA} = \left[\vec{x}_1(t)...\vec{x}_n(t)\right]\left[\vec{x}_1(0)...\vec{x}_n(0)\right]^{-1}$. In this method of evaluating e^{tA}, the matrix $M(t) = \left[\vec{x}_1(t)...\vec{x}_n(t)\right]$ plays an essential role. Indeed, $e^{tA} = M(t)M(0)^{-1}$.

(Continued)

Design Example 12.2 (Continued)

Definition (fundamental matrix solution): If $\vec{x}_1(t), \cdots, \vec{x}_n(t)$ are n linearly independent solutions of the n dimensional homogeneous linear system $d\vec{x}/dt = A\vec{x}$; we call $M(t) = \left[\vec{x}_1(t) \dots \vec{x}_n(t) \right]$ a *fundamental matrix solution* of the system.

Remark 1: The matrix function M(t) satisfies the equation $M'(t) = AM(t)$. Moreover, M(t) is an invertible matrix for every t. These two properties characterize fundamental matrix solutions.

Remark 2: Given a linear system, fundamental matrix solutions are not unique. However, when we make any choice of a fundamental matrix solution M(t) and compute $M(t)M(0)^{-1}$, we always get the same result.

Design Example 12.3

Evaluate e^{tA} for $A = \begin{Bmatrix} -7 & -9 & 9 \\ 3 & 5 & -3 \\ -3 & -3 & 5 \end{Bmatrix}$

Solution

We first solve $d\vec{x}/dt = A\vec{x}$. We obtain

$$\vec{x}(t) = C_1 e^{-t} \begin{Bmatrix} 3 \\ -1 \\ 1 \end{Bmatrix} + C_2 e^{2t} \begin{Bmatrix} -1 \\ 1 \\ 0 \end{Bmatrix} + C_3 e^{2t} \begin{Bmatrix} 1 \\ 0 \\ 1 \end{Bmatrix}.$$

This gives a fundamental matrix solution:

$$M(t) = \begin{Bmatrix} 3e^{-t} & -e^{2t} & e^{2t} \\ -e^{-t} & e^{2t} & 0 \\ e^{-t} & 0 & e^{2t} \end{Bmatrix}.$$

The matrix exponential is

$$e^{tA} = M(t)M(0)^{-1} = \begin{Bmatrix} 3e^{-t} & -e^{2t} & e^{2t} \\ -e^{-t} & e^{2t} & 0 \\ e^{-t} & 0 & e^{2t} \end{Bmatrix} \begin{Bmatrix} 3 & -1 & 1 \\ -1 & 1 & 0 \\ 1 & 0 & 1 \end{Bmatrix}^{-1}$$

$$= \begin{Bmatrix} 3e^{-t} - 2e^{2t} & 3e^{-t} - 3e^{2t} & -3e^{-t} + 3e^{2t} \\ -e^{-t} + 2e^{2t} & -e^{-t} + 2e^{2t} & e^{-t} - e^{2t} \\ e^{-t} - e^{2t} & e^{-t} - e^{2t} & -e^{-t} + 2e^{2t} \end{Bmatrix}$$

Design Example 12.4

Evaluate e^{tA} for $A = \begin{Bmatrix} -5 & -8 & 4 \\ 2 & 3 & -2 \\ 6 & 14 & -5 \end{Bmatrix}$

Solution: We first solve $d\vec{x}/dt = A\vec{x}$. We obtain

$$\vec{x}(t) = C_1 e^{-t} \begin{Bmatrix} 3 \\ -1 \\ 1 \end{Bmatrix} + C_2 e^{-3t} \begin{Bmatrix} -2 \\ 1 \\ 1 \end{Bmatrix} + C_3 e^{-3t} \begin{Bmatrix} -1-2t \\ \frac{1}{2}+t \\ t \end{Bmatrix}$$

This gives a fundamental matrix solution:

$$M(t) = \begin{Bmatrix} 3e^{-t} & -2e^{-3t} & -e^{-3t}-2te^{-3t} \\ -e^{-t} & e^{-3t} & \frac{1}{2}e^{-3t}+te^{-3t} \\ e^{-t} & e^{-3t} & te^{-3t} \end{Bmatrix}$$

The matrix exponential is

$$e^{tA} = M(t)M(0)^{-1}$$

$$= \begin{Bmatrix} 3e^{-t} & -2e^{-3t} & -e^{-3t}-2te^{-3t} \\ -e^{-t} & e^{-3t} & \frac{1}{2}e^{-3t}+te^{-3t} \\ e^{-t} & e^{-3t} & te^{-3t} \end{Bmatrix} \begin{Bmatrix} 3 & -2 & -1 \\ -1 & 1 & 1/2 \\ 1 & 1 & 0 \end{Bmatrix}^{-1}$$

$$= \begin{Bmatrix} 3e^{-t}-2e^{-3t}-8te^{-3t} & 6e^{-t}-6e^{-3t}-20te^{-3t} & 4te^{-3t} \\ -e^{-t}+e^{-3t}+4te^{-3t} & -2e^{-t}+3e^{-3t}+10te^{-3t} & -2te^{-3t} \\ e^{-t}-e^{-3t}+4te^{-3t} & 2e^{-t}-2e^{-3t}+10te^{-3t} & e^{-3t}-2te^{-3t} \end{Bmatrix}$$

Design Example 12.5

Evaluate e^{tA} for $A = \begin{Bmatrix} 9 & -5 \\ 4 & 5 \end{Bmatrix}$

Solution 1: (Use Diagonalization)

Solving $\det(A - \lambda I) = 0$, we obtain the eigenvalues of $A : \lambda_1 = 7 + 4i$, $\lambda_2 = 7 - 4i$.

Eigenvectors for $\lambda_1 = 7 + 4i$ are obtained by solving $[A - (7 + 4i)I]\vec{v} = 0$:

$$\vec{v} = v_2 \begin{Bmatrix} \frac{1}{2}+i \\ 1 \end{Bmatrix}. \tag{A1}$$

Eigenvectors for $\lambda_2 = 7 - 4i$: are complex conjugate of the vectors in (A1).

(*Continued*)

Design Example 12.5 (Continued)

The matrix A is now diagonalized: $A = PDP^{-1}$ with

$$P = \left\{ \begin{array}{cc} \frac{1}{2}+i & \frac{1}{2}-i \\ 1 & 1 \end{array} \right\}, D = \left\{ \begin{array}{cc} 7+4i & 0 \\ 0 & 7-4i \end{array} \right\}.$$

Now we have

$$e^{tA} = Pe^{tD}P^{-1} = \begin{bmatrix} \frac{1}{2}+i & \frac{1}{2}-i \\ 1 & 1 \end{bmatrix} \begin{bmatrix} e^{(7+4i)t} & 0 \\ 0 & e^{(7-4i)t} \end{bmatrix} \begin{bmatrix} -\frac{1}{2}i & \frac{1}{2}+\frac{1}{4}i \\ \frac{1}{2}i & \frac{1}{2}-\frac{1}{4}i \end{bmatrix}$$

$$= \begin{bmatrix} \left(\frac{1}{2}-\frac{1}{4}i\right)e^{(7+4i)t} + \left(\frac{1}{2}+\frac{1}{4}i\right)e^{(7-4i)t} & \frac{5}{8}ie^{(7+4i)t} - \frac{5}{8}ie^{(7-4i)t} \\ -\frac{1}{2}ie^{(7+4i)t} + \frac{1}{2}ie^{(7-4i)t} & \left(\frac{1}{2}+\frac{1}{4}i\right)e^{(7+4i)t} + \left(\frac{1}{2}-\frac{1}{4}i\right)e^{(7-4i)t} \end{bmatrix}.$$

Solution 2: (Use fundamental solutions and complex exponential functions)

A fundamental matrix solution can be obtained from the eigenvalues and eigenvectors:

$$M(t) = \left\{ \begin{array}{cc} \left(\frac{1}{2}+i\right)e^{(7+4i)t} & \left(\frac{1}{2}-i\right)e^{(7-4i)t} \\ e^{(7+4i)t} & e^{(7-4i)t} \end{array} \right\}.$$

The matrix exponential is

$$e^{tA} = M(t)M(0)^{-1} = \begin{bmatrix} \left(\frac{1}{2}+i\right)e^{(7+4i)t} & \left(\frac{1}{2}+i\right)e^{(7-4i)t} \\ e^{(7+4i)t} & e^{(7-4i)t} \end{bmatrix} \begin{bmatrix} \frac{1}{2}+i & \frac{1}{2}-i \\ 1 & 1 \end{bmatrix}^{-1}$$

$$= \begin{bmatrix} \left(\frac{1}{2}-\frac{1}{4}i\right)e^{(7+4i)t} + \left(\frac{1}{2}+\frac{1}{4}i\right)e^{(7-4i)t} & \frac{5}{8}ie^{(7+4i)t} - \frac{5}{8}ie^{(7-4i)t} \\ -\frac{1}{2}ie^{(7+4i)t} + \frac{1}{2}ie^{(7-4i)t} & \left(\frac{1}{2}+\frac{1}{4}i\right)e^{(7+4i)t} + \left(\frac{1}{2}-\frac{1}{4}i\right)e^{(7-4i)t} \end{bmatrix}.$$

Solution 3: (Use Fundamental Solutions and Avoid Complex Exponential Functions)

A fundamental matrix solution can be obtained from the eigenvalues and eigenvectors:

$$M(t) = \left\{ \begin{array}{cc} e^{7t}\left(\frac{1}{2}\cos 4t - \sin 4t\right) & e^{7t}\left(\cos 4t + \frac{1}{2}\sin 4t\right) \\ e^{7t}\cos 4t & e^{7t}\sin 4t \end{array} \right\}$$

Design Example 12.5 (Continued)

The matrix exponential is

$$
e^{tA} = M(t)M(0)^{-1} = \left\{ \begin{matrix} e^{7t}\left(\dfrac{1}{2}\cos 4t - \sin 4t \right) & e^{7t}\left(\cos 4t + \dfrac{1}{2}\sin 4t \right) \\[2ex] e^{7t}\cos 4t & e^{7t}\sin 4t \end{matrix} \right\} \left\{ \begin{matrix} 1/2 & 1 \\ 1 & 0 \end{matrix} \right\}^{-1}
$$

$$
= \left\{ \begin{matrix} e^{7t}\cos 4t + \dfrac{1}{2}e^{7t}\sin 4t & -\dfrac{5}{4}e^{7t}\sin 4t \\[2ex] e^{7t}\sin 4t & e^{7t}\cos 4t - \dfrac{1}{2}e^{7t}\sin 4t \end{matrix} \right\}.
$$

References

1 S. Lloyd, M. Mohseni, and P. Rebentrost, Quantum algorithms for supervised and unsupervised machine learning, arXiv:1307.0411.

2 E. Farhi, and H. Neven, Classification with Quantum Neural Networks on Near Term Processors, arXiv:1802.06002v2.

3 Lu, S. and Braunstein, S.L. (2013). Quantum decision tree classifier. *Quantum Inf. Process.*: 757–770.

4 S. Lloyd, Quantum algorithm for solving linear systems of equations, APS March Meeting Abstracts, (2010).

5 Aaronson, S. (2015). Read the fine print. *Nat. Phys.* **11** (4): 291.

6 Childs, A.M., Kothari, R., and Somma, R.D. (2017). Quantum algorithm for systems of linear equations with exponentially improved dependence on precision. *SIAM J. Comput.* **46**: 1920.

7 Clader, B.D., Jacobs, B.C., and Sprouse, C.R. (2013). Preconditioned quantum linear system algorithm. *Phys. Rev. Lett.* **110**.25.250504.

8 D. Dervovic, M. Herbster, P. Mountney, et al. Quantum linear systems algorithms: a primer, (2018), arXiv preprint arXiv:1802.08227.

9 S. Dutta, et al. Demonstration of a Quantum Circuit Design Methodology for Multiple Regression, arXiv preprint arXiv:1811.01726, (2018).

10 Rebentrost, P., Mohseni, M., and Lloyd, S. (2014). Quantum support vector machine for big data classification. *Phys. Rev. Lett.* **113**: 130503.

11 Li, Z., Lui, X., Xu, N., and Du, J. (2015). Experimental realization of a quantum support vector machine. *Phys. Rev. Lett.* **114**: 140504.

12 I. Kerenidis, A. Prakash, and D. Szilágyi, Quantum algorithms for Second-Order Cone Programming and Support Vector Machines, arXiv:1908.06720, (2019).

13 A. K. Bishwas, A. Mani, and V. Palade, Big Data Quantum Support Vector Clustering, arXiv:1804.10905, (2018).

14 T. Arodz, S. Saeedi, Quantum Sparse Support Vector Machines, arXiv:1902.01879, (2019).

15 C. Ding, T. Bao, and H. Huang, Quantum-Inspired Support Vector Machine, arXiv:1906.08902, (2019).

16 Anguita, D., Ridella, S., Rivieccio, F., and Zunino, R. (2003). Quantum optimization for training support vector machines. *Neural Netw.* **16**: 763–770.

17 Chelliah, B.J., Shreyasi, S., Pandey, A., and Singh, K. (2019). Experimental comparison of quantum and classical support vector machines. *IJITEE* **8**: 208–211.

18 M. Schuld, A. Bacharov, K. Svore and N. Wiebe, Circuit-centric quantum classifiers, arXiv:1804.00633v1 [quant-ph] (2018).

19 Schuld, M., Sinayskiy, I., and Petruccione, F. (2015). An introduction to quantum machine learning. *Contemp. Phys.* **56**: 172–185.

20 Grant, E., Benedetti, M., Cao, S. et al. (2018). *npj Quantum Inf.* **4** (65).

21 Shi, Y.-Y., Duan, L.-M., and Vidal, G. (2006). Classical simulation of quantum many-body systems with a tree tensor network. *Phys. Rev. A* **74**: 022320.

22 Vidal, G. (2008). Class of quantum many-body states that can be efficiently simulated. *Phys. Rev. Lett.* **101**: 110501.

23 Cincio, L., Dziarmaga, J., and Rams, M.M. (2008). Multiscale entanglement renormalization ansatz in two dimensions: quantum ising model. *Phys. Rev. Lett.* **100**: 240603.

24 Evenbly, G. and Vidal, G. (2010). Entanglement renormalization in noninteracting fermionic systems. *Phys. Rev. B* **81**: 235102.

25 Turkpence, D. et al. (2019). A steady state quantum classifier. *Phys. Lett. A* **383**: 1410.

26 Breuer, H.P. and Petruccione, F. (2007). *The Theory of Open Quantum Systems*. Oxford: Oxford University Press.

27 https://www.qutisgroup.com/wpcontent/uploads/2014/10/TFG-Cristian-Romero.pdf. Cristian Romero Garcia.

28 Cai, X.D., Wu, D., Su, Z.-E. et al. (2015). Entanglement-based machine learning on a quantum computer. *Phys. Rev. Lett.* **114**: 110504.

29 Y. Liu, X. Zhang, M. Lewenstein, and S. J. Ran, Entanglement-guided architectures of machine learning by quantum tensor network, arXiv:1803.09111, (2018).

30 Levine, Y., Sharir, O., Cohen, N., and Shashua, A. (2019). Quantum entanglement in deep learning architectures. *Phys. Rev. Lett.* **122**: 065301.

31 Farley, B. and Clark, W. (1954). Simulation of self-organizing systems by digital computer. *Trans. IRE Profess. Gr. on Inf. Theor.* **4**: 76.

32 P. Smolensky, Chapter 6: information processing in dynamical systems: foundations of harmony theory. Parallel Distributed Processing: Explorations in the Microstructure of Cognition, 1.

33 Deng, D.L., Li, X., and Sarma, S.D. (2017). Quantum entanglement in neural network states. *Phy. Rev. X* **7**: 021021.

34 Susskind, L. and Lindesay, J. (2004). *An Introduction to Black Holes, Information and the String Theory Revolution: The Holographic Universe*. World Scientific 200.

35 Q. Zhuang, and Z. Zhang, Supervised Learning Enhanced by an Entangled Sensor Network, arXiv preprint arXiv:1901.09566, (2019).

36 Kak, S.C. (1995). Quantum neural computing. *Adv. Imag. Elect. Phys.* **94**: 259.

37 Menneer, T. and Narayanan, A. (1995). Quantum-inspired neural networks. *Tech. Rep.* **R329**.

38 Perus, M. (1996). Neuro-quantum parallelism in brain-mind and computers. *Informatica* **20**: 173.

39 T. Menneer, Quantum artificial neural networks, PhD thesis, University of Exeter, (1998).

40 J. Faber and G. A. Giraldi, Quantum Models for Artificial Neural Networks, LNCC–National Laboratory for Scientific Computing.

41 Schuld, M., Sinayskiy, I., and Petruccione, F. (2014). The quest for a quantum neural network. *Quantum Inf. Process.* **13**: 2567.

42 N. Wiebe, A. Kapoor, and K. M. Svore, Quantum deep learning, arXiv:1412.3489, (2014).

43 M. V. Altaisky, Quantum neural network, arxiv:quantph/0107012, (2000).

44 Gupta, S. and Zia, R.K.P. (2001). Quantum neural networks. *J. Comput. Sys. Sci.* **63**: 355.

45 Zidan, M., Abdel-Aty, A.-H., El-shafei, M. et al. (2019). Quantum classification algorithm based on competitive learning neural network and entanglement measure. *Appl. Sci.* **9**: 1277.

46 Sagheer, A., Zidan, M., and Abdelsamea, M.M. (2019). A novel autonomous perceptron model for pattern classification applications. *Entropy* **21**: 763.

47 Lloyd, S. and Weedbrook, C. (2018). Quantum generative adversarial learning. *Phys. Rev. Lett.* **121**: 040502.

48 Kak, S. (1995). On quantum neural computing. *Inform. Sci.* **83**: 143.

49 Zak, M. and Williams, C.P. (1998). Quantum neural nets. *Int. J. Theor. Phys.* **37**: 651.

50 Y. Cao, G. G. Guerreschi, and A. A. Guzik, Quantum Neuron: an elementary building block for machine learning on quantum computers, arXiv:1711.11240, (2017).

51 S. Hayou, A. Doucet, and J. Rousseau, On the Impact of the Activation Function on Deep Neural Networks Training, arXiv:1902.06853, (2019).

52 F. Agostinelli, M. Hoffman, P. Sadowski, and P. Baldi, Learning Activation Functions to Improve Deep Neural Networks, arXiv:1412.6830, (2015).

53 I. Daubechies, R. DeVore, S. Foucart, B. Hanin, and G. Petrova, Nonlinear Approximation and (Deep) ReLU Networks, arXiv:1905.02199, (2019).

54 Neukart, F. and Moraru, S.A. (2013). On quantum computers and artificial neural networks. *Sig. Process. Res.* **2**: 1.

55 Schuld, M., Sinayskiy, I., and Petruccione, F. (2015). Simulating a perceptron on a quantum computer. *Phys. Lett. A* **7**: 660.

56 Alvarez-Rodriguez, U., Lamata, L., Montero, P.E. et al. (2017). Supervised quantum learning without measurements. *Sci. Rep.* **7**: 13645.

57 Wan, K.H., Dahlsten, O., Kristjánsson, H. et al. (2017). Quantum generalisation of feedforward neural networks. *npj Quantum Inf.* **3** (36).

58 Rebentrost, P., Bromley, T.R., Weedbrook, C., and Lloyd, S. (2018). Quantum Hopfield neural network. *Phys. Rev. A* 24 **98**: 042308.

59 J. S Otterbach, et al., Unsupervised Machine Learning on a Hybrid Quantum Computer, arXiv:1712.05771, (2017).

60 Lamata, L. (2017). Basic protocols in quantum reinforcement learning with superconducting circuits. *Sci. Rep.* **7**: 1609.

61 Tacchino, F., Macchiavello, C., Gerace, D., and Bajoni, D. (2019). An artificial neuron implemented on an actual quantum processor. *npj Quantum Inf.* **5** (26).

62 Hubel, D.H. and Wiesel, T.N. (1968). Receptive fields and functional architecture of monkey striate cortex. *J. Physiol.* **195** (1): 215–243. https://doi.org/10.1113/jphysiol.1968.sp008455.

63 Fan, J., Xu, W., Wu, Y., and Gong, Y. (2010). Human tracking using convolutional neural networks. *IEEE Trans. Neural Netw.* **21**: 1610.

64 M. Jaderberg, A. Vedaldi, and A. Zisserman, Deep Features for Text Spotting, Eur. Conf. Comput. Vis. (2014).

65 A. Toshev and C. Szegedy, Deep-pose: Human pose estimation via deepneural networks, CVPR, (2014).

66 J. Donahue, Y. Jia, O. Vinyals, J. Hoffman, N. Zhang, E. Tzeng, and T. Darrell, Decaf: A deep convolutional activation feature for generic, (2014).

67 C. Farabet, C. Couprie, L. Najman, and Y. LeCun, Learning hierarchical features for scene labeling, PAMI, (2013).

68 R. Zhao, W. Ouyang, H. Li, and X. Wang, Saliency detection by multicontext deep learning, in CVPR, (2015).

69 N. Aloysius and M. Geetha, A Review on Deep Convolutional Neural Networks, International Conference on Communication and Signal Processing, India, (2017).

70 Carleo, G. and Troyer, M. (2017). Solving the quantum manybody problem with artificial neural networks. *Science* **355**: 602.

71 van Nieuwenburg, E.P.L., Liu, Y.H., and Huber, S.D. (2017). Learning phase transitions by confusion. *Nat. Phys.* **13**: 435–439.

72 Maskara, N., Kubica, A., and Jochym-O'Connor, T. (2019). Advantages of versatile neural-network decoding for topological codes. *Phys. Rev. A* **99**: 052351.

73 Zhang, Y. and Kim, E.-A. (2017). Quantum loop topography for machine learning. *Phys. Rev. Lett.* **118**: 216401.

74 Carrasquilla, J. and Melko, R.G. (2017). Machine learning phases of matter. *Nat. Phys.* **13**: 431–434.

75 Wang, L. (2016). Discovering phase transitions with supervised learning. *Phys. Rev. B* **94**: 195105.

76 Biamonte, J., Wittek, P., Pancotti, N. et al. (2017). Quantum machine learning. *Nature* **549**: 195–202.

77 Dunjko, V., Taylor, J.M., and Briegel, H.J. (2016). Quantum enhanced machine learning. *Phys. Rev. Lett.* **117**: 130501.

78 E. Farhi, and H. Neven, Classification with quantum neural networks on near term processors, arXiv preprint arXiv: 1802.06002, (2018).

79 Huggins, W., Patil, P., Mitchell, B. et al. (2018). Towards quantum machine learning with tensor networks. *Quantum Sci. Tech.* **4**: 024001.

80 Cong, I., Choi, S., and Lukin, M.D. (2019). Quantum convolutional neural networks. *Nat. Phys.*

81 Jia, Z.-A., Yi, B., Zhai, R. et al. (2019). Quantum neural network states: a brief review of methods and applications. *Adv. Quantum Technol.*: 1800077.

82 Monterola, C. and Saloma, C. (2001). Solving the nonlinear schrodinger equation with an unsupervised neural network. *Opts. Exp.* **9**: 72.

83 Caetano, C., Reis, J. Jr., Amorim, J. et al. (2011). Using neural networks to solve nonlinear differential equations in atomic and molecular physics. *Int. J. Quantum Chem.* **111**: 2732.

84 Gao, X. and Duan, L.-M. (2017). Efficient representation of quantum many-body states with deep neural networks. *Nat. Commun.* **8**: 662.

85 A. P. Dash, S. Sahu, S. Kar, B. K. Behera, P. K. Panigrahi, Explicit demonstration of initial state construction in artificial neural networks usingNetKet and IBM Q experience platform, ResearchGate- DOI: 10.13140/RG.2.2.30229.17129 (2019).

86 Gardas, B., Rams, M.M., and Dziarmaga, J. (2018). Quantum neural networks to simulate many-body quantum systems. *Phys. Rev. B* **98**: 184304.

87 Mohseni, M. et al. (2017). Commercialize quantum technologies in five years. *Nature* **543** (7644): 171.

88 Edward Farhi, Jeffrey Goldstone, and Sam Gutmann. A quantum approximate optimization algorithm. arXiv preprint arXiv:1411.4028, 2014.

89 Harrow, A.W. and Montanaro, A. (2017). Quantum computational supremacy. *Nature* **549** (7671): 203.

90 Alejandro Perdomo-Ortiz, Marcello Benedetti, John Realpe-Gómez, and Rupak Biswas. Opportunities and challenges for quantum-assisted machine learning in near-term quantum computers. arXiv preprint arXiv:1708.09757, 2017.

91 Schuld, M., Sinayskiy, I., and Petruccione, F. (2015). Introduction to quantum machine learning. *Contemp. Phys.* **56** (2): 172–185.

92 Iordanis Kerenedis and Anupam Prakash. Quantum recommendation systems. arXiv preprint arXiv:1603.08675, 2016.

93 Wiebe, N., Braun, D., and Lloyd, S. (2012). Quantum algorithm for data fitting. *Phys. Rev. Lett.* **109** (5): 050505.

94 Schuld, M., Fingerhuth, M., and Petruccione, F. (2017). Implementing a distance-based classifier with a quantum interference circuit. *EPL (Europhysics Letters)* **119** (6): 60002.

95 McClean, J.R., Romero, J., Babbush, R., and Aspuru-Guzik, A. (2016). The theory of variational hybrid quantum-classical algorithms. *New J. Phys.* **18** (2): 023023.

96 Romero, J., Olson, J.P., and AspuruGuzik, A. (2017). Quantum autoencoders for efficient compression of quantum data. *Quantum Science and Technology* **2** (4): 045001.

97 Mitarai, K., Negoro, M., Kitagawa, M., and Fujii, K. (2018). Quantum circuit learning. *Phys. Rev. A* **98**: 032309. arXiv preprint arXiv:1803.00745.

98 G. Verdon, M. Broughton, and J. Biamonte. A quantum algorithm to train neural networks using low-depth circuits. arXiv preprint arXiv:1712.05304, 2017.

99 J.-L. Brylinski and R. Brylinski. Universal quantum gates, pp. 101–116, 2002.

100 Barenco, A., Bennett, C.H., Cleve, R. et al. (1995). Elementary gates for quantum computation. *Phys. Rev. A* **52** (5): 3457. arXiv: quant-ph/9503016 [quant-ph].

101 According to the laws of quantum mechanics we have to sum over the absolute square values of the amplitudes that correspond to basis states where the first qubit is in state 1. Using the standard computational basis, this is exactly the 'second half' of the amplitude vector, ranging from entry $2^{n-1} + 1$ to 2n.

102 Arjovsky, M., Shah, A., and Bengio, Y. (2016). Unitary evolution recurrent neural networks. *J. Mach. Learn. Res.* **48**.

103 Yoav Levine, David Yakira, Nadav Cohen, and Amnon Shashua. Deep learning and quantum entanglement: Fundamental connections with implications to network design. arXiv preprint arXiv:1704.01552, 2017.

104 Gian Giacomo Guerreschi and Mikhail Smelyanskiy. Practical optimization for hybrid quantum-classical algorithms. arXiv preprint arXiv:1701.01450, 2017.

105 Sushant Patrikar, Batch, Mini Batch & Stochastic Gradient Descent https://towardsdatascience.com/batch-mini-batch-stochastic-gradient-descent-7a62ecba642a, also see http://d2l.ai/chapter_optimization/minibatch-sgd.html.

106 Léon Bottou. Large-scale machine learning with stochastic gradient descent. In Proceedings of COMPSTAT'2010, pp. 177–186. Springer, 2010.

107 Childs, A.M. and Wiebe, N. (2012). Hamiltonian simulation using linear combinations of unitary operations. *Quantum Inf. Comput.* **12**: 901–924.

108 Li, J., Yang, X., Peng, X., and Sun, C.-P. (2017). *Phys. Rev. Lett.* **118**: 150503.

109 Schuld, M., Bergholm, V., Gogolin, C. et al. (2019). Evaluating analytic gradients on quantum hardware. *Phys. Rev. A* **99**: 032331. arXiv:1811.11184.

110 V. Bergholm, J. Izaac, M. Schuld, C. Gogolin, and N. Killoran (2018), arXiv:1811.04968.

111 J. G. Vidal and D. O. Theis (2018) Calculus on parameterized quantum circuits. arXiv:1812.06323.

112 Nicholas J. Higham and Awad H. Al-Mohy, Computing Matrix Functions, Manchester Institute for Mathematical Sciences 2010,The University of Manchester, ISSN 1749–9097. pp. 1–47.

113 Moler, C.B. and Van Loan, C.F. (2003). Nineteen dubious ways to compute the exponential of a matrix, twenty-five years later. *SIAM Rev.* **45** (1): 349.

114 Syed Muhammad Ghufran, The Computation of Matrix Functions in Particular, The Matrix Exponential, Master Thesis, University of Birmingham, England, 2009, 169 pp.

115 Nathelie Smalls, The exponential of matrices, Master Thesis, University of Georgia, Georgia, 2007, 49 pp

116 Jordan, S.P. (2005). Fast quantum algorithm for numerical gradient estimation. *Phys. Rev. Lett.* **95**: 050501.

117 Zhang, J., Vala, J., Sastry, S., and Whaley, K.B. (2003). A geometric theory of non-local two-qubit operations. *Phys. Rev. A* **67**: 042313. arXiv:quant-ph/0209120.

118 Zhang, J., Vala, J., Sastry, S., and Whaley, K.B. (2004). Optimal quantum circuit synthesis from Controlled-U gates. *Phys. Rev. A* **69**: 042309. arXiv:quant-ph/0308167.

119 Blaauboer, M. and de Visser, R.L. (2008). An analytical decomposition protocol for optimal implementation of two-qubit entangling gates. *J. Phys. A: Math. Theor* **41**: 395307, arXiv:cond-mat/0609750.

120 Drury, B. and Love, P. (2008). Constructive quantum Shannon decomposition from Cartan involutions. *J. Phys. A: Math. Theor* **41**: 395305, arXiv:0806.4015.

121 Watts, P., O'Connor, M., and Vala, J. (2013). Metric structure of the space of two-qubit gates, perfect entanglers and quantum control. *Entropy* **15**: 1963.

122 E. C. Peterson, G. E. Crooks, and R. S. Smith (2019), Fixed-depth two-qubit circuits and the monodromy polytope arXiv:1904.10541.

123 Nielsen, M.A. and Chuang, I.L. (2000). *Quantum Computation and Quantum Information*. Cambridge University Press.

124 R. S. Smith, M. J. Curtis, and W. J. Zeng (2016), A practical quantum instruction set architecture arXiv:1608.03355.

125 Rigetti, C. and Devoret, M. (2010). Fully microwave-tunable universal gates in superconducting qubits with linear couplings and fixed transition frequencies. *Phys. Rev. B* **81**: 134507.

126 Chow, J.M., Córcoles, A.D., Gambetta, J.M. et al. (2011). A simple all-microwave entangling gate for fixed-frequency superconducting qubits. *Phys. Rev. Lett.* **107**: 080502.

127 P. Krantz, M. Kjaergaard, F. Yan, T. P. Orlando, S. Gustavsson, and W. D. Oliver (2019), A quantum engineer's guide to superconducting qubits arXiv:1904.06560.

128 G. E. Crooks, QuantumFlow: A Quantum Algorithms Development Toolkit v0.9, https://quantumflow. readthedocs.io/. See the decompositions subpackage for a python implementation of canonical gate decomposition; and the gradients subpackage for implementations of parameter-shift and middle-out gradients of parameterized quantum circuits.

129 Makhlin, Y. (2002). Nonlocal properties of two-qubit gates and mixed states, and the optimization of quantum computations. *Quant. Info. Processing* **1**: 243.

130 Khaneja, N., Reiss, T., Kehlet, C. et al. (2005). Optimal control of coupled spin dynamics: design of NMR pulse sequences by gradient ascent algorithms. *J. Magn. Reson.* **172**: 296.

131 M. Arjovsky, A. Shah, and Y. Bengio. "Unitary Evolution Recurrent Neural Networks". ArXiv e-prints (Nov. 2015). arXiv: 1511.06464 [cs.LG].

132 V. Dunjko et al. "Super-polynomial and exponential improvements for quantumenhanced reinforcement learning". ArXiv e-prints (Oct. 2017). arXiv: 1710.11160 [quant-ph].

133 C. Trabelsi et al. "Deep Complex Networks". ArXiv e-prints (May 2017). arXiv: 1705.09792.

134 S. L. Hyland and G. Rätsch. "Learning Unitary Operators with Help From u(n)". ArXiv e-prints (July 2016). arXiv: 1607.04903 [stat.ML].

135 Yoo, S. et al. (Oct. 2014). A quantum speedup in machine learning: finding an N-bit Boolean function for a classification. *New J. Phys.* **16** (10): 103014. https://doi.org/10.1088/1367-2630/16/10/103014. arXiv: 1303.6055 [quant-ph].

136 Cybenko, G. (1989). Approximations by superpositions of sigmoidal functions mathematics of control signals and systems. *Math. Control Signals Syst.* **2**: 304–314.

137 Hornik, K. (1991). Approximation capabilities of multilayer feedforward networks. *Neural Netw.* **4** (2): 251–257. issn: 0893-6080. url: http://www.sciencedirect.com/science/article/pii/089360809190009T.

138 J. Romero et al. "Strategies for quantum computing molecular energies using the unitary coupled cluster ansatz". ArXiv e-prints (Jan. 2017). arXiv: 1701 . 02691 [quant-ph].

139 Sasaki, M. and Carlini, A. (2002). Quantum learning and universal quantum matching machine. *Phys. Rev. A* **66**: 022303.

140 Songfeng Lu et al, Quantum decision tree classifier, https://www.researchgate.net/publication/260526004_Quantum_decision_tree_classifier13,154].

141 Vatan, F. and Williams, C. (2004). Optimal quantum circuits for general two-qubit gates. *Phys. Rev. A* **69**: 032315, arXiv:quant-ph/0308006.

142 Leung, N., Abdelhafez, M., Koch, J., and Schuster, D. (2017). Speedup for quantum optimal control from automatic differentiation based on graphics processing units. *Phys. Rev. A* **95**: 042318.

13

QC Optimization

13.1 Hybrid Quantum-Classical Optimization Algorithms

Here, as the first step, we discuss a class of hybrid quantum-classical algorithms based on the variational approach. These algorithms provide an approximate solution to the problem at hand by encoding it in the state of a quantum computer. The operations used to prepare the state are not a priori fixed but, on the contrary, are subjected to a classical optimization procedure that modifies the quantum gates and improves the quality of the approximate solution. Whereas the quantum hardware determines the size of the problem and what states are achievable (limited, respectively, by the number of qubits and by the kind and number of possible quantum gates), it is the classical optimization procedure that determines the way in which the quantum states are explored and whether the best available solution is actually reached. In addition, the quantities required in the optimization, for example the objective function itself, have to be estimated with finite precision in any experimental implementation. Although it is desirable to have very precise estimates, this comes at the cost of repeating the state preparation and measurement multiple times. Here, we analyze the competing requirements of high precision and low number of repetitions, and study how the overall performance of the variational algorithm is affected by the precision level and the choice of the optimization method. Finally, we discuss the quasi-Newton optimization methods in the general context of hybrid variational algorithms and present quantitative results for the quantum approximate optimization algorithm (QAOA) along the lines presented in [1].

The class of hybrid quantum-classical algorithms that is the subject of this work is characterized by three distinct steps. The first one corresponds to the state preparation and is achieved by applying a sequence of gates, described by the corresponding set of parameter values, on an initial reference state. The second step is the measurement operation, in which one measures the quantum state, records the outcomes, and analyzes them to obtain the value of the objective function corresponding to the prepared state. The third step is the classical optimization iteration that, based on previous results, suggests new parameter values to improve the quality of the state. We pictorially illustrate these three parts and their interplay in Figure 13.1 (These steps have to be repeated until convergence or when a sufficiently good quality of the solution is reached: (i) state preparation involving quantum hardware capable of tunable gates characterized by parameters γ_n (blue), (ii) measurement of the quantum state and evaluation of the objective function, and (iii) iteration of the optimization method to determine promising changes in the state preparation. Notice that a single parameter, γ_n, may characterize more than one gate; for example, see γ_1 and γ_6 in the blue box. In practice, many state preparations and measurements are necessary before proceeding with a single update of the parameters.)

Artificial Intelligence and Quantum Computing for Advanced Wireless Networks, First Edition.
Savo G. Glisic and Beatriz Lorenzo.
© 2022 John Wiley & Sons Ltd. Published 2022 by John Wiley & Sons Ltd.

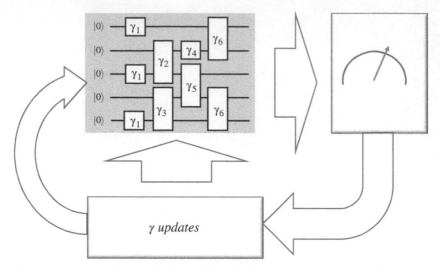

Figure 13.1 Illustration of the three common steps of hybrid quantum-classical algorithms (QAOA). *Source:* Modified from Guerreschi et al. [1].

As mentioned, the goal of variational algorithms is to find an approximate solution to certain problems. The quality of such an approximation is given by the value of the objective function that one desires to maximize (or minimize). The objective function is expressed as a quantum observable, noted here with $\hat{C}$, of the qubit register. It can be a genuinely quantum quantity, as is the case for the energy of molecular systems, or classical in nature, for example when it is associated with combinatorial optimization, scheduling problems, or financial modeling. Given the quantum register in state $|\varphi\rangle$, the objective function is given by the expectation value $\langle\varphi|\hat{C}|\varphi\rangle$.

The choice of the state ansatz specifies how state $|\varphi\rangle$ is prepared. In general, one applies a sequence of p gates $\hat{W}_1^p(\gamma) = \hat{W}_1^p\left(\gamma_1, \gamma_2, ..., \gamma_p\right)$:

$$\hat{W}_1^p(\gamma) = \hat{U}_p\left(\gamma_p\right)...\hat{U}_2(\gamma_2)\hat{U}_1(\gamma_1), \tag{13.1}$$

to a reference state $|\varphi_0\rangle$. Each gate is characterized by a parameter γ_n, and gates $\hat{U}_n(\gamma_n)$ and $\hat{U}_m(\gamma_m)$ do not have to commute for $n \neq m$. The final state is

$$|\gamma\rangle = |\gamma_1...\gamma_p\rangle = \hat{W}_1^p(\gamma)|\varphi_0\rangle. \tag{13.2}$$

For practical applications, it is helpful to express $\hat{C}$ as a linear combination of Hermitian operators that can be easily measured in experiments. In fact, it is always possible to express $\hat{C} = \sum_{v=1}^{k_C} c_v \hat{\sigma}_v^{(C)}$ as the weighted sum of products of a few Pauli matrices and impose the coefficients c_v to be real and positive (possibly including a minus sign in $\hat{\sigma}_v^{(C)}$). More general choices of $\hat{\sigma}_v^{(C)}$ are possible (i.e., not only products of Pauli operators), since the constraints come from experimental limitations. Finally, notice that, for most problems of interest, the number k_C of terms is polynomial in the number of qubits N, typically a quadratic, cubic, or quartic function. If the problem is classical, the observable $\hat{C}$ is diagonal in the computational basis and $\hat{\sigma}_v^{(C)}$ pairwise commute (even better, in this case $\hat{C}$ can be measured directly). In the general case, the explicit form of the objective function is

$$F_p(\gamma) = \langle \gamma | \hat{C} | \gamma \rangle = \sum_{v=1}^{k_C} c_v \langle \gamma | \hat{\sigma}_v^{(C)} | \gamma \rangle. \tag{13.3}$$

Observe that a single measurement of $|\gamma\rangle$ cannot directly provide the value $F_p(\gamma)$. Instead, it is computed by repeating the state preparation and measurement steps, and accumulating enough outcome statistics to estimate the expectation value of $\hat{C}$. We note with $F_{p,\varepsilon}(\gamma)$ the estimator within precision ε, meaning that it belongs to a stochastic distribution centered in $F_p(\gamma)$ and with standard deviation ε.

Considering each experimental repetition as independent, one can compute the number of repetitions M to achieve such a level of precision:

$$M \geq \frac{\text{Var}[\hat{C}]}{\varepsilon^2} = \frac{\sum_{v=1}^{k_C} c_v^2 \,\text{Var}\!\left[\hat{\sigma}_v^{(C)}\right]}{\varepsilon^2}, \tag{13.4}$$

where all variances of observables are with respect to the state $|\gamma\rangle$. Although the objective function and its finite-precision estimator $F_{p,\varepsilon}(\gamma)$ are the main quantities of interest, the optimization algorithms can be improved by providing additional information. In the next sections, we will explain how knowledge of the gradient can be exploited to find the values $(\gamma_1, ..., \gamma_p)$ that optimize $F_p(\gamma)$ and how to compute its repetition cost.

Finite difference derivatives: Several finite difference schemes can approximate the value of derivatives, depending on the required accuracy and the number of function evaluations needed. For quadratic accuracy in the finite increment (FN) δ, the formula for the central finite difference derivative is

$$\frac{\partial F_p(\gamma)}{\partial \gamma_n} = \frac{F_p\!\left(\gamma_1, ..., \gamma_n + \delta/2, ..., \gamma_p\right) - F_p\!\left(\gamma_1, ..., \gamma_n - \delta/2, ..., \gamma_p\right)}{\delta} + \mathcal{O}(\delta^2). \tag{13.5}$$

Substituting the estimators in the expression at the numerator, one has

$$\frac{F_{p,\varepsilon'}(\gamma_1, ..., \gamma_n + \delta/2, ...) - F_{p,\varepsilon'}(\gamma_1, ..., \gamma_n - \delta/2, ...)}{\delta} + \mathcal{O}(\delta^2) + \mathcal{O}\!\left(\frac{\varepsilon'}{\delta}\right), \tag{13.6}$$

where $\mathcal{O}(\delta^2)$ is related to the accuracy of the estimate, whereas $\mathcal{O}(\frac{\varepsilon'}{\delta})$ is related to its precision. Note that we used a precision ε' for the function estimates in the numerator, and it can differ from Eq. (13.8), the one considered in the following. Why is this flexibility necessary? First of all, it is questionable to require higher precision than accuracy, and this suggests the condition $\varepsilon' \geq \delta^3$. Second, ε' should be small enough to separate the values of the estimators at numerator by more than their common precision: $\sqrt{2}\varepsilon' \leq \delta \frac{\partial F_{p,\varepsilon'}(\gamma)}{\partial \gamma_n}$, where $\sqrt{2}$ comes from having summed the standard deviations in quadrature.

The first condition confirms that high precision is not necessary when δ is (relatively) large, but the second condition may cause problems near local maxima of the objective function. In those regions, each gradient component tends to zero, and this imposes such a high precision, meaning very small ε', that it can be achieved only with a large repetition cost, here quantified by

$$M \geq \frac{\text{Var}[\hat{C}]_{\gamma_n + \delta/2} + \text{Var}[\hat{C}]_{\gamma_n - \delta/2}}{2(\varepsilon')^2} \approx \frac{\text{Var}[\hat{C}]_{\gamma_n}}{(\varepsilon)^2}, \tag{13.7}$$

where the subscript attached to the variance clarifies the value of parameter γ_n for the corresponding state, and the approximated equivalence holds for small δ.

It was verified through numerical simulations [1] that imposing $\varepsilon' \leq \frac{\delta}{\sqrt{2}} \frac{\partial F_{p,\varepsilon'}(\gamma)}{\partial \gamma_n}$ increases the total repetition cost by several orders of magnitude. The advantage of using gradient-based optimization methods is nullified by this cost. To avoid such a situation, a lower bound to ε' was introduced that is directly related to the precision of function estimates: $\varepsilon' \geq \frac{1}{10}\varepsilon$. The constant $\frac{1}{10}$ is arbitrary, but has an intuitive meaning: To compute a single gradient component, at most a factor 10^2 more repetitions are required than those for a single function evaluation. In the numerical analysis in [1], ε' was determined according to the formula:

$$\varepsilon' = \max\left\{\delta^3, \frac{1}{10}\varepsilon, \min\left\{\varepsilon, \frac{\delta}{\sqrt{2}} \frac{\partial F_p(\gamma)}{\partial \gamma_n}\right\}\right\}. \tag{13.8}$$

The finite precision and accuracy of the gradient estimation affect the optimization process: [1] takes them into account in the numerical studies, together with the finite precision for the objective function.

Analytical gradient: It is possible to eliminate the bias in the gradient estimation by substituting the approximated formula in Eq. (13.6) with its analytical expression. Here, we derive the analytical form of the gradient components before discussing its repetition cost. For ease of notation, consider the operator

$$\hat{W}_n^k(\gamma) = U_k(\gamma_k)...U_{n+1}(\gamma_{n+1})U_n(\gamma_n) \tag{13.9}$$

that summarizes the state preparation circuit including only the steps $\{n, n+1, ..., k-1, k\}$, with $1 \leq n \leq k \leq p$. The operator $\hat{W}_1^p$ corresponds to the complete state preparation. Furthermore, it is helpful to write each gate $\hat{U}_n$ in term of its Hermitian generator $\hat{G}_n$:

$$\hat{U}_n(\gamma_n) = e^{-i\gamma_n \hat{G}_n}. \tag{13.10}$$

$\hat{G}_n$ is a Hermitian matrix that, similarly to $\hat{C}$, can be expressed as a linear combination of unitaries as $\hat{G}_n = \sum_\mu^{k_G} g_\mu \hat{\sigma}_\mu^{(G)}$. Observe that both k_G and $\hat{\sigma}_\mu^{(G)}$ should depend on the index n, but we omit it from the notation for readability. Again, g_μ can be taken to be real and positive, and the number of terms k_G can be realistically polynomial in the number N of qubits. Note, for example, that k_G is $\mathcal{O}(1)$ when $\hat{U}_n(\gamma_n)$ corresponds to a one- or two-qubit gate. The gradient components can be written as

$$\frac{\partial F_p(\gamma, \beta)}{\partial \gamma_n} = i\langle \phi_0 | \hat{W}_1^{n-1\dagger} \hat{G}_n \hat{W}_n^{p\dagger} \hat{C} | \gamma \rangle + \text{h.c.}$$

$$= -2 \sum_{\mu=1}^{k_G} \sum_{\nu=1}^{k_C} g_\mu c_\nu \Im\left[\langle \gamma | \hat{W}_n^p \hat{\sigma}_\mu^{(G)} \hat{W}_n^{p\dagger} \hat{\sigma}_\nu^{(C)} | \gamma \rangle\right], \tag{13.11}$$

where "h.c." refers to the Hermitian conjugate, and $\Im[*]$ denotes the imaginary part. Whereas the first line of the right-hand side is directly computable with a quantum emulator (i.e., in a classical simulation of the quantum system including operations not available in the quantum experiments), expressions like $\hat{W}_1^{n-1}\dagger \hat{G}_n \hat{W}_n^p \dagger \hat{C}$ are neither unitary operators nor Hermitian observables. Still, it is possible to evaluate such quantities with quantum circuits based on the second line of Eq. (13.11). There is no unique way to construct the estimator for the left-hand side of Eq. (13.11). It depends not only on the chosen decomposition of $\hat{C}$ and $\hat{G}_n$, but also on the exact way the terms are measured in

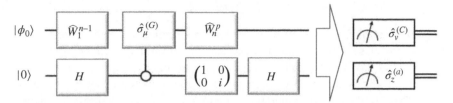

Figure 13.2 Quantum circuit to evaluate the n-th component of the gradient in hybrid quantum-classical algorithms, term by term. A single ancilla qubit, labeled *(a)* and included at the bottom, is required in addition to the N-qubit register. The expectation value of the observable $\hat{\sigma}_v^{(C)} \otimes \hat{\sigma}_z^{(a)}$ with respect to the state $|\psi_\mu\rangle$ at the end of the circuit corresponds to $-\Im\left[\left\langle \gamma | \hat{W}_n^p \hat{\sigma}_\mu^{(G)} \hat{W}_n^{p\dagger} \hat{\sigma}_v^{(C)} | \gamma \right\rangle\right]$. *Source:* Modified from Guerreschi et al. [1].

experiments. Different estimators for the same quantity exhibit different statistical variances, and the repetition cost varies accordingly (in the context of the Variational Quantum Eigensolver (VQE), see, for example, [2]). In the rest of this subsection, we consider fairly general decompositions, but also describe in detail the quantum circuit used to measure each term.

In addition to the quantum register with N qubits, we require a single ancilla qubit. Consider the circuit illustrated in Figure 13.2; it generates the final state $|\psi_\mu\rangle$ such that the expectation value of the observable $\hat{\sigma}_v^{(C)} \otimes \hat{\sigma}_z^{(a)}$ corresponds to $-\Im\left[\left\langle \gamma | \hat{W}_n^p \hat{\sigma}_\mu^{(G)} \hat{W}_n^{p\dagger} \hat{\sigma}_v^{(C)} | \gamma \right\rangle\right]$. The gradient components can be computed by summing up the expectation values of the different contributions for $\mu \in \{1, 2, ..., k_G\}$ and $v \in \{1, 2, ..., k_C\}$, with the appropriate weight c_v, g_μ [1].

At this point, it is important to make a few observations:

1) If $\hat{C}$ can be directly measured, one can avoid the summation over v and directly measure $\hat{C}$.
2) When $\hat{G}_n$ corresponds to an unitary operator, one can avoid the summation over μ by directly applying gate $\hat{G}_n$.
3) The roles of $\hat{\sigma}_\mu^{(G)}$ and $\hat{\sigma}_v^{(C)}$ are effectively interchangeable, and the proposed quantum circuit can be straightforwardly adapted to the case in which one applies $\hat{\sigma}_v^{(C)}$ to the quantum register and measures $\hat{\sigma}_\mu^{(G)}$. Analogously, the corresponding summation can be avoided if $\hat{C}$ corresponds to a unitary operator or $\hat{G}_n$ to a directly measurable observable.

In several hybrid variational algorithms, one or more of the conditions above are indeed satisfied: In the VQE (discussed in the introduction), the generators $\hat{G}_n$ are typically products of Pauli matrices and all commuting $\hat{\sigma}_v^{(C)}$ can be measured at the same point, whereas for the QAOA (analyzed in the following), $\hat{C}$ is obtained by measuring the qubit register in the computational basis. For specific variational algorithms, this fact greatly simplifies the following expression for the repetition cost and helps to considerably reduce the cost itself.

The repetition cost to estimate of the n-th component of the analytical gradient (AG) to a precision ε'' is

$$M \geq \frac{4}{(\varepsilon'')^2}\left\{\sum_{\mu=1}^{k_G}\sum_{v=1}^{k_C} g_\mu^2 c_v^2 \, \mathrm{Var}\left[\hat{\sigma}_v^{(C)}\right]\mu\right\}, \tag{13.12}$$

where the variance refers to the observable $\hat{\sigma}_v^{(C)}$ measured on the state $|\psi_\mu\rangle$ produced as the output of the quantum circuit in Figure 13.2.

13.1.1 QAOA

It is difficult to draw conclusions from the above discussion on optimization methods and their repetition cost for the general class of hybrid quantum-classical algorithms based on the variational approach. To analyze the interplay between precision, cost, and performance, one needs to focus on specific algorithms. Here, we study the QAOA, which was recently proposed to solve constraint satisfaction problems. These problems are important in many areas of science and technology, but, in their abstract form, involve functions of binary variables: simply posed, each instance of a constraint satisfaction problem comprises a number of clauses that have to be satisfied, and the central question is to determine the maximum number of clauses that can be simultaneously satisfied. An approximated solution is represented by the variable assignment that satisfies a number of clauses corresponding to a high fraction of the best case.

Following an established procedure to solve constraint satisfaction problems with quantum computers, one converts the classical objective function $C(z_1, ..., z_n)$, that is, the sum of all the clauses (each clause involves a subset of the N binary variables $z_i \in \{-1, 1\}$ for $i = 1, 2, ..., N$, and is equal to 1 if satisfied or null otherwise), into its quantum version. In practice, one substitutes the binary variable z_i with the Z Pauli operator of the i-th qubit $\hat{\sigma}_z^{(i)}$ (more formally, we include in $\hat{\sigma}_z^{(i)}$ the tensor product of identity operators acting on all other qubits):

$$\hat{C}\left(\hat{\sigma}_z^{(1)}, ..., \hat{\sigma}_z^{(n)}\right) = \sum_\alpha \hat{C}_\alpha\left(\hat{\sigma}_z^{(1)}, ..., \hat{\sigma}_z^{(n)}\right), \tag{13.13}$$

where the sum over α extends to all the clauses. The QAOA specifies how trial states are prepared: one initializes the qubit register in the state $|s\rangle = |+ + ... +\rangle$, corresponding to the balanced superposition of all the 2^N bit strings, and then repeatedly applies two quantum operations:

$$\hat{U}(\gamma) = \exp\left(-i\gamma\hat{C}\right)$$
$$\hat{V}(\beta) = ep\left(-i\beta\hat{B}\right), \tag{13.14}$$

with $\hat{B} = \sum_{i=1}^N \hat{\sigma}_x^{(i)}$. Every time an operation is applied, the parameters $\gamma \in [0, 2\pi[$ and $\beta \in [0, \pi[$ can take different values, so that the complete description of a p-depth circuit for state preparation is provided by the $2p$-dimensional array $(\gamma_1, \beta_1, ..., \gamma_p, \beta_p) = (\gamma, \beta)$. Observe that the notation differs slightly from that used in the previous sections and, in particular, the parameters are now labeled (γ, β) instead of γ alone and have the form $2p$. The specific QAOA reference state is $|\varphi_0\rangle = |s\rangle$.

To verify what is the average number of clauses satisfied by the N-qubit quantum state $|\gamma, \beta\rangle$, one needs to compute the expectation value of the observable $\hat{C}$ as defined in Eq. (13.13). In practice, this is achieved by measuring the qubit register in the computational basis, computing the corresponding value of the objective function C, and then averaging over several repetitions of the measurement. The final goal is to find the maximum value of $F_p(\gamma, \beta)$ as defined by

$$F_p(\gamma, \beta) = \langle \gamma, \beta | \hat{C} | \gamma, \beta \rangle, \tag{13.15}$$

over all the accessible states

$$|\gamma, \beta\rangle = \hat{V}\left(\beta_p\right)\hat{U}\left(\gamma_p\right)...\hat{V}(\beta_1)\hat{U}(\gamma_1)|s\rangle. \tag{13.16}$$

The advantage of QAOA over other hybrid algorithms is twofold: first, QAOA clearly defines the form of the quantum gates for state preparation and describes them with relatively few parameters [3–5]. Second, it has been proved that the exact solution is reachable for state preparation circuits that are deep enough (i.e., the limit $p \to \infty$ of $\max_{(\gamma, \beta)} F_p(\gamma, \beta)$ corresponds to the exact global solution [3]), in this way certifying the good choice of the state "ansatz." It is an open question to address the QAOA performance for small p, but there are arguments for moderate optimism [3, 4] (see also the design example in the following). Finally, since for QAOA all terms in $\hat{C}$ involve only Z Pauli operators, one can simply measure every qubit in the computational basis and compute

$$F_p(\gamma,\beta) = \sum_{z\in\{-1,1\}^N} p_z C(z) \tag{13.17}$$

where the probability $p_z = |\langle z|\gamma,\beta\rangle|^2$ is estimated through the relative frequency with which the N-bit string z appears among the measurement outcomes. In practice, $\hat{C}$ is directly observable in most, if not all, experimental setups.

The formulas for computing the repetition cost to estimate the objective function, the finite difference gradient, and the AG are direct specialization of the expressions in Eqs. (13.4), (13.8) and (13.12), respectively. Furthermore, the analytic form of the gradient components of type-γ is

$$\begin{aligned}\frac{\partial F_p(\gamma,\beta)}{\partial\gamma_n} &= i\langle s|\hat{W}_1^{n-1\dagger}\hat{C}\hat{W}_n^{p\dagger}\hat{C}|\gamma,\beta\rangle + \text{h.c.}\\ &= -2\sum_{\mu=1}^{K_C} c_\mu\Im\left[\langle\gamma,\beta|\hat{W}_n^p\hat{\sigma}_x^{(C)}\hat{W}_n^{p\dagger}\hat{C}|\gamma,\beta\rangle\right]\end{aligned} \tag{13.18}$$

where we have used the fact that $\hat{C}$ can be directly measured and that the generator $\hat{G}_n$ in this case corresponds to $\hat{C}$, whereas for the components of type-β it is

$$\begin{aligned}\frac{\partial F_p(\gamma,\beta)}{\partial\beta_n} &= i\langle s|\hat{W}_1^{n\dagger}\hat{B}\hat{W}_{n+1}^{p\dagger}\hat{C}|\gamma,\beta\rangle + \text{h.c.}\\ &= -2\sum_{i=1}^N \Im\left[\langle\gamma,\beta|\hat{W}_n^p\hat{\sigma}_x^{(i)}\hat{W}_n^{p\dagger}\hat{C}|\gamma,\beta\rangle\right]\end{aligned} \tag{13.19}$$

where we have used the explicit decomposition $\hat{B} = \sum_{i=1}^N \hat{\sigma}_x^{(i)}$.

Design Example 13.1

In [1], QAOA was applied to the Max-Cut problem on random 3-regular graphs. Each instance is defined by an undirected graph, and one is asked to color each of the N nodes with one of two colors (consider here the color labels $\{-1, 1\}$). Max-Cut refers to finding the coloring pattern such that the lowest possible number of vertices connect nodes with the same color. According to the notation in terms of binary variables, the vertex between node i and j corresponds to the clause $(1 - z_iz_j)/2$. In a 3-regular graph, each node has exactly three vertices. The algorithm is used for designing MAC protocol in wireless networks. Explicitly, and neglecting an additive constant, Eq. (13.13) becomes

$$\hat{C} = \sum_{\mu=(\mu_1,\mu_2)} \hat{C}_\mu = -\frac{1}{2}\sum_{\mu=(\mu_1,\mu_2)} \hat{\sigma}_z^{(\mu_1)}\hat{\sigma}_z^{(\mu_2)}, \tag{13.20}$$

in which each vertex μ is identified by the two nodes it connects, namely, (μ_1, μ_s). The rightmost side represents the decomposition of $\hat{C}$ that is used to estimate the AG (γ-type components)

(Continued)

Design Example 13.1 (Continued)

according to $k_C = 3N/2$, $c_\mu = 1/2$ and $\hat{\sigma}_\mu^{(C)} = -\hat{\sigma}_z^{(\mu_1)}\hat{\sigma}_z^{(\mu_2)}$. Two (classical) optimization methods are considered to identify the values of (γ, β) that maximize $F_p(\gamma, \beta)$: The Nelder–Mead (NM) [6] simplex method, which does not involve derivatives; and the quasi-Newton method with the Broyden–Fletcher–Goldfarb–Shanno (BFGS) [7] update rule (for the approximated inverse Hessian matrix). For the latter optimization, we implement either finite difference or AG. Although both methods are empirically demonstrated to be very effective, in presence of a non-convex objective function there is no guarantee of convergence toward the global maximum, as opposed to attraction by a local maximum. For this reason, we try to solve each instance by starting the optimization process from different randomly chosen initial values of (γ, β).

To summarize:

- One problem class: Max-Cut on random 3-regular graphs
- Multiple instances: Each characterized by a graph with N nodes and 3N/2 vertices
- Multiple optimization runs for each instances: Characterized by the initial values of (γ, β)
- Three different optimization algorithms: The gradient-free *NM* and the quasi-Newton with finite derivative (FD) or AG
- Multiple choices of precision ε, and possibly *FN* δ or precision ε'' (AG)

All numerical simulations in [1] are performed using qHiPSTER, a state-of-the-art quantum emulator [8, 9]. The effect of finite precision for all observable quantities is included by adding a stochastic contribution to the expectation value of the single observable (for example, each term of the sum in Eqs. (13.18) and (13.19) has a stochastic contribution). The stochastic contribution is drawn uniformly at random in $[-\widetilde{\varepsilon}, \widetilde{\varepsilon}]$, where $\widetilde{\varepsilon}$ denotes the precision of the corresponding observable. All data are computed for $N = 16$ qubits.

Single instance: The (randomly generated) Max-Cut instance was fixed, and the repetition cost and performance of the optimization algorithms were analyzed. To facilitate a comparison between distinct instances, the figure of merit of the "performance" was defined not through the maximum $F_p(\gamma, \beta)$ achieved during the optimization, but via the ratio of the number of satisfied clauses for the approximated solution $|\gamma, \beta\rangle$ to the maximum number of satisfiable clauses (i.e., the exact solution):

$$R_p(\gamma, \beta) = \frac{F_p(\gamma, \beta)}{\max_{z \in \{-1,1\}^N} C(z)}$$

Figure 13.3 [1] shows how the initial values of the parameters affect the optimization process. We observe that different optimization runs reach distinct states. In actual applications, one would select the run leading to the approximated solution with highest $R_p(\gamma, \beta)$ as the one generating the answer from the hybrid algorithm. For the repetition cost, it is tempting to consider only that of this post-selected optimization run, but such a consideration would be misleading. In the absence of a way to a priori select good initial values of (γ, β), one needs to explore several initial conditions (by contrast, see an alternative approach based on machine learning techniques in [9]) and, even more, one needs to determine when to stop exploring new initial conditions. In the study $N_r = 16$ runs per instance (per optimization method) was performed.

Figure 13.3 Fraction of satisfied clauses $R_7(\gamma, \beta)$ for circuits of depth $p = 7$ versus the repetition cost of the optimization run. Single instance (number 111 in the simulations), $N_r = 16$ runs of quasi-Newton method with $\varepsilon = 0.01$ and $\delta = 0.1$. *Source:* Modified from Guerreschi et al. [1].

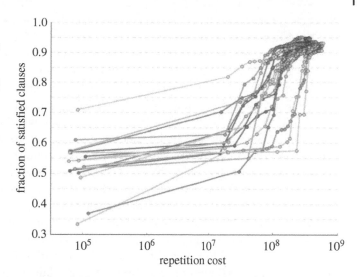

13.2 Convex Optimization in Quantum Information Theory

As an extension of the previous section, we now discuss more general problem of convex optimization in quantum information theory. The presentation adopted here assumes that the reader has a solid background in matrix theory. For readers with no such background, we provide an extensive list of references [10–53]. Due to the dense information presented here, the elaboration of such details within the main text would distract the reader from the main problems discussed in the section.

Convex optimization problems arise naturally in quantum information theory, often in terms of minimizing a convex function over a convex subset of the space of Hermitian matrices. In most cases, finding exact solutions to these problems is rather difficult if not impossible. As a compromise, a general method to solve the converse problem rather than find explicit solutions is introduced in [10]. That is, given a matrix in a convex set, a family of convex functions is determined whose functions are minimized at this point. This method, for example, allows us to find explicit formulas for the relative entropy of entanglement (REE) and the Rains bound, two well-known upper bounds on the distillable entanglement.

Convexity naturally arises in many segments of quantum information theory; the sets of possible preparations, processes, and measurements for quantum systems are all convex sets. Many important quantities in quantum information are defined in terms of a convex optimization problem, such as quantifying entanglement [11, 12]. Since the set of separable or unentangled states is convex, a measure of entanglement may be defined for entangled states outside this set, given a suitable distance measure, as the minimum distance to a state inside. If $\mathcal{D}$ is the set of all unentangled states, a measure of entanglement for a state ρ can be given by $E(\rho) = \min D(\rho \| \sigma)$, where $D(\rho \| \sigma)$ is a suitable distance (though not necessarily a metric) between two states ρ and σ [13]. Perhaps the most well-known of these quantities is the REE E_D, in which the choice of distance function is given by the relative entropy $D(\rho \| \sigma) = S(\rho \| \sigma)$, defined as $S(\rho \| \sigma) = \mathrm{Tr}[\rho(\log \rho - \log \sigma)]$.

On the problem of under what condition a closed formula for the REE exists, see [14]. Many other quantities in quantum information can be considered in terms of convex optimization problems. Defining H_n as the space of $n \times n$ Hermitian matrices, these problems are usually given in terms of a convex function $f: H_n \to [0, +\infty]$ and some convex subset $\mathcal{C} \subset H_n$. Then we can be looking for the condition when matrix $\sigma^\star \in \mathcal{C}$ minimizes f, defined by $f(\sigma^\star) = \min_{\sigma \in \mathcal{C}} f(\sigma)$, assuming that $f(\sigma)$ is finite for at least one $\sigma \in \mathcal{C}$.

Since f is a convex function, it is sufficient to show that $\sigma^\star$ is a semi-local minimum of f (see Theorem 13.1 below). That is, all of the directional derivatives of f at $\sigma^\star$ are nonnegative. Since the directional derivative is usually a linear function, denoted by $D_{f,\sigma^\star} : H_n \to \mathbb{R}$, the condition in Theorem 13.1 reduces to the fact that $D_{f,\sigma^\star}$ defines a supporting functional of $\mathcal{C}$ at $\sigma^\star$.

In general, finding a closed analytic formula for an optimal $\sigma^\star$ is difficult if not impossible, although, from the computational point of view, the complexity of finding a good approximation to $\sigma^\star$ is relatively easy, that is, polynomial, in terms of computation of the function f and the membership in $\mathcal{C}$. Such numerical optimization for the REE, for example, has been studied in [15].

However, rather than trying to directly solve these optimization problems, in this section we instead discuss methods to solve the converse problem, proposed in [10]. That is, given a matrix $\sigma^\star \in \mathcal{C}$, we will be alternatively looking for functions f achieving their minimum over $\mathcal{C}$ at $\sigma^\star$. Although this may seem trivial at first, these kinds of results can yield meaningful statements about finding closed formulas for certain quantities in quantum information [16].

Recent work has been done [16–18] that employs similar methods to determine an explicit expression for the REE for certain states. Given a state $\sigma^\star \in \mathcal{D}$, one can find all of the entangled states ρ for which $\sigma^\star$ is the *closest* separable state, thus minimizing the REE. We extend these results to find an explicit expression for the Rains bound [19], a quantity related to the REE, and show how these results can be generalized to other functions of interest in quantum information theory. For the presentation in the following, we need to recall some basic definitions from matrix theory [32]. Let M_n be the space of $n \times n$ matrices and H_n the subset of Hermitian matrices. We also define the subsets $H_{n,+,1} \subset H_{n,+} \subset H_n$, where $H_{n,+}$ is the cone of positive Hermitian matrices, and $H_{n,+,1}$ consists of the positive Hermitian matrices with unit trace. Note that $H_{n,+,1}$ coincides with the space of density matrices acting on an $n \times n$ quantum system, which may be composed of subsystems of dimensions $n_1 \times \cdots \times n_k = n$. Furthermore, let $H_{n,++} = H_n(0, +\infty)$ denote the set of Hermitian matrices whose eigenvalues are strictly positive. For $A, B \in H_n$, we denote by $A \leq B$ when $B - A \in H_{n,+}$ and $A < B$ when $B - A \in H_{n,++}$. With the Hilbert–Schmidt inner product given by $\langle A, B \rangle = \mathrm{Tr}[A^\dagger B]$, the space M_n becomes a Hilbert space and H_n becomes a real Hilbert space. A linear superoperator $\Lambda : M_n \to M_n$ is said to be *self-adjoint* if it is self-adjoint with respect to the Hilbert–Schmidt inner product, that is, $\mathrm{Tr}[\Lambda(A)^\dagger B] = \mathrm{Tr}[A^\dagger \Lambda(B)]$ for all $A, B \in M_n$.

While we will generally be using H_n as our Hilbert space, since this is the most interesting one in quantum information, the main theorem of this section also applies to any Hilbert space $\mathcal{H}$. Let $\mathcal{C} \subset \mathcal{H}$ be a convex set. We recall that a function $f : \mathcal{C} \to \mathbb{R}$ is said to be *convex* if [30]

$$f((1-t)A + tB) \leq (1-t)f(A) + tf(B) \tag{13.21}$$

for all $A, B \in \mathcal{C}$ and $t \in [0, 1]$, and f is *concave* if $-f$ is convex. Furthermore, a convex function $f : \mathcal{C} \to \mathcal{H}$ is said to be *operator convex* if the above relation holds as a matrix inequality. We call f strictly convex if $f((1-t)A + tB) < (1-t)f(A) + tf(B)$ for all $t \in (0, 1)$ and $A \neq B$. Instead of only considering functions $f : \mathcal{C} \to \mathbb{R}$, it is convenient to allow the range of f to be the extended real line $\mathbb{R}^{+\infty}$, defined as $\mathbb{R}^{+\infty} = (-\infty, +\infty]$. We can define the *domain* of f as $\mathrm{dom} f = f^{-1}(\mathbb{R})$, that is, the set of $\sigma \in \mathcal{C}$ such that $f(\sigma)$ is finite. A function $f : \mathcal{C} \to \mathbb{R}^{+\infty}$ is said to be *proper* if $\mathrm{dom} f \neq \emptyset$, and f is said to be convex if it is convex satisfying Eq. (13.21) on its domain. Furthermore, if f is convex then $\mathrm{dom} f \subset \mathcal{C}$ is a convex subset. Finally, a function $f : \mathcal{C} \to [-\infty, +\infty)$ is *concave* if $-f$ is convex on its domain [30].

Necessary/ sufficient conditions for optimization: Given a convex and compact subset $\mathcal{C} \subset \mathcal{H}$ and a convex function $f : \mathcal{C} \to \mathbb{R}^{+\infty}$, solving for an element $\sigma^\star$ in $\mathcal{C}$ that minimizes f is usually a rather difficult task. Yet, in the following theorem, we state a necessary and sufficient condition for $\sigma^\star$ to minimize f, one that involves convex combinations of the form $(1-t)\sigma^\star + t\sigma$ where $\sigma \in \mathcal{C}$. Here, we make use of the *directional derivative* of f at a point $A \in \mathcal{C}$. For A in the domain of f and $B \in \mathcal{H}$, this is defined by

$$f'(A;B) := \lim_{t \to 0+} \frac{f(A + tB) - f(A)}{t} \qquad (13.22)$$

if the limit exists. Since f is convex, this limit always either exists or is infinite. For example, if A is on the boundary of the domain of f, it is possible that $f'(A; B) = \pm\infty$. (For example if $C = H_{n,+}$ and $f(A) = \mathrm{Tr}(-\log A)$, then for $A, B \in H_{n,+}$ with $A \ngtr 0$ and $B > 0$ we have that $f'(A; B) = \infty$.) If A is in the interior of the domain, then $f'(A; B)$ is finite for all $B \in \mathcal{H}$.

Theorem 13.1 Let $\mathcal{H}$ be a Hilbert space, $C \subset \mathcal{H}$ a convex compact subset and $f: \mathcal{H} \to \mathbb{R}^{+\infty}$ a convex function. Then an element $\sigma^* \in C$ minimizes f over C, that is, $\min f(\sigma) = f(\sigma^*)$, if and only if for all $\sigma \in C$ we have $f'(\sigma^*; \sigma - \sigma^*) \geq 0$.

For the proof, see [10]. The main idea here is to turn the criterion in Theorem 13.1 into one that is more useful so that we may more easily determine if a given σ^* is optimal. In case the value of the directional derivative is linear in the choice of σ, the criterion $f'(\sigma^*; \sigma - \sigma^*) \geq 0$ can be recast in terms of a *supporting functional* for the convex set C. That is, a linear functional $\Phi: \mathcal{H} \to \mathbb{R}$ such that $\Phi(\sigma) \leq c$ for all $\sigma \in C$, and $c = \Phi(\sigma^*)$ for some $\sigma^* \in C$. Then the set $\{\sigma \in \mathcal{H} | \Phi(\sigma) = c\}$ is a *supporting hyperplane* tangent to C at the point $\sigma^* \in C$.

In a finite-dimensional Hilbert space, any linear functional can be written as $\Phi(\sigma) = \langle \varphi, \sigma \rangle$ for some $\varphi \in \mathcal{H}$. Since the Hilbert space considered here is H_n, the linear functionals are of the form $\Phi(\sigma) = \mathrm{Tr}[\varphi\sigma]$ for some matrix $\varphi \in H_n$. Conversely, every matrix $\varphi \in H_n$ defines a linear functional $\Phi: H_n \to \mathbb{R}$ by $\Phi(\sigma) = \mathrm{Tr}[\varphi\sigma]$.

Linear differential operator D_g: For applications in quantum information, we first examine functions $f: H_n(a, b) \to \mathbb{R}$ of the form $f(\sigma) = -\mathrm{Tr}[\rho g(\sigma)]$, where $\rho \in H_{n,+}$ is a matrix and $g: (a, b) \to \mathbb{R}$ is an analytic function that we can extend to matrices in $H_n(a, b)$. Since g is analytic, we may easily take the necessary derivatives to investigate the criterion in Theorem 13.1 (see [32]). We then extend this analysis to extended real-value functions $f: H_n \to \mathbb{R}^{+\infty}$ by considering carefully the cases when $\sigma \notin H_n(a, b)$, in which case $f(\sigma) = +\infty$ for most (but not necessarily all) $\sigma \notin H_n(a, b)$.

Let $g: (a, b) \to \mathbb{R}$ be an analytic function and $\Omega \subset \mathbb{C}$ an open set containing (a, b) such that g can be extended to $g: \Omega \to \mathbb{C}$, a function that is analytic on Ω. If $A \in M_n$ is an $n \times n$ matrix whose eigenvalues are contained in Ω, we may write [32]

$$g(A) = \frac{1}{2\pi i} \oint_\gamma g(s) [s1 - A]^{-1} ds, \qquad (13.23)$$

where γ is any simple closed recitifiable curve in Ω that encloses the eigenvalues of A. For a continuously differentiable family $A(t) \in H_n$ of Hermitian matrices, and t_0 such that the eigenvalues of $A(t_0)$ is contained in Ω, we have

$$
\begin{aligned}
2\pi i \frac{d}{dt} g(A(t)) \Big|_{t = t_0} &= \oint_\gamma g(s) \frac{d}{dt} \left([s1 - A(t)]^{-1} \right) \Big|_{t = t_0} ds \\
&= \oint_\gamma g(s) [s1 - A(t_0)]^{-1} A'(t_0) [s1 - A(t_0)]^{-1} ds,
\end{aligned}
\qquad (13.24)
$$

where $A'(t_0) = \frac{d}{dt} A(t) \big|_{t = t_0}$, and γ is any simple, closed rectifiable curve in Ω that encloses all the eigenvalues of $A(t_0)$. Since $A(t)$ is Hermitian, we may write it in terms of its spectral decomposition (in particular, at $t = t_0$) as $A(t_0) = \sum_{i=1}^n a_i |\psi_i\rangle \langle \psi_i|$, where $|\psi_i\rangle$ are the orthonormal eigenvectors of

$A(t_0)$ and a_i the corresponding eigenvalues. Then the matrix elements of $\frac{d}{dt}g(A(t))\big|_{t=t_0}$ in the eigenbasis of $A(t_0)$ are

$$\langle \psi_i | \left(\frac{d}{dt} g(A(t)) \bigg|_{t=t_0} \right) | \psi_j \rangle = \langle \psi_i | A'(t_0) | \psi_j \rangle \frac{1}{2\pi i} \oint_\gamma \frac{g(s)}{(s-a_i)(s-a_j)} \, ds$$

$$= \langle \psi_i | A'(t_0) | \psi_j \rangle \cdot \begin{cases} \dfrac{g(a_i) - g(a_j)}{a_i - a_j} & a_i \neq a_j \\ g'(a_i) & a_i = a_j. \end{cases} \qquad (13.25)$$

For a function $g\colon (a,b) \to \mathbb{R}$ and a Hermitian matrix A whose eigenvalues $\{a_1, ..., a_n\}$ are contained in (a,b), we define the matrix of the so-called *divided differences* [23] as

$$[T_{g,A}]_{ij} = \begin{cases} \dfrac{g(a_i) - g(a_j)}{a_i - a_j}; & a_i \neq a_j \\ g'(a_i); & a_i = a_j. \end{cases}$$

In the eigenbasis of $A(t_0)$, that is, assuming that $A(t_0)$ is diagonal, we may write $\frac{d}{dt}g(A(t))\big|_{t=t_0} = T_{g,A} \circ A'(t_0)$, where " $\circ$ " represents the Hadamard (entrywise) product of matrices. The entrywise product of $T_{g,A}$ with a matrix is a linear operator on the space of matrices, and for an arbitrary matrix $B \in M_n$ we write $D_{g,A}(B) = T_{g,A} \circ B$, where $D_{g,A}$ is a linear operator on the space of matrices such that $\frac{d}{dt}g(A(t))\big|_{t=t_0} = D_{g,A}(A'(0))$. This linear operator $D_{g,A}\colon M_n \to M_n$ is called the *Fréchet derivative* of g at A [23]. A function: $H_n(a,b) \to H_n$ is said to be *Fréchet differentiable* at a point A when its directional derivative

$$g'(A;B) := \lim_{t \to 0+} \frac{g(A + tB) - g(A)}{t}$$

is linear in B and coincides with the Fréchet derivative: that is, $D_{g,A}(B) = g'(A; B)$. Furthermore, as long as $g'(a_i) \neq 0$ for all eigenvalues a_i of A, the linear operator $D_{g,A}$ is invertible, since we may define a matrix $S_{g,A}$ as the element-wise inverse of $T_{g,A}$, namely

$$[S_{g,A}]_{ij} = \begin{cases} \dfrac{a_i - a_j}{g(a_i) - g(a_j)}; & a_i \neq a_j \\ 1/g'(a_i); & a_i = a_j. \end{cases}$$

such that $T_{g,A} \circ S_{g,A} \circ B = S_{g,A} \circ T_{g,A} \circ B = B$ for all matrices B. Then the inverse of the linear operator $D_{g,A}$ is given by $D_{g,A}^{-1}(B) = S_{g,A} \circ B$, such that $D_{g,A}^{-1}\big(D_{g,A}(B)\big) = D_{g,A}\left(D_{g,A}^{-1}(B)\right) = B$ for all matrices B.

In the following section, we consider the extended real-valued function $f\colon H_n \to \mathbb{R}^{+\infty}$, in which case it is important to also extend the definition of $D_{g,A}$ to matrices A whose eigenvalues are not in (a,b). The definition of $D_{g,A}$ is extended in the following manner. For $A \notin H(a,b)$, define the matrix $T_{g,A}$ as above on the eigenspaces of A with corresponding eigenvalues in (a,b), but to be zero otherwise A. Thus, in the eigenbasis of A, the matrix elements of $T_{g,A}$ are

$$[T_{g,A}]_{ij} = \begin{cases} \dfrac{g(a_i) - g(a_j)}{a_i - a_j} & a_i \neq a_j, \; a_i, a_j \in (a,b) \\ g'(a_i) & a_i = a_j \in (a,b)' \\ 0 & a_i \text{ or } a_j \notin (a,b) \end{cases}$$

such that $D_{g,A}(B) = T_{g,A} \circ B$. If $g'(a_i) \neq 0$ for all eigenvalues a_i of A in the interval (a, b), then we can define the *Moore–Penrose* inverse (or *pseudo-inverse*) of $D_{g,A}$. In the eigenbasis of A, this is given by $D_{g,A}^{\ddagger}(B) = S_{g,A} \circ B$ where $S_{g,A}$ is the matrix with matrix elements given in the eigenbasis of A as

$$
[S_{g,A}]_{ij} = \begin{cases} \dfrac{a_i - a_j}{g(a_i) - g(a_j)}; \; a_i \neq a_j, a_i, a_j \in (a, b) \\ 1/g'(a_i); \; a_i = a_j \in (a, b) \\ 0; \; a_i \text{ or } a_j \notin (a, b) \end{cases}
$$

such that $D_{g,A}\left(D_{g,A}^{\ddagger}(B)\right) = D_{g,A}^{\ddagger}\left(D_{g,A}(B)\right) = P_A B P_A$ for all matrices B, where P_A is the projection matrix that projects onto the eigenspaces of A whose corresponding eigenvalues are in (a, b). If $A \in H_n(a, b)$, then $D_{g,A}^{\ddagger}$ coincides with $D_{g,A}^{-1}$. Finally, we note that the linear differential operator $D_{g,A}$ is self-adjoint with respect to the trace inner product. Indeed, the matrix $T_{g, A}$ is Hermitian since A is Hermitian and $\mathrm{Tr}[C^{\dagger} D_{g, A}(B)] = \mathrm{Tr}[C^{\dagger}(T_{g, A} \circ B)] = \mathrm{Tr}[(T_{g, A} \circ C)^{\dagger} B] = \mathrm{Tr}[(D_{g, A}(C))^{\dagger} B]$, for all matrices B and C.

Optimization objective functions of form $f_{\rho}(\sigma) = -\mathrm{Tr}[\rho g(\sigma)]$: Given a matrix $\rho \in H_{n, +}$ we can now consider functions of the form $f_{\rho}(\sigma) = -\mathrm{Tr}[\rho g(\sigma)]$, which is convex as long as the function g: $(a, b) \to \mathbb{R}$ is concave. We can extend f_{ρ} to an extended real-valued convex function f_{ρ}: $H_n \to \mathbb{R}^{+\infty}$ in the following manner. If $\rho \in H_{n, ++}$ is strictly positive, then $f_{\rho}(\sigma) = +\infty$ whenever $\sigma \notin H_n(a, b)$. Otherwise, if $\rho \in H_{n, +}$ has at least one zero eigenvalue, in the eigenbasis of ρ we can write the matrices ρ and σ in block form as

$$
\rho = \begin{pmatrix} \widetilde{\rho} & 0 \\ 0 & 0 \end{pmatrix} \quad \text{and} \quad \sigma = \begin{pmatrix} \widetilde{\sigma} & \widetilde{\sigma}_{12} \\ \widetilde{\sigma}_{21} & \widetilde{\sigma}_{22} \end{pmatrix},
\tag{13.26}
$$

such that $\widetilde{\rho} \in H_{\widetilde{n}, ++}$, where $\widetilde{n}$ is the dimension of the support of ρ. Then, if all of the eigenvalues of $\widetilde{\sigma}$ are in (a, b), the matrix-valued function $g(\widetilde{\sigma})$ is well defined, and we can define $f_{\rho}(\sigma) = f_{\widetilde{\rho}}(\widetilde{\sigma}) = -\mathrm{Tr}[\widetilde{\rho} g(\widetilde{\sigma})]$. Otherwise, define $f_{\rho}(\sigma) = +\infty$ if $\widetilde{\sigma} \notin H_{\widetilde{n}}(a, b)$.

The standard formula for the relative entropy of ρ with respect to σ is recovered by choosing the function g: $(0, \infty) \to \mathbb{R}$ to be $g(x) = -S(\rho) + \log(x)$, where $S(\rho) = \mathrm{Tr}[\rho \log \rho]$ is a constant for a fixed ρ. That is, $f_{\rho}(\sigma) = \mathrm{Tr}[\rho(\log \rho - \log \sigma)] = S(\rho\|\sigma)$.

In particular, if $\sigma > 0$, then $f_{\rho}(\sigma) = S(\rho\|\sigma)$ is finite for all ρ, and $S(\rho\|\sigma) = +\infty$ if σ is zero on the support of ρ, that is, if $\langle \psi | \sigma | \psi \rangle = 0$ for some $|\psi\rangle$ such that $\langle \psi | \rho | \psi \rangle > 0$. We now show how to find the derivatives of the function f_{ρ}. If $\sigma \in H_n(a, b)$, then the directional derivative $f_{\rho}'(\sigma; \cdot) = D_{f_{\rho},\sigma}(\cdot)$ is a well-defined linear functional and $D_{f_{\rho},\sigma}(\tau) = -\mathrm{Tr}[\rho D_{g,\sigma}(\tau)]$, where $D_{g, \sigma}$ is the linear operator $D_{g, \sigma}$: $H_n \to H_n$ defined previously. If σ is in $dom f_{\rho}$ but $\sigma \notin H_n(a, b)$, then we can compute the directional derivatives as follows.

Given a concave analytic function g: $(a, b) \to \mathbb{R}$ and a matrix $\rho \in H_{n, +}$, consider the convex extended function f_{ρ}: $H_n \to \mathbb{R}^{+\infty}$ given by $f_{\rho}(\sigma) = -\mathrm{Tr}[\rho g(\sigma)]$. Let $\sigma \in dom f_{\rho}$ such that $\widetilde{\sigma}$, as defined in Eq. (13.26), is in $H_{\widetilde{n}}(a, b)$, and thus $f_{\rho}(\sigma) = f_{\widetilde{\rho}}(\widetilde{\sigma})$. Let $\tau \in H_n$ and define $\widetilde{\tau} \in H_{\widetilde{n}}$ as the block of τ on the support of ρ, analogous to Eq. (13.26), that is,

$$
\tau = \begin{pmatrix} \widetilde{\tau} & \widetilde{\tau}_{12} \\ \widetilde{\tau}_{21} & \widetilde{\tau}_{22} \end{pmatrix}.
$$

Since $H_n(a, b)$ is open, there exists an $\varepsilon > 0$ small enough such that $\widetilde{\sigma} + t\widetilde{\tau} \in H_{\widetilde{n}}(a, b)$ for all $t \in [0, \varepsilon)$, and thus $f_\rho(\sigma + t\tau)$ is finite for $t \in [0, \varepsilon)$. So, the directional derivative $f'_\rho(\sigma; \tau)$ exists for all $\tau \in H_n$ and is given by

$$f'_\rho(\sigma; \tau) = -\operatorname{Tr}[\rho D_{g,\sigma}(\tau)]. \tag{13.27}$$

If we consider ρ, σ and τ in block form as in Eq. (13.26) such that $\widetilde{\rho} > 0$, then $f_\rho(\sigma + t\tau) = f_{\widetilde{\rho}}(\widetilde{\sigma} + t\widetilde{\tau})$ for all $t \in [0, \varepsilon)$ and

$$\begin{aligned}
f'_\rho(\sigma; \tau) &= \lim_{t \to 0^+} \frac{f_{\widetilde{\rho}}(\widetilde{\sigma} + t\widetilde{\tau}) - f_{\widetilde{\rho}}(\widetilde{\sigma})}{t} \\
&= -\operatorname{Tr}\left[\widetilde{\rho} \lim_{t \to 0^+} \frac{g(\widetilde{\sigma} + t\widetilde{\tau}) - g(\widetilde{\sigma})}{t}\right] = -\operatorname{Tr}[\widetilde{\rho} g'(\widetilde{\sigma}; \widetilde{\tau})] = -\operatorname{Tr}[\widetilde{\rho} D_{g,\sigma}(\widetilde{\tau})].
\end{aligned}$$

Note that $\operatorname{Tr}\left[\widetilde{\rho} D_{g,\widetilde{\sigma}(\widetilde{\tau})}\right] = \operatorname{Tr}[\rho D_{g,\sigma}(\tau)]$, so this simplifies to the form in Eq. (13.27). We can now restate the criterion in Theorem 13.13.1 for functions of the form $f_\rho(\sigma) = -\operatorname{Tr}[\rho g(\sigma)]$ in terms of supporting functionals.

Theorem 13.2 Let $C \subset H_n$ be a convex compact subset, $\rho \in H_{n,+}$, and g: $(a, b) \to \mathbb{R}$ be a concave analytic function. As above, consider the convex extended real-valued function $f_\rho \colon H_n \to \mathbb{R}^{+\infty}$ given by $f_\rho(\sigma) = -\operatorname{Tr}[\rho g(\sigma)]$. Then a matrix $\sigma^\star \in C$ minimizes f_ρ over C if and only if

$$\operatorname{Tr}[D_{g,\sigma^\star}(\rho)\sigma] \leq \operatorname{Tr}[D_{g,\sigma^\star}(\rho)\sigma^\star] \tag{13.28}$$

for all $\sigma \in C$. Thus, the matrix $D_{g,\sigma^\star}(\rho) \in H_n$ defines a supporting functional of C at $\sigma^\star$ [10].

Note that the matrix $D_{g,\sigma^\star}(\rho) \in H_n$ defines a linear functional $\Phi \colon H_n \to \mathbb{R}$ given by $\Phi(\sigma) = \operatorname{Tr}[D_{g,\sigma^\star}(\rho)\sigma]$ such that the criterion $\Phi(\sigma) \leq \Phi(\sigma^\star)$ for all $\sigma \in C$ defines a supporting functional of C at the point $\sigma^\star \in C$. This acts as "witness" for C in the sense that, for $\varphi = D_{g,\sigma^\star}(\rho)$ and a constant $c = \operatorname{Tr}[\varphi\sigma^\star]$, if $\sigma \in H_n$ is a matrix such that $\operatorname{Tr}[\varphi\sigma] > c$, then $\sigma \notin C$. Furthermore, if $\sigma^\star$ is on the boundary of C, the hyperplane defined by the set of all matrices $\sigma \in H_n$ such that $\operatorname{Tr}[\varphi\sigma] = c$ is tangent to C at the point $\sigma^\star$. This criterion is useful in characterizing the function f_ρ, however, only if the linear functional Φ defined by φ is nonconstant on C; that is, if there exists at least one $\sigma \in C$ such that $\Phi(\sigma^\star)$ is strictly less than $\Phi(\sigma)$. This occurs only when $\sigma^\star$ lies on the boundary of C, which is proved in the following corollary. Here, we mean that an element $\sigma \in C$ is in the interior of C if for all $\sigma' \in C$ there exists a $t < 0$ with $|t|$ small enough such that $\sigma + t(\sigma' - \sigma)$ is in C, and σ is on the boundary of C otherwise. If the convex subset C is fulldimensional in H_n, then these notions coincide with the standard definitions of the interior and boundary of C. Otherwise, this coincides with the notions of the *relative interior* and *relative boundary* [20]

Corollary 13.3 Let define g, ρ, f_ρ, and C such that $\sigma^\star \in C$ optimizes f_ρ over C. If the linear functional $\Phi \colon C \to \mathbb{R}$ defined by $\Phi(\sigma) = \operatorname{Tr}[\varphi\sigma]$ is nonconstant on C, where $\varphi = D_{g,\sigma^\star}(\rho)$, then $\sigma^\star$ is a boundary point of C [10].

If $\sigma^\star$ is on the boundary of C, then characterizing all of the supporting functionals of C that are maximized by $\sigma^\star$ allows us to find all matrices ρ for which $\sigma^\star$ minimizes the function $f_\rho f(\sigma) = -\operatorname{Tr}[\rho g(\sigma)]$ over C.

Corollary 13.4 Let g, ρ, f_ρ, and C be defined as above and $\sigma^\star$ be a boundary point of C. In addition, assume that $g'(\lambda) \neq 0$ for all eigenvalues $\lambda \in (a, b)$ of $\sigma^\star$. Then f_ρ achieves a minimum at $\sigma^\star$ if and only if ρ is of the form $\rho = D_{g,\sigma^\star}^{\ddagger}(\varphi)$ as long as $0 \leq D_{g,\sigma^\star}^{\ddagger}(\varphi)$, where $\varphi \in H_n$ is zero outside of the support of $D_{g,\sigma^\star}$ and defines a supporting functional of C that is maximized by $\sigma^\star$, i.e. $\mathrm{Tr}[\varphi\sigma] \leq \mathrm{Tr}[\varphi\sigma^\star]$ for all $\sigma \in C$. The requirement that φ be zero outside of the support of $D_{g,\sigma^\star}$ means that $\langle\psi|\varphi|\psi\rangle = 0$ for every eigenvector $|\psi\rangle$ of $\sigma^\star$ with corresponding eigenvalue $\lambda \notin (a, b)$ [10].

13.2.1 Relative Entropy of Entanglement

For a quantum state ρ, the REE is a quantity that may be defined in terms of a convex optimization problem. The function that is to be optimized is the relative entropy $S(\rho\|\sigma)$, defined as

$$S\left(\rho\middle\|\sigma\right) = -S(\rho) - \mathrm{Tr}[\rho\,\log\,\sigma], \tag{13.29}$$

and $S(\rho) = -\mathrm{Tr}[\rho\,\log\,\rho]$ is the von Neuman entropy. For $\rho \in H_{n,+,1}$ and $\sigma \in H_{n,+}$, the relative entropy has the important properties that $S(\rho\|\sigma) \geq 0$ and $S(\rho\|\sigma) = 0$ if and only if $\rho = \sigma$. We can extend the range of $S(\rho\|\sigma)$ to $[0, +\infty]$ such that $S(\rho\|\sigma) = +\infty$ if the matrix ρ is nonzero outside the support of σ [24], that is, if $\langle\psi|\rho|\psi\rangle > 0$ for some $|\psi\rangle$ such that $\langle\psi|\sigma^\star|\psi\rangle = 0$. The REE of a state $\rho \in H_{n,+,1}$ was originally defined as $E_D(\rho) = \min_{\sigma \in D} S(\rho\|\sigma)$, where $D \subset H_{n,+,1}$ is the convex subset of separable states [13, 25]. The REE has not only been shown to be a useful measure of entanglement, but its value comprises a computable lower bound to another important measure of entanglement, the distillable entanglement [19, 26, 27], whose optimization over purification protocols is much more difficult than the convex optimization required to calculate the REE. In addition, the regularized version of the REE, defined as $E_D^\infty(\rho) = \lim_{k\to\infty} E_D(\rho^{\otimes k})/k$, plays a role analogous to entropy in thermodynamics [28] and gives an improved upper bound to the distillable entanglement [27]. Recall that $E_D^\infty(\rho) \leq E_D(\rho)$. Unfortunately, the computational complexity of computing the REE is high, since it is difficult to characterize when a state is separable [29].

Alternatively, the REE can be defined as $E_P(\rho) = \min S(\rho\|\sigma)$, where the optimization is instead taken over the convex set of states that are positive under partial transposition (PPT), denoted by P [19, 27]. This definition of the REE, as well as its regularized version E_P^∞, are also upper bounds to the distillable entanglement. Since P includes the separable states of quantum systems of any dimension [30], the quantities E_P and E_P^∞ are smaller than their D-based counterparts, so they offer improved bounds to the distillable entanglement. Because of this fact, along with the fact that the set of PPT states is much easier to characterize than the set of separable ones, that is, polynomially in the dimension of the state, we will primarily take E_P to be the REE for the remainder of this section.

Although we limit ourselves here to consideration of the sets of separable and PPT states, it is also possible to define a relative entropy with respect to any convex set of positive operators. That is, given any convex subset $C \subset H_{n,+}$, we can define the quantity $E_C(\rho) = \min_{\sigma \in C} S(\rho\|\sigma)$. Such quantities are useful in generalized resource theories in quantum information [31–33]. In such cases, the set of "free" states that may be used in a resource theory comprises a convex set, and the resourcefulness of a given state may be measured by its relative entropy to the set of free states. Many of the results derived here for E_P also hold true for relative entropies with respect to arbitrary convex sets C. There is no systematic method for calculating the REE with respect to either D or P, even for pure states, so it is worthwhile looking for cases for which an explicit expression for the REE may be obtained. From a given state $\sigma^\star$, a method to determine all entangled states $\rho \notin P$ whose REE may be given by $E_P(\rho) = S(\rho\|\sigma^\star)$ has been previously developed [16, 17]. In the following, using our notation from the previous section, we restate the results from Friedland and Gour [16] and omit the proofs.

Derivative of $Tr[\rho \log (A + tB)]$: For a fixed quantum state $\rho \in H_{n,+,1}$, the relative entropy $S(\rho\|\sigma)$ is minimized over $\mathcal{P}$ whenever the function $f_\rho(\sigma) = -\text{Tr}[\rho \log (\sigma)]$ is minimized. Thus, given a state $\sigma^\star$ on the boundary of $\mathcal{P}$ and taking $g(x) = \log (x)$ (which is operator concave [34]), we may use the analysis from the previous section to find states ρ such that the relative entropy $S(\rho\|\sigma) = f_\rho(\sigma)$ is minimized by $\sigma^\star$. Note that $g(x) = \log x$ is analytic on $(0, +\infty)$. Thus, for any matrix $A \in H_{n,+}$ that is zero outside the support of ρ, the directional derivative can be given as $f'_\rho(A; B) = D_{\log,A}(B)$, and this derivative exists for all $B \in H_n$. For simplicity, we define $L_A = D_{\log, A}$ as well as $S_A = S_{\log, A}$. Since $\frac{d}{dx} \log (x) = \frac{1}{x}$, the corresponding matrix S_A is given by

$$[S_A]_{ij} = \begin{cases} \dfrac{a_i - a_j}{\log (a_i) - \log (a_j)}; & a_i \neq a_j, a_i, a_j > 0 \\ a_i & a_i = a_j > 0 \\ 0 & a_i = 0 \text{ or } a_j = 0. \end{cases}$$

Finally, we note that $L_A(A) = P_A$ and also $L_A^{\ddagger}(1) = L_A^{\ddagger}(P_A) = A$ for all $A \in H_{n,+}$. This is a special property of the choice of function $g(x) = \log x$ that makes the relative entropy easy to study compared to arbitrary concave functions g.

A criterion for closest $\mathcal{P}$-states: A state $\sigma^\star \in \mathcal{P}$ that minimizes the relative entropy with ρ, that is, $E_{\mathcal{P}}(\rho) = S\left(\rho\|\sigma^\star\right)$, is said to be a _closest $\mathcal{P}$-state_ (C$\mathcal{P}$S) to ρ. Since $S(\rho\|\sigma) \geq 0$ for all matrices $\rho, \sigma \in H_{n,+}$, and $S(\rho\|\sigma) = 0$ if and only if $\rho = \sigma$, the REE of any state $\rho \in \mathcal{P}$ vanishes. Thus, the more interesting cases to analyze occur when $\rho \notin \mathcal{P}$. Before finding all states $\rho \notin \mathcal{P}$ that have the given state $\sigma^\star \in \mathcal{P}$ as a C$\mathcal{P}$S, we present some useful facts. Note that the function f_ρ is _proper_ on $\mathcal{P}$ for all states ρ. That is, there always exists a state $\sigma \in \mathcal{P}$ such that $f_\rho(\sigma)$ is finite. Indeed, the maximally mixed state $\frac{1}{n}1$ is always in $\mathcal{P}$, and $\text{Tr}\left[\rho \log \left(\frac{1}{n}1\right)\right]$ is finite for all $\rho \in H_{n,+}$. If a state $\sigma^\star \in \mathcal{P}$ is a C$\mathcal{P}$S to a state $\rho \notin \mathcal{P}$, and $\sigma^\star$ is not full rank, then ρ must be zero outside of the support of $\sigma^\star$. Otherwise, $f_\rho(\sigma^\star)$ is not finite, and thus $\sigma^\star$ is not optimal. Furthermore, since $\mathcal{P}$ is compact and f_ρ is bounded below, f_ρ attains its minimum value over $\mathcal{P}$ for all states ρ.

We also note that a C$\mathcal{P}$S of any non-PPT state $\rho \in \mathcal{P}$ must be on the boundary of $\mathcal{P}$ [16]. This agrees with the notion of the relative entropy as being a distance-like measure on the space of states. Note this fact is unique to the choice $g(x) = \log x$ in the minimization target $f_\rho(\sigma) = -\text{Tr}[\rho g(\sigma)]$, since in this case we have $\frac{d}{dx} \log x = \frac{1}{x}$ and thus $L_A(A) = P_A$ for all matrices $A \geq 0$.

We are now ready to state the criterion for a state $\rho \notin \mathcal{P}$ to have $\sigma^\star$ as a C$\mathcal{P}$S. Since $\sigma^\star$ is on the boundary of $\mathcal{P}$, there is a proper supporting functional at $\sigma^\star$ defined by a matrix $\varphi \in H_n$ of the form $\text{Tr}[\varphi\sigma] \leq \text{Tr}[\varphi\sigma^\star] = 1$. Here the condition that φ be _proper_ means that there exists at least one $\sigma \in \mathcal{P}$ that is zero outside the support of $\sigma^\star$ with $\text{Tr}[\varphi\sigma] < 1$. Hence $\varphi \neq P_{\sigma^\star}$, so we can restrict to supporting hyperplanes such that $\text{Tr}[(P_{\sigma^\star} - \varphi)^2] \neq 0$. For each such φ, we construct the family of states

$$\rho(\sigma^\star, \varphi, x) = (1-x)\sigma^\star + xL_{\sigma^\star}^{\ddagger}(\varphi), x \in (0, x_{\max}], \tag{13.30}$$

where, for a given $\sigma^\star$ and supporting functional defined by φ, the value $x_{\max}$ is the largest such that $\rho(\sigma^\star, \varphi, x_{\max})$ has no negative eigenvalues and is thus a valid quantum state. We consider the case when $\sigma^\star$ is singular separately from when $\sigma^\star$ is full rank.

Theorem 13.5 (Full-rank CPS). Let $\sigma^\star$ be a full-rank state on the boundary of $\in \mathcal{P}$. Then $\sigma^\star$ is a CPS to a state $\rho \notin \mathcal{P}$ if and only if ρ is of the form $\rho = \rho(\sigma^\star, \varphi, x)$ in Eq. (13.30), where φ defines a supporting functional of $\mathcal{P}$ at $\sigma^\star$ such that

$$Tr[\varphi\sigma] \le Tr[\varphi\sigma*] = 1 \text{ for all } \sigma \in \mathcal{P} \tag{13.31}$$

and $Tr[(1-\varphi)^2] = 1$, and $x \in (0, x_{max}]$, where x_{max} is the largest value of x such that $\rho(\sigma^\star, \varphi, x)$ is a positive semi-definite matrix [16].

Theorem 13.6 (Singular CPS). Let $\sigma^\star$ be a singular state on the boundary of $\in \mathcal{P}$. Then $\sigma^\star$ is a CPS to all states of the form $\rho = \rho(\sigma^\star, \varphi, x)$ in Eq. (13.31), where φ defines a supporting functional of $\mathcal{P}$ at $\sigma^\star$ of the form in Eq. (13.31) such that $Tr[(P_{\sigma^\star}\text{-}\varphi)^2] = 1$, and $x \in (0, \tilde{x}_{max}]$, where $\tilde{x}_{max} = min\{1, x_{max}\}$ and x_{max} is the largest value of x such that $\rho(\sigma^\star, \varphi, x)$ is a positive semi-definite matrix.

For a given $\sigma^\star$ on the boundary of $\mathcal{P}$, these conditions allow us to construct families of non-PPT states that have $\sigma^\star$ as a CPS. Indeed, each matrix φ defining a supporting functional of the form in Eq. (13.31) with $Tr[(P_{\sigma^\star}\text{-}\varphi)^2] = 1$ determines a different family. Fortunately, the boundary and the supporting functionals of the set of PPT matrices are easy to characterize. All matrices $\varphi \in H_n$ that define supporting functionals of $\mathcal{P}$ are of the form

$$\varphi = 1 - \sum_{i:\mu_i = 0} a_i |\phi_i\rangle\langle\phi_i|^\Gamma \tag{13.32}$$

with each $a_i \ge 0$, where $\sigma^{\star\Gamma} = \sum \mu_i |\phi_i\rangle\langle\phi_i|$ is the spectral decomposition of the partial transpose of $\sigma^\star$. The partial transpose operation is a self-adjoint linear operator on matrices with respect to the Hilbert–Schmidt inner product, so for each $\sigma \in \mathcal{P}$, $Tr[|\phi_i\rangle\langle\phi_i|^\Gamma\sigma] = \langle\phi_i|\sigma^\Gamma|\phi_i\rangle \ge 0$, since $\sigma^\Gamma \ge 0$, and so $Tr[\varphi\sigma] \le 1$ for all $\sigma \in \mathcal{P}$, and $Tr[\varphi\sigma\star] = 1$.

If $\sigma^\star$ is full rank, then $\sigma^\star$ is on the boundary of $\mathcal{P}$ if its partial transpose $\sigma^{\star\Gamma}$ has at least one zero eigenvector. The supporting functional of $\mathcal{P}$ at $\sigma^\star$ of this form is unique if $\sigma^{\star\Gamma}$ has exactly one zero eigenvector. Otherwise there exists a range of supporting functionals of $\mathcal{P}$ at $\sigma^\star$, and thus there is a range of families of entangled states $\rho(\sigma^\star, \varphi, x)$ that have $\sigma^\star$ as a CPS. Furthermore, if $\rho \notin \mathcal{P}$ is full rank, then its CPS is unique, owing to the strong concavity of the matrix function log and is proved in [16]. For a state $\rho \notin \mathcal{P}$ that has $\sigma^\star \in \mathcal{P}$ as the closest $\mathcal{P}$-state, a closed-form expression for the REE can be given by

$$E_\mathcal{P}(\rho) = -S(\rho) - Tr[\varphi(x)\sigma^\star \log(\sigma^\star)] \tag{13.33}$$

where $\varphi(x) = (1-x)1 + x\varphi$ and $\rho = \rho(\sigma^\star, \varphi, x)$ have the forms given in Eq. (13.30). (13.34)

13.3 Quantum Algorithms for Combinatorial Optimization Problems

Combinatorial optimization problems are specified by n bits and m clauses. Each clause is a constraint on a subset of the bits that is satisfied for certain assignments of those bits and unsatisfied for the other assignments. The objective function, defined on n bit strings, is the number of satisfied clauses, $C(z) = \sum_{\alpha=1}^m C_\alpha(z)$, where $z = z_1 z_2 \dots z_n$ is the bit string and $C_\alpha(z) = 1$ if z satisfies clause α and 0 otherwise. Typically, C_α depends on only a few of the n bits. Satisfiability asks if there is a string that satisfies every clause. *MaxSat* asks for a string that maximizes the objective function.

Approximate optimization asks for a string z for which $C(z)$ is close to the maximum of C. In this section, we present a general quantum algorithm for approximate optimization. We study its performance again in special cases of *Max-Cut* and also explore an alternative form of the algorithm geared toward finding a large independent set of vertices of a graph.

The quantum computer works in a 2^n dimensional Hilbert space with computational basis vectors $|z\rangle$, and we view Eq. (13.34) as an operator that is diagonal in the computational basis. Define a unitary operator $U(C, \gamma)$ which depends on an angle γ,

$$U(C,\gamma) = e^{-i\gamma C} = \prod_{\alpha=1}^{m} e^{-i\gamma C_\alpha}. \tag{13.35}$$

All of the terms in this product commute because they are diagonal in the computational basis and each term's locality is the locality of the clause α. Because C has integer eigenvalues, we can restrict γ to lie between 0 and 2π. Define the operator B, which is the sum of all single bit σ^x operators, as

$$B = \sum_{j=1}^{n} \sigma_j^x. \tag{13.36}$$

Now define the β-dependent product of commuting one bit operators

$$U(B,\beta) = e^{-i\beta B} = \prod_{j=1}^{n} e^{-i\beta \sigma_j^x} \tag{13.37}$$

where β runs from 0 to π. The initial state $|s\rangle$ will be the uniform superposition over computational basis states: $|s\rangle = \sum_z |z\rangle / \sqrt{2^n}$. For any integer $p \geq 1$ and $2p$ angles $\gamma_1 \dots \gamma_p \equiv \gamma$ and $\beta_1 \dots \beta_p \equiv \beta$ we define the angle-dependent quantum state $|\gamma, \beta\rangle = U(B, \beta_p)U(C, \gamma_p) \cdots U(B, \beta_1)U(C, \gamma_1)|s\rangle$.

Even without taking advantage of the structure of the instance, this state can be produced by a quantum circuit of maximum depth $mp + p$. Let F_p be the expectation of C in this state – $F_p(\gamma, \beta) = \langle \gamma, \beta | C | \gamma, \beta \rangle$ – and let M_p be the maximum of F_p over the angles: $M_p = max_{\gamma, \beta} F_p(\gamma, \beta)$. Note that the maximization at $p - 1$ can be viewed as a constrained maximization at p, so $M_p \geq M_{p-1}$. Furthermore, we will later show that $lim_{p \to \infty} M_p = max_z C(z)$.

These results suggest a way to design an algorithm. Pick a p and start with a set of angles (γ, β) that somehow make F_p as large as possible. Use the quantum computer to get the state $|\gamma, \beta\rangle$. Measure in the computational basis to get a string z and evaluate $C(z)$. Repeat with the same angles. Enough repetitions will produce a string z with $C(z)$ very near or greater than $F_p(\gamma, \beta)$. Unfortunately, it is not obvious in advance how to pick good angles.

If p does not grow with n, one possibility is to run the quantum computer with angles (γ, β) chosen from a fine grid on the compact set $[0, 2\pi]^p \times [0, \pi]^p$, moving through the grid to find the maximum of F_p. Since the partial derivatives of $F_p(\gamma, \beta)$ are bounded by $\mathcal{O}(m^2 + mn)$, this search will efficiently produce a string z for which $C(z)$ is close to M_p or larger. However, we show in the next section that if p does not grow with n and each bit is involved in no more than a fixed number of clauses, then there is an efficient classical calculation that determines the angles that maximize F_p. These angles are used to run the quantum computer to produce the state $|\gamma, \beta\rangle$ that is measured in the computational basis to get a string z. The mean of $C(z)$ for strings obtained in this way is M_p.

Fixed p algorithm: We now explain how for fixed p we can perform classical preprocessing and determine the angles γ and β that maximize $F_p(\gamma, \beta)$. This approach will work more generally, but we illustrate it for a specific problem, Max-Cut for graphs with bounded degree. The input is a graph with n vertices and an edge set $\{\langle jk \rangle\}$ of size m. The goal is to find a string z that makes $C = \sum_{\langle jk \rangle} C_{\langle jk \rangle}$, where $C_{\langle jk \rangle} = \left(-\sigma_j^z \sigma_k^z + 1 \right)/2$, as large as possible. Now

$$F_p(\gamma, \beta) = \sum_{\langle jk \rangle} \langle s | U^\dagger(C, \gamma_1) \cdots U^\dagger\left(B, \beta_p\right) C_{\langle jk \rangle} U\left(B, \beta_p\right) \cdots U(C, \gamma_1) | s \rangle. \tag{13.38}$$

Consider the operator associated with edges $\langle jk \rangle$, $U^\dagger(C, \gamma_1) \cdots U^\dagger(B, \beta_p) C_{\langle jk \rangle} U(B, \beta_p) \cdots U(C, \gamma_1)$. This operator only involves qubits j and k and those qubits whose distance on the graph from j or k is less than or equal to p.

To see this, consider $p = 1$ where the previous expression is $U^\dagger(C, \gamma_1) U^\dagger(B, \beta_1) C_{\langle jk \rangle} U(B, \beta_1) U(C, \gamma_1)$. The factors in the operator $U(B, \beta_1)$ that do not involve qubits j or k commute through $C_{\langle jk \rangle}$ and we get $U^\dagger(C, \gamma_1) e^{i\beta_1 \left(\sigma_j^x + \sigma_k^x\right)} C_{\langle jk \rangle} e^{-i\beta_1 \left(\sigma_j^x + \sigma_k^x\right)} U(C, \gamma_1)$.

Any factors in the operator $U(C, \gamma_1)$ that do not involve qubits j or k will commute through and cancel out. Return to Eq. (13.38); note that the state $|s\rangle$ is the product of σ^x eigenstates $|s\rangle = |+\rangle_1 | +\rangle_2 \ldots |+\rangle_n$, so each term in Eq. (13.38) depends only on the subgraph involving qubits j and k and those at a distance no more than p away. These subgraphs each contain a number of qubits that is independent of n (because the degree is bounded), and this allows us to evaluate F_p in terms of quantum subsystems whose sizes are independent of n. As an illustration, consider Max-Cut restricted to input graphs of fixed degree 3. For $p = 1$, there are only these possible subgraphs for the edge $\langle jk \rangle$:

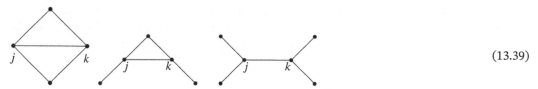

$$\tag{13.39}$$

We will return to this case later. For any subgraph G define the operator C_G which is C restricted to G, $C_G = \sum_{\langle \ell \ell' \rangle \in G} C_{\langle \ell \ell' \rangle}$, and the associated operator $U(C_G, \gamma) = e^{-i\gamma C_G}$. Also, define $B_G = \sum_{j \in G} \sigma_j^x$ and $U(B_G, \beta) = e^{-i\beta B_G}$.

Let the state $|s, G\rangle$ be $|s, G\rangle = \prod_{\ell \in G} |+\rangle_\ell$. Return to Eq. (13.38). Each edge $\langle j, k \rangle$ in the sum is associated with a subgraph $g(j, k)$ and makes a contribution to F_p of

$$\langle s, g(j, k) | U^\dagger\left(C_{g(j,k)}, \gamma_p \right) \cdots U^\dagger\left(B_{g(j,k)}, \beta_1 \right) C_{jk} U\left(B_{g(j,k)}, \beta_1 \right) \cdots$$
$$\cdots U\left(C_{g(j,k)}, \gamma_p \right) | s, g(j, k) \rangle \tag{13.40}$$

The sum in Eq. (13.38) is over all edges, but if two edges $\langle jk \rangle$ and $\langle j'k' \rangle$ give rise to isomorphic subgraphs, then the corresponding functions of (γ, β) are the same. Therefore, we can view the sum in Eq. (13.38) as a sum over subgraph types. Define

$$f_g(\gamma, \beta) = \langle s, g(j, k) | U^\dagger\left(C_{g(j,k)}, \gamma_1 \right) \cdots U^\dagger\left(B_{g(j,k)}, \beta_p \right) C_{\langle jk \rangle} U\left(B_{g(j,x)} \beta_p \right)$$
$$U\left(C_{g(j,k)}, \gamma_1 \right) | s, g(j, k) \rangle, \tag{13.41}$$

where $g(j, k)$ is a subgraph of type g. F_p is then

$$F_p(\gamma, \beta) = \sum_g w_g f_g(\gamma, \beta) \tag{13.42}$$

where w_g is the number of occurrences of the subgraph g in the original edge sum. The functions f_g do not depend on n and m. The only dependence on n and m comes through the weights w_g, and these are just read off the original graph. Note that the expectation in Eq. (13.41) only involves the qubits in subgraph type g. The maximum number of qubits that can appear in Eq. (13.40) comes when the subgraph is a tree. For a graph with maximum degree v, the numbers of qubits in this tree is

$$q_{\text{tree}} = 2 \left\lceil \frac{(v-1)^{p+1} - 1}{(v-1) - 1} \right\rceil, \tag{13.43}$$

(or $2p + 2$ if $v = 2$), which is independent of n and m. For each p there are only finitely many subgraph types.

Using Eq. (13.41), $F_p(\gamma, \beta)$ in Eq. (13.42) can be evaluated on a classical computer whose resources are not growing with n. Each f_g involves operators and states in a Hilbert space whose dimension is at most $2^{q_{\text{tree}}}$. Admittedly, for large p this may be beyond current classical technology, but the resource requirements do not grow with n.

To run the quantum algorithm, we first find the (γ, β) that maximizes F_p. The only dependence on n and m is in the weights w, and these are easily evaluated. Given the best (γ, β), we turn to the quantum computer and produce the state $|\gamma, \beta\rangle$ given by $|\gamma, \beta\rangle = U(B, \beta_p)U(C, \gamma_p)\cdots U(B, \beta_1)U(C, \gamma_1)|s\rangle$. We then measure in the computational basis and get a string z and evaluate $C(z)$. Repeating gives a sample of values of $C(z)$ between 0 and $+m$ whose mean is $F_p(\gamma, \beta)$. An outcome of at least $F_p(\gamma, \beta) - 1$ will be obtained with probability $1 - 1/m$ with order $m\log(m)$ repetitions.

Concentration: Still using Max-Cut on regular graphs as our example, it is useful to get information about the spread of C measured in the state $|\gamma, \beta\rangle$. If v is fixed and p is fixed (or grows slowly with n), the distribution of $C(z)$ is actually concentrated near its mean. To see this, calculate

$$\langle \gamma, \beta | C^2 | \gamma, \beta \rangle - \langle \gamma, \beta | C | \gamma, \beta \rangle^2$$

$$= \sum_{\langle jk \rangle, \langle j'k' \rangle} \left[\langle s | U^\dagger(C, \gamma_1) \cdots U^\dagger\left(B, \beta_p\right) C_{\langle jk \rangle} C_{\langle j'k' \rangle} U\left(B, \beta_p\right) \cdots U(C, \gamma_1) | s \rangle \right. \tag{13.44}$$

$$- \langle s | U^\dagger(C, \gamma_1) \cdots U^\dagger\left(B, \beta_p\right) C_{\langle jk \rangle} U\left(B, \beta_p\right) \cdots U(C, \gamma_1) | s \rangle \tag{13.45}$$

$$\left. \cdot \langle s | U^\dagger(C, \gamma_1) \cdots U^\dagger\left(B, \beta_p\right) C_{\langle j'k' \rangle} U\left(B, \beta_p\right) \cdots U(C, \gamma_1) | s \rangle \right].$$

If the subgraphs $g(j, k)$ and $g(j', k')$ do not involve any common qubits, the summand in Eq. (13.45) will be 0. The subgraphs $g(j, k)$ and $g(j', k')$ will have no common qubits as long as there is no path in the instance graph from $\langle jk \rangle$ to $\langle j'k' \rangle$ of length $2p + 1$ or shorter. From Eq. (13.43) with p replaced by $2p + 1$, we see that for each $\langle jk \rangle$ there are at most

$$2 \left\lceil \frac{(v-1)^{2p+2} - 1}{(v-1) - 1} \right\rceil \tag{13.46}$$

edges $\langle j'k' \rangle$ that could contribute to the sum in Eq. (13.45) (or $4p + 4$ if $v = 2$) and therefore

$$\langle \gamma, \beta | C^2 | \gamma, \beta \rangle - \langle \gamma, \beta | C | \gamma, \beta \rangle^2 \leq 2 \left\lceil \frac{(v-1)^{2p+2} - 1}{(v-1) - 1} \right\rceil \cdot m \tag{13.47}$$

since each summand is at most 1 in norm. For v and p fixed, we see that the standard deviation of $C(z)$ is at most on the order of $\sqrt{m}$. This implies that the sample mean of order m^2 values of $C(z)$ will be within 1 of $F_p(\gamma, \beta)$ with probability $1 - \frac{1}{m}$. The concentration of the distribution of $C(z)$ also means that there is only a small probability that the algorithm will produce strings with $C(z)$ much bigger than $F_p(\gamma, \beta)$.

Design Example 13.2

Max-Cut on 2-regular graphs: Regular of degree 2 (and connected) means that the graph is a ring. The objective operator is again given by $C = \sum_{\langle jk \rangle} C_{\langle jk \rangle}$, and its maximum is n or n – 1 depending on whether n is even or odd. We will analyze the algorithm for all p. For any p (less than n/2), for each edge in the ring, the subgraph of vertices within p of the edge is a segment of 2p + 2 connected vertices with the given edge in the middle. So, for each p, there is only one type of subgraph, a line segment of 2p + 2 qubits, and the weight for this subgraph type is n. The function given in Eq. (13.41) was numerically maximized in [52], and it was found that for p = 1, 2, 3, 4, 5, and 6 the maxima are 3/4, 5/6, 7/8, 9/10, 11/12, and 13/14 to 13 decimal places, from which it was concluded that M_p = n(2p + 1)/(2p + 2) for all p. So, the quantum algorithm will find a cut of size n(2p + 1)/(2p + 2) – 1 or bigger. Since the best cut is n, we see that our quantum algorithm can produce an approximation ratio that can be made arbitrarily close to 1 by making p large enough, independent of n. For each p the circuit depth can be made 3p by breaking the edge sum in C into two sums over $\langle j, j + 1 \rangle$ with j even and j odd. So this algorithm has a circuit depth independent of n.

Design Example 13.3

Max-Cut on 3-regular graphs: We now look at how the quantum approximate optimization algorithm, the QAOA, performs on Max-Cut on (connected) 3-regular graphs. The approximation ratio is $C(z)$, where z is the output of the quantum algorithm, divided by the maximum of C. We first show that for *p* = 1, the worst-case approximation ratio that the quantum algorithm produces is 0.6924 [52]. Suppose a 3-regular graph with *n* vertices (and accordingly 3n/2 edges) contains *T* "isolated triangles" and *S* "crossed squares," which are subgraphs of the form

$$(13.48)$$

The dotted lines indicate edges that leave the isolated triangle and the crossed square. To say that the triangle is isolated is to say that the three edges that leave the triangle end on distinct vertices. If the two edges that leave the crossed square are in fact the same edge, then we have a four-vertex disconnected 3-regular graph. For this special case (the only case where the analysis below does not apply), the approximation ratio is actually higher than 0.6924. In general, $3T + 4S \leq n$ because no isolated triangle and crossed square can share a vertex.

Return to the edge sum in $F_1(\gamma, \beta)$ of Eq. (13.38). For each crossed square there is one edge $\langle jk \rangle$ for which $g(j, k)$ is the first type displayed in Eq. (13.39). Call this subgraph type g_4 because it has four vertices. In each crossed square, there are four edges that give rise to subgraphs of the second type displayed in Eq. (13.39). We call this subgraph type g_5 because it has five vertices. All three of the edges in any isolated triangle have subgraph type g_5, so there are $4S + 3T$ edges with subgraph type g_5.

The remaining edges in the graph all have a subgraph type like the third one displayed in Eq. (13.39), and we call this subgraph type g_6. There are $\left(\frac{3n}{2} - 5S - 3T\right)$ of these, so we have

$$F_1(\gamma, \beta) = Sf_{g_4}(\gamma, \beta) + (4S + 3T)f_{g_5}(\gamma, \beta) + \left(\frac{3n}{2} - 5S - 3T\right)f_{g_6}(\gamma, \beta) \qquad (13.49)$$

The maximum of F_1 is a function of n, S, and T, $M_1(n, S, T) = max_{\gamma, \beta} F_1(\gamma, \beta)$. Given any 3-regular graph it is straightforward to count S and T. Then using a classical computer it is straightforward to calculate $M_1(n, S, T)$. Running a quantum computer with the maximizing angles γ and β will produce the state $|\gamma, \beta\rangle$, which is then measured in the computational basis. With order $n\log n$ repetitions, a string will be found whose cut value is very near or larger than $M_1(n, S, T)$.

To get the approximation ratio, we need to know the best cut that can be obtained for the input graph. This is not just a function of S and T. However, a graph with S crossed squares and T isolated triangles must have at least one unsatisfied edge per crossed square and one unsatisfied edge per isolated triangle, so the number of satisfied edges is $\leq(3n/2 - S - T)$. This means that for any graph characterized by n, S, and T the quantum algorithm will produce an approximation ratio that is at least $M_1(n, S, T)/(3n/2 - S - T)$. It is convenient to scale out n from the top and bottom of this relation. Note that M_1/n, which comes from F_1/n, depends only on $S/n \equiv s$ and $T/n \equiv t$, so we can write it as $M_1(1, s, t)/(3/2 - s - t)$, where $s, t \geq 0$, and $4s + 3t \leq 1$. It is straightforward to numerically evaluate this equation, and it was found [52] that it achieves its minimum value of 0.6924 at $s = t = 0$. So we know that on any 3-regular graph, the QAOA will always produce a cut whose size is at least 0.6924 times the size of the optimal cut. This $p = 1$ result on 3-regular graphs is not as good as known classical algorithms [53]. It is possible to analyze the performance of the QAOA for $p = 2$ on 3-regular graphs. However, it is more complicated than the $p = 1$ case, and we will show only partial results. The subgraph type with the most qubits is this tree with 14 vertices:

$$(13.50)$$

Numerically maximizing Eq. (13.41) with g given by Eq. (13.50) yields 0.7559 [52]. Consider a 3-regular graph on n vertices with $o(n)$ pentagons, squares, and triangles. Then all but $o(n)$ edges have Eq. (13.50) as their subgraph type. The QAOA at $p = 2$ cannot detect whether the graph is bipartite, that is, completely satisfiable, or if it contains many odd loops of length 7 or longer. If the graph is bipartite, the approximation ratio is 0.7559 in the limit of large n. If the graph contains many odd loops (length 7 or more), the approximation ratio will be higher.

13.4 QC for Linear Systems of Equations

Solving linear systems of equations is a common problem that arises both on its own and as a subroutine in more complex problems: given a matrix A and a vector $\vec{b}$, find a vector $\vec{x}$ such that $A\vec{x} = \vec{b}$. We consider the case where one does not need to know the solution $\vec{x}$ itself, but rather an approximation of the expectation value of some operator associated with $\vec{x}$, for example, $\vec{x}^\dagger M \vec{x}$

for some matrix M. In this case, when A is sparse, of dimension $N \times N$, and has condition number κ, classical algorithms can find $\vec{x}$ and estimate $\vec{x}^{\dagger} M \vec{x}$ in $\widetilde{O}(N\sqrt{\kappa})$ time. Here, we present a quantum algorithm for this task that runs in poly ($\log N, \kappa$) time, an exponential improvement over the best classical algorithm. The algorithm is known as the HHL algorithm (named after the authors of the original work: Aram Harrow, Avinatan Hassidim, and Seth Lloyd [54]).

Linear equations play an important role in virtually all fields of science and engineering. The sizes of the datasets that define the equations are growing rapidly over time, so that terabytes and even petabytes of data may need to be processed to obtain a solution. In other cases, such as when discretizing partial differential equations, the linear equations may be implicitly defined and thus be far larger than the original description of the problem. For a classical computer even to approximate the solution of N linear equations in N unknowns in general requires time that scales at least as N. Indeed, merely to write out the solution takes time of order N. Frequently, however, one is interested not in the full solution to the equations, but rather in computing some function of that solution, such as determining the total weight of some subset of the indices. We show that in some cases, a quantum computer can approximate the value of such a function in time that scales logarithmically in N, and polynomially in the condition number (defined below) and desired precision. The dependence on N is exponentially better than what is achievable classically, while the dependence on the condition number is comparable, and the dependence on error is worse. Thus, the algorithm can achieve useful, and even exponential, speed-ups in a wide variety of settings where N is large and the condition number is small. First, we sketch the basic idea of the algorithm, and then discuss it in a few iterations in more detail in the following sections.

Problem Statement Given a Hermitian $N \times N$ matrix A, and a unit vector $\vec{b}$, suppose we would like to find $\vec{x}$ satisfying $A\vec{x} = \vec{b}$. (Later, we discuss questions of efficiency as well as how the assumptions we have made about A and $\vec{b}$ can be relaxed.) First, the algorithm represents $\vec{b}$ as a quantum state $|b\rangle = \sum_{i=1}^{N} b_i |i\rangle$. Next, we use techniques of Hamiltonian simulation [55, 56] to apply e^{iAt} to $|b\rangle$ for a superposition of different times t. This ability to exponentiate A translates, via the well-known technique of phase estimation [57–59], into the ability to decompose $|b\rangle$ in the eigenbasis of A and to find the corresponding eigenvalues λ_j. Informally, the state of the system after this stage is close to $\sum_{j=1}^{N} \beta_j |u_j\rangle |\lambda_j\rangle$, where u_j is the eigenvector basis of A, and $|b\rangle = \sum_{j=1}^{N} \beta_j |u_j\rangle$. We would then like to perform the linear map taking $|\lambda_j\rangle$ to $C\lambda_j^{-1}|\lambda_j\rangle$, where C is a normalizing constant. As this operation is not unitary, it has some probability of failing, which will enter into our discussion of the runtime below. After it succeeds, we uncompute the $|\lambda_j\rangle$ register and are left with a state proportional to

$$\sum_{j=1}^{N} \beta_j \lambda_j^{-1} |u_j\rangle = A^{-1}|b\rangle = |x\rangle. \qquad (*)$$

An important factor in the performance of the matrix inversion algorithm is κ, the condition number of A, or the ratio between A's largest and smallest eigenvalues. As the condition number grows, A becomes closer to a matrix that cannot be inverted, and the solutions become less stable. Such a matrix is said to be "ill-conditioned." Our algorithms will generally assume that the singular values of A lie between $1/\kappa$ and 1; equivalently, $\kappa^{-2} I \le A^{\dagger} A \le I$. In this case, our runtime will scale as $\kappa^2 \log(N)/\varepsilon$, where ε is the additive error achieved in the output state $|x\rangle$. Therefore, the greatest advantage our algorithm has over classical algorithms occurs when both κ and $1/\varepsilon$ are poly log (N), in which case it achieves an exponential speedup. However, we will also discuss later some techniques for handling ill-conditioned matrices.

This procedure yields a quantum mechanical representation $|x\rangle$ of the desired vector $\vec{x}$. Clearly, to read out all the components of $\vec{x}$ would require one to perform the procedure at least N times. However, often one is interested not in $\vec{x}$ itself, but in some expectation value $\vec{x}^T M \vec{x}$, where M is some linear operator (the procedure also accommodates nonlinear operators as described below). By mapping M to a quantum mechanical operator, and performing the quantum measurement corresponding to M, we obtain an estimate of the expectation value $\langle x|M|x\rangle = \vec{x}^T M \vec{x}$, as desired. A wide variety of features of the vector $\vec{x}$ can be extracted in this way, including normalization, weights in different parts of the state space, moments, and so on.

A simple example where the algorithm can be used is to see if two different stochastic processes have a similar stable state [60]. Consider a stochastic process $\vec{x}_t = A\vec{x}_{t-1} + \vec{b}$, where the $i' - $th coordinate in the vector $\vec{x}_t$ represents the abundance of item i in time t. The stable state of this distribution is given by $|x\rangle = (I-A)^{-1}|b\rangle$. Let $\vec{x}'_t = A'\vec{x}'_{t-1} + \vec{b}'$, and $|x'\rangle = (I-A')^{-1}|b'\rangle$. To know if $|x\rangle$ and $|x'\rangle$ are similar, we perform the SWAP test between them [61]. We note that classically finding out if two probability distributions are similar requires at least $O(\sqrt{N})$ samples [62].

The strength of the algorithm is that it works only with $O(\log N)$-qubit registers, and one never has to write down all of A, $\vec{b}$ or $\vec{x}$. In situations (detailed below) where the Hamiltonian simulation and our nonunitary step incur only poly log (N) overhead, this means the algorithm takes exponentially less time than a classical computer would need even to write down the output. In that sense, the algorithm is related to classical Monte Carlo algorithms, which achieve dramatic speedups by working with samples from a probability distribution on N objects rather than by writing down all N components of the distribution. However, although these classical sampling algorithms are powerful, we will prove that in fact *any* classical algorithm requires in general exponentially more time than the quantum algorithms to perform the same matrix inversion task. The algorithm presented here was extended by [63] to solving nonlinear differential equations.

13.4.1 Algorithm in Brief

Going to a more detailed explanation of the algorithm, we want to first transform a given Hermitian matrix A into a unitary operator e^{iAt} that we can apply at will. This is possible (for example) if A is s-sparse and efficiently row computable, meaning it has at most s nonzero entries per row and given a row index these entries can be computed in time $O(s)$. Under these assumptions, [55] shows how to simulate e^{iAt} in time $\widetilde{O}(\log (N)s^2 t)$, where the $\widetilde{O}$ suppresses more slowly growing terms (described in [64]). If A is not Hermitian, define

$$C = \begin{pmatrix} 0 & A \\ A^\dagger & 0 \end{pmatrix} \tag{13.51}$$

As C is Hermitian, we can solve the equation $C\vec{y} = \begin{pmatrix} \vec{b} \\ 0 \end{pmatrix}$ to obtain $y = \begin{pmatrix} 0 \\ \vec{x} \end{pmatrix}$. Applying this reduction if necessary, the rest of the section assumes that A is Hermitian. We also need an efficient procedure to prepare $|b\rangle$. For example, if b_i and $\sum_{i=i_1}^{i_2} |b_i|^2$ are efficiently computable, then we can use the procedure of [65] to prepare $|b\rangle$. Alternatively, our algorithm could be a sub-routine in a larger quantum algorithm of which some other component is responsible for producing $|b\rangle$.

The next step is to decompose $|b\rangle$ in the eigenvector basis, using phase estimation [57–59]. Denote by $|u_j\rangle$ the eigenvectors of A (or equivalently, of e^{iAt}), and by λ_j the corresponding eigenvalues. Let

$$|\Psi_0\rangle := \sqrt{\frac{2}{T}}\sum_{\tau=0}^{T-1} \sin\frac{\pi\left(\tau+\frac{1}{2}\right)}{T}|\tau\rangle \tag{13.52}$$

for some large T. The coefficients of $|\Psi_0\rangle$ are chosen [57–59] to minimize a certain quadratic loss function [64]. Next, we apply the conditional Hamiltonian evolution $\sum_{\tau=0}^{T-1}|\tau\rangle\langle\tau|^C \otimes e^{iA\tau t_0/T}$ on $|\Psi_0\rangle^C \otimes |b\rangle$, where $t_0 = O(\kappa/\varepsilon)$. Fourier-transforming the first register gives the state

$$\sum_{j=1}^{N}\sum_{k=0}^{T-1}\alpha_{k|j}\beta_j|k\rangle|u_j\rangle, \tag{13.53}$$

where $|k\rangle$ are the Fourier basis states, and $|\alpha_{k|j}|$ is large if and only if $\lambda_j \approx 2\pi k/t_0$. Defining $\tilde{\lambda}_k := 2\pi k/t_0$, we can relabel our $|k\rangle$ register to obtain $\sum_{j=1}^{N}\sum_{k=0}^{T-1}\alpha_{k|j}\beta_j|\tilde{\lambda}_k\rangle|u_j\rangle$. Adding an ancilla qubit and rotating conditioned on $|\tilde{\lambda}_k\rangle$ yields $\sum_{j=1}^{N}\sum_{k=0}^{T-1}\alpha_{k|j}\beta_j|\tilde{\lambda}_k\rangle|u_j\rangle\left(\sqrt{1-C^2/\tilde{\lambda}_k^2}|0\rangle + \left(C/\tilde{\lambda}_k\right)|1\rangle\right)$, where $C= O(1/\kappa)$. We now undo the phase estimation to uncompute the $|\tilde{\lambda}_k\rangle$. If the phase estimation were perfect, we would have $\alpha_{k|j} = 1$ if $\tilde{\lambda}_k = \lambda_j$, and 0 otherwise. Assuming this for now, we obtain

$$\sum_{j=1}^{N}\beta_j|u_j\rangle\left(\sqrt{1-C^2/\tilde{\lambda}_k^2}|0\rangle + \left(C/\tilde{\lambda}_k\right)|1\rangle\right).$$

To finish the inversion, we measure the last qubit. Conditioned on seeing 1, we have the state $\sqrt{1/\left(\sum_{j=1}^{N}C^2|\beta_j|^2/|\lambda_j|^2\right)}\sum_{j=1}^{N}\beta_j(C/\lambda_j)|u_j\rangle$, which corresponds to $|x\rangle = \sum_{j=1}^{N}\beta_j\lambda_j^{-1}|u_j\rangle$ up to normalization. We can determine the normalization factor from the probability of obtaining 1. Finally, we make a measurement M whose expectation value $\langle x|M|x\rangle$ corresponds to the feature of $\vec{x}$ that we wish to evaluate.

Runtime and error analysis: We present an informal description of the sources of error; the exact error analysis and runtime considerations are presented in [64]. Performing the phase estimation is done by simulating e^{iAt}. Assuming that A is s-sparse, this can be done with error ε in time proportional to $ts^2(t/\varepsilon)^{o(1)} =: \tilde{O}(ts^2)$. The dominant source of error is phase estimation. This step errs by $O(1/t_0)$ in estimating λ, which translates into a relative error of $O(1/\lambda t_0)$ in λ^{-1}. If $\lambda \geq 1/\kappa$, taking $t_0 = O(\kappa/\varepsilon)$ induces a final error of ε. Finally, we consider the success probability of the post-selection process. Since $C = O(1/\kappa)$ and $\lambda \leq 1$, this probability is at least $\Omega(1/\kappa^2)$. Using amplitude amplification [66], we find that $O(\kappa)$ repetitions are sufficient. Putting this all together, we obtain the stated runtime of $\tilde{O}(\log[N]s^2\kappa^2/\varepsilon)$.

13.4.2 Detailed Description of the Algorithm

To produce the input state $|b\rangle$, we assume that there exists an efficiently implementable unitary B, which when applied to $|initial\rangle$ produces the state $|b\rangle$, possibly along with garbage in an ancilla register. We make no further assumption about B; it may represent another part of a larger algorithm, or a standard state preparation procedure such as [65]. Let T_B be the number of gates required to implement B. We neglect the possibility that B errs in producing $|b\rangle$ since, without any other way of producing or verifying the state $|b\rangle$, we have no way to mitigate these errors. Thus, any errors in producing $|b\rangle$ necessarily translate directly into errors in the final state $|x\rangle$. Next, we define the state

$$|\Psi_0\rangle = \sqrt{\frac{2}{T}} \sum_{\tau=0}^{T-1} \sin \frac{\pi\left(\tau + \frac{1}{2}\right)}{T} |\tau\rangle \tag{13.54}$$

for a T to be chosen later. Using [65], we can prepare $|\Psi_0\rangle$ up to error ε_Ψ in time poly log (T/ε_Ψ). One other subroutine we will need is Hamiltonian simulation. Using the reductions described in the previous section around Eq. (13.51), we can assume that A is Hermitian. To simuluate e^{iAt} for some $t \geq 0$, we use the algorithm of [55]. If A is s-sparse, $t \leq t_0$ and we want to guarantee that the error is $\leq \varepsilon_H$, then this requires time

$$T_H = O\left(\log(N)(\log^*(N))^2 s^2 t_0 9^{\sqrt{\log(s^2 t_0/\varepsilon_H)}}\right) = \tilde{O}\left(\log(N)s^2 t_0\right) \tag{13.55}$$

The scaling here is better than any power of $1/\varepsilon_H$, which means that the additional error introduced by this step is negligible compared with the rest of the algorithm, and the runtime is almost linear with t_0. Note that this is the only step where we require that A be sparse; as there are some other types of Hamiltonians that can be simulated efficiently [55, 56], this broadens the set of matrices we can handle.

The key subroutine of the algorithm, denoted U_{invert}, is defined as follows:

---

1) Prepare $|\Psi_0\rangle^C$ from $|0\rangle$ up to error ε_Ψ.
2) Apply the conditional Hamiltonian evolution $\sum_{\tau=0}^{T-1} |\tau\rangle\langle\tau|^C \otimes e^{\frac{iA\tau t_0}{T}}$ up to error ε_H.
3) Apply the Fourier transform to the register C. Denote the resulting basis states by $|k\rangle$, for $k = 0$, ... $T - 1$. Define $\tilde{\lambda}_k := 2\pi k/t_0$.
4) Adjoin a three-dimensional register S in the state.

$$|h(\tilde{\lambda}_k)\rangle^S := \sqrt{1 - f(\tilde{\lambda}_k)^2 - g(\tilde{\lambda}_k)^2}|nothing\rangle^S + f(\tilde{\lambda}_k)|well\rangle^S + g(\tilde{\lambda}_k)|ill\rangle^S,$$

   for functions $f(\lambda)$, $g(\lambda)$ defined below. Here "nothing" indicates that the desired matrix inversion has not taken place, "well" indicates that it has, and "ill" means that part of $|b\rangle$ is in the ill-conditioned subspace of A.
5) Reverse steps 1–3, uncomputing any garbage produced along the way.

The functions $f(\lambda)$, $g(\lambda)$ are known as filter functions [67], and are chosen so that for some constant $C > 1$: $f(\lambda) = 1/C\kappa\lambda$ for $\lambda \geq 1/\kappa$, $g(\lambda) = 1/C$ for $\lambda \leq 1/\kappa' := 1/2\kappa$ and $f^2(\lambda) + g^2(\lambda) \leq 1$ for all λ. Additionally, $f(\lambda)$ should satisfy a certain continuity property that we will describe in the next section. Otherwise the functions are arbitrary. One possible choice is

$$
f(\lambda) = \begin{cases} \dfrac{1}{2\kappa\lambda} & \text{when } \lambda \geq 1/\kappa \\[2mm] \dfrac{1}{2}\sin\left(\dfrac{\pi}{2}\cdot\dfrac{\lambda - \frac{1}{\kappa'}}{\frac{1}{\kappa} - \frac{1}{\kappa'}}\right) & \text{when } \dfrac{1}{\kappa} > \lambda \geq \dfrac{1}{\kappa'} \\[2mm] 0 & \text{when } \dfrac{1}{\kappa'} > \lambda \end{cases}
$$

$$
g(\lambda) = \begin{cases} 0 & \text{when } \lambda \geq 1/\kappa \\[2mm] \dfrac{1}{2}\cos\left(\dfrac{\pi}{2}\cdot\dfrac{\lambda - \frac{1}{\kappa'}}{\frac{1}{\kappa} - \frac{1}{\kappa'}}\right) & \text{when } \dfrac{1}{\kappa} > \lambda \geq \dfrac{1}{\kappa'} \\[2mm] \dfrac{1}{2} & \text{when } \dfrac{1}{\kappa'} > \lambda \end{cases}
$$

$$(13.56)$$

If U_{invert} is applied to $|u_j\rangle$ it will, up to an error we will discuss below, adjoin the state $|h(\lambda_j)\rangle$. Instead, if we apply U_{invert} to $|b\rangle$ (i.e., a superposition of different $|u_j\rangle$), measure S, and obtain the outcome "well," then we will have approximately applied an operator proportional to A^{-1}. Let $\widetilde{p}$ (computed in the next section) denote the success probability of this measurement. Rather than repeating $1/\widetilde{p}$ times, we will use amplitude amplification [66] to obtain the same results with $O\left(1/\sqrt{\widetilde{p}}\right)$ repetitions. To describe the procedure, we introduce two new operators:

$$R_{\text{succ}} = I^S - 2|\text{well}\rangle\langle\text{well}|^S,$$

acting only on the S register and

$$R_{\text{init}} = I - 2|\text{initial}\rangle\langle\text{initial}|.$$

The main algorithm then follows the amplitude amplification procedure: we start with $U_{\text{invert}}B|\text{initial}\rangle$ and repeatedly apply $U_{\text{invert}}BR_{\text{init}}B^\dagger U_{\text{invert}}^\dagger R_{\text{succ}}$. Finally, we measure S and stop when we obtain the result well." The number of repetitions would ideally be $\pi/4\sqrt{\widetilde{p}}$, which in the next section we will show is $O(\kappa)$. Although $\widetilde{p}$ is initially unknown, the procedure has a constant probability of success if the number of repetitions is a constant fraction of $\pi/4\widetilde{p}$. Thus, following [66], we repeat the entire procedure with a geometrically increasing number of repetitions each time: 1, 2, 4, 8, ..., until we have reached a power of two that is $\geq\kappa$. This yields a constant probability of success using $\leq 4\kappa$ repetitions. Putting everything together, the runtime is $\widetilde{O}(\kappa(T_B + t_0 s^2\log(N))$, where the $\widetilde{O}$ suppresses the more slowly growing terms of $(\log^*(N))^2$, $\exp\left(O\left(1/\sqrt{\log(t_0/\varepsilon_H)}\right)\right)$, and poly $\log(T/\varepsilon_\psi)$. In the next section, we will show that t_0 can be taken to be $O(\kappa/\varepsilon)$ so that the total runtime is $\widetilde{O}(\kappa T_B + \kappa^2 s^2\log(N)/\varepsilon)$

13.4.3 Error Analysis

In this section, we show that taking $t_0 = O(\kappa/\varepsilon)$ introduces an error of $\leq\varepsilon$ in the final state. The main subtlety in analyzing the error comes from the post-selection step, in which we choose only the part of the state attached to the |well⟩ register. This can potentially magnify errors in the overall state. On the other hand, we may also be interested in the non–post-selected state, which results from applying U_{invert} once to |b⟩. For instance, this could be used to estimate the amount of weight of |b⟩ lying in the ill-conditioned components of A. Somewhat surprisingly, we show that the error in both cases is upper-bounded by $O(\kappa/t_0)$. In this section, it will be convenient to ignore the error terms ε_H and ε_Ψ, as these can be made negligible with relatively little effort, and it is the errors from phase estimation that will dominate. Let $\tilde{U}$ denote a version of U_{invert} in which everything except the phase estimation is exact. Since $\left\| \tilde{U} - U_{invert} \right\| \leq O(\varepsilon_H + \varepsilon_\Psi)$, it is sufficient to work with $\tilde{U}$. Define U to be the ideal version of U_{invert} in which there is no error in any step. With this assumption, it can be shown that the following inequalities are valid [54]:

---

1) When no post-selection is performed, the error is bounded as $\left\| \tilde{U} - U \right\| \leq O(\kappa/t_0)$.

2) If we post-select on the flag register being in the space spanned by {|well⟩,|ill⟩} and define the normalized ideal state to be |x⟩ and our actual state to be $|\tilde{x}\rangle$, then $\left\| |\tilde{x}\rangle - |x\rangle \right\| \leq O(\kappa/t_0)$.

3) If |b⟩ is entirely within the well-conditioned subspace of A and we post-select on the flag register being |well⟩, then $\left\| |\tilde{x}\rangle - |x\rangle \right\| \leq O(\kappa/t_0)$.

The third claim is often of the most practical interest, but the other two are useful if we want to work with the ill-conditioned space, or estimate its weight.

Phase estimation calculations: Here we describe, in our notation, the improved phase estimation procedure of [57, 59], and discuss the concentration bounds on $|\alpha_{k|j}|$. Adjoin the state

$$|\Psi_0\rangle = \sqrt{\frac{2}{T}} \sum_{\tau=0}^{T-1} \sin \frac{\pi\left(\tau + \frac{1}{2}\right)}{T} |\tau\rangle.$$

Apply the conditional Hamiltonian evolution $\sum_\tau |\tau\rangle\langle\tau| \otimes e^{iA\tau t_0/T}$. Assume the target state is $|u_j\rangle$, so this becomes simply the conditional phase $\sum_\tau |\tau\rangle\langle\tau| e^{i\lambda_j t_0 \tau/T}$. The resulting state is

$$|\Psi_{\lambda_j t_0}\rangle = \sqrt{\frac{2}{T}} \sum_{\tau=0}^{T-1} e^{\frac{i\lambda_j t_0 \tau}{T}} \sin \frac{\pi\left(\tau + \frac{1}{2}\right)}{T} |\tau\rangle |u_j\rangle.$$

Defining $\delta := \lambda_j t_0 - 2\pi k$, we now measure in the Fourier basis, and find that the inner product with $\frac{1}{\sqrt{T}} \sum_{\tau=0}^{T-1} e^{\frac{2\pi i k \tau}{T}} |\tau\rangle |u_j\rangle$ is

$$
\begin{aligned}
\alpha_{k|j} &= \frac{\sqrt{2}}{T} \sum_{\tau=0}^{T-1} e^{\frac{i\tau}{T}(\lambda_j t_0 - 2\pi k)} \sin \frac{\pi\left(\tau + \frac{1}{2}\right)}{T} \\
&= \frac{1}{i\sqrt{2}T} \sum_{\tau=0}^{T-1} e^{\frac{i\tau\delta}{T}} \left(e^{\frac{i\pi(\lambda+1/2)}{T}} - e^{-\frac{i\pi(\lambda+1/2)}{T}} \right) \\
&= \frac{1}{i\sqrt{2}T} \sum_{\tau=0}^{T-1} e^{\frac{i\pi}{2T}} e^{i\tau\frac{\delta+\pi}{T}} - e^{-\frac{i\pi}{2T}} e^{i\tau\frac{\delta-\pi}{T}} = \frac{1}{i\sqrt{2}T} \left(e^{\frac{i\pi}{2T}} \frac{1 - e^{i\pi + i\delta}}{1 - e^{i\frac{\delta+\pi}{T}}} - e^{-\frac{i\pi}{2T}} \frac{1 - e^{i\pi + i\delta}}{1 - e^{i\frac{\delta-\pi}{T}}} \right) \\
&= \frac{1 + e^{i\delta}}{i\sqrt{2}T} \left(\frac{e^{-\frac{i\delta}{2T}}}{e^{-\frac{i}{2T}(\delta+\pi)} - e^{\frac{i}{2T}(\delta+\pi)}} - \frac{e^{-\frac{i\delta}{2T}}}{e^{-\frac{i}{2T}(\delta-\pi)} - e^{\frac{i}{2T}(\delta-\pi)}} \right) \\
&= \frac{(1 + e^{i\delta}) e^{-i\delta/2T}}{i\sqrt{2}T} \left(\frac{1}{-2i \sin\left(\frac{\delta+\pi}{2T}\right)} - \frac{1}{-2i \sin\left(\frac{\delta-\pi}{2T}\right)} \right) \\
&= -e^{i\frac{\delta}{2}\left(1 - \frac{1}{T}\right)} \frac{\sqrt{2} \cos\left(\frac{\delta}{2}\right)}{T} \left(\frac{1}{\sin\left(\frac{\delta+\pi}{2T}\right)} - \frac{1}{\sin\left(\frac{\delta-\pi}{2T}\right)} \right) \\
&= -e^{i\frac{\delta}{2}\left(1 - \frac{1}{T}\right)} \frac{\sqrt{2} \cos\left(\frac{\delta}{2}\right)}{T} \cdot \frac{\sin\left(\frac{\delta-\pi}{2T}\right) - \sin\left(\frac{\delta+\pi}{2T}\right)}{\sin\left(\frac{\delta+\pi}{2T}\right) \sin\left(\frac{\delta-\pi}{2T}\right)} \\
&= e^{i\frac{\delta}{2}\left(1 - \frac{1}{T}\right)} \frac{\sqrt{2} \cos\left(\frac{\delta}{2}\right)}{T} \cdot \frac{2 \cos\left(\frac{\delta}{2T}\right) \sin\left(\frac{\pi}{2T}\right)}{\sin\left(\frac{\delta+\pi}{2T}\right) \sin\left(\frac{\delta-\pi}{2T}\right)}
\end{aligned}
\tag{13.57}
$$

Following [57, 59], we make the assumption that $2\pi \leq \delta \leq T/10$. Further, using $\alpha - \alpha^3/6 \leq \sin\alpha \leq \alpha$ and ignoring phases, we find that

$$
|\alpha_{k|j}| \leq \frac{4\pi\sqrt{2}}{(\delta^2 - \pi^2)\left(1 - \frac{\delta^2 + \pi^2}{3T^2}\right)} \leq \frac{8\pi}{\delta^2}.
\tag{13.58}
$$

Thus, $|\alpha_{k|j}|^2 \leq 64\pi^2/\delta^4$ whenever $|k - \lambda_j t_0/2\pi| \geq 1$.

Design Example 13.4 QC FOR MULTIPLE REGRESSION

Multiple linear regression, one of the most fundamental supervised learning algorithms, has been studied already in Chapter 2. Remarkably, any multiple linear regression problem can be reduced to a linear system of equations problem as discussed in the previous section. However, finding a practical and efficient quantum circuit for the quantum algorithm in terms of elementary gate operations is still an open topic. Here, as a design example, we present a 7-qubit quantum circuit design based on the previous section and [54, 68, 69], to solve a three-variable regression problem, utilizing only basic quantum gates. First, we revisit the HHL algorithm and provide additional details.

(Continued)

Design Example 13.4 (Continued)

As described in the previous section, the HHL algorithm consists of three major steps that we will briefly summarize here with new details. Initially, we begin with a Hermitian matrix A and an input state $|b\rangle$ corresponding to our specific system of linear equations. We already know (see Section 13.4.1) that the assumption that A is Hermitian may be dropped without loss of generality. Since A is assumed to be Hermitian, it follows that e^{iAt} is unitary. Here iAt and $-iAt$ commute, and hence $e^{iAt}e^{-iAt} = e^{iAt-iAt} = e^{0} = I$. Moreover, e^{iAt} shares all its eigenvectors with A, and its eigenvalues are $e^{i\lambda_j t}$ if the eigenvalues of A are taken to be λ_j. Suppose that $|u_j\rangle$ are the eigenvectors of A, and λ_j are the corresponding eigenvalues. We recall that we assumed all the eigenvalues to be of magnitude less than 1 (spectral norm is bounded by unity). As the eigenvalues λ_j are of the form 0. $a_1 a_1 a_3 \cdots$ in binary [70, p. 222], we will use $|\lambda_j\rangle$ to refer to $| a_1 a_2 a_3 \cdots \rangle$. We know from the spectral theorem that every Hermitian matrix has an orthonormal basis of eigenvectors. So, in this context, A can be rewritten as $\sum_j \lambda_j |u_j\rangle\langle u_j|$ (via eigendecomposition of A) and $|b\rangle$ as $\sum_j \beta_j |u\rangle_j$.

Phase estimation: The quantum phase estimation algorithm performs the mapping $(|0\rangle^{\otimes n})^C |u\rangle^I |0\rangle^S \rightarrow |\widetilde{\varphi}\rangle^C |u\rangle^I |0\rangle^S$, where $|u\rangle$ is an eigenvector of a unitary operator U with an unknown eigenvalue $e^{i2\pi\varphi}$ [73]. $\widetilde{\varphi}$ is a t-bit approximation of φ, where t is the number of qubits in the clock register. The superscripts on the kets indicate the names of the registers that store the corresponding states. In the HHL algorithm, the input register begins with a superposition of eigenvectors – that is, $|b\rangle = \sum_j \beta_j |u_j\rangle$ instead of a specific eigenvector $|u\rangle$ – and for us the unitary operator is e^{iAt}. So, the phase estimation circuit performs the mapping

$$(|0\rangle^{\otimes n})^C |b\rangle^I \rightarrow \left(\sum_{j=1}^{N} \beta_j |u_j\rangle^I |\widetilde{\lambda}_j t_0 / 2\pi\rangle^C \right)$$

where the $\widetilde{\lambda}_j$'s are the binary representations of the eigenvalues of A to a tolerated precision. To be more explicit, here $\widetilde{\lambda}_j$ is represented as $b_1 b_2 b_3 \cdots b_t$ (t is the number of qubits in the clock register) if the actual binary equivalent of λ_j is of the form $\lambda = 0. b_1 b_2 b_3 \cdots$. To avoid the factor of 2π in the denominator, the evolution time t_0 is generally chosen to be 2π. However, t_0 may also be used to normalize A (by rescaling t_0) if the spectral norm of A exceeds 1. As discussed in the previous section, an important factor in the performance of the algorithm is the condition number κ. As κ grows, A tends more and more toward a noninvertible matrix, and the solutions become less and less stable. Matrices with large condition numbers are said to be ill-conditioned. The HHL algorithm generally assumes that the singular values of A lie between $1/\kappa$ and 1, which ensures that the matrices we have to deal with are well-conditioned. However, there are methods to tackle ill-conditioned matrices [64]. It is worth mentioning that in this step the clock-register-controlled Hamiltonian simulation gate U can be expressed as $\sum_{k=0}^{T} |\tau\rangle\langle\tau|^C \otimes e^{iA\tau t_0/T}$, where $T = 2^t$ (t is the number of qubits in the clock register) and evolution time $t_0 = \mathcal{O}(\kappa/\varepsilon)$. Interestingly, choosing $t_0 = \mathcal{O}(\kappa/\varepsilon)$ can at maximum error cause an error of magnitude ε in the final state [64].

$R\left(\widetilde{\lambda}^{-1}\right)$ *rotation:* A clock-register-controlled σ_y-rotation of the (ancilla qubit produces a normalized state of the form

Design Example 13.4 (Continued)

$$\sum_{j=1}^{N} \beta_j |u_j\rangle^I |\tilde{\lambda}_j\rangle^C \left(\sqrt{1 - \frac{C^2}{\tilde{\lambda}_j^2}} |0\rangle + \frac{C}{\tilde{\lambda}_j} |1\rangle \right)^S$$

These rotations, conditioned on the respective $\tilde{\lambda}_j$, can be achieved by the application of the

$$\exp\left(-i\theta\sigma_y\right) = \begin{cases} \cos\theta & -\sin\theta \\ \sin\theta & \cos\theta \end{cases}$$

operators, where $\theta = \cos^{-1}\left(\frac{C}{\tilde{\lambda}_j}\right)$. C is a scaling factor to prevent the controlled rotation from being unphysical [71]. That is, practically $C < \lambda_{\min}$ (minimum eigenvalue of A) is a safe choice, which may be more formally stated as $C = \mathcal{O}(1/\kappa)$ [64].

Uncomputation: In the final step, the inverse quantum phase estimation algorithm sets back the clock register to $(|0\rangle^{\otimes n})^C$ and leaves the remaining state as

$$\sum_{j=1}^{N} \beta_j |u_j\rangle^I \left(\sqrt{1 - \frac{C^2}{\tilde{\lambda}_j^2}} |0\rangle + \frac{C}{\tilde{\lambda}_j} |1\rangle \right)^S$$

Post-selecting on the ancilla $|1\rangle^S$ gives the final state $C\sum_{j=1}^{N}\left(\frac{\beta_j}{\lambda_j}\right)|u_j\rangle^I$ [71]. The inverse of the Hermitian matrix A can be written as $\sum_j \frac{1}{\lambda_j}|u_j\rangle\langle u_j|$, and hence $A^{-1}|b\rangle$ matches $\sum_{j=1}^{N}\frac{\beta_j}{\lambda_j}|u_j\rangle^I$.

This outcome state, in the standard basis, is component-wise proportional to the exact solution x of the system Ax =b [72]. The three processing steps of HHL algorithm are checked in Figure 13.4.

Linear regression utilizing the HHL: Linear regression models a linear relationship between a scalar response variable and one or more feature variables. Given an *n*-unit data set $\{y_i, x_{i1}, \cdots, x_{ip}\}_{i=1}^{n}$, a linear regression model assumes that the relationship between the dependent variable y and a set of p attributes, that is, $x = \{x_1, \cdots, x_p\}$ is linear [see Section 13.2]. Essentially, the model takes the form

$$y_i = \beta_0 + \beta_1 x_1 + \cdots + \beta_p x_{ip} + \varepsilon_i = x_i^T \beta + \varepsilon_i$$

where ε_i is the noise or error term. Here, i ranges from 1 to n. x_i^T denotes the transpose of the column matrix x_i, and $x_i^T \beta$ is the *inner product* between vectors x_i and β. These n equations may be more compactly represented in the matrix notation as $y = X\beta + \varepsilon$. Now, as our design example, we will consider a simple case with three feature variables and a bias β_0.

Let us say our datasets are

$$\left\{ -\frac{1}{8} - \frac{1}{8\sqrt{2}}, \sqrt{2}, -\frac{1}{\sqrt{2}}, -\frac{1}{2} \right\} \left\{ \frac{3}{8} + \frac{3}{8\sqrt{2}}, -\sqrt{2}, -\frac{1}{\sqrt{2}}, \frac{1}{2} \right\}$$

$$\left\{ -\frac{1}{8} - \frac{1}{8\sqrt{2}}, \sqrt{2}, -\frac{1}{\sqrt{2}}, -\frac{1}{2} \right\} \left\{ \frac{3}{8} + \frac{3}{8\sqrt{2}}, \sqrt{2}, \frac{1}{\sqrt{2}}, \frac{1}{2} \right\}$$

(Continued)

Design Example 13.4 (Continued)

Plugging in these datasets, we get the linear system:

$$\beta_0 - \sqrt{2}\beta_1 + \frac{1}{\sqrt{2}}\beta_2 - \frac{1}{2}\beta_3 = -\frac{1}{8} + \frac{1}{8\sqrt{2}}$$

$$\beta_0 - \sqrt{2}\beta_1 - \frac{1}{\sqrt{2}}\beta_2 + \frac{1}{2}\beta_3 = \frac{3}{8} - \frac{3}{8\sqrt{2}}$$

$$\beta_0 + \sqrt{2}\beta_1 - \frac{1}{\sqrt{2}}\beta_2 - \frac{1}{2}\beta_3 = -\frac{1}{8} - \frac{1}{8\sqrt{2}}$$

$$\beta_0 + \sqrt{2}\beta_1 + \frac{1}{\sqrt{2}}\beta_2 + \frac{1}{2}\beta_3 = \frac{3}{8} + \frac{3}{8\sqrt{2}}$$

(13.59)

To estimate β, we will use the popular "least squares" method, which minimizes the residual sum of squares $\sum_{i=1}^{N}(y_i - x_i\beta_i)^2$. If X is positive definite (and in turn has full rank), we can obtain a unique solution for the best fit $\hat{\beta}$, which is $(X^TX)^{-1}X^Ty$. It is possible that all the columns of X are not linearly independent and by extension X is not full rank. This kind of a situation might occur if two or more of the feature variables are perfectly correlated. Then X^TX would be singular, and $\hat{\beta}$ would not be uniquely defined. Nevertheless, techniques like "filtering" can be used to resolve the non-unique representations by reducing the redundant features. Rank deficiencies might also occur if the number of features p exceeds the number of datasets N. If we estimate such models using "regularization," then redundant columns should not be left out. The regulation takes care of the singularities. More importantly, the final prediction might depend on which columns are left out [72]. Equation (13.59) may be expressed in matrix notation as

$$
\begin{bmatrix}
-\sqrt{2} & 1 & \frac{1}{\sqrt{2}} & -\frac{1}{2} \\
-\sqrt{2} & 1 & -\frac{1}{\sqrt{2}} & \frac{1}{2} \\
-\sqrt{2} & -1 & \frac{1}{\sqrt{2}} & \frac{1}{2} \\
\sqrt{2} & 1 & \frac{1}{\sqrt{2}} & \frac{1}{2}
\end{bmatrix}
\begin{bmatrix}
\beta_1 \\ \beta_0 \\ \beta_2 \\ \beta_3
\end{bmatrix}
=
\begin{bmatrix}
-\frac{1}{8} + \frac{1}{8\sqrt{2}} \\
\frac{3}{8} + \frac{3}{8\sqrt{2}} \\
\frac{1}{8} + \frac{1}{8\sqrt{2}} \\
\frac{3}{8} + \frac{3}{8\sqrt{2}}
\end{bmatrix}
$$

Note that unlike common convention, our representation of X does not contain a column full of 1's corresponding the bias term. This representation is used simply because of the convenient form that we obtain for X^TX. The final result remains unaffected as long as $y = X\beta$ represents the same linear system.

Now

$$\text{and } X^TX = \frac{1}{4}
\begin{bmatrix}
15 & 9 & 5 & -3 \\
9 & 15 & 3 & -5 \\
5 & 3 & 15 & -9 \\
-3 & -5 & -9 & 15
\end{bmatrix}$$

Design Example 13.4 (Continued)

$$\mathbf{X}^T\mathbf{y} = \begin{bmatrix} \frac{1}{2} \\ \frac{1}{2} \\ \frac{1}{2} \\ \frac{1}{2} \end{bmatrix}.$$

Thus, we need to solve for $\hat{\beta}$ from $\mathbf{X}^T\mathbf{X}\hat{\beta} = \mathbf{X}^T\mathbf{y}$ [73].

13.5 Quantum Circuit

Having discussed the general idea behind the HHL algorithm and its possible application in drastically speeding up multiple regression, we now move on to the quantum circuit design meant to solve the 4×4 linear system $\mathbf{X}^T\mathbf{X}\hat{\beta} = \mathbf{X}^T\mathbf{y}$. For the sake of convenience, we will now denote $\mathbf{X}^T\mathbf{X}$ by $A, \hat{\beta}$ by x, and $\mathbf{X}^T\mathbf{y}$ by b. The circuit requires only seven qubits, with four qubits in the "clock register," two qubits in the "input register," and the remaining one as an "ancilla" qubit. At this point, it is necessary to mention that we specifically chose the form of the regression data points in the previous section such that A turns out to be Hermitian, has four distinct eigenvalues of the form $\lambda_i = 2^{i-1}$, and b has a convenient form that can be efficiently prepared by simply using two Hadamard gates.

$$\mathbf{A} = \frac{1}{4}\begin{bmatrix} 15 & 9 & 5 & -3 \\ 9 & 15 & 3 & -5 \\ 5 & 3 & 15 & -9 \\ -3 & -5 & -9 & 15 \end{bmatrix}$$

A is a Hermitian matrix with eigenvalues $\lambda_1 = 1$, $\lambda_2 = 2$, $\lambda_3 = 4$, and $\lambda_4 = 8$. The corresponding eigenvectors encoded in quantum states $|u_j\rangle$ may be expressed as

$$\begin{aligned} |u_1\rangle &= -|00\rangle - |01\rangle - |10\rangle + |11\rangle \\ |u_2\rangle &= +|00\rangle + |01\rangle - |10\rangle + |11\rangle \\ |u_3\rangle &= +|00\rangle - |01\rangle + |10\rangle + |11\rangle \\ |u_4\rangle &= -|00\rangle + |01\rangle + |10\rangle + |11\rangle \end{aligned}$$

(13.60)

Also, $b = \begin{bmatrix} \frac{1}{2} & \frac{1}{2} & \frac{1}{2} & \frac{1}{2} \end{bmatrix}^T$ can be written as $\sum_{j=1}^{j=4}\beta_j|u_j\rangle$ where each $\beta_j = \frac{1}{2}$. The implementation of the solution from Figure 13.4 is for our example shown in Figure 13.5. We will now trace through the quantum circuit in Figure 13.5 $|q_0\rangle$ and $|q_1\rangle$ are the input register qubits which are initialized to a combined quantum state

$$|b\rangle = \frac{1}{2}|00\rangle + \frac{1}{2}|01\rangle + \frac{1}{2}|10\rangle + \frac{1}{2}|11\rangle$$

which is basically the state-encoded format of b. This is followed by the quantum phase estimation step, which involves a Walsh–Hadamard transform on the clock register qubits $|j_0\rangle, |j_1\rangle, |j_2\rangle, |j_3\rangle$,

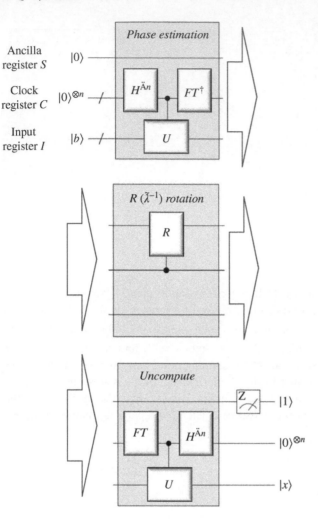

Figure 13.4 Processing steps of HHL algorithm.

clock-register-controlled unitary gates U^{2^0}, U^{2^1}, U^{2^2}, and U^{2^3} where $U = \exp(iAt/16)$, and an inverse quantum Fourier transform on the clock register. As discussed in the previous section, this step would produce the state $\frac{1}{2}|0001\rangle^C|u_1\rangle^I + \frac{1}{2}|0010\rangle^C|u_2\rangle^I + \frac{1}{2}|0100\rangle^C|u_3\rangle^I + \frac{1}{2}|1000\rangle^C|u_4\rangle^I$, which is essentially the same as $\sum_{j=1}^{N}\beta_j|u_j\rangle^I|\frac{\widetilde{\lambda}_j t_0}{2\pi}\rangle^C$, assuming $t_0 = 2\pi$. Also, in this specific example $|\widetilde{\lambda}_j\rangle = |\lambda_j\rangle$, since the four qubits in the clock register are sufficient to accurately and precisely represent the four eigenvalues in binary. As far as the endianness (the order or sequence of bytes of a word of digital data in computer memory) of the combined quantum states is concerned, we must keep in mind that in our circuit $|q_0\rangle$ is the *most* significant qubit (MSQ), and $|q_3\rangle$ is the *least* significant qubit (LSQ).

Next is the $R\left(\widetilde{\lambda}^{-1}\right)$ rotation step. We utilize an ancilla qubit $|s\rangle$ (initialized in the state $|0\rangle$), which gets phase-shifted depending upon the clock register's state. Let us take an example clock register state $|0100\rangle^C = |0\rangle_{q_0}^C \otimes |1\rangle_{q_1}^C \otimes |0\rangle_{q_2}^C \otimes |0\rangle_{q_3}^C$ (binary representation of the eigenvalue corresponding to $|u_3\rangle$, which is 4). In this combined state, $|q_1\rangle$ is in the state $|1\rangle$, whereas $|q_0\rangle$, $|q_2\rangle$, and $|q_3\rangle$ are all the in state $|0\rangle$. This state will trigger only the $R_y\left(\frac{8\pi}{2^r}\right)$ rotation gate, and none of the other phase shift

Figure 13.5 Quantum circuit for solving a 4 × 4 system of linear equation $Ax = b$.

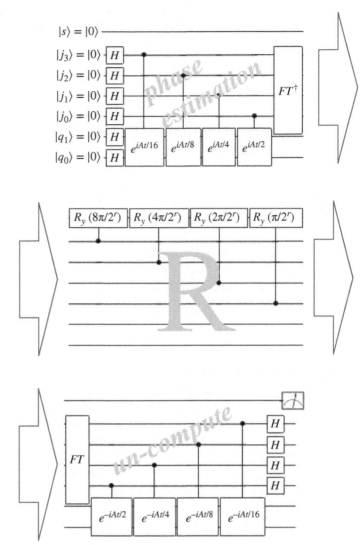

gates. Thus, we may state that the smallest eigenvalue states in C cause the largest ancilla rotations. Using linearity arguments, it is clear that if the clock register state had instead been $|b\rangle$, as in our original example, the final state generated by this rotation step would be $\sum_{j=1}^{N} \beta_j |u_j\rangle_I |\tilde{\lambda}_j\rangle^C \left(\left(1 - C^2/\tilde{\lambda}_j^2\right)^{1/2} |0\rangle + \frac{C}{\lambda_j} |1\rangle \right)^S$, where $C = 8\pi/2^r$. For this step, an a priori knowledge of the eigenvalues of A was necessary to design the gates. For more general cases of eigenvalues, one may refer to [69].

Then, as elaborated in the previous section, the inverse phase estimation step essentially reverses the quantum phase estimation step. The state produced by this step, conditioned on obtaining $|1\rangle$ in ancilla, is $\frac{8\pi}{2^r} \sum_{j=1}^{j=4} \frac{1/2}{2^{j-1}} |u_j\rangle$.

Upon writing in the standard basis and normalizing, it becomes $\dfrac{1}{\sqrt{340}}$ $(-|00\rangle + 7|01\rangle + 11|10\rangle + 13|11\rangle)$. This is proportional to the exact solution of the system $x = \dfrac{1}{32}[-1\ 7\ 11\ 13]^T$.

13.6 Quantum Algorithm for Systems of Nonlinear Differential Equations

In this section, we present the solutions of a set of n first-order nonlinear ordinary differential equations (ODEs) whose nonlinear terms are given by n polynomials $f_\alpha(z)$ in n variables $z_j, j = 1, 2, ..., n$, over $\mathbb{C}$. That is, we look for solutions $z(t)$ of the simultaneous set

$$
\begin{aligned}
\frac{dz_1(t)}{dt} &= f_1(z_1(t), z_2(t), ..., z_n(t)) \\
\frac{dz_2(t)}{dt} &= f_2(z_1(t), z_2(t), ..., z_n(t)) \\
&\ \ \vdots \\
\frac{dz_n(t)}{dt} &= f_n(z_1(t), z_2(t), ..., z_n(t)),
\end{aligned}
\tag{13.61}
$$

subject to the boundary condition $z(0) = b$. Standard results ensure that a solution to this initial value problem exists and is unique (see, e.g., [74]). Although we will mostly describe only the algorithm for *quadratic* systems, the extension to higher degrees is straightforward. Quadratically nonlinear equations can exhibit a wide variety of phenomena, including chaos and anomalous diffusion, and classical examples include the eponymous *Lorenz system* and the *Orszag–McLaughlin dynamical system*.

Along the lines presented in [75], we encode the variables $z_j(t)$ as the *probability amplitudes* of a quantum state of an $(n + 1)$-level quantum system:

$$
|\varphi\rangle = \frac{1}{\sqrt{2}}|0\rangle + \frac{1}{\sqrt{2}}\sum_{j=1}^{n} z_j |j\rangle,
\tag{13.62}
$$

where, to ensure that the state is normalized, we require $\sum_{j=1}^{n}|z_j|^2 = 1$. (Our constructions ensure that $|\varphi\rangle$ always remains normalized.) Although it is convenient to regard $|\varphi\rangle$ as the state of a single $(n + 1)$-level quantum system, when actually implementing the algorithm on a quantum computer we will encode $|\varphi\rangle$ as a state of $\log(n)$ qubits in the natural way.

We describe the procedure in two stages:

1) a method of implementing nonlinear transformations of the probability amplitudes of $|\varphi\rangle$
2) a quantum algorithm to implement Euler's method

A quantum algorithm: In this section, we describe a nondeterministic algorithm to prepare quantum states whose amplitudes are nonlinear functions of those of some input quantum state.

Suppose we want to implement a *quadratic* transformation on the probability amplitudes z_j of $|\varphi\rangle$. (We assume throughout that the initial state $|\varphi\rangle$ can be efficiently prepared on a quantum computer, for example, by using a combination of the methods of [54, 76].) Since the amplitudes are unknown, this is, in general, impossible, and, unfortunately, this is the generic setting when integrating ODEs as every point on the solution trajectory can be regarded as an initial condition for the system. But suppose we have two copies of $|\varphi\rangle$. In this case, the probability amplitudes of the tensor product are given by

$$|\varphi\rangle|\varphi\rangle = \frac{1}{2}\sum_{j,k=0}^{n} z_j z_k |jk, \tag{13.63}$$

where, for convenience, we set $z_0 = 1$ from now on. Evidently, every monomial $z_j^{l_j} z_k^{l_k}, l_j, l_k \leq 1$, of degree less than 2 appears (more than once) in this expansion. Suppose we want to iterate the transformation $z \to F(z)$, where

$$F(z) = \begin{pmatrix} f_1(z) \\ f_2(z) \\ \vdots \\ f_n(z) \end{pmatrix}, \tag{13.64}$$

and f_α, $\alpha = 1, 2, ..., n$, are quadratic polynomials $f_\alpha(z) = \sum_{k,l=0}^{n} a_{kl}^{(\alpha)} z_k z_l$, with $a_{kl}^{(\alpha)} = a_{lk}^{(\alpha)}$ and $f_0(z) = 1$. Thus, we aim to prepare the quantum state $|\varphi'\rangle = \frac{1}{\sqrt{2}}\sum_{\alpha=0}^{n} f_\alpha(z)|\alpha\rangle$, where, to simplify matters, we have assumed that the transformation is *measure preserving*, that is, $1 = \sum_{j=1}^{n}|z_j|^2 = \sum_{\alpha=1}^{n} f_\alpha^*(z) f_\alpha(z)$.

The measure-preservation assumption plays an important role in our constructions. However, if it is relaxed, our algorithm still proceeds unchanged; only the success probability is modified. To ensure that our method is efficient, we need to make several additional assumptions beyond measure preservation. The first assumption is that $|a_{kl}^{(\alpha)}| = O(1), k, l, \alpha = 1, 2, ..., n$. The second assumption is that the map F is *sparse*, which means that $|\{(k, l)|a_{kl}^{(\alpha)} \neq 0\}| \leq s/2, \alpha = 1, 2, ..., n$, and $|\{\alpha|a_{kl}^{(\alpha)} \neq 0\}| \leq s/2, k, l = 1, 2, ..., n$, where $s = O(1)$. Note that the assumption of sparsity means that each $f_\alpha(z)$ can only involve at most $s/2$ monomials and that each variable appears in at most $s/2$ polynomials $f_\alpha(z)$. The final assumption is that the Lipschitz constant for our system, that is, the number λ such that $\|F(x - y)\| \leq \lambda\|x - y\|$ in the ball $\|x\|^2 \leq 1$ and $\|y\|^2 \leq 1$, is $O(1)$. Although these assumptions are rather restrictive, as we discuss, there are many important systems that satisfy them. We also later describe how to relax these assumptions. It turns out that implementing the desired transformation will, in general, require that we make some destructive nonunitary transformation of the system's state. To understand what is required, we now set up the operator $A = \sum_{\alpha,k,l=0}^{n} a_{kl}^{(\alpha)}|\alpha 0\rangle\langle kl|$.

We now adjoin a qubit "pointer" P and use A to set up a Hamiltonian (this is essentially the von Neumann measurement prescription [77]): $H = -iA \otimes |1\rangle_P\langle 0| + iA^\dagger \otimes |0\rangle_P\langle 1|$. We now initialize our system in the state $|\varphi\rangle|\varphi\rangle|0\rangle_P$, and evolve according to H for a time $t = \varepsilon$. The evolution time needed depends crucially on the sparsity of H and the desired error [78]; roughly speaking, when the sparsity of A is some constant s we can efficiently simulate (in terms of log (n)), up to some prespecified precision, the evolution for any constant time t. After the evolution, the system ends up in the state

$$|\Psi\rangle = e^{i\varepsilon H}|\varphi\rangle|\varphi\rangle|0\rangle = \sum_{j=0}^{\infty}\frac{(i\varepsilon H)^j}{j!}|\varphi\rangle|\varphi\rangle|0\rangle$$
$$= |\varphi\rangle|\varphi\rangle|0\rangle + \varepsilon A|\varphi\rangle|\varphi\rangle|1\rangle - . \tag{13.65}$$

Now, noting that $A|\varphi\rangle|\varphi\rangle = \sum_{\alpha,k,l=0}^{n} a_{kl}^{(\alpha)} z_k z_l |\alpha\rangle|0\rangle/2 = |\varphi'\rangle|0\rangle/\sqrt{2}$, we measure $|\Psi\rangle$ on the ancilla qubit and post-select on "1"; we succeed with probability $\approx \varepsilon^2/2$ (thanks to the measure-preservation property; if our polynomial map is not measure preserving, then this success probability will be proportionally lower) and our posterior state is

$$\frac{\sqrt{2}}{\varepsilon}(\mathbb{I}\otimes\mathbb{I}\otimes\langle 1|)|\Psi\rangle = \frac{1}{\sqrt{2}}\sum_{\alpha,k,l=0}^{n} a_{kl}^{(\alpha)} z_k z_l |\alpha\rangle|0\rangle = |\varphi'\rangle|0\rangle. \tag{13.66}$$

If we fail, then we end up with some "poisoned" state $|\Psi'\rangle$ (this occurs with probability $\approx 1 - \varepsilon^2/2$), which we discard. In order to ensure, with high probability, that we end up with at least one copy of $|\varphi'\rangle$ we need to repeat this process on approximately $16/\varepsilon^2$ fresh pairs $|\varphi\rangle|\varphi\rangle$. It is an interesting question whether one can design H so that the poisoned state can be recovered and used again. Such a possibility would allow one to substantially reduce the resource requirements of the algorithm. Obviously, because the expansion Eq. (13.65) is truncated to first order, we do not exactly produce $|\varphi'\rangle$, but rather some approximation to $|\varphi'\rangle$. To correct this, we actually use the method described in [54] to implement the transformation

$$|\varphi\rangle|\varphi\rangle|0\rangle \rightarrow \sqrt{\mathbb{I} - \varepsilon^2 H^2}|\varphi\rangle|\varphi\rangle|0\rangle + i\varepsilon H|\varphi\rangle|\varphi\rangle|0\rangle \tag{13.67}$$

where $|\varepsilon| \leq 1/\|H\|$. Since H is sparse, we have, by Geršgorin's theorem [79], that $\|H\| \leq cs$, where c is a constant. This allows us to assume that when we succeed, we will obtain precisely a copy of $|\varphi'\rangle$, modulo only imperfections in the simulation of $e^{i\varepsilon H}$. If we want to iterate the polynomial map $z \rightarrow F(z)$ a constant (in n) number m times to produce the state $|\varphi(m)\rangle$, we need to start with $(16/\varepsilon^2)^m$ initial states. Thus, the total spatial resources required by this algorithm scale as $(16/\varepsilon^2)^m \log(n)$ because the cost of storing n variables via encoding in $|\varphi\rangle$ scales linearly with $\log(n)$. (See Proposition 1 in [63], for a precise statement of the spatial resource requirements of the algorithm.)

The simulation of the evolution e^{itH} on a quantum computer cannot be done perfectly; in Proposition 2, in [63] the errors that accumulate throughout the running of the polynomial iteration algorithm were quantified: if the evolution e^{itH} can be simulated up to error δ, then after m steps the final state will have accumulated an error no worse that $\delta(3\gamma)^{m+1}$. Thus, choosing the simulation error in such a way that $\delta < (3\gamma)^{-m}$ is satisfied will ensure that the m-th iteration is exponentially close the desired state. The costs [78] of simulation to this level of precision imply that the total running time T of our algorithm scales as $T \sim mpoly(\log(n)\log_*(n))s^2 9^{\kappa\sqrt{m}}$, where κ is some $O(1)$ constant and $\log^*(n) \equiv \min\left\{r \mid \log_2^{(r)}(n) < 2\right\}$ with $\log^{(r)}$ denoting the r-th iterated logarithm, and we have assumed that the transformation Eq. (13.67) is carried out in parallel on each of the remaining pairs in each iteration. Thus, the parallelized temporal scaling is subexponential in m and polynomial in $\log(n)$.

To complete the description of our iteration algorithm, we need to describe how to read out information about the solution. After m iterations, the system will be, up to some prespecified error, in the quantum state $|\varphi^{(m)}\rangle$ encoding the m-th iterate of F in the probability amplitudes. To access information about the solution, we need to make measurements of the system. In principle, any Hermitian observable $M = \sum_{j,k=0}^{n} M_{j,k}|j\rangle\langle k|$ may be measured to extract information. Through Hoeffding's inequality, we learn that we can estimate, using repeated measurements, the quantity $\langle M\rangle \equiv \sum_{j,k=0}^{n} \bar{z}_j M_{j,k} z_k$ to within any desired additive error. In practice, the observable M is measured using (a discretization of) von Neumann's measurement prescription [77, 80], so the evolution e^{itM} must be efficiently simulable on a quantum computer. Many natural such operators fall into this class, including via a quantum Fourier transform operator whose measurement statistics provide information on the sums $S_k = \sum_{j=1}^{n} x_j \exp\left(2\pi ijk/n\right)/\sqrt{n}$. As noted in [54], and as is evident from our construction here, measuring multiple copies of $|\varphi^{(m)}\rangle$ also makes it possible to extract information about polynomial functions of the solution.

The flexibility to measure efficiently implementable Hermitian operators to extract information about the solution provides the key to the exponential separation between the method described here and the best classical methods. Indeed, if we only wanted to learn one element z_j, for some j, of the m-th iteration, then there is actually an efficient classical algorithm with the same resource scaling. (This is similar to the situation with linear equations [81, 82], where if we only want to learn about one element of the solution vector of a well-conditioned sparse set of linear equations we can efficiently do this classically. Indeed, even if the system is badly conditioned, we can still learn about parts of the solution in the well-conditioned subspace.)

Solving nonlinear differential equations: In this section, we show how to use the method we have just described to integrate a sparse set of simultaneous nonlinear differential equations for any constant time. Suppose we want to integrate the system Eq. (13.61) with the initial condition z(0) = b, where f_j are sparse polynomials. We again assume that our system is measure preserving, which means that $\sum_{j=1}^{n} z_j^* f_j(z(t)) + z_j f_j^*(z(t)) = 0$ and that the Lipschitz constant is O(1). The simplest approach is to use *Euler's method* [83]: we pick some small step size h and iterate the map $z_j \rightarrow z_j + hz_j = z_j + hf_j(z)$.

While Euler's method is rather inconvenient in practice, especially for stiff ODEs, it does provide a basic proof of principle; more sophisticated methods such as fourth-order Runge–Kutta and predictor–corrector methods are essentially only *polynomially* more efficient. As the algorithm is precisely an implementation of Euler's method on the probability amplitudes, we can appeal to the standard theory [84] concerning its correctness and complexity; thus, our algorithm suffers from all the standard drawbacks of Euler's method, including a first-order decrease in error in terms of the step size h. Nevertheless, it will provide us with an algorithm scaling polynomially with $\log(n)$, where n is the number of variables. However, it should be noted that our method scales *exponentially* with the inverse step size. Thus, without modification, the algorithm is only suited to well-conditioned systems.

As we have indicated, the idea behind the approach is very simple: we integrate the system using Euler's method. Thus, given $|\varphi(t)\rangle$, we aim to prepare $|\varphi(t+h)\rangle = |\varphi(t)\rangle + h|\varphi(t)\rangle + O(h^2)$, where now

$$|\varphi'(t)\rangle = \frac{1}{\sqrt{2}} \sum_{\alpha=0}^{n} f_\alpha(z(t))|j = \frac{1}{\sqrt{2}} \sum_{\alpha,k,l=0}^{n} a_{kl}^{(\alpha)} z_k(t) z_l(t)|\alpha\rangle. \tag{13.68}$$

To implement this transformation, we suppose we have two copies of $|\varphi(t)\rangle$ and apply the method of the previous section to implement the polynomial transformation $z_\alpha \rightarrow z_\alpha + hf_\alpha(z(t))$. Note that this transformation is only measure preserving to O(h); the success probability will be diminished by a factor of $O(h^2)$, which can be made negligible by reducing h in the standard way.

So, to integrate the system Eq. (13.61) forward in time to $t = O(1)$, we begin by discretizing time into m steps. (Thus, our step size is $h = t/m$.) We next prepare $(16/\varepsilon^2)^m$ copies of $|\varphi(0)\rangle$, to produce approximately $(16/\varepsilon^2)^m$ copies of $|\varphi(t/m)\rangle$ in expected time poly($\log(n)$). We then iterate until we produce at least one copy of $|\varphi(t)\rangle$ in expected time poly $(m, \log(n))$ with probability greater than 1/3. The resources required by this approach scale polynomially with $\log(n)$ and *exponentially* with t and $1/h$.

References

1 G. G. Guerreschi, Practical optimization for hybrid quantum-classical algorithms, https://www.arxiv-vanity.com/papers/1701.01450

2 McClean, J.R., Romero, J., Babbush, R., and Aspuru-Guzik, A. (2016). The theory of variational hybrid quantum-classical algorithms. *New J. Phys.* **18**: 023023.

3 E. Farhi, J. Goldstone, and S. Gutmann, A Quantum Approximate Optimization Algorithm, arXiv:1411.4028 (2014).

4 E. Farhi and A. W. Harrow, Quantum Supremacy through the Quantum Approximate Optimization Algorithm, arXiv:1602.07674 (2016).

5 Yu-Hong Dai, A Perfect Example for The BFGS Method ftp://www.cc.ac.cn/pub/dyh/papers/bfgs-example.pdf

6 I. Fajfar, Á Búrmen and J Puhan, The Nelder–Mead simplex algorithm with perturbed centroid for high-dimensional function optimization, https://link.springer.com/article/10.1007/s11590-018-1306-2

7 J. Rafati, Quasi-Newton Optimization Methods for Deep Learning Applications, arXiv:1909.01994v1 [cs.LG] 4 Sep 2019

8 N. P. D. Sawaya, M. Smelyanskiy, J. R. McClean, and A. Aspuru-Guzik, Error sensitivity to environmental noise in quantum circuits for chemical state preparation, arXiv:1602.01857v2 (2016).

9 Wecker, D., Hastings, M.B., and Troyer, M. (2016). Learning to optimize variational quantum circuits to solve combinatorial problems. *Phys. Rev. A* **94**: 022309.

10 M. Girard, G Gour, and S Friedland, On convex optimization problems in quantum information theory, arXiv:1402.0034v2 [quant-ph] 25 Nov 2014

11 Plenio, M.B. and Virmani, S. (2005). An introduction to entanglement measures. *Quantum Inf. Comput.* **7** (1), arXiv:quant-ph/0504163.

12 Horodecki, R., Horodecki, M., and Horodecki, K. (2009). Quantum entanglement. *Rev. Mod. Phys.* **81**: 865, arXiv:arXiv:quantph/0702225v2.

13 Vedral, V. and Plenio, M.B. (1998). Entanglement measures and purification procedures. *Phys. Rev. A* **57**: 1619.

14 O. Krueger and R. F. Werner, (2005), Some Open Problems in QuantumInformation TheoryarXiv: quantph/0504166.

15 Zinchenko, Y., Friedland, S., and Gour, G. (2010). Numerical estimation of the relative entropy of entanglement. *Phys. Rev. A* **82**: 052336.

16 Friedland, S. and Gour, G. (2011). Closed formula for the relative entropy of entanglement in all dimensions. *J. Math. Phys.* **52**: 052201, arXiv:1007.4544.

17 Ishizaka, S. (2003). Analytical formula connecting entangled state and the closest disentangled state. *Phys. Rev. A* **67**: 060301, arXiv:quant-ph/0301107.

18 Miranowicz, A. and Ishizaka, S. (2008). Closed formula for the relative entropy of entanglement. *Phys. Rev. A* **78**: 032310, arXiv:0805.3134v3.

19 Rains, E.M. (1999). A rigorous treatment of distillable entanglement. *Phys. Rev. A* **60**: 173. arXiv: quantph/9809078.

20 Borwein, J.M. and Vanderwerff, J.D. (2010). *Convex Functions: Constructions, Characterizations and Counterexamples*. Cambridge University Press.

21 Borwein, J.M. and Lewis, A.S. (2006). *Convex Analysis and Nonlinear Optimization: Theory and Examples*. Springer.

22 Horn, R.A. and Johnson, C.R. (1994). *Topics in Matrix Analysis*. Cambridge University Press.

23 Bhatia, R. (1997). *Matrix Analysis, Graduate Texts in Mathematics*, vol. **169**. Springer.

24 Ohya, M. and Petz, D. (1993). *Quantum Entropy and Its Use*. Springer.

25 Vedral, V., Plenio, M.B., Rippin, M.A., and Knight, P.L. (1997). Quantifying entanglement. *Phys. Rev. Lett.* **78**: 2275, arXiv:quantph/9702027.

26 Bennett, C.H., DiVincenzo, D., Smolin, J., and Wootters, W. (1996). Mixed-state entanglement and quantum error correction. *Phys. Rev. A* **54**: 3824, arXiv:quantph/9604024.

27 Rains, E.M. (1999). Bound on distillable entanglement. *Phys. Rev. A* **60**: 179, arXiv:quantph/9809082.

28 Brandão, F. and Plenio, M.B. A reversible theory of entanglement and its relation to the second law. *Commun. Math. Phys.* **295**: 829, 2010, arXiv:0710.5827.

29 L. Gurvits, Classical deterministic complexity of Edmonds' Problem and quantum entanglement, in Proc. thirty-fifth ACM Symp. Theory Comput. - STOC '03 (ACM Press, New York, New York, USA, 2003) p. 10, arXiv:quant-ph/0303055.

30 Peres, A. (1996). Separability criterion for density matrices. *Phys. Rev. Lett.* **77**: 1413, arXiv:quantph/9604005v2.

31 Gour, G. and Spekkens, R.W. (2008). The resource theory of quantum reference frames: manipulations and monotones. *New J. Phys.* **10**: 033023, arXiv:0711.0043.

32 Brandão, F.G.S.L. and Plenio, M.B. (2010). *Commun. Math. Phys.* **295**: 791, arXiv:0904.0281v3.

33 Narasimhachar, V. and Gour, G. (2014). Phase-asymmetry resource interconversion via estimation. *Phys. Rev. A* **89**: 033859, arXiv:1311.4630.

34 Carlen, E.A. (March 16-20, 2009). Trace inequalities and quantum entropy:an introductory course. In: *Entropy and the Quantum: A School on Analytic and Functional Inequalities with Applications* (eds. R. Sims and D. Ueltschi), 73–140. Tucson, Arizona: American Mathematical Society.

35 Rains, E.M. (2000). Erratum: Bound on distillable entanglement. *Phys. Rev. A* **63**: 019902.

36 Rains, E.M. (2001). A semidefinite program for distillable entanglement. *IEEE Trans. Inf. Theory* **47**: 2921, arXiv:quant-ph/0008047.

37 Plenio, M.B. (2005). Logarithmic negativity: a full entanglement monotone that is not convex. *Phys. Rev. Lett.* **95**: 090503, arXiv:quant-ph/0505071.

38 Audenaert, K., De Moor, B., Vollbrecht, K.G.H., and Werner, R.F. (2002). Asymptotic relative entropy of entanglement for orthogonally invariant states. *Phys. Rev. A* **66**: 032310, arXiv:quant-ph/0204143.

39 Horn, R.A. and Johnson, C.R. (1985). *Matrix Analysis*. Cambridge University Press.

40 Harrow, A.W. and Montanaro, A. (2013). Testing product states, quantum Merlin-Arthur games and tensor optimization. *J. ACM* **60** (1), arXiv:1001.0017v6.

41 Choi, M.-D. (1975). Completely positive linear maps on complex matrices. *Linear Algebra Appl.* **10**: 285.

42 Montanaro, A. (2013). Weak multiplicativity for random quantum channels. *Commun. Math. Phys.* **319**: 535, arXiv:1112.5271v2.

43 Petz, D. (1986). Quasi-entropies for finite quantum systems. *Reports Math. Phys.* **23**: 57.

44 Petz, D. (2010). Quasi-entropies for finite quantum systems. *Entropy* **12**: 304.

45 Sharma, N. (2011). Equality conditions for the quantum f-relative entropy and generalized data processing inequalities. *Quantum Inf. Process.* **11**: 137, arXiv:0906.4755.

46 Hiai, F., Mosonyi, M., Petz, D., and Bény, C. (2011). Quantum f-divergences and error correction. *Rev. Math. Phys.* **23**: 691, arXiv:1008.2529v5.

47 Mosonyi, M. and Datta, N. (2009). Generalized relative entropies and the capacity of classical-quantum channels. *J. Math. Phys.* **50**: 072104.

48 Frank, R.L. and Lieb, E.H. (2013). Monotonicity of a relative Rényi entropy. *J. Math. Phys.* **54**: 122201, arXiv:1306.5358.

49 Müller-Lennert, M., Dupuis, F., Szehr, O. et al. (2013). On quantum Rényi entropies: a new generalization and some properties. *J. Math. Phys.* **54**: 122203, arXiv:1306.3142v2.

50 Beigi, S. (2013). Sandwiched Rényi divergence satisfies data processing inequality. *J. Math. Phys.* **54**: 122202, arXiv:1306.5920.

51 Datta, N. and Leditzky, F. (2014). A limit of the quantum Rényi divergence. *J. Phys. A Math. Theor* **47**: 045304, arXiv:1308.5961.

52 E. Farhi, J. Goldstone, and S. Gutmann, A Quantum Approximate Optimization Algorithm, https://arxiv.org/abs/1411.4028v1

53 Halperin, E., Livnat, D., and Zwick, U. (2004). MAX CUT in cubic graphs. *J. Algorithms* **53** (2): 169–185.

54 Harrow, A.W., Hassidim, A., and Lloyd, S. (2009). Quantum algorithm for linear systems of equations. *Phys. Rev. Lett.* **103**: 150502. arXiv:0811.3171v3 [quant-ph].

55 Berry, D.W., Ahokas, G., Cleve, R., and Sanders, B.C. (2007). Efficient quantum algorithms for simulating sparse Hamiltonians. *Comm. Math. Phys.* **270** (2): 359–371. arXiv:quant-ph/0508139.

56 A.M. Childs. On the relationship between continuous- and discrete-time quantum walk, 2008. arXiv:0810.0312.

57 Luis, A. and Peˇrina, J. (Nov 1996). Optimum phase-shift estimation and the quantum description of the phase difference. *Phys. Rev. A* **54** (5): 4564–4570.

58 R. Cleve, A. Ekert, C. Macchiavello, and M. Mosca. Quantum Algorithms Revisited, 1997. arXiv: quant-ph/9708016.

59 Buzek, V., Derka, R., and Massar, S. (1999). Optimal quantum clocks. *Phys. Rev. Lett.* **82**: 2207–2210. arXiv:quantph/9808042.

60 Luenberger, D.G. (1979). *Introduction to Dynamic Systems: Theory, Models, and Applications*. New York: Wiley.

61 Buhrman, H., Cleve, R., Watrous, J., and de Wolf, R. (2001). Quantum fingerprinting. *Phys. Rev. Lett.* **87** (16): 167902–167902. 1.

62 P. Valiant. Testing symmetric properties of distributions. In Proceedings of the 40th Annual ACM Symposium on Theory of computing (STOC), pages 383–392. ACM Press New York, NY, USA, 2008

63 Sarah K. Leyton and Tobias J. Osborne. A quantum algorithm to solve nonlinear differential equations, 2008. arXiv:0812.4423.

64 A.W. Harrow, A. Hassidim, and S. Lloyd. Quantum algorithm for solving linear systems of equations, 2008. arXiv:0811.3171.

65 L. Grover and T. Rudolph. Creating superpositions that correspond to efficiently integrable probability distributions. arXiv:quant-ph/0208112

66 G. Brassard, P. Høyer, M. Mosca, and A. Tapp. Quantum Amplitude Amplification and Estimation, volume 305 of Contemporary Mathematics Series Millenium Volume. AMS, New York, 2002. arXiv: quant-ph/0005055.

67 Hansen, P.C. (1998). *Rank-Deficient and Discrete Ill-Posed Problems: Numerical Aspects of Linear Inversion*. Philadelphia, PA: SIAM.

68 S. Dutta et al, Demonstration of a Quantum Circuit Design Methodology for Multiple Regression, arXiv:1811.01726v2 [quant-ph] 17 Nov 2018

69 Cao, Y., Daskin, A., Frankel, S.H. et al. (10 Aug 2013). Quantum circuits for solving linear systems of equations. *Mol. Phys.* **110**: 1675 (2012, arXiv:1110.2232v3 [quant-ph].

70 Nielsen, M.A. and Chuang, I.L. (2011). *Quantum Computation and Quantum Information: 10th Anniversary Edition*, 10e. New York: Cambridge University Press.

71 D. Dervovic, M. Herbster, P. Mountney, S. Severini, N. Usher, and L. Wossnig, Quantum linear systems algorithms: a primer arXiv e-prints (2018), arXiv:1802.08227 [quant-ph].

72 Buhlmann, P.B. and Van De Geer, S. (2011). *Statistics for High-Dimensional Data: Methods Theory and Applications*. Springer Science & Business Media.

73 Friedman, J., Hastie, T., and Tibshirani, R. (2001). *The Elements of Statistical Learning*, Springer Series in Statistics, vol. **1**. New York, NY, USA.

74 Arnold, V.I. (1992). *Ordinary Differential Equations, Springer Textbook.* Berlin: Springer-Verlag. MR 1162307 (93b,34001).

75 S.K. Leyton And T. J. Osborne, A Quantum Algorithm to Solve Nonlinear Differential Equations, https://arxiv.org/abs/0812.4423v1

76 Lov Grover and Terry Rudolph, Creating superpositions that correspond to efficiently integrable probability distributions, 2002; quant-ph/0208112.

77 Peres, A. (1993). *Quantum Theory: Concepts and Methods.* Dordrecht: Kluwer Academic Publishers Group. MR 95e:81001.

78 Berry, D.W., Ahokas, G., Cleve, R., and Barry, C. (2007). Sanders, efficient quantum algorithms for simulating sparse Hamiltonians. *Comm. Math. Phys.* **270** (2): 359–371; quant-ph/0508139. MR 2276450 (2007k,81028).

79 Horn, R.A. and Johnson, C.R. *Matrix Analysis.* Cambridge: Cambridge University Press, 1990. MR 91i:15001.

80 Andrew M. Childs, Enrico Deotto, Edward Farhi, Jeffrey Goldstone, Sam Gutmann, and Andrew J. Landahl, Quantum search by measurement, 66 (2002), no. 3, 032314; quantph/0204013.

81 Demko, S., Moss, W.F., and Smith, P.W. (1984). Decay rates for inverses of band matrices. *Math. Comp.* **43** (168): 491–499. MR 758197 (85m:15002).

82 Benzi, M. and Golub, G.H. (1999). Bounds for the entries of matrix functions with applications to preconditioning. *BIT* **39** (3): 417–438. MR 1708693 (2000h:65047).

83 Press, W.H., Teukolsky, S.A., Vetterling, W.T., and Flannery, B.P. (2007). *Numerical Recipes*, 3e. Cambridge: Cambridge University Press. MR 2371990.

84 Iserles, A. (1996). *A First Course in the Numerical Analysis of Differential Equations*, Cambridge Texts in Applied Mathematics. Cambridge: Cambridge University Press. MR 1384977 (97m:65003).

14

Quantum Decision Theory

In the conclusion of Part II, we discussed potential enablers for quantum communications (Qc) and possible applications of quantum computing (QC) in advanced wireless networks. We will start with a brief review of these possibilities and then revisit some of the most interesting solutions in more details in the form of design examples. This format is part of our effort to take the structure of textbooks to the next level; instead of having a set of problems for the exercises at the end of some of the chapters, we provide whenever possible throughout the book design examples, which require comprehensive engagement on the part of the students, most often a group of students. In our opinion, teamwork will be more prevalent form of the work at the beginning of their professional careers. This approach has attracted a lot of attention of the students at University of Massachusetts, here in Amherst.

14.1 Potential Enablers for Qc

A1. Quantum entanglement (Qe): One of the problems in Qc is the effective transmission of information over a noisy quantum channel, and there are several attempts in the literature to characterize the achievable rate of transmitting classical and quantum information over a noisy quantum channel. We have discussed this topic in Chapters 9 and 10, and here in addition we provide a review of the main contributions in the literature. For example, the achievable rate for the transmission of classical information over a noisy quantum channel is given by the Holevo–Schumacher–Westmorel (HSW) coding theorem [1], which generalizes Shannon's theorem in quantum settings. Also, regarding the transmission of quantum data over a quantum channel, the achievable rate is given by the Lloyd–Shor–Devetak (LSD) coding theorem [2, 3]. Subsequently, the article [4] investigated the case where both the classical and quantum information can be simultaneously transmitted over a quantum channel by employing a time-sharing strategy. Authors in [5] investigated the trade-offs for channel-coding both quantum and classical information over a noiseless entanglement-assisted quantum channel and proved that the proposed entanglement-assisted classical and quantum capacity theorem provides the achievable rates in the considered scenario. In addition to quantum-entanglement-based communication [5, 6], there are recent attempts in developing quantum-entanglement-assisted quantum turbo codes [7] and the squashed entanglement of a quantum channel, which is an additive function of a tensor product of any two quantum channels [8].

Artificial Intelligence and Quantum Computing for Advanced Wireless Networks, First Edition.
Savo G. Glisic and Beatriz Lorenzo.
© 2022 John Wiley & Sons Ltd. Published 2022 by John Wiley & Sons Ltd.

A2. Quantum hardware capacity: One of the crucial issues for the application of quantum technology in communications-related applications is the presence of harmful quantum perturbations, whose harmful effects can be mitigated by employing quantum error correction codes (QECCs) (discussed in Chapter 10 and [7]). The performance of QECCs can be enhanced by employing entanglement assistance in the context of a symmetric depolarizing channel [7]. In this regard, authors in [9] have provided a detailed analysis of the capacity of an entanglement-assisted quantum channel while considering realistic quantum devices, and also provided an EXtrinsic Information Transfer (EXIT) chart-based design methodology for the QECCs to enhance their performance in asymmetric quantum channels. With the help of simulation results, it has been demonstrated that the proposed EXIT chart-based techniques are useful tools to analyze and design quantum coding schemes. In the above context, the authors of [10] provided a comprehensive survey on the recent development of quantum-like models that can better represent the various factors involved in the human decision-making process, namely, ambiguity, uncertainty, emotions, and risks. Furthermore, the article [11] developed a quantum decision theory (QDT)-based approach for quantitative predictions in arbitrary scenarios, including ones where utility theory fails. In contrast to the previous quantum-like models, which mainly utilize several fitting parameters for the construction of some models to describe particular effects of a use case, the QDT model proposed in [11] is considered to be a generic theory applicable to any type of decision making, and its mathematical structure is common to both decision theory and quantum measurements. The proposed QDT model is based on the generalization of the von Neumann theory [11] of quantum measurements to the nonconclusive measurements and composite events comprising noncommutative operators.

A3. Quantum key distribution: The crucial problem in the traditional Vernam one-time pad cryptosystem is to deliver a secret key to two legitimate parties. This issue can be addressed by quantum key distribution (QKD), also called quantum cryptography, which provides a secret key to two legitimate parties in a Vernam one-time pad cryptosystem [12]. In this QKD approach, a quantum mechanism provides the unconditional guarantee of the security of the key. There are several QKD protocols available in the literature, namely, BB84, E91, B92, and BBM92, of which BB84 is the most popular and widely used QKD scheme. The QKD can be used to enhance security in various networks including optical networks, terrestrial wireless networks, and satellite networks. Recently, authors in [13] investigated the application of QKD in a satellite communication system to perform secure Qc between ground stations and the satellite. The performance of QKD in satellite networks gets degraded in the presence of high attenuation due to noise and atmospheric effects. To address this problem, suitable quantum error correction methods can be employed. Furthermore, the article [14] analyzed the feasibility of trust-free long-haul QKD in future Qc networks by combining measurement-device-independent QKD and a quantum repeater, which is considered as one of the key ingredients of trust-free networks.

Quantum Decision Theory QDT: The classical decision-making process is mostly based on expected utility theory, and its performance significantly degrades in scenarios involving risk and uncertainty [11]. In most of the classical decision-making process, the possibility of making correct predictions can be strongly affected by the nature of the surrounding environment, such as the unknown stochastic or varying environment. Furthermore, in scenarios with incomplete or partially reliable information or incomplete preference relations, any prediction is likely to be just partial and qualitative. To address this, QDT seems to be a promising approach and has been already investigated in some of the existing literature [10, 11]. Also, the process of representing all the steps of a decision process mathematically in order to allow quantitative prediction is significantly important not only for decision theory but also for developing artificial quantum intelligence, which can work only for the operations defined in mathematical terms [15].

A4. Quantum game theory (QGT): With the recent advances in quantum information and quantum computation, there has been a trend of formulating classical game theory using quantum probability amplitudes for analyzing the impact of quantum superposition, entanglement and interference on the agents' optimal strategies [16]. The QGT in general replaces the classical probabilities of game theory by quantum amplitudes by creating the possibility of new effects arising from entanglement or superposition. The main difference between the classical game and the quantum game is that classical games perform calculations in the probability space, whereas quantum games operate in Hilbert space. Quantum game-theoretic techniques can be utilized in investigating suitable solutions in Qc [17] and quantum information processing [18]. In this regard, the article in [16] provides an introduction to quantum theory along with some related works and discusses some well-known quantum games, including quantum penny flip, Eisert's quantum prisoners' dilemma and quantum Parrondo's games. Furthermore, the recent article in [19] analyzed the existing works on quantum games from three perspectives: co-authorship, co-occurrence, and co-citation, and also reviewed main quantum game models and applications.

A5. Quantum-proof randomness extractors (QPREs): For several applications in computation, information theory, and cryptography, randomness is a fundamental aspect, and the objective of randomness extraction is to transform the sources of correlated and biased bits into nearly uniform bits [20]. The extractors that can work in the presence of quantum side information are quantum proof; also, the extractors with one bit output are regarded as the quantum proof [21]. QPRE can be considered as an important building block for implementing classical and quantum cryptography in security applications [22]. The randomness extractors setting of this block provides a nice framework to study the capabilities and limitations of a quantum memory over the classical one. The study of the behavior of randomness extractors in scenarios with quantum adversaries can be based on the theory of operator spaces, which is also known as quantized functional analysis. The extractors in general approximately map a weakly random system into uniform random bits by utilizing perfectly random bits called the seed. There exists one interesting generalization of extractors, called condensers, which are considered to be an intermediate step toward building the extractors [23].

B. QC-assisted communications

B1. Quantum-assisted multi-user detection (QMUD): The practical implementation of classical optimal classical detectors such as maximum likelihood (ML) MUD is often limited by their very high implementation complexity. To address this, one of the promising approaches could be QMUD [24]. With the recent advances in quantum cryptography and quantum error correction, there have been substantial research efforts investigating the feasibility of QMUDs. In this regard, the article in [24] presents a comprehensive review and tutorial on quantum search algorithms and their applications. Furthermore, an ML QMUD was proposed by considering legitimate combinations of the users' transmitted symbols at the receiver, and it was shown that the performance of the proposed ML QMUD matches that of the classical QMUD.

B2. Quantum-aided multi-user transmission: In addition, the quantum search algorithm (QSA) can be utilized to reduce the complexity of vector perturbation precoding and enhance the performance of multi-user transmission in wireless networks. In this regard, authors of [25] proposed quantum-assisted particle swarm optimization (PSO) algorithms in both discrete and continuous modes with the objective of performing vector perturbation precoding and reducing the transmission power at the base station (BS) for rank-deficient multi-user systems while minimizing the average bit error rate (BER) for mobile users. Numerical results show that quantum-assisted precoding provides better BER performance as compared to the conventional PSO algorithm, while maintaining the same computational complexity. Also, the superiority of the quantum-assisted precoder over the classical precoder has been illustrated in scenarios with limited feedback of channel state information (CSI) from users to the BS. In this regard, low-complexity soft-output quantum-assisted MUD has been investigated in various settings by considering different multiple-access schemes including space division multiple access (SDMA), orthogonal frequency division multiple access (OFDMA), code division multiple access (CDMA), and interleave-division multiple access (IDMA) [26–28]. In a rank-deficient multiple-access system in which the number of users is higher than the number of receive antenna elements at the BS, low-complexity heuristic MUD does not provide the desired performance. Furthermore, the complexity of optimal maximum a posteriori probability (MAP) MUD increases exponentially with the number of users and the number of bits per transmit symbol. To address this, the authors of [28] employed quantum-search-assisted MUD to reduce the search space, and with this soft-input soft-output MUD approach, only a fixed subset of the best multi-level symbols having a near-optimal cost function needs to be evaluated to achieve near-optimal BER performance. Subsequently, the EXIT chart was utilized to design the proposed QMUD assuming the Gaussian distribution of the MUD's output, and the performance was evaluated for multi-carrier interleave-division multiple-access systems. Furthermore, another article [29] exploited the advantages of QMUD in the uplink of a multi-user system by considering the transmission of a video stream from a reference user to the BS. The employed QMUD detects the signals transmitted by all the users instead of considering other users' signals as interference.

B3 Quantum-assisted indoor localization: There is a recent trend of employing mmWave and visible light communications (VLC) technologies in indoor localization applications. One of the main issues with these technologies in practical applications is to achieve the desired localization accuracy. Also, it may not be possible to utilize the triangulation approach due to the limitations in the infrastructure and scenarios [30]. Although a fingerprinting-based localization method could be employed in both the radio frequency (RF)-based and VLC-based applications, the complexity of searching the fingerprinting database can be expensive for the scenarios requiring high accuracy. One of the promising approaches of addressing this complexity reduction issue is to employ a QSA, which aims to find the minimum entry in the unsorted database with N elements by utilizing only the $O(\sqrt{N})$ cost function evaluations (CFEs). In this regard, the authors of [30] showed the possibilities of utilizing QSA to reduce the computational complexity of mmWave-based and VLC-based localization algorithms while achieving the same performance as that of a full search.

B4 Quantum-assisted joint routing and load balancing: One of the crucial challenges in wireless networks involving mobile networking devices such as smartphones and tablets is to optimize the routing of message flow in order to maximize the utilization of bandwidth and power. One of the problems in achieving this is nodes' social selfishness, which makes nodes choose certain paths for optimizing specific utility but without considering the impact on the degradation of the overall network's performance [31]. This may lead to the creation of bottlenecks in the network flow, and to address this issue, the design of socially aware load balancing may be significantly useful, and it is important to consider nodes' user-centric social behavior in addition to the conventional conflicting objectives such as power consumption and path delay [82]. In this context, a multi-objective optimization approach can be utilized based on the socially aware Pareto-optimal routing. However, finding the set of Pareto-optimal solutions involves huge complexity since the problem is usually NP-hard. The recently emerging quantum technologies, including quantum computation [32] and quantum information processing, can significantly reduce the complexity of finding Pareto-optimal solutions by utilizing the concept of quantum parallelism (QP). As compared to hardware parallelism (HP) for complexity reduction (which provides complexity reduction on the order of $O(K)$, K being the number of independent parallel processes), QP can achieve a complexity reduction on the order of $O(\sqrt{N})$, N being the database length. In this regard, authors of [36] employed a multi-objective decomposition quantum optimization algorithm for the joint optimization of routing and load balancing in socially aware networks.

B5. Quantum-assisted channel estimation and detection: The performance enhancement of MIMO-OFDM systems with joint channel estimation and MUD has been depicted in several existing works [33, 34]. In this joint channel estimation and MUD process, QC can play a significant role, due to its inherent parallelism, in reducing the complexity, and for enhancing the estimation as well as detection performance [35]. In this regard, the authors of [35] proposed a quantum-aid repeated weighted boosting algorithm for channel estimation and employed in the uplink of multiple-input multiple-output (MIMO-OFDM) systems along with a MAP MUD and a near-optimal QMUD. The performance of the proposed quantum-based scheme was shown to be superior to that of the conventional repeated weighted boosting algorithm, and also the impacts of channel impulse response prediction filters, Doppler frequency, and the power delay profile of the channels were analyzed.

14.2 Quantum Game Theory (QGT)

Classical game theory has been extensively used in modeling resource allocation in multi-operator wireless networks, especially the multi-operator strategies for acquisition of the spectrum. This section concentrates on simultaneous move quantum games of two players. QGT models the behavior of strategic agents (players) with access to quantum tools for controlling their strategies. The simplest example is to envision a classical (ordinary) two-player two-strategy game G_C given in its normal form (a table of payoff functions; think of the prisoner dilemma) in which players communicate with a referee via a specific quantum protocol, and, motivated by this vision, construct a new game G_Q with greatly enlarged strategy spaces and a properly designed payoff system. The novel elements in this scheme consist of four axes:

1) Instead of the four possible positions confess, confess (CC), confess, deny (CD), deny, confess (DC), and deny, deny (DD), there is an infinitely continuous number of positions represented as different quantum mechanical states.
2) Instead of the two-point strategy space of each player, there is an infinitely continuous number of new strategies (this should not be confused with mixed strategies).
3) The payoff system is entirely different, since it is based on extracting real numbers from a quantum state that is generically a vector of complex numbers.
4) The fourth difference is apparently the most difficult to grasp, since it is a conceptually different structure that is peculiar to quantum mechanics and has no analogue in standard (classical) game theory related to quantum entanglement.

Its significance in game theory requires a nontrivial modification of one's mind and attitude toward game theory and choice of strategies. Although we have discussed the quantum entanglement in Chapter 9, in this section, where the classical game G_C is simple enough, it can be (and will) be explicitly defined. Moreover, it is possible to define a certain continuous real parameter $0 \leq \gamma \leq \pi/2$ such that for $\gamma = 0$ there is no entanglement, while for $\gamma = \pi/2$ entanglement is maximal.

Naturally, a substantial part of this section is devoted to settling of the mathematical and physical grounds for the topic of quantum games, including the definition of the four axes mentioned above, and the way in which a standard (classical) game can be modified to be a quantum game (sometimes this is referred to as *quantization of a classical game*). The connection between game theory and information science is briefly explained as well. Whereas the four positions of the classical game are formulated in terms of *bits*, the myriad positions of the quantum game are formulated in terms of *quantum bits*. Whereas the two strategies of the classical game are represented by a couple of simple 2×2 matrices, the strategies of a player in the quantum game are represented by an infinite number of complex unitary 2×2 matrices with unit determinant. The notion of entanglement is explained and exemplified, and the parameter controlling it is introduced. The quantum game is formally defined, and the notion of pure strategy Nash equilibrium (PSNE) is defined. With these tools, it is possible to investigate some important issues like existence of PSNE and its relationship with the degree of entanglement.

14.2.1 Definitions

Classical games: The standard notion of games as it appears in the literature will be referred to as a classical game, to distinguish it from the notion of a quantum game, which is the subject of this section. Usually, these games will be represented in their normal form (a payoff table). Except for the language used, nothing is new here.

Two-player two-decision games: Consider a two-player game with a pure strategy such as the prisoner's dilemma, which is now described. The formal definition is $\Gamma = \langle N = \{1, 2\}, A_i = \{C, D\}, u_i: A_1 \times A_2 \rightarrow \mathbb{R} \rangle$.

Each player can choose between two strategies C and D for Confess or Don't Confess deny. Let us modify the presentation of the game just a little bit in order to adapt it to the nomenclature of quantum games. When the two prisoners appear before the judge, he tells them that he assumes that they both will confess and lets them decide whether to change their position or leave it at C. This modification does not affect the conduct of the game. The only change is that instead of choosing C or D as strategy, the strategy to be chosen by each player is either to *replace C by D* or *leave C as it is*. Of course, if the judge were to tell the prisoner that he assumes prisoner 1 confesses and prisoner 2 does not, then the strategies will be different, but again, each one's strategy space has the two points {Don't replace, Replace}.

Now let us use notations other than C and D, say 0 and 1, or even better $|0\rangle$ and $|1\rangle$. This *notation* is very useful in analyzing quantum games. In summary, we have

$$\text{bit state } 0 = \begin{pmatrix} 1 \\ 0 \end{pmatrix} = |0\rangle, \text{ bit state } 1 = \begin{pmatrix} 0 \\ 1 \end{pmatrix} = |1\rangle. \tag{14.1}$$

Two-bit states: Looking at the game table, the prisoner's dilemma game table has four squares marked by (C,C), (C,D),(D,C), and (D,D). In our modified language, any square in the game table is called a *two-bit state*, because each player knows what is his bit value in this square. The corresponding four two-bit states are denoted as $(0, 0)$, $(0, 1)$, $(1, 0)$, and $(1, 1)$. In this notation (exactly as in the former notation with C and D), it is understood that the first symbol (from the left) belongs to player 1 and the second belongs to player 2.

Thus, in our language, when the prisoners appear before the judge, he tells them "your two-bit state at the moment is (0,0), and now I ask anyone to decide whether to replace his bit value from 0 to 1 or leave it as it is." Single-bit states have several equivalent notations as specified in Eq. (14.1), and two-bit states also have several different notations. In the vector notation of Eq. (14.1), the four two-bit states listed above are obtained as outer products of the two bits:

$$\begin{pmatrix} 1 \\ 0 \end{pmatrix} \otimes \begin{pmatrix} 1 \\ 0 \end{pmatrix} = \begin{pmatrix} 1 \\ 0 \\ 0 \\ 0 \end{pmatrix}, \quad \begin{pmatrix} 1 \\ 0 \end{pmatrix} \otimes \begin{pmatrix} 0 \\ 1 \end{pmatrix} = \begin{pmatrix} 0 \\ 1 \\ 0 \\ 0 \end{pmatrix},$$

$$\begin{pmatrix} 0 \\ 1 \end{pmatrix} \otimes \begin{pmatrix} 1 \\ 0 \end{pmatrix} = \begin{pmatrix} 0 \\ 0 \\ 1 \\ 0 \end{pmatrix}, \quad \begin{pmatrix} 0 \\ 1 \end{pmatrix} \otimes \begin{pmatrix} 0 \\ 1 \end{pmatrix} = \begin{pmatrix} 0 \\ 0 \\ 0 \\ 1 \end{pmatrix}. \tag{14.2}$$

Again, it is understood that the bit composing the left factor in the outer product belongs to player 1 (the column player) and the right factor in the outer product belongs to player 2 (the row player). Generalization to n-player two-decision games is straightforward. A set of n bits can exist in one of 2^n different configurations and is described by a vector of length 2^n, where only one component is 1, all the others being 0.

Ket notation for two-bit states: The vector notation of Eq. (14.2) requires a great deal of page space, a problem that can be avoided by using the ket notation. In this framework, the four two-bit states are respectively denoted as (see Chapter 8),

$$|0\rangle \otimes |0\rangle = |00\rangle, |0\rangle \otimes |1\rangle = |01\rangle,$$
$$|1\rangle \otimes |0\rangle = |10\rangle, |1\rangle \otimes |1\rangle = |11\rangle. \tag{14.3}$$

For example, in the prisoner's dilemma game, these four states correspond respectively to (C, C), (C, D), (D, C), and (D, D).

Classical strategy as an operation on bits: Now we come to the description of the classical strategies (replace or do not replace) using our information-theoretic language. Since we have agreed to represent bits as two-component vectors, the operation of each player on his own bit (replace or do not replace) is represented by a 2×2 real matrix. In classical information theory, operations on bits are referred to as *gates*. Here, we will restrict ourselves to the two simplest operations performed on bits, changing them from one configuration to another. An operation on a bit state that results in the same bit state is accomplished by the unit 2×2 matrices $\mathbf{1} = \begin{pmatrix} 1 & 0 \\ 0 & 1 \end{pmatrix}$. An operation on a bit state that results in the other bit state is accomplished by a 2×2 matrix denoted as $Y \equiv \begin{pmatrix} 0 & 1 \\ -1 & 0 \end{pmatrix}$

An important notational comment: The -1 in the matrix Y is designed to guarantee that $\det[Y] = 1$, in analogy with the strategies of the quantum game to be defined in the following sections. As far as the classical game is concerned, this sign has no meaning, because a bit state $|0\rangle$ or $|1\rangle$ is not a number; it is just a symbol, so that we can agree that for classical games, the vectors $\begin{pmatrix} 1 \\ 0 \end{pmatrix}$ and $\begin{pmatrix} -1 \\ 0 \end{pmatrix}$ represent the *same* bit, $|0\rangle$, and the vectors $\begin{pmatrix} 0 \\ 1 \end{pmatrix}$ and $\begin{pmatrix} 0 \\ -1 \end{pmatrix}$ represent the *same* bit, $|1\rangle$.

$$\begin{pmatrix} 1 & 0 \\ 0 & 1 \end{pmatrix} \begin{pmatrix} 1 \\ 0 \end{pmatrix} = \begin{pmatrix} 1 \\ 0 \end{pmatrix}, \begin{pmatrix} 1 & 0 \\ 0 & 1 \end{pmatrix} \begin{pmatrix} 0 \\ 1 \end{pmatrix} = \begin{pmatrix} 0 \\ 1 \end{pmatrix},$$

$$\begin{pmatrix} 0 & 1 \\ -1 & 0 \end{pmatrix} \begin{pmatrix} 1 \\ 0 \end{pmatrix} = \begin{pmatrix} 0 \\ -1 \end{pmatrix}, \begin{pmatrix} 0 & 1 \\ -1 & 0 \end{pmatrix} \begin{pmatrix} 0 \\ 1 \end{pmatrix} = \begin{pmatrix} 1 \\ 0 \end{pmatrix} \tag{14.4}$$

Written in ket notation, we have

$$\mathbf{1}|0\rangle = |0\rangle, \mathbf{1}|1\rangle = |1\rangle, Y|0\rangle = |1\rangle, Y|1\rangle = |0\rangle. \tag{14.5}$$

In the present language, the two strategies of each player are the two 2×2 matrices 1 (we will drop bold notation in the sequel) and Y, and the four elements of $A_1 \times A_2$ are the four 4×4 matrices

$$\mathbf{1} \otimes \mathbf{1}, \mathbf{1} \otimes Y, Y \otimes \mathbf{1}, Y \otimes Y. \tag{14.6}$$

In this notation, following the comment after Eq. (14.2), the left factor in the outer product is executed by player 1 (the column player) on his bit, whereas the right factor in the outer product is executed by player 2 (the row player). In matrix notation, each operator listed in Eq. (14.6) acts on a four-component vector as listed in Eq. (14.2).

Design Example 14.1

Consider the classical prisoner's dilemma with the normal form

Prisoner 1

		1 (C)	Y (D)
Prisoner 2	1 (C)	−4,−4	−6,−2
	Y (D)	−2,−6	−5,−5

$$\tag{14.7}$$

The entries stand for the number of years in prison. The formal definition of a classical game in the language of bits is

$$G_C = \langle N = \{1,2\}, \ | \ ij\rangle, A_i = \{1, Y\}, u_i : A_1 \times A_2 \to \mathbb{R}\rangle. \tag{14.8}$$

The two differences between this definition and the standard definition is that the players face an initial two-bit state $|ij\rangle$ $i, j = 0, 1$ presumed by the judge (usually $|00\rangle = (C, C)$), and the two-point strategy space of each players contains the two gates $(1, Y)$ instead of (C, D). Running a pure strategy classical two-player two-strategy simultaneous game given in its normal form (a 2×2 payoff matrix) consists of the following steps [97]:

1) A referee declares that the initial configuration is some fixed two-bit state. This initial state is one of the four two-bit states listed in Eq. (14.3). The referee's choice does not, in any way, affect the final outcome of the game; it just serves as a starting point. For definiteness, assume that the referee suggests the state $|00\rangle$ as the initial state of the game. We already gave an example: In the story of the prisoner's dilemma, it is like the judge telling them that he assumes that they both will confess.

2) In the next step, each player decides upon his strategy (1 or Y) to be applied on his respective bit. For example, if each player choses the strategy Y, we note from Eq. (14.4) that

$$Y \otimes Y|00\rangle = Y|0\rangle \otimes Y|0\rangle = |1\rangle \otimes |1\rangle = |11\rangle = |DD\rangle. \tag{14.9}$$

Thus, a player can choose to either leave his bit as suggested by the referee or to change it to the second possible state. As a result of the two operations, the two-bit state assumes its final form.

Design Example 14.1 (Continued)

3) The referee then "rewards" each players according to the sums appearing in the corresponding payoff matrix. Explicitly:

$$u_1(1,1) = u_2(1,1) = -4, u_1(1,Y) = u_2(Y,1) = -6,$$
$$u_1(Y,1) = u_2(1,Y) = -2, u_1(Y,Y) = u_2(Y,Y) = -4.$$

A PSNE is a pair of strategies $S_1^*, S_2^* \in \{1,Y\}^2$ such that

$$u_1(S_1, S_2^*) \leq u_1(S_1^*, S_2^*) \forall S_1 \neq S_1^*$$
$$u_2(S_1^*, S_2) \leq u_2(S_1^*, S_2^*) \forall S_2 \neq S_2^*.$$
(14.10)

In the present example, it is easy to check that, given the initial state $|00\rangle$ from the referee, the pair of strategies leading to NE is $(S_1^*, S_2^*) = Y \otimes Y$. However, this equilibrium is not *Pareto efficient*; that is, there is a strategy set S_1, S_2 such that $u_i(S_1, S_2) \geq u(S_1^*, S_2^*)$ for $i = 1, 2$. In the present example, the strategy set $I \otimes I$ leaves the system in the state $|00\rangle$ and $u_i(1,1) = -4 > u_i(Y,Y) = -5$.

Mixed strategy: This technique of operation on bits is naturally extended to treat mixed strategy games. Then, by operating on the bit state $\begin{pmatrix} 1 \\ 0 \end{pmatrix}$ by the matrix $p\mathbf{1} + (1-p)Y$ with $p \in [0, 1]$, we get the vector

$$\left[p \begin{pmatrix} 1 & 0 \\ 0 & 1 \end{pmatrix} + (1-p) \begin{pmatrix} 0 & 1 \\ 1 & 0 \end{pmatrix} \right] \begin{pmatrix} 1 \\ 0 \end{pmatrix} = \begin{pmatrix} p \\ 1-p \end{pmatrix},$$
(14.11)

which can be interpreted as a mixed strategy of choosing pure strategy $|1\rangle$ with probability p and pure strategy $|0\rangle$ with probability $1 - p$. Following our example, assuming player 1 choses 1 with probability p and Y with probability $1 - p$ and player 2 choses 1 with probability q and Y with probability $1 - q$, the combined operation on the initial state $|00\rangle$ is

$$[p\mathbf{1} + (1-p)Y] \otimes [q\mathbf{1} + (1-q)Y]|00\rangle = pq|00\rangle + p(1-q)|01\rangle + (1-p)q|10\rangle + (1-p)(1-q)|11\rangle.$$

Operations on a single qubit – quantum strategies: In Eqs. (14.5) and (14.6), we defined two classical strategies, $\mathbf{1}$ and Y, as operations on bits. According to Eq. (14.4), they are realized by 2×2 matrices $\mathbf{1} = \begin{pmatrix} 1 & 0 \\ 0 & 1 \end{pmatrix}$, $Y = \begin{pmatrix} 0 & 1 \\ -1 & 0 \end{pmatrix}$ and act on the bit vectors $|0\rangle = \begin{pmatrix} 1 \\ 0 \end{pmatrix}$ and $|1\rangle = \begin{pmatrix} 0 \\ 1 \end{pmatrix}$. In this subsection, we develop the quantum analogues: We are interested in operations on qubits (also referred to as single qubit quantum gates) that transform a qubit $|\psi\rangle = a|0\rangle + b|1\rangle$ into another qubit $a'|0\rangle + b'|1\rangle$.

There are some restrictions on the allowed operations on qubits. First, a qubit is a vector in two-dimensional Hilbert space, and therefore operations on a single qubit must be realized by complex 2×2 matrices. Second, we have seen (Chapter 8) that a qubit is a point on the Bloch sphere, and therefore the new qubit must have the same unit length (the radius of the Bloch sphere). In other words, the unit length of a qubit must be conserved under any operation. From what we learned in Chapter 8, this means that any allowed operation on a qubit is defined by a *unitary 2×2 matrix U*.

In the above notation a unitary operation on a qubit represented as a two-component vector $\begin{pmatrix} a \\ b \end{pmatrix}$ is defined as

$$U \begin{pmatrix} a \\ b \end{pmatrix} = \begin{pmatrix} U_{11}a + U_{12}b \\ U_{21}a + U_{22}b \end{pmatrix} \equiv \begin{pmatrix} a' \\ b' \end{pmatrix}, |a|^2 + |b|^2 = |a'|^2 + |b'|^2 = 1. \tag{14.12}$$

For reasons that will become clear later on, we will restrict ourselves to unitary transformations U with unit determinant, $\text{Det}[U] = 1$. The collection of all 2×2 unitary matrices with unit determinant forms a group under the usual rule of matrix multiplication. This is the Special Unitary $SU(2)$ group [98], which plays a central role in physics as well as in abstract group theory. The most general form of a matrix $U \in SU(2)$ is

$$U(\varphi, \alpha, \theta) = \begin{pmatrix} e^{i\varphi} \cos \dfrac{\theta}{2} & e^{i\alpha} \sin \dfrac{\theta}{2} \\ -e^{-i\alpha} \sin \dfrac{\theta}{2} & e^{-i\varphi} \cos \dfrac{\theta}{2} \end{pmatrix} \tag{14.13}$$

$$0 \le \varphi, \alpha \le 2\pi, 0 \le \theta \le \pi$$

Thus, in quantum games, the (infinite number of) quantum strategies of each player i = 1, 2 is the infinite set of his 2 × 2 matrices U(φ_i, α_i, θ_i) as defined in Eq. (14.13). The infinite collection of these matrices form the group SU(2) of unitary 2 × 2 matrices with unit determinant. Since the functional form of the matrix U(φ, α, θ) is given by Eq. (14.13), the strategy of player i is determined by his choice of the three angles γ_i = (φ_i, α_i, θ_i). Here, γ_i is just a short notation for the three angles. The three angles φ, α, and θ are referred to as Euler angles.

Although we have not yet defined the notion of a quantum game, we assert that, in analogy with Eq. (14.6) (which defines a player's classical strategies as operations on bits), the operation on qubits (such that each player acts with his 2×2 matrix on his qubit) is an implementation of each player's quantum strategy. The quantum strategy specified by the 2×2 matrix $U(\varphi, \alpha, \theta)$ as specified above has a geometrical interpretation. This is similar to the geometrical interpretation given to qubit as a point on the Bloch sphere, where the two angles (φ, θ) determine a point on the boundary of a sphere of unit radius in *three dimensions*. Such a (Bloch) sphere is a two-dimensional surface denoted by S^2. On the other hand, the three angles φ, α, and θ defining a quantum strategy determine a point on the surface of the unit sphere in *four-dimensional* space, $\mathbb{R}^4$ (the four-dimensional Euclidean space). The unit sphere is in this space is defined as the collection of points with Cartesian coordinates (x, y, z, w) restricted by the equation $x^2 + y^2 + z^2 + w^2 = 1$. This equality defines the surface of a three-dimensional sphere denoted by S^3 (this is impossible to represent by a figure). The equality is satisfied by writing the four Cartesian coordinates as

$$x = \sin \theta \sin \varphi \cos \alpha, y = \sin \theta \sin \varphi \sin \alpha, z = \sin \theta \cos \varphi, w = \cos \theta. \tag{14.14}$$

An alternative definition of a player's strategy is therefore as follows:

A strategy of player i in a quantum analog of a two-player two-strategy classical game is a point γ_i = (φ_i, α_i, θ_i) $\in$ S^3

Thus, instead of a single number 0 or 1 as a strategy of the classical game, the set of quantum strategies has a cardinality $\mathcal{N}^3$.

Classical strategies as special cases of quantum strategies: A desirable property from a quantum game is that the players can also reach their classical strategies. Of course, the interesting thing is that reaching classical strategies does not lead to Nash equilibrium, but the payoff awarded to players in a quantum game who use their classical strategies serves as a useful reference point. Therefore, we ask the question whether, by an appropriate choice of the three angles (φ, α, θ), the quantum strategy $U(\varphi, \alpha, \theta)$ is reduced to one of the two classical strategies 1 or Y. First, it is trivially seen that $U(0, 0, 0) = \mathbf{1}$. It is now clear why we have chosen the classical strategy that flips the state of a bit as $Y = \begin{pmatrix} 0 & 1 \\ -1 & 0 \end{pmatrix}$, and not as $\sigma_x = \begin{pmatrix} 0 & 1 \\ 1 & 0 \end{pmatrix}$, because Det $[U(\varphi, \alpha, \theta)] = \mathbf{1} \forall \varphi, \alpha,$ θ whereas Det $[\sigma_x] = -1$. On the other hand, we note that $(0, 0, \pi) = \begin{pmatrix} 0 & 1 \\ -1 & 0 \end{pmatrix} = Y$. The quantum game procedure to be described in the next section is such that the difference between σ_x and Y does not affects the payoff at all, and therefore we may conclude that the classical strategies are indeed obtained as special cases of the quantum strategies,

$$U(0, 0, 0) = \mathbf{1} = \begin{pmatrix} 1 & 0 \\ 0 & 1 \end{pmatrix}, \quad U(0, 0, \pi) = Y = \begin{pmatrix} 0 & 1 \\ -1 & 0 \end{pmatrix}. \tag{14.15}$$

Two-qubit states: In Eqs. (14.2) and (14.3), we represented two-bit states as tensor products of two one-bit states. Equivalently, a two-bit state is represented by a four-dimensional vector, three of whose components are 0 and one component is 1; see Eq. (14.2). Since each bit can be found in one of two states $|0\rangle$ or $|1\rangle$, there are exactly four two-bit states. With two-qubit states, the situation is dramatically different in two respects. First, as noted earlier, each qubit $a \,|\, 0\rangle + b \,|\, 1\rangle$ with $|a|^2 + |b|^2 = 1$ can be found in an infinite number of states. This is easily understood by noting that each qubit is a point on the two-dimensional (Bloch) sphere. Accordingly, once we construct two-qubit states by tensor products of two one-qubit states, we expect a two-qubit state to be represented by a four-dimensional vector of complex numbers. Second, and much more profoundly, there are four-dimensional vectors that are *not* represented as a tensor product of two two-dimensional vectors. That is, in contrast to the classical two-bit states, there are two-qubit states that are not represented as a tensor product of two one-qubit states. This is referred to as *entanglement* (see Chapter 8). In a two-player two-strategy classical game, each player has its own bit upon which he can operate (that is, choose his strategy). Below we shall define a quantum game that is based on a two-player two-strategy classical game. In such game, each player has its own qubit upon which he can operate by an $SU(2)$ matrix $U(\varphi, \alpha, \theta)$ (that is, choose his quantum strategy).

Outer (tensor) product of two qubits: In analogy with Eq. (14.2), which defines the four two-bit states, we define an outer (or tensor) product of two qubits $| \psi_1 \rangle \otimes | \psi_2 \rangle \in \mathcal{H}_2 \otimes \mathcal{H}_2$ using the notation for q-bits as follows: Let $|\psi_1\rangle = a_1 \,|\, 0\rangle + b_1 \,|\, 1\rangle$ and $|\psi_2\rangle = a_2 \,|\, 0\rangle + b_2 \,|\, 1\rangle$ be two qubits numbered 1 and 2. We define their outer (or tensor) product as (see Chapter 8)

$$| \psi_1 \rangle \otimes | \psi_2 \rangle = (a_1 \,|\, 0\rangle + b_1 \,|\, 1\rangle) \otimes (a_2 \,|\, 0\rangle + b_2 \,|\, 1\rangle)$$
$$= a_1 a_2 |0\rangle \otimes |0\rangle + a_1 b_2 |0\rangle \otimes |1\rangle + b_1 a_2 \,|\, 1\rangle \otimes \,|\, 0\rangle + b_1 b_2 \,|\, 1\rangle \otimes \,|\, 1\rangle \in \mathcal{H}_2 \otimes \mathcal{H}_2. \tag{14.16}$$

In terms of four-component vectors, the tensor products of the elements such as $|0\rangle \otimes |0\rangle$ are the same as the two-bit states defined in Eq. (14.2), and therefore in this notation we have

$$|\psi_1\rangle \otimes |\psi_2\rangle = a_1 a_2 \begin{pmatrix} 1 \\ 0 \\ 0 \\ 0 \end{pmatrix} + a_1 b_2 \begin{pmatrix} 0 \\ 1 \\ 0 \\ 0 \end{pmatrix} + b_1 a_2 \begin{pmatrix} 0 \\ 0 \\ 1 \\ 0 \end{pmatrix} + b_1 a_2 \begin{pmatrix} 0 \\ 0 \\ 0 \\ 1 \end{pmatrix} = \begin{pmatrix} a_1 a_2 \\ a_1 b_2 \\ b_1 a_2 \\ b_1 a_2 \end{pmatrix} \tag{14.17}$$

A tensor product of two qubits as defined above is an example of a two-qubit state, briefly referred to as *2qubits*. The coefficients of the four products in Eq. (14.16) (or, equivalently, the four vectors in Eq. (14.17)) are complex numbers referred to as *amplitudes*. Thus, we say that the amplitude of $|0\rangle \otimes |0\rangle$ in the 2qubits $|\psi_1\rangle \otimes |\psi_2\rangle$ is $a_1 a_2$, and so on. Using simple trigonometric identities, it is easily verified that the sum of the squares of the coefficients is 1:

$$|a_1 a_2|^2 + |a_1 b_2|^2 + |b_1 a_2|^2 + |b_1 b_2|^2 = 1. \tag{14.18}$$

We have seen in Eq. (14.17) that a tensor product of two qubits is a 2qubits that is written as a linear combination of the four basic 2qubits states:

$$|0\rangle \otimes |0\rangle \equiv |00\rangle, \ |0\rangle \otimes |1\rangle \equiv |01\rangle, \ |1\rangle \otimes |0\rangle \equiv |10\rangle, \ |1\rangle \otimes |1\rangle \equiv |11\rangle \tag{14.19}$$

From the theory of Hilbert spaces, we know the 2qubits defined in Eq. (14.19) form a basis in $\mathcal{H}_4$. This brings us to the following definition: A general 2qubits $|\Psi\rangle \in \mathcal{H}_4$ has the form

$$\begin{aligned} |\Psi\rangle &= a\,|0\rangle \otimes |0\rangle + b\,|0\rangle \otimes |1\rangle + c\,|1\rangle \otimes |0\rangle + d\,|1\rangle \otimes |1\rangle \\ &= a\,|00\rangle + b\,|01\rangle + c\,|10\rangle + d\,|11\rangle \ \text{with} \ |a|^2 + |b|^2 + |c|^2 + |d|^2 = 1. \end{aligned} \tag{14.20}$$

Note the difference between this expression and the outer product of two qubits as defined in Eq. (14.16), in which the coefficients are certain products of the coefficients of the qubit factors. In the expression, namely, Eq. (14.20), the coefficients are arbitrary as long as they satisfy the normalization condition. Therefore, Eq. (14.16) is a special case of Eq. (14.20), but not vice versa. This observation leads us naturally to the next topic: entanglement.

Entanglement is one of the most fundamental concepts in quantum information and in QGT. We have discussed it already in Chapter 8, and here we introduce some additional details by asking the following question: Let

$$\begin{aligned} |\Psi\rangle &= a\,|00\rangle + b\,|01\rangle + c\,|10\rangle + d\,|11\rangle, \\ &\text{with} \ |a|^2 + |b|^2 + |c|^2 + |d|^2 = 1, \end{aligned} \tag{14.21}$$

as already defined in Eq. (14.20) denote a general 2qubits. Is it always possible to represent it as a tensor product of two single-qubit states as in Eq. (14.16) or Eq. (14.17)? As we know from Chapter 8, the answer is no. A few counterexamples with two out of the four coefficients set equal to 0 are

$$|T\rangle \equiv \frac{1}{\sqrt{2}}(|01\rangle + |10\rangle), |S\rangle \equiv \frac{1}{\sqrt{2}}(|01\rangle - |10\rangle), |\psi_{\pm}\rangle \equiv \frac{1}{\sqrt{2}}(|00\rangle \pm i|11\rangle). \tag{14.22}$$

where the notations T = triplet and S = singlet are borrowed from physics. These four 2qubits are referred to as *maximally entangled Bell states*. We now have a definition:

A 2qubits $|\Psi\rangle$ as defined in Eq. (14.21) is said to be entangled iff it cannot be represented as a tensor product of two single-qubit states as in Eq. (14.16) or Eq. (14.17).

Entanglement is a pure quantum mechanical effect that appears in manipulating 2qubits. It does not occur in manipulations of bits. There are only four 2bit states as defined in Eq. (14.2), and all of them are obtained as tensor products of single-bit states, so that by definition they are not entangled. The concept of entanglement is of vital importance in many aspects of quantum mechanics. It led to a very long debate initiated by a paper written in 1935 by Albert Einstein, Boris Podolsky, and Nathan Rosen, referred to as the EPR paradox, which questioned the completeness of quantum mechanics. The answer to this paradox was given by John Bell in 1964. Entanglement plays a central role in quantum information, as discussed in Chapter 8. Here, we will see that it also plays a central role in QGT. Strictly speaking, without entanglement, QGT reduces to classical game theory.

Operations on 2qubits (2qubits gates): An important tool in manipulating 2qubits is operations transforming one 2qubits to another. Borrowing from the theory of quantum information, these are called two-qubit gates (see Chapter 8). Writing a general 2qubits as defined in Eq. (14.21) in terms of its four vector of coefficients,

$$|\Psi\rangle = a|00\rangle + b|01\rangle + c|10\rangle + d|11\rangle = \begin{pmatrix} a \\ b \\ c \\ d \end{pmatrix}, \tag{14.23}$$

a 2qubits gate is a unitary 4×4 matrix (with unit determinant) acting on the four vectors of coefficients, in analogy with Eq. (14.12),

$$\mathcal{U}\begin{pmatrix} a \\ b \\ c \\ d \end{pmatrix} = \begin{pmatrix} a' \\ b' \\ c' \\ d' \end{pmatrix}, \mathcal{U} \in SU(4), \tag{14.24}$$

$$a|^2 + |b|^2 + |c|^2 + |d|^2 = |a'|^2 + |b'|^2 + |c'|^2 + |d'|^2 = 1.$$

2qubits gates defined as outer product of two 1qubit gates: Let us recall that the two-player strategies in a classical game are defined as the outer product of each single-player strategy (1 or Y), defined in Eq. (14.6), that operates on two-bit states as exemplified in Eq. (14.9). Let us also recall that each player in a *quantum game* has a strategy $U(\varphi_i, \alpha_i, \theta_i)$ that is a 2×2 matrix as defined in Eq. (14.13). Therefore, we anticipate that the two-player strategies in a *quantum game* are defined as outer product of the two single-player strategies. Thus, a two-qubit gate of special importance is the outer product operation $\mathcal{U} = U_1 \otimes U_2$ where each player acts on his own qubit. Explicitly, the operation of $\mathcal{U} = U_1 \otimes U_2$ on $|\Psi\rangle$ given in Eq. (14.23) is

$$\mathcal{U}|\Psi\rangle = a[U_1|0\rangle] \otimes [U_2|0\rangle] + b[U_1|0\rangle] \otimes [U_2|1\rangle] \\ + c[U_1 \mid 1\rangle] \otimes [U_2 \mid 0\rangle] + d[U_1 \mid 1\rangle] \otimes [U_2 \mid 1\rangle]. \tag{14.25}$$

Again, before defining the notion of a quantum game, we assert that this operation defines the set of combined quantum strategies in analogy with the classical game set of combined strategies defined in Eq. (14.6). Thus, the (infinite numbers of) elements in the set $A_1 \times A_2$ of combined (quantum) strategies are 4×4 matrices, $U(\varphi_1, \alpha_1, \theta_1) \otimes U(\varphi_2, \alpha_2, \theta_2)$. These 4×4 matrices act on two-qubit states as defined above in Eq. (14.23). The single-qubit operations are defined in Eq. (14.12).

Just as we required the matrices U operating on a single-qubit state to have a unit determinant, that is $U \in SU(2)$, we require $\mathcal{U}$ also to have a unit determinant, that is, $\mathcal{U} \in SU(4)$, the group of 4×4 unitary complex matrices with unit determinant.

Entanglement operators (entanglers): We have already underlined the crucial importance of the concept of entanglement in quantum games. Therefore, of crucial importance for quantum game is an operation executed by an entanglement operator J that acts on a non-entangled 2qubits and turns it into an entangled 2qubits. Anticipating the importance and relevance of Bell's states introduced in Eq. (14.22) for quantum games, we search entanglement operators J that operate on the non-entangled state $|0\rangle \otimes |0\rangle = |00\rangle$ and create maximally entangled Bell states such as $|\psi_+\rangle$ or $|T\rangle$

as defined in [36]. For reason that will become clear later, we should require that J is unitary; that is, $J^\dagger J = J J^\dagger = \mathbf{1}_4$. With a little effort, we find

$$
J_1|00\rangle = \frac{1}{\sqrt{2}} \begin{pmatrix} 1 & 0 & 0 & i \\ 0 & 1 & -i & 0 \\ 0 & -i & 1 & 0 \\ i & 0 & 0 & 1 \end{pmatrix} \begin{pmatrix} 1 \\ 0 \\ 0 \\ 0 \end{pmatrix} = \frac{1}{\sqrt{2}} \begin{pmatrix} 1 \\ 0 \\ 0 \\ i \end{pmatrix} = \frac{1}{\sqrt{2}}(|00\rangle + i|11\rangle) = |\psi_+\rangle
$$

(14.26)

$$
J_2|00\rangle = \frac{1}{\sqrt{2}} \begin{pmatrix} 0 & 1 & 1 & 0 \\ 1 & 0 & 0 & 0 \\ 1 & 0 & 1 & 0 \\ 0 & 0 & 0 & 1 \end{pmatrix} \begin{pmatrix} 1 \\ 0 \\ 0 \\ 0 \end{pmatrix} = \frac{1}{\sqrt{2}} \begin{pmatrix} 0 \\ 1 \\ 1 \\ 0 \end{pmatrix} = \frac{1}{\sqrt{2}}(|01\rangle + |10\rangle) = |T\rangle \quad (14.27)
$$

It is straightforward to check that J_1 and J_2 as defined above are unitary and that the application of $J_1^\dagger$ instead of J_1 on the initial state $|00\rangle$ in Eq. (14.26) yields the second Bell's state $|\psi_-\rangle$ also defined in Eq. (14.22), while $J_2^\dagger | 00\rangle = | S\rangle$. There are, however, some subtle differences between J_1 and J_2 that will surface later on.

Partial entanglement operators: Intuitively, the Bell's states defined in Eq. (14.22) are *maximally entangled* because the two coefficients before the two-bit states (say, $|00\rangle$ and $|11\rangle$) have the same absolute value, $1/\sqrt{2}$. We may think of an entangled state where the weights of the two two-bit states are unequal; in that case, we speak of a *partially entangled state*. Thus, instead of the maximally entangled Bell states $|\psi_+\rangle$ and $|T\rangle$ defined in Eqs. (14.22), (14.26), and (14.27), we may consider the partially entangled states $|\psi_+(\gamma)\rangle$ and $|T(\gamma)\rangle$ that depend on a continuous parameter (an angle) $0 \leq \gamma \leq \pi$ defined as

$$
|\psi_+(\gamma)\rangle = \cos\frac{\gamma}{2}|00\rangle + \sin\frac{\gamma}{2}|11\rangle,
$$

$$
|\psi_+(0)\rangle = |00\rangle, \; |\psi_+(\pi)\rangle = |11\rangle, \; |\psi_+\left(\frac{\pi}{2}\right)\rangle = |\psi_+\rangle.
$$

(14.28)

$$
|T(\gamma)\rangle = \cos\frac{\gamma}{2}|01\rangle + \sin\frac{\gamma}{2}|10\rangle,
$$

$$
|T(0)\rangle = |01\rangle, \; |T(\pi)\rangle = |10\rangle, \; |T\left(\frac{\pi}{2}\right)\rangle = |T\rangle.
$$

(14.29)

The notion of partial entanglement can be put on a more rigorous basis once we have a tool to determine the degree of entanglement. Such a tool – called *Entanglement Entropy* – does exist, but it will not be detailed here. The reason for introducing partial entanglement is that it is intimately related to the existence (or the absence) of PSNE in quantum games, as will be demonstrated below. In the same way that we designed the entanglement operators J_1 and J_2 that upon acting on the two-bit state $|00\rangle$ yield the maximally entangled Bell's states $|\psi_+\rangle$ and $|T\rangle$, we need to design analogous partial entanglement operators $J_1(\gamma)$ and $J_2(\gamma)$ that upon acting on the two-bit state $|00\rangle$ yield the partilly entangled states $|\psi_+(\gamma)\rangle$ and $|T(\gamma)\rangle$. With a little effort, we find

$$
J_1(\gamma) = \begin{pmatrix} \cos\frac{\gamma}{2} & 0 & 0 & i\sin\frac{\gamma}{2} \\ 0 & \cos\frac{\gamma}{2} & -i\sin\frac{\gamma}{2} & 0 \\ 0 & -i\sin\frac{\gamma}{2} & \cos\frac{\gamma}{2} & 0 \\ i\sin\frac{\gamma}{2} & 0 & 0 & \cos\frac{\gamma}{2} \end{pmatrix}
$$

$$J_2(\gamma) = \begin{pmatrix} 0 & \cos\dfrac{\gamma}{2} & 0 & -\sin\dfrac{\gamma}{2} \\ \cos\dfrac{\gamma}{2} & 0 & -\sin\dfrac{\gamma}{2} & 0 \\ \sin\dfrac{\gamma}{2} & 0 & \cos\dfrac{\gamma}{2} & 0 \\ 0 & \sin\dfrac{\gamma}{2} & 0 & \cos\dfrac{\gamma}{2} \end{pmatrix} \tag{14.30}$$

14.2.2 Quantum Games

We come now to the heart of this section, that is, the description and search for PSNE in these games. The structures and rules of quantum games are different from those of classical games. There are, however, two points that connect a classical game with its quantum analogue. First, the quantum game is based on a classical game, and the payoffs in the quantum game are determined by the payoff function of the classical game. Second, the classical strategies are obtained as a special case of the quantum strategies. Depending on the entanglement operators J defined in Eq. (14.30), the players may even reach the classical square in the game table. In most cases, however, this will not lead to a Nash equilibrium. With all these complex numbers running around, it must be quite hard to imagine how this formalism can be connected to a game in which people have to make decisions and get tangible rewards that depend on their opponent's decisions, especially when these rewards are expressed in real numbers (dollars or years in prison). Whatever we do, at the end of the day, a passage to real numbers must occur. To show how it works, we start with an old faithful classical game (e.g., the prisoner's dilemma) and show how to turn it into a quantum game that still ends with rewarding its players with tangible rewards. This procedure is referred as *quantization of a classical game*. We will carry out this task in two steps. In the first step, we will consider a classical game and equip each player i with a quantum strategy (the 2×2 matrix $U(\varphi_i, \alpha_i, \theta_i)$ defined in Eq. (14.13)). At the same time, we will also design a new payoff system that translates the complex numbers appearing in the state of the system into a real reward. This first step leads us to a reasonable description of a game, but proves to be inadequate if we want to achieve a really new game, not just the classical game from which we started our journey. This task will be achieved in the second step.

Suppose we start with the same classical game described earlier in this section, which is given in its normal form with specified payoff functions as [97]

		Player 2	
		I	Y
Player 1	I	$u_1(I,I), u_2(I,I)$	$u_1(I,Y), u_2(I,Y,1)$
	Y	$u_1(Y,I), u_2(Y,I)$	$u_1(Y,Y), u_2(Y,Y)$

It is assumed that the referee already decreed that the initial state is $|00\rangle$, and asks the players to choose their strategies. There is, however, one difference: instead of using the classical strategies of either leaving a bit untouched (the strategy I) or operating on it with the second strategy Y, the referee allows each player $i = 1, 2$ to use his quantum strategy $U(\varphi_i, \alpha_i, \theta_i)$ defined in Eq. (14.13). Before we find out how all this will help the players, let us find out what will happen with the state of the system after such an operation. For that purpose, it is convenient to use the vector notations specified in Eq. (14.1) and let each player act on his own qubit with his own as strategy as explained through Eq. (14.25), thereby leading the system from its initial state $|00\rangle$ to its final state $|\Psi\rangle$ given by

$$
\begin{aligned}
|\Psi\rangle &= U_1 \otimes U_2 |00\rangle = U_1 |0\rangle \otimes U_2 |0\rangle \\
&= U_1 \begin{pmatrix} 1 \\ 0 \end{pmatrix} \otimes U_2 \begin{pmatrix} 1 \\ 0 \end{pmatrix} = \begin{pmatrix} [U_1]_{11} \\ [U_1]_{21} \end{pmatrix} \otimes \begin{pmatrix} [U_2]_{11} \\ [U_2]_{21} \end{pmatrix} \\
&= \begin{pmatrix} [U_1]_{11}[U_2]_{11} \\ [U_1]_{11}[U_2]_{21} \\ [U_1]_{21}[U_2]_{11} \\ [U_1]_{21}[U_2]_{21} \end{pmatrix}
\end{aligned}
\tag{14.31}
$$

With the help of Eq. (14.23), we may then write

$$
\begin{aligned}
|\Psi\rangle &= [U_1]_{11}[U_2]_{11}|00\rangle + [U_1]_{11}[U_2]_{21}|01\rangle \\
&\quad + [U_1]_{21}[U_2]_{11}|10\rangle + [U_1]_{21}[U_2]_{21}|11\rangle \\
&\equiv a\,|\,00\rangle + b\,|\,01\rangle + c\,|\,10\rangle + d\,|\,11\rangle.
\end{aligned}
\tag{14.32}
$$

From Eq. (14.13) it is easy to determine the dependence of the coefficients on the angles (that is, the strategies of the two players), for example, $a = [U_1]_{11}[U_2]_{11} = e^{i(\varphi_1 + \varphi_2)} \cos\dfrac{\theta_1}{2} \cos\dfrac{\theta_2}{2}$, and so on. Since $|\Psi\rangle$ is a 2qubits, then, as we have stressed in the text around Eq. (14.20) or Eq. (14.24) we have $|a|^2 + |b|^2 + |c|^2 + |d|^2 = 1$. This naturally leads us to suggest the following payoff system:

The payoff P_i of player i is calculated in a similar fashion to the calculation of payoffs in correlated equilibrium classical games, with the absolute value squared of the amplitudes a, b, c, d (which themselves are complex numbers) as the corresponding probabilities:

$$
P_i(\varphi_1, \alpha_1, \theta_1; \varphi_2, \alpha_2, \theta_2) = |a|^2 u_i(0,0) + |b|^2 u_i(0,1) + |c|^2 u_i(1,0) + |d|^2 u_i(1,1).
\tag{14.33}
$$

For example, a prisoner's 1 and prisoner's 2 years in prison in the prisoner's dilemma, game table, Eq. (14.7), are

$$
\begin{aligned}
P_1 &= -4|a|^2 - 6|b|^2 - 2|c|^2 - 5|d|^2, \\
P_2 &= -4|a|^2 - 2|b|^2 - 6|c|^2 - 5|d|^2.
\end{aligned}
\tag{14.34}
$$

The reader must have noticed that this procedure ends up in a classical game with mixed strategies. First, once absolute values are taken, the role of the two angles φ and θ is void because

$$
\begin{aligned}
|a|^2 &= \cos^2\frac{\theta_1}{2} \cos^2\frac{\theta_2}{2}, \ |b|^2 = \cos^2\frac{\theta_1}{2} \sin^2\frac{\theta_2}{2}, \\
|c|^2 &= \sin^2\frac{\theta_1}{2} \cos^2\frac{\theta_2}{2}, \ |d|^2 = \sin^2\frac{\theta_1}{2} \sin^2\frac{\theta_2}{2}.
\end{aligned}
\tag{14.35}
$$

What is more disturbing is that we arrive at an old format of classical games with mixed strategies. Since $\cos^2\dfrac{\theta}{2} + \sin^2\dfrac{\theta}{2} = 1$, we immediately identify the payoffs in Eq. (14.33) as those resulting from a mixed strategy classical game where a prisoner i chooses to confess with probability $\cos^2\dfrac{\theta_\lambda}{2}$ and to not confess with probability $\sin^2\dfrac{\theta}{2}$. In particular, the pure strategies are obtained as specified in Eq. (14.15). Thus, although the analysis of the first step taught us how to use quantum strategies and how to design a payoff system applicable to a complex state of the system $|\Psi\rangle$ as defined in Eq. (14.32), it did not prevent us from falling into the trap of triviality, in the sense that so far nothing is new.

The reason for this failure is at the heart of quantum mechanics. The initial state $|00\rangle$ upon which the players apply their strategies according to Eq. (14.31) in not entangled, since it is a simple outer product of $|0\rangle$ of player 1 and $|0\rangle$ of player 2; so, according to the definition of entanglement given after Eq. (14.22), it is not entangled. Thus, we arrive at the following:

> In order for a quantum game to be distinct from its classical analogue, the state upon which the two players apply their quantum strategies should be entangled.

That is where the entanglement operators J defined in Eqs. (14.26), (14.27), and (14.30) come into play. Practically, we ask the referee not only to suggest a simple initial state such as $|00\rangle$ but also to choose some entanglement operator J and to apply it to $|00\rangle$ as exemplified in Eqs. (14.26) and (14.27) in order to modify it into an entangled state. Only then are the players allowed to apply their quantum strategies, after which the state of the system will be given by $U_1 \otimes U_2 J \,|\, 00\rangle$, as compared with Eq. (14.31). There is one more task the referee should take care of. A reasonable desired property is that if, for some reason, the players choose to leave everything unchanged by taking $\gamma_i = (\varphi_i, \alpha_i, \theta_i) = (0, 0, 0)$, that is, $U_1 = U_2 = I$, then the final state should be identical to the initial state. This is easily achieved by asking the referee to apply the operator $J^{-1} = J^\dagger$ to the state $U_1 \otimes U_2 J \,|\, 00\rangle$ (that was obtained after the players applied their strategies to the entangled state $J \,|\, 00\rangle$). These modifications change things entirely, and turn the quantum game into a new game with complicated strategies; that is, it is much richer than its classical analogue. Let us then organize the game protocol as explained above by presenting a list of well-defined steps:

1) The starting point is some classical two-player two-strategy classical game given in its normal form (a table with utility functions) and a referee whose duty is to choose an initial two-bit state and an entanglement operator J.

2) The referee chooses a simple non-entangled 2qubits initial state, which, for convenience, we fix once and for all to be $|\psi_I\rangle = |\, 00\rangle$. As in the classical game protocol, the choice of this state does not affect the game in any form; it is just a starting point.

3) The referee then chooses an entanglement operator J and applies it to $|\psi_I\rangle$ to generate an entangled state $|\psi_{II}\rangle = J \,|\, \psi_I\rangle$ as exemplified in Eq. (14.26). This operation is part of the rules of the game; that is, it is not possible for the players to affect this choice in any way.

4) At this point every player applies his own transformation $U_i = U\,(\varphi_i, \alpha_i, \theta_i)$ to his own qubit. The functional dependence of U on the three angles is displayed in Eq. (14.13). This is the only place where the players have to make a decision. After the players have made their decisions, the product operation is applied to $|\psi_{II}\rangle$ as in Eq. (14.25), resulting in the state $|\psi_{III}\rangle = U_1 \otimes U_2 \,|\, \psi_{II}\rangle$.

5) The referee then applies the inverse of J (that is, $J^\dagger$ since J is unitary) and gets the final state

$$|\Psi\rangle = \overbrace{J^\dagger}^{\text{referee}} \overbrace{U_1 \otimes U_2 J}^{\text{players}} \overbrace{|\, 00\rangle}^{\text{referee}} = a \,|\, 00\rangle + b \,|\, 01\rangle + c \,|\, 10\rangle + d \,|\, 11\rangle, \qquad (14.36)$$

where the complex numbers a, b, c, and d with $|a|^2 + |b|^2 + |c|^2 + |d|^2 = 1$ are functions of the elements of U_1 and U_2; that is, following Eq. (14.13), they are functions of the six angles $(\varphi_1, \alpha_1, \theta_1; \varphi_2, \alpha_2, \theta_2)$.

6) The players are then rewarded according to the prescription given by Eq. (14.33).

Formal definition of a two-player pure strategy quantum game: We can now give a formal definition of a two-player two-strategy quantum game that is an extension of a classical two-player two-strategy game. The necessary ingredients of a quantum game should include the following:

1) A quantum system that can be analyzed using the tools of quantum mechanics, for example, a two-qubit system.
2) The existence of two players who are able to manipulate the quantum system and operate on their own qubits.
3) A well-defined strategy set for each player. More concretely, a set of unitary 2×2 matrices with unit determinant $U \in SU(2)$.
4) A definition of the payoff functions or utilities associated with the players' strategies. More concretely, we have in mind a classical two-player two-strategy game given in its normal form (a table of payoffs).

Definition 14.1 Given a classical game with two players and two pure strategies:

$$G_C = \langle N = \{1,2\}, \mid ij \rangle, A_i = \{I, Y\}, u_i : A_1 \otimes A_2 \to \mathbb{R} \rangle. \tag{14.37}$$

Its quantum (pure strategy) analogue is the game

$$G_Q = \langle N = \{1,2\}, \mid \psi_I \rangle, \{A_i\}, J, u_i, P_i \rangle. \tag{14.38}$$

Here, $N = \{1, 2\}$ is the set of (two) players, $|\psi_I\rangle$ is the initial state suggested by the referee (usually a simple two-bit state such as $|00\rangle$ as in the classical game), $A_i = U(\gamma_i) \equiv U_i$, is the infinite set of quantum pure strategies of player i on his qubit defined by the 2×2 matrix of Eq. (14.13), J is an entanglement operator defined by Eqs. (14.26), (14.27), and (14.36), $u_i(k, \ell)$ with $k, \ell = 0, 1$ are the classical payoff functions of the game G, and $P_i(U_1, U_2)$ are the quantum payoff functions defined in Eq. (14.33) in which the coefficients a, b, c, and d are complex numbers (also called amplitudes) that determine the expansion of the final state $|\Psi\rangle$ as a combination of two-bit states as in Eq. (14.36).

In addition, one should be aware of the following:

1) Since U is uniquely determined by the three angles $\gamma_i = (\varphi_i, \alpha_i, \theta_i)$ through Eq. (14.13), we may also regard γ_i as the strategy of player i. Thus, unlike the classical game where each player has but two strategies, in the quantum game the set of strategies of each player is determined by three continuous variables. As we have already mentioned, the set of strategies of a player corresponds to a point on S^3.
2) J is part of the rules of the game (it is not controlled by the players). The main requirement from J is that it is a unitary matrix and that after operating on the initial bit state (taken to be $|00\rangle$ in our case) the result is an entangled 2qubits.
3) As we stressed in connection with Eq. (14.37), the amplitudes are functions of the two strategies $\gamma_i = (\varphi_i, \alpha_i, \theta_i)$, (i = 1, 2) that are given analytically once the operations implied in Eq. (14.37) are properly carried out (see below).

Nash equilibrium in a pure strategy quantum game: A PSNE in a quantum game is a pair of strategies $(\gamma_1^*, \gamma_2^*) \in S^3 \otimes S^3$ (each represents three angles $\gamma_i^* = (\varphi_i^*, \alpha_i^*, \theta_i^*) \in S^3$), such that

$$\begin{aligned} P_1(\gamma_1, \gamma_2^*) &\leq P_1(\gamma_1^*, \gamma_2^*) \forall \gamma_1 \in S^3, \\ P_2(\gamma_1^*, \gamma_2) &\leq P_2(\gamma_1^*, \gamma_2^*) \forall \gamma_2 \in S^3. \end{aligned} \tag{14.39}$$

It is immediately realized that the concept of Nash equilibrium and its elucidation in a quantum game is far more difficult than in a classical game. If each player's strategy were dependent on a *single* continuous parameter, then the use of the method of best response functions could be effective, but here each player's strategy depends on *three* continuous parameters, and the method of response functions might be inadequate. One of the goals of this section is to alleviate this problem. Another important point concerns the question of cooperation. In the classical prisoner dilemma game, a player that chooses the don't-confess strategy (Y) forces his opponent to cooperate and choose Y (don't confess) as well, which leads to a PSNE (Y,Y). On the other hand, in the quantum game, the situation is quite different. By looking at the payoff expressions in Eq. (14.34) we see that prisoner 1 wants to reach the state where $|c|^2 = 1$ and $|a|^2 = |b|^2 = |d|^2 = 0$, whereas prisoner 2 wants to reach the state where $|b|^2 = 1$ and $|a|^2 = |c|^2 = |d|^2 = 0$. Surprisingly, as we shall see below, there are situations such that for every strategy chosen by prisoner 1, prisoner 2 can find the best response that makes $|b|^2 = 1$ and $|a|^2 = |c|^2 = |d|^2 = 0$, and vice versa, for every strategy chosen by prisoner 2, prisoner 1 can find the best response that makes $|c|^2 = 1$ and $|a|^2 = |b|^2 = |d|^2 = 0$. Since the two situations cannot occur simultaneously, there is no Nash equilibrium and no cooperation in this case.

The role of the entanglement operator J and classical commensurability: A desired property (although not crucial) of a quantum game is that the theory is as defined in Eq. (14.36) and includes the classical game as a special case. We already know from Eq. (14.15) that the classical strategies I and Y are obtained as special cases of the quantum ones, since $U(0, 0, 0) = I$ and $U(0, 0, \pi) = Y$. What we require here is that by using their classical strategies, the players will be able to reach the four classical states (the squares of the game table). For example, to reach the square (C,C) the coefficients a, b, c, and d in the final state $|\Psi\rangle$ at the end of the game (see Eq. 14.37) should be $|a|^2 = 1$, $b = c = d = 0$, and so on. For this requirement to hold, the entanglement operator J should satisfy a certain equality. We refer to this equality to be satisfied by J as *classical commensurability*. From the discussion around Eq. (14.15), we recall that in a classical game, the only operations on bits are implemented either by the unit matrix I (leave the bit in its initial state $|0\rangle$ or $|1\rangle$) or $Y = \begin{pmatrix} 0 & 1 \\ -1 & 0 \end{pmatrix}$ (change the state of the bit from $|0\rangle$ to $|1\rangle$ or vice versa). Thus, by choosing $U(0, 0, 0)$ or $U(0, 0, \pi)$, the players virtually use classical strategies. Therefore, classical commensurability implies

$$[Y \otimes Y, J] = 0, \text{ (classical commensurability)}, \tag{14.40}$$

where we recall that for two square matrices A, B with equal dimensions, the commutation relation is defined as $[A, B] = AB - BA$. Indeed, if this condition is satisfied and both U_1 and U_2 are classical strategies, then $[U_1 \otimes U_2, J] = 0$ because in this case $U_1 \otimes U_2 = I \otimes I$ or $I \otimes Y$ or $Y \otimes I$ or $Y \otimes Y$, and as we show below, all of the four operators commute with J. Consequently

$$|\Psi\rangle = J^\dagger U_1 \otimes U_2 J |00\rangle = J^\dagger J U_1 \otimes U_2 |00\rangle = U_1 \otimes U_2 |00\rangle, \tag{14.41}$$

that is what happens in a classical game. To prove that the four two-player classical strategies listed above do commute with J, we note that by direct calculations it is easy to show that J_1 defined in Eq. (14.26) satisfies classical commensurability because an elementary manipulation of matrices shows that J_1 can be written as

$$J_1 = e^{i\frac{\pi}{4}Y \otimes Y} = \frac{1}{\sqrt{2}}(I_4 + iY \otimes Y), \tag{14.42}$$

and this matrix naturally commutes with $Y \otimes Y$. On the other hand, J_2 defined in Eq. (14.27) does not satisfy classical commensurability as can be checked by directly inspecting the commutation relation $[Y \otimes Y, J_2] \neq 0$.

In general, entanglement shared between different players allows the players to obtain correlated outcomes even in the absence of communication. This leads to the quantum game sampling a larger space of probability distributions that can realize equilibria resembling classical correlated equilibria, which are only possible in classical games when the players receive advice

---

Design Example 14.2

Here, we reproduce some experimental results presented in [37]. Routing games are formulated as a collection of source–sink pairs in a directed graph. The flow on the graph represents traffic or information flow over a communication network. We model a non-atomic game where the information is divided in continuous units, with the total flow from the source to the sink normalized to 1. The players of the game can be interpreted as each infinitesimal unit of information at each node being routed through the network. Since each player acts independently in their own interest, it is natural to analyze this in a game-theoretic context.

Each edge in the graph has a time delay, or latency, L[f], associated with it, which is a function of the flow on that edge, f. The latency serves as the cost function of the game. The selfish routing case is where the players try to minimize their own latency, or equivalently, when they try to equalize the latency of each of their outgoing paths [38]. This leads to the Wardrop equilibrium (which is analogous to the Nash equilibrium in standard game theory) [39]. Analytically, the equilibrium flow, $\{f_e\}$, is the set of flows that satisfies [40] $\min \left(\sum_j \int_0^{f_j} L_j[z] dz \right)$, where the sum is over all j edges or channels. The total cost of a set of flows can be measured as the average cost for all the flows on a network and is given by the sum of the latency on each edge multiplied by the amount of flow on that edge: $C_T[f] = \sum_j f_j L[f_j]$.

The optimal flow, $\{f_o\}$, is the set of flows that produce the global minimum of C_T. This flow is optimal from a societal perspective as it minimizes the average cost. If it is not equal to the equilibrium flow, the optimal flow is only accessible if the players agree to cooperate through some central mechanism such as shared advice, or a contract. A useful metric in congestion games is the price of anarchy, (κ), which is the ratio of the total cost at the Wardrop equilibrium to the total cost of the optimum flow $\kappa = C_T[f_e]/C_T[f_o]$. The cost of the optimal flow does not change when the game is quantized; rather, the goal is to structure the game so that the price of anarchy approaches 1.

The counterintuitive Braess's paradox arises from the intuition that a new zero-cost link in a network will only improve the efficiency of the network. It is formulated on a four-node network with source s and sink t, as seen in Figure 14.1. The paths $s \rightarrow u$ and $v \rightarrow t$ have a latency equal to the amount of flow on the edge, while the paths $s \rightarrow v$ and $u \rightarrow t$ have a constant latency equal to 1.

If the path through nodes u and v does not exist, the equilibrium flow of the network is with the flow equally shared on the two possible paths, $s \rightarrow u \rightarrow t$ and $s \rightarrow v \rightarrow t$ with a $C_T = 3/2$. This is also the optimal flow, giving the network $\kappa = 1$. If one tries to improve the performance of the network by adding the bidirectional zero-cost edge between $u \rightarrow v$, the equilibrium flow actually

Design Example 14.2 (Continued)

Figure 14.1 Braess's paradox. *Source:* Modified from Solmeyer et al. [37].

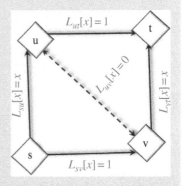

has a higher total cost of $C_T = 2$ as each player tries to take advantage of the lowest-cost path $s \rightarrow u \rightarrow v \rightarrow t$. The optimal flow is the same as the optimal flow without the central edge, and therefore $\kappa = 4/3$. In this example of paradox, the addition of a zero-cost edge increases the price of anarchy from 1 to 4/3. To quantize the game, one qubit is assigned to each node where a player has to choose which direction to route the information, s, u, and v in this case. The state of the players' qubits is initialized to $|000\rangle$. An N-qubit entangling operation is performed between the three nodes $J_N(\gamma) = e^{i\gamma\sigma_x \otimes^N}$. The amount of entanglement is parameterized by γ, which is maximal at $\gamma = \pi/2$ and zero at $\gamma = 0$.

Next, the players at each node apply an arbitrary unitary rotation to their qubits, which serves as their choice of strategy. An arbitrary rotation, similar to Eq. (14.13), can be written as

$$\hat{U}(\theta, \varphi, \alpha) = \begin{pmatrix} e^{-i\varphi} \cos \dfrac{\theta}{2} & e^{i\alpha} \sin \dfrac{\theta}{2} \\ -e^{-i\alpha} \sin \dfrac{\theta}{2} & e^{i\varphi} \cos \dfrac{\theta}{2} \end{pmatrix} \tag{14.43}$$

In practice, we place no restriction on the parameters θ, φ, or α since a winding in phase only produces redundant strategy choices, which does not compromise our analysis. Finally, an unentangling operation $J^\dagger(\gamma)$ is performed on the qubits, and the resulting state is measured.

For each qubit, the two possible measurement outcomes are associated with the two outgoing paths from the node, and the expectation value of the measured qubit determines the amount of information it routes along each path as a fraction of the information that enters the node. This determines the flow along each of the paths, which is then used to calculate the latencies along each path and the total cost of the flow. Symbolically, the flows are a function of the expectation values of the final state, $f[\langle \psi_f | \psi_f \rangle]$, which is a function of the player's strategy choices and the entangling parameter, $|\psi_f[\theta_s, \varphi_s, \alpha_s, \theta_u, \varphi_u, \alpha_u, \theta_v, \varphi_v, \alpha_v, \gamma]\rangle$.

To model selfish behavior, we simulate a repeated game where players update their strategy choice based on a no-regrets condition on their local latencies, which should converge on the Wardrop equilibrium [41]. The no-regrets condition states that an equilibrium is obtained if no player can improve their payoff by unilaterally altering their strategy choice. Thus, we allow the players to locally sample the cost function as they adjust each of the three parameters in their strategy choice in order to approximate the local slope of the cost function to update their strategy choice to minimize the difference between latencies of their two outgoing paths.

(Continued)

Design Example 14.2 (Continued)

After each round, they are given their expected cost function; that is, for player s, the difference in the latencies of the outgoing paths is $\delta L_s[|\psi_f\rangle] = L_{su}(f_{su}) - L_{sv}(f_{sv})$. Then the local derivative of the cost function is approximated by keeping all other eight strategy choice parameters fixed, and changing only one. For example, player s updates the parameter θ_s by computing $\delta L_{\theta s} = \delta L_s[|\psi_f\{\theta_s \to (\theta_s + d)]\rangle]$, where d is a small parameter. The players then update each of their strategy choices for the $(n+1)^{th}$ round of the game by adjusting the parameter to lower the latency differences of its outgoing paths with a learning parameter, or gain, M, that is: $\theta_s^{(n+1)} = \theta_s^{(n)} - M(\delta L_s - \delta L_{\theta s})$. This is done for all three strategy parameters $\{\theta, \varphi, \alpha\}$ of all three players $\{s, u, v\}$. The players initially choose a random $\{\theta, \varphi, \alpha\}$, and the game is repeated until an equilibrium is reached.

We simulate the full network from Figure 14.1, including the central 0 cost edge, as the graph with no central edge is already optimal with $\kappa = 1$, and cannot be improved with quantum players. An example run of the simulation is shown in Figure 14.2 [37]. The simulations are

(a)

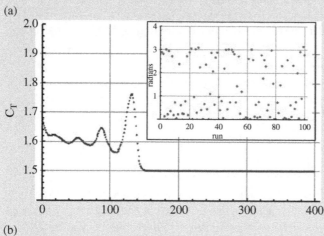

(b)

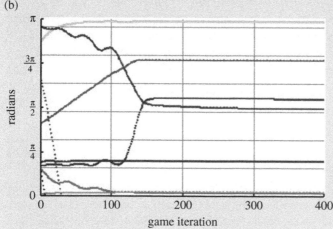

game iteration

Figure 14.2 Simulation results. *Source:* Modified from Solmeyer et al. [37].

Design Example 14.2 (Continued)

typically performed with 400 iterations, a gain of $M = 10$, and $d = 0.01$. The example shown is for a partially entangled initial state, $\gamma = \pi/4$. The total cost of the flow is plotted in Figure 14.2a, and the fact that the total cost is a fixed value shows that the algorithm does indeed lead to an equilibrium flow.

The graph in Figure 14.2b plots the values of the nine strategy parameters. The strategy parameters also reach stable values. Occasionally, strategy parameters can appear to run off and not stabilize, as do two that appear in Figure 14.2b. This can be either because they are irrelevant to the equilibrium, or because they maintain a fixed difference with respect to another strategy parameter, or they later converge outside of the bounds of the graph. Each of these possibilities was seen in different runs of the simulation. It is possible for parameters to be irrelevant to the game due to the structure of the strategy matrix (14.48), where, for example, when $\theta = 0$, α is undefined.

Each run of the simulation produces different final values for the equilibrium strategy parameters, though the cost at the equilibrium is always the same. The equilibrium value for one of the strategy parameters is shown for 100 different runs in the inset on the right of Figure 14.2a.

In Figure 14.3, we plot the cost at equilibrium found for simulations with varying amounts of entanglement. For $\gamma = 0$, the equilibrium flow is the same as in the classical case. This reflects the fact that it is a properly quantized game. This also proves that Braess's paradox remains in the quantum network even when a much wider set of strategy choices is allowed. The total cost at equilibrium has a minimum at $\gamma = \pi/4$ and is equal to the optimal cost, which resolves the paradox. It is interesting to note that at maximal entanglement, Braess's paradox is recovered, as the equilibrium flow again goes to the value in the classical game, with the price of anarchy approaching 1.33. The optimal value of entanglement to take full advantage of the quantum correlations is not the maximal entanglement, but rather, the half entanglement.

At $\gamma = \pi/4$, though the strategy choices may be different for each run of the simulation, the flow always converges to 0.5 flow on all edges (except for $u \rightarrow v$, which has $f_{uv} = f_{vu} = 0$), and thus has a total cost at equilibrium equal to the optimal cost and $\kappa = 1$.

Figure 14.3 Simulation results. *Source:* Modified from Solmeyer et al. [37].

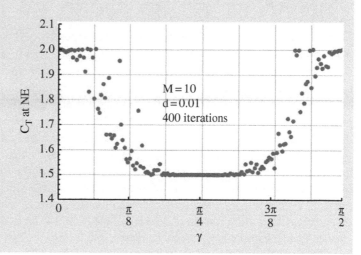

14.2.3 Quantum Game for Spectrum Sharing

System model: The system analyzed in this section has N channels and N users who must be assigned to one of those channels. The state of such a system in Dirac notation of some user j, where $j = 0, 1, N-1$, is $|c_j\rangle$, with $c_j = 0, 1, N-1$. Moreover, the state of the entire system $|\psi\rangle = |c_0\rangle \otimes |c_1\rangle \otimes \cdots \otimes |c_{N-1}\rangle = |c_0 c_1 \ldots c_{N-1}\rangle$. Thus, it must be understood that user 0 is assigned to channel c_0, user 1 is assigned to channel c_1, and so on. As an illustration, we present the simplest case of two users and two channels.

Two-user game: Let 0 and 1 be the indexes of two smart devices attempting to transmit information through two free channels, 0 and 1. The devices are assumed to be indistinguishable, and thus have identical transmission preferences. The states of the system are represented by vectors of a Hilbert space; more specifically, the vector position corresponds to the user, and the value in each position represents the user's assigned channel. Collisions are avoided when channels are not shared. For example, a desirable state is $|c_0 c_1\rangle = |10\rangle$, which specifies that user 0 is assigned to channel $c_0 = 1$; meanwhile, user 1 is assigned to channel $c_1 = 0$. If players play classically, the probabilities of each user and channel are all equal. The quantum equivalent for that case is $|\psi_C\rangle = (|00\rangle + |01\rangle + |10\rangle + |11\rangle)/2$. Then, according to the classic strategies, it is clear that they have (at best) a 50/50 chance of avoiding collisions, and no strategy can modify the system in order to avoid collisions completely. Therefore, it is a classic Nash equilibrium of the system. On the other hand, they can do better if they play quantum, because they can achieve a 100% probability of success. In order to take advantage of QC, a one-shot quantum game is proposed; it begins with the system in an entangled state, $|\psi_e\rangle = (|00\rangle - |11\rangle)/\sqrt{2}$, which is a linear combination of two of the four possible states. In this manner, the state $|00\rangle$ means that both users are assigned to channel 0; meanwhile, state $|11\rangle$ assigns both users to channel 1. In order to change the initial state, the players must apply a strategy which, mathematically, is represented by a two-dimensional operator that we call U. In general, players can choose to operate on their qubits using a classic or quantum U, in order to enhance their chances of winning. However, there is only one optimal quantum strategy (the Hadamard gate $U = H$) that modifies the system to a more favorable state for the two-user example. Given the condition that is applied by both players, the final state $|\psi_f\rangle$ is

$$|\psi_f\rangle = H^{\otimes 2} \cdot \frac{(|00\rangle - |11\rangle)}{\sqrt{2}} = \frac{(|01\rangle + |10\rangle)}{\sqrt{2}} \tag{14.44}$$

From $|\psi_f\rangle$, it follows that the system can only collapse to $(|01\rangle)$, where user 0 is assigned to channel 0 and user 1 is assigned to channel 1, or to $(|10\rangle)$, where user 0 is assigned to channel 1 and user 1 is assigned to channel 0. Thus, by quantum rules, a new Nash equilibrium arises, where the worst case is avoided and both users transmit successfully with probability 1. Furthermore, it is a Pareto-optimal solution because it is impossible to make any player better off without harming some other player. It is important to note that, because the studied network is composed of indistinguishable devices, the necessary condition that all players take the same actions is natural.

N-user game formulation: Usually, there are $N > 2$ users sharing a spectrum assumed to be divided into N channels. Because none of the users has information about other users, there is a high probability that more than one of them will take part in a collision. When that occurs, all those involved cannot transmit, resulting in a situation that must be avoided or, at least, minimized by means of appropriate spectrum allocation protocols. These types of problems are difficult to solve classically as the number of players increases; that is, they are included in the group referred to as nondeterministic polynomial (NP) problems. Accordingly, they cannot be solved in polynomial time, which generally results in inefficient solutions. We are facing a type of decision problem consisting of agents with similar objectives that compete for a limited number of resources. Therefore, the spectrum allocation problem may be modeled as a multiple-options minority game.

The cognitive radio (CR) concept implies that cognitive devices can make smart choices and access the spectrum holes left unused by primary users. Despite this promising idea, it is very important to take into account that the existence of those spectral holes is dynamic in size and limited in time, which causes difficulties in sensing, sharing, and allocating tasks. The first constraint determines how many users can transmit simultaneously. Meanwhile, the second constraint limits the time that users have to select the channel they will transmit in, and the time they have to transmit. As the number of CR users increases, the decision processes become more complex, thus limiting the time the users have to transmit. Taking the latter into account, an efficient spectrum allocation algorithm is absolutely necessary. Many researchers point to the use of game theory as the most appropriate technique to model (and consequently perform) resource sharing and allocation tasks. Following the same line of thought, we present here the use of a one-shot quantum game to minimize decision times and the number of collisions [42].

The model considers a cellular network in which each cell has a single cognitive BS and a group of CR users in its coverage range as shown in Figure 14.4.

The BSs are transceivers in charge of connecting the devices to other devices in the cell. To achieve this, they collect the CR user reports, and prepare to allocate the radio channels. It is assumed that the devices cooperatively sense the spectrum and record information about the spectrum holes, which will eventually be provided to the BSs. In the following, we focus on a quantum algorithm capable of managing the spectrum allocation based on probability amplitude amplification. More specifically, we present two cases of interest: the first one aims to avoid all users being assigned to the same channel, and the second one aims to enhance the probability of quantum states that assign different channels to users.

The quantum medium allocation evolves by following three basic steps:

1) The cognitive quantum BS assigns a set of qubits to the cognitive users in the cell range and prepares entangled state $|\psi_e\rangle$.

$$| \psi_e \rangle = \frac{1}{\sqrt{N}} \sum_{k=0}^{N-1} \omega_N^{kp} | kk \cdots k \rangle, \tag{14.45}$$

where $\omega_N = e^{2\pi i/N}$ and p is a tunable parameter that modifies the amplitude phase. Depending on p, it is possible to select BS preferences to avoid the least favorable case, $p = 1$, or, on the other hand, to enhance the optimum one, $p = (N(N-1))/2$.

Figure 14.4 Cognitive network architecture.

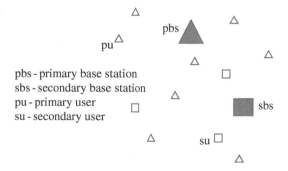

pbs - primary base station
sbs - secondary base station
pu - primary user
su - secondary user

2) Every node locally applies a one-shot strategy U to the initial state, which makes the system collapse to a new state.

$$\left| \psi_f \right\rangle = U^N \cdot \left| \psi_e \right\rangle, \tag{14.46}$$

3) The nodes of each cell measure the final state ψ_f to obtain the assigned channel.

In what follows, we present the quantum circuits for the case N = 4 and describe the main steps.

Quantum circuit description: Figure 14.5 shows a possible circuit to generate the entangled state $\left| \psi_e \right\rangle$. The system in the base state $\left| 00 \ldots 0 \right\rangle$ is modified by the action of gate R applied on the two upper qubits,

$$R = \frac{1}{\sqrt{2}} \left\{ \begin{matrix} 1 & 1 \\ -1 & 1 \end{matrix} \right\}$$

generating state $\left| \psi_1 \right\rangle = \dfrac{\left| 00000000 \right\rangle}{2} - \dfrac{\left| 01000000 \right\rangle}{2} - \dfrac{\left| 10000000 \right\rangle}{2} + \dfrac{\left| 11000000 \right\rangle}{2}$. Then, the two upper qubits of $\left| \psi_1 \right\rangle$ are the control lines of three *Ctrl — F* gates. A white circle in a control line indicates that the control qubit must be in state 0, whereas a black circle implies that the control must be in state 1 for F_k to be applied (see Figure 14.6). Note that the range of the system state is $N \cdot \log_2(N)$ and that $R^{\log_2(N)}$ must perform the rotation on the upper $\log_2(N)$ qubits in the more general case. The extension of the circuit to N is straightforward. Finally, the action of gates F_k on state $\left| \psi_1 \right\rangle$ yields

$$\left| \psi_e \right\rangle = \frac{\left| 00000000 \right\rangle}{2} - \frac{\left| 01010101 \right\rangle}{2} - \frac{\left| 10101010 \right\rangle}{2} + \frac{\left| 11111111 \right\rangle}{2} \tag{14.47}$$

Collision reduction: One of the main functions of CR is to provide a fair spectrum scheduling method among coexisting cognitive users. In this context, we discuss methods to improve the classic methods' ability to reduce the collision probability. The objective of the first method is to increase the probability of occurrence of the no-collision state. When one user cannot transmit because of a collision, he must wait for some time to re-manage the transmission request. System reliability and the network's quality of service improve if collisions are avoided. The second method focuses on wireless sensor networks, where the importance of all nodes being able to transmit is superseded by the importance of avoiding network downtime; here, the objective is to avoid the massive collisions that occur when all users are assigned to the same channel.

As was described earlier, the channel assignation procedure is the same in both cases. The base station prepares the entangled state of Eq. (14.45) with all the users in the cell, setting

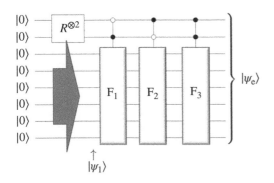

Figure 14.5 Circuit that generates the initial entangled state $\left| \psi_e \right\rangle$.

Figure 14.6 *Ctrl* − F_1 gate circuit, where $P_1 = \omega_N^{1p} \cdot I^{\otimes 6}$. Looking from top to bottom, the F_1 operation is performed on the last six lines only if the state of the first two upper lines is $|10\rangle$.

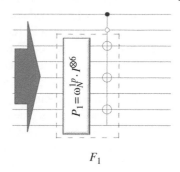

F_1

$p = N(N-1)/2$. After that, the users are positioned to perform their strategies. Strategy U, which each player applies, is represented by an $N \times N$ unitary matrix whose elements are $U_w = \left(e^{2\pi i/N}\right)^{r \cdot c}/\sqrt{N}$, where $r, c = 0, 1 \ldots N-1$ are the row and column indexes. Then, the final state is

$$|\psi_f\rangle = U^{\otimes N}|\psi_e\rangle = \left(\frac{1}{\sqrt{N}}\right)^{N+1} \sum_{k=0}^{N-1} \omega_N^{kp} |kk \cdots k\rangle,$$

$$|\psi_f\rangle = \left(\frac{1}{\sqrt{N}}\right)^{N+1} \sum_{k=0}^{N-1} \sum_{c_0=0}^{N-1} \cdots \sum_{c_{N-1}=0}^{N-1} \left(e^{\frac{2\pi i}{N}k \cdot p} e^{\frac{2\pi i}{N}k \cdot c_0} \cdots e^{\frac{2\pi i}{N}k \cdot c_{N-1}} |c_0 \cdots c_{N-1}\rangle\right)$$

Thus, the state coefficients can be expressed as

$$\alpha_{c_0 \cdots c_{N-1}} = \left(\frac{1}{\sqrt{N}}\right)^{N+1} \sum_{k=0}^{N-1} e^{\frac{2\pi i}{N}k \overbrace{(p + c_0 + c_1 + \cdots + c_{N-1})}^{m}} \tag{14.48}$$

Strategy to increase the optimum case probability: The fairness of the network implies that every user has a priori the same chances to transmit. In the language of games, the BS acts as the arbiter of the game because it assigns the qubits to the players and creates the entangled state. Later on, the players' strategies modify the state amplitudes and hence their chances to win. The players receive a reward, which in this case is to succeed in transmitting.

As set forth above, once spectrum holes are detected, the nodes must be assigned to one channel. Clearly, there are $N!$ possibilities that every player will be assigned to different states, with N being the number of cognitive users. Therefore, provided that all the cognitive users are indistinct, the probability that all of them transmit at the same time is $P_c = N!/N^N$ in the classic world; for example, $P_c = 2.4 \times 10^{-3}$ if $N = 8$. Such a low success probability can only be increased by means of statistical methods involving exploration and/or a previous knowledge of the network, which is hardly possible if the network is continuously changing. In this framework, we present the one-shot quantum game-based algorithm [42].

The m sum in the phase factor of Eq. (14.48) is analyzed in order to properly select p. Thereby, a proper use of quantum interference makes it possible to improve the players' chances. The case where $c_0 \neq c_1 \neq \cdots \neq c_{N-1}$ leads to $m = p + N(N-1)/2$. Thus, in order to guarantee the constructive interference, $p = N(N-1)/2$ and the phase factor is $e^{i2\pi k(N-1)}$. Finally, the probability of the most favorable case is $P_{best} = N \cdot N!/N^N$, which is N times larger than the classic one, $P_{best} = N \cdot P_c$. Clearly, the algorithm performance provides a more efficient use of the devices' energy, extending the time of communication and battery life. This point is even more important in the type of networks that are analyzed later in the chapter.

Strategy to avoid the most unfavorable situation: Wireless sensor networks are a type of autonomous communication network mainly deployed in areas where physical access is almost impossible. Every device installed at each node is a small computer in charge of monitoring physical and environmental conditions such as temperature and air pressure. The sensed data are sent to a base station for analysis. Although sensor networks were originally designed for military purposes, their applications now include area sensing, industrial monitoring, and health-care monitoring. One of the main challenges that communications engineers must face is optimization of the network's power consumption, because of the limited lifetime of the devices batteries and the impracticality of replacing them frequently. Therefore, in order to extend the network's lifetime, more efficient communication protocols are needed. Because collisions are the main cause of unnecessary energy consumption, we discuss a quantum algorithm that prevents the most unfavorable situation. When all users are assigned to the same channel, no transmissions will be performed. There are N of these worst-case possibilities from a total of N^N, so the probability of the worst-case possibility is $P_{worse} = N^{(1-N)}$ by means of classic computation, where the probability that any user will be assigned to any channel follows a uniform distribution.

Once the eventually free channels are identified, the channel allocation procedure begins. The quantum algorithm considers that the cognitive BSs have the extra ability to share a set of qubits with each node in the cell and to prepare the entangled state of Eq. (14.45), setting p so that the probability amplitude associated with states $|c, c, ..., c\rangle$ is reduced to zero. If players measure their state directly on $|\psi_e\rangle$, it will collapse to one of the worst cases. Otherwise, the users implement their strategies in order to change their chances. Let us note that $c_0 = c_1 = \cdots = c_{N-1} = c$ leads to $m = p + N \cdot c$ when all users apply U_w as before. Thus, in order to guarantee destructive interference, $p = 1$ can be chosen. Then, the probability amplitude coefficients are

$$\alpha_{cc\cdots c} = \left(\frac{1}{\sqrt{N}}\right)^{N+1} \sum_{k=0}^{N-1} e^{i2\pi kc} e^{\frac{2\pi i}{N}k} = 0.$$

By allowing at least one node to send information at a certain time slot by using the idle spectrum holes, the sensor network avoids downtime, a significant aspect regardless of the network structure. For instance, if the network uses a star topology, every node communicates directly with the BS. Because the nodes can communicate only through the BS, it represents a single point of failure (SPF) that makes this topology unreliable. However, owing to its simplicity, it is frequently chosen when the coverage areas are not too wide. In that case, the quantum BS must prepare a new allocation scheme by requesting information from the rest of the CR nodes. Although the SPF problem remains unsolved because there are many failure sources, the network reliability is improved under normal BS functioning owing to the one-shot characteristic of the algorithm, which allows at least one node of the star to always send information; this optimizes energy use. Meanwhile, in the case of multihop systems, each node can communicate directly and is able to take distinct paths to reach the data collector, which is advantageous as there is no SPF. On the other hand, these networks have an important disadvantage: high power consumption. To operate, they must draw more power because each node in a mesh must act as a BS. This issue is even more serious if the spectrum allocation task is not performed efficiently. Likewise, in our model, each node of the mesh must eventually prepare the allocation scheme following the procedure explained above, in order to exchange information gathered from the environment or from other nodes. The goal is to minimize the power consumption of mesh topologies by reducing collisions, which is made possible through this quantum allocation algorithm.

14.3   Quantum Decision Theory (QDT)

QDT is a recently developed theory of decision making based on the mathematics of Hilbert spaces, a framework known in physics for its application to quantum mechanics. This framework formalizes the concept of uncertainty and other effects that are particularly manifest in cognitive processes, which makes it well suited for the study of decision making. QDT describes a decision maker's choice as a stochastic event occurring with a probability that is the sum of an *objective utility factor* and a *subjective attraction factor*. We see the potential of using this methodology in modeling processes in *user behavioral microeconomics* for resource sharing in wireless networks. Recently developed concepts of dynamics wireless networks [43–45] where network can borrow the user terminal and employ it as an access point or a relay for temporally augmenting the network capabilities depends on the willingness of a user to participate in such a process. Besides the economic incentives offered by the network (utility), this will also depend on the individual characteristics of the user itself, its preferences. QDT offers a prediction for the average effect of subjectivity on decision makers, the quarter law. We demonstrate results on individual and aggregated (group) data, and show that the results are in good agreement with the quarter law at the level of groups. At the individual level, it appears that the quarter law could be refined in order to reflect individual characteristics. This section revisits the formalism of QDT [46] along with a concrete example and offers a practical guide to researchers who are interested in applying QDT to a dataset of binary lotteries in the domain of gains.

Let us start with a few elements of decision theory that help understand how QDT relates to classical theories of that field that are well known in the fields of psychology and behavioral economics. For this review, we consider how classical theories evaluate simple gambles. A simple gamble is a lottery that yields, for example, a 20% chance of winning $50 and an 80% chance of winning nothing. Although we have primarily in mind the users of wireless network making decisions on whether or not to participate in resource sharing with the network, in order to keep our presentation general, throughout this section, we call such gambles "prospects," "options," or "lotteries." A lottery (indexed by j) is characterized by a set of outcomes and their probability of occurrence, and is written as

$$L_j = \left\{ x_n, p_j(x_n) : \quad n = 1, 2, ..., N \right\}, \tag{14.49}$$

where p_j is a probability measure over the set of payoffs $\{x_n\}$ and thus belongs to the interval $[0, 1]$ and is normalized to one. In experimental settings, it is common for decision makers to have to choose between two simple gambles or between a gamble and a sure thing, as in "would you rather have a 20% chance of winning $50 (with an 80% chance of winning nothing), or get $10 for sure?" We call this a "decision task" (or "choice problem," or "game"). We write the former example as $L_1 = \{50, 0.2 \mid 0, 0.8 \mid 10, 0\}$, and $L_2 = \{50, 0 \mid 0, 0 \mid 10, 1\}$, where the vertical line separates different outcomes, and all amounts present in the decision task appear in both lotteries.In decision theory, such decision tasks serve as simple models for the more complex decisions we face in everyday life. In real situations, outcomes are often not expressed in monetary terms, and their probabilities are unknown. For instance, we are unable to assign a probability to the event that our happiness will increase if we get a new job and move, nor do we assign an exclusively quantitative value to this change of happiness. In our example of user resource sharing with the network, in addition to a monetary incentive by the network the user's decision might in addition depend on the state of the battery, whether or not she expects an important call for herself, concerns about the privacy and security, and so on. Nevertheless, it is the consensus of the field that simple choice problems such as the above elicit risk preferences, and we will focus on lotteries of that form.

A few risk elicitation methods are reviewed in [47]. The method used to generate our dataset is called "random lottery pair design" in the former review. This method, made popular by [48], consists in offering the decision maker a series of random lottery pairs in sequence. The dataset, used in this section, was produced as part of [49], and the tool created for that purpose was called Randomized Lottery Task (RALT) by its authors. In accordance with probability theory, [50] expressed the idea that it would be rational to choose the option with the highest expected value, given by the weighted sum

$$U(L_j) = \sum_n x_n p_j(x_n).$$ (14.50)

Later, work in [51] examined the relationship between the psychological and the objective value of money. The idea of a decreasing marginal value of wealth was introduced, which amounts to introducing a non-decreasing and concave utility function u transforming values in Eq. (14.50), giving an expected utility

$$\bar{U}(L_j) = \sum_n u(x_n) p_j(x_n).$$ (14.51)

It was proposed that $u(x) = \ln(x)$, to reflect that we become more indifferent to changes of wealth as the initial amount of wealth increases. For example, an increase of wealth from 1 to 4 million has a higher psychological value than an increase from 4 to 7 million.

The view that people should and will consistently choose the option with the highest expected utility given by Eq. (14.51) (with different forms of $u(x)$) remained dominant for a very long time. In [52], axioms of rational behavior are presented according to which rationality consists in maximizing an expected utility. Expected utility theory was the foundation of the rational-agent model, whereby people are represented by rational and selfish agents exhibiting tastes that do not change over time. This forms the foundation of the standard economic approach to decisions under risk and uncertainty [53].

Prospect theory [54] modifies expected utility theory in order to explain a collection of observations showing that people exhibit a variety of cognitive biases contradicting rationality, in particular the Allais paradox [55]. In prospect theory, the utility $\hat{U}(L_j)$ is given by

$$\hat{U}(L_j) = \sum_{n=1}^{N} v(x_n) w(p(x_n)),$$ (14.52)

where the value function $v(x)$ is constructed based on a reference point so that relative (and not absolute) wealth variations are considered in the expected utility $\hat{U}(L_j)$. The following parametric functions (interpreted below) were proposed in [56]:

$$v(x) = \begin{cases} x^\alpha, x \geq 0; \\ -\lambda(-x)^\beta, x < 0 \end{cases}; \quad w^+(p) = \frac{p^\gamma}{(p^\gamma + (1-p)^\gamma)^{1/\gamma}}; \quad w^-(p) = \frac{p^\delta}{\left(p^\delta + (1-p)^\delta\right)^{1/\delta}}$$ (14.53)

The two latter expressions distinguish between gains (+) and losses (−).

Other functional specifications have been formulated in so-called non-expected utility theories [57]. The ideas underlying the value and the probability weighting functions is that people exhibit diminishing sensitivity to the evaluation of changes in wealth in the domain of gains (encapsulated in the concavity of $v(x)$ for $x \geq 0$), the reverse effect in the domain of losses (loss aversion), and a subjective probability weighting that overweights small probabilities and underweights large probabilities (and can be different for gains and losses). Also, evaluation is relative to a neutral reference point (here $x = 0$), below which changes in wealth are seen as losses. This contrasts with standard utility theory, in which only the final state of wealth contributes to the utility evaluation. Parameters (here $\alpha, \beta, \gamma, \delta$) are fitted to experimental data to reflect the choices of groups or individuals, assuming that people prefer the option with the highest utility.

It was observed in [58] that decision making can be inherently stochastic; that is, the same decision maker may make a different decision when faced with the same question at different times. This idea was formalized in [59] by offering a form for the probability of choosing one option over another. Several functions have since been proposed for this so-called stochastic specification, stochastic error, or choice function [47, 56]. A probabilistic element can thus be integrated in prospect theory models, providing in principle a limit for the explanation and prediction power of such models [48, 60, 61].

Prospect theory is a fertile field of research that currently dominates decision theory [62]. However, some works [63, 64] point out that non-expected utility theories in general do not remove paradoxes, create inconsistencies, and always necessitate an ambiguous fitting that cannot always be done. In this context, QDT proposes an alternative perspective that may provide novel insights into decision making.

The main features of QDT are the following. First, as mentioned above, QDT derives from a complete, coherent theoretical framework that explicitly formalizes the concepts of uncertainty, entanglement, and order effects. In the framework of QDT, paradoxes of classical decision theory such as the disjunction effect, the conjunction fallacy, the Allais paradox, the Ellsberg paradox, or the planning paradox (to name just a few) have quantitative explanations [65–67]. Within QDT, behavioral biases result from interference caused by the deliberations of decision makers making up their mind [68].

Second, QDT is inherently a probabilistic theory, in the sense that it focuses on the fraction of people who choose a given prospect, or on the frequency with which a single decision maker does so over a number of repetitions of the same question. In the theoretical part of this section, we derive the following expression for the probability $p(L_j)$ that a prospect L_j is chosen by one or several decision makers:

$$p(L_j) = \frac{U(L_j)}{\sum_i U(L_i)} + q(L_j), \tag{14.54}$$

where $U(L_j)$ is the same utility as in Eq. (14.50), and $q(L_j)$ is the attraction factor; in this term are encompassed the "hidden variables" of decision theory, that is, feelings, contextual factors, subconscious processes, and so on. Eq. (14.54) can be derived from seeing prospects and cognitive states as vectors in a Hilbert space, as we show in the next section.

Lastly, QDT distinguishes itself from classical and other quantum-like decision theories by offering quantitative predictions. Specifically, the quarter law predicts that the average absolute value of $q(L_j)$ is 1/4 under the null hypothesis of no prior information. Besides explaining several paradoxes on binary lotteries [65–68], QDT has been developed in several directions. It provides expressions for discount functions employed in the theory of time discounting [69] and explains dynamical inconsistencies [65]. QDT also describes the influence of information and a surrounding society on individual decision makers [70, 71]. Although QDT has been developed to describe the behavior of human decision makers, it can also be used as a guide to create artificial quantum intelligence [15].

14.3.1 Model: QDT

Hilbert space formalism: This section shows how Eq. (14.54) can be derived from seeing prospects and a decision maker's state of mind as vectors in a complex Hilbert space in the simple, concrete case of a choice between two lotteries in the domain of gains. This section requires some knowledge of the mathematics of Hilbert spaces and quantum mechanics. After Eq. (14.54) is derived, the rest of this chapter does not require any such knowledge.

Prospects: We consider the *fruit fly* of decision theory [72], that is, the situation where subjects can choose between two lotteries in the domain of gains, denoted by L_1 and L_2 and expressed as

$$L_1 = \{x_n, p_1(x_n) : n = 1, 2, ..., N\},$$
$$L_2 = \{x_n, p_2(x_n) : n = 1, 2, ..., N\}. \tag{14.55}$$

An example is given below (Eq. 14.49).

Observables and Hilbert spaces: Let us introduce two observables A and B, represented by operators $\hat{A}$ and $\hat{B}$ acting on Hilbert spaces $\mathcal{H}_A$ and $\mathcal{H}_B$, respectively. Each observable can take on two values, $A = \{A_1, A_2\}$ and $B = \{B_1, B_2\}$. A_1 and A_2 represent the two options presented to the subjects of the experiment: when the lottery L_j is chosen, A takes the corresponding value A_j ($j = 1, 2$). B embodies an uncertainty [73]. For instance, B_1 (respectively, B_2) can represent the confidence (resp., the disbelief) of the decision maker that she correctly understands the empirical setup, that she is taking appropriate decisions, and that the lottery is going to be played out as announced by the experimenter. B thus encapsulates the idea that these choices involve an uncertainty for the decision maker, although it is not necessarily explicitly expressed in the setup. The eigenstates of each operator form an orthonormal basis of the associated Hilbert space, $\mathcal{H}_A = \text{span} \{|A_1\rangle, |A_2\rangle\}$, $\mathcal{H}_B = \text{span} \{|B_1\rangle, |B_2\rangle\}$. A decision maker's state is defined in the tensor product space $\mathcal{H}_{AB} = \mathcal{H}_A \otimes \mathcal{H}_B$, spanned by the tensor product states $|A_i\rangle \otimes |B_j\rangle (i, j \in \{1, 2\})$. For simplicity, we write $|A_i B_j\rangle$ without the tensor product sign: $\mathcal{H}_{AB} = \text{span} \{|A_1 B_1\rangle, |A_1 B_2\rangle, |A_2 B_1\rangle, |A_2 B_1\rangle\}$.

States: A decision maker is assumed to be in a *decision-maker state* $|\psi\rangle \in \mathcal{H}_{AB}$, which is a linear combination of the basis states $|\psi\rangle = \alpha_{11} |A_1 B_1\rangle + \alpha_{12} |A_1 B_2\rangle + \alpha_{21} |A_2 B_1\rangle + \alpha_{22} |A_2 B_2\rangle$, with $\alpha_{mn} \equiv \alpha_{mn}(t) \in \mathbb{C}$ for $m, n \in \{1, 2\}$. Each decision maker is characterized by his own set of time-dependent, nonzero coefficients $\{\alpha_{mn}(t)\}$, $m, n \in \{1, 2\}$. This superposition state reflects our indecision until we make a choice. The time dependence implies that the same individual may make different decisions when asked the same question at different times. The time evolution can be seen as due to endogenous processes in the decision maker's body and mind (e.g., breathing, digestion, feelings, thoughts) as well as exogenous factors (interactions with the surroundings). We assume that $|\psi\rangle$ is normalized, that is, $\langle \psi | \psi \rangle = |\alpha_{11}|^2 + |\alpha_{12}|^2 + |\alpha_{21}|^2 + |\alpha_{22}|^2 = 1$.

The *prospect states* are defined as product states $|\pi_j\rangle \in \mathcal{H}_{AB}$,

$$|\pi_j\rangle = |A_j\rangle \otimes \left\{ \gamma^j_{j1} |B_1\rangle + \gamma^j_{j2} |B_2\rangle \right\}$$
$$= \gamma^j_{j1} |A_j B_1\rangle + \gamma^j_{j2} |A_j B_2\rangle, \gamma^j_{kl} = 0, \forall j, k \neq j, l \in \{1, 2\}, \tag{14.56}$$

where $\gamma^j_{kl} \in \mathbb{C}$, $j, k, l \in \{1, 2\}$. Concretely,

$$|\pi_1\rangle = \gamma^1_{11} |A_1 B_1\rangle + \gamma^1_{12} |A_1 B_2\rangle, \gamma^1_{21} = 0, \gamma^1_{22} = 0$$
$$|\pi_2\rangle = \gamma^2_{21} |A_2 B_1\rangle + \gamma^2_{22} |A_2 B_2\rangle, \gamma^2_{11} = 0, \gamma^2_{12} = 0. \tag{14.57}$$

The prospect states are superposition states, each corresponding to the decision maker ultimately choosing either lottery with indefinite mixed feelings about the setup and context. The use of three indices in γ_{kl}^j is useful to distinguish options that are available to the decision maker as opposed to options that are excluded, as illustrated in the next section.

Probability measure: QDT assumes that the following process occurs: the decision maker approaches any question in a state $|\psi\rangle$. During her deliberations, she transits to either $|\pi_1\rangle$ or $|\pi_2\rangle$. If she transits to $|\pi_j\rangle(j = 1, 2)$, she chooses the lottery L_j. The experimenter observes the choice of the lottery L_j, but does not know whether B chose the value B_1 or B_2. The decision maker herself may remain undecided about B_1 or B_2. After the decision, the decision-maker state becomes $|\psi'\rangle$, a superposition state of the same form, but possibly with different coefficients than before, due to the time evolution. The same process is repeated when the next question is asked.

Hence, we identify the probability that the lottery L_j be chosen with the probability that $|\psi\rangle$ makes a transition to the superposition state $|\pi_j\rangle(j = 1, 2)$:

$$p(L_j) \approx \text{proba}\,(\psi \to \pi_j) = |\langle \psi \mid \pi_j\rangle|^2 (\, j = 1, 2). \tag{14.58}$$

The approximation sign is there because, a priori, one does not have $|\langle \psi \mid \pi_1\rangle|^2 + |\langle \psi | \pi_2 \rangle|^2 = 1$. This is because, formally, there are additional states in $\mathcal{H}_{AB}$ than just $|\pi_1\rangle$ and $|\pi_2\rangle$ to which the system can make a transition; for instance, $|\pi_3\rangle = \gamma_{11}^3 |A_1 B_1\rangle + \gamma_{12}^3 |A_1 B_2\rangle + \gamma_{21}^3 |A_2 B_1\rangle$. However, $|\pi_3\rangle$ does not correspond to any decision that can be made in the experimental setting. In practice, decision makers have to choose between L_1 and L_2 (alternatively, if they fail to answer properly, their data is discarded). This amounts to constraining the system such that $\sum_{j=1}^2 p(L_j) = 1$, which can be achieved by defining $p(L_j)$ as follows:

$$p(L_j) := \frac{|\langle \psi \mid \pi_j\rangle|^2}{|\langle \psi \mid \pi_1\rangle|^2 + |\langle \psi | \pi_2\rangle|^2}. \tag{14.59}$$

By defining the normalization quantity P, the former expression can also be written as

$$p(L_j) = \frac{1}{P}|\langle \psi \mid \pi_j\rangle|^2; P = |\langle \psi|\pi_1\rangle|^2 + |\langle \psi|\pi_2\rangle|^2. \tag{14.60}$$

Equation (14.59) ensures that $\sum_{j=1}^2 p(L_j) = 1$ and that $p(L_j) \in [0, 1](\forall j = 1, 2)$.

The probability $p(L_j)(j = 1, 2)$ is to be understood as the theoretical frequency of the prospect L_j being chosen a large number of times. Two types of setups can be put in place. The first setup involves a number of agents; in that case, $p(L_j)$ gives the fraction of agents expected to choose L_j. In the second setup, a single decision maker is faced with a number of decision tasks, among which the same decision task appears several times. This setup is designed such that each repetition of the same decision task can be assumed to be independent of previous occurrences. That is, we assume negligible memory and influence of previous decisions. In this second setup, the option L_j is chosen a fraction $p(L_j)$ of the time by the same decision maker. QDT treats these two setups similarly.

Utility and attraction factors: Let us examine the quantity $|\langle \psi \mid \pi_j\rangle|^2$.

$$\begin{aligned}
|\langle \psi \mid \pi_j\rangle|^2 &= \langle \psi \mid \pi_j\rangle\langle \pi_j \mid \psi\rangle = \left(\alpha^*_{j1}\gamma^j_{j1} + \alpha^*_{j2}\gamma^j_{j2}\right)\left(\alpha_{j1}\gamma^{j*}_{j1} + \alpha_{j2}\gamma^{j*}_{j2}\right) \\
&= |\alpha_{j1}|^2 |\gamma^j_{j1}|^2 + |\alpha_{j2}|^2|\gamma^j_{j2}|^2 + \alpha^*_{j1}\gamma^j_{j1}\alpha_{j2}\gamma^{j*}_{j2} + \alpha^*_{j2}\gamma^j_{j2}\alpha_{j1}\gamma^{j*}_{j1}.
\end{aligned} \tag{14.61}$$

In quantum mechanics, the last two terms in Eq. (14.61) correspond to an interference between different intermediate states as the system makes a transition from $|\psi\rangle$ to $|\pi_j\rangle$. In decision theory, this interference can be understood as originating from the decision maker's deliberations as she is in the process of weighing up options and making up her mind. These interference terms are encapsulated into what is called in QDT the *attraction factor*,

$$q(L_j) = \frac{1}{P}\left(\alpha^*_{j1}\gamma^j_{j1}\alpha_{j2}\gamma^{j*}_{j2} + \alpha^*_{j2}\gamma^j_{j2}\alpha_{j11}\gamma^{j*}_{j1}\right), \tag{14.62}$$

where P is the normalization quantity introduced in Eq. (14.60). The attraction factor is interpreted in QDT as a contextual object encompassing subjectivity, feelings, emotions, cognitive biases, and framing effects. The classical terms become the so-called *utility factor*:

$$f(L_j) = \frac{1}{P}\left(|\alpha_{j1}|^2\left|\gamma^j_{j1}\right|^2 + |\alpha_{j2}|^2\left|\gamma^j_{j2}\right|^2\right). \tag{14.63}$$

Equation (14.59) can then be rewritten as

$$p(L_j) = f(L_j) + q(L_j). \tag{14.64}$$

In the absence of interference effects, only the utility factor $f(L_j)$ remains in $p(L_j)$. When $q(L_j) = 0$, the standard classical correspondence principle [74] leads one to let $p(L_j)$ connect to more classical decision theories such as those mentioned in the introduction. The utility factor $f(L_j)$ has to take the form of a probability function, satisfying $\sum_j f(L_j) = 1$ and $f(L_j) \in [0, 1]$.

As the simplest non-parametric formulation connecting $f(L_j)$ to classical decision theories, the utility factor is equated with $f(L_j) = U(L_j)/\sum_i U(L_i)$, where $U(L_j)$ is an expected value or expected utility, as in Eqs. (14.50), (14.51), or (14.52). In this section, we use the simple non-parametric form given by Eq. (14.50), $U(L_j) = \sum_{n=1}^{N} p(x_n)x_n$, making it an expected value. A more general form for $f(L_j)$ has been used as

$$f(L_j) = \frac{U(L_j)\exp\{\beta U(L_j)\}}{\sum_i U(L_i)\exp\{\beta U(L_i)\}}, \tag{14.65}$$

where $\beta \geq 0$ is called the "belief parameter." Previous applications of QDT to empirical data use the case $\beta = 0$, which is also what we use in this section.

Let us examine the implications of conditions $\sum_j f(L_j) = 1$ and $f(L_j) \in [0, 1]$ when the utility factors are written as in Eq. (14.64). Imposing that the utility factors sum to one means that

$$|\alpha_{11}|^2\left|\gamma^1_{11}\right|^2 + |\alpha_{12}|^2\left|\gamma^1_{12}\right|^2 + |\alpha_{21}|^2\left|\gamma^2_{21}\right|^2 + |\alpha_{22}|^2\left|\gamma^2_{22}\right|^2 = P. \tag{14.66}$$

Based on its definition in Eqs. (14.60) and (14.61), the normalization coefficient P is explicited as

$$\begin{aligned} P = &|\alpha_{11}|^2\left|\gamma^1_{11}\right|^2 + |\alpha_{12}|^2\left|\gamma^1_{12}\right|^2 + |\alpha_{21}|^2\left|\gamma^2_{21}\right|^2 + |\alpha_{22}|^2\left|\gamma^2_{22}\right|^2 + \\ &+ \alpha^*_{11}\gamma^1_{11}\alpha_{j2}\gamma^{1*}_{12} + \alpha^*_{12}\gamma^1_{12}\alpha_{11}\gamma^{1*}_{j1} + \alpha^*_{21}\gamma^2_{21}\alpha_{22}\gamma^{2*}_{22} + \alpha^*_{22}\gamma^2_{22}\alpha_{21}\gamma^{2*}_{21}. \end{aligned} \tag{14.67}$$

From the definition of the attraction factors (Eq. 14.62), and using Eq. (14.66), this can be rewritten as

$$P = P + P(q(L_1) + q(L_2)), \tag{14.68}$$

which yields

$$q(L_1) + q(L_2) = 0, \tag{14.69}$$

since the attraction factors are not null by definition. The constraint that the utility factors sum to one thus imposes the constraint that the attraction factors sum to zero. The latter condition is the focus of the next section.

Quarter law – prediction of QDT regarding attraction factors: In this section, we recall the derivation of the so-called quarter law, which governs the typical amplitude of the attraction factors. Since $p(L_j)$ and $f(L_j)$ both sum to one over the $L = 2$ prospects, it follows from Eq. (14.64) that the attraction factors $q(L_j)$ sum to zero. Also, since $p(L_j)$ and $f(L_j)$ both take values in the interval $[0, 1]$, $q(L_j)$ lies in the interval $[-1, 1]$. In QDT, these two conditions are called the *alternation conditions:*

$$-1 \leq q(L_j) \leq 1, \quad \sum_{j=1}^{L} q(L_j) = 0. \tag{14.70}$$

Arising from interference effects between prospects in the mind of the decision maker, the attraction factor can be seen as a random quantity varying across decision makers and over time for a single decision maker. Thus, the choices made by different individuals or by the same person at different times constitute a number of realizations of q equal to L (the number of prospects in each decision task) multiplied by the number of choices made. Let us introduce $\varphi(q)$, the normalized distribution of q, as

$$\int_{-1}^{1} \varphi(q)dq = 1. \tag{14.71}$$

Because of the alternation conditions (Eq. 14.70), in the presence of $L = 2$ prospects, the distribution of q is symmetrical around zero and the mean of q is zero:

$$\int_{-1}^{1} \varphi(q)qdq = 0. \tag{14.72}$$

Let us define the quantities

$$q_+ = \int_0^1 \varphi(q)qdq, \text{ and } q_- = \int_{-1}^0 \varphi(q)qdq. \tag{14.73}$$

From the alternation conditions (Eq. 14.70) leading to Eq. (14.72), we have $q_+ + q_- = 0$. In the absence of any information, the variable q is equiprobable; that is, the distribution $\varphi(q)$ is uniform. From Eq. (14.71), it follows that $\varphi(q) = 1/2$. Put into Eq. (14.73), this yields $q_+ = 1/4$, $q_- = -1/4$.

Applied to a binary lottery choice, this yields the prediction that when L_1 is the most attractive prospect, we have $\bar{q}(L_1) = \dfrac{1}{4}$, $\bar{q}(L_2) = -1/4$, where the signs are reversed if L_2 is the most attractive prospect. In QDT, this is called the *quarter law* and constitutes a quantitative prediction regarding the average value of the attraction factors in any given experiment, under the assumption of no additional prior information. Several families of distributions $\varphi(q)$ yield the same average value of 1/4 for the attraction factor, which makes this result quite general, as pointed out in [73]. For example, this is true for the symmetric beta distribution,

$$\varphi(q) = \frac{\Gamma(2\alpha)}{2\Gamma^2(\alpha)} |q|^{\alpha-1}(1 - |q|)^{\alpha-1}, \tag{14.74}$$

defined on the interval $q \in [-1, 1]$, with $\alpha > 0$ and $\Gamma(\alpha)$ the gamma function. The beta distribution is employed in many applications, for example, in Bayesian inference as a prior probability distribution. The quarter law also follows from several other distributions normalized on the interval $[-1, 1]$, such as the symmetric quadratic distribution,

$$\varphi(q) = 6\left(|q| - \frac{1}{2}\right)^2, \tag{14.75}$$

and the symmetric triangular distribution,

$$\varphi(q) = \begin{cases} 2\,|\,q\,| & \text{if } 0 \le |\,q\,| \le \dfrac{1}{2}, \\ 2(1 - |\,q\,|) & \text{if } \dfrac{1}{2} < q \le 1. \end{cases} \tag{14.76}$$

Typical values of the attraction factors are derived in [76] in the general case of a decision involving more than two prospects.

Sign of attraction factor in the case of close utility factors: A rule has been developed in [73], giving the sign of the attraction factor for a binary decision task with close utility factors. This rule considers two lotteries $L_1 = \{x_i, p_1(x_i): \ i = 1, 2, ...\}$, $L_2 = \{y_j, p_2(y_j): j = 1, 2, ...\}$. Note that not all of the same amounts appear in the two prospects. The maximal and minimal gains are denoted as $x_{max} = \sup\{x_i\}$, $x_{min} = \inf\{x_i\}$, $y_{max} = \sup\{y_j\}$, $y_{min} = \inf\{y_j\}$. The gain factor $g(L_1)$ of the first prospect, the risk factor $r(L_2)$ of choosing the second prospect, and the quantity $\alpha(L_1)$ are then defined as follows:

$$g(L_1) = \frac{x_{max}}{y_{max}}$$

$$r(L_2) = \begin{cases} \dfrac{p_2(y_{min})}{p_1(x_{min})}, p_2(y_{min}) < 1 \\ 0, p_2(y_{min}) = 1 \end{cases} \tag{14.77}$$

$$\alpha(L_1) = g(L_1)r(L_2) - 1.$$

Using these quantities, the sign of the first prospect attraction factor, $q(L_1)$, is defined as

$$sgn\ q(L_1) = \begin{cases} +1, \alpha(L_1) > 0 \\ -1, \alpha(L_1) \le 0. \end{cases} \tag{14.78}$$

Design Example 14.3

In this section, we will combine results presented in [46] with a modified interpretation relevant for advanced wireless networks. In the original dataset analyzed in [46], subjects have to choose between one of two lotteries. One lottery, L_1, is risky: subjects can win either $50, with a probability p, or nothing, with a probability $1-p$. In the other lottery L_2, subjects get the sure amount x in $ (i.e., with probability 1). This can be seen as a "certain lottery." The condition $0 < x < 50$ is always ensured, otherwise there would be no point in choosing the risky lottery. The two lotteries are written

$$L_1 = \{0, 1 - p \mid x, 0 \mid y, p\}, \tag{14.79}$$

$$L_2 = \{0, 0 \mid x, 1 \mid y, 0\}. \tag{14.80}$$

with $0 < x < y$ and in the experiment, $y = 50. A practical interpretation relevant for dynamic wireless networks would be the following: subjects (users) make available their mobile phones to the network to be used as an augmented element of the network infrastructure under two different possible contracts. The benefits of such decisions will depend on how much the phone is used by the network, which depends on the amount of excessive traffic in the network, which

Design Example 14.3 (Continued)

is a random variable. Contract one, referred to as C_1, corresponding to lottery L_1, offers $50 if the phone is used by the network in the period T, which depends on whether or not the network has a need to use it in a given period. Let assume that that happens with probability p. If the phone is not used by the network in that period, the user gets nothing. An alternative is to have a flat price contract C_2, corresponding to lottery L_2, where the user gets $ x independent of whether the phone is used or not. Although we have concrete models in wireless networks using these algorithms, in the following we will retain the general notations L_1 and L_2 and the term *lottery* instead of *contract* so that the presented results can be also interpolated into other applications as well.

Note that the same amounts appear in both prospects. Writing L_1 as Eq. (14.79) means that one can get 0 with probability $1 - p$, x with probability 0, and y with probability p. Similarly, writing L_2 as Eq. (14.80) corresponds to gaining 0 with probability 0, x with probability 1, and y with probability 0. This way of expressing the two prospects captures the fact that decision makers compare the two lotteries as they are making up their mind.

14.3.1.1 Decision Tasks and Participants

In the original [46] dataset, a decision task is characterized by the values of the two parameters p (the probability of winning the fixed amount $50 in the risky lottery L_1) and x (the guaranteed payoff in the certain lottery L_2). In the experiment that generated the dataset, pairs of (p, x) values were randomly generated, and the corresponding decision tasks (L_1, L_2) were submitted to subjects.

Each of 27 participants was given 200 randomly generated decision tasks, in four runs of 50 questions each. This amounts to 5400 data points. Overall, the probability p was varied between 0.05 and 0.9 in steps of 0.05, and the sure amount x between 0 and 49 in steps of 1. At most 900 different (p, x) pairs could thus be generated. The detailed method used in the experiment is given in [49], including the description of conditions between which we do not differentiate in the present analysis.

The mean age of participants was 25.8 ± 3.6 years. Thirteen women (mean age 25 ± 3.3 years) and fourteen men (mean age 27 ± 3.7 years) were included in the study. The decisions were contextualized, in the sense that participants were asked to imagine a bank investment. Each decision was equally important, as participants were promised that they would receive, at the end of the experiment, the amount resulting from one randomly chosen decision task. All participants provided written, informed consent and were compensated for their participation.

Application of QDT to the dataset: We now describe how QDT specifically applies to the empirical dataset under study. The theoretical correspondence was carried out in the section that follows the introduction. Indeed, this section considers a decision problem whose structure corresponds to that of the decision tasks generating the dataset.

Utility factors: As stated earlier, we equate prospect utilities with the expected values given by Eq. (14.50); hence

$$U(L_1) = (1 - p)0 + 0 \cdot x + p \cdot 50 = 50p,$$
$$U(L_2) = 0 \cdot 0 + 1 \cdot x + 0 \cdot 50 = x. \tag{14.81}$$

Then, according to the definition of $f(L_j)$ as given before Eq. (14.65), $f(L_j) = U(L_j)/\sum_i U(L_i)$, the utility factors are given by

$$f(L_1) = \frac{U(L_1)}{U(L_1) + U(L_2)} = \frac{50p}{50p + x}, \tag{14.82}$$

$$f(L_2) = \frac{U(L_2)}{U(L_1) + U(L_2)} = \frac{x}{50p + x}. \tag{14.83}$$

Aggregation of decision tasks: Since QDT is a probabilistic theory, a decision task must be offered several times in order to obtain an empirical choice frequency approximating (L_j). As is the case of other datasets available to researchers, the present dataset was not generated with QDT in mind. We suggest in the discussion how decision tasks more suitable for testing QDT can be designed. There are several ways to aggregate the decision tasks:

(i) Only aggregate decisions presenting the same (p, x) values, that is, the same utilities $U(L_1)$, $U(L_2)$.

(ii) Aggregate decisions with close (p, x) values. For example, $(p = 0.1, x = 42)$ and $(p = 0.1, x = 45)$ present the same value of p and close values of x, and could be considered so similar as to represent the same decision task.

(iii) Aggregate decisions presenting the same utility factors $f(L_1)$, $f(L_2)$. For instance, the (p, x) pairs $A(p = 0.1, x = 42)$, $B(p = 0.1, x = 45)$, and $C(p = 0.05, x = 22)$ give respectively $f(L_1^A) = 0.106$, $f(L_1^B) = 0.1$, and $f(L_1^C) = 0.102$. Rounding these utility factors to the lowest 0.01, the three games A, B, and C are aggregated as three realizations of the same decision task characterized by a utility factor $f(L_1) = 0.1$.

The problem with only aggregating identical (p, x) pairs (option [i]) is that the available empirical dataset does not always present a sufficient number of realizations of each (p, x) pair to enable a meaningful probabilistic analysis. For instance, in [46]'s dataset, 10.7% of all (p, x) pairs were offered only once; 11.5% were offered twice; and 30.4% were offered three times or less. At most, one (p, x) pair was offered 126 times. Ignoring decision tasks with less than a minimum number of realizations is possible, but this means giving up a substantial amount of data.

Aggregation using a utility factor (option [iii]) partly resolves this problem. When rounding $f(L_1)$ to the lowest 0.01, no decision task characterized by its utility factor $f(L_1)$ was offered less than three times in [46], and only 1.3% of all values of $f(L_1)$ were submitted exactly three times. At most, a given value of $f(L_1)$ was submitted 274 times.

Probability: Empirically, we have access to the number of times, N_j, a prospect was chosen by one or several decision makers over the N times the same decision task was offered. The probabilities are related by $\sum_{j=1}^2 p(L_j) = 1$, utility factors by $\sum_j f(L_j) = 1$ and $f(L_j) \in [0, 1]$, and attraction factors for the two prospects ($j = 1, 2$) by Eq. (14.69), and the entire analysis can rest on the quantities associated with only one prospect. In what follows, we focus on the risky prospect, that is, $j = 1$. The empirical frequency is given by $p_{exp}(L_1) = N_1/N$, which approximates the probability $p(L_1)$. In what follows, we identify $p_{exp}(L_1)$ with $p(L_1)$. Let us introduce a random variable X such that, at the k-th realization of a given decision task,

$$X_k = \begin{cases} 1, \text{if the risky prospect is chosen,} \\ 0, \text{if the certain prospect is chosen.} \end{cases} \tag{14.84}$$

The probability $p(L_1)$ is thus the Bernoulli distribution of X. Let us additionally introduce the *retract* function, which retracts a variable z into an interval $[a, b]$:

$$\text{Ret}_{[a,b]}\{z\} = \begin{cases} a, z \leq a \\ z, a < z < b \\ b, z \geq b \end{cases} \tag{14.85}$$

Empirically, based on Eq. (14.64), the following relationship holds between the probability $p(L_1)$, the utility factor $f(L_1)$, and the attraction factor $q(L_1)$:

$$p(L_1) = \text{Ret}_{[0,1]}\{f(L_1) + q(L_1)\}, \tag{14.86}$$

where the retract function ensures that $p(L_1)$ lies in $[0, 1]$.

Attraction factors: The attraction factor can be deduced from experimental results as

$$q(L_1) = p(L_1) - f(L_1), \tag{14.87}$$

but only for $0 < p(L_1) < 1$, because of the retract function in Eq. (14.86). Indeed, for $p(L_1) = 0$ and $p(L_1) = 1$, $q(L_1)$ can have taken any value such that $f(L_1) + q(L_1) \leq 0$ or $f(L_1) + q(L_1) \geq 1$, respectively. Hence, the exact value of $q(L_1)$ that guided the decision maker(s) cannot be retrieved in these two cases; applying Eq. (14.87) may lead to over- or underestimation of $q(L_1)$.

Sign of attraction factors: The rule for the sign of the attraction factor in the case of close utility factors given by Eq. (14.78) applies to the lotteries written as

$$L_1 = \{50, p \mid 0, 1-p\}, \tag{14.88}$$

$$L_2 = \{y, 1\}. \tag{14.89}$$

One gets $r(L_2) = 0$, $\alpha(L1) = -1$, and sgn $q(L_1) = -1$. In other words, at and around $f(L_1) = f(L_2) = 0.5$, the risky prospect's attraction factor should be negative and the certain prospect should be preferred, in accordance with the principle of risk aversion.

Finally, Figure 14.7 presents empirical probability $p(L_1)$ (choice frequency of the risky prospect) as a function of the utility factor $f(L_1)$, for women (W) and men (M) separately. Each point aggregates decision tasks presenting the same value of $f(L_1)$ rounded to the lowest 0.01. The area of the markers is proportional to the number of decision tasks per point, which ranges from 1 to 140 for women and from 1 to 134 for men. The vertical dotted lines at $f(L_1) = 0.55$ and 0.66 relate to the transition, and the diagonal lines to the quarter law.

Similarly, Figure 14.8 presents empirical probability $p(L_1)$ (choice frequency of the risky prospect) as a function of the utility factor $f(L_1)$. Each point aggregates decision tasks presenting the same value of $f(L_1)$ rounded to the lowest 0.01. The area of the markers is proportional to the number of decision tasks per point and varies between 3 and 274.

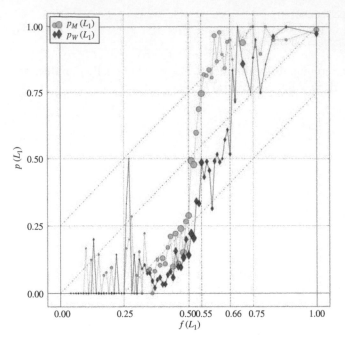

Figure 14.7 Empirical probability $p(L_1)$ (choice frequency of the risky prospect) as a function of the utility factor $f(L_1)$. *Source:* Favre et al. [46].

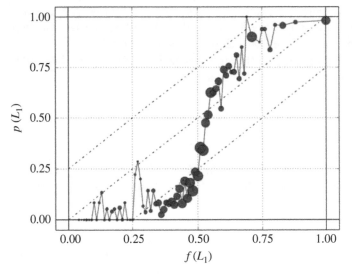

Figure 14.8 Empirical probability $p(L_1)$ (choice frequency of the risky prospect) as a function of the utility factor $f(L_1)$. *Source:* Favre et al. [46].

14.4 Predictions in QDT

In this section, QDT from the previous section is generalized to the games containing lotteries with gains as well as losses. The mathematical structure of the approach is based on the theory of quantum measurements, which makes this approach relevant both for the description of decision making of humans and the creation of artificial quantum intelligence. General rules are formulated allowing for the explicit calculation of quantum probabilities representing the fraction of decision makers preferring the considered prospects. This provides a method to quantitatively predict decision-maker choices, including the cases of games with high uncertainty for which the classical expected utility theory fails. The approach is applied to experimental results obtained on a set of lottery gambles with gains and losses. The predictions, involving no fitting parameters, are in very good agreement with experimental data. In addition, the use of quantum decision making [76] in game theory is described, and a principal scheme for creating quantum artificial intelligence is suggested.

In this section, we consider a set of events $\{A_n\}$ labeled by an index $n = 1, 2, ...$ Each event A_n is put into correspondence with a state $|n\rangle$ of a Hilbert space $\mathcal{H}_A$, with the family of states $\{|n\rangle\}$ forming an orthonormalized basis:

$$A_n \rightarrow |n\rangle \in \mathcal{H}_A = \text{span}\{|n\rangle\}. \tag{14.90}$$

There also exists another set of events $\{B_\alpha\}$, labeled by an index $\alpha = 1, 2,...$, with each event being in correspondence with a state $|\alpha\rangle$ of a Hilbert space $\mathcal{H}_B$, the family of the states $\{|\alpha\rangle\}$ forming an orthonormalized basis:

$$B_\alpha \rightarrow |\alpha\rangle \in \mathcal{H}_B = \text{span}\{|\alpha\rangle\}. \tag{14.91}$$

A pair of events from different sets forms a composite event $A_n \otimes B_\alpha$ represented by a tensor product state $|n\rangle \otimes |\alpha\rangle$,

$$A_n \otimes B_\alpha \rightarrow |n\rangle \otimes |\alpha\rangle \in \mathcal{H}, \tag{14.92}$$

in the Hilbert space

$$\mathcal{H} \equiv \mathcal{H}_A \otimes \mathcal{H}_B = \text{span}\{|n\rangle \otimes |\alpha\rangle\}. \tag{14.93}$$

An event A_n is called *operationally testable* if and only if it induces a projector $|n\rangle\langle n|$ on the space $\mathcal{H}_A$. The event set $\{A_n\}$ is assumed to consist of operationally testable events. A different situation occurs when we have an *inconclusive event* consisting of a set

$$\mathbb{B} \equiv \{B_\alpha, b_\alpha : \alpha = 1, 2, ...\} \tag{14.94}$$

of events B_α associated with amplitudes b_α that are random complex numbers. An inconclusive event corresponds to a state $|B\rangle$ in the space $\mathcal{H}_B$, such that

$$\mathbb{B} \rightarrow |B\rangle = \sum_\alpha b_\alpha |\alpha\rangle \in \mathcal{H}_{\mathrm{B}}. \tag{14.95}$$

The states $|B_\alpha\rangle$ are not orthonormalized, so the operator $|B\rangle\langle B|$ is not a projector.

A composite event is termed a prospect. Of major interest are the prospects composed of an operationally testable event and an inconclusive event:

$$\pi_n = A_n \otimes \mathbb{B}. \tag{14.96}$$

A prospect corresponds to a prospect state in the space $\mathcal{H}$,

$$\pi_n \rightarrow |\pi_n\rangle = |n\rangle \otimes |B\rangle \in \mathcal{H}, \tag{14.97}$$

and induces a prospect operator

$$\hat{P}(\pi_n) \equiv |\pi_n\rangle\langle\pi_n|. \tag{14.98}$$

The prospect states are not orthonormalized, and the prospect operator is not a projector. The given set of prospects forms a lattice

$$\mathcal{L} = \{\pi_n : n = 1, 2, \dots, N_L\}, \tag{14.99}$$

whose ordering is characterized by prospect probabilities to be defined below. The assembly of prospect operators $\{\hat{P}(\pi_n)\}$ constitutes a positive operator-valued measure. By its role, this set is analogous to the algebra of local observables in quantum theory. The strategic state of a decision maker in decision theory, or statistical operator of a system in physics, is a semipositive trace-one operator $\hat{\rho}$ defined on the space $\mathcal{H}$. The prospect probability is the expectation value of the prospect operator:

$$p(\pi_n) = \text{Tr}\hat{\rho}\hat{P}(\pi_n), \tag{14.100}$$

with the trace over the space $\mathcal{H}$. To form a probability measure, the prospect probabilities are normalized, $\sum_n p(\pi_n) = 1, 0 \leq p(\pi_n) \leq 1$. Taking the trace in Eq. (14.100), it is possible to separate out positive-defined terms from the sign-undefined terms, which respectively, are

$$f(\pi_n) = \Sigma_\alpha |b_\alpha|^2 \langle n\alpha \mid \hat{\rho} \mid n\alpha \rangle,$$
$$q(\pi_n) = \Sigma_{\alpha \neq \beta} b_\alpha^* b_\beta \langle n\alpha \mid \hat{\rho} \mid n\beta \rangle. \tag{14.101}$$

Then the prospect probability reads as

$$p(\pi_n) = f(\pi_n) + q(\pi_n). \tag{14.102}$$

The appearance of a sign-undefined term is typical for quantum theory, describing the effects of interference and coherence.

Note that the decision-maker strategic state has to be characterized by a statistical operator and not just by a wave function since, in real life, any decision maker is not an isolated object but a member of a society. An important role in quantum theory is played by the *quantum-classical correspondence principle*, according to which classical theory has to be a particular case of quantum theory. In the present consideration, this is to be understood as the reduction of quantum probability to classical probability under the decaying quantum term:

$$p(\pi_n) \to f(\pi_n), q(\pi_n) \to 0. \tag{14.103}$$

In quantum physics, this is also called *decoherence*, when quantum measurements are reduced to classical measurements. The positive-definite term $f(\pi_n)$, playing the role of classical probability, is to be normalized,

$$\sum_n f(\pi_n) = 1, 0 \leq f(\pi_n) \leq 1. \tag{14.104}$$

From the conditions following Eqs. (14.100) and (14.104), we get

$$\sum_n q(\pi_n) = 0, -1 \leq q(\pi_n) \leq 1, \tag{14.105}$$

which is called the *alternation law*.

In decision theory, the classical part $f(\pi_n)$ describes the utility of the prospect π_n, which is defined on rational grounds. In that sense, a prospect π_1 is more useful than π_2 if and only if $f(\pi_1) > f(\pi_2)$ (*more useful*). The quantum part $q(\pi_n)$ characterizes the attractiveness of the prospect, which is based on irrational subconscious factors. Hence, a prospect π_1 is more attractive than π_2 if and only if $q(\pi_1) > q(\pi_2)$ (*more attractive*).

And the prospect probability (Eq. 14.102) defines the summary preferability of the prospect, taking into account both its utility and attractiveness. So, a prospect π_1 is preferable to π_2 if and only if

$$p(\pi_1) > p(\pi_2) \text{ (preferable).} \tag{14.106}$$

The structure of the quantum probability (Eq. 14.102), consisting of two parts, one showing the utility of a prospect and the other characterizing its attractiveness, is representative of real-life decision making, where both these constituents are typically present. Quantum probability, taking into account the rationally defined utility as well as such an irrational behavioral feature as attractiveness, can be termed as *behavioral probability*.

It is worth stressing that QDT is an intrinsically probabilistic theory. This is different from sto-chastic decision theories, where the choice is assumed to be deterministic, while randomness arises due to errors in decision making. The probabilistic nature of QDT is not caused by errors in decision making, but it is due to the natural state of a decision maker, described by a kind of statistical oper-ator. Upon the reduction of QDT to a classical decision theory, it reduces to a probabilistic variant of the latter, since decisions under uncertainty are necessarily probabilistic [78]. As mentioned above, the description of a decision maker strategic state by a statistical operator, and not by a wave func-tion, emphasizes the fact that any decision maker is not an absolutely isolated object but rather a member of a society, who is subjected to social interactions [73, 75, 78, 79, 80]. When comparing theoretical predictions with empirical data, it follows from the logical structure of QDT that one has to compare the theoretically calculated probability (Eq. 14.102) with the fraction of decision makers preferring the considered prospect.

14.4.1 Utility Factors

In this section, we describe the general method for defining utility factors for a given set of lotteries containing both gains as well as losses [77]. Let a set of payoffs be given by $X_n = \{x_i : i = 1, 2, ..., N_n\}$, in which payoffs can represent either gains or losses, being respectively positive or negative. The probability distribution over a payoff set is a lottery $L_n = \{x_i, p_n(x_i) : i = 1, 2, ..., N_n\}$, with the nor-malization condition $\sum_i p_n(x_i) = 1$, $0 \leq p_n(x_i) \leq 1$. The lotteries are enumerated by the index $n = 1$, 2,..., N_L. Under a utility function $u(x)$, the expected utility of lottery L_n is $U(L_n) = \sum_i u(x_i) p_n(x_i)$ ($n = 1, 2, ..., N_L$). Utility functions for gains and losses can have different signs. Therefore, the expected utility can also be either positive or negative. When it is negative, one often uses the nota-tion of the lottery cost $C(L_n) \equiv - U(L_n) = |U(L_n)| (U(L_n) < 0)$. An expected utility is positive, when in its payoffs gains prevail. And it is negative, when losses overwhelm gains.

*) In our example of Dynamic Network Architecture, the contracts C_1 and C_2 described in Section 14.2, should be modified to include losses of the user including battery consumption of the mobile unit, uncertainty due to the security and privacy concerns etc.

As has been explained in Section 14.2, the choice between the given lotteries in any game is always accompanied by uncertainty related to the decision-maker hesitations with respect to the formulation of the game rules, understanding of the problem, and his ability to decide what he con-siders to be the correct choice. All these hesitations form an inconclusive event denoted above as B. Therefore, a choice of a lottery L_n is actually a composite event, or a prospect

$$\pi_n = L_n \otimes B \ (n = 1, 2, ..., N_L). \tag{14.107}$$

Here, we denote the action of a lottery choice and a lottery by the same letter L_n, which should not lead to confusion. The utility factor $f(\pi_n)$ characterizes the utility of choosing a lottery L_n. Since QDT postulates that the choice is probabilistic, it is possible to define the average quantity over the set of lotteries,

$$U = \sum_{n=1}^{N_L} f(\pi_n) U(L_n), \tag{14.108}$$

playing the role of a normalization condition for random expected utilities. The utility factor repre-sents a classical probability distribution and can be found from the conditional minimization of Kullback–Leibler information [81, 82]. The use of the Kullback–Leibler information for defining such a probability distribution is justified by the Shore–Jonson theorem [83], which states that there exists only one distribution satisfying consistency conditions, and this distribution is uniquely defined by the minimum of the Kullback–Leibler information, under given constraints. The role of the constraints here is played by the normalization conditions Eqs. (14.104) and (14.107). Then the information functional reads as

$$I[f] = \sum_{n=1}^{N_L} f(\pi_n) \ln \frac{f(\pi_n)}{f_0(\pi_n)}$$
$$+ \gamma \left[\sum_{n=1}^{N_L} f(\pi_n) - 1 \right] + \beta \left[U - \sum_{n=1}^{N_L} f(\pi_n) U_n \right],$$

where $f_0(\pi_n)$ is a prior distribution, $U_n \equiv U(L_n)$, and β and γ are Lagrange multipliers. As boundary conditions, it is natural to require that the utility factor of a lottery with asymptotically large expected utility tends to unity,

$$f(\pi_n) \to 1 \, (U_n \to \infty), \tag{14.109}$$

whereas the utility factor of a lottery with asymptotically large cost would go to zero:

$$f(\pi_n) \to 0 \, (U_n \to -\infty). \tag{14.110}$$

Also, the utility factors, as their name implies, have to increase together with the related expected utilities:

$$\frac{\delta f(\pi_n)}{\delta U_n} \geq 0. \tag{14.111}$$

Minimizing the information functional (Eq. 14.108) results in the utility factors

$$f(\pi_n) = \frac{f_0(\pi_n) e^{\beta U_n}}{\sum_n f_0(\pi_n) e^{\beta U_n}}, \tag{14.112}$$

with a non-negative parameter β.

If one assumes that the prior distribution is uniform, such that $f_0(\pi_n) = 1/N_L$, then one arrives at the utility factors of the logit form. However, the uniform distribution does not satisfy the boundary conditions (Eqs. 14.109 and 14.110). Therefore, a more accurate assumption, taking into account the boundary conditions, should be based on the Luce choice axiom [59, 84]. According to this axiom, if an n-th object, from the given set of objects, is scaled by a quantity λ_n, then the probability of its choice is $f_0(\pi_n) = \lambda_n / \sum_n \lambda_n$. In our case, the considered objects are lotteries, and they are scaled by their expected utilities. So, for the non-negative utilities, we can set $\lambda_n = U_n \, (U_n \geq 0)$, and for the negative utilities, $\lambda_n = 1/|U_n|, \, (U_n < 0)$. The last expression is chosen in order to comply with Luce's axiom together with the ranking of preferences with respect to losses.

In general, utilities can be measured in some units, say, in monetary units M. Then we could use dimensionless scales λ_n defined as U_n/M and M/U_n, for gains and losses, respectively. Obviously, expression $f_0(\pi_n) = \lambda_n / \sum_n \lambda_n$ is invariant with respect to the units in which λ_n is measured. Therefore, for simplicity of notation, we assume that utilities are dimensionless. Thus, the utility factor (Eq. 14.112), with prior $f_0(\pi_n) = \lambda_n / \sum_n \lambda_n$, is

$$f(\pi_n) = \frac{\lambda_n e^{\beta U_n}}{\sum_n \lambda_n e^{\beta U_n}} \, (\beta \geq 0). \tag{14.113}$$

In particular, when gains prevail, so that all expected utilities are non-negative, then

$$f(\pi_n) = \frac{U_n e^{\beta U_n}}{\sum_n U_n e^{\beta U_n}} \, (\forall U_n \geq 0). \tag{14.114}$$

On the other hand, when losses prevail, and all expected utilities are negative, then

$$f(\pi_n) = \frac{|U_n|^{-1} e^{-\beta |U_n|}}{\sum_n |U_n|^{-1} e^{-\beta |U_n|}} \, (\forall U_n < 0) \tag{14.115}$$

In the mixed case, where the utility signs can be both positive and negative, one has to employ the general form Eq. (14.114).

The parameter β characterizes the belief of the decision maker as to whether the problem is correctly posed. Under strong belief, one gets

$$f(\pi_n) = \begin{cases} 1, & U_n = \max_n U_n \\ 0, & U_n \neq \max_n U_n \end{cases} (\beta \to \infty), \tag{14.116}$$

which recovers the classical utility theory with the deterministic choice of a lottery with the largest expected utility. In the opposite case of weak belief, when uncertainty is strong, one has

$$f(\pi_n) = \frac{\lambda_n}{\sum_n \lambda_n} \ (\beta = 0). \tag{14.117}$$

To explicitly illustrate the forms of the utility factors, let us consider the often-met situation of two lotteries under strong uncertainty, thus considering the binary prospect lattice

$$\mathcal{L} = \{\pi_n : n = 1, 2\} \ (\beta = 0), \tag{14.118}$$

with a zero belief parameter. Then, if in both the lotteries gains prevail, we have

$$f(\pi_n) = \frac{U_n}{U_1 + U_2} \ (U_1 \geq 0, U_2 \geq 0). \tag{14.119}$$

When losses prevail in the two lotteries, then

$$f(\pi_n) = 1 - \frac{|U_n|}{|U_1| + |U_2|} \ (U_1 < 0, U_2 < 0). \tag{14.120}$$

And if one expected utility is positive, say that of the first lottery, while the other utility is negative, then the utility factor for the first lottery is

$$f(\pi_1) = \frac{U_1 \, |U_2|}{U_1 \, |U_2| + 1} \ (U_1 > 0, U_2 < 0), \tag{14.121}$$

and $f(\pi_2) = 1 - f(\pi_1)$. In this way, the utility factors are explicitly defined for any combination of lotteries in the given game, with the payoff sets containing gains as well as losses.

14.4.2 Classification of Lotteries by Attraction Indices

By definition, an attraction factor quantifies how each of the given lotteries is more, or less, attractive [77]. The attractiveness of a lottery is composed of two factors, possible gain and its probability. It is clear that a lottery is more attractive when it suggests a larger gain and/or this gain is more probable. In other words, a more attractive lottery is more predictable and promises a larger profit. On the contrary, a lottery suggesting a smaller gain or a larger loss and/or higher probability of the loss is less attractive. A less certain lottery is less attractive, since it is less predictable, which is referred to as uncertainty aversion or ambiguity aversion. In order to come up with an explicit mathematical formulation of these ideas, let us introduce, for a lottery L_n, the notation for the *minimal gain* $g_n \equiv \min \{x_i \geq 0 : x_i \in L_n\}$ and for the *minimal loss* $l_n \equiv \max_i \{x_i \leq 0 : x_i \in L_n\}$. These quantities characterize possible gains and losses in the given lotteries.

But payoffs are not the only features that attract the attention of decision makers. In experimental neuroscience, it has been discovered that, during the act of choosing, the main and foremost attention of decision makers is directed to the payoff probabilities [85]. We capture this empirical observation by considering different weights related to payoffs and to their probabilities in the characterization of the lottery's attractiveness. Specifically, the weight of a payoff x should be much smaller than the weight of its probability $p(x)$. We quantitatively formulate this by choosing weights proportional respectively to x for the payoff versus $10^{p(x)}$ for its probability. The later term is motivated by the decimal number system. This leads us to define the *lottery attractiveness* $a_n \equiv a_n(L_n) \equiv \sum_i x_i 10^{p_n(x_i)}$, while the related relative quantity can be termed the *attraction index* $\alpha_n = \alpha_n(L_n) \equiv a_n / \sum_m |a_m|$. The latter satisfies the normalization condition $\sum_n |\alpha_n| = 1$.

The notion of the lottery attraction index makes it straightforward to classify all lotteries from the considered game into more, or less, attractive. Thus a lottery L_1 is more attractive than L_2, and hence $q(\pi_1) > q(\pi_2)$ when the attraction index of the first lottery is larger than that of the second, $\alpha_1 > \alpha_2$. In the marginal case, when $\alpha_1 = \alpha_2 \geq 0$, the first lottery is more attractive if the probability of its minimal gain is smaller than that of the second lottery, $\alpha_1 = \alpha_2 \geq 0$, $p(g_1) < p(g_2)$.

For brevity, this will be denoted as $\alpha_1 - \alpha_2 = +0$. And in the other marginal case, where $\alpha_1 = \alpha_2 < 0$, the first lottery is more attractive if the probability of its minimal loss is larger than that of the second, $\alpha_1 = \alpha_2 \langle 0, p(l_1) \rangle p(l_2)$. This, for brevity, will be denoted as $\alpha_1 - \alpha_2 = +0$.

The criterion allows us to arrange all the given lotteries with respect to the level of their attractiveness.

For the particular case, of a binary prospect lattice (Eq. 14.118), the alternation property (Eq. 14.105) reads as $q(\pi_1) + q(\pi_2) = 0$. Therefore, the attraction factors have different signs, $q(\pi_1) = -q(\pi_2)$.

The sign of each of the attraction factors is determined by the sign of the difference $\Delta\alpha \equiv \alpha_1 - \alpha_2$.

If $\Delta\alpha$ is positive, then the attraction factor of the first prospect is positive and that of the second is negative. On the contrary, if $\Delta\alpha$ is negative, then the attraction factor of the first lottery is negative and that of the second is positive. In the marginal case, when $\alpha_1 = \alpha_2$, we shall use the notations accepted above and explained earlier: If the first lottery is more attractive, we shall write $\Delta\alpha = +0$, whereas when the second lottery is more attractive, this will be denoted as $\Delta\alpha = -0$.

Typical values of attraction factors: The criterion of the previous section allows us to classify all the lotteries of the considered game into more, or less, attractive. But we also need to define the amplitudes of the attraction factors. According to QDT, these values are probabilistic variables, characterizing irrational subjective features of each decision maker. For different subjects, they may be different. They can also be different for the same subject at different times [86]. Different game setups also influence the values of the attraction factors [87]. However, for a probabilistic quantity, it is possible to define its average or typical value.

General considerations: We consider N_G games, enumerated by $k = 1, 2, ..., N_G$, with N_L lotteries in each, enumerated by $n = 1, 2, ... N_L$. In addition, let the choice be made by a society of N decision makers, numbered by $j = 1, 2, ..., N$. In the k-th game, decision makers make a choice between N_L prospects π_{nk}. The typical value of the attraction factor is defined as the average

$$\bar{q} \equiv \frac{1}{N_G} \sum_{k=1}^{N_G} \frac{1}{N_L} \sum_{n=1}^{N_L} \left| \frac{1}{N} \sum_{j=1}^{N} q_j(\pi_{nk}) \right|. \tag{14.122}$$

Denoting the mean value of the attraction factor for a prospect π_n, as

$$|q(\pi_n)| \equiv \frac{1}{N_G} \sum_{k=1}^{N_G} \left| \frac{1}{N} \sum_{j=1}^{N} q_j(\pi_{nk}) \right|, \tag{14.123}$$

we can write

$$\bar{q} = \frac{1}{N_L} \sum_{n=1}^{N_L} |q(\pi_n)|. \tag{14.124}$$

For a large value of the product $N_G N_L N$, the distribution of the attraction factors can be characterized by a probability distribution $\varphi(q)$, which, in view of the property Eq. (14.105), is normalized as

$$\int_{-1}^{1} \varphi(q)dq = 1. \tag{14.125}$$

The average absolute value of the attraction factor can be represented by the integral

$$\bar{q} = \int_{0}^{1} \varphi(q)dq. \tag{14.126}$$

This defines the typical value of the attraction factor that characterizes the level of deviation from rationality in decision making [88].

If there is no information on the properties and specifics of the given set of lotteries in the suggested games, then one should resort to a non-informative prior, assuming a uniform distribution satisfying normalization (Eq. 14.125), which gives $\varphi = \dfrac{1}{2}$. Substituting the uniform distribution $\varphi = \dfrac{1}{2}$ into the typical value of the attraction factor (Eq. 14.126) yields $\bar{q} = 0.25$, which was named the "quarter law" in Section 14.2. However, it is possible to find a more precise typical value $\bar{q}$ by taking into account the available information on the given lotteries. For example, it is straightforward to estimate the level of uncertainty of the lottery set.

Choice between two prospects: When choosing between two lotteries with rather differing utilities, the choice looks quite easy – the lottery with the largest utility is preferred. But when two lotteries have very close utilities, the choice becomes difficult. The closeness of the lotteries, corresponding to two prospects π_1 and π_2, can be quantified by the relative difference

$$\delta f(\pi_1, \pi_2) = \frac{2\,|f(\pi_1) - f(\pi_2)\,|}{f(\pi_1) + f(\pi_2)} \times 100\%. \tag{14.127}$$

When the choice is between just two prospects whose utility factors are normalized according to the condition Eq. (14.104), $f(\pi_1) + f(\pi_2) = 1$, then the relative difference simplifies to $\delta f = 2\,|f(\pi_1) - f(\pi_2)| \times 100\%$ ($N_L = 2$). There have been many discussions concerning choices between similar alternatives with close utilities or close probabilities, such that the choice becomes hard to make [89–92]; such choices are referred to as "irresolute." One of the major problems is how to quantify the similarity or closeness of the choices. Several ways of measuring the distance between the alternatives f_1 and f_2 have been suggested, including the linear distance $|f_1 - f_2|$, as well as different nonlinear distances $|f_1 - f_2|^m$, with $m > 0$. It was proposed in [77] that the value of δf which serves as an upper threshold, below which the lotteries are irresolute, should not depend on the exponent m used in the definition of the distance. Therefore, in order for the exponent m not to influence the boundary value, one has to require invariance of the distance with respect to the exponent m at the threshold, so that the critical threshold value should obey the equality: $(\delta f_c)^m = \delta f_c$ for any $m > 0$. This can be expressed as $[\delta f_c(\pi_1, \pi_2)]^m = \delta f_c(\pi_1, \pi_2)$, where $\delta f_c(\pi_1, \pi_2)$ is measured in percent. This equation is valid for arbitrary m only for $\delta f_c(\pi_1, \pi_2) = 1\%$. Hence the critical boundary value equals 1%. Thus, the lotteries for which the *irresoluteness criterion* $\delta f(\pi_1, \pi_2) < 1\%$ is valid are to be treated as close, or similar, and the choice between them as irresolute.

The next question is how the irresoluteness in the choice influences the typical attraction factor. Suppose that the fraction of irresolute games equals ν. Then the following properties of the distribution $\varphi(q)$ over admissible attraction factors should hold. In the presence of irresolute games

($v > 0$) for which the irresoluteness criterion holds true, the probability that the attraction factor is zero is asymptotically small:

$$\lim_{q \to 0} \varphi(q) = 0 \ (v > 0). \tag{14.128}$$

In other words, this condition means that, on the manifold of all possible games, absolutely rational games form a set of zero measure. If not all games are irresolute ($v < 1$), the probability of the maximal absolute value of the attraction factor is asymptotically small:

$$\lim_{|q| \to 1} \varphi(q) = 0 \ (v < 1). \tag{14.129}$$

That is, on the manifold of all possible games, absolutely irrational games constitute a set of zero measure. Often employed as a prior distribution in standard inference tasks [93–95], the simplest distribution that obeys the two conditions Eqs. (14.128) and (14.129) is the beta distribution, which, under normalization (Eq. 14.125), is

$$\varphi(q) = \frac{|q|^{v}(1 - |q|)^{1-v}}{\Gamma(1 + v)\Gamma(2 - v)}. \tag{14.130}$$

Using this distribution, expression (14.135) gives the typical attraction factor value $\bar{q} = (1 + v)/6$. Note that the average of $\bar{q}$ over the two boundary values $v = 0$ and $v = 1$ gives

$$\frac{1}{2}\left(\frac{1}{6} + \frac{2}{6}\right) = \frac{1}{4},$$

thus recovering the non-informative quarter law. The expression $\bar{q} = (1 + v)/6$ can be used for predicting the results of decision making. For example, in the case of a binary prospect lattice, the difference in the attraction indices $\Delta\alpha \equiv \alpha_1 - \alpha_2$ defines the signs of the attraction factors, making it possible to assign the attraction factors $\bar{q}$ and $-\bar{q}$ to the considered prospects.

Choice between more than two prospects: When there are more than two prospects in the considered game, the following procedure to estimate the attraction factors is used in [77]. By using the classification of the prospects by the attraction indices, as described in the previous section, it is straightforward to arrange the prospects in descending order of attractiveness, $q(\pi_n) > q(\pi_{n+1})$ ($n = 1, 2, \ldots, N_L - 1$). Let the maximal attraction factor be denoted as $q_{\max} \equiv q(\pi_1) > 0$. Given the unknown values of the attraction factors, the non-informative prior assumes that they are uniformly distributed and at the same time they must obey the ordering constraint $q(\pi_n) > q(\pi_{n+1})$ ($n = 1, 2, \ldots, N_L - 1$). Then, the joint cumulative distribution of the attraction factors is given by

$$\Pr\left[q(\pi_1) < \eta_1, \ldots, q(\pi_{N_L}) < \eta_{N_L} \mid \eta_1 \leq \eta_2 \leq \ \leq \eta_{N_L}\right] =$$
$$= \int_0^{\eta_1} dx_1 \int_{x_1}^{\eta_2} dx_2 \ldots \int_{x_{N_L-1}}^{\eta_{N_L}} dx_{N_L}, \tag{14.131}$$

where the series $\eta_1 \leq \eta_2 \leq \ldots \leq \eta_{N_L}$ of inequalities ensures the ordering. It is then straightforward to show that the average values of the $q(\pi_n)$ are equidistant; that is, the difference between any two neighboring factors, on average, is independent of n, so that $\Delta \equiv \langle q(\pi_n)\rangle - \langle q(\pi_{n+1})\rangle = const.$

Taking their average values as determining their typical values, we omit the symbol $\langle . \rangle$ representing the average operator and use the previous equation to represent the n-th attraction factor as $q(\pi_n) = q_{\max} - (n - 1)\Delta$. From the alternation property (Eq. 14.105), it follows that $q_{\max} = (N_L - 1)\Delta/2$.

The total number of lotteries N_L can be either even or odd, leading to slightly different forms for the following expressions:

$$\Delta = \begin{cases} 4\bar{q}/N_L & (N_L \text{ even}) \\ 4\bar{q}N_L/(N_L^2 - 1) & (N_L \text{ odd}) \end{cases} \tag{14.132}$$

Then the maximal attraction factor becomes

$$q_{\max} = \begin{cases} 2\bar{q}(N_L - 1)/N_L & (N_L \text{ even}) \\ 2\bar{q}N_L/(N_L + 1) & (N_L \text{ odd}) \end{cases} \tag{14.133}$$

Therefore, formula $q(\pi_n) = q_{\max} - (n-1)\Delta$ yields the expressions for all attraction factors:

$$q(\pi_n) = \begin{cases} 2\bar{q}\dfrac{N_L + 1 - 2n}{N_L} & (N_L \text{ even}) \\ 2\bar{q}\dfrac{N_L(N_L + 1 - 2n)}{N_L^2 - 1} & (N_L \text{ odd}) \end{cases} \tag{14.134}$$

Let us denote the set of all attraction factors in the considered game as $Q_{N_L} \equiv \{q(\pi_n) : n = 1, 2, \dots N_L\}$. If there are only two lotteries, then we have $\Delta = 2\bar{q}, q_{\max} = \bar{q}\ (N_L = 2)$, and the attraction factor set is $Q_2 = \{\bar{q}, -\bar{q}\}$. In the case of three lotteries, $\Delta = 3\bar{q}/2, q_{\max} = 3\bar{q}/2\ (N_L = 3)$, and the attraction factor set is

$$Q_3 = \left\{ \frac{3}{2}\bar{q}, 0, -\frac{3}{2}\bar{q} \right\}.$$

All attraction factors can be defined in this way.

Design Example 14.4

Here, we present the set of experiments performed in [96] and also used for comparison in [77]. This collection of games, including both gains and losses, is a classical example showing the inability of standard utility theory to provide even qualitatively correct predictions as a result of the confusion caused by very close or coinciding expected utilities. Let us emphasize that the choice of these games has been done in [96] in order to stress that standard decision making cannot be applied for these games. This is why it is logical to consider the same games and to show that the use of QDT does allow us to not only qualitatively explain the correct choice, but also that QDT provides quantitative predictions for such difficult cases. In the set of games described below, each game consists of two lotteries L_n, with $n = 1, 2$. The number of decision makers is about 100.

Recall that, as explained in Section 14.3, the choice between lotteries corresponds to the choice between prospects (Eq. 14.116) including the action of selecting a lottery L_n under a set of inconclusive events B representing hesitations and irrational feelings. Therefore the choice, under uncertainty, between lotteries L_n is equivalent to the choice between prospects π_n. The choice under uncertainty for the case of a binary lattice can be characterized by the utility factors (Eqs. 14.119–14.121). We take the linear utility function, which is convenient because the utility factors are independent of the monetary units used in the lottery payoffs. The attraction factors are calculated by following the recipes described in the previous sections.

(Continued)

Design Example 14.4 (Continued)

The authors in [77] compare the prospect probabilities $p(\pi_n)$, theoretically predicted by QDT, with the empirically observed fractions [96] $p_{exp}(\pi_n) \equiv N(\pi_n)/N$ of the decision makers choosing the prospect π_n, with respect to the total number N of decision makers taking part in the experiments.

14.4.2.1 Lotteries with Gains [77]

G1. $(L_1 = \{2.5, 0.33 \mid 2.4, 0.66 \mid 0, 0.01\}, L_2 = \{2.4, 1\})$. The utilities of these lotteries are $U(L_1) = 2.5 \times 0.33 + 2.4 \times 0.66 + 0 \times 0.01 = 2.409$, $U(L_2) = 2.4 \times 1 = 2.4$. Their sum is $(L_1) + U(L_2) = 2.409 + 2.4 = 4.809$. The utility factors are close to each other, $f(\pi_1) = 2.409/4.809 = 0.501$, $f(\pi_2) = 2.4/4.809 = 0.499$. For the lottery attractiveness $a_n \equiv a_n(L_n) \equiv \sum_i x_i 10^{p_n(x_i)}$, we find $a_1 = 2.5 \times 10^{0.33} + 2.4 \times 10^{0.66} + 0^{0.1} = 16.32$, $a_2 = 2.4 \times 10^1 = 24$, which gives $a_1 + a_2 = 16.32 + 24 = 40.32$. The attraction indices $\alpha_n = \alpha_n(L_n) \equiv a_n / \sum_m |a_m|$ become $\alpha_1 = 16.32/40.32 = 0.405$, $\alpha_2 = 2.4/40.32 = 0.595$. Then the attraction difference is $\Delta\alpha = 0.405 - 0.595 = -0.19$. The negative attraction difference tells us that the first lottery is less attractive, $q(\pi_1) < q(\pi_2)$, which suggests that the second lottery is preferable, $\pi_1 < \pi_2$. The experimental results confirm this, displaying the fractions of decision makers choosing the respective lotteries as $p_{exp}(\pi_1) = 0.18$, $p_{exp}(\pi_2) = 0.82$. Thus, although the first lottery is more useful, having a larger utility factor, it is less attractive, which makes it less preferable.

G2. $(L_1 = \{2.5, 0.33 \mid 0, 0.67\}, L_2 = \{2.4, 0.34 \mid 0, 0.66\})$. The following procedure is the same as in the first game. Calculating the utility factors $f(\pi_1) = 0.503$, $f(\pi_2) = 0.497$, we again see that the lottery utilities are close to each other, so it is difficult to make the choice. For the lottery attractiveness, we have $a_1 = 16.57$, $a_2 = 5.25$, giving the attraction indices $\alpha_1 = 0.759$, $\alpha_2 = 0.241$, and the attraction difference $\Delta\alpha = 0.518$. Now the latter is positive, showing that the first lottery is more attractive, $q(\pi_1) > q(\pi_2)$, which suggests that the first lottery is preferable, $\pi_1 > \pi_2$. The experimental data for the related fractions are $p_{exp}(\pi_1) = 0.83$, $p_{exp}(\pi_2) = 0.17$, which agree with the expectation that the first lottery is preferable.

G3. $(L_1 = \{4, 0.8 \mid 0, 0.2\}, L_2 = \{3, 1\})$. We calculate in the prescribed way the utility factors $f(\pi_1) = 0.516$, $f(\pi_2) = 0.484$, lottery attractiveness, $a_1 = 25.24$, $a_2 = 30$, and the attraction indices $\alpha_1 = 0.457$, $\alpha_2 = 0.543$. The negative attraction difference $\Delta\alpha = -0.086$ implies that the first lottery is less attractive, $q(\pi_1) < q(\pi_2)$, which tells us that the second lottery should be preferable, $\pi_1 < \pi_2$. Again, this is in agreement with the experimental results $p_{exp}(\pi_1) = 0.2$, $p_{exp}(\pi_2) = 0.8$. The first lottery is less preferable, although it is more useful, having a larger utility factor.

G4. $(L_1 = \{4, 0.2 \mid 0, 0.8\}, L_2 = \{3, 0.25 \mid 0, 0.75\})$. Here, we have $f(\pi_1) = 0.516$, $f(A_2) = 0.484$, lottery attractiveness $a_1 = 6.34$, $a_2 = 5.33$, and the attraction indices $\alpha_1 = 0.543$, $\alpha_2 = 0.457$, and the positive attraction difference $\Delta\alpha = 0.086$. Hence, the first lottery is more attractive $q(\pi_1) > q(\pi_2)$, which suggests that the first lottery is preferable, $\pi_1 > \pi_2$. The experimental data $p_{exp}(\pi_1) = 0.65$, $p_{exp}(\pi_2) = 0.35$ confirm this expectation.

G5. $(L_1 = \{6, 0.45 \mid 0, 0.55\}, L_2 = \{3, 0.9 \mid 0, 0.1\})$. Here, the utility factors $f(\pi_1) = 0.5$, $f(\pi_2) = 0.5$ turn out to be equal, which makes it impossible to decide in the framework of classical decision theory based on expected utilities. Then we calculate the lottery attractiveness $a_1 = 16.91$, $a_2 = 23.83$, and the related attraction indices $\alpha_1 = 0.415$, $\alpha_2 = 0.585$. The negative attraction difference $\Delta\alpha = -0.17$ means that the first lottery is less attractive, $q(\pi_1) < q(\pi_2)$, and hence the second lottery is expected to be preferable, $\pi_1 < \pi_2$. This is confirmed by the empirical data $p_{exp}(\pi_1) = 0.14$, $p_{exp}(\pi_2) = 0.86$.

G6. ($L_1 = \{6, 0.001 \,|\, 0, 0.999\}$, $L_2 = \{3, 0.002 \,|\, 0, 0.998\}$). Again their utility factors are equal to each other, $(\pi_1) = 0.5, f(\pi_2) = 0.5$. The lottery attractiveness values $a_1 = 6.01$, $a_2 = 3.01$ yield the attraction indices $\alpha_1 = 0.666$, $\alpha_2 = 0.334$, whose positive attraction difference $\Delta\alpha = 0.332$ implies that the first lottery is more attractive, $q(\pi_1) > q(\pi_2)$, which suggests that the first lottery should be preferable, $\pi_1 > \pi_2$. The experimental results are $p_{exp}(\pi_1) = 0.73$, $p_{exp}(\pi_2) = 0.27$, in agreement with the expectation.

G7. ($L_1 = \{6, 0.25 \,|\, 0, 0.75\}$, $L_2 = \{4, 0.25 \,|\, 2, 0.25 \,|\, 0, 0.5\}$). Their equal utility factors, $f(\pi_1) = 0.5$, $f(\pi_2) = 0.5$, do not allow us to make a choice based on their utility. We calculate the lottery attractiveness $a_1 = 10.67$, $a_2 = 10.67$ and the attraction indices $\alpha_1 = 0.5$, $\alpha_2 = 0.5$. Here the attraction difference is zero, $\Delta\alpha = 0$, with the attraction indices being positive. Therefore, we resort to criterion $\alpha_1 = \alpha_2 \geq 0$, $p(g_1) < p(g_2)$, for which the minimal gains are $g_1^{min} = g_2^{min} = 0$. We find that $p_1(g_1^{min}) = 0.75 > p_2(g_2^{min}) = 0.5$. The marginal case, when $\alpha_1 = \alpha_2$ and $p_1(g_1^{min}) > p_2(g_2^{min})$, is denoted as $\Delta\alpha = -0$. This suggests that the first lottery is less attractive, according to the negative sign $\Delta\alpha = -0$. Thus, we find that $(\pi_1) < q(\pi_2)$, which suggests that the second lottery is preferable, $\pi_1 < \pi_2$. The experimental results give $p_{exp}(\pi_1) = 0.18$, $p_{exp}(\pi_2) = 0.82$.

14.4.2.2 Lotteries with Losses

G8. ($L_1 = \{-4, 0.8 \,|\, 0, 0.2\}$, $L_1 = \{-3, 1\}$). Here, we find the utility factors $f(\pi_1) = 0.484$, $f(\pi_2) = 0.516$, lottery attractiveness $a_1 = -25.24$, $a_2 = -30$, and the attraction indices $\alpha_1 = -0.457$, $\alpha_2 = -0.543$. The positive attraction difference $\Delta\alpha = 0.086$ means that the first lottery is more attractive, $q(\pi_1) > q(\pi_2)$, because of which we expect that the first lottery is preferable, $\pi_1 > \pi_2$. The experiments give $p_{exp}(\pi_1) = 0.92$, $p_{exp}(\pi_2) = 0.08$, confirming that the first lottery is preferable, although its utility factor is smaller.

G9. ($L_1 = \{-4, 0.2 \,|\, 0, 0.8\}$, $L_2 = \{-3, 0.25 \,|\, 0, 0.75\}$). With the utility factors $f(\pi_1) = 0.484$, $f(\pi_2) = 0.516$, *lottery attractiveness* $a_1 = -6.34$, $a_2 = -5.33$, and the attraction indices $\alpha_1 = -0.543$, $\alpha_2 = -0.457$, the attraction difference is negative, $\Delta\alpha = -0.086$. Since the first lottery is less attractive, $q(\pi_1) < q(\pi_2)$, we expect that the second lottery is preferable, $\pi_1 < \pi_2$. The empirical data are $p_{exp}(A_1) = 0.42$, $p_{exp}(\pi_2) = 0.58$.

G10. ($L_1 = \{-3, 0.9 \,|\, 0, 0.1\}$, $L_2 = \{-6, 0.45 \,|\, 0, 0.55\}$). Here the utility factors are equal, $f(\pi_1) = 0.5$, $f(\pi_2) = 0.5$, and hence both lotteries are equally useful. But the lottery attractiveness is different, $a_1 = -23.83$, $a_2 = -16.91$, yielding the attraction indices $\alpha_1 = -0.585$, $\alpha_2 = -0.415$. The negative attraction difference $\Delta\alpha = -0.17$ signifies that the first lottery is less attractive, $q(\pi_1) < q(\pi_2)$, which implies that the second lottery is preferable, $\pi_1 < \pi_2$. The experimental results are $p_{exp}(\pi_1) = 0.08$, $p_{exp}(\pi_2) = 0.92$.

G11. ($L_1 = \{-3, 0.002 \,|\, 0, 0.998\}$, $L_2 = \{-6, 0.001 \,|\, 0, 0.999\}$). The utility factors are again equal to each other, $f(\pi_1) = 0.5$, $f(\pi_2) = 0.5$, which makes it impossible to employ classical utility theory. But the lottery attractiveness $a_1 = -3.01$, $a_2 = -59.86$ and the attraction indices $\alpha_1 = -0.048$, $\alpha_2 = -0.952$ show that the attraction difference is positive, $\Delta\alpha = 0.904$. Therefore, the first lottery is more attractive, $q(\pi_1) > q(\pi_2)$, which suggests that the first lottery is preferable, $\pi_1 > \pi_2$. The experimental data are $p_{exp}(\pi_1) = 0.7$, $p_{exp}(\pi_2) = 0.3$.

G12. ($L_1 = \{-1, 0.5 \,|\, 0, 0.5\}$, $L_2 = \{-0.5, 1\}$). Here, we have again a situation where the equal utility factors, $f(\pi_1) = 0.5$, $f(\pi_2) = 0.5$, do not allow for the choice based on the lottery utilities. But calculating the lottery attractiveness $a_1 = -3.16$, $a_2 = -5$, and the attraction indices $\alpha_1 = -0.387$, $\alpha_2 = -0.613$, we see that the attraction difference is positive, $\Delta\alpha = 0.226$. This means that the first lottery is more attractive, $q(\pi_1) > q(\pi_2)$, and hence the first lottery is expected to be preferable, $\pi_1 > \pi_2$. The empirical results are $p_{exp}(\pi_1) = 0.69$, $p_{exp}(\pi_2) = 0.31$.

G13. $(L_1 = \{-6, 0.25 \mid 0, 0.75\}, L_2 = \{-4, 0.25 \mid -2, 0.25 \mid 0, 0.5\})$. The utility factors are again equal, $f(\pi_1) = 0.5$, $f(\pi_2) = 0.5$. For the lottery attractiveness we have $a_1 = -10.67$, $a_2 = -10.67$, and the attraction indices are also equal, $\alpha_1 = -0.5$, $\alpha_2 = -0.5$. Obtaining the zero attraction difference, $\Delta\alpha = 0$, with negative attraction indices, we have to involve the criterion $(\alpha_1 = \alpha_2 < 0, p(l_1) > p(l_2).)$. The minimal losses are $l_1^{min} = l_2^{min} = 0$, and we find $p_1(0) = 0.75 > p_2(0) = 0.5$. Consequently, the first lottery is more attractive, which can be denoted as $\Delta\alpha = +0$. The stronger attractiveness of the first lottery, when $q(\pi_1) > q(\pi_2)$, suggests that the first lottery should be preferable, $\pi_1 > \pi_2$. The experimental data are $p_{exp}(\pi_1) = 0.7$, $p_{exp}(\pi_2) = 0.3$.

G14. $(L_1 = \{-5, 0.001 \mid 0, 0.999\}, L_2 = \{-0.005, 1\})$. Although the utility factors are equal, $f(\pi_1) = 0.5$, $f(\pi_2) = 0.5$, the lottery attractiveness $a_1 = -5.01$, $a_2 = -0.05$ defines different attraction indices $\alpha_1 = -0.99$, $\alpha_2 = -0.01$. The negative attraction difference $\Delta\alpha = -0.98$ implies that the first lottery is less attractive, $q(\pi_1) < q(\pi_2)$. Thus, the second lottery is expected to be preferable, $\pi_1 < \pi_2$. The experimental results $p_{exp}(\pi_1) = 0.17$, $p_{exp}(\pi_2) = 0.83$ confirm this expectation.

References

1 Holevo, A.S. (1998). The capacity of the quantum channel with general signal states. *IEEE Trans. Inf. Theory* **44** (1): 269–273.

2 Devetak, I. (2005). The private classical capacity and quantum capacity of a quantum channel. *IEEE Trans. Inf. Theory* **51** (1): 44–55.

3 Lloyd, S. (1997). Capacity of the noisy quantum channel. *Phys. Rev. A Gen. Phys.* **55** (3): 1613–1622.

4 Devetak, I. and Shor, P.W. (2005). The capacity of a quantum channel for simultaneous transmission of classical and quantum information. *Commun. Math. Phys.* **256** (2): 287–303.

5 Hsieh, M.-H. and Wilde, M.M. (2010). Entanglement-assisted communication of classical and quantum information. *IEEE Trans. Inf. Theory* **56** (9): 4682–4704.

6 Hsieh, M.-H. and Wilde, M.M. (2010). Trading classical communication, quantum communication, and entanglement in quantum Shannon theory. *IEEE Trans. Inf. Theory* **56** (9): 4705–4730.

7 Wilde, M.M., Hsieh, M.-H., and Babar, Z. (2014). Entanglement-assisted quantum turbo codes. *IEEE Trans. Inf. Theory* **60** (2): 1203–1222.

8 Takeoka, M., Guha, S., and Wilde, M.M. (2014). The squashed entanglement of a quantum channel. *IEEE Trans. Inf. Theory* **60** (8): 4987–4998.

9 Nguyen, H.V., Babar, Z., Alanis, D. et al. (2016). EXIT-chart aided quantum code design improves the normalised throughput of realistic quantum devices. *IEEE Access* **4**: 10194–10209.

10 Ashtiani, M. and Azgomi, M.A. (2015). A survey of quantum-like approaches to decision making and cognition. *Math. Social Sci.* **75**: 49–80.

11 Yukalov, V.I. and Sornette, D. (2018). Quantitative predictions in quantum decision theory. *IEEE Trans. Syst. Man Cybern. Syst.* **48** (3): 366–381.

12 Inoue, K. (2006). Quantum key distribution technologies. *IEEE J. Sel. Top. Quantum Electron.* **12** (4): 888–896.

13 Sharma, V. and Banerjee, S. (2018). Analysis of quantum key distribution based satellite communication. In *Proceedings of the International Conference on Computing, Communication and Networking Technologies*, pp. 1–5.

14 Piparo, N.L. and Razavi, M. (2015). Long-distance trust-free quantum key distribution. *IEEE J. Sel. Top. Quantum Electron.* **21** (3): 123–130.

15 Yukalov, V.I. and Sornette, D. (2009). Scheme of thinking quantum systems. *Laser Phys. Lett.* **6** (11): 833–839. https://doi.org/10.1002/lapl.200910086.

16 Liu, W., Liu, J., Cui, M., and He, M. (2010). An introductory review on quantum game theory. In *Proceedings of the International Conference on Genetic and Evolutionary Computing*, pp. 386–389.

17 Brandt, H.E. (1999). Qubit devices and the issue of quantum decoherence. *Prog. Quantum Electron.* **22** (5–6): 257–370.

18 Lee, C.F. and Johnson, N.F. (2002). Exploiting randomness in quantum information processing. *Phys. Lett. A* **301** (5–6): 343–349.

19 Huang, D. and Li, S. (2018). A survey of the current status of research on quantum games. In *Proceedings of the 4th International Conference on Information Management*, May 2018, pp. 46–52.

20 Berta, M., Fawzi, O., Scholz, V., and Szehr, O. (2014). Variations on classical and quantum extractors. In *Proceedings of the IEEE International Symposium on Information Theory*, June/July 2014, pp. 1474–1478.

21 Konig, R.T. and Terhal, B.M. (2008). The bounded-storage model in the presence of a quantum adversary. *IEEE Trans. Inf. Theory* **54** (2): 749–762.

22 Berta, M., Fawzi, O., and Scholz, V.B. (2017). Quantum-proof randomness extractors via operator space theory. *IEEE Trans. Inf. Theory* **63** (4): 2480–2503.

23 Reingold, R.S.O. and Wigderson, A. (2006). Extracting randomness via repeated condensing. *SIAM J. Comput.* **35** (5): 1185–1209.

24 Botsinis, P., Ng, S.X., and Hanzo, L. (2013). Quantum search algorithms, quantum wireless, and a low-complexity maximum likelihood iterative quantum multi-user detector design. *IEEE Access* **1**: 94–122.

25 Botsinis, P., Alanis, D., Babar, Z. et al. (2016). Quantum-aided multi-user transmission in non-orthogonal multiple access systems. *IEEE Access* **4**: 7402–7424.

26 Botsinis, P., Alanis, D., Ng, S.X., and Hanzo, L. (2014). Low-complexity soft-output quantum-assisted multiuser detection for direct-sequence spreading and slow subcarrier-hopping aided SDMA-OFDM systems. *IEEE Access* **2**: 451–472.

27 Botsinis, P., Ng, S.X., and Hanzo, L. (2014). Fixed-complexity quantum-assisted multi-user detection for CDMA and SDMA. *IEEE Trans. Commun.* **62** (3): 990–1000.

28 Botsinis, P., Alanis, D., Babar, Z. et al. (2015). Iterative quantum-assisted multi-user detection for multi-carrier interleave division multiple access systems. *IEEE Trans. Commun.* **63** (10): 3713–3727.

29 Botsinis, P., Huo, Y., Alanis, D. et al. (2017). Quantum search-aided multi-user detection of IDMA-assisted multi-layered video streaming. *IEEE Access* **5**: 23233–23255.

30 Botsinis, P., Alanis, D., Feng, S. et al. (2017). Quantum-assisted indoor localization for uplink mmWave and downlink visible light communication systems. *IEEE Access* **5**: 23327–23351.

31 Li, Y., Su, G., Wu, D.O. et al. (2011). The impact of node selfishness on multicasting in delay tolerant networks. *IEEE Trans. Veh. Technol.* **60** (5): 2224–2238.

32 Alanis, D., Botsinis, P., Ng, S.X., and Hanzo, L. (2014). Quantum-assisted routing optimization for self-organizing networks. *IEEE Access* **2**: 614–632.

33 Prasad, R., Murthy, C.R., and Rao, B.D. (2015). Joint channel estimation and data detection in MIMO-OFDM systems: a sparse Bayesian learning approach. *IEEE Trans. Signal Process.* **63** (20): 5369–5382.

34 Zhang, J., Chen, S., Mu, X., and Hanzo, L. (2011). Joint channel estimation and multiuser detection for SDMA/OFDM based on dual repeated weighted boosting search. *IEEE Trans. Veh. Technol.* **60** (7): 3265–3275.

35 Botsinis, P., Alanis, D., Babar, Z. et al. (2016). Joint quantum assisted channel estimation and data detection. *IEEE Access* **4**: 7658–7681.

36 Landsburg, S.E. Nash Equilibria in Quantum Games, arXiv:1110.1351.

37 Solmeyer, N., Dixon, R., and Balu, R. (2016). Quantum routing games, arXiv:1709.10500v1 [quant-ph] 29 Sep 2017. *J. Phys.: Math. Theor.* **51** (45): 455304.

38 Roughgarden, T. (2007). Routing games. In: *Algorithmic Game Theory* (eds. N. Nisan, T. Roughgarden, E. Tardos and V.V. Vazirani), 461–484. Cambridge: Cambridge University Press.

39 Wardrop, J.G. (1952). Some Theoretical aspects of road traffic research. In *Proceedings of the Institution of Civil Engineers*, pt. II, Vol. 1, pp. 325–378.

40 Ozdaglar, A. (2008). Networks' challenge: where game theory meets network optimization. In *International Symposium on Information Theory*.

41 Fischer, S., Racke, H., and Vocking, B. (2006). Fast Convergence to Wardrop equilibria by adaptive sampling methods. In *Proceedings of 38th Symposium on Theory of Computing*, pp. 653–662.

42 Zabaleta, O.G., Barrangu, J.P., and Arizmendi, M. (2016). Quantum Game Application to Spectrum Scarcity Problems. arXiv:1608.07264v1 [quant-ph] 23 August 2016.

43 Shafigh, A.S., Glisic, S., Hossain, E. et al. (2019). User-centric distributed spectrum sharing in dynamic network architectures. *IEEE/ACM Trans. Netw.* **27** (1): 15–28.

44 Shafigh, A.S., Mertikopoulos, P., Glisic, S., and Fang, Y.M. (2017). Semi-cognitive radio networks: a novel dynamic spectrum sharing mechanism. *IEEE Trans. Cognit. Commun. Netw.* **3** (1): 15–28.

45 Khan, Z., Glisic, S., DaSilva, L.A., and Lehtomäki, J. (2011). Modeling the dynamics of coalition formation games for cooperative spectrum sharing in an interference channel. *IEEE Trans. Comput. Intell. AI Games Year* **3** (1).

46 Favre, M., Wittwer, A., Heinimann, H.R. et al. (2016). Quantum decision theory in simple risky choices. arXiv:1602.04058v2 [physics.soc-ph] 24 December 2016. *PLoS One* **11** (12): e0168045. https://doi.org/10.1371/journal.pone.0168045.

47 Harrison, G.W. and Rutström, Y.Y. (2008). Risk aversion in the laboratory. In: *Risk Aversion in Experiments (Research in Experimental Economics, Volume 12)* (eds. J.C. Cox and G.W. Harrison), 41–196. Emerald Group Publishing Limited https://doi.org/10.1016/S0193-2306(08) 00003-3.

48 Hey, J.D. and Orme, C. (1994). Investigating generalizations of expected utility theory using experimental data. *Econometrica* **62** (6): 1291–1326. https://doi.org/10.2307/2951750.

49 Wittwer, A.M.J. (2009). Human behaviour under the influence of pain and risk. Physiological and psychological aspects of unstable cognitive-affective states. Ph.D. thesis, ETH Zurich. doi: 10.3929/ethz-a-006037636, diss. ETH No. 18806.

50 Pascal, B. (1670). Pens'ees. Republished several times, for instance 1972 in French by Le Livre de Poche, and 1995 in English by Penguin Classics.

51 Bernoulli, D. (1738). Specimen theoriae novae de mensura sortis. Republished in 1954 as "Exposition of a New Theory on the Measurement of Risk". *Econometrica* **22** (1): 23–36. http://jstor.org/stable/1909829.

52 von Neumann, J. and Morgenstern, O. (1953). *Theory of Games and Economic Behavior*. Princeton, NJ: Princeton University.

53 Gollier, C. (2004). *The Economics of Risk and Time*. The MIT Press New Ed edition.

54 Kahneman, D. and Tversky, A. (1979). An analysis of decision under risk. *Econometrica* **47** (2): 263–292. http://www.jstor.org/stable/1914185.

55 Allais, M. (1953). Le comportement de l'homme rationnel devant le risque, critique des postulats et axiomes de l'ecole Americaine. *Econometrica* **21**: 503–546. http://www.jstor.org/stable1907921.

56 Tversky, A. and Kahneman, D. (1992). Advances in prospect theory: cumulative representation of uncertainty. *J Risk Uncertainty* **5**: 297–323. https://doi.org/10.1007/BF00122574.

57 Stott, H.P. (2006). Cumulative prospect theory's functional menagerie. *J. Risk Uncertainty* **32**: 101–130. https://doi.org/10.1007/s11166-006-8289-6.

58 Mosteller, F. and Nogee, P. (1951). An experimental measurement of utility. *J. Polit. Economy* **59**: 371–404. https://doi.org/10.1086/257106.

59 Luce, R.D. (1959). *Individual Choice Behavior: A Theoretical Analysis*. New York, NY: Wiley.

60 Harless, D.W. and Camerer, C.F. (1994). The predictive utility of generalized expected utility theories. *Econometrica* **62** (6): 1251–1290. https://doi.org/10.2307/2951749.

61 Murphy, R.O. and ten Brincke, R.H. (2014). Hierarchical maximum likelihood parameter estimation for cumulative prospect theory: Improving the reliability of individual risk parameter estimates. ETH Risk Center – Working Paper Series, ETH-RC-14-005. doi: https://doi.org/10.2139/ssrn.2425670.

62 Wakker, P. (2010). *Prospect Theory: For Risk and Ambiguity*. Cambridge, UK: Cambridge University Press https://doi.org/10.1017/CBO9780511779329.

63 Safra, Z. and Segal, U. (2008). Calibration results for non-expected utility theories. *Econometrica* **76** (5): 1143–1166. https://doi.org/10.3982/ECTA6175.

64 Al-Najjar, N.I. and Weinstein, J. (2009). The ambiguity aversion literature: a critical assessment. *Econ. Philos.* **25**: 249–284. https://doi.org/10.1017/S0266267109990289.

65 Yukalov, V.I. and Sornette, D. (2009). Processing information in quantum decision theory. *Entropy* **11**: 1073–1120. https://doi.org/10.3390/e11041073, special Issue 'Entropy and Information'.

66 Yukalov, V.I. and Sornette, D. (2010). Mathematical structure of quantum decision theory. *Adv. Complex Syst.* **13** (5): 659–698. https://doi.org/10.1142/S0219525910002803.

67 Yukalov, V.I. and Sornette, D. (2011). Decision theory with prospect interference and entanglement. *Theory Decision* **70**: 283–328. https://doi.org/10.1007/s11238-010-9202-y.

68 Yukalov, V.I. and Sornette, D. (2010). Entanglement production in quantum decision making. *Phys. Atomic Nuclei* **73**: 559–562. https://doi.org/10.1134/S106377881003021X.

69 Frederick, S., Loewenstein, G., and O'Donoghue, T. (2002). Time discounting and time preference: a critical review. *J. Econ. Lit* **40** (2): 351–401. https://doi.org/10.1257/002205102320161311.

70 Yukalov, V.I. and Sornette, D. (2014). Conditions for quantum interference in cognitive sciences. *Top. Cognit. Sci.* **6**: 79–90. https://doi.org/10.1111/tops.12065.

71 Yukalov, V.I. and Sornette, D. (2015). Role of information in decision making of social agents. *Int. J. Inf. Technol. Decision Making* **14** (5): 1129–1166. https://doi.org/10.1142/S0219622014500564.

72 Kahneman, D. (2011). *Thinking, Fast and Slow*. New York: ePUB ed., Farrar, Straus and Giroux.

73 Yukalov, V.I. and Sornette, D. (2014). Manipulating decision making of typical agents. *IEEE Trans. Syst. Man Cybern. Syst.* **44**: 1155–1168. https://doi.org/10.1109/TSMC.2014.2314283.

74 Bohr, N. (1920). Uber die Serienspektra der Element. *Zeitschrift f'ur Physik* **2** (5): 423–478. https://doi.org/10.1007/BF01329978.

75 Yukalov, V.I. and Sornette, D. (2014). Self-organization in nature and society as decision making. *Adv. Complex Syst.* **17** (3–4): 1450 016. https://doi.org/10.1142/S0219525914500167.

76 Yukalov, V.I. and Sornette, D. (2016). Quantitative predictions in quantum decision theory. *IEEE Trans. Syst. Man Cybern. Syst.* https://doi.org/10.1109/TSMC.2016.2596578.

77 Yukalov, V. and Sornette, D. (2018). Quantitative Predictions in Quantum Decision Theory. arXiv:1802.06348v1 [physics.soc-ph] 18 February 2018.

78 Guo, P. (2011). One-shot decision theory. *IEEE Trans. Syst. Man Cybern. A* **41**: 917–926.

79 Yukalov, V.I. and Sornette, D. (2016). Quantum probability and quantum decision making. *Philos. Trans. Roy. Soc. A* **374**: 20150100.

80 Brock, W.A. and Dauf, S.N. (2001). Discrete choice with social interactions. *Rev. Econ. Stud.* **68**: 235–260.

81 Kullback, S. and Leibler, R.A. (1951). On information and sufficiency. *Ann. Math. Stat.* **22**: 79–86.

82 Kullback, S. (1959). *Information Theory and Statistics*. New York: Wiley.

83 Shore, J.E. and Johnson, R.W. (1980). Axiomatic derivation of the principle of maximum entropy and the principle of minimum cross-entropy. *IEEE Trans. Inf. Theory* **26**: 26–37.

84 Luce, R.D. (1958). A probabilistic theory of utility. *Econometrica* **26**: 193–224.

85 Kim, B.E., Seligman, D., and Kable, J.W. (2012). Preference reversals in decision making under risk are accompanied by changes in attention to different attributes. *Front. Neurosci.* **6**: 109.

86 Blavatskyy, P.R. and Pogrebna, G. (2010). Models of stochastic choice and decision theories: why both are important for analyzing decisions. *J. Appl. Economet.* **25**: 963–986.

87 Holt, C.A. and Laury, S.K. (2002). Risk aversion and incentive effects. *Am. Econ. Rev.* **92**: 1644–1655.

88 Yukalov, V.I. and Sornette, D. (2015). Preference reversal in quantum decision theory. *Front. Psychol.* **6**: 01538.

89 Thurstone, L.L. (1927). A law of comparative judgment. *Psychol. Rev.* **34**: 273–286.

90 Krantz, D.H. (1967). Rational distance functions for multidimensional scaling. *J. Math. Psychol.* **4**: 226–245.

91 Rumhelhart, D.L. and Greeno, J.G. (1971). Similarity between stimuli: an experimental test of the Luce and Restle choice models. *J. Math. Psychol.* **8**: 370–381.

92 Lorentziadis, P.L. (2013). Preference under rsik in the presence of indistinguishable probabilities. *Oper. Res.* **13**: 429–446.

93 Devroye, L. (1986). *Non-Uniform Random Variate Generation.* New York: Springer.

94 MacKay, D.J.C. (2003). *Information Theory, Inference, and Learning.* Cambridge: Cambridge University.

95 Cover, T.M. and Thomas, J.A. (2006). *Elements of Information Theory.* Hoboken: Wiley.

96 Kahneman, D. and Tversky, A. (1979). Prospect theory: an analysis of decision under risk. *Econometrica* **47**: 263–292.

97 Avishai, Y. *Some Topics in Quantum Games*, arXiv:1306.0284v1 [quant-ph] 3 Jun 2013.

98 https://en.wikipedia.org/wiki/Representation_theory_of_SU(2).

15

Quantum Computing in Wireless Networks

In this chapter, we discuss several examples of wireless network design based on the tools enabled by quantum computing. Both satellite and terrestrial networks are considered. The integration of the two networks is presented in Figure 15.1

15.1 Quantum Satellite Networks

Quantum key distribution (QKD) has attracted much attention for secure communications across global networks. QKD over satellite networks can overcome the limitations of terrestrial optical networks, such as large attenuation over long-distance fiber channels and the difficulty of intercontinental domain communications. Different QKD networks (around the world) can intercommunicate through quantum satellites, which could give rise to a global quantum network in the near future. This raises a new resource allocation and management problem of QKD involving multiple satellite layers and distributed ground stations. Using existing schemes, a single satellite cannot perform QKD for ground stations for the whole day. Moreover, the research problem is more challenging due to limitations of satellite coverage: limited coverage time of low earth orbit (LEO) satellite, high channel losses of geostationary earth orbit (GEO) satellite, and so on. To overcome these limitations, a double-layer quantum satellite network (QSN) using a quantum key pool (QKP) to relay keys for ground stations is considered. It is an architecture of trusted-repeater-based double-layer QSNs comprising GEO and LEO satellites. Here, we also address the routing and key allocation (RKA) problem for key-relay services over QSNs. A specific joint GEO-LEO routing and key allocation (JGL-RKA) algorithm is discussed to solve the RKA problem. Within a design example, we will show simulation results confirming that the scheme can increase the success probability of key-relay services significantly. We also discuss the impact of different route selection mechanisms, the number of satellite links, satellite node capability, and service granularity on network performance.

Traditional security techniques mostly focus on the encryption of communication, where security depends on the mathematical complexity. However, encryption methodologies are becoming less reliable as eavesdroppers and attackers are gaining powerful computing ability. As discussed already in Chapters 8 and 11, quantum cryptography is a new cryptographic technology for generating random secret keys to be used in secure communication. Quantum cryptography can provide communication security based on the laws of quantum physics (e.g., the no-cloning theorem and the uncertainty principle). However, the quantum key has to be distributed over the communication network to be used by the senders and receivers.

Artificial Intelligence and Quantum Computing for Advanced Wireless Networks, First Edition.
Savo G. Glisic and Beatriz Lorenzo.
© 2022 John Wiley & Sons Ltd. Published 2022 by John Wiley & Sons Ltd.

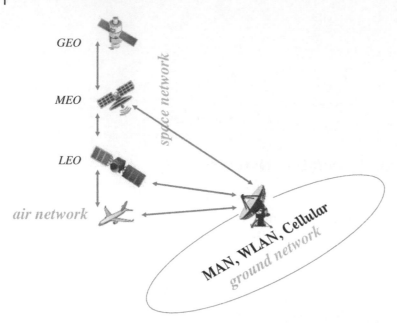

GEO

MEO

LEO

space network

air network

MAN, WLAN, Cellular
ground network

Figure 15.1 Integration of satellite and ground communication networks.

Reference [1] demonstrated the feasibility of QKD over optical networks. Such a QKD network can be constructed by distributing end-to-end secret (quantum) keys through trusted repeaters (e.g., based on the point-to-point BB84 protocol). References [2, 3] also reported such optical-fiber-based QKD networks, used to secure metropolitan and backbone networks. Recent studies discussed the integration of QKD and classical networks, such as QKD over wavelength division multiplexing (WDM) networks [4, 5] and QKD-enabled software-defined networks (SDN) [6]. Implementing QKD in terrestrial optical networks and distributing secret keys over a long distance (e.g., across the globe) is challenging. Single-photon signals transmitted over long-distance optical fiber suffer from high losses and depolarization. Hence, carrying the keys using optical fiber over long distances (e.g., 1000 KM) is not an effective solution [7].

To address these limitations, an experimented free-space QKD has been studied in recent years. In contrast to optical fibers, the free-space photon will experience negligible loss in vacuum, making it feasible to distribute secret keys over thousands of kilometers. Although the optical beam of a satellite-to-ground link can suffer from atmospheric loss, most of space is empty, which makes the channel loss less than that of a long fiber [7, 8]. The quantum satellite *Micius*, launched in 2016 for quantum communication experiments, has successfully demonstrated satellite-to-ground QKD using a single-photon source [9]. In 2017, a ground free-space QKD experiment was carried out at a telecom wavelength in daylight and demonstrated the feasibility of inter-satellite QKD in daylight [10, 11]. Therefore, satellite-based QKD is a promising method for distributing quantum keys between two ultra-long-distance parties on the ground. Since the coverage and flyover time of one satellite is limited, a group of quantum satellites can be used as trusted repeaters to serve the ground stations. Recently, researchers have proposed a "network of quantum satellites" to realize global-scale quantum communications [12, 13]. The authors of [10] proposed a QKD satellite network architecture based on quantum repeaters. The researchers also proposed the trusted-repeater-based satellite QKD Scheme [11–15]. Their scheme is based on the BB84 protocol since quantum repeaters are still far from implementation. Reference [16] investigates the possible schemes of free-space QKD using inter-satellite links and analyzes the properties of satellite–ground links. These studies motivated the concept presented here [17], which is a contribution toward advancement of the state of the art in satellite-based QKD networks.

Prior studies envision that a quantum-capable satellite constellation can be formed to construct global QKD (similar to traditional satellite constellations such as Iridium [18]). In recent proposals, quantum satellites use LEO to benefit from its low channel loss. But an LEO satellite can access a particular ground station only for a limited time of the day [19]. This limited coverage may lead to a shortage of secret keys between satellite and ground. By contrast, GEO satellites can access ground stations continuously, all day. However, their signal can suffer from high channel loss and limited key generation rate.

In 2017, German researchers successfully measured quantum signals that were sent from a GEO to a ground station [20]. Italian researchers have also demonstrated the feasibility of quantum communications between high-orbiting global navigation satellites and a ground station [21]. The Chinese Academy of Sciences has planned future projects to launch higher-altitude satellites [9–11]. According to researchers, the future quantum satellite constellation will comprise satellites in high and low orbits [22]. Thus, combining both GEO and LEO satellites to build QKD networks is a research direction worth exploring.

15.1.1 Satellite-Based QKD System

This section discusses the current and future state of technologies of free-space QKD and quantum satellites, including satellite-to-ground and inter-satellite QKD.

Free-space QKD: Similar to ground QKD, current free-space QKD experiments mostly implement the mechanism of transmitting individual-encoded polarized photons to generate secret keys between two communication parties (A and B), based on the BB84 protocol. The procedure of satellite-to-ground QKD consists of (i) quantum communication (quantum signal transmitted at 850 nm) and (ii) classical communication (classical optical signal transmitted at 1550 nm). These two communications are usually located at different working wavelengths over the same laser link. In the near future, quantum satellites will be able to conduct quantum communication and classical communication using a single integrated transponder [23]. Typically, the quantum signal is transmitted on downlinks, and the classical signal is transmitted on uplinks [9]. The single-polarized photons are transmitted in a quantum channel. The classical channel can be used for transmitting the measurement-basis signals and key-relay services, as well as data services in the future. For the inter-satellite quantum channel, the 1550 nm wavelength is used due to its higher efficiency in daylight [10]. To be compatible with classical communications, a multi-beam system is used in inter-satellite communications. With the onboard multi-beam transponders, quantum signals and data signals can be carried on different laser beams, in the same optical link.

Trusted-repeater-based satellite QKD: Quantum satellites can be used as trusted repeaters in generating secret keys for terrestrial nodes. Similar to terrestrial QKD networks, quantum satellites are considered trusted nodes – even more trusted than ground nodes – because the cost of eavesdropping over satellites is much higher than that with ground networks [15]. With a group of quantum satellites, real-time secret key distribution can be achieved between a pair of ground stations. Figure 15.2 illustrates the basic procedure of trusted-repeater-based satellite QKD.

The secret key KA can be transmitted from ground station (GS) A to ground station B by successively encrypting and decrypting on intermediate nodes. The XOR operation will be conducted on

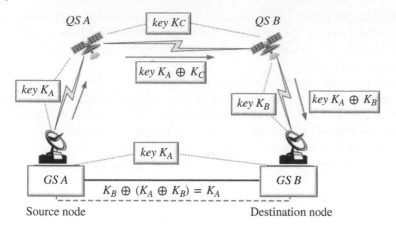

Figure 15.2 Principle of trusted-repeater-based satellite QKD. *Source:* Huang et al. [17].

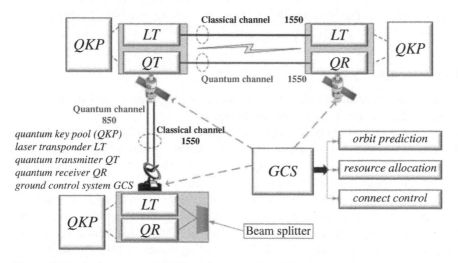

Figure 15.3 Basic structure of QKP-enabled satellite QKD system. *Source:* Huang et al. [17].

each link. Due to the long distance of the satellite links, the secret key rate is limited and the round-trip delay is high. To overcome these challenges, QKP can be constructed between satellite and ground and between the pair of satellites. Each pair of adjacent nodes generates and exchanges secret keys continuously and stores keys in QKPs. Figure 15.3 shows the basic structure of QKP-enabled satellite QKD system.

Each node has its quantum transceiver, laser transceiver, and QKP. The control system calculates the route selection and key assignment, and allocates them on each node. The controller can be connected to satellites by radio or optical links (the radio transceiver is omitted in the picture).

15.1.2 QSN Architecture

Based on the above analysis and technologies of satellite-based QKD, we present an architecture of global-scale QSNs as in [17].

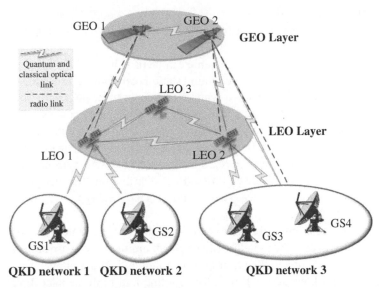

Figure 15.4 Architecture of double-layer quantum satellite networks (QSNs). *Source:* Huang et al. [17].

Double-layer QSN architecture: The number of secret keys in QKPs depends on the key generation rates and the duration of the key generation procedure. However, LEO satellites can only access a ground station for about 10–15 min in a satellite moving period due to their high-moving speed relative to Earth. Within the short coverage time, the secret keys in QKP between the LEO and ground stations may not be enough for key-relay services. On the other hand, GEO satellites stay at rest relative to Earth and cover a wider range due to the high orbit; therefore, they can perform QKD continuously (at the expense of much larger losses). GEOs can generate and store the keys for the entire day with lower secret key rates. The technologies of higher link efficiency including a larger telescope and better pointing system are being studied to increase the key rates on higher orbits [9]. To eradicate the limitations of single-layer satellite networks, a new architecture of double-layer QSNs is proposed in [17]. As shown in Figure 15.4, the network consists of at least two orbit layers of satellites.

In this section, we consider that satellite networks comprise both GEO and LEO. A hybrid of LEO and GEO satellite networks can combine the advantages of both satellite layers. In double-layer satellite networks, GEO and LEO can both establish access links to ground stations; LEO is the first choice to access satellites, and GEO is the alternative. Satellites in the same orbit layer are interconnected by inter-satellite links (ISLs). Also, satellites in different orbit layers could be interconnected by inter-orbit-links (IOLs). In the ground segment, QKD networks are distributed all over the world and interconnected by one or more satellites.

Topology design: In the design example, 66 LEO and 3 GEO satellites are set in the satellite constellation [17]. Similar to the Iridium system, the LEO layer consists of six orbits and satellites located uniformly in each orbit. The Sun-Synchronous Orbit (SSO) is adopted because it can cover the same area in each satellite period. The GEO layer consists of three GEO satellites located uniformly in the equator orbit. Since GEO satellites could provide long QKD performing time and a high coverage rate, it stores the generated keys in satellite–ground QKP.

With multiple pairs of transponders on board, a satellite can set up several simultaneous optical links with adjacent nodes and ground stations. However, considering the resource constraint of satellites, the establishment of inter-orbit layer links and access links should be scheduled efficiently. We will study the routing problem for the cases with and without GEO-LEO links in the following sections.

With limited transponders on satellite, a time-sharing scheme can be used in the QKD connection between GEO and ground, which means two or more ground stations can share a transponder on GEO. For example, if one transponder can access two ground stations in turn, GEO with four transponders can set up eight quantum satellite–ground links. In this section, we suppose one transponder can connect to two ground stations and each connection lasts for 30 min. As for key relaying, GEO can transmit XOR keys to ground stations and LEOs in radio links by broadcasts.

Routing and key assignment (RKA): In double-layer QSNs, it is necessary to design a customized RKA algorithm for key-relay services to schedule the end-to-end key distribution. The algorithm calculates the key-relay path for each key-relay service. Then it allocates bandwidth and quantum keys of each link along the service path.

We assume that key-relay services are originated from two nodes in different QKD networks or two distant nodes in the same QKD network. Each satellite can establish multiple free-space optical links with other satellites. GS are capable of handling four ground–satellite links simultaneously. The optical links can be set up in millisecond (ms) time. The routing and resource allocation problem over QSNs is stated as follows:

- Given:
  1) Terrestrial network topology: The geolocation information of GS in global networks
  2) Node and link property: The capacity of QKP between each pair of nodes and secret key rates in different types of links
  3) Satellite network topology: LEO and GEO satellites and respective ISLs, connectivity between satellites and ground stations
- Output: The routing, key, and bandwidth assignment results for key services at each instant.
- Goal: Schedule the routing, key, and bandwidth allocation for key-relay services and maximize the number of generated keys in a QSN.
- Constraints: Secret key rates, link durations, numbers of satellite–ground links, existence of GEO-LEO links, and numbers of secret keys in QKPs.

Figure 15.5 illustrates different route selection schemes in two scenarios of a double-layer QSN. Figure 15.5a describes the scenario with GEO-LEO links, and Figure 15.5b describes the scenario without GEO-LEO links. The bold lines represent the continuous links, and the dotted lines represent the intermittent links. The red arrows identify the routing using only LEO for accessing, and the green arrows identify the joint GEO and LEO access routing.

The latter scheme will be chosen when GS cannot access LEO. In the first scenario, the joint GEO and LEO routing can leverage two types of satellites to relay keys, while in the second scenario, it can only use LEO or GEO with the constraint of no GEO-LEO links. Given that the satellite network topology varies over time, the routing and resource allocation scheme should take the variation in link distance and link duration into consideration. In this section, we will handle the satellite routing problem based on the methodology of virtual topology [24].

We partition the satellite period (satellites move periodically) into many time slots where satellite connectivity remains unchanged. In such time slots, satellite topology can be regarded as static. That is, the dynamic topology is divided into a series of static virtual topologies.

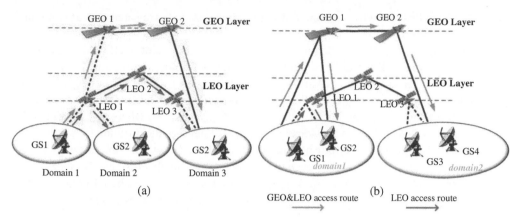

Figure 15.5 Route selection for key-relay services in two scenarios over the double-layer quantum satellite network (QSN): (a) with and (b) without GEO-LEO links. *Source:* Huang et al. [17].

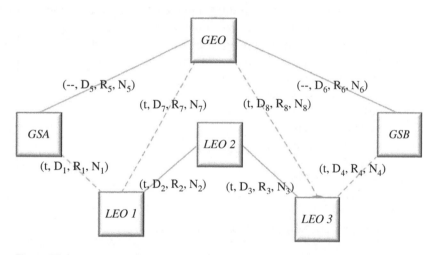

Figure 15.6 Contact and resource graph of quantum satellite network (QSN). *Source:* Huang et al. [17].

15.1.3 Routing and Resource Allocation Algorithm

Based on the double-layer QSN architecture, a JGL-RKA algorithm to solve the RKA problem is presented in [17].

Topology and resource graph: Since the movement of satellites is predictable and periodic, the connectivity relationship of all nodes can be calculated for a time slot. Thus, we can calculate a series of fixed topologies for each time slot. Although a topology graph is more accurate with smaller time slots, too many time slots may decrease the efficiency of route calculation. Thus, the time duration of a discrete topology was set as 1 minute in the 100 min of simulation. The period can be divided into n intervals as $\{[t_1, t_2), [t_2, t_3), \ldots, [t_{n-1}, t_n]\}$. The topology matrix is represented by $M = \{M_1, M_2, \ldots M_n\}$, where each M_k belongs to the interval $[t_{k-1}, t_k]$.

Based on the topology matrixes, the contact and resource graph of the QSN can be created. Figure 15.6 shows an example of the contact and resource graph. The solid lines represent continuous links, and the dotted lines represent intermittent links. Each link has several parameters (t, D_k, R_k, N_k), including the time instant t, link distance D, secret key rate of link R, and available secret keys N in QKP of the link between two nodes. This group of parameters identifies the state of link k at instant t. Each R of the link is calculated based on the link distance and link properties. For fixed links like GEO–ground links, their time is set as "–," as their key rates and link distances remain the same.

As the secret key of each QKP in each node is an important constraint of RKA, the remaining number of secret keys in QKPs should be updated in a timely fashion in a resource graph.

The number N_k of secret keys in QKP at the next instant is decided by the number of key generations and key consumptions in previous interval. At the start of each instant, the N_k of link k can be calculated from the secret key rate as follows: $N_k = N_{Last} + R_k \cdot \delta t$, where N_{Last} denotes the remaining number of secret keys of previous instant, and δt denotes the duration of a time slot.

According to [9, 10], the secret key rate of a link decreases linearly with the link distance. Therefore, we can describe the relationship between the key rate R and the link distance D as $R = R_{max} \cdot (D - D_{max})/(D_{min} - D_{max})$ with $D \in [D_{min}, D_{max}]$. D_{min} denotes the distance where key rate reaches the maximum value, and D_{max} denotes the distance where the key rate falls to zero.

Algorithm 1 Joint GEO-LEO Routing and Key Allocation Algorithm.

```
Input: r(s, d, N, B), L
Output: RKA solution for key services, updated network resource graph
Step 1      1:    for each key-relay services r(s, d, N, B), do
            2:        obtain the time-varying topology matrix and update
                      resource map for the current moment;
            3:        if L = = 1, then
            4:           call Algorithm 2:
            5:        end if
            6:        if L = = 0, then
            7:           call Algorithm 2;
            8:        end if
Step 2      9:    if S_S = = S_D, then
           10:        continue;
           11:    else
           12:        compute route path P WITH Dijkstra
           12:        algorithm;
           13:    end if
           14:    search available timeslots T(P) along the
           14:    path;
           15:    if T(P) ≠ ∅, then
           16:        select one time slot on each link;
           17:        search the remaining number N_k of secret
           19:        keys in each QKP;
           18:        if N < N_k, then
           19:           select N secret keys from QKPs on each link;
           20:        else
           21:           inter-satellite key assignment failed;
           22:        end if
           23:    else
           24:        inter-satellite routing failed;
           25:    end if
           26: end for
```

Source: Huang et al. [17]

Since the propagation environments of different type of links are different, the maximum key rate of different links should be set accordingly. The key rate of ISLs is higher than that of satellite–ground links as the optical signal will not experience atmospheric turbulence. In addition, key rates of LEO–ground links are higher than GEO–ground links due to the shorter transmission distance.

Algorithm: In order to solve the RKA problem, a JGL-RKA algorithm to select the access satellites and QKD route in QSNs was designed in [17]. In Step 1, Algorithm 1 obtains the time-varying topology matrix and updated resource map. The resource map is updated according to the key consumption and secret key rates of each link. Step 2 performs the access satellite selection to find an access satellite. This selection is executed for both source node and destination node. Two access-satellite-selecting algorithms under the scenarios with GEO-LEO links (Algorithm 2) and without GEO-LEO links (Algorithm 3) were proposed in [17]. In Algorithm 2, the terrestrial node searches for available LEOs as the access satellite and chooses the best one that satisfies wavelength and key requirements. If there is no available LEO, it attempts to select GEO as the access satellite. In Algorithm 3, the terrestrial node searches available LEOs as a priority selection. If there is no available LEO, the source and destination nodes both search GEOs as the access node because there are no GEO-LEO links. Third, the RKA algorithm is performed for calculating the inter-satellite path. If the source node and destination node have accessed the same satellite, inter-satellite route calculation is not required. The Dijkstra algorithm is used to calculate the shortest path between

---

Algorithm 2 Joint GEO-LEO Access Algorithm.

```
1:   for source and destination ground station, do
2:     search all accessible LEOs for ground node;
3:     for each satellite do
4:       choose the best one according to shortest distance;
5:       search the remaining number N_k of secret keys in
         satellite-ground QKP;
6:       if N < N_k then
7:         select the satellite as access node;
8:         break;
9:       else
10:          continue;
11:     end if
12:   end for
13:   if no LEO satellite has enough keys, then
14:       search all accessible GEOs for ground node;
15:       repeat lines 3-12;
16:       if no GEO satellite has enough keys then
17:           access satellite selecting failed;
18:       end if
19:   end if
20    end for
```

Source: Huang et al. [17]

Algorithm 3 Separated GEO and LEO Access Algorithm.

```
1:  for source and destination ground station, do
2:    search all accessible LEOs for ground node;
3:    for each satellite do
4:      choose the best one according to shortest distance;
5:        search the remaining number N_k of secret keys in
          satellite-ground QKP;
6:      if N < N_k then
7:        select the satellite as access node;
8:        break;
9:      else
10:       continue;
11:     end if
12:   end for
13: end for
14: if no access LEO for source or destination node then
15:    for source and destination ground station do
16:      search all accessible GEOs for ground node;
17:      repeat lines 3-13;
18:  if no access GEO for source or destination node then
19:      access satellite selecting failed;
20:  end if
21: end if
```

Source: Huang et al. [17]

---

source and destination nodes. Also, the First-Fit algorithm is used for times-slot and secret key allocation on each intermediate link for key services.

The JGL-RKA algorithm is considered as a two-step process: (i) satellite-to-ground routing and (ii) inter-satellite routing. In the scenario where GEO-LEO links exist, the joint GEO-LEO access algorithm is executed to select access satellites for pairs of ground nodes. Whereas if GEO-LEO links do not exist, the separated GEO and LEO access algorithm is executed to select access satellites for ground nodes.

The time complexities of Algorithm 2 (lines 3–5) and Algorithm 3 (lines 6–8) in Step 1 are $O(|L| + |G|)$. The complexity of Step 2 is $O(|L + G|^2 + |W| \cdot |L + G - 1|)$. Thus, the total time complexity of JGL-RKA algorithm is $O(|L + G|^2)$.

Notations:

- $G_t (V_t, E_t)$: Substrate topology of double-layer QSN at instant t, where V_t denotes the set of nodes and E_t denotes the set of optical links
- T: A period of satellite movement
- s: Source ground node of key-relay service
- d: Destination ground node of key-relay service
- $r(s, d, N, B)$: Key-relay service

- S_S: Source access satellite
- S_D: Destination access satellite
- *N:* Required number of secret keys of key-relay service
- *B:* Required time slot of key-relay service
- *L:* Integer variable that equals 1if there are GEO-LEO links in the double-layer QSN, and 0 otherwise
- *LN:* Maximum number of ground stations that can be connected to one GEO
- NG: Maximum threshold of ground–GEO QKP
- NS: Maximum threshold of inter-satellite QKP

Figure 15.7 shows illustrative results of the SP of key-relay services (SP) and access satellite selection (SP-a) versus traffic load under different topologies and route selections.

We observe that the SP decreases as the traffic load (in erlang) increases. We compare the SP under a double-layer topology with a single-layer topology without GEO. The scenarios with and without GEO-LEO links (denoted as GL links) are also compared. The result shows that the SP of key-relay services in a double-layer network is higher than that in a single-layer network. We can observe similar phenomena on SP-a. The reason for this is that double-layer QSNs can provide additional GEO choices for access satellite selection, leading to a higher SP in satellite–ground routing. On the other hand, the SP and SP-a over a topology with GL links is slightly higher than

Design Example 15.1[1]

To evaluate the performance of the JGL-RKA algorithm, the simulation is performed on a satellite topology with 66 LEO, 3 GEO, and a terrestrial network with 25 ground stations distributed across the globe (in major population centers). AGI STK[*)] is used to obtain the satellite trajectory and calculate the satellite topology matrix. The LEO constellation is similar to the Iridium system, where each LEO establishes four ISLs with adjacent satellites, including intra-orbit and inter-orbit links. GEO can set up links with LEO in its coverage. Both GEO and LEO can set up links with multiple satellites depending on their optical terminal numbers. It was assumed that LEO can connect to at most four ground stations simultaneously. In the simulation, it was assumed that each pair of nodes generates quantum keys until the number of stored keys exceeds the maximum capacity of QKP, which is related to the storage capacity of the satellite nodes. The key-relay requests are generated randomly among all terrestrial nodes according to the Poisson distribution. 100 000 key-relay services were considered in each simulation, and the holding time of each service was set as 30 s. The algorithm was implemented in C++ with Visual Studio 2017 on a computer with a 3.0 GHz Intel Core i5-7200U CPU and 16 GB RAM.

In order to evaluate the performance of the double-layer network and the JGL-RKA algorithm, the success probability (SP) of key-relay services in each scenario of simulation will be presented.

Simulation parameters [17]: Number of time slots on per link 16, Maximum secret key rate of inter-satellite link 1000 units of keys, Maximum secret key rate of LEO–ground link 400 units of keys, Maximum secret key rate of GEO–ground link 40 units of keys, key-relay service's time slot requirements 1, hold time of a key-relay service 30 s, interval of time slot of topology 1 minute, processing delay on satellite 20 ms.

---

1 *AGI: Systems Tool Kit (STK) – Analytical Graphics, Inc.*

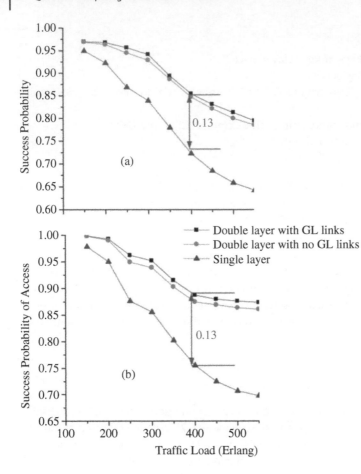

Figure 15.7 Success probability (SP) and SP-a versus traffic load under different topologies and route selections (LN = 10, NG = 2000, NS = 20 000, N = 20). (a) SP, (b) SP-a. *Source:* Huang et al. [17].

those over a topology without GL links. This is because route selection with GL links can provide more flexibility for access satellite selection. However, route selection without GL links allow only ground nodes access to satellites in the same layer.

Figure 15.8a presents the SP versus traffic load under different numbers of GEO–ground links. For these results, the number of LEO links is fixed. One can see that the SP gradually increases as the maximum number of GEO–ground links increases. This is because there are more accessible satellites for ground stations with more satellite–ground links. But the increase in GEO–ground links will increase the total links of the QSN. Therefore, there is a trade-off between the SP and the costs of the QSN.

Figure 15.8b illustrates the impact of QKP capacity on the SP. It can be observed that the SP increases with the increase in GEO–ground QKP (NG) capacity. However, the capacity of inter-satellite QKP (NS) remains unchanged. The increase in NG has little impact when the traffic load is low (150–200); the impact becomes large as the traffic load increases. This is because the higher capacity of QKPs can enable QKP to store more secret keys in a satellite period and provide more secret keys for ground stations. But when the threshold exceeds 2000, the SP will undergo little change as the threshold is enough for storing secret keys generated in one satellite period.

As for the impact of NS, we can see that the SP increases with the increase of capacity when traffic load is low (150–300). When traffic load becomes larger, the difference between the curves will

Figure 15.8 (a) Success probability (SP) versus traffic load with different numbers of GEO–ground links. (NG = 2000, NS = 20 000, N = 20). (b) SP versus traffic load with different capacities of QKP (LN = 10, N = 20, with GL links). *Source:* Huang et al. [17].

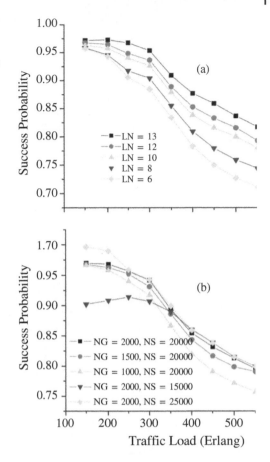

become quite small. The reason for this is that the SP of access satellite selection is the major impact factor of the SP when the traffic load is large. The increase in NS can decrease the BP of inter-satellite routing, which has a great impact on the SP when the traffic load is low. Therefore, the SP of different NS values is similar under a high traffic load.

Figure 15.9a illustrates that the SP will decrease dramatically when N increases. A higher secret key demand increases the consumption of secret keys in QKPs and reduces the SP of key-relay services. Figure 15.9b shows the average available satellites versus the different topologies. As the traffic load increases, the number of average available satellites decreases, owing to the higher key consumption of satellite–ground QKP. Compared with a single-layer network, there are more available satellites in a double-layer QSN, and the number of available satellites increases as the number of GEO–ground links (LN) increases. Figure15.9c illustrates the average hop number of the route path for key-relay services under different topologies. It can be observed that the hop number over a double-layer satellite network is lower than that of a single-layer network. The hop number becomes smaller over a double-layer network with GL links. Therefore, the scheme can lower the total hop number of the key-relay path and increase the security of the key relaying procedure. Also, we can see that the hop number decreases as the traffic load increases. A possible reason for this is that when the consumption of secret keys and time slots becomes larger, long route paths are more likely to fail than short route paths, as their requirement for link resources is larger.

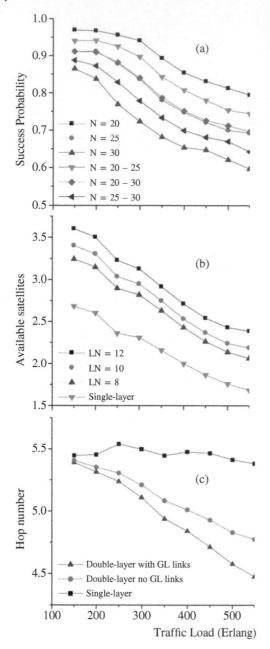

Figure 15.9 (a) Success probability (SP) versus traffic load with different N (LN = 10, NG = 2000, NS = 20 000). (b) Average available satellites under different topologies (c). Average hop number of route path for key-relay service under different topologies (LN = 10, NG = 2000, NS = 20 000, N = 20). *Source:* Huang et al. [17].

15.2 QC Routing for Social Overlay Networks

The widespread use of mobile networking devices, such as smartphones and tablets, has substantially increased the number of nodes in the operational networks. This applies especially in the case of dynamic network architectures, where the terminals can also be turned into the access points or relays when needed to augment network capabilities [25–28]. These devices often suffer from a lack of power and bandwidth. Hence, we have to optimize their message routing to maximize their capabilities. However, the optimal routing typically relies on a delicate balance of diverse and often conflicting objectives, such as the route's delay and power consumption. The network design also has to consider the nodes' user-centric social behavior, a topic that we discussed to some extent in Chapter 14. Hence, the employment of socially aware load balancing becomes imperative to avoid the potential formation of bottlenecks in the network's packet flow. In this section, we discuss new emerging algorithms that exploit quantum parallelism to its full potential by reducing the database correlations for performing multi-objective routing optimization, while at the same time balancing the tele-traffic load among the nodes without imposing a substantial degradation in the network's delay and power consumption. Furthermore, we also discuss a socially aware load balancing metric, namely, the normalized entropy of the normalized composite betweenness of the associated socially aware network, for striking a better trade-off between the network's delay and power consumption [29].

15.2.1 Social Overlay Network

We consider the social and wireless network overlay shown in Figure 15.10. In [29], this architecture is referred to as a twin-layer network. To elaborate further, the network is composed of a set of N_{MC} users, which from now on will be referred to as mesh clients (MCs) and by a set of N_{MR} wireless mesh routers (MRs).

The latter form the backbone of a wireless mesh network, which supports communications among the MCs. This network constitutes the bottom layer (underlay) of the network (WUN). On the other hand, the MCs are assumed to exhibit a specific social behavior, and hence they form a social overlay network (SON), which incorporates the upper layer (overlay) of the network. In [29], the locations of both the MCs and of the MRs are assumed to be random, obeying a uniform distribution within a (100×100) m^2 square block, which is the network's coverage area considered for this scenario, for the sake of approaching the fully-connected scenario in the WUN layer. Additionally, each of the MCs is exclusively served by its closest MR, which is denoted by the gray arrows

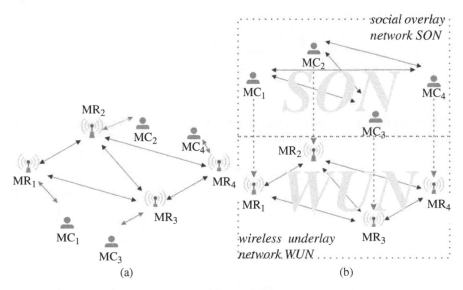

Figure 15.10 Social overlay network. *Source:* Alanis et al. [29].

in Figure 15.10. As far as the packet dissemination process is concerned, we assume that the source and destination nodes belong exclusively to the set of MCs. Therefore, the MRs of the WUN layer can only act as intermediate relays forwarding the packets of the source MC to the destination MC. Furthermore, the communication between MCs is only feasible via MRs. For instance, let us consider the case, where MC1 has to send a packet to MC3. Despite the fact that in Figure 15.10a MC1 and MC3 are quite close to each other, their communication can only be achieved through MR1 and MR3. Hence, the shortest route in terms of the number of hops that the packet can follow is the route $MC_1 \rightarrow MR_1 \rightarrow MR_3 \rightarrow MC_3$.

SON: As we have mentioned in the previous subsection, the MCs exhibit social behavior, increasing the probability of their communication with a specific set of other Ms. This set of MCs is often referred to in wireless sensor network (WSN) terminology as *friends*. Hence, the MCs' friendship status can be modeled by the binary friendship matrix F^o that defines the set of MCs that are friends of a specific MC in an overlay network. Naturally, the friendship matrix F_{MC} is symmetric, with all the elements of its diagonal being equal to zero. Equivalently, since each MC is associated with a specific MR in the UWN, a binary friendship matrix F^u may be defined in the context of MR as a cross-network metric. The elements $F_{u,ij}$ of the latter matrix indicate whether MR_i and MR_j are associated with a pair of MCs having a friendship relationship in the SON. We note that the F^u matrix is also symmetric; however, its diagonal elements may not be strictly equal to zero, corresponding the scenario where two friendly MCs are associated with the same MR. As for generating the F^u matrix, the authors in [29] have utilized the well-studied social relationship from [30] portrayed in Figure 15.11. To elaborate further, the MCs are randomly generated similarly to [30], and the sole constraint imposed is that of having a connected social graph to avoid the potential isolation of certain MCs. In this way, packet dissemination emerging from a specific MC to the rest of the MCs is enabled, regardless of whether they have a friendship relationship, by forwarding a packet on a friend-by-friend basis.

The social behavior of the MCs provides us with the capability of employing social network analysis (SNA) [31] tools for analyzing the performance of socially aware networks. In fact, the betweenness centrality B^c metric has been proposed by Freeman in [31] for quantifying the information flow of each node MR_k of the WUNs denoted as the node k^u (node k in the underlay network). In this context, each node has been considered to have a social friendship with the specific nodes it can reliably communicate with using a single hop. The betweenness centrality metric actually quantifies the usage of each node k^u as an intermediate relay. To be specific, the betweenness centrality B is defined as [31]

$$B^c(k^u) = \sum_{i=1, i \neq k}^{U} \sum_{j=1, j \neq k}^{U} g_{i^u, j^u}(k^u) / g_{i^u, j^u} \tag{15.1}$$

where $g_{i^u, j^u}(k^u)$ represents the number of times the node k^u is involved in the shortest routes – in terms of the number of hops – spanning the node i^u to the node j^u, while g_{i^u, j^u} denotes the number of the optimal routes and U corresponds to the total number of $u \in \mathcal{U}$ nodes (MRs). We note that the normalized betweenness centrality $\overline{B}^c(k^u)$, defined in Eq. (15.2), corresponds to the probability of k^u being used as a relay, and it is formulated as

$$\overline{B}^c(k^u) = B^c(k^u) / \sum_{i=1}^{U} B^c(i^u) \tag{15.2}$$

We can adapt the betweenness centrality to the context of overlay networks by defining the so-called composite betweenness centrality. Later, the friendship relationship is defined in a rather generic manner. To elaborate further, since the links between overlay nodes $o \in \mathcal{O}$(MCs) that share a

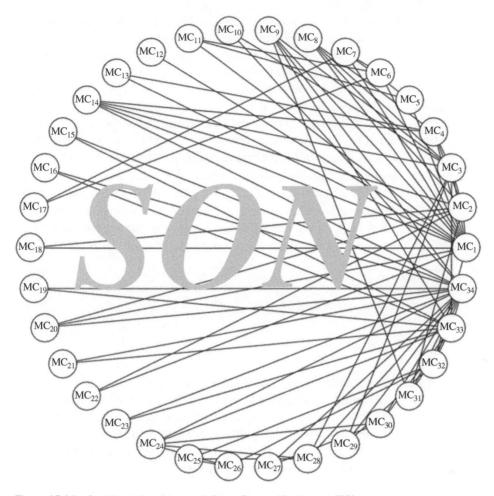

Figure 15.11 Social relationship graph form. *Source:* Alanis et al. [29].

friendship are established on an exclusive basis, the composite betweenness centrality calculation is restricted to these specific routes:

$$B^{\sigma}(k^u) = \sum_{i=1}^{O} \sum_{j=1, j \neq k}^{O} g_{i^o, j^o}(k^u) F_{i^o, j^o} / g_{i^o, j^o} \tag{15.3}$$

where F_{i^o, j^o} denotes the friendship relationship between i^o as well as j^o, and it is equal to the element of the i-th row and the j-th column of the F^o matrix. Additionally, the term $g_{i^o, j^o}(k^u)$ corresponds to the number of optimal routes between i^o and j^o involving k^u, while g_{i^o, j^o} is the total number of optimal routes for the same source and destination pair. In analogy with the normalized betweenness centrality, the normalized composite betweenness centrality $\overline{B}^{\sigma}(k^u)$ quantifies the probability of a specific k^u being used as an intermediate relay, in the context of the socially aware network considered. The latter metric is defined as

$$\overline{B}^{\sigma}(k^u) = B^{\sigma}(k^u) / \sum_{i=1}^{U} B^{\sigma}(i^u) \tag{15.4}$$

The vector $\overline{B}^{\sigma}$ contains the probability distribution of the specific *u-nodes* (MRs) being used as intermediate relays. Therefore, instead of optimizing a specific parameter, such as the sum-rate considered in [32], we can readily manipulate this distribution by selecting the appropriate routes. To guarantee fairness in terms of the forwarded tele-traffic load among the u nodes, we will consider the desired set of route solutions to be those that result in the normalized composite betweenness $\overline{B}^{\sigma}$ approaching the uniform distribution.

A direct approach to equally distributing the relayed load among the u nodes would be to minimize the standard deviation $\Sigma_{\overline{B}^{\sigma}}$ of the normalized composite betweenness. Nevertheless, there exist cases where none of the active routes utilize intermediate u nodes, which results in an all-zero normalized composite betweenness distribution, that is, we have $\overline{B}^{\sigma}(k^u) = 0, \forall k \in \{1, ..., U\}$. This kind of distribution yields a standard deviation equal to $\Sigma_{\overline{B}^{\sigma}} = 0$, which is optimal; however, these route solutions often exhibit poor performance in terms of their power consumption or bit error ratio (BER). Therefore, we will consider an alternative metric, namely, the *normalized entropy* $\overline{H}(\overline{B}^{\sigma})$ of the normalized composite betweenness, which is defined as follows [29]:

$$\overline{H}(\overline{B}^{\sigma}) = H(\overline{B}^{\sigma})/\log_2 U \tag{15.5}$$

where $H(\overline{B}^{\sigma})$ is Shannon entropy given by [33]:

$$H(\overline{B}^{\sigma}) = \sum_{k=1}^{U} \overline{B}^{\sigma}(k^u)/\log_2 \overline{B}^{\sigma}(k^u) \tag{15.6}$$

We note that the normalization factor of Eq. (15.5) is used to make the normalized entropy value independent of the number of u nodes, U, and bounds its value to the range [0, 1]. Explicitly, the entropy of a distribution can be viewed as a metric of proximity of a specific distribution to the uniform one. This could be justified by the fact that the entropy of a specific distribution is inversely proportional to the Kullback–Leibler divergence $D_{KL}(\overline{B}^{\sigma}\|\Omega)$ [34], where Ω denotes the uniform distribution of U events. This is formally expressed as follows [35]:

$$H(\overline{B}^{\sigma}) = \log_2 U - D_{KL}(\overline{B}^{\sigma}\|\Omega) \tag{15.7}$$

where the Kullback–Leibler divergency $D_{KL}(\overline{B}^{\sigma}\|\Omega)$ is defined as [35]:

$$D_{KL}(\overline{B}^{\sigma}\|\Omega) = \sum_{k=1}^{U} \overline{B}^{\sigma}(k^u) \log_2 [\overline{B}^{\sigma}(k^u)/\Omega(k^u)] \tag{15.8}$$

The Kullback–Leibler divergence constitutes an appropriate metric of the difference between two different distributions [35]. Hence, based on Eq. (15.7), the value of the divergence for the distributions $\overline{B}^{\sigma}$ and Ω is bound to the range [0, log2(U)]. The upper bound of this region denotes complete divergence of the examined distributions, while its lower bound yields a perfect convergence of the two distributions. This can equivalently be translated into normalized entropy $\overline{H}(\overline{B}^{\sigma})$ terms, where the perfect matching of the normalized composite betweenness distribution and the uniform distribution is achieved, when we have $\overline{H}(\overline{B}^{\sigma}) = 1$, whereas they are uncorrelated when $\overline{H}(\overline{B}^{\sigma}) = 0$. This metric circumvents the problem of the all-zero normalized composite betweenness distribution, since in this case its normalized entropy is equal to $\overline{H}(\overline{B}^{\sigma}) = 0$. Therefore, efficient load balancing relies upon maximization of the normalized entropy, leading to the optimization problem in terms of the active routes S formulated as

$$\underset{\forall S}{argmax} \ \overline{H}(\overline{B}^{\sigma}(S)) \tag{15.9}$$

The optimization problem of Eq. (15.9) is unconstrained, and hence it does not take into account any other quality of service (QoS) criteria, such as the network delay or power consumption. This results in the route solutions defined by Eq. (15.9) that either exhibit excessive delay or excessive power consumption or cannot be established at all owing to a maximum transmit power violation. These QoS criteria, which stem from the *wireless underlay network* (WUN), are presented in the next subsection. From a cross-network optimization perspective, they will be encapsulated in Eq. (15.9) in the form of a set of constraints, for the sake of guaranteeing an optimal performance in terms of the QoS criteria considered.

Wireless underlay network: As mentioned at the beginning of this section, the WUN network is composed of a specific set of the u-nodes (MRs) that facilitate communications among the o-nodes (MCs) by forwarding the respective packets, as portrayed in the bottom layer of Figure 15.10b. Their locations are random, which is typical for an ad hoc deployment, but then are considered to be stationary. By contrast, the o-nodes are mobile. Additionally, a rather strong line-of-sight (LoS) component [36] is assumed to be encountered by each i^u-node to j^u-node link, and thus only the link's path loss is taken into account. The path loss $L_{i,j}$ for a link between the nodes i^u and j^u is calculated using the classic path loss model, which is formally expressed as [37], $L_{i,j} = P_{i,j}^t / P_{i,j}^r = L_0 (d_{i,j}/d_0)^\alpha$, where α is the path loss coefficient ($\alpha = 3$ is used in what follows), $d_{i,j}$ is the Euclidean distance between the nodes i^u and j^u, L_0 is the reference path loss at the distance $d_0 = 1$ m, and $P_{i,j}^r$ and $P_{i,j}^t$ are the received and transmitted powers, respectively. The parameter L_0 can be expressed as [36] $L_0 = (4\pi d_0 f_c/c)^2$, where $f_c = 2.4$ GHz is used in what follows, and c is the speed of light. As far as the forwarding scheme is concerned, the Decode-and-Forward (DF) scheme was utilized in [29] due to its capability of encapsulating the routing information into the packet header. In this context, the modulation scheme adopted was quadrature phase shift keying (QPSK). As for the transmission environment, the links among the u-nodes are subjected to only additive white Gaussian noise (AWGN), while the links between the o-nodes and their associated u-nodes are established for transmission over Rayleigh fading channels. Additionally, an adaptive power control scheme was adopted, where each link, either between two u-nodes or between o-nodes and their associated u-nodes, can be successfully established as long as the link's BER is lower than a certain threshold P_{eth}. This constraint is imposed to guarantee that the packets are successfully recovered from the intermediate MRs, hence mitigating the need for retransmission. In our scenario, we have set this BER threshold to $P_{eth} = 10^{-2}$, which corresponds to the uncoded BER of each link, because powerful state-of-the-art channel coding schemes are capable of further reducing the BER to infinitesimally low values. Therefore, at each link we will attempt to match the link BER value to that of its threshold, hence minimizing the potential interference experienced by the rest of the nodes owing to excessive interferences. This yields an equivalent signal to noise plus interference ratio (SINR) threshold $\gamma_{i,jth}$ equal to

$$\gamma_{i,jth} = \frac{P_{i,j}^r}{N_0 + I_{\max}} = \begin{cases} \dfrac{2(1 - 2P_{eth})^2}{1 - (1 - 2P_{eth})^2}; & i \text{ or } j \text{ are } o - nodes \\ Q^{-1}(P_{eth}); & otherwise \end{cases} \quad (15.10)$$

where the function $Q^{-1}(\cdot)$ is the inverse of the Q-function, N_0 is the thermal noise power, and $I_{\max}$ is the maximum tolerable interference power level. The thermal noise power is set to $N_0 = -114$ dBm per bandwidth of W = 1 MHz. Therefore, based on the expression for $L_{i,j}$ and Eq. (15.10) the transmit power $P_{i,j}^{t,req}$ required for satisfying the BER threshold is equal to $P_{i,j}^{t,req}$. An additional constraint regarding the actual transmitters' maximum power level $P_{\max}^{t,act}$ is also imposed. In fact, it is considered to be upper-bounded to $P_{\max}^{t,act} = 20$ dBm, which is a typical value for the IEEE 802.11b/g protocol. Based on this constraint, we can define the adjacency matrix A as $a_{i,j} = h\left(P_{i,j}^{t,req} - P_{max}^{t,act}\right)$, where $a_{i,j}$ corresponds to the element of the matrix A located at the i-th row and the j-th column, while $h(\cdot)$ is the Heaviside function. Therefore, the actual transmitted power $P_{i,j}^{t,act}$ required for establishing the link between the nodes i and j is equal to $P_{i,j}^{t,act} = P_{i,j}^{t,req}/a_{i,j}$. Based on Eq. (15.10), the cost in terms of power for the link spanning the i-th node to the j-th one will be equal to the power required for achieving a BER equal to the threshold value should the required power be less or equal to the maximum transmit power value. Otherwise, the cost is set to $+\infty$, implying that the link cannot be established.

As far as the maximum tolerable interference power level I_{max} is concerned, it is defined as the maximum interference level that allows the u-nodes to establish at least a single link with the rest of the WUN with a probability of 99%. Therefore, its value can be determined from the cumulative density function (CDF) of the connectivity of the u-nodes versus the value of I_{max}. Having defined the physical layer parameters of the wireless mesh network (WMN) layer, let us now proceed by defining our multiple-objective optimization problem. First, let us consider the set of N_r active routes $S = [x^{(1)},. ..., x^{(i)}, ..., x^{(Nr)}]$, where $x^{(i)}$ is the i-th active route and corresponds to a unique pair of o-nodes. Since each o-node is associated with a unique u-node, each active route is defined as follows: $x^{(i)} = [k^o, l^u,. ..., m^u, n^o]$, where the i-th active route corresponds to a transmission from the k-th o-node k^o to the n-th o-node n^o, while the source and destination o-nodes are associated with the l-th u-node l^u and the m-th u-node m^u, respectively.

Let us define first the average route delay D, which is quantified as $D(S) = \sum_{i=1}^{N_r} D^{(i)}(S)/N_r$, where S is the set of the active routes, and $D^{(i)}(S)$ corresponds to the delay of the i-th active route. For the sake of simplicity, we have chosen to quantify the latter as the number of hops incorporated by the route $x(i)$. Hence, the route delay $D^{(i)}(S)$ is formulated as

$$D^{(i)}(S) = \sum_{j=1}^{|x^{(i)}|-1} \left(a_{x_j^{(i)},x_{j+1}^{(i)}}^{-1}\right) - 1 \tag{15.11}$$

where the factor $|x^{(i)}|$ denotes the number of nodes involved in the route $x^{(i)}$, and $x_j^{(i)}$ is the route's j-th node. In Eq. (15.11), the sum of the inverse of the adjacency matrix elements guarantees that all the route's links can be established. Otherwise, the route delay will be set to $D^{(i)}(S) = +\infty$, hence classifying the route $x^{(i)}$ as infeasible. We note that the nodes' specific buffer packet length could be readily encapsulated in Eq. (15.11) in order to account for delays the imposed by buffered packets. Apart from the average delay D, we also consider the routes' average power consumption P, which is quantified as $P(S) = \sum_{i=1}^{N_r} P^{(i)}(S)/N_r$, where $P^{(i)}(S)$ corresponds to the power consumption of the route $x(i)$, which is in turn formulated based on Eq. (15.11) as

$$P^{(i)}(S) = \sum_{j=1}^{|x^{(i)}|-1} \left(P_{x_j^{(i)},x_{j+1}^{(i)}}^{t,act}\right) \tag{15.12}$$

In Eq. (15.12), the adjacency matrix elements $a_{x_j^{(i)},x_{j+1}^{(i)}}^{-1}$ are taken into account with the aid of Eq. (15.11). To be specific, a route composed of links that cannot guarantee satisfaction of the-BER threshold will require a power set to $P^{(i)}(S) = +\infty$, based on Eq. (15.12). This is in line with the route's delay, which is at the same time set to $+\infty$. Therefore, we have encapsulated the BER constraint in both of our optimization objectives, which we will refer to as utility functions (UFs). Based on these UFs, let us now define the optimization *Utility Vector* (UV), which is used for jointly optimizing both the average delay and the average power consumption, as $f(x^{(1)},....,x^{(Nr)}) = f(S) = [D(S),P(S)]$.

15.2.2 Multiple-Objective Optimization Model

For the evaluation of the UV used for quantifying the performance of the overlay network defined previously, the Pareto dominance concept [38] was used in [29]. Let us first summarize few definitions useful for the formal representation of the optimization problem.

Definition 1 (Weak Pareto Dominance): A particular solution x_1, associated with the UV $f(x_1)$ $= [f_1(x_1),. ..., f_K(x_1)]$, where K corresponds to the number of optimization objectives, is said to weakly dominate another solution x_2 associated with the UV $f(x_2) = [f_1(x_2),. ..., f_n(x_2)]$, iff $f(x_1) \succeq f(x_2)$; that is, we have $f_i(x_1) \le f_i(x_2) \ \forall i \in \{1,. ..., K\}$ and $\exists j \in \{1,. ..., K\}$ such that $f_j(x_1) < f_j(x_2)$.

Definition 2 (Strong Pareto Dominance): A particular solution x_1 associated with the UV $f(x_1) = [f_1(x_1),. ..., f_K(x_1)]$, where K corresponds to the number of optimization objectives, is said to strongly dominate another solution x_2 associated with the UV $f(x_2) = [f_1(x_2),. ..., f_K(x_2)]$, iff $f(x_1) \succ f(x_2)$; that is, we have $f_i(x_1) < f_i(x_2) \ \forall i \in \{1,. ..., K\}$.

Now using Eq. (15.9) and the definition of UV from the previous section, we define the optimization problem as

$$S^{opf} = \arg \max_{\forall S_i \in S*} \overline{H}\,\overline{B}^{\sigma}(S_i)$$

$$\text{Subject to } \nexists j : f(S_j) \succeq f(S_i) \tag{15.13}$$

where S^{opf} represents the optimal (*opf* stands for "optimal Pareto front") active route allocation based on the constrained optimization problem, and $S*$ corresponds to the set containing all the potential sets of active routes, which are strictly composed of routes that visit each of the *u*-nodes at most once. In a nutshell, the optimization problem of Eq. (15.13) attempts to distribute the intermediate relay tele-traffic load among the *u*-nodes as close as possible to the ideal uniformly distributed load, while ensuring that the associated network performance is Pareto-optimal in terms of its average delay and power consumption. Assuming a total number of *u*-nodes is equal to N_u, the total number N of S* routes for a specific pair source and destination u-nodes is given by [39] $N = \sum_{i=0}^{N_u - 2}(N_u - 2)!/(N_u - 2 - i)!$ Therefore, for the sake of verifying whether a single set of active routes satisfies the optimization problem constraint, we have to perform precisely N Pareto dominance comparisons. Let us now consider that the total number of pairs of source and destination u-nodes is exactly $N_r = |S|$. Then the total number N_{tot} of sets of active routes is given by

$$N_{tot} = N^{N_r} = \left[\sum_{i=0}^{N_u - 2}(N_u - 2)!/(N_u - 2 - i)!\right]^{N_r},$$ and hence N_{tot} increases exponentially as the number of *u*-nodes N_u increases, and the constrained optimization problem defined in Eq. (15.13) is classified as NP-hard. Consequently, sophisticated quantum-assisted methods are required to confine the escalating complexity. Such algorithms are derived for example in [29, 39, 40]. These algorithms are based on quantum search algorithms (QSAs), which are discussed in detail in Chapter 11.

15.3 QKD Networks

QKD networks differ from traditional networks in several aspects.

Although theoretical and pioneering results have been published in the field of quantum repeaters and quantum relays [41–43], in practice they remain unachievable with current technology [44–46]. Therefore, communication is realized in a hop-by-hop [47] or key-relay manner [48, 49]. Both methods rely on the assumption that all nodes along the path between the sender and the receiver must be fully trusted, forming a trusted relay QKD network [47, 50, 51].

Nodes are connected with QKD logical links, referred to below as links, which employ two distinct channels: a quantum channel, which is used for transmission of raw cryptographic keys encoded in certain photon properties, and a public channel, used for verification and processing of the exchanged values. Each quantum channel is always a point-to-point connection between exactly two nodes [52], whereas public channels can be implemented as any conventional connection, which can include an arbitrary number of intermediate devices [53].

The key rate is interconnected with a length of optical fiber such that a longer distance implies a lower key rate due to absorption and scattering of photons [44, 54–57]. Although key rates of 1 Mbps and above have been achieved [58–61], such solutions are limited to very short distances. Therefore, both endpoints of the corresponding link implement key buffers (storages) of limited capacity, which are gradually filled at their maximum key rate with the processed cryptographic key, referred to below as key material, and subsequently used for encryption/decryption of data flow [52, 62]. Key material denotes the symmetric cryptographic keys that are generated during the QKD process, stored in buffers (storages), and used subsequently for cryptographic operations over user traffic. Without key material, cryptographic operations cannot be performed, and a link can be described as temporarily unavailable [50]. To provide information-theoretically secure (ITS) communication, the key tends to be applied with a one-time pad (OTP) cipher and authenticated using an ITS message authentication scheme such as Wegman–Carter when communicating over a public channel [63–65]. As a result, ITS communication requires more bits of key material than the length of the secured message [52]. The type of encryption algorithm used and the volume of network traffic to be encrypted determine the key storage emptying speed, referred to as the key consumption rate, which denotes the rate of key material being taken from buffers (storages) and used for cryptographic operations. Similarly, the charging key rate (or simply key rate) denotes the rate of new key material generation, that is, the rate at which new keys are added to the buffers (storages) [48, 52, 66].

To meet the requirement to bypass untrusted nodes, in practice, QKD networks are usually deployed as overlay point-to-point networks, which exhibit selfish behavior, acting strategically to optimize performance and resulting in dynamic and unpredictable link performance [52, 62, 67–69]. As discussed in the previous section, overlay networks use the existing underlying networks in an attempt to implement better service; one of their most important features is the independence of the path offered by Internet service providers (ISPs). The specific QKD problems and constraints described above pose significant challenges in QKD network design. However, by analyzing the characteristics of QKD networks, we note similarities with mobile ad hoc networks (MANET) [70–72]. First, we specify the main characteristics of QKD technology from a simple point of view. QKD links (described above), due to the features of quantum channels, are always implemented in point-to-point behavior, and they can be roughly characterized by two features: limited distance and a key rate that is inversely proportional to the distance [52]. Additionally, QKD links may become unavailable when there is not enough key material or when the public channel is congested [73]. Such behavior is similar to Wi-Fi links, which are limited in length and where the communication speed depends on the user's distance from the transmitter.

One of the main features of QKD networks is the absence of a quantum repeater or quantum router in practice; therefore, communication is usually performed on a hop-by-hop basis

[46, 52]. In MANET, communication takes place on a hop-by-hop basis, and mobile nodes are typically powered by batteries, making energy-aware solutions especially important. The nodes connect themselves in a decentralized, self-organizing manner with no authority in charge of managing and controlling the network [71, 74]. The battery power in MANET nodes can be easily linked to the amount of key material in QKD key storages. Given that a node without a power supply (empty batteries) is not an active member of the network, the same analogy is valid for QKD networks, where a node without available key material cannot be used for data transmission. The range limitations of wireless links can be mapped to the limitations in the length of QKD links, whereas the absence of dedicated network infrastructure (such as a router) is common to MANET and QKD. Here we recognize the significant similarity between these two technologies, requiring a new approach to addressing QKD network problems [75].

15.3.1 QoS in QKD Overlay Networks

The specific QKD constraints described above lead to the conclusion that this type of network provides weak support to QoS.

QoS models-1 – Integrated Service and QKD networks: The basic concept of the Integrated Service (IntServ) model is a per-flow resource reservation using the Signaling Resource ReSerVation Protocol (RSVP) before data transmission [76]. The IntServ model is not suitable for QKD networks [75] because of an inability to guarantee the reservation: When QoS is provided in an IP network, an IP router has complete control over its packet buffers and the output link bandwidth, and can directly schedule these resources. By contrast, in an overlay network, the node cannot directly access the available resources in the overlay path. It can rely only on measurement techniques, where high accuracy cannot be guaranteed, and it cannot directly control or reserve resources in the underlying network. The only thing that a node in a QKD network can do is to guarantee the resources of a quantum channel by reserving key material in key storages. However, considering the interdependence of public and quantum channels in a QKD link [73], such a reservation does not constitute an advantage.

Signaling: RSVP is an out-of-band signalization protocol, which means that signaling packets contend for network resources with data packets and consume a substantial amount of scarce key material and network resources.

Differentiated Service and QKD networks: Differentiated Service (DiffServ) uses Differentiated Services Code Point (DSCP) bits in the IP header and a base set of packet-forwarding rules known as per-hop-behavior. DiffServ is known as an edge-provisioning model, and it does not provide any QoS guarantees per se [77]. The application of DiffServ in its original form is limited in a QKD network due to the following:

Edge router selection: Existing QKD technology limits the deployment of a QKD network to the metropolitan scale [56, 58]. In such a network, it is necessary to clearly define the edge routers, which play a key role in the processing of traffic.

Lack of service level agreement (SLA): Each network node needs to comply with the rules for the classification and processing of traffic of different priorities. However, since the SLA concept is not defined in a QKD network, it is questionable how nodes of potentially different domains can negotiate traffic rules.

QoS signalization in QKD networks: In general, the QKD protocol that establishes a new key material consists of six successive stages: a physical exchange of quantum states between a pair of devices, extraction of the raw key (sifting), error rate estimation, reconciliation, privacy amplification, and authentication [78, 79]. Only the first stage is performed over a quantum channel; all other stages are performed over a public channel, resulting in communication referred to as QKD post-processing. Reference [75] proposes an extension of authenticated packets with signaling data, which provides an elegant way of tackling the problem of distribution of signaling information without introducing additional traffic overheads [80].

QoS routing in QKD networks: The following main design objectives for a routing protocol well suited for operation in dynamic QKD networks were specified in [75]:

- Reducing the consumption of scarce key material by choosing the shortest path considering both channels of the QKD link. The routing algorithm needs to find a balance between the requirements, since a path that meets the requirements of the public channel may not be suitable for the quantum channel, and vice versa [52, 73].
- Given that the main objective of QKD is to provide ITS (Information Technology & Services) communication, routing packets need to be encrypted and authenticated [52, 81]. This means that the number of routing packets needs to be minimized to preserve scarce key material.
- To prevent denial of service, it is necessary to minimize knowledge about the utilized routing path by reducing the broadcast of routing packets [82].
- The routing protocol should be scalable to different network sizes.
- Due to a low key charging rate and overlay networking mode, link interruptions are common in QKD networks. Hence, the routing protocol should be robust enough to find an adequate replacement path. In general, routing solutions can be divided into three broad categories: source, hierarchical, and distributed routing. The performance of source routing algorithms relies on the availability of precise link state information, whereas the dynamic nature of QKD networks makes the available link state information inherently imprecise. Given that the constant maintenance of link state information is mostly done by periodic flooding, this solution is inadequate for QKD networks. Although several examples exist of hierarchical network organization [83, 84], in our opinion, such organization is not suitable for QKD networks since the nodes of upper hierarchical levels represent a potentially easy target for an attack to disassemble the network. In distributed routing, the computation of the path is shared among network nodes on a periodic basis (proactive) or only when a routing path is requested (reactive). Proactive routing protocols mainly use the static update period time for keeping routes up to date, but QKD networks are dynamic. Therefore, in overlay networks, reactive routing performs better in terms of efficiency and stability than proactive routing [85, 86].

15.3.2 Adaptive QoS-QKD Networks

A possible solution to overcome the problems of providing QoS in a dynamic environment was presented in [75] as a flexible QoS model for QKD (FQKD) networks. The model avoids a centralized resource management scheme or reservation of resources mechanism. Instead, it turns to a distributed approach to control traffic loads by providing soft-QoS constraints without flow or session state information maintained in support of end-to-end communication. FQKD defines three roles for nodes in a QKD network: ingress, interior, and egress. Each node can perform any of these roles depending on its position in the network flow. A source node that sends data is referred to as an ingress node. Interior nodes are nodes that forward data to the final destination node, which is referred to as an egress node.

Network model: As shown in Figure 15.12, the network model consists of a sender-based classifier, waiting queues, local-node-based admission controller, crypto module, and dynamic regulation of admitted sessions at the MAC layer. The classifier is input at the ingress node to distinguish

Figure 15.12 Adaptive QoS-QKD network model. *Source:* Modified from Mehic et al. [75].

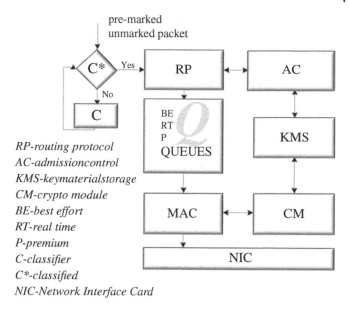

RP-*routing protocol*
AC-*admissioncontrol*
KMS-*keymaterialstorage*
CM-*crypto module*
BE-*best effort*
RT-*real time*
P-*premium*
C-*classifier*
C*-*classified*
NIC-*Network Interface Card*

between traffic classes by marking the DSCP field in the IP packet header. The system distinguishes between three traffic classes with corresponding DSCP values: best effort, real time, and premium class. For each class, separate waiting queues are defined and processed by priority. The packets are forwarded by interior nodes in per-hop behavior associated with the assigned DSCP value. Considering that nodes in QKD networks continuously generate new keys at their maximum rate [62], before setting the route, the routing protocol contacts the admission controller to filter those links to its neighbors that have sufficient resources to serve the classified network packet. The routing protocol calculates the path, and the packet is forwarded to the MAC layer for further processing. Otherwise, if no available link is found, the packet waits in the queue for reprocessing. In the system, additional waiting queues are installed between the L3 and L4 TCP/IP layer to avoid conflicts in decision making that could lead to inaccurate routing. Suppose the queues are implemented on the data link layer (L2) only and suppose that they are half filled with packets. Since the routing protocol used the routing metric that at the time t_1 of calculating the route had a different value from the time t_2 when the packet came online in the queue to be served, it follows that significant changes to the state of links in the time interval $\Delta t = t_2 - t_1$ could occur, which can lead to inaccurate and incorrect routing. Instead, by exploiting higher-level waiting queues, the packet for which the route is calculated will be directly forwarded to lower layers and immediately sent to the network. This implies the usage of one set of waiting queues (a set of three waiting queues for best-effort, real-time, and premium traffic classes) for all network interfaces. Using queuing at the L2 layer is not excluded, but additional attention is given to queues at a higher level due to the dynamic nature of the network.

Assuming the key rate is constant in time when the quantum channel has a fixed length [52, 62], it is evident that the key storage can be identified with the token bucket traffic-shaping mechanism. This simplifies the view of the admission controller, which behaves as the traffic conditioner. The volume of traffic over the QKD link is limited by the amount of key material in key storage that is used for encryption or authentication of data over that link. The key material storage of link k between nodes a and b can be represented using following parameters:

- The time measurement moment t
- The average key generation rate r_k, measured in bits per seconds and used to indicate the charging rate of the storage
- The key material storage depth $\overline{M}_k$ used to indicate the capacity of the storage (where the overbar indicates maximum)
- The current value $\widetilde{M}_k(t)$ representing the amount of key material in the storage at the time of measurement t, where it holds that $\widetilde{M}_k(t) \leq \overline{M}_k$
- The threshold value $\hat{M}_{a,b}(t)$ or simply $\hat{M}_k(t)$ described in greater detail below
- QKD is also known as quantum key growing [87, 88] or quantum key expansion [89], since it needs a small amount of key material pre-shared between parties (denoted as $\underline{M}_k$, where the underbar indicates minimum) to establish a larger amount of the secret key material. This pre-shared key material is used for QKD post-processing and authentication [65, 89]. The amount of key material over a time interval T depends on the key generation rate and the available amount of key material in the storage and can be calculated using Eq. (15.14). The average operational rate – that is, the rate at which packets can be served over an interval T – can be calculated using Eq. (15.15). As $T \rightarrow \infty$, the operational rate $A_k(T)$ approaches the charging key rate r_k.

$$D_k(t) \leq r_k T + \widetilde{M}_k(T) - \underline{M}_k(T) \qquad (15.14)$$

$$A_k(t) = \frac{D_k(t)}{T} = r_k + \frac{\widetilde{M}_k(T) - \underline{M}_k(T)}{T} \qquad (15.15)$$

The overall amount of traffic data that can be transmitted over link k in a time interval T can be calculated by dividing the value obtained from Eq. (15.14) and the ratio L_k, which is the quotient of the key length used for encryption with authentication and the length of the data message. Note that for ITS communication, which usually involves the OTP cipher and Wegman–Carter authentication, more bits of key material than the length of the data message are required ($L_k > 1$) [52]. An incoming packet is served from the queue only if there is enough key material in the storage. Otherwise, the packet remains in the queue waiting for storage to be charged. The length of the queue is limited, and traffic-shaping algorithms are in charge of packet management operations. To avoid blocking work due to the lack of the key material used to generate new key material, special attention is paid to the categorization of the traffic. If storage stops charging, the purpose of the link is lost. Therefore, the traffic generated by the post-processing application has the highest priority and is sorted in the premium queue. Only traffic from post-processing applications can use the key material when $\widetilde{M}_k(t) \leq \underline{M}_k$, while the traffic from the other two queues is served only when $\widetilde{M}_k(t) > \underline{M}_k$. The threshold value $\hat{M}$ is proposed to increase the stability of QKD links, where $\hat{M}_k(t) \leq \overline{M}_k$. The parameter is explained by considering the simple topology shown in Figure 15.13 [75] where node a needs to communicate with remote node e. Suppose the routing protocol uses only information about the state of its links with its neighbors. Then, assuming that all network links have the same performance of public channels, we consider only the state of key storages, which are marked next to the links as shown in Figure 15.13a. Upon reception of the packet from node a, the routing protocol on node b selects path b–c since the link b–d has a lower performance.

However, if node b does not consider the state of links that are more than one hop away, the traffic may get stuck on the link between nodes b and c as shown in Figure 15.13b.

To avoid such behavior, the threshold value $\hat{M}$ is used. Each node i calculates value $L_i = \sum_{k=0}^{N_i} \widetilde{M}_{i,k} / N_i$ summarizing the current values $\widetilde{M}$ of links to its neighbors and dividing it by the number of its neighbors N_i. Then, each node exchanges the calculated value of L_i with its

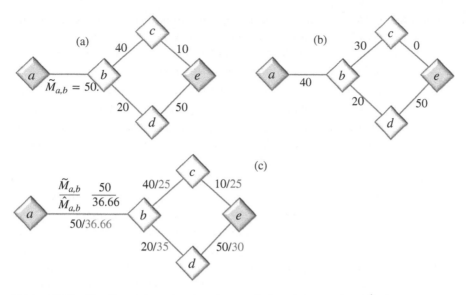

Figure 15.13 Simple topology showing the calculation of the threshold $\hat{M}$. *Source:* Modified from Mehic et al. [75].

neighbors. The minimum value $\hat{M}_{i,j} = \min\{L_i, L_j\}$ is accepted as a reference threshold value of the link. As shown in Figure 15.13c, node b calculates $L_b = 36.66$, while node c calculates $L_c = 25$. The threshold value of the link b-c is set to $\hat{M}_{b,c} = 25$, and it is included in link metric calculation as described in the next section. The higher the value of the threshold $\hat{M}$, the better the state of links that are more than one hop away.

QKD link metric: Popular metrics from conventional networks that describe the state of the communication link cannot be adequately used in QKD networks since they only describe the public channel. Therefore, we propose new metrics that clearly define the state of the QKD link taking into account its most essential features:

1) *The Quantum Channel Status Metric:* At the moment of serving the packet, the remaining key material in the key storage is the main factor contributing to the link's availability; this is because without key material, cryptographic operations cannot be performed, and secure communication over the link is not possible. Reference [75] uses $\ddot{Q}_{s,i} = \widetilde{M}_{s,i}^2 \cdot \hat{M}_{s,i} / \overline{M}_{s,i}^3$ to express the state of the quantum channel between nodes s and i, where $\ddot{Q}_{s,i}$ is the ratio of the squared amount of key material at the time of measurement ($\widetilde{M}_{s,i}^2$) multiplied by the threshold value ($\hat{M}_{s,i}$) and the cube of the capacity of the key storage ($\overline{M}_{s,i}^3$). Parameter $\ddot{Q}_{s,i}$ is in the range [0,1]; it highlights the current amount of key material on the closest links in relation to the amount of key material on links that are further away since more distant links are unreachable when links to neighbors are unavailable. Parameter $Q_{s,i}^m = 1 - \ddot{Q}_{s,i} / \exp(1 - \ddot{Q}_{s,i})$ is the utility function associated with the key material level of the link. Parameter $Q_{s,i}^m$ uses an exponential formula to address the fact that the lower the amount of key material in the storage, the more critical the situation, and the less time is left for the routing protocol to react. The value of $Q_{s,i}^m$ is normalized as a grade ranging from 0 to 1 as shown in Figure 15.14 [75], where a lower value means a better quantum channel state. In the example shown in Figure 15.13c, the routing protocol should favor the link b-d since $Q_{b,d}^m < Q_{b,c}^m$

2) *The Public Channel Status Metric:* Instead of using popular approaches from conventional or overlay networks [67, 90], we use the meta-data of keys, such as the time duration of the key establishment process, to assess the state of the public channel effectively. We define $P_{s,i}^m = \left(T_{s,i}^l + \Delta t\right)/\overline{T}_{s,i}$ to evaluate the state of the public channel between nodes s and i, where $T_{s,i}^l$ is the length of time spent on the establishment of the key material at the time of measurement, and $\overline{T}_{s,i}$ is the maximum time that can be allowed for the establishment of the key. $\overline{T}_{s,i} = 2 \cdot T_a$ is calculated as twice the average duration of the key material establishment process in the long run, denoted as T_a; Δt is used to describe the freshness of the information and is defined as the difference between the current time of the measurement and the time when the $T_{s,i}^l$ is recorded.

Note that T_a is not equal for all links of the network since it depends on the load of the network, types of quantum and network devices, QKD post-processing application, and the state of the public channel. The value of $P_{s,i}^m$ mainly falls in the range [0,1] where the lower value means a better public channel state. Values greater than 1 indicate that the link has a problem with establishing new key material, and such links should not be considered.

3) *The Overall QKD Link Status Metric:* Key material depletion is not the same for all links since it depends on the type of encryption algorithm used and the volume of network traffic to be encrypted. For example, a QKD link between nodes s and i having a low value of $Q_{s,i}^m$ may be suitable for a network flow encrypted with less secure algorithms that require less key material than OTP (such as the AES cipher), but it may not be suitable for encryption using OTP. Thus, a factor α that reflects the balance between the requirements is introduced in $R_{s,i}^m = \alpha Q_{s,i}^m + (1 - \alpha)P_{s,i}^m$ to compensate for this effect using the UFs of the quantum and public channel in the [0,1] range, where a lower value means a better overall link state. The parameter α takes a value in the [0,1] range; if the OTP cipher is used, we suggest the value of $\alpha = 0.5$. This means that both channels of the QKD link are considered equally. If the AES cipher is used, α can be set to a lower value to put a greater emphasis on the public channel due to its lower requirements for key material, depending on how frequently it is refreshed and how long the AES key is.

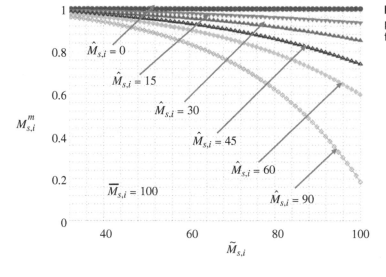

Figure 15.14 Network parameters. *Source:* Modified from Mehic et al. [75].

15.3.3 Routing Protocol for QKD Network

Driven by the similarities between the MANET and QKD networks discussed earlier, we present the Greedy Perimeter Stateless Routing Protocol for QKD networks (GRQ). The primary motivation for designing GRQ is to minimize the number of routing packets and to achieve high-level scalability by using distributed geography reactive routing.

We assume that all nodes know the geographical locations of all other network nodes they wish to communicate with. Therefore, there is no periodic flooding of the node location details, and we assume a location registration and lookup service that maps the node address to a location. Here, we do not deal with the implementation details of such a service, but we assume it can be implemented using internal or other communication channels [91]. As indicated earlier in this section, authenticated packets in QKD post-processing can be used to exchange information about the geographical position of nodes effectively. Although several experiments have been conducted regarding mobile QKD networking [8, 92–95], due to the high sensitivity of quantum equipment to various environmental factors and the relatively low key generation rates in free-space QKD links [96–98], here we assume that QKD networks are composed of static nodes representing secure access points. We follow the idea that "the greater the distance separating two nodes, the slower they appear to be moving with respect to each other" outlined in [99] to implement caching in GRQ, which is discussed further below.

GRQ sets up a network without hierarchical organization, which means that all nodes in the network are equally important. Nodes do not exchange routing tables, which significantly minimizes the consumption of scarce key material and reduces the probability of passive eavesdropping [82]. Route selection, that is, the decision regarding the next hop, is made in per-hop behavior such that the packet is moved closer to the destination based on the states of links in the local environment and on the geographical distance from the node. An eavesdropper is not able to intercept routing packets and find out the exact route to the destination, since it is not known at which node's network interface the packet will be forwarded until the last moment. GRQ uses two packet-forwarding algorithms: *greedy forwarding* and *recovery mode forwarding*.

Greedy forwarding: By definition, greedy forwarding entails forwarding to the neighbor geographically closest to the destination. An example of greedy forwarding is shown in Figure 15.15 [75], where ingress node a, which is surrounded by three adjacent nodes b, d, and k, needs to communicate with egress node g. Ingress node a forwards the packet to b, as the Euclidean distance between b and g is smaller than the distance between g and any of a's other neighbors. Such greedy forwarding is repeated on interior nodes, and it stops when the packet reaches its destination. GRQ aims to maximize network utilization by using different paths for different traffic classes. It uses the equation $F_{a,g,v} = (1 - \beta) \cdot R_{a,v} + \beta \cdot G_{v,d}$ to calculate the path to forward the packet, where $R_{a,v}$ denotes the state of the link between source node a and neighboring node v using $R_{s,i}^m = \alpha Q_{s,i}^m + (1 - \alpha) P_{s,i}^m$, and $G_{v,g}$ represents the Euclidean distance between neighboring node v and destination node g, for each node v that belongs to the set N_a of all neighbors of source node a, $\forall v \in N_a$. All routes toward the destination are sorted in descending order using the equation $F_{a,g,v} = (1 - \beta) \cdot R_{a,v} + \beta \cdot G_{v,d}$ and the route with the lowest value is used. GRQ uses the parameter β with a value in the [0,1] range to manage network utilization by choosing between forwarding along the geographically shortest route or the route that has the most available resources. We discuss simulation results for different values of β in the next design example.

Greedy forwarding relies on knowledge of the geographical location and state of links to neighbors, which results in a high level of network scalability. However, in some cases, the route to the destination requires forwarding the packet over a neighboring node that is geographically further

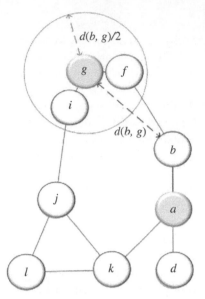

Figure 15.15 An example of greedy forwarding. *Source:* Modified from Mehic et al. [75].

from the destination than the node that forwards the packet. In cases when a local maximum occurs, an alternative recovery mode forwarding is used. To increase scalability and exclude routes that do not lead to the destination, a robust caching mechanism is used to preserve key material consumption. Consider the example shown in Figure 15.15, where we further suppose that link *b-f* is unavailable due to a lack of key material. When node *b* realizes there is only one interface available (the interface that was used to receive the packet from node *a*), it marks a "loop" field in the GRQ packet header and returns the packet to node *a*. Then, node *a* calculates the Euclidean distance *d(b,g)* between node *b* and destination node *g* and writes in its internal cache memory that it is not possible to route toward the region marked with a circle of radius *d(b,g)/2* and the center in node *g* along the path *a-b*. Upon receiving further requests for routing toward the node placed in the defined circle region, node *a* will ignore the route over node *b* and look for an alternative route. The validity of the cached record is set to a time interval defined as $T^c = \overline{T}_{b,g}/2$, where $\overline{T}_{b,g}$ is defined by $\overline{T}_{b,g} = 2 \cdot T_a$. The overall goal is to reduce the dynamics of the network topology changes using the scalable cache mechanism. In the next design example, we illustrate the impact of different values on cache validity. After the cached record expires, the node is allowed to try establishing the connection once again. If GRQ detects there is no neighbor closer to the destination, it enters recovery mode.

Recovery mode forwarding: This involves using the well-known right-hand rule, which states that the next edge from node *k* upon arriving from node *a* is edge (*k,j*), which is sequentially counterclockwise to edge (*a,k*) [100]. However, for the first forwarding, the packet is forwarded along edge (*a,k*), which is counterclockwise to node *a* from line $\overline{ag}$. The packet stays in recovery mode until it reaches a node that is closer to the destination than the node where forwarding in recovery mode started. To avoid routing loops, the GRQ header contains information about the IP address of the node at which the packet entered recovery mode and the outgoing interface that was used for the first forwarding. If the loop is detected by analyzing the packet header, the packet is returned to the previous node for rerouting and adding a new entry to the node's internal cache memory. If the public channel of link *j−i* is unavailable, there is no available path to destination *g*.

Source node a forwards the packet to node k, which forwards the packet to node j in greedy forwarding mode. Since link $j-i$ is unavailable, node j is not able to find any neighbor closer to the destination; so it enters recovery mode, sets the value of the field "*inRec*" to 1, writes its IP address to the header field "*recPosition*," writes the interface number that leads to node l in the "*recIF*" header field, and forwards the packet to node l since it is on the first edge counterclockwise about j from the line $\overline{jg}$ as required by the right-hand rule. Upon receipt of the packet, node l inspects the header and remains in recovery mode since node j in which the packet entered recovery mode is closer to the destination g. Then, the packet is forwarded to node k, which forwards the packet back to node j. When node j detects its IP address from the header field "*recPosition*," it adds a record to the internal cache memory stating that it is not possible to reach destination node g via node l by adding a record consisting of the triplet (i) IP address of hop l, (ii) the radius of circle region $d(l,g)/2$, and (iii) the value of the circle center, which is set to the location of node g. Given that there is no other interface available, node j sets the GRQ header field "loop" to 1 and returns the packet to node k, which adds a record to its cache memory stating that it is not possible to reach destination node g via node j. Then, node k sets the field "loop" to 2 and tries again with greedy forwarding where node j is excluded as the next hop. The packet is forwarded to node l, which forwards the packet to node j. Since node j does not have any other interface available, it will set the value of header field "loop" to 1, and return the packet to node l, which will add to its cache memory a record stating that it is not possible to reach destination node g over node j. The packet is returned to node k and then it is returned to node a. This procedure is repeated until a feasible path to the destination is found. Otherwise, if no available path is found, the packet is gradually returned to the source node, which is allowed to discard the packet while keeping updated records in the cache memory of other nodes. To make the routing operation easier, encryption and authentication are performed on the data link TCP/IP layer. For the details, see [75].

The simulation was performed using the QKD Network Simulation Model (QKDNetSim) [80] to deploy GRQ and DSDV, and NS-3-DCE v.1.9 was used to deploy the OSPFv2 routing protocol [107, 108]. The BRITE topology generator was used to generate random topologies according to

---

Design Example 15.2[2]

To ensure simulations are independent of the topology or characteristics of any specific network, in [75] random graphs were constructed. Random network topologies were generated using the Waxman model [101], which is recommended for small and medium-sized networks that include locality aspects, such as QKD networks [47, 77, 84]. Additionally, the Waxman model corresponds to the requirement for the implementation of QKD networks without hierarchical multi-plane organization [102] since it spreads nodes randomly on a grid and adds links randomly, such that the probability P_e of interconnecting two nodes in a single plane is parameterized by the Euclidean distance separating them, as $P_e(u, v) = \Theta \exp(-d(u, v)/\Omega\Lambda)$, where $d(u, v)$ is the Euclidean distance between nodes u and v, and Λ denotes the maximum possible distance between two nodes where $0 < \Omega, \Theta \leq 1$. The parameter choices are constrained to ensure $P_e(u, v) \in [0, 1]$. In all, 1290 simulations were performed with 30 randomly generated simulation seeds defining random network topologies and random values of the initial amount of key material in key storages. GRQ ($\beta = 0.6; T_a = 5$) was evaluated against Open Shortest Path First OSPFv2, which was used in other deployed QKD networks [52, 62, 103–105]; and against Destination-Sequenced Distance-Vector DSDV, which was used in [106].

---

2 To be reproduced by a student group

the Waxman model since it is supported under NS-3 and the source code is freely available [109]. NS-3-DCE and QKDNetSim were set to share the same seed file to generate random values, which enables the use of the same random topologies with the same configuration values in QKDNetSim and NS-3- DCE. Simulations include static networks with 10, 20, 30, 40, 50, 60, and 70 nodes that were randomly placed in a rectangular region and connected to QKD links with the following settings: minimum amount of key material 1 MB; maximum amount 100 MB; initial amount randomly generated in the [0.5, 25] MB range; maximum bandwidth of the link set to 10 Mbps; and the charging key rate set to 100 kbps with a charging key period of 7 s. The Waxman router model was used with the following parameter values: $m = 2$, $\Lambda = 100$, $\Omega = 0.4$, and $\Theta = 0.4$. The first node was set as the source of traffic, while the last randomly placed node was set as the desti-nation. The source node generated User Datagram Protocol (UDP) traffic with a 1 Mbps rate and a fixed packet size of 512 bytes that was encrypted using one-time pad (OTP) and authenticated using VMAC with a 32-bit authentication tag [63–65]. The duration of the simulation was 150 s, while the capacity of waiting queues per device on the L2 and L4 layers (used for GRQ only) was set to 1000 packets. The parameters not given here are the default parameters of QKDNetSim and NS-3-DCE. In following sections, as in [75], simulation results are presented using box-plot graphs.

Simulation result examples: Figure 15.16 shows the routing protocol overhead, measured by the number and average sizes of routing packets sent network-wide during the simulation for GRQ, DSDV, and OSPFv2. OSPFv2 is a widely deployed link state routing protocol that uses the periodic Link State Announcement (LSA) flooding mechanism to update link state databases describing the network topology [110]. By default, OSPFv2 floods LSA update information every 30 min, and it exchanges Hello packets to establish and maintain a neighbor relationship every 10 s. If a node does not receive a Hello message from a neighbor within a fixed dead interval of time that is set to a default of 40 s for point-to-point networks, OSPFv2 modifies its topology data-base entries to indicate that the neighbor is unavailable. DSDV is a proactive routing protocol that periodically broadcasts its routing table to its neighbors (every 15 s by default). Besides, DSDV uses triggered updates when the network topology suddenly changes. With the increase in the number of network nodes, the number of triggered packets is rising, which decreases the average size of the DSDV packets [90, 111]. By contrast, GRQ relies on knowledge of the

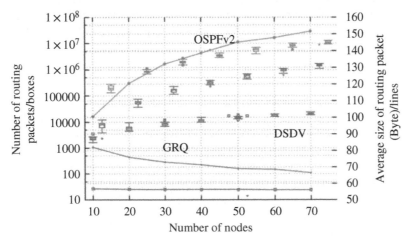

Figure 15.16 The number and average sizes of routing packets. *Source:* Modified from Mehic et al. [75].

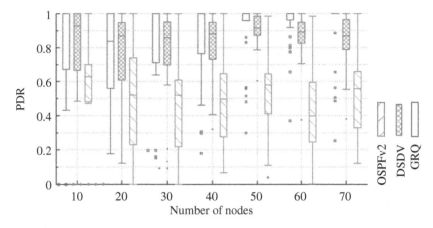

Figure 15.17 Packet delivery ratio (PDR). *Source:* Modified from Mehic et al. [75].

geographical position and state of links to neighbors, which provides a high level of network scalability.

As such, it periodically exchanges only $\hat{M}$ packets every time new key material is stored in key storages; the value was set to 7 s in the simulations. It is important to note that DSDV and OSPFv2 exchange their routing packets using UDP, whereas GRQ exchanges $\hat{M}$ values using TCP, so Figure 15.16 shows all packets including TCP SYN, TCP ACK, and TCP FIN. Several simulations were performed with $\hat{M} = 5$, 15, 20, and 30 s. The value of $\hat{M}$ is exchanged every time new key material is added to key storage. The data showed the same values, suggesting that a single exchange of a $\hat{M}$ value in a QKD post-processing period is adequate for the smooth operation of GRQ. In the simulations, values from GRQ packets were moved into the QKD command header as described later, while DSDV and OSPFv2 packets were sent using the standard QKD header [52]. Figure 15.16 shows that GRQ consumes the lowest amount of key material for cryptographic operations in routing packets.

The packet delivery ratio (PDR), calculated as the ratio of received and sent application packets, is used to assess the effectiveness of the routing protocol within the specified simulation environment. Figure 15.17 shows that Greedy Perimeter Stateless Routing Protocol for QKD (GPSRQ) networks is successful in finding available routes to the destination when compared to OSPFv2 and DSDV [111, 112]. Due to the significant value of the dead interval, OSPFv2 [110] is not able to react quickly to the changes in network topology, which results in a reduced PDR value. DSDV exchanges routing packets more often; this returns a higher PDR value, although it is still significantly lower than that of GPSRQ. It is important to note that in some simulation scenarios, PDR could not reach value "1" because it depends on the network conditions as defined by random values, such as the initial amount of key material in key storages. More precisely, because of the randomly assigned amount of the initial key material in the key buffers, several simulated scenarios were generated with little or no key available to establish a path to the destination regardless of which routing protocol is being used.

However, using the same seed files ensures identical network conditions for all tested protocols in all simulated scenarios. By increasing the number of nodes, the number of possible routes to the destination increases, which enables the GRQ protocol to produce significantly better results than those produced by the other two protocols.

References

1 Qi, B., Zhu, W., Qian, L., and Lo, H.-K. (2010). Feasibility of quantum key distribution through a dense wavelength division multiplexing network. *New J. Phys.* **12** (10) Art. no. 103042.

2 Patel, K.A., Dynes, J.F., Lucamarini, M. et al. (2014). Quantum key distribution for 10 Gb/s dense wavelength division multiplexing networks. *Appl. Phys. Lett.* **104** (5) Art. no. 051123.

3 S. Bahrani, M. Razavi, and J. A. Salehi, "Optimal wavelength allocation," in Proc. 24th Eur. Signal Process. Conf., Budapest, Hungary, Aug./Sep. 2016, pp. 483–487.

4 Cao, Y., Zhao, Y., Yu, X., and Wu, Y. (Nov. 2017). Resource assignment strategy in optical networks integrated with quantum key distribution. *IEEE/OSA J. Opt. Commun. Netw.* **9** (11): 995–1004.

5 Zhao, Y., Cao, Y., Wang, W. et al. (Aug. 2018). Resource allocation in optical networks secured by quantum key distribution. *IEEE Commun. Mag.* **56** (8): 130–137.

6 Cao, Y., Zhao, Y., Colman-Meixner, C. et al. (Nov. 2017). Key on demand (KoD) for software-defined optical networks secured by quantum key distribution (QKD). *Opt. Express* **25** (22): 26453–26467.

7 Nauerth, S., Moll, F., Rau, M. et al. (May 2013). Air-to-ground quantum communication. *Nature Photon.* **7** (5): 382–386.

8 Vallone, G., Bacco, D., and Dequal, D. (2015). Experimental satellite quantum communications. *Phys. Rev. Lett.* **115** (4) Art. no. 040502.

9 Liao, S.K., Cai, W.Q., and Liu, W.Y. (Sep. 2017). Satellite-to-ground quantum key distribution. *Nature* **549** (7670): 43–47.

10 Liao, S.-K. et al. (Aug. 2017). Long-distance free-space quantum key distribution in daylight towards inter-satellite communication. *Nature Photon.* **11** (8): 509–513.

11 Liao, S.-K., Cai, W.-Q., and Handsteiner, J. (2018). Satellite-relayed intercontinental quantum network. *Phys. Rev. Lett.* **120** (3) Art. no. 030501.

12 Bacsardi, L. (Aug. 2013). On the way to quantum-based satellite communication. *IEEE Commun. Mag.* **51** (8): 50–55.

13 Simon, C. (2017). Towards a global quantum network. *Nature Photon.* **11** (11): 678–680.

14 P. Wang, X. Zhang, and G. Chen, "Quantum key distribution for security guarantees over quantum-repeater-based QoS-driven 3d satellite networks," in Proc. IEEE Global Commun. Conf., Dec. 2014, pp. 728–733.

15 Bedington, R., Arrazola, J.M., and Ling, A. (2017). Progress in satellite quantum key distribution. *NPJ Quantum Inf.* **3** (1): 30.

16 M. Pfennigbauer, W. Leeb, and M. Aspelmeyer, "Free-space optical quantum key distribution using intersatellite links," in Proc. CNESIntersatellite Link Workshop, 2003.

17 D. Huang et al, Quantum Key Distribution Over Double-Layer Quantum Satellite Networks, IEEE Access, 2020 | Volume: 8 | IEEE

18 Pratt, S.R., Raines, R.A., Fossa, C.E., and Temple, M.A. (1999). An operational and performance overview of the IRIDIUM low earth orbit satellite system. *IEEE Commun. Surveys Tuts* **2** (2): 2–10, 2nd Quart.

19 Bourgoin, J.-P., Meyer-Scott, E., Higgins, B.L. et al. (2013). A comprehensive design and performance analysis of low earth orbit satellite quantum communication. *New J. Phys.* **15** (2) Art. no. 023006.

20 Günthner, K., Khan, I., Elser, D. et al. (Jun. 2017). Quantum-limited measurements of optical signals from a geostationary satellite. *Optica* **4** (6): 611–616.

21 Calderaro, L., Agnesi, C., Dequal, D. et al. (2018). Towards quantum communication from global navigation satellite system. *Quantum Sci. Technol* **4** (1) Art. no. 015012.

22 F. Yu. ScienceNet.cn, China. Accessed: Aug. 10, 2017. [Online]. Available: http://news.sciencenet.cn/htmlnews/2017/8/384831.shtm?id=384831

23 X. M. Liu and L. Zhang, "An on-board integrated system compatible with microwave, laser and quantum communication," CN Patent 103 873 151 A, May 10, 2014

24 Alagoz, F., Korcak, O., and Jamalipour, A. (Jun. 2007). Exploring the routing strategies in next-generation satellite networks. *IEEE Wirel. Commun.* **14** (3): 79–88.

25 Shafigh, A.S., Glisic, S., Hossain, E. et al. (2019). User-centric distributed spectrum sharing in dynamic network architectures. *IEEE/ACM Trans. Networking* **27** (1): 15–28.

26 Shafigh, A.S., Mertikopoulos, P., Glisic, S., and Fang, Y.M. (2017). Semi-cognitive radio networks: a novel dynamic spectrum sharing mechanism. *IEEE Trans. Cogn. Commun.* **3** (1): 97–110.

27 Khan, Z., Glisic, S., DaSilva, L.A., and Lehtomäki, J. (2011). Modeling the dynamics of coalition formation games for cooperative spectrum sharing in an interference channel. *IEEE Trans. Comp. Intel. AI* **3** (1): 17–30.

28 Lorenzo, B., Shafigh, A.S., Liu, J., González-Castaño, F.J., and Fang, Y. (2018). Data and spectrum trading policies in a trusted cognitive dynamic network architecture. *IEEE/ACM Trans. Networking* **26**, (3): 1502–1516.

29 Alanis, D., Hu, J., Botsinis, P. et al. (2016). Quantum-assisted joint multi-objective routing and load balancing for socially-aware networks. *IEEE Access* **4**: 9993–10028.

30 Zachary, W.W. (1977). An information flow model for conflict and fission in small groups. *J. Anthropol. Res.* **33** (4): 452–473.

31 Lin, C.Y. et al. (Sep. 2012). Social network analysis in enterprise. *Proc. IEEE* **100** (9): 2759–2776.

32 Li, X., Zhang, R., and Hanzo, L. (Apr. 2015). Cooperative load balancing in hybrid visible light communications and WiFi. *IEEE Trans. Commun.* **63** (4): 1319–1329.

33 Shannon, C.E. (Jul. 1948). A mathematical theory of communication. *Bell Syst. Tech. J.* **27** (3): 379–423.

34 Kullback, S. and Leibler, R.A. (Mar. 1951). On information and sufficiency. *Ann. Math. Stat.* **22** (1): 79–86.

35 van Erven, T. and Harremos, P. (Jul. 2014). Rényi divergence and Kullback–Leibler divergence. *IEEE Trans. Inf. Theory* **60** (7): 3797–3820.

36 Steele, R. and Hanzo, L. (1999). *Mobile Radio Communications: Second and Third Generation Cellular and WATM Systems*. Hoboken, NJ, USA: Wiley.

37 Hanzo, L., Ng, S.X., Webb, W., and Keller, T. (2004). *Quadrature Amplitude Modulation: From Basics to Adaptive Trellis-Coded, Turbo-Equalised and Space-Time Coded OFDM, CDMA and MC-CDMA Systems*. Hoboken, NJ, USA: Wiley.

38 Deb, K. (2005). Multi-objective optimization. In: *Search Methodologies* (eds. E.K. Burke and G. Kendall), 273–316. New York, NY, USA: Springer.

39 Alanis, D., Botsinis, P., Ng, S.X., and Hanzo, L. (2014). Quantum-assisted routing optimization for self-organizing networks. *IEEE Access* **2**: 614–632.

40 Alanis, D., Botsinis, P., Babar, Z. et al. (2015). Non-dominated quantum iterative routing optimization for wireless multihop networks. *IEEE Access* **3**: 1704–1728.

41 Collins, D., Gisin, N., and De Riedmatten, H. (2005). Quantum relays for long distance quantum cryptography. *J. Mod. Opt.* **52** (5): 735–753.

42 Dür, W., Briegel, H.-J., Cirac, J.I., and Zoller, P. (Jan. 1999). Quantum repeaters based on entanglement purification. *Phys. Rev. A, Gen. Phys.* **59** (1): 169–181.

43 Yuan, Z.-S., Chen, Y.-A., Zhao, B. et al. (Aug. 2008). Experimental demonstration of a BDCZ quantum repeater node. *Nature* **454** (7208): 1098–1101.

44 Salvail, L., Peev, M., Diamanti, E. et al. (Jan. 2010). Security of trusted repeater quantum key distribution networks. *J. Comput. Secur.* **18** (1): 61–87.

45 van Enk, S.J., Cirac, J.I., and Zoller, P. (Jan. 1998). Photonic channels for quantum communication. *Science* **279** (5348): 205–208.

46 Alléaume, R. et al. (2014). Using quantum key distribution for cryptographic purposes: a survey. *Theor. Comput. Sci.* **560**: 62–81.

47 Peev, M. et al. (2009). The SECOQC quantum key distribution network in Vienna. *New J. Phys.* **11** (7) Art. no. 075001.

48 C. Elliott and H. Yeh, "DARPA quantum network testbed," Raytheon BBN Technol. Cambridge, MA, USA, Tech. Rep., Jul. 2007.

49 Sergienko, A.A.V.A. (2005). *Quantum, Cryptography Communication*. Boca Raton, FL, USA: CRC Press.

50 Elliott, C. (Jul. 2002). Building the quantum network. *New J. Phys.* **4** (1): 46.

51 M. Marhoefer et al., "Applicability of quantum cryptography for securing mobile communication networks," Long-Term Dyn. Aspects Inf. Secur., Emerg. Trends Inf. Commun. Secur., 2007, pp. 97–111.

52 Kollmitzer, C. et al. (2010). *Application Quantum Cryptography*, vol. **797**. Cham, Switzerland: Springer.

53 M. Dianati and R. Alleaume, "Architecture of the secoqc quantum key distribution network," in Proc. 1st Int. Conf. Quantum, Nano, Micro Technol. (ICQNM), Jan. 2007, p. 13.

54 Alleaume, R. et al. (2009). Topological optimization of quantum key distribution networks. *New J. Phys.* **11** (7) Art. no. 075002.

55 Gisin, N., Ribordy, G., Tittel, W., and Zbinden, H. (Mar. 2002). Quantum cryptography. *Rev. Mod. Phys.* **74** (1): 145–195.

56 Scarani, V., Bechmann-Pasquinucci, H., Cerf, N.J. et al. (Sep. 2009). The security of practical quantum key distribution. *Rev. Mod. Phys.* **81** (3): 1301–1350.

57 Boaron, A. et al. (2018). Secure quantum key distribution over 421 km of optical fiber. *Phys. Rev. Lett.* **121** (19) Art. no. 190502.

58 Sasaki, M. et al. (Aug. 2011). Field test of quantum key distribution in the Tokyo QKD network. *Opt. Express* **19** (11): 10387–10409.

59 Dixon, A.R., Yuan, Z.L., Dynes, J.F. et al. (2010). Continuous operation of high bit rate quantum key distribution. *Appl. Phys. Lett.* **96** Art. no. 161102.

60 Korzh, B. et al. (2015). Provably secure and practical quantum key distribution over 307 km of optical fibre. *Nature Photon.* **9** (3): 163–168.

61 Wang, S. et al. (2012). 2 GHz clock quantum key distribution over 260 km of standard telecom fiber. *Opt. Lett.* **37** (6): 1008–1010.

62 Dianati, M., Alléaume, R., Gagnaire, M., and Shen, X. (Jan. 2008). Architecture and protocols of the future European quantum key distribution network. *Secur. Commun. Netw.* **1** (1): 57–74.

63 A. Abidin and J.-Å. Larsson, "Security of authentication with a fixed key in quantum key distribution," 2011, arXiv:1109.5168. [Online]. Available: https://arxiv.org/abs/1109.5168

64 Portmann, C. (Jul. 2014). Key recycling in authentication. *IEEE Trans. Inf. Theory* **60** (7): 4383–4396.

65 Wegman, M.N. and Carter, J.L. (Jun. 1981). New hash functions and their use in authentication and set equality. *J. Comput. Syst. Sci.* **22** (3): 265–279.

66 Mehic, M., Niemiec, M., and Voznak, M. (Dec. 2015). Calculation of the key length for quantum key distribution. *Elektronika Ir Elektrotechnika* **21** (6): 81–85.

67 Andersen, D., Balakrishnan, H., Kaashoek, F., and Morris, R. (Jan. 2002). Resilient overlay networks. *ACM SIGCOMM Comput. Commun. Rev* **32** (1): 66.

68 G. M. Lee and T. Choi, "Improving the interaction between overlay routing and traffic engineering," in NETWORKING 2008 Ad Hoc and Sensor Networks, Wireless Networks, Next Generation Internet (Lecture Notes in Computer Science), vol. 4982, A. Das, H. K. Pung, F. B. S. Lee, and L. W. C. Wong, Eds. Berlin, Germany: Springer, 2008, doi: 10.1007/978-3-540-79549-0_46.

69 Y. Liu, H. Zhang, W. Gong, and D. Towsley, "On the interaction between overlay routing and underlay routing," in Proc. IEEE 24th Annu. Joint Conf. IEEE Comput. Commun. Societies, vol. 4 Mar. 2005, pp. 2543–2553.

70 Fazio, P., De Rango, F., and Sottile, C. (Aug. 2016). A predictive cross-layered interference management in a multichannel MAC with reactive routing in VANET. *IEEE Trans. Mobile Comput.* **15** (8): 1850–1862.

71 Fazio, P., Tropea, M., De Rango, F., and Voznak, M. (Nov. 2016). Pattern prediction and passive bandwidth management for hand-over optimization in QoS cellular networks with vehicular mobility. *IEEE Trans. Mobile Comput.* **15** (11): 2809–2824.

72 De Rango, F., Fazio, P., Scarcello, F., and Conte, F. (Oct. 2014). A new distributed application and network layer protocol for VoIP in mobile ad hoc networks. *IEEE Trans. Mobile Comput.* **13** (10): 2185–2198.

73 Mehic, M., Maurhart, O., Rass, S. et al. (2017). Analysis of the public channel of quantum key distribution link. *IEEE J. Quantum Electron.* **53** (5) Art. no. 9300408.

74 De Rango, F., Guerriero, F., and Fazio, P. (Apr. 2012). Link-stability and energy aware routing protocol in distributed wireless networks. *IEEE Trans. Parallel Distrib. Syst.* **23** (4): 713–726.

75 Mehic, M. et al. (February 2020). A novel approach to quality-of-service provisioning in trusted relay quantum key distribution networks. *IEEE/ACM Trans. Networking* **28** (1): 168.

76 Zhang, L., Deering, S., Estrin, D. et al. (Sep. 1993). RSVP: a new resource ReSerVation Protocol. *IEEE Netw.* **7** (5): 8–18.

77 Ciurana, A. et al. (2014). Quantum metropolitan optical network based on wavelength division multiplexing. *Opt. Express* **22** (2): 1576–1593. https://doi.org/10.1364/OE.22.001576.

78 Bennett, C.H., Bessette, F., Brassard, G. et al. (Jan. 1992). Experimental quantum cryptography. *J. Cryptol.* **5** (1): 3–28.

79 Mehic, M., Partila, P., Tovarek, J., and Voznak, M. (May 2015). Calculation of key reduction for B92 QKD protocol. *Proc. SPIE, Quantum Inf. Comput. XIII, Int. Soc. Opt. Photon* **9500**: 95001J. https://doi.org/10.1117/12.2177149.

80 M. Mehic, A. Maric, and M. Voznak, "QSIP: A quantum key distribution signaling protocol," in Proc. Int. Conf. Multimedia Commun., Services Secur. Cham, Switzerland: Springer, 2017, pp. 136–147, doi: 10.1007/978-3-319-69911-0_1.

81 O. Maurhart, T. Lorunser, T. Langer, C. Pacher, M. Peev, and A. Poppe, "Node modules and protocols for the quantum-back-bone of a quantum key-distribution network," in Proc. 35th Eur. Conf. Opt. Commun., Sep. 2009, pp. 3–4

82 Rass, S. and König, S. (2012). Turning quantum cryptography against itself: how to avoid indirect eavesdropping in quantum networks by passive and active adversaries. *Int. J. Adv. Syst. Meas.* **5** (1): 22–33.

83 Xu, F. et al. (2009). Field experiment on a robust hierarchical metropolitan quantum cryptography network. *Chin. Sci. Bull.* **54** (17): 2991–2997.

84 Wang, S. et al. (Sep. 2014). Field and long-term demonstration of a wide area quantum key distribution network. *Opt. Express* **22** (18): 21739–21756.

85 Zhu, Y., Dovrolis, C., and Ammar, M. (Apr. 2006). Dynamic overlay routing based on available bandwidth estimation: a simulation study. *Comput. Netw.* **50** (6): 742–762.

86 D. G. Andersen, A. C. Snoeren, and H. Balakrishnan, "Best-path vs. Multi-path overlay routing," in Proc. ACM SIGCOMM Conf. Internet Meas. (IMC), Oct. 2003, pp. 91–100.

87 Cederlof, J. and Larsson, J.-Å. (Apr. 2008). Security aspects of the authentication used in quantum cryptography. *IEEE Trans. Inf. Theory* **54** (4): 1735–1741.

88 D. Dodson et al., "Updating quantum cryptography report ver. 1," 2009, arXiv:0905.4325. [Online]. Available: https://arxiv.org/abs/0905.4325

89 Sergienko, A., Pascazio, S., and Villoresi, P. (2010). *Quantum Communication and Quantum Networking*. Berlin, Germany: Springer https://doi.org/10.1007/978-3-642-11731-2.

90 Mehic, M. et al. (May 2016). On using multiple routing metrics with destination sequenced distance vector protocol for MultiHop wireless ad hoc networks. *Proc. SPIE, Model. Simul. Defense Syst. Appl. XI, Int. Soc. Opt. Photon* **9848**: 98480F. https://doi.org/10.1117/12.2223671.

91 J. Li, J. Jannotti, D. S. J. De Couto, D. R. Karger, and R. Morris, "A scalable location service for geographic ad hoc routing," in Proc. 6th Annu. Int. Conf. Mobile Comput. Netw., Aug. 2000, pp. 120–130.

92 S. Wijesekera, "Quantum cryptography for secure communication in IEEE 802.11 wireless networks," Ph.D. dissertation, Dept. Inf. Sci. Eng., Univ. Canberra, Canberra, ACT, Australia, 2011.

93 K. H. Sheikh, S. S. Hyder, and M. M. Khan, "An overview of quantum cryptography for wireless networking infrastructure," in Proc. Int. Symp. Collaborative Technol. Syst., (CTS), May 2006, pp. 379–385.

94 Schmitt-Manderbach, T. et al. (2007). Experimental demonstration of freespace decoy-state quantum key distribution over 144 km. *Phys. Rev. Lett.* (98) Art. no. 010504.

95 Yin, J. et al. (2017). Satellite-based entanglement distribution over 1200 kilometers. *Science* **356** (6343): 1140–1144.

96 Liao, S.K. et al. (2017). Space-to-ground quantum key distribution using a small-sized payload on Tiangong-2 space lab. *Chin. Phys. Lett.* **34** (9) Art. no. 090302.

97 Pugh, C.J. et al. (2017). Airborne demonstration of a quantum key distribution receiver payload. *Quantum Sci. Technol* **2** (2) Art. no. 024009.

98 Shimizu, K. et al. (2014). Performance of long-distance quantum key distribution over 90-km optical links installed in a field environment of Tokyo metropolitan area. *J. Lightwave Technol.* **32** (1): 141–151.

99 S. Basagni et al., "A distance routing effect algorithm for mobility (DREAM)," in Proc. 4th Annu. ACMIEEE Int. Conf. Mobile Comput. Netw., Oct. 1998, pp. 76–84

100 B. Karp and H. T. Kung, "GPSR: Greedy perimeter stateless routing for wireless networks," in Proc. 6th Annu. Int. Conf. Mobile Comput. Netw., Aug. 2000, pp. 243–254.

101 Waxman, B.M. (Dec. 1988). Routing of multipoint connections. *IEEE J. Sel. Areas Commun.* **6** (9): 1617–1622.

102 Klaus, W. et al. (2010). *Modeling and Tools for Network Simulation*. Berlin, Germany: Springer.

103 Y. Tanizawa, R. Takahashi, and A. R. Dixon, "A routing method designed for a quantum key distribution network," in Proc. 8th Int. Conf. Ubiquitous Future Netw. (ICUFN), Jul. 2016, pp. 208–214.

104 Y. Sun et al., "Quality of service realization method applied to quantum key distribution network," CN 102 394 745 B, Dec. 2012. [Online]. Available: https://patents.google.com/patent/CN102394745Ben?q=%22Quality+of+service+realization+method+applied+to+quantum+key+distribution+network%22&oq=%22Quality+of+service+realization+method+applied+to+quantum+key+distribution+network%22

105 C. Xianzhu, Y. Sun, and Y. Ji, "A QoS-supported scheme for quantum key distribution," in Proc. Int. Conf. Adv. Intell. Awareness Internet (AIAI), 2011, pp. 220–224.

106 Mehic, M., Fazio, P., Voznák, M., and Chromý, E. (2016). Toward designing a quantum key distribution network simulation model. *Adv. Electr. Electron. Eng.* **14** (4): 413–420.

107 Mehic, M., Maurhart, O., Rass, S., and Voznak, M. (2017). Implementation of quantum key distribution network simulation module in the network simulator NS-3. *Quantum Inf. Process* **16** (10): 253.

108 Riley, G.F. and Henderson, T.R. (2010). *The Ns-3 Network Simulator*, 15–34. Berlin, Germany: Springer.

109 A. Medina, A. Lakhina, I. Matta, and J. Byers, "BRITE: An approach to universal topology generation," in Proc. MASCOTS 9th Int. Symp. Modeling, Anal. Simulation Comput. Telecommun. Syst., Aug. 2001, pp. 346–353

110 J. T. Moy, OSPF Version 2 Internet Requests for Comment, document RFC 1247, 1991, pp. 1–124. [Online]. Available: https://tools.ietf.org/html/rfc1247

111 Perkins, E.C. and Bhagwat, P. (1994). Highly dynamic destination-sequenced distance-vector routing (DSDV) for mobile computers. *ACM SIGCOMM Comput. Commun. Rev.* **24** (4): 234–244.

112 Hobson, A. (1971). *Concepts in Statistical Mechanics*. Boca Raton, FL, USA: CRC Press.

16

Quantum Network on Graph

For security and high-data-rate reasons, the core network of 6/7G wireless technology will be based on the quantum network concept. Unlike classical network communication, during quantum communication, we pay more attention to the perfect state transfer (PST) during quantum communication, due to data congestion. To fully unleash the potential of quantum computing, several new challenges and open problems need to be addressed. From a routing perspective, the optimal routing problem, that is, the problem of jointly designing a routing protocol and a route metric ensuring the discovery of the route providing the highest quantum communication opportunities between an arbitrary couple of quantum devices, is crucial. In this chapter, the optimal routing problem is addressed for generic quantum network architectures comprising repeaters operating through single atoms in optical cavities. Specifically, we first model entanglement generation through a stochastic framework that allows us to jointly account for the key physical mechanisms affecting the end-to-end entanglement rate, such as decoherence time, atom-photon and photon-photon entanglement generation, entanglement swapping, and imperfect Bell state measurement (BSM). Then, we present the closed-form expression of the end-to-end entanglement rate for an arbitrary path and an efficient algorithm for entanglement rate computation. Finally, we present a routing protocol and discuss its optimality when used in conjunction with the entanglement rate as a routing metric.

16.1 Optimal Routing in Quantum Networks

To fully benefit from the advantages of the quantum technology, it is necessary to design and implement quantum networks [1, 2] and connect distant quantum processors through remote quantum entanglement distribution. However, despite the tremendous progress in quantum technologies, efficient long-distance entanglement distribution still constitutes to be a key issue, due to the exponential decay of the communication rate as a function of the distance [3, 4]. A solution for counteracting exponential decay loss is the adoption of quantum repeaters [5, 6]. Instead of distributing entanglement over a long link, entanglement will be generated through shorter links. A combination of entanglement swapping [7] and entanglement purification [8] performed at each quantum repeater enables extension of the entanglement over the entire channel. Now a simple question arises: when does a repeater ensure higher entanglement distribution over the direct long link?

Unlike classical information, quantum information (e.g., qubits) cannot be copied, due to the no-cloning theorem [9, 10]. Hence, quantum networks rely on the quantum teleportation process

Artificial Intelligence and Quantum Computing for Advanced Wireless Networks, First Edition.
Savo G. Glisic and Beatriz Lorenzo.
© 2022 John Wiley & Sons Ltd. Published 2022 by John Wiley & Sons Ltd.

(Chapter 8; [11]) as the unique feasible solution for transmitting a qubit without the need to physically move the physical particle storing such a qubit. The quantum teleportation of a single qubit between two different nodes requires (i) a classical communication channel capable of sending two classical bits and (ii) the generation of a pair of maximally entangled qubits, referred to as an Einstein–Podolsky–Rosen (EPR) pair, with each qubit stored at each remote node. In the following, the generation of an EPR pair at two different nodes is referred to as remote entanglement generation.

In a nutshell, the process of teleporting an arbitrary qubit, say qubit $|\varphi\rangle$, from quantum node v_i to quantum node v_j can be summarized as follows (see Chapter 8):

(i) An EPR pair, that is, a remote entanglement, is generated between v_i and v_j, with the first qubit $|\Phi_i\rangle$ stored at v_i and the second qubit $|\Phi_j\rangle$ stored at v_j; (ii) at v_i, a BSM of $|\Phi_i\rangle$ and $|\varphi\rangle$ is performed, and the two-bit measurement output is sent to v_j through the classical communication channel; and (iii) by manipulating the EPR pair qubit $|\Phi_j\rangle$ at v_j on the basis of the received measurement output, the qubit $|\varphi\rangle$ is obtained.

It is clear that the design of a routing metric for quantum networks poses several challenges:

Entanglement: As in classical networks, the transmission of quantum information is limited by the classical bit throughput necessary to transmit the output of the BSM. However, unlike classical networks, the transmission of quantum information requires the generation of a remote entanglement. Hence, a quantum routing metric must jointly account for both these limiting factors.

Decoherence: Not only is entanglement the most valuable resource for transmitting quantum information, but it is also a perishable resource. Indeed, due to the inevitable interactions with the external environment, a loss of the entanglement between the entangled entities occurs as time passes. Hence, a quantum routing metric must explicitly account for quantum decoherence.

Stochasticity: The physical mechanisms underlying entanglement generation are stochastic. Hence, a quantum routing metric must be able to effectively describe such a stochastic nature.

Due to the difficulties arising from entanglement generation and quantum decoherence, entanglement can be considered the key limiting factor for quantum information transmission. In fact, the qubit transmission rate between two quantum nodes is upper-bounded by the entanglement generation rate, since each qubit teleportation requires a successfully remote entanglement generation.

Hence, in this section, we design a routing metric for quantum networks based on the entanglement rate. By taking into account the aforementioned challenges, in this section, we discuss a route metric for quantum networks exhibiting the following attractive features:

1) The metric is entanglement aware; that is, it accounts for the need of remote entanglement generation in quantum information transmission.
2) The metric is accurate; that is, it accounts for all the physical mechanisms affecting the entanglement generation, such as decoherence time, atom-photon and photon-photon entanglement generation, entanglement swapping, and imperfect BSM.
3) The metric is stochastic; that is, it is able to effectively describe the stochastic nature of the physical mechanisms underlying the entanglement generation.

We first discuss a stochastic framework to model entanglement generation. In addition to what is presented in Chapter 8 and in [12–16], here we jointly account for all the key physical mechanisms affecting the end-to-end entanglement rate, such as decoherence time, atom-photon and photon-photon entanglement generation, entanglement swapping and imperfect BSM. Then, we discuss the closed-form expression of the entanglement rate, first through a link and then through an arbitrary path.

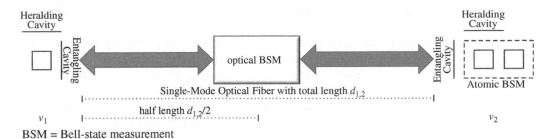

BSM = Bell-state measurement

Figure 16.1 Schematic illustration of the adopted quantum network architecture, operating through single atoms in optical cavities. The relative sizes of different components are not as shown, for the sake of clarity. *Source:* Caleffi [17].

We also present an efficient algorithm for entanglement rate computation that exhibits a linear time complexity. Finally, we describe a link-state-based routing protocol and discuss its optimality when used in conjunction with the entanglement rate as a routing metric by means of routing algebra theory.

Network architecture: We consider without loss of generality a wired quantum network composed of repeaters operating through single atoms in optical cavities as suggested in [17]. The entanglement generation is based on single-photon detection, and high-fidelity entangled pairs are created at the price of low entanglement generation success probabilities [12–16, 18–21]. A quantum repeater (Figure 16.1) consists of an atom storing a qubit and surrounded by two cavities: a *heralding cavity* and a *telecom-wavelength entangling cavity*.

The atoms (^{87}Rb rubidium isotopes) are individually excited by laser pulses, which allows entanglement between the atom and a telecom-wavelength photon. The heralding cavity is responsible for detecting the entanglement generation, whereas the entangling cavity is responsible for coupling the telecom-wavelength photon to the mode of a single-mode optical telecom fiber.

Once an atom-photon entanglement is locally generated at each node, a remote entanglement between two adjacent nodes is generated by entanglement swapping through *optical BSM* of the two photons. Finally, remote entanglement between non-adjacent nodes is generated by performing entanglement swapping at intermediate nodes through an *atomic BSM* operating on the atom pair stored at each intermediate node. Specifically, a cavity-assisted quantum gate operation is performed on the two atoms via reflection of a single photon originating from a cavity-based single-photon source (SPS). Subsequent detection of the atomic quantum states in suitable bases allows for an unambiguous determination of the two-particle Bell state. This results in an entangled state between the two non-adjacent nodes.

16.1.1 Network Model

We denote the quantum network with the graph $G = (V, E)$, with $V = \{v_i\}_{i=1}^N$ and $E = \{e_{i,j}, v_i, v_j \in V\}$ denoting the set of nodes and optical links, respectively. Given an arbitrary pair of nodes v_i and v_j, if $e_{i,j} \in E$ exists, then v_i and v_j are defined as *adjacent* nodes. Furthermore, $d_{i,j}$ and $T_{i,j}^c$ denote the length of the optical link and the average time required for a classical communication between node v_i and v_j, respectively. The route $r_{i,j}$ denotes a simple path between two arbitrary nodes v_i and v_j, that is, a finite ordered sequence of edges $(e_{\sigma_1,\sigma_2}, ..., e_{\sigma_{n-1},\sigma_n})$ in E so that $v_{\sigma_1} = v_i$, $v_{\sigma_n} = v_j$, and $\sigma_i \neq \sigma_j$ for any i, j. $T_{r_{ij}}^c = \sum_{i=1}^{n-1} T_{\sigma_i \sigma_{i+1}}^c$ denotes the average time required for a classical communication between nodes v_i and v_j through path $r_{i,j}$.

In the following, we will use some definitions:

1) *Local entanglement probability:* The *local entanglement generation probability* p_i denotes the probability of successfully generating an atom-photon entanglement at node $v_i \in V$.
2) *Local entanglement generation time:* The *local entanglement generation time* T_i denotes the average time required for successfully generating an atom-photon entanglement at node $v_i \in V$.
3) *Link entanglement probability:* The *link entanglement generation probability* $p_{i,j}$ denotes the probability of successfully generating an entanglement between two adjacent nodes v_i and v_j through optical link $e_{i,j}$.
4) *Link entanglement time:* The *link entanglement generation time* $T_{i,j}$ denotes the average time required for successfully generating an entanglement between two adjacent nodes v_i and v_j through optical link $e_{i,j}$.
5) *Link entanglement rate:* The *link entanglement rate* $\xi_{i,j}(T^{\mathrm{ch}})$ denotes the average number of successful entanglement generations within the unit time between two adjacent nodes v_i and v_j through optical link $e_{i,j}$, which can be successfully used for teleportation given the quantum memory coherence time T^{ch}.
6) *End-to-end entanglement probability:* The *end-to-end entanglement generation probability* $p_{r_{i,j}}$ denotes the probability of successfully generating a remote entanglement between two nodes v_i and v_j through route $r_{i,j}$.
7) *End-to-end entanglement time:* The *end-to-end entanglement generation time* $T_{r_{i,j}}$ denotes the average time required for successfully generating a remote entanglement between two nodes v_i and v_j through route $r_{i,j}$.
8) *End-to-end entanglement rate:* The *end-to-end entanglement rate* $\xi_{r_{i,j}}(T^{\mathrm{ch}})$ denotes the average number of successful entanglement generations within the unit time between two nodes v_i and v_j through route $r_{i,j}$, which can be successfully used for teleportation given the quantum memory coherence time T^{ch}.

Optimal quantum routing problem: Given the quantum network $G = (V, E)$ with coherence time T^{ch}, the goal is to choose, for an arbitrary source–destination pair $(v_i, v_j) \in V \times V$, the *optimal route* $r_{i,j}^*$, that is, the route ensuring the highest end-to-end entanglement rate $\xi_{r_{i,j}^*}(T^{\mathrm{ch}})$ between v_i and v_j.

16.1.2 Entanglement

Link entanglement: First, we observe that the local entanglement generation probability p_i at node i is affected by two main factors [16]: (i) successful generation of a herald photon and a telecom photon, assumed constant at each node since it is influenced by the isotope unwanted initial states and decay paths and (ii) the parasitic losses in the heralding and entangling cavity, assumed constant at each node since they are influenced by the detector technology. Hence, p_i can be written as $p_i = (p^{\mathrm{ht}} v^{\mathrm{h}} v^{\mathrm{t}})$ with p^{ht} denoting the photon generation probability, and v^{h} and v^{t} denoting the heralding and entangling detector efficiency, respectively. In the following, without loss of generality, we will omit the i-th node dependence from p_i for the sake of notational simplicity, that is, $p_i = p \, \forall \, v_i \in V$. Once a heralded local entanglement is generated at each node, the two photons must be sent to the BSM and measured, as shown in Figure 16.1. Hence, by using $p_i = (p^{\mathrm{ht}} v^{\mathrm{h}} v^{\mathrm{t}})$, the link entanglement generation probability $p_{i,j}$ is equal to [16]

$$p_{i,j} = \frac{1}{2} v^o \left(p e^{-d_{i,j}/(2L_0)} \right)^2 = \frac{1}{2} v^o p^2 e^{-d_{i,j}/L_0} \tag{16.1}$$

where v^o denotes the optical BSM efficiency (assumed constant at each node), $d_{i,j}$ denotes the length of link $e_{i,j}$, L_0 denotes the attenuation length of the optical fiber, and the term ½ accounts for the optical BSM capability of unambiguously identifying only two out of four Bell states.

The average time T_i required for a single atom-photon entanglement operation is equal to $T_i = \tau^p + \max\{\tau^h, \tau^t\} \forall v_i \in V$, with τ^p denoting the duration of the pulse required to excite the atom, and τ^h and τ^t denoting the time expectation for heralding-cavity and telecom-cavity output (again, assumed constant at each node without loss of generality).

Once an atom-photon entanglement operation is performed, the two photons must be sent to the optical BSM, and then an acknowledgment of the arrival of the photons must be sent back from the BSM to each node. If the first link entanglement attempt succeeds, the average time $T_{i,j}^s$ required for the successful attempt is equal to $T_{i,j}^s = \tau^p + \max\{\tau^h, \tau_{i,j}\}$, where the average time $\tau_{i,j}$ elapsed between the atom-photon entanglement generation and the ack reception is given by $\tau_{i,j} = \tau^t + d_{i,j}/2c_f + \tau^o + T_{ij}^c$ with c_f denoting the light speed in optical fiber, τ^o denoting the time required for the optical BSM, and $T_{i,j}^c$ denoting the time required for ack transmission over a classical communication link between nodes v_i and v_j. Otherwise, if the first attempt fails, an additional time τ^d is required for cooling the atom before starting a new local entanglement generation, and the total average time $T_{i,j}^f$ required for the failed attempt is equal to $T_{i,j}^f = \tau^p + \max\{\tau^h, \tau_{i,j}, \tau^d\}$.

With the above notations, the average time required to generate a remote entanglement between two adjacent nodes v_i and v_j is equal to [17] $T_{i,j} = (\bar{p}_{ij} T_{i,j}^f + p_{ij} T_{i,j}^s)/p_{ij}$ with $\bar{p}_{ij} = 1 - p_{ij}$ and $T_{i,j}^f$ and $T_{i,j}^s$ given above.

Based on this, the expected entanglement rate $\xi_{i,j}(T^{ch})$ between adjacent nodes v_i and v_j is equal to

$$\xi_{i,j}(T^{ch}) = \begin{cases} 0 & \text{if } T^{ch} < \tau_{i,j} \\ 1/T_{i,j} & \text{otherwise} \end{cases} \tag{16.2}$$

with T^{ch} denoting the quantum memory coherence time and $\tau_{i,j}$ given above.

End − to-end entanglement: Once an entanglement between adjacent nodes is obtained, remote entanglement between non-adjacent nodes can be generated by performing entanglement swapping at intermediate nodes through atomic BSM. By denoting as τ^a and v^a the duration and the efficiency of a single atomic BSM, respectively, the expected time required to generate a remote entanglement between two non-adjacent nodes v_i and v_j through route $r_{i,j}$ is given by [17] $T_{r_{i,j}} = T_{r_{\sigma_1,\sigma_n}}$ with T_{σ_l,σ_m}, for the arbitrary sub-route r_{σ_l,σ_m} recursively defined as

$$T_{r_{\sigma_l,\sigma_m}} = \begin{cases} \left(\max\left\{T_{r_{\sigma_l,\sigma_k}}, T_{r_{\sigma_k,\sigma_m}}\right\} + \tau^a + \max\left\{T_{r_{\sigma_l,\sigma_k}}^c, T_{r_{\sigma_k,\sigma_m}}^c\right\}\right)/v^a, \\ k = \left\lceil \dfrac{m+l}{2} \right\rceil \text{if } m > l+1 \\ T_{\sigma_l,\sigma_{l+1}}, \qquad \text{otherwise} \end{cases} \tag{16.3}$$

and with $T_{r_{\sigma_l,\sigma_m}}^c = \sum_l^{m-1} T_{\sigma_l,\sigma_{l+1}}^c$ Now, the expected entanglement rate $\xi_{r_{i,j}}(T^{ch})$ between nodes v_i and v_j through route $r_{i,j}$ is equal to

$$\xi_{r_{i,j}}(T^{ch}) = \begin{cases} 0 \text{ if } T^{ch} < \tau_{r_{i,j}} - \min_{l=1,n-1}\left\{T_{\sigma_l,\sigma_{l+1}}^s - \tau_{\sigma_l,\sigma_{l+1}}\right\} \\ \dfrac{1}{T_{r_{i,j}}} \text{ otherwise} \end{cases} \tag{16.4}$$

with T^{ch} denoting the quantum memory coherence time and $\tau_{r_{\sigma_l,\sigma_m}}$, recursively defined as

$$
\tau_{r_{\sigma_l,\sigma_m}} = \begin{cases} \max\left\{\tau_{r_{\sigma_l,\sigma_k}}, \tau_{r_{\sigma_k,\sigma_m}}\right\} + \tau^a + \max\left\{T^c_{r_{\sigma_l,\sigma_k}}, T^c_{r_{\sigma_k,\sigma_m}}\right\}, \\ k = \left\lceil \dfrac{m+l}{2} \right\rceil \text{if } m > l+1 \\ T^s_{\sigma_l,\sigma_{l+1}} \quad \text{otherwise} \end{cases} \tag{16.5}
$$

The parameter $\tau_{r_{\sigma_l,\sigma_m}}$ given in Eq. (16.5) denotes the average duration of the successful (last) round of link entanglement operations required to generate a remote entanglement between two non-adjacent nodes v_i and v_j through route $r_{i,j}$. It is straightforward to prove that, under the reasonable assumption that the BSM duration and efficiency are constant at each node, by maximizing the entanglement rate $\xi_r(T^{CH})$ we are maximizing the teleportation rate as well. Based on this, Algorithm 1 provides the pseudocode for computing the expected entanglement rate $\xi_{r_{i,j}}(T^{ch})$ between nodes v_i and v_j through route $r_{i,j}$, whereas *Algorithm 2* describes two auxiliary functions. Specifically, first Algorithm 1 computes the link entanglement generation time $T_{l,m}$ for any link $e_{l,m}$ with path $r_{i,j}$ (lines 4–11). Then, if path $r_{i,j}$ is made up of a single link (lines 13–16) and the time $\tau_{l,m}$ elapsed since the entanglement generation is smaller than the quantum memory coherence time T^{ch} (line 14), the entanglement rate $\xi_{r_{i,j}}(T^{ch})$ is obtained as the reciprocal of the link entanglement generation time $T_{l,m}$ (line 15). On the other hand, if path $r_{i,j}$ is made up of multiple links (lines 17–31), route $r_{i,j}$ is split into two sub-routes $r_{i,k}$ and $r_{k,i}$ at the intermediate node v_k (line 18). Then, the entanglement generation times $T_{r_{i,k}}$ and $T_{r_{k,j}}$ are recursively computed (lines 19–20) through function recT($\cdot$) given in Algorithm 2. Finally, if the time $\tau_{r_{i,j}} - \min\left\{T^s_{l,m} - \tau_{l,m}\right\}$ elapsed since the oldest entanglement generation is smaller than the quantum memory coherence time T^{ch} (line 28), the entanglement rate $\xi_{r_{i,j}}(T^{ch})$ is obtained as the reciprocal of the end-to-end entanglement generation time $T_{r_{i,j}}$ (line 29). We note that the computation of $\tau_{r_{i,k}}$ and $\tau_{r_{j,k}}$ represents the preliminary step for obtaining $\tau_{r_{i,j}}$ (lines 26–27), and both $\tau_{r_{i,k}}$ and $\tau_{r_{j,k}}$ are recursively computed (lines 29–24) through function recTau ($\cdot$) given in Algorithm 2.

Algorithm 1 exhibits a linear time complexity $\mathcal{O}(n \log n)$ with the number n of links belonging to the route [17].

16.1.3 Optimal Quantum Routing

Here, we present an optimal routing protocol for quantum networks based on the expected end-to-end entanglement rate $\xi_{r_{i,j}}(T^{ch})$. Toward this aim, the following preliminaries are needed.

Optimality: A route metric is considered *optimal* if there exists a routing protocol that, when used in conjunction with such a metric, always discovers the most favorable path between any pair of nodes in any connected network.

Strict monotonicity: A routing metric $W: R \rightarrow \mathbb{R}$ is strictly monotone if and only if $W(r_{i,j}) > W(r_{i,j} \oplus e_{j,k}) \forall r_{ij} \in R, e_{j,k} \in E$, with R denoting the set of simple paths in the arbitrary network, $\oplus$ being the operator that concatenates a simple path with a link, and $>$ denoting the ordering relation over the paths; that is, the higher the entanglement rate, the more preferable the path.

Strict isotonicity: A routing metric $W: R \rightarrow \mathbb{R}$ is strictly isotone if and only if $W(r_{i,j}) < W(\tilde{r}_{i,j}) \Rightarrow W(r_{i,j} \oplus e_{j,k}) < W(\tilde{r}_{i,j} \oplus e_{j,k})$, for any $r_{i,j}, \tilde{r}_{i,j} \in R$ and $e_{j,k} \in E$.

The route metric $W(r_{i,j}) = \nabla \xi_{r_{i,j}}(T^{CH}) \forall r_{i,j} \in R$, based on the end-to-end entanglement rate given in Eq. (16.4), is strictly monotone for any route $r_{i,j}$ [17]. We note that $W(r_{i,j})$, given above,

---

Algorithm 1 Expected Entanglement Rate.

1: $//D = \{d_{1,m} : e_{1,m} \in E\}$, $T^C = \{T^C_{1,m} : e_{1,m} \in E\}$
2: $//T^S = \{T^S_{1,m} : e_{1,m} \in E\}$, $T = \{T_{1,m} : e_{1,m} \in E\}$
3: **function** Xi(r_{ij}, D)
4:   **for** link $e_{1,m} \in r_{ij}$ **do**
5:     $p_{1,m} = \frac{1}{2}\nu_o p^2 e^{-d_{1,m}/L_0}$
6:     $T^c_{1,m} = d_{1,m}/(2c_f)$
7:     $t_{1,m} = \tau^t + \tau^o + d_{1,m}/(2c_f) + T^c_{1,m}$
8:     $T^S_{1,m} = \tau^p + \max\{\tau^h, \tau_{1,m}\}$
9:     $T^f_{1,m} = \tau^p + \max\{\tau^h, \tau_{1,m}, \tau^d\}$
10:     $T_{1,m} = \left((1-p_{1,m})T^f_{1,m} + p_{1,m}T^S_{1,m}\right)/p_{1,m}$
11:   **end for**
12:   $n = $ numLinks($r_{i,j}$)
13:   **if** $n = 1$ **then**
14:     **if** $\tau_{1,m} \leq T^{CH}$ **then**
15:       $\xi_{r_{i,j}} = 1/T_{1,m}$
16:     **end if**
17:   **else**
18:     $k = \lceil (n+1)/2 \rceil$
19:     $T_{r_{i,k}} = $ recT($r_{i,k}$, T, T^C)
20:     $T_{r_{k,j}} = $ recT($r_{k,j}$, T, T^C)
21:     $\widetilde{T} = \max\{T_{r_{i,k}}, T_{r_{k,j}}\}$
22:     $\widetilde{T}^C = \max\{T^C_{r_{i,k}}, T^C_{r_{k,j}}\}$ $//T^C_{r_{i,k}} = \sum_{e_{1,m} \in r_{i,k}} T^C_{1,m}$
23:     $T_{r_{i,j}} = (\widetilde{T} + \tau^a + \widetilde{T}^C)/\nu^a$
24:     $\tau_{r_{i,k}} = $ recTau($r_{i,k}$, T^S, T^C)
25:     $\tau_{r_{k,j}} = $ recTau($r_{k,j}$, T^S, T^C)
26:     $\widetilde{\tau} = \max\{\tau_{r_{i,k}}, \tau_{r_{k,j}}\}$
27:     $\tau_{r_{i,j}} = \widetilde{\tau} + \tau^a + T^C$
28:     **if** $\tau_{r_{i,j}} - \min_{e_{1,m} \in r_{i,j}}\{T^S_{1,m} - \tau_{1,m}\} \leq T^{CH}$ **then**
29:       $\xi_{r_{i,j}} = 1/T_{r_{i,j}}$
30:     **end if**
31:   **end if**
32:   **return** $\xi_{r_{i,j}}$
33: **end function**

Source: [17]

---

is strictly monotone for any realistic parameter setting, that is, $\nu^a < 1$ and $\tau^a > 0$. Nevertheless, even under the unrealistic assumption of $\nu^a = 1$ and $\tau^a = 0$, $W(r) = \xi_r(T^{CH})$ is still monotone; that is, $W(r) \geq W(r \oplus e) \forall r \in R$, $e \in E$, and the results derived in the subsequent steps continue to hold. The route metric $W(r_{i,j})$ given in Eq. (16.4) is not strictly isotone. Algorithm 3 provides the pseudocode for the optimal routing protocol; that is, the protocol is always able to converge to the optimal route r^*_{ij} between any pair of nodes v_i and v_j in any connected quantum network. Specifically,

---

Algorithm 2 Auxiliary Functions.

```
1: function recT(r_{a, b}, T, T^C)
2:   n = numLinks(r_{a, b})
3:   if n = 1 then
4:     T_{r_{a,b}} = T_{a,b} // T = {T_{l,m} : e_{l,m} ∈ E}
5:   else
6:     k = ⌈(a+b)/2⌉
7:     T_{r_{a,k}} = recT(r_{a,k}, T, T^C)
8:     T_{r_{k,b}} = recT(r_{a,k}, T, T^C)
9:     T̃ = max{T_{r_{a,k}}, T_{r_{k,b}}}
10:    T̃^C = max{T^C_{r_{a,k}}, T^C_{r_{k,b}}} // T^C_{r_{a,k}} = Σ_{e_{l,m}∈r_{a,k}} T^C_{l,m}
11:    T_{r_{i,j}} = (T̃ + τ^a + T̃^C)/v^a
12:  end if
13: end function
14: function recTau(r_{a, b}, T^s, T^C)
15:   n = numLinks(r_{a, b}, T^s, T^C)
16:   if n = 1 then
17:     τ_{r_{a,b}} = T^s_{a,b} = {T^s_{l,m} : e_{l,m} ∈ E}
18:   else
19:     k = ⌈(a+b)/2⌉
20:     τ_{r_{a,k}} = recTau(r_{a,k}, T^s, T^C)
21:     τ_{r_{k,b}} = recTau(r_{k,b}, T^s, T^C)
22:     τ̃ = max{τ_{r_{a,k}}, τ_{r_{k,b}}}
23:     T̃^C = max{T^C_{r_{a,k}}, T^C_{r_{k,b}}} // T^C_{r_{a,k}} = Σ_{e_{l,m}∈r_{a,k}} T^C_{l,m}
24:     τ_{r_{a,b}} = τ̃ + τ^a + T̃^C
25:  end if
26: end function
```

Source: [17]

Algorithm 3 implements a simple path enumeration algorithm adapted from [22]. At first (lines 4–9), the algorithm generates all the routes with no internal vertices (i.e., the simple paths composed of a single link), and it computes the entanglement rate along such routes through function Xi($\cdot$) given in Algorithm 1 (line 8). Then (lines 10–25), the algorithm concatenates two subsimple paths p_1 and p_2 between vertices $v_i - v_k$ and $v_k - v_j$, respectively, given that the resulting path $r = p_1 \oplus p_2$ between vertices v_i and v_j is simple, that is, given that the intersection of the vertices $V(p_1)$ of path p_1 with the vertices $V(p_2)$ of path p_2 is empty with the exception of vertex v_k (line 14). The entanglement rate along the concatenated path $r = p_1 \oplus p_2$ is computed through function Xi($\cdot$) given in Algorithm 1 (line 17), and the optimal path r^*_{ij} between vertices v_i and v_j is updated depending on the computed entanglement rate (lines 17–20).

The route metric $W(r_{i,j})$ given in Eq. (16.4) is optimal for any source–destination pair v_i, v_j when combined with the routing protocol given in Algorithm 3 [17]. The route metric $W(r_{i,j})$ given in Eq. (16.4) is not optimal when combined with any routing protocol based on the Dijkstra or

Algorithm 3 Optimal Path Selection.

1: $//D = \{d_{i,j}\}_{e_{i,j} \in E}$
2: **function** optimalPath (V, E, D)
3:   $w_{i,\ j} = 0 \,\forall\, v_i,\ v_j \in V$
4:   **for** link $e_{i,j} \in E$ **do**
5:     $R(i,\ j).\ append(e_{i,\ j})$
6:     $r^*_{i,j} = e_{i,j}$
7:     //Xi($\cdot$) defined in Algorithm 1
8:     $w_{i,j} = $ Xi$(e_{i,j},\ D)$
9:   **end for**
10:   **for** $v_k \in V$ **do**
11:     **for** $v_i \in V$ **do**
12:       **for** $v_j \in V$ **do**
13:         **for** path $p_1 \in R(i,\ k)$ and $p_2 \in R(k,\ j)$ **do**
14:           **if** $!(V(p_1)\ \&\ V(p_2)\ \&\ V\backslash\{k\})$
    then
15:             $r = p_1 \otimes p2$
16:             $R(i,\ j).\ append(r)$
17:             **if** Xi$(r,\ D) > w_{i,j}$ **then**
18:               $r^*_{i,j} = r$
19:               $w_{i,j} = $ Xi$(r,\ D)$
20:             **end if**
21:           **end if**
22:         **end for**
23:       **end for**
24:     **end for**
25:   **end for**
26:   **return** $\left\{r^*_{i,j},\ w_{i,j}\right\}_{v_i, v_j \in V}$
27: **end function**
Source: [17]

Bellman–Ford algorithms [17]. Algorithm 3 exhibits a time complexity equal to $\mathcal{O}(|V|^3\ |S||E|\ \log\ |E|)$, polynomial with the number $|V|$ of vertices, linear with the number $|E|$ of edges, and linear with the number $|S|$ of simple routes in G [17].

Design Example 16.1 [17]

Here, we present the evaluation results for both the link and the end-to-end entanglement rate by adopting the quantum repeater model shown in Figure 16.1. All the parameters have been set in agreement with experimental results [16, 19], but it was also noted in [17] that the analytical results derived in the previous sections continue to hold for any different parameter setting.

(Continued)

Design Example 16.1 [17] (Continued)

Parameters: $p^{ht} = 0.53$, $v^h = v^t = 0.8$, $v^a = 0.3904$, $L_0 = 22$km, $c_f = 2 * 10^8$ m/s, $\tau^p = 5.9$ μs, $\tau^h = 20$ μs, $\tau^t = 10$ μs, and $\tau^d = 100$ μs. In addition, $T^c_{i,j} = d_{i,j}/(2c_f)$ by neglecting the delay introduced by the optical amplifiers, and we set $\tau^o = \tau^a = 10$ μs analogously to τ^t and $v^a = 0.39$ analogously to v^o. Finally, we reasonably assume quantum memories with coherence time $T^{ch} = 10$ ms, since coherence times greater than 10 s have been already reported for the adopted qubit implementation (i.e., $^{87}R_b$) [23].

In Figure 16.2, we show the expected link entanglement rate $\xi_{i,j}(T^{ch})$ between adjacent nodes v_i and v_j given in Eq. (16.2) as a function of the optical link length $d_{i,j}$ for different values of the time τ^d required for atom cooling (ranging from 10 μs to 0.1 s). For a performance comparison, the approximation of the link entanglement rate recently proposed in [16], referred to as the *conventional rate*, is considered; the rate is approximated as $p_{i,j}/(d_{i,j}/c_f + \tau)$ with $\tau = 100$ μs and $v^o = 1$ (i.e. ideal optical BSM). First, we note that the approximation slightly differs from the exact closed-form expression derived in Eq. (16.2) when $\tau^d = \tau$. Furthermore, we note that the duty cycle duration significantly degrades the achievable rates.

In Figure 16.3, we show the expected end-to-end entanglement rate $\xi_{r_{i,j}}(T^{ch})$ between nodes v_i and v_j through route $r_{i,j}$ given in Eq. (16.4), with $r_{i,j} = \{e_{i,k}, e_{k,j}\}$ constituted by two links. In this experiment, the impact of the proportion between the link lengths $d_{i,k}$ and $d_{k,j}$ on the entanglement rate was evaluated.

Furthermore, the case in which there exists a direct link between v_i and v_j with length $d_{i,j} = d_{i,k} + d_{k,j}$, was also considered. Finally, for a performance comparison, we report the approximation of the end-to-end entanglement rate recently proposed in [16], referred to as the *conventional rate*, which is defined only for the case $d_{i,k} = d_{k,j}$. First, we note that the approximation significantly differs from the exact closed-form expression derived in Eq. (16.2) whenever $d_{i,k} \neq d_{k,j}$, with rates overestimated by roughly two order of magnitudes. Furthermore, we note that the exact closed-form expression derived in Eq. (16.4) is able to account for the rich dynamic

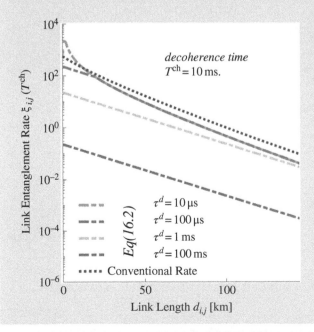

Figure 16.2 Expected link entanglement rate $\xi_{i,j}(T^{ch})$ between adjacent nodes v_i and v_j as a function of the optical link length $d_{i,j}$ for different values of the time τ^d required for atom cooling. Decoherence time T^{ch} equals 10 ms. Logarithmic scale for y axis. *Source:* Caleffi [17].

Design Example 16.1 [17] (Continued)

Figure 16.3 Expected end-to-end entanglement rate $\xi_{r_{i,j}}(T^{ch})$ between nodes v_i and v_j through route $r_{i,j} = \{e_{i,k}, e_{k,j}\}$ as a function of the total path length $d_{i,k} + d_{k,j}$ for different values of $d_{i,k}$. Atom cooling time τ^d and decoherence time T^{ch} are equal to 100 µs and 1 ms, respectively. *Source:* Caleffi [17]. (For more details see color figure in bins).

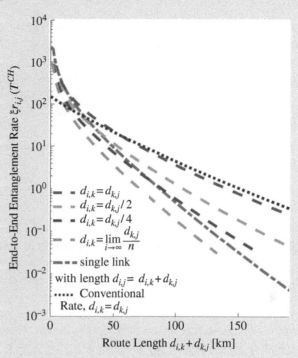

Figure 16.4 Minimum coherence time $\tau_{r_{i,j}}$ required for the successful utilization of an end-to-end entanglement between nodes v_i and v_j through route $r_{i,j} = \{e_{i,k}, e_{k,j}\}$ as a function of the total path length $d_{i,k} + d_{k,j}$ for different values of $d_{i,k}$. Atom cooling time τ^d is equal to 100 µs. Logarithmic scale for y axis. *Source:* Caleffi [17]. (For more details see color figure in bins).

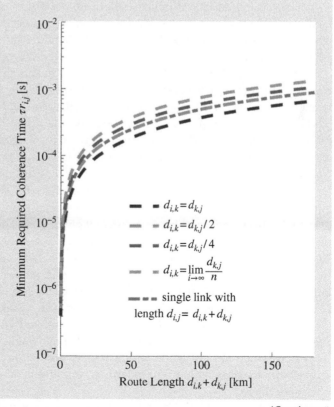

(Continued)

Design Example 16.1 [17] (Continued)

imposed by the ratio of the link lengths. As an example, at d = 200 km, the end-to-end entanglement rate can vary from 0.19 entanglements/second for $d_{k,j} = d_{i,k}$ to 0 entanglements/second for $d_{k,j} = 4d_{i,k}$ due to the decoherence effects.

Finally, in Figure 16.4, we report the minimum coherence time $\tau_{r_{ij}}$ required of the quantum memories for the successful utilization of an end-to-end entanglement between nodes v_i and v_j through route $r_{i,j} = \{e_{i,k}, e_{k,j}\}$ for the same simulation set of Figure 16.3. The analytical expression of $\tau_{r_{ij}}$ is given in Eq. (16.5). We first observe that the minimum coherence times are obtained by using a repeater positioned in the path median. Furthermore, quantum memories with coherence times exceeding the order of 10 ms can guarantee an end-to-end entanglement even for the larger values of path lengths.

16.2 Quantum Network on Symmetric Graph

Quantum state transfer from one location to another is a significant problem for quantum information processing systems. A quantum computer, which consists of different processing units, requires the quantum states to be transferred between its parts. Therefore, quantum state transfer is an important part of quantum computer design. There are various ways of achieving this task depending on the technology at hand [23].

Quantum communication through a spin chain was first considered by Bose [24] and since then it has been studied in depth [22, 25–31]. This procedure consists of interacting spins on a chain, whose dynamics is governed by Heisenberg, XX, or XY Hamiltonians. PST through a spin chain, in which adjacent spins are coupled by equal strength, can be achieved only over short distances [32, 33].

Quantum walks (QWs) have been introduced as a quantum analogue of classical random walks. A continuous-time QW has been suggested by Farhi and Gutmann [34] as a quantum algorithm to reach the n-th level of a decision tree faster than the classical random walk. The discrete-time QW has been introduced by Aharonov et al. [35] where the walker has a larger average path length than its classical counterpart. These properties of QWs have allowed the development of new quantum algorithms [36]. Many experimental systems for QWs have been implemented [37–53].

As already discussed so far throughout the book, entanglement is an indispensable resource for performing various quantum tasks (see [54] for a recent review, [55] and the references therein for entanglement preparation). Several schemes have been proposed [56–59] for the generation and distribution of entanglement between different systems, most of which involve an initial entangling of the two systems followed by spatial separation. Such spatially separated and entangled states can be used for quantum communication protocols, for example, quantum cryptography [60] and quantum teleportation [61]. The amount of entanglement degrades with an increase in spatial separation because of physical limitations and the noise effect. One way of circumventing this problem would be to generate entanglement when the two systems are spatially separated.

In this section, we will begin our discussion on quantum PST by considering a QW in the network represented by a symmetric graph. We believe that this would provide an easy-to-follow, introductory discussion of the problem where the routing decision in the network nodes is determined by the network topology itself. In the following, we will generalize the routing models by using random walk theory.

Discrete-time QW controlled by coins: In this section, we pay attention to discrete-time QW, where there are two spaces, a coin space denoted by H_c and a walker space denoted by H_w, respectively.

Design Example 16.2

The above method will be illustrated on both the butterfly network and the inverted crown network shown in Figures 16.5a and b, respectively [61]. At the beginning, assume that the initial state is $|\psi^0\rangle = |0\rangle(\alpha|0\rangle + \beta|1\rangle)$, where $\alpha|0\rangle + \beta|1\rangle$ is the coin state, $|\alpha|^2 + |\beta|^2 = 1$, the superscript 0 stands for the number of steps, and $|0\rangle$ is the initial position. Our purpose is to transmit the initial state $|\psi^0\} = \alpha|0\rangle + \beta|1\rangle$ from position $|0\rangle$ to a certain position $|x\rangle$ perfectly after n steps. In addition, during the quantum communication, the positions of state $\alpha|0\rangle$ and state $\beta|1\rangle$ are denoted by $|P_1\rangle$ and $|P_2\rangle$, respectively. Therefore, at the i-th step, the state can be written as $|\psi^i\rangle = \alpha|P_1^i\rangle|0\rangle + \beta|P_2^i\rangle|1\rangle$ [61].

Then, the whole space is the Hilbert space $H = H_c \otimes H_w$. In this scheme, the movement of the walker is controlled by the conditional shift operator as $S = \sum_x(|x+1\rangle\langle x| \otimes |0\rangle\langle 0| + |x-1\rangle\langle x| \otimes |1\rangle\langle 1|)$, which displays the summation over all possible positions (x is the node the state is located at). The whole process is under the control of the coin flipping operators and the conditional shift operator S. The coin flipping operator is denoted by $I \otimes C$, in which I is the identity operator controlling the walker, and C is the coin flipping operator applied to the coin state. In general, the coin flipping operators are the identity operator I and the Pauli operator σ_x. On the line, using identity operator I, the coin state will keep unchanged, and the walker will move in the same direction as the previous walker does. On the other hand, if we apply the Pauli operator σ_x on the line, the condition will be diametrically opposite to the previous one. Assuming that there is an arbitrary quantum input $|\psi_A\rangle$ at the source node A supposed to be transferred to the target node B, at target node B, the quantum output is $|\psi_B\rangle$. Then the state fidelity $F_B = |\langle\psi_A|\psi_B\rangle| = 1$ can be achieved, and the state transfer is called PST. This definition can be generalized to multiunicast communication.

1) *Perfect single-qubit states transfer (butterfly network):* Here, the initial state at A_1 is $|\varphi_1^0\rangle = |A_1\rangle(\alpha_1|0\rangle + \beta_1|1\rangle)$ where $|\alpha_1|^2 + |\beta_1|^2 = 1$. Similarly, the initial state at A_2 is $|\varphi_2^0\} = |A_2\rangle(\alpha_2|0\rangle + \beta_2|1\rangle)$ where $|\alpha_2|^2 + |\beta_2|^2 = 1$. The detailed process is described as follows. PST from source A_1 to target B_1 develops through the following steps: step 0 $|\varphi_1^0\rangle = |A_1\rangle(\alpha_1|0\rangle + \beta_1|1\rangle)$; step 1 $\rightarrow |\varphi_1^1\rangle = |C_1\rangle(\alpha_1|0\rangle \beta_1|1\rangle)$; step 2 $\rightarrow^I$ $|\varphi_1^2\rangle = \alpha_1|C_2\rangle|0\rangle + \beta_1|A_2\rangle|1\rangle$; step 3 $\rightarrow^I |\varphi_1^3\rangle = |B_1\rangle(\alpha_1|0\rangle + \beta_1|1\rangle)$.

From this, we can clearly learn about the whole process of PST from A_1 to B_1. In addition, we use $|\varphi_1^i\rangle$ to represent the state during the quantum communication, where the superscript i stands for the i-th step and the subscript 1 denotes that the state $|\varphi_1^i\rangle$ is transferred from source A_1 to target B_1. The symbols on the arrows are operators used in the corresponding step. First, the state $|\varphi_1^0\rangle$ is transmitted to C_1. Then, we apply the identity operator I to the coin state, getting the coin state $|\varphi_1^2\rangle$. Finally, we keep applying the identity operator I to the coin state, so that we can get the state $|\varphi_1^3\rangle$. Therefore, the initial state $|\varphi_1^0\rangle$ is perfectly transferred from source A_1 to target B_1 after three steps.

Similarly, the PST from source A_2 to target B_2 can be represented as step 0 : $|\varphi_2^0\rangle = |A_2\rangle(\alpha_2|0\rangle + \beta_2|1\rangle)$; step 1 $\rightarrow |\varphi_2^1\rangle = |C_1\rangle(\alpha_2|0\rangle + \beta_2|1\rangle)$;
step 2 $\rightarrow^I |\varphi_2^2\rangle = \alpha_2|A_1\rangle|0\rangle + \beta_2|C_2\rangle|1\rangle$; step 3 $\rightarrow^I |\varphi_2^3\rangle = |B_2\rangle(\alpha_2|0\rangle + \beta_2|1\rangle)$

2) *Perfect two-qubit states transfer (butterfly network):* In this case, the initial states at sources A_1 and A_2 are $|\Phi_1^0\rangle = |A_1\rangle(\alpha_1|00\rangle + \beta_1|10\rangle)$ and $|\Phi_2^0\rangle = |A_2\rangle(\alpha_2|00\rangle + \beta_2|10\rangle)$, respectively, with $|\alpha_1|^2 + |\beta_1|^2 = 1$ and $|\alpha_2|^2 + |\beta_2|^2 = 1$. Here, we apply the coin operator to the first particle. The detailed processes are given as follows. For the PST from source A_1 to target B_1, we have

$|\Phi_1^0\rangle = |A_1\rangle(\alpha_1|00\rangle + \beta_1|10\rangle); \xrightarrow{I_1} |\Phi_1^1\rangle = \alpha_1|C_1\rangle|00\rangle + \beta_1|B_2\rangle|10\rangle; \xrightarrow{I_1} |\Phi_1^2\rangle = |C_2\rangle(\alpha_1|00\rangle + \beta_1|10\rangle); \rightarrow |\Phi_1^3\rangle = |B_1\rangle(\alpha_1|00\rangle + \beta_1|10\rangle)$

Similarly, for the PST from source A_2 to target B_2, we have $|\Phi_2^0\rangle = |A_2\rangle(\alpha_2|00\rangle + \beta_2|10\rangle);$
$\xrightarrow{I_1} |\Phi_2^1\rangle = \alpha_2|B_1\rangle|00\rangle + \beta_2|C_1\rangle|10\rangle; \xrightarrow{I_1} |\Phi_2^2\rangle = |C_2\rangle(\alpha_2|00\rangle + \beta_2|10\rangle); \rightarrow |\Phi_2^3\rangle = |B_2\rangle(\alpha_2|00\rangle + \beta_2|10\rangle)$

3) *Perfect single-qubit states transfer (inverted crown network):* The initial single-qubit states are $|\psi_1^0\rangle = |A_1\rangle(\alpha_1|0\rangle + \beta_1|1\rangle)$, $|\psi_2^0\rangle = |A_2\rangle(\alpha_2|0\rangle + \beta_2|1\rangle)$ and $|\psi_3^0\rangle = |A_3\rangle(\alpha_3|0\rangle + \beta_3|1\rangle)$, respectively, where $|\alpha_i|^2 + |\beta_i|^2 = 1 (i = 1, 2, 3)$.

For the PST from source A_3 to target B_3 (see Figure 16.5b), we have $|\psi_3^0\rangle = |A_3\rangle(\alpha_3|0\rangle + \beta_3|1\rangle); \xrightarrow{I} |\psi_3^1\rangle = \alpha_3|C_1\rangle|1\rangle + \beta_3|C_2\rangle|0\rangle; \xrightarrow{I} |\psi_3^2\rangle = |B_3\rangle(\alpha_3|0\rangle + \beta_3|1\rangle)$. The symbols on the arrows are operators used in the corresponding step. In the beginning, we apply the identity operator I to the coin state; then the states are $|\psi_3^1\rangle$. Afterward, the operator I is applied to the coin state once again, and the states become $|\psi_3^2\rangle$. Thus, the initial state $|\psi_3^0\rangle$ is successfully transmitted from node A_3 to node B_3 after two steps.

Similarly, for the PST from source A_1 to target B_1, we have $|\psi_1^0\rangle = |A_1\rangle(\alpha_1|0\rangle + \beta_1|1\rangle); \rightarrow |\psi_1^1\rangle = |A_3\rangle(\alpha_1|0\rangle + \beta_1|1\rangle); \xrightarrow{I} |\psi_1^2\rangle = \alpha_1|C_2\rangle|0\rangle + \beta_1|A_2\rangle|1\rangle; \xrightarrow{I} |\psi_1^3\rangle = |B_1\rangle(\alpha_1|0\rangle + \beta_1|1\rangle)$.

Finally, for the PST from source A_2 to target B_2, we have $|\psi_2^0\rangle = |A_2\rangle(\alpha_2|0\rangle + \beta_2|1\rangle); \rightarrow |\psi_2^1\rangle = |A_3\rangle(\alpha_2|0\rangle + \beta_2|1\rangle); \xrightarrow{I} |\psi_2^2\rangle = \alpha_2|A_1\rangle|0\rangle + \beta_2|C_1\rangle|1\rangle; \xrightarrow{I} |\psi_2^3\rangle = |B_2\rangle(\alpha_2|0\rangle + \beta_2|1\rangle)$.

4) *Perfect two-qubit states transfer (inverted crown network):* The initial states at sources A_1, A_2, and A_3 are $|\Psi_1^0\rangle = |A_1\rangle(\alpha_1|00\rangle + \beta_1|10\rangle)$, $|\Psi_2^0\rangle = |A_2\rangle(\alpha_2|00\rangle + \beta_2|10\rangle)$, and $|\Psi_3^0\rangle = |A_3\rangle(\alpha_3|00\rangle + \beta_3|10\rangle)$, respectively, where $|\alpha_i|^2 + |\beta_i|^2 = 1 (i = 1, 2, 3)$. We apply the operator to the first coin state to realize the initial states transfer from the sources to the targets. The detailed processes are as follows:

For the PST from source A_3 to target B_3, we have $|\Psi_3^0\rangle = |A_3\rangle(\alpha_3|00\rangle + \beta_3|10\rangle); \rightarrow^{I_1} |\Psi_3^1\rangle = \alpha_3|C_2\rangle|00\rangle + \beta_3|C_1\rangle|10\rangle; \rightarrow^{I_1} |\Psi_3^2\rangle = |B_3\rangle(\alpha_3|00\rangle + \beta_3|10\rangle)$

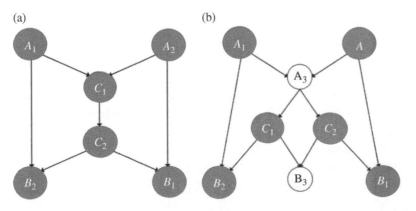

Figure 16.5 (a) Butterfly, (b) inverted crown network. *Source:* Xiu-Bo Chen et al. [61].

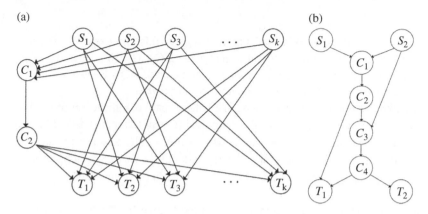

Figure 16.6 (a) The G_k network, (b) the grail network. *Source:* Xiu-Bo Chen et al. [61].

For the PST from source A_1 to target B_1, we have $| \Psi_1^0 \rangle = | A_1 \rangle (\alpha_1 | 00 \rangle + \beta_1 | 10 \rangle); \rightarrow | \Psi_1^1 \rangle = | A_3 \rangle (\alpha_1 | 00 \rangle + \beta_1 | 10 \rangle); \xrightarrow{I_1} | \Psi_1^2 \rangle = \alpha_1 | A_2 \rangle | 00 \rangle + \beta_1 | C_2 \rangle | 10 \rangle; \xrightarrow{I_1} | \Psi_1^3 \rangle = | B_1 \rangle (\alpha_1 | 00 \rangle + \beta_1 | 10 \rangle)$.

Finally, for the PST from source A_2 to target B_2, we have $| \Psi_2^0 \rangle = | A_2 \rangle (\alpha_2 | 00 \rangle + \beta_2 | 10 \rangle);$ $\rightarrow | \Psi_2^1 \rangle = | A_3 \rangle (\alpha_2 | 00 \rangle + \beta_2 | 10 \rangle)$; $\xrightarrow{I_1} | \Psi_2^2 \rangle = \alpha_2 | C_1 \rangle | 00 \rangle + \beta_2 | A_1 \rangle | 10 \rangle$; $\xrightarrow{I_1} | \Psi_2^3 \rangle = | B_2 \rangle (\alpha_2 | 00 \rangle + \beta_2 | 10 \rangle)$

The PST schemes described above can also be used in the networks shown in Figure 16.6.

16.3 QWs

In the previous section, we have introduced the basic concept of QW on a given network on a graph, and in order to further generalize this concept, we need to go back and review, to some extent, the basic theory of QWs.

Discrete QWs on a line (DQWL): This is the most studied model of discrete QWs. As its name suggests, these kinds of QWs are performed on graphs G composed of a set of vertices V and a set of edges E (i.e., G = (V, E)), and having two edges from each vertex. The main components of a coined DQWL are a walker, a coin, evolution operators for both walker and coin, and a set of observables:

Walker and coin: The walker is a quantum system living in a Hilbert space of infinite but countable dimensions $\mathcal{H}_p$. It is customary to use vectors from the canonical (computational) basis of $\mathcal{H}_p$ as "position sites" for the walker. So, we denote the walker as $| \text{position} \rangle \in \mathcal{H}_p$ and affirm that the canonical basis states $|i\rangle_p$ that span $\mathcal{H}_p$, as well as any superposition of the form $\sum_i \alpha_i | i \rangle_p$ subject to $\sum_i |\alpha_i|^2 = 1$, are valid states for |position⟩. The walker is usually initialized at the "origin"; that is, $|\text{position}\rangle_{initial} = | 0 \rangle_p$.

The coin is a quantum system living in a two-dimensional Hilbert space $\mathcal{H}_c$. The coin may take the canonical basis states $|0\rangle$ and $|1\rangle$ as well as any superposition of these basis states. Therefore, $| \text{coin} \rangle \in \mathcal{H}_c$, and a general normalized state of the coin may be written as $|\text{coin}\rangle = a | 0 \rangle_c + b | 1 \rangle_c$, where $|a|^2 + |b|^2 = 1$.

The total state of the QW resides in $\mathcal{H}_t = \mathcal{H}_p \otimes \mathcal{H}_c$. It is customary to use product states of $\mathcal{H}_t$ as initial states; that is, $|\psi\rangle_{initial} = | \text{position} \rangle_{initial} \otimes | \text{coin} \rangle_{initial}$.

16.3.1 DQWL

This is the most studied model of discrete QWs. As its name suggests, this kinds of QWs are performed on graphs G composed of a set of vertices V and a set of edges E (i.e., G = (V, E)), and having two edges associated with each vertex. The main components of a coined DQWL are a walker, a coin, evolution operators for both walker and coin, and a set of observables:

Walker and coin: The walker is a quantum system living in a Hilbert space of infinite but countable dimensions $\mathcal{H}_p$. It is customary to use vectors from the canonical (computational) basis of $\mathcal{H}_p$ as ("position sites") for the walker. So, we denote the walker as $|\,\text{position}\rangle \in \mathcal{H}_p$ and affirm that the canonical basis states $|i\rangle_p$ that span $\mathcal{H}_p$, as well as any superposition of the form $\sum_i \alpha_i \,|\,i\rangle_p$ subject to $\sum_i |\alpha_i|^2 = 1$, are valid states for $|\text{position}\rangle$. The walker is usually initialized at the "origin"; that is, $|\text{position}\rangle_{initial} = \,|\,0\rangle_p$.

The coin is a quantum system living in a two-dimensional Hilbert space $\mathcal{H}_c$. The coin may take the canonical basis states $|0\rangle$ and $|1\rangle$ as well as any superposition of these basis states. Therefore, $|\,\text{coin}\rangle \in \mathcal{H}_c$ and a general normalized state of the coin may be written as $|\text{coin}\rangle = a\,|\,0\rangle_c + b\,|\,1\rangle_c$, where $|a|^2 + |b|^2 = 1$.

The total state of the QW resides in $\mathcal{H}_t = \mathcal{H}_p \otimes \mathcal{H}_c$. It is customary to use product states of $\mathcal{H}_t$ as initial states; that is, $|\psi\rangle_{initial} = \,|\,\text{position}\rangle_{initial} \otimes \,|\,\text{coin}\rangle_{initial}$.

Evolution operators: The evolution of a QW is divided into two parts that closely resemble the behavior of a classical random walk. In the classical case, chance plays a key role in the evolution of the system. In the quantum case, the equivalent of the previous process is to apply an evolution operator to the coin state followed by a conditional shift operator to the total quantum system. The purpose of the coin operator is to render the coin state in a superposition, and the randomness is introduced by performing a measurement on the system after both evolution operators have been applied to the total quantum system several times. Among coin operators, customarily denoted by $\hat{C}$, the Hadamard operator has been extensively employed:

$$\hat{H} = \frac{1}{\sqrt{2}}\left(|\,0\rangle_c\langle 0\,| \, + \, |\,0\rangle_c\langle 1\,| \, + \, |\,1\rangle_c\langle 0\,| \, - \, |\,1\rangle_c\langle 1\,|\right) \tag{16.6}$$

For the conditional shift operator, use is made of a unitary operator that allows the walker to go one step forward if the accompanying coin state is one of the two basis states (e.g., $|0\rangle$), or one step backward if the accompanying coin state is the other basis state (e.g., $|1\rangle$). A suitable conditional shift operator has the form

$$\hat{S} = \,|\,0\rangle_c\langle 0\,|\otimes\sum_i |\,i+1\rangle_p\langle i\,| \, + \, |\,1\rangle_c\langle 1\,|\otimes\sum_i |\,i-1\rangle_p\langle i\,|\,. \tag{16.7}$$

Consequently, the operator on the total Hilbert space is $\hat{U} = \hat{S}\cdot\left(\hat{C}\otimes\hat{\mathbb{I}}_p\right)$ and a succinct mathematical representation of a discrete QW after t steps is

$$|\,\psi\rangle_t = \left(\hat{U}\right)^t |\,\psi\rangle_{initial}, \tag{16.8}$$

where $|\psi\rangle_{initial} = \,|\,\text{position}\rangle_{initial} \otimes \,|\,\text{coin}\rangle_{initial}$.

Observables: Several advantages of QWs over classical random walks are a consequence of interference effects between coin and walker after several applications of $\hat{U}$ (other advantages originate from quantum entanglement between walker(s) and coin(s) as well as partial measurement and/or interaction of coins and walkers with the environment.) However, we must perform a measurement at some point in order to know the outcome of our walk. To do so, we define a set of observables according to the basis states that have been used to define coin and walker.

Figure 16.7 Probability distributions of 100-step discrete quantum walks on a line (DQWLs).

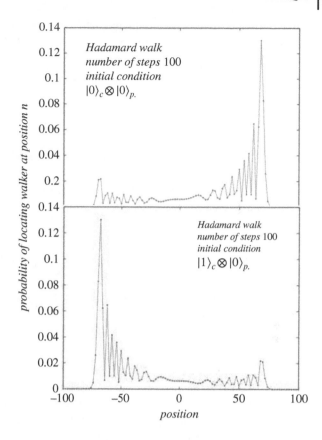

There are several ways to extract information from the composite quantum system. For example, we may first perform a measurement on the coin using the observable $\hat{M}_c = \alpha_0 \mid 0\rangle_c\langle 0 \mid + \alpha_1 \mid 1\rangle_c\langle 1 \mid$.

A measurement must then be performed on the position states of the walker by using the operator $\hat{M}_p = \sum_i a_i \mid i\rangle_p\langle i \mid$. Figure 16.7 shows the probability distributions of two 100-step DQWLs. Coin and shift operators for both QWs are given by Eqs. (16.6) and (16.7), respectively. The DQWLs from plots (a) and (b) have corresponding initial quantum states $\mid 0\rangle_c \otimes \mid 0\rangle_p$ and $\mid 1\rangle_c \otimes \mid 0\rangle_p$. The first evident property of these QWs is the skewness of their probability distributions, as well as the dependence of the symmetry of such a skewness from the coin initial quantum state ($\mid 0\rangle$ for upper plot and $\mid 1\rangle$ for lower plot). This skewness arises from constructive and destructive interference due to the minus sign included in Eq. (16.6). Also, we notice a quasi-uniform behavior in the central area of both probability distributions, approximately in the interval [−70, 70]. Finally, we note that regardless of their skewness, both probability distributions cover the same number of positions (in this case, even positions from −100 to 100. If the QW had been performed an odd number of times, then only odd position sites could have nonzero probability.)

16.3.2 Performance Study of DQWL

In the case of the Schrödinger approach, we take an arbitrary component $\mid \psi\rangle_n = (\alpha \mid 1\rangle_c + \beta \mid 0\rangle_c) \otimes \mid n\rangle_p$ of the QW, the tensor product of the coin and position components for a certain walker position. $\mid \psi\rangle_n$ is then Fourier-transformed in order to get a closed form of the coin amplitudes. Then, standard tools of complex analysis are used to calculate the statistical properties of the probability distribution computed from the corresponding coin amplitudes.

In the case of a combinatorial approach, we compute the amplitude for a particular position component $|n\rangle_p$ by summing up the amplitudes of all the paths that begin in the given initial condition and end up in $|n\rangle_p$. This approach can be seen as using a discrete version of path integrals.

Following a [62, 63] QW on an infinite line after t steps can be written as $|\psi\rangle_t = \hat{U}^t |\psi\rangle_{\text{initial}}$ (16.8) or, alternatively, as

$$\sum_k [a_k |0\rangle_c + b_k |1\rangle_c] |k\rangle_p \tag{16.9}$$

where $|0\rangle_c$, $|1\rangle_c$ are the coin state components, and $|k\rangle_p$ are the walker state components. For example, let us suppose we have $|\psi\rangle_0 = |0\rangle_c \otimes |0\rangle_p$ as the QW initial state, with Eqs. (16.6) and (16.7) as the coin and shift operators. Then, the first three steps of this QW can be written as

$$|\psi\rangle_1 = \frac{1}{\sqrt{2}}|0\rangle_c |1\rangle_p + \frac{1}{\sqrt{2}}|1\rangle_c |-1\rangle_p, |\psi\rangle_2 = \left(\frac{1}{2}|0\rangle_c + 0|1\rangle_c\right)|2\rangle_p + \left(\frac{1}{2}|0\rangle_c + \frac{1}{2}|1\rangle_c\right)|0\rangle_p$$

$$+ \left(0|0\rangle_c - \frac{1}{2}|1\rangle_c\right)|-2\rangle_p, |\psi\rangle_3 = \left(\frac{1}{2\sqrt{2}}|0\rangle_c + 0|1\rangle_c\right)|3\rangle_p + \left(\frac{1}{\sqrt{2}}|0\rangle_c + \frac{1}{2\sqrt{2}}|1\rangle_c\right)|1\rangle_p$$

$$+ \left(\frac{-1}{2\sqrt{2}}|0\rangle_c + 0|1\rangle_c\right)|-1\rangle_p + \left(0|0\rangle_c + \frac{1}{2\sqrt{2}}|1\rangle_c\right)|-3\rangle_p$$

Let us use the notation

$$\Psi(n, t) = \begin{pmatrix} \Psi_R(n, t) \\ \Psi_L(n, t) \end{pmatrix}$$

as the two-component vector of amplitudes of the particle being at point n and time t or, in operator notation $|\Psi(n+1, t)\rangle = \Psi_L(n, t)|1\rangle + \Psi_R(n, t)|0\rangle$. With this, we now analyze the behavior of a Hadamard walk at point n after $t + 1$ steps. We begin by applying the Hadamard operator given by Eq. (16.6) to those coin state components in positions $n - 1$, n, and $n + 1$:

$$\hat{H}(|\Psi(n-1,t)\rangle + |\Psi(n,t)\rangle + |\Psi(n+1,t)\rangle) = \frac{1}{\sqrt{2}}(|\Psi_L(n-1,t)\rangle|0\rangle + |\Psi_R(n-1,t)\rangle|0\rangle -$$
$$|\Psi_L(n+1,t)\rangle|1\rangle + |\Psi_R(n+1,t)\rangle|1\rangle - |\Psi_L(n-1,t)\rangle|1\rangle + |\Psi_R(n-1,t)\rangle|1\rangle$$
$$+ |\Psi_L(n+1,t)\rangle|0\rangle + |\Psi_R(n+1,t)\rangle|0\rangle + |\Psi_L(n,t)\rangle|0\rangle + |\Psi_R(n,t)\rangle|0\rangle$$
$$- |\Psi_L(n,t)\rangle|1\rangle + |\Psi_R(n,t)\rangle|1\rangle) \tag{16.10}$$

By applying the shift operator given by Eqs. (16.7)–(16.10), we get

$$\hat{U}\left(\hat{H}(|\Psi(n-1,t)\rangle + |\Psi(n,t)\rangle + |\Psi(n+1,t)\rangle)\right) =$$

$$\frac{1}{\sqrt{2}}(|\Psi_L(\mathbf{n},\mathbf{t})\rangle|0\rangle + |\Psi_R(\mathbf{n},\mathbf{t})\rangle|0\rangle - |\Psi_L(\mathbf{n},\mathbf{t})\rangle|1\rangle + |\Psi_R(\mathbf{n},\mathbf{t})\rangle|1\rangle - |\Psi_L(n-2,t)\rangle|1\rangle +$$
$$|\Psi_R(n-2,t)\rangle|1\rangle + |\Psi_L(n+2,t)\rangle|0\rangle + |\Psi_R(n+2,t)\rangle|0\rangle$$
$$- |\Psi_L(n-1,t)|1 + |\Psi_R(n-1,t)|1 + |\Psi_L(n+1,t)|0 + |\Psi_R(n+1,t)\rangle|0\rangle) \tag{16.11}$$

The bold font amplitude components of Eq. (16.11) are the amplitude components of $|\Psi(n, t+1)\rangle$, which can be written in matrix notation as

$$\Psi(n, t+1) = \begin{pmatrix} \dfrac{-1}{\sqrt{2}} & \dfrac{1}{\sqrt{2}} \\ 0 & 0 \end{pmatrix} \Psi(n+1, t) + \begin{pmatrix} 0 & 0 \\ \dfrac{1}{\sqrt{2}} & \dfrac{1}{\sqrt{2}} \end{pmatrix} \Psi(n-1, t) \tag{16.12}$$

With the new notation $M_- = \begin{pmatrix} \dfrac{-1}{\sqrt{2}} & \dfrac{1}{\sqrt{2}} \\ 0 & 0 \end{pmatrix}$ and $M_+ = \begin{pmatrix} 0 & 0 \\ \dfrac{1}{\sqrt{2}} & \dfrac{1}{\sqrt{2}} \end{pmatrix}$, we have

$$\Psi(n, t+1) = M_- \Psi(n+1, t) + M_+ \Phi(n-1, t) \tag{16.13}$$

Equation (16.13) is a difference equation with $\Psi(0,0) = \begin{pmatrix} 1 \\ 0 \end{pmatrix}$ and $\Psi(n,0) = \begin{pmatrix} 0 \\ 0 \end{pmatrix}$ $\forall n \neq 0$ as initial conditions $|\psi\rangle_0 = |0\rangle_c \otimes |0\rangle_p$. Our objective is to find analytical expressions for $\Psi_L(n, t)$ and $\Psi_R(n, t)$. To do so, we compute the discrete-time Fourier transform of Eq. (16.13).

For this, let $f: \mathbb{Z} \rightarrow \mathbb{C}$ be a complex function over the integers $\Rightarrow$ its discrete-time Fourier transform (DTFT) $\tilde{f}: [-\pi, \pi] \rightarrow \mathbb{C}$ is given by

$$\tilde{f} = \tilde{f}(e^{i\omega}) = \sum_{n=-\infty}^{\infty} f(n) e^{-in\omega}$$

and its inverse is given by

$$f(n) = \frac{1}{2\pi} \int_{-\pi}^{\pi} F(e^{i\omega}) e^{in\omega} d\omega$$

Ambainis et al. [62] employ the following slight variant of the DTFT: $\tilde{f}(k) = \sum_n f(n) e^{ik}$, where $f: \mathbb{Z} \rightarrow \mathbb{C}$ and $\tilde{f}: [-\pi, \pi] \rightarrow \mathbb{C}$. The corresponding inverse DTFT is given by

$$f(n) = \frac{1}{2\pi} \int_{-\pi}^{\pi} \tilde{f}(k) e^{-ik} dk \tag{16.14}$$

So, using $\tilde{f}(k) = \sum_n f(n) e^{ik}$ we have $\tilde{\Psi}(k, t) = \sum_n \Psi(n, t) e^{ikn}$ and using Eq. (16.13) we obtain

$$\tilde{\Psi}(k, t+1) = \sum_n (M_- \Psi(n+1, t) + M_+ \Psi(n-1, t)) e^{ikn} \tag{16.15}$$

After some algebra, we get $\tilde{\Psi}(k, t+1) = M_k \tilde{\Psi}(k, t)$, where

$$M_k = e^{-ik} M_- + e^{ik} M_+ = \frac{1}{\sqrt{2}} \begin{pmatrix} -e^{-ik} & e^{-ik} \\ e^{ik} & e^{ik} \end{pmatrix} \tag{16.16}$$

Thus

$$\tilde{\Psi}(k, t) = \begin{pmatrix} \tilde{\Phi}_L(k, t) \\ \tilde{\Psi}_R(k, t) \end{pmatrix} = M_k^t \tilde{\Psi}(k, 0),$$

$$\text{where } \tilde{\Psi}(k, 0) = \begin{pmatrix} 1 \\ 0 \end{pmatrix} \tag{16.17}$$

Our problem now consists in diagonalizing the (unitary) matrix M_k in order to calculate M_k^t. If M_k has eigenvalues $\{\lambda_k^1, \lambda_k^2\}$ and eigenvectors $|\Phi_k^1\rangle, |\Phi_k^2\rangle$, then

$$M_k = \lambda_k^1 |\Phi_k^1\rangle\langle\Phi_k^1| + \lambda_k^2 |\Phi_k^2\rangle\langle\Phi_k^2| \tag{16.18}$$

Using the mathematical properties of linear operators, we then find

$$M_k^t = (\lambda_k^1)^t |\Phi_k^1\rangle\langle\Phi_k^1| + (\lambda_k^2)^t |\Phi_k^2\rangle\langle\Phi_k^2| \tag{16.19}$$

It is shown in [62] that $\lambda_k^1 = e^{i\omega_k}$, $\lambda_k^2 = e^{i(\pi - \omega_k)}$, where

$$\omega_k \in \left[-\frac{\pi}{2}, \frac{\pi}{2}\right] \text{ and } \sin(\omega_k) = \frac{\sin k}{\sqrt{2}} \tag{16.20}$$

and

$$\Phi_k^1 = \frac{1}{\sqrt{2\left[(1 + \cos^2(k)) + \cos(k)\sqrt{1 + \cos^2 k}\right]}} \begin{pmatrix} e^{-ik} \\ \sqrt{2}\,e^{i\omega_k} + e^{-ik} \end{pmatrix} \tag{16.21a}$$

$$\Phi_k^2 = \frac{1}{\sqrt{2\left[(1 + \cos^2(\pi - k)) + \cos(\pi - k)\sqrt{1 + \cos^2(\pi - k)}\right]}} \begin{pmatrix} e^{-ik} \\ -\sqrt{2}\,e^{-i\omega_k} + e^{-ik} \end{pmatrix} \tag{16.21b}$$

From Eqs.(16.20), (16.21a), and (16.21b), we compute the Fourier-transformed amplitudes $\widetilde{\Psi}_L(n,t)$ and $\widetilde{\Psi}_R(n,t)$

$$\widetilde{\Psi}_L(n,t) = \frac{e^{-ik}}{2\sqrt{1 + \cos^2 k}}\left(e^{i\omega_k t} - (-1)^t e^{-i\omega_k t}\right) \tag{16.22a}$$

$$\widetilde{\Psi}_R(n,t) = \frac{1}{2}\left(1 + \frac{\cos k}{\sqrt{1 + \cos^2 k}}\right)e^{i\omega_k t} + \frac{(-1)^t}{2}\left(1 - \frac{\cos k}{\sqrt{1 + \cos^2 k}}\right)e^{-i\omega_k t} \tag{16.22b}$$

Using Eq. (16.22), we can get corresponding inverse discrete-time Fourier transform (DTFT) as [62]

$$\begin{aligned}
\Psi_L(n,t) &= \frac{1}{2\pi}\int_{-\pi}^{\pi} \frac{-ie^{ik}}{2\sqrt{1 + \cos^2 k}}\left(e^{-i(\omega_k t - kn)}\right)dk \\
\Psi_R(n,t) &= \frac{1}{2\pi}\int_{-\pi}^{\pi}\left(1 + \frac{\cos k}{\sqrt{1 + \cos^2 k}}\right)\left(e^{-i(\omega_k t - kn)}\right)dk
\end{aligned} \tag{16.23}$$

where $\omega_k = \sin^{-1}\left(\frac{\sin k}{\sqrt{2}}\right)$ and $\omega_k \in \left[\frac{-\pi}{2}, \frac{\pi}{2}\right]$.

Now we have an analytical expression for $\Phi_L(n, t)$ and $\Phi_R(n, t)$, and taking into account that $P(n, t) = |\Phi_L(n, t)|^2 + |\Psi_R(n, t)|^2$, we are interested in studying the asymptotical behavior of $\Phi(n, t)$ and $P(n, t)$. Integrals in Eq. (16.23) are of the form $I(\alpha, t) = \frac{1}{2\pi}\int_{-\pi}^{\pi} g(k)e^{i\varphi(k,\alpha)t}dk$, where $\alpha = n/t$ (=position/number of steps). The asymptotical properties of this kind of integral can be studied using the method of stationary phase [64, 65], a standard method in complex analysis. Using such a method, the authors of [62, 63] reported the following results:

For any constant $\varepsilon > 0$, and α in the interval $\left(\frac{-1}{\sqrt{2}} + \varepsilon, \frac{1}{\sqrt{2}} - \varepsilon\right)$, as $t \to \infty$, we have (uniformly in n)

$$p_L(n,t) \approx \frac{2}{\pi\sqrt{1 - 2\alpha^2 t}}\cos^2\left(-\omega t + \frac{\pi}{4} - \rho\right),$$

$$p_R(n,t) \frac{2(1 + \alpha)}{\pi(1 - \alpha)\sqrt{1 - 2\alpha^2 t}}\cos^2\left(-\omega t + \frac{\pi}{4}\right)$$

where $\omega = \alpha\rho + \theta$, $\rho = \arg\left(-B + \sqrt{\Delta}\right)$, $\theta = \arg\left(B + 2 + \sqrt{\Delta}\right)$, $B = \frac{2\alpha}{1 - \alpha}$, and $\Delta = B^2 - 4(B + 1)$.

For $n = \alpha t \to \infty$ with α fixed and $\alpha \in \left(-1, -1/\sqrt{2}\right) \cup \left(1/\sqrt{2}, 1\right) \Rightarrow \exists c > 1$ for which $p_L(n, t) = O(c^{-n})$ and $p_R(n, t) = O(c^{-n})$.

16.4 Multidimensional QWs

Here, we continue our discussion on quantum random walks by introducing into the model more details related to the physical aspects of the process. To illustrate this and give an intuition for what follows, we start with an example taken from [35]. Imagine a particle on a line whose position is described by a wave packet $| \psi_{x_0} \rangle$ localized around a position x_0; that is, the function $\langle x | \psi_{x_0} \rangle$ corresponds to a wave packet centered around x_0. Let P be the momentum operator. The translation of the particle, corresponding to a step of length l, can be represented by the unitary operator $U_l = \exp(-iPl/\hbar)$, so that $U_l | \psi_{x_0} \rangle = | \psi_{x_0-l} \rangle$. Now let us also assume that the particle has an additional dimension of movement, a spin -½ degree of freedom. Let S_z represent the operator corresponding to the z component of the spin and denote the eigenstates of S_z by $| \uparrow \rangle$ and $| \downarrow \rangle$, so that $S_z | \uparrow \rangle = (\hbar/2) | \uparrow \rangle$ and $S_z | \downarrow \rangle = -(\hbar/2) | \downarrow \rangle$. From now on, we will use $\hbar = 1$ in order to simplify the notation.

A spin -½ particle is usually described by a 2-vector $| \Psi \rangle = \left(| \widetilde{\psi}^{\uparrow} \rangle ; | \widetilde{\psi}^{\downarrow} \rangle \right)^T$, where the first part is the component of the wave function of the particle in the spin$- | \uparrow \rangle$ space, and the second one is the component in the $| \downarrow \rangle$-space. Normalization requires that $\left\| | \widetilde{\psi}^{\uparrow} \rangle \right\|^2 + \left\| | \widetilde{\psi}^{\downarrow} \rangle \right\|^2 = 1$. To emphasize the tensor structure of the space of the particle, we will write this in a slightly different but equivalent way as $| \Psi \rangle = \alpha^{\uparrow} | \uparrow \rangle \otimes | \psi^{\uparrow} \rangle + \alpha^{\downarrow} | \downarrow \rangle \otimes | \psi^{\downarrow} \rangle$, where we normalize the two wave functions $\langle \psi^{\uparrow} | \psi^{\uparrow} \rangle = \langle \psi^{\downarrow} | \psi^{\downarrow} \rangle = 1$, so that $|\alpha^{\uparrow}|^2 + |\alpha^{\downarrow}|^2 = 1$. The tensor product $\otimes$ separates the *two dimensions (degrees of freedom)*, spin and space, and will allow us to view the resulting correlations between these two degrees of freedom more clearly. The time development corresponding to a translation by l on the larger state-space of the spin-½ particle can now be described by the unitary operator $U = \exp(-2iS_z \otimes Pl)$. This operator induces a kind of conditional translation of the particle depending on its internal spin degrees of freedom. In particular, if the spin of the particle is initially in the state $|\uparrow\rangle$ so that its wave function is of the form $|\uparrow\rangle \otimes | \psi_{x_0}^{\uparrow} \rangle$, then application of U transforms it to $|\uparrow\rangle \otimes | \psi_{x_0-l}^{\uparrow} \rangle$, and the particle will be shifted to the right by l. If the spin of the particle is in the state $| \downarrow \rangle$, that is, the total wave function is given by $|\downarrow\rangle \otimes | \psi_{x_0}^{\downarrow} \rangle$, then the translation operator will transform it to $|\downarrow\rangle \otimes | \psi_{x_0+l}^{\downarrow} \rangle$ and the particle will be shifted to the left. More interesting behavior occurs when the initial spin state of the particle, localized in x_0, is not in an eigenstate of S_z, but in a superposition $| \Psi_{\text{in}} \rangle = (\alpha^{\uparrow}|\uparrow\rangle + \alpha^{\downarrow}|\downarrow\rangle) \otimes |\psi_{x_0}\rangle$.

Application of the translation operator U will induce a superposition of positions $U|\Psi_{\text{in}}\rangle = \alpha^{\uparrow}|\uparrow\rangle \otimes |\psi_{x_0-l}\rangle + \alpha^{\downarrow}|\downarrow\rangle \otimes |\psi_{x_0+l}\rangle$. If at this point we decide to *measure* the spin in the S_z basis, the particle will be either in the state $|\uparrow\rangle \otimes | \psi_{x_0-l} \rangle$ localized around $x_0 + l$ with probability $p^{\uparrow} = |\alpha^{\uparrow}|^2$ or in the state $|\downarrow\rangle \otimes | \psi_{x_0-l} \rangle$ localized around $x_0 - l$ with probability $p^{\downarrow} = |\alpha^{\downarrow}|^2$. This procedure corresponds to a (biased) random walk of a particle on the line: we can imagine that a biased coin with probabilities of head/tail $p^{\uparrow}/p^{\downarrow}$ is flipped. Upon head, the particle moves right; and upon tail, the particle moves left. After this step, the particle is on average displaced by $l(p^{\uparrow} - p^{\downarrow})$. If we repeat this procedure T times (each time measuring the spin in the basis $\{| \uparrow \rangle, | \downarrow \rangle\}$ and re-initializing the spin in the state $\alpha^{\uparrow} | \uparrow \rangle + \alpha^{\downarrow} | \downarrow \rangle$), the particle will be displaced on average by an amount $\langle x \rangle = Tl(p^{\uparrow} - p^{\downarrow}) = Tl(|\alpha^{\uparrow}|^2 - |\alpha^{\downarrow}|^2)$, and the variance of its distribution on the line will be $\sigma^2 = 4Tl|\alpha^{\uparrow}|^2|\alpha^{\downarrow}|^2 = 4Tl^2 p^{\uparrow} p^{\downarrow}$.

This is exactly what we obtain if the particle performs a (biased) random walk on the line. We can imagine that the spin of the particle takes the role of a coin. This coin is "flipped," and the outcome determines the direction of the step in the random walk of the particle.

Now let us consider the following modification of this procedure. Instead of measuring the spin in the eigenbasis of S_z we will measure it in some rotated basis, given by two orthogonal vectors $\{|s_+\rangle,$

$|s_-\rangle\}$. Alternatively, we can *rotate* the spin by some angle θ before measuring it in the S_z eigenbasis. Let us take a more formal approach, and set up some more of the language used in quantum information theory. If we identify

$$|\uparrow\rangle = \begin{pmatrix} 1 \\ 0 \end{pmatrix}; \; |\downarrow\rangle = \begin{pmatrix} 0 \\ 1 \end{pmatrix}; \tag{16.24}$$

we can write

$$S_z = \frac{1}{2} \begin{pmatrix} 1 & 0 \\ 0 & -1 \end{pmatrix} = \frac{1}{2}(|\uparrow\rangle\langle\uparrow| - |\downarrow\rangle\langle\downarrow|) \tag{16.25}$$

A rotation of the spin can be described by the matrix

$$R(\theta) = \begin{pmatrix} \cos\theta & -\sin\theta \\ \sin\theta & \cos\theta \end{pmatrix} \tag{16.26}$$

Note that this is not the most general unitary transformation on a two-level system. A general (normalized) unitary is given by two parameters (θ, ϕ).

Let us denote the measurement in the S_z basis by M_z. To explore the effect of the suite of operations $M_z R(\theta) U$ on the initial state $|\Psi_{\text{in}}\rangle$, we have to slightly rewrite the operator U:

$$\begin{aligned} U &= \exp(-2iS_z \otimes Pl) \\ &= \exp[-i(|\uparrow\rangle\langle\uparrow| - |\downarrow\rangle\langle\downarrow|) \otimes Pl] \\ &= (|\uparrow\rangle\langle\uparrow| \otimes \exp(-iPl))(|\downarrow\rangle\langle\downarrow| \otimes \exp(iPl)) \end{aligned} \tag{16.27}$$

The second equality follows from the fact that $|\uparrow\rangle\langle\uparrow| \otimes Pl$ and $|\downarrow\rangle\langle\downarrow| \otimes Pl$ commute, together with the observation that $|\uparrow\rangle\langle\uparrow|$ and $|\downarrow\rangle\langle\downarrow|$, are projectors, so that $|\uparrow\rangle\langle\uparrow|^k = |\uparrow\rangle\langle\uparrow|$ and $|\downarrow\rangle\langle\downarrow|^k = |\downarrow\rangle\langle\downarrow|$ when we expand the exponential. The equality $\exp(A + B) = \exp(A)\exp(B)$ is true if A and B commute, that is,

AB = BA. Now

$$U|\Psi_{\text{in}}\rangle = \left(\alpha^\uparrow |\uparrow\rangle \otimes \exp(-iPl) + \alpha^\downarrow |\downarrow\rangle \otimes \exp(iPl)\right)|\psi_{x_0}\rangle \tag{16.28}$$

and applying $R(\theta)$ from the left gives

$$\left[\left(\alpha^\uparrow \cos\theta \exp(-iPl) - \alpha^\downarrow \sin\theta \exp(iPl)\right)|\uparrow\rangle + \left(\alpha^\uparrow \sin\theta \exp(-iPl) + \alpha^\downarrow \cos\theta \exp(iPl)\right)|\downarrow\rangle\right] \otimes |\psi_{x_0}\rangle \tag{16.29}$$

If the width Δx of the initial wave packet is much larger than the step length l, we can approximate $\exp(\pm iPl)|\psi_{x_0}\rangle \approx (I \pm iP0|\psi_{x_0}\rangle)$. With this in mind, we can establish the state of the particle after the measurement M_z:

$$M_z R(\theta) U|\Psi_{\text{in}}\rangle = \begin{cases} |\uparrow\rangle \otimes (I - iPl\delta^\uparrow)|\psi_{x_0}\rangle; \\ |\downarrow\rangle \otimes (I - iPl\delta^\downarrow)|\psi_{x_0}\rangle; \end{cases} \tag{16.30}$$

with probabilities $p^\uparrow = |\alpha^\uparrow \cos\theta - \alpha^\downarrow \sin\theta|^2$, $p^\downarrow = |\alpha^\uparrow \sin\theta + \alpha^\uparrow \cos\theta|^2$ and displacements

$$l\delta^\uparrow := l\frac{\alpha^\uparrow \cos\theta + \alpha^\downarrow \sin\theta}{\alpha^\uparrow \cos\theta - \alpha^\downarrow \sin\theta}; l\delta^\downarrow := l\frac{\alpha^\uparrow \sin\theta - \alpha^\downarrow \cos\theta}{\alpha^\uparrow \sin\theta + \alpha^\downarrow \cos\theta} \tag{16.31}$$

If the width Δx of the initial wave packet is much larger than $l\delta^\uparrow$ and $l\delta^\downarrow$, we can again approximate $(I - iPl\delta^{\uparrow,\downarrow}) \mid \psi_{x_0}\rangle \approx \exp(-iPl\delta^{\uparrow,\downarrow}) \mid \psi_{x_0}\rangle = \mid \psi_{x_0 - l\delta_{\uparrow,\downarrow}}\rangle$.

Now, it is crucial to note that the displacement of the particle in one of the two cases, $l\delta^\uparrow$ say, can be made much *larger* than l. For instance, we may choose $\tan\theta = \mid\alpha^\uparrow/\alpha^\downarrow\mid(1 + \varepsilon)$ with $l/\Delta x \ll \mid\varepsilon\mid \ll 1$. Then the displacement of the particle in case we measured $\mid\uparrow\rangle$ will be $l\delta^\uparrow \approx -2l/\varepsilon$, which can be several orders of magnitude larger than l. However, this event is "rare": the probability of measuring $\mid\uparrow\rangle$ is $p^\uparrow \approx \mid\alpha^\uparrow\alpha^\downarrow\mid^2\varepsilon^2$. For the same choice of parameters, the probability of measuring $\mid\downarrow\rangle$ is $p^\downarrow \approx 1 - \mid\alpha^\uparrow\alpha^\downarrow\mid^2\varepsilon^2$, and the displacement in that event is $\delta^\downarrow \approx l(\mid\alpha^\uparrow\mid^2 - \mid\alpha^\downarrow\mid^2) + O(l\varepsilon)$. For the average displacement $p^\uparrow l\delta^\uparrow + p^\downarrow l\delta^\downarrow$, we get as before $l(\mid\alpha^\uparrow\mid^2 - \mid\alpha^\downarrow\mid^2)$, and similarly the variance of the walk will be unchanged. We have the effect that even though our translation operation displaces by only l, in some (rare) cases the particle will jump much further than l.

This is strikingly different from any classical behavior. Quantum mechanics allows us to post-select events that cannot be observed classically. Even though these events are rare events, we cannot create a classical setup that allows us to observe such an effect. In what follows, we will expand and show how variations on this phenomenon might be useful in the context of modern quantum information processing.

16.4.1 The Quantum Random Walk

In order to use analogies with the discussions in the previous sections, we will start by defining our model in one dimension, on the line or the circle. However, the definitions carry over to the general case with slight modifications, which we will mention later.

Let $\mathcal{H}_P$ be the Hilbert space spanned by the positions of the particle. For a line with grid length 1, this space is spanned by basis states $\{\mid i\rangle : i \in Z\}$; if we work on a circle of size N, we have $\mathcal{H}_P = \{\mid i\rangle : i = 0...N - 1\}$. States in this basis will take the role of the wave function $\mid\psi\rangle$ with $\mid i\rangle$ corresponding to a particle localized in position i. We will not be concerned any more about the width of the distribution of the wave function – our model describes unitary transformations of the states of a finite Hilbert space $\mathcal{H}$, and the notion of a particle is used only to guide our intuition from now on. Yet later, when we talk about the physical implementation of the quantum random walk, we will see that we can approximate the states of this mathematical model by particles (atoms, photons, etc.) with wave functions of finite width.

The position Hilbert space $\mathcal{H}_P$ is augmented by a "coin" space $\mathcal{H}_C$ spanned by two basis states $\{\mid\uparrow\rangle, \mid\downarrow\rangle\}$, which take the role of the spin-½ space in the previous section. States of the total system are in the space $\mathcal{H} = \mathcal{H}_C \otimes \mathcal{H}_P$ as before. The conditional translation of the system (taking on the role of $\exp(-2iS_z \otimes Pl)$) can be described by the following unitary operation:

$$S = \mid\uparrow\rangle\langle\uparrow\mid \otimes \sum_i \mid i + 1\rangle\langle i\mid + \mid\downarrow\rangle\langle\downarrow\mid \otimes \sum_i \mid i - 1\rangle\langle i\mid; \tag{16.32}$$

where the index i runs over Z in the case of a line or $0 \leq i \leq N - 1$ in the case of a circle. In the latter case, we always identify 0 and N, so all arithmetic is performed modulo N. S transforms the basis state $\mid\uparrow\rangle \otimes \mid i\rangle$ to $\mid\uparrow\rangle \otimes \mid i + 1\rangle$ and $\mid\downarrow\rangle \otimes \mid i\rangle$ to $\mid\downarrow\rangle \otimes \mid i - 1\rangle$.

The first step of the random walk is a rotation in the coin space, which in analogy with the classical random walk we will call a "coin flip" C. The unitary transformation C is very arbitrary, and we can define a rich family of walks with different behavior by modifying C. For the moment, we will want C to be "unbiased" in the following sense. Assume we would initialize the walk in a localized state $\mid 0\rangle$ with the coin in one of the basis states, say $\mid\uparrow\rangle$. If we chose to measure the coin register of the walk in the (standard) basis $\{\mid\uparrow\rangle, \mid\downarrow\rangle\}$ after one iteration (coin flip C followed by translation S), we want to obtain the classical probability distribution of the unbiased walk, namely, a translation to the right ($|1\rangle$) with probability ½ and a step to the left ($|-1\rangle$) otherwise. A frequently used balanced unitary coin is the so-called Hadamard coin H

$$H = \frac{1}{2^{1/2}} \begin{pmatrix} 1 & 1 \\ 1 & -1 \end{pmatrix} \tag{16.33}$$

It is easy to see that the Hadamard coin is balanced:

$$|\uparrow\rangle \otimes |0\rangle \xrightarrow{H} \frac{1}{2^{1/2}} (|0\rangle + |1\rangle) \otimes |0\rangle$$

$$\xrightarrow{S} \frac{1}{2^{1/2}} (|\uparrow\rangle \otimes |1\rangle + |\downarrow\rangle \otimes |-1\rangle) \tag{16.34}$$

Measuring the coin state in the standard basis gives each of $\{|\uparrow\rangle \otimes |1\rangle, |\downarrow\rangle \otimes |-1\rangle\}$ with probability $1/2$. After this measurement, there is no correlation left between the positions. If we continued the QW with such a measurement at each iteration, we obtain the plain classical random walk on the line (or on the circle). In the quantum random walk, we will of course not measure the coin register during intermediate iterations, but rather keep the quantum correlations between different positions and let them interfere in subsequent steps. The quantum random walk of T steps is defined as the transformation U^T, where U, acting on $\mathcal{H} = \mathcal{H}_C \otimes \mathcal{H}_P$, is given by $U = S \cdot (C \otimes I)$.

To illustrate the departure of the QW from its classical counterpart, let us evolve the walk (without intermediate measurements) for some steps starting in the initial state $|\Phi_{in}\rangle = |\downarrow\rangle \otimes |0\rangle$ and study the induced probability distribution on the positions.

$$|\Phi_{in}\rangle \xrightarrow{U} \frac{1}{2^{1/2}} (|\uparrow\rangle \otimes |1\rangle - |\downarrow\rangle \otimes |-1\rangle)$$

$$\xrightarrow{U} \frac{1}{2} (|\uparrow\rangle \otimes |2\rangle - (|\uparrow\rangle - |\downarrow\rangle) \otimes |0\rangle + |\downarrow\rangle \otimes |-2\rangle)$$

$$\xrightarrow{U} \frac{1}{2(2^{1/2})} (|\uparrow\rangle \otimes |3\rangle + |\downarrow\rangle \otimes |1\rangle + |\uparrow\rangle \otimes |-1\rangle - 2|\downarrow\rangle \otimes |-1\rangle - 1|\downarrow\rangle \otimes |-3\rangle).$$

$$\tag{16.35}$$

After $T = 100$ steps of the QW starting in $|\downarrow\rangle \otimes |0\rangle$, the probability distribution looks as shown already in lower part of Figure 16.7. One can clearly discern a two-peaked distribution. The first thing to notice is that the quantum random walk induces an asymmetric probability distribution on the positions; it is "drifting" to the left. This asymmetry arises from the fact that the Hadamard coin treats the two directions $|\uparrow\rangle$ and $|\downarrow\rangle$ differently; it multiplies the phase by -1 only in the case of $|\downarrow\rangle$. Intuitively, this induces more cancelations for paths going rightward (destructive interference), whereas particles moving to the left interfere constructively. There are two ways to mend this asymmetry. Inspecting Eq. (16.34), which describes the first step of the Hadamard walk starting in $|\uparrow\rangle \otimes |0\rangle$ (instead of in $|\Phi_{in}\rangle = |\downarrow\rangle \otimes |0\rangle$ as in Eq. (16.35)) and iterating the walk in Eq. (16.34) more, we see that the walk starting in $|\uparrow\rangle \otimes |0\rangle$ has a drift to the right side, exactly opposite to the walk in Eq. (16.35), as indicated in upper part of Figure 16.7. To obtain a symmetric distribution, we can start the walk in a superposition of $|\uparrow\rangle$ and $|\downarrow\rangle$ and make sure that these two drifts do not interfere with each other. This can be achieved starting in the symmetric state $|\Phi_{sym}\rangle = 2^{-1/2}(|\uparrow\rangle + i|\downarrow\rangle) \otimes |0\rangle$. Since the Hadamard walk does not introduce any complex amplitudes, the

Figure 16.8 The probability distribution obtained from a computer simulation of the Hadamard walk with a symmetric initial condition [66]. The number of steps in the walk was taken to be 100. Only the probability at the even points is plotted, since the odd points have probability zero. *Source:* Nayak and Vishwanath [66].

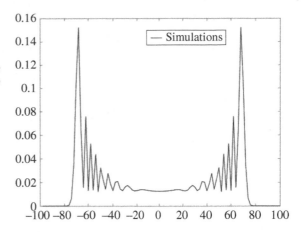

trajectories from $|\uparrow\rangle$ will stay real, and the ones from $|\downarrow\rangle$ will be purely imaginary; they will hence not interfere with each other, making the total distribution symmetric.

Another solution to eliminate asymmetry of the walk is to use a different (balanced) coin, namely

$$Y = \frac{1}{2^{1/2}} \begin{pmatrix} 1 & i \\ i & 1 \end{pmatrix} \tag{16.36}$$

It is not hard to see that this coin treats $|\uparrow\rangle$ and $|\downarrow\rangle$ in the same way and does not bias the walk, independently of its initial coin state. Figure 16.8 shows the probability distribution on the positions of a symmetric QW [66].

16.4.2 Quantum Random Walks on General Graphs

Various aspects of quantum random walks on graphs and in higher dimensions have recently been studied in [67–72]. As a start, let us define the random walk for d-regular graphs first. These are graphs with vertex degree d; that is, each vertex has d outgoing edges. The coin Hilbert space $\mathcal{H}_P$ is of dimension d. For every vertex, let us internally label all the outgoing edges with $j \in 1 \ldots d$ such that each edge has a distinct label. Let us call e_v^j an edge $e = (v, w)$ that on v's end is labeled by j. The state associated with a vertex v pointing along an edge labeled j is $|j\rangle \otimes |v\rangle$ (corresponding to $|\uparrow\rangle \otimes |i\rangle$ on the line or circle). Now we can define a conditional shift operation S

$$S|i\rangle \otimes |v\rangle = \begin{cases} |j\rangle \otimes |w\rangle; & \text{if } e_v^j = (v, w), \\ 0, & \text{otherwise:} \end{cases} \tag{16.37}$$

S moves the particle from v to w if the edge (v, w) is labeled by j on v's side. If the graph is not regular, we can still define S in the same way if we let d be the maximum degree of any vertex in the graph. Figure 16.9 shows a graph and a valid labeling.

The coin flip C is now a d-dimensional unitary transformation, which gives a lot of freedom in the choice of the coin-flip operation. The choice of C will have to be guided by the specifics and symmetries of the random walk we wish to obtain. We have already seen that even in the simple case of a walk on a line, the choice of the coin operator can have a serious impact on the shape of the resulting distribution, and this effect is only amplified in higher dimensions [69].

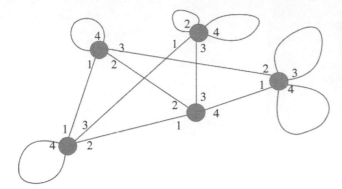

Figure 16.9 A graph with various degrees and a labeling of the edges for each vertex. Note that the label associated with an edge (v, w) can be different at v's end from that at w's end. Self-loops have been added to the graph to make it regular so that a single four-dimensional coin can be used.

If the graph is not regular, that is, if the vertices have varying degrees, we can use one of several tricks to define a random walk with a coin. We can add self-loops to each vertex of degree less than d (d is the maximal degree) and include them in the labeling (with the same label on both its ends), as in Figure 16.9. The shift applied to a self-loop will just keep the walk in place. Another option is to retain the irregularity of the graph and use different coin operators $C_{d'}$ (of different dimensions) for vertices of degree $d' \leq d$. In that case, the coin operation has to be conditioned on the position of the particle and can no longer be written in the separable form $(C \otimes I)$. However, whenever we can define the corresponding classical walk, we are able to define the QW and implement it efficiently on a quantum computer.

If we wish to retain the property in general graphs that the coin is balanced (i.e., every direction is obtained with equal probability if we measure the coin space), we can use the following coin that generalizes H:

$$
DFR = \frac{1}{d^{1/2}} \begin{pmatrix} 1 & 1 & 1 & \cdots & 1 \\ 1 & \omega & \omega^2 & \cdots & \omega^{d-1} \\ & & \ddots & & \\ 1 & \omega^{d-1} & \omega^{2(d-1)} & \cdots & \omega^{(d-1)(d-1)} \end{pmatrix}
\tag{16.38}
$$

The name of the coin "DFT" comes from "discrete Fourier transform." This transformation is a cornerstone in quantum algorithms and a building block for algorithms such as factoring. It has the property that it is efficiently implementable on a quantum computer. We will specify this statement more in the following text. Here, $\omega = \exp(2\pi i/d)$ is a d-th root of unity. Clearly, the unitary DFT coin transforms each direction into an equally weighted superposition of directions such that after measurement each of them is equally likely to be obtained (with probability $1/d$).

Figure 16.10 shows the hypercube in three dimensions, an example where a non-balanced coin is used. The vertices of the d-dimensional hypercube can be enumerated by d-bit strings of 0's and 1's. Two vertices given by two-bit strings are connected whenever they differ by exactly one bit (e.g., 001101 and 011101). If we define the *Hamming distance* $d_H(x, y)$ between two-bit strings x and y to be the minimum number of bits that need to be flipped to obtain y from x, then the hypercube connects all vertices of Hamming distance $d_H = 1$. The number of 1's in a bit string is called its *Hamming weight*.

The labeling of the edges of the hypercube can be chosen such that for each edge the labels from both sides coincide. Such labeling allows one to color the edges of a graph (with colors 1, 2, ..., d) such that the colors of the incident edges of a vertex are all different. It is a well-known fact from

Figure 16.10 The hypercube in d = 3 dimensions. Vertices correspond to 3-bit strings. Edges are labeled by 1, 2, 3 (boxed) according to which bit needs to be flipped to get from one vertex of the edge to the other.

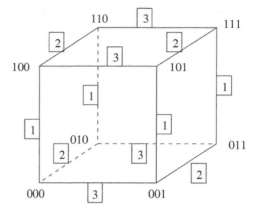

Figure 16.11 The classical simple random walk on the three-dimensional hypercube reduced to the walk on a line of four points. In the original walk, the transition probabilities are 1/3. If we bundle nodes of the same Hamming weight w_H to a single point on the line, we obtain a biased random walk on the line. The new transition probabilities for the walk on the line are indicated. For the walk on the d-dimensional hypercube, we can reduce the graph to a line of d + 1 vertices. The transition probability from vertex i to vertex i + 1 in the general case is given by $p_{i,i+1} = (d - i)/d$ and from i + 1 to i by $p_{i+1,i} = (i + 1)/d$.

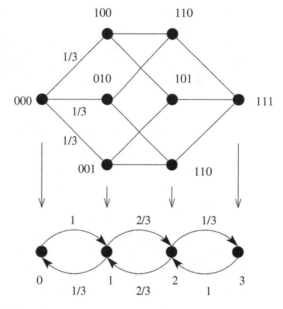

graph theory that every graph of maximum degree d can be consistently edge-colored with at most d + 1 colors. In the case of the d-dimensional hypercube, only d colors are needed.

The classical simple random walk on the hypercube (where in each step a neighboring vertex is chosen with probability 1/d) has a high symmetry. If we start the walk in the vertex 00 ... 0, for example, then all d vertices of Hamming weight 1 can be interchanged without modifying the random walk. Similarly, all vertices of equal distance from the starting vertex, that is, of equal Hamming weight, can be interchanged without changing the walk. This implies that all vertices of the same Hamming weight have the same weight in the probability distribution of the random walk. This allows us to "cumulate" all the vertices of the same Hamming weight into a single vertex and to reduce the symmetric random walk on the hypercube to a biased random walk on the line, as shown in Figure 16.11 for a three-dimensional hypercube. Such a reduction to the line will substantially simplify the analysis of the random walk when we are interested in questions like the speed of propagation of the random walk to the opposite corner.

If we wish to retain this symmetry property for the quantum random walk, it can be shown [67] that the only coins that are unitary and permutation symmetric are of the following form:

$$G_{a,b} = \begin{pmatrix} 1 & b & b & ... & b & b \\ b & a & b & ... & b & b \\ b & b & a & ... & b & b \\ & & & ... & & \\ b & b & b & ... & a & b \\ b & b & b & ... & b & a \end{pmatrix} \qquad (16.39)$$

where a and b are real, $1 - (2/d) \le |a| \le 1$, and $b = \pm(1 - a)$. Among all these coins, we will pick the coin G with $a = (2/d)\text{-}1$ and $b = 2/d$ and will sometimes call it the Grover coin (see Chapter 11). Among all coins $G_{a,b}$, this is the coin which is the farthest away from the identity operator ($G_{1,0} = I$). G is not a balanced coin because the probability of not changing directions ($p = [1 - (2/d)]^2$) is different from the probability of flipping to one of the $d - 1$ other directions ($p = 4/d^2$). If we start the QW in an equal superposition of all the directions and measure the coin space H_C after each iteration, the resulting (classical) walk will have a higher propensity to go back and forth on the same edge than to switch directions. However, the permutation invariance will allow us to reduce the QW on the hypercube to a QW on the line. This would not be possible if we used the d-dimensional DFT coin, for example. We will return to this graph later in the chapter.

16.4.3 Continuous-Time Quantum Random Walk

The discrete-time model of quantum random walks is only one way to intersperse quantum effects with random walks. Another route to generalize the phenomenon described above has been taken in [34, 73]. Although at the outset this concept seems remote from the discrete-time random walk we have described so far, in what follows we will see the similarities between the two approaches. The continuous-time random walk takes place entirely in the position space H_P. No coin space is needed and no coin is flipped. The intuition behind this model comes from continuous-time classical Markov chains. Let us illustrate this with the simple classical random walk on a graph with vertex set V. A step in the classical random walk can be described by a matrix M that transforms the probability distribution over V. The entries M_{ij} give the probability of going from i to j in one step of the walk. Let $p^t = \left(p_1^t, p_2^t, ...,p_{|V|}^t\right)$ be the probability distribution over the vertices of V at time T. Then $p_i^{t+1} = \sum_j M_{ij}p_j^t$, which means $p^{t+1} = Mp^t$.

The entries of M_{ij} are nonzero only if there is a nonzero probability of going from i to j, that is, when i and j are connected. The entry M_{ij} is the probability of going from i to j and is equal to $1/d_i$ (in the so-called "simple" random walk), where d_i is the degree of i. For instance, the matrix M for a simple random walk on a circle of N vertices is given by

$$M = \frac{1}{2} \begin{pmatrix} 0 & 1 & 0 & ... & 0 & 1 \\ 1 & 0 & 1 & 0 & ... & 0 \\ 0 & 1 & 0 & 1 & ... & 0 \\ & & \ddots & & & \\ 0 & ... & 1 & 0 & 1 & 0 \\ 0 & ... & 0 & 1 & 0 & 1 \\ 1 & 0 & ... & 0 & 1 & 0 \end{pmatrix} \qquad (16.40)$$

It transforms an initial state $p^0 = (1, 0, \ldots, 0)$, corresponding to a starting position of 0, to $p^1 = \left(0, \frac{1}{2}, \ldots, 0, \frac{1}{2}\right), p^2 = \left(\frac{1}{2}, 0, \frac{1}{4}, 0, \ldots, 0, \frac{1}{4}, 0\right), p^3 = \left(0, \frac{3}{8}, 0, \frac{1}{8}, 0, \ldots, 0, \frac{1}{8}, 0, \frac{3}{8}\right)$, and so on.

The process given by the iterations of M transforms the state at integer times only. To make the process continuous in time, we can assume that transitions can occur at all times and the jumping rate from a vertex to its neighbor is given by γ, a fixed, time-independent constant. This means that transitions between neighboring nodes occur with probability γ per unit time. The infinitesimal generator matrix H of such a process is given by

$$
\begin{aligned}
H_{ij} &= -\gamma; i \neq j \text{ and } i \text{ and } j \text{ connected;} \\
&= 0; \; i \neq j \text{ and } i \text{ and } j \text{ not connected;} \\
&= d_{i\gamma} \, i = j
\end{aligned}
\tag{16.41}
$$

If $p_i(t)$ denotes the probability of being at vertex i at time t; then the transitions can be described by a differential equation $dp_i(t)/dt = -\sum_j H_{i,j} p_j(t)$. Solving the equation, we obtain $p(t) = \exp(-Ht)p(0)$. Note the similar structures of H and M. In the theory of classical Markov chains, many connections between the discrete and continuous-time models can be made, and many of the quantities of interest, such as mixing times and absorption probability, exhibit similar behavior in both cases.

The idea in [34] was to carry this construction over to the quantum case. Their key idea is that the generator matrix will become the *Hamiltonian* of the process generating an evolution $U(t)$ as $U(t) = \exp(-iHt)$. If we start in some initial state $|\Psi_{in}\rangle$, evolve it under U for a time T and measure the positions of the resulting state, we obtain a probability distribution over the vertices of the graph as before.

With this definition in place, [34] studied the penetration of graphs by the quantum random walk. In [73], a finite graph is given where classical and QWs give an exponential separation in the *expected hitting time*. We will give this example here to illustrate yet another aspect of the difference between classical and quantum random walks, this time examining the expected hitting time of certain nodes in a graph. The expected hitting time between two points S and T in a graph is the time it takes the random walk on average to reach T starting at S. The graph G_n consists of two n-level binary trees glued together at their leaves, as seen in Figure 16.12.

We start the random walk at the root of the left tree. Rather than the hitting time, we study a slightly modified related quantity: the probability of hitting the root of the other (right) tree as a function of time. In other words, we are interested in how long it takes to propagate from the leftmost vertex to the rightmost vertex as a function of n.

Consider the classical random walk first. The vertices of G_n can be grouped in columns indexed by $j \in \{0, 1, \ldots, 2n\}$. Column 0 contains the root of the left tree, column 1 contains the two vertices connected to that root, and so on. Note that column n contains the 2^n vertices in the middle of the graph, and column $2n$ is the root at the right.

As in the example of the hypercube in Figure 16.11, the symmetry of the walk allows us to reduce it to a random walk on a line. We need only keep track of the probabilities of being in the columns. In the left tree, for $0 < j < n$, the probability of stepping from column j to column $j + 1$ is twice as great as the probability of stepping from column j to column $j - 1$. However, in the right tree, for $n < j < 2n$, the probability of stepping from column j to column $j + 1$ is half as great as the probability of stepping from column j to column $j - 1$. This means that if you start at the left root, you quickly move to the middle of the graph, but then it takes a time exponential in n to reach your destination. More precisely, starting in column 0, the probability of being in column $2n$ after any number of steps is less than 2^{-n}. This implies that the probability of reaching column $2n$ in a time that is polynomial in n must be exponentially small as a function of n.

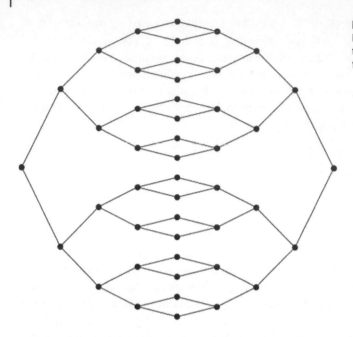

Figure 16.12 The graph G_4. Two binary trees of $n = 4$ levels are glued together at their leaves in a symmetric fashion. *Source:* Childs et al. [74].

We now analyze the QW on G_n [77] starting in the state corresponding to the left root and evolving with the Hamiltonian given by Eq. (16.41). With this initial state, the symmetries of H keep the evolution in a $(2n + 1)$-dimensional subspace of the $(2^{n+1} + 2^n - 2)$-dimensional Hilbert space. This subspace is spanned by states $|\tilde{j}\rangle$ (where $0 \leq \tilde{j} \leq 2n$), the uniform superposition over all vertices in column j, that is,

$$|\tilde{j}\rangle = \frac{1}{N_j^{1/2}} \sum_{a \in column\, j} |a\rangle \tag{16.42}$$

where

$$N_j = \begin{cases} 2^j & 0 \leq j \leq n \\ 2^{2n-j}, & n \leq j \leq 2n \end{cases} \tag{16.43}$$

In this basis, the nonzero matrix elements of H are

$$\langle \tilde{j} | H | \tilde{j} \pm 1 \rangle = -2^{1/2} \gamma; \tag{16.44}$$

$$\langle \tilde{j} | H | \tilde{j} \rangle = \begin{cases} 2\gamma, & j = 0, n, 2n, \\ 3\gamma, & \text{otherwise,} \end{cases} \tag{16.45}$$

shown in Figure 16.13 (for $n = 4$) as a quantum random walk on a line with $2n + 1$ vertices.

As a first attempt to solve this reduced problem, we can approximate the walk on this finite line by a walk on an infinite and furthermore homogeneous line by extending the Hamiltonian and replacing all diagonal entries of 2 by 3 as seen in Figure. 16.14.

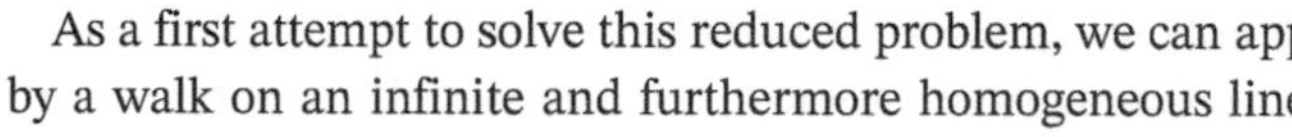

$$\underset{2}{\bullet} \overset{-\sqrt{2}}{\underset{3}{\bullet}} \overset{-\sqrt{2}}{\underset{3}{\bullet}} \overset{-\sqrt{2}}{\underset{3}{\bullet}} \overset{-\sqrt{2}}{\underset{2}{\bullet}} \overset{-\sqrt{2}}{\underset{3}{\bullet}} \overset{-\sqrt{2}}{\underset{3}{\bullet}} \overset{-\sqrt{2}}{\underset{3}{\bullet}} \overset{-\sqrt{2}}{\underset{2}{\bullet}}$$

Figure 16.13 The elements of the Hamiltonian of the quantum random walk on G_n when reduced to the line for $n = 4$. For convenience, g is set to 1.

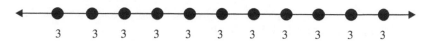

Figure 16.14 Approximation of the finite line by an infinite homogeneous line. The diagonal elements of H are all set equal to 3. The off-diagonal elements connecting the vertices are still $-2^{1/2}$.

By solving this modified problem, the solution can readily be given in terms of Bessel functions [74] for a much more complete treatment. It can be seen that the speed of propagation of the random walk on the infinite homogeneous line is linear in time T. In other words there are constants $a < b$ such that when $T \in [an, bn]$, then the probability of measuring the walk at a distance of $2n + 1$ from the starting point (i.e., at the root of the right tree starting from the root of the left tree) is on the order of $1/n^{1/2}$.

16.4.4 Searching Large-Scale Graphs

S − T connectivity: Let us illustrate how random walks help solve the $s − t$ (source-target) connectivity problem. Given an undirected graph G with a vertex set V of size $|V|$, the problem is to decide whether two vertices s and t are connected or not. This problem is a natural abstraction of a number of graph search problems used in the study of large-scale communication networks.

It is easy to see that a standard graph search algorithm that keeps track of all the vertices the search has visited can do the job in a time linear in the number of edges of the graph. Let us assume now that our computer (e.g., a mobile device) is limited in memory and can keep track only of a few vertices at a time. It can perform a random walk on the vertices of the graph starting in s. At each step of the walk, the computer chooses one of the adjacent edges with equal probability and moves to the vertex that is connected to the current position by that edge. If the computer reaches t in the course of the walk, it outputs YES. If it never sees t after $T = |V|^3$ steps, it outputs NO.

Clearly, the machine will never output YES when s and t are not in the same connected component. It turns out that a simple random walk on a graph with $|V|$ vertices has at least probability 1/2 of hitting any given vertex starting from any other in $|V|^3$ steps. This means that our machine will be making an error with probability 1/2 when it outputs NO. We can make this probability arbitrarily small by repeating the algorithm several times. Assume that s and t are connected. Then the error probability of an algorithm that iterates the above procedure k times is simply the probability of outputting NO k times. Since we assume that each iteration is independent of the previous one, this probability is given by $(1/2)^k$. If we want to make this probability very small (ε), we need to repeat the algorithm approximately $k = \log(1/\varepsilon)$ times.

2-SAT: Let us give another computational problem that can be solved by random walks on graphs, namely, 2-SAT. Let us define more generally the class of decision problems called SAT. In an instance of SAT, we are given a set of logical clauses $C_1,. ..., C_m$. The Boolean inputs are the variables $X_1, X_2,. ..., X_n$, which can take the values 0 or 1. They can appear in either uncomplemented (X_i) or complemented ($\neg X_i$) form in the clauses. A clause is said to be satisfied (SAT) if at least one of the variables in it is true: an unnegated variable X_i is true if $X_i = 0$, and a negated variable $\neg X_i$ is true if $X_i = 1$. For example, the clause $C = X_1 \vee \neg X_2 \vee X_3$ is not satisfied only if $X_1 X_2 X_3 = 101$. We want to know if all the clauses can be satisfied simultaneously by some assignment of 0 and 1 for $X_1, ..., X_n$ (then we say that the formula $C_1 \wedge C_2 \wedge .. \wedge C_m$ is satisfiable and output YES). The class 2-SAT is the class of all SAT decision problems where each clause contains only two variables. For example, take the following instance of 2-SAT on X_1, X_2, X_3: $\Phi(X_1, X_2,$

$X_3) = (X_1 \lor \neg X_2) \land (\neg X_1 \lor X_3) \land (X_2 \lor X_3) \land (\neg X_1 \lor \neg X_3)$. The underlying decision problem has the answer YES, and a satisfying assignment is $X_1 X_2 X_3 = 110$.

Let us now give a random walk algorithm that solves 2-SAT in a time that is proportional to n^2. To simplify matters, imagine that our formula is satisfiable and that it has a single truth assignment (in the above example, this is 110). The algorithm picks a random assignment of 0, 1 for the variables $X_1, ..., X_n$. It checks the clauses one by one if they are satisfied until it either runs out of clauses (this means the assignment was satisfied; the algorithm stops and outputs YES) or it finds a clause C that is not satisfied. Assume the two variables in the clause are X_i and X_j. In the true assignment, one of these two variables must be flipped (0 1). Now the algorithm chooses one of the two variables X_i or X_j randomly and flips it. This is the new assignment, and the algorithm restarts a new checking of the clauses one by one, and so on. Let us see what happens to the Hamming distance between the true assignment (110 in our example) and the current assignment of the algorithm when we flip X_i or X_j. In the true assignment, one of the variables X_i, X_j must be flipped (since it satisfies the clause C). So, with probability 1/2, the algorithm flips the right variable. In this case, the Hamming distance between the new assignment and the true assignment has decreased by 1. Or the algorithm flips the wrong variable, in which case the Hamming distance increases by 1. So we are faced with a random walk on the Hamming distances with transition probabilities 1/2. It is well known that such a walk on a line of length n will hit the corner with high probability after $T \sim n^2$ steps. Figure 16.15 illustrates the algorithm for our example.

Although this random walk algorithm is not the optimal one to solve 2-SAT, it is very instructive. Many randomized algorithms can be viewed as random walks. The efficiency of these random algorithms is then closely related to the expected *hitting time* from one vertex (the initial state) to another (the solution). In fact, the best-known algorithm for 3-SAT [75] relies on a sophisticated version of this random walk idea. If a quantum random walk could improve the hitting time on certain graphs, this could give rise to efficient quantum algorithms for problems that cannot be solved efficiently on a classical computer. It is yet another incentive to study the behavior of quantum random walks.

Classical random walks: Let us state without proofs some known facts about random walks on graphs [76]. A simple random walk on an undirected graph, $G(V, E)$, is described by repeated

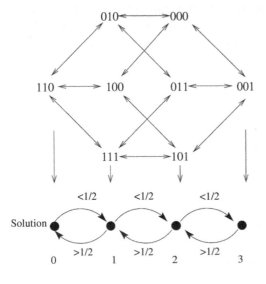

Figure 16.15 A random walk on assignments to the 2-SAT formula of our example. Each step increases or decreases the Hamming distance to the true assignment 110 by 1. This gives rise to a random walk on the line.

applications of a stochastic matrix M, where $M_{ij} = 1/d_i$ if (i, j) is an edge in G and d_i the degree of i (we use the notation introduced earlier in this section). If G is connected and non-bipartite, then the distribution of the random walk, $p^T = M^T p^0$, converges to a stationary distribution π that is independent of the initial distribution p^0. For a d-regular G (all nodes have the same degree, d), the limiting probability distribution is uniform over the nodes of the graph.

In many computational problems, the solution can be found if we are able to sample from a set of objects according to some distribution. This problem is often approached by setting up a random walk on a graph whose nodes are the objects we want to sample from. The graph and the walk are set up in such a way that the limiting distribution is exactly the distribution we wish to sample from. To sample, we now start the walk in some random initial point and let it evolve. This type of algorithm is only efficient if the random walk approaches the limiting distribution fast.

There are many definitions that capture the rate of convergence to the limiting distribution. A survey can be found in [77]. A frequently used quantity is the mixing time, given by $M_\varepsilon = min \{T \mid \forall t \geq T; \ p^0 : \|p^t - \pi\| \leq \varepsilon\}$, where we use the total variation distance to measure the distance between two distributions p, q: $\|p - q\| = \sum_i |p_i - q_i|$. It turns out that the mixing time is related to the gap between the largest eigenvalue $\lambda_1 = 1$ of the stochastic matrix M and the second-largest eigenvalue λ_2 in the following way [77]

$$\frac{\lambda_2}{(1 - \lambda_2) \ log \ 2\varepsilon} \leq M_\varepsilon \leq \frac{1}{(1 - \lambda_2)} \left(max_i \ log \ \pi_i^{-1} + log \ \varepsilon^{-1} \right) \tag{16.46}$$

This powerful theorem provides a very useful connection between mixing times and the second-largest eigenvalue λ_2 of the transition matrix M. In particular, it shows that λ_2 is the only eigenvalue of M that really matters to determine the mixing behavior of the walk. This will be very different in the quantum case.

Circle: It is well known that for the simple random walk on an N-circle, the mixing time is the quadratic $M_\varepsilon \sim N^2 \ log \ (1/\varepsilon)$. Similarly, the expected time T we need to run the walk such that starting at a vertex i we hit a certain vertex j with probability close to 1 is $T \sim N^2$.

Hypercube: For the d-dimensional hypercube defined above, the mixing time scales with d as $M_\varepsilon \sim d \ log \ d \ log \ (1/\varepsilon)$. The expected hitting time T from one corner of the hypercube, say 00. ... 0, to its opposite, 11. ... 1, scales exponentially with the dimension d as $T \sim 2^d$. We will see a sharp quantum improvement here.

Quantum random walks – the circle: The first and perhaps easiest finite graph to explore with quantum random walks is the circle of N vertices [78]. This example has most of the features of walks on general graphs.

Recall that any classical random walk approaches a stationary distribution independent of its initial state; the classical random walk loses its memory. This cannot be true for the quantum random walk. All transformations are unitary and hence reversible, and therefore the walk can never lose its recollection of the initial state and therefore it does not converge to a stationary distribution. To be able to speak of mixing toward a stationary distribution, we have to introduce some "forgetting" into the definitions. There is a standard way to do this, the so-called Cesàro limit. Instead of studying the probability distribution p^t induced by the random walk after a measurement at time t and its limit as t grows, we pick a time s, $0 < s \leq t$, uniformly at random. That is, our probability distribution c^t is an average distribution over all measurement results between 1 and t: $c^t = (1/t)\sum_{s=1}^{t} p^s$. With these definitions in place, it is not very hard to see that c^t converges to a stationary distribution. We will show this below for the Hadamard walk on the circle [78] (also to give an idea about the kind of calculations involved in these types of problems), but the result is true for all finite graphs.

In order to analyze the behavior of the QW, we follow its wave-like patterns using the eigenvectors and eigenvalues of the unitary evolution U_t. To observe its classical behavior, we collapse the wave vector at time t, $| \Psi_t \rangle = U^t | \Psi_0 \rangle$, into a probability vector p^t. The probability of measuring the particle in position i at time t, $p_i^t = |\langle \uparrow, i | \Psi_t \rangle|^2 + | \langle \downarrow, i | \Psi_t \rangle|^2$, where we write $| \uparrow, i \rangle$ short for $| \uparrow \rangle \otimes | i \rangle$ and similarly for $| \downarrow, i \rangle$. Let $\{(\lambda_k, | v_k \rangle): k = 1..2N\}$ be the eigenvalues and eigenvectors of U. Note that $\lambda_k^* = \lambda_k^{-1}$ because U is unitary. Expanding the initial state $| \Psi_0 \rangle = \sum_{k=1}^{2N} a_k | v_k \rangle$, we obtain $| \Psi_t \rangle = U^t | \Psi_0 \rangle = \sum_{k=1}^{2N} a_k \lambda_k^t | v_k \rangle$. Putting this all together, we get for the i-th component

$$c_i^t = \frac{1}{t} \sum_{s=1}^t \sum_{\alpha=\uparrow,\downarrow} \sum_{k,l=1}^{2N} a_k a_l^* \left(\lambda_k \lambda_l^*\right)^S \langle \alpha, i | v_k \rangle \langle v_l | \alpha, i \rangle \qquad (16.47)$$

In the limit $t \to \infty$, we have

$$\frac{1}{t} \sum_{s=1}^t \left(\lambda_k \lambda_l^*\right)^S \to \begin{cases} 1; & \lambda_k = \lambda_l, \\ \lim_{t \to \infty} \dfrac{1}{t\left(1 - \left(\lambda_k \lambda_l^*\right)\right)} = 0; & \lambda_k \neq \lambda_l, \end{cases} \qquad (16.48)$$

and hence

$$c_i^t \overset{t \to \infty}{\to} \sum_{\alpha=\uparrow,\downarrow} \sum_{k,l=1; \lambda_k=\lambda_l}^{2N} a_k a_l^* \langle \alpha, i | v_k \rangle \langle v_l | \alpha, i \rangle =: \pi_i \qquad (16.49)$$

In the case of non-degenerate eigenvalues λ_k, Eq. (16.48) simplifies further to $\pi_i = \sum_{\alpha=\uparrow,\downarrow} \sum_{k=1}^{2N} |a_k|^2 |\langle \alpha, i | v_k \rangle|^2$.

Equations (16.47) and (16.49) already reveal some crucial differences between classical walks and QWs. Whereas in the classical case the stationary distribution π_j is independent of the initial state of the walk, in the QW this is not the case in general, as is demonstrated by the presence of the expansion coefficients a_k in the expression for π_i. However, in the case of the circle (and many other graphs from a family called Cayley graphs), the stationary distribution is uniform and independent of the staring state as long as this state is localized in one position [78]. Cayley graphs are graphs corresponding to Abelian groups: the group is given by a set of generators. Each node of the graph represents an element of the group, and two nodes are connected if the corresponding elements can be obtained from each other by applying one of the generators. Another remarkable difference is the dependence of the mixing time, the rate of convergence to π, on *all* eigenvalues of U. Remember that in the classical case the mixing time was governed only by the second-largest eigenvalue of the transition matrix M. As can be seen from Eq. (16.47), the rate of convergence to π in the quantum case is governed by the terms

$$\frac{1}{t} \sum_{s=1}^t \left(\lambda_k \lambda_l^*\right)^S = \frac{1 - \left(\lambda_k \lambda_l^*\right)^t}{t\left(1 - \left(\lambda_k \lambda_l^*\right)\right)} \leq \frac{1}{t | \lambda_k - \lambda_l |} \qquad (16.50)$$

All of these sums over pairs of eigenvalues enter Eq. (16.47), and so the mixing time is determined by all $|\lambda_k - \lambda_l|$. It is possible to bound the mixing time M_ε of the quantum random walk on the circle as $M_\varepsilon \leq (N \log N)/\varepsilon^3$ with some additional calculus [78]. This gives a nearly quadratic speedup over the classical walk on the circle, which mixes in a time that is proportional to N^2. We have found yet another "quantum advantage": any algorithm that uses a random walk on a circle can be made quadratically faster on a quantum computer!

We might ask if there are graphs for which we can achieve even more drastic speedups. In computer science, the transition between an easy and a hard problem is made between polynomial time and exponential time. Problems that take exponential time to solve are hard (the resources to solve them do not scale well with their size) problems that take only polynomial amount of time are "easy." The interesting question is now: can we find graphs such that the QW mixes exponentially faster than its classical counterpart? Unfortunately, the answer is no in all but possibly very contrived cases. As shown by Aharonov et al. [78] the QW mixes at most quadratically faster. Yet this is not the end of all hopes for exponential speedup, as we will see in the next section.

The hypercube: It is possible to calculate the eigen spectrum of several matrices U corresponding to a random walk on a graph with some coin C. Moore and Russell [67] analyzed the mixing time of the walk on the hypercube along the lines of the previous paragraph, both in the discrete-time case as well as in the continuous one. Their results for the mixing time are not very encouraging, though. The hypercube is one of the graphs that mixes fast to the uniform distribution in the classical case already (it belongs to a class of so-called expander graphs, which all share this property), namely, $M_\varepsilon \sim d \log d$.

The discrete-time QW turns out to do worse: its mixing time M_ε is at least $d^{3/2}/\varepsilon$. Even more dramatically, the continuous-time QW on the hypercube does not converge to the uniform distribution at all.

We have mentioned another quantity of crucial interest in the study of random walks: the expected hitting time. We have already shown the importance of fast hitting to solve some algorithmic problems. It is here that we may hope to achieve great quantum advantage: the classical random walk on the hypercube takes exponential time to hit its opposite corner.

In the quantum world, the notion of hitting can be made precise in several ways [68]. In order to know whether a walk hits a certain point, measurements need to be made, yet we do not wish to measure the position of the walk completely in order to not kill its quantum coherences and make it classical. In [68] two ways to define hitting time are presented: either we can wait for a certain time T (which we somehow determine in advance) and then measure the walk. If the probability of being in the node of interest is close to 1, we can call T a hitting time. To circumvent the problem of knowing T in advance, we can alternatively use a definition similar to the absorbing wall. At each step, a measurement is performed that only determines if the walk is in the node of interest or not. If it is found there, the walk is stopped. We will call T a hitting time if the walk has stopped before time T with high probability. In the classical case, all these notions of hitting time from one corner of the hypercube to its opposite are exponential in d. Kempe [68] shows that the behavior of the quantum discrete-time walk is indeed crucially different: the expected hitting time (both notions) from a corner to its opposite turns out to be polynomial in the dimension d. This is an exponential separation of the classical and quantum behavior, similar to what we have seen on the graph G_n for the continuous-time QW. It remains to be seen how this speedup can be harnessed algorithmically.

An oracle separation: The first successful attempt to make an algorithmic statement using exponentially faster quantum hitting times is given in [74]. They provide a so-called oracle separation using the example described in Section 16.4.3. We have seen that the continuous-time QW penetrates the glued trees from root to root exponentially faster than the classical walk. This can be made into an exponential separation of classical and quantum query complexity in an oracle problem. This means the following: we are given an oracle (in the form of a black box that we cannot open) that we can query with some input to get a specific answer. For instance, in database search setups, the oracle encodes a database with one marked item (like a telephone book where we happen to know one specific phone number and wish to know whom it belongs to).

Given the input string x (a possible name) as a query, the oracle will reply 0 if x is not marked (does not belong to the phone number) or 1 if it is the item we are looking for. Imagine that each such query costs a fixed amount; it is our task then to minimize the number of queries. It has been

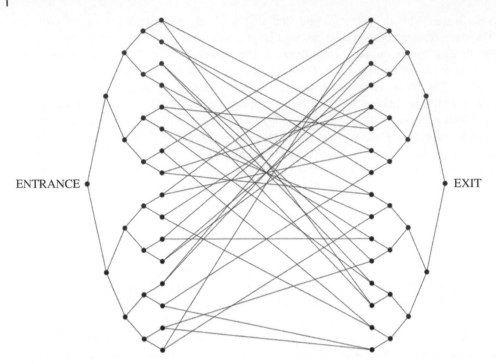

Figure 16.16 The modified graph of Figure 16.12. A big random cycle has been inserted between the two binary trees. This makes the classical task of penetrating the graph from root to root exponentially hard [74]. *Source:* Childs et al. [74].

shown that a quantum computer (which can ask a query "in superposition") can find the marked item with only $N^{1/2}$ queries, where N is the number of items, whereas any classical algorithm will require on the order of N queries.

In [74] an oracle was constructed that encodes a graph similar to the one in Figure 16.12. It turns out that there are classical algorithms (random walks that keep track of the valence of vertices they visit) that can penetrate the graph of Figure 16.12 in polynomial time. To make the task classically hard, the graph has to be modified by inserting a huge cycle between the trees, as in Figure 16.16.

The oracle now encodes the structure of the graph: every node of the graph has a name unknown to us. We are given the name of the right root and wish to find the name of the left root. Queried with the name of some vertex, the oracle outputs the names of the neighbors of this vertex. Classically, this oracle has to be queried exponentially many times in n (the number of levels of the tree) to obtain the name of the root of the left tree starting with the name of the root of the right tree. Intuitively, the best way to proceed is to ask the oracle for the names of the neighbors of the root. With the answer, we ask for the names of the neighbors of one of these neighbors, and so on, making our way through the graph in the form of a random walk. We have seen that it takes an expected time that is exponential in n for the classical random walk to hit the opposite root. It can be shown [74] that this naive way of making our way through the graph is the best a classical algorithm can do. Using the continuous quantum walk (QW) to find the succession of (quantum) queries to the oracle, the problem can be solved with only polynomially many queries using a quantum computer [74]. For this problem, we have found an exponential separation between classical and quantum power based on quantum random walks.

References

1 Kimble, H.J. (Jun. 2008). The quantum internet. *Nature* **453** (7198): 1023–1030.

2 Nguyen, H.V., Viet, H., Babar, Z. et al. (2017). Towards the quantum internet: generalized quantum network coding for large-scale quantum communication networks. *IEEE Access* **5**: 17288–17308.

3 Sun, Q.-C., Mao, Y.-L., Chen, S.-J. et al. (Oct. 2016). Quantum teleportation with independent sources and prior entanglement distribution over a network. *Nature Photon.* **10** (10): 671–675.

4 Yin, J., Cao, Y., Li, Y.-H. et al. (2017). Satellite-based entanglement distribution over 1200 kilometers. *Science* **356** (6343): 1140–1144.

5 Briegel, H.-J., Dür, W., Cirac, J.I., and Zoller, P. (Dec. 1998). Quantum repeaters: the role of imperfect local operations in quantum communication. *Phys. Rev. Lett.* **81**: 5932–5935.

6 Dür, W., Briegel, H.-J., Cirac, J.I., and Zoller, P. (Jan. 1999). Quantum repeaters based on entanglement purification. *Phys. Rev. A, Gen. Phys.* **59**: 169–181.

7 Żukowski, M., Zeilinger, A., Horne, M.A., and Ekert, A.K. (1993). 'Event-ready detectors' bell experiment via entanglement swapping. *Phys. Rev. Lett.* **71**: 4287–4290.

8 Deutsch, D. et al. (Sep. 1996). Quantum privacy amplification and the security of quantum cryptography over noisy channels. *Phys. Rev. Lett.* **77**: 2818–2821.

9 Wootters, W.K. and Zurek, W.H. (1982). A single quantum cannot be cloned. *Nature* **299** (5886): 802–803.

10 Dieks, D. (1982). Communication by EPR devices. *Phys. Rev. A, Gen. Phys.* **92** (6): 271–272.

11 Bennett, C.H., Brassard, G., Crépeau, C. et al. (Mar. 1993). Teleporting an unknown quantum state via dual classical and Einstein-Podolsky-Rosen channels. *Phys. Rev. Lett.* **70**: 1895–1899.

12 T. Bacinoglu, B. Gulbahar, and O. B. Akan, "Constant fidelity entanglement flow in quantum communication networks," in Proc. IEEE Global Telecommun. Conf. GLOBECOM, Dec. 2010, pp. 1–5.

13 Van Meter, R. et al. (Dec. 2013). Path selection for quantum repeater networks. *Netw. Sci.* **3** (1): 82–95.

14 Bratzik, S., Abruzzo, S., Kampermann, H., and Bruß, D. (Jun. 2013). Quantum repeaters and quantum key distribution: the impact of entanglement distillation on the secret key rate. *Phys. Rev. A, Gen. Phys* **87**: 062335.

15 Bernardes, N.K., Praxmeyer, L., and van Loock, P. (Jan. 2011). Rate analysis for a hybrid quantum repeater. *Phys. Rev. A, Gen. Phys* **83**: 012323.

16 Uphoff, M., Brekenfeld, M., Rempe, G., and Ritter, S. (Mar. 2016). An integrated quantum repeater at telecom wavelength with single atoms in optical fiber cavities. *Appl. Phys. B Lasers Opt.* **122** (3): 46.

17 Caleffi, M. (2017). Optimal routing for quantum networks. *IEEE Access* **5**: 2229.

18 Radnaev, A.G. et al. (2010). A quantum memory with telecom-wavelength conversion. *Nat. Phys.* **6** (11): 894–899.

19 Hofmann, J. et al. (2012). Heralded entanglement between widely separated atoms. *Science* **337** (6090): 72–75.

20 Ritter, S. et al. (2012). An elementary quantum network of single atoms in optical cavities. *Nature* **484** (7393): 195–200.

21 Borregaard, J., Kómár, P., Kessler, E.M. et al. (Jul. 2015). Long-distance entanglement distribution using individual atoms in optical cavities. *Phys. Rev. A, Gen. Phys* **92**: 012307.

22 Lemr, K., Bartkiewicz, K., Cernoch, A., and Soubusta, J. (2013). Resource-efficient linear-optical quantum router. *Phys. Rev. A* **87**: 062333.

23 Nikolopoulos, G.M. and Jex, I. (2014). *Quantum State Transfer and Network Engineering*. Berlin: Springer.

24 Bose, S. (2003). Quantum Communication through an Unmodulated Spin Chain. *Phys. Rev. Lett.* **91**: 207901.

25 Subrahmanyam, V. (2004). Entanglement dynamics and quantum-state transport in spin chains. *Phys. Rev. A* **69**: 034304.

26 W'ojcik, A., Luczak, T., Kurzy'nski, P. et al. (2007). Multiuser quantum communication networks. *Phys. Rev. A* **75**: 022330.

27 Di Franco, C., Paternostro, M., and Kim, M.S. (2008). Perfect state transfer on a spin chain without state initialization. *Phys. Rev. Lett.* **101**: 230502.

28 Chudzicki C and Strauch F W 2010 Parallel State transfer and efficient quantum routing on quantum networks *Phys. Rev. Lett.* **105** 260501

29 Paganelli, S., Lorenzo, S., Apollaro, T.J.G. et al. (2013). Routing quantum information in spin chains. *Phys. Rev. A* **87**: 062309.

30 Zwick, A., Alvarez, G.A., Stolze, J., and Osenda, O. (2011). Robustness of spin-coupling distributions for perfect quantum state transfer. *Phys. Rev. A* **84**: 022311.

31 Zwick, A., Alvarez, G.A., Stolze, J., and Osenda, O. (2012). Spin chains for robust state transfer: modified boundary couplings versus completely engineered chains. *Phys. Rev. A* **85**: 012318.

32 Christandl, M., Datta, N., Ekert, A., and Landahl, A.J. (2004). Perfect state transfer in quantum spin networks. *Phys. Rev. Lett.* **92**: 187902.

33 Christandl, M., Datta, N., Dorlas, T.C. et al. (2005). Perfect transfer of arbitrary states in quantum spin networks. *Phys. Rev. A* **71**: 032312.

34 Farhi, E. and Gutmann, S. (1998). Quantum computation and decision trees. *Phys. Rev. A* **58**: 915.

35 Aharonov, Y., Davidovich, L., and Zagury, N. (1993). Quantum random walks. *Phys. Rev. A* **48**: 1687.

36 Kempe, J. (2003). Quantum random walks: an introductory overview. *Contemp. Phys.* **44**: 307.

37 Travaglione, B.C. and Milburn, G.J. (2002). Include the below article title: implementing the quantum random walk. *Phys. Rev. A* **65**: 032310.

38 Dür, W., Raussendorf, R., Kendon, V.M., and Briegel, H.J. (2002). Quantum walks in optical lattices. *Phys. Rev. A* **66**: 052319.

39 Sanders, B.C., Bartlett, S.D., Tregenna, B., and Knight, P.L. (2003). Quantum quincunx in cavity quantum electrodynamics. *Phys. Rev. A* **67**: 042305.

40 Xue, P., Sanders, B.C., and Leibfried, D. (2009). Quantum walk on a line for a trapped ion. *Phys. Rev. Lett.* **103**: 183602.

41 Bouwmeester, D., Marzoli, I., Karman, G.P. et al. (1999). Optical Galton board. *Phys. Rev. A* **61**: 013410.

42 Du, J., Li, H., Xu, X. et al. (2003). Experimental implementation of the quantum random-walk algorithm. *Phys. Rev. A* **67**: 042316.

43 Côt'e, R., Russell, A., Eyler, E.E., and Gould, P.L. (2006). Quantum random walk with Rydberg atoms in an optical lattice. *New J. Phys.* **8**: 156.

44 Perets, H.B., Lahini, Y., Pozzi, F. et al. (2008). Realization of quantum walks with negligible decoherence in waveguide lattices. *Phys. Rev. Lett.* **100**: 170506.

45 Karski, M., Förster, L., Choi, J.M. et al. (2009). Quantum walk in position space with single optically trapped atoms. *Science* **325**: 174.

46 Schmitz, H., Matjeschk, R., Schneider, C. et al. (2009). Quantum walk of a trapped Ion in phase space. *Phys. Rev. Lett.* **103**: 090504.

47 Schreiber, A., Cassemiro, K.N., Potoček, V. et al. (2010). Photons walking the line: a quantum walk with adjustable coin operations. *Phys. Rev. Lett.* **104**: 050502.

48 Z¨ahringer, F., Kirchmair, G., Gerritsma, R. et al. (2010). Realization of a quantum walk with one and two trapped ions. *Phys. Rev. Lett.* **104**: 100503.

49 Broome, M.A., Fedrizzi, A., Lanyon, B.P. et al. (2010). Discrete single-photon quantum qalks with tunable decoherence. *Phys. Rev. Lett.* **104**: 153602.

50 Peruzzo, A., Lobino, M., Matthews, J.C.F. et al. (2010). Quantum walks of correlated photons. *Science* **329**: 1500.

51 Sansoni, L., Sciarrino, F., Vallone, G. et al. (2012). Two-particle Bosonic-Fermionic quantum walk via integrated photonics. *Phys. Rev. Lett.* **108**: 010502.

52 Schreiber, A., G'abris, A., Rohde, P.P. et al. (2012). A 2D quantum walk simulation of two-particle dynamics. *Science* **336**: 55.

53 Ghosh, J. (2014). Simulating Anderson localization via a quantum walk on a one-dimensional lattice of superconducting qubits. *Phys. Rev. A* **89**: 022309.

54 Horodecki, R., Horodecki, P., Horodecki, M., and Horodecki, K. (2009). Quantum entanglement. *Rev. Mod. Phys.* **81** (2): 865–942. https://doi.org/10.1103/RevModPhys.81.865.

55 Brougham, T., Kostak, V., Jex, I. et al. (2011). Entanglement preparation using symmetric multiports. *Eur. Phys. J. D* **61** (1): 231–236. https://doi.org/10.1140/epjd/e2010-10337-2.

56 Cabrillo, C., Cirac, J.I., Garcia-Fernandez, P., and Zoller, P. (1999). Creation of entangled states of distant atoms by interference. *Phys. Rev. A.* **59** (2): 1025–1033. https://doi.org/10.1103/PhysRevA.59.1025.

57 Plenio, M.B., Huelga, S.F., Beige, A., and Knight, P.L. (1999). Cavity-loss-induced generation of entangled atoms. *Phys. Rev. A.* **59** (3): 2468–2475. https://doi.org/10.1103/PhysRevA.59.2468.

58 Duan, L., Lukin, M.D., Cirac, J.I., and Zoller, P. (2001). Long distance quantum communication with atomic ensembles and linear optics. *Nature (London)* **414**: 413–418. https://doi.org/10.1038/35106500.

59 Bose, S. and Home, D. (2002). Generic entanglement generation, quantum statistics, and complementarity. *Phys. Rev. Lett.* **88**: 050401. https://doi.org/10.1103/PhysRevLett.88.050401.

60 Ekert, A.K. (1991). Quantum cryptography based on Bell's theorem. *Phys. Rev. Lett.* **67** (6): 661–633. https://doi.org/10.1103/PhysRevLett.67.661.

61 Chen, X.-B. et al. (2019). Quantum network communication with a Novel Discrete-time quantum walk. *IEEE Access* https://doi.org/10.1109/ACCESS.2018.2890719.

62 A. Ambainis, E. Bach, A. Nayak, A. Vishwanath, and J. Watrous. One-dimensional quantum walks. In Proceedings of the 33th ACM Symposium on The Theory of Computation (STOC'01) ACM, pp. 60–69, 2001.

63 A. Nayak and A. Vishwanath. Quantum walk on the line. quant-ph/0010117.

64 Bender, C. and Orszag, S. (1978). *Advanced Mathematical Methods for Scientists and Engineers. International Series in Pure and Applied Mathematics.* McGraw-Hill, Inc.

65 Bleistein, N. and Handelsman, R. (1975). *Asymptotic Expansions of Integrals.* Holt, Rinehart and Winston.

66 Nayak, A., and Vishwanath, A., 2000, DIMACS Technical Report 2000–43 and Los Alamos preprint archive, quant-ph/0010117.

67 Moore, C., and Russell, A., 2002, Proceedings of RANDOM 2002, edited by J. D. P. Rolim and S. Vadhan (Cambridge, MA: Springer), pp. 164–178.

68 Kempe, J., 2002, lanl-arXiv quant-ph/0205083.

69 Mackay, T.D., Bartlett, S.D., Stephenson, L.T., and Sanders, B.C. (2002). *J. Phys. A Math. Gen.* **35**: 2745.

70 Yamasaki, T., Kobayashi, H., and Imai, H., 2002, Unconventional Models of Computation, Third International Conference, UMC 2002, Kobe, Japan, 15–19 October, Vol. 2509, Lecture Notes in Computer Science, edited by C. Calude, M. J. Dinneen, and F. Peper (Berlin: Springer), pp. 315–330.

71 Tamon, C. (2002). Non-uniform mixing in continuous quantum walks. *Quantum Physics* lanl-arXiv quant-ph/0209106.

72 Shenvi, N., Kempe, J., and Whaley, K.B. (2003). A quantum random walk search algorithm. *Phys. Rev. A* https://arxiv.org/pdf/quant-ph/0210064.pdf.

73 Childs, A., Farhi, E., and Gutmann, S., 2002, Quantum Information Processing, 1, 35; lanl-report quant-ph/0103020.

74 Childs, A. M., Cleve, R., Deotto, E., Farhi, E., Gutmann, S., and Spielman, D. A., 2002 Exponential algorithmic speedup by a quantum walk, Proceedings of the Thirty-Fifth ACM Symposium on Theory of Computing - STOC '03, 2002. lanl-report quant-ph/0209131.

75 Scho¨ning, U., 1999, 40th Annual Symposium on Foundations of Computer Science (New York, NY: IEEE), pp. 17–19.

76 Feller, W. (1968). *An Introduction to Probability Theory and its Applications*. New York: Wiley.

77 Lovasz, L., and Winkler, P., 1998, Microsurveys in Discrete Probability, Vol. 41, DIMACS Series on Disc. Mathematics and Theoretical Computer Science, edited by D. Aldous and J. Propp (Providence, RI: AMS), pp. 85–134

78 Aharonov, D., Ambainis, A., Kempe, J., and Vazirani, U., 2001, Proceedings of the 33th STOC (New York, NY: ACM), pp. 50–59.

17

Quantum Internet

Finally, in this chapter, we discuss current progress in building up a quantum internet [1–4] intended to enable the transmission of quantum bits (qubits) between distant quantum devices to achieve the tasks that are impossible using classical communication. For example, with such a network we can implement cryptographic protocols like long-distance quantum key distribution (QKD) [5, 6], which enables secure communication. Apart from QKD, many other applications in the domain of distributed computing and multi-party cryptography [7] have already been identified at different stages of quantum network development [8].

Like the classical internet, a quantum internet consists of network components like physical communication links, and eventually routers [2, 9–11]. However, due to fundamental differences between classical and quantum bits, these components in a quantum network behave rather differently than their classical counterparts. For example, qubits cannot be copied, which rules out retransmission as a means to overcome qubit losses [12]. To nevertheless send qubits reliably, a standard method is to first produce quantum entanglement between a qubit held by the sender and a qubit held by the receiver. Once this entanglement has been produced, the qubit can then be sent using quantum teleportation [12, 13]. This requires, in addition, the transmission of two classical bits per qubit from the sender to the receiver. Importantly, teleportation consumes the entanglement, meaning that it has to be re-established before the next qubit can be sent. When it comes to routing qubits in a network, one hence needs to consider routing entanglement [1, 14–17].

An important tool for establishing entanglement over long distances is the notion of entanglement swapping. If two nodes A and B are both connected to an intermediary node r, but not directly connected themselves by a physical quantum communication channel such as fiber, then they can nevertheless create entanglement between themselves with the help of r. First, A and B each individually create entanglement with r. This requires one qubit of quantum storage at A and B to hold their end of the entanglement, and 2qubits of quantum storage at r. Node r then performs an *entanglement swap* [13, 18–20; also Section 16.1], destroying its own entanglement with A and B, but instead creating entanglement between A and B. This process can be understood as node r teleporting its qubit entangled with A onto node B using the entanglement that it shares with B. In turn, using this process iteratively, node r can, with the assistance of A and B, also establish entanglement with nodes that are far away in the physical communication network. Any node r capable of storing qubits can thus simultaneously be entangled with as many nodes in the network as it can store qubits in its quantum memory. Such a node may function as an entanglement router by taking decisions such as for which of its neighbors it should perform an entanglement swap operation for sharing an entangled link between a source s and a destination e (see [21] for a longer introduction).

Artificial Intelligence and Quantum Computing for Advanced Wireless Networks, First Edition.
Savo G. Glisic and Beatriz Lorenzo.
© 2022 John Wiley & Sons Ltd. Published 2022 by John Wiley & Sons Ltd.

As already elaborated across Part II of the book, in the domain of quantum information we use the term *quantum state* to represent the state of a multi-qubit quantum system. A pure n-qubit quantum state $|\psi_n\rangle$ can be mathematically described as a unit vector in a Hilbert space $\mathcal{H}$ of dimension 2^n. The entangled target state $|\psi^+\rangle = (|00\rangle_{AB} + |11\rangle_{AB})/\sqrt{2}$ is a pure quantum state of 2qubits A and B. An n-qubit mixed state ρ_n on $\mathcal{H}$ is a Hermitian operator with unit trace. ρ_n is called a density matrix. A mixed state is a generalization of a pure state that can model noisy quantum states, and the density matrix representation ρ of a pure state $|\psi\rangle$ is $|\psi\rangle\langle\psi|$, where $\langle\psi|$ is the transpose of the complex conjugate of $|\psi\rangle$. In this section, we use the quantity known as *fidelity* to measure the closeness between two quantum states. The fidelity between a target pure state $|\psi\rangle$ and a mixed state ρ is defined as $F(\rho, |\psi\rangle\langle\psi|) = \langle\psi|\rho|\psi\rangle$. The mixed state ρ has a unit trace and $|\psi\rangle$ is a unit vector, which implies $0 \leq F(\rho, |\psi\rangle\langle\psi|) \leq 1$. Moreover, $F(\rho, |\psi\rangle\langle\psi|) = 1$ if and only if $\rho = |\psi\rangle\langle\psi|$. This implies that two states with high fidelity are close to each other. In this section, we mostly consider depolarizing channels, and for this type of channel, if a node r performs a noise-free entanglement swap operation between two entangled links with fidelity F_1, F_2, then the fidelity of the resulting entangled state is at least $F_1 F_2$[21].

A quantum network may generate entanglement on demand only when a request arrives, which is referred to as the *on-demand* model. In this case, the routing problem reduces to routing entanglement on the physical communication graph ($G_{\mathrm{ph}} = (V, E_{\mathrm{ph}})$) corresponding to the fibers (or free-space links) connecting the quantum network nodes. This means that entanglement is produced by two nodes connected in G_{ph} followed by entanglement swapping operations along a path in this graph. Two such neighbor nodes in G_{ph} are called physical neighbors of each other. However, we may also pre-establish entanglement between two nodes that do not share a physical connection, in anticipation of future requests. Such pre-shared entanglement forms a *virtuallink* [21]. Two such nodes that are not directly connected by a physical link but share an entangled link or a virtual link are called *virtual neighbors* of each other. Here, we consider routing on the *virtual graph* given by pre-shared entanglement ($\mathcal{G} = (V, \mathcal{E})$). This virtual graph may have a much lower diameter than the underlying physical one. Such virtual links are in spirit similar to forming an overlay network in peer-to-peer networks, with the important distinction that the graph is highly dynamic: each virtual link can be used only once, and it must be re-established before further use. This can be a very time-consuming process. In addition, due to the short lifetimes of quantum memories, the virtual graph is continuously changing as virtual links expire after some time even if they have not been used.

Of course, on both graphs, one can nevertheless apply classical algorithms to select a path from the sender to the receiver, along which entanglement swapping is performed to create an end-to-end link. The performance of the centralized shortest path routing algorithms is highly dependent on the network topology. If the topology changes rapidly, then keeping the routing tables up to date becomes challenging. This type of situation also occurs in classical delay-tolerant networks. Usually, for this type of network, the distributed routing algorithms always perform better than the centralized shortest path algorithm. Hence, in this section, we address the routing problem by modifying existing classical distributed routing algorithms. The main challenge in designing such algorithms is that the nodes need to decide which operation to perform (entanglement generation or entanglement swap) based on local information. Analyzing those routing algorithms for multiple demands is also a challenging task. In this section, we use the mathematical tools from classical routing theory for computing the latency of these routing algorithms for single source–destination pairs. We present some numerical simulations for illustration of the performance in the case of multiple source–destination pairs.

17.1 System Model

Here we are interested in computing the latency of a demand. Let a routing algorithm $\mathcal{A}$ takes $T_{A, i, j}$ time steps to distribute $D_{i, j}$ number of entangled links between the source node i and destination node j. If $|D|$ denotes the number of nonzero entries in D, then with respect to a routing algorithm $\mathcal{A}$ we define the *average latency (AL)* as AL $= \sum_{i, j} T_{A, i, j}/|D|$, where $T_{A, i, j}$ denotes the latency to distribute the $D_{i, j}$ entangled link between the nodes i and j. In this section, for a graph G, we use $dist_G(u, v)$, $diam_G$, $Neigh_G(u)$ to denote the hop distance between two nodes u, v in G, the diameter of G, and the set of neighbors of u, respectively.

Discrete time model: In this chapter, we consider a simplified discrete time model where each time step is equivalent to the communication time between two neighboring nodes in the physical graph $G_{ph} = (V, E_{ph})$. Here, we assume that the distance between any two physical neighbor nodes $u, v \in V$ is upper-bounded by $dist_{phys}$, that is, the maximum length of a physical communication link is d_{th}. This implies in the discrete time model each time step is equivalent to $dist_{phys}/c$ time units, where c is the speed of light in the communication channel.

Quantum Network: Each node in the network has the following features:

1) Each node has a unique ID, which carries the information about its location in the physical graph.
2) The nodes are capable of generating the cap number of Einstein–Podolsky–Rosen (EPR) pairs in parallel with each of its neighbors.
3) Each node is capable of storing the created entangled state. However, we assume that the storage is noisy and the fidelity of the stored entangled state decays with each time step. If any entangled link is not being used for T_{th} time steps, then the corresponding nodes will not use that link for entanglement swapping or for teleportation.
4) After T_{th} time steps, each node throws away the stored entangled state and starts generating a new entangled state.
5) In this section, we assume that $T_{th} \gg diam_{G_{ph}}$; that is, the storage time for quantum memory is much higher than the classical communication time between any two nodes in the network.
6) Each node stores information about the physical graph topology.
7) Each node stores information (if available) about its both virtual neighbors (if any) and physical neighbors.
8) The distance between two virtual neighbors in $G_{ph} = (V, E_{ph})$ is upper-bounded by d_{th}.

Long-distance entanglement creation: This is a well-studied subject [22–26]. For a detailed review, we refer to [27]. In this section, we are interested in a basic model. Due to the threshold time T_{th}, the entanglement distribution time scales exponentially with the distance between the source–destination pair. However, with this type of entanglement generation scheme, we can guarantee on the end-to-end fidelity of the shared entangled links. It is important to note that this model is a trivial one. One can reduce this exponential scaling to a polynomial one by other techniques like *entanglement distillation* or *quantum error correction* [28–30]. The concepts of these techniques have been discussed in Chapter 10. In this section, our main focus is on the decision-making procedure for routing, not the physical means of entanglement generation. However, our routing algorithms are designed in such a manner that it can work with any entanglement generation procedure. In other words, the conclusions we draw in this chapter about the routing algorithms also hold for other entanglement generation procedures.

The entanglement generation protocol between two nodes s, e with $\text{dist}_{G_{\text{ph}}}(s, e) = d$ that we use in this section can be subdivided into two parts:

- *Elementary link creation*, where the nodes in $\text{path}_{G_{\text{ph}}}(s, e)$, which are connected directly by a physical link, create entangled links between themselves. Usually, the created links are stored in a quantum memory.
- The next part is called *longer link creation*, where the intermediate nodes perform an *entanglement swap* operation and share an entangled link between the end nodes as discussed in Chapter 16, Section 16.1.

In practice, photon loss in the optical fiber and other imperfections of the network components make the entanglement generation procedure a probabilistic but heralded one. This implies that the elementary link creation procedure can produce a signal that certifies the successful creation of the entangled link. In order to model this here, we assume that *elementary link creation* can be performed with probability $P_0 \in [0, 1]$ within a single time step. For an example of P_0 that takes into account the repeater technology based on the nitrogen-vacancy (NV) center, we refer to [31]. In this chapter, inspired by certain physical implementations [32], we assume that the *entanglement swap* operation is a deterministic one. We make the simplifying assumption that the time for this operation is negligible.

According to our simplified model, s, e can share an entangled state if and only if all the elementary links are being created within the time step T_{th}. Of course, after the creation of the elementary entangled links the nodes need to communicate each other about it, and it will cost some time steps. However, in the last section, we assume that T_{th} is much larger than this classical communication time. So, for the sake of simplicity, we remove the classical communication time from our calculation. This implies that the probability of creating an entangled link between s, e within the T_{th} time step is at least $\left(1 - (1 - P_0)^{T_{\text{th}}}\right)^d$. As a consequence, the expected entanglement distribution time increases exponentially with d. As mentioned before, this is a simplified model for entanglement generation, but it is useful to guarantee the end-to-end fidelity of the shared entangled state.

Noisy quantum storage: The stored quantum state in quantum memory devices decoheres with time. Here, we assume a simplified pessimistic model where the qubits decohere under the effect of symmetric depolarizing noise with the parameter p. This type of quantum channel can be described as a completely positive trace-preserving map $\varepsilon\colon \mathcal{H}^{\otimes 2} \to \mathcal{H}^{\otimes 2}$.

The noise operator for a 2qubit state $\rho_{0,\,se} = |\psi^+\rangle_{s,\,e}\langle\psi^+|$, shared between s, e, is denoted as ε, and on this specific state (not in general) it acts as follows: $\varepsilon(\rho_{0,se}) := p^2 \rho_{0,\,se} + (1 - p^2)I_4/4$, where I_4 is a 4×4 identity matrix. If at time step $t - 1$ the stored state is $\rho_{t-1,\,se}$, then at time step t the stored state would be $\rho_{t,se} = \varepsilon(\rho_{t-1,se})$. By solving this recursive relation on time steps t, we get

$$\rho_{t,se} = p^{2t}\rho_{0,se} + \left(1 - p^{2t}\right)\frac{I_4}{4}. \tag{17.1}$$

We can rewrite the above expression as $\rho_{t,se} = \left(\frac{1}{4} + \frac{3}{4}p^{2t}\right)\rho_{0,se} + \frac{3}{4}\left(1 - p^{2t}\right)\rho_{0,se}^{\perp}$, where $\rho_{0,se}^{\perp}$ is orthogonal to $\rho_{0,se}$. This implies the fidelity of the stored state after t time steps is $F\left(\rho_{t,se}, \rho_{0,se}\right) = \frac{1}{4} + \frac{3}{4}p^{2t}$.

Entangled links with low fidelity make quantum communication very noisy. In order to protect the information from noise, we fix a threshold value, F_{th}, for the fidelity. According to this model, each entangled link can be stored inside the quantum memory for T_{th} time. This implies $\rho_{T_{\text{th}},se}$ should satisfy the following condition: $F\left(\rho_{T_{\text{th}},se}, \rho_{0,se}\right) > F_{\text{th}}$. By substituting the value of $F\left(\rho_{T_{\text{th}},se}, \rho_{0,se}\right)$ from the previous section, we can get the following bound, up to time T_{th}:

$$T_{\text{th}} \geq \frac{1}{2 \log p} \, \log \left[\frac{4F_{\text{th}}}{3} - \frac{1}{3}\right]. \tag{17.2}$$

Continuous network: In this model, each of the nodes u in $G_{\text{ph}} = (V, E_{\text{ph}})$ keeps the information about its $|\, \text{Neigh}_{G_{\text{ph}}}(u)\,|$ physical neighbors and $O(k)$ virtual neighbors. According to the model, for any long-distance neighbor v of u, $\text{dist}_{G_{\text{ph}}}(u, v) \leq d_{\text{th}}$. Each of the nodes establishes and maintains virtual entangled links with all of its neighbors using the entanglement generation procedure discussed in the following. After some fixed time interval (T_{th}), the nodes again start to generate all of the links, irrespective of whether there is any demand or not. Borrowing ideas from classical complex network theory, we give a more precise description of the following families of continuous network models:

1) Deterministically chosen virtual neighbors: In the later sections, we give a specific strategy for choosing virtual neighbors for ring, grid, and recursively generated graph topologies.
2) Randomly chosen virtual neighbors:

   a) Virtual neighbors are chosen following a uniform distribution: In this network, any node u choses another node $v\big(\text{dist}_{G_{\text{ph}}}(u, v) > 1\big)$ as a neighbor with probability P_{choose}, where

$$P_{\text{choose}}(u, v) := \begin{cases} \dfrac{1}{N_{\leq d_{\text{th}}}(G_{\text{ph}})}, & \text{dist}_{G_{\text{ph}}}(u, v) \leq d_{\text{th}} \\ 0 & \textit{otherwise}, \end{cases} \tag{17.3}$$

   where $N_{\leq d_{\text{th}}}(G)$ denotes the number of nodes at a distance at most d_{th} from a node u.

   b) Virtual neighbors are chosen following a power-law distribution: In this network, any node u choses another node v (such that $\text{dist}_{G_{\text{ph}}}(u, v) > 1$) as a neighbor with probability P_{choose}, where

$$P_{\text{choose}}(u, v) := \begin{cases} \dfrac{1}{\beta_u} \dfrac{1}{\text{dist}_G^{\alpha}(u, v)}, & \text{dist}_G(u, v) \leq d_{\text{th}} \\ 0 & \textit{otherwise}, \end{cases} \tag{17.4}$$

   where $\beta_u = \sum_{v' \in V} P_{\text{choose}}(u, v')$ and $\alpha > 0$.

On-demand network: In this model, each node u in the physical graph $G_{\text{ph}} = (V, E_{\text{ph}})$ has only $|\, \text{Neigh}_{G_{\text{ph}}}(u)\,|$ neighbors. In the on-demand network, there are no pre-shared entangled links, and each node has information about the entire physical network topology. This implies that if a demand arises, then the source node can compute the shortest path from a source to a destination and starts generating entangled links between the source and destination along that path.

17.1.1 Routing Algorithms

In this section, we present three different kinds of distributed routing algorithms [33]. The entire routing procedure between any two nodes in the quantum network can be subdivided into following three phases: (i) *path discovery phase*, (ii) *entanglement reservation phase*, and (iii) *entanglement distribution phase*. These steps of the routing procedure are summarized in in Algorithm 1. Among the above three phases, all the routing decisions are made within the first two phases. In this section, in all of the routing algorithms, we focus on different types of path discovery algorithms. Moreover, the algorithms reserve the entangled links while discovering the path. The reservation of the links is useful to prevent the utilization of those links by other demands. After the path discovery and link reservation, if all of the entangled links are available along the path, then the intermediate nodes perform an entanglement swap (in parallel) between the links. If there are not enough links available between two neighbors in the path, then the demand waits until all the missing links are generated. If this missing link generation time exceeds T_{th}, then all of the reserved links along the path expire. In this case, the demand waits until all links along the path are being generated. In all the routing algorithms, we assume that each node has the complete information about the physical network topology. However, due to the fragile nature of the entangled links, it is difficult to keep track of the current topology of the virtual graph. Here, we assume that each node has all the information about the virtual links it shares with its neighbors. During the path discovery, each node decides the next hop on the basis of the physical graph topology and the information it has about the shared entangled links with its neighbors. Both the algorithms try to minimize the average waiting time. Designing such algorithms becomes challenging when there are not enough entangled links available between two neighbors u, v. At that moment, for a demand, if v is an optimal neighbor of u to reach a destination node e, then the routing algorithm has two options: (i) select the path via v and generate a sufficient number of links between u, v, or (ii) u tries to select another neighbor with whom it already shares a sufficient number of entangled links.

Algorithm 1 Distributed Routing Algorithms ($s, e, \mathcal{G}, D, cap$)

1: $round = \left\lceil \frac{D_{s,e}}{cap} \right\rceil$

2: $i = 1$ ▷ Path discovery phase

3: **while** $i \leq round$ **do**

4:     $CommPath_{s,e} = PathDisc(s, e, \mathcal{G}, D_{s,e})$ ▷
$CommPath_{s,e} = \{s = u_0, u_{1...}, u_{d-1} = e\}$

5:     **if** in $CommPath_{s,e}$ some of the neighbor nodes do not have enough entangled links **then**

6:        Generate all the links.

7:     **else**

8:        $j = 1$ ▷ communication Phase

9:        **while** $j \leq d - 2$ **do**

10:           $EntSwap(u_0, u_j, u_{j+1})$

11:           $j = j + 1$

12:     $dem = dem - cap$

13:     $i = i + 1$

Source: Chakraborty [33].

The classical greedy routing algorithm [34, 35] always chooses the first option. However, this is not always a good option for routing in a quantum internet. However, a slight modification of the greedy algorithm can give better performance. In Algorithm 2, we describe the modified version of the greedy routing algorithm in detail. Algorithm 3, a path discovery algorithm, is a best-effort algorithm, and it utilizes the second option. The aim of this algorithm is to utilize all the existing entangled links before generating a new one. In the next two sections, we give a detailed description of both of the algorithms.

Algorithm 2 Modified Greedy: PathDisc(*s*, *e*, $\mathcal{G}$, $D_{s,e}$)

```
1: u_curr = s
2: CommPath_s,e = {s}
3: while u_curr ≠ e do
4:     u = arg min_{v∈Neigh_g(u_curr)} dist_{G_ph}(v, e)
```

5:      **if** $\left(\begin{array}{c} (i)\, \text{There are not enough links available between } u, u_{\texttt{curr}} \\ \text{and} \\ (ii)\, \text{dist}_{G_{ph}}(e, u_{\texttt{curr}}) < \text{dist}_{G_{ph}}(u, u_{\texttt{curr}}) + \text{dist}_{G_{ph}}(u, e) \end{array}\right)$

       then

```
6:         u = arg min_{v∈Neigh_g(u_curr), dist_{G_ph}(v, u_curr) = 1} dist_{G_ph}(v, e)
7:     CommPath_s,e = CommPath_s,e ∪ {u}
8:     u_curr = u
9: return (CommPath_s,e)
```

Source: Chakraborty [33].

Modified greedy routing: In classical network theory, greedy routing has been deeply studied for discovering near-optimal paths using only local information [34, 35]. On the basis of the information of its neighbors, each node decides the next hop of a demand. Here, each node tries to jump to as close as possible to the destination node. The virtual neighbors are very useful for making such jumps. One big disadvantage of using the classical greedy routing algorithm for entanglement distribution is that while discovering the path, it does not take into account whether sufficient entangled links are available between two virtual neighbors. If the links are not present, then the request or demand has to wait until all of the missing links are generated. This might increase the latency. For example, for a demand, u is the last node discovered in the path and v is a neighbor of u that is closest to the destination e. If the number of entangled links available between u, v is insufficient and if $\text{dist}_{G_{ph}}(u, v) \geq \text{dist}_{G_{ph}}(u, e)$, then it is not a good idea for u to put v in the path. Here, we use a slightly modified version of the algorithm proposed in [35] so that it can handle this type of problem. In the modified *Algorithm 2*, a node u puts the virtual neighbor v in the path closest to e if at least one of the following two cases are satisfied (see step 5 of the Algorithm 2).

- If the amount of available entangled links between them is greater than $D_{s,\,e}$.
- If $dist_{G_{ph}}(u, e) = dist_{G_{ph}}(u, v) + dist_{G_{ph}}(v, e)$, where $G_{ph} = (V, E_{ph})$ is a physical graph, u is the current node, and v is its virtual neighbor that is the closest to the destination e.

If none of these two conditions were satisfied, then u chooses its physical neighbor closest to e as the next hop. The details of the algorithm are described in Algorithm 2.

Algorithm 3 Local Best Effort: PathDisc(*s*, *e*, $\mathcal{G}$, $D_{s,e}$)

```
1: u_curr = s
2: CommPath_s, e = {s}
3: while u_curr ≠ e do
4:     u = arg min_{v∈Neigh_g(u_curr), g(v, u_curr) ≥ D_s,e} dist_{G_ph}(v, e)
```

(*Continued*)

Algorithm 3 (Continued)

5: **if** $\begin{pmatrix} (i)\ \text{No such } u \text{ exists} \\ \text{or} \\ (ii)\ \text{dist}_{G_{ph}}(u_{curr},\ e) > \text{dist}_{G_{ph}}(u,\ e) \end{pmatrix}$ **then**

6: $\quad u = \arg\min_{\substack{v \in \text{Neigh}_{\mathcal{G}}(u_{curr}) \\ \text{dist}_{G_{ph}}(v,\ u_{curr}) = 1}} \text{dist}_{G_{ph}}(v,\ e)$

7: $\quad CommPath_{s,\ e} = CommPath_{s,e} \cup \{u\}$

8: $\quad u_{curr} = u$

9: retun$(CommPath_{s,e})$

Source: Chakraborty [33].

Local best-effort routing: The local best-effort routing algorithm is a distributed algorithm where each node tries to jump as close as possible to the destination node, using existing entangled links. Unlike the greedy algorithm in this one, a node u first prepares a set of neighbors with whom it shares more than $D_{s,\ e}$ amount of entangled links. Then, from that set, u chooses the next hop v such that v is closest to e and $\text{dist}_{G_{ph}}(u, e) < dist_{G_{ph}}(v, e)$ (see step 4 of the *Algorithm 3*). If no such neighbor exists, then it chooses its physical neighbor that is the closest to the destination (see step 6 of the Algorithm 3). Algorithm 3 describes the procedure in more detail.

Algorithm 4 NoN Local Best Effort: PathDisc($s, e, \mathcal{G}, D_{s,e}$)

1: $u_{curr} = s$

2: $CommPath_{s,\ e} = \{s\}$

3: $d = \text{dist}_{G_{ph}}(s,\ e)$

4: **while** $u_{curr} \neq e$ **do**

5: $\quad U' = \{u' \in \text{Neigh}_{\mathcal{G}}(u) : \mathcal{G}(u_{curr},\ u') \geq D_{s,e}\}$

6: $\quad$ **for** all $u' \in U'$ **do**

7: $\quad\quad u = \arg\min_{\substack{v \in \text{Neigh}_{\mathcal{G}}(u') \\ \mathcal{G}(v,\ u') \geq D_{s,e}}} \text{dist}_{G_{ph}}(v,\ e)$

8: $\quad\quad$ **if** $\begin{pmatrix} (i)\ \text{No such } u \text{ exists} \\ \text{or} \\ (ii)\ \text{dist}_{G_{ph}}(u_{curr},\ e) > \text{dist}_{G_{ph}}(u,\ e) \end{pmatrix}$ **then**

9: $\quad\quad\quad u = \arg\min_{\substack{v \in Neigh_{\mathcal{G}}(u_{curr}) \\ \text{dist}_{G_{ph}}(v,\ u_{curr}) = 1}} \text{dist}_{G_{ph}}(v,\ e)$

10: $\quad\quad$ **if** $d < \text{dist}_{G_{ph}}(u,\ e)$ **then**

11: $\quad\quad\quad d = \text{dist}_{G_{ph}}(u,\ e)$

12: $\quad\quad\quad u_{next} = u'$

13: $\quad$ **if** $U' = \varphi$ **then**

(Continued)

Algorithm 4 (Continued)

14:     for all $\begin{pmatrix} u'' \in Neigh_{\mathcal{G}}(u) \\ \textbf{and} \\ dist_{G_{ph}}(u_{curr}, u'') = 1 \end{pmatrix}$ **do**

15:         $u = \arg\min_{\substack{v \in Neigh_{\mathcal{G}}(u'') \\ \mathcal{G}(v, u'') \geq D_{s,e}}} dist_{G_{ph}}(v, e)$

16:         **if** $\begin{pmatrix} (i)\,\text{No such}\,u\,\text{exists} \\ \textbf{or} \\ (ii)\,dist_{G_{ph}}(u_{curr}, e) > dist_{G_{ph}}(u, e) \end{pmatrix}$ **then**

17:             $u = \arg\min_{\substack{v \in Neigh_{\mathcal{G}}(u_{curr}) \\ dist_{G_{ph}}(v, u_{curr}) = 1}} dist_{G_{ph}}(v, e)$

18:         **if** $d < dist_{G_{ph}}(u, e)$ **then**
19:             $d = dist_{G_{ph}}(u, e)$
20:         $u_{next} = u''$
21:     $CommPath_{s,\,e} = CommPath_{s,\,e} \cup \{u_{next}\}$
22:     $u_{curr} = u_{next}$
23: return$(CommPath_{s,\,e})$

Source: Chakraborty [33].

NoN local best-effort routing: we are interested in studying the behavior of the local best-effort algorithm when the nodes have information about its neighbors as well as the neighbors of the neighbors in the virtual graph. In the literature of classical complex networks, this type of algorithm is known as the NoN routing algorithm. In [36, 37], it has been shown that this type of algorithm gives better advantages for routing in certain kind of physical graphs. For example, in ring (C_n) and grid networks (Grid$_{n \times n}$) if virtual neighbors are chosen following a power law distribution, then the classical NoN routing algorithm can discover a path with expected length $\log_2 n /$ $(\log_2 \log_2 n)$ [36–38]. Here we adopt the idea of the classical NoN routing algorithm into the local best effort algorithm. As it is a local best effort algorithm, during the path discovery, the current node u_{curr} first prepares a set of neighbors U' with whom it shares more than $D_{s,\,e}$ amount of entangled links (see step 5 of the Algorithm 4). Then, from that set, the algorithm finds a node u' such that it has a neighbor u that is the closest (compare to the neighbors of the nodes in U') to the destination e and the available entangled links between u, u' is more than $D_{s,\,e}$. If no such u exists, then the algorithm just chooses u from the physical neighbors of u' (see steps 6–12 of the Algorithm 4). If the set U' is empty, then the algorithm chooses the next hop among its physical neighbors (SEE the steps 14–20 of the Algorithm 4). For more details, we refer the reader to Algorithm 4.

17.1.2 Quantum Network on General Virtual Graph

The performance analysis of the distributed routing algorithms in a general virtual graph is a challenging task. However, due to the greedy nature of the routing algorithms in [33], an upper bound on the latency of a demand for all of the proposed routing algorithms has been derived.

> For any physical graph G_{ph} and a demand matrix D with $|D| = 1$, for any source and destination pair s, e, with $D_{s,e} = 1$, for both the modified greedy and local best effort algorithms the expected waiting times are upper-bounded by $O\left(P^{-\text{diam}_{G_{ph}}}\right)$ for the on-demand model and $O\left(d_{th}\text{diam}_{G_{ph}}\right)$ for the continuous model, where $P = \left(1 - (1 - P_0)^{T_{th}}\right)$, that is, the probability of creating an entangled link between two neighbor nodes (in G) within the T_{th} time step [33].

In the continuous model, the pre-shared entangled links are temporary in nature, and one link can only be used once. If $D_{s,e} > cap$, then in this model it is a better idea to find different edge-disjoint paths between s and e and use each path to distribute cap number of entangled links. An upper bound on $D_{s,e}$, such that the nodes do not need to wait for the creation of new entangled links, is derived in [33].

> In the continuous network model, for any virtual graph G, and for a demand matrix D with $|D| = 1$, if mincut G denotes the minimal cut of the graph G, then any two nodes s, e in G can distribute at least mincut $G.cap$ number of EPR pairs before regenerating any new entangled link [33].

The fragile nature of the entangled links affects the network topology. Due to this feature, if $|D| > 1$, then the topology of the network changes rapidly, and sometimes it might become disconnected. This triggers an interesting question regarding the performance of the routing algorithms. The next section focuses on this problem.

17.1.3 Quantum Network on Ring and Grid Graph

Here we consider two physical graphs, a ring network C_n and a grid network $Grid_{n' \times n'}$. For the ring network, each node in the network has a unique ID from $\{0, 1, \ldots, n - 1\}$. For the grid network, we assume that each node has node ID $u = (u_a, u_b)$, where $u_a, u_b \in \{0, 1, \ldots, n' - 1\}$. For the simplicity of our calculation, we assume for the ring network, $n = 2^m$ for some positive integer m and $d_{th} = 2^l$ for some positive integer $l \leq m$. In the next subsections, we define how to choose the virtual neighbors in the continuous model and in the on-demand model.

Continuous Model–Virtual G with deterministically chosen entangled links: In this model, for the ring network, each node chooses its virtual neighbors with a deterministic strategy. If any node with node ID x is of the form $2^i y$, where i, y are nonnegative integers and y is an odd number or 0, then that node has min $(2i, 2log_2 d_{th})$ virtual neighbors. The node IDs of those virtual neighbors are $x + 2$ $(mod n)$, $x + 2^2 (mod\ n),\ldots, x + 2^{\min\ (i, log_2 d_{th})}\ (mod\ n)$ and $x + n - 2(mod n)$, $x + n - 2^2\ (mod\ n),\ldots,$ $x + n - 2^{\min\ (i, log_2 d_{th})}\ (mod\ n)$. One can also find this type of virtual network topology in [21], although in this work the network was constructed only for $d_{th} = \text{diam}_{G_{ph}}$. An example of such a network is presented in Figure 17.1.

Similarly, for the grid network, each node with node ID $u = (u_a, u_b)$ of the form $(2^i x, 2^j y)$, where i, j are nonnegative integers and x, y are positive odd numbers or zero, chooses $k = \min (2 \min (i, j), 2log_2 d_{th})$ virtual neighbors. The node IDs of those virtual neighbors are $(u_a + 2(\ mod\ n+1), u_b)$, $(u_a + 2^2\ (mod\ +1), u_b),\ldots, (u_a + 2^k\ (mod\ n+1), u_b)$ and $(u_a, u_b + 2(mod n + 1), (u_a, u_b + 2^2\ (mod\ n + 1)),\ldots,$ $(u_a, u_b + 2^k\ (mod\ n + 1))$. An example of such a network is presented in Figure 17.2.

Randomly chosen virtual neighbors: In this model, for both of the network topologies, each node $u \in V$ has $k = log_2 d_{th}$ virtual neighbors (other than the physical neighbors), and each of such

Figure 17.1 Quantum internet graph G with deterministically chosen virtual links. Here, each of the virtual links is denoted by a dotted line. In this example, d_{th} = 2. Nodes with even node id are of the form 2y, and so each such node has two virtual neighbors, and nodes with odd node ID have no long-distance neighbor. *Source:* Chakraborty [33].

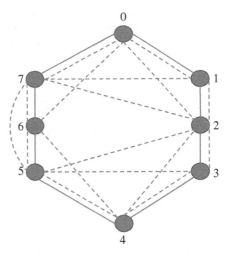

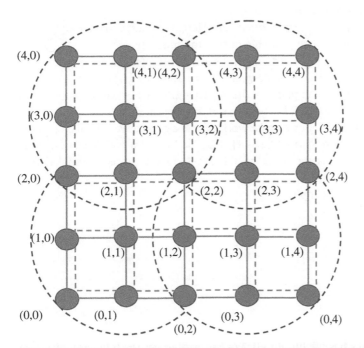

Figure 17.2 Quantum internet graph G with deterministically chosen virtual links. Here each of the virtual links is denoted by a dotted line. In this example, d_{th} = 2. Nodes with even node ID are of the form 2y, so each such node has two virtual neighbors, and nodes with an odd node ID have no long-distance neighbor. *Source:* Chakraborty [33].

neighbors v is chosen independently without replacement, following the distribution $P_{choose}(u, v)$. For the ring network, if $P_{choose}(u, v)$ follows the power law distribution, then the diameter of the virtual graph is optimal: $\alpha = 1$. In the simulation presented in [33], $\alpha = 1$ was used. For the grid network, the diameter of the virtual graph is optimal for $\alpha = 2$ [32]. In this section, we assume $\alpha = 2$.

Table 17.1 Expected number of entanglement swaps for ring and grid network with single source–destination pair.

Models	Greedy routing	NoN routing
Deterministically chosen virtual links	$O\left(\dfrac{n}{d_{th}} + \log d_{th}\right)$	$O\left(\dfrac{n}{d_{th}} + \log d_{th}\right)$
Virtual links chosen with power-law distribution	$O\left(\dfrac{n}{d_{th}} + \log d_{th}\right)$	$O\left(\dfrac{n}{d_{th}} + \dfrac{\log d_{th}}{\log \log d_{th}}\right)$
Virtual links chosen with uniform distribution	$O\left(\dfrac{n}{d_{th}} + \dfrac{d_{th}}{(\log d_{th})^2}\right)$	$O\left(\dfrac{n}{d_{th}} + \dfrac{d_{th}}{(\log d_{th})^2}\right)$

Source: Chakraborty [33].

On-demand model: In the on-demand model, the nodes do not have any virtual neighbors. So, for this model, the simulation is run with the physical graphs.

Lower bound on the fidelity for single source–destination pair: Here, we assume that for all types of virtual graphs, all of the pre-shared links are available during the routing.

In the continuous model with $d_{th} > 2$, if the virtual graphs are constructed from a physical network (G_{ph}) like a ring (C_n) or a grid ($Grid_{n \times n}$) topology, if $|D| = 1$ and for all $i, j \in [0, n-1]$ and if $D_{i,j} \in \{0, 1\}$, then for any source–destination pair s, e, the expected number of required entangled swap operations for sharing an entangled link between s, e is as given in Table 17.1 [33].

Another result can be stated as follows: For a ring network C_n and a grid network $Grid_{n \times n}$, in the continuous model, if $|D| = 1$ and for some $s, e \in [0, n-1]$, if $D_{s,e} = 1$ then for both local best effort and modified greedy routing algorithms the expected fidelity, F, of the shared entangled link between s, e is lower-bounded by

Deterministic and Power Law Virtual Graphs

$$F^{O\left(\dfrac{n}{d_{th}} + \log d_{th}\right)} \tag{17.5}$$

Uniform Virtual Graphs

$$F^{O\left(\dfrac{n}{d_{th}} + \dfrac{d_{th}}{(\log d_{th})^2}\right)}, \tag{17.6}$$

where each of the pre-shared links has fidelity F [33]. We can further get the following result by replacing d_{th} by the diameter of C_n and $Grid_{n \times n}$.

For a ring network C_n and a grid network $Grid_{n \times n}$, in the continuous model with $d_{th} = \lceil n/2 \rceil$, if $|D| = 1$ and for some $s, e \in [0, n-1]$, if $D_{s,e} = 1$ then for both local best effort and modified greedy routing algorithms the expected fidelity of the shared entangled link between s, e is lower-bounded by

$F^{O(\log n)}$ for deterministic and power law virtual graphs and by $F^{O\left(n/(\log n)^2\right)}$ for uniform virtual graphs, where each of the pre-shared link has fidelity F.

Design Example 17.1

Performance of Greedy Routing Algorithm with Multiple Source–Destination Pairs on Ring Network
At this point, it would be instructive to develop programs to simulate the algorithms presented so far. As a reference point, we present several samples of the results published in [33]. The presented results cover the study of the performance of the greedy routing algorithm when we have multiple source–destination pairs. The average entanglement distribution time for all of the models using MATLAB simulations are evaluated.

Simulation parameters: For the simulation, C_{32} and *Grid* 5×5 are used as the physical graphs. The dist$_{phys}$ = 10 km, was assumed, which implies that each time step is equivalent to $10/c \approx$ 0.00006 s (c denotes the speed of light in the optical fiber). It is assumed that the threshold fidelity F_{th} is 0.8 and $p = 0.9993$. If we plug in all the values of these parameters in Eq. (17.2), we get $T_{th} \approx 1000$ steps, which is equivalent to 0.06 s. Note that the maximum classical communication time between any two nodes in both grid and ring network is on the order 10^{-5} s, which is much less than T_{th}. This makes the classical communication time negligible compared to the memory storage time.

In present-day practical implementations for basic heralded entanglement link generation the value of P_0 exceeds the order of 10^{-4} [39, 40]. Here, for the analysis of worst-case scenario, we assume $P_0 = 0.0003$. If we plug in the values of all the parameters in the expression $\left(1 - (1 - P_0)^{T_{th}}\right)$, then we get the result that the probability of generating an entangled link between two physical neighbor nodes within the time window T_{th} is at least 0.25.

On top of the physical graph, we construct the virtual graph using the techniques proposed in the previous sections. For each virtual graph, first we fix $|D|$ and then randomly generate the demand matrix D. Once we generate the demand matrix, then for each value of $D_{i,j}$ we compute the latency for entanglement distribution and update the topology of the virtual graph. For each value of $|D|$ we take 10 000 samples of D and compute the *AL* by taking the average over all the samples. In the simulation, it was also assumed that $D_{i,j} \leq cap$. For routing in the continuous model, first the nodes discover a path from a source to a destination and reserve the entangled links along the path. If all of the required entangled links are available, then the intermediate nodes just perform entanglement swap operation, otherwise the demand waits until all of the virtual links along the path are being generated. During the path discovery and entanglement reservation phase, it is assumed that there is no collision between two demands for reserving the same link. One can easily overcome this assumption by adding some priority corresponding to each demand. The nodes distribute an entangled link between a source and a destination using the procedure proposed in the previous sections. For each demand, we compute the waiting time, which is composed of the path discovery time, the time for generating missing entangled links, and the communication time for informing all the nodes in the path of the performance of the entanglement swap operation.

For the randomly chosen virtual neighbor models, we should first sample the neighbors and construct the corresponding virtual graph from the physical graphs. We take 100 such samples of virtual graphs and for each such sample graph, we compute the average latency *AL* by taking the average over all the samples of $|D|$ and virtual graphs. On the basis of this setup, Figure 17.3 shows a comparison of different routing algorithms on the deterministic virtual graphs, with $D_{i,j} = 1$ and $cap = 1$.

(Continued)

Design Example 17.1 (Continued)

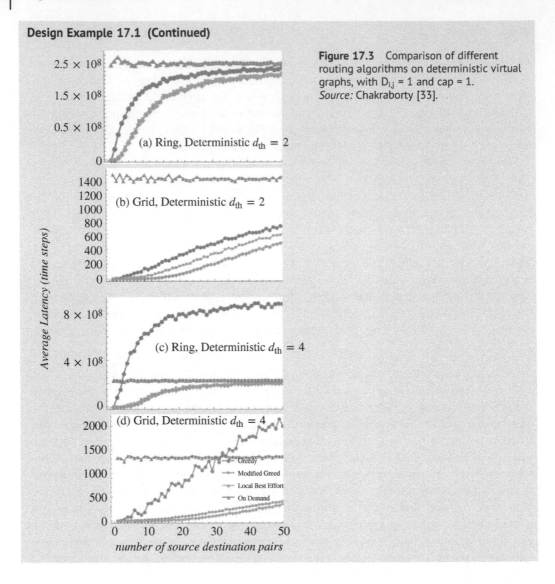

Figure 17.3 Comparison of different routing algorithms on deterministic virtual graphs, with $D_{i,j} = 1$ and cap = 1. *Source:* Chakraborty [33].

17.1.4 Quantum Network on Recursively Generated Graphs (RGGs)

Here, we focus on entanglement pre-sharing and routing models in more general graphs. The topology of a large real-life internet network is far more complex than a ring or grid, and it always grows with time. However, in most of the cases, the global pattern of a complex system emerges from the patterns observed in smaller subsystems. These phenomena can also be observed in the classical internet. The recursive graph is one of the best ways to model this kind of object [41, 42]. In general, recursive graphs are constructed from a base graph G_0, and at each recursive step, the current graph G_t is substituted by another graph G_{t+1}. The substitution rules remain the same for the entire evolution. Tensor product graphs are one example of such graphs [43]. Here, we study a model of the RGG, where a new graph is generated by substituting the edges of the old graph. One can find an example of such graphs in [21]. Here, we use the term *edge substitution* to describe this operation. It is defined as follows.

Edge substitution of a graph: Let $G_0 = (V_0, E_0)$ and $H = (V_H, E_H)$ be two graphs. The edge substitution of a graph G_0 with respect to H is an operation where each edge $(u, v) \in E_0$ (where $, v \in V_0$) is substituted by another graph $(\{u, w_{uv}\}, \{(u, w_{uv})\}) \cup G_{uv} \cup (\{v, w'_{uv}\}, \{(v, w'_{uv})\})$, where $w_{uv}, w'_{uv} \in G_{uv}$ and $G_{uv} = (V_{uv}, E_{uv})$ is isomorphic to H and $\text{dist}_{G_{uv}}(w_{uv}, w'_{uv}) = \text{diam}_H$. If $G_1 = (V_1, E_1)$ denotes the new substituted graph; then

$$V_1 = V_0 \bigcup_{(u,v) \in E_0} V_{uv} \tag{17.7}$$

$$E_1 = (E_0 - (u, v)) \bigcup_{(u,v) \in E_0} [(u, w_{uv}) \cup E_{uv} \cup (v, w'_{uv})].$$

We construct recursive graphs using the following rules:

1) The base graph $G_0 = (V_0, E_0)$ represents a quantum internet graph with physical links.
2) Let the physical graph at recursive step l be $G_l = (V_l, E_l)$.
3) Let $\mathcal{P}$ be a set of graphs. If any subgraph $\widetilde{G}_l \subseteq G_l$ is isomorphic to any graph in $\mathcal{P}$, then we perform edge substitution of $\widetilde{G}_l$ with respect to $H = (V_H, E_H)$. Suppose $\widetilde{G}_{l+1} = \left(\widetilde{V}_{l+1}, \widetilde{E}_{l+1}\right)$ denotes the substituted graph.
4) At recursive step $l + 1$, if the physical graph with physical links is $G_{l+1} = (V_{l+1}, E_{l+1})$, then

$$V_{l+1} = V_l \bigcup_{\tilde{G}_l \subseteq G_l - G_{l-1}; \; \tilde{G}_l \cong P} \widetilde{V}_{l+1} \text{ and } E_{l+1} =$$

$$\left(E_l - \left(\bigcup_{\tilde{G}_l \subseteq G_l - G_{l-1}; \; \tilde{G}_l \cong P} \widetilde{E}_l\right)\right) \bigcup_{\tilde{G}_l \subseteq G_l - G_{l-1}; \tilde{G}_l \cong P} \widetilde{E}_{l+1}$$

Regular recursively generated graphs (RRGG): A RGG with respect to an initial graph $G_0 = (V_0, E_0)$, a set of graphs $\mathcal{P}$, and a substitution graph $H = (V_H, E_H)$ is called regular if $G_0 = H$ is a regular graph and $\mathcal{P} = \{H\}$. Here, we focus on studying RRGG with $G_0 = H = C_n$ and $\mathcal{P} = \{C_n\}$.

17.1.5 Recursively Generated Virtual Graph

The main motivation for studying recursive graph is to understand the behavior of a hierarchical topology for a quantum network. Here, we are also interested in studying the quantum internet if the nodes from different levels of the hierarchy have different entanglement generation capabilities. It is assumed that for any RRGG $G_l = (V_l, E_l)$ if any node $v \in V_{l'} - V_{l'-1}$, for some $0 \le l' \le l - 1$, then it can pre-share an entangled link with any node within $d_{th}(\text{diam}_{G_{l-l'-1}} + 2)$ distance from itself. The nodes $v \in G_l - G_{l-1}$ can create entangled links within d_{th} distance from itself.

The detailed construction of the virtual graph $\mathcal{G}_l = (V_l, \mathcal{E}_l)$ is as follows:

1) Let $G_0 = (V_0, E_0)$ be a physical graph that is isomorphic to C_n. We construct the corresponding virtual graph $\mathcal{G}_0 = (V_0, \mathcal{E}_0)$ using the same procedure proposed in the previous section.
2) Let $G_{l-1} = (V_{l-1}, E_{l-1})$ denote the physical graph at the $(l-1)$-th level of recursion.
3) At the l-th level, if any subgraph $\widetilde{G}_{l-1}$ of G_{l-1} is isomorphic to C_n, then for all of the edges of $\widetilde{G}_{l-1}$ we perform edge substitution with respect to the graph $\mathcal{G}_0$. Let $\widetilde{\mathcal{G}}_l = \left(V_l, \widetilde{\mathcal{E}}_l\right)$ denotes the substituted graph.
4) This implies that, if at the l-th level the virtual graph is denoted by $\mathcal{G}_l = (V_l, \mathcal{E}_l)$, then $\mathcal{E}_l = \mathcal{E}_{l-1} \bigcup_{\tilde{G}_l \subseteq G_l - G_{l-1}; \tilde{G}_l \cong P} \widetilde{\mathcal{E}}_l$. Examples of the RRGG with $G_0 = H = C_8$ and $\mathcal{P} = \{C_8\}$ are presented in Figures 17.4 and 17.5.

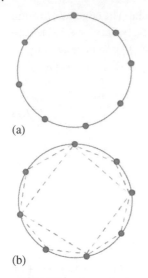

(a)

(b)

Figure 17.4 Recursively generated physical graph and virtual graph at the 0-th level of the recursive step: (a) RRGG with $G_0 = H = C_8$ and $\mathcal{P} = \{C_8\}$, at the 0-th level of the recursive step, (b) recursively generated deterministic virtual graph $\mathcal{G}_0$ with $d_{th} = 2$ corresponding to the physical graph G_0 shown in Figure 17.4a. Here the green lines marked by diamonds represent the pre-shared entangled state.
Source: Chakraborty [33].

The graph in Figure 17.4a represents the physical graph at the recursive step 0. From there we construct the deterministic virtual graph $\mathcal{G}_0$ with $d_{th} = 2$ using the techniques explained above. Later, in Figure 17.5a, we construct the physical graph by performing edge substitution corresponding to each of the edges in G_0. To improve the representation, in Figure 17.5a we color the nodes at G_0 red. One can note that, as a result of the edge substitution, between two red nodes there is a C_8. The virtual graph $\mathcal{G}_1$ in Figure 17.5b is constructed from $\mathcal{G}_0$ and G_1. In Figure 17.5b, all the edges of G_0 are substituted by a graph isomorphic to $\mathcal{G}_0$. Here also we color the nodes from G_0 red. Further, in $\mathcal{G}_1$, we keep the virtual links between the red nodes from $\mathcal{G}_0$. In Figure 17.5b, we denote these links by green dashed lines.

Understanding the properties of this type of network is useful to get an upper bound on the latency for distributing an entangled link between a source and destination pair using all of the routing algorithms described so far. In the previous section, we assume that for any RRGG $G_l = (V_l, E_l)$ if any node $v \in V_{l'} - V_{l'-1}$, for some $0 \leq l' \leq l - 1$, then it can pre-share entangled link with any node within $d_{th}(\text{diam}_{G_{l-l-1}}, + 2)$ distance from itself.

It was shown in [33] that the assumption holds for the recursively generated virtual graphs.

In the recursively generated virtual graph $\mathcal{G}_l = (V_l, \mathcal{E}_l)$, generated from an RRGG $G_l = (V_l, E_l)$, if for any two nodes $u, v \in V_l$, $\text{dist}_{G_l}(u, v) = 1$, then $\text{dist}_{\mathcal{G}_l}(u, v) \leq d_{th}(\text{diam}_{G_{l-l-1}}, + 2)$ if $\forall 1 \leq l' \leq l - 1, v \in V_{l'} - V_{l'-1}$ and $\text{dist}_{\mathcal{G}_l}(u, v) \leq d_{th}$ if $v \in V_l - V_{l-1}$ [33]

So, in the continuous model, if a single source–destination pair would like to generate a single entangled link, then the latency is on the order of the diameter of the physical graph. Here, we have another useful result for the computation of the diameter of an RRGG at the l-th step of the recursion [33]:

For any RRGG $G_l = (V_l, E_l)$ where $l \geq 1$ and $G_0 = (V_0, E_0) = C_n$ is the base graph and $\mathcal{P} = \{C_n\}$,

$$\text{diam}_{G_l} = \text{diam}_{G_0}(\text{diam}_{G_{l-1}} + 2). \tag{17.8}$$

By using the recursive relation in Eq. (17.8), we get the following upper bound on the latency for entanglement distribution in RRGG:

In the continuous model, for a virtual graph $\mathcal{G}_l = (V_l, \mathcal{E}_l)$ corresponding to any RRGG $G_l = (V_l, E_l)$ with $G_0 = (V_0, E_0) = C_n$ as base graph and $\mathcal{P} = \{C_n\}$, if $|D| = 1$ and for all $i, j \in V_l$ and if $D_{i,}$

$j \in \{0, 1\}$ then for any source destination pair s, e, the latencies of the routing algorithms 2–4 are upper-bounded by

$$O\left(\left(\frac{n}{2}\right)^{l+1}\right). \tag{17.9}$$

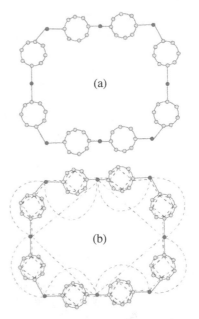

17.2 Quantum Network Protocol Stack

Here, we present a protocol stack model for breaking down the complexity of entanglement-based quantum networks along the lines presented in [44]. The focus is on the structures and architectures of quantum networks and not on concrete physical implementations of network elements. The quantum network stack is constructed in a hierarchical manner comprising several layers, similar to the classical network stack, and quantum networking devices operating on each of these layers are identified. The layers' responsibilities range from establishing point-to-point connectivity over intra-network state generation graph, to inter-network routing of entanglement. In addition, several protocols operating on these layers are presented. The existing intra-network protocols are extended for generating arbitrary graph states to ensure reliability inside a quantum network, where in this case reliability refers to the capability to compensate for devices failures. In addition, a routing protocol for quantum routers that enables arbitrary graph states to be generated across network boundaries is presented as well. This protocol, in correspondence with classical routing protocols, can compensate dynamically for failures of routers, or even of complete networks, by simply re-routing the given entanglement over alternative paths. We also discuss how to connect quantum routers in a hierarchical manner to reduce complexity, as well as reliability problems arising in connecting these quantum networking devices. At this point, we will assume that the reader is familiar with the seven-layer OSI protocol stack in classic networks, and so we will not introduce that topic.

Figure 17.5 Recursively generated physical graph and virtual graph at the first level of the recursive step: (a) RRGG with $G_0 = (V_0, E_0) = H = C_8$ and $\mathcal{P} = \{C_8\}$, at the first level of the recursive step. Here, red nodes correspond to the nodes from the graph G_0 in Figure 17.4. (b) Recursively generated deterministic virtual graph $\mathcal{G}_1$ with $d_{th} = 2$ corresponding to the physical graph G_0 shown in 17.5a. Here, green dashed lines denote the pre-shared entangled links from $\mathcal{G}_0$, and black dashed lines denote the newly generated pre-shared entangled links. *Source:* Chakraborty [33].

17.2.1 Preliminaries

Dijkstra's algorithm and Steiner trees: Here, we briefly recall two important algorithms in graph theory, which we will use here frequently. The first algorithm is Dijkstra's algorithm [45] which is used to determine the shortest path between two vertices $a \in V$ and $b \in V$ of a graph $G = (V, E)$. For that purpose, it uses a cost function, $E \to \mathbb{R}+$, that associates a certain cost with every edge in the graph. The algorithm is a greedy algorithm, which evaluates at each step whether a shorter path to a vertex is available. One may generalize Dijkstra's algorithm by not only finding the shortest path to one particular $b \in V$ but also finding a shortest path from $a \in V$ to any vertex $b \in B \subseteq V$. We denote Dijkstra's algorithm throughout this chapter by Dijkstra (a, B), where $a \in V$ and $B \subseteq V$.

The second algorithm we use in this section constructs an approximation of a so-called Steiner tree [46] on a graph. A Steiner tree on a graph $G = (V, E)$ is defined for a subset of vertices $S = \{v_1, \ldots, v_k\}$ as a tree that connects the nodes of S with minimal cost. The choice of the cost function $f: E \rightarrow \mathbb{R}_+$ depends on the discussed application. The tree is allowed to also contain vertices that are not an element of S. If $S = V$, the algorithm derives a minimal spanning tree. An algorithm for approximating a Steiner tree for S on $G = (V, E)$ with weighted edges is described in *Protocol 1* [44].

The problem of determining a Steiner tree has been shown to be NP-complete in the rectilinear case [47].

Protocol 1   Steiner (*S*, *x*)

Require: Set of nodes $S \subseteq V$
Require: Starting node $x \in S$
 1: $T = (T_S = \emptyset,\ E_S = \emptyset)$
 2: $T_S = \{x\}$
 3: **while** $T_S \neq S$ **do**
 4: d_i... distances to T_S
 5: **for each** x in $S \backslash T_S$ **do**
 6: d_i = Dijkstra(x, Ts)
 7: **end for**
 8: x' = arg min d_i
 9: $T_S = T_S \cup \{x'\}$
10: $E_S = E_S \cup \{\text{Path to}\, x'\}$
11: **end while**
12: **return** T

Source: Pirker and Dür [44].

Graph states and GHZ (Greenberger–Horne–Zeilinger) state: Graph states [48–51] are an important subclass of multipartite entangled quantum states. These states are associated with a classical graph $G = (V, E)$ where the vertices of V correspond to qubits and the edges in E indicate correlations among the vertices in V. In particular, for a graph $G = (V, E)$ (where $|V| = n$) we define the graph state $|G\rangle$ as the common +1 eigenstate of the correlation operators $K_a = X_a \otimes_{\{a,b\} \in E} Z_b$, where X and Z denote the Pauli matrices and the subscripts indicate on which qubit the Pauli operator acts on. We call two graph states $|G\rangle$ and $|G'\rangle$ LU-equivalent if there exist unitaries $U_1, \ldots, U_n$ such that $|G\rangle = U_1 \otimes \ldots \otimes U_n | G'\rangle$.

In the following, we discuss several important operations on graph states that we will use frequently here [48, 50]. The first operation is local complementation, which acts just locally on the qubits of the graph state and transforms the graph state according to the following rule: if a local complementation at vertex a is applied, then the subgraph induced by the neighborhood of a is inverted. We further require in this work Pauli measurements of the qubits of a graph state.

A measurement in the Z basis effectively removes the measured vertex from the graph, thereby also removing all the incident edges. Depending on the measurement outcome, some local Pauli corrections may have to be applied. A measurement in the Y basis corresponds to the following transformation of the graph state: first, a local complementation at the measured qubit is done, followed by removal of the corresponding qubit and all its incident edges. Again, depending on the outcome, some local Pauli corrections may be required.

Finally, we discuss GHZ states. An n-qubit GHZ state reads as $| \mathrm{GHZ}_n \rangle = (| 0 \rangle^{\otimes n} + | 1 \rangle^{\otimes n})/\sqrt{2}$. This state is Local Unitary (LU) equivalent to a fully connected graph or a star graph state; see, for example, [52]. Here, we usually depict GHZ states using a star graph with a chosen root node. In particular, we use the term GHZ state of size n, or its state $|\mathrm{GHZ}_n\rangle$, synonymously for the LU equivalent star graph state with n vertices.

An interesting property of GHZ states is that if one combines two GHZ states via a Bell measurement, then the result is again a GHZ state, up to local Pauli corrections. In other words, measuring a qubit of $|\mathrm{GHZ}_n\rangle$ and a qubit of $|\mathrm{GHZ}_m\rangle$ with a Bell measurement leads (up to LU) to the state $|\mathrm{GHZ}_{m+n-2}\rangle$. We will use this property extensively in this section. In principle, one can also use a different measurement setup to transform the state $|\mathrm{GHZ}_n\rangle$ and $|\mathrm{GHZ}_m\rangle$ to the state $|\mathrm{GHZ}_{m+n-1}\rangle$; see, for example, [53].

Quantum networks: Here, we will first provide additional information on the work done on quantum networks that rely on quantum repeaters [31, 54–68]. As discussed in the previous section, most of these approaches assume a network of quantum repeaters sharing Bell pairs with each other. However, in general, the goal of a quantum network should be to generate arbitrary states between remote clients rather than Bell pairs alone. For many applications, however, it suffices to be able to generate a specific class of states. Graph states [48, 50] play an important role in this respect, and the generation of arbitrary graph states among clients has been identified as a desirable goal for quantum networks [69, 70]. This is what we will require from our network in the following. For that purpose, several different approaches regarding the entanglement structure may be pursued, which include (i) the usage of a central master node that creates the state locally and teleports it to clients via Bell pairs shared between the central node and all others; (ii) establishment of pairwise entanglement between all of the network nodes first, followed by combining or merging it in an appropriate manner; and (iii) generation of the target state directly in a distributed manner by using multipartite states.

Approaches (i) and (ii) are far better understood than (iii), due to in-depth knowledge about bipartite entanglement and quantum repeater networks. Using a central master node that creates the requested graph state and teleports it to clients, thereby consuming Bell pairs, basically suffices to generate any arbitrary entangled state between the clients. However, this approach has one significant drawback: if the central master node fails, then the whole network goes down. This motivates a decentralized approach, leading to quantum repeater networks. In a network of quantum repeaters sharing bipartite entanglement, depending on the requested target state between the clients of the network, the intermediate quantum repeaters employ entanglement distillation and swapping operations (or other kinds of repeater protocols) to establish the required long-distance Bell pairs that will be merged to generate the target state. In order to establish these long-distance Bell pairs, routing in the repeater network needs to be done. Recently, several quantum routing protocols for bipartite quantum repeater networks were presented [71–77]]. In this context, the goal of a routing protocol is to determine a way of combining short-distance Bell pairs to establish a long-distance Bell pair in the most resource-efficient way. Reference [31] studies the application of Dijkstra's algorithm to quantum repeater networks, where the cost associated with an edge in the repeater network, that is, a small-scale Bell pair, depends on several physically motivated parameters, for example, the Bell-pair generation rate and transmittance. A routing algorithm for ring- and sphere-type network topologies of repeater networks has been proposed in [71]. In [61] a routing protocol for a two-dimensional cluster-type network relying on Bell pairs was proposed. Another algorithm for optimal routing in an end-to-end setting was subject of study in [77]. Routing using an entanglement gradient in quantum networks was studied in [75]. Reference [76] constructs a so-called base graph that represents the optimal entanglement structure of a repeater network to determine optimal paths, and a method for adapting this graph, for example, due to node failures, was studied in [78]. In [73] lower and upper bounds on the end-to-end capacities in arbitrarily complex quantum networks for single and multipath routing strategies for a single sender and a single receiver, but also for multiple senders and multiple receivers ultimately sharing bipartite states among each other simultaneously, were established. Finally, in [60] the routing of Bell pairs in memory-free, two-dimensional quantum networks was investigated, where intermediate workstations either generate Bell pairs or perform entanglement swapping, both in configurable directions, thereby achieving routing for establishing Bell pairs in the network.Routing protocols using multipartite quantum states received far less attention. Recently, it was shown that routing on a cluster state, which is shared among network nodes, using local complementation and measurements in the X basis provides an advantage compared to routing based on Bell pairs [79]. Here, the main goal was to generate one or several Bell pairs simultaneously from the cluster state. In addition, they show that by slightly modifying the protocol it can be used to generate GHZ states from the cluster state. An algorithm that is closely related to routing which uses multipartite states was presented in [80]. The algorithm decides whether a certain stabilizer state (which includes graph states) can be transformed into another stabilizer state by using single-qubit Clifford operations, single-qubit Pauli measurements, and classical communication. In [81] the complexity of such transformations between graph states was studied, and it was shown that this task is in general NP-complete.

Here, we follow mainly the entanglement-based multipartite approach to quantum networks as presented in [70]. Therefore, we recall several concepts that were introduced there. Clients are assumed to be of minimal functionality (single-qubit unitaries and single-qubit measurements), connect to quantum network devices by sharing entanglement with them, for example in the form of Bell pairs. The network devices, that is, routers and switches, use an internal multipartite quantum state, which we refer to as the device state, to connect their clients. Finally, networking devices connect to each other by sharing multipartite entangled quantum states, referred to as the network state. This is illustrated in Figure 17.6. In the example, three switches (boxes with multiple vertical arrows) and a router (the box with diagonal arrows) connect in a network via GHZ states of decreasing size (black lines indicate entanglement). Internally, each of these networking devices again uses GHZ states of decreasing size to connect three clients each. In this example, the clients connect via Bell pairs to the network devices. Observe that the entanglement structure of the network is different from the physical channel configuration (red arrows).

The aim of the network is to generate arbitrary graph states between its clients on demand. Because the clients have only minimal functionality, the quantum network devices have to carry out the generation of the target state.

Since the target state is not known prior to a request, the state of the static phase, that is, the network and device states, need to be such that any graph state can be generated from them using only LOCC (local operations and classical communication), without generating additional entanglement. All state combinations, that is, device state and network state, that satisfy this criterion – that is, that any arbitrary graph state can be generated from them using only LOCC – may serve as a device state and network state, respectively. In [61], two different types of multipartite states for

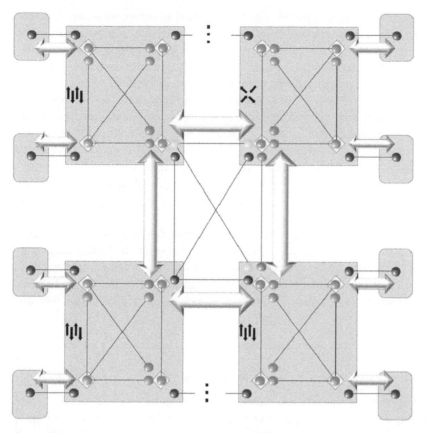

Figure 17.6 Network example with three switches (boxes with multiple vertical arrows) and a router (the box with diagonal arrows) connected in a network via Greenberger–Horne–Zeilinger (GHZ) states of decreasing size (black lines indicate entanglement). *Source:* Pirker and Dür [44]. (For more details see color figure in bins).

device and network states were identified: multiple copies of GHZ states (more precisely, the LU-equivalent star graph states) of decreasing size, or m-partite, fully connected graph states with decoration qubits on each edge (decorated graph state). The number m corresponds to the number of network devices that will connect.

Because we will use the GHZ architecture of quantum networks, we clarify this architecture further. In particular, if m network devices connect in this architecture, then the network state corresponds up to local unitaries to $\otimes_{i=2}^{m} | GHZ_i \rangle^{\otimes c_i}$, where c_i denotes the number of clients that connect to network device i. We observe that multiple copies of each GHZ state $| GHZ_i \rangle$ are mandatory for the network state to enable arbitrary graph states in the network; see [70] for a detailed discussion. Furthermore, we do not claim that the state to $\otimes_{i=2}^{m} | GHZ_i \rangle^{\otimes c_i}$ is optimal; it is just a state from which arbitrary graph states (by including the device states) can be generated in a network using LOCC only. However, depending on the desired target states of the network, only a subset of these states may be required for graph state generation.

We also relate the work of [70] to the phases of the previous section as follows: The static phase corresponds to the entanglement structure in the devices and across the network, that is, the network states. These states are generated during the dynamic phase, where the networking devices utilize the quantum channels to distribute the required entanglement. One way of doing this is to use the quantum network configuration protocol (QNCP) as discussed in [47]. In the adaptive phase, the clients request a graph state from the network, and the quantum network devices manipulate the states of the static phase in such a way that the target state is established between requesting clients. For that purpose, the quantum networking devices apply controlled Z gates (CZ gates), measurements in the Y or Z basis, and Bell measurements to connect the network and the device state.

Finally, we also comment on why following a direct multipartite approach is indeed beneficial compared to using Bell pairs between network devices in the setting considered here. If network devices share only Bell pairs among each other, then, depending on the requested graph states, the network devices have to apply more CZ gates, Bell measurements, and single-qubit measurements in the Y or Z basis in contrast to a multipartite approach. Observe that if these operations are noisy, a state of smaller fidelity will result compared to directly using multipartite quantum states; see [82]. Furthermore, such a direct multipartite approach offers a storage advantage compared to bipartite schemes [70, 82].

Most works on quantum networks, in the bi- and multipartite case, do not clearly specify which quantum task has to be done by which node in the network at which time. In particular, how to organize and classify quantum networking devices depending on their (yet-to-be-defined) capabilities is not fully known yet. However, similar problems arising in quantum repeater networks have, for example, been addressed in [83], which resulted in a stack model for quantum repeater architectures.

Assumptions

For the rest of this section, we make the following assumptions:

1) We restrict ourselves to discrete variable systems in terms of qubits.
2) Quantum networking devices can apply controlled phase gates, Bell-state measurements, and single-qubit Pauli matrices and measurements.
3) All quantum operations and measurements are assumed to be noiseless. However, we will later discuss possibilities of relaxing this assumption.
4) Bell-state measurements are deterministic. We discuss approaches and techniques for dealing with nondeterministic Bell-state measurements later.
5) Quantum network devices have quantum memories. We also discuss later the possibilities of dealing with noise in quantum memory as well.
6) Local quantum states are free, which means that quantum networking devices have the capability to create quantum states locally.

These assumptions correspond to the points 1–3 and 5–7 of the checklist of [84]. We do not require point 4, since all the operations to which the network devices apply are Clifford operations, for which several fault-tolerant computing schemes exist [85, 86].

Relation to other stack and network models: The approach used here is closely related to the works of [52, 83] as follows. Work in [83] introduces a protocol stack for quantum repeater networks, which establishes single entangled links, that is, a Bell pairs, between two nodes of a network. By contrast, the stack we present here aims to construct arbitrary graph states rather than single links among the clients of the network. This allows the clients of the quantum network to immediately execute more complex protocols, such as conference key agreement or even distributed quantum computation using graph states. The stack of [83] may appear inside layer 2 of the quantum network stack considered here.

Work in [52] introduces architectures for single quantum networks, but does not deal with their reliability and issues of connecting different networks to each other. Nevertheless, the GHZ architecture therein provides an efficient architecture for quantum networks that reduces storage requirements for network devices by a factor of two compared to direct bipartite architectures using Bell pairs. However, when connecting several networks, the graph state generation process across network boundaries becomes very complex. In order to simplify this process, the concept of region routing is introduced here. Region routing establishes a virtual network state across requesting network devices, which tremendously simplifies the graph state generation process. In other words, the output of region routing is a GHZ network state between the requesting network devices, which enables them to directly employ the state linking protocols of layer 3, to fulfill the graph state request. Some improvements of the protocols for GHZ architectures of [52] as examples of reliability and routing are presented later as well.

17.2.2 Quantum Network Protocol Stack

In classical computer networks, communication in a network follows the OSI layer model. This model vertically breaks down the complexity of networks into several layers. Each of these layers takes data (in the form of a packet) from the layer above, and passes it, after optionally prepending the packet by additional descriptive information, to the layer below. In contrast to the classical network stack, where descriptive information is added, we assume that qubits of neighboring layers in the quantum network stack can be accessed and combined.

The quantum network protocol stack for quantum networking devices proposed in [44] is depicted in Figure 17.7. Each layer has a specific goal, meaning that we break down the responsibilities in a quantum network vertically by clearly defining the objectives of a particular layer. One important feature of such a stack is that different layers can be evolved and studied independently. More specifically, changing protocols at higher layers of the stack does not imply changes to the lower layers; that is, lower layers do not depend on concrete implementations of higher layers. As already shown in the figure, depending on the layer a network device operates on, it has access to more or fewer layers of the quantum network stack.

The main motivation of following such a stack model in networking is abstractions. The key concept that stack models exploit in the form of layers is abstraction. In particular, layers introduce boundaries for complexities, as high-level layers do not have to deal with all the details of low-level protocols. For example, a developer of a quantum conference key agreement protocol will not have to deal with how the networks generate the graph state that the key agreement protocol requires. It simply commands the networks to generate such a state between its communication partners, without worrying about all the necessary quantum operations needed to construct the state, how to establish (possibly long-distance) entanglement, or the underlying physical implementations (which may also be different between networks). This example highlights the necessity (and also the power) of abstractions in networks, which is reflected in the quantum network stack discussed here.

For vendors and experimentalists, it is of the utmost importance to establish such a standardized and technology-independent view in quantum networks, as it provides the community with a set of common protocols and specifies which quantum networks devices can build upon. For example, for quantum network vendors, it is necessary to know which operations, protocols, and responsibilities a quantum network device has (needs to have) in a network. Without such a common notion or common understanding of a quantum network, interoperability of different network devices is not achievable.

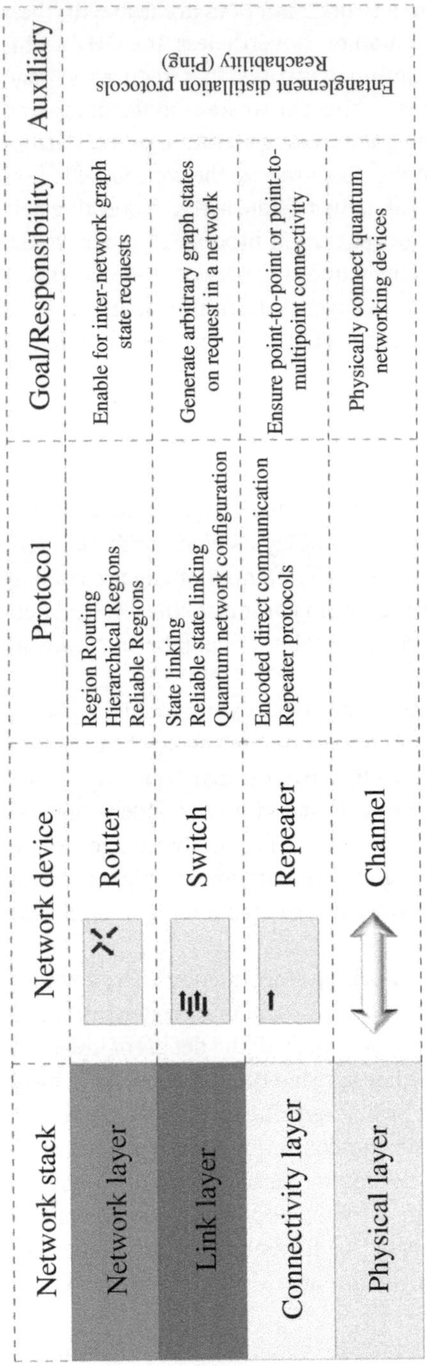
Network stack
Network device
Protocol
Goal/Responsibility
Auxiliary
Network layer
Router
Region Routing
Hierarchical Regions
Reliable Regions
Enable for inter-network graph state requests
Link layer
Switch
State linking
Reliable state linking
Quantum network configuration
Generate arbitrary graph states on request in a network
Connectivity layer
Repeater
Encoded direct communication
Repeater protocols
Ensure point-to-point or point-to-multipoint connectivity
Physical layer
Channel
Physically connect quantum networking devices
Entanglement distillation protocols
Reachability (Ping)

Figure 17.7 A quantum network protocol stack comprising four layers: physical layer (channel configuration), a connectivity layer (for ensuring connectivity for high-fidelity entangled states between network devices), a link layer (comprising a single network by sharing a multipartite entangled network state), and a network layer (connecting quantum network routers). *Source:* Pirker and Dür [44].

We also elaborate how such a network stack may work in terms of calls and procedures from a programming point of view. In principle, there are two different approaches: synchronous or asynchronous.

In a synchronous approach, a high-level layer instructs, or invokes, an operation of a low-level layer and waits until it receives a response. For example, in a synchronous approach, the connectivity layer invokes the operation for establishing short-link entanglement of the physical layer and waits until it responds.

In an asynchronous approach, high-level layers invoke operations of low-level layers, but they do not wait for the response of the low-level layer. Instead, the low-level layer notifies the high-level layer by publishing an event that the operation completed. For example, in an asynchronous approach, the connectivity layer invokes the operation for establishing short-link entanglement of the physical layer. However, in the asynchronous case, the connectivity layer does not wait for a response of the physical layer. Instead, the physical layer notifies the connectivity layer when the short-link entanglement was established. Such architectural approaches are also referred to as event-driven systems, since the components of a system communicate with each other via events.

In the following subsections, we elaborate on each of these layers in detail. Before that, we want to emphasize that if a client of a quantum network has sufficient capabilities, then it may work even on top of the network layer of Figure 17.7, which means that it can act as a router or switch in the network. Observe that in such a case, the protocols itself remain unchanged. Furthermore, a client can employ verification techniques and applications to the final states after graph state generation.

In what follows, we provide a complete example of how the layers of the quantum network protocol stack work together for a particular request

Layer 1—Physical Layer: This layer corresponds to the quantum channels connecting the interacting quantum network devices, for example, optical fibers or free space channels. It is responsible for forwarding qubits from one network device to the other, without applying any error correction or distillation mechanisms. The setting of layer 1 is depicted in Figure 17.8

At layer 1, quantum channels connect quantum networking devices. Neighboring quantum networking devices operating on layer 2 utilize the quantum channels to create long-distance entangled quantum states. In general, the entanglement structure at layer 2 is independent of the physical channel configuration of layer 1. Because this layer deals with the interfacing to the quantum channels of the network, it is also responsible for converting between quantum memory and quantum channel technologies. For example, a quantum network device may store qubits in an ion trap or NV center, but for transmission the quantum network device uses an optical setup. Therefore, this layer has to deal with the conversion between these different technologies. Importantly, the layers above do not have to deal with these interfacing and technology-dependent concerns. The physical layer encapsulates these implementation-specific interfacing details.

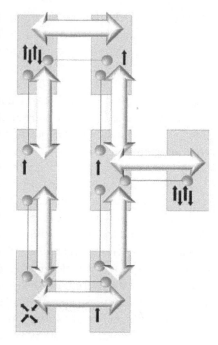

Figure 17.8 Setting of layers 1 and 2. *Source:* Pirker and Dür [44].

Quantum network devices will use different communication technologies at the physical layer. Therefore, quantum network converters that convert between different technologies, or transmission strategies, will be necessary for a full quantum internet. For example, if two networks use different frequencies in an optical setup for transmitting qubits, a converter has to translate between those different transmission strategies.

Finally, we point out that, since this layer is responsible for connecting network devices at the lowest level, the physical layer is responsible for establishing short-link entanglement. For that purpose, several different schemes exist. Some of them do not reveal whether an entangling attempt was successful or not, but some of them, referred to as heralding schemes, provide such a mechanism. Heralding schemes therefore have the advantage that network devices recognize successful entangling attempts, which enables the physical layer to repeat entangling attempts until success. Regarding the distribution protocol for short entanglement, quantum network devices may use any protocol that enables heralding such as Meet-in-the-middle or Sender-Receiver of [81], parts of the multiplexing protocol of [55] or the protocols of [87–89] in the case of optical transmission setups. Such protocols can run until entanglement attempts complete successfully, which the physical layer then reports to the connectivity for further processing.

This loose coupling between layers perfectly fits into stack models, in which high-level layers do not care about how lower layers fulfill their tasks; they only care that tasks are completed (by whatever means). In particular, the connectivity layer (which will be responsible for generating long-distance entanglement) assumes that short-link entanglement was generated, but the connectivity layer will not be concerned about how it was generated.

Layer 2– Connectivity Layer: This layer tackles errors due to imperfections in the quantum channels of layer 1. The techniques for establishing long-distance quantum communications reside on this layer. In particular, concrete technologies include quantum repeaters, bipartite [31, 56–68,

90–97] or multipartite [82, 98], but also the direct transmission of encoded quantum states [99–102] or percolation approaches [103, 104] that generate entanglement structures in a noisy quantum network of networking devices by applying techniques from percolation theory. The main purpose of devices operating on this layer is to enable point-to-point or point to-multipoint long-distance connectivity without any notion of requests. This functionality is crucial for the dynamic phase of a quantum network, where network devices have to (re-) establish long-distance entanglement, that is, network states, required in the static phase. Observe that if quantum repeaters are in use, the entanglement structure in terms of Bell pairs can be independent (or different from) of the configuration of quantum channels at layer 1.

The notion of success here depends on the protocol the connectivity layer employs. For example, in the case of quantum repeaters that use recurrence-type entanglement distillation, the long-distance entanglement attempt can fail if the distillation step of the recurrence-type protocol fails. However, quantum repeaters detect such a failure due to classical outcomes during protocol execution, which enables them to repeat the distillation step until the complete distillation protocol successfully completes. Furthermore, if Bell-state measurements are nondeterministic, the repeater protocol may also fail to perform entanglement swapping. However, several different protocols exist to deal with nondeterministic Bell state measurements and recognize successful entanglement attempts for quantum-optical implementations [105, 106]. Higher layers, that is, devices operating on a higher layer such as switches or routers utilize this layer to establish multipartite entangled quantum states within a network or between several independent networks; see Figure 17.8.

The layer above, that is, the link layer, is independent of the protocol that this layer uses. It simply instructs this layer to perform certain tasks within the network, such as establishing a long-distance Bell pair or a GHZ state between other high-level networking devices. Such instructions may also involve several devices of this layer across the network. Such an abstraction enables quantum network administrators to easily change protocols. For example, the link layer is not aware of whether the network devices use quantum repeaters, send encoded states across the quantum channels, or rely on techniques from entanglement percolation to generate entanglement. Since the layers above (link and network layer) are completely decoupled from the connectivity layer, devices at layer 2 can apply enhanced techniques, such as finding optimal paths in quantum repeater networks by routing, without affecting the upper layers of our stack.

Layer 3 – Link Layer: The link layer defines the boundaries of a quantum network in terms of an entangled, distributed, multipartite network state that the networking devices of a quantum network share in the static phase. This layer utilizes the connectivity layer to establish the entangled network state during the dynamic phase, which therefore also enables long-distance quantum networks. Once the dynamic phase completes, the link layer devices (switches) share multipartite entangled states that comprise the network state; see Figure 17.9. (The network devices of layer 3 request and combine the entangled states from layer 2 to create the network state (green nodes). Depending on client requests, this network state is consumed during graph state generation. On layer 4, quantum routers connect quantum networks via multipartite entangled quantum states (red nodes). In this figure, the quantum routers connect via GHZ network states).

We thus end up in the static phase. We observe that the entanglement structure can be completely different from the underlying configuration of quantum channels and devices or protocols operating at layer 2. Concrete instances of networks may connect in the static phase via, for example, GHZ states or decorated graph states, as proposed in [70].The link layer orchestrates and coordinates the process of generating the network state, utilizing the connectivity layer in the dynamic phase, and is responsible for generating arbitrary graph states between the clients of the network during the adaptive phase via a so-called linking protocol; see Figure 17.7. The linking protocol is responsible

Figure 17.9 Settings of layers 3 and 4. *Source:* Pirker and Dür [44]. (For more details see color figure in bins).

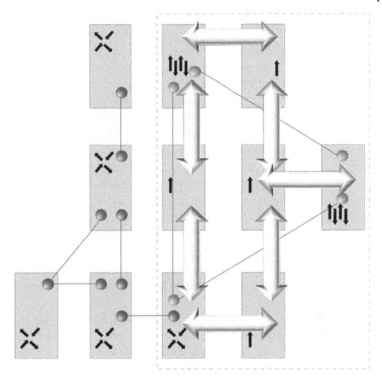

for transforming the entangled network state and device-internal states using only LOCC to the requested graph state, which consumes the entanglement of the network state. These linking protocols depend on the network state. For example, for GHZ or decorated architectures, devices at this layer may invoke the linking protocols of [70] to create the requested graph state.

In addition, the link layer also has the capability to invoke entanglement distillation protocols for two-colorable graph states [107–110] which ensures that the network state has a sufficiently high fidelity. In addition, it uses the auxiliary protocols for entanglement swapping and merging states.

Layer 4 – Network Layer: The network layer is responsible for generating and manipulating inter-network entanglement to enable graph state requests spanning several different quantum networks. The network devices operating on this layer are quantum routers. They are connected with each other via multipartite entangled quantum states in so-called regions in the static phase, similar to quantum networks at the link layer. The corresponding states depend on the protocol of this layer. The overall setting is illustrated in Figure 17.9 Regions connect in the same fashion as quantum networks do. More specifically, quantum routers in the same region share a multipartite entangled quantum state with each other, such as a GHZ network state, but in contrast to a switch, a quantum router may be part of several regions at the same time. In addition, a router may also be part of a quantum network of the link layer, thereby providing an entry point to that quantum network from the viewpoint of other networks. We outline available operations and protocols below, and discuss them in more depth later for regions connecting via GHZ states. Observe that lower layers, such as link or connectivity layer, are independent of the protocols and considerations of the network layer. The network layer is responsible for enabling graph state requests across network boundaries in the adaptive phase. Therefore, some sort of routing between different quantum networks needs to be done. More precisely, to enable graph state requests across networks, a quantum routing protocol should establish a "virtual network state" between the quantum networks that are part of a graph state request. The topology of the virtual network state will depend on the routing protocol. Note, however, that this only involves local manipulation of entangled states that are already present in the network from the static phase, and no generation of additional entanglement is required. Hence, these requests can typically be fulfilled fast. Once routing finishes, the routers use this virtual network state of the network layer to establish a network state between the requesting network devices inside their respective networks. Routers achieve this by combining the virtual network state of layer 4 with the inner network state of layer 3 by local operations, for example, in terms of Bell measurements for GHZ states or controlled phase gates and measurements in the Y basis for decorated architecture. However, the output of the routing protocol creates a full network state among the requesting network devices. It might be necessary to transform the output state of routing into an appropriate form to combine it with the intra-network states. We note that the link layer itself is not involved in this routing process. We discuss a routing protocol for regions using GHZ network states and approaches for simplifying the complexity in regions and introducing reliability for connecting routers using GHZ network states in regions later. Finally, the network layer can also invoke entanglement distillation protocols for two-colorable graph states, and techniques for entanglement swapping and merging from the set of auxiliary protocols at all layers.

Auxiliary protocols: As illustrated in Figure 17.7, each layer has access to some auxiliary protocols. The network devices use these protocols to, for example, to (i) generate high-fidelity entangled quantum states, (ii) check whether network devices operating at the same layer are still reachable, (iii) perform entanglement swapping or merging, (iv) employ techniques for error correction, or (v) classically monitor the status of the network using the techniques of (i)–(iv). Depending on the layer a quantum network device operates on, it will use different subsets of the aforementioned protocol types.

The protocols of (i) are entanglement distillation protocols. The layers use these protocols to generate high-fidelity entangled quantum states across the network by transforming several noisy input states to fewer, but more entangled copies. We can associate with each layer one class of entanglement distillation protocols. For example, layer 2 may use entanglement distillation protocols for Bell pairs [101, 111], whereas layer 3 and layer 4 need access to the entanglement distillation protocols for two-colorable graph states [107–109] or CSS (named after Calderbank, Shor, and Steane) states [110].

The protocols of (ii) address reachability in quantum networks. In entanglement-based quantum networks, there are different forms of reachability. At a basic level, this is about the (classical) reachability of the corresponding network device. However, this is not sufficient; also, the presence of the required entangled states needs to be ensured. We discuss this issue in detail later.

Entanglement swapping and merging, that is, protocol type (iii), are operations that are crucial for repeater architectures, but also for the modification of entangled states on the link and network layer. Entanglement swapping corresponds to a Bell measurement that is applied to one qubit of two Bell states each plus the classical communication of the measurement outcome. Such a measurement re-establishes a Bell pair between outer nodes and is usually used to generate long-distance Bell pairs. It may also be used to combine 2 GHZ states into a single larger GHZ state. By contrast, merging connects two graph states into a single graph state in a well-defined, protocol-dependent manner. This technique emerges especially at the link layer, at which network devices execute linking protocols to generate graph states that clients request. Such protocols include controlled phase gates, as well as single qubit measurements. Observe that the realization of such operations (Bell state measurements, controlled phase gates, single qubit measurements) depend on the physical implementation technology. Therefore, these types of auxiliary protocols may include fault-tolerant quantum computational elements to deal with noise. In addition, the network devices may employ different strategies for dealing with nondeterministic gates and measurements, such as [112] for optical implementations or [113, 114].

The techniques of (iv) correspond to quantum error correcting codes, which networking devices may use to not only tackle channel noise and loss that occur during the dynamic phase, but also to store qubits that are part of larger entangled states for a longer time in quantum memory in the static phase.

The techniques of (v) monitor the health status of the stack layers, also across device boundaries. For that purpose, we use the protocols of (i) to ensure that the fidelity of quantum states is sufficiently high. Monitoring the fidelity of quantum states is in general difficult; however, devices may employ parameter estimation techniques to statistically infer the fidelity of the entire ensemble of quantum states by employing measurements to a Sub ensemble. Furthermore, the protocols of (ii) may be used on a regular basis to decide whether network devices are reachable. If devices do not respond to these reachability requests, the remaining network devices conclude that they are no longer part of the network, thereby invoking recovery mechanisms. Additional auxiliary protocols may be added on demand. We emphasize the importance of these kind of protocols in a network stack, since monitoring the health status of a network as well as recovery from failures are indispensable mechanisms to operate a fully functioning network.

17.2.3 Layer 3 – Reliable State Linking

In this section, we discuss how to achieve reliability at the link layer using multipartite entanglement, which is very important for the static phase of a quantum network. The term *reliability* in our case means that parts of the entanglement structure in a quantum network remain intact, that is, usable for other devices, if one network device disconnects without performing any further operation. Before discussing the reliability of multipartite networks, we review its problems arising in bipartite networks using Bell pairs. In this case, reliability depends greatly on the topology of the distributed Bell pairs. For example, consider a quantum network with a central master node sharing Bell states with all clients. Clearly, if this central master node disappears, all Bell pairs are lost, and hence, no further communication is possible. In a fully bipartite approach, where all quantum network devices connect to each other via Bell states in a decentralized manner, and clients only connect to these network devices, we note that the problem of reliability disappears. The failure of a node affects only the entangled pairs the node is part of; all other Bell pairs remain undisturbed.

Here, we consider the GHZ architecture within networks for our reliability protocols in quantum networks; see [70]. Recall that in this architecture network devices that reside within the same network share multiple copies of GHZ states of decreasing size. The network state $\aleph$ connecting m devices is, up to several copies of the states, LU equivalent to the state $\aleph = \otimes_{i=2}^{m} | \text{GHZ}_i \rangle$. In particular, the network state corresponds to the star graph states that one obtains by transforming each GHZ state $|\text{GHZ}_i\rangle$ of $\aleph$ to a star graph state of size i via local unitaries. Due to this LU equivalence, we often use in the remainder of this work the term GHZ state to refer to the corresponding star graph state. If a network device leaves the network, it measures all of its leaf qubits of the GHZ states of $\aleph$ in the Z basis and the root qubits of its associated GHZ states in the X basis. These measurements simply reduce the sizes of all the GHZ states connecting the devices, thereby preserving entanglement in the network.

We now illustrate why it may be a problem to directly use star graph states without any further modification as the network state. For that purpose, consider the GHZ state $|\text{GHZ}_i\rangle$, and suppose one network device disconnects from the network without performing the protocol for leaving the network on his qubits of the network state. Such a disconnect corresponds to tracing out all the qubits of that particular network device. The state after tracing out any qubit of the 1 GHZ state of $\aleph$ results in $\mathrm{tr}_j[|\mathrm{GHZ}_i\rangle\langle\mathrm{GHZ}_i|] = (|0\rangle\langle0|^{\otimes(i-1)} + |1\rangle\langle1|^{\otimes(i-1)})/2$, which is a separable state. Therefore, losing one qubit due to a disconnect will destroy the entanglement between all other network devices that are part of that GHZ state. The situation is shown in Figure 17.10. (If one of the network devices disappears, then at least one GHZ state is completely lost (gray vertices indicate entanglement lost), as disconnecting corresponds to tracing out a qubit from a GHZ state, which results in a separable state. The green vertices are not affected by the disconnect.) As depicted in the figure, depending on which network device disconnects, we may even lose all network states. In particular, if one of the network devices that connect via $|\mathrm{GHZ}_2\rangle$ (i.e., N_3 or N_4) disappears, all network states will be lost, since these network devices store one leaf of each GHZ state of $\aleph$.

Because we cannot predict which network device will fail or disconnect, we have to find solutions that are able to deal with the disconnect of any of the network devices such that the functionality for the remaining system is preserved. Nevertheless, we find that schemes using multipartite entanglement are still more beneficial in terms of storage size compared to a full bipartite approach. In the following, we discuss two protocols as a proof of principle that tackle the effect of failing network devices.

Reliable state linking – symmetrization: In general, several copies of each GHZ state in $\aleph$, which comprises the network state, are mandatory to enable for arbitrary graph state requests in a network.

The first solution is to symmetrize the network state. In particular, we circularly shift the parties of the network with respect to their assignment to leaves and roots of the GHZ states of $\aleph$. The situation is summarized in Figure 17.11a. Static phase: The first solution to tackle device failures is to rotate the full network state, that is, cyclically shift the parties. For m network devices, cyclically shifting the network state m times results in m different configurations. More specifically, we

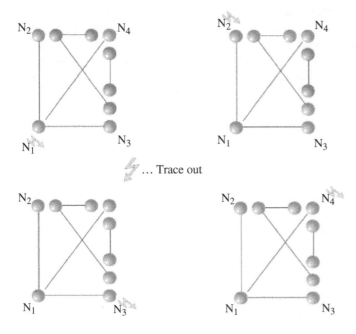

... Trace out

Figure 17.10 Greenberger–Horne–Zeilinger (GHZ) states are very fragile. *Source:* Pirker and Dür [44]. (For more details see color figure in bins).

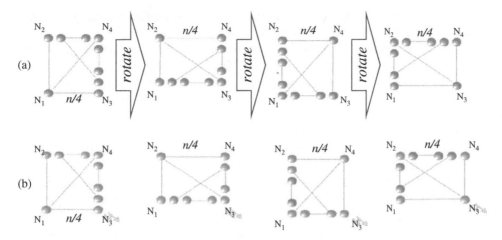

Figure 17.11 (a) Static phase, (b) adaptive phase. *Source:* Pirker and Dür [44]. (For more details see color figure in bins).

split the n copies of GHZ into m configurations, where each configuration is obtained by cyclically shifting the root-leaf assignment in GHZ. A further extension might be a full symmetrization among the network devices. (b) Adaptive phase (Figure 17.11b): If one network device disconnects, then there exists at least one configuration that ensures full connectivity among the remaining devices,which implies that at least n/m copies of the network state of GHZ remain intact. But there also exist other configurations that remain partially intact.)

Observe that by symmetrizing the root-leaf assignment in the state of $\aleph$, each network device stores several roots of each GHZ state $|\text{GHZ}_i\rangle$ where $2 \leq i \leq m$ and m denotes the number of devices in the network. We call the state obtained after one cyclic-shifting step a configuration.

The crucial observation is that if one network device disconnects, there exists one configuration for which the disconnecting device holds the root of the largest GHZ state $|\text{GHZ}_m\rangle$ of $\aleph$. All other network devices connect in this configuration via the states $|\text{GHZ}_i\rangle$ where $2 \leq i \leq m - 1$. Therefore, the disconnect of this network device only destroys the largest GHZ state in that configuration, whereas all other states in this configuration remain intact. The situation is summarized in Figure 17.11.

Furthermore, as we discuss in the figure, we propose to distribute n copies of the state of $\aleph$. Because the number of network devices, that is, m, is constant (unless a network device leaves the network, which we assume to happen rarely as in classical networks), at least n/m copies of the state in $\aleph$ remain intact. Therefore, by increasing the number of copies n, the network administrator is able to attain higher reliability for the quantum network. For example, by letting $n = 2m$ the network administrator ensures that if one of the network devices fails, at least two full copies of the network state of $\aleph$ remain intact for further processing. We also observe that in the case of symmetrization, the protocol for leaving the network for a network device does not change.

Several variants of such a symmetrization approach are possible. For example, instead of symmetrizing GHZ states of different sizes, it is worth considering, as proposed above, to symmetrize GHZ states of constant size in a uniform way across the network devices. Although such an approach is beneficial in terms of reliability, it introduces an additional overhead in terms of resources, that is, qubits that the network devices have to store, to ensure the goal of a quantum network that generates arbitrary graph states between clients. Another variant – in order to tackle arbitrary losses, including failures of multiple network devices – is to use a full symmetrization according to all possible permutations of network devices with GHZ states of decreasing size.

Reliable state linking – shielding: The second solution to ensure reliability in a quantum network is to introduce shielding qubits into the star graph states comprising the network state. In the following, when referring to a GHZ state $|GHZ_i\rangle$, we mean the corresponding star graph state of size i. To achieve reliability, we place on each edge of the GHZ states $|GHZ_i\rangle$ in $\aleph$ one additional qubit (which we call the shielding qubit of that edge in the GHZ state), except the Bell pair, of the network state. We consider the graph state corresponding to this decorated graph, where we use the star graph to represent the initial GHZ state. This shielding qubit belongs to the network device that holds the root of the respective GHZ state; see Figure 17.12. (a) Static phase: The second solution to achieve reliability in a quantum network using entanglement in the form of GHZ states is to introduce shield qubits. We place on each edge of every GHZ state (represented by a star graph) one qubit and consider the resulting graph state. Only the Bell pair needs no decoration, as entanglement vanishes if either of the two nodes fails. (b) Adaptive phase (Figure 17.12b): Because tracing out a qubit commutes with Z measurements on other qubits, the remaining devices just have to measure the shield qubits to the disconnected device in the Z basis. The remaining devices will still have a full network state.

In terms of stabilizers, we uniquely describe the corresponding graph state resulting in shielding the GHZ states $|GHZ_i\rangle$ for $2 \leq i \leq m$, where m denotes the number of network devices, as the eigenstate of the family of operators $K_j = X_j \otimes_{k \in N_j} Z_k$, where j denotes the vertices of the graph state in the static phase of Figure 17.12, and N_j the neighborhood of vertex j.

To create a shielded GHZ state i, network device i locally prepares a star graph state of size i, as well as long-distance Bell pairs to the network devices $1 \leq j \leq i - 1$ using the connectivity layer. Finally, network device i merges its local star graph state with the Bell pairs, which results in the state of K_j. Alternatively, if the connectivity layer uses the transmission of encoded states,

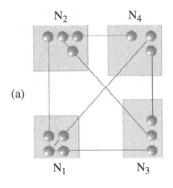

(a)

Figure 17.12 (a) Static phase, (b) adaptive phase. *Source:* Pirker and Dür [44]. (For more details see color figure in bins).

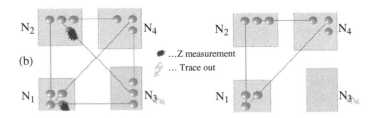

(b)

☀ ...Z measurement

⚡ ... Trace out

network device i prepares the shielded GHZ state locally and transmits the leaf qubits as encoded states to the network devices $1 \leq j \leq i - 1$.

During network operation, the link layer detects network device failures by using classical ping messages; see "monitoring protocol" later in this section. For example, if a network device is not responding to the ping requests, then all other network devices assume that the unreachable network device has disconnected. The crucial observation for the shielded GHZ states of Figure 17.12 is that if a network device disconnects, which corresponds to a trace of its qubits, the remaining network devices preserve their states by measuring all the shielding qubits to the disconnecting network device in the Z basis. This can easily be seen since the trace out operation commutes with the Z measurement of neighboring qubits, which effectively decouples the part of the shielded GHZ network states corresponding to the disconnecting network device; see Figure 17.12. Because we assume that operations are deterministic, the recovery operation from an unexpected disconnect is also deterministic.

However, if no error occurs, the networking devices can reduce the shielded GHZ states to a GHZ state by measuring the shielding qubits in the Y basis, which establishes wires to other network devices; see, for example, [70]. Observe that, depending on the measurement outcomes, some Pauli corrections may be necessary.

In the following, we compare the number of qubits necessary in this shielded GHZ approach to a full bipartite solution, using Bell pairs alone, because this scheme automatically ensures reliability in quantum networks.

In [70] it was shown that the number of qubits of a GHZ network state for a network of m devices connecting $c_1, \dots, c_m$ clients after expanding the network state to all connected clients is $M_M = \sum_{i=2}^{m} \left[c_i \left(1 + \sum_{k=1}^{i-1} c_k \right) \right]$. We explain M_M as follows: Network device i connects to the network devices $1, \dots, i-1$ via c_i copies of the GHZ state $|\text{GHZ}_i\rangle$. Each copy of that GHZ state corresponds to the adjacency of one client of network device i to the $c_1, \dots, c_{i-1}$ clients located at the network devices $1, \dots, i-1$. To take into account all these adjacencies, the network devices $1, \dots, i-1$ expand each of the c_i copies of the GHZ state $|\text{GHZ}_i\rangle$ to $|\text{GHZ}_{1 + \sum_{k=1}^{i-1} c_k}\rangle$ via Bell measurements. We refer to this state also as an expanded network state.

Recall that we decorate each edge of the GHZ network state $|\text{GHZ}_m\rangle, \dots, |\text{GHZ}_3\rangle$ once, and that device i has c_i copies of the state $|\text{GHZ}_i\rangle$. Therefore, the total number of qubits that have to be stored including the shielding qubits is $M_S = \sum_{i=2}^{m} \left[c_i \left(1 + \sum_{k=1}^{i-1} c_k \right) \right] + \sum_{i=3}^{m} c_i (i-1)$.

For the number of qubits necessary in following a direct bipartite approach, one finds [70] that $M_B = 2 \sum_{i=1}^{m-1} c_i \sum_{j=i+1}^{m} c_j$ qubits are required in all. The number of qubits of the shielded GHZ network state and the bipartite approach for various scenarios are compared in Table 17.2.

From Table 17.2, we find that even though it seems at first glance that shielding the GHZ network state will introduce a large overhead, it still results in better performance in terms of qubits to be stored compared to a direct bipartite approach. The reason for this is that we place qubits only on the edges of the network state before expansion, and not for the expanded network state. In contrast to symmetrization, shielding requires shielded GHZ states instead of GHZ states as a network state. These shielded GHZ states impose an additional overhead in terms of quantum memory compared to the symmetrization technique. Nevertheless, at the same time, shielding is more effective in the case of device failures, as all states of the network remain intact after a device failure. Finally, we note that the protocol for leaving a network changes slightly in the case of reliable state linking with shielding. In particular, if a network device leaves the network, it first measures all of its shielding qubits in the Y. Then it executes the protocol for leaving a GHZ network.

Table 17.2 Comparison of the number of qubits that have to be stored in a direct bipartite approach using Bell pairs alone to the shielded GHZ network state, and the GHZ network state without shielding with different number of clients $c_i = c$ and m devices.

c	m	M_B	M_S	M_M
$c = 3$	$m = 5$	180	129	102
	$m = 10$	810	564	432
	$m = 15$	1890	1299	987
$c = 5$	$m = 5$	500	315	270
	$m = 10$	2250	1390	1170
	$m = 15$	5250	3215	2695
$c = 7$	$m = 5$	980	581	518
	$m = 10$	4410	2576	2268
	$m = 15$	10 290	5971	5243

Source: Pirker and Dür [44].

17.2.4 Layer 4 – Region Routing

In this section, we discuss protocols operating on layer 4 of the quantum network stack and use GHZ network states to connect routers into regions. Recall that the purpose of this layer is to enable inter-network graph state requests by LOCC.

We start by discussing a routing protocol for the adaptive phase in quantum networks for quantum routers, which may connect in a highly irregular manner. Next, we introduce a way to reduce the size of network states appearing in the static phase for connecting routers in a region, which also reduces the complexity of the regions. Finally, we discuss how to achieve reliability for connecting routers in regions.

Region routing: We start with a brief review of classical routing protocols. In classical routing, there exist protocols using metrics (such as Routing Information Protocol (RIP) [115]) and the so-called link state protocols (such as Open Shortest Path First (OSPF) [116]). Protocols using metrics internally construct a so-called routing table. Each table entry is a key–value pair with the key corresponding to a network address and values corresponding to the distance and interface port of the router to which packets will be forwarded.

Link-state protocols operate in a different manner. They internally construct a global view of the network topology, that is, a weighted graph where the weight of an edge corresponds to the distance or cost between two nodes of the network. Depending on the destination IP address of an incoming packet, routers compute a minimal cost path through the network by using Dijkstra's algorithm. The protocol that we present here follows a similar approach as the link-state protocols in classical networks.

Before we start with the protocol description, we first recall that we abstract quantum networks via routers as in classical networks. The router provides, according to the stack of Figure 17.7, an entry point to a quantum network. For simplicity, we assume that there is only one router in each network. Several routers in one network can be taken into account as follows: If there are two routers, then there exists at least one part of the network state that connects those routers. One of the routers can teleport all of its qubits that belong to another region to the other, thereby providing a single-entry point to the network under consideration.

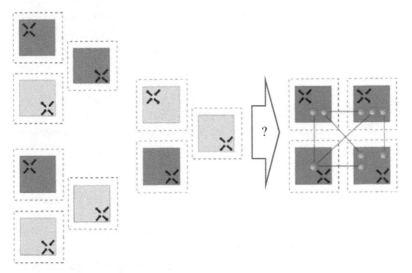

Figure 17.13 The goal of a quantum routing protocol. *Source:* Pirker and Dür [44].

In the previous section, we identified the goal of the network layer – and therefore also of routing – as follows: Routing protocols in quantum networks should establish a virtual network state across routers, as this enables routers of networks to combine the virtual network state with the respective inner network states of each router to fulfill graph state requests across network boundaries. The situation is summarized in Figure 17.13 (A routing protocol should generate a "virtual network state" between routers of different quantum networks that are involved in a request. After that, the routers combine the virtual network state with the inner network state to transfer the entanglement to the requesting devices. This enables the networking devices to directly apply the graph state linking protocol of layer 3 to complete the request.)

Now we discuss a routing protocol that achieves the above goal. For that purpose, we assume that routers of networks connect via GHZ network states in regions. Such a scenario corresponds to the case when a network administrator defines which routers will connect in a region. Such a configuration of routers in regions, and thus also the configuration of network states, may be highly irregular. We stress that such a scenario is very important for practical settings, as it enables network administrators to define network boundaries and which networks connect to each other in regions. The network administrator may have knowledge about the traffic that clients in quantum networks produce and tries to minimize the overall entanglement cost associated with network states. The goal of the routing protocol is now as follows: Clients, possibly located in different networks, wish to generate a particular graph state. The aim of the region routing protocol is to establish a virtual network state across the routers of networks involved in a request; see Figure 17.14. (A region – indicated by dashed lines – connects routers (boxes) via a GHZ network state. A router may be part of several regions. If clients of specific networks request a graph state, the region routing protocol shall establish a virtual network state among the routers of these networks. This state can then be used to generate a network state between graph states requesting quantum network devices.)

In order to generate such a virtual network state, Dijkstra's algorithm is used (which some works on routing for quantum repeater networks also use, e.g., [74]) and the algorithm for determining a Steiner tree as discussed earlier. We remark that Steiner trees have also been used in [117] for deriving fundamental limitations on quantum broadcast channels. These algorithms require the

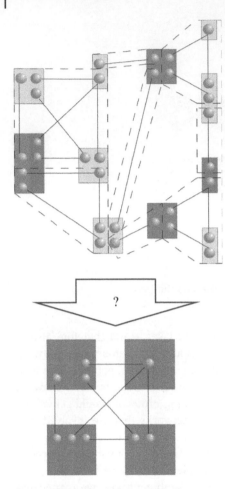

Figure 17.14 Regions and how they connect. *Source:* Pirker and Dür [44].

definition of a cost function C for the edges of the graph. For illustrative purposes, we use the number of states the routing protocol consumes as cost; that is, each edge in the graph has unit cost. We discuss more appropriate cost functions later. The input to the region routing protocol is a set of networks (or more precisely, the routers of the networks) that connect via regions. Each router corresponds to a vertex in the graph corresponding to the configuration of regions. Suppose a subset $S = \{N_1, \ldots, N_k\}$ of the vertices request a graph state. Then we perform the following algorithm: In step 1 of *Protocol 2*, the routers transform the configuration of states connecting the regions to a classical graph by merging all qubits of a router to a single node. However, observe that the routers have to keep track of the states (which correspond to edges in the graph) that the Steiner tree algorithm selects internally. The routers further optimize the consumption of states by minimizing the multipartite entanglement they select between regions for a request. An alternative approach for the step is to generate the classical graph that the Steiner tree algorithm requires by associating a qubit with a vertex in the classical graph, and creating an edge for every possible Bell measurement that can, in principle, connect two regions. Observe that the while-loop of *Protocol 2* creates one of the $k - 1$ GHZ states of the virtual network state. Steps 3–5 create one part of the GHZ network state with the root located at v' by using a Steiner tree between the remaining routers in S. A complete example for the routing protocol is provided in the Design Example 17.2.

Protocol 2 Region Routing(*S*)

Require: Set of nodes $S \subseteq V$, V set of networks
1: Transform the graph of vertices (networks) to a classical graph, where qubits belonging to the same network fusion into one vertex. We denote this graph by $G' = (V, E)$.
2: **while** $S \neq \emptyset$ **do**
3: Select $v \in S$
4: T = Steiner (S, v)
5: Generate $|\text{GHZ}_{|S|}\rangle$ with root at v according to T
6: $S = S \backslash \{v\}$
7: **end while**

Source: Pirker and Dür [44].

Note that *Protocol 1* presented earlier, to determine a Steiner tree, requires the usage of a specific cost function. This cost function should take into account the cost of generating and combining bipartite or multipartite states at different layers. Channel noise as well as noise in local operations are relevant for the performance of entanglement distillation protocols and the combination of different states (e.g. via entanglement swapping or merging), and hence determine the cost. An appropriate choice of cost function remains a subject of research, but note that using multipartite entangled states can also be beneficial in this respect [107–109].

Hierarchical regions: One obvious way of connecting quantum networks in a region is to connect them all in the same way that a quantum network connects its devices, that is, in a single region. In that case, only Z measurements on the GHZ states connecting the networks are necessary to establish the state depicted in Figure 17.13. However, such an approach has one serious drawback: The size of the network state will increase with the number of networks, that is, the number of routers. In particular, to connect n routers in a single region, the largest GHZ state connecting them is of size n. In a practical realization, the size of GHZ states might however be limited. The reason is that GHZ states suffer from noise and decoherence and are in fact become fragile with increasing size n [118, 119]. The approach discussed in the previous section might also be impractical. The network administrator plays a key role, as he defines which routers will connect in a region. This determines the topology of the network, and a proper knowledge of the underlying traffic is crucial for an efficient choice. However, if the administrator does not have this knowledge prior to region design, or there are unexpected fluctuations, the topology might be inefficient. The method considered here is an automatic and efficient scheme for connecting routers into regions in a hierarchical manner. The key element is to use only GHZ states of limited size and arrange the regions in a hierarchical manner. This avoids the problem of large, fragile GHZ states. In addition, regions can be arranged on demand, for example, optimized with respect to expected traffic. We note that such a hierarchic arrangement was also implicitly assumed in [52, 53]. The features of such hierarchical graphs and their properties in a network structure have recently been analyzed in detail in [120].

In our case, regions connect via a GHZ network state, and we fix the maximum number of routers m that are part of such a region. This effectively limits the size of the GHZ network state connecting the routers. Regarding fragility, we remark that in fact a three-qubit GHZ state can accept more local depolarizing noise per particle than a Bell pair – only for larger particle numbers there is an increased fragility [98]. The situation for the case of $m = 3$ is depicted in Figure 17.15. (The figure depicts the state for connecting nine networks in hierarchical regions for m = 3. The entire network of routers is broken down into smaller regions, again sharing a network state, with size of at most 3 (green). Each router of a region connects again to the next hierarchical level

via a GHZ network state (red)).

We can also view these hierarchical regions as substructures inside the network layer of the quantum networking stack. In other words, the hierarchical layers may be considered high layers in the stack. We call a router that connects regions at different hierarchical levels also a designated router (DR). These routers enable routers/networks located at regions at different levels of the hierarchy to be reached. The process of establishing and connecting routers in regions can be done automatically: If a new router starts, it simply classically discovers all the routers previously appeared. Then, the DRs check if the new router fits into any of the existing regions. If so, then the new router will be added to that region. If not, a new hierarchical level is created, thereby creating an m-ary tree of

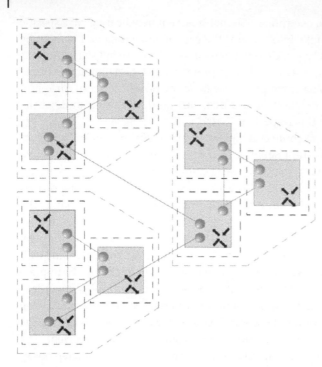

Figure 17.15 The state for connecting nine networks in hierarchical regions for m = 3. *Source:* Pirker and Dür [44]. (For more details see color figure in bins).

regions. Note that, in principle, one can also choose the position of routers in the hierarchy with respect to certain parameters, such as traffic. This enables one to place the routers of networks with many requests in the same region, thereby optimizing the regions between quantum networks. We also observe that such a hierarchy of regions decreases the complexity of the region routing protocol.

Reliable regions: Here, we discuss the reliability of regions. In principle, since regions connect via GHZ network states, they will suffer from similar problems as quantum networks at layer 3 if a router disconnects. The schemes we discussed earlier enable the failure of network devices to be compensated in a network, leaving the remaining devices within the network with a functional network state. However, in the setting of regions, the situation is more involved since the failure of one router at the boundary of a region will also disable all other routers of the same region from generating graph states to other regions. This problem can be solved by symmetrizing inside regions. In that direction, suppose m regions connect with a GHZ network state. Instead of distributing the qubits of the GHZ network states to a particular router of each region, we symmetrize the GHZ states inside the respective regions. For example, in the case of the regions $A,..., M$, we distribute the qubits of the largest GHZ to different routers inside the regions $A, ..., M$. In particular, for region A, we can assign the qubits to $|A|$ different routers, and in region B, we can distribute the qubits to $|B|$ different routers, and so on. The scheme is illustrated in Figure 17.16 (Symmetrizing is done with respect to all possible permutations of routers residing in different regions. Observe that the inter-region entanglement is still of the GHZ type.)

Figure 17.16 Symmetrizing a network state between regions (shown for a three-qubit GHZ state). *Source:* Pirker and Dür [44].

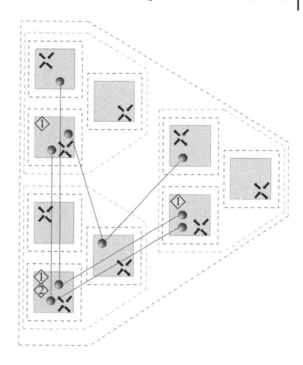

Design Example 17.2 Region Routing [44]

Here, we illustrate the region routing *Protocol 2* for the concrete example shown in Figure 17.17. In this example, four clients of four different networks want to share a graph state. The region routing protocol will establish a virtual network state among the respective routers. The first step in the Steiner tree construction for the first router is shown in Figure 17.17 (Clients of the networks *N1*,..., *N4* want to generate a graph state. The configuration of routers (boxes) in regions (dashed lines) is shown at the top of the figure. There are four regions of size two, three regions of size three (one includes *N1*, and the other one includes *N2* and *N3*), and one of size four. Observe that networks may be part of several regions, such as *N1*, which connect at one router; see the discussion above. In the bottom of the figure, we depict the first step of the protocol: It starts with *S* = {*N1*,..., *N4*}, and selects *N1* to be the root of the first Steiner tree. Then, in the first step of the Steiner tree computation, *N2* is chosen to be closest network to *N1*, and the path is added to the Steiner tree (red edge)).

(Continued)

Design Example 17.2 Region Routing [44] (Continued)

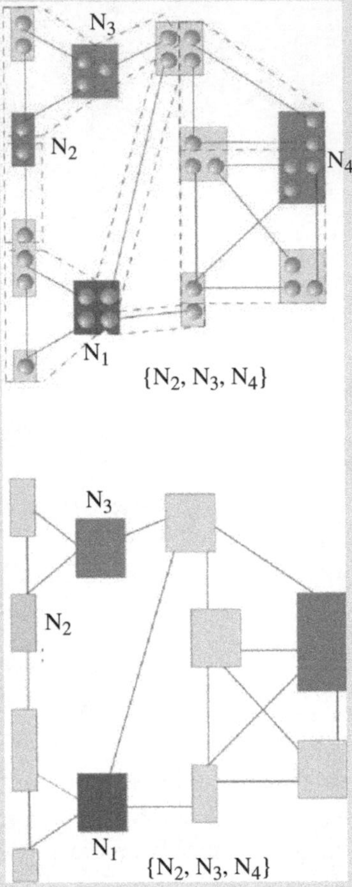

Figure 17.17 Example network for illustration of Protocol 2. *Source:* Pirker and Dür [44]. (For more details see color figure in bins).

This result in a total of $|A| \cdot |B|....|M|$ different M–qubit GHZ states. Observe that the GHZ type of entanglement between the regions $A, ..., M$ is preserved by this symmetrization. The same procedure is also applied to the smaller GHZ states between regions. This technique will introduce complexity to the region routing protocol, and therefore one may use only one specific permutation in regular operation mode, for example, the configuration $A_1, ..., M_1$. All other permutations are only used in the case of route failures.

The approach presented in this section can be considered as a proof of principle for achieving reliability between regions, and other approaches may yield better results. For example, one may consider applying quantum error correction codes for the erasure channel (see chapter 10 in [121]) in the context of reliable regions. In such a scenario, each qubit of the GHZ state between regions could be encoded in a logical qubit of the quantum error correction code for the erasure channel, and the physical qubits comprising the logical qubit distributed among the routers inside the region. This allows failures of router inside regions to be compensated for. However, in order to recover from a failure, the remaining routers within a region have to communicate and collaborate

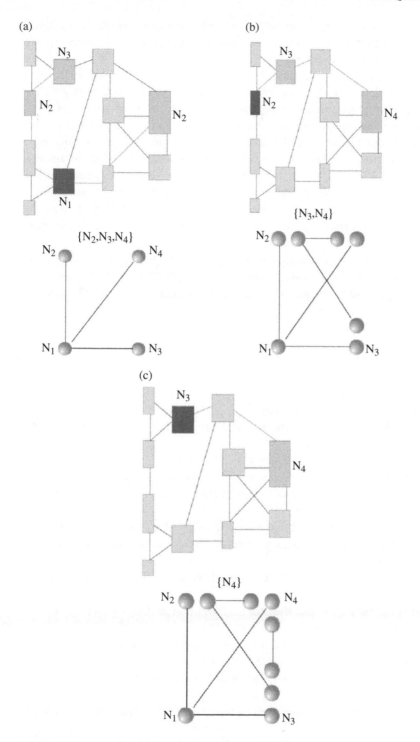

Figure 17.18 (a) Generating the state |GHZ₄⟩, (b) generating the state |GHZ₃⟩, (c) generating a Bell pair.
Source: Pirker and Dür [44].

to restore the GHZ state between regions, which will necessarily consume entanglement inside a region. Finally, we emphasize that we do not claim optimality of the symmetrizing approach used in this section to achieve reliability between regions.

After the first Steiner tree construction finishes, the algorithm transforms the Steiner tree to a GHZ state as follows: If the degree of the root vertex r selected by the protocol is larger than one, it combines all qubits into one (by, e.g., preparing a local GHZ state of size $\deg(r) + 1$, and performing at most r Bell measurements), thereby again obtaining a GHZ state of size $\deg(r) + 1$. All nodes that are not target networks employ Bell measurements to their qubits which have been selected for the Steiner tree. If a target node t is not a terminal node, then it locally creates a GHZ state of size $\deg(t) + 1$, keeps one qubit, and performs at most t Bell measurements of all qubits that are part of the Steiner tree. Observe that it may be necessary that some routers to measure qubits in the Z basis to shape the GHZ states in regions. In the next step, the *Protocol 2* removes N_1 from the set of target networks S, and we perform the same procedure for the remaining network nodes in S.

The final state after the routing protocol is depicted in Figure 17.18. (Figure 17.18a shows generation of the state $|GHZ_4\rangle$, Figure 17.18b shows generation of the state $|GHZ_3\rangle$, and Figure 17.18c shows generation of a Bell pair. After the protocol finishes, the router shares the full GHZ network state.)

References

1 Van Meter, R. (2014). *Quantum Networking*. Wiley.
2 Lloyd, S., Shapiro, J.H., Wong, F.N. et al. (2004). Infrastructure for the quantum internet. *ACM SIGCOMM Comp. Comm. Rev.* **34** (5): 9–20.
3 Kimble, H.J. (2008). The quantum internet. *Nature* **453** (7198): 1023.
4 Castelvecchi, D. (2018). The quantum internet has arrived (and it hasn't). *Nature* **554** (7692): 289.
5 Bennett, C.H. and Brassard, G. (2014). Quantum cryptography: public key distribution and coin tossing. *Theor. Comput. Sci.* **560** (P1): 7–11.
6 Ekert, A.K. (1991). Quantum cryptography based on bell theorem. *Phys. Rev. Lett.* **67** (6): 661.
7 Broadbent, A. and Schaffner, C. (2016). Quantum cryptography beyond quantum key distribution. *Des. Codes Crypt.* **78** (1): 351–382.
8 Wehner, S., Elkouss, D., and Hanson, R. (2018). Quantum internet: a vision for the road ahead. *Science* **362** (6412): eaam9288.
9 Van Meter, R., Ladd, T.D., Munro, W., and Nemoto, K. (2009). System design for a long-line quantum repeater. *IEEE/ACM Trans. Netw.* **17** (3): 1002–1013.
10 Simon, C., De Riedmatten, H., Afzelius, M. et al. (2007). Quantum repeaters with photon pair sources and multimode memories. *Phys. Rev. Lett.* **98** (19): 190503.
11 Sangouard, N., Dubessy, R., and Simon, C. (2009). Quantum repeaters based on single trapped ions. *Phys. Rev. A* **79** (4): 042340.
12 Nielsen, M.A. and Chuang, I. (2002). *Quantum Computation and Quantum Information*. Cambridge University Press.
13 Bennett, C.H., Brassard, G., Crepeau, C. et al. (1993). Teleporting an unknown quantum state via dual classical and einstein-podolsky-rosen channels. *Phys. Rev. Lett.* **70** (13): 1895.
14 Caleffi, M. (2017). Optimal routing for quantum networks. *IEEE Access* **5**: 22 299–22 312.
15 Gyongyosi, L. and Imre, S. (2018). Decentralized base-graph routing for the quantum internet. *Phys. Rev. A* **98** (2): 022310.

16 Van Meter, R., Satoh, T., Ladd, T.D. et al. (2013). Path selection for quantum repeater networks. *Netw. Sci.* **3** (1–4): 82–95.

17 Perseguers, S., Lapeyre, G. Jr., Cavalcanti, D. et al. (2013). Distribution of entanglement in large-scale quantum networks. *Rep. Prog. Phys.* **76** (9): 096001.

18 Zukowski, M., Zeilinger, A., Horne, M.A., and Ekert, A.K. (1993). "Eventready-detectors" bell experiment via entanglement swapping. *Phys. Rev. Lett.* **71**: 4287–4290.

19 Goebel, A.M., Wagenknecht, C., Zhang, Q. et al. (2008). Multistage entanglement swapping. *Phys. Rev. Lett.* **101** (8): 080403.

20 Bennett, C.H., Brassard, G., Popescu, S. et al. (1996). Purification of noisy entanglement and faithful teleportation via noisy channels. *Phys. Rev. Lett.* **76**: 722.

21 E. Schoute, L. Mancinska, T. Islam, I. Kerenidis, and S. Wehner, "Shortcuts to quantum network routing," arXiv preprint arXiv:1610.05238, 2016.

22 Cabrillo, C., Cirac, J.I., Garcia-Fernandez, P., and Zoller, P. (1999). Creation of entangled states of distant atoms by interference. *Phys. Rev. A* **59** (2): 1025.

23 Barrett, S.D. and Kok, P. (2005). Efficient high-fidelity quantum computation using matter qubits and linear optics. *Phys. Rev. A* **71** (6): 060310.

24 Jones, C., Kim, D., Rakher, M.T. et al. (2016). Design and analysis of communication protocols for quantum repeater networks. *New J. Phys.* **18** (8): 083015.

25 Nemoto, K., Trupke, M., Devitt, S.J. et al. (2016). Photonic quantum networks formed from nv-centers. *Sci. Rep.* **6**: 26284.

26 van Dam, S.B., Humphreys, P.C., Rozpedek, F. et al. (2017). Multiplexed entanglement generation over quantum networks using multi-qubit nodes. *Quantum Sci. Technol.* **2** (3): 034002.

27 Munro, W.J., Azuma, K., Tamaki, K., and Nemoto, K. (2015). Inside quantum repeaters. *IEEE J. Sel. Top. Quantum Electron.* **21** (3): 78–90.

28 Briegel, H.-J., Dur, W., Cirac, J.I., and Zoller, P. (1998). Quantum repeaters: the role of imperfect local operations in quantum communication. *Phys. Rev. Lett.* **81** (26): 5932.

29 Ionicioiu, R. and Munro, W.J. (2010). Constructing 2d and 3d cluster states with photonic modules. *Int. J. Qantum Inf.* **8** (01n02): 149–159.

30 Muralidharan, S., Li, L., Kim, J. et al. (2016). Optimal architectures for long distance quantum communication. *Sci. Rep.* **6**: 20463.

31 Van Meter, R., Satoh, T., Ladd, T.D. et al. (2013). Path selection for quantum repeater networks. *Netw. Sci.* **3**: 82.

32 F. Rozpedek, R. Yehia, K. Goodenough, M. Ruf, P. C. Humphreys, R. Hanson, S. Wehner, and D. Elkouss, "Near-term quantum repeater experiments with nv centers: overcoming the limitations of direct transmission," arXiv preprint arXiv:1809.00364, 2018.

33 K. Chakraborty, Distributed Routing in a Quantum Internet , arXiv:1907.11630v1 [quant-ph] 26 Jul 2019

34 Kleinberg, J.M. (2000). Navigation in a small world. *Nature* **406** (6798): 845.

35 Kleinberg, J. (1999). *The Small-World Phenomenon: An Algorithmic Perspective*. Tech. Rep: Cornell University.

36 M. Naor and U. Wieder, "Know thy neighbor's neighbor: better routing for skip-graphs and small worlds," in International Workshop on Peerto-Peer Systems. Springer, 2004, pp. 269–277.

37 G. S. Manku, M. Naor, and U. Wieder, "Know thy neighbor's neighbor: the power of lookahead in randomized p2p networks," in Proceedings of the thirty-sixth annual ACM symposium on Theory of computing. ACM, 2004, pp. 54–63.

38 D. Coppersmith, D. Gamarnik, and M. Sviridenko, "The diameter of a long range percolation graph," in Proceedings of the thirteenth annual ACM-SIAM symposium on Discrete algorithms. Society for Industrial and Applied Mathematics, 2002, pp. 329–337.

39 F. Rozpedek, R. Yehia, K. Goodenough, M. Ruf, P. C. Humphreys, R. Hanson, S. Wehner, and D. Elkouss, "Near-term quantum repeater experiments with nv centers: overcoming the limitations of direct transmission," arXiv preprint arXiv:1809.00364, 2018.

40 Sinclair, N., Saglamyurek, E., Mallahzadeh, H. et al. (2014). Spectral multiplexing for scalable quantum photonics using an atomic frequency comb quantum memory and feed-forward control. *Phys. Rev. Lett.* **113** (5): 053603.

41 Comellas, F., Fertin, G., and Raspaud, A. (2004). Recursive graphs with smallworld scale-free properties. *Phys. Rev. E* **69** (3): 037104.

42 Hammack, R., Imrich, W., and Klavzar, S. (2011). *Handbook of Product Graphs*. CRC Press.

43 Hui, P., Crowcroft, J., and Yoneki, E. (2011). Bubble rap: Social-based forwarding in delay-tolerant networks. *IEEE Trans. Mob. Comput.* **10** (11): 1576–1589.

44 Pirker, A. and Dür, W. (2019). A quantum network stack and protocols for reliable entanglement-based networks, arXiv:1810.03556v2 [quant-ph]. *New J. Phys.* **21**: 2019.

45 Dijkstra, E.W. (1959). A note on two problems in connexion with graphs. *Numer. Math.* **1**: 269.

46 Hwang, F.K., Richards, D.S., and Winter, P. (1992). *The Steiner Tree Problem*. Elsevier.

47 Garey, M. and Johnson, D. (1977). The rectilinear Steiner tree is NP-complete. *SIAM J. Appl. Math.* **32**: 826.

48 Hein, M., Eisert, J., and Briegel, H.J. (2004). Multiparty entanglement in graph states. *Phys. Rev. A* **69**: 062311.

49 Guehne, O., T'oth, G., Hyllus, P., and Briegel, H.J. (2005). Bell Inequalities for Graph States. *Phys. Rev. Lett.* **95**: 120405.

50 M. Hein, W. Ds¨ur, J. Eisert, R. Raussendorf, M. van den Nest, and H.-J. Briegel, "Entanglement in Graph States and its Applications. In: Proceedings of the International School of Physics" Enrico Fermi" on" Quantum Computers, Algorithms and Chaos"," (2006), arXiv:quant-ph/0602096.

51 T'oth, G., G¨uhne, O., and Briegel, H.J. (2006). Two-setting Bell inequalities for graph states. *Phys. Rev. A* **73**: 022303.

52 Pirker, A., Walln¨ofer, J., and D¨ur, W. (2018). Modular architectures for quantum networks. *New J. Phys.* **20**: 053054.

53 Walln¨ofer, J., Zwerger, M., Muschik, C. et al. (2016). Two dimensional quantum repeaters. *Phys. Rev. A* **94**: 052307.

54 Muralidharan, S., Li, L., Kim, J. et al. (2016). Efficient long distance quantum communication. *Sci. Rep.* **6**: 20463.

55 Munro, W., Harrison, K., Stephens, A. et al. (2010). From quantum multiplexing to high-performance quantum networking. *Nat. Photonics* **4**: 792.

56 Epping, M., Kampermann, H., and Bruß, D. (2016). Robust entanglement distribution via quantum network coding. *New J. Phys.* **18**: 103052.

57 Hayashi, M. (2007). Prior entanglement between senders enablesperfect quantum network coding with modification. *Phys. Rev. A* **76**: 040301.

58 Van Meter, R. (2014). *"Quantum Error Correction-Based Repeaters," in Quantum Networking*, 219–236. Wiley.

59 Pant, M., Krovi, H., Englund, D., and Guha, S. (2017). Rate-distance tradeoff and resource costs for all-optical quantum repeaters. *Phys. Rev. A* **95**: 012304.

60 S. Das, S. Khatri, and J. P. Dowling, Robust quantum network architectures and topologies for entanglement distribution , ArXiv e-prints (2017), arXiv:1709.07404 [quant-ph].

61 M. PantH. KroviD. TowsleyL. TassiulasL. JiangP. BasuD. Englundand S. Guha, Routing entanglement in the quantum internet, ArXiv e-prints (2017) arXiv:1708.07142 [quant-ph].

62 Munro, W.J., Azuma, K., Tamaki, K., and Nemoto, K. (2015). Inside Quantum Repeaters. *IEEE J. Sel. Top. Quantum Electron.* **21**: 78.

63 Munro, W.J., Van Meter, R., Louis, S.G.R., and Nemoto, K. (2008). High-Bandwidth Hybrid Quantum Repeater. *Phys. Rev. Lett.* **101**: 040502.

64 Sangouard, N., Simon, C., de Riedmatten, H., and Gisin, N. (2011). Quantum repeaters based on atomic ensembles and linear optics. *Rev. Mod. Phys.* **83**: 33.

65 Guha, S., Krovi, H., Fuchs, C.A. et al. (2015). Rate-loss analysis of an efficient quantum repeater architecture. *Phys. Rev. A* **92**: 022357.

66 S. Pirandola, Capacities of repeater-assisted quantum communications, ArXiv e-prints (2016), arXiv:1601.00966 [quant-ph].

67 Meter, R.V. and Touch, J. (2013). Designing Quantum Repeater Networks. *IEEE Commun. Mag.* **51**: 64.

68 Van Meter, R., Ladd, T.D., Munro, W.J., and Nemoto, K. (2009). System Design for a Long-Line Quantum Repeater. *IEEE/ACM Trans. Netw.* **17**: 1002.

69 R. Van Meter, J. Touch, and C. Horsman, Recursive Quantum Repeater Networks, arXiv.org > quant-ph > arXiv:1105.1238. (2011).

70 A. Pirker, J. Wallnˉofer, and W. Dˉur, Modular architectures for quantum networks, arXiv.org > quant-ph > arXiv:1711.02606

71 E. Schoute, L. Mancinska, T. Islam, I. Kerenidis, and S. Wehner, Shortcuts to quantum network routing arXiv preprint arXiv:1610.05238 (2016).

72 S. Das, S. Khatri, and J. P. Dowling, Robust quantum network architectures and topologies for entanglement distribution, ArXiv e-prints (2017), arXiv:1709.07404 [quant-ph].

73 S. Pirandola, End-to-end capacities of a quantum communication network, ArXiv e-prints (2016) arXiv:1601.00966 [quant-ph].

74 Van Meter, R., Satoh, T., Ladd, T.D. et al. (2013). Path selection for quantum repeater networks. *Netw. Sci.* **3** (82): 82–95.

75 Gyongyosi, L. and Imre, S. (2017). Entanglement-Gradient Routing for Quantum Networks. *Sci. Rep.* **7**: 14255.

76 Gyongyosi, L. and Imre, S. (2018). Decentralized base-graph routing for the quantum internet. *Phys. Rev. A* **98**: 022310.

77 Caleffi, M. (2017). Optimal Routing for Quantum Networks. *IEEE Access* **5**: 22299.

78 L. Gyongyosi and S. Imre, Topology Adaption for the Quantum Internet, ArXiv e-prints (2018), arXiv:1809.02928 [quant-ph].

79 F. HahnA. Pappaand J. Eisert, Quantum network routing and local complementation, ArXiv e-prints (2018) arXiv:1805.04559 [quant-ph].

80 Dahlberg, A. and Wehner, S. (2018). Transforming graph statesusing single-qubit operations. *Philos. Trans. Royal Soc. Lon. A* **376**.

81 A. Dahlberg, J. Helsen, and S. Wehner, How to transform graph states using single-qubit operations: computational complexity and algorithms, ArXiv e-prints (2018), arXiv:1805.05306 [quant-ph].

82 J. Wallnˉofer, A. Pirker, M. Zwerger, and W. Dˉur, Multipartite state generation in quantum networks with optimal scaling, ArXiv e-prints (2018) arXiv:1806.11562 [quant-ph].

83 Meter, R.V. and Touch, J. (2013). Designing Quantum Repeater Networks. *IEEE Commun. Mag.* **51** (64): 64–71.

84 DiVincenzo, D.P. The Physical Implementation of Quantum Computation. *Fortschritte der Phy.* **48**: 771.

85 Chamberland, C., Iyer, P., and Poulin, D. (2018). Fault-tolerant quantum computing in the Pauli or Clifford frame with slow error diagnostics. *Quantum* **2**: 43.

86 Chao, R. and Reichardt, B.W. (2018). Fault-tolerant quantum computation with few qubits. *Npj Quantum Inf.* **4**: 42.

87 Jones, C., Kim, D., Rakher, M.T. et al. (2016). Design and analysis of communication protocols for quantum repeater networks. *New J. Phys.* **18**: 083015.

88 van Dam, S.B., Humphreys, P.C., Rozpkedek, F. et al. (2017). Multiplexed entanglement generation over quantum networks using multi-qubit nodes. *Quantum Sci. Technol.* **2**: 034002.

89 Zwerger, M., Pirker, A., Dunjko, V. et al. (2018). Long-Range Big Quantum-Data Transmission. *Phys. Rev. Lett.* **120**: 030503.

90 Briegel, H.-J., D̈ur, W., Cirac, J.I., and Zoller, P. (1998). Quantum Repeaters: The Role of Imperfect Local Operations in Quantum Communication. *Phys. Rev. Lett.* **81**: 5932.

91 D̈ur, W., Briegel, H.-J., Cirac, J.I., and Zoller, P. (1999). Quantum repeaters based on entanglement purification. *Phys. Rev. A* **59**: 169.

92 Sangouard, N., Dubessy, R., and Simon, C. (2009). Quantum repeaters based on single trapped ions. *Phys. Rev. A* **79**: 042340.

93 Muralidharan, S., Li, L., Kim, J. et al. (2016). Optimal architectures for long distance quantum communication. *Sci. Rep.* **6**: 20463.

94 Munro, W., Harrison, K., Stephens, A. et al. (2010). From quantum multiplexing to high-performance quantum networking. *Nat. Photonics* **4**: 792.

95 Azuma, K., Tamaki, K., and Lo, H.-K. (2015). All-photonic quantum repeaters. *Nat. Commun.* **6**: 6787.

96 Pirandola, S., Laurenza, R., Ottaviani, C., and Banchi, L. (2017). Fundamental limits of repeaterless quantum communications. *Nat. Commun.* **8**: 15043 EP.

97 Epping, M., Kampermann, H., and Bruß, D. (2016). Robust entanglement distribution via quantum network coding. *New J. Phys.* **18**: 103052.

98 Walln̈ofer, J., Zwerger, M., Muschik, C. et al. (2016). Two-dimensional quantum repeaters. *Phys. Rev. A* **94**: 052307.

99 E. Knill and R. Laflamme, Concatenated Quantum Codes, eprint arXiv:quantph/9608012 (1996), quant-ph/9608012.

100 Zwerger, M., Briegel, H.J., and D̈ur, W. (2014). Hybrid architecture *for* encoded measurement-based quantum computation. *Sci. Rep.* **4**: 5364.

101 Muralidharan, S., Kim, J., L̈utkenhaus, N. et al. (2014). Ultrafast and Fault-Tolerant Quantum Communication across Long Distances. *Phys. Rev. Lett.* **112**: 250501.

102 Ewert, F., Bergmann, M., and van Loock, P. (2016). Ultrafast Long-Distance Quantum Communication with Static Linear Optics. *Phys. Rev. Lett.* **117**: 210501.

103 Acin, A., Cirac, J.I., and Lewenstein, M. (2007). Entanglement percolation in quantum networks. *Nat. Phys.* **3**: 256.

104 Rudolph, T. (2017). Why I am optimistic about the silicon-photonic route to quantum computing. *APL Photonics* **2**: 030901.

105 van Enk, S.J., Cirac, J.I., and Zoller, P. (1997). Ideal quantum communication over noisy channels: a quantum optical implementation. *Phys. Rev. Lett.* **78**: 4293.

106 van Enk, S.J., Cirac, J.I., and Zoller, P. (1998). Photonic channels for quantum communication. *Science* **279**: 205.

107 D̈ur, W., Aschauer, H., and Briegel, H.-J. (2003). Multiparticle Entanglement Purification for Graph States. *Phys. Rev. Lett.* **91**: 107903.

108 Aschauer, H., D̈ur, W., and Briegel, H.-J. (2005). Multiparticle entanglement purification for two-colorable graph states. *Phys. Rev. A* **71**: 012319.

109 D̈ur, W. and Briegel, H.J. (2007). Entanglement purification and quantum error correction. *Rep. Prog. Phys.* **70**: 1381.

110 Chen, K. and Lo, H.-K. (2007). Multi-partite quantum cryptographic protocols with noisy GHZ states. *Quantum Info. Comput.* **7**: 689.

111 Deutsch, D., Ekert, A., Jozsa, R. et al. (1996). Quantum privacy amplification and the security of quantum cryptography over noisy channels. *Phys. Rev. Lett.* **77**: 2818.

112 Browne, D.E. and Rudolph, T. (2005). Resource-efficient linear optical quantum computation. *Phys. Rev. Lett.* **95**: 010501.

113 Kieling, K., Rudolph, T., and Eisert, J. (2007). Percolation, renormalization, and quantum computing with nondeterministic gates. *Phys. Rev. Lett.* **99**: 130501.

114 Zaidi, H.A., Dawson, C., van Loock, P., and Rudolph, T. (2015). Near-deterministic creation of universal cluster states with probabilistic Bell measurements and three-qubit resource states. *Phys. Rev. A* **91**: 042301.

115 G. S. Malkin, Flaws in RIPv2 packet's authenticationm, draft-etienne-ripv2-auth-flaws-00.txt "RIP Version 2," RFC 2453 (1998).

116 J. Moy, "OSPF Version 2," RFC 2328 (1998).

117 B̈auml, S. and Azuma, K. (2017). Fundamental limitation on quantum broadcast networks. *Quantum Sci. Technol.* **2**: 024004.

118 D̈ur, W. and Briegel, H.-J. (2004). Stability of Macroscopic Entanglement under Decoherence. *Phys. Rev. Lett.* **92**: 180403.

119 Hein, M., D̈ur, W., and Briegel, H.-J. (2005). Entanglement properties of multipartite entangled states under the influence of decoherence. *Phys. Rev. A* **71**: 032350.

120 A. Bapat, Z. Eldredge, J. R. Garrison, A. Desphande, F. T. Chong, and A. V. Gorshkov, Unitary Entanglement Construction in Hierarchical Networks, ArXiv e-prints (2018), arXiv:1808.07876 [quant-ph].

121 Grassl, M., Beth, T., and Pellizzari, T. (1997). Codes for the quantum erasure channel. *Phys. Rev. A* **56**: 33.

Index

Artificial Intelligence and Quantum Computing for Advanced Wireless Networks, First Edition.
Savo G. Glisic and Beatriz Lorenzo.
© 2022 John Wiley & Sons Ltd. Published 2022 by John Wiley & Sons Ltd.